MW01598519

# Corporate Taxes

*WORLDWIDE SUMMARIES*
*2004–2005*

# Corporate Taxes

*WORLDWIDE SUMMARIES*
*2004–2005*

WILEY

**John Wiley & Sons, Inc.**

# Information Guide Series

This Guide is one of a series on business conditions
in the countries in which PricewaterhouseCoopers firms
have offices or carry out work, and is based on the
latest available information from these offices.

---

To obtain a copy of a title in the
Information Guide series, contact
your local PricewaterhouseCoopers
office, or call (800) 579-1646.

This series is available in print, on
CD-ROM, and on the Internet at
*www.pwc.com*

---

This Guide, *Corporate Taxes — Worldwide Summaries,* supersedes the 2003–2004 edition.

# PricewaterhouseCoopers Organization—Practice Firms Worldwide

To Our Readers:

I take great pleasure in introducing the 2004–2005 edition of the PricewaterhouseCoopers annual information guide, *Corporate Taxes—Worldwide Summaries.* This edition has information on 113 countries and territories. All entries, unless otherwise stated, present tax rates and rules in effect at January 1, 2004.

Part of the PricewaterhouseCoopers information guide series, which also includes *Individual Taxes—Worldwide Summaries,* this book exemplifies the breadth and depth of expertise offered by the worldwide PricewaterhouseCoopers network.

PricewaterhouseCoopers (*www.pwc.com*) provides industry-focused assurance, tax, and advisory services for public and private clients. More than 120,000 PricewaterhouseCoopers people in 139 countries connect their thinking, experience, and solutions to build public trust and enhance value for clients and their stake-holders. The tax practices in our worldwide network are able to provide a full range of services to meet the needs of our clients and their businesses.

PricewaterhouseCoopers refers to the network of member firms of PricewaterhouseCoopers International Limited, each of which is a separate and independent legal entity. Each of these firms is ready to help with your tax and business problems, wherever in the world you might need assistance. Don't hesitate to contact us.

Yours sincerely,

Paul Boorman
Global Tax Leader, PricewaterhouseCoopers

# Foreword

This Guide has been prepared to provide a summary of basic information about corporate taxes in 113 countries and territories. It is designed to outline briefly the corporate tax rates and certain major features of the tax laws that affect corporate taxation in the countries covered. For most countries, the tax summary is supplemented by a sample corporate tax calculation to illustrate the basic rules.

In a guide of this nature it is not possible to provide detailed rules on which to base specific action. When more detailed information is required on a country, reference should be made to the specific laws, regulations and tax treaties of the country; and/or to tax advisers.

**Unless otherwise indicated, the tax rates and rules in effect at January 1, 2004 have been used.**

# Table of Contents

## PwC contact

For additional information on taxation in Antigua and Barbuda, contact:

Charles W. Walwyn
PricewaterhouseCoopers
Old Parham Road
St. John's, Antigua
Telephone: (1) (268) 462 3000
Fax: (1) (268) 462 1902
e-mail: charles.walwyn@ag.pwc.com

## Significant developments

The government has repealed the 3% tax levied on the gross profits of international business corporations.

The following amendments to the Income Tax Act have been made by the government and were gazetted on April 3, 2003.

- Audited accounts—All incorporated entities will be required to file audited accounts commencing with the year of assessment 2004, that is, for all fiscal years ending in 2003.

- Rate of income tax—The rate is to be reduced to 35% from 40%. Any company with financial year ending March 31, 2003 or earlier will pay taxes at the rate of 40%. Companies with a financial year ending after March 31, 2003, but before March 31, 2004, will be required to prorate its income between the period prior to April 1, 2003 and the period after March 31, 2003. Companies with a financial year ending March 31, 2004 or later will be taxed at 35%.

- Rate of withholding tax—The rate of withholding tax on mortgage or debenture interest, or any rent or allocated branch expenses, or annuity or other annual payment paid to nonresident corporations is to be reduced to 25% from 40%. Interest payments on bank deposits made to nonresident individuals will not be subject to withholding tax. Interest payments on bank deposits made to nonresident corporations will be taxed at the rate of 25%.

- Hotel incentives—The erection of new hotels, and the extension of existing hotels, commenced after January 2003, shall qualify the owner for an exemption from the payment of income tax for specific periods based on bedroom capacity. New hotels consisting of 100 or more rooms qualify for a 25-year income tax exemption. For existing hotels, the addition of 30–49 rooms qualifies the hotel for a seven-year exemption, the addition of 50–99 rooms qualifies the hotel for a 15-year exemption and the addition of 100 or more rooms qualifies the hotel for a 25-year exemption.

- Amendments targeted at closely-held and owner managed corporations, as follows.

  No deduction for interest on loans owing to shareholders, directors, their spouses, children or relatives, or to any related parties. Only interest paid to banks and financial institutions licensed under the Financial Institutions (Non-Banking) Act on loans borrowed at commercial rates and terms would be allowed as a deduction.

  Restriction on rents paid—Rents paid by a company to shareholders, directors, their spouses, children or relatives, or to any related parties in excess of 5% of the otherwise chargeable profits of the company would not be allowed as a deduction.

Restriction on compensation—Salaries, wages, director's fees and other payments made for services rendered by the shareholders, directors, their spouses, children or relatives in excess of 25% of otherwise chargeable profits would not be allowed as a deduction.

- Branch offices—A resident branch of a foreign company shall be regarded as a separate company and shall be taxed on the same basis as that of a locally registered corporation.

The current Commissioner of Inland Revenue is now claiming the following in respect of the existing legislation.

1. Dividends paid to a nonresident and non-CARICOM company are subject to withholding tax at a rate of 25%.
2. Capital gains are taxable and should be included in ordinary income and taxed at 35%.

The current tax treatment of dividends and capital gains has been challenged.

## Taxes on corporate income

*Corporation tax*/Corporation tax is imposed at a rate of 35%.

## Corporate residence

A corporation is deemed to be resident if it is incorporated in Antigua, if it is registered as an external company doing business in Antigua, or if the central management and control of its business are exercised in Antigua.

## Other taxes

*Life insurance premium tax*/A premium tax of 3% is levied on the premium income (net of agent's commission) of all life insurance companies, whether resident or nonresident.

*General insurance premium tax*/A premium tax of 3% is levied on the premium income, excluding motor business (net of agent's commission), of all general insurance companies, whether resident or nonresident.

*Stamp tax on transfer of property*/Stamp tax is levied on the value of property as assessed by the Chief Valuation Officer, as follows.

| | % |
|---|---|
| Vendors who are citizens of Antigua | 7.5 |
| Vendors who are noncitizens of Antigua | 7.5 |
|   In addition, land value appreciation tax at the rate of 5% is assessed on the difference between the value of property when purchased and the value of property at the time of sale. | |
| Purchasers who are citizens of Antigua | 2.5 |
| Purchasers who are noncitizens of Antigua | 2.5 |
|   In addition, 5% of the value of property with reference to a license required to hold property in Antigua. | |

*Stamp tax on transfer of shares*/Stamp tax is levied on the value of consideration for the sale of shares or debentures issued by or on behalf of a company. It is payable by the vendor at the rate of 2.5%. Noncitizens must obtain a license (at a cost of EC$400) to hold shares or be a director in a company that owns land or has a lease on land in excess of five acres for a period greater than five years.

*Property tax*/Property tax is levied at graduated rates on the basis of the market value of the real property, its use (residential or commercial) and its zone.

As a general guide, the following applies.

Residential buildings—up to 1/2 of 1% of the taxable value, with surcharges of 5% to 20% depending on the zone.

Commercial buildings
- Hotels—1/2 of 1% of taxable value.
- Other—3/4 of 1% of taxable value.

Land—outside of the capital, based on acreage (up to EC$200 per acre); within the capital, 1% of taxable value (EC$50 per sq ft).

*Value-added tax*/There is no VAT.

*Hotel tax*/Hotel tax is levied on the accommodation charge at graduated rates per night in respect of each guest residing in a hotel or guest house for a night or part thereof. The tax ranges from a rate of EC$2.50 to EC$10.00 per room night

*Guest tax*/A guest tax of 6.5% is payable in respect of every item on the hotel bill.

*Guest levy*/A guest levy of 2% is payable in respect of every item on the hotel bill.

## Branch income

Branch income is taxed on the same basis and at the same rate as that of corporations. Withholding tax is not applicable on the transfer of after-tax profits to the head office.

Recharges of expenses from the head office to the branch will be subject to withholding tax at a rate of 25% if the recharged amounts cannot be specifically attributed to the branch. The recharge cannot be based on a percentage allocation.

## Income determination

*Inventory valuation*/Inventories are generally stated at the lower of cost or net realizable value. FIFO and average cost methods of valuation are generally used for book and tax purposes. However, the Commissioner of Inland Revenue will normally accept a method of valuation that conforms to standard accounting practice in the trade concerned. LIFO is not permitted for tax or book purposes.

*Capital gains*/Capital gains are not subject to tax.

At the time of going to press, the Commissioner of Inland Revenue is claiming that capital gains of companies should be included in ordinary income and taxed at a rate of 40%.

*Intercompany dividends*/Dividends received by a company resident in Antigua from another company resident in Antigua are taxed at the rate of 40%. Credit is given to the recipient for the tax on the dividend in computing the tax liability.

*Foreign income*/An Antiguan corporation is taxed on foreign branch income as earned and on foreign dividends as received. Double taxation is avoided by means of foreign tax credits where active tax treaties exist and through deduction of foreign income taxes in other cases (United Kingdom and CARICOM). There is also relief from Commonwealth taxes.

*Stock dividends*/An Antiguan corporation may distribute a tax-free stock dividend proportionately to all shareholders.

## Deductions

*Depreciation and depletion*/Depreciation allowed for tax purposes is computed by the diminishing-balance method at prescribed rates. Initial allowances are granted on industrial buildings and in respect of capital expenditure incurred on plant and machinery by a person carrying on a trade or undertaking, as defined. In addition, an annual allowance of 2% is granted on all buildings. Conformity between book and tax depreciation is not required. Gain on the sale of depreciated assets is taxable as ordinary income up to the amount of tax depreciation recaptured.

*Net operating losses*/Income tax losses may be carried forward for six years following the year in which the loss was incurred. However, the chargeable income of a company in any one income year may not be reduced by more than one-half by losses brought forward. No carryback of losses is permitted.

*Payments to foreign affiliates*/An Antiguan corporation may claim a deduction for royalties, management fees and interest charges paid to foreign affiliates, provided the payments are equal to or less than what the corporation would pay to an unrelated entity. The deductibility of any payments to a foreign affiliate will be subject to an arm's length test.

## Group taxation

Group taxation is not permitted.

## Tax incentives

*Inward investment and capital investment*/Tax incentives are available under the following legislation.

1. Fiscal Incentives Ordinance 1975: This ordinance provides to manufacturers of an "approved product" exemption from taxes for varying periods, up to a maximum of 15 years. After the period of exemption, relief by way of tax credits of up to 50% of income tax paid on profits derived from certain export sales may be obtained. The net losses arising during the tax holiday period (i.e., the excess of accumulated tax losses over total profits) may be carried forward and relieved against profits following the expiration of the tax holiday in accordance with the normal rules for setoff of losses.

2. Hotel Aids Ordinance 1952: Under the Income Tax Ordinance, a hotel licensed under the Hotel Aids Ordinance is exempt from income tax for a period of five years following the year in which the construction or extension of the hotel is completed. Prior approval must be sought from the Cabinet. Thereafter, capital expenditure as defined may be set off against profits of the hotel at the rate of 20% in each of any five of the eight years immediately following the tax holiday period. Prior approval must be sought from the Cabinet.

3. International Business Corporations Act 1982: An international business company pays tax at 3% of gross profit. This legislation covers, in addition to companies, banks, gaming, and insurance companies.

**Other incentives**/Approved manufacturing, agricultural, and tourist ventures are permitted to import building materials and equipment free of customs duties.

## Withholding taxes

Tax is currently withheld from income as follows.

| Recipient | Dividends | Interest | Rentals | Management fees, royalties, and other payments to a nonresident | Interest on bank deposits |
|---|---|---|---|---|---|
| | % | % | % | % | % |
| Resident corporations and individuals | Nil | Nil | Nil | Nil | Nil |
| Nonresident corporations | Nil | 25 | 25 | 25 | 25 |
| Nonresident individuals | Nil | 20 | 20 | 25 | Nil |

At the time of going to press, the rate of withholding taxes on dividends is the subject of an Appeal. The current Commissioner of Inland Revenue is claiming that a rate of 25% should apply to dividends.

Where a nonresident lends money at arm's length for the purpose of promoting industrial, commercial, scientific, housing, or other development, the rate of withholding tax is 10%. Prior approval must be sought from the Commissioner of Inland Revenue and it is recommended that Cabinet approval also be obtained.

Withholding taxes become due at the time of payment or accrual and must be paid within seven days thereof.

**Tax treaties**/There is a tax treaty with the United Kingdom, and a double taxation agreement between member states of CARICOM.

## Tax administration

**Returns**/Taxes are assessed on a fiscal-year basis. The taxpayer files an information return, and the authorities subsequently raise an assessment. If a return is not filed on a timely basis the authorities have the power to issue estimated assessments. Also, if a return is not filed on a timely basis the authorities have the power to issue estimated assessments. There is a 5% penalty for late filing (minimum of EC$500). The taxpayer can object to assessments raised within 30 days, and ask the Commissioner of Inland Revenue to review and revise. In the event that the objection is unsuccessful, the taxpayer may appeal to the Tax Appeal Board. The Commissioner of Inland Revenue has the power to enforce the collection of tax prior to the determination of any objection or appeal. The Commissioner also has the discretion to order a stay on the collection and payment of the whole or part of any assessed tax until such time as the objection or appeal is finalized if it would be unjust not to do so. Assessments for the past six years may be reviewed and revised.

**Payment of tax**/Advance tax is payable in monthly installments based on the tax chargeable in the previous fiscal year. The standard amount of each installment is determined as one-twelfth of the tax chargeable in the previous fiscal year. If the assessment for the prior year has not been finalized, the Commissioner of Inland Revenue can raise an assessment based on the Commissioner's best judgment.

The balance of tax due after deduction of advance tax, as notified in the assessment, is payable at the time of submitting the annual financial statements, which must not be later than three months after the financial year end or one month of service of the assessment.

Tax is deemed to be in default if not paid within 30 days of the date on which it becomes due and payable. A penalty of 20% and interest of 1% per month is charged on unpaid taxes in default.

## CORPORATION TAX CALCULATION

Year ended December 31, 2004

| | | |
|---|---:|---:|
| Net income before taxation | | EC$ 1,000,000 |
| Add: | | |
| Book depreciation | 250,000 | |
| Bad debts previously written off, now recovered | 5,000 | |
| General provision for bad debts (1) | 10,000 | |
| Legal expenses re increase in share capital | 4,500 | |
| Legal fees re purchase of a capital asset | 5,000 | |
| Charitable donations not under covenant | 3,000 | |
| Increase in provision for maintenance of plant and equipment | 15,000 | |
| Balancing charge | 2,500 | 295,000 |
| | | 1,295,000 |
| Deduct: | | |
| Annual allowances (2) | 200,000 | |
| Gain on disposal of fixed assets | 5,000 | 205,000 |
| Taxable income | | EC$ 1,090,000 |
| Income tax at 35% (3) | | EC$ 381,500 |
| Less: | | |
| Credit for tax on local dividends | 1,000 | |
| Credit for tax on foreign income | 1,500 | (2,500) |
| | | EC$ 379,000 |

Notes:

1. Only specific write-offs are allowed.
2. Granted in place of book depreciation.
3. The tax is payable at the time of filing the tax return or within one month of service of the notice of assessment.
4. Exchange rate of the Eastern Caribbean dollar officially pegged at US$1 = EC$2.67.

## PwC contact

For additional information on taxation in Argentina, contact:

Jorge San Martín
Price Waterhouse & Co.
Cerrito 268
1010 Buenos Aires, Argentina
Telephone: (54) (1) 4370 6700, 4381 8181/7373/7282
Fax: (54) (11) 4370 6800, 4383 6339, 4382 2793
LN address: Jorge A. San Martin@SOACAT
e-mail: jorge.a.san.martin@ar.pwc.com

## Significant developments

The Public Emergency Law No. 25,561 (Official Gazette January 7, 2002) and regulatory decrees have introduced important reforms to the exchange rate system, including implementation of exchange restrictions (restrictions for certain transactions in foreign currency, for transferring funds abroad), abolition of the Convertibility Law (end of parity US$1 = AR$1), and establishment of a floating exchange rate for the peso in relation to the U.S. dollar. These measures will have an impact on the tax system.

Law No. 25,585 (Official Gazette May 15, 2002) introduced for Argentine companies the obligation to pay wealth tax determined on all their shares either held by individuals residing in Argentina, or outside the country, or held by other companies residing abroad. Reimbursement from shareholders may be requested.

Law No. 25,784 (Official Gazette October 21, 2003) introduced amendments to the income tax law relating to thin-capitalization and transfer pricing regulations.

Law No. 25,795 (Official Gazette November 2003) introduced changes to Law on Tax Procedures (Law No. 11,683) relating to penalties on several tax infringements and responsibility of members of joint ventures, among others.

## Taxes on corporate income

***Profits tax***/The rate of profits tax on net taxable business profits is 35%. Corporations resident in Argentina are subject to tax on Argentine and foreign-source income. They are able to claim any similar taxes actually paid abroad on foreign-source income as a tax credit.

The 1998 tax reform introduced a new tax on minimum notional income. The rate is 1% on the value of fixed and current assets. Income tax is creditable against the tax settlement arising from the tax return of the same fiscal year. In addition, payment of this tax, not offset by income tax, will be treated as payment on account of income tax chargeable during a maximum period of ten years.

## Corporate residence

Corporate residence is determined on the basis of centers of activity and is unaffected by place of incorporation or management. Centers of activity in Argentina of non-Argentine corporations are treated as permanent establishments.

# Argentina

## Other taxes

***Value-added tax***/The current general rate of 21% is applied on the sales value of products and services (including professional services), with a few specific exceptions. This tax is applicable to imports. Exports are tax exempt.

VAT paid on purchases, final imports, and rental of automobiles not considered as inventory and VAT derived from services relating to repair, maintenance, and use of those automobiles cannot be computed by the purchaser as a credit. The same tax treatment applies to other services such as those provided by restaurants, hotels, and garages.

The above-mentioned restrictions do not apply when the engagement of these services is aimed at the holding of conferences, congresses, conventions, or similar events directly related to the specific activity of the contracting party.

***Turnover tax (gross income tax)***/Each of the 24 jurisdictions into which Argentina is divided imposes a tax on gross revenues from the sale of goods and services. Most industries and exports of goods are exempt from this tax. Rates, rules, and assessment procedures are determined locally.

Wealth tax is payable by Argentine companies with effect for fiscal year 2003 on all shares issued by them and owned either by individuals, regardless of residence or owned by companies residing abroad. The Argentine company has the status of a "substitute responsible" toward their shareholders, and must determine and pay the wealth tax at a rate of 0.5% on the value of the shares as per December 31 of each year. However, the company is allowed to request reimbursement from the shareholders.

***Excise tax***/A wide variety of items (other than exports) is taxed at varying rates.

***Tax on credits and debits on bank accounts***/This new tax is levied at a rate of 0.6% on the amounts credited or debited on the taxpayer's bank accounts. Transactions made in banks without using a bank account, and any disposal of one's own or a third party's funds, are subject to a tax rate of 1.2%.

## Branch income

The rate of profits tax on net taxable profits from Argentine sources and from activities performed abroad by the branch is 35%.

## Income determination

***Inventory valuation***/Inventory valuation is based on the latest purchase. Thus, LIFO may not be elected for tax purposes. Conformity between book and tax reporting is not required.

***Capital gains***/Capital gains and losses attract normal profits tax treatment, except that losses from the sale of shares and other equity interests may be offset only against the same type of income.

***Intercompany dividends***/These dividends are not included in the tax base by the recipient if distributed by an Argentine company. However, see "Withholding taxes" below. Tax is levied if the dividends are distributed by a foreign company.

***Foreign income***/Foreign income received or held undistributed abroad by resident corporations is subject to tax.

**Stock dividends**/These dividends are tax exempt if distributed by an Argentine company. However, see "Withholding taxes" below. Tax is levied if the dividends are paid by a foreign company.

## Deductions

**Depreciation and depletion**/Depreciation is generally computed on a straight-line basis over the technically estimated useful life of the assets, or, alternatively, over their standard useful lives (e.g., machinery and equipment—ten years; furniture—ten years). Depreciation of buildings and other constructions on real estate is 2% per annum on cost (on a straight-line basis), unless it can be proved that useful life is less than 50 years.

Depreciation of automobiles whose original cost exceeds AR$20,000 is not deductible. Related expenses (gasoline vouchers, insurance, rentals, repairs and maintenance, etc.) are deductible up to an amount of AR$7,200 per car per year.

Conformity between book and tax depreciation is not required.

Profit or loss on the sale of depreciated property is determined with reference to cost less depreciation, restated for inflation as at March 1992, and is included in ordinary taxable income.

Percentage depletion is available for natural resources (mines, quarries, woods).

**Net operating losses**/The available life of losses is five years.

**Payments to foreign affiliates**/Transactions between related parties should be at arm's length. This principle was included in the new transfer pricing rules introduced by the 1998 tax reform and was extended to transactions with companies located in low or no tax jurisdictions, by tax reform of October 2003. The tax authorities will determine income by applying one of six methodologies: comparable uncontrolled price, resale price, added cost, profit distribution, residue from profit distribution, and net margin of the transaction. Payments to foreign affiliates or related parties and to companies located in low or no tax jurisdictions that represent income of Argentine source are tax deductible, provided they are paid before the due date for filing the tax return and the corresponding withholding is paid to the tax authorities.

Technical assistance and services that involve transfer of technology should be covered by agreements duly registered with the National Institute of Intellectual Property for information purposes. These transactions are governed by the Transfer of Technology Law (Law No. 22,426).

**Taxes**/Except for profits tax and the tax on minimum notional income, all taxes are deductible.

**Other significant items**/As follows.
1. Donations—When made to societies and associations expressly exempt from assessment to profits tax, donations are admissible deductions up to a maximum of 5% of the donor's net taxable profits, provided certain requirements are fulfilled.
2. Representation expenses—If adequately documented, representation expenses are admissible deductions up to 1.5% of the amount of salaries accrued during the fiscal year.

# Argentina

3. Directors' fees—Amounts up to the greater of 25% of after-tax profit or AR$12,500 per individual are deductible in the financial year to which they refer, provided they are approved and available for the director before the due date of the tax return, or in a later year of payment.

4. Although the Convertibility Law is no longer in place, the adjustment for inflation for tax purposes is not yet in force. There is a strong debate regarding the reinforcement of this procedure for fiscal years ended up to December 2002. No final decision has been taken yet. The wholesale price index for 2002 was 120% and for 2003 was 20%.

5. Thin capitalization—The 1998 tax reform established thin-capitalization rules, which have been amended by tax reform of October 2003, Law No. 25,784. Except for financial institutions governed by Law No. 21,526, interest deductibility will be subject to a test to determine whether interest can be deducted in the same fiscal year or whether it can be transferred to subsequent fiscal years. Recently, Law No. 25,784 has limited the rule to those interests from loans granted by nonresidents' bank entities which additionally have control over the local debtor and which debt exceeds twice the net equity of such local debtor. The portion of nondeductible interest will be treated as dividend.

## Group taxation

Group taxation is not permitted.

## Tax incentives

*Inward investment*/Law No. 23,614, Law No. 23,658, and Decree No. 2054/92 regulate the mechanisms for the replacement of investment incentives, such as those established by Law No. 21,608. The exemption, suspension, and deferment of taxes granted under the incentive schemes have been replaced by the granting of tax credit bonds, which are delivered by the government by means of a current account based on the theoretical fiscal cost declared by the companies and insofar as the investment objectives stated for recent years have been reached. In addition, the system allows companies to renounce the benefits by paying 40% of the taxes that were originally waived as a result of the industrial promotion scheme and 100% of the amounts offset against the current account mentioned above. This mechanism implies a significant reduction of industries in these schemes, since only those in a position to comply with the objectives included in each investment project will remain.

*Mining activity*/Law No. 24,196/93 created an investment regime for mining activity and is applicable to natural and legal persons. Mining ventures included within this regime enjoy fiscal stability (i.e., tax rates will remain basically the same) for a term of 30 years, except for VAT, which will adjust to the general regime. Furthermore, the regime grants incentives for profits tax, tax on assets, import duties, and any other tax for introduction of certain assets. Additionally, Law No. 25,429 (which amends Law No. 24,196/93) sets forth the possibility to obtain a VAT reimbursement during the exploring stage.

Law No. 24,402 establishes a regime under which credit lines are granted for the financing of VAT on the purchase or definitive import of new capital goods available for all export products industries or on infrastructure works for the mining industry.

Interest is payable by the national government. In addition, the law provides for a regime to obtain the advanced recovery of VAT that applies exclusively to the mining sector. It permits the return of tax amounts paid within 60 days of the investment, purchase, or import.

*Forestry*/Law No. 25,080 established an investment regime for plantation, protection, and maintenance of forests. It contains rules similar to those for mining activity tax incentives.

*Export incentives*/Exports are exempt from value-added and excise taxes. The temporary importation of raw materials and intermediate and packaging goods for the manufacture of products for export is free from duties with the obligation of offering sufficient guaranties for the import.

*Export taxes*/Export taxes were introduced in March 2002, with rates ranging from 5% to 20% depending on the products exported.

## Withholding taxes

In general terms, withholding tax is not applicable to dividends, regardless of the recipient. Gains on the sale of shares are also exempt. As from January 1, 1999, income tax withholding at a rate of 35% is applicable on dividends or other profits distributed by the company if the corresponding amounts have not been subject to income tax in the hands of the company. Other payments to residents and to nonresidents are subject to withholding rates as follows.

| Recipient | Interest (1) | Royalties (1, 2) |
|---|---|---|
| | % | % |
| Resident corporations | 6 or 28 (3) | 6 (4) |
| Resident individuals | 6 or 28 (3) | 6 (4) |
| Nonresident corporations and individuals: | | |
| Nontreaty | 15.05 or 35 | 21 or 28 |
| Treaty: | | |
| Australia | 12 | 10 or 15 |
| Austria | 12.5 | 15 |
| Belgium | 0 or 12 (5) | 3, 5, 10, or 15 |
| Bolivia | 15.05 or 35 | 21 or 28 |
| Brazil | 15.05 or 35 | 21 or 28 |
| Canada | 12.5 | 3, 5, 10, or 15 |
| Chile | 15.05 or 35 | 21 or 28 |
| Denmark | 12 (5) | 3, 5, 10, or 15 |
| Finland | 15 | 3, 5, 10, or 15 |
| France | 15.05 or 20 (6) | 18 |
| Germany | 10 or 15 (7) | 15 |
| Italy | 15.05 or 20 (6) | 10 or 18 |
| Netherlands | 12 | 3, 5, 10, or 15 |
| Norway | 12.5 (8) | 3, 5, 10, or 15 |
| Spain | 12.5 | 3, 5, 10, or 15 |
| Sweden | 12.5 | 3, 5, 10, or 15 |
| Switzerland | 12 | 3, 5, 10, or 15 |
| United Kingdom | 12 (5) | 3, 5, 10, or 15 |

The numbers in parentheses refer to the following numbered Notes.

# Argentina

Notes:

1. Withholding from payments of interest and royalties to nonresidents is based on a flat rate of 35% applied to an assumed percentage gross profit margin. This margin is not contestable, but the resultant rate may be limited by bilateral treaty. Under the 1998 tax reform, the general margin for interest paid for credits obtained abroad is 100%. However, a margin of 43% is applicable (1) if the debtor is a local bank, (2) if the creditor is a foreign financial institution located in a country not considered as a low or no tax jurisdiction or in countries that have signed an agreement with Argentina for exchange of information and have no bank secret, which are under the supervision of the respective central bank, (3) if the interest is paid on a loan dedicated to the purchase of tangible assets other than cars, (4) if the interest is paid on debt certificates (private bonds) issued by local companies and registered in certain countries that have signed an agreement with Argentina for the protection of investments, and (5) on interest paid on time deposits with local banks. "Royalties" covers a variety of concepts. The rates given in this column relate specifically to services derived from agreements ruled by the Foreign Technology Law, as follows.

   a. Technical assistance, technology, and engineering not obtainable in Argentina—21% (35% on assumed profit of 60%).

   b. Cession of rights or licenses for invention patents exploitation and technical assistance obtainable in Argentina—28% (35% on assumed profit of 80%).

      (On nonregistered agreements the rate is 31.5% (profit of 90% is assumed) or 35% (profit of 100% is assumed), depending on the case.)

   Several other concepts of "royalties" are subject to rates that, in turn, may be limited by treaty. A broad sample of these concepts and the nontreaty effective rates is set forth in Note 2.

2. Payments to nonresidents (only) for "royalties," rentals, fees, commissions, and so on, in respect of the following are subject to withholding at the rates given below on the basis of assumed gross profit margins (Note 1) unless limited by treaty. The treaty concerned should be consulted to determine any limitation in each case.

|  | % |
|---|---|
| Freight and passenger bookings (other than those covered by special treaties), news and feature services, insurance underwriting | 3.5 |
| Containers | 7.0 |
| Copyright | 12.25 |
| Rental of movable assets | 14.0 |
| Motion picture, video and sound tape rentals and royalties; radio, television, telex, and telefax transmissions; any other means for projection, reproduction, transmission, or diffusion of image or sound; sale of assets located in Argentina (9, 10) | 17.5 |
| Rental of real estate (9) | 21.0 |
| Any other Argentine-source income (unless the nonresident is or was temporarily resident) | 31.5 |

3. The higher tax rate is applicable on nonregistered taxpayers. On interest paid to corporations by financial entities or stock exchange/open market brokers, income tax must be withheld at 3% (10% if not registered); individuals are tax exempt.

4. Resident corporations and individuals who are registered for tax purposes are subject to 6% withholding (28% if not registered).

5. Interest is exempt if paid on credit sales of machinery or other equipment, specific bank loans at preferential rate or loans by public entities.

6. The treaty limits taxation of interest to 20% (registered).

7. The 10% rate is applicable to interest on credit sales of capital equipment, any bank loan or any financing of public works; otherwise 15%.

8. Interest paid on loans with guarantee of the Norwegian Institute for Credit Guarantees, or paid in relation to imports of industrial equipment is tax exempt.

9. Deduction of actual costs and expenses may be optionally exercised.

10. Gains on the sale of shares are exempt, except for companies, permanent establishments, or other entities residing abroad whose main activity based on their statutes consists of investments to be made outside of their country of formation. These entities are subject to income tax withholding at the definite flat rate of 17.5%.

## Tax administration

*Returns*/Tax is assessed on a fiscal-year, self-assessment basis. The due date for filing the profits and the notional income tax return is during the second week of the fifth month after the fiscal year end.

*Payment of tax*/Installment payments on account of profits tax must be made in the course of the tax year. The installment payments must be made at a monthly basis beginning in the first month after the due date of filing of the tax returns.

## Exchange control regime

As a result of the devaluation of the Argentine peso, several regulations were issued to limit the transfer of money abroad, and they have been made more flexible up to date.

Regulations referring to the entrance of funds to the country, the obligation of liquidation of foreign currency in the Exchange Market of payments of exports of goods and services, remain in force. The terms to comply with the liquidation obligation vary between 60 and 360 days.

There are no restrictions for the payment abroad of interest, dividends or profits, royalties and other commercial payments duly supported by the corresponding documentation. Payment abroad for other concepts may be subject to prior approval from the Central Bank.

# Argentina

## *CORPORATION TAX CALCULATION*

Fiscal year ended December 31, 2003

| | | |
|---|---:|---:|
| Net income before taxes (1, 2) ............................................................ | | AR$ 1,000,000 |
| Add: | | |
|    Adjustment of inventories valuation...................................... | 90,000 | |
|    Adjustment of depreciation of fixed assets.......................... | 73,600 | |
|    Nondeductible interest.......................................................... | 2,000 | |
|    Provision for bad debts ........................................................ | 8,400 | 174,000 |
| | | 1,174,000 |
| Deduct: | | |
|    Royalties to affiliate for prior years, paid after | | |
|       previous tax filing............................................................ | 80,000 | |
|    Actual bad debts................................................................... | 2,000 | 82,000 |
| Taxable income ................................................................................... | | AR$ 1,092,000 |
| Determination of profits tax (35% on 1,092,000)................................... | | AR$ 382,200 |

Notes:

1.  Net income before taxes is that arising from historical cost and fixed asset accounting restatement. Adjustments for inventories, depreciation, and inflation vary according to tax rules. Statutory financial statements incorporate an integral restatement to current purchasing power, which is omitted for tax computation purposes and not contemplated above.
2.  Branch taxable income would be similarly determined.
3.  Exchange rate of the peso at March 23, 2004: US$1 = AR$2.83.

## PwC contact

For additional information on taxation in Australia, contact:

Ann M. Previtera
PricewaterhouseCoopers
201 Sussex Street
Sydney, New South Wales 2000
Australia
Telephone: (61) (2) 8266 2946
Fax: (61) (2) 8266 5658
e-mail: ann.previtera@au.pwc.com

## Significant developments

Australia is still experiencing the aftermath of major tax reform. Some details are given below.

The transitional period for certain concessions for groups electing into Australia's tax consolidation regime ends on June 30, 2004. From July 1, 2002, 100% owned companies and some trusts may elect to be taxed as a consolidated group if they are ultimately held by a single entity resident in Australia that is taxed as a company. Australian subsidiaries that are 100% owned by a foreign company and that have no common Australian head company between the nonresident parent and the Australian-resident subsidiaries are also allowed to consolidate. Significant details of how this regime applies are still being developed. Previously available group relief is repealed subject to some exceptions. See "Group taxation."

At the time of writing, the federal government is proposing to release a further exposure draft of legislation that replaces the existing rules for the tax treatment of asset financing by tax preferred or tax exempt entities. The government proposes that the new rules will be introduced by July 1, 2004, and apply to transactions entered into after the date of enactment.

The first cut of the long-awaited reform of the foreign exchange rules, including comprehensive currency conversion rules and "functional currency" rules has been legislated with effect from July 1, 2003. See "Other significant items."

## Taxes on corporate income

Companies are subject to federal tax on their income at a flat rate of 30%. There are no state or municipal taxes on income.

## Corporate residence

A company is a resident of Australia for income tax purposes if it is incorporated in Australia or, if not incorporated in Australia, it carries on business in Australia and either (1) its central management and control are in Australia or (2) its voting power is controlled by shareholders who are residents of Australia.

## Other taxes

*Goods and services tax*/The federal government levies goods and services tax (GST) at a rate of 10%, and distributes the revenue to state governments. The GST is a value-added tax (VAT) applied at each level in the manufacturing and marketing chain and applies to most goods and services, with registered suppliers getting credits for GST on inputs acquired to make taxable supplies. Food, with some significant exceptions, exports and most health, medical and educational supplies, and some other supplies are "GST-free" (the equivalent of "zero-rated" in other VAT jurisdictions) and so not subject to GST. A registered supplier of a GST-free supply can recover relevant input tax credits, although the supply is not taxable. Residential rents, the second or later supply of residential premises, most financial supplies, and some other supplies are "input-taxed" ("exempt" in other VAT jurisdictions) and are not subject to GST, but the supplier cannot recover relevant input tax credits, except that financial suppliers may obtain a reduced input tax credit of 75% of the GST on the acquisition of certain services. Health insurance is GST-free. Life insurance is input taxed. General insurance is taxed. "Reverse charges" may apply to services or rights supplied from offshore, where the recipient is registered or required to be registered, and uses the supply solely or partly for a noncreditable supply.

*Luxury car tax*/Luxury car tax is levied by the federal government at the rate of 25% of the value of the car that exceeds the luxury car tax threshold, and is payable on the GST-exclusive value above the threshold. No input tax credit is available for luxury car tax, regardless of whether the car is used for business or private purposes.

*Wine equalization tax*/The federal government levies wine equalization tax (WET) at the wholesale level at a rate of 29% in addition to GST, and it applies to wine from grapes and fruit and certain vegetable wines. Retailers do not get an input tax credit for WET. Certain rebates are available to assist small winemakers.

*Import and excise duties*/Imports into Australia are subject to duties under the Australian Customs Tariff. Except for textile, clothing, and footwear items and motor vehicles, the top duty rate is 5%. Excise duties are imposed at high levels and on beer, spirits, liqueurs, tobacco, cigarettes, and petroleum products. There is a cleaner fuels grants scheme.

*Fringe benefits tax*/The federal government levies fringe benefits tax (FBT) on employers at the rate of 48.5% on the grossed-up value of noncash fringe benefits provided to employees and their associates by the employer or associates. The grossing-up of the value ensures tax neutrality between providing benefits and cash remuneration. FBT is deductible for income tax purposes. There are some exemptions, including for some minor benefits, remote area housing in certain circumstances and for specified relocation costs, and there are some concessional valuation rules, in particular for living-away-from-home benefits. Car fringe benefits are taxed under two valuation methods.

*Stamp duty*/All states and territories impose stamp duty on a wide variety of transactions at different rates. All jurisdictions impose stamp duty on real estate conveyances, but most exempt conveyances of goods (not associated with other property) from stamp duty. Corporate reconstruction exemptions are available and advice from a stamp duty specialist should usually be obtained where substantial stamp duty may be imposed, because the amount of duty may depend on the form of the transaction.

*Payroll tax*/States and territories impose on employers a tax on their payroll, widely defined but with small differences between jurisdictions. There is an exemption for employers with an annual payroll below a certain level, after taking into account grouping rules. In New South Wales currently the rate is 6% and the annual exemption threshold is A$600,000. In Victoria currently the rate is 5.25% and the annual exemption threshold is A$550,000. A variety of rates and thresholds apply in other jurisdictions.

*Insurance tax*/States impose duties which may be substantial on insurance premiums.

*Debits tax*/Some states and territories, but not New South Wales, levy a tax on debits to accounts kept with banks and nonbank financial institutions. Some jurisdictions are proposing to abolish debits tax, in general by July 1, 2005.

*Land tax*/All states and territories (except the Northern Territory) impose a tax based on the unimproved capital value of land.

*Local municipal taxes*/Local taxes, including water, sewerage, and drainage charges are levied based on the unimproved capital value of land and include a charge for usage, for example, water usage.

*Superannuation guarantee levy*/The federal government effectively requires employers to contribute 9% of an employee's earnings base, subject to limited exceptions, to a registered superannuation fund or retirement savings account on behalf of the employee. Failure to make these contributions will result in the employer being liable for a nondeductible superannuation guarantee charge.

No level of Australian government imposes a social security levy.

## Branch income

Branch profits are subject to ordinary corporate rates of taxation, and there is no withholding on repatriated profits.

## Income determination

*Inventory valuation*/Inventory may generally be valued at cost (full absorption cost), market selling value or replacement price. Where, because of obsolescence or other special circumstances, inventory should be valued at a lower amount, the lower valuation may generally be chosen, provided it is a reasonable valuation. Special rules apply, however, regarding the valuation of trading stock for certain companies joining a consolidated group. LIFO is not an acceptable basis of determining cost, nor is direct costing in respect of manufactured goods and work-in-progress.

Conformity is not required between book and tax reporting. For tax purposes inventory may be valued at cost, market selling value or replacement price, regardless of how inventory is valued for book purposes. Those who choose to come within the simplified tax system (STS) for small-business taxpayers (broadly defined as taxpayers with an "STS average turnover" of less than A$1 million for the year and depreciating assets with tax depreciation written down values at the end of that year of less than A$3 million) may ignore the difference between the opening and closing value of trading stock if on a reasonable estimate this is not more than A$5,000.

*Capital gains*/Capital gains tax applies to assets acquired on or after September 20, 1985. Capital gains realized on the disposal of such assets are included in assessable income and are subject to tax at the company tax rate, if the disposal is by a company. In order to determine the quantum of any gain, the cost base is indexed according to price movements since acquisition, as measured by the

# Australia

official Consumer Price Index until September 30, 1999 (provided the asset has been held for at least 12 months). There is no indexation of the cost base for price movements after October 1, 1999. Disposals of plant and equipment are subject to general rules rather than the capital gains tax rules, with indexation of the cost base frozen as at September 30, 1999 for relevant assets, and the excess of disposal proceeds over the frozen indexed cost base being taxed as a balancing adjustment. Capital losses are allowable as deductions only against capital gains and cannot be offset against other income. In calculating capital losses there is no indexation of the cost base.

Residents of Australia are liable for the tax on gains on the disposal of assets wherever situated, subject to relief from double taxation if the gain is derived and taxed in another country. Nonresidents are liable for tax on gains on the disposal of assets having a "necessary connection with Australia," defined broadly as including land or a building situated in Australia, assets used in carrying on a business through a permanent establishment in Australia, shares in Australian private companies, interests in resident trusts, interests owned in partnership assets that are taxable Australian assets, and shareholdings of 10% or more in the issued capital of Australian public companies.

The government has announced proposals to exempt Australian resident companies (and controlled foreign companies—see below) from capital gains tax on capital gains made on the disposal of nonportfolio interests in foreign companies with an underlying active business. At the time of writing, legislation to give effect to this announcement had not yet been released.

Rollover relief is available for scrip-for-scrip takeovers between companies (and also trusts) provided at least 80% of the target entity is acquired; this rollover is not limited to listed or Australian entities. "Demerger" rollover relief is available where the head entity of a group transfers ownership of one or more of its subsidiaries to its shareholders provided at least 80% of the interests in the demerged entity are acquired by the owners of the head entity of the group and they receive interests in the demerged entity in the same proportion as their original interests. There are other requirements. The government is currently considering proposals to counter the avoidance of Australian capital gains tax by nonresidents who dispose of an interposed entity holding Australian assets rather than the assets themselves. Under the proposal, Australian tax would not apply to the gain on the sale of the interposed entity if the gain was subject to tax in broad-exemption listed countries (Canada, France, Germany, Japan, New Zealand, the United Kingdom, and the United States) or would have been subject to tax in such a country except for recognized rollover relief. However, at the time of writing, no legislation dealing with this proposal has been introduced.

Rollover relief from capital gains tax is available on the transfer of assets between companies sharing 100% common ownership, provided the transfer is between nonresident companies, or between a nonresident company, on the one hand, and, on the other hand, a member of a consolidated group or multiple entry consolidated (MEC) group, or a resident company that is not a member of a consolidatable group. See "Group taxation."

*Intercompany dividends*/A "gross-up and credit" mechanism applies to franked dividends (dividends paid out of profits which have been subject to Australian tax) received by Australian companies from July 1, 2002. The corporate shareholder grosses up the dividend received for tax paid by the paying company (i.e., franking credits attaching to the dividend) and is then entitled to a tax offset. Subject to certain transitional provisions, dividends paid from July 1, 2000 to another resident company that are unfranked (because they are paid out of profits not subject to Australian tax) are taxable, unless they are paid before July 1, 2003 within a wholly owned group, or within a group that has chosen to be consolidated for tax purposes. Dividends paid between companies within a tax consolidated group are ignored for the purposes of determining the taxable income of the group.

To compensate for the removal of the intercorporate dividend rebate for dividends paid on or after July 1, 2000, a tax deduction is potentially available to certain nonresident-owned companies resident in Australia if the dividend they receive is taxed because of the operation of the new rules and is received from a company in which they hold at least 10% of the voting power. The deduction is allowed to the extent that the dividend is on-paid to a nonresident 100% parent company. Certain other conditions must also be satisfied. Foreign dividends are not eligible for a tax rebate but are tax exempt if received from a foreign affiliate resident in a comparable tax country where the Australian-resident company has a voting power of at least 10% in the foreign affiliate. An exemption from tax also applies to the repatriation of income of a nonresident entity in which Australian residents hold interests where the income has been previously attributed to those residents and taxed in Australia (see below).

Dividends paid out of "disqualifying accounts" (i.e., share capital accounts or, subject to certain exceptions, asset revaluation reserves) are not rebatable and are unfrankable.

Where a company transfers an amount to a share capital account from another account, the capital account will become a tainted share capital account. Until it becomes "untainted," any distribution debited to such an account is treated as an unfrankable and nonrebatable dividend.

A dividend imputation system allows Australian corporations to pass tax credits to individual resident shareholders, certain superannuation entities, life insurance companies in respect of their superannuation business and certain registered organizations such as registered trade unions and friendly societies, in respect of Australian tax imposed on profits from which dividends (including stock dividends treated as dividends) are paid.

A resident corporation receiving a franked dividend, that is, a dividend paid out of Australian taxed profits, may further distribute the imputed tax credits to its own resident shareholders. Franked dividends paid to nonresidents are exempt from dividend withholding tax

Companies that are effectively wholly owned by nonresidents (known as "exempting companies") may provide franking benefits only in limited circumstances. However, nonresident shareholders in receipt of franked dividends from exempting companies continue to be exempt from dividend withholding tax.

There is legislation designed to prevent the selective streaming of franking credits to different shareholders. Selection plans under which shareholders are given a choice of a tax-free bonus share (stock dividend), unfranked dividend or franked dividend in lieu of another dividend are no longer effective. Under debt and equity classification rules there may be situations where interest income is treated as if it were a dividend. Similarly, dividends paid on shares that are debt interests will not be frankable or rebatable.

# Australia

The dividend imputation system operates in the following way. The franking account is credited with tax paid. The corporate entity paying a dividend may determine the extent to which a dividend is franked, subject to antistreaming rules and benchmarking rules that limit the ability to change the franking percentage in later periods. As indicated above, generally from July 1, 2002, fully franked intercompany dividends are effectively untaxed under a "gross-up and credit" method as the intercompany dividend rebate with respect to franked dividends is repealed. A proposal that would have allowed franking credits for foreign dividend withholding tax on dividends received, has been dropped in favor of negotiating lower dividend withholding tax rates in tax treaties.

A shareholder is entitled to franking credits on dividends only in respect of ordinary shares held "at risk" for at least 45 days (90 days for preference shares). There is an exemption from these franking credit trading rules for individuals, provided the imputation rebates received in the year of income do not exceed A$5,000 and the individual is not obliged to make a payment related to the dividend.

*Foreign income/* The basis on which the foreign income of corporations resident in Australia is taxed is set out below. A number of measures relating to the taxation of international arrangements have been foreshadowed by the government, although at the time of writing, legislation to give effect to these measures and the date of effect had not been released. Some of these measures are also highlighted below.

1. In general, nonactive income of foreign entities controlled by Australian residents is attributed to those residents if the entity is resident in a broad-exemption listed country (see the table below) and the nonactive income is concessionally taxed, or if the entity is resident in other countries and the entity earns more than 5% of its income from nonactive sources ("active income test"). It is proposed from July 1, 2004 that income and gains of an entity resident in a broad-exemption listed country will only be attributable if it is of a type listed in regulations. Regulations to give effect to this proposal have yet to be released.

2. There is an exemption from tax for the repatriation of income previously taxed on attribution.

3. There is an exemption from Australian tax for dividends received by a resident company from foreign affiliates resident in a broad-exemption listed country or limited-exemption listed country (see the table below), where the resident company has a (nonportfolio) voting interest of at least 10% in the foreign affiliate. The government proposes to extend this exemption to all foreign nonportfolio dividends, but at the time of writing, legislation to give effect to that proposal had not been released.

4. There is an exemption from tax for the branch profits of a resident company from carrying on business through a permanent establishment in a broad-exemption listed country where the income is subject to tax rules comparable to those of Australia and in other listed countries where the income is active income or an active-income test is satisfied. The government proposes to extend this exemption to certain branch profits and gains derived in all foreign countries, although at the time of writing, legislation to give effect to that proposal had not been released.

5. Foreign income of Australian resident corporations that is not exempt (as broadly described above) is subject to tax, but a credit for foreign tax is allowed to the extent of Australian tax payable on foreign income computed in three separate classes: passive income, offshore banking income, and other income.

6. There are also measures to deal with passive foreign investment funds (FIFs) (including interests in foreign companies, foreign trusts, and foreign life insurance policies). Essentially, and subject to important qualifications, the FIF rules tax (attribute) increases or deemed increases in the value of interests held by Australian residents in offshore entities (wherever located), except for some categories that are specifically exempted. Investments in foreign companies listed on approved stock exchanges that are principally engaged in certain active businesses are exempt. There are several other exemptions.

The broad-exemption listed countries and limited-exemption listed countries are shown in the following tables.

## Broad-exemption listed countries

| | | |
|---|---|---|
| Canada* | Japan | United Kingdom |
| France* | New Zealand | United States |
| Germany* | | |

*Country where currently certain entities may be treated as deriving designated concession income to a greater extent than provided for by the rules applying generally to broad-exemption listed countries. As highlighted above, the government has announced that changes will be made to the types of income which will be liable to attribution in broad-exemption listed countries.

## Limited-exemption listed countries

| | | |
|---|---|---|
| Argentina | Israel | Russian Federation |
| Austria | Italy | Saudi Arabia |
| Bangladesh | Kenya | Singapore |
| Belgium | Kiribati | Slovak Republic |
| Brazil | Korea, Rep. of | Solomon Islands |
| Brunei | Luxembourg | South Africa |
| Bulgaria | Malaysia | Spain |
| China, P.R.* | Malta | Sri Lanka |
| Czech Republic | Mexico | Sweden |
| Denmark | Myanmar | Switzerland |
| Fiji | Netherlands | Taiwan |
| Finland | New Caledonia | Thailand |
| French Polynesia | Norway | Tokelau |
| Greece | Pakistan | Tonga |
| Hungary | Papua New Guinea | Turkey |
| Iceland | Philippines | Tuvalu |
| India | Poland | Vietnam |
| Indonesia | Portugal | Western Samoa |
| Iran | Romania | Zimbabwe |
| Ireland, Rep. of | | |

*Does not include Hong Kong Special Administrative Region.

***Stock dividends*/**Stock dividends, or the issue of bonus shares, as they are known under Australian law, are in general not taxed as a dividend, and the tax treatment is the spreading of the cost base of the original shares across the original shares and the bonus shares. However, if a company credits its share capital account with profits when issuing bonus shares, this will "taint" the share capital account (if it is not already a tainted share capital account), causing the bonus share issue to be a dividend. Certain other rules may apply to bonus share issues, depending on the facts.

## Deductions

***Depreciation and depletion*/**A capital allowances regime allows a deduction for the decline in value of depreciating assets held by a taxpayer. The "holder" of the asset is entitled to the deduction and may be the economic, rather than the legal, owner. A "depreciating asset" is an asset that has a limited effective life and can reasonably be expected to decline in value over the time it is used, but does not include land, trading stock or, subject to certain exceptions, intangible assets. Deductions are available for certain other capital expenditure.

Intangible assets that are "depreciating assets" (if they are not trading stock) include the following.

- Certain mining, quarrying, or prospecting rights and information.
- Items of intellectual property.
- "In-house" software.
- Indefeasible rights to use an international telecommunications submarine cable system.
- Spectrum licenses under radio communications legislation.
- Data casting transmitter licenses.

Goodwill is not a depreciating asset, for which tax amortization is available.

Taxpayers that do not qualify as small-business must depreciate the asset over its useful life (known as "effective life"), using either straight-line (known as the "prime cost" method) or diminishing-value method (straight-line rate multiplied by 150%).

Taxpayers may self-determine the effective life of a unit of plant or may choose the effective life contained in a published determination of the Commissioner of Taxation. Accelerated depreciation rates may apply for plant and equipment that was acquired, or the construction of which began, before 11:45 a.m. AEST on September 21, 1999, except for an item owned by a subsidiary member of a tax consolidated group, where under tax consolidation rules the tax cost of the item has increased, when reset. Intangible depreciating assets in general have a legislated effective life.

Nonsmall-business taxpayers are able to choose to write off all items costing less than A$1,000 through a low-value pool at a diminishing-value rate of 37.5%.

For those who choose to come within the STS for small-business taxpayers (broadly defined as taxpayers with an "STS average turnover" of less than A$1 million for the year and depreciating assets with tax depreciation written down values at the end of that year of less than A$3 million) a simplified depreciation system applies with more attractive depreciation rates.

"Project pool" rules allow expenditure that does not itself form part of a depreciating asset to be deductible over the life of a project that is carried on for a taxable purpose. Items included in the rules include the following.

- Amounts paid to create or upgrade community infrastructure for a community associated with the project.
- Site preparation costs for depreciating assets (except horticultural plants in certain circumstances).
- Amounts incurred for feasibility studies for a project.
- Environmental assessment costs applicable to the project.
- Amounts incurred to obtain information associated with the project.
- Amounts incurred in seeking to obtain a right to intellectual property.
- Costs of ornamental trees or shrubs.

Certain capital expenditure if it is incurred on or after July 1, 2001 and under a contract entered into on or after that date, can be written off on a straight-line basis over a period of five years, including the following provided the business was, or will be, carried on for a taxable purpose.

- Business structure establishment costs, including costs of incorporating a company, setting up a partnership or trust and costs of obtaining relevant information in connection with the business structure.
- Converting a business structure to a different structure.
- Equity-raising costs such as prospectus and underwriting costs.
- Takeover defense costs.
- Costs of unsuccessfully attempting a takeover.
- Costs of liquidating a company through which the taxpayer carried on a business.
- Costs to stop carrying on a business.

Special rates apply for primary producer assets, such as horticultural plants, water and land care assets, and the treatment of expenditure on R&D (see "Tax incentives") and on certain Australian films (expenditure on certain Australian films may be deducted either over one or two years).

A "luxury car" cost limit applies for depreciating the cost of certain passenger motor vehicles (A$57,009, cost limit for 2003/2004).

Expenditure on the development of "in-house" software may be allocated to a "soft development pool" and written off over three years, starting in the year after the expenditure was incurred (40% in year 2, 40% in year 3, and 20% in year 4). Amounts spent on acquiring computer software or the right to use it (except where the acquisition is for developing in-house software) is treated as incurred on acquiring a depreciating asset, deductible in the first year it is first used or installed ready for use. The effective life is two and one-half years. "Shrink-wrapped" software acquired or manufactured for sale is treated as trading stock.

A loss arising on the sale of a "depreciating asset" (depreciated value of the asset less sale consideration) is an allowable deduction. A gain on the sale of a "depreciating asset," to the extent of depreciation recaptured, is taxed as ordinary income. Gains exceeding the amount of depreciation recaptured are also taxed as ordinary income after deducting the cost base. (This cost base includes indexation for inflation up to September 30, 1999 if the asset was acquired before 11:45 A.M. AEST on September 21, 1999, and has been held for at least 12 months.)

The cost of income-producing structural improvements the construction of which started after February 26, 1992 is eligible for write-off for tax purposes on the same basis as that of income-producing buildings, that is, at a rate of 2.5% per annum.

Subject to exceptions referred to below, capital expenditure incurred after September 15, 1987 in the construction or improvement of nonresidential buildings used for producing assessable income is amortized over 40 years at an annual 2.5% rate. Capital expenditure on the construction of buildings used for short-term traveler accommodation (e.g., hotels, motels) and industrial buildings (typically, factories) is amortized over 25 years at an annual 4% rate where construction commenced after February 26, 1992. The cost of eligible building construction that commenced after August 21, 1984 and before September 16, 1987 (or construction contracted before September 16, 1987) is amortized over 25 years at an annual 4% rate. There is no recapture of the amortized amount upon disposal of the building, except where the expenditure is incurred after May 13, 1997, in which case recapture will apply, subject to certain transitional rules.

Similar provisions apply in relation to income-producing residential buildings on which construction commenced after July 17, 1985.

The cost of consumables may be either written off immediately, or as used. The following expenditure attracts an immediate 100% deduction: environmental protection activities, dealing with pollution and waste; money paid for the issue of shares in a "film licensed investment company"; "land care" operations; exploring or prospecting for minerals; mine site rehabilitation.

Tax depreciation is not required to conform with book depreciation.

Percentage depletion based on gross income or other noncost criteria is not available.

**Net operating losses**/Primary production losses for all income years and other losses incurred in 1989/1990 and subsequent income years may be carried forward indefinitely, subject to compliance with tests of continuity of more than 50% of ultimate stock ownership or, alternatively, "same business." For consolidated group companies the ability to carry forward these losses is determined by a modified version of these tests. Also see "Group taxation." Companies (including tax consolidated groups) can choose the proportion of their carry forward and current year losses to be deducted in a year. Making this choice deals with the situation where untaxed franked dividends and the imputation credit on such dividends would otherwise absorb carry forward and current year losses.

**Payments to foreign affiliates**/A corporation can deduct royalties, management service fees and interest charges paid to nonresidents, provided the amounts are commercially realistic. Debt and equity rules classify financial arrangements as either debt or equity interests, focusing on economic substance rather than legal form and taking into account related schemes, and extending beyond shares the interests in a company that are equity for tax purposes. In this situation, interest expense on nonshare equity would be treated as a dividend, which is potentially frankable, and would be nondeductible for the paying company/group. Thin capitalization measures apply to the total debt of the Australian operations of multinational groups (including branches of those groups). The measures cover investment into Australia of foreign multinationals and outward investment of

Australian-based multinationals, and include a safe-harbor debt-to-equity ratio of 3:1; interest deductions are denied to the extent that borrowing exceeds the safe-harbor ratio. Where borrowing exceeds the safe-harbor ratio, multinationals are not affected by the rules if they can satisfy the arm's length test (that the borrowing could have been borne by an independent entity). A further alternative test is available for outward investing entities based on 120% of their worldwide debt. The thin capitalization rules apply to inward investment into Australia, where a foreign entity carries on business through an Australian permanent establishment or has direct investments in Australia or in broad terms five or fewer nonresidents have at least 50%, or a single nonresident has at least 40% of an Australian entity that has incurred interest expenses that might otherwise be deductible against its Australian taxable income. Separate rules apply to financial institutions. To facilitate their inclusion in the rules, branches are required to prepare financial accounts.

*Taxes*/In general, GST input tax credits, GST and adjustments under the GST Act are disregarded for income tax purposes. Other taxes, including property, payroll, fringe benefits, and other business taxes, excluding income tax, are deductible to the extent they are incurred in producing assessable income or necessarily incurred in carrying on a business for this purpose, and are not of a capital or private nature.

*Other significant items*/Where expenditure for services is incurred in advance, deductibility of that expenditure will be prorated over the period during which the services will be provided, up to a maximum of ten years. Exceptions apply if the totality of services is provided within 13 months of the date of the expenditure and the prepayment is incurred by small businesses or outside of a business, for example, by an individual in respect of what a government press release refers to as "a standard negatively geared investment, such as rental property or shares."

The amount of a commercial debt "forgiven" (other than an intra-group debt within a tax consolidated group) that is not otherwise assessable or does not otherwise reduce an allowable deduction is applied to reduce the debtor's carryforward tax deductions for revenue tax losses, capital losses, undeducted capital losses, undeducted capital expenditure, and other capital cost bases in a certain order. Any amount not so applied is not assessable to the debtor. "Forgiveness" includes the release, waiver or extinguishment of a debt other than by full payment in cash, and the lapsing of the creditor's recovery right by reason of a statute of limitations. The net forgiven amount may in certain circumstances be apportioned among a nonconsolidated group of companies related to the debtor.

General value shifting rules apply to shifts of value, direct or indirect, in respect of loan and equity interests in companies or trusts. Circumstances in which these rules may apply include where there is a direct value shift under a scheme involving equity or loan interests, or where value is shifted out of an asset by the creation of rights in respect of the asset, or where there is a transfer of assets or the provision of services for a consideration other than at market value. The value shifting rules may apply to the head company of a tax consolidated group or MEC group for value shifts also involving entities outside the group, but not to value shifting between group members, which the tax consolidation rules address.

From July 1, 2003 new legislation replacing previous rules ensures foreign currency gains and losses are recognized when realized, regardless of whether there is a conversion into Australian dollars, and are included in or deducted from ordinary income, subject to limited exceptions. There are exceptions to the timing and characterization aspects of the realization approach where the foreign currency gain or loss is closely linked to a capital asset. Rollover relief is available for the issuer of a succession of short-term foreign currency bill or securities, to the extent that money remains outstanding under the facility. To reduce compliance costs with foreign currency denominated bank accounts caused by the FIFO approach mandated in the rules, taxpayers may elect to disregard gains or losses on low balance transaction accounts that satisfy a *de minimis* exemption, or may elect for retranslation by annually restating the balance of the account by reference to deposits, withdrawals, and the exchange rates at the beginning and end of each year. Entities or parts of entities, satisfying certain requirements, are able to choose to account for their activities in a currency other than Australian dollars for income tax purposes as an intermediate step to translating the result into Australian dollars.

## Group taxation

From July 1, 2002, a tax consolidation regime applies for income tax and capital gains tax purposes for companies, partnerships and trusts ultimately 100% owned by a single head company (or certain entities taxed like a company) resident in Australia. Australian resident companies that are 100% owned (either directly or indirectly) by the same foreign company and that have no common Australian head company between them and the nonresident parent are also allowed to consolidate as a multiple entry consolidated group (MEC group). The group that is consolidated for income tax purposes may differ from the group that is consolidated for accounts or for GST purposes. Groups that choose to consolidate must include all 100%-owned entities under an "all-in" rule and the choice to consolidate is irrevocable. However, "eligible tier-1 companies" (being Australian resident companies that have a nonresident shareholder) that are members of a potential MEC group, are not all required to join a MEC group, when it forms, or may form two or more separate MEC groups, if they so choose, of which the same foreign "top company" is the 100% owner. If an eligible tier-1 company joins a particular MEC group, all 100% subsidiaries of the company must also join the group.

While the rules for forming and joining MEC groups allow more flexibility than with consolidated groups, the ongoing rules for MEC groups are more complex, particularly for tax losses and on the disposal of interests in eligible tier-1 companies, which are subject to cost pooling rules. From July 1, 2003, subject to transitional rules for groups with substituted accounting periods and certain exceptions, existing group relief concessions regarding the transfer of losses, capital gains tax rollovers and the intercorporate dividend rebate for unfranked dividends are repealed. See previously under "Capital gains" for the exception with regard to capital gains tax rollovers.

Consolidated groups file a single tax return, ignoring all intra-group transactions. When a consolidated group acquires 100% of an Australian resident entity, so that it becomes a subsidiary member, the cost base of certain assets (in general, those that are nonmonetary) of the joining member are reset for all tax purposes, based on the purchase price plus the entity's liabilities, subject to certain adjustments. In this way acquisitions of 100% of an Australian resident entity by a consolidated group is the tax equivalent of acquiring its assets. Subject to certain tests being passed, tax losses of the joining member may be transferred to the head company, and may be utilized subject to a loss factor, which is broadly the market value of the joining member divided by the market value of the group (including the joining member). The value of the loss factor (referred to as "the available fraction") that applies for transferred losses may reduced by capital injections (or the equivalent) into the group. Franking credits, foreign tax credits and tax losses remain with the group when a member exits, and the cost base of shares in the exiting member is calculated based on the tax value of its assets at the time of exit, less liabilities subject to certain adjustments.

Generally, members of the group are jointly and severally liable for group income tax debts on the default of the head company unless the group liability is covered by a tax sharing agreement (TSA) that satisfies certain legislative requirements. A member who enters into a TSA can achieve a clean exit from the group where a payment is made to the head company in accordance with the TSA. Groups choosing to consolidate during the transitional period of the regime (i.e., July 1, 2002 to June 30, 2004) may be able to make use of more favorable transitional rules for the determination of values of assets and liabilities and the claiming of losses incurred by group members before consolidation. At the time of writing more than 250 pages of tax consolidation legislation have been enacted. However, the Treasury released 30 papers on December 4, 2003 proposing amendments that will be retroactive to July 1, 2002, clarifying aspects of the regime.

## Tax incentives

*Inward investment*/Depending on the nature and size of the investment project, state governments have given rebates from payroll, stamp and land taxes on an ad hoc basis and for limited periods.

*Capital investment*/Incentives for capital investment are as follows.

1.  Accelerated deductions for capital expenditures on the exploration for and extraction of petroleum and other minerals are available and for certain expenditure of primary producers.

2.  Deductions apply to eligible R&D expenditure of up to 125%. To qualify the company must lodge a registration application with the Industry Research & Development Board not later than ten months after the end of the relevant income year. The concessional deduction may be retrospectively cancelled, if subsequent exploitation of the results is not on normal commercial terms and is not "of the kind to be expected of hypothetical persons dealing with each other at arm's length and from positions of similar or like or roughly equivalent bargaining power." Expenditure in acquiring or gaining access to technology, known as "core technology expenditure," is deductible at 100% if the purpose is to carry on eligible R&D. For technology acquisitions occurring after July 23, 1996 the deduction in any year cannot exceed one-third of the amount of expenditure incurred in that year on R&D related to that core technology. Undeducted "core technology expenditure" may be carried forward for deduction in future years, subject to the same requirements. From July 1, 2001, there is an R&D tax offset for certain small companies and a 175% premium rate deduction for certain expenditure years where companies increase their R&D expenditure over a three year period. From July 1, 2002, the concessional deduction is only available for expenditure on a project whose details are set out in an R&D plan that has previously been approved by the company's board of directors or an authorized person. Special grant programs assist corporations in the conduct of research and development in

Australia. These grants are awarded on a discretionary basis and usually cover up to 50% of the R&D costs. Within a consolidated regime, R&D is claimed by the head entity on behalf of the group.

3. Nonresident pension funds that are tax-exempt in their home jurisdiction, are residents of Canada, France, Germany, Japan, the United Kingdom, the United States, or some other prescribed country, and satisfy certain Australian registration requirements are exempt from income tax on the disposal of investments in certain Australian venture capital equity held at risk for at least 12 months. From July 1, 2002 this exemption is extended to other tax-exempt nonresident investors, including managed funds and venture capital fund-of-funds vehicles and taxable nonresidents holding less than 10% of a venture capital limited partnership. These investors are able to invest in eligible venture capital investments through an Australian resident venture capital limited partnership or through a nonresident venture capital limited partnership. The exemption applies to investors from the United States, United Kingdom, Japan, Germany, Canada, Finland, France, Italy, the Netherlands, New Zealand, Norway, Sweden, and Taiwan. Certain activities such as property development, investment in passive entities, retailing and some elements of financial services are excluded from eligibility.

4. Specific tax measures apply to pooled development funds (PDFs). PDFs are investment companies established to provide equity capital to small- and medium-size enterprises. PDFs are taxed on their net income at 25%, except for income from small- and medium-size enterprises, which is taxed at 15%. PDFs are entitled to imputation credits on the receipt of franked dividend income. Dividends from PDFs are tax exempt. Gains on the sale of shares in a PDF are exempt from tax, and losses are not deductible.

5. The taxable income derived from pure offshore banking transactions by an authorized offshore banking unit in Australia is taxed at the rate of 10%.

Other incentives

1. Exports—Cash grants for export-market development expenditure are available to eligible businesses seeking to export Australian-source goods and services.

2. Government purchasing preference—The state and federal governments informally provide preference for goods manufactured in Australia and New Zealand in their purchasing decisions on a case-by-case basis.

## Withholding taxes

| Recipient | Dividends (1) | Interest (2) | Royalties (3) |
|---|---|---|---|
| | % | % | % |
| Resident corporations or individuals ........ | Nil | Nil | Nil |
| Nonresident corporations or individuals: | | | |
| Nontreaty ................................................ | 30 | 10 | 30 |
| Treaty: | | | |
| Argentina ........................................... | 10/15 (4) | 12 | 10/15 (5) |
| Austria ............................................... | 15 | 10 | 10 (6) |
| Belgium.............................................. | 15 | 10 | 10 (6) |
| Canada .............................................. | 5/15 (7) | 10 (7) | 10 (6) |
| China, P.R. (8) ................................... | 15 | 10 | 10 (6) |
| Czech Republic.................................. | 5/15 (9) | 10 | 10 |
| Denmark ............................................ | 15 | 10 | 10 (6) |
| Fiji...................................................... | 20 | 10 | 15 (6) |
| Finland............................................... | 15 | 10 | 10 (6) |
| France................................................ | 15 | 10 | 10 (6) |
| Germany ............................................ | 15 | 10 | 10 (6) |
| Hungary ............................................. | 15 | 10 | 10 (6) |
| India................................................... | 15 | 15 | 10/15 (10) |
| Indonesia .......................................... | 15 | 10 | 10/15 (11) |
| Ireland, Rep. of.................................. | 15 | 10 | 10 (6) |
| Italy.................................................... | 15 | 10 | 10 (6) |
| Japan................................................. | 15 | 10 | 10 (6) |
| Kiribati............................................... | 20 | 10 | 15 (6) |
| Korea, Rep. of ................................... | 15 | 15 | 15 (6) |
| Malaysia............................................. | 15 (12) | 15 | 15 (6) |
| Malta.................................................. | 15 (13) | 15 | 10 (6) |
| Mexico (14) ........................................ | 15 (15) | 10/15 (16) | 10 (6) |
| Netherlands ....................................... | 15 | 10 | 10 (6) |
| New Zealand...................................... | 15 | 10 | 10 (6) |
| Norway............................................... | 15 | 10 | 10 (6) |
| Papua New Guinea ............................ | 15/20 (17) | 10 | 10 (6) |
| Philippines ........................................ | 15/25 (18) | 15 | 15/25 (19) |
| Poland................................................ | 15 | 10 | 10 (6) |
| Romania ............................................ | 5/15 (20) | 10 | 10 |
| Russian Federation (21)...................... | 5/15 (22) | 10 | 10 (23) |
| Singapore .......................................... | 15 | 10 | 10 (6) |
| Slovak Republic ................................. | 15 | 10 | 10 |
| South Africa ....................................... | 15 | 10 | 10 |
| Spain ................................................. | 15 | 10 | 10 (6) |
| Sri Lanka ........................................... | 15 | 10 | 10 (6) |
| Sweden.............................................. | 15 | 10 | 10 (6) |
| Switzerland ........................................ | 15 | 10 | 10 (6) |
| Taiwan................................................ | 10/15 (24) | 10 | 12.5 (6) |
| Thailand............................................. | 15/20 (25) | 10/25 (26) | 15 (6) |
| United Kingdom (27) .......................... | 0/5/15 (28) | 0/10 (29) | 5 (6) |
| United States (30)............................... | 0/5/15/30 (31) | 0/10/15 (32) | 5 (6) (33) |
| Vietnam.............................................. | 10/15 (34) | 10 | 10 (6) |

The numbers in parentheses refer to the following numbered Notes.

# Australia

Notes:

1. Dividends paid to nonresidents are exempt from dividend withholding tax except when paid out of a company that has not borne Australian tax (i.e., unfranked dividends). Dividends include those stock dividends that are taxable. The rates shown apply to dividends on both portfolio investments and substantial holdings. Unfranked dividends paid to nonresidents are exempt from dividend withholding tax to the extent that the dividends are paid out of certain foreign-source dividend income and the company has specified an "FDA (foreign dividend account) declaration percentage" (i.e., declared by the company to have been paid out of an account in relation to these dividends) in relation to the dividend.

   The government has announced that, subject to a review and further consultation, the current FDA will be replaced by a foreign income account that extends relief from Australian dividend withholding tax on nonportfolio dividends to all types of foreign-source income (including portfolio dividends, foreign branch profits and capital gains) passing to nonresident investors. There is also a deduction from July 1, 2000 in certain cases to compensate for the company tax on inter-entity distributions where these are on-paid by holding companies to a 100% parent that is a nonresident (see "Intercompany dividends").

2. Australia's interest withholding tax rate is limited to 10% of gross interest although the treaty may allow for a higher maximum limit. An exemption from withholding tax can be obtained for interest on certain public issues or widely held issues of debentures. Provisions exist to ensure that discounts and other pecuniary benefits derived by nonresidents on various forms of financings are subject to interest withholding tax.

   Interest paid to nonresidents by offshore banking units is exempt from interest withholding tax where offshore borrowings are used in offshore banking activities (including lending to nonresidents). An offshore borrowing is defined as a borrowing from (1) an unrelated nonresident in any currency or (2) a resident or a related person in a currency other than Australian currency.

3. Royalties paid to nonresidents (except in respect of a permanent establishment in Australia of a resident of a treaty country) are subject to 30% withholding tax (on the gross amount of the royalty), unless a double taxation agreement (DTA) provides for a lesser rate.

4. For Australian-sourced dividends paid to a person who directly holds at least 10% of the voting power of the company, the limit is 10% (although note that Australia does not impose withholding tax on franked dividends). For Argentinean-sourced dividends paid to a person who holds at least 25% of the capital in the company, the limit is 10%. A 15% limit applies to other dividends.

5. Source-country tax is limited to 10% of the gross amount of royalties in relation to copyright of literary, dramatic, musical, or other artistic work; the use of industrial or scientific equipment; the supply of scientific, technical or industrial knowledge; assistance ancillary to the above; or certain forbearances in respect of the above. Source-country tax is limited to 10% of the net amount of royalties for certain technical assistance; in all other cases it is limited to 15% of the gross amount of royalties.

6. Tax is limited to the indicated percentage of gross royalty.

7. Under a protocol signed on January 23, 2002 the maximum withholding tax rate on interest is 10%. The Protocol adopts a 5% dividend withholding tax rate to franked dividends paid by an Australian resident company and in the case of dividends paid by a Canadian resident company (other than a nonresident owned investment corporation) to a company that holds directly at least 10% of the voting power in the dividend company. Otherwise the maximum withholding tax rate on dividends will continue to be 15%. The protocol has effect in Australia in relation to dividends, interest, and royalties on or after January 1, 2003.

8. Except Hong Kong and Macau.

9. To the extent that dividends are franked because they are paid out of profits that have borne Australian tax, they are exempt from dividend withholding tax. See note (1). The treaty between Australia and the Czech Republic allows Australia to impose a 5% withholding tax on the franked part of a dividend in certain circumstances. In the Czech Republic a rate of 15% applies to the gross amount of dividends if the dividends are paid to a company which holds directly at least 20% of the capital of the company paying the dividend.

10. The source-country limit under the Indian agreement is 10% for royalties paid in respect of the use of or rights to use industrial, commercial or scientific equipment or for the provision of consulting services related to such equipment. In other cases the limit is 15%.

11. The source-country limit under the Indonesian agreement is 10% for royalties paid in respect of the use of or the right to use any industrial, commercial, or scientific equipment or for the supply of scientific, technical, industrial, or commercial knowledge or information, and it is 15% in other cases.

12. Malaysia and Australia signed a Second Protocol to its DTA which entered into force on July 23, 2003. The Second Protocol updates the Dividend Article to reflect current treaty practice, that is, upon entry into force, a nil dividend withholding tax rate will apply to franked dividends paid by an Australian resident company to an entity that holds directly at least 10% of the voting power in the dividend paying company, otherwise a 15% withholding tax rate applies. In relation to dividends paid by a company resident of Malaysia, no withholding tax applies. The Second Protocol has effect in Australia in relation to any year of income beginning on or after July 1, 2004 and has effect in respect of Malaysian tax for any year of assessment beginning on or after January 1, 2004 (other than tax sparing provisions which apply retrospectively). Before those times, the DTA limits withholding tax on dividends paid by Australian resident companies to 15% and a nil rate applies in respect of dividends paid by Malaysian companies.

13. Source country tax in Malta is limited to the tax chargeable on the profits out of which the dividends are paid.

14. The agreement between Australia and Mexico was signed on September 9, 2002 and was about to enter into force at the time of writing. The Agreement will have effect in respect of Australian and Mexican withholding taxes for dividends, interest, and royalties paid or credited on or after January 1, 2004. The dates of effect for Australian income tax and other Mexican taxes is July 1, 2004.

15. A nil dividend withholding tax rate will apply to franked dividends paid (in Mexico, those dividends that have been paid from the net profit account) to

a company that holds directly at least 10% of the voting power in the dividend paying company. In all other cases, a 15% withholding tax rate will apply to dividends.

16. Source-country tax is limited to 10% when interest is paid to a bank or an insurance company, derived from bonds and securities that are regularly and substantially traded on a recognized securities market, paid by banks (except where the prior two criteria apply) or paid by the purchaser to the seller of machinery and equipment in connection with a sale on credit. It is 15% in all other cases.

17. For Australian-source dividends, the limit is 15%. Where dividends are sourced in Papua New Guinea, the limit is 20%.

18. Source-country tax is limited to 15% where relief by way of rebate or credit is given to the beneficial owner of the dividend. In any other case, source-country tax is limited to 25%.

19. Source-country tax is generally limited to 15% of gross royalties if paid by an approved Philippines enterprise; in all other cases to 25% of the gross royalties.

20. Source-country tax (Australia) is limited to 5% where a dividend is paid to a Romanian resident company that holds directly at least 10% of the capital of the Australian company paying the dividend to the extent that the dividend is fully franked. Source-country tax (Romania) is limited to 5% where a dividend is paid to an Australian resident company that holds directly at least 10% of the capital of the Romanian company paying the dividend if the dividend is paid out of profits that have been subject to Romanian profits tax; in other cases it is limited to 15%.

21. The agreement between Australia and the Russian Federation entered into force on December 17, 2003. The treaty has effect in Australia for all Australian taxes covered by the treaty for income and profits of years of income beginning on or after July 1, 2004. In the case of Russia, the treaty will have effect for taxable years and periods beginning on or after January 1, 2004.

22. Source country tax is generally limited to 15%. However, a rate of 5% applies where the dividends have been fully taxed at the corporate level, the recipient is a company which has a minimum direct holding in the paying company and has invested a minimum of A$700,000 or the Russian ruble equivalent in the paying company; and where the dividends are paid by a company that is a resident in Russia, the dividends are exempt from Australian tax.

23. The agreement with the Russian Federation is the first of Australia's new treaties to include spectrum licenses in the definition of royalties.

24. Source-country tax (Taiwan) is limited to 10% of the gross amount of the dividends paid to a company which holds at least 25% of the capital of the company paying the dividends. A rate of 15% applies in all other cases. To the extent that dividends are franked because they are paid out of profits that have borne Australian tax, they are exempt from dividend withholding tax. See Note (1). The treaty allows Australia to impose a 10% withholding tax on the franked part of a dividend.

25. The source-country limit where the recipient has a minimum 25% direct holding in the paying company is 15% if the paying company engages in an "industrial undertaking"; 20% in other cases.

26. The source-country limit is 10% when interest is paid to a financial institution; it is 25% in all other cases.

27. A new United Kingdom and Australia agreement entered into force on December 17, 2003. The new agreement has effect for Australian and United Kingdom withholding taxes in relation to dividends, interest and royalties on or after July 1, 2004. The dates of effect for Australian fringe benefits tax and income tax are respectively April 1, 2004 and July 1, 2004.

28. Source-country tax is generally limited to 15%. However, an exemption applies for dividends paid to a publicly listed company which controls 80% or more of the voting power in the company paying the dividend, and a 5% limit applies to dividends paid to other companies with voting power of 10% or greater in the dividend paying company.

29. Source-country tax is generally limited to 10%. However, generally nil interest withholding tax is payable where interest is paid to a financial institution or a government body exercising governmental functions.

30. The United States and Australia renegotiated the treaty and a protocol has effect for withholding taxes in relation to payments made on or after July 1, 2003. For other taxes covered by the protocol, it has effect in respect of income, profits or gains of years of income beginning on or after July 1, 2004.

31. Source-country tax is generally limited to 15%. Exceptions are: no source country tax is chargeable on dividends to a beneficially entitled company, that satisfies certain public listing requirements, and holds 80% or more of the voting power in the company paying the dividend; a 5% limit applies to dividends paid to other companies with voting power of 10% or greater in the dividend paying company; no limit applies to U.S. tax on dividends paid on certain substantial holdings of Australian residents in U.S. real estate investment trusts (REITs). In practical terms U.S. tax on these dividends is increased from 15% to the current U.S. domestic law rate of 30%. The 15% rate is retained for REIT investments made by certain listed Australian property trusts subject to the underlying ownership requirements not exceeding certain levels. Existing investments in REITs by listed Australian property trusts acquired before March 26, 2001 are protected from the increased rate.

32. Source-country tax is generally limited to 10%. However, generally nil interest withholding tax is payable where interest is paid to a financial institution or a government body exercising governmental functions. Rules consistent with U.S. tax treaty policy and practice will allow interest to be taxed at a higher 15% rate (the rate that generally applies to dividends) and for tax to be charged on intra-entity interest payments between a branch and its head office.

33. Amounts derived from equipment leasing (including container leasing) are excluded from the royalty definition.

34. Source-country tax is limited to 15% (Australia) and 10% (Vietnam).

## Tax administration

***Returns***/A corporation (including the head company of a tax consolidated group) generally lodges a tax return on the basis of a July 1 to June 30 year of income. However, a corporation may apply to adopt a substitute year of income, for example, January 1 to December 31. A return is lodged under a self-assessment system that allows the Australian Taxation Office (ATO) to rely on the information stated on the return. Where a corporation is in doubt as to its tax liability regarding a specific item, it can ask the ATO to consider that item prior to assessment.

*Payment of tax*/A pay-as-you-go (PAYG) installment system applies to companies other than those whose annual tax is less than A$8,000 that are not registered for GST. Companies are obliged to pay installments of tax for their current income year by the 21st days of the fourth, seventh, and tenth months of that year and by the 21st day of the month immediately following that year. Installments are calculated on a quarterly basis by applying an "installment rate" to the amount of the company's actual "ordinary income" (ignoring deduction) for the previous quarter. The installment rate is notified to the taxpayer by the ATO and determined by reference to the tax payable for the most recent assessment. The ATO may notify a new rate during the year on which subsequent installments must be based. Taxpayers can determine their own installment rate, but there may be penalty tax if the taxpayer's rate is less than 85% of the rate that should have been selected.

Final assessed tax is payable on the first day of the sixth month following the end of that income year or such later date as the Commissioner of Taxation allows by a published notice.

## *CORPORATION TAX CALCULATION*

Income year ended December 31, 2004 (in lieu of the normal Australian income year ending June 30, 2005) (1)

Resident public company

Net income before taxes:

| | | |
|---|---:|---:|
| Australian trading income | A$ 974,500 | |
| Capital gain on sale of shares after indexing cost for inflation (up until September 30, 1999) | 10,000 | |
| Fully franked dividends from resident corporation | 7,000 | |
| Foreign income (net of 30,000 foreign taxes paid) from business carried on at a permanent establishment in listed comparable tax country: 100,000 (exempt) | Nil | |
| Dividends from portfolio investment in the United States (net of 1,500 withholding tax) | 8,500 | A$ 1,000,000 |

Add:

| | | |
|---|---:|---:|
| Gross-up for tax paid on fully franked dividend | 3,000 | |
| Foreign taxes withheld from dividends | 1,500 | |
| Depreciation charged in accounts in excess of amount allowable for tax purposes | 100,000 | |
| Nondeductible building costs charged in accounts as repairs | 15,000 | |
| Provision for doubtful debts | 50,000 | 169,500 |
| | | 1,169,500 |
| Deduct—Research and development concession | | 15,250 |
| (61,000 actual expenditure at 25%) | | |
| Taxable income | | A$ 1,154,250 |

| | | |
|---|---:|---:|
| Income tax on 1,154,250 at 30% | | A$ 346,275 |

*Less:*

| | | |
|---|---:|---:|
| Tax offset on fully franked dividends from resident corporations | 3,000 | |
| Foreign tax credit (lesser of foreign taxes paid or Australian tax payable on gross nonexempt foreign income) 1,500 foreign taxes paid versus 3,000 Australian tax payable on gross nonexempt foreign income (10,000 at 30%) | 1,500 | (4,500) |
| Australian tax due | | A$ 341,775 |

Notes:

1. The corporate tax calculation for the income year ended December 31, 2003 is based on Australian tax laws as amended to January 1, 2004.
2. Exchange rate of the Australian dollar at January 1, 2004: US$1 = A$1.32732.

# Austria

## PwC contact

For additional information on taxation in Austria, contact:

Friedrich Roedler
PwC PricewaterhouseCoopers Wirtschaftsprüfung und Steuerberatung GmbH
Erdbergstraße 200
A–1030 Vienna, Austria
Telephone: (43) (1) 501 88 0
Fax: (43) (1) 501 88 601
e-mail: friedrich.roedler@at.pwc.com

## Significant developments

A number of relevant tax law amendments were recently adopted in Austria. Major changes regard the international participation exemption, the preferential treatment of undistributed profits for individuals, as well as the creation of new forms of investment incentives. The changes will be reflected in more detail in the sections below. Furthermore, a major tax reform has been announced for 2005 providing for a reduction of the Austrian CIT (corporate income tax) rate to 25%, and some other measures which will significantly increase Austria's attractiveness as a business location.

## Taxes on corporate income

*Corporation tax* **(Körperschaftsteuer)**/Profits are taxed at a flat rate of 34%. There is also a minimum corporate income tax, payable by companies in a tax loss position. The minimum corporate income tax amounts to €437.50 for limited liability companies (GmbH) and €875 for stock corporations (AG) for each full quarter of a year. To promote the foundation of new companies the minimum corporate income tax is in both cases reduced to €273 for the first four quarters. The minimum corporate income tax is credited against future taxable profits.

## Corporate residence

A corporation is resident for tax purposes if either it is registered in Austria or its center of effective management is in Austria.

## Other taxes

*Value-added tax* **(Mehrwertsteuer)**/VAT is chargeable on the sale of most goods and services except exports. The standard rate is 20%. A certain limited range of goods and services is taxed at 10%. Normally, VAT is wholly recoverable for corporations except those engaged in special business activities, that is, banking, insurance, and holding companies.

*Capital transfer tax* **(Gesellschaftsteuer)**/Capital transfer tax is imposed at a rate of 1% on the initial contribution of capital, other contractual or voluntary contributions in cash or in kind and certain hybrid instruments.

## Branch income

Branches of foreign corporations are taxed in the same way as Austrian corporations, except that intercompany dividends received by branches of non-EU corporations are not tax exempt (see below), and tax losses can be carried forward only under certain circumstances. As of 2001, a domestic permanent establishment of a foreign company may generally prepare and keep its books and records abroad (with certain restrictions).

## Income determination

*Inventory valuation/*In general, inventories are valued at the lower of cost or market. If specific identification during stock movements is not possible, other methods (e.g., LIFO and FIFO) are permitted only if it can be shown that they are in accord with the facts. Conformity between commercial book keeping and tax reporting is required.

*Capital gains/*No special treatment applies to capital gains except as stated below.

*Intercompany dividends/*Dividends received from an Austrian corporation are excluded from the tax base. Under the ("amended") foreign participation exemption, applicable as of the beginning of 2004, dividends received from a foreign company are tax exempt, if the Austrian company holds at least 10% of the issued share capital for a minimum holding period of one year. As a general rule, capital gains and capital losses are tax neutral, that is, a deduction of capital losses is under this general rule no longer available. However, the parent company can execute an (irrevocable) option for each single participation acquired to treat both capital gains and capital losses taxable (spread over a period of seven years). In case of presumed tax avoidance, the participation exemption for dividends and capital gains is replaced by a tax credit ("switch-over-clause"). The credit system will be applied in particular if the foreign subsidiary does not meet an active-trade-or-business test and a "subject to tax" condition (this means that the abroad profits must be subject to a minimum income tax rate of 15%).

A deduction of the financing costs for the tax-exempt investment is not allowable. The domestic and foreign participation exemptions are available only to Austrian resident corporations and to branches of EU corporations, not to branches of non-EU corporations.

*Foreign income/*Resident corporations are taxed on their worldwide income. If a double taxation treaty is in force, double taxation is mitigated either through an exemption or by granting a tax credit equal to the foreign withholding tax at the maximum. However, if the source of the income is a nontreaty country, exemption or a tax credit shall be available based on unilateral relief.

Special rules for taxing undistributed income of foreign subsidiaries are applicable only in the case of foreign investment funds.

*Stock dividends/*A conversion from revenue reserves/retained earnings to capital by a company does not lead to taxable income for the shareholder. However, capital reductions are treated as taxable income if within ten years prior to the capital reduction the above-mentioned increase in capital was repaid to the shareholder. Otherwise, they are tax exempt.

# Austria

## Deductions

***Depreciation and depletion***/Only the straight-line method is permitted, whereby the cost is evenly spread over the useful life of an asset. For certain assets, depreciation rates are prescribed by the tax law, as follows.

|                                   | %    |
|-----------------------------------|------|
| Buildings (industrial use)        | 3.0  |
| Buildings (banking, insurance)    | 2.5  |
| Other buildings                   | 2.0  |
| Cars                              | 12.5 |

Goodwill arising in the course of an asset deal must be amortized over 15 years. Goodwill arising as a result of a corporate merger cannot be amortized.

Tax depreciation is not required to conform to book depreciation. If depreciated property is sold, the difference between tax value and sale proceeds is taxed as a profit or loss in the year of sale. Rollover relief is available for new purchases under certain circumstances. For natural resources, cost depletion is available.

Tax losses incurred in 1991 and subsequent years can be carried forward without any time limit. However, from 2001 onward, tax loss carryforwards can be applied against taxable income only up to a maximum of 75% of taxable income for any given year (except in case of compensation with profits derived in the course of restructuring, sale or liquidation of a company which also in the future can be fully offset against tax loss carryforwards).

***Payments to foreign affiliates***/Basically there are no restrictions on the deductibility of royalties, interest, and service fees paid to foreign affiliates, provided they are at arm's length. There are no specific thin-capitalization rules. Payments to affiliates that are not at arm's length are regarded as constructive dividends, that is, they are not deductible, and a withholding tax of up to 33.3% is charged.

***Taxes***/ Taxes on income and other personal taxes, as well as VAT insofar as it relates to nondeductible expenditures, are nondeductible. Other taxes, such as payroll or capital transfer taxes, are deductible.

***Other significant items***/ The deductibility of entertainment expenses is restricted to advertising expenses. The deductibility of costs for business lunches is generally limited to 50% of actual expenses incurred. Lump-sum accruals or provisions are not deductible for tax purposes.

Austrian businesses have the option to deduct deemed interest on equity increases. The deemed interest is calculated on the amount by which the equity of a business has increased as compared to the highest average during the preceding seven years. As the amount of interest deducted is subject to a flat tax of 25% imposed at the level of the company (not the shareholder), the tax effect is usually rather low. This provision will probably be canceled in the course of the envisaged tax reform 2005 for corporations.

## Group taxation

There are no general provisions for group taxation. However, Austrian resident companies may be taxed as a unit under the *Organschaft* concept (i.e., parent-subsidiary relationship with at least 75% shareholding by the parent company; business and organizational integration of the subsidiary into the parent company; profit and loss takeover agreement). The *Organschaft* concept should be replaced by a modern system of group taxation under the envisaged tax reform for 2005.

## Tax incentives

A training allowance of 20% is granted for training expenditure incurred by an employer for his employees. The training allowance can be claimed for external training expenditures and for in-house, if there is a dedicated in-house training department. Alternatively, a training tax bonus payment of 6% can be claimed (e.g., in a loss situation).

In order to enhance the investments of the years 2002 to 2004, a temporary tax incentive has been introduced in autumn 2002 and extended in 2003. A tax bonus payment of the tax authorities can be applied for in the amount of 10% of any increase in investments in certain qualifying assets, as compared to the average relating investments of the past three years (so-called *Investitionszuwachsprämie*). Exemptions apply for buildings, low-value assets, cars and assets not used in an Austrian permanent establishment (PE).

*Inward investment/* There are no special tax incentives for encouraging inward investment. For investment in certain regions, government grants and subsidies are available (to be negotiated).

*Other incentives/*Research and development (R&D) costs are fully deductible when incurred. In addition, an R&D allowance of 25% of qualifying R&D expenses (under certain instances 35%) can be deducted. Alternatively (e.g., in a loss situation), a R&D tax premium payment of 8% can be used for these expenditures.

For buildings an extra depreciation of 7% is possible under certain conditions, if the company starts to build the respective building between January 1, 2002 and December 31, 2003.

# Austria

## Withholding taxes

| Recipient | Dividends (1, 2) | Interest (3) | Royalties, licenses (4) |
|---|---|---|---|
| | % | % | % |
| Resident corporations | Nil/25 (5) | Nil/25 | Nil |
| Resident individuals | 25 (6) | Nil/25 | Nil |
| Nonresident individuals | | | |
| Nontreaty: | | | |
| Nonresident corporations and business enterprises | 25 | Nil | 20/Nil (4) |
| Individuals | 25 | Nil | 20 |
| Treaty: | | | |
| Argentina (7) | 15 | 0 | 15 |
| Armenia (8) | 15/5* | 0 | 5 |
| Australia | 15 | 0 | 10 |
| Azerbaijan | 15/10*15* (9) | 0 | 10/5 (10) |
| Belarus (11) | 15/5* | 0 | 5 |
| Belgium | 15 | 0 | 10x |
| Belize (12) | 15/5* | 0 | 0 |
| Brazil | 15 | 0 | 25/15/10 |
| Bulgaria | 0 | 0 | 0 |
| Canada | 15/5+ | 0 | 10 |
| China, P.R. | 10/7* | 0 | 10/6 (13) |
| Croatia | 15/0+ | 0 | 0 |
| Cuba (32) | 15/5* | 0 | 5/0 (33) |
| Cyprus | 10 | 0 | 0 |
| Czech Republic | 10 | 0 | 5 |
| Denmark | 10 | 0 | 10x |
| Egypt | 10 | 0 | 0/films 20 |
| Estonia (14) | 15/5* | 0 | 5/10 (15) |
| Finland (16) | 10/0+ | 0 | 10 |
| France | 15/0+ | 0 | 0 |
| Germany (17) | 15/5+ | 0 | 0 |
| Greece | 25 (18) | 0 | 10x |
| Hungary | 10 | 0 | 0 |
| India (19) | 10 | 0 | 10 |
| Indonesia | 15/10* | 0 | 10 |
| Iran (20) | 10/5* | 0 | 5 |
| Ireland, Rep. of | 10/0* | 0 | 10x |
| Israel | 25 | 0 | 10 |
| Italy | 15 | 0 | 10x |
| Japan | 20/10** | 0 | 10 |
| Korea, Rep. of (21) | 15/5* | 0 | 10/2 (22) |
| Kuwait (23) | 0 | 0 | 10 |
| Kyrgyzstan (24) | 15/5* | 0 | 10 |
| Liechtenstein | 15 | 0 | Up to 10 |
| Luxembourg | 15/5* | 0 | 10x |
| Malaysia | 10/5* | 0 | 10/15 films |
| Malta | 15 | 0 | 10 |
| Morocco (25) | 10/5* | 0 | 10 |

| Recipient | Dividends (1, 2) | Interest (3) | Royalties, licenses (4) |
|---|---|---|---|
| | % | % | % |
| Nepal | 15/10+/5** | 0 | 15 |
| Netherlands | 15/5* | 0 | 10x |
| Norway | 15/5* | 0 | 0 |
| Pakistan | 25/10* | 0 | 20 |
| Philippines | 25/10+ | 0 | 15 |
| Poland | 10 | 0 | 0 |
| Portugal | 15 | 0 | 5/10x |
| Romania | 15 | 0 | 10 |
| Russia (26) | 15/5* (27) | 0 | 0 |
| Russian Federation (30) | 0 | 0 | 0 |
| Singapore (28) | 10/0+ | 0 | 5 |
| Slovakia | 10 | 0 | 5 |
| Slovenia | 15/5* | 0 | 10 |
| South Africa | 15/5* | 0 | 0 |
| Spain | 15/10** | 0 | 5 |
| Sweden | 10/5* | 0 | 10x |
| Switzerland | 15/0+ (29) | 0 | 5 |
| Thailand | 25/10* | 0 | 15 |
| Tunisia | 20/10* | 0 | Up to 15 |
| Turkey | 25 | 0 | 10 |
| Ukraine | 10/5+ | 0 | 0/5 films |
| United Kingdom | 15/5* | 0 | 10x |
| United States (31) | 15/5+ | 0 | 0/10 films |
| Uzbekistan | 15/5+ | 0 | 5 |

The numbers in parentheses refer to the following numbered Notes.

Notes:

1. Dividends—Dividend distributions attributable to a prior release of paid-in surplus or other shareholder contributions (qualified as capital reserve) are regarded as a repayment of capital, that is, no withholding tax will be applied. At the shareholder level, dividends received and reclassified as capital repayment will reduce the tax basis in shares. To the extent the tax basis would become negative, such dividend is treated as a taxable capital gain (unless taxation is eliminated by a tax treaty). Further, in accordance with the Parent/Subsidiary Directive, an exemption from withholding tax is granted for the distribution of profits by an Austrian corporation to an EU parent company if the parent holds a participation of at least 25% (as of January 1, 2004: 10% subject to the condition of reciprocity) during an uninterrupted period of at least one year (before January 1, 2004: two years).

2. Under some treaties the amount of withholding tax is dependent on the proportion of issued share capital held by the recipient. Where this is the case, all rates are given. Those marked + indicate a holding of 10%, * 25% and ** 50%.

3. Interest—Interest on bank deposits in Austrian schillings or foreign currency on bank accounts and bonds in foreign currency (issued after December 31, 1988) and on bonds denominated in Austrian schillings (issued after December 31, 1983) is subject to a 25% withholding tax.

If the recipient is an individual, this withholding tax is final (no further income taxation and inheritance taxation). Companies receiving interest can achieve an exemption from withholding tax through a written declaration from the recipient to the bank or other depository that such interest forms part of the recipient's business income (*Befreiungserklärung*). Interest income received by nonresidents without a permanent establishment in Austria is generally not subject to withholding taxation. Mortgage secured loans are subject to withholding tax.

4. Royalties, etc.—Where paid to countries marked with "x," the rate is nil unless more than 50% of the issued share capital of the company paying the royalties is held by the recipient, in which case the rate given applies. For Portugal, the rate of withholding tax is 5%, but 10% where more than 50% of the issued share capital is held by the recipient. Under the EU Interest and Royalty Directive as implemented into Austrian tax law, license payments effected by a domestic company shall be exempt from 20% domestic withholding tax, if the licensor is a qualifying EU resident company holding either a *direct* participation of at least 25% (licensor holding minimum 25% stake in licensee and vice versa qualify) or direct participation of a third company of at least 25% in licensor and licensee (licensor and licensee being direct sister companies) and minimum holding period of one year is met (when the payment is made) and royalty complies with the arm's length principle.

5. If the recipient holds a participation of less than 25% in the distributing company, the dividends are subject to a 25% withholding tax. As dividends distributed from an Austrian corporation to another Austrian corporation are generally not subject to tax (see "Income determination, Intercompany dividends"), the withholding tax is credited against corporation income tax upon assessment of the respective tax year of the recipient corporation.

6. Withholding tax on dividends from Austrian companies is final, that is, there is no further income taxation on the recipient.

7. The dividends may be taxed only in the source state and are tax exempt in the receiving state.

8. The new treaty was signed on February 27, 2002 and will presumably enter into force at the beginning of the fiscal year 2004 or 2005.

9. A rate of 5% for shares of at least 25% and worth at least US$250.000, 10% for shares of at least 25% and worth at least US$100,000, 15% for shares of below 25%.

10. A rate of 5% for industrial licenses and know how not older than three years.

11. The new treaty was signed on May 16, 2002 and enters into force at the beginning of the fiscal year 2003.

12. The new treaty was signed on May 8, 2002 and enters into force at the beginning of the fiscal year 2004.

13. Industrial, commercial, or scientific equipment—6%.

14. The new treaty enters into force at the beginning of the fiscal year 2003.

15. A rate of 5% for leasing of mobile goods and 10% for other licenses.

16. The new treaty enters into force at the beginning of the fiscal year 2002.

17. The new treaty enters into force at the beginning of the fiscal year 2003.

18. The treaty does not restrict the taxation right of the source country. Thus a 25% withholding tax according to domestic law is applicable.

19. The new treaty enters into force at the beginning of the fiscal year 2002.
20. The new treaty was signed on March 12, 2002 and will presumably enter into force at the beginning of the fiscal year 2004 or 2005.
21. The endorsement was signed on May 28, 2001 and entered into force at the beginning of the fiscal year 2003.
22. A rate of 2% for license income from industrial, commercial, or scientific use.
23. The new treaty was signed on July 13, 2002 and will presumably enter into force at the beginning of the fiscal year 2004 or 2005.
24. The new treaty was signed on September 18, 2001 and entered into force at the beginning of the fiscal year 2004.
25. The new treaty was signed on February 27, 2002 and will presumably enter into force at the beginning of the fiscal year 2004 or 2005.
26. The new treaty enters into force at the beginning of the fiscal year 2003.
27. A rate of 5% if capital share amounts to at least 10% worth at least US$100,000.
28. The new treaty was signed on October 22, 2002 and enters into force at the beginning of the fiscal year 2003.
29. For dividend distributions retroactive as of January 1, 2000.
30. The treaty applies to Armenia, Belarus, Georgia, Kyrgyzstan, Moldova, Russia, Tajikistan, Turkmenistan, and Ukraine. With Russia a new treaty has been ratified (see note 26). Under this treaty a withholding tax up to 5% in case of capital share of at least 10% worth at least US$100,000 and up to 15% in all other cases is levied.
31. This treaty contains a limit to the tax relief caused by the treaty.
32. The treaty was signed on June 26, 2003 and will presumably enter into force at the beginning of the fiscal year 2005.
33. Copyright license fees in connection with literature and art are free of withholding tax if they are subject to taxation in the country of residence.

## Tax administration

*Returns/* The tax year in Austria is the calendar year. A company's financial year may deviate. In such cases the basis of tax assessments for the calendar year is the financial year ending therein. Assessments are issued once the tax office has reviewed the return.

*Payment of tax/*Corporate income tax is prepaid in quarterly installments during the year, with a final settlement when the assessment is issued. Prepayments of corporate income tax are generally levied at a rate of 20% above the tax for the preceding year (unless the taxpayer can provide reasonable assurance that its tax charge for the current year will be lower). Interest is applied on underpayments (as well as overpayments) of tax.

# Austria

### *CORPORATION TAX CALCULATION*

Calculation valid for the year ending December 31, 2003

## Assumptions

The following is an example of a corporate income tax computation of a GmbH (limited liability corporation) on the basis of the following assumptions:

1. The GmbHs income, after charging all expenditures and all taxes except taxes on income, amounts to €100,000.
2. R&D expenditure amounts to €10,000; an allowance of €2,500 can be claimed in addition to the deduction of R&D expenses.
3. Deemed interest on equity increase amounts to €7,500 under the assumptions that the company has realized a profit of €100,000 in each of the preceding seven years, that profits have been retained and that additional shareholder equity of €100,000 has been contributed to the company in the middle of the current year.

## Tax computation

| | | |
|---|---:|---:|
| Net income before taxes | | € 100,000 |
| Less: | | |
| R&D allowance | 2,500 | |
| Deemed interest on equity increase | 7,500 | 10,000 |
| | | 90,000 |
| Add: | | |
| Fees for advisory board members (50% of €8,000) | 4,000 | |
| Donations and contributions | 2,400 | |
| Allocation to lump-sum accruals | 4,000 | 10,400 |
| Taxable income | | € 100,400 |
| Corporation tax thereon at 34% | | € 34,136 |
| 25% corporation tax on deemed interest | | 1,875 |
| Total of corporation tax | | € 36,011 |

Note:

Exchange rate of the euro at March 6, 2004: US$1 = €0.81853.

## PwC contact

For additional information on taxation in Azerbaijan, contact:

Zaid Sethi
PricewaterhouseCoopers
The Landmark Building
96 Nizami Street, 5th Floor
370010 Baku, Azerbaijan
Telephone: (994 12) 97 25 15
Fax: (994 12) 97 74 11
e-mail: zaid.sethi@az.pwc.com

## Significant developments

The tax code was introduced effective January 1, 2001. The latest changes were made to the tax code effective from January 1, 2004. Details are given below.

## Taxes on corporate income

Profit tax at the rate of 24% is imposed on domestic enterprises, as well as permanent establishments of nonresidents.

The code stipulates payment of simplified tax for enterprises not registered as value-added tax (VAT) payers, except for enterprises producing excisable goods, credit and insurance organizations and investment funds, and professional participants of the securities market. The rate of tax is 4% of gross revenue for Baku City, and 2% for other regions of Azerbaijan.

There are other types of tax regimes, called the "oil consortia tax regime" and "export pipelines tax regime."

The oil consortia regime applies to all foreign investors involved in a production sharing agreement (PSA), including foreign oil companies functioning as contractors, and foreign service companies providing services to the contractor or the operating company. Oil companies operating under PSAs have their own separate tax regimes. As of March 18, 2004, there are 23 signed and ratified PSAs, each with its own separate taxation regime. Each PSA contains a tax article, which outlines the taxation regime for that particular agreement. While many of the tax terms of PSAs may be similar to other PSAs, there are a number of differences other than merely different rates of tax or different reporting requirements. Additionally, tax protocols, which provide specific guidance regarding the procedures for payment of taxes and filing of reports, are negotiated with the Ministry of Taxes and other executive authorities. The PSAs set out the tax regimes that are applicable to each contractor party and the operating company and also address the tax regimes that are applicable to subcontractors, in particular foreign subcontractors that gain contracts for the conduct of hydrocarbon activities. However, as already mentioned above, it is the taxation protocols that act as tax instructions which set out the tax rules and compliance mechanisms.

The export pipelines regime is similar to the PSA tax regime. The major difference is that foreign incorporated service suppliers are not subject to any corporate income tax.

# Azerbaijan

## Corporate residence

A resident enterprise is any legal entity established and performing its entrepreneurial activity or being managed in Azerbaijan in accordance with the legislation of the Azerbaijan Republic.

A permanent establishment (PE) of a foreign legal entity is subject to taxation with respect to the income attributable to such PE. A PE is an establishment of a foreign legal entity, through which it fully or partially performs commercial activity (for these purposes, a PE may be considered a management unit, office bureau, agency, construction site, etc.) for not less than 90 consecutive days within any 12-month period. Activities of auxiliary or preparatory nature (e.g., exclusively storing or exhibiting goods or products belonging to a nonresident entity, purchasing goods, or collecting data by a nonresident enterprise for own purposes, etc.) do not create a PE.

## Other taxes

*Branch profit tax*/Foreign legal entities carrying out business activities through a representative office or branch office are subject to branch profit tax at 10% on their net profits when such profits are repatriated.

## Income determination

Profit tax is computed on the basis of an enterprise's taxable profits. Profits are defined as the difference between the worldwide gross income of a taxpayer and deductions. A nonresident enterprise operating in Azerbaijan through a PE shall pay tax on its gross income generated from Azerbaijan sources in relationship with the PE, less the amount of deductions incurred with respect to such income.

The gross income of a nonresident enterprise generated from Azerbaijan sources, and not connected with the PE, shall be taxed at the source of payment without expenses being deducted.

A nonresident enterprise generating income through the assignment of property not connected with a PE shall pay tax on said gross income received during a calendar year from an Azerbaijan source, after deducting expenses for the said period which relate to such income.

*Foreign tax credit for residents*/Azeri legal entities are taxed on worldwide profit. However, any tax paid overseas up to the amount that would be calculated under Azeri law will be allowed to offset the Azeri profits tax. The tax credit may not exceed the tax that would be imposed on such income in Azerbaijan.

*Dividends from Azeri sources*/Dividends received from Azeri sources, and previously taxed at the source of payment, are not included in the taxable profits of the recipient of the income.

*Taxes withheld at source*/If a resident enterprise or a PE of a nonresident has received interest, royalties, or rental fees taxable at the source of payment in Azerbaijan, it is entitled to credit the tax deducted from the source of payment, providing the documents supporting the tax deduction are in place.

## Deductions

*Deductible expenses*/All expenses connected with the obtaining of income, except for nondeductible expenses, are deductible from income.

*Nondeductible expenses*/Nondeductible expenses are as follows.

• Capital expenses.

• Expenses connected with noncommercial activity.

• Entertainment and meal expenses, accommodation and other expenses of a social nature incurred for the employees.

*Limitation of deductions for certain expenses*/Interest paid on loans obtained overseas, or from an associated enterprise, is deductible at no more than 125% of the rate determined by the inter-bank credit auction.

The amount of repair expenses deductible is limited to an amount, determined by a decree of the Cabinet of Ministers, of the balance value of each category of fixed assets. An amount exceeding the above limits shall be taken as an increase of the residual balance value of fixed assets in the category.

The portion of actual business trip expenses exceeding the norm established by the Cabinet of Ministers shall not be deducted from income.

Depreciation is calculated according to the following rates.

• For buildings and structures—up to 7%.

• For machines, equipment, and computing equipment—up to 25%.

• Transport means—up to 25%.

• Working cattle—up to 20%.

• Expenses incurred for geological and exploration works, as well as for preparatory works for the production of natural resources—25%.

• Intangible assets—10%.

• Other fixed assets—20%.

There is an accelerated cost recovery system for capital expenditures for production purposes incurred within a reporting period. The expenditures are subject to a depreciation deduction of up to two times the normally applicable rates. Capital investment of a production purpose is defined as capital construction and reconstruction in a new construction form of buildings and workshops involved in the process of production of goods, expansion and technical outfitting of enterprises engaged in activity, as well as the acquisition of units, equipment, transportation facilities used in production, fixed assets, and other objects (or parts).

*Deductions of allocations to reserve insurance funds*/A legal entity engaged in insurance activity is entitled to deduct allocations to reserve insurance funds within the norms established by the legislation of the Azerbaijan Republic.

*Net operating losses*/Taxable losses incurred by legal entities may be carried forward for five years in equal installments, or within 20% of profit of the current year.

## Tax incentives

The rate of profit tax of production enterprises belonging to public organizations of invalids where the total number of employees includes a minimum of 50% of invalids shall be reduced by 50%. In determining the right to such privileges, invalids performing under a contract of substitution, subcontract and those of civil and legal nature are not included into the average number of employees.

# Azerbaijan

## Withholding taxes

Payments from resident enterprises and PEs of nonresidents are subject to withholding tax at the following rates.

- Dividends paid by resident enterprises—at 10%.
- Interest paid by resident or PE of nonresident or on behalf of such establishment (except for interest paid to resident banks or permanent establishments of nonresident banks)—at 10%.

Income received from Azerbaijan sources not attributable to a permanent establishment (base) of a nonresident in Azerbaijan is subject to withholding tax at the following rates.

- Dividends and interest—10%.
- Payments in respect of leasing operations of resident enterprises, PEs of nonresident enterprises (or on behalf of such establishment) or entrepreneurs, including financial leasing operations, as well as insurance payments by a resident enterprise, PE of nonresident enterprise (or on behalf of such an establishment) or entrepreneur under the agreements on risk insurance or reinsurance—4%.
- Payments by a resident enterprise, PE of nonresident enterprise (or on behalf of such an establishment) or entrepreneur for the communication or transportation services during the provision of international communication or international shipments between Azerbaijan and other states—6%.
- Payments by a resident enterprise, PE of nonresident enterprise (or on behalf of such an enterprise) or entrepreneur in connection with other incomes from Azerbaijan sources (income from the assignment of goods, performance of works and provision of services; rental fees; income from immovable property in Azerbaijan, including income from the assignment of participating share in such a property; income from the lease of movable property used in Azerbaijan; other income attributable to an activity in Azerbaijan)—10%.

## Tax administration

*Returns*/Resident enterprises, and PEs of nonresidents, shall file a profit tax return for a calendar year by April 1 of the following year, and upon the liquidation of a legal entity or a PE of nonresident, within 30 days after the adoption of decree on liquidation. A nonresident that has no PE in Azerbaijan, and receives income subject to tax withholding at the source of payment (except for dividends and interest), can file a tax return in respect of the said income and expenses, connected with the generation of the said income, for purposes of reassessment of profit tax at the rate of 24%.

Should the taxpayer apply for an extension of the period for filing of the profit tax return prior to the expiration of the filing terms, and at the same time settle the full tax amount to be paid, the filing terms shall be deemed prolonged for up to three months. The prolongation of the terms for filing of the return shall not modify the terms of tax payment.

*Withholding tax reporting*/Legal entities and entrepreneurs withholding tax at the source of payment are obliged to file the withholding tax report with the tax authority within 20 days following the end of the reporting quarter.

*Tax payments*/Taxpayers shall make current tax payments of profit tax by the 15th day of the month following the end of the calendar quarter. Payments are determined either (1) as 25% of tax for the past fiscal year, or (2) by multiplying the amount of actual income through the quarter by a ratio representing a specific portion of tax in gross income for the previous year.

## Exchange rate

Exchange rate of the manat at 18 March 2004: US$1 = AZM4,927.

# Bahamas

## PwC contact

For additional information on taxation in the Bahamas, contact:

Kevin D. Seymour
PricewaterhouseCoopers
P.O. Box F-42682
Freeport, Grand Bahama, Bahamas
Telephone: (1) (242) 352-8471
Fax: (1) (242) 352-4810
e-mail: kevin.d.seymour@bs.pwc.com

## Absence of taxation

Income tax is not imposed on corporations in the Bahamas.

## Note

The Bahamian dollar (Bah$1.00) is at parity with the U.S. dollar.

## PwC contact

For additional information on taxation in Bahrain, contact:

Elham Hassan, Country Senior Partner
PricewaterhouseCoopers
BMB Centre, 4th Floor
Diplomatic Area
P.O. Box 21144
Manama, Bahrain
Telephone: (973) 17 540554
Fax: (973) 17 540556
LN address: Elham Hassan/AE/ABAS/PwC@EMEA-ME
e-mail: elham.hassan@bh.pwc.com

## Significant developments

There have been no significant tax or regulatory developments in the past year.

## Taxes on corporate income

With the exception of certain specific taxes on oil-producing and exploration companies, there are no taxes in Bahrain on income, sales, capital gains, or estates. There are no taxes or withholding taxes on interest, dividends, fees, or other remittances. Companies are allowed to transfer accumulated profits and capital without restrictions

## Note

Exchange rate (selling) of the dinar at January 1, 2004: US$1 = BD0.37715.

# Barbados

## PwC contact

For additional information on taxation in Barbados, contact:

R. Charles D. Tibbits
PricewaterhouseCoopers
The Financial Services Centre
Bishop's Court Hill, St. Michael
P.O. Box 111
Bridgetown, Barbados, W.I.
Telephone: (1) (246) 431 2700, 436 7000
Fax: (1) (246) 436 1275, 429 3747, 430 9231
LN address: Charles Tibbits/BB/TLS/PWC
e-mail: charles.tibbits@bb.pwc.com

## General note

This entry is repeated from the 2003/2004 edition. For more up-to-date
information consult the contact listed above or Jacqueline Collette at
jacqueline.collete@us.pwc.com.

## Significant developments

The government of Barbados has announced its intention to reduce the rate of
corporation tax from 37.5% to 36% for income year 2003, with further reductions
to 25% by 2006.

A new Tourism Development Act replacing the Hotel Aids Act became effective
from August 31, 2002. In addition to broadening the scope of activities that may
benefit from it, the Tourism Development Act increased the number of concessions
available to operators in the tourism industry.

Barbados is currently negotiating further double taxation agreements with
Botswana and Italy.

## Taxes on corporate income

*Corporation tax*/Corporation tax is levied at the flat rate of 37.5% (subject to
enabling legislation, effective income year 2003, this rate will be reduced to 36%)
on companies, excluding insurance companies and companies subject to differing
rates of corporation tax under specific pieces of incentive legislation. In lieu of
corporation tax, life insurance companies are taxed at 5% on gross investment
income.

## Corporate residence

A corporation is deemed to be resident in Barbados if it is incorporated in
Barbados or if it is managed and controlled in Barbados.

## Other taxes

*Life insurance premium tax*/This tax is levied at the following rates on gross
direct premium income.

| | Percentage of premium income | |
|---|---|---|
| | **New business** | **Renewal business** |
| | % | % |
| Resident companies | 5 | 3 |
| Foreign companies | 5 | 5 |

**General insurance premium tax**/This tax is levied at the following rates (as a percentage of premium income) for both resident companies and foreign companies.

| | % |
|---|---|
| Property | 3.75 |
| Other | 3.00 |

**Property transfer tax**/This tax is assessed at 10% on the gross consideration for sales of real estate or interests in real estate and for the transfer of shares or debentures issued by or on behalf of a company.

An exemption of Bds$50,000 of the gross sales proceeds for the sale of shares or debentures and Bds$125,000 of the gross sales proceeds for the sale of land on which a building exists is granted to the vendor. Transfers of shares that are listed on the Barbados Stock Exchange or where there is no change in beneficial ownership are also exempted from property transfer tax.

**Land tax**/Land tax is levied on the site value of land, or the improved value where a building exists, at the following rates.

1. On unimproved sites
   a. Value up to Bds$10,000: 0.8% to maximum of Bds$50.
   b. Thereafter: 0.8%.
2. Improved value
   a. A dwelling house used exclusively as a residence.
      i. Up to Bds$350,000: 0.1%.
      ii. $350,001 to $850,000: 0.65%.
      iii. Thereafter: .75%.
   b. All other properties: 0.7%.

Land tax for hotels and for residential properties owned by pensioners is calculated on 50% of the improved value of the property, and for certain villas committed to the tourism rental pool, at 75% of the improved value of the property.

**Tax on bank assets**/An annual charge of 0.2% is payable on the average domestic assets of licensed banks.

**Value-added tax**/VAT is applicable to a wide range of goods and services. The standard rate is 15%. Hotel accommodation bears a rate of 7.5%.

A number of services, including financial services, sale of real estate, public transportation, medical services, and education, are exempt. Intergroup transactions are taxable. Certain supplies are zero-rated, including exports, basic food items, some drugs, crude oil, and supplies of a few items to the international financial services sector.

# Barbados

## Branch income

Branches are taxed on the same basis as corporations. In addition, a 10% withholding tax on the transfer or deemed transfer of after-tax profits to the head office is assessed, unless a double taxation treaty overrides.

## Income determination

*Inventory valuation*/Inventories are generally stated at the lower of cost or net realizable value. FIFO or average values are generally used for book and tax purposes. LIFO is not acceptable for tax purposes. The Inland Revenue will normally accept a method of valuation that conforms to standard accounting practice in the trade. Conformity between book and tax values is expected.

*Capital gains*/Capital gains are not taxed.

*Intercompany dividends*/Dividends between two companies resident in Barbados are not taxed in the hands of the recipient. Dividends paid to a nonresident company are subject to 15% withholding tax unless a double taxation treaty overrides or exemption is granted under specific legislation.

*Foreign income*/A Barbados corporation is taxed on foreign branch income as earned and on foreign dividends as received. Double taxation is avoided by means of foreign tax credits or an exemption where double taxation agreements exist or by deductions for foreign income taxes in other cases.

*Stock dividends*/A Barbados corporation can distribute a tax-free bonus issue of stock proportionately to all stockholders.

## Deductions

*Depreciation and depletion*/Depreciation for tax purposes is computed on a straight-line basis at prescribed rates. These rates generally vary from 10% to 33.33%. The process is accelerated by additional initial allowances in the year of acquisition. Alternative allowances, known as investment allowances, are granted for machinery and equipment investment by manufacturers. These allowances are in lieu of initial allowances and are not deducted from cost in calculating the written-down value carried forward. Manufacturers may also claim an additional annual allowance on machinery and equipment (manufacturing allowance) equal to 50% of the regular annual allowance calculated using the prescribed rates. Like investment allowances, manufacturing allowances are not deducted from cost in calculating the written-down value carried forward. A depreciation allowance is granted on industrial buildings (4%). An allowance is also granted on commercial buildings at 1% of land tax improved value. Conformity between book and tax depreciation is not required. Gains on sales of depreciable assets are taxable as ordinary income up to the amount of tax depreciation recaptured, and losses on sales below depreciated value are deductible.

For oil and gas companies, depending on certain circumstances, a depletion allowance of 20% or 10% is given in addition to annual depreciation on prescribed types of capital expenditure.

*Net operating losses*/No carryback is allowed for corporation tax losses. Losses can be carried forward for nine years, except for those of insurance companies. Losses of general insurance companies can be carried forward for five years, whereas those of life insurance companies cannot be carried forward.

*Payments to foreign affiliates*/A Barbados corporation can claim a deduction for royalties, management fees, and interest charges paid to foreign affiliates, provided the payments are no greater than what it would pay to an unrelated party.

*Taxes*/Taxes on income are not deductible.

## Group taxation

Trading losses incurred during an income year may be offset wholly or in part against the profits of another company of the same group for the same income year. Two companies are considered members of the same group where one is a 75% subsidiary of the other company or both companies are 75% subsidiaries of a third company. Trading losses surrendered to group companies must exclude capital allowances. Companies operating under legislation pertaining to the international financial services sector are not eligible for group loss relief.

## Tax incentives

Tax incentives are available as follows.

1. Fiscal Incentives Act

   Provides to manufacturers of an "approved product" full exemption from taxes and duties for varying periods up to a maximum of 15 years. (See also items (8) and (9) below.)

2. Tourism Development Act

   Provides that a qualifying tourism product may offset expenditure on construction or the provision of certain amenities against its profits. This right arises in the year in which the expenditure is incurred, and unabsorbed expenditure can be carried forward for a period of up to 20 years depending on the value of the expenditure. Trading losses must be offset against trading profits before the qualifying expenditure may be utilized.

   It also provides for a deduction of 150% of certain expenditure on marketing and training and certain loan interest, in the computation of taxable income. Also available is an investment tax credit of 20% to 30% for certain capital expenditure. These credits can be carried forward for a period of 15 years where they exceed the tax payable. Dividends paid to the shareholder of a tourism product are exempted from withholding tax.

3. International Business Companies Act

   International business companies resident in Barbados but deriving income solely from outside Barbados are taxed at the following rates.

   |  | % |
   |---|---|
   | From 0 to Bds$10,000,000 | 2.5 |
   | Bds$10,000,001 to Bds$20,000,000 | 2.0 |
   | Bds$20,000,001 to Bds$30,000,000 | 1.5 |
   | Over Bds$30,000,000 | 1.0 |

   Exchange control freedom is granted to these companies, as well as duty-free concessions on certain imports. An annual license fee of Bds$500 is payable. No withholding tax is levied on remittances of dividends, royalties, interest, management fees, fees, or other income paid to a person outside Barbados. International business companies may also claim a credit for taxes paid outside Barbados, provided that this does not reduce the company's rate of tax in Barbados to less than 1%.

4. International Financial Services Act

   Provides for the establishment of international banking, trust administration and other related or ancillary services by eligible companies incorporated in Barbados or branches of qualified foreign banks. An annual license fee of Bds$25,000 is payable. International financial service entities are exempt from exchange control and are granted duty-free concessions on certain imports. Profits and gains are taxed as for international business companies. No withholding taxes are levied on remittances of dividends, interest, or fees. International financial services entities may also claim a credit for taxes paid outside Barbados, provided that this does not reduce the entities' rate of tax in Barbados to less than 1%.

5. Exempt Insurance Act

   Provides for the operation in Barbados of companies insuring risks outside the island and for companies that manage the former. Both types of companies are exempt from exchange control regulations and from corporation tax. There is an annual license fee of Bds$5,000. No withholding tax is levied on remittances of dividends or interest.

6. Societies with Restricted Liabilities Act (SRL)

   An SRL is a hybrid entity that can be recognized as a corporation or partnership in the United States depending on the nature of its organizational documents. The entity has limited liability and a maximum duration of 50 years. Membership units are known as quotas. Societies qualifying under this Act may apply for a license to operate as international SRLs and as such are granted preferential tax rates and concessions. Profits and gains are taxed at the same rates as for international business companies. No withholding tax is levied on any distributions, interest or other income paid to nonresidents. International SRLs are granted duty-free concessions on certain imports, and no exchange control requirements are applicable.

   Entity mobility is also a prominent feature of this legislation. Qualifying societies organized overseas can be continued under the Act.

7. Shipping Incentives Act

   Provides for income tax concessions to be granted to an approved shipping company in respect of profits or gains accruing during the concession period.

8. Export allowance

   This is a rebate of tax under the Income Tax Act in respect of income from export sales outside CARICOM. The maximum tax credit on eligible sales is 93%, which is available when eligible sales exceed 81% of total sales.

9. Market development allowance for export sales or the tourist industry

   150% of certain expenditure on research and development for export sales outside CARICOM or on tourism development is deductible.

10. Foreign currency credit

   A credit is available for net foreign currency earnings from construction projects or professional services undertaken outside CARICOM or international insurance business. The credit varies, depending on the ratio of foreign currency earnings to total earnings, but ranges from 35% to 93% of corporation tax otherwise payable on such foreign currency earnings.

11. Capital investment

    Capital expenditure on plant and machinery by manufacturers or by a company that exports outside CARICOM (Caribbean Community) qualifies for total depreciation allowances of 170% or 190% of actual costs. In the case of an agricultural enterprise a cash rebate may be claimed.

12. International Trust Act (ITA)

    This Act is aimed at permitting the use of Barbados trusts for purposes previously made possible in many zero-tax financial centers. An international trust is taxed in Barbados as an individual resident but one not domiciled in Barbados. This allows the trust to take advantage of a network of tax treaties while not subjecting its foreign earnings to Barbados tax unless they are remitted there. The Act exempts trusts from exchange control and withholding tax requirements. No registration is required.

13. Special Development Areas Act

    This Act provides relief for approved developers carrying out work in certain defined areas and to persons financing such work (other than a commercial bank). Persons financing such work are exempt from income tax on interest received. Approved developers are exempt from import duties and value-added tax on inputs for the construction or renovation of buildings; withholding taxes on repatriation of interest; land tax; and property transfer tax payable by vendors. An approved developer pays corporation tax at the rate of 30% and is granted initial and annual allowances on industrial buildings of 40% and 6%, respectively, and on commercial buildings of 20% and 4%, respectively.

14. Qualifying insurance companies

    Companies registered under the Insurance Act that derive at least 90% of their premiums from outside CARICOM and at least 90% of whose risks originate outside CARICOM may obtain a certificate of qualification. Such companies are entitled to the same exemptions from withholding taxes and exchange controls as exempt insurance companies. They are also entitled to the foreign currency credit described above, which may reduce their corporation tax rate from 37.5% to 2.625% for general insurance business. The rate on gross investment income applicable to life insurers may fall from 5% to 0.35%.

15. Small Business Development Act

    Companies incorporated under the Companies Act with at least 75% of their shares owned locally and having share capital of not more than Bds$1,000,000, annual sales not in excess of Bds$2,000,000 and not more than 25 employees may obtain approval as a small business. Such companies pay corporation tax at a reduced rate of 25% and are exempted from the payment of import duties on equipment imported for use in the business and from stamp duty on all documents related to the business that must be registered. In addition, 120% of certain expenditure directly related to the development of the business is deductible for tax purposes. Investors in such businesses are exempt from withholding tax on interest and dividends earned on their investment.

# Barbados

## Withholding taxes

***Dividends, interest, royalties, and other payments***/Withholding taxes are levied as follows.

| Recipient | Dividends | Interest | Rentals | Management fees, royalties |
|---|---|---|---|---|
| | % | % | % | % |
| Resident corporations and individuals ............... | Nil/12.5/40 (1)(2) | 12.5 (3) | Nil | Nil |
| Nonresident corporations and individuals: | | | | |
| Nontreaty ........................... | 15 | 15 | 40 | 15 |
| Treaty: | | | | |
| Canada........................... | 15 | 15 (4) | 40 | 5/10 (5) |
| China, P.R. ..................... | 5 | 10 | 40 | Nil/10 (6) |
| Cuba .............................. | 15/5 (7) | 10 | 40 | Nil/5 (8) |
| Finland ........................... | 15/5 (9) | 5 | 40 | 5 |
| Malta .............................. | 15/5 (10) | 5 | 40 | 15/5 (11) |
| Norway ........................... | 15/5 (9) | 5 | 40 | 5 |
| Sweden .......................... | 15/5 (9) | 5 | 40 | 5 |
| Switzerland..................... | Nil | 15 | 40 | Nil |
| United Kingdom.............. | Nil (12) | 15 (4) | 40 | Nil/15 (13) |
| United States.................. | 15/5 (14) | 5 | 40 | Nil/5 (15) |
| Venezuela ...................... | 10/5 (16) | 15/5 (17) | 40 | 10 (18) |
| CARICOM ...................... | Nil | 15 | 40 | 15 |

The numbers in parentheses refer to the following numbered Notes.

Notes:

1. Dividends paid to corporations are not subject to withholding tax, except for dividends paid on preference shares issued before January 1, 1975, which are subject to withholding tax at 40%. Dividends paid to individuals out of pre-July 1992 retained earnings are grossed up by 15% and included in taxable income. A 15% dividend tax credit is permitted on this income. Those paid from profits earned after July 1992 are subject to a final tax of 12.5%.

2. There is no withholding tax on dividends paid out of exempt profits under the Fiscal Incentives Act.

3. Interest paid to pensioners over the age of 60 is exempt from withholding tax.

4. This rate applies provided that the interest is subject to tax in the other territory.

5. The rate is 5% for management fees and 10% for royalties, provided that the income is subject to tax in the other territory.

6. Management fees are exempt, and the rate is 10% for royalties.

7. The rate is 15% for portfolio dividends, 5% for holdings of at least 25%.

8. Management fees are exempt and the rate is 5% for royalties, except for copyright royalties in respect of author's rights, which are exempt if the beneficial owner is liable to tax on them.

9. The rate is 15% for portfolio dividends, 5% for holdings of at least 10%.

10. The rate is 15% for portfolio dividends, 5% for holdings of at least 5%.

11. The rate is 15% for management fees, 5% for royalties, except for copyright royalties in respect of any literary, artistic, or scientific work, which are exempt.

12. Dividends are exempt from withholding tax if they are subject to tax in the other territory.

13. Management fees are exempt provided that they are subject to tax in the other territory. Withholding tax applies only to royalties in respect of cinematographic or television films. All other royalties are exempt from withholding tax, provided that they are subject to tax in the other territory.

14. The rate is 15% for portfolio dividends, 5% for holdings of at least 10%. Dividends paid by a regulated investment company will bear withholding tax at a rate of 15%, regardless of the percentage of shares held by the recipient. Dividends paid by a real estate investment trust (REIT) will qualify for the 5% withholding tax rate only if the beneficial owner is an individual holding less than 10% of the shares in the REIT. Otherwise, a 30% withholding tax rate will apply.

15. Management fees are exempt and the rate is 5% for royalties.

16. The rate is 10% for portfolio dividends, 5% for holdings of at least 5%.

17. The rate is 5% if the recipient is a bank, 15% in other cases.

18. Royalties and technical assistance fees are subject to withholding tax at 10%.

## Tax administration

*Returns*/Corporate tax returns are prepared on a fiscal-year basis. Returns are submitted by March 15 in the year following the end of the fiscal period for companies with year-ends between January 1 and September 30 and by June 15 in the year following the end of the fiscal period for companies with year-ends between October 1 and December 31. A self-assessment method is employed.

*Payment of tax*/Corporate tax is paid in installments. For companies with year-ends between January 1 and September 30, 50% of the previous year's liability is payable by September 15, and the remaining balance of tax, as disclosed in the tax return, is paid upon filing (March 15). For companies with year-ends between October 1 and December 31, 50% of the previous year's liability is paid in two installments, one by December 15 and the other by March 15. The remaining balance of tax, as disclosed in the tax return, is paid upon filing (June 15). It is possible to apply for a reduction in the installments if lower profits are anticipated in the current year when compared with those of the preceding year.

# Barbados

## *CORPORATION TAX CALCULATION*

Year ended December 31, 2002 (a fiscal-year basis)

| | | |
|---|---:|---:|
| Net income before corporation tax | | Bds$ 1,000,000 |
| Add: | | |
|   Book depreciation | 250,000 | |
|   Nonallowable expenses: | | |
|     Legal fees in respect of acquisition | | |
|       of a capital asset | 5,000 | |
|     Charitable donations not under covenant | 3,000 | |
|     Increase in provision for maintenance of plant | | |
|       and equipment | 17,000 | 275,000 |
| | | 1,275,000 |
| Deduct: | | |
|   Annual allowances (Note 1) | 200,000 | |
|   Local dividends received | 40,000 | |
|   Preference dividends paid (Note 2) | 100,000 | 340,000 |
| Taxable income | | Bds$ 935,000 |
| Corporation tax at 37.5% | | Bds$ 350,625 |

Notes:

1. Granted in place of book depreciation.
2. Preference dividends paid on preferred stock issued prior to January 1, 1975 are subject to withholding tax at the rate of 40%, and the gross dividend is allowed as a deduction for corporation tax.
3. Exchange rate of the Barbados dollar is officially pegged at US$1 = Bds$2.

## PwC contact

For additional information on taxation in Belgium, contact:

Frank Dierckx
PricewaterhouseCoopers Tax Consultants sccrl-bcvba
Woluwedal, 18
B–1932 Sint-Stevens-Woluwe, Belgium
Telephone: (32) (2) 710 42 11, 710 43 24 (direct)
Fax: (32) (2) 710 42 99
e-mail: frank.dierckx@be.pwc.com

## Significant developments

The corporate tax reform, which was announced on October 17, 2000, has been introduced by the law of December 24, 2002. Its aim is twofold: a change in the Belgian corporate tax regime and the introduction of a new ruling practice.

The modifications resulting from the tax reform are applicable as from tax year 2004 (financial years ended on December 31, 2003 and later), except for the 10% tax on liquidation surpluses, which is applicable to profits (deemed) attributed or made payable since January 1, 2002. However, the 10% tax does not apply if the liquidation was closed prior to March 25, 2002. The new provisions related to the ruling practice are effective as from January 1, 2003. As far as the new provisions regarding the Belgian coordination centers are concerned, a Royal Decree will determine when these provisions take effect.

## Taxes on corporate income

*Basic rate*/Until tax year 2003 (financial years ended on December 30, 2003 and earlier), the corporate income tax rate is 39%. This rate is increased by a 3% crisis tax levied on the 39%, which leads to an effective corporate tax rate of 40.17%. As from tax year 2004, the corporate tax will be levied at a rate of 33%, increased by the aforesaid 3% crisis tax, which leads to a 33.99% rate.

*Reduced rates*/When taxable income does not exceed a certain ceiling, a progressive scale of reduced rates applies.

Until tax year 2003, if the taxable income is lower than €322,500, the following scale applies.

| | |
|---|---|
| €0 up to €25,000 | 28% |
| €25,001 up to €89,500 | 36% |
| €89,501 up to €322,500 | 41% |

As from tax year 2004, if the taxable income is lower than €322,500, the following scale will apply.

| | |
|---|---|
| €0 up to €25,000 | 24.25% |
| €25,001 up to €90,000 | 31.00% |
| €90,001 up to €322,500 | 34.50% |

The 3% crisis tax is also levied on the aforesaid reduced corporate tax.

Even if their taxable income does not exceed the aforesaid ceilings, certain companies are excluded from the reduced rate and thus always subject to the basic corporate income tax rate, as follows.

# Belgium

1. Finance companies, that is, companies that own participations whose investment value exceeds, at the closure date of the annual accounts, 50% of the paid-up capital, possibly revalued, or 50% of the paid-up capital plus taxable reserves and recorded (taxable or tax free) capital gains of the companies that want to benefit from the reduced rates. Participation that exceeds 75% of the paid-up capital of the companies held is not taken into account for the purpose of this computation.
2. Companies held by another company (or companies) for 50% or more.
3. Companies that distribute dividends exceeding 13% of their paid-up capital.
4. Companies that, per taxable period, do not attribute a tax deductible remuneration of at least €24,500 to at least one key individual (*dirigeant d'entreprise/bedrijfsleider*) who can fall in one of the following categories.
   a. Directors, managers (*gérant/zaakvoerders*), liquidators, or any other individual person exercising a similar function in a company (e.g., an active partner).
   b. An individual person exercising in a company, outside of an employment contract, an activity or a managerial function of a commercial, technical, or financial nature or that relates to a day-to-day management.

   As from tax year 2005, the above mentioned amount of €24,500 will be increased as follows.
   - For tax year 2005: €27,000.
   - For tax year 2006: €30,000.
   - For tax year 2007: €33,000.
   - As from tax year 2008: €36,000.

   However, a company that has not attributed a remuneration of an amount of at least €24,500 (increased as from tax year 2005) to at least one key individual as defined above can nevertheless apply the reduced tax rates provided the taxable income is less than €24,500 (increased as from tax year 2005) and the remuneration attributed amounts to at least the taxable profit.
5. Companies belonging to a group that also holds a coordination center.

**Surcharge**/A surcharge is due on the final corporate tax amount upon assessment. For tax year 2004, this surcharge is equal to 6.75%. However, such surcharge can be avoided if sufficient advance payments are made in a timely fashion. The advance tax payments can be made in quarterly installments no later than the 10th day of the fourth, seventh, and tenth month of the financial year, and on the 20th day of the last month of the financial year. In the situation where the company's financial year ends on December 31, the due dates for the advance tax payments are April 10, July 10, October 10, and December 20. Advance payments give rise to a tax credit. The tax credit amounts to 9%, 7.5%, 6%, or 4.5% of the advance tax payment made, depending on whether such payment has been made in the first, second, third, or fourth period (percentages applicable for tax year 2004). If the total amount of credits exceeds the surcharge, no surcharge is due, but the excess of credits is not further taken into account for the final tax computation.

**Secret commissions tax**/A special assessment of 309% (300%, plus 300% of the crisis tax, i.e., 9%) is applicable to the so-called secret commissions, that is, to any expense consisting of the following.

- Commission, brokerage, trade, or other rebates, occasional or nonoccasional fees, bonuses or benefits in kind forming professional income for the beneficiaries.
- Remuneration or similar indemnities paid to personnel members or former personnel members of the paying company.
- Lump-sum allowances granted to personnel members in order to cover costs proper to the paying company, when the beneficiary of the expense is not properly identified by means of forms to be filed with the Belgian tax authorities.

According to a law published in November 2002, the secret commission tax is no longer applicable if the paying entity demonstrates that the aforesaid payments have been reported in the beneficiary's Belgian tax return. This new law is effective as of tax year 2003 (financial years ended on December 31, 2002 and later). The 309% rate is also applicable to hidden profits that are not part of the property of the company, with the exception of certain specific hidden reserves.

The special assessment of 309% and the expenses themselves are, however, fully deductible for corporate income tax purposes.

*Corporate income tax credit*/Corporations subject to the corporate income tax at the reduced corporate income tax rates get a tax credit fixed at 7.5% of the positive difference between the amount (at year-end) of the current year's capital paid in cash, and the highest capital that has been used in the past as a basis for allowing the income tax credit or the highest capital of the three preceding tax years, with a maximum of €19,850 per financial year.

## Corporate residence

A company that is not excluded from the scope of Belgian corporate income tax (e.g., nonprofit organizations) is considered to be a resident of Belgium for tax purposes if it has its registered office, its principal place of business, or its seat of management in Belgium. The "seat of management" has been defined by Belgian case law as the place from where directing impulsions emanate or the place where the company's effective management and central administration abide, meaning the place where the corporate decision-making process actually takes place.

## Other taxes

*Value-added tax*/VAT is payable on supplies of goods and on services rendered in Belgium as well as on importation and intra-community acquisitions of goods made in Belgium. VAT rates are as follows.

|  | % |
|---|---|
| Standard rate | 21 |
| Reduced rate applicable to cable TV, social houses, coal, etc. | 12 |
| Reduced rate applicable to basic necessary goods, flowers, and work to private immovable property 15 years old as well as (as from January 1, 2000 until December 31, 2005) to work to private immovable property five years old and to labor intensive services | 6 |
| Periodicals and newspapers | 6* |

*Reduced to 0 under conditions.

# Belgium

The following services/goods are, however, exempt from VAT (among others).

1. Medical, legal, social, and cultural services.
2. Renting of immovable property.
3. Sale of real estate. However, in case of buildings considered as new for VAT purposes, VAT is applicable.
4. Insurance services.
5. Most banking and financial services.

***Registration duty*/**Purchases and transfers of real estate located in Belgium, including buildings (except new buildings, which are subject to VAT—see above), are subject to registration duty at the rate of 12.5% on the transfer price or higher fair market value (except in the Flemish Region, where the applicable rate is 10%). Setting up of Belgian companies and increases in capital of Belgian companies are subject to 0.5% registration duty on subscribed capital or capital increase. However, the contribution (in property or usufruct) to a Belgian or foreign company by a physical person of real estate located in Belgium that is wholly or partially used as a dwelling is subject to a registration duty of 12.5% (10% in the Flemish Region).

The aforesaid registration duty of 0.5% is not levied upon the contribution to a Belgian company of a universality of goods (e.g., by way of a merger or a division) or of a line of business (i.e., a separate business unit that is able to function in an economically active manner, as an autonomous whole) provided the following conditions are met.

- The contributing company's registered office or seat of management is located in an EU member state.
- All assets and liabilities of the company or line of business are contributed.
- The contribution is exclusively remunerated by shares to which voting rights are attached (a remuneration in cash is allowed, up to a maximum of 10% of the nominal value of the attributed shares).

Provided these conditions are met, only a fixed registration duty of €25 is due.

Also, the contribution into a Belgian company of shares of an EU-resident company is exempt from the 0.5% registration duty, and is subject to only a fixed amount of €25 provided that, after the contribution, the acquiring company (the Belgian company) holds at least 75% of the capital of the company, the shares of which have been contributed, and that the contribution is remunerated by new shares of the acquiring company (a maximum compensation in cash of 10% can take place). In case the percentage of 75% is reached in different steps (contributions), the exemption from registration tax will only apply as from that contribution which leads to the above 75% percentage (and for all further contributions).

It should be noted that Belgian tax law does not foresee any recapture rule with respect to the aforesaid capital duty exemptions.

***Stamp duty*/**Stamp duties are due on transactions relating to public funds that are concluded or executed in Belgium, irrespective of their (Belgian or foreign) origin, to the extent that a professional intermediary intervenes in these transactions. Exemptions (amongst others for nonresidents) are available.

## Branch income

Branch profits are subject to the basic tax rate for Belgian corporations (increased by the 3% crisis tax) plus the possible surcharge for absence/insufficiency of advance payments (see above). Transfers of branch profits to the head office abroad do not give rise to further taxation in Belgium. Branches can benefit from the reduced corporate income tax rates under the applicable conditions (see above) with the following specifications.

1. To determine whether the €322,500 ceiling of taxable income is exceeded, and whether the "€24,500 (increased as from tax year 2005) remuneration" requirement is satisfied, reference needs to be made to the branch's results only.

2. All other conditions must be satisfied at the level of the foreign company taken as a whole.

Capital gains realized on real estate located in Belgium by nonresident companies are subject to a professional withholding tax at the basic tax rate. Such withholding tax can be offset against the final Belgian nonresident corporate income tax. Any balance is refundable.

## Income determination

*Inventory valuation*/Belgian accounting law provides for four methods of inventory valuation (method based on the individualization of the price of each item, method of the weighed average prices, LIFO method, and FIFO method). All these methods are accepted for tax purposes.

*Capital gains*/Capital gains are subject to the standard corporate income tax rate. Capital gains realized on tangible fixed assets and on intangible fixed assets on which depreciation has been accepted for tax purposes and that have been held for more than five years can, however, be subject to a deferred and spread taxation regime, provided the proceeds of the transfer are reinvested in tangible or intangible assets (subject to depreciation) in Belgium within three years (or five years in case of reinvestments in buildings, vessels or aircraft). If all the above conditions are complied with, the taxation of the capital gain is spread over the depreciation period (allowed for tax purposes) of the asset(s) that is acquired to fulfill the reinvestment obligation. Deferred and spread taxation occurs at the basic corporate income tax rate.

Capital gains realized on shares are exempt if dividends from such shares would, in case of distribution, meet the so-called taxation conditions under the participation exemption regime (see below). The "minimum participation condition" provided under that regime need not be satisfied.

*Intercompany dividends*/Dividends received by a Belgian company are first included in its taxable basis, on a gross basis when the dividends are received from a Belgian company or on a net basis, that is, after deduction of the foreign withholding tax, when they are received from a foreign company.

Then, a dividend-received deduction of 95% of the above amount can be applied under certain conditions. That deduction is, however, limited in case and to the extent it would lead to a tax loss. An excess, if any, cannot be carried forward and is thus definitely lost. However, recent case law would allow a company to defend that tax losses carried forward that may arise to the extent of the excess part of the dividend-received deduction. The Belgian participation exemption regime will

# Belgium

probably have to be amended so as to comply with the Directive, but the Belgian tax authorities have not, so far, changed their position in this respect.

Until tax year 2003, the dividend-received deduction is subject to the following.

- A "minimum participation condition"—The recipient company must have, at the moment of attribution, a participation of at least 5% or an acquisition value of at least €1,200,000 in the distributing company. That condition does, however, not apply to dividends received by insurance companies, credit institutions, stock exchange companies or investment companies, nor to dividends attributed by intercommunal organizations or by investment companies.
- A "taxation condition"—In a nutshell, the dividend income received must have been subject to tax at the level of the distributing company or its subsidiaries.
- There is no minimum period of ownership in order to qualify for the deduction.
- The "taxation condition" is based on five so-called exclusion rules and certain exceptions to these rules. Basically, the exclusion rules apply to the following.
  1. Tax haven companies, that is, companies that are not subject to Belgian corporate income tax or to a similar foreign tax, or that are established in a country where the common taxation system is notably more advantageous than in Belgium.
  2. Finance, treasury, or investment companies that, although they are subject in their country of tax residency to a taxation system similar to that of Belgium, as mentioned under point 1 above, nevertheless benefit from a taxation system that deviates from the one commonly applicable.
  3. Offshore companies, that is, companies receiving income (other than dividend income) that originates outside their country of tax residency, that is, the country where such income is subject to a separate taxation system that deviates substantially from the common one.
  4. Companies having branches that benefit from a taxation system notably more advantageous than the Belgian nonresident corporate taxation system.
  5. Intermediary holding companies, that is, companies (with the exception of investment companies) that redistribute dividend-received income, which, on the basis of regulations mentioned under points 1 through 4 above, would not qualify for the dividend-received deduction for at least 90% of its amount in case of direct holding.

There are numerous exceptions to these exclusion rules that need to be analyzed on a case-by-case basis.

The recent Belgian corporate tax reform has brought some amendments to the participation exemption regime, which are applicable as from tax year 2004, as follows.

  1. As to the minimum participation condition, the following applies.
     - The minimum shareholding percentage is increased to 10%, while the minimum shareholding acquisition value stays €1,200,000.
     - Additional conditions are added, that is, the beneficiary of the dividend must have been holding the full legal ownership of the underlying shares for at least one year prior to the dividend distribution, or commit to hold it for a minimum of one year (share-per-share test). Furthermore, the shares should be booked as "financial fixed assets."

2.  As to the taxation condition, the following applies.

    - Countries where the minimum level of (nominal or effective) taxation is below 15% qualify as tax havens for the application of the regime (a list of tainted countries has been set down by Royal Decree). The common tax legislations applicable to companies residing in the EU are, however, deemed not to be notably more advantageous than in Belgium.
    - The rules denying the participation exemption for dividends originating from profits obtained through low-taxed branch offices have been tightened.

Generally speaking, interest charges relating to the acquisition of shares are tax deductible. However, there is a specific antidividend stripping rule. Interest payments are indeed not tax deductible in Belgium up to the amount of dividends derived from any shareholding qualifying for the dividend received deduction, when said shareholding has not been held for at least one year. This rule is, however, not applicable with respect to shareholdings in group companies or in other affiliated companies. According to the Parliamentary Works, the provision is also not applicable with respect to shares acquired upon setting up or capital increase of a company. For the rule to apply, the interest charge does not need to be directly connected with the acquisition of the shareholding in question. As from tax year 2004, the aforesaid provision is abolished (and therefore at arm's length interest charges are in principle tax deductible, without any restriction—see however next paragraph).

**Thin capitalization**/The deduction of interest paid by a Belgian company or branch can be partially denied when the beneficial owner of such interest is not subject to tax, or is subject with respect to the interest received to a tax regime that is significantly more advantageous than the ordinary Belgian income tax system. In that case, the interest charge is considered as a disallowed expense to the extent that the outstanding total amount of loans (on which the interest is calculated), other than fixed interest securities, from such beneficiary exceeds seven times the sum of taxable reserves (at the start of the financial year) and paid-up capital (at the end of the financial year) of the interest paying company.

**Special thin capitalization rule**/Interest due on advances or loans (other than bonds) granted to a Belgian company by shareholders (natural persons only) of that company, or by any person acting as a director, manager, (*gérant*/*zaakvoerder*), liquidator or exercising a similar function in that company, or by the spouse or minor children of such persons, is recharacterized into dividend income (and is therefore not tax deductible) to the extent that the following applies.

1.  The interest rate exceeds the applicable market rate.
2.  The amount of such advances or loans exceeds the sum of the paid-up capital (at year-end) and taxable reserves (at the start of the financial year) of the Belgian company.

Interest due on advances granted by a Belgian resident company subject to corporate income tax and acting as a director, manager (*gérant*/*zaakvoerder*), liquidator, and so on, is excluded from the above limitation.

**Foreign income**/A Belgian resident company is subject to corporate tax on its worldwide income. However, notwithstanding the aforesaid, the following applies.

- Until tax year 2003, in case there is no double tax treaty applicable (see list below), income realized abroad by foreign branches is taxable in Belgium at a reduced rate equal to one-quarter of the normal corporate income tax (i.e.,

10.04%), provided that this income has been taxed abroad. As from tax year 2004, this provision is no longer applicable. As a result, foreign source profits not exempted from taxation by virtue of a double tax treaty will now be taxed at the basic corporate tax rate in Belgium (i.e., 33.99% as from tax year 2004). Income realized by foreign branches located in countries with which Belgium has concluded a double tax treaty is exempt from Belgian corporate income tax.

- Unless a more advantageous provision (e.g., so-called tax sparing provision) would apply based on a double tax treaty concluded by Belgium (see list below), a foreign tax credit is granted under Belgian tax law with respect to foreign royalty income, provided that this income has effectively been subject to taxation in its source country. This foreign tax credit is equal to 15/85 of the net frontier amount (i.e., after deduction of foreign withholding tax) of the royalty. The foreign tax credit is included in the taxable basis of the recipient company (grossing-up). It is only creditable against Belgian income tax to the extent that said foreign income is included in the taxable basis of the Belgian company. Excess of foreign tax credit, if any, is not refundable.

- Unless a more advantageous provision (e.g., so-called tax sparing provision) would apply based on a double tax treaty concluded by Belgium (see list below), the Belgian beneficiary of foreign interest income is entitled to a foreign tax credit under Belgian tax law, provided that this income has effectively been subject to taxation in its source country. The computation of the foreign tax credit is based on the net frontier interest income (i.e., after deduction of foreign withholding tax) and is determined based on the following formula.

First fraction

$[A / (100 - A)] \times B$

Where:

A = Foreign withholding tax actually levied, expressed as a percentage of the income to which it relates, with a maximum of 15%. The foreign withholding tax in the denominator is equal to the numerator of the fraction, and thus the maximum value of the fraction is 15/85. If the foreign withholding tax is borne by the debtor of the income (instead of the recipient), the denominator remains at 100.

B = Net interest received.

The amount determined using the first fraction must again be multiplied by a second fraction equal to the following:

Second fraction

$(C - D) / C$

Where:

C = Total income of the Belgian recipient (excluding capital gains).

D = Interest and royalties paid by the Belgian recipient.

The tax credit computed as described above is included in the taxable base of the Belgian lender (grossing-up). It is creditable against the corporate income tax due but is not refundable in case of excess.

- Undistributed income of subsidiaries, whether or not foreign, is not subject to any Belgian income tax.

***Bonus shares—Stock dividends***/Distribution of bonus shares to the shareholders in compensation for an increase of the share capital by incorporation of existing reserves is in principle tax-free. The situation may be different if the shareholder has the choice between cash or stock dividend.

## Deductions

***Depreciation***/Depreciation booked on an asset is tax deductible to the extent that it results from a devaluation of this asset, and that this devaluation really took place during the taxable period concerned. The depreciation methods that are accepted by Belgian tax law are the straight-line method (linear method) and the double-declining method. In the latter case, the depreciation annuity may not exceed 40% of the acquisition value. The double-declining method may not be used for intangible fixed assets, cars, minibuses and cars for mixed purposes and for assets, the use of which has been transferred to a third party (e.g., in case of operational leasing). Depreciation rates are based on the estimated lifetime of the assets concerned. However, intangible fixed assets have to be depreciated over a period of at least five years for tax purposes (except R&D expenses, for which the minimum depreciation period is three years). Euro software can nevertheless be depreciated over less than five years when subject to "abnormal" decreases in value that relate directly to the transition to Euro currency or when the software has been acquired or manufactured specifically to cope with the transition to Euro.

Note also that Belgian accounting and tax laws allow depreciation of goodwill arising at the occasion of an asset deal. For Belgian tax purposes, the depreciation period, which very much depends on the elements included in the goodwill, is minimum five years (according to the Minister of Finance, "clientele" should be depreciated over a period of 10 to 12 years), and the straight-line method must be applied. The aforesaid accounting and tax depreciation is not available in case of a merger or a demerger that occurs tax-free (i.e., that, among others, follows the continuity principle from an accounting perspective).

Until tax year 2003, a taxpayer is allowed to deduct a full annuity as depreciation for the financial year in which an asset is acquired, irrespective of the date of acquisition. The new law contains a provision stating that for the year of acquisition of an asset, only the pro-rata of an annuity can be accepted as depreciation for income tax purposes (to be computed on a daily basis). This provision does, however, not apply to companies subject to reduced rates. However, ancillary expenses incurred at the time of acquisition will have to be depreciated in the same way as the asset to which they relate (thus no full deduction in the year of acquisition, except for the companies benefiting from the reduced tax rates).

***Net operating losses***/Tax losses can be carried forward without any limitation in time. However, in case of change in control of a Belgian company (e.g., if the shares of this company are transferred and along with them the majority of the voting rights), the amount of tax loss carryforward available in that company (before the change of control) can no longer be offset against future profits, unless the change can be justified by legitimate needs of a financial or economic nature in the hands of the loss realizing company (i.e., evidence must be brought that the change is not purely tax driven). The condition of legitimate needs of a financial or economic nature is considered to be fulfilled when the employees and activities of the company are maintained by the new shareholder or when the company's control is acquired by a company belonging to the same consolidated group of companies as the former controlling company.

There is no tax loss carryback provision under Belgian tax law.

# Belgium

***Payments to foreign affiliates***/A Belgian corporation can claim a deduction for royalties, management service fees and interest charges paid to foreign affiliates, provided such amounts are at arm's length. However, when such payments are made, directly or indirectly, to a foreign person or entity or to a foreign branch, which is not subject to tax or is subject, with respect to the payments received, to a tax regime that is notably more advantageous than the Belgian tax regime on such income, there is a reversal of the burden of proof. Such charges will be disallowed unless the Belgian enterprise can prove that the payments are reasonable and that they correspond to genuine and real transactions.

Fees, commissions, and so on, paid to beneficiaries located in foreign countries, which are not properly reported on Form 281.50 and Summary Form 325.50, will in principle be subject to the secret commission tax, whatever the country the beneficiary of those payments is resident. However, recent case law would allow a company to defend the position that such reporting should not be made, to the extent that the payments are not subject to Belgian income tax in the hands of the beneficiary.

***Disallowed expenses***/As a general rule, expenses are tax-deductible in Belgium provided that they are incurred in order to maintain or to increase taxable income, that they are incurred or have accrued during the taxable period concerned, and that evidence of the reality and the amount of such expenses is provided by the taxpayer. Notwithstanding the aforesaid rule, the following expenses are not tax deductible in Belgium (this list is not limitative).

- Belgian (resident or nonresident) corporate income tax (including advance tax payments, any surcharge imposed in case of insufficient advance tax payments and any interest for late payment of the corporate income tax), Belgian movable withholding tax as well as any foreign tax credit granted in relation with foreign movable withholding tax. Immovable withholding tax, secret commission tax and foreign taxes, however, are considered as tax deductible.
- Any administrative and judicial fines or penalties (except for VAT proportionate fines).
- A total of 25% of car related expenses (except for fuel expenses, financial costs incurred in relation with cars and car telephone expenses, that remain fully tax deductible).
- A total of 50% of restaurant expenses (incurred in Belgium), representation expenses and business gifts (there are exceptions).
- Advantages granted to employees for social reasons (e.g., hospitalization insurance premiums, gifts of a small value, lunch vouchers).
- Capital losses on shares (except in the case of liquidation, up to the amount of paid-up capital of the liquidated company).
- As from tax year 2004, regional taxes and contributions, including penalties, increases, ancillary expenses and interest for late payment will no longer be tax-deductible (exceptions will however apply).

The following are also not tax deductible in Belgium.

- Interest, royalties, or fees paid or attributed—directly or indirectly—to nonresident taxpayers or foreign branches that are not subject to tax or are subject—with respect to the income received—to a notably more favorable tax regime than the Belgian tax regime on such income, unless the Belgian taxpayer can prove that those payments are made with respect to real and genuine transactions and provided that the payments do not exceed normal limits for such transactions.

- Interest paid, to the extent that it exceeds an amount corresponding to the market rate, taking into account factual circumstances proper to the appraisal of the risk linked to the operation, and particularly the financial situation of the debtor and the duration of the loan. The latter test is, however, not applied with respect to interest paid to a Belgian based financial institution.

*Provisions—bad debt reserve*/Provisions and bad debt reserve are tax deductible provided that the following applies.

- They are set up to cover clearly identified losses and charges and, thus, not to cover "general" risks, that have been rendered probable by events which took place during the taxable period concerned.
- They are booked at the end of the financial year in one or more separate accounts of the balance sheet.
- They are reported on a specific form enclosed with the tax return.
- They relate to losses and charges that are deductible for Belgian tax purposes.

## Group taxation

Belgium does not apply any tax consolidation mechanism. Note, however, that it is contemplated to have such mechanism implemented by 2010 for Belgian companies.

## Tax incentives

*Coordination centers*/A qualifying coordination center is a Belgian company or a Belgian branch of a foreign company the meets the following.

- That is part of an international group (certain size criteria apply).
- That carries out activities (limited to support and financial services) only for the benefit of group members (e.g., advertising and sales promotion, collection and supply of information, insurance and reinsurance, scientific research, relations with national and international authorities, accounting centralization, administration and data processing, all preparatory and auxiliary activities, reinvoicing, factoring, leasing, financing, etc.).
- That complies with certain employment requirements.

The Belgian Coordination Centers (BCC) agreement is in principle granted for a period of ten years (see, however, below).The taxable basis of the currently existing coordination centers is determined by applying a certain percentage (in general 8%) on the total amount of operational expenses, not including salary expenses, financial expenses and income tax expenses. The so-determined taxable income may, however, not be lower than an alternative taxable basis that is equal to all disallowed expenses and abnormal or benevolent advantages received by the coordination center. No deduction for investments or losses can be claimed.

Coordination centers are exempted from real estate tax and registration tax. Dividends distributed, as well as interest and royalties paid by coordination centers, are generally exempt from withholding tax.

An annual tax of €10,000 per full-time employee working in the coordination center on January 1 of each year, with an annual maximum of €100,000 per coordination center, is due at the latest on March 31 of each year.

# Belgium

The BCC regime has recently been redrafted in order to take into account the European Code of Conduct as well as the European state aid rules.

Under the new regime, the taxable basis of the BCCs will be determined on a cost-plus basis, whereby "cost" will be defined as full cost (and thus includes personnel and financial costs). The taxable profit will no longer be calculated as a fixed percentage of the costs but will be determined on a case-by-case basis and safeguarded by an Advance Pricing Agreement. The so-called alternative basis may still apply.

The tax on BCCs of €100,000 maximum is maintained, but may be credited against the corporate tax to be paid (although not refundable).

Finally, the exemption of Belgian real estate tax is abolished. The exemptions of movable withholding tax and of registration tax are, however, maintained.

On January 21, 2003, the Ecofin Council agreed that for BCCs recognized until December 31, 2000, their special tax regime could run until maximum December 31, 2010. As a result, BCC's recognized before 2000 will enjoy their ten-year-recognition period. However, they will not be able to renew their agreement under the old BCC regime up to 2010. Therefore, once the agreement expires, the renewal will have to be asked under the new BCC regime.

Finally, it has to be noted that the European Commission has decided that the old BCC regime is to be considered as a legitimate state aid which is not compliant with EU legislation. The Commission has ordered Belgium to discontinue the scheme, closing immediately to new entrants and phase it out with respect to existing beneficiaries not later than December 31, 2010. As the Commission had initially approved the regime, the beneficiaries are not required to pay back the tax advantages they have received in the past.

***Distribution centers***/A distribution center can be set up either as a Belgian company or as a Belgian branch of a foreign company. It must form part of a Belgian or foreign group of dependent companies (but not necessarily of a multi-national group) and be involved exclusively in authorized activities, which can be classified in three categories: agency activities, treatment of goods (without, however, any creation of added value) and administration activities. A distribution center, in performing its activities, may not bear any business risk or only insignificant risks.

In principle, distribution centers are subject to the ordinary taxation system that applies to branches and corporations. However, a distribution center is not deemed to grant any abnormal or benevolent advantages (and thus no tax adjustment will be operated at the level of such center) if, and as long as, its turnover is not lower than the sum of the following items.

- The purchase price of raw materials, supplies, merchandise, and finished products that were purchased for the account of group members.
- The costs of services rendered by third parties to the distribution center within the scope of its allowed activities, provided that those services are rendered at a normal price.
- 105% of all operating costs (excluding the above-mentioned costs, the nondeductible expenses and the taxable provisions and reserves).

If the amount of turnover is lower than the total of the above-mentioned items, the difference between both amounts is reported in the taxable basis of the distribution center as an abnormal or benevolent advantage granted.

*Service centers*/A Belgian company or a Belgian branch that forms part of a group of related companies may qualify as a service center, provided that its activities, rendered for the sole benefit of the group, are limited to the following.

1. Activities of a preparatory and/or auxiliary nature.
2. Activities providing information to customers (e.g., call centers, help desks).
3. Activities providing a "passive" contribution to sales: The service center will act in the name of and on behalf of group companies.
4. Activities implying an "active" participation in sales of goods or delivery of services. The service center will act in its own name but on behalf of group companies.

In principle, the service center is subject to the ordinary taxation system applied to branches and corporations. However, it can be accepted that the service center does not grant any (taxable) abnormal or benevolent advantage if the following applies.

- According to the cost-plus method (applying to service centers performing activities listed under (1), (2), and (3) above), the turnover is not lower than the sum of the following items.
  - Costs of services that, in the framework of the allowed activities of the service center, are supplied by third parties for the benefit of the center, insofar as the services might have been invoiced directly to the companies of the group to which the center belongs and the services are invoiced by the provider at a price including a normal profit margin.
  - Personnel costs, including all expenses related to personnel.
  - A total of 105% to 115% of all operating costs (excluding the above-mentioned costs, the nondeductible expenses and the taxable reserves and provisions).
- According to the resale-minus method (applying to service center actively involved as intermediaries—see (4) above), the following applies.
  - The turnover is not lower than the total amount of operating costs (excluding the nondeductible expenses and the taxable reserves and provisions).
  - The effective margin (being the difference between the turnover realized and the turnover ceded back to the group members) is higher than the margin required under the resale-minus ruling granted by the Belgian tax authorities (knowing that the minimum margin required is always lower than 5%).

Both methods described above can be combined. Such combination requires an allocation of operational expenses to determine which expenses relate to which activities.

As from January 1, 2003, in order to obtain the application of the service center and distribution center regimes, one will have to file a ruling request based on the ruling practice embodied in the new tax law. Such request will have to be backed up with a benchmarking study. The transfer pricing ruling granted based on such procedure will most likely take the form of a cost-plus ruling applicable on all the costs incurred by the center and will be applicable during five financial years.

*Investment deduction*/The percentage of the standard investment deduction was reduced to zero for investments as from March 27, 1992. However, qualifying small- and medium-size companies that are subject to Belgian resident or nonresident corporate income tax can still claim an investment deduction (3% for tax year 2004) on investments up to €6,800,000 per financial year. This basic percentage of 3% is increased by 10.5 percentage points for energy-saving investments and investments used for research and development and by 5 percentage points for investments made in innovation companies. The same increased investment deduction (plus 10.5% and possibly 5%) also applies to new licenses (not already used for business purposes in Belgium) acquired by companies. The aforesaid increased investment deductions can be claimed by all companies (whatever the size).

### Simplified "spread" investment deduction method

Enterprises employing less than 20 persons on the first day of the financial year in which the investment takes place can elect to use the simplified "spread" investment deduction method, whereby the investment deduction rate is fixed at 3%, increased by 7.5% of the annual depreciation charge (irrespective of the category of the investment), totaling 10.5%.

Enterprises, irrespective of the number of personnel employed, can also elect to use the simplified "spread" method for investments in assets used for research and development of new products and technologies. The investment deduction rate is fixed at 3% increased by 17.5% of the annual depreciation charge, totaling 20.5%.

### Investment deduction carryforward

In case of insufficiency or absence of taxable profits, the investment deduction can be carried forward without any limitation in time or in amount. However, the following restrictions apply as to the maximum amount of investment deduction carried forward that is tax deductible in a given year.

| Amount carried forward | Deductible amount |
| --- | --- |
| Up to €743,440 | Transferred amount |
| €743,441 to €2,973,770 | €743,440 |
| Over €2,973,770 | 25% of transferable amount |

Under certain conditions the investment deduction carryforward can be lost after a change of ownership (see "Net operating losses" above).

***Tax deduction for scientific personnel***/A tax deduction of €11,990 is granted for each additional scientific researcher employed in Belgium. The same incentive is extended to each employee expanding the technical possibilities of the enterprise, the head of integrated quality control or the head of export. The number of qualifying personnel is calculated per additional staff member employed on a full-time basis (part-time employees equaling full-time employees also qualify).

The deduction has furthermore been increased to €23,980 for highly qualified researchers (i.e., researchers with a doctorate and who can justify a ten years' service). A clawback applies if the number of qualifying personnel is decreased.

***Additional personnel***/An exemption of €4,460 is granted to companies that used to employ less than 11 persons on December 31, 1997 and which hire additional staff in Belgium with gross daily income of not more than €79.82.

***Tax exempted investment reserve***/As from tax year 2004, small- and medium-sized enterprises will be allowed to establish a tax-exempt reserve up to 50% of the increases of the taxable retained earnings, before calculation of the reserve for investments. The increase in taxable retained earnings that is taken into account for the calculation of the contribution to the investment reserve will be limited to €37,500 per taxable period, resulting in a maximum contribution to the investment reserve of €18,750 per taxable period.

## Withholding taxes

Domestic corporations and branches of foreign corporations paying dividends, interest, royalties, and/or certain rentals are required to withhold tax. The standard rates applicable under Belgian tax law are fixed at 25% for dividends and 15% for interest, royalties, and certain rentals. However, some withholding tax reductions/exemptions are foreseen under Belgian domestic tax law.

1. A reduced Belgian withholding tax of 15% applies to dividend distributions relating to nonpreference shares subscribed in cash, issued as from January 1, 1994 and which, upon issuance, are nominative or have been deposited with a financial institution in Belgium, on condition that the distributing company does not irrevocably renounce its right to benefit from the reduced rate of withholding tax.

2. A reduced Belgian withholding tax of 15% is foreseen for dividend distributions relating to nonpreference shares issued as from January 1, 1994 in the context of a public offering (i.e., shares quoted on the stock exchange) on condition that the distributing company does not irrevocably renounce its right to benefit from the reduced rate of withholding tax.

3. Under certain conditions, a reduced withholding tax of 15% applies to dividend distributions made by small- and medium-size companies quoted on a stock market or of which part of the capital has been contributed by a PRIVAK (Private Equity Bevak)/PRICAF (Private Equity SICAF) (a company that must also be quoted on a stock market) as defined by the 1997 law (a company with the sole objective of collective investment in companies—SICAV (*Société d'Investissment à Capital Variable*)/SICAF (*Société d'Investissment à Capital Fixe*)/SIC (*Société d'Investissment à Capital*)—whose shares are not quoted on a stock market and in growth companies).

4. A withholding tax exemption on dividends is foreseen if both the receiving and distributing companies are subject to Belgian corporate income tax, if the receiving company holds a minimum shareholding of at least 25% for at least one year in the capital of the subsidiary and if certain formalities are complied with. In case the one-year holding requirement is not fulfilled at the time of distribution, the distributing company should provisionally withhold the amount of withholding tax due (but it does not have to be paid to the tax authorities). Once the one-year holding requirement is met, the provisionally withheld tax amount can be paid out to the parent company. If the one-year holding requirement is eventually not complied with (e.g., because the Belgian participation is disposed of by the parent company before the one-year holding requirement is met), then the Belgian company has to pay the amount provisionally withheld increased with interest for late payment (at an annual rate of 7%) to the competent services of the Belgian tax authorities.

5. A withholding tax exemption is also foreseen for the distribution of profits made by a Belgian subsidiary to an EU parent company if both the parent and subsidiary have a legal form that is mentioned in the Annex to the EU Directive, if both are subject to corporate income tax and if the parent

company holds during an uninterrupted period of at least one year a shareholding of at least 25% in the capital of the distributing company. The same procedure as that described under point 4 above applies in case the one-year holding requirement is not met at the moment of the dividend distribution.

6. While in the past an exemption was available, a 10% tax is now applicable to profits that are attributed or made payable as a result of the (partial) liquidation of a company or the acquisition by a company of its own shares; however, the exemption of Belgian withholding tax is maintained for liquidation proceeds distributed by a SICAV, for dividends resulting from tax-free mergers and for liquidation proceeds resulting from the redemption of own shares by a company listed on a regulated stock exchange. If the conditions of 4 and 5 above apply, an exemption is also available. This 10% tax is applicable to profits attributed or made payable as from January 1, 2002, except in the case of the liquidation of a company—if the liquidation was closed prior to March 25, 2003.

7. Belgian domestic tax law also provides for a withholding tax exemption on the following movable income sourced in Belgium (this list is not exhaustive).

   a. Income from deposits allocated or attributed to nonresident savers by Belgian banks.

   b. Income from bonds, treasury bonds, or other similar titles of which the beneficiaries are identified as financial institutions.

   c. Income from receivables (this includes income from commercial receivables) or loans of which the beneficiaries are identified as financial institutions or professional investors. "Professional investors" are defined as any Belgian resident company or branch not being a financial institution or any equivalent. As a result, interest payments between two Belgian companies are exempted from withholding tax.

   d. Income from bonds paid by a Belgian resident financial institution or by a Belgian resident company to nonresident savers, provided that such bonds are registered on a nominal basis with the debtor of the income during the entire period to which the interest relates.

   e. Income from bonds and loans granted by "eligible quoted companies" and "eligible intra muros financial companies" to nonresidents (under conditions).

   f. Interest payments between a Belgian company and an EU tax resident company in case of direct or indirect shareholding of at least 25% for an uninterrupted period of at least one year (i.e., transposition of EU interest and royalty directive in Belgian tax law).

With respect to payments made to nonresident corporations or individuals, withholding tax exemptions and/or reductions can also be found in the double taxation treaties concluded by Belgium.

| Recipient | Dividends | Interest | Royalties, certain rentals |
|---|---|---|---|
| | % | % | % |
| Nonresident corporations and individuals: | | | |
| Nontreaty | 25 | 15 | 15 |
| Treaty: | | | |
| Algeria | 15 | 0, 15 | 5, 15 |
| Argentina | 10, 15 | 0, 12 | 3, 5, 10, 15 |
| Australia | 15 | 10 | 10 |
| Austria | 15 | 0, 15 | 10 |
| Bangladesh | 15 | 0, 15 | 10 |
| Belarus | 5, 15 | 0, 10 | 5 |
| Brazil | 15 | 10, 15 | 10, 15, 25 |
| Bulgaria | 10 | 0, 10 | 5 |
| Canada | 5, 15 | 0, 10, 15 | 0, 10 |
| China, P.R. (1) | 10 | 0, 10 | 0, 10 |
| Cyprus | 10, 15 | 0, 10 | 0 |
| Czech Republic | 5, 15 | 0, 10 | 0, 5, 10 |
| Denmark | 15 | 15 | 0 |
| Egypt | 15, 20 | 15 | 15, 25 |
| Estonia | 5, 15 | 0, 10 | 5, 10 |
| Finland | 5, 10, 15 | 10 | 5 |
| France | 10, 15 | 15 | 0 |
| Germany | 15 | 0, 15 | 0 |
| Greece | 15 | 10 | 5 |
| Hungary | 10 | 0, 15 | 0 |
| Iceland | 5, 15 | 0, 10 | 0 |
| India | 15 | 10, 15 | 20 |
| Indonesia | 15 | 10, 15 | 10 |
| Ireland, Rep. of | 15 | 15 | 0 |
| Israel | 15 | 15 | 10 |
| Italy | 15 | 0, 15 | 5 |
| Ivory Coast | 15 | 16 | 10 |
| Japan | 5, 15 | 10 | 10 |
| Kazakhstan | 0, 5, 15 | 0, 10 | 10 |
| Korea, Rep. of | 15 | 0, 10 | 10 |
| Kuwait | 0, 10 | 0 | 10 |
| Latvia | 5, 15 | 0, 10 | 5, 10 |
| Lithuania | 5, 15 | 0, 10 | 5, 10 |
| Luxembourg | 10, 15 | 0, 15 | 0 |
| Malaysia | 15 | 10 | 10 |
| Malta | 15 | 0, 10 | 10 |
| Mauritius | 5, 10 | 0, 10 | 0 |
| Mexico | 5, 15 | 0, 10, 15 | 10 |
| Mongolia | 5, 15 | 0, 10 | 5 |
| Morocco | 15 | 15 | 5, 10 |
| Netherlands | 5, 15 | 0, 10 | 0 |
| New Zealand | 15 | 10 | 10 |
| Nigeria | 12.5, 15 | 12.5 | 12.5 |

# Belgium

| Recipient | Dividends | Interest | Royalties, certain rentals |
|---|---|---|---|
| | % | % | % |
| Norway | 5, 15 | 0, 15 | 0 |
| Pakistan | 15 | 0, 15 | 15, 20 |
| Philippines | 10, 15, 20 | 0, 10, 15 | 15, 25 |
| Poland | 10 | 0, 10 | 10 |
| Portugal | 15 | 0, 15 | 10 |
| Romania | 5, 10, 15 | 0, 10, 15 | 5, 10 |
| Russia | 10 | 0, 10 | 0, 15 |
| Senegal | 15 | 15 | 10 |
| Singapore | 15 | 15 | 0, 15 |
| Slovak Republic | 5, 15 | 0, 10 | 5 |
| Slovenia | 5, 15 | 0, 10 | 5 |
| South Africa | 5, 15 | 0, 10 | 0 |
| Spain | 0, 15 | 15 | 5 |
| Sri Lanka | 15 | 0, 10 | 10 |
| Sweden | 5, 15 | 0, 10 | 0 |
| Switzerland | 10, 15 | 0, 10 | 0 |
| Thailand | 15, 20 | 0, 10, 25 | 5, 15 |
| Tunisia | 15 | 0, 15 | 5, 15, 20 |
| Turkey | 15, 20 | 0, 15 | 10 |
| USSR (former) (2) | 15 | 0, 15 | 0 |
| Ukraine | 5, 15 | 0, 2, 10 | 0, 10 |
| United Arab Emirates | 0, 5, 10 | 0, 5 | 0, 5 |
| United Kingdom | 5, 10 | 15 | 0 |
| United States | 5, 15 | 0, 15 | 0 |
| Uzbekistan | 5, 15 | 0, 10 | 5 |
| Venezuela | 5, 15 | 0, 10 | 5 |
| Vietnam | 5, 10, 15 | 0, 10 | 5, 10, 15 |
| Yugoslavia (former) (3) | 10, 15 | 15 | 10 |

Notes:

1. Not applicable to Hong Kong.
2. The USSR treaty is still applicable to Armenia, Azerbaijan, Georgia, Kyrgyzstan, Moldova, Tajikistan, and Turkmenistan.
3. The treaty concluded with ex-Yugoslavia is still applicable to Bosnia-Herzegovina, Croatia, Macedonia, and Serbia Montenegro.

Income tax treaties in effect on March 15, 2004 are listed above. The following are tax treaties signed or under renegotiation but not yet entered into force: Albania, Armenia, Brazil, Cameroon, Canada, Croatia, Ecuador, Gabon, Georgia, Guinea, Hong Kong, Luxembourg, Peru, Poland, San Marino, Saudi Arabia, and Singapore.

## Tax administration

*Returns*/As a general rule, the annual corporate (resident or nonresident) tax return cannot be filed less than one month as from the date where the annual accounts have been approved, and not later than six months after the end of the period to which the tax return refers. For instance, assuming that the accounting year has been closed on December 31, 2003, the corporate tax return needs to be filed in principle by June 30, 2004 at the latest.

*Payment of tax*/Corporate income tax is payable within two months following the issue of the tax assessment. Since January 1, 1999, interest for late payment amounts to 7% per annum (legal interest).

## *CORPORATION TAX CALCULATION*

Tax year 2004 (i.e., accounting year ended on December 31, 2003 or between January 1, 2004 and December 30, 2004)

## Assumptions

|  | € |
|---|---|
| Accounting profit before tax | 7,560,000 |
| General provisions for risks and charges | 241,000 |
| Penalties | 7,500 |
| Abnormal or benevolent advantage | 42,600 |
| Car expenses | 53,000 |
| Dividend income received | 390,000 |
| Tax loss carryforward | 785,000 |
| Recoverable withholding tax on interest income | 75,000 |

The company made the following advance payments:

| | |
|---|---|
| 1st advance payment | 750,000 |
| 2nd advance payment | 500,000 |
| 3rd advance payment | 100,000 |
| 4th advance payment | 100,000 |

## Determination of the taxable basis

| | | | | |
|---|---|---|---|---|
| Taxable reserves | | | | |
| Accounting profit before tax | | | | 7,560,000 |
| General provisions for risks and charges | | | | 241,000 |
| Disallowed expenses | | | | |
| Penalties | 100% | 7,500 | 7,500 | |
| Abnormal or benevolent advantage | 100% | 42,600 | 42,600 | |
| Car expenses | 25% | 54,000 | 13,500 | |
| Total | | | | 7,864,600 |
| *Less*—Dividend-received deduction | | | | |
| (95% x 390,000) | | | | (370,500) |
| *Less*—Tax loss carry forward | | | | (785,000) |
| Taxable basis | | | | 6,709,100 |

## Computation of corporate income tax

| Bonus for advance payments | | % | Bonus |
|---|---|---|---|
| 1st advance payment | 750,000 | 9 | 67,500 |
| 2nd advance payment | 500,000 | 7.5 | 37,500 |
| 3rd advance payment | 100,000 | 6 | 6,000 |
| 4th advance payment | 100,000 | 4.5 | 4,500 |
| Total | 1,450,000 | | 115,500 |

# Belgium

## Computation of taxes

|  | € |
|---|---:|
| Corporate income tax (33.99% x 6,709,100)............................................. | 2,280,423 |
| *Less*—Withholding tax on interest income................................................ | (75,000) |
|  | 2,205,423 |
| Increase for insufficient advance payments: |  |
| Surcharge (6.75% x 2,205,423) ........................................ 148,866 | 33,366 |
| *Less*—Bonus for advance payments ................................ (115,500) |  |
|  | 2,238,789 |
| *Less*—Advance payments....................................................................... | (1,450,000) |
| Tax Due ............................................................................................... | 788,789 |

Note:

Exchange rate of the Euro at January 1, 2004: US$1 = €0.793903.

## PwC contact

For additional information on taxation in Bermuda, contact:

Richard E. Irvine
PricewaterhouseCoopers
P.O. Box HM 1171
Hamilton HMEX
Bermuda
Telephone: (1) (441) 295 2000
Fax: (1) (441) 295 1242
LN address: Richard Irvine/TLS/PwC@Americas-BM
e-mail: richard.e.irvine@bm.pwc.com

## Absence of income taxation

Bermuda does not impose a tax on income or capital gains on corporations in Bermuda, nor does Bermuda impose any withholding taxes on payments by Bermuda corporations.

## Note

Exchange rate of the Bermuda dollar at January 1, 2004: US$1.00 = Bd$1.00.

# Bolivia

## PwC contact

For additional information on taxation in Bolivia, contact:

Rosa Talavera
PricewaterhouseCoopers S.R.L.
Avenida Mariscal
Santa Cruz & Yanacocha
Edificio Hansa, 19th floor
La Paz, Bolivia
Telephone: (591-2) 2408181
Fax: (591-2) 211 2752
e-mail: rosa.talavera @bo.pwc.com

## General note

The information in this entry is current as of January 2004. For subsequent developments consult the contact listed above.

## Taxes on corporate income

Pursuant to Law No. 1606, issued on December 22, 1994, all companies are subject to a 25% tax on corporate income. The taxable base is the profit arising from financial statements prepared in accordance with generally accepted financial principles, adjusted for tax purposes, as per the requirements established in the tax law and regulations.

On November 25, 1996, Law No. 1731 introduced an additional corporate income tax at a rate of 25%, which affects only extractive activities (mining and oil/gas). The additional tax is calculated on the same basis as the normal tax, except that two additional deductions are allowed, for up to 33% of the accumulated investment as from 1991, and 45% of the gross revenue of each extractive operation (e.g., a field, a mining site) with a ceiling of Bs360 million approximately (currently approximately US$46 million) for each extractive operation.

*Special industries*/Pursuant to law No. 1777, dated March 17, 1997, all mining companies are subject to the general income tax and to a special form of royalty called the "complementary mining tax." The corporate income tax is a payment in advance of the complementary mining tax, so that the effective tax burden for companies is the higher of the two taxes.

*Taxes on liberal professionals*/Liberal professionals (lawyers, economic or engineering advisers, accountants, etc.) are subject to corporate tax at a rate of 12.5% on their revenue net of value-added tax (VAT). Liberal professionals can offset 50% of the calculated tax by VAT paid on purchases for their personal consumption.

## Corporate residence

All corporate entities operating in Bolivia must register a corporate residence within the country, which is the corporate residence for tax purposes.

## Other taxes

*Value-added tax/*The 1986 tax reform (Law No. 843) introduced a VAT on all goods and services sales at the rate of 10%. Effective from March 1, 1992, the VAT rate is 13%.

*Tax on gross income/*The tax on gross income was introduced by Law No. 843 to tax gross income arising from the performance of any economic activity, except exports. The tax rate is 3%. The annual corporate income tax paid at the end of each fiscal year is considered payment on account of the gross income tax until it is completely used. This means that corporations annually pay either the corporate income tax or the tax on gross income, whichever is higher.

*Taxes on specific assets/*Property, real estate, and cars are subject to a tax based on their tax value calculated at rates depending on their value in the records.

*Taxes on specific consumer goods (excise tax)/*Specific goods are taxed at the following rates.

| | % |
|---|---|
| Vehicles (except those of high capacity and weight, which will pay a 10% rate excise tax) | 18 |
| Tobacco products | 50 |

| | Bs |
|---|---|
| Soft drinks | 0.20/liter |
| Beer, wines, and liquors | 1.61/liter |
| Alcohols | 0.79/liter |
| Whiskey | 6.7/liter |

*Special tax on hydrocarbons and derived products/*This tax is charged on the production or import of gasoline, diesel oil, and lubricating oil and grease. The rates are as follows.

| | Bs |
|---|---|
| Aviation gasoline | 0.34/liter |
| Premium gasoline | 2.58/liter |
| Special gasoline | 1.24/liter |
| Diesel oil (national) | 1.03/liter |
| Diesel oil (imported) | 0.46/liter |
| Lubricating oil/grease | 1.87/liter |
| Jet fuel (national) | 0.09/liter |
| Jet fuel (international) | 0.32/liter |
| Fuel oil | 0.29/liter |

## Branch income

Branch income is subject to the same tax as corporate income.

## Income determination

According to Law No. 1606 and Supreme Decree 24051, all income of Bolivian source is taxable, regardless of periodicity. Taxable income is determined on the basis of financial statements adjusted for depreciation, uncollectable credits, directors' fees, travel expenses, contributions, and expenses for employees' benefit that exceed certain limits.

# Bolivia

*Foreign income*/Resident corporations are taxed only on their Bolivian income.

## Deductions

As a general principle, all expenses necessary to obtain income and to preserve the source that generates the taxable income will be admitted.

The following items are not deductible, according to Law No. 1606.

1. Owner's or stockholders' personal withdrawals.
2. Owner's or stockholders' living expenses.
3. Individual service fees for which withholding tax has not been paid.
4. Amortization of trademarks and other intangible assets unless a price has been paid to acquire them.
5. Interest paid to related parties, to the extent it exceeds the rate of LIBOR plus 3%, for foreign operations of the official lending rate for local loans. Furthermore, in order to be deductible, interest paid to related parties may not exceed 30% of that paid to third parties.
6. Depletion in the hydrocarbon sector.
7. Income tax.
8. Taxes paid in the acquisition of capital assets. These are to be included in the cost of the asset and depreciated.
9. Provisions not specifically authorized by the tax law and regulations.

*Net operating losses*/Tax loss carryforward is permitted with no time limit.

*Payments to foreign affiliates*/According to Law No. 1606, payments to foreign affiliates are subject to a 12.5% withholding tax with no restriction.

*Taxes*/All taxes effectively paid by the corporation as a direct taxpayer are deductible. The income tax and any transaction tax set off against income tax are not deductible from taxable income.

*Other significant items*/Donations will not be deductible unless made to nonprofit organizations that are not subject to the tax. These donations will be deductible up to a maximum of 10% of the donor's net taxable profit. Provisions for employees' severance payments are also deductible, provided they are paid prior to the annual income tax filing due date.

## Tax incentives

*Inward and capital investments*/No incentives are granted to domestic or foreign investment.

*Other incentives*/Following Supreme Decree No. 21060, all foreign exchange transactions are legal, and a system of free-floating exchange rates was established.

Export activities benefit from reimbursements for VAT and customs duties paid in the process of producing the goods to be exported.

*Regional tax incentives*/New investments in manufacturing in the departments of Oruro and Potosí are entitled to tax exemptions granted by Laws Nos. 876 and 877, respectively. New regulations for these laws were approved by Supreme Decree No. 25305 dated February 18, 1999, as shown below.

New manufacturing industries in Oruro and Potosí are not exempt from VAT on their sales. However, as stated above, VAT is not payable on machinery imported prior to start-up. Industries in Oruro and Potosí must withhold the complementary VAT from employees, as well as the 12.5% tax on dividends paid to foreign shareholders and partners in accordance with the general tax law.

|  | Conditions of exemption |
|---|---|
| Import tariffs and VAT on imported machinery | On machinery imported exclusively for the new industry until start-up of operations. |
| Import tariffs and VAT on imported inputs | They do not replace domestic inputs of the same kind and are destined to a transformation process. The exemption is granted for the first five years of operation. |
| Transaction tax | For five years as from the start-up of operations. |

## Withholding taxes

**Payments to residents**/Dividend payments to resident individuals or companies are not subject to 13% retention.

**Payments to nonresidents**/Dividends, transfers of profits to the head office, interest, royalties, and fees for advice of any kind payable to nonresidents are subject to a 12.5% withholding tax (25% on 50% of amount paid, which the law presumes is Bolivian-source income).

## Tax administration

**Returns**/Tax is assessed on a fiscal-year, self-assessment basis. Tax returns must be accompanied by financial statements. The fiscal year varies according to activity. Banks and commercial and other service activities close at December 31; industrial concerns, including oil companies, at March 31; agribusiness and forestry at June 30; and mining at September 30.

**Payment of tax**/Tax is payable in one annual payment, except in the case of mining activities, for which advance payments are required.

# Bolivia

## *CORPORATION TAX CALCULATION*

Fiscal year ended December 31, 2003

| | | |
|---|---:|---:|
| Net book income (1) | | Bs 1,000,000 |
| Add: | | |
| Income tax provision | 250,000 | |
| Adjustment of inventories valuation | 80,300 | |
| Adjustment of depreciation of fixed assets technically revalued after 12/31/94 | 75,600 | |
| Provisions not accepted for tax purposes | 32,800 | 438,700 |
| | | 1,438,700 |
| Deduct: | | |
| Foreign-source revenue | 25,000 | |
| Dividends received from companies subject to income tax | 70,000 | 95,000 |
| Taxable income | | Bs 1,343,700 |
| Determination of profits tax (25% on 1,343,700) | | Bs 335,925 |

Notes:

1. Net book income is that according to financial statements prepared in accordance with generally accepted accounting principles.

2. Branch taxable income would be similarly determined.

3. Exchange rate of the boliviano at January 1, 2004: US$1 = Bs7.5936.

## PwC contact

For additional information on taxation in Botswana, contact:

D.K.U. Corea
PricewaterhouseCoopers
P.O. Box 1453
Gaborone, Botswana
Telephone: (267) 3952011
Fax: (267) 3973901
[No e-mail]

## Significant developments

New legislation has been introduced for taxation of International Financial Services Centre (IFSC) companies. See "Taxes on corporate income."

## Taxes on corporate income

Company tax is imposed at a rate of 15% for nonmanufacturing companies and 5% for manufacturing companies. Additional company tax is imposed at a rate of 10%. IFSC companies are taxed at a flat rate of 15% with no additional company tax component. Companies must apply for a certificate in order to be classified as IFSC companies, which deal only in specified services and only with nonresidents.

## Corporate residence

Corporate residence is determined on the basis that a company's registered office or place of incorporation is in Botswana or it is managed and controlled in Botswana.

## Other taxes

There are no other taxes on income.

## Branch income

Company tax at the rate of 25% is payable on branch profits.

## Income determination

*Inventory valuation*/Inventories are valued at cost less such amounts, if any, that the Commissioner of Taxes believes are reasonable as representing the amount by which the value of such stock has been diminished because of damage, deterioration, obsolescence, or other cause. Although not expressly excluded by legislation, LIFO has not been accepted in practice by the tax authorities.

*Capital gains*/Gains on specified capital assets (immovable property and marketable securities, including shares in private companies) are included in taxable income in the hands of the corporate taxpayer. Acquisition costs of immovable property are subject to a 10% compound annual addition for inflation for the period from acquisition to June 30, 1982, and thereafter to an inflation addition based on the increase in the consumer price index to the date of sale. For other gains, no inflation allowances are granted, but the taxable gain is set at one-half of the total gain.

# Botswana

The aggregate amount of capital losses is set off against the aggregate of capital gains in the same tax year. Any excess of loss is deducted from aggregate gains over losses accruing in the succeeding tax year only. Capital losses cannot, in any circumstances, be deducted against other income.

*Intercompany dividends*/Dividend income is not subject to tax. A withholding tax of 15% is deducted from dividend payments.

*Foreign income*/Resident corporations are not generally taxed on a worldwide income basis. However, interest arising from the South African rand monetary area is taxable in Botswana; relief is given for any withholding tax imposed on such income.

## Deductions

*Depreciation and depletion*/Annual and capital allowances available are as follows.

1. Companies other than mining companies:

   Annual taxation allowances for expenditure incurred on machinery and equipment before June 30, 1982 can be claimed up to 100%. This allowance may be for any proportion of previously unclaimed expenditure. For expenditure incurred on machinery and equipment after June 30, 1982, annual allowances are granted, calculated on cost by the straight-line method on the basis of the expected useful lives of the individual assets. Guidelines are provided for expected useful lives of different categories of assets, which vary from four to ten years. Book depreciation is not required to conform to tax depreciation. The capital allowance claimable on a company motorcar is restricted to a maximum of P100,000.

   An initial allowance of 25% of cost is granted on certain industrial buildings. All industrial and commercial buildings (excluding residential properties) are granted a 2.5% annual allowance based on cost or, in the case of an industrial building on which an initial allowance has been claimed, the original cost less the initial allowance.

   Balancing allowances and charges are brought to account on the disposal of assets on which allowances have been claimed. Where disposal value of an item of machinery or equipment exceeds the difference between expenditure incurred on the asset and allowances granted, the whole amount is taxable as corporate income, or the balancing charge can be offset against further additions of new equipment, thus providing rollover relief.

   However, there is no rollover relief on motorcars except where the cars are used in a car rental or taxi service business.

2. Mining companies:

   Mining capital allowances are ascertained by dividing the residual capital expenditure by a number equal to the estimated number of whole years during which mining operations may be expected to continue. This number of years is not to exceed ten.

*Net operating losses*/Losses may be carried forward for five years, with the exception of farming, mining, and prospecting operations, for which there is no time limit. There is no allowance for carrybacks.

**Payments to foreign affiliates**/Royalties, interest, and service fees paid to foreign affiliates are generally deductible, provided such amounts are at arm's length and withholding tax is paid.

**Taxes**/Any taxes paid are specifically disallowed in computing a company's taxable income.

**Other significant items**/An allowance is granted for dwelling houses erected for employees by a business other than a mining business. The amount of the allowance is the lower of cost or P5,000 for each dwelling house constructed.

A deduction of 200% of the cost of approved training expenditure is allowed.

As of February 13, 1984 companies with shareholders having 5% or more of the equity, either directly or indirectly, are classified as close companies, and there are additional tax regulations in respect of these shareholders.

Small companies, that is, resident private companies whose gross income does not exceed P300,000, may elect that the company be taxed as a partnership.

Expenses incurred by the company for having its shares listed on the Exchange are deductible in determining the chargeable income of the company.

## Group taxation

There are no concessions for group taxation, other than for wholly owned subsidiary companies of the Botswana Development Corporation.

## Tax incentives

**Inward investment**/To encourage investment in Botswana, extra tax reliefs on revenue or capital account will be granted for specific business development projects if the government is satisfied that such projects are beneficial to Botswana.

**Capital investment**/Under a financial assistance policy (FAP) introduced with effect from May 1982, a phased five-year reimbursement of unskilled labor costs is available, as are capital grants for new projects.

## Withholding taxes

Tax at the rate of 15% must be deducted from dividends paid to residents. Withholding taxes at the following rates must be deducted from payments to nonresidents unless a double taxation agreement exists.

|  | % |
|---|---|
| Interest | 15 |
| Dividends | 15 |
| Payments due under certain construction contracts | 3 |
| Payments for royalties, management or consultancy fees | 15 |
| Payments for entertainment fees | 10 |

# Botswana

Botswana has tax agreements with the following countries, which provide for withholding at the rates shown.

| Treaty | Dividends | Interest | Royalties | Management and Consultancy fees |
|---|---|---|---|---|
| | % | % | % | % |
| Mauritius......................... | (1) | 12 | 12.5 | 15 |
| South Africa.................... | 15 | 15 | 15 | Nil |
| Sweden........................... | 15 | 15 | 15 | 15 |
| United Kingdom ............. | 15 | 15 | 15 | Nil |

Note:

A rate of 5% if 25% or more of the share capital is held by a Mauritius company; otherwise 10%.

## Tax administration

*Returns*/Botswana has a fiscal year ending on June 30. However, a business may select its own accounting year, which may end on a date other than June 30. This accounting year is accepted for the computation of the company's taxable income, which will be the last accounting period prior to June 30.

The system is one that requires all taxpayers to file tax returns in standard format (providing information relating to taxable income earned). Self-assessment, which means that the return submitted constitutes the assessment, was introduced with effect from July 1, 2001.

*Payment of tax*/Under the self-assessment tax procedures, if the tax payable for a tax year exceeds P50,000, then the tax is required to be paid in equal quarterly installments over the period of the 12 months ending on the company's financial year-end date. Where the tax is less than P50,000, then the tax is payable on or before September 30 following the end of the relevant tax year (June 30).

## CORPORATION TAX CALCULATION

### Nonmanufacturing company

Fiscal year ending June 30, 2003

| | | |
|---|---:|---:|
| Net income before taxation | | P 1,000,000 |
| Add: | | |
|     Depreciation | 50,000 | |
|     Loss on disposal of machinery and equipment | 5,000 | |
|     Donations | 1,000 | |
|     Balancing charge | 35,000 | 91,000 |
| | | 1,091,000 |
| Less: | | |
|     Profit on disposal of industrial buildings | 33,000 | |
|     Initial allowance: | | |
|         Industrial buildings—25% on cost | 100,000 | |
|     Annual allowances: | | |
|         Commercial buildings at 2.5% on cost | 5,000 | |
|         Industrial buildings at 2.5% on cost | 10,000 | |
|         Plant and machinery at 15% on cost | 60,000 | |
|         Office equipment at 10% on cost | 2,000 | |
|     Residential accommodation for employees: | | |
|         Two houses, restricted to | 10,000 | |
|     Approved training expenditure (Additional 100% of | | |
|         cost of 20,000) | 20,000 | 240,000 |
| | | 851,000 |
| Add—Taxable capital gain on disposal of property | | 49,000 |
| Taxable income | | P 900,000 |
| Tax thereon—25% of 900,000 (Note 1) | | P 225,000 |

Notes:

1. Company tax at a rate of 15% plus additional company tax at a rate of 10%.
2. Exchange rate of the pula at February 25, 2004: US$1 = P4.7733.

# Brazil

## PwC contacts

For additional information on taxation in Brazil, contact:

Nélio B. Weiss
Raimundo L. M. Christians
PricewaterhouseCoopers Auditores Independentes
Centro Empresarial Água Branca
Av. Francisco Matarazzo, 1400 - Torre Torino
05001-903 São Paulo, SP, Brazil
Telephone: (55) (11) 3674-2000
Fax: (55) (11) 3674-2040
e-mail: nelio.weiss@br.pwc.com
          raimundo.christians@br.pwc.com

## Significant developments

As per Constitutional Amendment 42, issued on December 31, 2003, the Manaus Free Trade Zone is maintained for an additional ten-year period, that is, until 2023. Additionally, the application of the Provisional Contribution on Financial Transactions (CPMF) was extended until December 31, 2007. CPMF is applied at the rate of 0.38%.

Brazil has ratified the Convention to Avoid Double Taxation with Chile.

Services provided by nonresidents to Brazilian entities are now subject to the municipal service tax (ISS) at rates ranging from 2% to 5%. The Brazilian entity is responsible (on behalf of the nonresident) to withhold and remit the tax to the municipal authorities.

The cumulative effect of the COFINS tax was revoked and its rate increased to 7.6% (previously 3.0%). To eliminate the cumulative effect of this contribution, taxpayers are now allowed to use credits arising from previous transactions (i.e., COFINS applicable on inputs utilized in manufacturing or items acquired for resale).

Importation of goods and services will, as of May 1, 2004, be subject to PIS and COFINS (in addition to all other taxes imposed on import transactions). PIS and COFINS will be imposed on the Brazilian entity or individual (the importer of goods or services) and will apply at the rates of 1.65% and 7.6%, respectively. The contributions paid upon import transactions will generally be creditable.

The Brazilian tax authorities clarified that capital gains triggered upon the sale of Brazilian assets (such as shares of a Brazilian entity) from a nonresident seller to a nonresident buyer are, as from February 2004, subject to a 15% Brazilian withholding income tax. The rate is increased to 25% if the beneficiary is located in a tax haven jurisdiction (as defined by Brazilian legislation).

## Taxes on corporate income

*Income tax*/Federal income tax is paid at the rate of 15% on taxable income.

Corporate income tax is generally computed on the basis of annual taxable income. For tax purposes the company's year-end is December 31. A different year-end for corporate purposes is irrelevant.

*Surcharge*/Taxpayers are also subject to a surcharge of 10% on annual taxable income in excess of R$240,000 (approximately US$85,000).

*Social contribution*/All legal entities are subject to a social contribution to the federal government at the rate of 9%, which is not deductible for income tax purposes. The tax basis is the profit before income tax, after some adjustments.

Whenever the tax basis is negative (loss), it may be carried forward without any time limitation. However, the negative basis compensation may not reduce the tax basis by more than 30% of its amount prior to the compensation itself.

## Corporate residence

A corporation is considered resident in Brazil if it has been incorporated in Brazil, and its tax domicile is where its head office is located.

## Branch income

Profits of branches of foreign corporations are taxable at the normal rates applicable to local corporations.

## Income determination

There must be conformity between book and tax reporting.

*Inventory valuation*/Brazilian income tax regulations require that inventory may be valued at the actual average cost or by the cost of the most recently acquired or produced goods. Rulings to the effect that LIFO is not acceptable have been given.

*Capital gains*/Capital gains are taxed as ordinary income. However, profits on certain long-term sales of permanent assets may be computed for tax purposes on a cash basis. Profits on long-term contracts may be computed on a percentage-of-completion basis. When these contracts are entered into with the government or government-owned companies, the profit may be recognized on a cash basis for tax purposes.

Except during the year when incurred, capital losses may be offset only against capital gains. Unused capital losses are treated similarly to income tax losses with regard to limits on use and carryforward period.

*Foreign income*/Brazilian resident companies are taxed on worldwide income. Foreign branch profits and foreign subsidiary profits are taxed at the date of the financial statements in which the profits are calculated, regardless of remittance. Double taxation could be avoided by means of foreign tax credits.

*Stock dividends*/Stock dividend distributions are not subject to withholding tax.

*Financial income*/Fixed-rate interest income from short-, medium-, or long-term financial market transactions is subject to withholding income tax at the rate of 20%. Nonfixed financial gains related to stock/commodities exchange and/or futures market transactions are subject to withholding income tax at the rate of 20%. The total income or gain is considered taxable income, and the tax withheld may be offset against the total tax due by the corporate taxpayer.

*Interest on net equity*/Companies can pay interest (calculated on a pro rata basis and up to a given rate known as the "long-term interest rate" (TJLP) of approximately 10% per annum, (applicable rate at the beginning of 2004) to

# Brazil

partners and/or share/quotaholders, based on the company's net equity. Such interest, which may not exceed the highest of 50% of the annual profits or 50% of the accumulated earnings and profits, is deductible for both income tax and social contribution purposes and is subject to 15% tax at source. Whenever the beneficiary is a legal entity subject to normal income tax in Brazil, the tax withheld at source may be taken by the recipient as a tax credit against the normal corporate income tax due or the tax due at source on distributions of interest. If the beneficiary is a Brazilian resident individual, such interest will not become subject to any further tax.

## Deductions

***Depreciation and depletion/***Depreciation is allowable on a straight-line basis over the useful life of the asset. The annual rates normally allowable are 10% for machinery, equipment, furniture and installations; 20% for vehicles; and 4% for buildings. Accelerated depreciation is allowed for companies with a two- or three-shift operation by increasing normal rates by 50% and 100%, respectively.

Allowable depreciation for tax purposes must be booked, except in certain situations in which tax incentives apply.

Depletion allowances are allowed for natural resources on a useful-life basis. Special incentive depletion allowances are granted for mining operations. These special allowances are based on gross income, except for operations starting after December 1987.

***Net operating losses/***Tax losses may be carried forward without any time limitation. However, the tax loss compensation may not reduce taxable income by more than 30% of its amount prior to the compensation itself. Tax loss is defined as the accounting loss adjusted for tax purposes. There is no carryback.

***Payments to foreign affiliates and related companies/***Royalties and technical service fees payable to foreign companies with a direct or indirect controlling interest in the Brazilian company are deductible for tax purposes (observing applicable deduction limits), provided the contract has been duly registered by the National Institute of Industrial Property (INPI) and approved by the Brazilian Central Bank. There is no restriction on the deductibility of interest provided the contract has been approved by the Brazilian Central Bank. However, on unregistered related-party loans the deductible interest may not exceed that calculated using the six-month U.S. dollar deposit LIBOR (London interbank offered rate) rate plus 3%.

***Transfer pricing/***Transfer pricing rules apply to all import and export transactions between related parties and also between Brazilian residents and any residents in tax havens.

***Losses on bad debts/***Losses are tax deductible, depending on the amounts, time overdue and administrative and/or legal actions taken. Losses arising from intercompany transactions are not tax deductible.

***Taxes/contributions/***Taxes, contributions, and related costs, such as late-payment interest, are deductible for tax purposes on the accrual basis. This rule does not apply to taxes/contributions being or to be challenged by the taxpayer at any level of litigation, which are deductible for tax purposes only on a cash basis.

## Group taxation

Consolidated tax returns are not permitted.

## Tax incentives

*Inward investment*/Total or partial exemption from duty and excise tax on imported equipment is granted on certain approved investment projects.

*Regional incentives*/Income tax exemption or reduction is also available for companies set up in specified regions within Brazil, primarily the North and Northeast regions. These incentives are designed to accelerate the development of certain less-developed regions and industries considered to be of importance to the economy.

*Capital investment*/Approved investment projects are granted accelerated depreciation on nationally produced equipment and access to low-cost financing. Sales of some capital equipment are exempt from state sales tax.

*Other incentives*/Brazilian corporate taxpayers can only apply a percentage of their income tax liability on deposit for reinvestment and investment in their own approved investment projects. These approved investment projects are normally granted total or partial income tax exemption. Excise and sales and service tax exemptions are granted to exporters of manufactured goods.

## Other taxes

*Import tax*/Import tax (*Imposto de importação,* or II) is levied on the CIF (cost, insurance and freight) price. The rate depends on the degree of necessity and is defined by the product's tax code according to the Harmonized System (Mercosur Common Nomenclature—NCM). The rates tend to be in the range from 10 to 20%, although there are many exceptions subject to higher or lower rates.

*Value-added tax*/VAT is payable on imports, sales, and transfers of goods and products in the form of a federal excise tax (*Imposto sobre produtos industrializados,* or IPI) at various rates in accordance with the nature of the product (normally around 10% to 15%, but in certain cases ranging to over 300%) and a state sales and service tax (*Imposto sobre as operações relativas à circulação de mercadorias, e sobre a prestação de serviços de transporte interestadual e intermunicipal e de comunicação,* or ICMS) of from 7% to 25%. Except for services related to freight and transportation, communications, and electric energy, which are subject to ICMS, income from services rendered is normally subject to a municipal service tax (*Imposto sobre serviços de qualquer natureza,* or ISS)—which is not a VAT—from 2% to 5%.

*COFINS*/COFINS (*Contribuição para o financiamento da seguridade social*) levied at 7.6% is a monthly federal social assistance contribution calculated as a percentage of revenue. A new enacted COFINS credit system is meant to ensure the tax is applied only once on the final value of each transaction. However, some taxpayers (such as financial institutions, telecommunication companies, cooperatives and companies which opt to calculate Brazilian corporate income tax and social contribution on net income using a "Presumed Profit" method) are still subject to the previous COFINS system, that is, COFINS is applied at 3% and no credit system is allowed.

*PIS*/PIS (*Progama de Integracao Social*) levied at 1.65% is also a federal social contribution calculated as a percentage of revenue. A new enacted PIS credit system is meant to ensure the tax is applied only once on the final value of each transaction. However, some taxpayers (such as financial institutions, telecommunication companies, cooperatives and companies which opt to calculate Brazilian corporate income tax and social contribution on net income using a "Presumed Profit" method) are still subject to the previous PIS system, that is, PIS is applied at 0.65% and no credit system is allowed.

*PIS and COFINS on imports*/Importation of goods and services, as from May 1, 2004, are subject to PIS and COFINS (in addition to all other taxes imposed on import transactions). PIS and COFINS will be imposed on the Brazilian entity or individual (the importer of goods or services) and will apply at the rates of 0.65% and 7.6%, respectively. The contributions paid upon import transactions will generally be creditable.

*CPMF*/CPMF (*Contribuição provisória sobre movimentações financeiras* (Provisional Contribution on Financial Transactions)) is a contribution levied on withdrawals from bank accounts at 0.38% of the amount withdrawn. The contribution is withheld from bank accounts weekly and is deductible for purposes of income tax and social contribution on net income.

*IOF*/IOF (*Imposto sobre operações de crédito, cãmbio e seguro e sobre operações relativas a títulos e valores mobiliários,* or Financial Transactions Tax) is a tax levied primarily on certain financial transactions such as loans, foreign exchange operations, insurance and securities and transactions with gold (as a financial asset) and foreign exchange instruments. The applicable rate will vary depending on the transaction.

*CIDE*/CIDE (*Contribuição de intervenção no domínio econômico,* or Contribution to the Economic Intervention Domain) is a contribution levied on remittances made by corporate taxpayers for royalties and for administrative and technical services provided by nonresidents. CIDE is payable by the local entity and therefore not creditable to the nonresident. CIDE does not represent a liability to the foreign recipient.

## Withholding taxes

*Profits*/Dividends distributed to resident or nonresident beneficiaries (individuals and/or legal entities) relating to periods beginning on or after January 1, 1996 are not subject to withholding income tax. Profits/dividends distributed from earnings and profits relating to periods ended up to December 31, 1995 are subject to withholding income tax at the rate of either 25% or 15%, depending on the year to which they relate and residence status of the recipient.

The withholding tax rate applicable to payments for services rendered by nonresident companies or individuals is generally 15% but can be increased to 25% in certain cases.

Certain types of income paid by Brazilian companies to nonresident recipients are subject to withholding tax, as follows.

| Recipient | Dividends (1) | Interest | Royalties |
|---|---|---|---|
| | % | % | % |
| Nonresident companies and individuals: | | | |
| Nontreaty ................................................ | 0 (2) | 15 (2) | 15 (2) |
| Treaty (2): | | | |
| Argentina............................................ | 25 | 25 | 25 |
| Austria................................................ | 15 | 15 | 25, 15, 10 |
| Belgium .............................................. | 15 | 15, 10 | 25, 15, 10 |
| Canada .............................................. | 15 | 15, 10 | 25, 15 |
| Chile .................................................. | 10, 15 | 15 | 15 |
| China, P.R. ........................................ | 15 | 15 | 25, 15 |
| Czechoslovakia ................................. | 15 | 15, 10 | 25, 15 |
| Denmark ............................................ | 25 | 15 | 25, 15 |
| Ecuador.............................................. | 15 | 15 | 25, 15 |
| Finland ............................................... | 10 | 15 | 25, 15, 10 |
| France................................................ | 15 | 15, 10 | 25, 15, 10 |
| Germany ............................................ | 15 | 15, 10 | 25, 15 |
| Hungary ............................................. | 15 | 15, 10 | 25, 15 |
| India .................................................. | 15 | 15 | 25, 15 |
| Israel (3)............................................ | 10, 15 | 15 | 15, 10 |
| Italy ................................................... | 15 | 15 | 25, 15 |
| Japan ................................................ | 12.5 | 12.5 | 25, 15, 12.5 |
| Korea, Rep. of ................................... | 15 | 15, 10 | 25, 15 |
| Luxembourg ....................................... | 25, 15 | 15, 10 | 25, 15 |
| Netherlands........................................ | 15 | 15, 10 | 25, 15 |
| Norway ............................................... | 15 | 15 | 25, 15 |
| Philippines.......................................... | 25, 15 | 15, 10 | 25, 15 |
| Paraguay (3) ...................................... | 10 | 15 | 15 |
| Portugal.............................................. | 10, 15 | 15 | 15 |
| Slovak Republic.................................. | 15 | 15, 10 | 25, 15 |
| Spain.................................................. | 15 | 15, 10 | 25, 15, 10 |
| Sweden .............................................. | 25, 15 | 25, 15 | 25, 15 |
| Ukraine (3) ........................................ | 10, 15 | 15 | 15 |

Notes:

1. Note that the remittance of dividends is not subject to taxation in Brazil, since January 1, 1996.

2. Treaty rates in excess of those in force for nontreaty countries are automatically reduced. Payments of income to nonresidents in nontreaty countries that tax income at less than 20% are subject to withholding tax at 25% (except for dividends).

3. These treaties were signed, but still need to be ratified.

Additional information:

• Brazil has been negotiating tax treaties with Romania, Switzerland, the United Kingdom, the United States, and Venezuela.

• The treaty concerned should be consulted to confirm that the tax reduction is applicable in each case.

# Brazil

## CORPORATION TAX CALCULATION

Tax year ending December 31, 2004

| | |
|---|---:|
| Net profit before taxes........................................................................ | R$ 11,000,000 |
| Less—Dividends received (1)............................................................... | 1,000,000 |
| Net taxable income for both income tax and social contribution ............. | R$ 10,000,000 |

Taxes thereon:
Federal income tax:

| | |
|---|---:|
| Basic income tax at 15%.................................................................. | R$ 1,500,000 |
| Surcharge—10% from 240,000 to 10,000,000.................................. | 976,000 |
| Total federal income tax (2)............................................................. | R$ 2,476,000 |

Social contribution on profits:

| | |
|---|---:|
| Tax—10,000,000 x 9% ...................................................................... | R$ 900,000 |

Notes:

1. Dividends received from other Brazilian companies, including affiliated companies, are not subject to withholding income tax and excluded from the tax calculation.

2. Entities are allowed to elect quarterly or annual basis tax computation. For entities using the yearly calculation, any income tax due is payable up to the last working day of March following the year-end (subject to interest); however, prepayments are required.

3. Capital gains are included in net income and, after offsetting any current and/or brought-forward capital losses, taxed at the normal corporate rate.

4. The income tax/social contribution may be computed in three different ways, as follows.

   a. On a "presumed taxable income" basis:

   Only corporate taxpayers with gross annual revenues of not over R$48 million in the preceding year may opt for this income tax computation method. The tax rate of 25% is imposed on a percentage of monthly gross revenues (from the sale of goods/products/services) plus capital gains and money-market income, less some minor adjustments such as unconditional discounts and canceled sales. The taxable basis for other diversified activities is determined according to the proportionate amount of gross revenue.

| Type of activity | Taxable basis as a percentage of gross revenues |
|---|:---:|
| | % |
| In general | 8.0 |
| Oil and gas, lubricants, etc. (retail) | 1.6 |
| Transportation (except cargo) | 16.0 |
| Rendering of services (except for hospitals) | 32.0 |
| Business intermediation | 32.0 |
| Real estate management | 32.0 |
| Consulting in general and factoring | 32.0 |

The social contribution liability, at the rate of 9%, presumes a taxable basis equal to 12% of the sum of gross monthly revenues, capital gains and money market income and equal to 32% of services rendered.

b. On an "arbitrary" basis: Established solely at the discretion of the tax authorities, should the taxpayer fail to comply with the regulations for keeping records and/or computing taxable income;

c. On an "actual taxable income" basis: This basis is computed in accordance with the corporate records and adjusted for tax purposes in line with the applicable regulations. Legal entities with the following characteristics/activities must utilize this method.

    i. Annual gross revenues in the preceding calendar year of more than R$48 million.

    ii. Financial institutions in general, leasing companies, insurance companies, and nonprivate pension funds.

    iii. Legal entities that have profits, income, or capital gains from abroad.

    iv. Legal entities benefiting from income tax incentives (reduction or exemption).

    v. Legal entities that have made the monthly payments on an estimated basis during the tax year.

    vi. Legal entities that render services related to credit and market assistance, credit management, risks and selection, management of receivables and payables assistance or factoring.

These corporate taxpayers estimate their monthly tax payments (income tax and social contribution) by using the computation rules applicable for the presumed taxable income basis. Payments are due on the last working day of the subsequent month. A final balance sheet and statement of income must be drawn up at year-end and the annual tax liability (including income tax surcharge) computed. At this time, nominal gains from money market as well as from transactions in the stock/commodities exchange and/or futures market must be considered, and taxes withheld at source are treated as tax credits. Any difference between the final tax liability computed at year-end and the amounts estimated and paid in advance or withheld at source will either be paid up to the last working day of the month of March (subject to interest) or claimed as a tax credit. The taxpayer may at any time suspend or reduce the monthly advance payments upon proof that amounts already paid or withheld at source exceed what is due on actual taxable income for the same period.

Alternatively, the above-listed corporate taxpayers may draw up quarterly financial statements, calculate the appropriate taxable income and pay the income tax (including surcharges) and the social contribution thereon up to the last working day of the subsequent month. Taxes paid under this alternative are considered final, and the annual financial statements are not required for tax purposes.

5. Amounts have been rounded.
6. Exchange rate of the Brazilian real at March 21, 2004: US$1 = R$2.902.

# British Virgin Islands

## PwC contact

For additional information on taxation in the British Virgin Islands, contact:

Meade Malone
PricewaterhouseCoopers
Box 3339
Road Town, Tortola
Telephone: (1) (284) 494 4388, 494 4727 (direct)
Fax: (1) (284) 494 3088
e-mail: pwcabacus@surfbvi.com

## Taxes on corporate income

Except for International Business Companies, which are completely exempt from any form of taxation in the British Virgin Islands (BVI), the key issue with respect to BVI company taxation is whether the company is resident or nonresident. (For further information on tax liability and rates, see below.)

Resident corporations are taxed at a rate of 15% on net income. A resident company can be defined as a foreign trading company if it derives at least 90% of its income from trading exclusively outside the territory. If this is the case, a tax rate of 1% is applicable to this income.

A resident investment holding company is liable to BVI tax as follows.

1. On investment income that arises outside the territory and is exempt from tax, other than by reason of a double taxation treaty, in the jurisdiction where it arises, the rate is 1%.

2. On investment income that arises outside the territory and is taxed in the jurisdiction where it arises, the company rate is 15%. However, unilateral relief is available to reduce the amount payable in the BVI by the tax paid in the foreign jurisdiction.

Where there is a specific double taxation agreement, the provisions of the agreement prevail over the above terms.

A company can be incorporated as a nonresident company under the Companies Act (Cap. 285) or the International Business Companies (IBC) Ordinance, as amended. If the company is incorporated as an IBC, it is exempt from income tax; however, an annual license fee must be paid.

## Corporate residence

A company is defined in the BVI Tax Ordinance as resident in the BVI if the control and management of the company are exercised in the territory. In practice, this is determined by the place of residence of the majority of the directors and the place at which policy decisions are made, including where meetings of directors are held.

If the company is not resident, tax is payable only on earned income arising outside the BVI that is remitted to the BVI.

## Earned income and investment income

The BVI Tax Ordinance defines earned income and investment income as follows.

1. Earned income is income from any trade, business, profession, employment, or vocation in the form of gains or profits.

2. Investment income is income in the form of dividends from stocks or shares; interest from government securities, bank deposits or loans; or other income of a similar nature.

## Other taxes

No income or capital gains taxes apply upon liquidation. The taxable status of a company is not affected by liquidation. It is not possible to carry back a loss sustained by liquidation. Shareholders are not taxed on any distributions they receive following a liquidation.

## Withholding taxes

Dividends and interest are exempt from withholding tax as long as the Commissioner is satisfied that they do not exceed normal rates.

## Tax administration

*Returns*/A company must file a return of income with the Commissioner of Inland Revenue each year. The Commissioner issues tax returns at the beginning of each calendar year. These returns must be completed and submitted to the Commissioner by April 30.

*Payment of tax*/Tax is payable in two equal installments: the first payment within 30 days of the date of assessment and the second within 90 days.

## Note

The monetary unit is the U.S. dollar.

# Brunei Darussalam

## PwC contact

For additional information on taxation in Brunei, contact:

Kin C. Lee
PricewaterhouseCoopers
No. 1, 4th floor, Wisma Setia
Jalan Pemancha
Bandar Seri Begawan BS8811
Negara Brunei Darussalam
Telephone: (673) (2) 228593, 228595
Fax: (673) (2) 228594
LN address: Kin Chee Lee@Price Waterhouse-Asia
e-mail: kin.chee.lee@bn.pwc.com

## Significant developments

Major changes to the Income Tax Act, CAP 35, effective from June 1, 2001, include the following.

- Permanent establishment is now defined.
- Further deductions are allowed for expenses relating to the following.
  - Trade fairs, exhibition or trade missions, or the maintenance of overseas trade offices.
  - Export market development expenditure and certain advertising expenses.
  - Expenditure on research and development.
  - Write-down allowance for approved know-how and patents.
- Time within which payment of tax is to be made is reduced to 30 days (previously two months) after service of the notice of assessment.
- The penalty for nonpayment of tax is 5% of the tax payable if tax is not paid within 30 days after service of the notice of assessment. An additional penalty of 1% of the tax outstanding shall be payable for each completed month that the tax remains unpaid if tax is not paid within 60 days of the imposition of the first penalty. Such additional penalty shall not exceed 12% of the amount of tax outstanding.
- There is now no time limit with regard to the penalty for making an incorrect return.
- Previously, deductions of tax from interest due under a charge, or debenture or loan interest, only applied to interest paid to companies not resident in Brunei. Such deductions will now also apply to persons not resident in Brunei.

## Taxes on corporate income

Corporation taxes are imposed at a flat rate of 30%, with no state or municipal taxes on income.

## Corporate residence

The tax residence of a corporation is determined by the place of incorporation, as well as by the place where management and control are exercised, and this is generally taken to mean where the directors meet and exercise de facto control.

## Other taxes

Income from petroleum operations is subject to tax under the Income Tax (Petroleum) Act as amended.

## Branch income

Tax rates on branch profits are the same as on corporate profits, and no tax is withheld on remittance of profits to the head office.

## Income determination

*Inventory valuation/*There are no special rules as to which basis of valuation of inventories (stock-in-trade) should be adopted in the case of a continuing business, as long as the basis is consistent from one year to another.

*Capital gains/*There is no tax on capital gains. Where there is a series of transactions, the tax authorities may take the view that a business is being carried on and attempt to assess the gains as profits of the corporation.

*Intercompany dividends/*Except for dividends received from a corporation in Brunei that are excludable, dividends accruing in, derived from or received in Brunei by a corporation are included in taxable income. No tax is deducted at source on dividends paid by a Brunei corporation.

*Foreign income/*A company resident in Brunei is taxed on foreign income when received in Brunei. Double taxation with Commonwealth countries is avoided by means of unilateral relief on income arising from those Commonwealth countries that offer reciprocal relief. The maximum relief cannot exceed one-half the Brunei rate.

*Stock dividends/*Stock dividends are not taxable.

## Deductions

*Depreciation and depletion/*Depreciation is allowable on industrial buildings (straight-line basis) and on machinery and equipment (reducing-balance basis) at specified rates for all types of business. Tax depreciation is not required to conform to book depreciation. Gains on depreciable property are taxed as ordinary income to the extent depreciation has been allowed.

*Net operating losses/*Loss carryforward is allowed for up to six years. Loss carryback is allowed for one year. Carryforward of depreciation allowances is permitted without restriction. No carryback of depreciation allowances is permitted.

*Payments to nonresidents, including foreign affiliates/*Such payments are deductible, provided they are fair and reasonable. Interest paid to a nonresident person or corporation is subject to withholding tax at 20%.

*Taxes/*Generally speaking, income taxes are not deductible in determining corporate income. However, income tax paid on foreign income remitted into Brunei is, by concession, allowed as a deduction.

A tax credit is given under Brunei's tax treaties with the United Kingdom and Indonesia. Commonwealth tax relief is given on income arising from Commonwealth countries that provide reciprocal relief. However, the maximum relief cannot exceed one-half the Brunei rate of tax on the same income.

*Other significant items*/As there is no personal income tax in Brunei, remuneration to directors is not taxed but may still be deductible, provided it is fair and reasonable.

## Group taxation

There is no group relief.

## Tax incentives

*Inward investment*/The following incentives are available.

1. Pioneer industries—Corporations making investments in line with Brunei's economic development objectives are granted exemptions from income tax and import duties on specified materials for periods of up to five years, based on the level of investment. The relief period may be extended if certain conditions are met.

2. Foreign loans—Interest on approved foreign loans from a nonresident person is exempt from tax.

*Capital investment*/Expansion enterprises—An approved enterprise is granted tax exemption for up to five years, based on the increased capital expenditure incurred.

## Withholding taxes

Domestic corporations are required to withhold tax at 20% on interest paid to a nonresident person or corporation. There are no other withholding taxes.

## Tax administration

*Returns*/The tax year is the calendar year. The corporation files a return of income, and it is assessed by the Collector of Income Tax. The tax assessment is normally issued in February of each year, relating to the taxable income of the preceding year.

*Payment of tax*/Assessed tax is normally payable within 30 days after the notice of assessment is served.

## *CORPORATION TAX CALCULATION*

Fiscal year ended December 31, 2003 (year of assessment 2004)

| | | | |
|---|---:|---:|---:|
| Net income before taxes per profit and loss account (income statement)............................................................... | | | B$ 1,000,000 |
| Add: | | | |
| Depreciation charged in accounts (1) ................................ | 150,000 | | |
| Amounts transferred to provisions ..................................... | 200,000 | | |
| Donations not approved...................................................... | 5,000 | | |
| Legal fees (capital nature)................................................. | 15,000 | 370,000 | |
| | | 1,370,000 | |
| Less: | | | |
| Profit on sale of fixed assets............................................. | 30,000 | | |
| Expenditure charged against provisions ............................ | 300,000 | | |
| Directors' fees debited to profit and loss— | | | |
| Appropriation account..................................................... | 50,000 | 380,000 | |
| Adjusted profit.................................................................... | | 990,000 | |
| Less: | | | |
| Capital allowances at Inland Revenue rates (1) ................. | 120,000 | | |
| *Less*—Balancing charge on sale of fixed | | | |
| assets (2) ...................................................................... | (2,000) | 118,000 | |
| | | B$ 872,000 | |
| Tax thereon at 30% ............................................................ | | B$ 261,600 | |

Notes:

1. The rates of depreciation for book and tax purposes are often not the same, and adjustment for tax purposes is therefore necessary.
2. Refers to gains on depreciable property, which are taxable to the extent of tax depreciation previously allowed.
3. The Brunei dollar (B$) is interchangeable with the Singapore dollar.
4. Exchange rate of the Brunei dollar at March 15, 2004: US$1 = B$1.70838.

# Bulgaria

## PwC contact

For additional information on taxation in Bulgaria, contact:

Irina Tsvetkova
PricewaterhouseCoopers—Legal and Tax Consultants
9-11 Maria Louisa Blvd
1000 Sofia, Bulgaria
Telephone: (359) (2) 91 003; 985 08 126
Fax: (359) (2) 98 03 228
LN domain: Irina Tsvetkova/BG/TLS/PwC@EMEA-BG
e-mail: irina.tsvetkova@bg.pwc.com

## Tax on corporate income

In general, all companies are subject to corporate income tax. As of January 1, 2004, corporate income is taxed at the rate of 19.5%. Companies undertaking certain types of activities described by law (mostly restaurant and hotel services, hairdressers, etc.) with a turnover for the previous year below BGN50,000 (about US$31,388) pay a flat business tax, the amount depending on the type and size of the business, instead of business income.

Municipality tax is repealed as of January 1, 2003. Bulgarian resident entities are taxed on a worldwide basis. Nonresident entities are taxed on their Bulgarian-source income. Nonbusiness organizations (including governmental) are taxed on their businesslike activities.

The Bulgarian Law on Commerce provides for the following types of entities.
1. Limited liability company.
2. Joint stock company, which may be public or private.
3. General partnership.
4. Limited partnership.
5. Partnership limited by shares, which may be private or public.
6. Foreign business entities may register a branch in Bulgaria.

## Corporate residence

A corporation is resident in Bulgaria for tax purposes if it is registered in Bulgaria. Foreign legal entities with headquarters abroad and registered correspondingly are nonresidents for Bulgarian tax purposes, but their Bulgarian branches or registered in Bulgaria permanent establishments (PE) are treated as Bulgarian resident companies for tax purposes.

## Other taxes

*Tax on insurance and reinsurance premiums*/Insurance companies pay a special one-time (final) tax on insurance/reinsurance premiums and on any other kind of income, and are not obliged to pay corporate income taxes separately for their activities other than insurance or reinsurance.

The tax base is the difference between the following.
1. The sum of all insurance, reinsurance, and other premiums (even if not related to insurance) within a given month, reduced by the gross amount of

reinsurance premiums assigned to other reinsurance companies and insurance premiums paid back to clients.

2. The income from all other activities, including not related to insurance.

If the tax base is a negative figure, it is deductible from the tax base in the subsequent months.

The rate of the special tax for insurance companies is 7%. For life assurance the tax is 2%.

The same tax is levied on premiums received by a foreign insurance company through a permanent establishment in Bulgaria.

***Taxation of company expenses***/Entertainment and representation expenses, business gifts that do not bear the trademark of the donating company, sponsorships, and donations, when accounted for as expenses, are subject to taxation at 20%. Donations accounted for as expenses that are made in favor of registered religions and/or non-profit organizations operating in public benefit and registered with the Ministry of Justice are taxed at the rate of 15%. Social expenses and benefits in-kind for the staff, as well as expenses for maintenance, repair and usage of cars, are taxed at 20%. Expenses for maintenance and repair of cars used for core-business, as well as for administrative activities will not be subject to 20% tax for the part referring to the core business activities. The taxes are final, and both the taxes and the expenses are deductible expenses for the purposes of the corporate income tax.

***Value-added tax***/VAT was introduced on April 1, 1994. In general it follows the provisions of the Sixth EU Directive.

The tax base includes the agreed price, customs and excise duties, if any, and some other expenses (such as commission, packing, transport, insurance costs charged by the supplier to the purchaser).

The VAT rate is currently 20%. The export of goods and a limited number of services is subject to VAT at a zero rate. Within the meaning of the VAT Act, export of goods is exportation abroad or to the free zones, free warehouses and duty-free outlets. However, supply to customs warehouses does not qualify for export. There are three types of exempt supplies, as follows.

1. Supplies of services, which, according to the statutory "place of supply" rules, are provided outside the territory of Bulgaria.
2. Supplies of goods in customs warehouses within the scope of the respective customs procedure.
3. Supplies exempt due to their subject, such as financial services, insurance, gambling, educational and health services, transfer of ownership of land, and so on.

***Excise duties***/The Excise Duty Act was introduced on April 1, 1994. The system is harmonized with the VAT legislation. Excise duties are not due on goods and services for export. The duties are calculated as either percentage of the producer's sales price/customs value or as a flat amount per unit.

Excise duty is levied on a limited group of goods and services, mainly coffee and tea, certain types of cars, petrol and diesel fuel, heavy oil, beer and hard drinks, tobacco products, and gambling. Wine is still defined as excisable goods, though the rate is BGN0 as of January 1, 2003.

*Property tax*/Taxpayers are individuals and legal entities that are owners of immovable property, that is, land and buildings. For individuals, the property tax rate is 0.15% on the taxable value of the property, determined by the relevant method. If the owner of the real estate is a company, the tax base of nonresidential property is its acquisition cost.

A garbage collection fee is payable for immovable property too, at a rate determined by the local municipal council annually,

## Branch income

Although branch offices are not deemed legal persons, branches of nonresident companies have separate balance sheets and profit and loss accounts, and therefore are subject to corporate income tax at the standard rate of 19.5%, and to other general taxes (VAT, property tax).

Representative offices of foreign entities are not allowed to carry out business activities, and are not subject to corporate income taxation. A representative office registered under the Foreign Investments Act may perform only those activities that are not regarded as "economic activities," that is, marketing activities normally carried out by a representative office and auxiliary to the activities of its head office. Representative offices do not constitute permanent establishments of the nonresident entities, unless they engage in business activities in breach of the law.

## Income determination

*Inventory valuation*/Inventory valuation and revaluation will be determined according to the national accounting standards. Companies can choose the method of inventory valuation, but have to apply the chosen method consistently throughout the accounting period. As of January 1, 2003, companies can alternatively apply the international accounting standards, while certain types of companies, including banks and insurance companies are obliged to do so.

Inventories have to be stock-counted at least once annually.

Tangible and intangible fixed assets have to be stock-counted at least once within a two-year period. Inventories at the end of the year are to be valued at the lower of their cost or net realizable value at the balance sheet date. The difference is regulated for tax purposes.

*Capital gains*/Only realized capital gains are included in corporate income and taxed at the full corporate tax rate. Exchange rate gains and losses are reported in the profit and loss account and reflected in the assessment of taxable profit.

*Intercompany dividends*/Intercompany dividend payments between Bulgarian companies are deductible in full from the tax base of the recipient company (participation exemption, regardless of the size of the shareholding) except for special purpose investment companies. Dividends distributed by Bulgarian companies to foreign shareholders are subject to 15% withholding tax under the domestic legislation (see below for exceptions under double tax treaties [DTTs]).

*Foreign income*/Income derived outside Bulgaria by resident legal entities and Bulgarian branches of nonresidents is included in the taxable base for the purpose of corporate income tax, regardless of whether such income is subject to taxation abroad. In instances where the provisions of a DTT are applicable, a tax credit or exemption for the foreign tax paid may be allowed. There is also a unilateral tax credit which cannot exceed the amount of the tax that would be payable in Bulgaria for the same type of income. Undistributed income of foreign subsidiaries of a Bulgarian resident company is not taxed.

**Stock dividends**/Stock dividends do not entail withholding tax (c.f., cash dividends paid out to individuals and foreign entities).

## Deductions

**Depreciation and depletion**/For accounting purposes, depreciation is calculated in accordance with the straight-line, the progressive, or the declining method of depreciation. Accounting regulations permit Bulgarian companies to establish a depreciation schedule for each tangible and intangible fixed asset on the basis of the method chosen by the company. However, for tax purposes only the straight-line method applies. Depletion is not specifically regulated for tax purposes. With certain exceptions, shortages and wastes of inventory as well as scrapping of fixed assets are regulated for corporate tax purposes.

**Net operating losses**/The taxpayer has the right to carry forward losses incurred in an accounting period over the following five years. The loss subject to carry forward is the financial result (profit or loss) after tax adjustment (without the effect of the loss subject to carried forward itself). Carryforward of foreign-source losses can be offset only against income from the same source. Loss carryback is not permitted.

**Payments to foreign affiliates**/Payments to foreign affiliates may be subject by the tax authorities to recalculation in accordance with the arm's length principle. Market prices would apply, and deviations from such prices will not be tolerated, except for interest payments—25% deviation from the statutory interest is allowable. With regard to interest payable by local companies to either local or foreign persons, thin-capitalization rules also apply (they also apply to nonaffiliated companies). The tax deductibility of interest expense less interest income is restricted to 75% of the accounting profit of the company, exclusive of interest income and expense. In case of accounting loss the difference between interest expense and income is regulated for corporate tax purposes. Interest on bank loans and interest under financial lease agreements is subject to thin capitalization regulations only when the agreements are between related parties. The rules will not apply where the debt/equity ratio does not exceed 2:1 for the respective tax period.

**Other significant items**/Companies may also deduct the following costs for tax purposes.

1. The tax allowable depreciation costs (actually booked depreciation costs are added back to the taxable income).
2. Grants extended to Bulgarian educational and cultural institutions, within certain limits.
3. Capital gains from shares in listed public companies and tradable rights in shares realized on a regulated Bulgarian securities market.
4. Other specific items.

As of January 1, 2003, all expenses incurred by companies for provision for liabilities which reduce the financial result will be regulated for corporate tax purposes.

# Bulgaria

## Group taxation

There is no specific legislation on group taxation. All companies are assessed on individually assessable profits and losses. However, tax antiavoidance rules cover transfer pricing and related party transactions.

## Major tax incentives

*Agricultural producers*/Companies and cooperatives performing agricultural activities enjoy 60% corporate income tax relief for income related to nonprocessed agricultural production, provided that they reinvest that granted-back tax in the same activities.

*Bankruptcy proceedings*/Legal entities whose bankruptcy proceedings are terminated by an effective court decision introducing a rehabilitation plan are granted full relief for corporate income tax for the part of the financial result which relates to the plan. The relief is conditional on fulfilling the obligations under the plan.

*Special tax incentives for investments in depressed regions*/Entities investing in regions with a high unemployment rate (it is deemed high if it exceeds one and a half times the average unemployment rate for the country for the preceding year) enjoy a reduction of the corporate income tax provided the following.

- The investment is in the form of acquisition, modernization or reconstruction of fixed tangible assets such as buildings, equipment, transmitters, electricity transmitters, and telecommunication lines, machines, production facilities, cars (but not passengers cars), computers, and software.
- The funds for the investment are generated from the contributions made by shareholders for acquisition of new shares (including on incorporation) or increases in the capital of the company making the investments.

If the requirements for the tax reduction are met the annual corporate tax is reduced by an amount representing 10% of the amount of the share contributions used in the above manner.

The incentive is enjoyed in the year when the investment in the above-mentioned assets is made.

The amount of the reduction of corporate income tax is accounted for as reserves and if greater than the corporate tax in the respective year it can be used to reduce the corporate tax in the following five years.

In addition, companies can reduce their financial result with the mandatory social security contributions paid by and for the account of the employer during the current year, multiplied by the percentage of the increase of the "average number of employees"[1] of the company in the current year compared to that in the previous year. The reduction cannot exceed the difference between the effectively paid-in

---

[1] "The average number of the employees" for a respective year is the sum of the average number of the employees for each month divided by 12. The average number of the employees for each month is calculated as the sum of the number of the employees for each day of the month (including the holidays) is divided by the number of the days of the respective month.

The number of the employees during the holidays is considered equal to the number of the employees during the previous working day.

mandatory social security contributions (due for the account of the employer) in the current year, and the same mandatory social security contributions due for the previous year. The incentive is available to companies that open jobs in high unemployment regions, and do not have outstanding tax liabilities and mandatory insurance liabilities as at December 31 of the year for which the incentive applies.

The corporate income tax is granted back to companies for income related to their production activities, including inward processing, provided the following.

- The offices of the company, the assets, subject to registration for tax purposes under the rules of the Tax Procedure Code are allocated entirely in regions with unemployment rate that exceeds one and a half times the average unemployment rate for the country for the previous year. The Minister of Finance annually updates a list of these regions.
- Eighty percent of the average annual number of the employees of the company for the tax period in which the relief is applied resides in the respective region of high unemployment.
- The company does not have outstanding tax liabilities and mandatory insurance liabilities for the calendar year for which the incentive is used.

The tax granted back is accounted for as reserves. It has to be invested in tangible and intangible fixed assets and materials employed in the production activity, or in wages of the employees, not later than the end of the calendar year following the year in which the tax was granted back. The incentive is available, provided that the above criteria are met. If as a result of increase of the employment rate a municipality drops out of the approved list (mentioned in the bullets above), companies entitled to use the incentive retain their right to use it for the next five years, following the year when the respective municipality dropped out of the list. If a company satisfied the requirements to use the incentive in a year prior to the year when the municipality dropped out of the list, but it did not carry out production activities (due to preparatory work) the company will be entitled to use the incentive if it starts performing production activities in the following year. The company would be entitled to use the incentive for a period of five years as of the year the production activities started. The fulfillment of the above criteria is evidenced in attachments to the annual corporate tax return of the company.

*Investment funds*/Companies that have been licensed as investment funds under the Bulgarian Public Offer of Securities Act enjoy full corporate tax relief for their profits derived from trading of securities. Withholding tax at the rate of 15% applies to dividends distributed by investment funds.

Special investment companies licensed under the Special Investment Purpose Companies Act are exempt from corporate income tax.

## Withholding taxes

Bulgarian companies are required to withhold tax on payments of dividends and liquidation proceeds; interest (including that incurred under finance lease agreements and on bank deposits); royalties; fees for technical services; payments for use of properties; payments made under operating leasing, franchising and factoring agreements; management fees; gains from transfer of immovable property; and capital gain payments to nonresidents. Capital gains from securities will not be subject to withholding tax if resulting from shares in listed companies and tradable rights in such shares on a regulated Bulgarian securities market.

# Bulgaria

Dividends and liquidation proceeds are taxed also where payments are made to resident individuals and nonprofit organizations. (For details on dividend payments between domestic companies see "Intercompany dividends" above.) Dividends capitalized into shares (stock dividends) are not subject to withholding tax. As of January 1, 2004 income (other than dividends) accrued by a permanent establishment of a foreign person to other parts of its enterprise, located outside the country is subject to withholding tax. This rule applies for income subject to taxation with 15% withholding tax except income from dividends. The general rate under the domestic legislation is 15%. DTTs may reduce the rate.

*Dividends*/When a dividend is paid to a nonresident company, it is subject to withholding tax at a rate of 15%, unless the rate is reduced by an applicable DTT. No differentiation is made between portfolio and substantial holdings for purposes of this withholding tax on dividends.

*Interest*/A 15% rate applies to interest (including interest from bank deposits) transferred abroad, unless the rate is reduced by an applicable DTT.

Interest on borrowings by the government or the Bulgarian National Bank from international financial institutions will not be taxable, if the respective loan agreements contain relevant exemption arrangements (international treaties override domestic legislation).

Royalties payable to foreign persons are taxed at a rate of 15% at source, unless the rate is reduced by an applicable DTT.

The capital gains tax and the withholding tax on remittances for technical services and other payments are also imposed at 15%, if not reduced by an applicable DTT.

The following is a summary of the main parameters of the Bulgarian DTTs as of January 1, 2004.

| Recipient | Dividends | Interest | Royalties | Capital gains |
|---|---|---|---|---|
| | % | % | % | % |
| Albania (3, 6, 9) | 5/15 | 10/0 | 10 | 0/15 |
| Armenia (1, 6) | 5/10 | 10/0 | 10 | 0 |
| Austria (12) | 0 | 0 | 0 | 0 |
| Belarus (6) | 10 | 10/0 | 10 | 0 |
| Belgium (6) | 10 | 10/0 | 5 | 0 |
| Canada (9, 16) | 10/15 | 10 | 10 | 0/15 |
| China (2, 6, 9, 18) | 10 | 10/0 | 7/10 | 0/15 |
| Croatia | 5 | 5 | 0 | 0 |
| Cyprus (3, 9) | 5/10 | 7 | 10 | 0/15 |
| Czech Republic (9, 11) | 10 | 10/0 | 10 | 0/15 |
| Denmark (3) | 5/15 | 0 | 0 | 0 |
| Finland (4, 9, 12) | 10 | 0 | 0/5 | 0/15 |
| France (5) | 5/15 | 0 | 5 | 0 |
| Georgia (6) | 10 | 10/0 | 10 | 0 |
| Germany | 15 | 0 | 5 | 15 |
| Greece | 10 | 10 | 10 | 0 |
| Hungary (6) | 10 | 10/0 | 10 | 0 |
| India (6) | 15 | 15/0 | 15/20 | 15 |
| Indonesia (6) | 15 | 10/0 | 10 | 0 |
| Ireland (3, 9) | 5/10 | 5 | 10 | 0/15 |
| Israel (19, 20, 21, 22) | 10/7.5–12.5 | 0/5/10 | 7.5–12.5 | 7.5–12.5 |

| Recipient | Dividends | Interest | Royalties | Capital gains |
|---|---|---|---|---|
| | % | % | % | % |
| Italy | 10 | 0 | 5 | 0 |
| Japan (3, 6) | 10/15 | 10/0 | 10 | 15 |
| Kazakhstan (8, 9) | 10 | 10 | 10 | 0/15 |
| Lebanon (6) | 5 | 7/0 | 5 | 0 |
| Luxembourg (3) | 5/15 | 10 | 5 | 0 |
| Macedonia (3, 6, 9) | 5/15 | 10/0 | 10 | 0/15 |
| Malta (12, 17) | 0/30 | 0 | 10 | 0 |
| Moldova (3, 6, 9) | 5/15 | 10/0 | 10 | 0/15 |
| Mongolia | 10 | 10 | 10 | 15 |
| Morocco (5, 9) | 7/10 | 10 | 10 | 0/15 |
| The Netherlands (3, 7, 9) | 5/15 | 0 | 0/5 | 0/15 |
| Norway | 15 | 0 | 0 | 0 |
| North Korea (6) | 10 | 10/0 | 10 | 15 |
| Poland (6) | 10 | 10/0 | 5 | 0 |
| Portugal (3, 6) | 10/15 | 10/0 | 10 | 0 |
| Romania (3, 6) | 10/15 | 15/0 | 15 | 0 |
| Russian Federation (6) | 15 | 15/0 | 15 | 0 |
| Singapore (6) | 5 | 5/0 | 5 | 0 |
| Slovak Republic | 10 | 10 | 10 | 0 |
| South Korea (5, 6) | 5/10 | 10/0 | 5 | 0 |
| Spain (3) | 5/15 | 0 | 0 | 0 |
| Sweden (9) | 10 | 0 | 5 | 0/15 |
| Switzerland (3, 10, 13) | 5/15 | 10/0 | 0/5 | 0 |
| Syria | 10 | 10/0 | 18 | 0 |
| Thailand (9, 14, 15) | 10 | 10/15 | 5/15 | 0/15 |
| Turkey (3, 6, 9) | 10/15 | 10/0 | 10 | 0/15 |
| Ukraine (3, 6, 9) | 5/15 | 10/0 | 10 | 0/15 |
| United Kingdom | 10 | 0 | 0 | 0 |
| Vietnam (6, 9) | 15 | 10/0 | 15 | 0/15 |
| Yugoslavia (3) | 5/15 | 10 | 10 | 0 |
| Zimbabwe (3, 6, 9) | 10/20 | 10/0 | 10 | 0/15 |

Notes:

1. The lower rate applies to dividends paid out to a nonresident, which is the direct owner of at least US$40,000, forming part of the capital of the company making the payment.

2. The withholding tax on royalties for use (or right to use) of industrial, commercial, or scientific equipment is reduced to 7%.

3. The lower rate applies to dividends paid out to a foreign company, which controls directly at least 25% of the share capital of the payer of the dividends. In the specific cases of the different countries more requirements may be in place.

4. There is no withholding tax on royalties for the use (or the right to use) of scientific or cultural works.

5. The lower rate applies to dividends paid out to a foreign company, which controls directly at least 15% of the share capital of the payer of the dividends.

6. There is no withholding tax on interest when paid to public bodies (government, the Central bank, governmental institutions).

# Bulgaria

7. A rate of 5% on royalties is applicable in case the Netherlands applies withholding tax under their domestic law.
8. Up to 10% branch tax may be imposed on permanent establishment profits.
9. The 15% rate on capital gains from securities applies in specific cases pointed out in the respective treaty.
10. The zero rate on interest applies if the loan is extended by a bank.
11. The zero rate on interest applies if the interest is paid to public bodies (government, municipality, the Central bank or any financial institution owned entirely by the government), to residents of the other country when the loan or the credit is guaranteed by its government, or if the loan is extended by a company for any equipment or goods.
12. The Council of Ministers has stated its intention to re-negotiate the DTTs with Austria, Malta, and Finland.
13. A rate of 5% on royalties will apply if the Swiss Confederation introduces in its domestic law withholding tax on royalties paid to nonresidents.
14. The 10% rate on interest applies if the interests are received from a financial institution, including an insurance company.
15. The 5% rate on royalties applies if the royalties are paid for the use of copyright for literal, art, or scientific work.
16. The lower rate applies to dividends paid out to a foreign company, which controls directly at least 10% of the share capital of the payer of the dividends.
17. The 0% rate applies to dividends payable by a Bulgarian resident entity to an entity resident in Malta. The 30% rate applies to dividends payable by a Maltese entity to a Bulgarian entity.
18. There are indications that there may be some amendments to the Treaty, which are not yet officially promulgated in Bulgaria.
19. The 10% rate applies to dividends, distributed by companies that enjoy a reduced or zero corporate income tax by virtue of a tax incentive for investments. In all other cases the rate is equal to one-half of the applicable rate as per the national legislations of Bulgaria and Israel, nevertheless the withholding tax rate may not be less than 7.5% and more than 12.5%.
20. The 5% rate applies to interest payable to banks or other financial institutions. The zero rate applies to interest payable to certain public bodies (governments, municipalities, Central Banks) or to residents of the other country when the loan or credit is guaranteed, insured or financed by a public body of that country or by the Israeli international Trade Insurance Company. The 10% rate applies in all other cases.
21. The rate on royalties is equal to 1/2 of the applicable rate as per the national legislations of Bulgaria and Israel, nevertheless the withholding tax rate may not be less than 7.5% and more than 12.5%.
22. The rate on capital gains from securities is equal to 1/2 of the applicable rate as per the national legislations of Bulgaria and Israel, nevertheless the withholding tax rate may not be less than 7.5% and more than 12.5%. However, capital gains from transfers of shares in entities, whose real estate properties exceed 50% of their assets, are taxed in the country in which the real estate is located.

Under some DTTs technical service payments fall within the definition of royalty payments and are taxed accordingly.

Bulgaria has also signed DTTs with Algeria, Kuwait, and Mongolia, which the Bulgarian Parliament has ratified. It is awaited for these DTTs to be promulgated in the State Gazette in order to become applicable in Bulgaria.

## Tax administration

*Returns*/Annual profit must be declared no later than March 31 of the year following the financial (tax) year. The financial and tax years coincide with the calendar year. The annual balance sheet and profit and loss account of entities that meet certain criteria (number of employees, legal form, net sales proceeds, etc.), are to be audited by a chartered accountant and submitted to the Tax Office at the place of residence of the legal entity, together with the tax return. The self-assessment principle is applied.

*Payment of tax*/If a company ended up the preceding financial year with a taxable profit, it is liable for advance corporate income tax payments each month in the current year at the rate of 19.5%. The monthly taxable base for the second, third and fourth quarters is one-twelfth of the annual taxable profit for the preceding year multiplied by a coefficient determined in the State Budget Act for the current year. However, the taxable base for the advance payments during the first quarter is one-twelfth of the taxable profit of the company for the year before the preceding year multiplied by a coefficient defined in the State Budget Act for the current year.

Corporate taxpayers having a tax loss or zero taxable result in the previous year and companies established during the current year make quarterly advance payments during the current fiscal year. The base of the quarterly advance payments is the profit for the corresponding period accumulated from the beginning of the current year.

Overpayment of corporate tax is offsettable against advance and annual payments of the respective taxes due for the next period. The difference between the annual tax declared in the corporate income tax return and the advance tax paid for the corresponding year must be paid by the deadline for submitting the tax return—March 31 of the following year.

# Bulgaria

## *CORPORATION TAX CALCULATION*

Calendar year ended December 31, 2003. (Fiscal year ending December 31, 2003.)

### Assumptions

The company is a subsidiary of a foreign company. No tax exemption is available (see "Tax incentives" above).

### Tax computation in BGN

| | | | |
|---|---|---:|---:|
| (1) | Financial result in the profit and loss account | | BGN 10,000 |
| | Less: | | |
| (2) | Dividends received from Bulgarian resident companies | 150 | |
| (3) | Loss carried forward | 100 | |
| (4) | Tax depreciation costs | 100 | |
| (5) | Total deductions ((2) + (3) + (4)) | | 350 |
| | Plus: | | |
| (6) | Accounting depreciation costs | 230 | |
| (7) | Daily business trip allowances exceeding tax-deductible limits | 270 | |
| (8) | Other nondeductible costs | 950 | |
| (9) | Total of add-backs ((6) + (7) + (8)) | | 1,450 |
| (10) | Taxable profit ((1) − (5) + (9)) | | BGN 11,100 |
| (11) | Corporate tax (19.5% of (10)) | | BGN 2,164.5 |

Note:

Official exchange rate at March 16, 2004: US$1 = BGN1.58367.

Note that the amounts added/deducted above are just for illustrative purposes and do not represent an exhaustive list of all the relevant items as per the Bulgarian law.

## PwC contact

For additional information on taxation in Cambodia, contact:

Jean Loi
PricewaterhouseCoopers (Cambodia) Ltd.
124 Norodom Boulevard
Phnom Penh, Cambodia
Telephone: (855) (23) 218 086
Fax: (855) (23) 211 594
e-mail: jean.loi@kh.pwc.com

## Significant developments

The Law on the Amendment to the Law on Taxation (new Law on Taxation) and the Law on the Amendments to the Law on Investment (new Law on Investment) were passed by the National Assembly in March 2003 and became effective on January 1, 2004.

The specific tax rate for telecommunication services and air transportation of passengers increased from 2% to 10% with effect from January 1, 2004.

## Taxes on corporate income

*Corporate tax*/Cambodia's taxation rules vary according to the taxpayer's regime. "Real" regime taxpayers will include most large or incorporated taxpayers. The majority of foreign investors will fall into the real regime. Unless otherwise noted, the discussion is therefore restricted to real regime taxpayers.

Resident taxpayers are subject to tax on worldwide income/profits, while nonresidents are taxed on Cambodian sourced income/profits only. Residents earning foreign-sourced profits and income can receive credits for foreign taxes paid. A permanent establishment (PE) is taxable on its Cambodian source income only.

Resident taxpayers include companies organized, managed, or having their principal place of business in Cambodia. An internationally-recognized PE definition exists in the old and new Law on Taxation.

The standard rate of tax on profit for companies and permanent establishments is 20%. A preferential rate of 9% may be granted pursuant to investment incentives granted by the Council for the Development of Cambodia (CDC). The 9% preferential rate will be phased out over five years after the implementation of the new Law on Investment, that is, by 2008. Oil and gas, and certain mineral exploitation activities, are subject to tax at the rate of 30%. Insurance activities are taxable at the rate of 5% on the gross premium income.

*Additional tax on profit on dividend distribution*/With effect from January 1, 2004, a dividend-paying company is required to make an additional tax on profit on dividend distribution at the time of a dividend distribution if the profit was previously subject to the 9% or 0% tax on profit.

A shareholder is entitled to establish a special dividend account from which the relevant dividend may be paid without further additional tax on profit obligations.

A dividend will be exempt from tax in the hands of the shareholder if the additional tax on profit and withholding tax (for nonresident shareholders) have been paid.

# Cambodia

## Other taxes

In addition to the tax on profit, the following taxes may affect certain investors.

*Minimum tax*/Real-regime taxpayers are subject to a separate minimum tax, unless the taxpayer has been granted the status of an "investment enterprise" (i.e., registered with the CDC). The minimum tax is an annual tax with a liability equal to 1% of the turnover of the taxpayer for the year in question. The tax is due irrespective of the taxpayer's profit or loss position.

*Value-added tax*/VAT is applicable to real-regime entities, and is charged at 10% on the price of supply of most goods and services. Most exports of goods, and most services rendered outside Cambodia are zero-rated. Some supplies are exempt, with the main categories being public postal service, medical and dental services, electricity, transportation of passengers by wholly state-owned public transportation systems, insurance services, and primary financial services. Strict record-keeping requirements exist.

*Specific tax on certain merchandise and services*/The specific tax, with rates ranging from 0% to 33.33%, is a form of excise tax that applies to the importation, or domestic production and supply of, certain goods and services. Specific tax due on domestically produced goods is generally applied to the "ex-factory selling price." For imported goods the tax is due on the cost, insurance, and freight (CIF) value inclusive of customs duty. For hotel and telecommunication services, the tax is payable on the invoice prices. For international air transport of passengers, the tax is payable on the air ticket value issued in Cambodia for travel within and outside Cambodia.

*Import and export duties*/Import duties are levied on a wide range of products at rates ranging from 0% to 35%, although exemptions may be available as an investment incentive. As a requirement of Cambodia's membership in Association of South East Asian Nations (ASEAN), various import duties have been reduced as part of the Common Effective Preferential Tariffs program. Export duties are levied on a limited number of items, such as timber and certain animal products (including most seafood).

*Tax on house and land rent*/Businesses (other than real-regime entities) that rent land, buildings, certain equipment, storage facilities, and so forth, are subject to the tax on house and land rent. The tax is levied at 10% of the rental fee. This tax may not apply where the tax on profit has been withheld from the rental payment.

*Patent tax*/Registered businesses must pay a (relatively nominal) patent tax on initial business registration and annually thereafter. Patent tax is levied with reference to turnover or estimated turnover.

*Fiscal stamp tax*/Fiscal stamp tax is paid on certain official documents and, perhaps more important for foreign investors, certain advertising postings and signage. Amounts vary according to factors such as the location of the signage, illumination and "nationality" of any words.

*Tax for public lighting*/The tax for public lighting (TPL) applies to the distribution of tobacco and alcohol products. TPL is imposed on all chains of supply at the rate of 3% on the value of the taxable products inclusive of other taxes (but not VAT for real-regime taxpayers). The tax is payable on a monthly basis.

*Tax on unused land*/Land in towns and other specified areas that have no construction, or a construction site not in use, or in some cases certain built-upon land, is subject to the tax on unused land. The tax is calculated at 2% of the market value of the land per square meter, as determined by the Commission for Evaluation of Unused Land, as at June 30 each year. The first 1,200 square meters of land are free of tax. The owner of the land is required to pay the tax by September 30 each year. Failure to pay the tax will be subject to penalty or risk of losing the land to the state.

*Registration tax (property transfer tax)*/Certain documents relating to the establishment, dissolution or merger of a business, or to the transfer of title to certain assets (such as land and vehicles) are subject to registration tax, which is generally levied at 4% of the transfer value.

*Tax on means of transportation*/This tax imposes a number of statutory fees on the registration of certain transportation vehicles, including trucks, buses, motor vehicles, and ships.

## Branch income

Tax rates for branch income are the same as those for corporate profits.

## Income determination

*Inventory valuation*/Inventory can be valued at weighted-average cost, FIFO, or current value at the close of the period, where this value is lower than the purchase price or production cost. Work-in-progress should be valued at production costs.

*Capital gains*/Capital gains form part of taxable profit.

*Intercompany dividend*/Intercompany dividends may be exempt from tax (see "Withholding taxes" below).

*Foreign income*/Residents are taxed on their worldwide income/profits. Tax credits are available for foreign taxes suffered.

*Stock dividends*/Stock dividends appear to be subject to withholding tax as dividends.

*Other significant items*/None.

## Deductions

*Depreciation*/Property should be depreciated at rates according to four classes of assets as specified in the tax legislation. Land is not considered a depreciable asset. The straight-line or the declining-balance method is specifically required to be used for each class of assets. Special depreciation is available to assets purchased by a CDC-licensed investment, and used in manufacturing and processing (not defined). The special depreciation regime allows the use of accelerated 40% depreciation in the year of purchase or first use of assets.

*Net operating losses*/Tax losses may be carried forward for up to five years, subject to certain criteria, including a change in ownership, or the receipt of a unilateral tax assessment by the tax authority. Carryback of losses is not available.

*Payments to foreign affiliates*/Certain losses suffered on sales to (51%) related parties are nondeductible. Other discretionary transfer pricing provisions are present where there is a 20% common ownership.

# Cambodia

*Taxes*/Deductible taxes may be subtracted from the profits of the period of tax payment. Nondeductible taxes include taxes that are not a charge to the enterprise (e.g., personal taxes) and the tax on profits.

*Other significant items*/Interest deductibility in any year is limited to the amount of interest income plus 50% of the net noninterest income for the year. The excess nondeductible interest expense can be carried forward to the following tax years indefinitely.

## Group taxation

There is no provision for group taxation.

## Tax incentives

*Inward investment*/Most investments will require registration with the Ministry of Commerce (MoC) and other relevant ministries. The CDC may also be approached for the purposes of seeking investment incentives. CDC licensing is, however, not mandatory (except for certain large, politically sensitive, etc. projects), and may in fact not be available for certain investments, especially those in trading and services.

The investment incentives available have been significantly changed following the implementation of the new Law on Investment. The amended regime of incentives that primarily consist of a tax on profit holiday of up to six years, and import duty exemptions.

Under the new Law on Investment, all CDC licensed companies are required to obtain a certificate of compliance from the CDC on an annual basis in order to continue enjoying the investment incentives.

*Capital investment*/None.

*Other incentive*/None.

## Withholding taxes

The new Law on Taxation has amended the rates and scope of the withholding tax effective from January 1, 2004. Withholding tax needs only be withheld on payments made by resident taxpayers. The withheld tax constitutes a final tax when withheld in respect of nonresidents.

| Payment/recipient | % |
|---|---|
| Interest paid by a resident taxpayer: | |
| Resident, other than a Cambodian bank | 15 |
| Nonresident | 14 |
| Interest paid by a resident taxpayer bank: | |
| Resident individual on nonfixed term savings accounts | 4 |
| Resident individual on fixed term savings | 6 |
| Rent: | |
| Resident | 10 |
| Nonresident | 14 |
| Payments for services: | |
| Nonreal regime resident taxpayer | 15 |
| Nonresident for "management and technical services" (not defined) | 14 |
| Royalties: | |
| Resident | 15 |
| Nonresident | 14 |
| Dividend: | |
| Nonresident | 14 |

Withholding tax is required to be remitted by the payer on a monthly basis by the 15th day of the succeeding month.

At the time of writing, Cambodia had not negotiated any double taxation agreements.

## Tax administration

***Returns and payment of tax***/Returns for the tax on profit are to be filed annually within three months of year-end. The standard tax year is the calendar year, although different accounting year-ends may be granted upon application. The 1% prepayments of tax on profit are due on a monthly basis by the 15th day of the succeeding month. Cambodian incorporated companies are technically required to adopt the Cambodian Chart of Accounts as their accounting system. Failure to do so can result in the issuing of a unilateral tax assessment.

# Cambodia

## *CORPORATION TAX CALCULATION*

Calendar year ended December 31, 2003

| | | |
|---|---:|---:|
| Net profit before tax per accounts........................................................... | | CR 1,000,000 |
| Add back/deduct: | | |
| Nondeductible provisions at year end.................................. | 110,000 | |
| Nondeductible taxes............................................................ | 60,000 | 170,000 |
| | | 1,170,000 |
| Deduct—Provisions previously added back ........................................... | | 120,000 |
| Taxable basis for tax on profit................................................................ | | CR 1,050,000 |
| Tax on profit at 20% ............................................................................. | | CR 210,000 |

Note:

Average exchange rate of the riel at January 1, 2004: US$1 = CR4,087.1.

## PwC contact

For additional information on taxation in Canada, contact:

Bill Bower
PricewaterhouseCoopers LLP
1 Robert Speck Parkway
Suite 1100
Mississauga, ON L4Z 3M3, Canada
Telephone: (1) (905) 949 7331
Fax: (1) (905) 949 7335
LN address: Bill Bower/CA/TLS/PwC
e-mail: bill.bower@ca.pwc.com

## Significant developments

Corporate income tax rates have generally tended to decline in 2003 and more reductions are planned.

## General note

The following information is based on actual and proposed legislation as of January 1, 2004. It is assumed that the proposed legislation will become law.

## Taxes on corporate income

*Federal income tax*/The following rates apply for December 31, 2003 year-ends. The federal rate before surtax (and after the provincial abatement) on other income (see below) was reduced from 25% to 23% on January 1, 2003 and to 21% on January 1, 2004. As a result, the net federal tax rate on other income decreased to 22.1% on January 1, 2004. This rate reduction does not apply to the first Can$300,000 of active business income earned in Canada of Canadian-controlled private corporations, manufacturing and processing income, resource income (see below), income benefiting from refundable tax provisions and income of mutual fund and investment corporations, because such income already benefits from preferential rates.

| | Manufacturing and processing | Other |
|---|---|---|
| | % | % |
| Basic rate | 38.0 | 38.0 |
| Less—Provincial abatement (1) | 10.0 | 10.0 |
| Federal rate before surtax | 28.0 | 28.0 |
| Federal surtax of 4% (2) | 1.1 | 1.1 |
| | 29.1 | 29.1 |
| Less—General rate reduction | — | 5.0 |
| Profits deduction | 7.0 | — |
| Net federal tax rate | 22.1 | 24.1 |
| "Typical provincial rate" (3) | 11.0 | 12.5 |
| Total rate (4) | 33.1 | 36.6 |

# Canada

Notes:

1. The basic rate of federal tax is reduced by a 10% abatement to allow the provinces and territories room to impose corporate income taxes. The abatement is available in respect of taxable income allocated to Canadian provinces and territories. Taxable income allocable to a foreign jurisdiction is not eligible for the abatement and is normally not subject to provincial or territorial taxes.

2. A 4% surtax is calculated on the basic rate less the provincial abatement. Reductions to the federal rate before surtax on other income do not effect the federal surtax.

3. Provincial taxes apply in addition to federal taxes. Provincial tax rates are noted below.

4. For small Canadian-controlled private corporations, a federal rate of 13.1% applies to the first Can$225,000 of active business income. After taking into account the "typical" provincial rate (of 5.5%), the total rate on such income is 18.6%. For such corporations, a federal rate of 22.1% is levied on active business income between Can$225,000 and Can$300,000. The Can$225,000 threshold increased to Can$250,000 on January 1, 2004 and will further increase to Can$250,000 on January 1, 2005 and to Can$300,000 on January 1, 2006. Investment income (other than most dividends) of Canadian-controlled private corporations is subject to tax at the federal rate calculated for other income, or 29.1%, in addition to a refundable federal tax of 6-2/3%, for a total federal rate of 35.8%.

**Provincial income tax**/All provinces and territories impose income tax on income allocable to a permanent establishment in the province or territory. Income is generally allocated to a province or territory by using a two-factor formula based on gross revenue and on salaries and wages. Provincial and territorial income taxes are not deductible for federal income tax purposes. The rates given apply for December 31, 2003 year-ends. The rates do not take into account provincial tax holidays, which reduce or eliminate tax in limited cases.

| | Manufacturing and processing | Other income (1) |
|---|---|---|
| | % | % |
| Alberta (2) | 12.6 | 12.6 |
| British Columbia | 13.5 | 13.5 |
| Manitoba (3) | 16.0 | 16.0 |
| New Brunswick (4) | 13.0 | 13.0 |
| Newfoundland and Labrador | 5.0 | 14.0 |
| Northwest Territories | 12.0 | 12.0 |
| Nova Scotia | 16.0 | 16.0 |
| Nunavut | 12.0 | 12.0 |
| Ontario (5) | 11.0 | 12.5 |
| Prince Edward Island | 7.5 | 16.0 |
| Quebec (6) | 8.9 | 8.9 |
| Saskatchewan (7) | 10.0 | 17.0 |
| Yukon Territory | 2.5 | 15.0 |

Notes:

1. In all provinces and territories, the first Can$225,000 of active business income of a small Canadian-controlled private corporation is subject to

reduced rates that range from 2.5% to 8.9%, depending on the jurisdiction. The Can$225,000 threshold increased to Can$250,000 on January 1, 2004 and further increase to Can$250,000 on January 1, 2005 and to Can$300,000 on January 1, 2006. The Can$225,000 threshold is higher in some provinces.

2. Alberta's rate decreased from 13% to 12.5% on April 1, 2003 and is expected to further decrease to 11.5% on April 1, 2004. Furthermore, Alberta indicated that it intends to reduce the rate to 8% when this is affordable.

3. Manitoba's rate decreased from 16.5% to 16% on January 1, 2003 and to 15.5% on January 1, 2004. The rate will further decrease to 15% on January 1, 2005.

4. New Brunswick's rate decreased from 14.5% to 13% on January 1, 2003.

5. The lower Ontario rate applies to profits from manufacturing and processing, and from farming, mining, logging, and fishing operations carried on in Canada and allocated to Ontario. On January 1, 2004, Ontario's manufacturing and processing rate increased to 12% and its general corporate rate increased to 14%. Plans to decrease these rates to 8% by January 1, 2006 have been repealed.

   Ontario corporations that, on an associated basis, have either gross revenue over $10 million or total assets over $5 million are subject to a corporate minimum tax. The tax, which is levied at a rate on 4% of adjusted book income, is payable only to the extent that it exceeds the regular Ontario income tax liability.

6. The Quebec rate applies to active business income from manufacturing and nonmanufacturing activities. The rate on inactive income is 16.3%. The rates include a 1.6% Youth Fund surtax, which applied from March 15, 2000 to March 14, 2003, inclusive.

7. Saskatchewan's manufacturing and processing rate is reduced from 17% to as low as 10%, depending on the extent to which the corporation's income is allocated to the province.

## Corporate residence

As a general rule, corporations resident in Canada are subject to Canadian income tax on their worldwide income. As a result of special provisions in the Income Tax Act, almost all corporations incorporated in Canada are resident in Canada. A corporation not incorporated in Canada may be considered resident in Canada if its central management and control are exercised in Canada.

A corporation incorporated in Canada will cease to be a Canadian resident if it is granted articles of continuance in a foreign jurisdiction, or if it is a predecessor corporation in a cross-border amalgamation. Similarly, a foreign corporation will become resident in Canada if it is continued in Canada or is a predecessor corporation of an amalgamated corporation that is resident in Canada.

Nonresident corporations are subject to income tax on income derived from carrying on a business in Canada and on capital gains arising upon the disposition of taxable Canadian property. Taxable Canadian property includes, among other things, real estate situated in Canada, both capital and noncapital property used in carrying on a business in Canada and shares in Canadian resident corporations that are not listed on a stock exchange. In certain circumstances, shares in Canadian-resident corporations that are listed on a stock exchange, shares in nonresident corporations and interests in nonresident trusts will be considered taxable Canadian property.

Withholding tax at a rate of 25% is imposed on interest, dividends, rents, royalties, certain management and technical service fees, and similar payments made by a Canadian resident to a nonresident of Canada.

Canadian income tax and withholding tax can be reduced or eliminated if Canada has a treaty with the nonresident's country of residence. A list of treaties that Canada has negotiated and applicable withholding tax rates is provided below.

## Other taxes

**Goods and services tax**/The federal goods and services tax (GST) is levied at a rate of 7%. It is a value-added tax (VAT) applied at each level in the manufacturing and marketing chain and applies to most goods and services. However, the tax does not apply to sales of zero-rated goods, such as exports and groceries, or to tax-exempt supplies, such as certain services provided by financial institutions.

Generally, businesses pay GST on their purchases and charge GST on their sales, and remit the net amount (i.e., the difference between the GST collected and the input tax credit for the tax paid on purchases). Suppliers of zero-rated goods and services are entitled to input tax credits. Suppliers of tax-exempt goods are not entitled to input tax credits in respect of such goods.

**Harmonized sales tax**/New Brunswick, Newfoundland and Labrador, and Nova Scotia harmonized their sales tax systems with the GST and impose a single sales tax rate of 15%. The 15% rate includes an 8% provincial sales tax component and the 7% GST. It is imposed on essentially the same base as the GST.

**Retail sales tax**/British Columbia, Manitoba, Ontario, Prince Edward Island, and Saskatchewan levy retail sales tax at rates ranging from 6% to 10% on most purchases of tangible personal property for consumption or use in the province and on the purchase of specific services.

Quebec's sales tax is structured essentially in the same way as the GST. Quebec has widened its sales tax base to include most of the goods and services subject to the GST. The general Quebec sales tax rate is 7.5%. Quebec administers the GST in that province.

Only Prince Edward Island and Quebec levy the retail sales tax on prices that include the GST.

Alberta and the territories do not impose a retail sales tax. As mentioned above, New Brunswick, Newfoundland and Labrador, and Nova Scotia levy a harmonized sales tax, which includes a provincial sales tax.

**Other provincial and local taxes**/Municipalities throughout Canada also levy property taxes. All provinces and territories impose land transfer taxes or registration fees on the purchase of real property within their boundaries.

**Federal capital taxes**/Federal capital taxes are imposed at the following rates for December 31, 2003 year-ends. Federal capital taxes are not deductible for income tax purposes, but may be reduced as discussed below.

| Corporations affected | Tax | Rate |
|---|---|---|
| All corporations | Large Corporations Tax (Part I.3 Tax) (1) | 0.225% |
| Banks, trust and loan corporations, and life insurance companies | Financial Institutions Capital Tax (Part VI Tax) (2) | 1.25% |

Notes:

1. Part I.3 Tax applies to both taxable Canadian corporations and nonresident corporations that have a permanent establishment in Canada. The Part I.3 Tax will be eliminated over five years. The rate decreased from 0.225% to 0.2% on January 1, 2004 and will further decrease to 0.175% on January 1, 2005, 0.125% on January 1, 2006, 0.0625% on January 1, 2006 and nil on January 1, 2008.

   The tax is imposed on taxable capital employed in Canada over Can$10 million (the Can$10 million threshold must be allocated among related corporations; associated corporations in the case of Canadian-Controlled Private Corporations). The Can$10 million threshold increased to Can$50 million, effective for taxation years ending after 2003.

   Taxable capital is based on the company's financial statements. The tax base includes share capital, retained earnings and other surpluses, and loans and advances. It is reduced by an allowance for investments in other corporations, excluding financial institutions. Different rules apply when determining the taxable capital of financial institutions (e.g., banks, insurance companies, trust companies, and investment dealers).

   The Part I.3 Tax is not deductible in computing income for tax purposes. It is reduced by the portion of the federal surtax liability that is the corporation's Canadian surtax liability. Any unused Canadian surtax liability can be applied to reduce Part I.3 Tax for the previous three and next seven years. After 2003, the unused surtax credits will be calculated as if the Part I.3 Tax rate and the capital tax threshold remained 0.225% and Can$10 million, respectively.

2. Part VI Tax applies when taxable capital employed in Canada exceeds $200 million. A reduced rate of 1% applies to capital between Can$200 and Can$300 million. The thresholds are shared among related financial institutions. The tax is not deductible in computing income for tax purposes. It is reduced by the corporation's federal income tax liability, net of any federal surtax claimed against the Part I.3 liability. Any unused federal income tax liability can be applied to reduce Part VI Tax for the previous three and the next seven years. In effect, the tax constitutes a minimum tax on financial institutions.

*Provincial capital taxes*/Each of the provinces, except Alberta, imposes a tax on capital employed within the province. The tax is deductible for federal income tax purposes, but the federal government has proposed to place limits on deductibility. Implementation has been delayed by one year until 2005, representing the twelfth annual delay. As an interim measure, any increase in these taxes, with certain exceptions, is not deductible.

Provincial capital taxes are imposed at the following rates for December 31, 2003 year-ends. Exemptions and reduced rates apply in certain cases.

# Canada

| | General | Banks, trust and loan corporations |
|---|---|---|
| | % | % |
| Alberta .................................................................... | — | — |
| British Columbia ................................................... | — | 1.00 or 3.00 |
| Manitoba (1)........................................................... | 0.30 or .50 | 3.00 |
| New Brunswick....................................................... | 0.30 | 3.00 |
| Newfoundland and Labrador............................... | — | 4.00 |
| Nova Scotia (2)...................................................... | 0.25 | 3.00 |
| Ontario (3).............................................................. | 0.30 | 0.90 or 0.72 |
| Prince Edward Island............................................ | — | 3.00 |
| Quebec (4) ............................................................. | 0.60 | 1.45 |
| Saskatchewan (5).................................................. | 0.60 | 3.25 |

Notes:

1.  Manitoba's general capital tax rate includes a surcharge of 0.2% for corporations with taxable paid-up capital exceeding $10 million, for an effective rate of 0.50%.

2.  Nova Scotia's general capital tax is scheduled to expire on March 31, 2006, two years later than previously announced.

3.  Ontario had proposed reducing all of its capital tax rates on January 1, 2004 and eliminating its capital taxes by January 1, 2008. However, the changes scheduled for January 1, 2004 are not proceeding and, capital taxes are unlikely to be eliminated later, as proposed.

4.  Quebec had planned to reduced its general capital tax rate to 0.3% by January 1, 2007, however the decrease will not proceed. Quebec financial institution capital rate includes a 1.2% base rate, a 1.6% Youth Fund surtax on financial institution capital taxes, that applied to March 14, 2003, inclusive, and a 0.25% compensatory tax on paid-up capital. A compensatory tax of 2% of payroll also applies. Quebec had planned to reduced the base rate to 0.6% by January 1, 2007, however the decrease will not proceed.

5.  Saskatchewan imposes a capital tax surcharge on large resource corporations., in addition to the general capital tax. Saskatchewan's rate for financial institutions that have taxable paid-up capital of $400 million or less is 0.7%.

All provinces and the territories impose a premium tax on insurance companies (both life and nonlife). In addition, Manitoba and Nova Scotia impose a capital tax on all insurance companies, while Ontario and Quebec impose a capital tax on life insurance companies only. Quebec also levies a compensatory tax on insurance premiums at a rate of 0.35%.

***Provincial payroll taxes***/Manitoba, Newfoundland and Labrador, Ontario and Quebec employers are subject to payroll tax. Maximum rates range from 1.95% to 4.3%. The tax is deductible for federal income tax purposes, but as for provincial capital taxes (see above) the federal government is proposing to place limits on deductibility. In addition, Quebec employers with payroll of at least Can$250,000 must allot 1% of payroll to training or to a provincial fund. The Can$250,000 threshold will increase to Can$1,000,000, however the effective date for this increase has not been announced. Employers in the Northwest Territories and Nunavut must deduct from employees' salaries a payroll tax equal to 1% of employment earnings.

## Branch income

A nonresident corporation will be subject to income tax at normal corporate rates on profits derived from carrying on a business in Canada. However, Canada's tax treaties generally restrict taxation of a nonresident's business income to the portion allocable to a permanent establishment located in Canada.

In addition, a special 25% "branch tax" applies to a nonresident's after-tax profits that are not invested in qualifying property in Canada. The branch tax essentially is equivalent to a nonresident withholding tax on funds repatriated to the foreign head office. In the case of a company resident in a treaty country, the rate at which the branch tax is levied may be reduced to the withholding tax rate on dividends prescribed in the relevant tax treaty (generally 5%, 10%, or 15%). Some of Canada's treaties prohibit the imposition of branch tax or provide that branch tax is payable only on earnings in excess of a threshold amount. The branch tax does not apply to banks and transportation, communications, and iron-ore mining companies. Except in special circumstances it also does not apply to nonresident insurers.

Whether or not a treaty applies, a nonresident corporation that has a permanent establishment in Canada will be subject to federal capital taxes, and provincial capital taxes may also apply.

## Income determination

*Inventory valuation*/In most cases, all the property included in an inventory may be valued at fair market value, or each item may be valued at its cost or fair market value, whichever is lower. Most well-established and reasonable approaches to inventory costing may be used for tax purposes, with the exception of LIFO. Conformity between methods used for book and tax reporting is not mandatory, but the method chosen should be used consistently for tax purposes. Inventory must be valued at the commencement of the year at the same amount as at the end of the immediately preceding year.

*Capital gains*/One-half of a capital gain constitutes a taxable capital gain, which is included in the corporation's income and taxed at ordinary rates. Capital losses are deductible, but generally only against capital gains. Any excess of allowable capital losses over taxable capital gains in the current year may be carried back three years and forward indefinitely to be applied against net taxable capital gains from those years, except in the case of an acquisition of control. No particular holding period is required. Intent is a major factor in determining whether the gain or loss is income or capital in nature. Complex transitional rules ensure that gains and losses accrued to the end of 1971 have no tax effect. (Capital gains were not taxable before 1972.)

*Intercompany dividends*/Dividends received by one Canadian corporation from another Canadian corporation generally may be deducted in full in determining taxable income. However, dividends on certain preferred shares are an important exception to this rule and are taxed at full corporate rates. The intent is to limit the opportunity to transfer benefits of accumulated deductions or losses from the entity that incurred the expense to preferred share investors.

Dividends on most preferred shares are subject to a 10% tax in the hands of the recipient, unless the payer elects to pay a 40% tax (instead of a 25% tax) on the dividends paid. The payer can offset the tax against its income tax liability. The tax is not imposed on the first Can$500,000 of taxable preferred-share dividends paid in a taxation year. It also does not apply to dividends paid to a shareholder with a "substantial interest" in the payer (i.e., 25% of the votes and value).

Dividends received by private corporations (or public corporations controlled by one or more individuals) from Canadian corporations are subject to a special refundable tax of 33-1/3%. The tax is not imposed if the recipient is connected to the payer (i.e., the recipient owns more than a 10% interest in the payer) unless the payer was entitled to a refund of tax in respect of the dividend. The tax is refundable when the recipient pays dividends to its shareholders on the basis of Can$1 for every Can$3 of dividends paid.

*Foreign income*/Corporations resident in Canada are subject to Canadian federal income taxes on their worldwide income, including income derived directly from carrying on business in a foreign country, as earned. In addition, resident corporations may be currently taxable on certain passive income earned by foreign subsidiaries and other foreign affiliates. Relief from double taxation is provided through Canada's international tax treaties and foreign tax credits and deductions for foreign taxes paid on income derived from non-Canadian sources.

Foreign investment income earned directly, other than dividends, is taxed as earned, with foreign tax credits available in respect of foreign withholding taxes. Dividends received by private corporations from nonconnected foreign corporations are subject to the special refundable tax of 33-1/3% referred to above, to the extent that the dividends are deductible in determining taxable income.

The tax treatment of foreign dividends depends on whether the payer corporation is a foreign affiliate of the recipient. A foreign corporation is considered a foreign affiliate of a Canadian corporation if the Canadian corporation owns, directly or indirectly, at least 1% of any class of the outstanding shares of the foreign corporation *and* the Canadian corporation and related persons (together) own directly or indirectly at least 10% of any class of the outstanding shares of the foreign corporation.

Dividends received from foreign corporations that are not foreign affiliates are taxed when received, with foreign tax credits available in respect of foreign withholding taxes. Dividends received from foreign affiliates are, subject to certain limitations, permitted to flow between corporations on a tax-free basis. The limitations pertain to the nature of the earnings from which the dividends were paid, the underlying foreign taxes paid and withholding tax paid.

Canadian corporations are taxed on certain investment income (foreign accrual property income) of controlled foreign affiliates (more than 50% owned) as it is earned, whether or not distributed.

*Stock dividends*/If the payer is resident in Canada, stock dividends are treated for tax purposes in the same manner as cash dividends. The taxable amount of a stock dividend is the increase in the paid-up capital of the payer corporation because of the payment of the dividend. Stock dividends received from a nonresident are exempt from this treatment. Instead, the shares received have a cost base of zero.

## Deductions

*Depreciation*/Depreciation for tax purposes (capital cost allowance) is computed on a pool basis, with relatively few separate classes (pools) of property. Annual allowances are generally determined by applying a prescribed rate to each class on the declining-balance basis. For example, the prescribed annual rate on most machinery and equipment is 20%, on automotive equipment 30% and on most buildings 4%. In the year of acquisition, only one-half of the amount otherwise allowable may be claimed on most classes of property. Generally, a capital cost allowance may not be claimed until the taxation year when the property is available for use. The taxpayer may claim any amount of capital cost allowance up to the maximum. Capital cost allowance previously claimed may be recaptured if assets are sold for proceeds that exceed the undepreciated cost of the class.

*Mining and oil and gas activity*/Mining and oil and gas companies are generally allowed a 100% deduction for exploration costs. Development costs are deductible at the rate of 30% on a declining-balance basis. Capital property costs are subject to the depreciation rules noted above under "Depreciation." In addition, in certain cases, assets acquired for a new mine or major expansion benefit from accelerated depreciation up to 100% of the income from the new mine.

Provinces levy mining taxes and royalties on mineral extraction and on oil and gas production. Under recent amendments that are being phased in over five years, these levies are now partially deductible for income tax purposes, and will become mostly deductible by 2007. In the interim, a special deduction is also allowed (the resource allowance) equal to a prescribed percentage of resource profits calculated before deducting interest and exploration/development costs. This allowance will be eliminated in 2007.

Investment tax credits are available federally (and in some provinces) for prescribed mineral exploration expenditures. The federal credit in 2004 is 15% for individuals making qualified 'flow-through' share investments, and 10% for corporations (see below). These credits can be used to offset current taxes payable or carried over to certain previous or subsequent taxation years.

Mining and oil and gas activities are currently taxed at higher corporate tax rates than other businesses in Canada. However, recent amendments will lower this rate to the net federal tax rate (see above) by 2007.

*Net operating losses*/Net operating losses generally may be carried back three tax years and forward seven tax years. Special rules may prohibit the use of losses from other years when there has been an acquisition of control of the corporation.

*Losses from a business or property*/Draft legislation that applies to taxation years commencing after 2004 allows a loss from a business or property to be claimed only if there is a "reasonable expectation of profit" from that business or property. The new rules would apply to limit the deductibility of interest and other expenses.

*Payments to foreign affiliates*/Royaltles, management fees, and similar payments to affiliated nonresidents are deductible expenses to the extent that they are incurred to earn income of the Canadian company and do not exceed a reasonable amount (in most cases, this is fair market value).

*Interest*/Interest on borrowed money used for earning business or property income or interest in respect of an amount payable for property acquired to earn income is deductible, provided the interest is paid pursuant to a legal obligation and is reasonable in the circumstances.

# Canada

Thin capitalization rules may limit interest deductions where debt owing to certain nonresident shareholders exceeds two times the corporation's equity.

*Taxes*/Neither federal nor provincial income taxes are deductible in determining income subject to tax. The tax treatment of federal capital taxes and provincial payroll and capital taxes is discussed above.

*Scientific research*/Current and capital expenditures on scientific research in Canada are deductible (expenditures on buildings acquired after 1987 are excluded, however). Similarly, current expenditures on scientific research outside Canada are deductible. Any unclaimed expenditures for research in Canada can be carried forward indefinitely.

Capital expenditures claimed may be subject to recapture upon the disposition of the research properties.

A federal investment tax credit of 20% is provided for research expenditures incurred in Canada (35% for qualifying Canadian-controlled private corporations). Several provinces also provide tax incentives to taxpayers that carry on research and development activities.

*Other significant items*/Reporting requirements apply to taxpayers with offshore investments. The rules impose a significant compliance burden for taxpayers with foreign affiliates. Failure to comply could result in substantial penalties.

Canadian taxpayers dealing with nonresident related parties are required to follow the arm's length principle to determine any amount needed for Canadian tax purposes. Documentation requirements and transfer pricing penalties apply.

Draft legislation that will change the tax treatment of interests held in foreign investment entities (FIEs) became effective for taxation years beginning after 2002. In general, taxpayers subject to the new rules must include in income either an inclusion based on a prescribed rate of interest, their share of the actual income and capital gains of the FIE, or any change in the fair market value of the interest in the FIE from the previous year.

Transfers of losses and other deductions between unrelated corporate taxpayers are severely limited after an acquisition of control.

Three-quarters of capital expenditures for goodwill and certain other intangible properties may be amortized at a maximum annual rate of 7% on a declining-balance basis. A portion of proceeds may be taxable as recapture or as a gain on disposition. Charitable donations made to registered Canadian charitable organizations are deductible in computing taxable income to the extent of 75% of net income. A five-year carryforward is provided.

## Group taxation

Group taxation is not permitted.

## Tax incentives

*Inward investment*/Substantial regional development incentives are available under various federal and provincial programs to encourage corporations to locate their manufacturing facilities in areas of slow economic growth.

*Capital investment*/In specified regions of Canada a 10% investment tax credit is available for different forms of capital investment.

## Withholding taxes

Canada is continually renegotiating and extending its network of treaties, some with retroactive effect. This table is a summary only. The applicable treaty should be consulted to determine the withholding tax rate that applies in a particular circumstance.

| Recipient | Dividends (1) % | Interest (2) % | Royalties (3) % |
|---|---|---|---|
| Resident corporations and individuals ......................... | Nil | Nil | Nil |
| Nonresident corporations and individuals: | | | |
| Nontreaty ................................. | 25 | 25 | 25 |
| Treaty: | | | |
| Algeria ..................................... | 15 | 15 | 0 or 15 |
| Argentina ................................. | 10 or 15 (5) | 12.5 | 3, 5, 10 or 15 |
| Australia (4) ............................ | 5 or 15 (5) | 10 | 0 or 10 |
| Austria ..................................... | 5 or 15 (5) | 10 | 0 or 10 |
| Bangladesh.............................. | 15 | 15 | 10 |
| Barbados ................................. | 15 | 15 | 10 |
| Belgium (6) .............................. | 5 or 15 (5) | 10 | 0 or 10 |
| Brazil ....................................... | 15 or 25 (5) | 15 | 15 or 25 |
| Bulgaria ................................... | 10 or 15 (5),(7) | 10 | 0 or 10 (7) |
| Cameroon (8).......................... | 15 | 15 | 15 |
| Chile (7) .................................. | 10 or 15 (5) | 15 | 15 |
| China, P.R. (9)......................... | 10 or 15 (5) | 10 | 10 |
| Croatia ..................................... | 5 or 15 (5) | 10 | 10 |
| Cyprus ..................................... | 15 | 15 | 10 |
| Czech Republic (4) .................. | 5 or 15 (5) | 10 | 10 |
| Denmark .................................. | 5 or 15 (5) | 10 | 0 or 10 |
| Dominican Republic ................. | 18 | 18 | 18 |
| Ecuador ................................... | 5 or 15 (5) | 15 | 10 or 15 (7) |
| Egypt ....................................... | 15 | 15 | 15 |
| Estonia (10) ............................. | 5 or 15 (5) | 10 | 10 |
| Finland..................................... | 10 or 15 (5) | 10 | 10 |
| France ..................................... | 5 or 15 (5) | 10 | 0 or 10 |
| Gabon (11)............................... | 15 | 10 | 10 |
| Germany .................................. | 5 or 15 (5) | 10 | 0 or 10 |
| Guyana .................................... | 15 | 15 (8) | 10 |
| Hungary.................................... | 5 or 15 (5) | 10 | 10 |
| Iceland ..................................... | 5 or 15 (5) | 10 | 0 or 10 |
| India ........................................ | 15 or 25 (5) | 15 | 10, 15 or 20 |
| Indonesia ................................ | 10 or 15 (5) | 10 | 10 |
| Ireland, Rep. of (12) ................ | 5 or 15 (5) | 0 or 10 | 0 or 10 |
| Israel........................................ | 15 | 15 | 15 |
| Italy (13) .................................. | 5 or 15 (5) | 10 | 0, 5 or 10 |
| Ivory Coast .............................. | 15 (8) | 15 | 10 |
| Jamaica ................................... | 15 (8) | 15 | 10 |
| Japan ....................................... | 5 or 15 (5) | 10 | 10 |
| Jordan ...................................... | 10 or 15 (5) | 10 | 10 |
| Kazakhstan (10)....................... | 5 or 15 (5) | 10 | 10 |

# Canada

| Recipient | Dividends (1) | Interest (2) | Royalties (3) |
|---|---|---|---|
| | % | % | % |
| Kenya | 15 or 25 (5) | 15 | 15 |
| Korea, Rep. of | 15 | 15 | 15 |
| Kuwait (4) | 5 or 15 (5) | 10 | 10 |
| Kyrgyzstan (10) | 15 (7) | 15 (7) | 0 or 10 |
| Latvia (10) | 5 or 15 (5) | 10 | 10 |
| Lebanon (11) | 5 or 15 (5) | 10 | 5 or 10 |
| Lithuania (10) | 5 or 15 (5) | 10 | 10 (7) |
| Luxembourg | 5 or 15 (5),(8) | 10 | 0 or 10 |
| Malaysia | 15 (8) | 15 | 15 |
| Malta | 15 (8) | 15 | 10 |
| Mexico | 10 or 15 (5) | 15 | 15 |
| Moldova (4) | 5 or 15 (5) | 10 | 10 |
| Mongolia (4) | 5 or 15 (5) | 10 | 5 or 10 |
| Morocco | 15 | 15 | 5 or 10 |
| Netherlands | 5 or 15 (5) | 10 | 0 or 10 |
| New Zealand | 15 | 15 | 15 |
| Nigeria | 12.5 or 15 (5) | 12.5 | 12.5 |
| Norway (4) | 5 or 15 | 10 | 0 or 10 |
| Pakistan (8) | 15 | 15 | 15 |
| Papua New Guinea | 15 (8) | 10 | 10 |
| Peru (4), (7) | 10 or 15 (5) | 15 | 15 |
| Philippines | 15 (8) | 15 | 10 (8) |
| Poland | 15 | 15 | 10 |
| Portugal | 10 or 15 (5) | 10 | 10 |
| Romania | 15 | 15 | 10 or 15 |
| Russia (10) | 10 or 15 (5) | 10 | 0 or 10 |
| Senegal (4), (8) | 15 | 15 | 15 |
| Singapore | 15 | 15 | 15 |
| Slovak Republic | 5 or 15 (5) | 10 | 0 or 10 |
| Slovenia (4) | 5 or 15 (5) | 10 | 10 |
| South Africa | 5 or 15 (5) | 10 | 6 or 10 |
| Spain | 15 | 15 | 10 |
| Sri Lanka | 15 | 15 | 10 |
| Sweden | 5 or 15 (5) | 10 | 0 or 10 |
| Switzerland | 5 or 15 (5) | 10 | 0 or 10 |
| Tanzania | 20 or 25 (5) | 15 | 20 |
| Thailand | 15 (8) | 15 (8) | 5 or 15 |
| Trinidad and Tobago | 5 or 15 (5) | 10 | 10 |
| Tunisia | 15 | 15 | 15 or 20 |
| Ukraine (10) | 5 or 15 (5) | 10 | 10 |
| United Arab Emirates (11) | 5 or 15 (5) | 10 | 0 or 10 |
| United Kingdom (14) | 5 or 15 (5) | 10 | 10 |
| United States (15) | 5 or 15 (5) | 10 | 0 or 10 |
| Uzbekistan (10) | 5 or 15 (5) | 10 | 5 or 10 |
| Venezuela (7), (11) | 10 or 15 (5) | 10 | 5 or 10 |
| Vietnam | 5,10 or 15 (5) | 10 | 7.5 or 10 |
| Zambia | 15 | 15 | 15 |
| Zimbabwe | 10 or 15 (5),(8) | 15 | 10 |

Notes:

1. Dividends—In its treaty negotiations, Canada is prepared to accept a withholding tax rate of 5% on "direct dividends," that is, dividends paid by a Canadian affiliate to a foreign parent or other corporation with a substantial interest in the affiliate.

2. Interest—Interest paid on certain arm's length, long-term (five-year) indebtedness may not be subject to any withholding tax. Interest on certain debt obligations may be exempt from source-country tax (e.g., interest paid on government bonds, debentures, or similar obligations). There is explicit provision in most treaties for higher withholding tax on interest in excess of fair market values in non-arm's length circumstances. A nil rate of tax may apply in certain circumstances.

3. Royalties—In its treaty negotiations, Canada is prepared to eliminate the withholding tax on arm's length payments in respect of rights to use patented information or information concerning scientific experience. It is also willing to negotiate exemptions from withholding tax for payments for the use of computer software.

   Canada does not levy withholding tax on "cultural royalties," other than payments in respect of motion picture and television films, and so on. Different rates may apply in the case of immovable property (e.g., payments that relate to Canadian natural resources). There is explicit provision in most treaties for higher withholding tax on royalties in excess of fair market value in non-arm's length circumstances. A nil rate of tax may apply in certain circumstances.

4. A treaty and/or protocol was recently ratified and entered into force. Its provisions apply for the purposes of nonresident withholding tax to amounts paid or credited after, and for other taxes to taxation years beginning after the following dates.

   • December 31, 2002 with respect to Australia, the Czech Republic, Kuwait, Moldova, Mongolia, Norway, and Slovenia.

   • December 31, 2003 with respect to Peru and Senegal.

5. The lower (lowest for Vietnam) rate applies where the beneficial owner of the dividend is a company that owns/controls a specified interest in the paying company. The nature of the ownership requirement, the necessary percentage (10%, 20%, or 25%) and the relevant interest (e.g., capital, shares, voting power, equity percentage) vary by treaty.

6. A new treaty with Belgium was recently signed. Upon ratification, its provisions will apply.

   • For purposes of nonresident withholding tax, to amounts paid or credited after December 31 of the calendar year the treaty is ratified.

   • For other taxes, for taxation years beginning after December 31 of the calendar year the treaty is ratified.

   Under the new treaty, the withholding tax rate will change as follows.

   • Be reduced from 15% to 5% on dividends paid to a company that owns at least 10% of the payer's voting stock (the rate will remain 15% on other dividends).

   • Be reduced from 15% to 10% on interest, but certain interest payments will be exempt.

   • Remain 10% on royalties, but certain copyright royalties and royalties for the use of computer software will be exempt.

7. If the other contracting state concludes a treaty with another country providing for a lower withholding tax rate, the lower rate will apply, within limits in some cases.

8. The rate(s) indicated applies to payments arising in Canada. Other rules may apply to payments that arise in the other contracting state.

9. Canada's treaty with China does not apply to Hong Kong.

10. The treaty status of the republics that comprise the former U.S.S.R. is as follows.

    • Estonia, Kazakhstan, Kyrgystan, Latvia, Lithuania, Russia, Ukraine, and Uzbekistan—New treaties entered into force (see table for rates).

    • Azerbaijan—Negotiations are underway.

    • Other republics—No negotiations are underway.

    Azerbaijan, Belarus, Tajikistan, Turkmenistan, and Uzbekistan have indicated that they will not honor the treaty with the former U.S.S.R. and therefore, Canada will impose a maximum 25% rate of withholding on dividends, interest, royalties until a new treaty enters into force. For all other republics that comprise the former U.S.S.R., the status of the former treaty with the U.S.S.R. is uncertain. Since the situation is subject to change, Canadian taxpayers are advised to consult with the CCRA as transactions are carried out.

11. The treaty has been signed, but is not yet in force. Absent a treaty, Canada imposes a maximum 25% rate of withholding on dividends, interest, and royalties.

12. A new treaty with Ireland was recently signed. Upon ratification, its provisions will apply.

    • For purposes of nonresident withholding tax, to amounts paid or credited after December 31 of the calendar year if the treaty is ratified.

    • For other taxes, for taxation years beginning after December 31 of the calendar year the treaty is ratified.

    Under the new treaty, the withholding tax rate will change as follows.

    • Be reduced from 15% to 5% on dividends paid to a company that owns at least 10% of the payer's voting stock (the rate will remain 15% on other dividends).

    • Be reduced from 15% to 10% on interest, but certain interest payments will be exempt.

    • Be reduced from 15% to 10% on royalties, but certain royalties for the use of computer software and certain copyright royalties will be exempt.

13. A new treaty with Italy was recently signed. Upon ratification, its provisions will apply.

    • For purposes of nonresident withholding tax, to amounts paid or credited after December 31 of the calendar year the treaty is ratified.

    • For other taxes, for taxation years beginning after December 31 of the calendar year the treaty is ratified.

    Under the new treaty, the withholding tax rate will change as follows.

    • Be reduced from 15% to 5% on dividends paid to a company that owns at least 10% of the payer's voting stock (the rate will remain 15% on other dividends).

- Be reduced from 15% to 10% on interest, but certain interest payments will be exempt.
- Will remain 10% on royalties, but certain royalties for the use of computer software will be subject to a rate of 5% and certain copyright royalties will be exempt.

14. A new protocol to the tax treaty with the United Kingdom was recently signed. Upon ratification, its provisions will apply in Canada as follows.
    - For purposes of nonresident withholding tax, to amounts paid or credited after December 31 of the calendar year the treaty is ratified.
    - For other taxes, for taxation years beginning after December 31 of the calendar year the treaty is ratified.

    Other rules apply in the United Kingdom. Under the new protocol, the withholding tax rate will change as follows.
    - Be reduced from 10% to 5% on dividends paid to a company that controls at least 10% of the payer's voting stock (the rate will remain 15% on other dividends).
    - Remain 10% on interest, but certain interest payments will be exempt.
    - Will remain 10% on royalties, but certain copyright royalties and royalties for the use of computer software, a patent or know-how will be exempt.

15. Canada and the U.S. have agreed to recommend changes to the Canada/U.S. treaty that will change as follows.
    - For individuals—ensure the appropriate tax treatment of an emigrant's gains.
    - For corporations—clarify the effects on a company's residence of "continuance" (or "continuation") from one country into the other.

## Tax administration

**Returns**/Both the federal and the provincial corporation tax systems operate on an essentially self-assessing basis. The tax year of a corporation, which is normally the fiscal period it has adopted for accounting purposes, may not exceed 53 weeks. The tax year need not be the calendar year. Once selected, the tax year cannot be changed without approval from the tax authorities.

**Payment of tax**/Corporate tax installments are due on the last day of each month. Any balance payable is generally due on the last day of the second month following the end of the tax year.

# Canada

## CORPORATION TAX CALCULATION

Fiscal year ended December 31, 2003

### Assumptions

1. The corporation is an Ontario entity, with Canadian manufacturing and processing profits of Can$300,000, capital gains of Can$60,000 and foreign nonbusiness income (i.e., investment income), other than dividends from foreign affiliates, of Can$40,000, from which Can$6,000 profits tax has been paid to the foreign country.
2. The corporation is not to a private corporation, for which the calculation of federal income tax might differ substantially.

### Income

| | | |
|---|---:|---:|
| Net income per financial statements (before income taxes) | | Can$ 1,000,000 |
| Add—Depreciation and amortization charged in accounts | | 325,000 |
| | | 1,325,000 |
| Deduct: | | |
| Capital cost allowance claimed | 400,000 | |
| Gain on sale of depreciable property credited in accounts | 50,000 | |
| Nontaxable half of capital gain on sale of investments | 30,000 | 480,000 |
| Net income for income tax purposes | | 845,000 |
| Deduct—Dividends received from: | | |
| Taxable Canadian corporations | 35,000 | |
| Foreign affiliates out of exempt surplus | 25,000 | 60,000 |
| Taxable income | | Can$ 785,000 |

## Income tax

### *Federal*

| | | |
|---|--:|--:|
| Basic tax—38% of taxable income | Can$ | 298,300 |
| Deduct—Provincial abatement (10% of $785,000 ) | | (78,500) |
| Net amount | | 219,800 |
| Add—Corporate surtax—4% | | 8,792 |
| | | 228,592 |

Deduct:
|  |  |  |
|---|--:|--:|
| Manufacturing and processing tax credit | | |
|   (7% of 300,000 ) | 21,000 | |
| General rate reduction (5% of $485,000) (1) | 24,550 | |
| Foreign nonbusiness income tax credit | | |
|   (Lesser of 40,000 ÷ 785,000 x 228,592 | | |
|   (i.e., 11,648) or 6,000) | 6,000 | 51,250 |
| Federal income tax | | 177,342 |

### *Provincial*

| | |
|---|--:|
| Ontario income tax (12.5% of 785,000) | 98,125 |
| Deduct—Manufacturing and processing tax credit | |
|   (1.5% of 300,000) | 4,500 |
| | 93,625 |
| Total federal and provincial tax | Can$ 270,967 |

Notes:
1. The general rate reduction does not apply to manufacturing and processing income.
2. Exchange rate of the Canadian dollar at January 1, 2004: US$1 = Can$ 1.2934.

# Cayman Islands

## PwC contact

For additional information on taxation in the Cayman Islands, contact:

David Walwyn
PricewaterhouseCoopers
P.O. Box 258 GT
Grand Cayman, B.W.I.
Telephone: (1) (345) 949 7000
Fax: (1) (345) 949 7352
e-mail: david.walwyn@ky.pwc.com

## Absence of taxation

Income tax is not imposed on corporations in the Cayman Islands.

## Note

Exchange rate of the Cayman Islands dollar is fixed at US$1 = CI$0.83.

# Channel Islands, Guernsey (including Alderney)

## PwC contact

For additional information on taxation in Guernsey, contact:

Tony Mancini
PricewaterhouseCoopers
P.O. Box 321
Le Truchot
St. Peter Port
Guernsey
Channel Islands
GY1 4ND
Telephone: (44) (1481) 727777
Fax: (44) (1481) 711075
LN address: Tony Mancini@EMEA-UK-TLS
e-mail: tony.mancini@uk.pwc.com

## Significant developments

Proposals are currently in place for a corporate tax reform to take effect from January 1, 2008. An outline strategy and consultation paper is not expected until December 2004, and the following changes to the system are proposals only.

1. A 0% tax rate for companies generally, to be introduced from 2008.
2. A 10% tax rate for financial services businesses, also to be introduced from 2008. These would include banks, fiduciaries, insurance company managers and fund managers but not insurance companies or funds themselves.
3. Exempt company status and international company status (see below) to be abolished from January 1, 2008, after which companies currently subject to these regimes would qualify for the 0% or 10% rate as appropriate.
4. The international loan business concession, under which loan business referred to Guernsey banks from affiliated entities outside the Island qualifies for a concessional 2% rate, to be abolished with effect from January 1, 2008.
5. Special, but as yet unspecified, rules to be introduced to ensure that residents of Guernsey are taxed on a proportion of the profits of companies in which they have a beneficial interest.

## Taxes on corporate income

At present, individuals and companies pay income tax at a rate of 20% on taxable income.

*Exempt companies*/Any company, whether incorporated in Guernsey or in any other jurisdiction, may make a claim to be exempt from Guernsey taxation and for all purposes be treated as not resident in the Island if either of the following conditions hold.

1. The company is a Collective Investment Fund.
2. No Guernsey resident individual/company has an interest in the company. (Interest for this purpose is interpreted very widely.)

An exempt company is subject to a fixed levy of £600 per annum.

*International companies*/International companies (IC) pay tax at a negotiated rate on profits from international activities. An IC can establish a presence in Guernsey and is regarded as resident in the Island. Beneficial ownership must

# Channel Islands, Guernsey (including Alderney)

be in the hands of nonresidents of Guernsey, and the company must conduct international trading activities that generate income exclusively from nonresidents. One of the initial procedures before such a company commences an operation in Guernsey will be for the Administrator to discuss with the applicant or applicant's agent the business plan, including the proposed sources of income, and to determine the tax rate to be applied. The rate of tax is determined on a case-by-case basis, normally prior to the incorporation of the company, and must be greater than 0% but not more than 30%, with the proviso that the tax being collected is in excess of the exempt company fee. In light of the proposed corporate tax reforms referred to above, tax rates are currently being fixed for periods of up to four years, that is, to December 31, 2007.

## Corporate residence

All Guernsey-registered companies are regarded as resident in the Island, unless granted exempt company status. In addition, a company will be treated as resident in Guernsey (regardless of where it is incorporated) if central management and control is exercised by persons resident in the Island.

## Other taxes

*Dwellings profit tax*/A tax is levied at 100% of the inflation-adjusted profit arising from the disposal of an interest in a Guernsey dwelling. This tax extends to the profits arising from the outright sale, the granting of a lease and the sale of a right of usufruct in a dwelling. A number of exemptions are available.

## Branch income

Branch income is taxed at the standard 20% rate. No further tax is withheld on the transfer of profits abroad.

## Income determination

*Inventory valuation*/Inventory is valued at the lower of historical cost or net realizable value. Use of LIFO is not permitted. Generally, there are no material differences between accounts prepared on a normal accounting basis and those prepared on a tax basis.

*Capital gains*/Capital gains are not subject to tax.

*Intercompany dividends*/Dividends from Guernsey-resident companies may be paid net with an attached tax credit, so that the recipient is treated as having paid the tax. If the parent company is an investment holding company, relief for management expenses may be obtained by reclaiming tax paid at source on income to the extent of justifiable management expenses, regardless of the proportion of shares owned.

*Foreign income*/Resident corporations are subject to tax on their worldwide income. Income tax is levied on foreign branch income when earned, and on investment income from foreign dividends, interest, rents, and royalties. Double taxation is mitigated either through unilateral relief (by giving credit for foreign taxation at up to three-quarters of the effective Guernsey rate) or by treaty relief.

*Stock dividends*/Stock dividends may be treated as income.

*Other significant items*/None.

## Deductions

**Depreciation and depletion**/Depending on the life of an asset, annual allowances (depreciation) are available on machinery and equipment, including vehicles, on diminishing-balance or on straight-line tests at varying standard rates. Obsolescence allowance is given when, on disposal, proceeds of sale are less than the unclaimed annual allowances on machinery and equipment that are being replaced. Any surplus of realization value of an asset over its tax written down value is subject to tax, up to the total amount of the allowances claimed.

Limited allowances are applicable to freehold buildings, but not to the depletion of natural resources.

**Net operating losses**/Trading losses may be carried back one year against total income as an aggregate loss, offset against total current income, or carried forward and offset against income from the same trade. Losses resulting from balancing allowances on cessation may be carried back for two years, and unclaimed annual allowances may be treated as a current year loss.

**Payments to foreign affiliates**/Guernsey-source royalties and long-term interest are subject to taxation at source. Relief is obtained by the retention of the tax deducted. Short interest, unless owed to an authorized bank, is not deductible, unless the advance in respect of which it is paid is used wholly and exclusively for the purposes of the trade. Other fees must be paid on an arm's-length basis.

**Taxes**/Local income tax paid is not deductible in computing taxable income.

**Other significant items**/Normally, business deductions that are incurred wholly and exclusively for the purposes of the trade are allowed.

## Group taxation

To benefit from group loss relief, companies must be in the same group, have co-terminus year ends and must either be incorporated in Guernsey, or carrying on a business in Guernsey through a permanent establishment.

A claim for group loss relief must be made by the claimant company within two years after the end of the calendar year in which the relevant accounting period ended, and must be accompanied by a declaration by the surrendering company that it consents to the surrender.

## Tax incentives

In view of the low rate of tax, no special incentives are available to local businesses. (However, see "Exempt companies" and "International Companies" above.) Premiums from group companies received by a captive insurance company can be treated as mutual income, and as such are exempt from taxation. Alternatively, the captive insurance company may opt to be taxed according to the graduated-scale method, in which a proportion of the investment income is taxed on a sliding scale. In addition, captive insurance companies may opt for exempt company status.

## Withholding taxes

A standard rate applies on long-term interest, royalties and all other sources where the corporation is acting as agent for or making payment to a nonresident liable to Guernsey taxation on that income.

## Tax administration

**Returns**/The tax year is the calendar year. The system relies on the filing of a return of information with the Island tax authority, which then raises an assessment.

**Payment of tax**/In Guernsey, tax is payable in two installments, on June 30 and December 31 in the year of assessment. Where liabilities have not been determined, this may necessitate initially raising estimated assessments based on prior-year figures, and raising a final assessment when the figures are agreed.

### CORPORATION TAX CALCULATION

### Trading Company

| | | |
|---|---:|---:|
| Profit per accounts for the year ended December 31, 2003 | | £ 1,000,000 |
| Add: | | |
| Depreciation | 25,000 | |
| Disallowable legal fees | 1,000 | |
| Charitable donations | 500 | 26,500 |
| | | 1,026,500 |
| Less: | | |
| Bank interest | 15,000 | |
| Computer software capitalized (100% allow) | 3,500 | (18,500) |
| Adjusted profit | | 1,008,000 |
| **Year of Charge 2004** | | |
| Adjusted profit as computed | | 1,008,000 |
| Less—Annual allowances | | (30,000) |
| | | 978,000 |
| Add—Bank interest (provisional) (1) | | 15,000 |
| Assessable income | | 993,000 |
| Tax @ 20% | £ | 198,600 |

Notes:

1. Bank interest is assessed on a current year basis while business profits are assessed on a prior year basis. The bank interest provisionally assessable for the Year of Charge 2004 is therefore an estimate based on the 2003 figure, and will be revised to actual once 2004 interest receipts are known.

# Channel Islands, Guernsey (including Alderney)

## Investment Company

All amounts are in pounds sterling.

|  | Gross | Tax | Net | Gross/ Grossed | Management expenses | Assessable income |
|---|---|---|---|---|---|---|
| U.S. dividends ..... | 100,000 | 30,000 | 70,000 | 82,353 | 5,086 | 77,267 |
| French dividends......... | 100,000 | 25,000 | 75,000 | 88,235 | 5,449 | 82,786 |
| Guernsey dividends......... | 200,000 | 40,000 | 160,000 | 200,000 | 12,352 | 187,648 |
| U.K. dividends (see W2 below) ............. | 100,000 | 10,000 | 90,000 | 90,000 | 5,557 | 84,443 |
| U.K. loan interest. | 50,000 | 11,000 | 39,000 | 48,750 | 3,012 | 45,738 |
| Guernsey bank interest............ | 25,000 | — | 25,000 | 25,000 | 1,544 | 23,456 |
|  | 575,000 | 116,000 | 459,000 | 534,338 | 33,000 | 501,338 |

| | |
|---|---|
| Guernsey income tax @ 20% ................................................................... | 100,268 |
| *Less:* | |
| Credit for Guernsey tax (W1) ................................................................ | (40,000) |
| Double taxation relief (W2)................................................................... | (9,148) |
| Unilateral relief (W3) ............................................................................ | (24,008) |
| Tax payable.......................................................................................... | 27,112 |

| | |
|---|---|
| Management expenses | |
| Directors' fees ..................................................................................... | 15,000 |
| Audit fee .............................................................................................. | 2,500 |
| Bank charges........................................................................................ | 500 |
| Administration expenses ...................................................................... | 15,000 |
| | 33,000 |

### W1—Credit for Guernsey Tax
Guernsey dividends are treated as paid out of taxed income, and a claim for the full amount of the 20% underlying tax credit is allowed.

### W2—Double taxation relief
U.K. income (excluding dividends) is covered by the double taxation agreement between Guernsey and the U.K.

U.K. loan interest has had basic rate U.K. tax deducted at 22%
(50,000 – 11,000 = 39,000)

For double taxation purposes the net income is 'grossed up' at the Guernsey tax rate of 20%: 39,000 x 100/80 = 48,750 (less management expenses) – 3,012 = 45,738 assessable income

Double tax relief is then calculated as 20% of the net assessable income:
45,738 x 20% = 9,148

### W3—Unilateral relief
Relief is given for overseas (other than United Kingdom or Jersey) tax suffered at up to 15% (i.e., three quarters of the Guernsey effective rate).

U.S. dividends have suffered withholding tax of 30%   (100,000 – 30,000 = 70,000)
French dividends have suffered withholding tax of 25%   (100,000 – 25,000 = 75,000)

# Channel Islands, Guernsey (including Alderney)

The net dividends received are grossed up at 15%, and relief is given at 15% of the net assessable income after deduction of apportioned management expenses.

For example,

$$70,000 \times 100/85 = 82,353 \quad \text{(less management expenses)} - 5,086 = 77,267$$
$$75,000 \times 100/85 = 88,235 \quad \text{(less management expenses)} - 5,449 = 82,786$$

| | | | |
|---|---|---|---|
| 77,267 | x | 15% | = | 11,590 |
| 82,786 | x | 15% | = | 12,418 |
| Unilateral relief available | | | 24,008 |

U.K. dividends and debenture interest are not covered by the double taxation agreement with the United Kingdom, and as such no double tax relief is available. The net amount of dividends received is treated as the assessable income (less management expenses), as follows.

| Gross | Tax | Net | Gross/ Grossed | Management expenses | Assessable income |
|---|---|---|---|---|---|
| 100,000 | 10,000 | 90,000 | 90,000 | 5,557 | 84,443 |

Tax is then calculated at 20% of the assessable income = 16,888.

Exchange rate of the pound sterling at January 1, 2004: US$1 = £0.560003.

## PwC contact

For additional information on taxation in Jersey, contact:

Jane Stubbs
PricewaterhouseCoopers
Twenty-Two Colomberie
St. Helier, Jersey JE1 4XA
Channel Islands
Telephone: (44) (1534) 838200
Fax: (44) (1534) 767556
e-mail: jane.stubbs@uk.pwc.com

## General note

This entry is repeated from the 2003/2004 edition. For more up-to-date information consult the contact listed above or Jacqueline Collette at jacqueline.collete@us.pwc.com.

## Significant developments

The main changes include:

Although not part of the EU's fiscal territory or bound by EU law, Jersey has given commitments to cooperate with the EU in relation to its Savings Directive which will require automatic exchange of information in respect of EU resident individuals who receive interest from Jersey paying agents from January 1, 2002.

Jersey has also committed to change certain of their practices highlighted by the EU Code of Conduct review, potentially giving effect to the discontinuance of exempt companies from around 2010 and also international business companies, although exisitng arrangements will likely be honored for the time scale already agreed.

The States of Jersey have also announced the future reduction in the income tax rate of companies down to 0%, other than utilities or those working within the finance industry. The reduced tax rate applicable to the latter and also the time scale have not yet been announced although it is likely to be within a period of five years. The drop in tax rates may result in an additional tax burden on shareholders for instance at the point of the corporate distribution.

## Taxes on corporate income

*Income tax*/Corporations pay income tax at a rate of 20% on taxable income.

*Exempt companies*/A company that is resident in the Island, whether incorporated in Jersey or in any other jurisdiction, may make a claim to be exempt from Jersey taxation and for all purposes be treated as not resident in the Island if the following conditions are met.

1. The company is a Collective Investment Fund; or
2. No Jersey resident individual has an interest in the company. (Interest for this purpose is interpreted very widely.); and
3. The company does not trade through an established place of business in Jersey.

An exempt company is liable to a fixed levy of £600 per annum.

*International Business Company* **(IBC)**/An IBC will be resident in Jersey for tax purposes, but its special status modifies the impact of the Income Tax Law in a number of ways. Profits from its international activities will be subject to tax at tiered rates that range from 2.0% on the first £3 million of profit to 0.5% on profits that exceed £10 million. From 1997, the IBC may make an application to have its international profits taxed at one single rate of tax, being not less than 2 pence in the pound. Losses cannot be carried forward. As with exempt companies, beneficial ownership must be in the hands of non-Jersey residents. An IBC must make a £1,200 tax payment on account each year. This payment cannot be refunded, even if the IBC makes losses.

## Corporate residence

All Jersey-registered companies are regarded as tax resident in the Island unless the company is granted exempt-company status.

A company is also deemed resident in Jersey if management and control of the company is exercised on the Island. Normally, this will be the case if the majority of the board of directors is resident in Jersey or if board meetings are held on the Island.

## Other taxes

None.

## Branch income

Branch income is taxed at the standard 20% rate. No further tax is withheld on the transfer of profits abroad.

## Income determination

*Inventory valuation*/Inventory is valued at the lower of historical cost or net realizable value. LIFO is not permitted. Generally, there are no material differences between accounts prepared on a normal accounting basis and those prepared on a tax basis.

*Capital gains*/Capital gains are not subject to tax.

*Intercompany dividends*/Intercompany dividends are taxed at source and are not further liable to tax in the hands of the recipient. If the parent company is an investment holding company resident in Jersey, relief for management expenses may be obtained by reclaiming tax paid at source on income to the extent of justifiable management expenses, regardless of the proportion of shares owned.

*Foreign income*/Income tax is levied on foreign branch income when earned and on foreign dividends, interest, rents, and royalties. Double taxation is mitigated by either the granting of unilateral relief to the extent of taxing foreign income net of foreign taxes or by treaty relief (United Kingdom and Guernsey only), which gives credit for foreign tax. Treaty relief does not apply to UK-source dividends or debentures. Concessional credit relief might be granted in certain limited circumstances upon application.

*Stock dividends*/Stock dividends are not treated as income.

*Other significant items*/None.

## Deductions

*Capital allowances*/Capital allowances are available by the diminishing-balance method on machinery and equipment, including vehicles, at a rate of 25%. For this purpose, all such assets are pooled, and the allowance is calculated by reference to the value of the pool. On disposal of an asset, the lower of cost and sale proceeds of the asset is deducted from the pool. A balancing charge is levied if the proceeds exceed the balance of the pool. Motor vehicles costing more than £20,000 and greenhouses are subject to special rules and are not pooled with other assets.

By concession, an alternative is to claim for the full cost of replacement in the year of replacement. The capital allowances are not applicable to buildings or the depletion of natural resources.

*Net operating losses*/Trading losses may be offset against total profits of the same accounting period and/or for accounting periods ending after January 1, 1992, carried back and set against income of the same trade of the previous accounting period. Unrelieved trading losses may be carried forward and set against the income from the same trade in future accounting periods.

*Payments to foreign affiliates*/Patent royalties, long-term interest, and annual payments are generally subject to taxation at source, and relief is obtained by retention of the tax deducted. Short interest, unless owed to an authorized bank, is not normally deductible, unless the advance in respect of which it is paid is used wholly and exclusively for the purposes of the trade. Other fees must be paid on an arm's-length basis.

*Taxes*/Local income tax paid is not deductible in computing taxable income.

*Other significant items*/Normally, business deductions are allowed if they are incurred wholly and exclusively for the purpose of the trade.

## Group taxation

Group taxation is not permitted. Although the income tax law contains no provisions for group relief, it is possible to mitigate the situation by way of reasonable management fees charged against profits of the profitable company in favor of a loss-making company. It is advisable to obtain prior approval for this from the Comptroller of Income Tax.

## Tax incentives

There are generally no special incentives for locally owned businesses in view of the low rate of tax and opportunity presented by the exempt company and IBCs discussed above.

## Withholding taxes

A standard rate (20%) applies on annual payments, such as long-term interest, and on Jersey source patent royalties.

## Tax administration

*Returns*/The tax year is the calendar year. The system relies on the filing of a return of information with the Island tax authority, which then raises an assessment.

# Channel Islands, Jersey

*Payment of tax*/In Jersey, tax is payable in arrears during the year following the year of assessment. Tax paid after a prescribed date (usually early in the December following the year of assessment) incurs a 10% surcharge.

## CORPORATION TAX CALCULATION

### Trading company

Year of assessment 2004 based on accounts for the year ended December 31, 2003

| | | |
|---|---:|---:|
| Net profit before tax | | £ 1,000,000 |
| Add: | | |
|     Donations | 100 | |
|     Legal expenses re lease | 1,000 | |
|     Depreciation | 10,000 | 11,100 |
| | | 1,011,100 |
| Less—Capital (depreciation) allowances | | 11,100 |
| | | 1,000,000 |
| Taxation at 20% | | 200,000 |
| | | 800,000 |
| Dividends free of tax (gross 500,000) | | (400,000) |
| Carried to reserve | | £ 400,000 |

### Investment company

Year of assessment 2003 based on accounts for the year ended December 31, 2003

| | | |
|---|---:|---:|
| Dividends received | | £ 100,000 |
| Less—Foreign withholding taxes | | 30,000 |
| | | 70,000 |
| Management expenses | | 20,000 |
| | | 50,000 |
| Taxation at 20% (on net dividends) | 14,000 | |
| *Less*—Relief for management expenses | (4,000) | 10,000 |
| | | 40,000 |
| Dividends free of tax (gross 25,000) | | (20,000) |
| Carried to reserve | | £ 20,000 |

Note:
Exchange rate of the pound sterling at December 31, 2002: US$1 = £0.6651.

## PwC contact

For additional information on taxation in Chile, contact:

Julio Pereira G.
PricewaterhouseCoopers
Avda. Andrés Bello 2711
Cuarto Piso
Santiago, Chile
Telephone: (56) (2) 9400151
Fax: (56) (2) 9400503
e-mail: julio.pereira@cl.pwc.com

## General note

This entry is repeated from the 2003/2004 edition. For more up-to-date information consult the contact listed above or Jacqueline Collette at jacqueline.collete@us.pwc.com.

## Significant developments

There have been several significant tax developments in the past year. An Investment Platform Law was approved, establishing new rules that exempt corporations with foreign capital from the provisions of the Income Tax Law on income obtained outside Chile, provided they fulfill certain requirements. The useful life of assets that may benefit from accelerated depreciation was reduced from 5 to 3 years. Legislation was approved which allows exemption from tax on gain on the sale of traded shares of Chilean stock corporations under certain circumstances. A Free Trade Agreement was signed with the European Community, and another was agreed with the United States. Several tax treaties have been agreed which are still pending ratification by the Chilean Congress.

## Taxes on corporate income

*First Category tax*/The basic tax on income of a Chilean corporation engaged in commerce, mining, fishing, or industry is the First Category income tax, which is assessed at a rate of 16.5%. Nondomiciled and nonresident shareholders and partners are subject to a 35% withholding of Additional tax on distributions or remittances, with a 16.5% credit granted, provided amounts distributed were subject to the First Category tax. This results in an effective tax rate of 35%. The income tax rate, which is 16.5% for calendar year 2003, will rise to 17% for calendar year 2004.

## Corporate residence

Companies constituted in Chile are considered to be domiciled in the country.

## Other taxes

*Value-added tax*/Value-added tax is payable on transfers and services at a rate of 18%. The same tax is applicable to imports.

*Special taxes*/Alcoholic and nonalcoholic beverages and certain luxury items, such as jewels, are subject to additional sales taxes, ranging from 13% to 70%.

## Branch income

Branches are subject to the First Category income tax, assessed at a rate of 16.5%. They are also subject to a 35% Additional tax on amounts remitted or withdrawn during a given calendar year, less the 16.5% credit, payable in April of the year following distribution. At the time of distribution there is a 35% withholding less the 16.5% credit, which is offset against the tax due in April. Thus, the tax burden for a branch is 35%.

## Income determination

*Inventory valuation*/LIFO is not allowed. Inventories must be valued in accordance with monetary correction provisions, basically by adjusting raw material content and direct labor to replacement cost (which is generally the most recent cost), but excluding indirect costs. No conformity is required between book and tax reporting for income determination.

*Capital gains*/Capital gains are subject to normal taxation unless special provisions, such as those pertaining to gains on the sale of shares or monetary correction on capital repayments, establish exemptions.

*Intercompany dividends*/Dividends received from Chilean corporations are exempt from the First Category tax.

*Foreign income*/Resident corporations are subject to taxes on their worldwide income. In general, foreign income and dividends received by a domestic corporation are subject to Chilean taxation in the financial year when received.

A tax credit for taxes paid abroad is granted, subject to the regulations of the Income Tax Law.

Branches of foreign corporations are taxed on their income without regard to the results of the head office.

*Stock dividends*/Stock dividends are not taxed.

## Deductions

*Depreciation and depletion*/Depreciation rates are calculated on the estimated useful life of the assets. The normal periods of depreciation for new assets working under normal conditions are as follows: heavy machinery, 15 years; trucks, 7 years; factory buildings, in general, 20 years to 40 years. At the request of the Foreign Investment Committee or the taxpayer, the Internal Revenue Service (IRS) may reduce the normal useful life.

Taxpayers have the right to apply accelerated depreciation up to one-third of the normal useful life with regard to new or imported fixed assets, provided the normal period of depreciation is equal to or more than three years.

According to the new Law No 19,738, published on June 19, 2001, accelerated depreciation can only be used to reduce the taxable basis of the First Category tax. For the purpose of the taxation applicable to distributions, accelerated depreciation is not considered.

No conformity is required between book and tax depreciation.

Annual depreciation is taken by the straight-line method. Gains or losses at book value on the sale of fixed assets are considered operational profits or losses.

Normally, the sale will not be subject to sales tax unless they are sold before 12 months from the date of acquisition. For tax purposes, depletion for natural mineral resources is allowed on a unit-of-production basis.

Amortization of goodwill is not allowed for tax purposes.

*Net operating losses*/An indefinite carryforward of losses is allowed. Consistent with monetary correction, losses are carried forward, adjusted by the cost-of-living increase. No carrybacks are allowed, except in the case where a taxpayer has retained tax profits and has a subsequent tax loss.

*Payments to foreign affiliates*/The deductibility of payments made abroad for the use of trademarks, patents, formulas, and consulting and similar services is limited to a maximum of 4% of the income derived from sales and services in the corresponding year, unless the royalty is subject in the country of the beneficiary to income tax over 30%.

Transfer pricing regulations are in line with general OECD (Organization for Economic Cooperation and Development) principles.

*Taxes*/Taxes imposed by Chilean laws are deductible, provided they are related to the normal activities of the company. However, income taxes and special contributions for promotion or improvement are not deductible.

*Other significant items*/Deductions for allowable grants may not exceed 2% of the taxable income or 1.6% of the net equity of the company at the end of the period. Charges in respect of monetary correction, including exchange losses, are deductible, provided they arise from credits used for the company's business.

## Group taxation

Consolidated returns are not allowed.

## Tax incentives

*Inward investment*/The principal incentives are the following.

1. Tax benefits and other incentives for companies operating in the northernmost and southernmost parts of the country.
2. Tax benefits to forestry companies.

*Capital investment*/The principal incentives to encourage foreign capital contributions are statutory guarantees covering the repatriation of capital, remittance of profits, nondiscrimination toward foreign investment, and access to the foreign exchange market for remittance purposes. In general, foreign investors are subject to the same legislation as national investors. A guaranteed income tax rate of 42% may be granted for 10 years or, provided the capital investment project exceeds US$50 million, 20 years.

The Andean Pact is not in force in Chile.

*Other incentives*/The principal incentives for exports are as follows.

1. Reimbursement of taxes paid in the importation or acquisition of goods required in the export activity.
2. Chile has signed free-trade agreements with Mexico, Canada, and the European Community and has joined Mercosur with associate member status. All these agreements provide for reduced customs duties.

# Chile

## Withholding taxes

Dividends paid to a nonresident recipient are subject to a 35% withholding of Additional tax, with a credit available that is equivalent to the income tax effectively paid at the corporate level, corresponding to the First Category tax paid by the corporation. This credit is added to the amount that is distributed to form the taxable base for the Additional tax. Consequently, the tax burden for a nonresident recipient of dividends, including taxes at the company level, is 35%.

Branches are subject to a 35% Additional tax on amounts remitted or withdrawn, less the 16% credit. See "Branch income."

In the case of a foreign investor that has applied for the 42% tax invariability, the effective tax burden is also 42%.

Interest and royalties paid to nonresidents are generally subject to a flat 35% and 30% Additional withholding tax, respectively. Interest on loans granted by foreign banking or other financial institutions is subject to a sole 4% Additional withholding tax, provided the credit has been approved by the Central Bank.

*Tax treaties*/Chile and Argentina ratified a treaty in 1986 to avoid double taxation, following the Andean Pact model. Double taxation agreements with Mexico and Canada were ratified by Congress and are in force as of January 1, 2000. A free trade agreement between the European Community (EC) and Chile was signed and is in force as of February 1, 2002, the date on which it was ratified by Congress. A free trade agreement with the United States was also signed, leaving only ratification by the Chilean Congress. Double tax treaties have been agreed with Denmark, Brazil, Peru, Ecuador, Poland, and Norway and are pending ratification by the Chilean Congress.

## Tax administration

*Returns*/The tax year coincides with the calendar year. The tax system is one of self-assessment by the taxpayer, with occasional auditing by the tax authorities. Tax returns must be filed with the IRS before April 30 of each year on income of the previous calendar year. Tax returns constitute a self-assessment.

*Payment of tax*/Taxes are payable at the time of submitting the annual tax return in April of each year. Taxpayers, in general, are subject to monthly advance payments on account of their yearly income taxes. The difference between the advance payments and the final tax bill is payable in cash at the time of filing the tax return. If prepayments exceed the final tax bill, the excess is reimbursed by the Treasury.

### *CORPORATION TAX CALCULATION*

Payable on 2003 income

## Domestic corporation

| | | |
|---|---:|---:|
| Net income before taxes (1) | C$ | 1,000,000 |
| Taxable income | C$ | 1,000,000 |
| First Category tax—16.5% | | 165,000 |
| Available for distribution | C$ | 835,000 |
| Additional tax—35% on 1,000,000 (2) | C$ | 350,000 |
| *Less*—16.5% credit on 1,000,000 | | (165,000) |
| Net Additional tax | C$ | 185,000 |
| Total taxes: | | |
| First Category tax | C$ | 165,000 |
| Additional tax | | 185,000 |
| | C$ | 350,000 |

## Branch of foreign corporation

| | | |
|---|---:|---:|
| Taxable income | C$ | 1,000,000 |
| First Category tax—16.5% | | 165,000 |
| Available for distribution | | 835,000 |
| Withholding (payable on distribution or remittance) | | |
| Distribution | C$ | 835,000 |
| Plus credit | | 165,000 |
| Taxable income for Additional tax | C$ | 1,000,000 |
| Additional tax—35% | C$ | 350,000 |
| *Less*—Credit | | (165,000) |
| Net Additional tax | C$ | 185,000 |
| Total taxes: | | |
| First Category tax | C$ | 165,000 |
| Additional tax | | 185,000 |
| | C$ | 350,000 |

Notes:
1. Net income before tax is adjusted for price-level restatement, opening equity and fixed assets in accordance with variations in the consumer price index, foreign currency receivables and payables at the closing rates of exchange, and inventories at replacement value.
2. The Additional tax is assessed on amounts effectively distributed, withdrawn or remitted.
3. Exchange rate of the peso at January 2, 2003: US$1 = C$718.73.

# China, People's Republic of

## PwC contact

For additional information on taxation in the People's Republic of China, contact:

Cassie Wong
PricewaterhouseCoopers
18th floor, Beijing Kerry Centre
1 Guang Hua Lu
Chao Yang District
Beijing 100020
People's Republic of China
Telephone: (86) (10) 6561 2233
Fax: (86) (10) 8529 9000
e-mail: cassie.wong@cn.pwc.com

## Significant developments

Pursuant to the closer economic partnership agreement signed between the governments of the Mainland China and the Hong Kong Special Administrative Region, starting from January 1, 2004, 374 categories of goods of Hong Kong origin may enjoy customs duty exemption upon importation into China. In addition, certain service sectors (including distribution, logistics and warehousing, banking and insurance, tourism, construction and real estate, etc.) may gain earlier access to China market at loosen capital and regulatory requirements.

However, starting from January 1, 2004, royalty being defined to include payment for patents, trademarks, copyright, distribution and resale rights and other similar payment relating to goods imported into China, may be regarded as part of the dutiable value of goods and levied for customs duties by China customs.

Late last year, a circular on adjustment of the value-added tax (VAT) refund rates was issued. Except for a few items such as wheat flour, maize flour, and cuts of ducks and geese, the export VAT refund rate for most goods were reduced by an average of 3% to 12% on January 1, 2004.

In January 2004, the State Administration of Taxation (SAT) started a VAT reform campaign in three provinces of Northeastern China. Subject to the official approval from the State Council for the VAT reform, enterprises from eight selected industrial sectors may claim their input VAT incurred in purchases of fixed assets against output VAT of regular sales.

Separately, there is another encouraging move made by the SAT. It has been confirmed that the tax principles for foreign investment enterprises (FIEs) are applicable to FIEs converted from domestic enterprises in the wake of mergers and acquisitions. Particularly, cumulative loss bought forward from the preacquisition period can be used to offset profit derived in the post-acquisition period.

Meanwhile, the SAT allows intra-China transfer pricing corresponding adjustment. This eliminates the possible double taxation happened in transfer pricing adjustment during transfer pricing audit. However, adjustments involving cross-border transactions are not under the protection of this new requirement.

## Corporate residence

Foreign enterprises are taxed on profits earned from trade or business activities carried out through an establishment or place of business in China. Foreign investment enterprises, as Chinese-incorporated companies, are taxed on their worldwide income.

## Other taxes

*Turnover taxes*/On January 1, 1994 China introduced a new turnover tax system consisting of three taxes—VAT, business tax, and consumption/excise tax. Under the new system the sale or importation of goods and the provision of repairs, replacement, and processing services are subject to VAT. Other services provided in China and the transfer of real property and intangible assets are subject to business tax.

VAT is charged at a standard rate of 17%. The sale of certain necessity goods and the importation of certain special equipment could be exempt from VAT or be subject to VAT at a reduced rate of 13%, as specified in the VAT regulations. With effect from January 1, 2001, exports of all foreign investment enterprises are effectively tax exempt under the "exempt, credit, refund" mechanism. However, this does not mean that all input VAT will be refunded; this depends on the type of product.

VAT is typically a recoverable tax, except for VAT incurred at the importation or local purchase of fixed assets. Such VAT is generally treated as part of the cost of the fixed assets and depreciated. However, input VAT incurred in purchases of fixed assets by enterprises of eight selected industrial sectors in Northeastern China may be recovered by offsetting against output VAT of regular sales when the VAT reform policy is finally approved by the State Council.

Business tax rates are 3% or 5%, except for the leisure and entertainment industry, which may attract a rate of up to 20%.

Consumption/excise tax was also introduced to tax 11 categories of goods, including cigarettes, alcoholic beverages, and certain luxury items.

Business tax and consumption/excise taxes are not recoverable but are deductible as expenses for income tax purposes.

*Real estate tax*/A real estate tax is assessed on land and buildings according to the standard value on the basis of a general market evaluation.

## Branch income

A branch is taxed under the normal provisions of the income tax law at the branch level. There is no further tax upon remittance of branch profits.

## Income determination

Taxable income is defined as "net income in a tax year after deduction of costs, expenses and losses in that year." The accrual method of accounting should be used.

*Inventory valuation*/Inventory is valued at cost. Under the tax regulations, inventory can be valued in accordance with one of the following methods: FIFO, shifting-average, LIFO, or weighted-average method. Approval from the local tax authorities must be obtained before changes can be made in the method of valuing inventory.

*Capital gains*/Foreign enterprises that do not have an establishment or place of business in China, and those that do have an establishment or place of business but generate income not effectively connected with that establishment or place of business, are subject to a 10% withholding tax on gains sourced in China, unless the tax is further reduced by a taxation treaty. An additional land appreciation tax is levied on gains generated from the disposal of real property rights. The tax rates range from 30% to 60%, depending on the amount of the gain.

*Intercompany dividends*/If a foreign investment enterprise invests in another enterprise in China, the dividends obtained from that enterprise may be excluded from the investing enterprise's taxable income. Any expenses and losses incurred in the investment are not deductible.

*Foreign income*/The worldwide income of a foreign investment enterprise and its branches both within and outside China is taxable. A foreign tax credit is allowed for income taxes paid on foreign-source income. For foreign enterprises with an establishment or a place of business in China, foreign income effectively connected with the establishment or place of business is taxable, with deduction of foreign taxes paid as expenses.

In addition, transfer pricing will be subject to stringent review by the tax bureaus. Recently, joint efforts from tax bureaus of different provinces have been taken to target investment of multinational enterprises.

## Deductions

*Depreciation*/Fixed assets with useful lives of two years or less, and items that cost RMB2,000 or less, can be expensed. Other fixed assets must be capitalized and depreciated in accordance with the income tax regulations. Depreciation is calculated by the straight-line method. Under special circumstances, an application may be made to the tax authorities to use accelerated methods of depreciation. Under the straight-line method, cost less residual value is depreciated over the useful lives of the assets. Residual value is estimated at 10% of cost under the regulations. The regulations provide minimum useful lives for the following assets.

| | Years |
|---|---|
| Houses and buildings | 20 |
| Trains, ships, machines, equipment, and other facilities used in production | 10 |
| Electronic equipment, means of transportation other than ships and trains, furniture, fittings, and other appliances | 5 |

For enterprises engaged in petroleum exploitation, depreciation of fixed assets resulting from investments made during and after the development stage may be computed according to the composite-life method, without retaining the residual value. The minimum depreciation period for these assets is six years.

*Amortization of intangible assets*/A deduction is allowed for amortization of intangible assets, such as patents, proprietary technology, trademarks, copyrights, the right to the use of sites, and other intangibles. Intangible assets that are contributed as investment by a foreign enterprise with a provision for time limit of use should be amortized according to the time limit. Those not subject to such provisions are to be amortized over a period of not less than ten years. Organization expenses incurred during the preparation period can be amortized over a period of not less than five years. Offshore oil projects can amortize exploration expenses over a period of not less than one year after commencement of commercial production.

*Net operating losses*/Operating losses can be carried forward for a period of no longer than five years.

***Payments to foreign affiliates***/Royalties and interest charges paid by a foreign investment enterprise to foreign affiliates are tax deductible, provided the amounts are on an arm's length basis. A management fee paid to a foreign affiliate may not be deductible.

***Taxes***/Income tax and local surtax charges are nondeductible items in determining an enterprise's taxable income. Other taxes, such as irrecoverable VAT, business tax, consumption/excise tax, real estate tax, and property gains tax, are deductible in calculating the net taxable income.

***Head office expenses***/A deduction can be claimed by a foreign enterprise with an establishment or a place of business for reasonable overhead expenses that are relevant to production and business operation paid to the head office, provided the following documents are submitted with its tax return.

1. A report documenting the total amount, categories of expenses, and allocation basis.
2. An audited statement of head office expenses.

## Group taxation

Group taxation is not permitted. However, a combination of profits and losses for different projects/activities of a single legal entity is permitted in a single tax return.

## Tax incentives

***Inward investment***/Foreign investment enterprises of a production nature that expect to operate in China for more than ten years can apply for an exemption from income tax for two years, beginning from the first profit-making year, and a 50% tax reduction in the following three years. Starting from January 1, 2002, income derived from projects funded by additional capital injection is entitled to receive a tax holiday similar to a newly formed foreign investment enterprise if the projects fall within the "Encouraged" category of the new Industry Catalogue and the additional capital injection amount can reach either of the following.

- At least US$60 million.
- At least US$15 million and at least 50% of the original registered capital.

A range of other reductions and exemptions is available, subject to certain criteria. A reduced income tax rate of 15% may be possible for productive foreign investment enterprises in the Economic and Technological Development Zones and for enterprises engaged in production or business operations in the Special Economic Zones. A tax rate of 24% is possible for productive foreign investment enterprises located in the different economic open zones, depending on the location of the project.

***Capital investment***/Where a foreign investor of a foreign investment enterprise reinvests its share of profit or capital reserve or enterprise development and expansion reserve, it may obtain a tax rebate of 40% of the income tax paid by the enterprise and attributable to the foreign investor if the profit or capital reserve or enterprise development and expansion reserve is reinvested for a period of at least five years. The reinvestment must be either in the original venture by increasing its registered capital or in another foreign investment enterprise. If the foreign investor reinvests its profits in an export-oriented or technologically advanced enterprise for a period of at least five years, the investor may receive a full refund of the income tax already paid on the reinvested amount.

Meanwhile, utilization of foreign investors' attributable portion of statutory reserve, including capital reserve and enterprise development and expansion reserve to increase the registered capital of a foreign investment enterprise is entitled to an income tax refund.

## Withholding taxes

No withholding tax is levied on business profits remitted overseas as dividends to foreign investors by foreign investment enterprises.

*Corporations resident in nontreaty countries*/Subject to the exception noted above for dividends from foreign investment enterprises, foreign enterprises without establishments in China will be subject to a withholding tax of 10% on gross income from interest, lease of property, royalties, and other China-source nonbusiness income, with the following exceptions.

1. Withholding tax on proprietary technology usage fees may be exempt, subject to approval.
2. A temporary exemption from withholding tax applies to dividends/gains generated from China B shares.
3. Dividends from China enterprises other than foreign investment enterprises are subject to a statutory rate of 20% withholding tax (which is subject to a concessionary rate of 10%).

*Corporations resident in treaty countries*/Withholding taxes are as follows (as of December 2003).

| | Dividends | Interest (1) | Royalties (2) |
|---|---|---|---|
| | % | % | % |
| Armenia | 10, 5 (3) | 10 | 10 |
| Australia | 15 | 10 | 10 |
| Austria | 10, 7 (4) | 10, 7 (7) | 10, 6 |
| Bahrain | 5 | 10 | 10 |
| Bangladesh | 10 | 10 | 10 |
| Barbados | 5 | 10 | 10 |
| Belarus | 10 | 10 | 10 |
| Belgium | 10 | 10 | 10, 6 |
| Brazil | 15 | 15 | 25, 15 (8) |
| Bulgaria | 10 | 10 | 10, 7 |
| Canada | 15, 10 (12) | 10 | 10 |
| Croatia | 5 | 10 | 10 |
| Cuba | 10, 5 (3) | 7.5 | 5 |
| Cyprus | 10 | 10 | 10 |
| Czech Republic | 10 | 10 | 10 |
| Denmark | 10 | 10 | 10, 7 |
| Egypt | 8 | 10 | 8 |
| Estonia | 10, 5 (3) | 10 | 10 |
| Finland | 10 | 10 | 10, 7 |
| France | 10 | 10 | 10, 6 |
| Germany | 10 | 10 | 10, 7 |
| Greece | 10, 5 (3) | 10 | 10 |
| Hong Kong Special Administrative Region | Not covered in the arrangement | | |
| Hungary | 10 | 10 | 10 |

| | Dividends | Interest (1) | Royalties (2) |
|---|---|---|---|
| | % | % | % |
| Iceland | 10, 5 (3) | 10 | 10, 7 |
| India | 10 | 10 | 10 |
| Indonesia | 10 | 10 | 10 |
| Iran | 10 | 10 | 10 |
| Ireland, Rep. of | 10, 5 (4) | 10 | 10, 6 |
| Israel | 10 | 10, 7 (7) | 10, 7 |
| Italy | 10 | 10 | 10, 7 |
| Jamaica | 5 | 7.5 | 10 |
| Japan | 10 | 10 | 10 |
| Kazakstan | 10 (14) | 10 | 10 |
| Korea, Rep. of | 10, 5 (3) | 10 | 10 |
| Kuwait | 5 | 5 | 10 |
| Kyrgizastan | 10 | 10 | 10 |
| Laos | 5 | 5 (in Laos) 10 (in Mainland China) | 5 (in Laos) 10 (in Mainland China) |
| Latvia | 10, 5 (3) | 10 | 10 |
| Lithuania | 10, 5 (3) | 10 | 10 |
| Luxembourg | 10, 5 (3) | 10 | 10, 6 |
| Macao | 10 | 10, 7 (7) | 10 |
| Macedonia | 5 | 10 | 10 |
| Malaysia | 10 | 10 | 15 (10), 10 |
| Malta | 10 | 10 | 10 |
| Mauritius | 5 | 10 | 10 |
| Moldova | 10, 5 (3) | 10 | 10 |
| Mongolia | 5 | 10 | 10 |
| Morocco | 10 | 10 | 10 |
| Nepal | 10 | 10 | 15 (9) |
| Netherlands | 10 | 10 | 10, 6 |
| New Zealand | 15 | 10 | 10 |
| Nigeria | 7.5 | 7.5 | 7.5 |
| Norway | 15 | 10 | 10 |
| Oman | 5 | 10 | 10 |
| Pakistan | 10 | 10 | 12.5 |
| Papua New Guinea | 15 | 10 | 10 |
| Philippines | 15, 10 (13) | 10 | 15 (10), 10 |
| Poland | 10 | 10 | 10, 7 |
| Portugal | 10 | 10 | 10 |
| Qatar | 10 | 10 | 10 |
| Romania | 10 | 10 | 7 |
| Russia | 10 | 10 | 10 |
| Seychelles | 5 | 10 | 10 |
| Singapore | 12, 7 (6) | 10, 7 (7) | 10 |
| Slovak Republic | 10 | 10 | 10 |
| Slovenia | 5 | 10 | 10 |
| South Africa | 5 | 10 | 10, 7 |
| Spain | 10 | 10 | 10, 6 |
| Sri Lanka | 10 | 10 | 10 |

# China, People's Republic of

| | Dividends | Interest (1) | Royalties (2) |
|---|---|---|---|
| | % | % | % |
| Sudan | 5 | 10 | 10 |
| Sweden | 10, 5(3) | 10 | 10, 7 |
| Switzerland | 10 | 10 | 10, 6 |
| Thailand | 20, 15 (5) | 10 | 15 |
| Trinidad and Tobago | 10, 5 (6) | 10 | 10 |
| Tunisia | 8 | 10 | 10, 5 (15) |
| Turkey | 10 | 10 | 10 |
| Ukraine | 10, 5 (3) | 10 | 10 |
| United Arab Emirates | 7 | 7 | 10 |
| United Kingdom | 10 | 10 | 10, 7 |
| United States | 10 | 10 | 10, 7 |
| Uzbekistan | 10 | 10 | 10 |
| Venezuela | 10, 5 (11) | 10, 5 (7) | 10 |
| Vietnam | 10 | 10 | 10 |
| Yugoslavia | 5 | 10 | 10 |

Source: State Administration of Taxation, China

In addition to the above tax treaties, a number of these countries have entered into investment protection treaties with China.

Notes:

- This table is a summary only, and does not reproduce all the provisions relevant in determining the application of withholding taxes in each tax treaty/arrangement.
- The former Czechoslovak Socialist Republic is divided into Czech Republic and Slovak Republic.
- The former Yugoslavia is divided into Bosnia, Croatia, Macedonia, Serbia, Slovenia, and Yugoslavia.
- There is no tax treaty signed between China and Bosnia and Serbia.

The numbers in parentheses refer to the following numbered Notes.

1. Nil on interest paid to government bodies. Reference should be made to the individual tax treaties.
2. The lower rate on royalties applies for the use of or right to use any industrial, commercial, or scientific equipment.
3. The lower rate applies to dividends paid by a company (not a partnership) and received by a company owning at least 25% of the capital of the paying company.
4. The lower rate applies to dividends paid by a company and received by a company owning at least 25% of the voting shares of the paying company.
5. The lower rate applies to dividends paid by a company (not a partnership) and received by a company owning at least 25% of the shareholding of the paying company.
6. The lower rate applies to dividends paid by a company and received by a company owning at least 25% of the shareholding of the paying company.
7. The lower rate applies to interest paid to banks or financial institutions.
8. The higher rate applies to trademarks.

9. The tax rate may be reduced to a lower rate if Nepal agrees to a lower tax rate with any other countries.

10. The higher rate applies to artistic royalties/cinematographic films and tapes for television or broadcasting.

11. The lower rate applies where the beneficial owner of the dividend is a company (not a partnership) that owns at least 10% of the shareholding of the paying company.

12. The lower rate applies where the beneficial owner of the dividend is a company that owns at least 10% of the voting stock of the paying company.

13. The lower rate applies where the beneficial owner of the dividend is a company that owns at least 10% of the shareholding of the paying company.

14. A branch profits tax in Kazakstan may be applied to net taxable income less income tax.

15. The lower rate applies to technology or economic research or technology subsidies.

## Tax administration

**Returns**/The tax year commences on January 1 and ends on December 31. Enterprises are required to file their income tax returns and final accounting statements within four months after the end of the tax year, together with an audit certificate of a registered public accountant in China. Information on related party transactions must be filed with the annual tax return.

**Payment of tax**/Enterprises are required to pay provisional taxes on a quarterly basis within 15 days after the end of each quarter. Three options are available to the taxpayer in computing the provisional tax: (1) actual quarterly profits, (2) one-quarter of the taxable income of the preceding year, or (3) other formulas approved by the local tax authorities. The final settlement must be made within five months after the end of each tax year.

# China, People's Republic of

## *CORPORATION TAX CALCULATION*

Year ended December 31, 2003

| | | | |
|---|---:|---|---:|
| Net income before taxes and depreciation | | RMB | 1,000,000 |
| Add: | | | |
| Donations other than for public welfare and relief purposes in China | 1,000 | | |
| Entertainment expenses in excess of limit permitted for tax purposes | 1,000 | | |
| Depreciation charged in accounts | 15,000 | | |
| Amounts transferred to provisions | 4,000 | | |
| Interest on capital | 7,000 | | |
| Management fee paid to affiliates | 10,000 | | 38,000 |
| Adjusted taxable income | | RMB | 1,038,000 |
| Less: | | | |
| Depreciation at rates approved by the Ministry of Finance | 14,000 | | |
| Expenditure charged against provisions | 2,000 | | |
| Amortization of organization expenses | 7,200 | | 23,200 |
| Adjusted taxable income | | RMB | 1,014,800 |
| Income tax at 30% | | RMB | 304,440 |
| Local surtax at 3% on taxable income | | | 30,444 |
| Total income tax payable | | RMB | 334,884 |

Note:

Exchange rate of the renminbi as of January 1, 2004: US$1 = RMB8.2766.

## PwC contacts

For more information on taxation in Colombia, contact:

María Helena Díaz Méndez
Carlos M. Chaparro
Calle 100 No. 11-A-35, Piso Tercero
Bogotá, Colombia
Telephone: (57) (1) 6340555, ext. 368
Fax: (57) (1) 6104626
e-mail: maria.helena.diaz@co.pwc.com
        carlos.chaparro@co.pwc.com

## General note

This entry is repeated from the 2003/2004 edition. For more up-to-date information consult the contact listed above or Jacqueline Collette at jacqueline.collete@us.pwc.com.

## Taxes on corporate income

The corporate income tax rate for calendar (fiscal) year 2003 is 38.5% and 36.7% for later years (up from 35%). The increase will only apply to taxpayers with a filing requirement. Tax paid on the increase will not be deductible. Actual taxable income is compared with an imputed net taxable income equal to 6% of net equity, and income tax is assessed on the greater. This procedure does not apply when documentary proof is furnished that the company was in the preproduction stage or that other circumstances limited the company's profits as force majeure facts. Further, companies going through certain anti-bankruptcy procedures and companies in liquidation status (the latter for the first three years only) are exempted from using imputed taxable income.

As from taxable year 1998, in no case can income tax liability, after subtracting credits, be less than 75% of that determined under the presumptive income system upon net equity.

## Corporate residence

Corporate residence is determined by place of incorporation.

For income tax purposes, companies incorporated under foreign laws and with main domicile abroad are considered "foreign companies."

## Other taxes

*Value-added tax*/A consumer tax that operates in effect as a VAT is levied at 16% (as from January 2001) on the value of goods and services unless they are specifically exempt. Sales and imports of certain motor vehicles are now subject to rates of 38%, where some others will gradually be subject to rates of 21%, 23%, and 2%. Exports of goods and services are zero-rated. However, effective 2005 export of services will trigger VAT at 2%. However, unless an exemption is available, imports do generate VAT.

*Remittance tax*/Interest, commissions, fees, royalties, rentals, branch profits, and compensation for personal services remitted abroad are subject to a 7% remittance tax. An exemption is granted in some cases of interest on foreign currency loans or credits registered with the Colombian Central Bank.

As a general rule, the remittance tax is collected through withholding at source when effecting the transfer abroad or credit to account, whichever occurs first.

**Municipal tax**/Most major cities have a municipal tax based on gross income (industry and trade tax). It is a local tax levied by municipalities on the gross income derived from industrial and commercial activities as well as the rendering of services. The municipalities are entitled to set their own rates, within the limits set forth in the law: on industrial activities, from 0.2% to 0.7%; on commercial and service activities, from 0.2% to 1.0%.

**Property (predial) tax**/A local property tax is levied on land and buildings, based on an estimated commercial value.

**Stamp tax**/This tax is payable at the rate of 1.5% on all public and private documents whose value exceeds COP53,000,000 (approximately US$17,900) provided other legal requirements are met. This rate applies also to documents of undetermined amount.

**Motor vehicle tax**/An annual motor vehicle tax is payable on the commercial value determined by the competent authorities.

**Tax on financial transactions**/Law 633/2000 treats the so-called impost on financial transactions or GMF (*Gravamen a los Movimientos Financieros*) as a new tax of a permanent character and instantaneous accrual, payable by among others, the users of the financial system and the entities which form it, as well as by the Central Bank (*Banco de la República*).

The triggering factor for the GMF is the performance of financial transactions whereby resources deposited in current or savings accounts as well as deposit accounts at the Central Bank are disposed of, the drawing of bank checks, and other acts.

The GMF rate is set at three per mil of the total amount of the financial transaction whereby resources are disposed of, and the tax is not deductible from the gross taxable income of taxpayers.

## Branch income

Branch income is taxed at the same rate as corporate income, 38.5% for 2003 and 36.7% for 2004 and later years. (Formerly, the tax rate was 35%; tax paid on the increase for 2003 and 2004 will not be deductible.) In addition, for 1998 and later years, profits after income tax are subject to a 7% remittance tax. This tax is presumed to have accrued in the year in which profits were earned. However, inasmuch as the profits are reinvested in Colombia, the remittance tax will be deferred. Furthermore, reinvestment of profits (holding same in company's net assets) for five years will give rise to exemption of the remittance tax. There is reinvestment of profits and an increase in the net equity or net assets, owned in the country, when same are held in the company's equity.

## Income determination

Effective 2003, inventories are again subject to inflation adjustments.

*Capital gains*/Capital gains tax is assessed on the sale of fixed assets owned for more than two years. The rate is 35%. For companies, as from 1992, capital gains are taxed as ordinary operating income.

*Intercompany dividends*/Gross dividends received by a Colombian corporation from another domestic company are exempt from income and capital gains taxes if distributed out of profits that have already been taxed at the distributing entity level.

*Foreign income*/Domestic corporations are taxed on their worldwide income. Foreign income, net of related expenses incurred abroad or locally, is taxed at the corporate rate. Foreign companies' branches are taxed only on Colombian income.

*Stock dividends*/Stock dividends are not taxed in Colombia in certain cases, most notably if they were already taxed to the corporation that issued them or when the stocks are quoted on the stock market. In the case of nonresident or nondomiciled shareholders, dividends are taxed at 7% when paid out of profits that were already taxed at the distributing entity level. Otherwise, an additional 35% income tax applies, for a net effective rate of 39.55%. The 7% income tax can be deferred or forgiven if dividends are reinvested in Colombia for at least five years.

*Other significant items*/Some donations can be taken as an income tax deduction, with a limit of 30% of the actual taxable income.

## Deductions

*Depreciation and depletion*/Fixed assets are fully depreciable, and normal estimated useful lives are as follows.

|  | Years |
| --- | --- |
| Buildings (including pipelines) | 20 |
| Vessels, trains and planes, machinery and equipment, furniture and fixtures | 10 |
| Vehicles and computers | 5 |

As from 1992 the cost of fixed assets and accumulated depreciation must be adjusted for the effects of annual inflation, and the adjusted cost of fixed assets must be depreciated.

Depreciation rates can be increased by 25% for each additional eight-hour shift (and proportionately for fractions) that the asset has been in use during the year. When tax depreciation exceeds book depreciation, establishment of a reserve equivalent to 70% of the difference is mandatory. Recapture of depreciation on the sale of depreciated property is taxed at 35%.

Amortization of deferred expenses is granted over a minimum period of five years. As from 1996, amortization of assets related to some concession contracts and joint ventures must have the same term as the contract. Per the New Mining Code, the costs of exploration for and exploitation of oil and gas deposits and other natural resources, and acquisition and exploitation of mines, can be amortized on the basis of the straight-line system over a period of not less than five years, or it is also possible to use the system of technical operating units. When the investments made in exploration turn out to be unsuccessful, the amount thereof can be amortized in the year in which such condition is determined and the following two years.

*Net operating losses*/Net operating losses (adjusted for inflation) incurred up to 2002 may be carried forward to the following five years. Losses incurred as from 2003 onward can be carried forward over an eight-year term. New provisions limit the amount of losses that can be deducted yearly. Further, the "passing" of losses to profit-making entities through mergers and spin-offs is now subject to certain limitations, including that the participating entities in the reorganization have the same business purpose. There is no loss carryback.

**Payments to foreign affiliates**/From 1996, direction and administrative expenses, royalties, and the costs of exploitation or acquisition of all kinds of intangibles that are charged by head offices and foreign affiliates are permitted as tax deductions, provided that the corresponding withholdings for income and complementary remittance tax have been made. Other payments are subject to the general rules for expenses incurred abroad.

**Expenses abroad**/In general, expenses abroad are limited to 15% of the taxpayer's net income computed before deducting such expenses, whenever they are not subject to income tax withholding. However, when they have to be capitalized, the tax law provides exceptions to the above rule, wherein the expenses thus incurred are fully deductible from the income tax liability.

Effective 2003, deduction of costs and expenses incurred to companies or individuals located or incorporated in tax haven countries is restricted. Under the recent bill, a deduction will be available to the extent income and remittance tax have been effectively withheld. Tax haven countries are those as designated by the Organization for Economic Cooperation and Development (OECD) or the Government of Colombia. It is expected that regulations will be promulgated to develop this new rule.

**Taxes**/Effective 2003, 80% of the industry and commerce tax and real estate tax liabilities effectively paid are deductible. Although not entirely clear, it appears that deduction will not be available for registry tax, motor vehicle tax or stamp tax. The deductible tax liability cannot be treated simultaneously as a cost and as an expense of the corresponding company.

**Exchange differences**/Accounts payable in foreign currency are adjusted at the year-end exchange rate and on the date of payment. Exchange differences resulting from adjustment of payables by branches or affiliates to their home/head office or parent companies are not tax deductible, save if they are originated in "short term loans" for import of goods.

**Interest**/Corporations are entitled to deduct (either as cost or as expense) interest paid to financial institutions or to third parties. Interest and finance-related costs (including exchange differences) are not deductible when related to debts recorded by agencies, branches, subsidiaries, or companies operating in Colombia in favor of their foreign home offices, agencies, branches, or subsidiaries domiciled abroad. However, among other exceptions, interest derived from short-term imports of merchandise and raw material of which the home offices, branches, agencies, or subsidiaries act as suppliers is deductible from the income tax liability.

## Group taxation

Group taxation is not permitted.

## Tax incentives

**Inward investment**/Effective 2003, new tax exemptions are created for a number of businesses including (1) sale of electricity based on, among others, wind resources, (2) hotel services at new or refurbished facilities, (3) seismic services, among others. Further, if dividends or branch profits are reinvested for at least five years, the 7% tax will be forgiven. The conditions under which reinvestment qualifies for this benefit have beem substantially relaxed over the past few years.

*Capital investment*/Pursuant to Act 633/2000 (effective as from 2001), for taxpayers with deductible or offsettable "value-added tax" (VAT) balances paid upon the acquisition or nationalization of fixed assets, it is provided that the right to claim such balances is held (as a deduction or as a tax setoff, depending on each taxpayer's specific case) in the following tax period.

*Other incentives*/Exporters of products other than crude oil and its derivatives, rawhide and coffee and those exporting to Ecuador, Bolivia, or Venezuela receive CERTS (income tax credit certificates) in Colombian pesos, which vary from 2% to 8%, depending on the type of goods exported. A tax credit equivalent to 35% of the value of the certificates can, up to 2002, be claimed in the income tax calculation. In this case the minimum tax limit (75%, as explained under "Taxes on corporate income") decreases by up to 70% in the case of certificates thus issued (it would be effective as from 2001 instead of the 50% applicable up to December, 2000). Effective the last quarter of 2002, no CERTS incentives will be available since the government took down the benefit to 0%.

Revenue on certain businesses will enjoy an income tax exemption. Among others, these include electricity based on, among others, wind resources (exempt for 15 years), hotel services at new or refurbished facilities (exempt for 30 years), eco-tourism services (exempt for 20 years), seismic services (exempt for 5 years).

For years 2003 up to 2004, VAT paid on the import or purchase of industrial machinery can be credited against VAT liabilities. Where the importer or purchaser doe not have any VAT liabilities (i.e., it sells exempted goods and services), input VAT can be credited against income tax liability.

## Withholding taxes

On payments to nondomiciled corporations and nonresident individuals, the following payments are subject to withholding tax.

1. Dividends—The withholding tax rate for 1996 and later years is 7%. The effective rate is 39.55% when dividends have not already been subject to tax on the company that distributes them. Tax is withheld when dividends are paid or have been credited to the recipient's account. There is no remittance tax on dividends.

2. Technical services, technical assistance, and consulting—Tax withholding is as follows.

   Regardless if rendered in Colombia or abroad, the payments made for consulting, technical services, and technical assistance, rendered by nonresident or nondomiciled entities, are deemed as national source income subject to a 10% income and remittance tax withholding.

3. Royalties—As from 1998, royalties are subject to 35% income tax withholding plus an additional remittance tax of 7% (effective rate is 39.55%).

4. Interest on loans—Interest related to foreign trade or obtained abroad by Colombian or foreign companies performing activities considered of interest to Colombia's economic and social development is exempt from income tax and remittance tax withholding.

5. Remuneration paid to nonresident employers (different than the services mentioned above, set forth in point 2.)—As from 1996, payments to

nonresidents are subject to an income tax withholding of 35% and a remittance tax withholding of 7%, calculated after deduction of income tax withholding inasmuch as they have to file an income tax return. However, if they were not obliged to file an income tax return, their final tax liability would be the withholding at source performed by the employer.

*Tax treaties*/Some double taxation treaties are in effect, especially with Andean Pact countries. Most of the tax treaties in force deal with international air and maritime transportation.

As discussed above, effective 2003, payments of any nature that qualify as domestic income to companies or individuals resident or incorporated in tax haven countries will be subject to income tax withholding at 35% plus remittance tax at 7%. These rates prevail over those listed above if and when the recipients is a resident or is incorporated or located in a tax haven country as dictated by the OECD or the government of Colombia.

## Tax administration

*Returns*/The taxable period is the calendar year, and no exceptions are permitted. The tax amount is self-assessed; however, the tax authorities can reassess the tax amount within two years from the date of filing of the return (except when it comes to returns where tax losses originate or offset, for which a five-year statute of limitations is now applicable). In certain cases, provided the taxpayer meets certain requirements including assessing a greater income tax liability than that of previous years, the statute of limitations reduces to ten months (except where the return originates a loss).

*Payment of taxes*/For tax purposes, corporations are divided into "large taxpayers" and "other taxpayers." Large taxpayers must file their 2002 tax return from February 1, 2003 to April 11, 2003 (depending on the tax identification number); other taxpayers file from February 1, 2003 to April 7, 2003, depending on their tax identification number.

## Transfer Pricing

Effective January 1, 2004, transfer pricing rules apply to all taxpayers on both domestic and cross-border transactions with related parties.

The law calls for the rules to impact on income and complementary tax only (therefore, other taxes such as stamp tax, gross receipts tax, etcetera, are not to be affected by any price adjustment).

In developing the rules, Colombia has taken the OECD approach that six methods must be used to determine an "arm's length" price. These include (1) comparable uncontrolled price method, (2) resale-price method, (3) cost-plus method, (4) profit split method, (5) residual profit split method, and (6) transactional net margin method. While not explicitly stated, it can be held that Colombia will apply the international rule of the "best method," as a guide to taxpayers required to use arm's length prices.

Advance pricing arrangements (APAs) are envisaged as well. While developing regulations are expected to be issued soon, the Act provides that APAs can apply to the tax period in which they are negotiated, the immediately preceding year, and the three years immediately following. The Colombian tax administration retains its audit capabilities regardless of the APAs, which may be construed as a mere verification process by the Colombian tax administration that the taxpayer is actually applying arm's-length prices.

In the event of cross-border pricing examinations, the Act subjects the acceptability of a foreign tax administration adjustment to (1) the existence of a tax treaty between that jurisdiction and Colombia and (2) the approval of the adjustment by the Colombian tax administration. If these two requirements are met, the taxpayer resident in Colombia can file an amendment return without incurring any penalties. While needed in the context of transfer pricing rules to avoid double taxation, this rule is potentially inapplicable since Colombia does not currently have any international tax treaties other than the Andean Pact Double Taxation Treaty (and certain other air and maritime double taxation treaties).

Legislation does not address how adjustments on domestic transactions will be dealt with. Clearly, this is a loophole that requires close attention unless the upcoming regulations address it.

Transactions such as dispositions of tangible or intangible assets, services, financing, etcetera, are to be subjected to the new rules.

Taxpayers subject to transfer pricing rules are required to prepare, gather and keep (over a five-year term) certain required documentation which will be the basis to prove that the prices they have are arm's-length. Also, an informative transfer pricing return will need to be filed once a year.

OECD guidelines, to the extent consistent with domestic rules, are to be applied by both the tax administration and taxpayers in construing the new rules.

Taxpayers subject to an in compliance with the transfer pricing rules will not be subject to the existing limitations on transactions between related parties.

# Colombia

## *CORPORATION TAX CALCULATION*

Calendar year 2003

|  |  | (In COP thousands) |
|---|---:|---:|
| Net commercial profits before taxes ............................................... |  | 600,000 |
| Add: |  |  |
| Penalties ................................................................................... | 64,000 |  |
| Provision for industry and commerce tax ...................................... | 20,000 |  |
| Provision for inventory losses ...................................................... | 8,000 |  |
| Nondeductible expenses.............................................................. | 1,200 |  |
| Other nondeductible provisions ................................................... | 4,500 |  |
| Total items that increase income for tax purposes or decrease tax loss.................................................................. |  | 97,700 |
| Deduct: |  |  |
| Payment of industry and commerce tax (80%)............................. | 16,000 |  |
| Nontaxable dividends received by another company ................... | 124 |  |
| Provision for recuperation of nondeductible receivables .............. | 3,400 |  |
| Provision for contingency used .................................................... | 23 |  |
| Total items that decrease income for tax purposes or increase tax loss................................................................... |  | (19,547) |
| Net income................................................................................... |  | 678,153 |
| Net tax payable (38.5% of 678,153) .............................................. |  | 261,088 |

Notes:

The exchange rate of the peso at March 13, 2003: US$1 = COP2,960.

## PwC contact

For additional information on taxation in the Democratic Republic of Congo, contact:

Benjamin Nzailu Basinsa
PricewaterhouseCoopers
B.P. 10195
Kinshasa 1, D.R.C.
Telephone: (243) 44.435 – 40.239
Fax: (243) (88) 00075
e-mail: bnzailu.pricewa@ic.cd

## General note

This entry is repeated from the 2003/2004 edition. For more up-to-date information consult the contact listed above or Jacqueline Collette at jacqueline.collete@us.pwc.com.

## Taxes on corporate income

*Profits tax*/Taxable income from Congo sources is subject to a 40% profits tax. The petroleum and mining industries are closely controlled, and each venture has its own tax provisions fixed by an agreement signed with the government.

## Corporate residence

The rule of the territoriality of income is applied. Therefore, corporate residence is irrelevant. Congo taxes both domestic and foreign companies having a permanent establishment in Congo on income derived from professional, commercial, agricultural, and real estate activities carried out in Congo. Foreign companies are deemed to have a permanent establishment if either of the following is true.

1. They possess in the country any material installations, such as a place of effective management control, branches, factories, workshops, agencies, shops, offices, laboratories, purchase or sales departments, depots, rented buildings, or any other permanent or fixed installations of a productive nature.

2. In the absence of such material installations, they carry on directly under their name a business activity during a period equal to at least six months, and this activity cannot be considered as assistance to a domestic company.

Companies having their principal center of production in Congo must be incorporated in Congo.

# Congo, Democratic Republic of

## Other taxes

*Sales taxes*/Sales tax is levied at the following rates.

| | % |
|---|---|
| Imports: | |
| On cost, insurance, freight (CIF) value plus import duties | |
| All goods matched with a custom duty of 5% and 15% | 3 |
| Other goods and products | 13 |
| Exports: | |
| On net foreign currency repatriation arising from export of mineral products, crude oil, coffee, lumber (duties are also payable) | 3 |
| Gold and diamond from working relating to crafts | 0.25 |
| Local manufacture: | |
| On wholesale price: | |
| Local product, identical or similar to imported goods matched with a custom duty of 5% and 15% | 3 |
| Other products | 13 |
| Construction works: | |
| On three-quarters of gross billing | 18 |
| Local services: | |
| On gross billing | 18 |
| Imported services: | |
| On gross billing | 30 |
| Carriage of passengers by air, sea, rail, and road, especially for interurban: | |
| Domestic lines | 6 |
| Foreign lines | 15 |

*Tax on rent income*/The gross rent income is subject to a 22% tax (*contribution sur les revenus locatifs*). The main amount of this tax is withheld by the tenant before paying his rent. The amount to withhold is 20% of the rent.

*Employment tax*/Employment tax (*contribution exceptionnelle sur les rémunérations* [CER]) is levied at 25% on the total remuneration of all non-Congolese employees. This tax is calculated on the same base as that used for the *contribution professionnelle sur les rémunérations* (CPR), but it cannot be taken as a deduction in determining taxable profit.

From June 1997, non-Congolese natives of neighboring countries are assimilated to Congolese as regards to individual tax (CPR).

*Payroll tax (social security)*/Both employers and employees contribute to a national pension scheme. However, the contributions and the benefits are negligible.

*Educational tax*/Educational tax is levied at 1% of total gross remuneration of all employees.

*Property tax*/Land and buildings are taxed at various rates according to the nature and location of property. The amounts of taxes are fixed in "Francs fiscal" (Ff) as indicated below (today 1Ff = US$1).

1. For buildings
   a. Villa: 0.30 Ff to 1.50 Ff per square meter ($m^2$) according to the location;
   b. Other buildings: from 4 Ff to 75 Ff by level according to status of owners (companies or individual) and location; from 11 Ff to 75 Ff for apartments; from 1.5 Ff to 11 Ff for other buildings.
2. For land: from 1.5 Ff to 30 Ff according to location.

*Registration duty*/Transfers of real or immovable properties and property rights are subject to registration duties ranging from 10% to 15%, depending on the circumstances of transfer.

Formation and extension of the life of limited companies (*sociétés par actions à responsabilités limitée* [SARLs]) and increase of capital are subject to 10% registration duty on subscribed capital, capital at the time of life extension or capital increase.

*Branch income*/Branches of foreign corporations are subject to profits tax at the rate of 40% on taxable profits. The portion of distributed profit is subject to a withholding tax at the rate of 20%.

## Income determination

*Inventory valuation*/Inventory for tax reporting purposes must agree with the books. Tax regulations on inventory valuation are as follows: FIFO and the weighted-average method are the most usual accepted bases. To date, the Revenue Department has permitted the LIFO method, particularly in the mining industry, but there is no special ruling on this.

*Capital gains*/Realized capital gains and losses are treated as ordinary trading profits and losses for tax purposes. Unrealized capital gains reported in the books are exempt from tax if they are credited directly to a capital reserve account, as long as they are not treated as profits (i.e., distributed).

*Intercompany dividends*/Dividends received from locally based subsidiaries or other corporations are excluded from taxable income to the extent of 90% of the effective revenues. Dividends from foreign-based subsidiaries or other corporations are not taxable in Congo.

*Foreign income*/Income is subject to profits tax only when it arises from activities carried out in Congo or from capital invested or real estate located in the country. Foreign-source profits (e.g., income from foreign investments or from foreign branches or subsidiaries) are not taxable. The present tax administration seems at times to contest the nontaxability of foreign income, although this is counter to the spirit of the 1969 tax reform.

*Stock dividends*/Stock dividends are excluded from the profit tax base.

## Deductions

*Depreciation and depletion*/Depreciation is tax deductible only to the extent recorded in the books. Depreciation on a straight-line basis over the estimated life of the assets is the most usual method, but other methods may be acceptable if proved to be more suitable in the particular circumstances.

Annual depreciation rates generally accepted by the Revenue Department are as follows.

|  | % |
|---|---|
| Buildings | 3–5 |
| Furniture/office equipment | 10–15 |
| Machinery/vehicles | 20–25 |
| Small tools | 33 |

The excess of sale price over the net book value (as eventually revalued in accordance with the provisions of revaluations law) is taxed at normal trading income.

During the period of tax holiday, depreciation is deemed to have been taken annually at 10% of the total depreciable assets.

Under the mining legislation, mineral and oil concession holders may claim a depletion allowance. The maximum allowable charge is 15% of the gross sales, but this charge cannot exceed 50% of the net profit. The allowance must be reinvested within two years.

*Net operating losses*/Losses may be carried over for two years. There is no loss carryback.

*Payments to foreign affiliates*/Royalties and service fees are allowable only if proved to relate to genuine transactions and to be of an amount commensurate with the service rendered. To qualify for deduction, the service must be unobtainable in Congo. In general, assistance fees should be substantially less than 5% of turnover (sales).

*Interest*/Interest payable on loans from foreign affiliates is deductible, provided the rates are reasonable.

*Taxes*/Employment tax is no longer deductible in determining taxable profit. Other taxes, except the tax on profits, are deductible.

*Other significant items* include the following.

1. Provisions for expenses or losses not yet incurred, for example, provisions for bad debts, stock obsolescence, bonuses, exchange losses, and future maintenance, are not tax deductible. A deduction is permitted in respect of amounts subsequently paid or written off.
2. Remuneration and interest on loans paid to partners in a private limited company (*société de personnes à responsabilité limitée* [SPRL]), are not deductible. However, partners are not liable to individual taxes.
3. Head office overheads and expenses incurred outside Congo may not be allocated to Congolese branch income.

## Group taxation

Group taxation is not permitted.

## Tax incentives

*Inward investment and capital investment*/The investment code provides foreign investors with tax and other advantages and guarantees the right of transfer of dividends, royalties, and loans. The code provides for a general regime and for special advantages for small and medium-sized companies and small and medium-sized industries.

*General regime*/As to eligibility, investors are required to apply to the *Agence Nationale pour la Promotion des Investissements* (ANAPI [National Agency for Investments Promotion]) and must meet the following criteria.

1. Be a Congolese company.
2. A minimum investment equivalent to US$200,000.
3. Pledge to respect the regulation in relation with the protection of the environment and the conservation of the nature.

4. Pledge to train national staff to specialized technical functions and to the executive functions and responsibilities.

5. Ensure a rate of added value of not less than 35%.

Benefits conferred under the general regime are as follows.

Investments agreed will have benefits provided for a duration of the following.

- Three years when investment is done in economic region A (Kinshasa City).
- Four years when done in economic region B (Province of Bas-Congo and Cities of Lubumbashi, Likasi, and Kolwezi).
- Five years when done in economic region C (other where in D.R.C.).

1. For general regime, exclusions include the following.
   a. Custom duties and sales tax on new equipment, material, and spare parts. The list of goods not to be taxed will be attached to the document of agreement signed by ministers.
   b. Corporate tax for new investments.
   c. Registration duties related to company formation or increase in capital.
   d. Property tax.
   e. Duties and sales tax on export.
   f. Sales tax on equipment and materials manufactured in Congo and on services rendered for construction works.

   These benefits are conferred only one time.

2. For small and medium-sized companies and industries: benefits are the same as provided in the general regime. These companies and industries are authorized to deduct from their taxable profit expenses for staff training, protection, and preservation of nature. They are also allowed to apply the degressive system for depletion (*amortissements selon le mode dégressif*).

## Withholding taxes

Dividends and other profit distributions, unless paid to an active partner in a private limited company (SPRL), are subject to a withholding tax (which is a final tax) of 20%. Royalties and interest payments to nonresidents are subject to the same withholding tax of 20%. A standard deduction of 30% on gross royalties is allowed to arrive at the taxable basis.

*Tax treaties*/The government has not ratified any tax treaties. It is understood that some countries accept preindependence treaties negotiated with Belgium as still valid for income arising in Congo.

## Tax administration

*Returns*/The calendar year must be used for tax purposes. The tax return must be filed by March 31 of the subsequent year.

*Payment of tax*/Tax is payable by installments on the basis of the amount of the previous year's assessment as follows: before September 1, 40%; before December 1, 40%; before April 1, 20%. The first two installments are obligatory, even if the current profits do not justify such amounts. The third may be reduced or omitted altogether, depending on the final tax calculation.

The balance is payable within 30 days following the receipt of the final assessment raised by the tax authorities (usually in May-June).

## CORPORATION TAX CALCULATION

Year ending December 31, 2002

| | | |
|---|---:|---:|
| Profit shown on accounts ................................................................... | | CDF 1,000,000 |
| Add back: | | |
|    Depreciation ................................................................... | 100,000 | |
|    Bad or doubtful debts not proven irrecoverable ................ | 50,000 | |
|    Fines, interest, or other tax penalties ................................ | 20,000 | |
|    Reserves or provisions not representing | | |
|       identifiable liabilities ...................................................... | 70,000 | 240,000 |
| Total ............................................................................................. | | 1,240,000 |
| Deduct: | | |
|    Excess depreciation in previous years to the extent | | |
|       now allowable ............................................................. | 50,000 | |
|    Bad or doubtful debts previously disallowed, | | |
|       now proved irrecoverable ............................................. | 20,000 | |
|    Loss for year before last ................................................... | 400,000 | |
|    Loss for last year .............................................................. | 200,000 | 670,000 |
| Taxable profit................................................................................. | | 570,000 |
| Profits tax at 40% ......................................................................... | | 228,000 |
| Withholding tax: | | |
|    Assumed dividend ............................................................. | 150,000 | |
|    Directors' fees.................................................................. | 50,000 | 200,000 |
| Withholding tax at 20% ................................................................. | | 40,000 |

Note:
1. Official exchange rate at December 31, 2002 US$1 = CDF385.

## PwC contact

For additional information on taxation in Costa Rica, contact:

Gerardo Cásares Alvarado
Price Waterhouse
Edificio Price Waterhouse
Barrio Los Yoses
San José, Costa Rica
Telephone: (506) 224-15 55
Fax: (506) 253-40 53
e-mail: gerardo.casares@cr.pwc.com

## General note

This entry is repeated from the 2003/2004 edition. For more up-to-date information consult the contact listed above or Jacqueline Collette at jacqueline.collete@us.pwc.com.

## Significant developments

There have been no significant tax or regulatory developments regarding corporate taxation in the past year.

## Taxes on corporate income

Taxable income is taxed at a 30% rate. Only for the current year this rate will be 36%.

However, the law establishes special regulations for small companies, those corporations whose gross income does not exceed CRC39,617,000; for this category the following tariffs will be applied: 10% (only for the current year this rate will be 12%) on taxable income up to CRC19,695,000; 20% (only for the current year this rate will be 24%) on taxable income over CRC17,960,000, but not over CRC39,617,000; 30% (only for the current year this rate will be 36%) on the excess.

## Corporate residence

In most cases, the place of incorporation is regarded by Costa Rican authorities as the corporate residence. However, income taxes on corporations in Costa Rica are levied on local income irrespective of the place of incorporation, since any business not registered under Costa Rican laws that carries on industrial, agricultural or commercial activity is subject to taxation in the same way as a registered business. To these corporations doing business in Costa Rica, the "permanent establishment" rules apply.

At the same time, under the Costa Rican Income Tax Law certain transactions (income and expenses) may be regarded as performed outside Costa Rica and, therefore, as not subject to income taxes. Under this situation, corporations may have their residence in Costa Rica and perform the central management function of other nonresident affiliates from Costa Rica and not be subject to taxes, as long as the registered entity performs no income-generating activities within the country and all local disbursements are subject to reimbursement from an outside source. The tax administration is trying strongly to set up rules in order to control and eventually to tax the cost centers.

# Costa Rica

## Other taxes

*Franchise tax*/The payments realized abroad for the use of a franchising will be subject to remittances abroad, with a withholding tax of 25%. Only for the current year this rate will be 27.5%.

*Capital gains tax*/At present, there is no capital gains tax on the sale of real estate or securities when such sales are not a habitual activity. There is capital gain tax, at the regular rate, on the sale of depreciable assets when the sales price of them is higher than their adjusted basis.

*Sales tax*/Sales tax was decreased to 13% effective April 1996. It is applied at all stages in the sale of merchandise or the invoicing of certain services. The tax is levied on sales of merchandise within the national territory (except sales of land, buildings, exports, and certain basic necessity items, such as medicines and veterinary products); the value of services performed by restaurants, bars, motels, printing services, social and recreational clubs, and painting and repair shops; and imports consisting of merchandise for personal use or consumption or to satisfy commercial needs.

*Selective consumption tax*/The selective consumption tax rates range from 10% to 75% and are applied to goods that are considered nonessential. The tax base is the cost, insurance, freight (CIF) price plus import duties for imported items and sales value for articles produced in Costa Rica. The tax is levied at only one stage in the sale of merchandise, payment of the tax being required at the time of importation or, for articles produced in Costa Rica, within 15 days after the month of the sale.

*Property tax*/Each local government is in charge of real estate appraisal. The tax to be applied throughout Costa Rican territory is 0.25% of the appraised value registered in the respective Municipality at the moment of origin of the tax liability. The first CRC6,147,000 is exempt if the taxpayer owns only one property within the country.

*Real estate transfer tax*/Real estate transferred is taxed at 1.51%.

## Branch income

Branch income is subject to income tax at the rates applicable for corporate income taxes. There is a withholding tax of 15% from dividends distributed within the country, and a 15% tax in lieu of a dividend withholding tax is assessed on profits transferred abroad. Only for the current year this rate will be 16.5%. There are tax holidays under certain circumstances.

## Income determination

*Inventory valuation*/Inventories are generally stated at cost and can be valued at the compound average cost method, FIFO, LIFO, retailer method, or specific identification method. Since all entities must keep legal records, any adjustment resulting from different methods of inventory valuation for tax purposes and financial purposes should be recorded.

*Capital gains*/Capital gains and losses on the disposition of all fixed assets or shares of other companies are excluded for income tax purposes if such dispositions are not a habitual activity.

*Intercompany dividends*/Dividends between domestic subsidiaries and other domestic corporations are not subject to any taxes. There are no ownership requirements to qualify for this exclusion.

*Foreign income*/Foreign-source income is not taxable.

*Stock dividends*/Stock dividends are subject to income tax at 15% (only for the current year this rate will be 16.5%); 5% if the stock is registered at an approved Costa Rican stock market (only for the current year this rate will be 6%).

Dividends paid in form of stock/Dividends paid in form of stock are allowed and exempt from taxes.

## Deductions

*Depreciation and depletion*/The straight-line and sum-of-the-years-digits methods of depreciation are allowed.

|  | % |
|---|---|
| Buildings | 2 to 6 |
| Machinery and equipment | 7 to 15 |
| Furniture and fixtures | 10 |
| Vehicles | 10 to 20 |
| Agricultural plantations | 10 to 50 |

The Tax Administration, at the request of the taxpayer, could adopt technically acceptable special depreciation methods in cases duly justified by the taxpayer. In addition, the Tax Administration could authorize, through general resolution, accelerated depreciation methods on new assets, acquired by corporations with monetary activities requiring constant technological update, higher installed production capacity and productive reconversion processes, in order to maintain and strengthen their competitive advantage.

Percentage depletion is permitted up to 5% of net income before taxes of each fiscal year.

*Net operating losses*/Losses incurred by industrial and agricultural enterprises may be deducted from the taxable profits of the following three and five years, respectively. Loss carrybacks are not allowed.

*Payments to foreign affiliates*/Corporations can claim deductions for royalties, technical and management service fees, and interest charges paid to foreign affiliates, provided a tax of 25% (27.5% for the current year) for royalties, franchisings, and other services, and 15% (16.5% for the current year) for interest is withheld. However, the deductions for technical and management service fees cannot exceed 10% of gross sales in the aggregate if paid to the parent company.

*Taxes*/With the exception of sales tax, selective consumption tax, specific taxes over consumption and special duties over them established by law, penalties and interest paid over any tax obligation, and the income tax itself, all other taxes are deductible expenses when determining taxable income.

*Other significant items*/None.

## Group taxation

Not applicable.

# Costa Rica

## Tax incentives

*Free zones*/Entities established at free zones may enjoy exemption from import duties on goods, income tax, sales tax, export tax, selective consumption tax, property tax (if registered under this regime before June 19, 1995), real estate transfer tax, and withholding tax on payments abroad, plus the discretionary use of foreign currency generated abroad. However, these incentives will be affected by the rules established by the World Trade Organization (WTO), in force in the year 2009.

*Other incentives*/Other incentives are available as follows:

1. Drawback industries—Special benefits exist for industries that import semimanufactured materials for assembly in Costa Rica and export finished products. Benefits consist of duty-free import of raw materials for subsequent export as manufactured products. Machinery for these industries may also be imported duty-free.

2. Tourism development—The Incentive Law for Tourism Development grants several tax benefits, such as exemption from import duties on goods and from property tax for companies dedicated to tourism, but only for those corporations with a signed tourism agreement before April 3, 1992; therefore, such incentives are no longer being given by the Costa Rican government, but could actually be enjoyed by corporations under the situation abovementioned. Also, this law states that 50% of the amount invested in tourism through the purchase of nominative shares of corporations established in the country with a signed tourism agreement before April 3, 1992 may be taken as a tax credit with previous authorization from the Tourism Regulatory Commission.

## Withholding taxes

*Payments to nondomiciled foreign corporations or individuals*/Taxes are withheld as follows:

1. Dividends—15%. Only for the current year this rate will be 16.5%.

   Withholding depends on the origin or source of the retained earnings. Total or partial exemption will be authorized by the tax authorities to the extent that a foreign tax credit is totally or partially disallowed to the taxpayer in the taxpayer's country of residence. This exemption will not be allowed, however, if this type of income is not taxable to the taxpayer in the country of residence.

2. Interest and other financial expenses—15%. Only for the current year this rate will be 16.5%.

   No tax is withheld if the recipient is a bank or a financial institution recognized as a First Class Bank by the Central Bank of Costa Rica or a supplier of merchandise. Interest or financial expenses paid to parties other than those mentioned above are subject to a 15% withholding tax. Only for the current year this rate will be 16.5%.

   An 8% withholding tax (only for the current year this rate will be 8.8%) applies to interest on bearer documents issued by financial entities registered at the Central Bank's General Auditor's Office or stock exchange. No withholding applies to interest paid on securities issued by the Workmen's Bank or the Mortgage Housing Bank and its authorized institutions or on foreign currency securities issued by the state banks.

3. Special tax on banks and nonresident financial entities. Banks or nonresident financial entities being part of a local financial group are payers of taxes established in this article. The taxpayers mentioned in the above paragraph should pay, in lieu of tax on remittances abroad, a local currency tax equivalent to US$125,000 per annum. The tax period will run from January 1 to December 31 of each year. Only for the current year this rate will be US$300,000.

4. Royalties, patents, trademarks, franchises, and formulas—These payments are subject to a 25% withholding tax. Only for the current year this rate will be 27.5%.

5. Technical service and management fees— A 25% tax is withheld from these fees. Only for the current year this rate will be 27.5%.

6. Personal services from a Costa Rican source are subject to the following withholdings: employees—10%; directors—15% (17.5% for the current year); others, depending on the nature of the services rendered—30% (33% for the current year).

7. Transportation and communication services—Fees for these services are subject to an 8.5% withholding tax (9.25% for the current year).

*Tax treaties*/Costa Rica is a full member of the Central American Common Market, which guarantees free trade among the countries of the area. Additionally, it is part of the Caribbean Basin Region, by means of which a large amount of Costa Rican products may enter the United States free of duties under the Caribbean Basin Initiative (CBI). It also has a free-trade bilateral treaty in force with Mexico (1994), and has signed free-trade bilateral treaties with the Dominican Republic (1998) and Chile (1998), which have been approved by the Costa Rican Parliament; however, in the Dominican Republic case, the agreement is pending approval. Currently under negotiation are free-trade agreements with the United States, Canada, and Panama. These agreements aim to provide favorable conditions for the exchange of merchandise between contracting parties.

The only tax treaty in force between Costa Rica and the United States, effective since February 12, 1991, established as its principal benefits for Costa Rica access to Section 936 funds from Puerto Rico and U.S. tax deductibility of business expenses related to conventions held in Costa Rica.

## Tax administration

*Returns*/With certain exceptions, all corporations must file by December 15 a tax return on the basis of a fiscal year ended on September 30. Entities with an operating period of less than four months may present a return together with the following year's tax return. The present legislation contemplates that other fiscal year-ends may be adopted with the prior approval of the tax authorities.

The tax system is one of self-assessment with occasional auditing by the tax authorities.

*Payment of tax*/In March, June and September all corporations must prepay installments that total 75% of the average income taxes paid in the last three fiscal years. Failure to pay at these dates results in the accrual of interest unless the taxpayer has requested on a timely basis that the tax authorities eliminate the corresponding payments. Any amount owed in excess of the installments should be paid by December 15.

# Costa Rica

## *CORPORATION TAX CALCULATION*

Fiscal year ended September 30, 2001

|  | Case A | Case B |
|---|---:|---:|
|  | CRC | CRC |
| Income before taxes | 11,000,000 | 1,100,000,000 |
| Add—Nondeductible expenses: | | |
| Depreciation of fixed assets in excess of authorized rates | 50,000 | 5,000,000 |
| Reserve for severance compensation | 40,000 | 4,000,000 |
| Loss on sale of land | 30,000 | 3,000,000 |
|  | 11,120,000 | 1,112,000,000 |
| Less: | | |
| Nontaxable dividends received | 10,000 | 1,000,000 |
| Profit on sale of investments | 20,000 | 2,000,000 |
| Operating loss carryover | 50,000 | 5,000,000 |
| Reinvestment of profit in capital assets for expansion of production facilities by companies engaged in agricultural or agroindustrial activities | 10,000 | 1,000,000 |
| Taxable income | 11,030,000 | 1,103,000,000 |
| Tax thereon (1) | 1,103,000 | 330,900,000 |

Notes:

1. The normal tax rate is 30% (Case B) (36% for the current year). The rate is reduced for a "small company," which is defined by the Income Tax Law as a corporation that does not receive more than CRC39,617,000 in the fiscal year. Receipts up to CRC19,695,000 (Case A) are taxed at 10% (12% for the current year). Receipts in excess of that amount and up to CRC39,617,000 are taxed at 20% (24% for the current year) and in excess of the latter amount at 30% (36% for the current year).
2. Exchange rate of the colón at April 21, 2003: US$1 = CRC390.82.

## PwC contact

For additional information on taxation in Croatia, contact:

Iain McGuire
PricewaterhouseCoopers d.o.o.
Alexandera von Humboldta
410000 Zagreb, Croatia
Telephone: (385) (1) 6328 888
Fax: (385) (1) 6111 556
e-mail: iain.mcguire@hr.pwc.com

## General note

This entry is repeated from the 2003/2004 edition. For more up-to-date information consult the contact listed above or Jacqueline Collette at jacqueline.collete@us.pwc.com.

## Significant developments

The new Corporate Income Tax Law and Personal Income Tax Law was introduced on January 1, 2001.

The General Tax Law, which establishes a general legal framework for the tax system in Croatia, was introduced on January 1, 2001.

The Tax Advisory Law, which sets the framework for providing tax advisory services, was introduced on January 1, 2001.

Amendments to the Law on Excise Duties for Personal Cars, Other Motor Vehicles, Vessels, and Aircraft introduced higher excise duties on January 1, 2002.

The Law on the Amendments to the Law on Excise Duty on Tobacco Products introduced higher excise duties on cigarettes and other tobacco products on January 1, 2002.

The Law on the Amendments to the Law Excise Duty on Oil Derivatives introduced higher excise duties on oil derivatives on October 13, 2000. (Changes were made in the administrative procedure.)

The Law on the Amendments to the Law on Excise Duty on Beer introduced higher excise duties on beer on January 1, 2002. (Changes were made in the administrative procedure.)

The Law on the Amendments to the Law on Excise Duty on Alcohol introduced highor excise duties on alcohol on January 1, 2002. (Changes were made in the administrative procedure.)

The Law on the Amendments to the Law on Excise Duty on Coffee introduced higher excise duties on coffee on June 1, 2000. (Changes were made in the administrative procedure.)

The Law on the Amendments to the Law on Excise Duty on Cars, Other Motor Vehicles, Boats, and Aircrafts introduced higher excise duties on cars and other motor vehicles, on January 1, 2002. (Changes where made in the administrative procedure.)

# Croatia

## Taxes on corporate income

*Profit tax*/Profit tax is paid by enterprises engaged in independent activities on a long-term basis for the purpose of deriving profit; branches of foreign enterprises; enterprises that control shares in capital (unless the object of investment itself pays profit tax); and natural persons who choose to pay profit tax instead of personal income tax. The tax base is the difference between revenue and expenditures, adjusted for increasing and decreasing items. Croatian residents pay profit tax on profit derived in Croatia and abroad, and nonresidents, for example, branches, pay profit tax only on profits derived in Croatia.

The profit tax base is reduced by the following items.

- Material costs, such as raw materials.
- Costs of services (both productive and nonproductive) including items such as production, transportation, maintenance of goods, facilities and equipment, research and development, advertising, management services, utility services, and any such other services that may constitute a basis for the generation of revenue.
- Depreciation costs.
- Employee costs.
- Employee reimbursements.
- Provisions for pensions and severance compensations, natural resource renewal costs, warranty periods, and litigation costs.
- Value adjustments of fixed and current assets.
- Financing costs.
- Donations in kind or in cash.
- Other operating costs (professional association membership fees, administrative and legal costs, technical literature costs, fines, and all other expenses incurred in connection with the derivation of income by the taxpayer).

The profit tax base is increased by the following items.

- Depreciation costs exceeding the maximum amount allowed for tax purposes.
- A total of 70% of entertainment and promotion costs (this includes entertainment; gifts with or without the stamped mark of the firm or product; holiday, sporting, recreation and leisure costs; hire of cars, vessels, aircraft, or holiday houses; and similar expenses).
- Fines.
- A total of 30% of costs incurred in connection with owned or hired motor vehicles or other means of personal transportation used by executive officers, managers, and other employed person. Where the use of the means of transport for personal transportation is defined as pay, the tax base will only be increased by 30% of insurance costs.
- Donations exceeding 2% of revenue generated in the preceding year, unless these expenses have been incurred under special programs and pursuant to decisions passed by the competent ministry.
- Expenses resulting from asset losses exceeding the levels determined by the Croatian Chamber of Commerce or Croatian Chamber of Small Business in the meaning of the regulations on value-added tax, and the pertinent tax calculated on these losses.

- Hidden profit payments (increases in expenses or decreases in revenues resulting from the withdrawal of assets and use of services by the company owners or co-owners for private purposes).

*Local taxes*/Local authorities are entitled to levy a business name tax up to the kuna equivalent of approximately US$290.

## Corporate residence

Profit tax is payable by enterprises engaged in independent activities in Croatia on a long-term basis for the purpose of deriving a profit, including Croatian domestic entities, branches of foreign enterprises, and domestic business units of foreign entities.

## Other taxes

*Value-added tax*/VAT was introduced on January 1, 1998 at a rate of 22%. VAT is a consumption tax and has a neutral effect on enterprises by operation of the input and output mechanism. Accordingly, the tax burden is borne by the final consumer. A VAT-registered entity must calculate its VAT liability or refund and submit a monthly (by the end of the following month) VAT return to the relevant Tax Authority Office or a quarterly VAT return if the taxpayer is classified as small. An annual VAT return must be submitted by April 30 of the following year.

Where the amount of input tax credits exceeds the entity's VAT liability, a taxpayer is entitled to a refund of the difference or may choose to use the difference as a VAT prepayment.

VAT payers are defined as entrepreneurs that deliver goods or perform services in Croatia. An "entrepreneur" is a legal entity or a natural person that continuously and independently performs an activity for the purpose of deriving profit. In addition to those that may be regarded as "normal" taxpayers, domestic enterprises receiving imported services from foreign enterprises and legal entities and individuals that issue invoices or receipts including VAT without authorization are also liable to pay VAT.

A taxpayer is required to be registered for VAT where turnover in the previous year exceeded HRK85,000. Voluntary registration is also possible.

VAT is also payable on the sale of new buildings.

The VAT base for goods and services supplied domestically is the consideration received. Where no consideration is provided, for instance where goods are exchanged, the VAT base is the market value of the good or service. The VAT base of imports is the customs value as prescribed by customs regulations, increased by customs duties, import duties, special taxes, and other fees paid during customs clearing.

VAT paid to the customs office at the time of import can be credited to the taxpayer's VAT account and offset against any domestic VAT liability. If goods are exempt from import duty, they will also be VAT exempt. A VAT entity must self-assess VAT on imported services provided by a foreign entity. This VAT can be reclaimed through the VAT return as described above.

For services, the place of supply is in general taken to be the place as prescribed by the 1977 EU Directive.

# Croatia

Pursuant to amendments made to the VAT Law and Regulations on November 1, 1999, goods and services provided by a public cinema as well as certain other consumer goods are VAT free. As of this date, VAT-registered entities are required to account for inventories at their sales price. VAT-registered entities are required to issue an invoice (R-1 or R-2) which clearly illustrates the VAT base amount and the rate of VAT charged (0% or 22%) as well as the tax amount as a separate figure.

*Real estate tax*/The acquisition of real estate is subject to taxation. "Real estate" includes agricultural, construction, and other land as well as residential, commercial, and other buildings. Transactions include the sale, exchange, and any other means of acquiring real estate for consideration.

Tax is charged at 5% of the market value of the real estate on the contract date.

*Excise duties*/There are a number of excise duties levied on specific products. They are levied at a fixed amount and are payable by the producer or importer. VAT is applied after which the fixed amounts are added. The following list is not exhaustive.

1. Oil derivatives—Tax ranging from 0 to HRK2.4 per liter as of July 1, 2000.
2. Tobacco products—Tax on cigarettes ranging from HRK5.0 to HRK8.90 per packet; from HRK1.10 to HRK38.00 for other types of tobacco products.
3. Beer—HRK200.00 per hectoliter for both domestic and imported beer; HRK60.00 per hectoliter for nonalcoholic beer.
4. Soft drinks—HRK40 per hectoliter for domestically produced brands and imported soft drinks. Some soft drinks, including mineral water and natural fruit juices, are exempt.
5. Alcohol—HRK60 per liter of content of absolute alcohol in alcoholic drinks.
6. Imported coffee—HRK5.00 to HRK20.00 per kilogram.
7. Imported cars—At least 15% of the amount paid for used cars and at least HRK5,000 for new cars, depending on the price of the car.
8. Imported motorcycles—At least HRK5,000, depending on the price of the motorcycle.
9. Imported boats—HRK6,000 to HRK24,000 without cabin and HRK15,000 to HRK90,000 with cabin and also depending on the length of the vessel.
10. Imported aircraft—HRK7,000 to HRK175,000, depending on the number of seats in the aircraft.

As of November 1, 1999, excise duties were introduced on luxury goods at a rate of 30%. This duty is applied on the sales price (excise duty base) excluding VAT, in addition to VAT of 22%. The obligation of calculating and paying excise duties rests with the manufacturer and importer of the luxury goods. The following are deemed to constitute taxable trade in luxury goods: delivery of products to the buyer by the manufacturer or importer, purchase of goods for own needs, and deficit of goods.

Excise duty applies to jewelry and complementary products (diamonds, gems, goldsmith's and filigree products, etc.); watches (including straps and bangles if partially or completely made out of or plated with precious metals); fur and reptile-skin clothes and footwear; fireworks; arms; articles made of ivory, coral and the like; and pocket and desktop lighters made of precious metals.

*Chamber of Commerce contribution*/Employers pay a mandatory contribution to the Croatian Chamber of Commerce. The amount is a monthly fee between HRK55 and HRK5,500 depending on the size of the company and 1/12 of 0.01% of the annual income stated in the profit and loss statement.

*Water consumption tax*/Employers pay water consumption tax of 0.76% of the gross amount of salary paid.

*Social security*/The employer's social security contribution, covering pensions and health care, is 16.22% of an employee's salary, and 0.85% must be paid into an unemployment fund.

## Branch income

Foreign corporations carrying on business in Croatia are taxed on their Croatian source income at a 20% rate.

## Income determination

*Inventory valuation*/Inventories are generally valued at the lower of their acquisition cost or net realizable value. Taking into consideration the accounting principles set out in the Accounting Act and the International Accounting Standards (IAS), a company can choose to adopt the most favorable method.

*Capital gains*/Capital gains or losses are covered by the profit tax regime. They are either an increasing or decreasing item to the profit tax base.

*Intercompany dividends*/Intercompany dividends are treated as income under the profit tax regime but are not included in the tax base.

## Deductions

*Depreciation*/Most companies depreciate assets on a straight-line basis; this is because depreciation calculated this way at the prescribed rates is recognized for tax purposes. Companies are, however, free to use any depreciation method defined in the IAS and to estimate the useful lives of all fixed assets in accordance with their accounting policies. However, depreciation expenses in excess of the amount allowed for tax purposes are taxable. The value adjustment of tangible fixed assets rarely occurs in practice, except in the case of financial assets and claims.

As of January 2001, the law allows taxpayers to partly or wholly write off plant and equipment acquired or built during the tax period. Plant and equipment are taken to be acquired in the period in which it is installed or ready for use. Plant and equipment includes: tools of trade, information technology infrastructure including software, furniture and fittings and motor vehicles (excluding vehicles that may be used for personal uses). If the taxpayer writes off a portion of a depreciable asset, the remaining undepreciated portion will be depreciated at the rate prescribed by law.

Land and forests are not depreciated

Goodwill paid on the acquisition of a business must be amortized over five years. Goodwill started to appear in the balance sheets of some Croatian companies following privatization, but it does not really reflect goodwill. It is usually the difference between the estimated statistical value of assets and liabilities and their book value. Companies that have disclosed goodwill in the balance sheet are allowed to depreciate fixed assets at an accelerated rate and thus pay less profit tax.

*Tax losses*/Tax losses can be carried forward for up to five years. Protective interest is no longer applied to tax losses. If a taxpayer does not utilize a tax loss within five years, the tax loss will expire.

# Croatia

*Payments to foreign affiliates*/The treatment of payments made to foreign affiliates is dealt with through the mechanism of the profit tax base. The profit tax base is increased for any concealed profit payments made. The Tax Administration may audit the expenditure of nonresident taxpayers, examining expenditure on goods and services abroad as well as management, intellectual property and other fees and payments that may have the character of profit transfer. If the Tax Administration discovers that transactions have been used to conceal profit transfers, the difference between the declared price/fee and the average market price/fee will be added back to the taxpayer's tax base.

## Group taxation

There are no grouping provisions in Croatia.

## Tax incentives

The Corporate Profit Tax Act provides the following relief and incentives for taxpayers.

1. Investment Incentives.

   Profits derived from investments may be subject to the following corporate income tax rate reductions for a period of up to ten years where certain conditions including the following employment and investment criteria are met.

   | Investment (Mil HRK) | Employees | Applicable Tax Rate |
   |---|---|---|
   | 10–20 | 30–50 | 7% |
   | 20–60 | 50–75 | 3% |
   | More than 60 | 75+ | 0% |

2. Employment incentives.

   Where a taxpayer employs a "new employee" as defined by the Profit Tax Act, the taxpayer is entitled to claim a double deduction in respect of the salary expenses for a period of one year given that certain conditions are satisfied. A new employee is defined as an employee as follows.

   • With whom an indefinite employment contract has been drawn up;
   • Who has been secured employment after being registered as unemployed for a minimum period of a month.
   • Who has given up the right to retire.
   • Who is being employed for the first time.

3. Concessions for taxpayers in regions under special state care.

   Taxpayers performing their business activities in a region under special state care, as defined by the Law on Regions Under Special State Care, and who employ more than five persons on a permanent basis, with more than 50% of such employees having their permanent residence in a region under special state care, are entitled to a 75% corporate income tax reduction, depending on the region.

4. Concessions and exemptions for taxpayers in the territory of the city of Vukovar.

   Taxpayers performing their business activities within the territory of the city of Vukovar and who employ more than five people on a permanent basis (with more than 50% of such employees having their residence and abode within the territory of the city of Vukovar), are exempt from paying corporate income tax in the 2000 and in the subsequent five years and, thereafter, shall pay profit tax at a rate of 25% of the prescribed rate.

5. Concessions and exemptions for taxpayers operating in free zones.

   Users of a free zone, as defined in the Free Zone Act, pay profit tax in the amount of 50% of the statutory tax rate.

   Any free zone beneficiary who, within the territory of such free zone, constructs or participates in the construction of any facilities by investing funds in excess of HRK1 million shall, after investing such funds, be exempted from profit tax in the year of investment and in the next five subsequent years. However, no such exemption shall exceed the level of invested funds.

   The Government of the Republic of Croatia may increase concessions wherever it determines that specific zones or the performance of specific activities in such zones are of particular economic interest to the Republic of Croatia.

   For the performance of activities in free zones located within the territory of the Vukovar and Srijem County, no profit tax shall be paid for five years from the beginning of the performance of such activities. After that, the profit tax shall be paid in the amount of 25% of the statutory tax rate.

## Withholding tax

Taxpayers who pay fees for the use of intellectual property rights (the right to reproduction, patents, licenses, copyrights, designs or models, manufacturing procedures, production formulas, blueprints, plans, industrial or scientific experience, and such other rights), or fees for market research services, tax consulting services, legal, auditing or such other services, dividends, shares in profit, or interest to foreign legal entities, natural persons excluded, shall, when making the payment, calculate and withhold tax at a rate of 15%.

Tax is not withheld from interest payments that are as follows.

- For sales made on credit for equipment used by the taxpayer in the ordinary course of business.
- For the sale of goods on credit sale to the taxpayer.
- On any loan granted by a foreign bank.

## Tax administration

All profit tax taxpayers are obliged to submit an annual profit tax return to the Tax Authorities no later than four months after the end of the tax period for which profit tax is assessed. Every taxpayer is required to make monthly profit tax installments (on the last day of each month) on the basis of the previous year's tax return. In the first year of operation, the installment payments are assessed on the basis of the entity's income in the first three months of operation.

Profit tax is assessed at the end of the calendar year, and the assessed amount, less any installments made, is payable by April 30 of the following year. If a domestic taxpayer has paid tax abroad on profit derived abroad, the tax paid will be included in its profit tax, up to the amount of tax paid abroad where no double tax treaty exists with the country in question.

The Ministry of Finance administers taxation matters through the Tax Administration and the Financial Police. These organizations have responsibilities and powers defined by law.

# Croatia

## *CORPORATION TAX CALCULATION*

| | | |
|---|---:|---:|
| Income as defined by the law | | HRK 1,400,000.00 |
| Expenditures as defined by the law | | 1,200,000.00 |
| Taxable base increase according to the law | 135,000.00 | |
| Taxable base decrease according to the law | 25,000.00 | |
| Loss carried forward | 110,000.00 | |
| Tax relief | 0.00 | |
| Taxable base | | 200,000.00 |
| Tax at 20% | | 40,000.00 |
| Taxes paid abroad | | 15,000.00 |
| Tax payable | HRK | 25,000.00 |

Note:

Exchange rate of the kuna at March 3, 2003: US$1 = HRK7.0934.

## PwC contact

For additional information on taxation in Cyprus, contact:

Panikos N. Tsiailis
PricewaterhouseCoopers Cyprus
Julia House
3 Themistoclis Dervis Streeta
CY-1066 Nicosia, Cyprus
Telephone: (357) (22) 555000
Fax: (357) (22) 555001
Mail address: P.O. Box 21612
            CY-1591 Nicosia, Cyprus
e-mail: panikos.n.tsiailis@cy.pwc.com

## Significant developments

As from January 1, 2003, a new tax regime applies in Cyprus. The new legislation aims to conform with European Union law and the EU Code of Conduct, and abide by Cyprus' commitment to the Organization for Economic Cooperation and Development (OECD) to eliminate harmful tax practices.

With the new legislation, Cyprus maintains and enhances its competitiveness as an international financial center. It remains a perfect location for investments to and from Russia and Central and Eastern Europe. At the same time, ultimately having the lowest tax regime in the EU, it becomes a stepping stone for investments to and from the European Union.

The new tax legislation includes some very beneficial tax provisions, such as the following.

- Exemption from tax on any gains arising from disposal of securities.
- Transitional period up to December 31, 2005 for companies existing as at December 31, 2001 (under conditions).
- No withholding taxes on any payments made out of Cyprus to nonresidents.
- Exemption from tax on dividends and profits from permanent establishments abroad (with certain limitations).
- Introduction of group relief.
- No time limitation on carryforward of losses.
- Tax exemption of profits arising from mergers, acquisitions, reorganizations.

## Taxes on corporate income

*Corporation tax*/The corporate tax rate is 10% on taxable income. For years 2003 and 2004 only, an additional tax of 5% is imposed on taxable profits over C£1 million.

*International business entities*/International business entities that derive their income from sources outside Cyprus, and which had income from activities as at December 31, 2001 (or expected to have income which was not earned by December 31, 2001 due to the nature of its activities) may opt to be taxed at the rate of 4.25% until December 31, 2005. In such a case, certain tax exemptions and other beneficial provisions of the new legislation will not be available, such as group relief, tax free reorganizations and tax exemption of gains on disposals of shares, of profits from permanent establishments abroad and of dividends.

# Cyprus

*Life insurance companies*/When the tax payable on profits arising from life insurance business does not exceed 1.5% of the gross amount of premiums, the difference is paid in addition to corporation tax.

*International Collective Investment Schemes*/The International Collective Investment Schemes (ICIS) Law 1999 provides the required legal framework for the registration, regulation of operations, and supervision of ICISs.

An ICIS can take the following legal forms.

1. International fixed capital company.
2. International variable capital company.
3. International unit trust scheme.
4. International investment limited partnership.

The sole object of an ICIS is the collective investment of funds of the unit holders.

ICISs are exempt from tax on profits arising on disposal of securities. Dividend income is also exempt (with minor limitations) whereas interest income is taxed at the rate of 10%.

ICISs set up in Cyprus can utilize the double taxation treaty network of Cyprus.

## Corporate residence

All companies managed and controlled in Cyprus are treated as resident in Cyprus. As from 2003, incorporation in Cyprus is not a criterion for tax residence.

## Other taxes

*Defense contribution*/A contribution for the defense of the Republic is imposed on certain types of income. Dividends are generally exempt from defense contribution (subject to certain rarely applicable limitations mentioned below). Interest income which is 50% exempt from income tax is subject to defense contribution at the rate of 10%. Rental income (reduced by 25%) is subject to defense contribution at the rate of 3%.

*Value-added tax*/The standard rate of VAT is 15%. Exports, food, medicines, and certain other essential goods and services are zero-rated. Some supplies are exempt, the main categories being rents, insurance, financial services, education, and health and welfare.

International business entities are no longer outside the scope of VAT. However, the activities of most international business companies would fall outside the scope of VAT and thus there is no obligation for registration.

*Social security*/Employed persons are compulsorily insured under a state-administered Social Insurance Fund. Contributions to this are borne by both employer and employee.

The employer's contributions are made as a percentage of earnings to the following funds.

|  | % |
|---|---|
| Social Insurance Fund | 6.3 |
| Redundancy Fund | 1.2 |
| Training Development Fund | 0.5 |
| Social Cohesion Fund | 2.0 |
|  | 10.0 |

With the exception of the Social Cohesion Fund, the maximum amount of monthly earnings on which the contributions are made is C£1,911. These contributions are an allowable deduction for corporation tax purposes.

International business entities are exempt from contributing to any of the above-mentioned funds in respect of their expatriate employees.

*Immovable property tax*/Immovable property is subject to property tax, which is levied on the market value of the property as at January 1, 1980, and is payable by the end of September each year. The tax rates vary from 0 per thousand to 3.5 per thousand on values of up to C£500,000, and 4 per thousand on any excess. This tax is an allowable deduction for corporation tax purposes.

## Branch income

The rate of tax on branch profits is the same as on corporate profits. No further tax is withheld on a transfer of profits to a foreign head office.

## Income determination

*Inventory valuation*/Inventories are generally stated at the lower of cost and net realizable value. LIFO is not permitted for taxation purposes. FIFO is permitted. Conformity between book and tax reporting is not required.

*Capital gains*/Capital gains tax is imposed at the rate of 20% on gains arising from the disposal of immovable property situated in Cyprus, and of shares in companies (other than companies whose shares are listed in any recognized stock exchange) that own immovable property. Liability is confined to gains accruing since January 1, 1980. The costs that are deducted from gross proceeds on the disposal of immovable property are its market value at January 1, 1980, or the costs of acquisition and improvements of the property, if made after January 1, 1980, as adjusted for inflation up to the date of disposal on the basis of the consumer price index in Cyprus.

*Intercompany dividends*/All dividends are excluded from the taxable income of the recipient company.

*Foreign income*/Resident corporations are subject to tax on their worldwide income. However, foreign-branch income, as well as dividend income from abroad, is exempt from taxation in Cyprus (with some minor limitations). Where foreign income is taxed in Cyprus, double taxation is avoided either through unilateral relief by giving credit for foreign taxation or by treaty relief. This credit cannot exceed the Cyprus income tax imposed on the same income.

*Stock dividends*/A Cyprus corporation can distribute tax free a dividend of common stock (bonus shares) proportionately to all common stock shareholders

*Other significant items*/None.

## Deductions

*Depreciation and depletion*/Depreciation is computed on a straight-line basis at rates that vary, depending on the life and type of asset. Tax depreciation is not required to conform to book depreciation. Gains on the sale of depreciated property are taxable as ordinary income to the extent of depreciation allowed.

Depletion is computed on the cost of natural resources properties, based mainly on the output from the source during the year.

# Cyprus

*Net operating losses*/Tax losses can be carried forward and set off against taxable profits of future years. Carrybacks are not permitted.

*Payments to foreign affiliates*/A Cyprus corporation can claim a deduction for royalties and interest charges paid to foreign affiliates, and a reasonable amount of head office expenses of an overseas company, provided such expenditures can be justified as having been incurred in the production of the income. In the case of insurance companies, the amount of head office expenses should not exceed 3% of the net premiums in Cyprus for general insurance business, and 2% for life insurance business.

*Taxes*/Taxes that are deducted in computing profits for corporation tax purposes include VAT not recovered, the employer's share of contributions to the Social Insurance Fund, and immovable property tax.

*Other significant items*/Charitable donations or contributions made for educational, cultural, or other charitable purposes to the Republic, or to approved charitable institutions, are wholly deductible, provided that these expenses are supported with relevant vouchers. Voluntary contributions to the Special Fund for the Relief of Displaced Persons, which is under the control of the Accountant General, are tax deductible without limit.

Any expenditure on scientific research of a capital nature for which no capital allowance is granted is allowed as a deduction from taxable income, and spread equally over the year in which it has been incurred and the five subsequent years. Scientific expenditure of a revenue nature is deducted in the year incurred.

Any expenditure incurred on the acquisition of patents and patent rights is allowed as a deduction from taxable income, and spread equally over the life of the patents or patent rights.

## Group taxation

Group relief provisions allow, subject to certain conditions, companies of the same group to transfer losses from the loss making companies to profitable companies. A group includes only Cypriot resident companies with a 75% direct or indirect holding relationship.

## Tax incentives

The following tax incentives exist.

1. Dividends earned from foreign investments are exempt from income tax in Cyprus. Dividend income is also exempt from defense contribution provided the company receiving the dividend owns at least 1% of the company paying the dividend. This exemption does not apply if both of the following conditions are met.
   a. More than 50% of the paying company's activities result directly or indirectly in investment income.
   b. The foreign tax is significantly lower than the tax rate payable in Cyprus.
2. Profits from permanent establishments abroad are exempt from income tax. This exemption does not apply if both of the following conditions are met.
   a. More than 50% of the foreign permanent establishment's activities result directly or indirectly in investment income.

    b. The foreign tax on the income of the foreign permanent establishment is significantly lower than the tax rate payable in Cyprus.

3. For ship-owning companies, the profits derived by the owner of a Cyprus ship from its operation, as well as the salaries and benefits of the captain, the officers, and the crew, are fully exempt from corporation and income tax. In addition, there is no tax on dividends paid by a ship-owning company, no estate tax on the inheritance of shares, and no capital gains tax on the sale or transfer of a ship or shares in a ship. Local or international ship management and crew management businesses have an option to be taxed either at the rate of 4.25% or at rates equal to 25% of the rates used to calculate tonnage tax of vessels under management that are registered outside Cyprus. This treatment applies until 2020.

## Reorganizations

Transfers of assets and liabilities between companies can be effected without tax consequences within the framework of a reorganization. Reorganizations include mergers, demergers, transfers of activities, and exchanges of shares.

## Withholding taxes

Cyprus does not impose any withholding tax on dividends, interest, and royalties paid by Cyprus companies. Otherwise, withholding tax is imposed as follows.

### Paid from Cyprus

|  | Dividends (1) | Interest | Royalties |
|---|---|---|---|
|  | % | % | % |
| Nontreaty countries | Nil | Nil | Nil |
| Treaty countries: |  |  |  |
| Austria | 10 | Nil | Nil |
| Belarus | 5 (2) | 5 | 5 |
| Belgium | 10 (3) | 10 (4, 5) | Nil |
| Bulgaria | 5 (6) | 7 (4) | 10 |
| Canada | 15 | 15 (7) | 10 (8) |
| China, P.R. | 10 | 10 | 10 |
| Czech Republic | 10 | 10 (4) | 5 (9) |
| Denmark | 10 (3) | 10 (4) | Nil |
| Egypt | 15 | 15 | 10 |
| France | 10 (10) | 10 (11) | Nil (12) |
| Germany | 10 (3) | 10 (4) | Nil (12) |
| Greece | 25 | 10 | Nil (13) |
| Hungary | Nil | 10 (4) | Nil |
| India | 10 (10) | 10 (11) | 10 (14) |
| Ireland, Rep. of | Nil | Nil | Nil (13) |
| Italy | Nil | 10 | Nil |
| Kuwait | 10 | 10 (4) | 5 (9) |
| Malta | 15 | 10 | 10 |
| Mauritius | Nil | Nil | Nil |
| Norway | Nil | Nil | Nil |
| Poland | 10 | 10 (4) | 5 |
| Romania | 10 | 10 (4) | 5 (9) |
| Russia | 5 (15) | Nil | Nil |

# Cyprus

| | Dividends (1) | Interest | Royalties |
|---|---|---|---|
| | % | % | % |
| Singapore.......................................... | Nil | 10 (4, 16) | 10 |
| Slovak Republic............................... | 10 | 10 (4) | 5 (9) |
| South Africa .................................... | Nil | Nil | Nil |
| Sweden ............................................ | 5 (3) | 10 (4) | Nil |
| Syria................................................. | Nil (3) | 10 | 10 |
| Thailand .......................................... | 10 | 15 (17) | 5 (18) |
| U.S.S.R. (former) (19)...................... | Nil | Nil | Nil |
| United Kingdom................................ | Nil | 10 | Nil (12) |
| United States .................................. | Nil | 10 (11) | Nil |
| Yugoslavia (former) ........................ | 10 | 10 | 10 |

## Received in Cyprus

| | Dividends | Interest | Royalties |
|---|---|---|---|
| Treaty countries: | % | % | % |
| Austria ............................................ | 10 | Nil | Nil |
| Belarus ........................................... | 5 (2) | 5 | 5 |
| Belgium............................................ | 10 (3) | 10 (4, 5) | Nil |
| Bulgaria ........................................... | 5 (6) | 7 (4, 20) | 10 (20) |
| Canada............................................ | 15 | 15 (7) | 10 (8) |
| China, P.R........................................ | 10 | 10 | 10 |
| Czech Republic................................ | 10 | 10 (4) | 5 (9) |
| Denmark........................................... | 10 (3) | 10 (4) | Nil |
| Egypt ............................................... | 15 | 15 | 10 |
| France ............................................. | 10 (10) | 10 (11) | Nil (12) |
| Germany........................................... | 10 (3) | 10 (4) | Nil (12) |
| Greece............................................. | 25 (21) | 10 | Nil (13) |
| Hungary........................................... | 5 (3) | 10 (4) | Nil |
| India................................................. | 10 (10) | 10 (11) | 15 (22) |
| Ireland, Rep. of .............................. | Nil | Nil | Nil (13) |
| Italy................................................. | 15 | 10 | Nil |
| Kuwait.............................................. | 10 | 10 (4) | 5 (9) |
| Malta................................................ | Nil | 10 | 10 |
| Mauritius.......................................... | Nil | Nil | Nil |
| Norway ............................................ | Nil (23) | Nil | Nil |
| Poland ............................................. | 10 | 10 (4) | 5 |
| Romania .......................................... | 10 | 10 (4) | 5 (9) |
| Russia ............................................. | 5 (15) | Nil | Nil |
| Singapore ........................................ | Nil | 10 (4, 16) | 10 |
| Slovak Republic ............................... | 10 | 10 (4) | 5 (9) |
| South Africa..................................... | Nil | Nil | Nil |
| Sweden............................................ | 5 (3) | 10 (4) | Nil |
| Syria ................................................ | Nil (3) | 10 (7) | 10 |
| Thailand........................................... | 10 | 15 (17) | 5 (18) |
| U.S.S.R. (former) ............................ | Nil | Nil | Nil |
| United Kingdom ............................... | 15 (24) | 10 | Nil (12) |
| United States .................................. | 5 (10) | 10 (11) | Nil |
| Yugoslavia (former)......................... | 10 | 10 | 10 |

The numbers in parentheses refer to the following numbered Notes.

Notes:

1. Under Cyprus legislation, there is no withholding tax on dividends paid by a Cyprus company to nonresidents of Cyprus.
2. If investment is less than €200,000, dividends are subject to 15% withholding tax, which is reduced to 10% if the recipient company controls 25% or more of the paying company.
3. A rate of 15% if received by a company controlling less than 25% of the voting power.
4. Nil if paid to the government of the other state.
5. No withholding tax is imposed for interest on deposits with banking institutions.
6. This rate applies to companies holding directly at least 25% or the share capital of the company paying the dividend. In all other cases, the withholding tax is 10%.
7. Nil if paid to a government or for export guarantee.
8. Nil on literary, dramatic, musical, or artistic work.
9. This rate applies for patents; trademarks; designs or models; plans; secret formulas or processes; any industrial, commercial, or scientific equipment; or information concerning industrial, commercial, or scientific experience.
10. A rate of 15% if received by a company controlling less than 10% of the voting power.
11. Nil if paid to a government, bank, or financial institution.
12. A rate of 5% on film and TV royalties.
13. A rate of 5% on film royalties.
14. Treaty rate 15%; therefore, restricted to Cyprus legislation rate.
15. A rate of 10% if dividend paid by a company in which the beneficial owner has invested less than US$100,000.
16. A rate of 7% if paid to a bank or financial institution.
17. A rate of 10% on interest received by a financial institution or when it relates to sale on credit of any industrial, commercial, or scientific equipment or of merchandise.
18. This rate applies for any copyright of literary, dramatic, musical, artistic, or scientific work. A 10% rate applies for industrial, commercial, or scientific work. A 10% rate applies for industrial, commercial, or scientific equipment. A 15% rate applies for patents, trademarks, designs or models, plans, secret formulas, or processes.
19. Armenia, Kyrgyzstan, Moldova, Tajikistan, Turkmenistan, and Ukraine apply the USSR/Cyprus treaty.
20. This rate does not apply if the payment is made to a Cyprus international business entity by a resident of Bulgaria owning at least 25% of the share capital of the Cyprus entity.
21. The treaty provides for withholding taxes on dividends, but Greece does not impose any withholding tax in accordance with its own legislation.
22. A rate of 10% for payments of a technical, managerial, or consulting nature.
23. A rate of 5% if received by a company controlling less than 50% of the voting power.

24. This rate applies to individual shareholders, regardless of their percentage of shareholding. Companies controlling less than 10% of the voting shares are also entitled to this rate.

## Tax administration

**Returns/**Tax returns must be filed on a calendar-year basis. Business organizations are required to prepare accounts and pay their tax on a self-assessment basis on or before August 1 of the year that follows the year of assessment.

**Payment of tax/**Corporate entities must pay provisional tax on the current year's income in three equal installments on August 1, September 30, and December 31. A final payment must be made on or before August 1 of the following year on a self-assessment basis to bring the total installment payments of the tax to the total actually due according to the tax return.

## CORPORATION TAX CALCULATION

Calendar year 2004

| | | |
|---|---:|---:|
| Net profit before taxation........................................................... | | C£ 1,000,000 |
| Add: | | |
| Depreciation charged in the accounts.................................... | 250,000 | |
| Increase during year in general provision for doubtful debts (only the amount specifically required would be allowed)............................................. | 50,000 | |
| Profit on sale of equipment (balancing addition per tax computation)........................................................ | 120,000 | 420,000 |
| | | 1,420,000 |
| Deduct: | | |
| Profit on sale of investments................................................ | 10,000 | |
| Profit on sale of equipment per books ............................... | 100,000 | |
| Capital (depreciation) allowance.......................................... | 300,000 | 410,000 |
| Profits chargeable to corporation tax....................................... | | C£ 1,010,000 |
| Corporation tax thereon: | | |
| 1,000,000 at 10%.................................................................. | | C£ 100,000 |
| 10,000 at 15%...................................................................... | | 1,500 |
| | | C£ 101,500 |

Note:

Exchange rate of the Cyprus pound at January 1, 2004: US$1 = C£0.483.

## PwC contacts

For additional information on taxation in the Czech Republic, contact:

Zuzana Vanecková
Antoni Turczynowicz
Lorenz Bernhardt
Stephen Booth
PricewaterhouseCoopers
Katerinská 40
120 00 Prague 2
Czech Republic
Telephone: (420) 251 151 111
Fax: (420) 251 156 111
e-mail: zuzana.vaneckova@cz.pwc.com
      antoni.turczynowicz@cz.pwc.com
      lorenz.bernhardt@cz.pwc.com
      stephen.booth@cz.pwc.com

## General note

Tax legislation applicable in the Czech Republic (CR) generally has features that can be expected from a modern tax system. Recently, the Czech tax legislation has undergone considerable amendment, especially with respect to the EU harmonization process.

## Significant developments

A major amendment to the Income Tax Act came into effect from January 1, 2004, with certain other provisions expected to come into effect on May 1, 2004, the day of the CR's accession in the EU. The amendment is the result of the harmonization of Czech law with EU regulations and also part of the reform of public finances.

The amendment implements four EU tax directives into Czech tax legislation, all of which were prerequisites for accession: the parent/subsidiary directive, the merger directive, the savings directive, and the royalties/interest directive.

Provisions regarding public finance reform include the tax treatment of the sale of a business; rules governing the carry forward of tax losses; asset depreciation and related issues; changes to thin capitalization rules; several changes to the tax treatment of financial transactions; changes to the determination of the tax base; stricter rules regarding the tax treatment of receivables and changes related to the recent amendment of the Accounting Act.

## Taxes on corporate income

The rate of corporate income tax for 2004 and fiscal years which began in 2003 is 28%. Corporate income tax applies to the profits of all companies, including branches of foreign companies. Corporate partners in general partnerships and corporate general partners in a limited partnership are subject to corporate income tax on their share of the profits in the partnership.

## Corporate residence

A company is a resident in the Czech Republic if it is registered or has its place of management in the Czech Republic.

# Czech Republic

## Other taxes

The following taxes may apply in addition to the corporate income tax.

*Value-added tax*/VAT is charged at 22% (19% from May 1, 2004) on the supply of goods and most services within the Czech Republic. Some services and goods are taxed at a rate of 5%. Exports are generally exempt with credit. Some supplies are exempt without credit. The main categories are the lease of real estate (with some exceptions), financial and insurance services, radio and TV broadcasting, education, health and welfare. As of May 1, 2004, the Czech Republic will become part of the EU Single market. A number of new rules will be introduced as of that date, including reverse charge VAT.

*Road tax*/This tax is payable on vehicles used for commercial purposes. Foreign vehicles cease to be liable for road tax with effect from May 1, 2004. Rates depend on engine capacity and vehicle size, and range from CZK 1,200 to CZK 4,200 per year for passenger vehicles and from CZK 1,800 to CZK 50,400 for commercial vehicles.

*Real estate tax*/This tax is payable by the owner of land or buildings. It is based on area, location and usage.

*Transfer taxes*/Real estate transfer tax is levied on the transferor of real estate at a rate of 3% on the greater of the transaction price or the officially appraised value. Inheritance and gift taxes are levied to the recipient of property transferred by inheritance or gift. The inheritance tax rates range from 0.5% to 20%, and the gift tax rates range from 1% to 40% of the value of the transferred property.

*Excise tax*/Excise tax is charged on the production or import of tobacco products, wines, spirits, beer, and mineral oils

## Branch income

A foreign company can trade through a Czech branch. The basis of taxation is the same as for corporations. For nontrading branches it may be possible to negotiate the basis on which profits are attributed to the branch with the tax authorities. A branch is liable for tax on its attributable profits at the standard corporate rate of 28% for 2004.

## Income determination

*Inventory valuation*/Stock (i.e., inventory) is valued at the purchase price or own cost incurred, using the FIFO or weighted-average mean methods of valuation. LIFO is not acceptable. Currently, stock provisions are generally not deductible.

*Capital gains*/There is no special capital gains tax law. Capital gains are taxable under the Income Tax Law at the same rate applicable to ordinary income.

Capital losses on the sale of fixed assets are, with some exceptions, tax deductible.

Capital losses on the sale of investment instruments are tax deductible with the exception of promissory notes, nonhedging derivates and certain interests and share stakes in a joint stock company. A special three-year carryforward of losses exists for nonhedging derivates.

***Stock dividends*/**A stock dividend paid by a Czech company will be liable for flat withholding tax at 15% and will not be included in the general tax base of the recipient (if also a Czech company). The applicable withholding tax may be reduced under the terms of the relevant double taxation treaty with the Czech Republic.

***Intercompany dividends*/**No withholding tax will be applicable at the source from dividends received from Czech subsidiaries, if the conditions for the EU parent/subsidiary directive application are fulfilled. The conditions are holding of at least 25% in the subsidiary for at least two years, legal form of joint stock company or limited liability company on the Czech side and appropriate legal form listed in the Directive on the foreign side. Dividends are in such case exempt from taxation also on the side of the recipient. If the conditions for exemption are not fulfilled, 15% Czech withholding tax is applicable for domestic transaction, and lower rates according to international tax treaties are applicable in cross-border transactions. The relief in the form of deduction of half the withholding tax against the corporate income tax liability of the payer has been abolished with effect from January 1, 2004.

***Foreign income*/**Companies resident in the Czech Republic are taxed on their worldwide income. A Czech corporation is taxed on foreign branch income when earned, and on foreign dividends when received. The foreign dividends are tax-exempt if the transaction fulfills conditions for the application of the EU parent/subsidiary directive. If the foreign dividends are not exempt, they are taxed at a flat 15% tax rate in a separate tax base. No distinction is made in the Czech Republic between income received from treaty or nontreaty countries, unless a respective treaty provides otherwise. Tax paid on dividends in a nontreaty country is a tax-deductible expense. Credit relief is available for foreign tax paid only under double taxation treaties, but excess foreign tax credits are tax-deductible in the following tax year.

No current legislation exists to tax the undistributed income of foreign subsidiaries.

***Exchange gains and losses*/**All exchange gains and losses, including calculations at the year end, will be booked as realized and will be tax deductible/taxable, except for exchange gains and losses from securities and interests that are not revaluated to fair value, or the revaluation to fair value is recorded to equity. In these cases, the exchange gains and losses are booked to equity until disposal of the respective assets.

***Reserves and provisions*/**Tax-deductible reserves can be created for repairs of tangible fixed assets whose statutory depreciation period is six years or longer (buildings). The reserve has to be created in at least two tax periods. Provisions for bad debts can be created against receivables fulfilling certain conditions. These can be created in the amount of 20% of the value of receivables that are more than six months overdue. If a judicial or arbitration proceeding is commenced to claim the unpaid receivable, the provision can reach 100% of the receivable value after 36 months have passed, since the receivable reached maturity. Bankruptcy or settlement proceedings initiated against the debtor entitle the creditor to create 100% tax-deductible provisions against the receivables from the debtor, provided that the receivables were claimed in the proceedings in time. There are special regimes for creation of loan provisions and reserves for banks and insurance companies.

# Czech Republic

***Statutory reserve fund***/A joint stock company must transfer at least 5% of its net profits, after-tax and other statutory post-tax disbursements to a nondistributable reserve fund annually until the value of the fund reaches at least 20% of the equity of the company. A limited liability company must transfer at least 5% of its net profits to a nondistributable reserve fund each year until the value of the fund reaches at least 10% of the equity. Special rules apply for the first years of existence and profit of a company.

The above-stated rates reflect the minimum legal limits, and can be increased by the memorandum of association or articles of association.

A branch of a foreign company is not required to set up a reserve fund.

## Deductions

***Depreciation***/Tax depreciation is calculated on an asset-by-asset basis on a straight-line or accelerated basis at statutory rates. In both cases, depreciation in the first year is lower than for subsequent years. The company may choose which method to apply to a new asset, but once made, the choice cannot be altered. All assets are classified into six groups, which determine the number of years over which the asset will be written off, as follows.

| Group and types of assets | Write-off period |
|---|---|
| | (Years) |
| 1—Cars, vans, hand tools, computers | 4 |
| 2—Fixtures and fittings, certain mobile machinery | 6 |
| 3—Plant and machinery, goodwill | 12 |
| 4—Motors, fixed constructions other than buildings | 20 |
| 5—Buildings | 30 |
| 6—Certain buildings used for administrative purposes | 50 |

Straight-line depreciation rates and a formula and coefficients for calculating accelerated depreciation are specified in the legislation.

Low value fixed assets (input price less than CZK 40,000) cannot be written of immediately but have to be depreciated over their lifespan.

Intangible assets purchased in 2004 (input price more than CZK 60,000) and later shall be depreciated for tax purposes over specified statutory periods (48 months to 72 months). Intangible assets acquired before this date are depreciated according to tax depreciation rules applicable at that time.

An entity may interrupt depreciation or use lower rates of straight-line depreciation charges.

Assets that are the subject of a financial lease may be written off by the lessor over the term of the lease if certain conditions relating to minimum term and residual value are met.

An entity is permitted an additional deduction from its tax base of 10% (or 15% in certain cases) of the initial price of certain new tangible assets, provided the entity is the first owner or first lessee of the asset. There are some limitations regarding the availability of these deductions. This deduction is not available for passenger cars.

Accounting depreciation must be determined by taking into account the term of usage of the fixed asset, the relation of its usage to revenues, and so on. The difference between accounting and tax depreciation is reflected in the tax return.

*Travel expenses and meal allowances*/Payments for travel expenses and meal allowances that are made to employees in excess of statutory limits are not tax deductible.

*Net operating losses*/Losses incurred in a tax year can be carried forward as relief against taxable profits incurred in the next five tax years (carryforward for the next seven years will be used for the last time for tax loss as assessed in 2003). In addition, the following rules were introduced in 2004.

The tax loss expires if a substantial change of ownership in persons directly participating in the capital or control of the company occurs compared to the period in which the tax loss was generated. The change is understood to be substantial if more than 25% of the registered capital or voting rights are transferred to a different legal entity or individual.

The restriction does not apply if the company can prove to the tax authorities that at least 80% of the current ordinary revenues in the year in which the tax losses could be utilized are generated from the same activity as the activity performed in the taxable period when the respective tax loss was generated. Extraordinary revenues should not be taken into account when carrying out this test.

If the company is in doubt as to whether the restrictions on offsetting the tax losses brought forward should apply, it is entitled to submit a written request to the Czech tax authorities for a binding ruling.

The above restriction (the same business test) applies to all tax losses carried forward, regardless of their date of recognition.

Any capital loss realized on the sale of securities that was treated as tax nondeductible in the 1999, 2000, or 2001 fiscal years can be used to reduce the tax base of the taxpayer in 2002 or the following years, but no later than in the third year following the year in which the capital loss was realized.

*Payments to foreign affiliates*/Generally, deductions can be claimed for royalties and for management service and interest charges paid to foreign affiliates, provided such amounts do not exceed what would be paid to unrelated entities. Interest deductions will be limited where the credits and loans are provided by a related entity and the recipient has a debt/equity ratio greater than 4:1 (6:1 in the case of banks and insurance companies).

*Taxes*/Road tax, real estate tax, and most other taxes, with the exception of gift and inheritance taxes, are deductible, as are social security contributions paid by an employer on behalf of employees. If an employer bears income tax on behalf of employees, this is not deductible for corporate income tax purposes.

*Other deductions*/Fees paid to directors and members of other statutory bodies of companies for their services are not deductible. Certain charitable donations are deductible. The minimum deductible donation is CZK 2,000, and the maximum is 5% of the tax base.

## Group taxation

There is currently no system of group taxation in the Czech Republic, and each company in a group is taxed individually.

# Czech Republic

## Tax incentives

***High-tech and manufacturing investment incentives***/The Czech Republic offers
a comprehensive package of incentives for large-scale investment projects.
Incentives were first offered in 1998, and since May 2000 they have been codified
under the Investment Incentives Act. Available incentives include the following.

1. Corporate income tax relief.
2. Financial support for job creation.
3. Financial support for training/re-training.
4. Site support and industrial zones.
5. Exemptions from customs, import duties and VAT (under separate legislation
   related to investment incentives.

Only Czech entities (including subsidiaries of foreign companies) are eligible
for these incentives. New manufacturing facilities must be constructed or existing
facilities expanded. There must be at least CZK 200 million (approximately
US$7.6 million) of investment into assets. A minimum CZK 100 million must be
covered by the recipient's own equity. In regions with high unemployment, the
minimum investment is reduced to CZK 100 million (approximately US$3.5 million),
of which CZK 50 million must come from the recipient's own equity. The
minimum investment must be paid within three years. Investment into machinery
must account for at least 40% of the total investment. The project must be
environmentally friendly.

***Investment incentives in strategic services and technology centers***/On
February 20, 2004 the government approved a new program to support strategic
services and technology centers. This program is focused primarily on investments
in human capital, as well as the training or retraining of skilled staff. Certain
investments in tangible fixed assets are still required.

Strategic services projects require a minimum investment of CZK 30 million over
three years, of which at least CZK 15 million must come from the investor's own
equity. The project must create at least 50 new jobs. Technology centers require
a minimum investment of CZK 15 million over three years, of which at least
CZK 7.5 million must come from the investor's own equity. The project must create
at least 15 new jobs.

Investors who are granted incentives can claim a business subsidy of up to 50% of
eligible business costs for a maximum of ten years. Subsidies to cover the costs of
training and re-training are available for a maximum of three years. Subsidies are
granted based on the location, size, and nature of the project. Investors who qualify
as small and medium enterprises can receive increased levels of subsidies by up
to 10% to 20%.

## Withholding taxes

Czech corporations are required to withhold tax on payments of dividends, interest,
and royalties as follows.

| Recipient | Dividends (1) | Interest (2) | Royalties (3) |
|---|---|---|---|
| | % | % | % |
| Resident corporations ........................ | 0/15 | 0/15 | 0 |
| Resident individuals ........................... | 15 | 15 | 0 |
| Non-resident corporations, individuals: | | | |
| Nontreaty: | | | |
|    Corporations................................. | 0/15 | 0/15 | 1/25 (4) |
|    Individuals .................................... | 15 | 15 | 1/25 (4) |
| Treaty: | | | |
|    Albania ......................................... | 5/15 | 0/5 | 10 |
|    Australia ....................................... | 5/15 | 10 | 10 |
|    Austria ......................................... | 10 | 0 | 0/5 |
|    Belarus......................................... | 10 | 0/5 | 10 |
|    Belgium ........................................ | 5/15 | 10 | 0/5/10 |
|    Brazil ........................................... | 15 | 10/15 | 15/25 |
|    Bulgaria........................................ | 10 | 0/10 | 10 |
|    Canada......................................... | 5/15 | 0/10 | 10 |
|    China, P.R. ................................... | 10 | 0/10 | 10 |
|    Croatia ......................................... | 5 | 0 | 10 |
|    Cyprus.......................................... | 10 | 0/10 | 0/5 |
|    Denmark........................................ | 15 | 0 | 0/5 |
|    Egypt............................................ | 5/15 | 0/15 | 15 |
|    Estonia ......................................... | 5/15 | 0/10 | 10 |
|    Finland ......................................... | 5/15 | 0 | 0/1/5/10 |
|    France .......................................... | 10 | 0 | 0/5 |
|    Germany ....................................... | 5/15 | 0 | 5 |
|    Greece .......................................... | Local rates | 0/10 | 0/10 |
|    Hungary ........................................ | 5/15 | 0 | 10 |
|    Iceland ......................................... | 5/15 | 0 | 10 |
|    India ............................................ | 10 | 0/10 | 10 |
|    Indonesia...................................... | 10/15 | 0/12.5 | 12.5 |
|    Ireland ......................................... | 5/15 | 0 | 10 |
|    Israel ........................................... | 5/15 | 0/10 | 5 |
|    Italy ............................................. | 15 | 0 | 0/5 |
|    Japan ........................................... | 10/15 | 0/10 | 0/10 |
|    Kazakhstan ................................... | 10 | 0/10 | 10 |
|    Korea, Rep. of............................... | 5/10 | 0/10 | 0/10 |
|    Latvia .......................................... | 5/15 | 0/10 | 10 |
|    Lebanon ....................................... | 5 | 0 | 5/10 |
|    Lithuania ...................................... | 5/15 | 0/10 | 10 |
|    Luxembourg ................................. | 5/15 | 0 | 0/10 |
|    Macedonia..................................... | 5/15 | 0 | 10 |
|    Malaysia ....................................... | 0/10 | 0/12 | 12 |
|    Malta ........................................... | 5 | 0 | 5 |
|    Mexico.......................................... | 10 | 0/10 | 10 |
|    Moldova........................................ | 5/15 | 5 | 10 |
|    Mongolia....................................... | 10 | 0/10 | 10 |
|    Netherlands................................... | 0/10 | 0 | 5 |
|    Nigeria.......................................... | 12.5/15 | 0/15 | 15 |
|    Norway ......................................... | 5/15 | 0 | 0/5 |
|    Philippines..................................... | 10/15 | 0/10 | 10/15 |

# Czech Republic

| Recipient | Dividends (1) | Interest (2) | Royalties (3) |
|-----------|:---:|:---:|:---:|
| | % | % | % |
| Poland | 5/10 | 0/10 | 5 |
| Portugal | 10/15 | 0/10 | 10 |
| Romania | 10 | 0/7 | 10 |
| Russia | 10 | 0 | 10 |
| Singapore | 5 | 0 | 10 |
| Slovak Republic | 5/15 | 0 | 0/5 |
| Slovenia | 5/15 | 0/5 | 10 |
| South Africa | 5/15 | 0 | 10 |
| Spain | 5/15 | 0 | 0/5 |
| Sri Lanka | 15 | 0/10 | 0/10 |
| Sweden | 0/10 | 0 | 0/5 |
| Switzerland | 5/15 | 0 | 10 |
| Thailand | 10 | 0/10 | 5/10/15 |
| Tunisia | 10/15 | 0/12 | 5/15 |
| Turkey | 10 | 10 | 10 |
| Ukraine | 5/15 | 5 | 10 |
| United Arab Emirates | 0/5 | 0 | 10 |
| United Kingdom | 5/15 | 0 | 0/10 |
| United States | 5/15 | 0 | 0/10 |
| Uzbekistan | 10 | 0/5 | 10 |
| Venezuela | 5/10 | 0/10 | 12 |
| Vietnam | 10 | 0/10 | 10 |
| Yugoslavia (former) | 5/15 | 0 | 10 |

Notes:

1. The lower rate applies mostly to cultural royalties.
2. The lower rate applies to lease contracts under which the lessee has the right to purchase the leased asset at the end of the lease period, provided the lease is of a certain minimum duration.
3. The lower rate applies if the recipient is a company that owns at least a certain amount of the capital or a certain amount of the voting shares of the company paying the dividend directly (mostly 25%).
4. The lower rate applies mostly in situations when the interest is received by the government or a state-owned institution or is paid by the government.

Arrangements regarding double taxation involving the former Soviet Republics, except the Baltic republics, Belarus, Kazakhstan, Moldova, Russia, Ukraine, and Uzbekistan, continue to be governed by the CMEA (COMECON) multilateral tax treaties for legal entities and physical persons. These treaties provide for a nil rate of withholding on dividends, interest, and royalties.

As a part of the Czech Republic's economic plan, it is working toward double taxation agreements with countries that are or will be its most important trading partners.

## Tax administration

*Returns*/A corporation can opt for a calendar year or an accounting year as its fiscal year. A combined tax and accounting return must be made by the end of the third month following the end of the fiscal year. This deadline may be extended if the return is prepared and submitted under a power of attorney by a registered tax adviser and the tax authorities have been so advised, or if the entity is required to have a Czech statutory audit. Any outstanding tax must be paid on the same date the tax return is filed.

**Payment of tax**/Corporate income tax must be paid quarterly or semi-annually in advance. Installments are based on the last known tax liability (for the preceding tax period) or, if the taxpayer is notified by the Financial Office, on the expected tax liability. Installment payments are not required if the last known tax liability did not exceed CZK 30,000. After the tax return is filed, the final tax liability is known, any outstanding tax is paid and new installment payments for the current year are calculated.

## CORPORATION TAX CALCULATION

Calendar year ending December 31, 2003
(Under legislation as of January 1, 2004)

| | | |
|---|---:|---:|
| Net profit before taxes shown by the accounts | | CZK 1,000,000 |
| Add: | | |
| Accounting depreciation | 300,000 | |
| Entertainment | 35,000 | |
| Excess travel expenses | 30,000 | 365,000 |
| | | 1,365,000 |
| Less: | | |
| Tax depreciation | 280,000 | |
| Czech-source dividends | 10,000 | 290,000 |
| Total taxable income | | CZK 1,075,000 |
| Tax payable—At 28% | | CZK 301,000 |
| Foreign tax credits | | (10,000) |
| Total tax payable | | CZK 291,000 |

Exchange rate of the CZK, Czech crown (koruna), as of January 1, 2004:
US$1 = CZK 25.7460.

# Denmark

## PwC contact

For additional information on taxation in Denmark, contact:

Henrik Meldgaard
PricewaterhouseCoopers
Strandvejen 44
DK-2900 Hellerup, Denmark
Telephone (45) 39 45 94 32
Fax: (45) 39 45 95 71
LN domain: henrik.meldgaard@dk.pwc.com or hme@pwc.dk

## Significant developments

Significant developments for the last year are incorporated in the text below.

## Taxes on corporate income

The company tax rate is 30%. Tax is payable on account during the income year. Underpaid tax is payable by November the following year with a surtax of 10%. Overpaid tax is refunded by November the following year with interest of 4.2%.

## Corporate residence

A corporation is resident in Denmark for tax purposes if it is incorporated in Denmark and registered in the Companies Register as having a Danish place of business. Further, non-Danish companies having their management and control in Denmark will be taxable in Denmark. In this connection, management and control is where the decisions concerning the daily company operations are taken.

A recent proposed change of law affects the tax residence of otherwise Danish resident companies that have "checked the box" under U.S. tax law. Generally, such a company is treated as a Danish branch of the U.S. parent company

## Other taxes

*Value-added tax*/The general VAT rate is 25% of the price charged (exclusive of VAT).

Stamp tax is payable on a few documents, for example, a deed of transfer of real estate (0.6% of the transfer sum). There is no stamp duty on transfer of shares.

*Hydrocarbon income tax*/This is a special corporate income tax levied over and above the ordinary corporation tax on profits from the exploration and extraction of oil and gas on the Danish continental shelf. Corporation tax is deductible in computing the hydrocarbon tax.

*Miscellaneous taxes*/Employer's tax (social security charges). The employer's contribution to ATP (*Arbejdsmarkedets till Aegspension,* old-age pension) charges is DKK 1,789 per annum.

Companies that are exempt from VAT pay an employer's tax, which is calculated on the total annual salary cost. The rate can be up to 9.13%, which is the rate for banks and other financial institutions, the most significant sector paying the employer's tax. This tax is deductible for tax purposes.

Other than those, employer's social security taxes are minimal.

A social security charge of 8% on salaries and wages is borne by employees. An additional 1% charge is made for a compulsory pension saving.

*Environmental taxes*/Danish companies must pay environmental taxes introduced to reduce industrial carbon-dioxide pollution. In general, companies can receive a refund for the costs of pollution control, and the individual company will benefit or be penalized accordingly. A company with a branch that requires heavy consumption of energy will be likely to suffer a significant increase in tax costs. Transition rules allow companies with heavy energy consumption a few years to adjust to the new regime.

## Branch income

Branches and permanent establishments of foreign companies are taxed under the same rules and rates as apply to Danish resident companies. There is no branch remittance tax or the like. See also "Other significant items" under "Deductions."

## Income determination

In general, taxable profits are determined on the basis of a set of accounts prepared under Danish accounting principles. Typical timing differences include depreciation of machinery and equipment, amortization of goodwill and other intangibles, reserves and work in progress.

*Capital gains*/Gains and losses realized on the sale of tangible and intangible assets, including goodwill, are generally included in taxable income. However, gains realized on the sale of shares are tax-exempt if held for more than three years. This applies regardless of the degree of participation. Losses on the sale of shares are not tax deductible but can be offset against taxable gains on other shares realized if held for less than three years. Special rules apply to investment in subsidiaries in low-tax jurisdictions ("§2a shares").

Gains realized on the sale of real estate property are taxable whereas losses are not tax deductible unless the property is a building qualifying for tax depreciation. A loss realized on the sale of land and other buildings can only be utilized against taxable profits on sale of real estate properties in the same year or can be brought forward indefinitely.

Gains and losses on financial instruments are included in taxable income according to a mark-to-market principal, which is mandatory. There are special rules for losses on certain share-based contracts.

*Intercompany dividends*/Dividends received from domestic or foreign shareholdings are tax exempt, provided the Danish company holds at least 20% of the total share capital in a consecutive period of at least one year within which period the actual shareholder approval of the dividend payment must occur. Dividends received from companies in which the recipient holds less than a 20% interest (or more than 20% but for less than 12 months) are subject to corporation tax. In such cases, 66% of the dividends received is included in taxable income.

If shares are held in a foreign company that has more than one-third of its gross income or assets from financial sources (interest, securities, etc.) and pays a foreign corporation tax less than three quarters of the corresponding Danish level, the above-mentioned rules only apply provided the Danish company holds at least 25% of the share capital or more than 50% of the votes in the foreign company and has done so either from the very first acquisition or for the last three years. Otherwise, 100% of the dividend received would be taxable.

***Foreign income***/A Danish corporation is taxed on its worldwide income, subject to tax treaty relief or domestic law credit relief for foreign taxes incurred.

The income of a foreign subsidiary may be subjected to Danish taxation through a Danish tax grouping with its Danish parent company. See "Incentives."

Financial type income of a foreign subsidiary may have to be taxed in the hands of its Danish parent company if the subsidiary constitutes a Controlled Foreign Corporation (CFC). See "CFC Rules" below.

***CFC rules***/According to the Danish CFC rules, a Danish company has to include in its taxable income the financial net income of a foreign subsidiary that qualifies as a CFC.

A foreign subsidiary can be a CFC if (1) the Danish company together with other group member companies directly or indirectly owns at least 25% of the capital or controls more than 50% of the voting rights in the subsidiary; (2) more than one-third of the subsidiary's taxable profits as assessed under Danish tax law are derived from financial sources; and (3) in that year the subsidiary pays foreign corporation tax at less than three quarters of the corresponding Danish level.

***Stock dividends***/Stock dividends may be distributed to shareholders free of tax provided that they are in proportion to their existing shareholdings.

## Deductions

***Depreciation and depletion***/Tax depreciation is not in conformity with book depreciation.

Annual depreciation allowances on all fixed assets other than those related to real estate and buildings may be claimed under the declining balance method at up to 25% per year. The depreciation base is the cost of fixed assets less (1) sales proceeds of disposals and (2) depreciation allowances previously claimed. For ships, the depreciation rate is 20% in the year of construction and 12% in subsequent years.

Depreciation allowances on buildings (other than residential buildings and office buildings not adjoining an industrial building) may be claimed at up to 5% on a straight-line basis.

Advance allowances of up to 15% may also be claimed on the agreed aggregate cost of fixed assets (except buildings) ordered in excess of DKK 1,155,800. After October 2000 advance allowances are available only for ships.

Amortization of the cost of acquisition or exploitation of natural resources is subject to special rules.

Acquired goodwill can be amortized at up to one-seventh a year on a straight-line basis. Certain restrictions regarding the depreciable value of goodwill apply in the case of intra-group transactions. Goodwill on the purchase of shares cannot be amortized for tax purposes.

Costs related to purchase of patents, know-how and rights/licenses to utilize such intangibles can either be fully expensed in the year of acquisition or amortized over at up to 14.7% per annum on a straight-line basis.

All depreciation recaptured on the sale of buildings or the sale of all ships or all machinery and equipment will become subject to tax.

**Net operating losses**/Tax losses incurred after 2001 may be carried forward indefinitely, whereas losses incurred before 2002 can only be carried forward for five years. Tax loss carryforwards can be restricted or cancelled if more than 50% of the shares or votes change hands, or if the company receives a general debt forgiveness from creditors other than group member companies.

**Payments to foreign affiliates**/A Danish corporation can claim a deduction for royalties and specific service fees paid to foreign affiliates, provided such amounts are equal to what it would pay an unrelated entity (arm's-length principle). Interest at normal commercial rates paid to foreign affiliates will generally be allowed as a deduction, provided the company is not thinly capitalized, see "Other significant items."

**Taxes**/Taxes are nondeductible for income tax purposes, except employer's taxes, duties and VAT.

**Other significant items**/Following the European Court of Justice (ECJ) court ruling on Lankhorst-Hohorst, Danish thin capitalization rules are now in the process of being changed so as to apply to loans both from domestic and foreign group member companies. In general, a Danish company can claim full relief for intercompany interest costs so long as its overall debt/equity ratio is less than 4 to 1. For purposes of measuring this ratio, special consolidation rules apply where there are more than one Danish group member company. Intercompany debt in excess of the 4 to 1 debt/equity ratio counts as equity for purposes of measuring the ratio; in many cases, this rule has the effect of allowing interest relief for 80% of the excess debt. Other than that, there is no recharacterization of interest as dividend.

Furthermore, Danish transfer pricing rules apply to transactions between related parties, for example, intergroup transactions, whether the transactions are made between residents or nonresidents. The rules apply when a company or person directly or indirectly owns more than 50% of the share capital/50% of the voting rights in another company.

Companies are obliged to disclose certain information regarding type and volume of intra-group transactions in the annual tax return. Companies are obliged to maintain transfer pricing documentation substantiating that intragroup transactions are conducted in accordance with arm's length-principles.

Restructuring such as mergers, demergers, shares-exchanges, drop-down of assets, and so on, can in some cases be carried out tax-free. Formation, merger, reorganization, and liquidation expenses are mostly nondeductible.

## Incentives

**Group taxation**/A Danish group of companies may file a group tax return if there is 100% ownership for the full financial period. Following a proposed change of law, such ownership can also be by a foreign parent company resident within the EU or in a state with which Denmark has a tax treaty. Tax grouping is a simple combination (adding together) of individual taxable profits and losses. Also, foreign subsidiaries can be included in a Danish tax grouping; this can be beneficial if the foreign subsidiary is in a tax loss position. There are rules to provide for a

# Denmark

claw-back of foreign tax losses under certain circumstances but as a minimum an interest-free deferral of Danish tax payment can be achieved.

*Other incentives*/There are minor categories of state subsidies available. As a general rule, the subsidies must be applied for, and the amounts received constitute taxable income.

## Withholding taxes

*On payments to foreign corporations and nonresident aliens*/The domestic rate of withholding tax is 28% on dividends and 30% on royalty payments. No withholding tax applies to payments of interest. However, a proposed change of law introduces 30% withholding tax on interest and capital gains paid on loans from a foreign group member company; an exemption applies where (1) the foreign group member company (the creditor) is resident in a state with which Denmark has a tax treaty, or (2) the foreign group member company (the creditor) is resident within the EU and at least 25% of the share capital of both companies are held directly by the same EU resident parent company, or by the other company, for at least 12 months.

Dividends paid to a parent company in another EU member state are exempt from withholding tax provided that the parent company holds at least 20% of the share capital for at least 12 months. The same applies to a parent company in a state other than an EU member state provided that there is a tax treaty between Denmark and that country and that the parent company is eligible for treaty protection in respect of the dividend.

In other cases, foreign recipients of Danish-source dividends have to file a special certificate to either have the withholding rate reduced to any lower rate afforded by the relevant double taxation treaty or to obtain a refund of any excess withholding tax.

A proposed change of law introduces 0% withholding tax on royalty payments comprised by EU-directive 2003/49/EF. As of January 1, 2004 royalty payments from a Danish company to a receiving associated company in another EU-member state are no longer subject to Danish withholding tax, provided that the companies have been associated (25% direct or indirect ownership) for a continuous period of at least 12 months within which period the royalty is paid. The rules do not apply to royalty payments from a Danish company to a permanent establishment (PE) of an associated company, if the PE is in Denmark or in a nonmember state.

| Recipient | Treaty type | Dividend tax limited to | | |
| --- | --- | --- | --- | --- |
| | | Qualifying companies | | Others |
| | | % | | % |
| Resident corporations................... | | Nil | (2b) | 28 |
| Resident individuals....................... | | 28 | (2a) | 28 |
| Nontreaty: | | | | |
|   Nonresident corporations........... | | Nil | (2b) | 28 |
|   Nonresident individuals.............. | | 28 | (2a) | 28 |
| Treaty: | | | | |
|   Argentina (3)............................. | (1b) | Nil | (2b) | 15 |
|   Australia .................................. | (1b) | Nil | (2b) | 15 |
|   Austria (4)................................ | (1d) | Nil | (2b) | 10 |
|   Bangladesh .............................. | (1b) | 10/Nil | (2d)/(2b) | 15 |

# Denmark

| | | Dividend tax limited to | | |
|---|---|---|---|---|
| Recipient | Treaty type | Qualifying companies | | Others |
| | | % | | % |
| Belgium | (1b) | Nil | (2b) | 15 |
| Brazil (4) | (1d) | Nil | (2b) | 25 |
| Bulgaria | (1b) | Nil | (2b) | 15 |
| Canada | (1b) | Nil | (2b) | 15 |
| China, P.R. | (1b) | Nil | (2b) | 10 |
| CIS (4) | (1b) | Nil | (2b) | 15 |
| Cyprus | (1b) | Nil | (2b) | 15 |
| Czech Republic | (1b) | Nil | (2b) | 15 |
| Egypt | (1b) | Nil | (2b) | 20 |
| Estonia | (1b) | Nil | (2b) | 15 |
| Faroe Islands | (1a) | Nil | (2d) | 15 |
| Finland | (1a) | Nil | (2d) | 15 |
| France (4) | (1c) | Nil | (2a) | Nil |
| Germany | (1a) | 5/Nil | (2d)/(2b) | 15 |
| Greece (3) | (1b) | Nil | (2b) | 18 |
| Greenland | (1a) | Nil | (2b) | 28 |
| Hungary | (1b) | Nil | (2b) | 15 |
| Iceland | (1a) | Nil | (2d) | 15 |
| India | (1b) | Nil | (2b) | 25 |
| Indonesia | (1b) | Nil | (2b) | 20 |
| Ireland, Rep. of | (1b) | Nil | (2b) | 15 |
| Israel (4) | (1d) | Nil | (2b) | 15 |
| Italy | (1b) | Nil | (2b) | 15 |
| Jamaica | (1b) | Nil | (2b) | 15 |
| Japan | (1b) | Nil | (2b) | 15 |
| Kenya | (1a) | Nil | (2b) | 28 |
| Korea, Rep. of | (1a) | Nil | (2b) | 15 |
| Latvia | (1b) | Nil | (2b) | 15 |
| Lithuania | (1b) | Nil | (2b) | 15 |
| Luxembourg | (1b) | Nil | (2d) | 15 |
| Macedonia | (1b) | Nil | (2b) | 15 |
| Malaysia (4) | (1b) | Nil | (2a) | Nil |
| Malta | (1b) | Nil | (2b) | 15 |
| Mexico | (1b) | Nil | (2b) | 15 |
| Morocco | (1b) | Nil | (2b) | 25 |
| Netherlands (4, 5) | (1b) | Nil | (2d) | 15 |
| New Zealand | (1b) | Nil | (2b) | 15 |
| Norway | (1b) | Nil | (2d) | 15 |
| Pakistan | (1b) | Nil | (2b) | 15 |
| Philippines | (1a) | Nil | (2b) | 15 |
| Poland | (1b) | Nil | (2b) | 15 |
| Portugal | (1b) | Nil | (2b) | 10 |
| Romania | (1b) | Nil | (2b) | 15 |
| Russia | (1a) | Nil | (2b) | 10 |
| Singapore | (1b) | Nil | (2b) | 10 |
| Slovak Republic | (1b) | Nil | (2b) | 15 |
| Slovenia | (1a) | Nil | (2b) | 15 |
| South Africa | (1b) | Nil | (2b) | 15 |

# Denmark

| Recipient | Treaty type | Dividend tax limited to | | Others |
|---|---|---|---|---|
| | | Qualifying companies | | |
| | | % | | % |
| Spain | (1a) | Nil | (2b) | 15 |
| Sri Lanka | (1b) | Nil | (2b) | 15 |
| Sweden | (1a) | Nil | (2d) | 15 |
| Switzerland | (1a) | Nil | (2a) | Nil |
| Tanzania | (1b) | Nil | (2b) | 15 |
| Thailand | (1b) | Nil | (2b) | 10 |
| Trinidad and Tobago | (1a) | Nil | (2b) | 20 |
| Tunisia | (1b) | Nil | (2b) | 15 |
| Turkey | (1b) | Nil | (2b) | 20 |
| Uganda | (1b) | Nil | (2b) | 15 |
| Ukraine | (1b) | Nil | (2b) | 15 |
| United Kingdom (6) | (1b) | Nil | (2b) | 15 |
| United States (3) | (1b) | 5/Nil | (2b)/(2d) | 15 |
| Venezuela | (1b) | Nil | (2b) | 15 |
| Vietnam | (1b) | Nil/5 | (2b)/(2c) | 15 |
| Yugoslavia (4,7) | (1b) | Nil | (2b) | 15 |
| Zambia | (1a) | Nil | (2b) | 15 |

| Recipient | Treaty type | Interest | Royalty* |
|---|---|---|---|
| | | % | % |
| Resident corporations | | Nil | Nil |
| Resident individuals | | Nil | Nil |
| Nonresident corporations and individuals: | | | |
| Nontreaty | | Nil | 30 |
| Treaty: | | | |
| Argentina | (1b) | | 3/5/10/15 |
| Australia | (1b) | | 10 |
| Austria | (1d) | | 10/Nil |
| Bangladesh | (1b) | | 10 |
| Belgium | (1b) | | Nil |
| Brazil | (1d) | | 25/15 |
| Bulgaria | (1b) | | Nil |
| Canada | (1b) | | Nil/10 |
| China, P.R. | (1b) | | 10 |
| CIS | (1b) | | Nil |
| Cyprus | (1b) | | Nil |
| Czech Republic | (1b) | | 5 |
| Egypt | (1b) | | 20 |
| Estonia | (1b) | | 10/5 |
| Faroe Islands | (1a) | | Nil |
| Finland | (1a) | | Nil |
| France | (1c) | | Nil |
| Germany | (1a) | | Nil |
| Greece | (1b) | | 5 |
| Greenland | (1a) | | 10 |
| Hungary | (1b) | | Nil |

| Recipient | Treaty type | Interest | Royalty* |
|---|---|---|---|
| | | % | % |
| Iceland | (1b) | | Nil |
| India | (1b) | | 20 |
| Indonesia | (1b) | | 15 |
| Ireland, Rep. of | (1b) | | Nil |
| Israel | (1d) | | 10 |
| Italy | (1b) | | 5 |
| Jamaica | (1b) | | 10 |
| Japan | (1b) | | 10 |
| Kenya | (1a) | | 20 |
| Korea, Rep. of | (1a) | | 10/15 |
| Latvia | (1b) | | 5/10 |
| Lithuania | (1b) | | 5/10 |
| Luxembourg | (1b) | | Nil |
| Macedonia | (1b) | | 10 |
| Malaysia | (1d) | | 0/30 |
| Malta | (1b) | | Nil |
| Mexico | (1b) | | 10 |
| Morocco | (1b) | | 10 |
| Netherlands | (1b) | | Nil |
| New Zealand | (1b) | | 10 |
| Norway | (1b) | | Nil |
| Pakistan | (1b) | | 12 |
| Philippines | (1b) | | 15 |
| Poland | (1b) | | 5 |
| Portugal | (1b) | | 10 |
| Romania | (1b) | | 10 |
| Russia | (1a) | | Nil |
| Singapore | (1b) | | 10 |
| Slovak Republic | (1b) | | 5 |
| Slovenia | (1a) | | 5 |
| South Africa | (1b) | | Nil |
| Spain | (1a) | | 6 |
| Sri Lanka | (1b) | | 10 |
| Sweden | (1a) | | Nil |
| Switzerland | (1a) | | Nil |
| Tanzania | (1b) | | 20 |
| Thailand | (1d) | | 5/15 |
| Trinidad and Tobago | (1a) | | 15 |
| Tunisia | (1h) | | 15 |
| Turkey | (1b) | | 10 |
| Uganda | (1b) | | 10 |
| Ukraine | (1b) | | 10 |
| United Kingdom | (1b) | | Nil |
| United States | (1b) | | Nil |
| Venezuela | (1b) | | 5/10 |
| Vietnam | (1b) | | 5/15 |
| Yugoslavia | (1b) | | 10 |
| Zambia | (1a) | | 15 |

*Limited to certain royalties

# Denmark

The numbers in parentheses refer to the following numbered Notes.

Notes:

1. Treaty types are defined as follows.
   a. Type C (tax credit). The tax abatement is the lower of (1) the tax paid in the foreign country and (2) the amount of Danish tax in the proportion to the total Danish tax that the net foreign income bears to the company's taxable income in Denmark.
   b. Type C/e. This type is similar to the Organization of Economic Cooperation and Development (OECD) Model Convention, for example, the main rule is the credit method, but certain types of income, such as international transportation, sale of capital assets used in international transportation and income from employment in the public sector, are exempted.
   c. Type E (tax exemption). The tax abatement is equal to the amount of Danish tax in the proportion to total Danish tax that the net foreign income bears to the company's taxable income in Denmark, whether higher or lower than the tax paid in the foreign country.
   d. Type E/e. Tax exemption except for certain forms of income, such as dividends, interest, and royalties, and income from shipping and aviation, for which special rules apply.
   e. Type E/C. Denmark uses the E/e type; the other country uses the C type.
2. A qualifying company is one whose shareholding in the Danish subsidiary is as follows.
   a. No minimum shareholding required.
   b. At least 20%. In this case Denmark does not operate a system of withholding tax on dividends when the parent company holds at least 20% of the share capital in the Danish subsidiary for at least 12 months and the distribution of dividend takes place within that period.
   c. A company that has invested at least US$12 million in the company.
   d. At least 10%.
3. In addition to income tax treaties listed above, treaties in respect of sea and/or air transport are in effect with Argentina, Greece, Hong Kong, Jordan, Kuwait, Lebanon, and the United States.
4. Presently, Denmark has a treaty with the former USSR, which will still apply for the Commonwealth of Independent States and Georgia. Denmark has a new treaty with Estonia, Latvia, Lithuania, Russia and Ukraine. Azerbaijan, Kazakhstan, Moldova and Tadzhikistan have informed the Danish authorities that they do not wish to honor the former USSR treaty.

   Negotiations are in progress with the following countries concerning new treaties or revision of old treaties: Austria, Brazil, Chile, France, Hong Kong, Israel, Malaysia, the Netherlands, Nigeria, Turkmenistan, Uzbekistan, and Yugoslavia.
5. The protocol with the Netherlands Antilles extending the Netherlands treaty to the Antilles has been cancelled.
6. The old U.K. treaty included some former British territories. Denmark has terminated the treaty regarding all former British territories effective from January 1, 1993.

7. Because of the political climate within the former Yugoslavia it is very uncertain whether the existing treaty will remain in force. The treaty includes Croatia and Yugoslavia. Denmark has a new treaty with Slovenia and Macedonia.

## Tax administration

**Returns**/Tax returns are completed on the basis of audited accounts with tax adjustment. Tax returns should be filed no later than six months after the end of the accounting year. Corporations with an accounting year-end in the period January 1 to March 31 must file a tax return no later than July 1 in the same calendar year. The tax system, in practice, is based on self-assessment. Tax assessments are made automatically by the tax authorities on the basis of the tax return. However, the tax authorities may subsequently audit the tax return. The general statute of limitation is May 1 in the fourth calendar year after that of the end of the relevant accounting period. As regards transfer pricing issues, the period is a further two years, that is, until May 1 in the sixth year.

**Payment of tax**/Corporation tax must be paid on a current-year basis in two equal installments due on March 20 and November 20. The authorities will ask for payments of 50% of the average of the last three years' final income tax. In addition, voluntary payments can be made. Underpaid tax is payable by November 20 of the following year with a surtax of 10%. Overpaid tax is refunded by November 20 of the following year with interest of up to 4%.

# Denmark

## *CORPORATION TAX CALCULATION*

Calendar year 2004

| | | |
|---|---:|---:|
| Income before tax (including foreign source income at DKK 250,000) | | DKK 1,050,000 |
| Less—Depreciation allowances claimed in excess of book depreciation | | 100,000 |
| Taxable income | | DKK   950,000 |
| Tax thereon at 30% | | DKK   285,000 |
| Less: | | |
| Foreign tax credit | | |
| (The lesser of 285,000 x 200,000/950,000 = 60,000 or 50,000) | | 50,000 |
| Income tax payable | | 235,000 |
| Ordinary payment on account tax: | | |
| March 20, 2004 | 70,000 | |
| November 20, 2004 | 70,000 | (140,000) |
| Voluntary on account: | | |
| March 20, 2004 | 40,000 | |
| November 20, 2004 | 30,000 | (70,000) |
| Supplement due taxpayer | | |
| (1% of 40,000 paid in March) | (400) | |
| Supplement owed by taxpayer | | |
| (1% of 30,000 paid in November) | 300 | (100) |
| Tax due | | 24,900 |
| 10% surtax | | 2,490 |
| Payable November 20, 2005 | | DKK   27,390 |

Notes:

The following assumptions have been made:

1.  The following assumptions have been made:

    | | | |
    |---|---:|---:|
    | Income before tax including net income from branch in foreign country | | DKK 1,050,000 |
    | Net income from branch in foreign country | 250,000 | |
    | Less Income tax paid by branch in foreign country | (50,000) | DKK   200,000 |
    | Depreciation allowances claimed in excess of book depreciation | | DKK   100,000 |

2.  Exchange rate at March 15, 2004: US$1 = DKK 6.0858.

## PwC contacts

For additional information on taxation in the Dominican Republic, contact:

Freddy Perez
Ramón Ortega
PricewaterhouseCoopers
Lope de Vega Esq. John F. Kennedy
Edificio Banco Nova Scotia, Third Floor
Santo Domingo, República Dominicana
Telephone: (809) 567 7741
Fax: (809) 541 1210
LN address: Freddy Perez@Americas-Carib
                    Ramon Ortega@Americas-Carib

## Taxes on corporate income

The Dominican Tax Code provides for a 25% corporate tax rate.

Effective on January 1, 2004, the minimum tax ceased to be in force. In consequence the 1.5% on gross revenue will continue to exist as an advanced income tax to be offset against tax liabilities.

## Corporate residence

A company is resident when it is incorporated in the Dominican Republic, and when its central management and control are exercised in the country. However, a company not incorporated in the Dominican Republic is subject to tax when it has a permanent establishment in the Dominican Republic.

## Other taxes

***Internal and consumption taxes collected at Customs upon importation***/These taxes are assessed at various rates in addition to customhouse duties.

***Selective consumption tax***/The selective consumption tax ranges from 19.5% to 78%, and is applied on the consumption of domestic manufactures (alcohol products and cigars), on imported goods that are considered to be nonessential, and on certain types of services, such as insurance, international air transportation, long-distance telephone calls, and hotel rooms.

***Value-added tax***/VAT is applied to industrialized goods, imports and the services. The rate is 12%. A zero-rate applies to exports, and a 6% to advertisement services.

Exemptions include living essentials, goods already subject to similar taxes and also certain services.

***Real estate transfer tax***/This tax is assessed at a basic rate of 4%, with a 12% surcharge (4.48% overall).

***Stamp taxes***/Stamp taxes are imposed on most government-related documents.

***Transitory contribution***/*Contribución Solidaria Transitoria* (CST) Law 01 and 02 of the year 2004 has introduced a temporary tax on exported goods and services amounting to 5% on the gross earnings derived from those exports. This temporary tax became in force on January 1, 2004 for a six-month period. This tax can be neither compensated nor offset with any other Dominican tax.

## Branch income

Branch profits are levied at the same rates as corporate profits. There is no withholding tax on branch profit remittances to the home office.

## Income determination

*Inventory valuation*/LIFO is the method of inventory valuation accepted for fiscal purposes. Exceptionally, other methods may be authorized upon request.

Conformity between book and tax reporting is not required.

*Capital gains*/Capital gains are taxable. Ordinary (taxable) income embraces the sale of assets used in the conduct of a business.

*Intercompany dividends*/Dividends are tax-exempt. There is a 25% withholding imposed on cash dividends that serve as an advance tax payment or as a credit against future tax payable for the company distributing the dividends.

*Foreign income*/Dominican-resident companies are subject to taxation on income from Dominican sources and on foreign dividends and interest.

*Stock dividends*/Stock dividends are not subject to taxation.

## Deductions

*Depreciation and depletion*/Depreciation allowances on fixed assets are determined by the diminishing-balance method at the following rates.

| Class | % |
| --- | --- |
| Buildings | 5 |
| Furniture, fixtures, computers, vehicles, etc. | 25 |
| Other assets not specified | 15 |

Depletion of mines is based on units produced.

*Net operating losses*/Losses may be carried forward for a maximum of three tax periods.

*Payments to foreign affiliates*/Payments to foreign affiliates for royalties, interest, or service fees are deductible, subject to a 25% withholding tax rate.

*Taxes*/Except for tax on income, inheritances, and donations and compensation-in-kind, all taxes are deductible.

*Other significant items*/For tax purposes, the following significant items should be considered.

1. Bad debts are deductible only in the year the loss is suffered. Authorization may be obtained to follow an alternate method allowing deduction only in the year charges qualify as doubtful, up to 4% of the balance of the clients accounts receivable at year-end.
2. Amortization of intangible assets, such as patents, author's rights, drawings, franchises, and contracts without set expiration date, is not deductible.
3. Changes in method of record accounting are not allowed without advance approval.
4. Bonuses to employees are deductible if they are paid within the year or 120 days after year-end.

## Group taxation

Group taxation is not permitted.

## Tax incentives

The Tax Code revokes all tax incentive laws (except those for offshore, that is, free-zone, operations for export). Qualified projects under, Forestry, Energy, Agroindustrial, and Industrial Free Zone Operations Laws will continue to enjoy tax benefits for the period granted, in accordance with the approved Resolution.

A Law of Tourism incentive was enacted in year 2001 (Law 158-01) granting full or partial tax exemptions on investments and projects carried out in developing zones or areas within the country.

## Withholding taxes

Dividends in cash to resident and nonresident individuals and corporations are subject to a withholding tax of 25%.

On payments to foreign corporations that are not permanently established in the Dominican Republic and to nonresident individuals, the withholding tax is as follows.

|  | Interest | Royalties | Technical assistance |
|---|---|---|---|
|  | % | % | % |
| Nontreaty (basic)............................................ | 15 (1) | 25 | 25 |
| Treaty (Canada) ............................................. | 18 (2) | 18 | 18 |

Notes:

1. The rate provided corresponds to interests paid to financial institutions. If interest is paid to nonfinancial institutions, the applicable rate will be 25% according to the domestic law.

2. Since the tax rate established by the domestic law is lower than the one determined by the treaty, the 15% withholding tax will apply to all payments on interest (loans) to Canadian financial institutions.

## Tax administration

*Returns*/The company's tax return must be filed and paid within 120 days from the closing of the tax period.

Tax returns are the self-assessment type, and must be filed on forms supplied by the Income Tax Department.

*Payment of tax*/The balance of any tax due must be paid no later than the due date for filing the return.

*Advance payments (general rule)*/Each month legal entities will pay an advance income tax of 1.5% of their monthly gross income corresponding to the fiscal year in question. However, those companies whose income tax due in the previous period represented an effective rate greater than 1.5% of the gross income will pay 1/12 part of the total of the tax effectively paid in the last fiscal year declared. When the liquidated tax does not exceed the 1.5% of the gross income paid as advance during the fiscal period, the said advance payments shall become a final income tax payment.

# Dominican Republic

*Advance payments for agroindustrial corporations and corporations with annual income lower than RD$ 6 million*/Three advance payments based on the income tax of the preceding year are mandatory, with the first 50% in the 6th month, the next 30% in the 9th month, and the final 20% in the 12th month of the tax year.


## CORPORATION TAX CALCULATION

Year ending December 31, 2003

| | | |
|---|---:|---:|
| Pretax income | | RD$ 1,000,000 |
| Add—Nondeductible expenses: | | |
| Charitable contribution in excess | | |
| of the 5% on taxable income | 25,000 | |
| Tax on compensation-in-kind (120,000 at 25%) | 30,000 | 55,000 |
| | | 1,055,000 |
| Deduct: | | |
| Net dividends from domestic operation | 50,000 | |
| Carryover loss (less than three years) | 100,000 | 150,000 |
| Taxable income | | RD$ 905,000 |
| Tax at 25% | | RD$ 226,250 |

Note:

Official exchange rate of the peso at January 7, 2004: US$1 = RD$40.50.

# Ecuador

## PwC contact

For additional information on taxation in Ecuador, contact:

Luciano Almeida
Price Waterhouse & Co.
Carchi 702 y Av. 9 de Octubre. Third floor
P.O. Box 09-01-5820
Guayaquil, Ecuador
Telephone: (593) (4) /228 1555
Fax: (593) (4) 239 3471
Quito, Ecuador
Telephone: (593) (2) 256 4142/223 2632
Fax: (593) (2) 2567 096
LN address: Luciano Almeida/EC/TLS/PwC@SOACAT
e-mail: luciano.almeida@ec.pw-co.com

## Significant developments

No significant developments occurred during 2003.

## Taxes on corporate income

Taxes on corporate income are levied at the following rates.

|  | % |
|---|---|
| On distributed or undistributed profits of local corporations and branches | 25.0 |
| For oil companies with risk service contracts: | |
| On distributed profits | 44.4 |
| On undistributed profits (under certain investment conditions) | 25.0 |
| For oil companies with other types of contract (on distributed or undistributed profits) | 25.0 |
| On reinvested profits | 15.0 |

## Corporate residence

Corporate residence is determined by the place of incorporation. For foreign branches, it is the place stated in the domiciliary deed.

## Other taxes

*Municipal assets tax*/The municipal assets tax is levied at the rate of 0.15% on total assets less current liabilities and contingencies.

*Property tax*/This tax is calculated by the city government and it represents a specified percentage, approximately 1.6%, of the taxable value of the property, which is equivalent to the commercial value less a general reduction of 40%. These assessed values are established by valuations made every five years by the city government, for both urban and rural properties.

*Value-added tax*/This tax is levied at the rates of either 12% or 0% on the owner-ship transfer of goods, import of goods and services rendered. Goods and services, which are subject to 0% rate, are explicitly listed in the law. Local taxes paid on the purchase of goods and services are compensated by taxes accrued by the local selling of goods or services; differences are payable, or carried forward as tax credits. Such tax credits are also available on exports of goods or services.

# Ecuador

Companies designated by the government as special taxpayers are required to withhold 30% of VAT applicable on their purchases of goods and 70% of VAT applicable on their purchase of services. Special taxpayers and companies are obligated to withhold 100% of VAT on payments made to individuals.

*Special consumption tax*/This tax is imposed at a 5.15% rate on certain automobiles and 10.30% on airplanes, helicopters, and boats. The tax on cigarettes, alcoholic beverages, and soft drinks ranges from 10.30% to 77.25%. For telecommunication services the tax is imposed at the rate of 15%. It must be paid monthly and is collected upon sales.

## Branch income

Distributed or retained branch profits (as well as reinvested profits of oil companies operating under risk service contracts) are taxed at the aforementioned 25% rate. No further taxes are payable when profits are remitted to headquarters. Reveinvested profits are levied at 15% income tax rate.

## Income determination

*Inventory valuation*/The valuation of inventories is not specifically treated in the tax law. However, the law refers to generally accepted accounting principles and tax authorities have endorsed official pronouncements based on International Accounting Standards and Ecuadorian Accounting Standards (NEC). Inventories are carried at cost. LIFO, FIFO, actual and average methods are used. The average method is the preferred valuation method.

*Capital gains*/Capital gains and financial yields (stock certificates, debentures, bonds, bank and finance company mortgage bonds, and similar instruments) paid to local (or foreign) businesses are subject to income tax (no exemptions are applicable). Occasional gains from stock sales are tax exempt, gains from investment funds and investment trusts are exempt as well. Gains on sale of fixed assets are added to the taxable base and levied at regular income tax rates, except gains emerging from occasional real state sales, which are tax-exempt.

*Intercompany dividends*/Dividends received by an Ecuadorian company from other domestic company are exempt from income taxes. The same treatment applies to dividends received, by a branch of a foreign company, from a domestic company.

*Foreign income*/Businesses incorporated under Ecuadorian law are subject to income taxes regardless where the income is generated. Any foreign–source income subject to foreign taxes would be credited or deductible against Ecuadorian income tax.

*Stock dividends*/The distribution of stock dividends is not subject to tax.

*Other significant items*/None.

## Deductions

*Depreciation and amortization*/Straight-line depreciation at rates specified by law applies. The director of the Internal Revenue Service of Ecuador would authorize higher rates of depreciation in cases such as obsolescence, excessive use, and faster wear out of assets.

Depreciation rates are as follows.

|  | % |
|---|---|
| Real estate (except land), aircrafts, naval crafts, and similar | 5 |
| Facilities, machinery, equipment and furniture | 10 |
| Vehicles, trucks and tractors used for construction | 20 |
| Computer equipment and software | 33 |

Depreciation rates apply to the cost of assets.

**Net operating losses**/The carrying forward of losses is allowed to a maximum of five years, with an amortization limit of 25% per year over the taxable base. There is no loss carryback.

**Payments to foreign affiliates**/In most cases, payments made abroad are deductible, as long as withholding of income taxes has been performed (at the rate of 25% over the taxable base). Professional fee, royalties, commissions or any payment made abroad is withheld at a rate of 25% over the taxable base. Payments on imports are deductible and are not subject to withholding of income taxes.

**Taxes**/Taxes, rates, levies and contributions to the social security system, which will help to generate revenues, are deductible. Interests and fines paid as penalties caused by delays on the payments of tax obligations, as well as income taxes payments, are not deductible for income tax calculation purposes.

**Other significant items**/Tax law refers to other deductions, from which the most important are as follows.

1. Organization, experimentation and preoperational expenses—These expenses are to be amortized over five years at the rate of 20% per year.
2. Interests of debts incurred for business purposes.
3. Foreign loan interests are deductible to the extent that they do not exceed the maximum rates established by the Ecuadorian Central Bank (ECB). Interest on foreign loans not registered in the ECB is nondeductible.
4. Intangible assets are amortized either within the terms specified in the contract or over a 20-year period.

**Statutory profit sharing**/According to the Ecuadorian Labor Code, companies must distribute 15% of their pre-tax earnings among their employees. This profit sharing is deductible for corporate income tax purposes.

## Group taxation

Group taxation is not permitted.

## Tax incentives

The president of the republic has the authority to grant special tax treatments to less developed areas. These incentives include tax exemptions or special deductions for income tax purposes.

Duty-free treatment is authorized for the imports of equipment, merchandise and materials of production to be re-exported. These companies may be 100% foreign owned. The application of this legislation has been limited.

Legislation also grants full exemption from import and virtually all other significant duties and taxes for a maximum holiday period of 20 years to companies involved

# Ecuador

in offshore (free-zone) operations for export. The tax holiday applies to free-zone administrators and users. Application of this legislation has been limited.

Companies can make annually voluntarily donations to municipalities and some charitable organizations up to a maximum of 25% of the payable income.

## Withholding taxes

Revenues from occasional services provided by nonresident individuals are levied at 25% of the total revenue. Payments made abroad to nonresident individuals and companies are subject to a 25% withholding tax. Withholding tax will apply on 100% of the total payment made for professional services rendered outside Ecuador (or occasional services rendered in Ecuador by nonresident individuals).

Other payments made abroad, different than dividends or profits, are subject to 25% income tax withholding. Withholding tax is not applied on loan interest remitted abroad, as long as the loan has been registered at the ECB. The rates at which the loan has been contracted should not exceed the rates set by the ECB.

The Internal Revenue Service of Ecuador will establish periodically withholding percentages on local payments, which will not be greater than 10%. For the year 2004, local payments (including interest paid by financial institutions) are subject to 1%, 5%, or 8% withholding.

*Tax treaties*/Ecuador has adopted Decision 40 of the Andean Community (former Andean Pact), which provides relief from double taxation for individuals or companies located in these countries. Furthermore, Ecuador has similar tax treaties with Brazil, Canada, France, Germany, Italy, Mexico, Romania, Spain, and Switzerland. A double taxation treaty with Chile has been signed.

## Tax administration

*Returns*/The fiscal year is the calendar year, from January 1 to December 31. The tax system operates on basis of self-assessment, with subsequent inspection by the tax authorities.

*Payment of tax*/Tax filing deadlines begin on April 10 and go up to April 28. The due tax dates are determined by the ninth digit of the company's Tax Identification Number (TIN).

Corporations must pay in advance income tax based on the difference between 50% of the previous year's tax less withholdings for that year. Advance payments are made in two equal payments in July and September. Differences between advance payments and the income tax returns must be paid. If difference is in favor of taxpayers, they need to request a reimbursement to the Internal Revenue Service of Ecuador.

## CORPORATION TAX CALCULATION

*All companies other than risk service companies*

Fiscal year 2003

| | | |
|---|---|---|
| Net Income before taxes and 15% employees' statutory profit sharing. (Data: $800 cash dividend, $3,200 occasional capital gains from stock sales, accumulated tax losses-previous years 2000–2001 $25,000 and reinvesting decision USD 10,000) | | $100,000 |
| Less—15% employees' statutory profit participation (SPP) (1) | | 15,000 |
| Profit after SPP | | 85,000 |
| (–) Cash Dividends | 800 | |
| (–) Gains on Stock sales | 3,200 | |
| Exempt income | 4,000 | |
| (+) Provision for depreciation in excess of amounts allowed | 1,800 | |
| (+) Interest and fines on income tax of a previous year paid in connection with tax examination | 500 | |
| Nondeductible items | 2,300 | |
| Other nondeductible items | 800 | |
| (+) 15% SPP applicable to exempt income | 600 | |
| (+) 5% Non-deductible expenses related to exempt income | 200 | |
| Taxable base | | 84,100 |
| Deduct: | | |
| Other deductions allowed by law | 21,025 | |
| (–) Loss carried forward (max. 25%) | 21,025 | |
| Taxable profits | | 63,075 |
| Tax payable (10,000 reinvested profits at 15%) | | 1,500 |
| Tax payable (63,075 – 10,000 at 25%) | | 13,268 |
| Less: | | |
| Taxes withheld | 6,500 | |
| Advanced payments from FY 2002 | 3,000 | (9,500) |
| Net tax payable | | $  5,268 |

Notes:

1. Nondeductible items and exempt income are not considered in the calculation of SPP.
2. Since 2000, the Ecuadorian currency system is based on the U.S. dollar.

# Estonia

## PwC contacts

For additional information on taxation in Estonia, contact:

Aare Kurist
Tax Department
AS PricewaterhouseCoopers
Pärnu mnt 15
10141 Tallinn, Estonia
Telephone: (372) (6) 141 800
Fax: (372) (6) 141 900
e-mail: aare.kurist@ee.pwc.com

A copy of all documents/inquiries should be sent to:

Cameron G. Greaves
TLS Baltic States Leader
PricewaterhouseCoopers SIA
K. Valdemara 19
Riga, LV-1010, Latvia
Telephone: (371) 7094400
Fax: (371) 7830055
e-mail: cameron.greaves@lv.pwc.com

## Significant developments

The Income Tax Law, effective from January 1, 2000, provides exemption from income tax on undistributed corporate profits, but imposes tax on all distributions (both actual and deemed), including dividends and other profit distributions, fringe benefits, gifts, donations, and representation expenses, as well as expenses and payments not related to business. From January 1, 2003, dividends between Estonian resident companies became subject to 26/74 income tax on the level of the distributing company. In order to avoid the double taxation of dividends, Estonian companies may deduct the income tax paid on dividends received from other domestic companies from the income tax payable on dividends distributed. Such deduction, however, is only allowed when dividends are received from domestic subsidiaries where the company receiving dividends holds at least 20% of the share capital at the time of distribution.

According to the Amendment to the Income Tax Law, it is expected that the income tax rate (which in 2004 is 26/74 on gross up basis or flat 26%) will be reduced as follows.

- To 24/76 or 24% in 2005.
- To 22/78 or 22% in 2006.
- To 20/80 or 20% in 2007.

## Taxes on corporate income

Estonian corporate tax on distributed profits in 2004 is 26/74 (approximately 35%, which may be misleading as a tax rate). As undistributed profits of companies are not taxed with the corporate tax on an annual basis, in comparison with other tax systems the effective Estonian tax rate is 26%. For example, where the company has profits available in the amount of 100, it can distribute dividends in the amount of 74, and must pay deferred corporate tax on distributions in the amount of 26. No local income taxes are imposed in Estonia.

## Corporate residence

A corporation is resident in Estonia for tax purposes if it is established under Estonian law. A permanent establishment (including an Estonian branch) of a foreign entity is deemed to be a nonresident taxpayer.

*Permanent establishment/*Irrespective of the fact that a nonresident has not established a subsidiary or a branch in Estonia, it may still be deemed to have a permanent establishment in Estonia. A permanent establishment is one of the following.

1. A fixed place of business through which the business of a nonresident is wholly or partly carried on in Estonia.
2. A nonresident for which any person has, and habitually exercises, in Estonia an authority to conclude contracts in its name.

The income of a nonresident taxpayer received through a permanent establishment is calculated as the income that it might be expected to make if it were a distinct and separate taxpayer engaged in the same or similar activities under the same or similar conditions.

## Other taxes

*Value-added tax/*The supply and import of goods and services are subject to VAT at the standard rate of 18%. The VAT rate on the export of goods and certain services (e.g., international transport) is 0% (i.e., zero-rated). Some supplies are exempt, such as medical services, banking, and insurance. A reduced 5% VAT rate applies to books, hotel accommodation services, the treatment of dangerous waste, and certain listed medicines and medical equipment.

Goods include movables, immovables, animals, and electric and thermal energy. If the taxable turnover of a newly established corporation exceeds EEK250,000 in a year, it is required to register for VAT with the local Tax Board. The taxation period as fixed in the VAT Law is a calendar month, and the VAT is to be declared and paid on or before the 20th day of the following month. It is also possible to register voluntarily for VAT if this will enable the taxpayer (Estonian corporation or permanent establishment of a foreign entity) to recover surplus input VAT, incurred as a result of its business which is subject to VAT. The new VAT Law drafted in accordance with the principles of EU Directives is effective from May 1, 2004.

*Excise tax/*Excise taxes are levied on tobacco, alcohol, packages, and motor fuel.

*Heavy vehicle tax/*From January 1, 2004, heavy vehicle tax will apply to trucks and heavy vehicles for freight transport with a weight of 12 tons or more that are registered with the Estonian National Motor Vehicle Register.

*Local taxes/*Municipalities are authorized to introduce local taxes, most notably advertising tax, motor vehicle tax, parking fee, and sales tax.

## Branch income

From January 1, 2000, permanent establishments of foreign entities (including branches), in the same manner as resident corporations, are subject to income tax only in respect of distributions (both actual and deemed), including dividends and other profit distributions, fringe benefits, gifts, donations, and representation expenses, as well as expenses and payments not related to business. The transfer of the assets of a branch to its head office or to other third persons are

# Estonia

also treated as distributions, unless other assets are granted or services are provided to the permanent establishment in exchange for these assets. However, there are no detailed rules for attribution of profits to permanent establishments.

## Income determination

*Inventory valuation*/Inventories are valued at acquisition cost or net realizable value, whichever is lower. The FIFO and weighted-average cost methods are permitted.

*Capital gains*/Capital gains are taxed as ordinary income; there is no separate capital gains tax. Gains derived by resident corporations are not subject to tax until further distributions are made (or deemed made).

Gains derived by nonresidents from the disposal of property located in Estonia or registered in any Estonian register, as well as the disposal of rights in real estate, are generally subject to 26% income tax. However, gains from the disposal of shares of Estonian corporate entities are subject to 26% tax only if the nonresident disposed of 10% or more of the shares in the company, and 75% of its assets are represented by real estate or buildings in Estonia.

*Intercompany dividends*/From January 1, 2003, dividends paid to resident corporations are subject to 26/74 income tax. For relief from double taxation, a corporate recipient of dividends that holds not less than 20% of the shares or votes of the distributing corporation at the time of the dividend distribution may deduct the income tax paid on dividends received, when making further distributions to its shareholders.

*Foreign income*/Resident corporations are taxed on their worldwide income. Until December 31, 2002, unilateral relief for corporations under the Income Tax Law provided that if the resident corporation had received dividends from abroad within the preceding 12 months, the underlying foreign tax credit was available for both the tax withheld on dividends and any corporate tax paid on underlying profits. However, in no case was this underlying credit permitted to exceed 26/74 of the dividends received.

From January 1, 2003, the underlying foreign tax credit will be available only to resident corporations that hold at least 20% of the shares or votes of the corporation distributing dividends. The 12-month timing restriction for the use of the underlying credit has been abolished. A per-country limitation will apply to the underlying tax credit.

In Estonia the principal method of avoiding double taxation under tax treaties is the credit method; in the case of dividends, a credit may also be granted for the underlying corporate tax of a company in which an Estonian corporation owns at least 10% of its shares having full voting rights. Under no circumstances may double taxation relief exceed the Estonian tax attributable to such income.

## Deductions

*Depreciation and depletion*/As there is no annual net taxation of corporate profits, corporate entities are not subject to tax depreciation rules. The tax depreciation calculated under the previous income tax laws cannot be taken into account for income tax payable after January 1, 2000.

*Net operating losses*/Losses carried forward under the previous tax laws cannot be set off or carried forward against taxable payments under the existing income tax legislation.

*Payments to foreign affiliates*/Payments to foreign affiliates may be subject to various withholding taxes. Estonian taxpayers are subject to 26/74 income tax on nonbusiness-related expenses or payments.

*Taxes*/The 26/74 income tax must be paid on fines and late payment interest imposed in relation to tax arrears. All taxes are deductible for income tax purposes.

*Other significant items*/Benefits in-kind are taxable to the employer furnishing the benefits. Income tax at 26/74 is due on gifts and donations made to individuals, nonresidents, resident companies, and nonprofit associations and foundations not included in the list issued by the government.

Income tax at 26/74 is due on gifts and donations given to nonprofit associations and foundations on the list issued by the government, to registered churches and political parties and to certain state or local government institutions, to the extent that such expenses exceed 3% of the social tax base for the calendar month in which the payments are made. Representation expenses are taxed with income tax at 26/74 to the extent that the monthly total of such expenses exceeds EEK500 plus 2% of the social tax base (excluding benefits in-kind) for the calendar month in which the payments are made. These annual limitations may be adjusted by the taxpayer on a monthly basis.

Income tax at 26/74 is payable in respect of expenses and payments not related to business (including various transactions with entities in low-tax jurisdictions, where the income tax rate is less than 2/3 of the equivalent Estonian income tax rate applicable to individuals engaged in business, which is currently 26%).

## Group taxation

There is currently no concept of group taxation in Estonia for income tax purposes, and each company in a group is taxed separately. Intra-group charges between resident companies are currently not usually subject to challenge by the tax authorities provided that these can be substantiated.

## Tax incentives

*Capital investments*/The regional income tax incentives introduced for underdeveloped regions of Estonia in 1998 were abolished from January 1, 2000. Corporate entities may not deduct from their taxable payments the losses attributable to this incentive. Tax incentives granted under income tax laws prior to 1994 to qualifying companies with foreign investment are also now ineffective.

## Withholding taxes

Withholding requirements do not apply to payments to resident corporations and permanent establishments of foreign entities. Payments subject to withholding taxes include the following.

1. Dividends paid to all nonresident individuals and to foreign legal entities that own less than 25% (from May 1, 2004—20%) of the share capital of a resident company—26%. Dividends paid to legal entities in low-tax jurisdictions are subject to 26% withholding tax, irrespective of their participation in the corporation distributing dividends. It should be noted that

the tax on distributions (26/74, see above) is not regarded as a withholding tax and that the withholding taxes referred to herein apply in addition to the tax on distributions. Under the accession treaty with the EU, Estonia may apply the tax on distributions to dividends until December 31, 2008.

2. Interest paid by resident credit institutions and branches of nonresident credit institutions to resident and nonresident individuals is exempt from income tax. Interest paid by other institutions to resident individuals and nonresidents is subject to 26% withholding tax, except certain interest paid to nonresident credit and financial institutions that is exempt from withholding tax. From May 1, 2004, interest paid to non-residents (other than entities in low-tax jurisdictions) is expected to be exempt from Estonian withholding tax.

3. Royalties paid to resident individuals—26% and to nonresidents—15%. From May 1, 2004, arm's-length royalties paid to associated corporations resident in the EU member state or their permanent establishments in the EU are expected to be exempt from Estonian withholding tax.

4. Payments to nonresidents for services provided in Estonia, including management and consultancy fees—15%. All payments made for services to the entities in low-tax jurisdictions are subject to 26% withholding tax, irrespective of where the services were provided.

5. Rental payments to nonresident and resident individuals—26%. However, payments for the use of industrial, commercial or scientific equipment are subject to reduced 15% withholding tax.

6. Payments to nonresident artists or sportsmen for personal activities rendered in Estonia or to third persons for such activities of nonresident artists or sportsmen—15%.

7. Directors' fees to members of management or supervisory boards—26%.

Estonia has effective double taxation treaties with Armenia, Austria, Belarus, Belgium, Canada, Czech Republic, Denmark, Finland, France, Germany, Iceland, Ireland, Italy, Kazakhstan, Latvia, Lithuania, Malta, Moldova, the Netherlands, Norway, People's Republic of China, Poland, Sweden, Ukraine, the United Kingdom, and the United States. Treaties have also been signed with Croatia, Hungary, Portugal, Romania, Russia, Slovak Republic, Spain, Switzerland, and Turkey, but these are awaiting ratification. The following rates apply to dividends, interest and royalties paid to a recipient resident in a tax treaty country. The lower of the domestic and the treaty rate is given.

| Recipient | Dividends (1) | Interest (2) | Royalties |
|---|---|---|---|
| | % | % | % |
| Nontreaty | 0/26 | 26 | 15 |
| Treaty: | | | |
| Armenia (11) | 0/15 | 10 | 10 |
| Austria (10) | 0/15 | 10 | 5/10 (4, 12) |
| Belarus | 0/10 | 10 | 10 |
| Belgium (11) | 0/15 | 10 | 5/10 (4, 12) |
| Canada | 0/15 | 10 | 10 |
| People's Republic of China (3) | 0/10 | 10 | 10 (12) |
| Czech Republic | 0/15 | 10 | 10 (12) |
| Denmark | 0/15 | 10 | 5/10 (4, 12) |
| Finland | 0/15 | 10 | 5/10 (4, 12) |
| France (5) | 0/15 (6) | 10 | 5/10 (4, 12) |

| Recipient | Dividends (1) | Interest (2) | Royalties |
|---|---|---|---|
| | % | % | % |
| Germany (7)........................................ | 0/15 | 10 | 5/10 (4, 12) |
| Iceland............................................... | 0/15 | 10 | 5/10 (4) |
| Ireland, Republic of............................ | 0/15 | 10 | 5/10 (4, 12) |
| Italy (8) ............................................. | 0/15 (6) | 10 | 5/10 (4, 12) |
| Kazakhstan (8).................................... | 0/15 | 10 | 15 |
| Latvia................................................ | 0/15 | 10 | 5/10 (4, 12) |
| Lithuania ............................................ | 0/15 | 0 | 0 |
| Malta (11) .......................................... | 0/15 | 10 | 10 (12) |
| Moldova ............................................. | 0/10 | 10 | 10 |
| Netherlands (7)................................... | 0/15 | 10 | 5/10 (4, 12) |
| Norway............................................... | 0/15 | 10 | 5/10 (4) |
| Poland................................................ | 0/15 | 10 | 10 (12) |
| Sweden.............................................. | 0/15 | 10 | 5/10 (4, 12) |
| Ukraine .............................................. | 0/15 | 10 | 10 |
| United Kingdom .................................. | 0/15 | 10 | 5/10 (4, 12) |
| United States (3)................................. | 0/15 (9) | 10 | 5/10 (4) |

The numbers in parentheses refer to the following numbered Notes.

Notes:

1. The rate is nil if the corporate shareholder owns at least 25% (20% from 1.05.2004) of the capital of the Estonian company (domestic law).

2. From July 1, 1998, interest received by nonresident companies from a resident bank or other financial institution is subject to a rate of 26% (domestic law). Most treaties provide for an exemption for certain types of interest (e.g., interest paid to the state, local authorities, the central bank, export credit institutions, and in relation to sales on credit). From May 1, 2004, interest paid to non-residents (other than entities in low-tax jurisdictions) is expected to be exempt from Estonian withholding tax.

3. The treaties with China and the United States came into effect on January 1, 2000.

4. The lower rate applies to royalties paid for the use of industrial, commercial, or scientific equipment.

5. The treaty with France came into effect from May 1, 2001 but is applied retroactively from 1996.

6. The rate is 5% if the corporate shareholder owns 10% to 24% of the capital of the Estonian company.

7. The treaties with Germany and the Netherlands are applied retroactively from 1994 and 1995, respectively.

8. The treaties with Italy and Kazakhstan came into effect on January 1, 2001.

9. The rate is 5% if the corporate shareholder owns 10% to 24% of voting shares of the Estonian company.

10. The treaty with Austria came into effect on January 1, 2003.

11. The treaties with Armenia, Belgium, and Malta came into effect from January 1, 2004.

12. From May 1, 2004, arm's length royalties paid to associated corporations resident in the EU member state or their permanent establishments in the EU are expected to be exempt from Estonian withholding tax.

# Estonia

## Tax administration

*Returns*/The tax period is a calendar month. The tax return for income subject to 26/74 income tax or any withholding tax is required to be submitted by the 10th day of the month during which the payment or taxable expense was made.

Instead of financial statements, resident corporations and permanent establishments of foreign entities must submit to the tax authorities a signed original of their annual accounts within six months of the end of their financial year. Resident corporations and permanent establishments of foreign entities will no longer be required to submit annual income tax returns.

*Payment of tax*/The income tax must be remitted to the local tax authorities by the tenth day of the month following the payment or taxable expense. There are no longer monthly corporate income tax installments.

## *CORPORATION TAX CALCULATION*

For January 2004

| | | |
|---|---:|---:|
| Profit available for distribution ...................................... | EEK 1,000,000 | |
| Dividends distributed and paid to resident individual or nonresident shareholders in January 2004 ......................................................... | 740,000 | |
| 26/74 income tax on income distributed ................................................... | | EEK 260,000 |
| Dividends received by nonresident corporation owning at least 25% of the share capital of the company distributing dividends ............................... | 740,000 | |
| Representation expenses made in January 2003.......... | 10,000 | |
| Limit—EEK500 plus 2% of the social tax base (payroll) of December 2003...................................... | 6,500 | |
| Amount over the limit .................................................... | 3,500 | |
| 26/74 income tax on the amount exceeding the limit ............................................................................. | | 1,230 |
| Nonbusiness expenses incurred and payments made in January 2004 ............................................. | 5,000 | |
| 26/74 income tax on nonbusiness expenses ........................................... | | 1,757 |
| Total income tax for January 2004, payable on or before February 10, 2004 ................................................................. | | EEK 262,987 |

Note:

Exchange rate of the kroon at March 18, 2004: US$1 = EEK 12.6475.

The Estonian kroon (EEK) is pegged to the euro at the rate: €1 = EEK 15.6466.

# Faroe Islands

## PwC contact

For additional information on taxation in Faroe Islands, contact:

Ole Guldborg Nielsen
Rasmussen & Weihe
Statsautoriserad grannskodarafelag P/F
Á Gladsheyggi
P.O.Box 30
FO-110 Tórshavn
Faroe Islands
Telephone: (298) 35 17 00
Fax: (298) 35 17 01
e-mail: rasmussen@rasmussen.fo

## Significant developments

There have not been any significant changes in the taxation in 2003.

However, legislation regarding "thin capitalization" and "transfer pricing" has been put before the government in December 2003. It is likely that the legislation will be passed early in 2004 and will be set into force from the day the legislation pass.

The legislation regarding transfer pricing is by and large a copy of the Danish legislation, which again is built on the Organization of Economic Cooperation and Development's (OECD's) model arrangement. These rules apply between related parties, no matter whether the transactions are between residents or nonresidents. The definition of related parties is when a company or person directly or indirectly owns at least 50% of the share capital or possess 50% of the voting rights in another company. Companies are obliged to maintain documentation, substantiating that intragroup transactions are conducted in accordance with arm's length principles.

The legislation regarding thin capitalization also stipulates that all transactions between related parties must be based on arm's length basis. The guidelines in the Danish regulations, which the proposal is built on, to decide whether or not the ratio of equity/intercompany financing to external financing is considered to be out of proportion, is when the ratio exceeds 1:4. If so, part of the interest expense is not deductible.

## Taxes on corporate income

The company tax rate is 20%. (For income in connection with production (first sale) of hydrocarbons, special rules apply). The tax deriving from the income year ended in 2003 will be due in three equal parts in the months of October, November, and December 2004.

Note that for entities with a registered and paid up capital of less than DKK80,000, the tax rate is 49%. A Faroese limited company will always have a registered and paid up capital of DKK80,000 or more, but this special tax rate for companies with a registered and paid up capital less than DKK80,000 will apply for branches of foreign companies, provided the foreign company has a registered and paid up capital less than DKK80,000.

## Taxes on incomes from hydrocarbon exploration

Whereas the corporation tax rate is 20%, licensees are subject to an income tax of 27% of income derived from production (first sale) of hydrocarbons. In addition, licensees shall pay a royalty of 2% of the revenue of the hydrocarbons sold. Furthermore, a special tax on "super-normal profits" exists.

In principle, the taxable income of a licensee is calculated in accordance with the provisions in the Tax Act.

However, royalties are not incorporated in the tax legislation, and are, as such, not regarded as a tax. They are therefore deductible when computing the taxable income (and also the taxable income for special tax).

As the main rule, the administrative requirements in the general tax legislation also apply for companies or individuals who are tax liable according to the Hydrocarbon Tax Act. However, a number of special rules are laid down in the Hydrocarbon Tax Administration Act.

## Corporate residence

A corporation is resident in Faroe Islands for tax purposes if it is incorporated in Faroe Islands and registered in the Companies Register as having a place of business in Faroe Islands.

## Other taxes

*Value-added tax*/The VAT rate is 25% of the price charged (exclusive of VAT).

*Stamp taxes*/There are few stamp taxes, and the amounts are insignificant.

*Hydrocarbon tax*/A hydrocarbon tax was instituted by new legislation in April 1999, and an amendment has been set into force on March 7, 2000.

*Employer's taxes*/For unemployment security and other social security, the employer is obliged to pay 1.50% of salaries and wages. Companies that are exempt from VAT pay an employer's tax calculated on the total annual cost of salaries and wages. The rate can be up to 5%, which is the rate for banks and other financial institutions, the most significant sector paying the employer's tax. These taxes are deductible for income tax purposes.

Social security charges of 1.50% on salaries and wages are borne by employees.

## Branch income

The tax on branch income is the same as on corporate profits. The employer's taxes also apply to branches. No tax is withheld on transfers of profits to a foreign head office.

## Income determination

*Inventory valuation*/Inventories are generally stated at the lower of cost or market value (replacement cost). Obsolete stock with an anticipated sales value below cost can be valued at the anticipated sales value.

*Capital gains*/Capital gains and losses on bonds and shares, options, debt and dividends are not included in the ordinary corporate taxable income. A special income statement stipulating the capital gains and losses should be filed at the same time as the ordinary income statement.

# Faroe Islands

Capital gains are taxed at a flat tax rate of 20%. Capital losses can only be deducted in the assessment of capital gains. However, capital losses may under certain circumstances be deducted from the ordinary taxable income.

Certain interim provisions apply for shares acquired before the new legislation was set in force.

Interest is treated as ordinary taxable income.

When computing capital gains on real estate, the original cost will be adjusted with the change in the price index since the property was acquired. Capital gain arising from normal inflation is thus not taxed.

*Intercompany dividends*/Dividends received from companies are taxed at a rate of 20%. The company declaring the dividend is obliged to withhold and pay this tax. However, provided the recipient company owns at least 25% of the total share capital, dividends from a domestic company are tax exempt and do not have to be withheld.

If the recipient is a foreign company, the dividend-paying company has to withhold tax at a rate of 20%. If the parent company is situated in a country where there is established a double tax treaty (for instance the Nordic countries), the withholding tax might be refunded/exempted. (See also "Withholding taxes.")

*Foreign income*/Faroese corporations are taxed on their worldwide income. A corporation can claim relief for taxes imposed by foreign countries on income that is included in ordinary taxable income in Faroe Islands. Foreign dividends received by a Faroese corporation should be included in the special income statement and will be taxed at a rate of 20%. The same rules apply as for intercompany dividends; for example, if the recipient holds more than 25% of the share capital, dividends will be tax-exempt.

Undistributed income of a subsidiary is not taxed in Faroe Islands.

*Stock dividends*/Stock dividends (bonus shares) are not possible.

## Deductions

*Depreciation and depletion*/Annual depreciation allowances on fixed assets other than buildings may be claimed by the diminishing-balance method at a rate of up to 30%. The depreciation base is the cost of fixed assets less (1) sales proceeds of disposals and (2) depreciation allowances previously claimed.

Depreciation allowances on buildings (other than those used for dwelling purposes) may be claimed on the straight-line basis. Depreciation may be claimed at a rate of 7% (industrial buildings) or 4% (office and other buildings) per annum for the first ten years, and after that at a rate of 2% (1%) until accumulated depreciation is 100%.

An advance allowance of up to 45% (though not in excess of 15% a year) may be claimed on a contract for the building of a ship.

All depreciation recapture on the sale of fixed assets, buildings, or ships is included in ordinary taxable income.

Tax depreciation need not be in conformity with book depreciation.

There are special rules regarding natural resources, and these are regulated in the Hydrocarbon Tax Act.

*Net operating losses*/Tax losses may be carried forward for five years. Loss carryback is not permitted. Special rules apply regarding hydrocarbon taxation. The Hydrocarbon Tax Act allows for loss carryforward for 20 years.

*Payments to foreign affiliates*/A Faroese corporation can claim a deduction for royalties and specific service fees paid to foreign affiliates, provided such amounts are equal to what it would pay to an unrelated entity. Interest at normal commercial rates paid to foreign affiliates is also allowed as a deduction.

*Taxes*/Taxes are not deductible for income tax purposes, except for employer's taxes.

*Other significant items*/Goodwill can be amortized over ten years for tax purposes. Formation, merger, reorganization, and liquidation expenses are mostly nondeductible.

## Group taxation

A Faroese corporation may obtain permission to be taxed jointly with one or more wholly owned domestic subsidiaries, provided certain conditions are fulfilled. Losses in one of the companies dating from before the joint taxation can be set off only against profits in the same company.

## Incentives

*Inward investment*/Provided certain conditions are fulfilled, it is possible to get subsidies or guarantees from a public fund (the Business Development Fund). Also, there is a publicly owned Industrial Development Institute that invests in Faroese businesses, whether by share capital or by loans.

*Capital investment*/There are no incentives available to encourage capital investment.

*Other incentives*/For shipping companies with ships registered in the Faroese International Ships Register (FAS) (and their crews therefore being liable to taxation in the Faroe Islands) there is a subsidy of 28% of total crew wages.

This subsidy is also available for Faroese shipping companies that bare-boat charter foreign ships (whereas the crewmembers become subject to taxation in the Faroe Islands).

## Withholding taxes

A Faroese corporation distributing dividends is obliged to withhold 20% tax on dividends to corporations, and 35% tax on dividends to individuals, no matter whether the recipient is resident or nonresident. However, the obligation to withhold the tax does not apply for any part of the total dividend that is distributed to a parent corporation situated in the Faroe Islands (owning 25% or more of the total share capital).

A 25% withholding tax is levied on royalties paid from Faroe Islands to a recipient abroad. However, in double taxation treaties, Faroe Islands has waived the right to tax royalties from sources in Faroe Islands. The royalty tax applies to industrial royalties and licenses but not to artistic royalties or lease payments.

There is no withholding tax on payments of interest.

# Faroe Islands

Faroe Island has entered into a tax treaty with the Nordic countries. It is a tax credit type of treaty, where the tax abatement is the lower of (1) the tax paid in the foreign country or (2) the amount of Faroese tax in proportion to total Faroese tax that the net foreign income bears to the company's taxable income in the Faroe Islands. The term "qualifying company" used in the schedule below for "Resident and nontreaty" means a company whose shareholding in the Faroese subsidiary is at least 25%. Under "Treaty" it means a company whose shareholding in the Faroese subsidiary is at least 10%.

| Recipient | Dividends | | Interest | Royalties |
|---|---|---|---|---|
| | Qualifying companies | Other | | |
| | % | % | % | % |
| Resident and nontreaty: | | | | |
| Resident corporations.................................. | 0 | 20 | Nil | Nil |
| Resident individuals.................................... | — | 35 | Nil | Nil |
| Nontreaty/nonresident corporations............ | 20 | 20 | Nil | Nil |
| Nontreaty/nonresident individuals............... | — | 35 | Nil | Nil |
| Treaty: | | | | |
| Denmark...................................................... | 0 | 15 | Nil | Nil |
| Finland ....................................................... | 0 | 15 | Nil | Nil |
| Iceland........................................................ | 0 | 15 | Nil | Nil |
| Norway ....................................................... | 0 | 15 | Nil | Nil |
| Sweden ...................................................... | 0 | 15 | Nil | Nil |

Note:

Recipient qualifying companies situated in a "treaty country" will have to apply for a refund of the withholding tax (20%) regarding dividends.

## Tax administration

**Returns**/Tax returns should be filed at June 1 in the year following the end of the accounting year. The tax system, in practice, is based on self-assessment. Tax assessments are automatically made by the tax authorities on the basis of the tax return. However, the tax authorities may subsequently audit the tax returns.

**Payment of tax**/The tax must be paid in three equal installments on October 20, November 20, and December 20 in the year following the end of the accounting year.

The payment of withholding tax regarding dividends must be paid no less than 14 days after the resolution is made at the ordinary general meeting.

## *CORPORATION TAX CALCULATION*

Calendar year 2003 (or accounting year ended in 2003)

| | | |
|---|---|---:|
| Income before tax | DKK | 1,000,000 |
| Add income tax paid by foreign branch | | |
| (on net income of 200,000) | | 50,000 |
| | | 1,050,000 |
| Less depreciation allowances claimed in excess | | |
| of book depreciation | | 100,000 |
| Taxable income | DKK | 950,000 |
| Tax thereon at 20% | DKK | 190,000 |
| *Less* foreign tax credit | | |
| (lesser of (1) 190,000 x 200,000/950,000 = 40,000 or | | |
| (2) foreign tax paid 50,000) | | (40,000) |
| Income tax payable | DKK | 150,000 |
| Payable October 20, 2004 | DKK | 50,000 |
| Payable November 20, 2004 | DKK | 50,000 |
| Payable December 20, 2004 | DKK | 50,000 |

Note:

The following assumptions have been made.

| | |
|---|---:|
| Income before tax (including net income after tax from branch in foreign country) | 1,000,000 |
| Net income from branch in foreign country | 200,000 |
| Income tax paid by branch in foreign country | 50,000 |
| Depreciation allowances claimed in excess of book depreciation | 100,000 |

Exchange rate of the krone at January 1, 2004: US$1 = DKK5.921.

# Fiji

## PwC contact

For additional information on taxation in Fiji, contact:

Jerome Kado
PricewaterhouseCoopers
Level 8, Civic Tower
262 Victoria Parade
(GPO Box 200)
Suva, Fiji
Telephone: (679) 331 3955
Fax: (679) 330 0981
LN address: Jerome Kado@AsiaPac
e-mail: jerome.kado@fj.pwc.com

## Significant developments

The government has increased the corporate income tax rate to 31% from the previously legislated 30%.

Amendments have been made to the antiavoidance provisions to further discourage tax avoidance.

The government has amended the various trust provisions of the Fiji Income Tax Act.

A new binding ruling system has been introduced from January 1, 2004.

Legislation has been introduced to effect the above and other proposed changes to the Fiji tax regime that were announced in the 2004 National Budget address. These changes are proposed to take effect from January 1, 2004 and are highlighted below.

## Taxes on corporate income

Normal tax is payable on taxable income at the following rates.

|  | % |
| --- | --- |
| Nonresident shipping companies in respect of outgoing business from Fiji | 2 |
| Mutual insurance companies in respect of life insurance income and Nonmutual insurance companies to the extent their life insurance business is deemed to be mutual | 30 |
| Other nonresident companies carrying on business in Fiji (e.g., branch profits) | 31 |
| Other companies | 31 |

## Corporate residence

A company incorporated in Fiji is resident in Fiji. A company not incorporated in Fiji is resident in Fiji if it carries on business in Fiji and either its practical management and control are in Fiji, or its voting powers are controlled by shareholders who are residents of Fiji.

## Other taxes

*Resident interest withholding tax*/A withholding tax of 31% is deductible from payments to or accrual of interest for resident depositors by banks and other financial institutions. However, this tax is not payable where the depositor provides a tax identification number to the financial institution, or where interest received does not exceed $F120.

**Land sales tax**/The profits arising from the sale of undeveloped land in Fiji, if not included in taxable income for income tax purposes, may be subject to land sales tax at rates ranging from 6.5% to 30%.

**Excise tax**/Excise tax is payable on tobacco and alcohol products manufactured in Fiji.

**Value-added tax**/The government increased the rate of VAT from 10% to 12.5%, effective from January 1, 2003. The supply of financial services, residential accommodation and education by an approved institution is exempt. The supply of exports and international transportation is zero-rated. General insurers, agents, and brokers are now proposed to be subject to VAT (these supplies are currently exempt).

The once-off dwelling home refund will now be first offset against any other tax liability of the taxpayer with effect from January 1, 2004.

VAT refunds will be first offset against other tax liabilities prior to the refunds being made with effect from January 1, 2004.

## Branch income

The tax rate on branch profits, 31%, is the same as the rate on profits of a resident corporation, 31%. There is no further withholding of tax on the repatriation of branch profits.

## Income determination

**Inventory valuation**/Inventories are normally valued at the lower of cost and net realizable value. While FIFO is acceptable, LIFO is not, for either book or tax purposes. Conformity between book and tax reporting is not required. There are no special provisions for valuing inventories or determining inventory flows.

**Capital gains**/Currently, capital gains are not subject to tax, although gains realized from the sale or other disposition of property acquired for the purpose of resale, or as part of a profit-making undertaking or scheme, are taxable as ordinary income.

**Intercompany dividends**/Resident corporations may exclude from taxable income dividends received from a company incorporated in Fiji. There are no ownership requirements for this exclusion.

**Foreign income**/Resident corporations are taxed on their worldwide income. Pursuant to the ruling in a recent case, the foreign income sourced from a nontreaty country would be subject to income tax in Fiji, with credits available for tax paid on such income. Income derived from a treaty country is taxed according to the treaty. A credit is allowed in Fiji for foreign tax paid on the foreign income, limited to the lesser of the Fiji tax payable or the overseas tax paid on such income. There are no special provisions for taxing undistributed income of foreign subsidiaries.

**Stock dividends**/Bonus shares are tax free, except where paid out of revenue profits of investment or service-type companies. Tax-free stock dividends issued by private companies become taxable upon realization of shares.

*Other significant items*/Where a foreign-controlled business in Fiji produces less income than might be expected, the revenue authorities may determine the income for tax purposes. A person normally residing outside Fiji that disposes of an interest in land in Fiji held directly or through a shareholding in a company may be assessed to income tax on the profit on that disposal.

## Deductions

*Depreciation and depletion*/Depreciation is calculated on the prime cost on the straight-line basis. The rates of depreciation are based on the estimated life of the asset. Upon disposal of an asset, recapture of depreciation claimed is taxable or the excess of tax written-down value over sale proceeds is deductible. The taxpayer has an option to set off recapture of depreciation against the cost of replacement assets. Conformity between book and tax depreciation is not required.

There are seven broad bands of depreciation rates for assets acquired after January 1, 1998, and the prescribed effective life of the asset is used to determine the relevant depreciation rate.

An optional 20% loading, which applies on the broadband rate, may be claimed. Buildings have been subject to new depreciation rates from January 1, 2001. It has been proposed that accelerated depreciation for buildings will be extended to December 31, 2007.

It was announced in the 2004 National Budget that renewable energy plant and water storage facilities also qualify for accelerated depreciation.

Assets acquired before January 1, 1998 will continue to be depreciated at the former rates.

Accelerated depreciation is available on capital expenditure on buildings constructed between certain specified dates that are to be used for agricultural, commercial or industrial purposes or on multistory, multiunit residential buildings, as well as on other capital expenditure considered of benefit to the economic development of Fiji. Up to one-fifth of the expenditure may be claimed in each of any five years of an eight-year period.

Capital expenditure aimed at economizing on the consumption of fuel, electricity or its derivatives or on an asset using energy sources indigenous to Fiji may be eligible for accelerated depreciation at varying rates or for an investment allowance (in addition to normal depreciation) of up to 40% of expenditure.

The cost of the acquisition of a mining lease or tenement and the cost of development of mines may be written off in equal installments in any five of the first or last eight years of a nine-year period, commencing with the year in which the expenditure was incurred.

A deduction for depletion of other natural resources is not available.

*Thin capitalization*/The government is considering introduction of thin-capitalization rules. The commercial sector was invited to make representations in this regard.

*Net operating losses*/From 2001, losses may be carried forward for eight years (previously six years), provided the company can demonstrate a minimum 51% continuity of shareholding between the year of loss and the year of claim and there is no substantial change in or cessation of the trade. Notwithstanding the change in ownership, losses may also be carried forward where a company carries on the same business in the carried forward year as it did in the loss year. Loss carrybacks are not permitted.

Losses incurred in agricultural or pastoral pursuits may be carried forward indefinitely.

**Donations**/From January 1, 2002, a 100% deduction for cash donations up to a maximum of $F50,000 is allowable (previously the tax deduction was limited to 50% of the cash donation subject to a maximum claim of $F2,000 for individuals and $F5,000 for companies).

**Payments to foreign affiliates**/Subject to the normal rules of deductibility, a deduction can be claimed for royalties, management service fees, and interest charges.

**Taxes**/Taxes levied on income are not deductible.

**Other significant items**/Provisions for expenses not yet incurred, for example, provisions for bad debts, bonuses or future maintenance, are not tax deductible. A deduction is permitted in respect of amounts subsequently paid or written off.

Employers contributing above the basic minimum statutory contribution to approved funds or the Fiji National Provident Fund can now claim the excess as a deduction.

## Group taxation

Group taxation is not permitted.

## Tax incentives

The tax incentives are designed primarily to promote export sales and to encourage the development of industries that are considered of benefit to the economic development of Fiji.

**Export income deduction**/From 2001, a deduction for export income is allowed in accordance with the following.

| Year of assessment | Percentage of export income to be deducted |
|---|---|
| 2001 and 2002 | 100% |
| 2003 and 2004 | 75% |
| 2005 and 2006 | 50% |
| 2007 and 2008 | 25% |
| 2009 and every thereafter | 0% |

From January 1, 2002, "export income" means profit derived by a taxpayer from the business of exporting goods and services, and the Commissioner of Inland Revenue may, where separate records for export income are not maintained, determine such income on the basis of a formula as set out in the legislation.

From January 1, 2004, the definition of "export income" has been clarified to mean "net profit."

The export income deduction will not be available for reexports.

From January 1, 2004, the 5th Schedule of the Income Tax Act—"Export Incentives," has been repealed. However, the existing concession areas are expected to continue to enjoy concessions under this schedule until expiry.

# Fiji

*Investment allowance*/From 2001, an investment allowance equal to 40% of the qualifying expenditure is available as a deduction for agricultural, forestry or marines resources business; or an information technology business; or a rural manufacturing business. This allowance may be claimed in addition to normal depreciation. A qualifying expenditure means expenditure of $F50,000 or more incurred in any of the years from the year of assessment 2001 to year of assessment 2005, for the purpose of acquiring a capital asset(s).

*Employment taxation scheme*/Salary and wages paid in the first 12 months period qualifying for the 150% deduction has been extended to 2004.

*Capital investment*/These incentives are available to the hotel, tourism, and mining industries.

1. Hotel industry—Approved capital expenditure incurred in building, renovating or expanding a hotel is subject to an investment allowance of 55% of the approved expenditure, in addition to normal depreciation. Any unused investment allowance can be carried forward indefinitely.

   Under the Short Life Investment Package (SLIP) the following concessions are available.
   a. Carryforward of losses to eight years.
   b. Duty-free entry of all capital equipment, plant and machinery.
   c. Permission to generate own electricity, the excess to be sold to the Fiji Electricity Authority.
   d. Tax holiday period of 20 years.

   A minimum investment of $F40 million is required to qualify for SLIP.

   A new package known as Half-Slip was introduced with effect from July 1, 1998. The minimum investment required is $F10 million to $F40 million, which entitles the investors to all of the benefits listed above, except that the tax holiday period is reduced to ten years. The exemption from tax for hotel developer profits derived up until December 31, 2005 and SLIP has been extended to December 31, 2005.

2. Mining industry—An approved mining company will for a specified period be exempt from income tax or taxed at a lower rate. The holder of a valid prospecting license may write off approved expenditure on prospecting for minerals against income from all sources. An investment package developed in consultation with the mining industry was announced by Government in the 2002 National Budget address. In addition to the eight-year loss carryforward period and reduced corporate tax rates, the package also includes (a) waiver of the 3% export tax; (b) duty-free importation of capital plant and equipment for two years from the date of approval; and (c) royalties based on the price of gold.

*Other incentives*/Other incentives include the following.

1. An export promotion incentive—This is available in the form of a tax deduction equal to 150% of expenditure approved by the Fiji Islands Trade and Investment Bureau for promotion and marketing of products eligible for the export incentive.

2. Filmmaking and audiovisual incentives—From January 1, 2001, new incentives are available for filmmaking and for the development of the audio-visual industry in Fiji. These incentives include the following.

- Availability of an exemption from tax or tax at a reduced rate on the income of nonresident employees of an approved nonresident company engaged or intending to be engaged in making a film in Fiji.
- Availability to a resident entity (excluding an entity holding a broadcast license in television or radio in Fiji or with substantial shareholdings in the same) of a deduction of up to 150% of monies expended on audiovisual production in respect of income in the year the monies are expended. "Audiovisual productions" includes production for exhibition or sale of theatrical films, broadcast television, direct-to-video and video disk program, audio recording, computer software and interactive websites.
- Exemption from tax on the income derived by a taxpayer from the commercial exploitation of a copyright until the taxpayer has received from the commercial exploitation a return of up to 60% of the monies expended. The monies expended must be of a capital nature and in relation to the audio-visual production costs in respect of a qualifying audio-visual production.
- Tax concessions are also available for residents of areas of land which the appropriate government minister may declare as a studio city zone.
- Legislation has been introduced for a tax rebate to be available under the Film Making and Audio Visual Incentives legislation.

Note: The production of computer software, interactive websites and other e-commerce and telecommunications operations will not be accorded a tax deduction under the Film Making and Audio Visual Incentives legislation, unless they are directly in connection with audio visual production.

3. Dividends — Any dividend from a company incorporated in Fiji, received or accrued to a resident company other than a unit trust, is exempt from tax.

4. Tax on land sales — Nonresidents of Fiji would no longer be taxed on profit from the sale of land acquired purely for investment purposes. However, profit from the business of buying and selling land is subject to tax.

5. South Pacific Games 2003 tax rebate — In support of the South Pacific Games in 2003, a tax rebate of 200% is available for corporate and individual sponsorships in respect of any cash donation made between January 1, 2002 and December 31, 2003 to the South Pacific Games Infrastructure Fund, 2003 South Pacific Games Organizing Committee and South Pacific Games Organizing Committee Limited.

6. From January 1, 2004, a 150% deduction is available to a taxpayer purchasing and donating motor vehicles to the Fiji Police Force; provided that the maximum cost of the vehicle on which claims are to be made shall not exceed $50,000.

7. From January 1, 2004, a 200% deduction is available to a taxpayer in respect of any cash donation made exceeding $100,000 between January 1, 2004 and December 31, 2006 to a sports fund for the purposes of sports development in the Fiji Islands.

8. From January 1, 2004, a 150% deduction is available on expenses incurred in reorganizing a company for the purpose of listing on the South Pacific Stock Exchange.

# Fiji

## Withholding taxes

| Recipient | Dividends | Interest | Royalties | Know-how, Management fees |
|---|---|---|---|---|
| | % | % | % | % |
| Resident individuals ............. | Nil (2) | 31 (1) | Nil | Nil |
| Nonresident corporations and individuals: | | | | |
| Nontreaty ........................... | 15 | 10 | 15 | 15 |
| Treaty: | | | | |
| Australia ......................... | 20 | 10 | 15 | 15 |
| Japan ............................. | 15 | 10 | 10 | 15 |
| Korea, Rep. of ................. | 10 or 15 (3) | 10 | 10 | 10 |
| Malaysia .......................... | 15 | 15 | 15 | 15 |
| New Zealand .................... | 15 | 10 | 15 | 15 |
| Papua New Guinea .......... | 17 | 10 | 15 | 15 |
| United Kingdom................ | 15 | 10 | 15 | 15 |

Notes:

1. Applies to interest (over $F120) on savings and deposits with commercial banks and other financial institutions, unless the taxpayer has provided a tax identification number to the financial institution.

2. Any dividend that has been paid or credited in favor of a resident individual in respect of shares of a company listed on the Suva Stock Exchange is not subject to tax.

3. The rate is 10% of gross amount of dividends if the beneficial owner is a company (other than a partnership) that holds directly at least 25% of the capital of the company paying the dividends. The rate is 15% in all other cases.

It was announced in the 2004 National Budget that the provisional tax rate would be increased from 15% to 30% with effect from January 1, 2004. The Fiji Institute of Accountants has made a submission to the government on this issue. In view of this, the Fiji Islands Revenue and Customs Authority has temporarily put on hold the increase of the rate to 30%.

Dividend Regulations were introduced from January 1, 2001 as a partial form of imputation whereby dividends may be taxed at reduced rates if the income source of the dividends has been subject to tax in the hands of the company.

## Tax administration

*Returns*/Tax is assessed on income derived during the calendar year preceding the year of assessment. Returns are therefore generally accepted on a calendar-year basis, although approval is also given to use a fiscal-year basis. For purposes of assessment of returns completed on a fiscal-year basis, the calendar year in which more than one-half of the fiscal year falls is deemed to be the calendar year in which the income is derived. The Fiji tax system is not based on self-assessment. Returns of income contain information on the basis of which assessments are raised by the tax authorities.

A Tax Agent Lodgement Program was introduced in 2003 to spread the lodgement of tax returns. In conjunction with this program, the advance tax payments will be increased to 100% in three installments by the seventh month after the end of the taxpayer's fiscal year end as follows.

1st advance—Due on the last day of the financial year.

2nd advance—Due three months after the end of the taxpayer's fiscal year end.

3rd advance—Due seven months after the end of the taxpayer's fiscal year end.

**Penalties**/From January 1, 2004, administrative penalty provisions have been amended for non-lodgement of tax returns and for the nonlodgement of annual summaries in relation to Pay As You Earn (PAYE) and Gambling Turnover Tax Summaries.

From January 1, 2004, a new provision has been introduced to allow for distress of business assets once a company goes into liquidation.

**Binding rulings**/A new binding ruling system has been introduced from January 1, 2004.

## CORPORATION TAX CALCULATION

Calendar year 2004

### Statement of taxable income

| | | |
|---|---:|---:|
| Net book profit before income tax | | $F 1,000,000 |
| Add—Provisions disallowed: | | |
| Leave pay and passages | 5,000 | |
| Doubtful debts | 4,000 | |
| Depreciation per accounts | 350,000 | |
| Development expenses written off | 50,000 | |
| Loss on sale of fixed assets per accounts | 500 | 409,500 |
| | | 1,409,500 |
| Deduct: | | |
| Depreciation for tax purposes: | | |
| Annual | 44,500 | |
| Loss on sale of fixed assets for tax purposes | 1,000 | |
| Expenditure charged to provisions: | | |
| Leave pay and passages | 7,500 | 53,000 |
| | | 1,356,500 |
| Deduct—Tax losses from prior years | | 200,000 |
| Taxable income | | $F 1,156,500 |

### Tax payable

| | | |
|---|---|---:|
| Normal tax at 31% | $F | 358,515 |
| Deduct—Advance payments | | (246,720) |
| Tax due on assessment | $F | 111,795 |

Notes:

1. The corporate tax calculation for the income year ending December 31, 2004 is based on Fijian tax laws in effect on January 2, 2004.

2. Exchange rate (bank selling) of the Fiji dollar at January 2, 2004: US$1 = $F1.7141.

# Finland

## PwC contacts

For additional information on taxation in Finland, contact:

Martti Virolainen
PricewaterhouseCoopers Oy
P.O. Box 1015
FIN-00101 Helsinki, Finland
Telephone: +358 9 2280 1481
Fax: + 358 9 657 120
e-mail: martti.virolainen@fi.pwc.com

Arja Björklund (VAT)
PricewaterhouseCoopers Oy
P.O. Box 1015
FIN-00101 Helsinki, Finland
Telephone: +358 9 2280 1805
Fax: + 358 2280 1820
e-mail: arja.bjorklund@fi.pwc.com

## General note

This entry is repeated from the 2003/2004 edition. For more up-to-date information consult the contact listed above or Jacqueline Collette at jacqueline.collete@us.pwc.com.

## Significant developments

The Finnish income tax system is expected to undergo some changes in the coming years. The working group on reform completed its report in November 2002. The most significant proposals for reform concern the taxation of dividend income, share conveyances between companies belonging to the same group, and the depreciation system. However, no political decisions have yet been made regarding the proposed reform and therefore for the present it is not clear the extent to which the proposed changes will be implemented.

## Taxes on corporate income

The corporate tax rate is 29%.

## Corporate residence

A company is deemed to be resident where it is incorporated (registered).

## Other taxes

*Value added tax*/VAT legislation entered into force in Finland on June 1, 1994. On January 1, 1995 Finland joined the EU and the Finnish VAT legislation was amended to conform to the 6th VAT Directive.

VAT is payable on the sale of goods and services when relating to business activities and import of goods. However, there are certain exemptions (e.g., heathcare services, financial services). The standard rate of VAT is 22%. A rate of 17% is applied to foodstuffs and animal feed (restaurant services and alcohol excluded). A rate of 8% applies to medicines, books, cinema performances, sports activities, passenger transport, and hotel accommodation. Subscriptions to newspapers and periodicals are zero-rated.

A taxable person can deduct the input VAT included in the purchase price of goods or services acquired from another taxable person for taxable business activities. However, input VAT cannot be reclaimed on the following goods and services:

1. Motorcars and their operating costs, such as petrol, repair, and maintenance costs. However, if the motorcar is used solely for taxable business activities, for example, rental or transportation activities, the input VAT can be reclaimed.
2. Entertainment costs.
3. Company housing and real estate used for leisure activities and their operating costs.
4. Gifts.

**Real estate tax**/Municipalities impose a real estate tax. The tax is levied on the taxable value of buildings and land. The tax rate, which is determined by the municipal council, ranges from 0.22% to 0.5% for permanent dwellings and from 0.5% to 1.0% for other real estate. The tax is deductible for income tax purposes if the real estate is used for business.

## Branch income

Tax rates on branch profits are the same as on corporate profits. No tax is withheld on transfers of profits to the head office. As a general rule, a branch is taxed on profits attributable to it, provided the branch constitutes a permanent establishment in Finland.

## Income determination

**Inventory valuation**/Inventories may be written down to the lowest of direct first in, first out (FIFO) cost, replacement cost, or net realizable value. Conformity between book and tax reporting is required.

**Capital gains**/Capital gains and losses are generally included in taxable income; that is, sales proceeds are included in the taxable income, and the undepreciated balance of the asset sold is deducted in the sales year. However, the entire stock of machinery and equipment is treated as a single item, and the capital gain on machinery and equipment is entered as income indirectly by deducting the selling price from the remaining value of the stock of machinery and equipment.

**Intercompany dividends**/The amount of dividends plus 29/71 of the dividend received by a Finnish corporation from another Finnish corporation, whether or not a subsidiary, are included in taxable income. This 29/71 share (imputation credit) corresponds to the minimum income tax that the company distributing a profit will have to pay. (Note that if the tax payable by a company under the normal tax rules is less than 29/71 of the distributed dividend, the difference will be levied as a compensatory tax. If the company's income tax exceeds 29/71 of the dividends distributed, the difference (tax surplus) can be utilized in dividend distributions during the following ten years if the tax based on the taxable income is smaller than the minimum tax.)

**Income from controlled foreign corporations**/New controlled foreign corporations (CFC) legislation came into force at the beginning of 1995. A Finnish shareholder resident for tax purposes in Finland can be taxed on income of a foreign entity (e.g., company, trust), even though profits have not been distributed from the foreign entity to the Finnish shareholders. CFC legislation is not applied

# Finland

to corporations carrying out industrial activities, similar production activities or ship-owning activities in a foreign country, or selling or marketing activities directly serving the above-mentioned industrial or production activities or ship owning in the foreign country. Corporations resident in a country with which Finland has a double taxation treaty are mainly outside the scope of CFC legislation if the tax rate in the country of residence does not substantially differ from tax rates in Finland and the company does not benefit from any special tax incentives. The provisions of the legislation will be applied only if the actual tax rate in the foreign country is less than three-fifths of the tax rate in Finland and the foreign entity is controlled by Finnish residents; that is, Finnish residents own a total of at least 50% of the share capital or at least 50% of the voting power in the foreign entity. The taxable income of the foreign entity can be allocated only to a Finnish shareholder that owns directly or indirectly more than 10% of the share capital of the foreign entity or whose proportion of the total return of the foreign entity is at least 10%.

**Foreign income**/A Finnish corporation is taxed on foreign-branch income as earned and on foreign dividends when received. Double taxation is avoided either by treaties or by foreign tax credits.

The principal method of avoiding double taxation in treaties is the credit method, although the exemption method is still applied in a few older treaties. Under virtually all tax treaties concluded by Finland, foreign dividends are exempt from taxation in Finland. This still holds true, despite the introduction of the new imputation system, because of an addition in the Act on Taxation of Business Income, Section 6, which came into force at the beginning of 1995. According to Section 6, foreign dividends are exempt from tax in Finland if the Finnish shareholder owns at least 25% of the share capital or has at least 10% of the voting power in the distributing corporation, provided that Finland has a tax treaty with the country of residency of the distributing corporation and the treaty has been in force since January 1, 1995. In cases where a tax treaty is not applicable, the foreign national tax may be credited against Finnish national tax payable on the same income. However, no underlying tax credit is allowed.

A provision effective as of the beginning of 2000 allows foreign dividends exempt from tax paid to a Finnish company to be redistributed to the company's foreign shareholders without the part of the dividend distributed to the foreign shareholders to be taken into account when the amount of the minimum tax is calculated. However, this applies only if the amount of dividend distributed to the foreign shareholders does not exceed the amount of foreign dividend exempt from tax received (unless there is dividend surplus that can be used to cover the difference). If the amount of dividend distributed abroad is smaller than the foreign dividend exempt from tax received, the difference (dividend surplus) can be utilized in later distributions to the foreign shareholders during the ten subsequent years. This modification does not apply if the dividend is redistributed to a corporate body controlled directly or indirectly by a Finnish resident or if this nonresident shareholder is entitled to imputation credit. The modification applies only if the foreign company paying the dividend would be subject to such taxation in its country of residency and the Finnish CFC legislation would not apply.

**Stock dividends**/Stock dividends (bonus shares) may be issued to stockholders free of tax.

## Deductions

*Depreciation and depletion*/Maximum annual rates of depreciation calculated on net book value (declining-balance method) are 25% for machinery and equipment and 4% to 20% for buildings and other construction, depending on the type and estimated life of the asset. Net book value is defined as cost less accumulated depreciation and, in the case of machinery and equipment, proceeds on disposal of the assets. The straight-line method is applied to certain intangible assets and capitalized expenditures and to assets with long economic use, such as dams. Tax depreciation is limited to the cumulative charges made in the books.

The capital cost of mines, sandpits, quarries, and peat bogs is written off in proportion to the quantities extracted. Short-lived items (the economic life of which is three years or less) may be written off immediately. Land is not a depreciable asset.

*Net operating losses*/Losses may be carried forward for ten subsequent years. Loss carrybacks are not allowed.

*Payment to foreign affiliates*/A Finnish corporation may claim a deduction for royalties, service fees, and interest charges paid to foreign affiliates, provided the underlying transaction is beneficial to it and the amounts paid are equal to what it would pay an unrelated entity.

*Taxes*/No income taxes are deductible when determining taxable income. However, the real estate tax is deductible.

## Group taxation

Group contributions between affiliated Finnish companies are deductible for income tax purposes under certain conditions.

## Tax incentives

It is possible for small and medium-sized companies carrying on certain production activity or tourism in developing areas to make use of increased depreciation.

## Withholding taxes

Finnish corporations paying certain types of income are required to apply the following withholding tax rates on payments to foreign corporations and nonresident aliens (see Note 1).

| Recipient | Dividends (2) | | Investment fund profit share | Royalties |
|---|---|---|---|---|
| | Portfolio* | Substantial** | | |
| | % | % | % | % |
| Resident corporations.................. | 0 | 0 | 0 | 0 |
| Resident individuals...................... | 0 | 0 | 29 | 0–60 |
| Nonresident corporations and individuals: | | | | |
| Nontreaty........................... | 29 | 29 | 29 | 29 |
| Treaty: | | | | |
| Argentina ....................... | 0 | 0 | 29 | 3, 5, 10, 15 (3) |

# Finland

| Recipient | Dividends (2) | | Investment fund profit share | Royalties |
|---|---|---|---|---|
| | Portfolio* | Substantial** | | |
| | % | % | % | % |
| Australia........................ | 0 | 0 | 29 | 10 |
| Austria ........................... | 0 | 0 | 0 | 5 |
| Barbados ...................... | 15 | 5 | 29 | 0, 5 (4) |
| Belgium ......................... | 15 | 0 | 0 | 0, 5 (4) |
| Brazil ............................. | 0 | 0 | 29 | 10, 15, 25 (5) |
| Bulgaria ........................ | 10 | 10 | 0 | 0, 5 (4) |
| Canada.......................... | 15 | 10 | 29 | 0, 10 (4) |
| China, P.R..................... | 0 | 0 | 29 | 7, 10 (6) |
| Croatia........................... | 15 | 5 | 0 | 10 |
| Czech Republic............. | 0 | 0 | 0 | 0, 1, 5, 10 (7) |
| Denmark........................ | 15 | 0 | 0 | 0 |
| Egypt ............................. | 10 | 10 | 29 | 25 |
| Estonia .......................... | 5 | 0 | 29 | 5, 10 (8) |
| France ........................... | 0 | 0 | 0 | 0 |
| Germany........................ | 15 | 0, 25 (9) | 0 | 0, 5 (4) |
| Great Britain ................. | 0 | 0 | 0 | 0 |
| Greece........................... | 13 | 0 | 0 | 0, 10 (4) |
| Hungary......................... | 15 | 5 | 0 | 0, 5 (4) |
| Iceland........................... | 15 | 0 | 0 | 0 |
| India .............................. | 0 | 0 | 29 | 15 (10) |
| Indonesia....................... | 15 | 10 | 29 | 10, 15 (11) |
| Ireland, Rep. of ............. | 15 | 0 | 0 | 0 |
| Israel.............................. | 0 | 0 | 0 | 10 |
| Italy................................ | 15 | 0 | 0 | 0, 5 (4) |
| Japan............................. | 15 | 10 | 0 | 10 |
| Korea, Rep. of............... | 15 | 10 | 0 | 10 |
| Latvia............................. | 5 | 0 | 29 | 5, 10 (8) |
| Lithuania........................ | 5 | 0 | 29 | 5, 10 (8) |
| Luxembourg................... | 15, 29 (12) | 0, 29 (12) | 0 | 0, 5, 29 (5, 12) |
| Malaysia ........................ | 15 | 5 | 29 | 5 |
| Malta.............................. | 0 | 0 | 0 | 0 |
| Mexico ........................... | 0 | 0 | 29 | 10 |
| Morocco......................... | 15 | 15 | 0 | 10 |
| Netherlands ................... | 0 | 0 | 0 | 0 |
| New Zealand.................. | 15 | 15 | 29 | 10 |
| Norway .......................... | 15 | 0 | 0 | 0 |
| Pakistan......................... | 0 | 0 | 29 | 10 |
| Philippines .................... | 29 | 15 | 29 | 15, 25 (13) |
| Poland ........................... | 0 | 0 | 0 | 0, 10 (4) |
| Portugal ......................... | 15 | 0 | 0 | 10 |
| Romania ........................ | 0 | 0 | 0 | 2, 5, 5 (14) |
| Russia ........................... | 0 | 0 | 0 | 0 |
| Singapore ...................... | 15 | 5 | 29 | 10 |
| Slovak Republic ............ | 0 | 0 | 0 | 0, 1, 5, 10 (7) |
| Slovenia......................... | 15 | 5 | 0 | 10 |
| South Africa................... | 0 | 0 | 0 | 0 |
| Spain ............................. | 15 | 0 | 0 | 5 |

| Recipient | Dividends (2) | | Investment fund profit share | Royalties |
|---|---|---|---|---|
| | Portfolio* | Substantial** | | |
| | % | % | % | % |
| Sri Lanka ..................... | 15 | 15 | 0 | 10 |
| Sweden......................... | 15 | 0 | 0 | 0 |
| Switzerland.................. | 5 | 0 | 0 | 0 |
| Tanzania ...................... | 20 | 20 | 0 | 20 |
| Thailand....................... | 29 | 15, 20 (15) | 29 | 15 |
| Turkey.......................... | 20 | 15 | 29 | 10 |
| Ukraine ........................ | 0 | 0 | 0 | 0, 5, 10 (16) |
| United Arab Emirates..... | 0 | 0 | 0 | 0 |
| United States................ | 15 | 5 (17) | 0 | 0, 5 (5) |
| Uzbekistan.................... | 0 | 0 | 0 | 0, 5, 10 (18) |
| Zambia ......................... | 15 | 5 | 29 | 0, 5, 15 (5, 19) |

*Individuals and corporations

**Qualifying corporations (20).

Notes:

According to the internal law of Finland, interest paid to a nonresident is usually exempt from taxation in Finland. Therefore, the tax rates mentioned in tax treaties apply only in the case that the interest is paid for a permanent loan in lieu of the contribution of capital.

1. Each tax treaty should be studied carefully because there are often exceptions to general rules.
2. Imputation credit can be obtained only if provided in a treaty. This kind of provision is included in the treaty between Finland and the Republic of Ireland. The withholding tax rate for imputation credit is 29%, unless a tax treaty provides otherwise. If the conditions in the EU Parent/Subsidiary Directive are fulfilled, inter alia, a shareholding of at least 25%, the withholding tax dividend is nil.
3. The rate is 10% on industrial royalties, 5% on artistic royalties, and 3% on royalties to news agency.
4. Tax is not levied on literary, scientific, or artistic royalties (for film royalties, see text of the treaty).
5. The rate is 10% on the use of films, literary, scientific, or artistic works, 25% on the use of trademarks or royalties paid for usufructs and 15% on other royalties.
6. The rate is 7% on industrial, scientific, and commercial royalties and 10% on other royalties.
7. Tax is not levied on literary, scientific, or artistic royalties (for film royalties, see text of the treaty). The rate is 1% for finance lease of equipment and 5% for operating lease of equipment and computer software.
8. The rate is 5% on royalties paid for the use of industrial, commercial, or scientific equipment and 10% on other royalties.
9. The rate is 29%, if the recipient is a silent partner.
10. A lower tax in certain cases.
11. The rate is 10% on film, literary, scientific, and artistic royalties.

12. The rate is 29% if the recipient is a special holding company.
13. The rate is 15% on films; tapes used in television or radio broadcasts; use of copyright of literary, artistic or scientific works; or royalty paid for usufruct.
14. The rate is 2.5% on royalties paid for the use of industrial, commercial, or scientific equipment or computer software.
15. The rate is 15% if the payer is also an industrial enterprise.
16. The rate is 5% for the use of a secret process or for know-how, and there is no tax for computer software or patents.
17. The holding requirement of 10% (of the shares) is calculated on the voting stock in circulation (see Note 20).
18. The rate is 5% for the use of a secret process or for know-how; the rate is 10% on literary, scientific or artistic royalties.
19. Tax is not levied on literary, scientific, or artistic royalties (for film royalties, see text of the treaty); the rate is 5% on royalties from films and tapes.
20. Generally, corporations with a holding of at least 25% of the shares qualify. However, in some cases, a holding of 10%, 20%, or a certain period of holding is required.

## Tax administration

***Returns***/The tax year is the calendar year. A company having a financial year other than the calendar year is taxed for the financial year or the financial years ending during the calendar year. A company must file a tax return within four months from the end of the financial year.

***Payment of tax***/Income taxes are due for payment after the tax assessment of the local tax office. However, limited liability companies should calculate and pay the tax for the tax year when filing the tax return. If the company has paid advance tax payments during the tax year and the advance tax exceeds the amount of final tax payable for the financial period, the company is entitled to a refund of the excess. If the tax is not paid to the tax authorities when the tax return is filed, interest of 5.5% per annum is payable on the unpaid amount (in 2003). The interest is not tax deductible. If an excess amount of final tax is refunded to the company after the tax return is filed, interest of 1.5% per annum is paid to the company (in 2003). The interest is not taxable income.

## *CORPORATION TAX CALCULATION*

Fiscal year ending December 31, 2002

| | | |
|---|---:|---:|
| Net income before taxes (1) | | € 1,000,000 |
| Add—Nondeductible items charged in the accounts: | | |
| Nonbusiness expenses | 20,000 | |
| Gifts and donations in excess of 25,000, or noncharitable | 20,000 | |
| Disallowed entertainment expenses (50%) | 20,000 | 60,000 |
| | | 1,060,000 |
| Deduct—Dividends from foreign subsidiaries | | 80,000 |
| Taxable income | | € 980,000 |
| Corporate income tax—29% of 980,000 | | € 284,200 |

Notes:
1. Net income includes cash dividends of €56,800 plus a tax credit of €23,200. The amount of tax credit is credited to the company as a preliminary tax. See "Intercompany dividends" above.
2. Exchange rate at March 6, 2003: US$1 = €0.913836.

# France

## PwC contact

For additional information on taxation in France, contact:

Jean-Luc Pierre
Landwell & Associés
32, rue Guersant
75017 Paris
France
Telephone: (33) (1) 56 57 83 92
Fax: (33) (1) 56 57 49 51
e-mail: jean-luc.pierre@fr.landwellglobal.com

## Significant developments

The finance act for 2004 has substantially amended the taxation of corporate dividends in France. The dividend tax credit (*avoir fiscal*) will no longer be granted in respect of dividends paid from January 1, 2004, to companies. The equalization tax (*précompte*) will be eliminated for distributions from January 1, 2005 onward. Dividends paid in 2005 out of profits realized over five years ago, or that were not subject to corporate tax at the standard 33.33% rate, will be subject to a special 25% tax, refundable over three years.

Moreover, the finance act has eliminated the time limit on the carryforward of losses by companies. This provision applies to losses incurred in fiscal years from January 1, 2004, and to losses currently being carried forward.

The European Union (EU) interest and royalties directive has also been transposed into French law. Consequently, no liability for withholding tax arises in France in respect of certain interest or royalties payments made by a French resident company, or a French permanent establishment of a company resident in another EU member state to an EU affiliated company.

## Taxes on corporate income

The only tax levied on corporate income is the corporate income tax. For fiscal years ending in 2004, the applicable rate is 33.33%, plus a 3% surtax of the normal corporate tax (including the ordinary tax of 33.33%), and a 3.3% social contribution on benefits assessed on the corporate tax amount from which €763,000 is withdrawn before reduction by the *avoir fiscal* credit and any foreign tax credit.

A reduced tax of 19% applies in certain situations (see "Capital gains" below).

No tax is levied on income at the regional or local level.

A withholding tax is levied on French branches of foreign non-EU corporations at the rate of 25%, or a reduced tax treaty rate (e.g., for the United States, 5%) on net profits. Refund (limited or full) of tax may be claimed to the extent that the taxable amount exceeds the dividend(s) actually distributed by the foreign corporation during the 12 months following the close of the fiscal year concerned, or the dividends are distributed to residents of France.

## Corporate residence

A corporation is resident in France if either it has been incorporated in France, or it has its registered seat in France. For this purpose, France is defined as metropolitan France (excluding Monaco, but including the continental shelf),

Corsica and the overseas departments (French Guyana, Guadeloupe, Martinique, Réunion, St. Barthélémy, and St. Martin).

## Other taxes

**Turnover taxes**/Value-added tax (VAT) is imposed on goods sold and services rendered in France. The normal rate is 19.6%. Other rates of 5.5% and 2.1% apply to specific sales and services. Exports and certain specific services invoiced to non-French residents are zero-rated.

**Business tax**/The rate of local business tax varies. The tax is assessed on the rental value of fixed business assets.

## Branch income

Tax rates on branch profits are the same as on corporate profits. However, as a principle, branch profits are deemed to be distributed to the head office. The total corporate tax burden on a subsidiary's profits distributed to the U.S. parent is now the same as on income of a U.S. company's French branch.

Profits realized in France by foreign corporations whose head offices are located in a European country are not subject to withholding taxes, provided that certain conditions are met (effective head office in a European country; foreign corporation subject to corporate taxation).

## Income determination

**Inventory valuation**/Inventories must be valued at the lower of cost or market. Cost must be determined in accordance with the FIFO or the average-cost method. The LIFO method is prohibited.

**Capital gains**/Capital gains are generally taxable as ordinary income, regardless of whether assets have been held for more or less than two years.

However, capital gains resulting from the sale of shares in subsidiaries held for at least two years, as well as royalties derived from the licensing of patents and patentable know-how, still qualify as long-term and may continue to benefit from the reduced rate of 19% (increased by the 3% surtax and the social contribution on benefits).

Long-term capital gains less the 19% tax thereon must be appropriated to a special reserve. The balance of corporate income tax (14.33%, plus the 3% surtax and the social contribution on benefits) becomes payable if this reserve is distributed to shareholders, but not if it is offset against operating losses or later long-term capital losses, contributed to share capital, or distributed upon liquidation.

**Intercompany dividends**/French parent companies (i.e., companies incorporated in France and holding qualifying shares that represent at least 5% of the issued capital of subsidiaries, French or foreign) have the option of excluding 95% of the subsidiaries' net dividends from corporate income tax (a 5% charges and expenses portion must be added back to the parent company's taxable results).

**Foreign income**/Resident corporations are taxed on their French-source income only, which excludes profits from activities carried out abroad through foreign branches. Foreign income is not taxable until actually due to French resident corporations. As a result, undistributed income of foreign subsidiaries is not taxable. The only exception is provided by Article 209 B of the Tax Code, whereby French corporations are required to include in their taxable income profits made by their more-than-10%-owned foreign subsidiaries and branches established in a country where they are subject to a privileged tax regime. The 10% holding is to be appraised as direct or indirect control of shares and voting rights. The existence of a low-tax regime is to be determined by looking at the specific tax burden borne by the nonresident entity.

When foreign income is due, and therefore becomes taxable, double taxation is partly avoided as follows.

1. For dividends, through the participation exemption.
2. For other income (interest, royalties, fees) by granting a tax credit at least equal to foreign withholding tax. However, if the source of income is a country with which there is no tax treaty, the credit is replaced by a deduction.

*Stock dividends*/The French tax treatment varies, depending on the definition of "stock dividends."

Where the shareholder is given the choice between the receipt of cash or the grant of additional shares as a distribution, such a distribution is treated as an ordinary dividend distribution for the recipient shareholder.

Where the concept refers to the increase in capital by means of a capitalization of reserves, there is no impact as far as the shareholder is concerned. However, the distributing company is subject to a fixed registration tax of €230.

## Deductions

*Depreciation and depletion*/In general, the straight-line-over-useful-life method must be used for all depreciable assets. The basis of depreciation is the cost of fixed assets.

Declining-balance depreciation is allowed for new machinery and equipment, and other qualifying assets having a useful life of three years or more. The rates are equal to straight-line rates multiplied by coefficients (1.25, 1.75, or 2.25), that vary according to the useful life of the asset. The basis of depreciation is net book value.

Special accelerated rates are applicable to investments in fixed assets, such as the following.

1. Immovable installations used for purification of industrial water or air (100% in the first year for installations completed before January 1, 2006).
2. Equipment aimed at saving energy (100% in the first year when acquired or completed before January 1, 2007).
3. Equipment used for producing renewable energy (100% in the first year when acquired or completed before January 1, 2007).
4. Industrial and commercial buildings located in certain depressed areas.
5. Software (100% in the first 12-month period).

*Net operating losses*/For tax purposes, the distinction between ordinary losses (carried forward for a maximum of five years), and losses corresponding to deferred depreciation, has been eliminated by the finance act for 2004. Companies subject to corporate tax can to carry forward their losses for an unlimited period of time. This provision applies to losses incurred in fiscal years after January 1, 2004, and to losses currently being carried forward.

Businesses may also elect a form of carryback. Losses of a given fiscal year may be offset against undistributed taxable profits of the three preceding years. The lower of the tax paid on these profits or the potential tax savings represented by the tax loss of the fiscal year is a tax credit. Such credit may be offset against corporate income tax of the following five fiscal years, and thereafter any excess credit may be refunded in cash.

*Payments to foreign affiliates*/Payments to foreign affiliates are allowed, as long as they meet the arm's-length test. If they do not, Article 57 of the Tax Code provides that income directly or indirectly transferred to the foreign affiliate, through either the increase or the reduction of the purchase or sales price of goods and services, or through any other means, may be added back to taxable income. For the purpose of this provision, foreign affiliates are defined as parent or sister companies.

Where the payments are made to tax haven companies, the French taxpayer must prove that the transaction is bona fide and that the amount due is not exaggerated.

Some specific limitations are also imposed on the payment of interest to shareholders, as follows.

1. The interest rate paid to any shareholder, whether French or foreign, is limited to the average effective annual rate charged by financial institutions for variable loans to companies for a period of more than two years (5.05% for the year 2003).

2. Any interest paid on the portion of a loan that exceeds 1.5 times the share capital of the paying company is disallowed when paid to a foreign corporate shareholder that has the effective management control of the debtor company, or that controls at least 50% of the paying company. This limitation does not apply to foreign parent companies located in EU countries and in certain countries with which a double tax treaty has been signed.

*Taxes*/Most taxes, including unrecoverable VAT, registration taxes and business tax, are deductible. The major exception is the corporate income tax and related penalties.

## Group taxation

French corporations and their 95%-owned domestic subsidiaries may elect to file one single tax return, thus allowing offset of losses of one group corporation against the profits of a related corporation.

Other group consolidation systems are available with the prior authorization of the Ministry of Finance, as follows.

1. *Bénéfice consolidé*—The 50%-owned subsidiary consolidation system allows the combined reporting of profits and losses of all controlled branches, subsidiaries, and partnerships, whether French or foreign.

2. *Bénéfice mondial*—Worldwide tax consolidation allows French corporations to include in their French tax return the results of their foreign activities carried out by branches.

## Tax incentives

*Inward investments*/No particular incentive is available to foreign investors in France. However, the government offers a comprehensive program of tax incentives (e.g., accelerated depreciation of industrial and commercial buildings,

# France

business-tax holiday) and development subsidies to encourage investment in underdeveloped areas.

Capital investment is encouraged only through the declining-balance method of depreciation for capital expenditure.

*Investment in research*/Qualifying research expenses may give rise to a tax credit that can be offset against corporate income tax. The standard credit is equal to 45% of the excess of expenses incurred during a given year over the average of those of the two preceding years, and 5% of the expenses incurred, with a maximum of €8 million per year.

## Withholding taxes

Payments to resident corporations and individuals are not subject to withholding taxes.

Payments to nonresident corporations and individuals are subject to withholding taxes, as shown below.

(Note: The withholding tax rate on distributions to certain EU corporate shareholders, subject to certain conditions, was reduced to nil as from 1992. See the details in the explanation of Columns 3 and 4 below.)

| | Dividends | | |
| Column 1 | Column 2 | Column 3 | Column 4 |
| | Individuals and nonparent | Parent | Shareholding required to be a |
| Country of residence | companies | companies | parent |
| | % | % | % |
| Nontreaty......................................... | 25 | 25 | — |
| Treaty: | | | |
| Algeria.......................................... | 15 | 5 | 10 |
| Argentina...................................... | 15 | 15 | — |
| Armenia......................................... | 15 | 5 | 10 |
| Australia ...................................... | 15* (1, 2) | 15 | — |
| Austria.......................................... | 15* (1) | 0 | 10 |
| Bahrain.......................................... | 0 | 0 | — |
| Bangladesh ................................. | 15 | 10 | 10 |
| Belgium ........................................ | 15* (2) | 10 | 10 |
| Benin............................................. | 25 | 25 | — |
| Bolivia........................................... | 15 | 15 | 10 |
| Botswana...................................... | 12 | 5 | 25 |
| Brazil ............................................ | 15* (1) | 15* (1) | — |
| Bulgaria......................................... | 15 | 5 | 15 |
| Burkina Faso ............................... | 15* (1) | 15* (1, 3) | — |
| Cameroon..................................... | 15 (4) | 15 | — |
| Canada.......................................... | 15 | 5 | 10 |
| Quebec...................................... | 15 | 10 | 10 |
| Central African Republic............... | 25 | 25 | — |
| China, P.R. ................................... | 10 | 10 | — |
| Comoro Islands ........................... | 15/25 | 15/25 | — |
| Congo, Rep. of (5) ....................... | 20 | 15 | 10 |

| | Dividends | | |
|---|---|---|---|
| **Column 1** | **Column 2** | **Column 3** | **Column 4** |
| | Individuals and nonparent | Parent | Shareholding required to be a |
| **Country of residence** | **companies** | **companies** | **parent** |
| | % | % | % |
| Croatia......................................... | 15 | 5 | 25 |
| Cyprus......................................... | 15 | 10 | 10 |
| Czech Republic ........................... | 10 | 10 | — |
| Denmark...................................... | 0 | 0 | — |
| Ecuador....................................... | 15 | 15 | — |
| Egypt........................................... | 15 | 5 | 10 |
| Estonia ....................................... | 15* | 5 | 10 |
| Finland ....................................... | 15* (6) | 0 | 10 |
| Gabon (5) .................................... | 15* (1) | 15* (1, 3) | — |
| Germany...................................... | 0 (7) | 0 | 10 |
| Ghana ......................................... | 15* (4) | 5 | 10 |
| Greece ........................................ | 25 | 25 | — |
| Hungary....................................... | 15 | 5 | 25 |
| Iceland........................................ | 15 (1) | 5 | 10 |
| India ........................................... | 10* (1) | 10 | 10 |
| Indonesia.................................... | 15 | 10 | 25 |
| Iran............................................. | 20 | 15 | 25 |
| Ireland, Rep. of ........................... | 15 | 10 | 50 |
| Israel .......................................... | 15 | 5 | 10 |
| Italy ............................................ | 15 (1) | 5 (1, 8) | 10 |
| Ivory Coast (Côte d'Ivoire) (5)....... | 15* | 15 | 10 |
| Jamaica....................................... | 15 | 10 | 10 |
| Japan .......................................... | 15* | 5, 0 (9) | 15 |
| Jordan ......................................... | 15 | 5 | 10 |
| Kazakhstan.................................. | 15 | 5 | 10 |
| Korea, Rep. of.............................. | 15* (4) | 10 | 10 |
| Kuwait.......................................... | 0 | 0 | — |
| Latvia.......................................... | 15* | 5 | 10 |
| Lebanon ...................................... | 0 | 0 | — |
| Lithuania..................................... | 15* | 5 | 10 |
| Luxembourg................................. | 15* (1) | 5 | 25 |
| Holding company (10)............... | 25 | 25 | — |
| Macedonia................................... | 15 | 5 | 25 |
| Madagascar................................. | 25 | 15 | 25 |
| Malawi ........................................ | 25 | 25 | — |
| Malaysia ..................................... | 15* (1) | 5 | 10 |
| Mali ............................................ | 15* (1) | 15* (1, 3) | — |
| Malta .......................................... | 15* | 5 | 10 |
| Mauritania .................................. | 25 | 25 | — |
| Mauritius..................................... | 15* | 5 | 10 |
| Mayotte....................................... | 15/25 (11) | 15/25 (11) | — |
| Mexico........................................ | 15 (1, 3) | 0/5 | 10 |
| Monaco ....................................... | 25 | 25 | 10 |
| Mongolia..................................... | 15 | 5 | 10 |

# France

| Column 1 | Dividends | | |
| --- | --- | --- | --- |
| | Column 2 | Column 3 | Column 4 |
| Country of residence | Individuals and nonparent companies | Parent companies | Shareholding required to be a parent |
| | % | % | % |
| Morocco | 15/0 (12) | 15/0 (12) | — |
| Netherlands | 15* (1, 13) | 5 | 25 |
| New Caledonia | 15* (2) | 5 | — |
| New Zealand | 15* (9) | 15 | — |
| Niger | 15* (1) | 15* (1, 3) | — |
| Nigeria | 15 | 12.5 | 10 |
| Norway | 15* (1, 10) | 0 | 10 |
| Oman | 0 | 5 (14, 15) | 25 |
| Pakistan | 15 (4) | 10 | 10 |
| Philippines | 15 | 10 | 10 |
| Poland | 15 | 5 | 10 |
| Polynesia, French | 25 | 25 | 25 |
| Portugal | 15 | 15 | — |
| Qatar | 0 | 0 | — |
| Romania | 10 | 10 | — |
| Russia (16) | 15/10 (17) | 15/10 (17) | — |
| Russian Federation | 15 | 15 | — |
| St. Pierre & Miquelon | 15 (1) | 5 | — |
| Saudi Arabia | 0 | 0 | — |
| Senegal | 15* (1) | 15* (1, 10) | — |
| Singapore | 15* (1) | 10 | 10 |
| Slovakia | 10 | 10 | — |
| South Africa | 15 | 5 | 10 |
| Spain | 15* (1) | 0 | 10 |
| Sri Lanka | 25 | 25 | — |
| Sweden | 15* (1) | 0 (1, 3) | 10 |
| Switzerland (18) | | | |
| A (19) | 15* | 0 (18) | 10 (18) |
| B (20) | 15* (18) | 15/0 (18) | 10 (18) |
| C (21) | 25 | 25 | — |
| Thailand | 25 | 20/15 (22) | 25 |
| Togo | 15* (1) | 15* (1, 3) | — |
| Trinidad and Tobago | 15 | 10 | 10 |
| Tunisia | 25 | 25 | — |
| Turkey | 20 (1) | 15 | 10 |
| Ukraine (23) | 15 | 15/5/0 | — |
| United Arab Emirates | 0 | 0 | — |
| United Kingdom | 15* (1) | 5 | 10 |
| United States | 15* | 5 | 10 |
| Uzbekistan | 10 | 5 | 10 |
| Venezuela | 15* (1)/5 | 0 | 10 |
| Vietnam | 15 | 5 | 10 |
| Zambia | 25 | 25 | 50 |
| Zimbabwe | 15 | 10 | 25 |

| Column 1 | Interest<br>Column 5 | Royalties<br>Column 6 | Distributions<br>Column 7 |
|---|---|---|---|
| Country of residence | For instruments<br>other than<br>borrowings | | Automatically<br>levied on<br>after-tax profits<br>of permanent<br>establishments |
| | % | % | % |
| Nontreaty (24, 25, 26) ................... | 15<br>(27) | 33.33 | 25 |
| Treaty: | | | |
| Algeria ..................................... | 10 | 10 | 0 |
| Argentina ................................. | 15/0 | 18 | 5 |
| Armenia .................................... | 10/0 | 10/5 | 5 |
| Australia................................... | 10 | 10 | 15 |
| Austria...................................... | 0 | 0 | 0 |
| Bahrain ..................................... | 0 | 0 | 25 |
| Bangladesh ............................... | 10 (14) | 10 | 15 |
| Belgium..................................... | 15 | 0 | 10 |
| Benin......................................... | 15 | 0 | 25 (28) |
| Brazil......................................... | 10 to 15 | 10/15/25 (29) | 15 |
| Bolivia ....................................... | 15/0 | 15 | 0 |
| Botswana .................................. | 10 | 10 | 0 |
| Bulgaria..................................... | 0 | 5 | 5 |
| Burkina Faso ............................. | 15 | 0 | 25 (28) |
| Cameroon .................................. | 0 to 15 | 15 | 15 |
| Canada ...................................... | 10 (14, 30) | 10 (31) | 5 |
| Quebec ............................... | 10 | 10 | 5 |
| Central African Republic............ | 15 | 0 | 25 (28) |
| China, P.R. ................................ | 10/0 (14) | 6/10 (32) | 0 |
| Comoro Islands ......................... | 10 to 15 | 33.33 | 25 (28) |
| Congo, Rep. of .......................... | 0 | 15 | 15 |
| Croatia ...................................... | 0 | 15 | 15 |
| Cyprus ...................................... | 0 to 10 (14) | 0 (33) | 0/25 (34) |
| Czech Republic ......................... | 0 | 5/0 (35) | 10 |
| Denmark .................................... | 0 | 0 | 0/25 (34) |
| Ecuador .................................... | 0/10/15 (36) | 15 | 15 |
| Egypt......................................... | 15 | 15/25 (37) | 5 |
| Estonia...................................... | 10/0 | 5/10 | 0 |
| Finland ...................................... | 10/0 (14) | 0 | 15 |
| Gabon ....................................... | 15 | 10 (38) | 25 (28) |
| Germany .................................... | 0 | 0 | 0 |
| Ghana ....................................... | 10 | 10 | 0 |
| Greece ...................................... | 0 | 5 | 0/25 (34) |
| Hungary .................................... | 0 | 0 | 5 |
| Iceland ...................................... | 0 | 0 | 5 |
| India.......................................... | 10 | 0 | 0 |
| Indonesia .................................. | 0/10/15 (14) | 10 | 10 |
| Iran .......................................... | 0/15 (14) | 10 | 15 |
| Ireland, Rep. of......................... | 0 | 0 | 0/25 (34) |

# France

| Column 1 | Interest | Royalties | Distributions |
|---|---|---|---|
| | Column 5 | Column 6 | Column 7 |
| Country of residence | For instruments other than borrowings | | Automatically levied on after-tax profits of permanent establishments |
| | % | % | % |
| Israel ........................................ | 10/0 (14) | 10/0 (33) | 5/10 |
| Ivory Coast (Côte d'Ivoire)......... | 15 | 10 (38) | 0 |
| Italy .......................................... | 0/10 (14) | 5 (35) | 0 |
| Jamaica..................................... | 0/10 | 10 | 10 |
| Japan ........................................ | 0/10 (14) | 10 | 0 |
| Jordan........................................ | 0/15 (14) | 5/15/25 (39) | 5 |
| Kazakhstan ............................... | 0/10 | 10 | — |
| Korea, Rep. of .......................... | 10 (14) | 10 | 5 |
| Kuwait ....................................... | 0 | 0 | 25 |
| Latvia ........................................ | 10/0 | 5/10 | 0 |
| Lebanon..................................... | 0 | 33.33 | 25 |
| Lithuania ................................... | 10/0 | 5/10 | 0 |
| Luxembourg ............................... | 10 | 0 | 0/5 (35) |
| Holding company (10) ........... | 10 to 15 | 33.33 | 25 |
| Macedonia ................................. | 0 | 0 | 25 |
| Madagascar ............................... | 0/15 (14) | 10/15 (40, 41) | 25 |
| Malawi........................................ | 15 | 0/33.33 (31) | 10 |
| Malaysia..................................... | 15 (14) | 10 (41) | 15 |
| Mali ........................................... | 15 | 0 | 25 (28) |
| Malta ......................................... | 0/10 | 10 | 10 |
| Mauritania ................................. | 15 | 0 | 25 (28) |
| Mauritius ................................... | 0/15 | 15/0 (35) | 15 |
| Mayotte ..................................... | 0 | 0 | 25 (28) |
| Mexico....................................... | 0/15 | 15 (32) | 0 |
| Monaco ...................................... | 15 | 33.33 | 25 |
| Mongolia .................................... | 0/10 | 5 | 0 |
| Morocco ..................................... | 10/15 | 5/10 (42) | 25 |
| Namibia...................................... | 0/10 | 10 | 0 |
| Netherlands................................ | 10/0 (14) | 0 | 0 |
| New Caledonia........................... | 0 | 10 (35) | 10 |
| New Zealand .............................. | 10/0 (14) | 10 | 15 |
| Niger ......................................... | 15 | 0 | 25 (28) |
| Nigeria ...................................... | 12.5 (14) | 12.5 | 0 |
| Norway....................................... | 0 (14) | 0 | 0 |
| Oman ......................................... | 0 | 0 | 25 |
| Pakistan .................................... | 10/0 | 10 | 0 |
| Philippines ................................ | 0/15 (14) | 15 | 10 |
| Poland........................................ | 0 | 10/0 (35) | 25 |
| Polynesia, French....................... | 0 | 33.33 | 25 (28) |
| Portugal ..................................... | 12 (14) | 5 | 0/15 (34) |
| Qatar.......................................... | 0 | 0 | 25 |
| Romania..................................... | 0/10 | 0 | 0 |

| Column 1 | Interest | Royalties | Distributions |
|---|---|---|---|
| | Column 5 | Column 6 | Column 7 |
| Country of residence | For instruments other than borrowings | | Automatically levied on after-tax profits of permanent establishments |
| | % | % | % |
| Russia | 0 (14) | 0 | 0 |
| Russian Federation | 10/0 | 0 | 25 |
| St. Pierre and Miquelon | 0 | 10 (35) | 10 |
| Saudi Arabia | 0 | 0 | 25 |
| Senegal | 15/0 | 0 | 0 |
| Singapore | 0/10 (14) | 0/33.33 (43) | 15 |
| Slovakia | 0 | 5/0 (35) | 10 |
| South Africa | 0 | 0 | 0 |
| Spain | 10 | 5 (44) | 0 |
| Sri Lanka | 0/10 (14) | 10/0 (45) | 25 |
| Sweden | 0 | 0 | 0 (35) |
| Switzerland (18) | | | |
| A (19) | 0 (18) | 5/0 (18, 46) | 0 (18) |
| B (20) | 0 (18) | 5/0 (18, 46) | 0 (18) |
| C (21) | 0 to 15 | 33.33 | 0 (18) |
| Thailand | 0/3/10 | 0/5/15 (42) | 25 |
| Togo | 15 | 0 | 25 (28) |
| Trinidad and Tobago | 0/10 (14) | 0/10 (32) | 10 |
| Tunisia | 0/12 (14) | 5/15/20 (47) | 25 (28) |
| Turkey | 15/0 | 10 | 7.5 |
| Ukraine | 10/0 | 0/5/10 | 25 |
| United Arab Emirates | 0 | 0 | 0 |
| United Kingdom | 0 | 0 | 0 (34) |
| United States | 0 (48) | 5/0 (49) | 5 |
| Uzbekistan | 5 | 0 | 0 |
| Venezuela | 0/5 (14) | 5 | 0 |
| Vietnam | 0 | 10 | 0 |
| Zambia | 15 | 0/33.33 (31) | 10 |
| Zimbabwe | 10/0 | 10 | 0 |

## Explanation of columns

**Column 2/**Companies not qualifying as parents and individuals are subject to the withholding tax rates indicated in this column. Where the *avoir fiscal* is available—for dividends paid until December 31, 2003 if the recipient is an individual shareholder, and for *avoir fiscal* refunded until December 31, 2004 if the recipient is a corporate shareholder—the availability is marked with an asterisk in the column. The withholding tax is levied on the gross dividend plus the *avoir fiscal*. The treaty with Italy (effective since 1992) provides for the refund of half of the *avoir fiscal* to parent companies (see Note 8 below).

**Columns 3 and 4/**Column 3 indicates the withholding tax rate for dividends paid to a foreign "parent" company. To be considered a parent company, the foreign company must hold a specified percentage of the French company's share capital or voting rights. These minimum percentages range from 0% to 50%, as indicated

# France

in Column 4, and certain other conditions must be met (see each treaty). If no percentage is indicated, either no minimum shareholding is required, or the tax treaty does not reduce the withholding tax rate of 25%.

For an explanation of the use of the asterisk in Column 3, see the explanation for Column 2 above.

As from 1992, no withholding tax is levied on dividends paid to an EU parent company by a French company actually subject to corporate tax, provided the following is the case.

1. The EU parent company has held a minimum of 25% of the capital of the distributing company directly and continuously for at least two years.
2. It is the effective beneficiary of the dividends.
3. It has its effective seat of management in an EU state and is not deemed to be domiciled outside the EU under an applicable tax treaty.
4. It has one of the legal forms enumerated by the relevant Directive.
5. It is subject to corporate income tax in the member state where it has its effective seat of management without exemption, or an option available.

*Column 5*/French domestic law exempts interest on most types of debt from withholding tax. Minor exceptions to this general rule include interest on current accounts, claims and certain coupon bonds. French tax treaties often reduce the withholding rate to nil in even these instances.

Moreover, as from January 1, 2004, there is no requirement to withhold income tax on interest and royalties paid to EU companies if all the following conditions are met.

- The payer is a French resident company or a French permanent establishment of a company resident in another EU member state.
- The recipient of the income is an EU resident company.
- The payer and the recipient are 25% associates, which means that either
  - One holds directly 25% or more of the capital or voting rights in the other; or
  - A third company (wherever resident in the EU) holds directly 25% or more of the capital or voting rights in them both.

*Column 7*/Withholding tax is automatically imposed on after-tax profits of a permanent establishment unless certain conditions are met. The rate is 25% or the reduced tax treaty rate.

Notes:

1. *Avoir fiscal* is granted only if recipients are subject to income tax on payment in their own country. In this case, the tax is withheld on the gross dividend (including *avoir fiscal*).
2. *Avoir fiscal* is granted only to individual shareholders.
3. If the dividend is not taxable in the recipient's country, the *avoir fiscal* is not granted and the withholding tax is levied at 25%.
4. *Avoir fiscal* is granted only to nonparent companies holding less than 10%.
5. The French authorities are granting a special rebate for dividends sent to Congo, Ivory Coast (*Côte d'Ivoire*), and Gabon.
6. To qualify for payment of the *avoir fiscal,* a Finnish company must be subject to corporate income tax in its country on the dividend and *avoir fiscal*.

7. A rate of 15% is applicable for dividends distributed by certain companies.

8. A rate of 50% of the *avoir fiscal* is refunded to qualified Italian parent companies.

9. The dividend withholding tax rate is eliminated if the recipient owns 15% or more in votes or value of the distributing corporation and is (a) a company regularly traded on either the Japanese or the French stock market, (b) a company more than 50% owned by the government of either country, (c) an individual or a quoted company resident in either country, or (d) any combination of (a), (b), and (c).

10. The 1929-type Luxembourg holding companies are not entitled to any of the benefits of the France-Luxembourg tax treaty.

11. A 25% rate applies if dividends are not included in the income taxed to either corporate or income tax.

12. No withholding tax applies if dividends are taxable in Morocco.

13. *Avoir fiscal* is granted only to nonparent companies holding less than 5%.

14. Full or partial exemption is applicable when specific conditions provided by the treaty are met.

15. These are taxed when attached to a permanent establishment in France.

16. The November 26, 1996 tax treaty came into force February 9, 1999.

17. The 5% rate applies to dividends when three conditions are fulfilled, as follows. (1) The effective recipient of the dividends must have invested at least €76,000 in the company that pays these dividends. (2) The recipient must be a company liable for corporate tax. (3) This latter company must be exempt from corporate tax. The rate is 10% when only condition (1) or conditions (2 and 3) are fulfilled. In all other cases the rate is 15%.

18. An addendum signed on July 22, 1997 modifies the provisions of the French–Swiss tax treaty relating to dividends, interest and royalties, and provides for the removal of the 5% withholding tax on profits realized by French permanent establishments of Swiss resident companies.

19. The rate indicated applies to Swiss resident companies controlled by Swiss residents.

20. The rate indicated applies to Swiss resident companies that are controlled by non-Swiss residents (Article 11.2.b ii) and meet the conditions of Article 14 of the tax treaty. In the case of column 3, the 15% rate applies to these companies, provided both the recipient and the distributing company are not quoted on a stock exchange. If these conditions are not met, the tax exemption applies.

21. The rate indicated applies to Swiss resident companies controlled by non-Swiss residents but not complying with Article 14 of the tax treaty.

22. The 15% rate applies to dividends paid to an industrial company.

23. A tax treaty between France and Ukraine was signed on January 31, 1997 and came into force November 1, 1999. The 5% rate applies to gross dividends if the effective recipient is a Ukrainian company that holds directly or indirectly at least 10% of the French company's capital. The rate is 0% if the participation exceeds 50% and €762,245, or guaranteed by Ukraine. It is 15% in all other cases.

24. Nontreaty recipients of royalties and management fees are subject to a 33.33% withholding rate. Where a treaty exists, management fees are exempt

from withholding tax unless they are included in the definition of royalties subject to withholding tax.

25. In France, the withholding tax is levied on a provisional basis, at 25% of the net profit. This amount is reduced to the extent it exceeds the dividends actually paid by the company during the previous 12 months, and the amount of dividends paid to residents of France. Consequently, if the foreign head office undertakes not to distribute dividends in a given year, the after-tax profits of its French branch are not subject to withholding tax even when they are transferred abroad.

26. Withholding tax on interest on loans with a contract is 0%, while withholding on other interest is in a range from 15% to 50%. For treaty rates, consult the individual entry in the table.

27. The withholding tax rate can be 60% for certain securities if the investor's identity is not disclosed.

28. The withholding tax is levied on the following amount—French net profit divided by the total foreign company net profit, multiplied by the amount of the distribution.

29. The rate of 10% is applicable on royalties for the use of literary, artistic, or scientific works, including films, 25% on royalties for the use of trademarks, and 15% otherwise.

30. Exemption is granted only to recipients actually subject to income tax on the payment in their own country.

31. No withholding tax is applicable on a royalty arising from the use of or the right to use literary, artistic, or scientific works (excluding film).

32. Withholding tax is reduced to 6% for royalties paid for the lease of industrial, commercial, or scientific equipment.

33. A rate of 5% (Cyprus) and 10% (Israel) is applicable on royalties paid for the use or the right of the use of films.

34. Profits realized in France by foreign corporations whose head offices are located in a European country are not subject to withholding taxes if certain conditions concerning the foreign corporation are met (effective head office in a European country; foreign corporation subject to corporate taxation).

35. No withholding tax is applicable on a royalty arising from the use or the right to use literary, artistic or scientific works.

36. The rate is reduced to 10% in certain circumstances (for equipment or bank loans) mentioned in the treaty, or nil in other circumstances.

37. The rate of 25% is applicable on royalties paid for the use of trademarks.

38. No withholding tax is levied on certain royalties paid in the field of audiovisual techniques.

39. The 5% rate is levied on royalties paid for the use of literary, artistic, and scientific works. The 25% rate is levied on royalties paid for the use of trademarks.

40. The rate of 15% is applicable on royalties paid for the use of industrial property and trademarks.

41. A rate of 33.33% is applicable on royalties paid for the use of or the right to use films.

42. The rate of 5% is applicable on royalties paid for the use of literary, artistic, or scientific works, excluding films.

43. The rate of 33.33% is applicable on royalties paid for the use of literary and artistic works, including films, and for information concerning commercial experience.

44. No withholding tax is levied on royalties paid for the use of or the right to use literary or artistic works, excluding films and recordings.

45. No withholding tax is levied on royalties paid for the use of or the right to use copyrights or films; 10% withholding tax where the royalties become payable for the first time on or after the date of entry into force of the convention, that is, November 18, 1982.

46. No withholding tax is levied on royalties paid for the use of or the right to use industrial, commercial, or scientific equipment.

47. The rate of 20% is applicable on royalties paid for the use of trademarks, 15% for the use of industrial property, and 5% for the use of literary, artistic, or scientific works.

48. Taxed in certain circumstances provided by the treaty.

49. No withholding tax is applicable on a royalty arising from the use of or the right to use literary, artistic, or scientific works, films, recordings, or computer software.

## Tax administration

**Returns**/A corporate income tax return must be filed each year three months after the fiscal year-end, which may be different from the calendar year-end. The tax due is self-assessed.

**Payment of tax**/Payment of tax is made during the fiscal year by way of four installments totaling 33.33% of the taxable income of the preceding year. The balance, if any, is due not later than three and one-half months after the year-end. A provisional amount of the first 3% surtax (3% of the preceding year's regular corporate tax liability) plus the social contribution on benefits' installment must be paid. Any remainder is due three and one-half months after the year-end.

# France

## CORPORATION TAX CALCULATION

Calendar year 2004

|  | | (In millions of euros) |
|---|---:|---:|
| Net book profit (1) | | 1,600,861 |
| Add: | | |
|     Corporate income tax | 331,189 | |
|     Nondeductible items | 147,950 | |
|     2004 accrued liabilities deductible on a cash basis | 95,000 | 574,139 |
| | | 2,175,000 |
| Deduct: | | |
|     Foreign branch profits | 400,000 | |
|     Long-term gain submitted to the 19% reduced rate | 400,000 | |
|     Intercompany dividends (2) | 182,500 | |
|     2004 accrued liabilities | 150,000 | |
| Tax loss carryforward | 300,000 | |
| | | 1,432,500 |
| Net taxable at 33.33% | | 742,500 |
| Corporate income tax thereon at 33.33% | | 247,475 |
| Less—Tax credits: | | |
|     On intercompany dividends | 0 | |
|     On other dividends (3) | 0 | |
|     On foreign-source interest | 10,000 | |
| | 10,000 | |
|     Limited to 10,000 at 66.66% (4) | 6,667 | 6,667 |
| Net liability at 33.33% | | 240,808 |
| Long-term capital gain (400,000) at 19% (5) | | 76,000 |
| Total regular tax liability | | 316,808 |
| Surtax of 3% (6): | | |
|     33.33% liability before reduction by tax credits (6) | 247,475 | |
|     19% liability | 76,000 | |
|     Base for surtax | 323,475 | |
|     Surtax at 3% | | 9,704 |
| Social contribution on benefits at 3.3% (7) | | 10,675 |
| Total tax payable | | 337,187 |

Notes:

1. Net book profit is determined as follows:

|  | (In millions of euros) |
|---|---|
| Pretax profit | 1,263,674 |
| Corporate income tax provided in the books | (337,187) |
| Net book profit | 1,600,861 |

Including:

| | | |
|---|---|---|
| Foreign branch income | | 400,000 |
| Capital gain on sale of shares: | | |
| Purchase price | 1,000,000 | |
| Selling price | (1,300,000) | 300,000 |
| Royalties from licensing of patents | | 100,000 |
| Accrued liabilities deductible on a cash basis (vacation pay reserve, contingencies): | | |
| At December 31, 2003 | | 150,000 |
| At December 31, 2004 | | 95,000 |
| Dividends from qualifying subsidiaries: | | |
| French subsidiary | | 100,000 |
| U.S. subsidiary (net of 5% withholding tax) | | 95,000 |
| Other dividends from French sources | | 60,000 |
| Foreign-source interest (net of 10% withholding tax) | | 90,000 |
| Nondeductible items (tax on company cars, penalties) | | 147,950 |
| Tax loss carryforward at December 31, 2003 | | 300,000 |

2. Intercompany dividends are tax exempt (except a 5% charges and expenses portion; see Note 8):

|  | (In millions of euros) |
|---|---|
| Cash dividends recorded in the books | 195,000 |
| Net deductible from taxable income | 182,500 |

3. Tax credits resulting from dividends not used in 2004 will be lost.
4. Tax credits cannot be used for tax-exempt intercompany dividends. Other income benefiting from tax credits is usually booked net of such credits. Since tax credits are taxable, the actual credit usable against corporate income tax liability must be reduced accordingly For a corporate income tax rate of 33.33%, theoretical credit is multiplied by 66.66%.
5. See "Capital gains" above.
6. The 3% surtax is applied to the total regular tax liability before reduction by *avoir fiscal* credit and foreign tax credit.
7. The social contribution on benefits is computed on the following (in millions of euros).
   a. A total of .763 is deducted from the base for surtax (323,475 − 0.763) = 323,474.
   b. 323,474 x 3.3% = 10,675.

8. The 5% charges and expenses portion is computed on the following (in millions of euros).
   a. The French subsidiary dividends, including the *avoir fiscal* (for FY 2004, but not for FY 2005)—(100,000 + 50,000) x 5% = 7,500.
   b. The U.S. subsidiary dividends including the withholding tax—(95,000 + 5,000) x 5% = 5,000.
   c. The intercompany dividends deductible—195,000 – 12,500 = 182,500.
9. Exchange rate of the Euro at January 2, 2004: US$1 = €0.7942.

## PwC contact

For additional information on taxation in Germany, contact:

Andrew Miles
PricewaterhouseCoopers GmbH
Marie-Curie-Str. 24-28
D–60439 Frankfurt (Main), Germany
Telephone: (49) (69) 9585 6345
Fax: (49) (69) 9585 6422
LN address: Andrew Miles/DE/TLS/PwC@EMEA-DE
e-mail: andrew.miles@de.pwc.com

## Significant developments

The thin capital rules now apply to companies in domestic as well as in foreign ownership. All holding company privileges have been withdrawn. A total of 40% of the annual income over €1 million is precluded from offset against losses brought forward. Enhanced related-party transfer pricing documentation rules are now in force.

## Taxes on corporate income

*Corporation tax* (**Körperschaftsteuer**)/German business profits are subject to two taxes, corporation tax and trade tax. Corporation tax is levied at a uniform rate of 25% and is then subject to a surcharge of 5.5% (the "solidarity levy").

*Trade tax* (**Gewerbesteuer**)/The effective rate varies by location from— generally—just under 12% to just under 20% (around 18% for most larger cities). This tax is deductible as an expense for corporation tax.

## Corporate residence

A corporation is resident in Germany for tax purposes if either its place of incorporation or its main place of management is in Germany.

## Other taxes

*Value-added tax*/Proceeds of sales and services effected in Germany are subject to value-added tax (VAT) at the standard rate of 16% (7% on certain transactions). The taxpayer is generally entitled to offset against the VAT payable the amount of such tax charged by suppliers or paid on imports. Taxes on fuel, electric power, insurance, and some other products and services are not a compliance issue for most businesses, although they can be a significant additional cost factor.

## Branch income

Both corporation tax and trade tax are imposed on the taxable income of a foreign company's German branch. The rates are the same for branches as for resident German companies, although the withholding tax on dividend distributions by German companies is not deducted from profits transferred by a German branch to its foreign head office.

## Income determination

*General*/In principle, conformity between book and tax reporting is required. However, major differences between the two can arise, such as where accruals or write-downs are made in the legal accounts but are not accepted for tax purposes.

*Inventory valuation*/Inventories are normally valued at the lowest of actual cost, replacement cost, and net realizable value. However, any write-downs below actual cost must be for specific reasons. If specific identification of the inventories is not possible, valuation at either standard or average cost is acceptable. The LIFO method is accepted provided it is also used in the statutory financial statements. Theoretically, FIFO is unacceptable unless its assumption accords with the facts, although in practice the condition is often fulfilled.

*Long-term liabilities and accounts*/Noninterest bearing long-term liabilities other than advance payments received must be discounted at 5.5% per annum. A similar provision applies to refurbishment and other accruals which accumulate over time.

*Capital gains*/Capital gains from the sale of investments in other companies are exempt. Corresponding losses are not deductible. The nondeductible directly related expenses are fixed at 5% of the tax-free gain. It is possible to postpone the taxation of part or all of the gains on real estate by offsetting it against the cost of replacement items.

*Dividends*/Dividends received are exempt, other than portfolio dividends for trade tax. Banks do not enjoy this exemption on dividends from securities held for trading. The nondeductible directly related expenses are fixed at 5% of the tax-free income.

*Foreign income*/Income, except dividends, received by a German corporation from foreign sources is included in taxable income for corporation tax unless a tax treaty provides for exemption. Double taxation is avoided by means of foreign tax credits or, at the taxpayer's option, by a deduction of the foreign taxes as an expense.

Irrespective of any tax treaty, income charged to trade tax is reduced by income or dividends included therein that flow from a foreign branch or partnership. Antiavoidance rules are in force with respect to subsidiaries in low-tax countries in certain lines of business.

*Stock dividends*/In principle, a declaration of stock dividends (by converting reserves to capital stock) by a company will not lead to taxable income for the shareholder or to other tax effects. Subsequent capital reductions will, however, be treated as cash dividends in most circumstances. There is no longer any German tax reason for distributing a stock dividend as opposed to merely leaving accumulated profits on the books to be carried forward. As regards current year profits, the decision therefore depends upon the situation in the investor's home country. There is a moratorium until December 31, 2005 on dividends as a method of releasing the tax credit inherent in any remaining 2000 and prior year earnings.

## Deductions

*Depreciation, amortization, and depletion*/Depreciation on moveable fixed assets is normally calculated by either the straight-line or the declining-balance method over the anticipated useful life. The annual declining-balance rate may not exceed twice the straight-line rate or be more than 20%. The residual value of the asset is taken into account only if it is material, while gains on a sale are treated as normal business income. Buildings are amortized on a variety of straight-line or reducing rate systems designed to reach a full write-down between 25 and 50 years depending on the age of the building and on whether the taxpayer was its first owner. Intangibles are amortized straight-line over their estimated useful lives—goodwill over 15 years. In addition to normal depreciation, special depreciation is deductible for tax purposes in certain limited circumstances. Apart from depreciation on the straight-line and declining-balance bases, other methods are allowed if commercially reasonable, including depreciation based on output or amortization (depletion) based on the gradual exhaustion of the investment in a mine.

**Net operating losses**/Losses are carried forward without time limit. For corporation (but not trade) tax there is an optional carry back to the previous year of up to €511,500. The loss relief claimable in any one year is limited to €1 million plus 60% of current income exceeding that amount. The remaining 40% of income over €1 million is charged to trade and corporation taxes at current rates— referred to as "minimum" taxation. The loss carry-forward ceases on change of "business identity." This is assumed if a single shareholder acquires more than half the voting rights and the then level of assets doubles within the following five years.

**Payments to foreign affiliates**/A German corporation can claim a deduction for royalties, management service fees and, within limits, interest charges (if not profit related) paid to foreign affiliates, provided such amounts are at arm's length. Detailed provisions define this. All aspects of intercompany or other related-party trading now fall under strict and extensive documentation requirements, breach of which can lead to serious penalties. Interest paid to affiliates is restricted by a debt/equity ratio of 1.5:1 and is disallowed altogether on related-party finance of intra-group acquisitions. The debt/equity ratio does not apply if the total related-party interest charge for the year does not exceed €250,000.

**Taxes**/All taxes borne are deductible except for corporation tax itself and VAT on nondeductible expenses. Late payment interest and similar charges are also not deductible.

**Special features for trade tax**/There are a number of adjustments between the incomes chargeable to trade and corporation taxes. The most significant are the trade tax disallowance of one-half of the long-term loan interest (except for banks) and of rental or leasing payments abroad for moveable assets.

## Group taxation

If a German parent holds more than 50% of the voting rights in a domestic subsidiary, the two may conclude a formal five-year, court registered profit pooling agreement. The ensuing relationship is then referred to as an *Organschaft*. Effectively the annual results of an *Organschaft* are pooled in the accounts and tax returns of the parent. Profits and losses within a group can therefore be offset, but there is no provision for the elimination of intra group profits from the total tax base.

## Incentives

**Tax incentives**/None.

**Other incentives**/Investment grants of 10% or 12.5% are available on capital investment in new manufacturing facilities in the eastern part of Germany. The investment must be completed during 2004. Local authorities may offer facilities on favorable terms, such as the provision of cheap land on industrial estates.

# Germany

## Withholding taxes

Domestic corporations paying certain types of income are required to withhold tax as follows. See Note 1.

| Recipient of German-source income | Dividends (1) | Royalties | Rentals from movable assets |
|---|---|---|---|
| | % | % | % |
| Resident corporations and individuals ..................................... | 20 | — | — |
| Nonresident corporations and individuals (2): | | | |
| EU corporations (1) .............................. | — | — | — |
| Non-treaty ........................................... | 20 | 25 | 25 |
| Treaty (3): | | | |
| Argentina (4)................................... | 15/25 | 15 | — |
| Australia ......................................... | 15 | 10 | 10 |
| Austria ............................................ | 5 (15) | — | — |
| Bangladesh .................................... | 15 | 10 | 10 |
| Belgium .......................................... | 15 | — | — |
| Bolivia............................................. | 10/25 | 15 | 15 |
| Brazil .............................................. | 15 | 15 (25) | 15 |
| Bulgaria (4)..................................... | 15/20 | 5 | 5 |
| Canada (5) ..................................... | 5/15 | 10 | 10 |
| China, P.R. (4) ............................... | 10/20 | 10 | 7 |
| Cyprus ............................................ | 10 (15) | 0 (5) (6) | — |
| Czech Republic............................... | 5 (15) | 5 | 5 |
| Denmark.......................................... | 15 (5) | — | — |
| Ecuador........................................... | 15 | 15 | 15 |
| Egypt (4).......................................... | 15 | 25 (15) | 15 |
| Estonia ........................................... | 5/15 | 10 | 5 |
| Finland ............................................ | 10 (15)/20 | 5 | 5 |
| France (4) ....................................... | 5 (10)/20 | — | — |
| Greece ............................................ | 10 | — | — |
| Hungary (7) ..................................... | 5 (15)/20 | — | — |
| Iceland............................................. | 5 (15) | — | — |
| India (4)........................................... | 10/25 | 10 | 10 |
| Indonesia......................................... | 10 (15) | 10 | 10 |
| Iran ................................................. | 15 (20) | 10 | 10 |
| Ireland, Rep.of ............................... | 15 | — | — |
| Israel .............................................. | 20 | 5 | 5 |
| Italy ................................................ | 15 (10) | 5 (8) | 5 |
| Ivory Coast (5)................................ | 15/20 | 10 | 10 |
| Jamaica........................................... | 10 (15) | 10 | 10 |
| Japan (7) ........................................ | 15/20 | 10 | 10 |
| Kazakhstan (4) ............................... | 5/15 | 10 | 10 |
| Kenya ............................................. | 15 | 15 | 15 |
| Korea, Rep. of................................. | 5/15 | 10 | 2 |
| Kuwait (4) ....................................... | 15/20 | 10 | 10 |
| Latvia (4) ........................................ | 5/15 | 10 | 5 |
| Liberia ............................................ | 10 (15) | 20/10 | 10 |
| Lithuania (4) ................................... | 5/15 | 10 | 5 |

| Recipient of German-source income | Dividends (1) | Royalties | Rentals from movable assets |
|---|---|---|---|
| | % | % | % |
| Luxembourg | 5 | 5 | 5 |
| Malaysia | 5 (15) | 10/25 | 10 |
| Malta | 5 (15) | — | — |
| Mauritius | 5 (15) | 15 | 15 |
| Mexico | 5 (15) | 10 | 10 |
| Mongolia | 5/10 | 10 | 10 |
| Morocco | 5 (15) | 10 | 10 |
| Namibia (4) | 10 (15)/20 | 10 | 10 |
| Netherlands | 15 | — | — |
| New Zealand (4) | 15/20 | 10 | 10 |
| Norway | 15 | — | — |
| Pakistan (4) | 10 (15)/20 | 10 | 10 |
| Papua-New Guinea (not yet in force) | 15 | 10 | 10 |
| Philippines (4) | 10 (15) 20 | 10 (15) (9) | 10 |
| Poland (4, 26) | 5 (15)/20 [5/15] | — [5] | — [5] |
| Portugal (4) | 15/20 | 10 | 10 |
| Romania | 10 (15) | 10 | 10 |
| Russia | 5/15 | — | — |
| Singapore | 10 (15) | — | — |
| Slovak Republic | 5 (15) | 5 | 5 |
| South Africa | 7.5 (15) | — | — |
| Spain | 15 | 5 | 5 |
| Sri Lanka (4) | 15/20 | 10 | 10 |
| Sweden (4) | 15/25 (5) | — | — |
| Switzerland (1, 4) | 0/15 | — | — |
| Thailand | 15 (20) | 15/5 | 15 |
| Trinidad and Tobago (9) | 10 (20) | 0/10 | 10 |
| Tunisia | 10 (15) | 10/15 | — |
| Turkey (4) | 15 (20)/20 | 10 | 10 |
| Ukraine | 5/10 | 5 | — |
| U.S.S.R. (4, 11) | 15/20 | — | — |
| United Arab Emirates (4) | 5 (15)/20 | — | — |
| United Kingdom | 15 | — | — |
| United States | 5/15 | — | — |
| Uruguay (4) | 15/20 | 15 (10) | 15 |
| Uzbekistan | 5/15 | 3 (5% on cultural royalties) | 3 |
| Venezuela | 5 (15) | 5 | 5 |
| Vietnam | 15 (10, 5) | 7.5 (10) | 10 |
| Yugoslavia (4, 12) | 15/20 | 10 | 10 |
| Zambia | 5 (15) | 10 | 10 |
| Zimbabwe (4) | 10 (20)/20 | 7.5 | 7.5 |

# Germany

| Recipient of German-source income | Interest on (13) | |
|---|---|---|
| | Convertible or profit-sharing bonds | Loans secured on German property (14) |
| Resident corporations and individuals (13) | 30 | — |
| EU corporations (1) | — | — |
| Nonresident corporations and individuals: | | |
| Nontreaty | 25 | 25 |
| Treaty: | | |
| Argentina (15) | 15/10/25 | 15/10 |
| Australia | 10 | 10 |
| Austria | 25 | — |
| Bangladesh | 10/25 | 10 |
| Belgium (16) | 15/0 | 15/0 |
| Brazil (17) | 15/10 | 15/10 |
| Bulgaria (4) | 0/25 | — |
| Canada | 10/25 | 10 |
| China, P.R. (4) | 10/25 | 10 |
| Cyprus | 10 | 10 |
| Czech Republic | — | — |
| Denmark | — | — |
| Ecuador | 15/10 | 15/10 (18) |
| Egypt | 25 | 25 |
| Estonia (4) | 10/25 | 10 |
| Finland | — | — |
| France | — | — |
| Greece | 10 | 10 |
| Hungary | — | — |
| Iceland | — | — |
| India (19) | 15/25/10 | 15/10 |
| Indonesia | 10 | 10 |
| Iran | 15 | 15 |
| Ireland, Rep. of | — | — |
| Israel | 15 | 15 |
| Italy | 10/25 | 10 |
| Ivory Coast | 15/25 (20) | 15 |
| Jamaica (21) | 12.5/10 | 12.5/10 |
| Japan | 10 | 10 |
| Kazakhstan (4) | 10/25 | 10 |
| Kenya | 15 | 15 |
| Korea, Rep. of | 25 | 10/0 (22) |
| Kuwait (4) | 0/25 | — |
| Latvia (4) | 10/25 | 10 |
| Liberia (23) | 20/10 | 20/10 |
| Lithuania (4) | 10/25 | 10 |
| Luxembourg | — | — |
| Malaysia | 15 | 15 |

| Recipient of German-source income | Interest on (13) | |
|---|---|---|
| | Convertible or profit-sharing bonds | Loans secured on German property (14) |
| Malta ............................................................ | — | — |
| Mauritius....................................................... | 25 | 25 |
| Mexico (24)................................................... | 15 | 15 |
| Mongolia....................................................... | 10/25 | 10 |
| Morocco ....................................................... | 10 | 10 |
| Netherlands .................................................. | — | — |
| New Zealand (4) ........................................... | 10/25 | 10 |
| Norway ......................................................... | — | — |
| Pakistan........................................................ | 20 | 10 |
| Papua New Guinea........................................ | 10 | 10 |
| Philippines (15)............................................. | 25/15/10 | 15/10 |
| Poland (4, 26)............................................... | 0/25 [5 - nonbanks - or 25] | — [5 - nonbanks] |
| Portugal (20)................................................. | 15/25/10 | 15/10 |
| Romania........................................................ | 10 | 10 |
| Russia .......................................................... | —/25 | — |
| Singapore..................................................... | 10 | 10 |
| Slovakia........................................................ | — | — |
| South Africa.................................................. | 10 | 10 |
| Spain............................................................ | 10 | 10 |
| Sri Lanka (4)................................................. | 10/25 | 10 |
| Sweden ........................................................ | — | — |
| Switzerland................................................... | 30 | — |
| Thailand (25) ................................................ | 25/10 | 25/10 |
| Trinidad and Tobago (25) .............................. | 15/10 | 15/10 |
| Tunisia ......................................................... | 10 | 10 |
| Turkey (4) ..................................................... | 15/25 | 15 |
| Ukraine......................................................... | 2/5/25 | 2/5 |
| U.S.S.R. (11) ................................................ | 5/25 | 5/25 |
| Uzbekistan.................................................... | 5 | 5 |
| United Kingdom ............................................ | — | — |
| United States (4) .......................................... | 0/25 | — |
| Uruguay (4) .................................................. | 15/25 | — |
| Venezuela..................................................... | 5 | 5 |
| Yugoslavia (4, 12)......................................... | 0/25 | — |
| Zambia ......................................................... | 10 | 10 |
| Zimbabwe (4) ............................................... | 10/25 | 10 |

Notes:

1. The lower rate given applies to dividends paid to a corporation with at least a 25% holding. Some treaties reduce the 25% threshold. Dividends to EU corporate shareholders on holdings of at least 25% are free of withholding tax, regardless of the provisions of the treaty. This privilege has also been agreed with Switzerland.

2. Dividends to nonresident individuals are usually taxed at the lower rate given in the table.

3. If the treaty provides for a rate less than 20% on dividends, specific application for the lower treaty rate or for refund of the excess must be made.

4. The rate of 25% applies to income derived from right or debt claims participating in profits (mostly including income of a sleeping partner from participation as such or from a *partiarisches Darlehen* and *Gewinn-obligationen*) that is deductible in determining the profits of the debtor.

5. The treaty with Canada provides for 10% on royalties for films, rentals, and franchises. There is no withholding tax on royalties for copyrighted works (on other than films) or on royalties for the use of software, patents, or information.

6. Withholding (Cyprus—at the reduced rate of 5%) is levied on royalties for the use of or the right to use cinema films and video tapes for television. Other royalties are tax exempt.

7. The rate of 25% applies to income derived from a silent partnership.

8. No withholding tax is levied on royalties for the use of or the right to use any copyright of literary, artistic, or scientific work, including films or tapes for television or broadcasting.

9. The withholding tax on royalties for literature, films, and other works of art is 15%.

10. No withholding tax is levied on royalties for the use of or the right to use any copyright, excluding cinema films or tapes for television or broadcasting.

11. Reference dividends, see Note 4 for the rate of 25%. This treaty continues in force with Armenia, Azerbaijan, Belarus, Georgia, Kyrgyzstan, Moldavia, Tajikistan, and Turkmenistan.

12. This treaty continues in force with Bosnia and Herzegovina, Croatia, Macedonia, Serbia and Montenegro, and Slovenia.

13. Interest paid abroad on instruments other than convertible or profit sharing bonds or mortgage loans is generally free of withholding tax. Bond or mortgage interest paid abroad is also often free of withholding tax under the treaty where the recipient is a government institution or state bank. Bank, but not other, interest paid to resident corporations and individuals is subject to a withholding tax of 30%.

14. Tax on loans secured on German property is not imposed by means of withholding tax but by way of an assessment to corporation tax at 25% of the interest income net of attributable expenses. The tax authorities can order a creditable withholding tax of 25% in specific cases, if they feel that ultimate collection of the corporation tax due may be in doubt.

15. The withholding tax on profit-sharing bonds is 25%; the rate of 10% applies in respect of sales of goods on credit, bank loans and convertible bonds; in all other cases, the rate of 15% applies.

16. German withholding tax on interest is levied at the reduced rate of 15%. No withholding is imposed where the recipient is a Belgian enterprise or on a corporate shareholder holding directly or indirectly at least 25% of the paying German company's shares.

17. The withholding rate is normally 15% but is reduced to 10% if the recipient is a resident bank and the loan is for at least seven years for certain specified purposes.

18. The reduced rate of 10% applies in respect of bank loans and credit sales.
19. The rate of 10% applies to loans from banks, and 15% applies to loans from all other creditors. See Note 4 for the rate of 25%.
20. The withholding tax rate on convertible bonds is 15%; on profit-sharing bonds, 25%.
21. The reduced rate of 10% applies where the recipient is recognized as a bank according to the laws of Jamaica.
22. The nil rate applies to interest on credit sales and on loans guaranteed under government sponsored export credit guarantee arrangements.
23. The rate of 10% applies to loans from banks; 20% applies to loans from all other creditors.
24. 10% on interest paid to banks after December 31, 1998.
25. The reduced rate of 10% applies where the recipient is a bank.
26. A new Polish treaty was signed on May 14, 2003 but has not yet been ratified. The withholding tax rates are shown in [ ].

## Tax administration

**Returns**/Returns are filed for each calendar year and reflect the financial statements for the business year ending in that calendar year. Assessments are issued once the tax office has reviewed the return.

**Payment of tax**/Taxes are payable in quarterly installments during the year, with a final settlement when the assessment is issued. The quarterly installments are based on the estimated ultimate liability. Usually, this is the total tax due shown by the last assessment issued as adjusted by any rate changes in the meantime.

# Germany

## *CORPORATION TAX CALCULATION*

2004 (Business year ending on or before December 31, 2004)

### Assumptions

1. Entity's taxable income after charging all expenditure and all taxes, except taxes on income, amounts to €1 million.
2. There are no disallowable charges for corporation tax. For trade tax, long-term loan interest of €120,000.
3. The effective rate of trade tax is 15%.

### Trade tax

| | |
|---|---:|
| Profit before taxes on income | € 1,000,000 |
| Add—Disallowable items: | |
| Long-term interest (€120,000 x 50%) | 60,000 |
| Profits subject to trade tax | 1,060,000 |
| Tax thereon at the rate of 15% | 159,000 |

### Corporation tax

| | |
|---|---:|
| Profit before taxes on income | € 1,000,000 |
| Less—Trade tax as computed above | 159,000 |
| Profits subject to corporation tax | 841,000 |
| Corporation tax of 25% | 210,250 |
| Solidarity levy of 5.5% | 11,564 |
| **Total tax burden** | 380,814 |

Note:

The fixed exchange rate at March 2, 2004: US$1 = €.823602.

## PwC contacts

For additional information on taxation in Ghana, contact:

Charles A. Egan
PricewaterhouseCoopers
P.M.B. CT. 42
Cantonments, Accra, Ghana
Telephone: (233) (21) 506217/8
Fax: (233) (21) 506216
e-mail: charles.a.egan@gh.pwc.com

## General note

This entry is repeated from the 2003/2004 edition. For more up-to-date information consult the contact listed above or Jacqueline Collette at jacqueline.collete@us.pwc.com.

## Significant developments

A new law known as the Internal Revenue Act 2000 is in force effective January 1, 2001.

## Taxes on corporate income

National income tax is payable on the following.

1. Income accruing in, derived from, brought into, or received in Ghana in respect of gains or profits from a trade, business, profession, or vocation.
2. Dividends, interest, or discounts.
3. Any charge or annuity.
4. Royalties, premiums, and any other profits arising from property, including rents.
5. Receipts, including royalties and deferred payments of any kind.

The corporate tax rate is 32.5% for all categories of companies other than companies listed on the Ghana Stock Exchange (30%), companies engaged in nontraditional export and rural banking (8%), bank lenders to the agricultural and leasing sectors (20%), and companies in the hotel industry (25%).

## Corporate residence

Corporate residence is determined by where the trade, business, profession, or vocation is carried on, so that where a nonresident corporate body carries on any trade, business, profession, or vocation in Ghana (part of the operations of which may be carried on outside Ghana), the full gains or profits of the trade, business, profession, or vocation are deemed to be derived from Ghana.

If the corporate body's activities are carried on entirely outside Ghana, the mere supply of goods or services to Ghana does not constitute carrying on trade or business in Ghana.

## Other taxes

*Gift tax*/The gift tax rate is nil up to GHC500,000 and 10% thereafter, where the value of the gift exceeds GHC500,000.

*Value-added tax/service tax*/Entertainment; betting; accommodation and food in hotels; food in restaurants and snack bars; and advertisements, which formerly attracted a 15% service tax, are now subject to VAT at 12.5%. Most professional services are also subject to 12.5% VAT. These include the following.

| | |
|---|---|
| Management services | Insurance brokerage and other services |
| Financial, tax, and economic consulting | Engineering and technical services |
| Accounting services | Courier services |
| Legal services | Provision of satellite television |
| Architectural services | Mobile cellular phone services |
| Services rendered by surveyors | |

Exports of goods and services are zero rated. Unless specifically exempt, supplies of all goods and services attract VAT.

*Capital gains*/Capital gains in excess of GHC500,000 are subject to tax at 10% thereafter. However, gains on stocks and shares listed on the Ghana Stock Exchange and those resulting from a merger, amalgamation, reorganization, reconstruction, and so on, are, for the time being, exempt from tax.

*Other taxes*/Other taxes include customs and excise duties, rent tax, and real estate (property) tax. A 2.5% transaction and expenditure tax is to be introduced.

## Branch income

The rates on branch profits are the same as on corporate profits. However, the profits for the period deemed to arise in connection with the operations of the branch may, at the discretion of the tax authorities, be computed by reference to the total consolidated profits of the whole group, taking into account the proportion that the turnover of that branch bears to the total consolidated turnover of the group. When repatriating branch profits, the amount to be repatriated attracts an additional tax of 10%.

## Income determination

*Inventory valuation*/There is no statutory guidance on the principles of stock valuation for income tax purposes. Any method of valuation of stock (inventory) and work-in-progress based on sound accounting principles is acceptable, provided it is adopted and consistently applied from one period to another. In practice, inventory is normally valued for tax purposes at the lower of cost and net realizable value.

*Capital gains*/A capital gains tax is payable by every person, including a corporate body, on any capital gain accruing or derived from the realization of any chargeable asset, including buildings of a permanent or temporary nature; business and business assets, including goodwill; land other than agricultural land; and any assets declared as chargeable by legislative instrument made under the law. See "Capital gains" above.

*Intercompany dividends*/The gross dividends received by one Ghanaian company from another, whether or not a subsidiary of the company, are normally exempt from corporate income tax if the dividends were taxed in the first instance.

*Foreign income*/Resident corporations are taxed on their foreign income as and when it is brought into or received in Ghana. Foreign income is taxed together with other income derived in Ghana, and double taxation is avoided by either treaties or foreign tax credits. There are no special rules for taxing undistributed income of foreign subsidiaries.

*Stock dividends*/The issue of stock dividends is permitted under Section 74 (1) of the Ghana Companies Code 1963, Act 179. It is, however, subject to income tax, at the dividend tax rate of 10%.

Rental income of a company other than a real estate company from any residential or commercial premises is taxed at a final tax of 10%.

*Other significant items*/Specific exemptions from tax include the following.
1. Income of a local authority.
2. Income of a statutory or registered building society.
3. Income of an ecclesiastical, charitable, or educational institution.
4. Income of organizations formed for the purpose of promoting social or sporting amenities not for profit.
5. Income accruing from a farming enterprise for a limited period.
6. Income of a registered trade union.
7. Income of rural banks for the first ten years of operations.
8. Gain or profit from the business of operating ships or aircraft by nonresident corporate bodies.
9. Investment income of a pension or provident society.
10. Income or profit of any registered cooperative society.
11. Income of a company engaged in the construction and sale or leasing of residential and commercial premises during the first five years following commencement of operations of the company.

## Deductions

*Depreciation and depletion*/Depreciation of capital assets in the accounts of a business is not an allowable deduction in computing taxable profits. It is replaced by capital allowances at statutorily prescribed rates. These allowances are available on capital expenditure for the following types of depreciating assets used in a trade. Depreciable assets have been grouped in classes as below, and the following rates apply:

| Class | Assets included | Rate |
| --- | --- | --- |
| 1 | Computers and data handling equipment | 40% |
| 2 | 1. Automobiles, trailers, plant and machinery used in manufacturing.<br>2. Plantation expenditure. | 30% |
| 3 | 1. Mineral and petroleum exploration rights, locomotives, water transportation equipment in respect of mineral and petroleum in year of operations.<br>2. Buildings, structures, and works of permanent nature used in respect of mineral and petroleum exploration.<br>3. Plant and machinery used in mining or petroleum operations. | 80% of cost in year of purchase, 50% of written down value (WDV)* annually thereafter. |
| 4 | Locomotives, water transportation equipment, aircraft equipment not included in other class. | 20% |
| 5 | Buildings, structures and works of a permanent nature other than those mentioned in class 3 above. | 10% |

| Class | Assets included | Rate |
|---|---|---|
| 6 | Intangible assets (e.g., goodwill). | Useful life |

*WDV is sum total of 5% of cost of previous year's additions to class 3 assets + additions for year + WDV brought forward from previous year to current year.

Allowances are granted only on the following conditions.

1. The taxpayer must own the asset.
2. Capital expenditure must be incurred.
3. The asset must be used in the trade.
4. The asset must be in use up to the end of the basis period.

Depreciation allowances are granted for every year in which the asset is in use. In some cases, balancing allowances and charges are made where use continued until immediately before disposal of the asset.

For intangibles such as patents, trademarks, and copyrights, the law allows them to be depreciated over their useful life.

For capital expenditure for acquisition of Ghanaian mineral concessions and related interest in land, an annual write-down allowance is allowed of 80% of the costbase added to the pool during the basis period and 50% of the balance of the pool, if any.

**Net operating losses**/Losses can be carried forward and deducted from assessable income of the five years immediately succeeding the year in which the loss was incurred. This provision only covers mining, manufacturing for export and farming companies.

**Payments to foreign affiliates**/There are no special restrictions on the deductibility of royalties, interest, and service fees paid to foreign affiliates, provided they are expenses incurred wholly, exclusively, and necessarily in the production of the income, although the commissioner may disallow certain transactions if of the opinion that they are artificial or fictitious.

**Taxes**/No taxes are deductible in determining taxable income.

**Other significant items**/No special deductions are allowed. Principal nondeductible items include the following.

1. Domestic or private expenses, including cost of travel between residence and place of business or employment.
2. Any disbursement or expense not being wholly and exclusively paid or expended for the purpose of acquiring income.
3. Capital withdrawn or any sum employed or intended to be employed as capital.
4. Capital employed in improvement.
5. Any sum recoverable under an insurance contract of indemnity.
6. Rent of or any expense in connection with premises or a part of premises not occupied or used for the purpose of producing business income.
7. Any amount paid or payable in respect of any income tax, profits tax, or similar tax, whether due within or outside Ghana.
8. Any payment to a provident, savings, or other society or fund unless specifically allowed by the tax commissioner.

9. Any sum payable by way of mortgage or debenture interest by any person to a nonresident person, except where tax has been deducted and accounted for.

10. Depreciation of any fixed assets of a permanent nature.

## Group taxation

No form of combined reporting of results of operations by a group or affiliates is permitted.

## Tax incentives

*Inward investment*/There are various incentives for encouraging investments in the country under the Ghana Investments Promotion Centre Act 1994, particularly in the areas of agriculture, manufacturing industries engaged in export trade or using predominantly local raw materials or producing agricultural equipment, and so on, construction and building industries, mining, and tourism. Incentives generally include exemption from customs import duties on plant and machinery, reduced corporate income tax rates, more favorable investment and capital allowances on plant and machinery, reduction in the actual corporate income tax payable, where appropriate, retention of foreign exchange earnings where necessary, guaranteed free transfer of dividends or net profits, foreign capital, loan servicing and fees, and charges in respect of technology transfer and guarantees against expropriation by the government.

*Capital investment*/There are currently no special incentives.

## Withholding taxes

Withholding taxes are as follows.

|  | % |
|---|---|
| From employees' monthly salaries | * |
| On fees to directors or board members | 15 |
| On fees to part-time teachers, lecturers, examiners | 15 |
| On dividends payable to shareholders | 10 |
| On interest from debentures, stocks, bonds, treasury bills, discounts, and annuities, other than interest earned by banks and other financial institutions and interest earned on government stocks, bonds, and treasury bills | 10 |
| General contracts for work done and services rendered, including rent (in excess of GHC500,000) | 5 |
| Commissions to insurance/sales agents | 15 |
| Royalties, management, and technical services fees | 15 |
| On commissions of lotto agents | 7.5 |

*Graduated tax rates as per regulations made under the Decree.

These taxes apply to both resident and nonresident recipients.

## Tax administration

*Returns*/The tax year runs from January 1 to December 31. Corporations with financial periods other than the calendar year are taxed on their financial period ending during the calendar year. There are separate provisions for commencement and cessation of business.

The tax administration system is an information return system, with subsequent assessment being issued by the tax authorities. Upon request to the Internal

Revenue Service, a taxpayer is given Income Tax Form 22A for completion and submission to the IRS. This form provides the relevant information for determining taxable income and is filed by either the taxpayer or an appropriate agent.

Companies are expected to submit a return four months after the end of the financial year. They may file an application for extension of filing time not to exceed two months. Upon satisfying certain conditions, companies may now file tax returns in the foreign currency of their parent companies.

The following are to be furnished together with a return.

1. Certified statement of turnover for the period covered by the return.
2. Copy of certified accounts of the business for the period.
3. An estimate of the tax due on the income declared and remittance of the tax so computed.

**Assessments**/An assessment may be made on the company after the beginning of each year of assessment. If the return is considered incorrect and inadequate, additional assessments may be made as often as necessary. The tax authorities may make a provisional assessment before a return is filed, which can serve as a tax credit against the final assessment based on the return.

**Payment of tax**/Where the assessment has been finalized, the tax is payable within 30 days after service of the notice. At the discretion of the tax commissioner, the time for payment may be extended. Without notice or demand from the commissioner, a taxpayer is required to pay not less than the total of the tax paid or payable in respect of the preceding year of assessment. This may be paid by equal quarterly installments at the end of March, June, September, and December in each year of assessment, but such payments are not deemed to be the actual tax payable.

Where tax is not paid by the due date, a penalty is assessed of interest at the rate of Bank of Ghana rediscount rate plus 5% on the amount unpaid calculated from the date on which the tax became payable until the date on which the payment is made.

## *CORPORATION TAX CALCULATION*

Fiscal year ending December 31, 2002.

| | | | |
|---|---|---|---|
| Profits for the year before taxes, as per accounts | | GHC Million | 1,000 |
| Add—Nondeductible items charged in accounts: | | | |
| Depreciation | 100 | | |
| Loss on disposal of fixed assets | 150 | | |
| Capital expenditure charged directly to income | 200 | | |
| Gifts and donations | 75 | | |
| Nonbusiness expenses | 100 | | |
| General provision for doubtful debts | 100 | | 725 |
| | | | 1,725 |
| Deduct—Profit on disposal of fixed assets | | | 25 |
| Adjusted profit | | | 1,700 |
| Deduct—Capital allowances: | | | |
| Capital allowance | 200 | | |
| Balancing allowance | 10 | | 210 |
| Chargeable income | | GHC Million | 1,490 |
| Income tax payable at 32.5% (1) | | GHC Million | 484.25 |

Notes:

1. Exchange rate of the cedi at March 5, 2003: US$1 = GHC8,500.00.

# Greece

## PwC contact

For additional information on taxation in Greece, contact:

Mary Psylla
268 Kifissias Avenue
152 32 Halandri
Athens, Greece
PricewaterhouseCoopers Business Solutions SA
Telephone: (30) (10) 6874 543
Fax: (30) (10) 6874 444
e-mail: mary.psylla@gr.pwc.com

## Significant developments

New provisions regarding the tax audit system have been introduced, aiming to render the tax audit procedure more objective and introducing a point-system base penalty system, whereby taxable profits may be increased depending on the number of tax violations assessed.

Furthermore, new incentive law provisions have increased the extent to which companies carrying out new investments may exempt part of their nondistributed profits from the annual corporate income tax.

In addition, recent announcements in the press indicate an intention to reduce tax rates (regarding nondistributed profits) for corporations to 25%.

## Taxes on corporate income

Effective for financial years ending June 30, 1992 and thereafter, corporations (*Société Anonyme* (SAs)) and limited liability companies (*Eteria Periorismenis Efthinis* (EPEs)) are taxed on total annual profits before distribution of dividends, profits, fees to directors, and profits to employees/workers. Profits are taxed only at the company level. There is no withholding tax on dividends or profits otherwise distributed, and no income tax in the name of the EPE members. If total annual profits of SAs and EPEs include dividends or profits from participations in other companies, these profits are deducted to arrive at taxable profits of SAs and EPEs. If total annual profits include tax-free income or income taxed on the basis of special regulations with exhaustion of the related tax liability (for companies other than banks operating in Greece most such categories have been abolished, with the main exception of sales of shares in SA companies), taxable profits are adjusted accordingly.

Corporate income tax rate is set at 35%.

The above rates are reduced by 40% for profits of companies derived from activities carried out on islands with less than 3,100 inhabitants.

## Corporate residence

Corporate residence is in practice determined by place of incorporation, although the commercial case law indicates that the decisive criterion that prevails is the place of effective management. However, subject to related tax treaty provisions, foreign corporations are subject to Greek taxation if operations, such as maintaining inventories from which orders are filled; maintaining offices, warehouses, factories, and so on; carrying out any other operations for the purposes of exploiting natural resources; processing raw materials or agricultural products in their own factories or through third parties; or providing services of a technical or scientific nature (surveys, designs, or research), are carried on in Greece.

## Other taxes

*Value-added tax*/The standard rate is 18%. There is a reduced rate of 8% on basic necessities (4% on books, newspapers, and periodicals). Supplies of goods and services to individuals and legal entities subject to VAT and established in European Union (EU) countries (intra-Union supplies) are exempt from VAT. Exports of goods and certain services to non-EU countries are also exempt.

*Contribution tax on capital accumulation*/A 1% tax contribution is imposed on capital accumulation (i.e., formation of business companies and joint ventures, capital increase, etc.) by (1) business companies and joint ventures; (2) cooperatives of all degrees and any other form of company, legal entity, or union of persons or society aiming to make profits; and (3) branches of foreign companies (unless of EU origin). An additional 0.1% duty in favor of the Competition Committee is imposed on capital accumulation of corporations.

*Real estate tax*/As from January 1, 1997 a real property tax is assessed on all property owners except those owning certain categories of property, that is, farming or stock farming expanses, mining rights, timber plantations, and buildings and machinery used in business operations, including hotels. New buildings are exempt for a maximum period of seven years. In addition, certain categories of owners are exempt, such as the Greek state, state corporations, including social security funds and utilities, embassy and consular property of foreign governments, and hotels for one-half of their land's value. For legal entities the tax rate is 0.7%, and is applicable to taxable value in excess of €243,600.

*Share transfer tax*/A 5% transfer tax is levied when legal entities, domestic or foreign, transfer shares not listed on the Athens Stock Exchange. This provision is effective as from November 17, 1999. The tax of 5% is calculated on the real value of the shares transferred as defined by a decision of the Minister of Finance. Reduced rates (1.2% and 2.4%) apply to transfers between relatives, depending on the proximity of the relation.

A tax at the rate of 0.3% (increased to 0.6% for sales of shares made from October 8, 1999 and thereafter, and decreased again to 0.3% for sales of shares made from January 1, 2001 and thereafter) is imposed on sales of shares listed on the Athens Stock Exchange. This tax is calculated on the sales value of shares as shown in the table prepared by the brokerage company, and is borne by the seller of the shares (individuals, corporations, other legal entities, and other groups regardless of citizenship, place of permanent residence or permanent establishment). This is effective for sales of shares on the Athens Stock Exchange as from the second day after the publication of the new law in the Government Gazette (February 19, 1998). Effective January 1, 1999 and thereafter, the above transaction tax of 0.6% (0.3% as from January 1, 2001) is also imposed on the sale of shares listed on a foreign stock exchange or other internationally recognized exchange made by domestic companies or foreign companies having a permanent establishment in Greece.

*Mobile telephone subscribers duty*/Effective as of February 1, 1998 a duty is charged to all subscribers of mobile telephone companies. This duty is calculated monthly and ranges from €1.5 to €6 per month, depending on the value of the subscriber's account.

***Special tax on real estate***/As of January 1, 2003, legal entities owning real estate property in Greece are subject to a special annual tax of 3% on the "objective" (i.e., determined by the Ministry of Finance) value of such property. This provision is mainly directed against property held, directly or indirectly, by offshore companies and the tax avoidance of transfer and inheritance taxes by the real owners. In this context exemptions apply to listed companies, companies with registered shares up to the individual shareholder, companies for which the income derived from the real estate property does not exceed the income from other activities, EU banks, insurance companies, investment funds, and so on.

An exemption from stamp duty on loans provided by Greek banks has been extended to any loan granted by bank, whether resident or nonresident.

## Branch income

Profits of branches of foreign companies are subject to income tax at the rate of 35%. No tax is withheld on post tax profit transferred to the foreign home office. However, if there is a remittance of profits abroad, the taxable profits must be increased by the portion of remitted profits corresponding to tax-free income or income taxed on the basis of special regulations after being increased by the applicable tax (grossed up).

## Income determination

***Inventory valuation***/Inventories are stated at the lower of cost or market (replacement value). LIFO, while permitted, is not used in practice. Conformity is required between book and tax reporting of inventory.

***Capital gains***/Capital gains derived from sales of any rights connected with the operations of an enterprise (such as the right of leasing or subleasing, trademarks or patents and similar rights, including profits from the sale of commercial passenger cars and trucks licenses) are subject to income tax at 20%. The same applies to realized goodwill, including gains on a business sold as a whole or a branch. Said gains are further taxed at the corporate income tax (CIT) rate, a tax credit being provided for the 20% already paid at the time of the transfer.

Goodwill realized through mergers of domestic companies carried out using incentive laws is not taxable.

Gains on the sale of shares listed on the Athens Stock Exchange are not taxable if they are set aside to cover losses from future sales. Gains on the sale of shares (parts) of EPEs, partnerships, including percentages of participation in a society of civil code doing business or in a joint venture, are taxed at a rate of 20%. Effective January 1, 1999 and thereafter, gains from the sale of shares listed on a foreign stock exchange or other internationally recognized exchange are also exempt from the capital gains tax but are subject to share transfer tax.

***Intercompany dividends***/Effective for financial years ending June 30, 1992 and thereafter, SAs and EPEs are taxed on their annual profit before distributions. Consequently, profits are taxed only at the company level, and there is no withholding on dividends or profits otherwise distributed. If total annual profits of SAs and EPEs include dividends or profits from participation in other domestic companies (SAs, EPEs, partnerships, and joint ventures), these profits are deducted to arrive at taxable profits of SAs and EPEs.

***Foreign income***/Resident corporations are taxed on their worldwide income. Foreign income received by a domestic corporation is taxed together with other income. If related income tax is withheld abroad, a tax credit is available up to the amount of the applicable Greek income tax.

***Stock dividends***/Greek legislation does not expressly recognize dividends in kind. Stock dividends could be treated for income tax purposes as though they were cash dividends, although the tax authorities may claim that a taxable share transfer has taken place.

***Other significant items***/Interest earned from interest-bearing securities (bonds and Treasury bills) issued on January 1, 1998 and thereafter by the Greek state, and interest earned from interest-bearing titles issued in Greece on January 1, 1998 and thereafter by the European Investment Bank, the International Financing Organization, the International Bank for Reconstruction and Development, the European Bank for Reconstruction and Development, and the Asian Development Bank is subject to a withholding tax of 10% (7.5% for those issued within calendar year 1997). Effective January 1, 1999, interest earned from Greek government bonds by nonresidents of Greece is exempt from taxation. Corporate bonds have the same treatment. Interest earned on deposits with banks operating in Greece is subject to income tax at the rate of 15% (previously 10%), withheld at source. Special tax incentives have been provided to financial transactions carried out in the context of asset securitizations.

Interest earned from any kind of deposits in foreign exchange by nonresidents of Greece with banks operating in Greece, the Postal Savings Bank or the Loan and Consignment Fund, including interest from deposits of banks with each other, including their obligatory or nonobligatory deposits with the Bank of Greece (central bank) and interest from deposits of the Postal Savings Bank and the Loan and Consignment Fund with the Bank of Greece, will remain tax-free. Interest earned from interest-bearing securities (bonds and Treasury bills) issued up to December 31, 1996 by the Greek state will also remain tax-free. Interest earned from interest-bearing titles issued in Greece up to December 31, 1996 by the European Investment Bank, the International Financing Organization, the International Bank for Reconstruction and Development, the European Bank for Reconstruction and Development, and the Asian Development Bank will remain tax-free as well.

Effective as of January 1, 1998, investment companies and mutual fund management companies are required to pay a tax of 0.3%, calculated (1) in the case of investment companies on the average of their investments, increased by their cash and cash equivalents at current prices as they appear in the quarterly investment tables, and (2) in the case of mutual funds on the half-yearly average of their entire net assets. In addition, income tax is imposed on the returns resulting from contracts or transactions on derivatives of financial products made by investment companies and mutual funds. This tax is calculated at the rate of 0.3% on the daily average of the "basis" amounts (notional amounts) relating to the transactions or contracts on the above derivatives.

Opportunities for a tax beneficial step-up of the historical value of real estate to market value is provided to listed companies, credit and insurance institutions, as well as 95% subsidiaries thereof.

# Greece

## Deductions

***Depreciation and depletion***/Depreciation of tangible assets is compulsory for financial years ending after December 30, 1997 (not compulsory for financial years ended within the period from January 1, 1992 through December 30, 1997). Fixed assets with acquisition value of up to €600 each may be written off to profit and loss in the year acquired or when used in operations. Effective for profits resulting from financial accounting years ending December 31, 1999 and thereafter, computer hardware and software may be written off to profit and loss in the year used in operations. Depreciation is computed on the basis of the straight-line method or the declining-balance method on the acquisition value, increased by any additions and improvements. The straight-line method or the declining-balance method must be used consistently. After January 1, 2003, and for fixed assets of the same category, the company may elect between a maximum and a minimum depreciation rate, which was stipulated in the Presidential Decree 299 issued as at November 4, 2003.

Preoperating expenses, including interest, may be amortized over a maximum period of five years, but once the method is established, it is binding.

There are no provisions for depletion.

***Net operating losses***/Losses can be carried forward five years. Carrybacks are not permitted.

***Payments to foreign affiliates***/Royalties, interest, and service fees paid to foreign affiliates are deductible expenses under certain requirements and conditions.

***Taxes***/Taxes other than income tax and real estate tax are recognized as deductible expenses only if supported by related tax returns and payment receipts.

***Other significant items***/Donations to the government, municipalities, religious organizations, and certain institutions are deductible expenses under certain requirements and conditions.

As of January 1, 2003, depreciation for fixed assets acquired from offshore companies, as well as service fees and other purchases from offshore companies, are not tax deductible.

As of January 1, 2003, bad debt write offs will be recognized as tax deductible on the basis of specific stringent conditions that are  clarified in a Ministerial Decision issued  at December 11, 2003.

## Group taxation

Group taxation is not permitted.

## Tax incentives

***Inward investment***/Foreign investments earmarked for the promotion of national production, or otherwise contributing to the economic development of the country has obtained a freezing of income tax rates for a specified period not exceeding ten years at a rate of 25% for investments exceeded the amount of €30 million.

***Capital investment***/Incentives for capital investment are available as follows.

New investors in eligible companies (i.e., manufacturing, handicraft, mining, and agricultural companies; companies/laboratories engaged in applied industrial, energy, mining, agricultural, etc., research; companies developing software;

commercial companies; international trade companies; companies providing advanced technology services; hotels; and tourist companies) making eligible investments in areas D, C, and B are entitled to 100%, 70%, and 40% income tax exemption (tax-free reserve), respectively, on the amount of the assisted expenditure and the amount of new machinery and other equipment whose use is obtained through leasing as from April 15, 1998. This incentive may be granted in conjunction with an interest subsidy on the investment loans of the assisted investment. In area A, except as noted in the law, old investors are not entitled to an income tax exemption and interest subsidy on the investment loans. The old business vehicles making eligible investments in areas D, C, and B are also entitled to 100%, 70%, and 40% income tax exemption (tax-free reserve), respectively, on the amount of the assisted expenditure and the amount of new machinery and other equipment whose use is obtained through leasing as from April 15, 1998. There is a wide range of exceptions to the general rules governing the granting of incentives.

Companies subject to incentive laws (manufacturing companies, enterprises involved in advanced technology, etc.) as well as commercial companies, are entitled, under certain conditions, to tax-free reserves formed from the profits of the accounting years 2004 until 2008, at a percentage up to 35% of the total nondistributed profits, as declared in the annual corporate income tax return filed by the date set in the law. Such a reserve should, within the next three years, be utilized in productive investments. (The special quantitative condition applies as to utilization in the first year). The part of reserve covered within this three-year period may be capitalized on a tax-free basis.

Especially for the accounting year 2003, the said reserve is calculated up to 50% on the remaining balance of profits for 2003 after the subtraction of profits 2002.

Reserves may be formed from the annual profits declared per the income tax return (less dividends distributed, directors' fees and appropriation for legal reserve) in the year the assets were acquired or subsequent years. Tax-free reserves under various investment laws may be capitalized entirely or partially. Companies will increase in the same financial year their share capital by the equivalent amount through the payment of cash by old or new shareholders. Reserves so capitalized are taxed at the rate of 5% for companies having shares quoted on the Athens Stock Exchange, and 10% for all other companies. The payment of this tax terminates the income tax liability of the company and its shareholders as regards the capitalized reserve.

If the assets concerned are sold within five years, or the reserve is distributed, the amount of the tax exemption is added back to the taxable profits. If in any year the company's books are found to be incorrect by the tax authorities, the amount of the tax exemption of that particular year is added back to the taxable profits.

Enterprises that have received investment and interest subsidies from the government are not entitled to the above tax-free reserves for subsidized investments.

*Other incentives*/Up to December 31, 2003, exporting companies are permitted to make a deduction from their taxable income equivalent to 1% of their annual gross sales up to €8,804,109, and 0.5% for sales exceeding such amount without supporting documents for meeting special expenses for which, because of their nature, the receipt of supporting documents is not feasible. For companies exporting any kind of products, as well as hotel companies deriving income from foreign customers, the relevant rates are 2% up to gross sales of €2,201,127, 1% between the former amount and €8,804,109, and 0.5% for any exceeding amount. Special uniform rates apply to oil products exporting companies (0.5%), international route transport companies (1%), and new publishers (2%). For the latter the incentive has been extended up to December 31, 2008.

SAs with shares not listed on the Athens Stock Exchange that come from a merger with or absorption of other companies of any legal form are taxed on their profits as shown on the first balance sheet after the completion of the transformation at the rate in force at the time of filing their tax return reduced by 10 percentage units; and on their profits shown on the second balance sheet they are taxed at the rate in force at the time of filing their tax return reduced by 5 percentage units. These provisions apply under certain requirements and conditions described in the law. The reduction of the corporate tax rate by 10 and 5 percentage units also applies, under the same requirements, to those SAs with shares listed on the Athens Stock Exchange that absorb one or more SAs with shares listed or not listed on the Athens Stock Exchange.

The government provides income tax and certain other tax and customs duty exemptions to foreign enterprises established under Law 89/1967. The activities of these enterprises must be conducted outside Greece. In addition, to protect the traditional local shipping industry, the government exempts Greek shipping enterprises from income tax. These exemptions do not apply to foreign commercial/manufacturing companies that are established in Greece under Law 89/1967 as from January 1, 2002. For foreign commercial/manufacturing companies that have been established in Greece under Law 89/1967 up to December 31, 2001, the above exemptions will continue to be in force up to December 31, 2005.

## Withholding taxes

| Recipient | Dividends | Interest | Royalties |
|---|---|---|---|
| | % | % | % |
| Resident individuals and companies............ | (1) | 20, 15 (2) | Nil |
| Nonresident individuals and companies: | | | |
| Nontreaty..................................................... | (1) | 35, 15 (2) | 20 (3) |
| Treaty: | | | |
| Albania (4).............................................. | 5 (5) | 5, Nil (6) | 5 |
| Armenia.................................................. | 10 (8) | 10 | 5 |
| Austria.................................................... | (1) | Nil, 10 (7) | Nil, 10 (7) |
| Belgium.................................................. | 25 (8) | 15 | 5 |
| Bulgaria (9)............................................ | 40 (8) | 10 | 10 |
| Croatia (10)............................................ | 5, 10 (11) | 10 | 10 |
| Cyprus.................................................... | 25 (8) | 10 | Nil, 5 (12) |
| Czech Republic...................................... | (1) | 10 | 10 |
| Denmark................................................. | 38 (8) | 8 | 5 |
| Finland................................................... | 47 (8) | 10 | 10 |
| France.................................................... | (1) | 10 | 5 |
| Georgia.................................................. | 8 (8) | 8 | 5 |
| Germany................................................. | 25 (8) | 10 | Nil |
| Hungary.................................................. | 45 (8) | 10 | 10 |
| India....................................................... | (1) | 35 | (3) |

| Recipient | Dividends | Interest | Royalties |
|---|---|---|---|
| | % | % | % |
| Israel (13) | (1) | 10 | 10 |
| Italy | 35 (8) | 10 | 5 (14) |
| Korea, Rep. of (8) | 15 (8), (15) | 8 | 10 |
| Luxembourg | 38 (8) | 8 | 7 (16) |
| Netherlands | 35 (8) | 10 (17) | 7 (16) |
| Norway | 40 (8) | 10 | 10 |
| Poland | (1) | 10 | 10 |
| Portugal | 15 | 15 | 10 |
| Romania | 45 (8) | 10 | 7 (16) |
| Slovak Republic | (1) | 10 | 10 |
| Slovenia | 10 (8) | 10 | 10 |
| South Africa | 5 (8) (21) | 8 | 7 (16) |
| Spain | 10, 5 (18) | 8 | 6 |
| Sweden | (1) | 10 | 5 |
| Switzerland | 35 (8) | 10 | 5 |
| Ukraine | 10 (8) | 10 | 10 |
| United Kingdom | (1) | Nil | Nil |
| Uzbekistan | 8 (8) | 10 | 8 |
| United States | (1) | Nil, 37.5 (19) | Nil, 10 (20) |

Notes:

1. A corporation is taxed on its total annual profits before distributions. Consequently, the profits are taxed only at the company level, and there is no withholding tax on dividends and profits otherwise distributed.

2. Interest earned on deposits with banks operating in Greece is subject to income tax at the rate of 15% withheld at source. Interest earned from bonds and treasury bills issued on January 1, 1997 and thereafter by the Greek state and interest earned from interest-bearing titles issued in Greece on January 1, 1997 and thereafter by the European Investment Bank, the International Financing Organization, the International Bank for Reconstruction and Development, the European Bank for Reconstruction and Development, and the Asian Development Bank are subject to income tax at 7.5% (10% for those issued on January 1, 1998 and thereafter). Interest earned by nonresidents on Greek government bonds after January 1, 1999 is exempt from income tax. Corporate bonds have the same treatment as government bonds.

3. Tax withholding is 20% for all payments of royalties and service fees.

4. The treaty is effective for income earned as from January 1, 2001.

5. The rate of 5% applies in case the person (individual or legal entity) that collects the dividends is also the beneficiary of them.

6. The exemption (nil rate) applies in case the entity that pays the interest is the government of the contracting state or some local authority of it or the interest is paid to the government of the other contracting state or some local authority or "vehicle" or organization of it (including financial organizations) that fully belongs to the other contracting state or to a local authority of it or the interest is paid to some other "vehicle" or organization (including financial organizations) in connection with loans that are granted in implementation of an agreement that has been concluded between the contracting states.

7. The rate of 10% is applicable only to majority (over 50%) shareholders.

8. Effective for financial years ending June 30, 1992 and thereafter the withholding tax rates on dividends provided by the double taxation treaties do not apply because the internal law regulations provide for more favorable tax treatment than the double taxation treaties (i.e., no withholding tax on dividends).

9. The treaty is in force as from January 1, 2002 (i.e., it is effective for income earned from January 1, 2002).

10. The treaty is in force.

11. The rate of 5% applies in case the beneficiary is a company (excluding a personal company) and directly holds, at least, 25% of the capital of the paying company and the rate of 10% applies in all other cases.

12. The rate of 5% is applicable only to film rentals.

13. The treaty is effective for income earned as from January 1, 1999.

14. Exemption (nil rate) applies to payments of any kind received as a consideration for the use or the right to use any copyright of literary, artistic, or scientific work, including cinematograph films, or films and tapes for television or radio broadcasting.

15. A rate of 5% is applicable to shareholders of 25% and above.

16. The rate is 5% if the royalties consist of payments of any kind received as a consideration for the use of or the right to use any copyright of literary, artistic, or scientific work, including cinematograph films.

17. If interest is paid to a bank or another financial institution, the tax withholding rate should not exceed 8%.

18. The rate is 5% when the beneficiary owns (unless it is a partnership) at least 25% of the distributing company and 10% in all other cases.

19. The exemption (i.e., nil rate) applies to the extent the rate of interest does not exceed 9% per annum; the rate of 37.5% (35% for income earned in the year 2002) applies to the portion of interest exceeding 9%. In addition, the 37.5% (35% for income earned in the year 2002) rate applies to interest payable to a U.S. corporation holding more than 50% of the share capital of a Greek company.

20. The rate of 10% is applicable only to film rentals.

21. The rate of 5% applies in case the beneficiary is a company (excluding a personal company) and directly holds, at least, 25% of the capital of the paying company and the rate of 15% applies in all other cases.

## Tax administration

*Returns*/Income tax returns of Greek SAs, EPEs and branches of foreign companies are filed on a special form within four months and ten days from the end of their financial year, which can be on either June 30 or December 31. By a decision of the Minister of Finance, the filing date for SAs may be extended a few days, depending on the last digit (figure) of their tax registration number. Branches and subsidiaries (at least 50% participation) of foreign companies may follow the financial year of the parent company. A Greek company that is at least 50% held by another Greek company that is in turn a subsidiary of a foreign company that has participation with the same or higher percentage may also follow the financial year of the foreign parent company. The income tax return constitutes the basis for assessment.

**Payment of tax**/Income tax and tax prepayment (55% [60% for banks operating in Greece] of the current year's income tax less tax withheld at source) based on the tax return are paid in eight equal monthly installments, the first of which should be paid upon filing. A discount of 2.5% is granted if total tax assessed is paid in a lump sum at the time of filing (within the time limit).

## CORPORATION TAX CALCULATION

Manufacturing company with registered shares not listed on the Stock Exchange.

Fiscal year ended December 31, 2003

### Assumptions

| | |
|---|---:|
| Net profit per profit and loss statement | € 500,000,000 |
| Income from interest taxed at 10% | 40,000,000 |
| Income from interest taxed at 15% | 20,000,000 |
| Nondeductible expenses | 50,000,000 |
| Appropriation to tax-free reserves | 100,000,000 |
| Proposed dividends | 200,000,000 |
| Proposed directors fees | 20,000,000 |
| Advance tax paid in 2003 | 60,000,000 |

### Taxable income

| | | |
|---|---:|---:|
| Net profit per profit and loss statement | | 500,000,000 |
| Add—Nondeductible expenses (provisions, fines, etc.) | | 50,000,000 |
| | | 550,000,000 |
| Deduct: | | |
| Appropriation to tax-free reserves | 100,000,000 | 100,000,000 |
| | | 450,000,000 |
| Taxable profits | | 450,000,000 |
| Corporate income tax at 35% | | € 157,500,000 |

### Payment of corporate income tax in 2004

| | | |
|---|---:|---:|
| Balance of 2003 corporate tax: | | |
| Corporate tax liability as above | 157,500,000 | |
| Less—Advance paid in 2003 | (60,000,000) | |
| Less—Withholding tax of 10% corresponding to interest (40,000,000 x 10%) | (4,000,000) | |
| Less—Withholding tax of 15% corresponding to interest (50,000,000 x 15%) | (7,500,000) | 86,000,000 |
| Advance payment of 2004 corporate tax (55% of corporate income tax as above) | | 86,625,000 |
| Total payment of tax in 2004 (Note 1) | | € 172,625,000 |

# Greece

Notes:

1. The balance of 2003 corporate tax (€86,000) and the advance payment at 55% (€86,625,000) are payable in eight equal monthly installments; the first installment must be paid on the due date of the return, which is four months and ten days after the company's financial year-end. If the entire amount of tax due (€172,625,000) is paid in a lump sum on the date the return is due for filing a 2.5% discount is given.
2. Exchange rate of the Euro at March 16, 2004: US$1 = €0.815.

## PwC contacts

For additional information on taxation in Guatemala, contact:

Oscar Cordon
Edgar Mendoza
PricewaterhouseCoopers
Edificio Tívoli Plaza
6a Calle 6-38, Zone 9
Guatemala City, Guatemala
Telephone: (502) (2) 345080
Fax: (502) (2) 331-8345
LN domain: Oscar.Cordon@gt.pwc.com
e-mail: edgar.mendoza@gt.pwc.com

## General note

The information in this entry is current as of January 2004. For subsequent developments, consult the contacts listed above.

## Taxes on corporate income

A rate of 31% is applicable to a company's taxable income from Guatemalan sources.

## Corporate residence

The place of incorporation determines corporate residence.

## Other taxes

*Stamp tax*/Except for transactions taxed with value-added tax (VAT) and other minor exceptions, a stamp tax must be paid on all documents covering legal transactions that originate locally or are received from abroad. Letters of credit and acceptances involving international transfers of funds are generally exempt from the stamp tax, as are documents subject to VAT (see below). The normal stamp tax rate of 3% is calculated on the face value of the documents or the gross value of the transaction.

*Tax on interest income*/Interest income earned by domiciled persons is subject to a flat 10% withholding tax. The interest so taxed is to be included by taxpayers in their income tax returns as nontaxable income.

*Social security contribution*/Corporations contribute 12.67% of their monthly payroll to social security. However, employees contribute 4.83% of their monthly salary to the same issue.

*Payment of incentive bonus to employees*/An addition to normal compensation is to be paid to all employees, as determined by an incentives plan commonly agreed on between the corporation and the labor force. This incentive bonus is tax exempt for the corporation. It is treated as a deductible item.

*Value-added tax*/A 12% VAT is levied on the sale or transfer of merchandise, chattels, and real estate; on nonpersonal services rendered; on the rental of goods and chattels; and on imports. The tax base is determined as follows.

1. Sale of goods: Sale price less standard commercial discount plus any other charges included in the invoice.

2. Services: Price of the service less standard commercial discount plus cost of goods used in the service.
3. Imports: Value declared for customs duties.
4. Rentals: Amount of the rent.

The following are exempt from VAT.

1. Imported machinery, equipment, and other goods related to the activities or services of legally constituted and registered cooperatives.
2. Temporary imports, as defined, by individuals and legal persons.
3. Imports by diplomatic and consular missions accredited to the Guatemalan government.
4. Banking services.
5. The creation, issuance, circulation, and transfer of stocks and bonds of all kinds.
6. Interest derived from bonds and other obligations issued by mercantile partnerships and offered on an authorized stock exchange.
7. Exports.
8. Contributions and donations to nonprofit educational, cultural, benevolent, and security service entities.

VAT charged to customers is set off against VAT paid to suppliers, and the net debit amount is paid to the tax authorities on a monthly basis. A credit amount is carried over to the following month. Refunds are made only to exporters of goods.

*Real estate taxes*/Real estate taxes are assessed annually at Q3 per thousand on declared property values of from Q2,000 to Q20,000, at Q6 per thousand on values from Q20,000 to Q70,000, and at Q9 per thousand on values in excess of Q70,000.

## Branch income

Tax rates on branch profits are the same as on corporate profits.

## Income determination

*Inventory valuation*/LIFO is accepted for tax purposes. Inventories are to be stated at average cost or at cost determined by the FIFO method. Conformity between book and tax reporting is generally required.

*Capital gains*/Capital gains taxes are equivalent to 10% of such gains as a flat tax. Tax is due with the year-end return. Capital losses can be netted only against capital gains.

*Intercompany dividends*/Dividends from domestic subsidiaries and other domestic corporations are not subject to income tax withholdings if Guatemalan income tax has been paid. However, a 3% stamp tax must be paid upon dividend payment.

*Foreign income*/Foreign-source income received by a domestic corporation is generally exempt from Guatemalan income tax.

*Stock dividends*/Stock dividends are permitted by the Commercial Code and are subject to a 3% stamp tax upon dividend payment.

## Deductions

*Depreciation*/Depreciation is generally computed on a straight-line basis. Upon request by the taxpayer, the tax authorities may authorize other depreciation methods. The maximum annual rates admitted as deductible expenses as follows.

|  | % |
| --- | --- |
| Buildings and improvements | 5 |
| Machinery and equipment | 20 |
| Furniture and fixtures | 20 |
| Vehicles | 20 |
| Tools | 25 |
| Trees and vegetable species | 15 |
| Computer equipment and software | 33.33 |
| Goods not specifically regulated | 10 |

Tax depreciation must conform to book depreciation.

*Net operating losses*/Only new companies or corporations may carry forward operating losses during their first five years of operations. These losses can be offset only against net income of the next years following that when they were sustained. Losses may not be carried back.

*Payments to foreign affiliates*/Deduction for royalties will be allowed up to 5% of gross income. Charges for technical service fees are deductible up to 1% of gross income or 15% of total salaries paid to Guatemalans, whichever is the larger.

*Taxes*/All taxes other than income tax and VAT are deductible.

## Group taxation

Group taxation is not permitted.

## Tax incentives

Exemption from payment of import duties on machinery and equipment and on raw and packaging materials and from income tax is available for those corporations classified as exporting companies. These exemptions also apply to free-trade zones.

*Capital investment*/Individuals or juridical persons may deduct from net income up to 5% of total profits of the annual tax period reinvested in the acquisition of plant, machinery, and equipment directly linked to the production process and destined to generate taxable income. This reinvestment must be made during the five months following the close of the annual tax period to which the deduction for plant, machinery, and equipment applies.

## Withholding taxes

On payments to nondomiciled foreign corporations or individuals.

|  | % |
| --- | --- |
| Dividends, profit participations, earnings, and other benefits (1) | 0 |
| Commissions, salaries | 10 |
| Interest (2) | 10 |
| Professional fees, royalties, technical service fees | 31 |

# Guatemala

Notes:
1. For taxpayers that have not been paying corporate income tax, there is a 10% withholding tax.
2. Interest income is tax exempt whenever the related foreign-exchange proceeds are directly sold into the Guatemalan banking system, and they are paid to a financial or banking institution.

*Tax treaties*/None.

## Tax administration

*Returns*/In general, the fiscal year runs from July 1 of one year to June 30 of the following year. Corporate taxpayers may request authorization to use the calendar year as their tax year. The tax system may best be described as one of information filing.

*Payment of tax*/All corporate taxpayers are required to prepay their estimated annual income tax liability in three quarterly installments. These advance payments must be made; one of the following procedures for computing estimated quarterly tax liability may be chosen.
1. Tax on income shown by partial closure of accounts or computation of presumed liquidation of operations at the end of each quarter.
2. Tax on 5% of overall gross income earned during the corresponding quarter of the preceding year (5% of the 31% income tax rate = 1.5%).
3. Tax equivalent to one-fourth of the tax paid for the immediately preceding tax year.
4. Tax on 5% of gross revenue is applicable for individual and corporation obtaining income from technical, professional or scientific services; any type of service, lease of movable and immovable property.

## *CORPORATION TAX CALCULATION*

Fiscal year ending December 31, 2003

| | | |
|---|---:|---:|
| Total income ................................................................................ | | Q 10,000,000 |
| Add—Nondeductible expenses: | | |
| Depreciation of fixed assets in excess | | |
| of authorized rates...................................................... | 100,000 | |
| Provision for doubtful accounts in excess (3%) of the | | |
| accounts receivable balance at year-end....................... | 20,000 | |
| Provision for severance payments in | | |
| excess of 8.33% of annual salaries ............................. | 15,000 | |
| Royalties paid in excess of 5% of gross income .............. | 10,000 | |
| Technical service fees paid (from overseas) | | |
| in excess of 1% of gross income ................................. | 9,000 | 154,000 |
| | | 10,154,000 |
| Less—Deductible expenses: | | |
| Cost of sales ................................................................. | 7,000,000 | |
| Salaries and wages......................................................... | 300,000 | |
| Rentals.......................................................................... | 150,000 | |
| Taxes and contributions.................................................. | 100,000 | |
| Interest and discounts .................................................... | 80,000 | |
| Insurance premiums........................................................ | 2,000 | |
| Depreciation.................................................................. | 200,000 | |
| Maintenance.................................................................. | 7,000 | |
| General expenses .......................................................... | 300,000 | 8,139,000 |
| Net taxable income................................................................ | | Q  2,015,000 |
| Income tax payable at 31%..................................................... | | Q   624,650 |

Note:

Exchange rate of the quetzal at January 31, 2004: US$1 = Q8.10.

# Guyana

## PwC contact

For additional information on taxation in Guyana, contact:

Ronald M. Alli
Jack A. Alli Sons & Co.
145 Crown Street
Queenstown, Georgetown, Guyana
Telephone: (592) (22) 62904, 66532, 37065-7
Fax: (592) (22) 53849
e-mail: jasco@guyana.net.gy
      ronald.alli@jaasco.com

## Significant developments

Tax holidays have been reinstituted for certain developmental or risk-bearing enterprises and economic activities in specified regions of the country.

Revised provisions have been enacted for interest and penalties for late payment of taxes due and late submission of tax returns.

## Taxes on corporate income

For the year of assessment 2004 (the accounting year ended during 2003) corporation tax is to be paid at a rate of 45% of chargeable income of a commercial company, and at the rate of 35% in the case of any other company (see "Minimum tax on corporate income" below).

A commercial company means a company for which at least 75% of the gross income is derived from trading in goods manufactured by others, and includes any commission agency, any telecommunications company, any corporate body licensed or otherwise authorized by law to carry on banking business in Guyana, and any company carrying on a Guyana insurance business, other than long-term insurance business, as defined in section 2 of the Insurance Act.

Petroleum and mining companies may, by Ministerial Order affirmed by the National Assembly, have all provisions of the Income Tax and Corporation Tax Acts waived, modified, adopted, or qualified as may be specified in the Order.

***Minimum tax on corporate income***/Where the actual corporation tax liability of a commercial company as computed at 45% of chargeable income is less than 2% of the turnover of the company in the year of income immediately preceding the year of assessment applicable, the Corporation Tax Act provides for the payment of corporation tax (referred to as minimum tax) at the rate of 2% of turnover.

Certain exemptions from minimum tax are provided.

1. Commercial companies with a turnover of less than G$1,200,000.
2. Companies carrying on insurance business.
3. Companies exempt from corporation tax.
4. Noncommercial companies.

Minimum tax paid in excess of the actual corporation tax liability is to be carried forward for setoff against the corporation tax liability for the succeeding year or years, to the extent this liability is in excess of the 2% of turnover minimum tax for the relevant year.

## Corporate residence

Corporate residence is determined by reference to location of central management and control of the business of a company, whether or not the company is incorporated in Guyana.

## Other taxes

*Property tax*/Property tax is payable on net property values of a company with assets acquired prior to January 1, 1991 included at the market values at January 1, 1991. As of January 1, 1999, the first G$1,500,000 of net property is exempt. A rate of 0.5% applies on the next G$5 million, and a rate of 0.75% thereafter.

*Other taxes*/Other revenue is raised in the form of a consumption tax on locally manufactured goods that are not exported, customs duties, purchase tax and consumption tax on importation of goods, local rates on property, and a wide range of stamp taxes. A 1994 revision of the duties and taxes payable on importation of materials and equipment has reduced or zero-rated consumption tax on a number of imported materials and equipment items.

*Hotel services tax*/Hotels, with accommodation greater than 16 rooms, are subject to accommodation and services tax of 10%.

## Branch income

Tax rates on branch income are the same as on corporate income. Branch income is subject to withholding tax regardless of whether the income is remitted to the head office, with the provision that branch income that is reinvested in Guyana to the satisfaction of the Commissioner will not be subject to withholding tax. The provision for withholding tax on branch income is amended by double taxation agreements with Canada, the United Kingdom, and certain CARICOM (Caribbean Community) territories.

## Income determination

*Inventory valuation*/Inventories are generally stated at the lower of cost or net realizable value. FIFO or average-cost methods are generally used for book and tax purposes. However, the Inland Revenue will normally accept a method of valuation that conforms to standard accounting practice in the trade. Book and tax conformity of inventory valuation is generally required.

*Capital gains*/Short-term gains, which are gains arising upon the disposal of capital assets within 12 months of acquisition, are subject to tax at corporate rates.

Long-term gains, which are gains arising upon disposal of capital assets between 1 and 25 years after acquisition, are subject to capital gains tax at a rate of 20% to the extent they exceed G$1,000. Capital assets held for more than 25 years are not subject to capital gains tax upon subsequent disposal.

Capital losses in excess of G$1,000 are allowed as an offset to capital gains, and may be carried forward for a period of 24 years.

The market value at January 1, 1991 of assets held prior to that date is taken into consideration when computing capital gains.

*Intercompany dividends*/Dividends received from a local company are excluded from further corporate taxes, since withholding taxes have been deducted at source (see "Withholding taxes" below).

# Guyana

**Bank interest**/Interest earned from banks and financial institutions is exempt from corporate taxes, since withholding taxes are deducted at source (see "Withholding taxes" below).

**Foreign income**/A resident company is taxable on its worldwide income, whether or not received in Guyana. A nonresident company is taxable on income directly or indirectly accruing in or derived from Guyana.

Double taxation is normally avoided by means of foreign tax credits where a tax treaty exists. In the absence of a treaty, there are provisions for the granting of relief.

**Stock dividends**/A Guyanese corporation may distribute bonus shares tax free to shareholders.

## Deductions

**Depreciation and depletion**/Tax depreciation (wear-and-tear allowance) is generally computed by either the straight-line or the reducing-balance method, depending on the business and type of asset involved, at prescribed rates set out in the Inland Revenue regulations.

Accelerated tax depreciation is allowed to certain trades, including depreciation on industrial buildings and hotels, in the form of initial allowances on capital expenditure in the year of acquisition.

Tax depreciation is not required to conform to book depreciation.

Gains on the sale of assets on which initial allowances were granted are subject to corporate taxes to the extent of tax allowances received (balancing charge), and the excess is subject to capital gains tax. Gains on the sale of other depreciated assets are subject to capital gains tax.

Allowances are granted for the depletion of natural resource properties at rates approved by the Inland Revenue.

**Net operating losses**/Losses may be carried forward indefinitely to be set off against future profits arising from the sources from which the losses arose. The profits of any year for each source may not be reduced by more than one-half by losses brought forward, except those losses brought forward from tax holiday periods, losses incurred in the petroleum and the gold and diamond mining industries and losses brought forward by commercial companies subject to minimum tax, which may be utilized without limitation.

Loss carrybacks are not permitted.

**Payments to foreign affiliates**/A Guyanese corporation may claim a deduction for royalties and interest charges paid to foreign affiliates, provided such amounts are reasonable and necessary, having regard to the requirements of the trade. Deduction for management charges is restricted to the lesser of the management charge or 1.0% of sales or gross income of any company.

Payments to foreign affiliates are subject to withholding tax (see "Withholding taxes" below).

**Taxes**/Property tax is not a deductible item in computing corporate chargeable income.

*Other significant items*/Payments made under deeds of covenant are deductible to the extent of 10% of the company's taxable income. Deeds of covenant must be for a period exceeding two years.

Amounts donated to the government of Guyana for public purposes or to prescribed organizations of a national or international character are allowable deductions.

## Group taxation

Group taxation is not permitted.

## Tax incentives

*Inward investment*/The following incentives are available.

1.  Tax holidays: With effect from December 31, 1998, the Income Tax (In Aid of Industry) Act provides that a company (other than a gold or diamond mining company or a petroleum company) which carries on business that in the Minister's opinion is wholly of a developmental or risk-bearing nature, and likely to be instrumental to the development of the resources of and beneficial to Guyana, or which carries on an economic activity which demonstrably creates new employment in specified regions of Guyana, is exempt from corporate taxes for periods of up to ten years. Profits may be distributed free of tax to shareholders during the holiday period and for two years thereafter. Net losses may be carried forward without limitation to offset income arising after the end of the holiday period.
2.  Hotels: Qualifying hotels may be entitled to accelerated depreciation provisions for capital investment (see also below).
3.  Approved mortgage finance companies and building societies: The profits of approved companies and societies are exempt from corporate taxes.
4.  Petroleum (Exploration and Production) Act 1986/Mining Act 1989: Petroleum and mining companies may be entitled to exemptions from or modifications of the requirements of the Corporate Taxes Act.

*Capital investment*/Initial allowances to industries entitled to accelerated tax depreciation may exceed 70% for certain categories of equipment.

*Export allowances*/Companies registered in Guyana that have made export sales of manufactured, processed, or agricultural products are entitled to export allowances that may be as much as 50% of the export profit, which occurs where the percentage of export sales in relation to total sales exceeds 61%. Products that do not qualify for this allowance are bauxite, gold, diamonds, petroleum, sugar, rum, molasses, rice, timber, lumber, and shrimp. Companies making export sales to certain CARICOM countries do not qualify for the allowance.

*Agricultural allowances*/Companies engaged in land development for agricultural purposes will be allowed to deduct the cost of this development over ten years.

# Guyana

## Withholding taxes

Withholding taxes are payable at the following rates (to be withheld at source; see Note 1).

| | Resident individual | Resident company | Nonresident company | Nonresident individual |
|---|---|---|---|---|
| | % | % | % | % |
| Dividends................................ | Nil | Nil | 20 | 20 |
| Bank interest........................... | 20 | 20 | 20 | 20 |
| Other interest (2, 3)................. | Nil | Nil | 20 | 20 |
| Royalties, management fees/charges, rent (3)........... | Nil | Nil | 20 | 20 |
| Contracts, including subcontracts (3) ................... | Nil | Nil | 10 (4) | Nil |
| Discounts on Treasury bills (5) .................. | 20 | 20 | 20 | 20 |

The numbers in parentheses refer to the following numbered Notes.

Notes:

1. The Minister may reduce the rate of withholding tax.
2. Interest on approved loans, trade accounts, and temporary bank loans is exempt from withholding tax.
3. Resident individuals or companies are subject to income or corporate tax provisions on income from contracts, royalties, management fees, rent, or other interest, and nonresident individuals are subject to income tax provisions on contract income.
4. The nonresident company is to be given credit for the withholding tax deducted from its contract payments in computing the corporation tax payable in Guyana by the nonresident company. A penalty of an amount equal to the amount of tax to be withheld on contract payments is to be charged if the taxes are not so withheld.
5. Credit is given for the withholding tax deducted from Treasury bills discounted.

*Tax treaties*/Guyana has double taxation treaties with Canada, the United Kingdom, and certain CARICOM territories, and the rates applied, if the recipient is the beneficial owner of the income, do not exceed the maximum rates stated above. There is an exchange of information agreement on taxes with the United States.

## Tax administration

*Returns*/Tax returns must be filed in specified form by April 30 of the year following the accounting year-end. Accounting year-ends that do not coincide with the calendar year-end must be approved by the Inland Revenue.

The system is one of self-assessment.

*Payment of tax*/Corporate bodies are required to pay corporation tax in quarterly installments on March 15, June 15, September 15, and December 15 of the year of income, calculated at the prevailing rate on one of the following.

1. On estimates based on the chargeable income or, for commercial companies, 2% of turnover of the preceding year, whichever is greater.

2. On a current-year basis if the Inland Revenue deems this appropriate.
3. On any amount agreed between the taxpayer and the Inland Revenue.

Any shortfall of taxes after accounting for quarterly installments should be met by April 30 following the year of income.

## CORPORATION TAX CALCULATION

Year of assessment 2004—Accounting year ended November 30, 2003

### Noncommercial company

| | | |
|---|---:|---:|
| Net profit before taxes per financial statements | | G$ 1,000,000 |
| Add: | | |
| Depreciation | 140,000 | |
| Various other disallowable items | 129,000 | 269,000 |
| | | G$ 1,269,000 |
| Less: | | |
| Dividends received from company resident in Guyana (not liable to corporate taxes in recipient company's hands) | 16,000 | |
| Government of Guyana—Prize money on premium bonds—Tax-exempt | 5,000 | |
| Profit on disposal of fixed asset (1) | 22,000 | 43,000 |
| Adjusted profits | | 1,226,000 |
| Less—Wear-and-tear allowances (2) | | 176,000 |
| Chargeable income | | G$ 1,050,000 |
| Corporate tax at 35% | | G$ 367,500 |
| Less—Advance quarterly payments (3/15/03 6/15/03, 9/15/03, 12/15/03) of 50,000 each | | (200,000) |
| Net balance due | | G$ 167,500 |

Notes:

1. Gains from the disposal of fixed assets occurring between 1 and 25 years after acquisition are subject to capital gains tax. (See "Capital gains" above.)
2. Wear-and-tear allowances are granted in place of depreciation at rates approved by the Commissioner of Inland Revenue.
3. Exchange rate of the Guyanese dollar at January 1, 2004: US$1 = G$179.

# Honduras

## PwC contact

For additional information on taxation in Honduras, contact:

Jorge Alberto Fú Padgett
PriceWaterhouseCoopers Honduras
Colonia Loma Linda Norte
Bloque F— Calle Diagonal Gema No. 1
Tegucigalpa, Honduras
Telephone: (504) 231 19 11, 239 87 08/ 239 87 09
Fax: (504) 31 19 06
e-mail: jorge.fu@hn.pwc.com

## Note

The following information on taxation in Honduras is accurate as of January 1, 2004. For subsequent developments, consult the contact listed above.

## Taxes on corporate income

The corporate tax rate is currently 25%. In addition, there is a 5% solidarity tax levied on all companies whose taxable income is in excess of HNL1 million. This solidarity tax will be in effect throughout the 2004, 2005, and 2006 fiscal years.

## Corporate residence

The place of incorporation is regarded by Honduran authorities as the corporate residence. However, income taxes on resident corporations are levied on local income irrespective of the place of incorporation

## Other taxes

*Net assets tax*/A net assets tax at a rate of 1% applies to all of a company's assets. The income tax paid the year before constitutes a credit for this tax.

*Value-added tax*/VAT is levied on the sales and import of goods and on the rendering of services at a general rate of 12% (15% rate for alcohol and tobacco products).

*Local sales taxes*/All cities have local sales taxes based on volume sales.

## Income determination

*Inventory valuation*/Inventories are generally stated at the lower of cost or market. LIFO is permitted only in special cases for both book and tax purposes.

*Capital gains*/Net gains are taxed with a 10% of income tax. Capital losses are allowed only as offset of capital gains in the same period.

*Intercompany dividends*/Dividends are nontaxable.

## Deductions

*Depreciation and depletion*/Depreciation is computed on a straight-line basis over useful life. Tax depreciation is not required to conform to book depreciation but must be recorded in the books to be deductible. Depreciation not taken in any given period is lost. Depletion is computed on the cost of natural resource properties, based on annual production according to an economic study and with previous authorization from the tax authorities.

***Net operating losses***/Losses incurred by agroindustrial, mining, manufacturing, and tourism enterprises may be deducted from the taxable profits of the following three years in which there are profits, at a maximum rate of 50% per year.

***Payments to foreign affiliates***/Deduction for reasonable charges for royalties, management services, and interest paid to foreign affiliates can be claimed. The corresponding withholding tax must be withheld. Reimbursement of expenses to foreign affiliates is not normally subject to withholding tax. Interest is not deductible if paid to a shareholder and is subject to withholding taxes if the payee is a nondomiciled or nonresident entity.

***Taxes***/Certain taxes to which a company is subject, such as municipal taxes, are deductible. VAT and income tax are not deductible.

## Group taxation

Group taxation is not permitted.

## Tax incentives

Honduran laws encourages foreign investment through tax and tariff incentives, and the establishment of Industrial Free Zones and Industrial Processing Zones, which provide foreign investors with a wide array of benefits. Some of the benefits offered by these industrial zones are the following.

1. Unrestricted currency conversion.
2. Duty free importation of capital goods, raw materials, and supplies employed in the production of goods.
3. A 100% foreign ownership.
4. No government income, sales, or corporate taxes.
5. Unrestricted repatriation of profits and capital at any time.
6. Low-cost skilled and unskilled labor.
7. A wide range of low-cost raw material.

Foreign firms located in industrial zones enjoy the same right as Honduran firms.

To diversify the economy, the government encourages the production of fruits and vegetables for exportation, petroleum exploration, mining, tourism, fishing activities, wood commodities, metalworking, leather goods, and electronics and apparel assembly.

In addition to the initiatives mentioned above, the Honduran government has established a set of incentives aimed at the tourism sector with the creation of the Tourism Incentive Law (*Ley de Incentivos al Turismo*). Some of the benefits offered by this law are the following.

1. A ten-year exoneration of income tax.
2. Duty free importation of capital goods, raw materials, and supplies employed in the construction of the project.
3. Duty free importation of capital goods, raw materials, and supplies employed in the promotion of the project.
4. Tax exonerations on events and cultural presentations.
5. Exoneration of municipal taxes for projects involved on the restoration and conservation of natural and historic resources.

# Honduras

## Withholding taxes

***On payments to domiciled corporations***/Interest and royalties to domiciled corporations and individuals are not subject to withholding.

***On payments to nondomiciled foreign corporations or individuals***/The following rates of withholding apply to payments to nondomiciled foreign corporations or individuals.

| Income source | Tax rate % |
| --- | --- |
| Real estate rent | 30 |
| Royalties from mining operations | 10 |
| Salaries paid for services | 35 |
| Profit transfers from branch office to head office | 15 |
| Royalties | 25 |
| Interest paid on commercial operations, bonds, securities, or negotiable instruments and other types of obligations | 5 |
| Interest obtained from operation of airplanes, ships, and vehicles | 10 |
| Income obtained from operation of telecommunication companies | 5 |
| Insurance premiums | 15 |
| Income obtained from public shows | 30 |
| Films and videotapes for cinemas, TV, video clubs, and cable TV | 10 |
| Any other income not mentioned previously | 20 |

***Tax treaties***/Honduras has no tax treaties.

## Tax administration

***Returns***/With certain exceptions, all corporations must file by April 30 a tax return on the basis of the fiscal year ended December 31.

***Payment of tax***/All entities are required to reflect in the annual return their estimated tax for the following year. The computation is based on the tax paid for the current year and must be paid in three equal quarterly payments, with the balance to accompany the next annual return.

## CORPORATION TAX CALCULATION

Fiscal year ending in 2003

| | |
|---|---:|
| Net income before taxes | Lps 1,908,350 |
| Nondeductible expenses: | |
| (+) Interest on loans from stockholders | 193,888 |
| (+) Loss on sale of fixed assets | 121,910 |
| (+) Depreciation of fixed assets in excess of authorized rates | 40,000 |
| (+) Tax fines, surcharges | 7,000 |
| Subtotal | Lps 2,271,148 |
| Nontaxable income: | |
| (–) Dividends received | 51,000 |
| (–) Interest | 20,500 |
| Taxable income | Lps 2,199,648 |
| Income tax (25%) | 549,912 |
| (–) *Less* quarterly advance payments | 130,000 |
| Total income tax payable | Lps 419,912 |
| Solidarity tax (5% of taxable income in excess of HNL 1 million) | Lps 59,982 |
| (–) *Less* quarterly advance payments | Lps 10,000 |
| Total solidarity tax payable | Lps 49,982 |

Note:

Exchange rate as of April 27, 2004: US$1 = Lps18.03.

# Hong Kong

## PwC contact

For additional information on taxation in Hong Kong, contact:

Rod Houng-Lee
PricewaterhouseCoopers
21/F Edinburgh Tower
The Landmark
15 Queen's Road Central
Hong Kong
Telephone: (852) 2289 2472
Fax: (852) 2810 9888
e-mail: rod.houng-lee@hk.pwc.com

## Significant developments

The following measures proposed by the former Financial Secretary in the 2003–2004 budget speech delivered on March 5, 2003 were enacted into law and became effective in 2003–2004.

- The profits tax rate for corporations was increased from 16% to 17.5%.
- The rate of deeming assessable profits for certain payments made to nonresidents, such as royalties, was increased from 10% to 30%.
- The maximum limit for deduction of donations to approved charities was increased from 10% to 25% of assessable profits.
- The tax concession in respect of qualifying debt instruments was made.

The Financial Secretary did not propose any significant tax measures in the budget speech delivered on March 10, 2004, other than reconfirming the government's view that it is necessary in the long term to introduce a goods and services tax (GST) to broaden the tax base and secure a stable source of public revenue. The Financial Secretary announced that the government has set up an internal committee to conduct a detailed and comprehensive study on the implementation of a GST in Hong Kong. It is not expected that such a tax would be implemented before 2008.

## Taxes on corporate income

*Profits tax*/Profits tax is payable by every corporation carrying on a trade, profession or business in Hong Kong on profits arising in or derived from Hong Kong at the company rate of 17.5% (16% for 2002/2003). One-half of this normal tax rate is applicable to the assessable profits of a corporation derived from the business of reinsurance of offshore risks as a professional reinsurer. In addition, income from certain qualifying debt instruments are also subject to a concessionary rate of 50% of this normal tax rate, or are exempt from tax, depending on the date of issue and maturity period of the debt instruments.

## Corporate residence

Corporate residence is determined by reference to the place of central management and control. However, for Hong Kong profits tax purposes, the source of income rather than residence is the decisive factor in determining taxability.

## Other taxes

*Capital duty*/A fee of HK$1 for every HK$1,000, or part thereof, of the nominal share capital, or increase in nominal share capital, applies. The fee is capped at HK$30,000 on each occasion.

*Stamp duty*/Stamp duty is charged at 0.2% on stock transactions, payable half by the vendor and half by the purchaser. The duty also applies to certain other documents, in particular for conveyance on sale of immovable property in Hong Kong, and the lease of immovable property in Hong Kong.

*Value-added tax*/There is presently no VAT or other broad-based consumption tax in Hong Kong.

*Dutiable commodities*/There is no tariff on general imports. However, there is a duty on liquors, tobacco, hydrocarbon oil, and methyl alcohol. This is prepaid by the seller and included in the price.

## Branch income

The rate of tax for branch profits is the same as that for corporations. There are three methods of assessing the Hong Kong profits of a corporation with a permanent establishment (branch) in Hong Kong and a head office outside, as follows.

1.  If accounts are maintained for the Hong Kong operation, the assessment will be based on the profits arising in or derived from Hong Kong as disclosed by these accounts, provided they reflect the true profits of the branch. These profits are taxable at the company rate.

2.  Where the Hong Kong operation accounts do not disclose the true profits arising in or derived from Hong Kong applicable to the Hong Kong operation, the assessment to profits tax will be computed by reference to the total profits, wherever made. The computation is based on assessing a portion of the total profits, determined by the ratio of turnover in Hong Kong to total turnover. This portion of profits will be regarded as profits arising in or derived from Hong Kong and taxed as such. In the case of a bank, Hong Kong profit is computed according to the proportion of Hong Kong assets over total assets if the assessor does not accept the branch accounts. Alternatively, the assessor may estimate the profits of the Hong Kong branch.

3.  Where the assessor considers the adoption of method (2) to be impracticable or inequitable, the assessor may then compute the profits arising in or derived from Hong Kong on a fair percentage of the turnover in Hong Kong.

A permanent establishment is stated to mean a branch, management or other place of business and an agency if the agent has, and habitually exercises, a general authority to negotiate and conclude contracts on behalf of his principal or has a stock of merchandise from which he regularly fills orders on his behalf.

## Income determination

*Inventory valuation*/Inventory may be stated at the lower of cost or market value. LIFO may not be used for tax purposes. FIFO must be consistently applied.

The Inland Revenue Department does not regard as obligatory the valuation of shares and securities held as trading stock to be at the lower of cost or market value. Either a valuation on a consistent basis of cost or a consistent basis of the lower of cost or market value is regarded as a valid basis acceptable to the

# Hong Kong

Department. In the banking and securities industries, securities (including debt and equity securities) held for dealing purposes are usually carried at market value, with fluctuations in values of such securities taken to the profit and loss account, irrespective of whether the profits or losses are realized. This basis, if consistently applied, is acceptable for taxation purposes for businesses in these industries.

There are special provisions for valuation upon cessation of a business under which inventory is valued at market value, unless it is sold to a person carrying on business in Hong Kong who may deduct a corresponding amount as the cost of the inventory in computing assessable profits.

*Capital gains*/Gains from realization of capital assets are not taxed.

*Intercompany dividends*/Dividends from sources either inside or outside Hong Kong are not taxable in Hong Kong.

*Foreign income*/Resident corporations are not taxed on their worldwide income. Foreign-source income, whether or not remitted to Hong Kong, is not taxed.

*Stock dividends*/Hong Kong corporations may declare bonus issues, which are not taxable in the hands of the recipient.

*Royalties*/Royalties paid or accrued to a nonresident for the use of or right to use in Hong Kong a trademark, patent, design, copyright material, secret process or other property of a similar nature, or for the use in Hong Kong of cinema or television tape or any sound recording are deemed to be taxable in Hong Kong. A total of 30% of the sum receivable is deemed to constitute profits subject to tax at the company rate of 17.5%. This gives an effective rate of 5.25% on such royalties paid to nonresidents. (For 2002/2003, only 10% of the sum receivable is deemed to constitute profits subject to tax at the company tax rate.)

Where such royalties are received or accrued from an associated corporation, however, 100% of the sum is deemed to constitute profits taxable at the rate of 17.5% (16% for 2003/2004), unless the Commissioner is satisfied that no person carrying on business in Hong Kong has at any time owned the property in respect of which the sum is paid.

*Banks and financial institutions*/Interest accruing to a bank or financial institution will be deemed to be sourced and taxable in Hong Kong if the interest arises through or from the carrying on of business in Hong Kong by the bank or financial institution.

Profits on the disposal or redemption of overseas certificates of deposit or bills of exchange are also deemed to be sourced and taxable in Hong Kong where they arise through or from the carrying on of business in Hong Kong by a bank or financial institution.

*Interest*/Interest income accruing on or after June 22, 1998 to a corporation carrying on business in Hong Kong and derived from any deposit placed in Hong Kong with a financial institution is exempt from profits tax, unless the deposit secures a borrowing the interest expense on which is deductible. This exemption does not, however, apply to interest accruing to a financial institution.

## Deductions

*Depreciation and depletion*/Deductions are allowable for certain capital expenditure, such as for the purchase of patent rights or rights to any industrial information or techniques likely to assist in the manufacture or processing of goods or materials, for use in Hong Kong, unless these rights were purchased from an associate. Legal fees and other expenses incurred in borrowing money are deductible if the interest expense itself is deductible.

Deductions are also allowable for depreciation in connection with capital expenditure incurred on the construction of buildings or structures and in the provision of machinery and plant for trade or business purposes.

1. Industrial buildings and structures—An initial allowance of 20%, in addition to an annual allowance of 4% of the cost of construction or cost of purchase from a developer, is granted for an industrial building or structure occupied for the purpose of a qualifying trade. Provision is made for balancing allowances or charges in the year of assessment in which the building is disposed of to adjust the written-down value of the building to the disposal price. Balancing charges are restricted to the total of initial and annual allowances previously given.

2. Commercial buildings and structures—An annual allowance of 4% of the capital expenditure incurred on the construction has applied since April 1, 1998. A balancing allowance or charge applies upon sale.

3. Renovation or refurbishment—A deduction is allowed for capital expenditure on the renovation or refurbishment of a building or structure, other than a domestic building or structure. The deduction is allowed as to 20% of the expenditure in the year when the expenditure is incurred, and 20% in each of the four succeeding years.

4. Machinery and plant—An initial allowance of 60% of the capital expenditure on machinery and plant is given for the year of assessment during the basis period in which the expenditure is incurred.

   An annual allowance is also given for depreciation at three prescribed rates on the reducing value of each of the three depreciation rate "pools." The three prescribed rates are 10%, 20%, and 30%, and the reducing value of each of the three depreciation rate pools is original cost less initial and annual allowances and sales proceeds. Some examples of prescribed machinery and equipment and the rates of annual allowance applicable to each are as follows: ships, junks and sampans (10%); room air-conditioning units (20%); aircraft (30%); and motor vehicles (30%). The annual allowance for machinery and equipment not included in the prescribed list is 20%.

   Provision is made for balancing charges when machinery and plant within one of the three depreciation rate pools are sold or disposed of and the reducing value of that pool is less than the sale price. In addition, balancing allowances or charges may be applicable upon cessation of business. Otherwise, sales proceeds are subtracted in calculating the reducing value on which the annual allowance is based. An immediate 100% write-off applies for "prescribed fixed assets," which covers certain machinery or plant used specifically and directly for any manufacturing process, computer hardware (other than that which is an integral part of machinery or plant), computer software, and computer systems. This concession is not, however, available for a fixed asset in which any person holds rights as a lessee under a lease.

5. Book depreciation is adjusted for tax purposes in accordance with the above depreciation allowances granted by the Inland Revenue Ordinance.

6. There is no provision in the Inland Revenue Ordinance for deduction in respect of depletion of natural resources.

*Net operating losses*/Losses incurred in an accounting year are carried forward indefinitely until set off against future profits of the business, but a corporation carrying on more than one business may have losses in one trade set off against profits of the other, with any balance being carried forward. There are antiavoidance provisions to prevent the utilization of losses in a corporation purchased for that purpose.

*Payments to foreign affiliates*/Royalties and service fees payable by a Hong Kong corporation to foreign affiliates are deductible provided they are incurred in the production of profits chargeable to tax and for the purpose of producing such profits. If the payments are in excess of arm's length payments, there may be problems in satisfying these statutory requirements. There are no special restrictions on the deductibility of these items. Interest payable to a foreign affiliate is not deductible if the recipient is not chargeable to Hong Kong tax.

*Interest*/Deduction of interest expense is allowable if the borrowing is made for the purpose of producing profits chargeable to tax and the interest falls into one of the following categories.

1. Interest on money borrowed by a financial institution.
2. Interest on money borrowed by a public utility company.
3. Interest payable to a nonfinancial institution where the corresponding interest income is chargeable to Hong Kong tax.
4. Interest on money borrowed from a financial institution, but not secured or guaranteed by a deposit with a financial institution made by the borrower (or a related person or corporation) the interest income on which is not chargeable to Hong Kong tax.
5. Interest on money borrowed wholly and exclusively to finance (i) plant and machinery that qualifies for tax depreciation allowances or (ii) trading stock used in the production of taxable profits. If, however, the lender is a related person or corporation, this interest is not deductible even if condition (i) or (ii) is met.
6. Interest payable by a corporation (i) on debentures listed on a stock exchange in Hong Kong or any other stock exchange recognized by the Hong Kong tax authorities; or (ii) to the holder of any instrument issued in the course of carrying on business that is marketable in Hong Kong or in a major financial center approved by the Commissioner, or issued under any arrangement where an invitation to the public has been authorized by the Securities Commission; or (iii) on money borrowed from an associated corporation where the money in the hands of the associated corporation arose entirely from the proceeds of an issue of debentures or such instrument as is described in (ii).

*Taxes*/Taxes paid on corporate income are generally not deductible for the purpose of calculating assessable profits. The Commissioner generally accepts that a foreign tax which is an expense that must be borne regardless of whether or not a profit is derived, as opposed to a charge on the profits themselves, is deductible under the general deduction provision. Where a person carrying on a trade or business in Hong Kong is deemed to be subject to profits tax on interest income and other similar gains, for example, from the sale of a certificate of deposit, which otherwise would not be subject to profits tax, a deduction is allowed for taxes of substantially the same nature paid in another jurisdiction in respect of that same income.

*Other significant items*/A deduction is allowed for donations to approved charities made in the basis period for a year of assessment if such donations are not less than HK$100. The deduction is limited to 25% of the assessable profits. For 2002/2003, the deduction was limited to 10% of the assessable profits.

## Group taxation

There are no group provisions in Hong Kong.

## Tax incentives

*Inward investment*/None.

*Capital investment*/None.

*Other incentives*/One-half of the normal profits tax rate applies to the assessable profits of a corporation derived from the business of reinsurance of offshore risks as a professional reinsurer. In addition, interest and gains on sale of certain qualifying debt instruments are subject to a concessionary rate of 50% of the normal profits tax rate, or are exempt from tax, depending on the date of issue and maturity period of the debt instruments. There are no compulsory distribution requirements or additional tax on undistributed profits under current law. Profits can be accumulated in a Hong Kong holding company without tax implications. Investment companies are not liable to tax on dividends or on gains from realization of capital investments.

The operations of clubs and trade associations, insurance companies, aircraft-owners and ship-owners (including charter hire) are subject to special tax provisions. For ship owners, from April 1, 1998, tax exemption on a reciprocal basis is applicable for a resident of a territory outside Hong Kong that is deemed to be carrying on business in Hong Kong because that entity's ships call at any location within the waters of Hong Kong.

## Withholding taxes

There is no withholding tax on dividends, interest, or royalties. However, the 5.25% (1.6% for 2002/2003) or 17.5% (16% for 2002/2003) tax on royalties received by nonresidents (see above) is in effect similar to a withholding tax.

Resident consignees are required to furnish quarterly returns to the Inland Revenue Department showing the gross proceeds from sales on behalf of their nonresident consignors, and to pay to the Commissioner a sum equal to 0.5% of such proceeds. The Department normally accepts this as satisfying the Hong Kong tax obligations of the nonresident.

*Tax treaties*/Hong Kong has entered into few treaties. These can be grouped under four headings: full scope tax treaties; arrangement with the People's Republic of China; shipping income; and air services.

*Full scope tax treaties*/Hong Kong has entered into a full scope tax treaty with Belgium. The procedures to bring the treaty into force have not yet been completed. The following is the withholding tax rates under the treaty: dividends, 0%/5%/15%; royalties, 5%; interest, 10%. The 5% or 15% withholding tax rate on dividends applies where the shareholding is at least 10%, or less than that, respectively. The withholding tax on dividends will be nil where the recipient has directly held at least 25% of the shares of the payor company for an uninterrupted period of at least 12 months as at the dividend payment date.

**Arrangement with the People's Republic of China**/An arrangement has been entered into between the People's Republic of China and the Hong Kong Special Administrative Region for the avoidance of double taxation on income. It applies in Hong Kong with respect to income derived in any year of assessment commencing on or after April 1, 1998. Where a resident of Hong Kong derives income from mainland China, the amount of tax paid there in respect of that income will be allowed as a credit against any Hong Kong tax imposed on that resident in respect of the same income. The amount of credit, however, shall not exceed the amount of the Hong Kong tax computed with respect to that income.

**Shipping income**/Under an agreement with the United States, the governments of the United States and Hong Kong exempt from tax the gross income derived from the international operation of ships by individuals who are residents of the other territory, and corporations that are incorporated or managed and controlled in the other territory.

The exemption granted to Hong Kong corporations by the United States applies only when either of the following conditions holds.

1. The corporation's stock is traded primarily and regularly on an established stock market in Hong Kong, the United States, or another country that grants an equivalent exemption to U.S. corporations.
2. More than 50% of the value of the corporation's stock is owned directly or indirectly by individuals who are residents of Hong Kong, or of a country that grants an equivalent exemption to U.S. corporations, or by a corporation organized in a country that grants an equivalent exemption to U.S. corporations and whose stock is traded primarily and regularly on an established stock market in that country, the United States or another country that grants an equivalent exemption to U.S. corporations.

The exemption provided by Hong Kong to U.S. corporations follows identical criteria.

The shipping income to which the agreement applies is the gross income arising from the international operation of ships, including the following.

1. Income from the rental of ships.
2. Income from the rental of containers.
3. Income from participation in marine transport pools.
4. Gains from the sale of ships by a person engaged primarily in the international operation, lease or rental of ships. International aircraft operations are specifically excluded from the scope of the agreement.

Hong Kong has entered into separate agreements with the United Kingdom and Netherlands for the avoidance of double taxation on revenues arising from the business of shipping transport. The procedures required to bring these agreements into force have been completed. In addition, shipping agreements with the following countries have been entered into but the procedures required to bring the agreements into force have not yet been completed: Germany, Norway, and Singapore.

*Air services*/Agreements between Hong Kong and a number of countries provide that revenues, gross receipts, income, or profits derived from the operation of an aircraft in international traffic by an airline of one country that are subject to tax in that country are exempt from income and profits tax in the other country on a reciprocal basis. The countries for which the procedures required to bring these agreements into force have been completed are Belgium, Canada, the People's Republic of China, Denmark, Germany, Israel, South Korea, Mauritius, Netherlands, New Zealand, Norway, Sweden and United Kingdom. In addition, airline agreements with the following countries have been entered into but the procedures required to bring the agreements into force have not yet been completed: Bangladesh, Croatia, Estonia, Macao Special Administrative Region, Russian Federation, and Singapore.

## Tax administration

*Returns*/The tax year ends on March 31, but the basis of assessment is the actual profit of the accounting year ending within the year of assessment. The system is one of information filing, with assessment after the return has been examined by the Inland Revenue. Taxpayers may be subject to field audit at a later date.

*Payment of tax*/The dates of payment of tax are determined by the Commissioner and reported to the taxpayer in the assessment. A system of provisional tax payments applies, whereby estimated payments are made on account of profits being derived during a year, the estimate normally being based on the previous year's tax liability. The final tax liability for a year is subsequently determined after lodgment of the return.

## *CORPORATION TAX CALCULATION*

Fiscal year 2003/2004, year ending March 31, 2004

| | | |
|---|---:|---:|
| Net income before taxes | | HK$ 1,000,000 |
| Add: | | |
| Depreciation charged in accounts | 14,000 | |
| Donations to nonapproved charities | 1,000 | |
| Capital losses | 4,000 | |
| Renovations to rented premises | 2,000 | |
| Amounts transferred to provisions | 5,000 | |
| Legal fees (capital nature) | 3,000 | 29,000 |
| | | 1,029,000 |
| Deduct: | | |
| Profits not arising in or derived from Hong Kong | 125,000 | |
| Depreciation at Inland Revenue rates | 16,000 | |
| Dividend received | 3,000 | |
| Capital profits | 2,000 | |
| Purchase cost of patent/know-how | 2,000 | |
| Expenditure incurred and charged against provisions | 2,000 | |
| Renovation or refurbishment deduction (20%) | 400 | |
| Legal fees re borrowing | 1,600 | 152,000 |
| Adjusted profit for tax purposes | HK$ | 877,000 |
| Tax at 17.5% | HK$ | 153,475 |

Note:

Exchange rate of the Hong Kong dollar at January 1, 2004: US$1 = HK$7.80.

# Hungary

## PwC contact

For additional information on taxation in Hungary, contact:

Gabriella Erdös
PricewaterhouseCoopers Kft
Wesselényi u. 16.
H–1077 Budapest, Hungary
Telephone: (36) (1) 461 9130
Fax: (36) (1) 461 9110
e-mail: gabriella.erdos@hu.pwc.com

## Significant developments

Hungary has ratified the treaty with the European Union (EU) whereby it joins the EU as of May 1, 2004. Hungary has been changing its national legislation to conform to EU legislation, and also comply with all the accession criteria. As a part of this harmonization procedure, tax legislation has changed significantly. Some changes will enter into force on the date of EU accession, and some have already entered into force as of January 1, 2004. The most significant changes are as follows.

- Tax incentives are generally available on the basis of permission granted by the government in connection with development programs which exceed HUF3 billion investment value (HUF1 billion in underdeveloped areas). The investment must have commenced on or after January 1, 2004. Under this incentive, companies may utilize a predefined percentage, called the "intensity level" (between 35% and 75%), of their investment value against the corporate tax liabilities they generate. The incentive is available for ten years following the year of the completion of the investment project, or in the year of the completion of the investment project and the following nine years.

- From the date of joining the EU, Hungary has become part of the European Single Market and the Customs Union. This means that there are no longer any customs borders between the old EU member states, the other accession countries, and Hungary. As a financial consequence, companies are no longer obliged to issue customs documents, do customs reporting or to pay the import customs duties previously levied on goods moving between the new and old member states of the EU and Hungary. Customs formalities (importation and exportation) remain in place only for trade with countries that are not members of the enlarged EU.

- As of May 1, 2004, the supply of goods to taxable persons registered in another member state of the EU is exempt from pre-charged VAT. The purchaser, however, must declare and pay the VAT effective in the target member-state in the reverse charge mechanism.

- For intra-Community acquisitions, and also for importation from third countries, Hungarian taxable persons pay the VAT burden in the reverse charge system, assessing and deducting VAT in the same VAT return without any cash-flow effect, if they are entitled to deduct input VAT on the purchase in question.

- As of January 1, 2004, the reduced VAT rate is 15% instead of the former 12%, and the zero rate on some medical supplies was increased to 5%. Postal and banking services, stock exchange transactions, gambling and other supplies are still exempt from VAT without a credit on input VAT.

- From January 1, 2004, interest and royalty payments are exempt from withholding tax under domestic law.
- From May 1, 2004, the date of EU accession, dividends paid by a Hungarian subsidiary company to an EU-resident company will be exempt from dividend tax if the EU-resident company has held at least 25% participation in the subsidiary company for two years. However, if the 25% participation does not exist at the time of dividend payment, the dividend tax need not be deducted if a third party guarantees to undertake the tax payment.
- As of January 1, 2004, a new tax, called the research and development innovation contribution, has been introduced. It is calculated on the same tax base as the local business tax, and its rate is 0.2% in 2004 (0.25% in 2005).
- The changes in the local tax law have ended the municipalities' ability to provide permanent tax incentives. Also, limited-term tax incentives will not be applicable from January 1, 2007.
- From January 1, 2003, the taxation of mergers, transfers of assets and business units, and exchanges of shares are regulated in accordance with EEC Directive 90/434. Thus, if these operations meet the prescribed criteria, the taxation of capital gains relating to the assets transferred can be deferred to date of the actual disposal of the assets. With effect from the date of Hungary's EU accession, concerning these transactions no tax disadvantage can arise for companies registered in an EU member state, in comparison to companies registered in Hungary.

If any international treaty, including treaties on the avoidance of double taxation, provides otherwise, the provisions of the treaty apply, including cases whereby a transaction would not be subject to tax under Hungarian national law, but would be subject under the treaty; the provisions of the treaty would prevail and would trigger a tax liability.

Hungarian offshore companies enjoying a favorable tax rate of 4% can no longer be newly established. The already established offshore companies can operate until January 1, 2006, applying the add-ups and deductions to the tax base as of December 31, 2002. Majority control by entities that have not previously been shareholders or a related party is disallowed, as are mergers.

The method used to establish the price that is applied vis-à-vis related parties should be documented, as should the facts and circumstances supporting the arm's length nature of the price. Related parties are defined in the corporate income tax act and in principle cover all intra-group companies. The government decree elaborating the details of this documentation requirement was issued and follows OECD (Organization for Economic Cooperation and Development) and EU guidelines. The documentation regulations must be applied to contracts concluded or amended after September 1, 2003. However, these requirements will be extended to all valid contracts from January 1, 2005. The documentation should be available by the due date of filing the tax returns.

## Taxes on corporate income

*Corporation tax*/Corporation tax is levied at a single rate of 16%. Hungarian offshore companies enjoy a preferential rate of 4%.

*Local taxes*/Every municipality is entitled to levy local tax. Local taxes are capped by law. Local taxes are deductible for Hungarian corporate income tax purposes, and they are not considered as an "income tax" in the application of tax treaties. The local business tax rate is capped at 2%. The base of the local business tax is net sales revenue plus 50% of interest income, reduced by materials cost, the cost of goods sold, mediated services and subcontractors' work.

## Corporate residence

A corporation is resident for tax purposes if it is incorporated in Hungary.

Foreign entities can only perform business activities within the territory of Hungary by way of registering as any of the three following forms of business.

1. Corporations.
2. Branches.
3. Commercial representative offices.

From February 1, 1999, certain business activities were exempted from the above rule. These activities are as follows.

- Activities requiring technical expertise (with the exception of auditing, bookkeeping, accounting, and legal services).
- Construction and installation performed on the basis of a foreign trade contract.
- Management.
- Artistic performance, education at universities, and professional sports activities.
- Activities limited to the sale of goods and provision of services acquired in the territory of Hungary by using a commercial card issued abroad and without actual presence in Hungary.
- Business activities that can be performed without registration in Hungary if it is specifically provided by law or government decree.

From May 1, 2004, the range of exempt activities was broadened. In practice, foreign companies can perform any business activity in Hungary, simply registering for VAT without the establishment of a branch, if the Corporate Tax Act does not require the corporate tax presence of the company. For non-EU companies, VAT registration can be done by an appointed fiscal representative.

Foreign companies may establish branch offices in Hungary with effect from June 16, 1998. A branch office is an organizational unit of a foreign company without legal personality, vested with financial autonomy, and registered as an independent form of company in the Hungarian company registration records as a branch office of the foreign company. A branch office is regarded as established when it has been entered in the company registration records, and it may commence entrepreneurial activities after such registration. Branch offices are regarded as resident entities. They may not perform representative or agency activities on behalf of the foreign company or any other nonresident party. The foreign parent must continuously provide the assets required for the operation of the branch office and the settlement of its liabilities.

The employees of a branch office are in a legal relationship with the foreign company, and the foreign parent exercises an employer's rights.

A branch office is considered dissolved upon its removal from the company registration records.

# Hungary

The provisions of the Hungarian accounting law apply to branch offices, which must prepare reports based on the principles of double-entry bookkeeping. A statutory audit is also required.

## Other taxes

*Value-added tax*/VAT is payable on sales of goods and the provision of services. VAT is also payable on the importation and intra-Community acquisition of goods and on the purchase of certain services provided to a Hungarian company by foreign suppliers.

The relevant rates are shown below.

|  | % |
| --- | --- |
| General rate | 25 |
| Food, essential goods, and certain services | 15 |
| Some medicines | 5 |
| Export | 0 |

Certain services are exempt, including most land transactions; letting residential property; medical, cultural, sporting, and educational services; financial services and insurance. In the case of industrial site and office rental, the VAT exemption is optional.

As of May 1, 2004, a VAT deduction will be available for the business-related proportion of purchases made partially for nonbusiness purposes.

*Stamp tax*/Acquisition and contribution-in-kind of immovable property are subject to a 10% duty. Immovable property used as a dwelling is subject to 2% to 6% duty.

*Registration tax*/Registration tax is imposed on cars, replacing the previously applied consumption tax.

*Excise tax*/Excise tax is imposed on grape wine, spirits, champagne, beer, tobacco, and fuel at fixed charges per liter or per number.

*Social security*/The employer's social security contributions amount to 29%, and its unemployment contributions to 3% of the employee's employment income, for a total of 32%. Fringe benefits are subject to either the 29% social security contribution or, in the absence of an insurance (i.e., employment) relationship, 11% health tax. In the absence of a compulsory insurance relationship, neither the employer's social security contribution, nor the health tax contribution, need be paid in respect of remuneration paid by a foreign company, or a partially or wholly foreign-owned entity, to a foreign employee. Other contributions (training fund) are 1.5% of the total salary paid to all employees, including foreign individuals employed by Hungarian employers. Business representation above the threshold of HUF2.5 million (app. US$12,000) and business gifts are subject to 44% personal income tax and 11% health-care tax.

## Income of branch offices

Though branch offices are regarded as permanent establishments, the rules discussed under "Permanent establishment" below do not apply to them. Branch offices must determine their tax base according to the general rules applicable to Hungarian companies. That is, corporate income tax at a rate of 16% is payable on the profit for the year, calculated on the basis of the Hungarian accounting system as adjusted by specific provisions of the corporate income tax and dividend withholding tax act.

Dividend tax at a rate of 20% applies to deemed dividends payable to the founders of a branch office. The majority of treaties, however, treat deemed dividends from branch offices as entrepreneurial income that is taxable in the state where the recipient of such income is resident. Some treaties, such as the France-Hungary and Canada-Hungary treaties, would allow Hungary to tax deemed dividends of branch offices payable to the other country.

## Permanent establishment

A foreign corporation carrying on business in Hungary is taxed on its Hungarian-source profit. Permanent establishments must use the accrual basis for accounting. If the profit is less than 12% of expenses incurred, 12% of such expenses are deemed to be the tax base in the case of foreign corporations seated in nontreaty countries.

At least 5% of revenue earned through the assistance of the permanent establishment is deemed to be revenue attributable to the permanent establishment.

The definition of "permanent establishment" is similar to that in the tax treaties, but somewhat wider.

## Income determination

*Corporate income tax base*/The corporate income tax base should be calculated by adjusting the accounting profit by add-ups and deductions as provided by the corporate income tax and dividend withholding tax act. (See "Corporate tax calculation" below)

*Inventory valuation*/Inventories are generally valued at the lower of cost and market. Cost may be determined on the basis of FIFO or average cost.

*Capital gains*/Capital gains (losses) are treated as ordinary income (losses). For tax purposes, capital gains (losses) on the sale of depreciable assets are calculated on the basis of tax depreciation.

*Intercompany dividends*/Except in the case of controlled foreign companies, dividends received are tax-free income. Dividends paid abroad are subject to withholding tax.

*Foreign income*/Income (other than dividends) earned from a foreign source is taxable, unless a tax treaty provides for an exemption. Foreign tax credit is available with respect to income taxes paid abroad up to the Hungarian tax payable on the creditable income.

*Stock dividends*/Where a corporation's after-tax profit is used to increase its registered capital, no withholding tax is due. However, subsequent capital reduction would trigger this liability, as would a distribution of stock.

## Deductions

*Depreciation and depletion*/Depreciation that is accounted for as expenditure, and thus included in the accounting profit, should be added to the corporate tax base. The depreciation recalculated with the rate prescribed in the corporate income tax act reduces the tax base, even if the tax depreciation is higher than the accounting depreciation.

Depreciation of tangibles is deductible by the straight-line method on the basis of the cost (plus related charges) from the time when the asset is first used for income-earning purposes. The rates are as follows.

|  | % |
| --- | --- |
| Computers and other high-tech machinery | 33 |
| Vehicles | 20 |
| Other tangible assets | 14.5 |
| Buildings (long-life structure) | 2 |

Additionally, goodwill paid on the acquisition of a business must be amortized over five years or a longer period of time.

Tax depreciation can be accelerated in 2003 and in 2004 by applying 50% instead of 33% or 14.5% rate to computers, computer accessories, and new tangible assets that are purchased or produced in 2003 or 2004.

***Net operating losses/***Except in the case of financial institutions, as of January 1, 2004, loss carryforwards can be utilized without time limitation, subject to the following.

- If the tax base of the previous two tax years was also negative, the loss can be carried forward with permission from the tax authority.
- If the ratio of net sales revenues to the total of costs and expenditures does not exceed 50% in the fourth year of operation and afterward, the loss can be carried forward with permission from the tax authority.

When offsetting losses are brought forward from prior years against profit, losses from the earliest years are to be considered first (FIFO principle). Losses cannot be carried back.

***Payments to foreign entities/***There is no specific restriction as to the deductibility of consideration due to foreign entities. If the parties are considered as related parties under the definition of the Hungarian Corporate Income Tax Act, the Hungarian tax office is entitled to adjust the Hungarian party's tax base to reflect the market price (arms' length price). Consideration due for services is deductible only if the actual performance of the services is supported and the Hungarian taxpayer can prove that it benefits from the service.

The consideration paid to a controlled foreign company (CFC) is not deductible for corporate tax, unless the taxpayer is able to prove that it serves the purposes of business operations. According to the definition of CFC, the existence of real economic presence, the portion of the actual tax liability reported and paid, and the profit before tax, are decisive as to whether a foreign company is considered as a controlled foreign company. An existing treaty on the avoidance of double taxation shifts the burden of proof to the Hungarian tax office for the nonexistence of a real economic presence, but does not automatically relieve a foreign entity registered in a treaty country from Hungarian CFC rules.

A total of 50% of the interest income in excess of interest expense vis-à-vis the same related party is an additional deduction from the tax base. A total of 50% of the interest expenditure in excess of interest income vis-à-vis the same related party increases the tax base. Taxpayers can opt for not making the add-up to the tax base on the basis of a formal letter issued to the affected related party.

A total of 50% of royalty income is deductible from the corporate tax base.

Tax depreciation of future investments can be deducted from the current tax base rather than from the tax base, which will include the accounting depreciation by labeling part of the accounting reserve as "investment reserve" up to 25% of the accounting profit, with a maximum HUF500 million per year.

**Taxes**/Local taxes, including local business tax, consumption taxes, and social security contributions are all tax deductible.

**Other significant items**/Interest expense incurred on any loan granted by any entity (other than Hungarian or foreign banks) is subject to a thin-capitalization rule. The maximum debt-to-equity ratio is 3:1. Thus, interest expense incurred on a loan that exceeds three times the net equity of the company is not deductible from the corporate tax base.

Limited deductions are allowed for doubtful debts and bad debts only if supported by qualified third party documents that the receivable cannot be collected. Writing down expired receivables is not allowable for tax purposes.

Employee benefits and the fringe benefit tax payable on them are tax deductible.

## Group taxation

There is no group taxation in Hungary. From a VAT perspective, group treatment was introduced for the financial sector as of May 1, 2004.

## Tax incentives

Allowances targeting small and medium-sized companies employing less than 250 people have been introduced with effect from January 1, 2001.

New tax incentives are licensed by the government on the basis of a request supported by an investment program that results in investing over HUF3 billion or HUF1 billion (the latter in underdeveloped or preferential areas in Hungary) started after December 31, 2002. Under this incentive, companies may utilize a predefined percentage, called the "intensity level" (between 35% and 75%), of their investment value against the 80% of the corporate liabilities they generate. The tax incentive applies to the year in which the investment is commenced or to the year in which the investment is put into operation, depending on the company's choice, and to the subsequent nine tax years.

This incentive can only be applied if, from the second year onward, any of the following applies.

- The annual average number of staff exceeds the average number of staff in the tax year preceding the year of commencement of the investment project by at least 100 persons, or 50 persons in the case of investments in underdeveloped areas.
- The total amount of annual wage cost exceeds the annual wage cost in the tax year preceding the year of commencement of the investment project, by at least 600 times the Hungarian minimum wage, or 300 times the Hungarian minimum wage in the case of investments in underdeveloped areas.
- More than 30% of the suppliers are Hungarian small or medium-sized companies.

# Hungary

## Withholding taxes

From January 1, 2004, interest and royalty payments are exempt from withholding tax under domestic law. Payments to resident corporations are not subject to withholding taxes.

For foreign corporations in treaty countries, withholding taxes are payable as follows.

| | Dividends | Interest (1) | Royalties |
|---|---|---|---|
| | % | % | % |
| Albania.............................................................. | 5/10 (2) | Nil | 5 |
| Australia............................................................ | 15 | 10 | 10 |
| Austria .............................................................. | 10 | Nil | Nil |
| Belarus*............................................................ | 5/15 (2) | 5 | 5 |
| Belgium............................................................. | 10 | 15 (3) | Nil |
| Bosnia-Herzegovina (4)..................................... | 10 (5) | Nil | 10 |
| Brazil................................................................. | 15 | 10/15 (6) | 15 (7) |
| Bulgaria ............................................................ | 10 | 10 | 10 |
| Canada ............................................................. | 5/15 (8) | 10 | 10 |
| China, P.R. (9).................................................. | 10 | 10 | 10 |
| Croatia.............................................................. | 5/10 (10) | Nil | Nil |
| Cyprus .............................................................. | 5/15 (2) | 10 (11) | Nil |
| Czech Republic.................................................. | 5/15 (2) | Nil | 10 |
| Denmark ........................................................... | 5/15 (2) | Nil | Nil |
| Egypt ................................................................ | 15/20 (2) | 15 | 15 |
| Estonia*............................................................ | 5/15 (2) | 10 (12) | 5/10 (13) |
| Finland.............................................................. | 5/15 (2) | Nil | 5 |
| France............................................................... | 5/15 (2) | Nil (14) | Nil |
| Germany ........................................................... | 5/15 (2) | Nil | Nil |
| Greece.............................................................. | 10 | 10 | 10 |
| India................................................................. | 15 (15) | 15 | 40 (16) |
| Indonesia .......................................................... | 15 | 15 | 15 |
| Ireland, Rep. of................................................. | 5/15 (17) | Nil | Nil |
| Israel................................................................ | 5/15 (17) | Nil | Nil |
| Italy.................................................................. | 10 | Nil | Nil |
| Japan................................................................ | 10 | 10 | 10 (18) |
| Kazakhstan ....................................................... | 5/15 (2) | 10 | 10 |
| Korea, Rep. of .................................................. | 5/10 (2) | Nil | Nil |
| Kuwait............................................................... | Nil | Nil | 10 |
| Luxembourg....................................................... | 5/15 (2) | Nil | Nil |
| Macedonia ........................................................ | 5/15 (19) | Nil | Nil |
| Malaysia............................................................ | 10 | 15 | 15 |
| Malta................................................................. | 5/15 (2) | 10 | 10 |
| Moldova ............................................................ | 5/15 (2) | 10 | Nil |
| Mongolia ........................................................... | 5/15 (2) | 10 | 5 |
| Morocco............................................................ | 12 | 10 | 10 |
| Netherlands ...................................................... | 5/15 (2) | Nil | Nil |
| Norway.............................................................. | 10 | Nil | Nil |
| Pakistan............................................................ | 15/20 (2) | 15 | 15 |
| Philippines ........................................................ | 15/20 (2) | 15 (20) | 15 |
| Poland............................................................... | 10 | 10 | 10 |

| | Dividends | Interest (1) | Royalties |
|---|---|---|---|
| | % | % | % |
| Portugal | 15 | 10 | 10 |
| Romania | 5/15 (10) | 15 | 10 |
| Russia | 10 | Nil | Nil |
| Singapore | 5/10 (2) | Nil/5 (21) | 5 |
| Slovak Republic | 5/15 (2) | Nil | 10 |
| Slovenia (22) | 10 (5) | Nil | 10 |
| South Africa | 5/15 (2) | Nil | Nil |
| Spain | 5/15 (2) | Nil | Nil |
| Sweden | 5/15 (2) | Nil | Nil |
| Switzerland | 10 | 10 | Nil |
| Thailand | 15/20 (23) | 10/25 (24) | 15 |
| Tunisia | 10/12 (2) | 12 (20) | 12 |
| Turkey | 10/15 (2) | 10 | 10 |
| Ukraine | 5/15 (2) | 10 | 5 |
| United Kingdom | 5/15 (2) | Nil | Nil |
| United States | 5/15 (25) | Nil | Nil |
| Uruguay | 15 | 15 | 15 (26) |
| Vietnam | 10 | 10 | 10 |
| Yugoslavia (to the former parts) (27) | 10 (18) | Nil | 10 |
| Yugoslavia | 5/15 (2) | 10 | 10 |

*Treaty concluded, but provisions cannot currently be applied.

Notes:

1.  Interest paid by the National Bank of Hungary and the Hungarian state, as well as late payment interest and interest paid vis-à-vis related parties exceeding the interest calculated on an arm's-length basis, is not subject to Hungarian withholding tax.

2.  The lower rate applies if the recipient has a stake of at least 25% in the distributing company.

3.  Interest paid in respect of (a) commercial claims (including claims represented by negotiable instruments) and installment payments for the delivery or supply of goods and/or services, (b) current accounts or registered loans placed by a financial institution, and (c) funds and deposits not represented by bearers' securities placed at any of the financial institutions (including public credit institutions) is exempt.

4.  The former treaty between Hungary and Yugoslavia applies until a new treaty enters into force.

5.  In the case of a partnership the general rate, currently 20%, applies.

6.  A rate of 10% applies to bank loans used for industrial purposes, research and development, or public works.

7.  A rate of 25% applies to royalties in respect of the use of or the right to use trademarks. Presently, 18% must be withheld from such payments made from Hungary.

8.  The lower rate applies if the recipient has control, directly or indirectly, of 25% of the voting rights in respect of the distributing company.

9.  The China-Hungary Treaty does not apply to Hong Kong.

10. The lower rate applies if the recipient has a stake of at least 40% in the distributing company.

11. Interest on a loan provided through deferred payments or guaranteed by central banks or municipalities is exempt.

12. Interest paid (a) to the Estonian state, the municipalities, the central, export-import and export credit insurance banks, or (b) on loans guaranteed or insured by any of the contracting states, or the above mentioned organizations in the contracting states, or (c) in respect of indebtedness.

13. The lower rate applies to royalties for the use of industrial, commercial, or scientific equipment, or for transmission by satellite, cable optic fiber, or similar technology.

14. Under Article 11 of the France-Hungary treaty, Hungary may tax interest arising in Hungary and paid to a resident of France. However, the Finance Ministry has stated that there was a mistake in the wording. The Hungarian tax office issued a ruling stating that Hungary does not tax this interest. The Finance Ministry will approach the French authorities in order to resolve the issue.

15. If the dividend distribution is due to an initial public offering or a new tranche of shares resulting in a stake of 10% in the distributing company, 15% applies. Otherwise, the general rate, currently 20%, applies.

16. A rate of 20% applies to technical service fees.

17. The lower rate applies if the recipient has a stake of at least 10% in the distributing company.

18. Cultural royalties are exempt.

19. The lower rate applies if the recipient (other than a partnership) has a stake of at least 25% in the distributing company.

20. Interest paid in respect of a loan provided by the government or a governmental agency, municipalities, central banks, or any institution acting on behalf of these organizations is exempt.

21. A 5% rate applies if the recipient is the beneficial owner of the interest. The interest is exempt if it is paid by one government to the other, or by one bank to another bank, provided that the recipient is also the beneficial owner of the interest.

22. The treaty between Hungary and Yugoslavia applies until a new treaty enters into force.

23. The lower rate applies if the recipient has a stake of 25% in the distributing company that carries out industrial activities.

24. A rate of 10% applies if the recipient of the interest is a financial institution, including an insurance company.

25. The lower rate applies if the recipient has voting stock of at least 10% in the distributing company.

26. A rate of 10% applies to technical service fees.

27. The treaty between Hungary and Yugoslavia applies to the former parts of the Socialist Federal Republic of Yugoslavia until new treaties are concluded.

## Tax administration

*Returns*/Corporation tax must be calculated by reference to the accounting year, which is either the calendar year or the group's accounting year. Returns must be lodged within 150 days following the last day of the accounting year. The tax payable is determined by self-assessment.

**Payment of tax**/Installments generally must be reported and paid quarterly or monthly (above HUF5 million tax payable), and at least 90% of the final payment is due by the 20th day of the last month of the accounting year. The difference is due when the return is filed.

## CORPORATION TAX CALCULATION

| | | |
|---|---:|---:|
| Accounting profit | | HUF 1,000,000 |
| Add: | | |
| Depreciation as per the accounts | 300,000 | |
| Bad debt provision reducing the previous year's tax base | 90,000 | |
| Bad debt provisions made in the given year | 80,000 | 470,000 |
| | | 1,470,000 |
| Deduct: | | |
| Tax depreciation | 220,000 | |
| Dividends received | 80,000 | |
| Bad debts as allowed | 40,000 | 340,000 |
| Taxable income | | HUF 1,130,000 |
| Corporation tax at 16% | | HUF 180,800 |
| Tax due | | HUF 180,800 |
| On distribution: | | |
| Accounting profit before tax | | HUF 1,000,000 |
| Corporation tax | | 180,800 |
| Profit after tax | | 819,200 |
| Dividend declared/proposed (1) | | 700,000 |
| Balance sheet profit | | HUF 119,200 |

Notes:

1. The general dividend withholding tax rate is 20%, reduced by the provisions of the treaty (if any).

2. Exchange rate of the Hungary forint at January 1, 2004: US$ 1 = HUF211.37.

# India

## PwC contact

For additional information on taxation in India, contact:

Nityanand Gupta
PricewaterhouseCoopers Pvt. Ltd.
Sucheta Bhawan (Gate no. 2, IInd Floor)
11-A, Vishnu Digamber Marg
New Delhi-110 002, INDIA.
Telephone: 0091 11 23232916
Fax: 0091 11 23210594, 96
e-mail: nityanand.gupta@in.pwc.com

## Significant developments

1. Tax on foreign companies reduced to 41% (including surcharge at 2.5%).
2. Long-term capital losses can be set off only against long-term capital gains in the same year or in the subsequent eight years.
3. The dividend/income distribution tax has been reintroduced. Indian companies/specified mutual funds again liable to pay distribution tax at the rate of 12.8125% (including surcharge at 2.5%) on the amount distributed on or after April 1, 2003. Correspondingly, such dividend/income is exempt from tax in the hands of shareholders/unit holders.

## Taxes on corporate income

*Income tax/*The year for tax purposes must end on March 31. The rate applicable to an Indian company for fiscal year 2004/2005, corresponding to the taxpayer's financial year ended March 31, 2004, is 35.875% (including surcharge at 2.5%). Foreign companies are taxed at the rates cited under "Withholding taxes" below.

*Minimum alternative tax/*Both resident and nonresident companies are liable to pay tax on their book profits where the tax liability of the year is less than 7.50% of the adjusted book profits. The minimum alternative tax (MAT) liability is fixed at 7.50% of the adjusted book profits, resulting in an effective tax rate of 7.6875% (applying surcharge of 2.5%). Sick companies are not subject to MAT. Export profits of undertakings set up in free-trade zones and 100% export-oriented undertakings would be exempt from MAT during the tax holiday period. Nontaxable profits from the export of goods and software are also exempt from MAT.

## Corporate residence

A company is resident if it is an Indian company or if during the relevant year the control or management of its affairs is situated wholly in India. A company that does not fulfill both of these conditions is nonresident.

## Other taxes

All states impose sales tax. The central government imposes sales tax on interstate sales. Excise tax is levied on most of goods manufactured. Service tax is levied on certain types of services rendered.

All companies are liable to wealth tax at 1% of the value of specified net assets exceeding in the aggregate Rs1,500,000.

## Branch income

Branches of foreign companies are taxed on their income that is received in India or that accrues or arises in India at the rates applicable to foreign companies (see "Withholding taxes" below). There is no withholding tax on remittance of profits to the head office.

## Income determination

*Inventory valuation*/Inventories are generally valued at the lower of cost or market price. Normally, there is conformity between book and tax reporting. FIFO and average cost are acceptable, provided they are consistently applied.

*Capital gains*/A short-term capital gain arises on the sale of an asset within three years of its acquisition (within one year in the case of shares, listed securities, units of specified mutual funds or of the Unit Trust of India) and is taxed at the rates applicable to business income. Other capital gains (called long-term gains) are determined after increasing the cost by prescribed inflation factors and are taxed at 20.5%. In the case of foreign companies, capital gains on the transfer of shares or debentures in Indian companies are computed (without adjustment for inflation factors) in the foreign currency in which the shares or debentures were acquired, and the capital gains reconverted into Indian rupees are taxed at 41% in the case of short-term gains and 20.5% in the case of long-term gains.

In respect of long-term capital gains arising on sale of securities listed in India, or units of specified mutual funds or of the Unit Trust of India, taxpayers can either choose the above methodology of indexation and pay tax at 20.5% or pay 10.25% on the gain amount computed without inflation adjustment. In the case of overseas financial organizations (offshore funds), long-term capital gains arising on the transfer of units of specified mutual funds or of the Unit Trust of India that are acquired in foreign currency are taxable at 10.25% on the gross amount. Similarly, long-term capital gains earned by nonresidents in India on the transfer of bonds or Global Depository Receipts of Indian companies (issued abroad in accordance with government guidelines/approved schemes and acquired in foreign currency) are taxable at 10.25% on the gain amount. In the case of foreign institutional investors investing in the Indian capital market, short-term gains are taxable at 30.75% and long-term gains at 10.25%. Long-term capital gains from sale of shares in a government approved enterprise wholly engaged in specified infrastructure sectors is exempt from tax, subject to fulfillment of prescribed conditions.

Long-term capital losses can be set off only against long-term capital gains. Similarly, long-term capital losses that are carried forward can be set off only against long-term capital gains. Losses arising from short-term capital assets can be set off against any capital gains (long-term or short-term). Gains and losses (computed in the manner indicated under "Depreciation and depletion" below) arising on the sale of depreciable assets are classified as short-term capital gains/losses, and are taxed at the same rates as business income.

*Intercompany dividends*/dividends declared, distributed or paid by a domestic company on or after April 1, 2003 attract a dividend distribution tax at the rate of 12.8125% in the hands of the company.

Income received by overseas financial organizations (offshore funds) from units of specified mutual funds or of the Unit Trust of India that are purchased in foreign currency, as well as interest received by nonresidents on bonds issued abroad by Indian companies following government guidelines and acquired in foreign currency, are taxable at 10.25% on the gross amount. Dividends (other than dividend declared, distributed or paid by a domestic company on or after April 1, 2003) and interest earned by foreign financial institutions from investments in the Indian capital market are taxable at 10.25% on the gross amount.

Income distributed on or after April 1, 2003 by specified mutual funds/the Unit Trust of India is exempt from tax in the hands of the recipient. The distributing fund/the Unit Trust of India is liable to pay distribution tax on such distributed income at the rate of 12.8125%. However, income distributed by an open-ended equity oriented fund during the period April 1, 2003 to March 31, 2004 is not liable to such income distribution tax.

*Foreign income*/A resident company is taxed on its worldwide income. A nonresident company is taxed only on income that is received in India or that accrues or is deemed to accrue in India.

Under the Indian tax code, nonresidents are charged tax on certain incomes deemed to accrue or arise in India from any "business connection" that the nonresident might have in India. The Finance Act 2003 has clarified that where a nonresident carries on a business activity through a person who exercises in India an authority to conclude contracts on behalf of the nonresident, habitually maintains in India a stock of goods or merchandise from which the person delivers goods or merchandise on behalf of the nonresident, or habitually secures orders in India mainly on behalf of the nonresident, such activities shall be deemed to constitute "business connection" of the nonresident in India.

Double taxation of foreign income is avoided through treaties that generally provide for deduction of the lower of foreign tax or Indian tax on the doubly taxed income from tax payable in India in the case of residents. Similar relief is allowed unilaterally where no treaties exist. Undistributed income of a nonresident subsidary is not subject to tax.

*Stock dividends*/Stock dividends (bonus shares) may be distributed, and are not taxed at the time of receipt in the hands of the recipient equity shareholders.

## Deductions

*Depreciation and depletion*/Depreciable assets are grouped in blocks, and each block is eligible for depreciation at a prescribed rate (20% to 100% for machinery, 5% to 100% for buildings, 25% for intangible assets, 15% for furniture and fittings) on the opening written-down value plus acquisitions, less moneys payable in respect of deletions during the year ("Deletion" is reduction through sale, discarding, demolition, or destruction). In the year of acquisition, depreciation is restricted to one-half of the prescribed rate if the acquired asset is used for less than 180 days. If money receivable on the transfer (less expenses incurred wholly and exclusively in connection with transfer) exceeds the opening written-down value plus acquisitions of the block concerned, the excess is taxed as a short-term capital gain at the same rates as business income. An additional depreciation of 15% on the original cost of new machinery or plant (other than ships and aircraft) acquired and installed after March 31, 2002 will be allowed to a new industrial undertaking in the year in which it begins manufacture. Existing industrial undertakings which achieve substantial expansion during any financial year by way of increase in installed capacity of 25% or more will also be allowed such additional depreciation in that year.

Power generating companies have been given the option either to use the reducing-balance method provided under the normal schedule or to charge depreciation on the straight-line basis. The straight-line rates are basically aligned to power companies' book depreciation rates. Under the amended provisions, terminal adjustment and recapture provisions are applicable for power companies' assets.

Book depreciation need not conform to tax depreciation.

No depletion is allowed on the cost of natural resource properties. Know-how, patents, licenses, franchises, and similar intangible assets form part of the block, which is eligible for depreciation at the prescribed rate (25%), as explained above.

**Net operating losses**/Losses may not be carried back. Loss carry forward is allowed as follows.

| | |
|---|---|
| Unabsorbed depreciation | Unlimited |
| Other business losses | 8 years |
| Capital losses | 8 years |

**Payments to foreign affiliates**/Royalties, interest, and technical or management service fees can be paid to foreign affiliates only with prior approval of the authorities or through designated bankers if prescribed guidelines are followed. Indian companies can claim deductions for such payments, provided they are not of a capital nature and are incurred wholly and exclusively for the purpose of the business. The tax paid by the Indian companies on behalf of a foreign company on royalties or technical service fees shall be included in the total income of the foreign company in respect of agreements entered into on or after June 1, 2002.

Hitherto royalties and fee for technical services accruing to a nonresident from Indian sources were taxed on gross basis at the rate of 20%, subject to certain conditions. The Finance Act 2003 has introduced a new provision whereby such income in pursuance of an agreement entered into after March 31, 2003 shall be taxed on net basis in accordance with the provisions of the domestic law provided the right, property, or contract in respect of which the aforesaid income is received is effectively connected with the following.

1. The business of the nonresident carried on in India through a permanent establishment.
2. Professional services rendered by the nonresident from a fixed place in India.

However, no deduction shall be allowed in respect of any expenditure which is not wholly or exclusively incurred for the business of such permanent establishment or fixed place of profession in India or in respect of any amount paid by the permanent establishment to its head office or to any of its offices.

**Transfer pricing**/The Finance Act 2001 has introduced new legislation on transfer pricing. As per this new code, income arising from all "international transactions" between "associated enterprises" would have to be computed on an "arm's length basis." Sharing of costs (between associated enterprises) relating to any benefit, service, etc., would also have to be undertaken on an "arm's length basis." The expressions "international transactions" and "associated enterprises" have been defined which are on lines similar to Organization for Economic Cooperation and Development (OECD) Model Tax Convention. The various alternative methods for computation of the arm's length price of a transaction have been prescribed.

Detailed rules relating to transfer pricing regulation have been announced.

*Taxes*/All taxes relating to business (other than income tax and wealth tax) incurred during a year ending March 31 are deductible in that year, provided they are paid by the following October 30. Otherwise, they are deductible in the year of payment.

## Group taxation

Group taxation is not permitted.

## Tax incentives

*Inward investment*/New industrial undertakings located in specified "backward" states and districts (which begin to manufacture or produce articles or items on or before March 31, 2004) are entitled to 100% deduction of profits for the first five or three years of operation, depending on their Category, followed by a partial tax deduction of 30% (for companies) of the profits for the next five years. The list of backward districts has been streamlined into Category A and B districts, depending upon the current level of infrastructure development in these areas. The initial tax holiday period is five years in case of Category A districts, and three years in case of Category B districts. Similar incentive is also applicable to hotels (which started functioning on or before March 31, 2000) satisfying prescribed conditions. The profits of an undertaking engaged in developing and building a housing project, scientific research, commercial production or refining of mineral oil, or setting up and operating a cold chain facility for agricultural produce, or engaged in the integrated business of handling, storage and transportation of food grains are also eligible for tax holiday subject to fulfillment of prescribed conditions. The period of tax holiday ranges from single project completion based deduction (applicable for housing projects) to five to ten years deduction, and the percentage of deduction varies from 30% to 50% to 100% in initial years, to 30% in later years. The number of initial and later years varies from sector to sector. A 50% deduction of profits is available for a period of five years to undertakings engaged in building, owning and operating a multiplex theatre or convention center satisfying prescribed conditions.

Deduction is available to enterprises carrying on the business of power generation or transmission or distribution, providing telecommunication services, or developing or operating and maintaining a notified infrastructure facility or an industrial park or special economic zone with respect to 100% profits for any ten consecutive years falling within the first 15 years of operation (20 years in the case of infrastructure projects except ports, airports, inland waterways and inland ports). The term telecommunication services has been defined to include radio-paging, domestic satellite services, network of trunking, and broadband network and internet services. The term "infrastructure facility" includes roads, bridges, highways, airports, ports, inland waterways and inland ports, rapid rail transport systems, irrigation projects, and water supply projects. However, for telecom's undertakings the deduction is 100% of profits for the initial five years followed by a partial deduction of 30% (for companies) of the profits for the later five years.

The Finance Act 2003 has introduced a special deduction of 100% of profits for the first five years and 30% of the profits (for companies) for the next five years, in case of setting up of new undertakings or substantial expansion of existing undertakings in the states of Himachal Pradesh, Uttaranchal, Sikkim, and north-eastern states. The deduction is available for specified/nonprohibited articles or items, and subject to prescribed conditions.

Currently, 100% of export profits (previously 90%) of a new industrial undertaking satisfying prescribed conditions established in a free-trade zone, software technology park, or electronic hardware technology park, or a 100% export-oriented undertaking are exempt from income tax for ten years, commencing with the year of manufacture. However, this exemption is only available until taxpayer's financial year 2008/2009. The tax exemption is also available to new undertakings engaged in the manufacture or production of articles or things or computer software in any special economic zone. The tax exemption is 100% for the first five years commencing with the year of manufacture, 50% for next two years, and thereafter up to 50% for the next three years, subject to the fulfillment of certain conditions concerning creation of a specified reserve and its utilization.

*Other tax incentives*/Indian companies and other residents are allowed the following tax incentives.

1. In the case of export of goods (other than mineral oils, specified minerals, and ores) and computer software (including technical services provided outside India for its development or production), where proceeds are received within a specified time in convertible foreign exchange, no income tax is payable on export profits computed in a prescribed manner. The benefit of this deduction has been extended to the export of film/television/music/television news software or telecasting rights, subject to fulfillment of prescribed conditions.

   A gradual phasing out of all export concessions has been enacted. The above-mentioned tax concessions on export income are only available until financial year 2003/2004 in a phased-out manner. The quantum of tax concession computed above would be further limited to 30% for financial year 2003/2004. No deduction is available from taxpayer's financial year 2004/2005 onwards.

2. Indian companies and other residents are allowed a deduction of the income received in convertible foreign exchange from foreign governments or foreign enterprises for the use outside India of any patent, invention, design, or registered trademark. The deduction in financial year 2003/2004 would be 10%. No deduction is available from taxpayer's financial year 2004/2005 onward. The excess and any other royalties are taxable in full, subject to credit for the foreign tax withheld or paid up to a maximum of the Indian tax on the royalties or fees.

3. Similarly, deduction is allowed in respect of the profits derived from the construction of any building, dam, road, bridge, or other structure outside India or from the assembly or installation of machinery or plant outside India if the proceeds are received in convertible foreign exchange within a specified time. The deduction for financial year 2003/2004 would be 10%. No deduction is available from taxpayer's financial year 2004/2005 onwards.

4. In the case of approved hotels, tour operators and travel agents being an Indian company or other resident in India, deduction is allowed of the profit from services to foreign tourists that is earned in convertible foreign exchange (plus amounts transferred to a specified reserve out of the balance of such

profits), subject to prescribed conditions. The deduction for financial year 2003/2004 would be 15%. No deduction is available from taxpayer's financial year 2004/2005 onwards.

## Withholding taxes

*Residents*/For resident companies, interest is subject to a 20.5% rate (including surcharge of 2.5%). Professional and technical service fees are subject to a 5.125% rate (including surcharge of 2.5%).

For other residents, specified types of interest are subject to a 10% rate (as increased by surcharge of 10%, if applicable), and nonspecified types of interest are subject to a 20% rate (as increased by surcharge of 10%, if applicable).

*Nonresident companies*/Rates are as follows.

| Type of transaction | Withholding % |
| --- | --- |
| Special rates | |
| Income from units and long-term capital gains from specified foreign currency units held by offshore funds (1) | 10 |
| Dividends (other than by domestic companies) and long-term capital gains from bonds or shares issued abroad by Indian companies in accordance with government guidelines and acquired in foreign currency (1) | 10 |
| In the case of foreign financial institutions: | |
| Dividends (other than dividends by domestic companies)/interest (2) | 20 |
| Short-term capital gains | 30 |
| Long-term capital gains | 10 |
| General rates | |
| Dividends (other than dividends by domestic companies) (2 | 20 |
| Interest on foreign currency loans and debts | 20 |
| Royalties and technical service fees (3) | 30/20 |
| Long-term capital gains (4) | 20 |
| Other income | 40 |

Notes:

1. The above rates are to be further enhanced by a surcharge of 2.5%.
2. Dividends declared, distributed or paid after April 1, 2003 by a domestic company is exempt from tax in the hands of the shareholder. The companies will be liable to pay dividend distribution tax of 12.8125% on such dividend.

   Also, income distributed on or after April 1, 2003 by specified mutual funds or the Unit Trust of India is exempt from tax in the hands of the recipient. The distributing fund/the Unit Trust of India is liable to pay distribution tax on such distributed income at the rate of 12.8125%.
3. A reduced rate of 20.5% applies under government approved agreements or agreements in accordance with declared government policy made after May 31, 1997. In respect of contracts entered into after March 31, 2003 where the foreign company carries on business in India through a permanent establishment (PE)/fixed place, such income is taxable on net basis at 41%.
4. A reduced rate of 10.25% (without inflation adjustment) may be opted for by the taxpayer in case of long-term capital gains arising on sale of securities listed in India. Long-term capital gains from sale of shares in a government-

approved enterprise wholly engaged in specified infrastructure sectors are exempt from tax, subject to fulfillment of prescribed conditions. Lower treaty rates are listed below.

5. Interest income arising on long-term finance provided to specified infrastructure sectors is exempt from tax subject to fulfillment of prescribed conditions. Such enterprise should be wholly engaged in the said infrastructure activity and the same should be approved by the Central Government. Any long-term capital gain arising on sale of shares of such infrastructure enterprise is also exempt from tax.

**Other nonresidents**/Any income is subject to a 30% rate (or lower treaty rates mentioned below). However, in the case of nonresident Indians the rate is 20% on investment income and 10% on long-term capital gains arising upon the sale of specified assets purchased in foreign currency. A surcharge of 10% is to be applied to these rates, if applicable.

**Treaty rates**/Some tax treaties provide for lower withholding rates from certain types of income, as follows.

| Treaty recipient | Dividends (1) | Interest | Royalties | Technical service fees |
|---|---|---|---|---|
| | % | % | % | % |
| Australia | 15 | 15 | 20 (2, 3) | 20 (2, 3) |
| Austria | 10 | 10 | 10 | 10 |
| Bangladesh | 15 (4) | 10 | 10 | (5) |
| Belarus | 15 (4) | 10 | 15 | 15 |
| Belgium | 15 | 15 (6) | 20 | 20 |
| Brazil | 15 | 15 | 15 (7) | (5) |
| Bulgaria | 15 | 15 | 20 (7) | 20 |
| Canada | 25 (4) | 15 | 20 (2, 3) | 20 (2, 3) |
| China, P.R. | 10 | 10 | 10 | 10 |
| Cyprus | 15 (4) | 10 | 15 | 10 |
| Czech Republic | 10 | 10 | 10 | 10 |
| Denmark | 25 (4) | 15 (6) | 20 | 20 |
| Egypt | (14) | (14) | (14) | (5, 14) |
| Finland | 15 | 10 | 20 (2, 3) | 20 (2, 3) |
| France (9) | 10 | 10 | 10 | 10 |
| Germany | 10 | 10 | 10 | 10 |
| Greece | 41 (10) | 20 | 30 (8) | (5) |
| Hungary | 20 (11) | 20 (6) | 40 (8) | 20 (12) |
| Indonesia | 15 (4) | 10 | 15 | (5) |
| Ireland | 10 | 10 | 10 | 10 |
| Israel | 10 | 10 | 10 | 10 |
| Italy | 25 (4) | 15 | 20 | 20 |
| Japan | 15 | 15 (6) | 20 | 20 |
| Jordan | 10 | 10 | 20 | 20 |
| Kazakhstan | 10 | 10 | 10 | 10 |
| Kenya | 15 | 15 | 20 | (5) |
| Korea, Rep. of | 20 (4) | 15 (6) | 15 | 15 |
| Kyrgyzstan | 10 | 10 | 15 | 15 |
| Libya | 41 (10) | 20 | 30 (8) | (5) |
| Malaysia | 41 (10) | 20 | 30 (8) | (5) |

# India

| Treaty recipient | Dividends (1) | Interest | Royalties | Technical service fees |
|---|---|---|---|---|
| | % | % | % | % |
| Malta | 15 (4) | 10 | 15 | 10 |
| Mauritius | 15 (4) | 20 | 15 | (5) |
| Mongolia | 15 | 15 | 15 | 15 |
| Morocco | 10 | 10 | 10 | 10 |
| Namibia | 10 | 10 | 10 | 10 |
| Nepal | 15 (4) | 15 (6) | 15 | (5) |
| Netherlands (9) | 10 | 10 | 10 | 10 |
| New Zealand | 20 | 15 | 30 (8) | 30 (8) |
| Norway | 25 (9, 11) | 15 (6) | 20 (9) | 20 (9, 12) |
| Oman | 12.5 (4) | 10 | 15 | 15 |
| Philippines | 20 (4) | 15 (6) | 15 | (5) |
| Poland | 20 (13) | 15 | 22.5 | 22.5 |
| Portugal | 15 (4) | 10 | 10 | 10 |
| Qatar | 10 (4) | 10 | 10 | 10 |
| Romania | 20 (4) | 15 | 22.5 | 22.5 |
| Russian Federation | 10 | 10 | 10 | 10 |
| Singapore | 15 (4) | 15 (6) | 15 (3) | 15 (3) |
| South Africa | 10 | 10 | 10 | 10 |
| Spain | 15 | 15 | 20 (3, 9) | 20 (3, 9) |
| Sri Lanka | 15 | 10 | 10 | (5) |
| Sweden (9) | 10 | 10 | 10 | 10 |
| Switzerland (9) | 15 | 15 | 20 (2, 3) | 20(2, 3) |
| Syria | 41 (10) | 7.5 | 10 | (5) |
| Tanzania | 15 (4) | 12.5 | 20 | (5) |
| Thailand | 20 (4) | 25 (6) | 15 | (5) |
| Trinidad and Tobago | 10 | 10 | 10 | 10 |
| Turkey | 15 | 15 (6) | 15 | 15 |
| Turkmenistan | 10 | 10 | 10 | 10 |
| Ukraine | 15 (4) | 10 | 10 | 10 |
| United Arab Emirates | 15 | 12.5 (5) | 10 (5) | (5) |
| United Kingdom | 15 | 15 (6) | 20 (2, 3) | 20 (2, 3) |
| United States | 25 (4) | 15 (6) | 20 (2, 3) | 20 (2, 3) |
| Uzbekistan | 15 | 15 | 15 | 15 |
| Vietnam | 10 | 10 | 10 | 10 |
| Zambia | 15 (4) | 10 | 10 | (5) |

The numbers in parentheses refer to the following numbered Notes.

Notes:

The numbers in parentheses refer to the notes below.

1. Effective from April 1, 2003 dividend distribution tax has been reintroduced. The tax is levied on the company distributing dividends at the rate of 12.5% to be further enhanced by a surcharge of 2.5%.

2. In the treaties with Australia, Canada, Finland, Switzerland, the United Kingdom, and the United States, 15% for royalties and fees for included services where the payer is the government, a political subdivision or a public sector company (not in the case of Finland and the United Kingdom). In other cases the rate will drop from 20% to 15% five years after the treaty has taken effect (in case of Finland, after 2001).

3. On rentals of equipment and fees for services ancillary and subsidiary to the enjoyment of such property, 10% for Australia, Canada, Finland, Singapore, Spain, Switzerland, the United Kingdom, and the United States.

4. On intercorporate dividends where recipient has specified minimum holding, the following apply.

   a. A rate of 5% — Mauritius, Qatar, United Arab Emirates, and Zambia.

   b. A rate of 10% — Bangladesh, Belarus, Cyprus, Indonesia, Malta, Nepal, Oman, Portugal, Singapore, Tanzania, and Ukraine.

   c. A rate of 15% — Canada, Denmark, Italy, Republic of Korea, the Philippines, Romania, and the United States.

   d. A rate of 15% — Thailand.

5. The treaties with Bangladesh, Brazil, Egypt, Greece, Indonesia, Kenya, Libya, Malaysia, Mauritius, Nepal, the Philippines, Sri Lanka, Syria, Tanzania, Thailand, United Arab Emirates, and Zambia do not have any separate article for technical service fees. However, the domestic tax rate applicable to technical service fees is 20.5% under agreements entered into after May 31, 1997.

6. On interest, the following apply.

   a. A rate of 5% — Banks in the case of the United Arab Emirates.

   b. A rate of 10% — Banks in the cases of Belgium, Denmark, Japan, Republic of Korea, Nepal, Turkey, and the United Kingdom.

   c. A rate of 10% — The Philippines, Thailand, Turkey, and the United States for financial institutions and insurance companies; Singapore for financial institutions carrying on banking business,

   d. A rate of 15% — Loans given or debts created after treaty or protocol came into force in the cases of Hungary and Norway.

7. On royalties — 15% for specified copyright royalties in the case of Bulgaria; 25% for use of trademarks in the case of Brazil.

8. A reduced rate of 20.5% applies under government-approved agreements or agreements in accordance with declared government policy made after May 31, 1997. In respect of contracts entered into after March 31, 2003 where the foreign company carries on business in India through a PE/fixed place, such income will be taxable on net basis at 41%.

9. Treaties with Belgium, France, the Netherlands, Spain, Sweden, and Switzerland provide that if India subsequently agrees to a lower withholding rate with any OECD country, the lower rate is to apply. There is a similar provision in the treaty with Norway if India subsequently agrees to a lower withholding rate with any country. India has signed a treaty with Germany, which prescribes a lower withholding rate of 10% on dividends, interest, royalties, and technical service fees. Accordingly, the rates in respect of dividends (other than those paid by an Indian company), interest, royalties, and technical service fees with regard to France, the Netherlands, Sweden and Switzerland are revised to 10%. Similarly, in the cases of Belgium, Norway and Spain the reduced rate of 10% applies to royalties and fees for technical services.

10. A reduced rate of 20.5% can be applied if withholding order for such rate is obtained. The tax rates of 41% and 20.5% are inclusive of 2.5% surcharge.

11. On intercorporate dividends on new contributions (not bonus shares) after the treaty or protocol came into force, provided the recipient has the specified minimum holding: 15% for Hungary, Netherlands, and Norway.

12. Treaty rate for technical service fees mentioned in respect of Hungary and Norway applies only in the case of contracts entered into after the treaties came into force.

13. On intercorporate dividends on new contributions (not bonus shares) after the treaty or protocol came into force, 15% for Poland.

14. No rates have been specified in the treaty and hence taxed as per the domestic laws.

**Treaty countries**/The status of India's tax treaties as on January 1, 2004 is as follows.

### Comprehensive

| | | |
|---|---|---|
| Australia | Japan | Romania |
| Austria | Jordan | Russian Federation |
| Bangladesh | Kazakhstan | Singapore |
| Belarus | Kenya | South Africa |
| Belgium | Korea, Rep. of | Spain |
| Brazil | Kyrgyzstan | Sri Lanka |
| Bulgaria | Libya | Sweden |
| Canada | Malaysia | Switzerland |
| China, P.R. | Malta | Syria |
| Cyprus | Mauritius | Tanzania |
| Czech Republic | Mongolia | Thailand |
| Denmark | Morocco | Trinidad and Tobago |
| Egypt | Namibia | Turkey |
| Finland | Nepal | Turkmenistan |
| France | Netherlands | Ukraine |
| Germany | New Zealand | United Arab Emirates |
| Greece | Norway | United Kingdom |
| Hungary | Oman | United States |
| Indonesia | Philippines | Uzbekistan |
| Ireland | Poland | Vietnam |
| Israel | Portugal | Zambia |
| Italy | Qatar | |

### Restricted—Airlines

| | | |
|---|---|---|
| Afghanistan | Kuwait | Saudi Arabia |
| Ethiopia | Lebanon | Yemen |
| Iran | Pakistan | |

## Tax administration

**Returns**/Accounts for tax purposes must be made up to March 31. The return must be filed, in the case of companies, by the following October 31. Self-assessment is necessary in furnishing the return.

**Payment of tax**/Tax is payable in advance in specified installments in the financial year (April to March) immediately preceding the fiscal year in respect of the income of the accounting year ending March 31. Any balance of tax due on the basis of the return must be paid on a self-assessment basis before filing the return.

## *CORPORATION TAX CALCULATION*

The computation assumes that the taxpayer is an Indian company.

| | | |
|---|---:|---:|
| Book profit (before provisions for taxation and proposed dividend) ......... | | Rs 1,000,000 |
| Less: | | |
| Dividends received from: | | |
| Indian companies ........................................................ | 90,000 | |
| Foreign companies ........................................................ | 10,000 | |
| Long-term capital gains on sale of nondepreciable | | |
| fixed assets, including investments (assuming all | | |
| listed securities) ............................................................ | 15,000 | 115,000 |
| | | 885,000 |
| Add: | | |
| Depreciation per accounts............................................... | 150,000 | |
| Donations....................................................................... | 12,000 | |
| Provision for bad and doubtful debts (1) ............................ | 100,000 | |
| Preliminary expenses charged in accounts........................ | 45,000 | |
| Expenditure on patent rights or copyrights charged | | |
| in accounts ................................................................ | 28,000 | |
| Unpaid statutory dues, bonuses/commissions due to | | |
| employees, interest due to financial institutions, | | |
| contributions to employees' retirement funds (2)............. | 50,000 | |
| Cash payments in excess of Rs20,000 (20% disallowed) ... | 55,000 | 440,000 |
| | | 1,325,000 |
| Less: | | |
| Capital expenditure on scientific research (3) ..................... | 100,000 | |
| Depreciation admissible for tax purposes (4) | | |
| (including depreciation on patent rights/copyrights)........ | 220,000 | |
| Preliminary expenses (one-fifth of 45,000) ........................ | 9,000 | 329,000 |
| Income from business...................................................... | | 996,000 |
| Add—Income from other sources: Gross dividends | | |
| (Foreign company) (5)........................................................ | | 10,000 |
| Gross Total Income ......................................................... | | 1,006,000 |
| Less—Chapter VIA deductions: | | |
| Exempt donations .......................................................... | | 6,000 |
| Export profits (6)............................................................. | | 15,728 |
| Tax holiday—30% of 498,000 (7) ...................................... | 149,400 | 171,128 |
| Income (other than long-term capital gains)........................... | | 834,872 |
| Long-term capital gains .................................................. | | 15,000 |
| Total taxable income ....................................................... | Rs | 849,872 |
| Income tax at 35% on 834,872 .............................. | Rs | 292,205 |
| Income tax at 10% on long-term capital gain of 15,000 (8) .................... | | 1,500 |
| Basic tax........................................................................ | | 293,705 |
| Add—Surcharge (at 2.5%) ................................................. | | 7,343 |
| Gross tax........................................................................ | | 301,048 |
| *Less*—Tax withheld on foreign dividends (9) ......................... | | (1,500) |
| Net tax payable.............................................................. | Rs | 299,548 |

Notes:

1. Actual bad debts written off in the accounts are deductible in full.
2. Statutory dues, bonuses, and commissions to employees, interest paid to financial institutions and banks and amounts payable to employees for their accumulated leave balance are deductible only on a cash basis, unless paid within the time allowed for filing the return.
3. Capital expenditure on scientific research, other than research connected with land, related to the business is allowable in full in the first year. Weighted deductions are permitted in respect of contributions for scientific research to approved institutions, as well as for expenditure incurred by specified industries on approved in-house research facilities.
4. Depreciation is allowable on blocks of fixed assets at the rates specified by the rules on the basis of written-down value.
5. Any dividend declared, distributed or paid on or after April 1, 2003 by a domestic company, whether out of current or accumulated profit, is liable to a dividend distribution tax of 12.8125% to be paid by domestic company. Such dividend is exempt from tax in the hands of the shareholders.
6. A deduction is allowed in respect of profits derived from the export of specified goods. The deduction is calculated according to the following formula:

    (Export turnover ÷ Total turnover) x Income from business

    The deduction computed above is reduced by 30% for accounting year 2003/2004 on account of gradual phasing-out of tax concessions on export profits. If the above formula results in a deduction of (say) Rs52,425, the permissible deduction would be 30% of this figure, that is, Rs15,728.
7. Assuming that 50% of income is from a new industrial undertaking that began manufacturing in financial year 1994/1995.
8. Capital gains arising on sale of long-term listed securities can be taxed at a reduced rate of 10.25% without availing indexation benefits, at the option of the taxpayer.
9. Foreign tax paid is less than the Indian tax on the foreign dividend.
10. Exchange rate of the rupee at January 1, 2004: US$1 = Rs45.595.

## PwC contact

For additional information on taxation in Indonesia, contact:

Firdaus Asikin
Tax Partner to Kantor Akuntan Publik
Drs Hadi Sutanto & Rekan
Gedung PricewaterhouseCoopers
Jalan HR Rasuna Said Kav. C-3
Kuningan
Jakarta 12940, Indonesia
Telephone: (62) (21) 521 2901-6
Fax: (62) (21) 521 2911-2
e-mail: firdaus.asikin@id.pwc.com

## General note

This entry is repeated from the 2003/2004 edition. For more up-to-date information consult the contact listed above or Jacqueline Collette at jacqueline.collete@us.pwc.com.

## Significant developments

Indonesia is currently facing serious economic problems. The Asian economic crisis of 1997 and subsequent political turmoil suffered by Indonesia in 1998 has reversed 30 years of rapid economic growth. In 1998 Indonesia became totally reliant on support from the International Monetary Fund, the World Bank, and other international financial institutions for the survival of its economy. This situation continues in 2002.

In 1998, inflation ran about 70%, and bank interest rates were higher than 60%. Since August 1997 the Indonesian rupiah has lost 80% of its value against other currencies. This has caused a significant increase in unemployment and a significant decrease in the standard of living.

In 2000, certain economic indicators showed improvement. These included GDP growth of 4.8%, export increase of 25.6%, bank interest rates of 18% and inflation rate of 9.35%. Nevertheless, the Indonesian rupiah, although it was relatively stable up to mid-2000, deteriorated up to the first quarter of 2001. In April 2001, the prevailing exchange rate was Rp10,500 per US$1, which was close to the worst condition in 1997–1998. The change of the president from Abdulrachman Wahid to Megawati in August 2001 gave rise to new optimism so that the rupiah recovered to Rp8,900 per US$1. However, as no significant progress was made, the rupiah grew weak again and in February 2002 the exchange rate was Rp10,150 per US$1. On average, the 2002 exchange rate was approximately Rp9,000 per US$1. By the end of February 2003, the rate was Rp8,900 per US$1.

## Taxes on corporate income

*Corporate tax*/Corporate entities are taxed at the following rates.

| | Taxable Income | Rate | Tax |
|---|---|---|---|
| | Rp | | Rp |
| On the first ....................................... | 50,000,000 | 10% | 5,000,000 |
| On the next..................................... | 50,000,000 | 15% | 7,500,000 |
| Over ............................................. | 100,000,000 | 30% | — |

Certain gross income is subject to a "final" tax as follows.

|  | % |
|---|---|
| Rent of land and building | 6.0 |
| Construction contracting services provided by small enterprises | 2.0 |
| Construction planning, supervision and consulting services provided by small enterprises | 4.0 |
| Sale of shares listed on an Indonesian stock exchange | 0.1 |
| Listing of shares on an Indonesian Stock Exchange (see "Capital gains") | 0.5 |
| Interest on time and saving deposits placed on bank operating in Indonesia | 20.0 |
| Interest on bonds listed on an Indonesian stock exchange | 15.0 |

Expenses relating to gross income subject to "final" tax are not deductible.

## Corporate residence

Corporate entities established in accordance with Indonesian laws are subject to corporate income tax on income from all sources. A foreign company that has a permanent establishment in Indonesia has the same tax obligations as an Indonesian resident company. The definition of "permanent establishment" is broad and includes a place of management, branch, representative office, agent or expert, factory or workshop, and construction or mining project. It is the permanent establishment (not the parent company) that is treated as the domestic taxpayer and subject to tax on its worldwide income. However, as a result of the "force of attraction" principle, the income attributable to business activities undertaken by the parent company in Indonesia that are of the same type as those of the permanent establishment may also be taxable.

## Other taxes

*Value-added tax*/VAT is imposed on importers, manufacturers, wholesalers, retailers, providers of most services, and users of intangible goods and services originating from outside the customs area within the customs area.

The rate of VAT is currently 10%, but the VAT law permits amendments within the range of 5% to 15%. Exports of goods are taxed at 0%.

*Sales tax on luxury goods*/Sales tax is imposed once only, upon the delivery or sale of specified luxury goods by a manufacturer or upon import. The tax rates range from 10% to 75%.

*Land and buildings tax*/The effective rate is 0.1% or 0.2% on the government-determined sales value.

## Branch income

Tax rates on corporate profits apply also to branch profits. A 20% withholding tax is payable on branch profits after corporate tax, regardless of whether these profits are remitted to the home country. However, concessional rates of withholding tax are applicable where a tax treaty is in force (see "Withholding taxes").

## Income determination

***Inventory valuation***/Inventories may be valued at average cost or FIFO. Once a method is adopted, it must be applied consistently.

***Capital gains***/Capital gains or losses are in principle recognized for tax purposes and taxed at the normal rates shown above. Sales of shares listed on Indonesian stock exchanges are not subject to normal income tax. They are subject only to a final withholding tax of 0.1% from the gross sales consideration. An additional final tax of 0.5% applies to the share value of founder shares at the time an initial public offering takes place, irrespective of whether the shares are held or sold. Shareholders can elect not to pay this tax, in which case the actual gain will be subject to normal tax at the time the shares are sold.

***Intercompany dividends***/Dividends received from Indonesian companies by companies incorporated in Indonesia are exempt from income tax if the receiving companies own at least 25% of the outstanding shares in the paying companies and have business activities other than shareholding. Otherwise, the dividends are taxable at the normal rates. Where the recipient is not resident in Indonesia, a withholding rate of 20% applies, subject to variation by tax treaties (see "Withholding taxes").

***Foreign income***/Foreign branch income of an Indonesian resident is included in taxable income. If the income has been subject to foreign tax, a tax credit is granted. The amount of allowable tax credit is the lower of actual foreign tax payable and the amount applicable where Indonesian tax rates are applied.

There are regulations requiring that undistributed profits of companies controlled 50% or more by Indonesian residents but incorporated in certain overseas countries be deemed distributed within seven months after year-end. This does not apply to offshore companies listed on a recognized overseas stock exchange.

***Stock dividends***/Stock dividends (bonus shares) are subject to withholding tax (resident recipient 15%, nonresident recipient 20% unless reduced by treaty) except when they are paid out of a share premium (*agio*) account. If withholding tax applies, it is a prepayment of income tax for a recipient domiciled in Indonesia and a final tax for a nonresident.

***Exchange gains and losses***/Gains and losses arising from currency fluctuations are generally recognized on an accrual basis.

## Deductions

***Depreciation and amortization***/"Depreciable/amortizable property" means both tangible and intangible property with a useful life of more than one year, except land that is owned and used in business or owned for the production, recovery, and securing of income. Depreciation may be calculated by the straight-line method or the declining-balance method on the individual asset basis. Once a method is chosen, it should be applied consistently. In calculating depreciation, depreciable property is divided into the following classes.

# Indonesia

| Class | Depreciation rate | |
| | Straight-line method | Declining-balance method |
| --- | --- | --- |
| | % | % |
| Property: | | |
| Useful life of 4 years | 25 | 50 |
| Useful life of 8 years | 12.5 | 25 |
| Useful life of 16 years | 6.25 | 12.5 |
| Useful life of 20 years | 5 | 10 |
| Buildings: | | |
| Permanent | 5 | — |
| Nonpermanent | 10 | — |

Special rules apply for assets used in certain business fields and/or certain areas. Tax depreciation need not conform to book depreciation.

The cost incurred for acquiring the rights with a beneficial life of more than one year for mining, oil and natural gas concessions; forest concessions; and other rights to exploit natural resources should be amortized by the production-unit method. Except for the right to acquire oil and natural gas concessions, the depletion rate used should not exceed 20% per annum.

*Net operating losses*/Losses may be carried forward for a maximum period of five years or, for specific types of businesses and/or companies investing in certain areas specially covered by a Minister of Finance decree, not more than ten years. Loss carrybacks are not permitted.

*Payments to foreign affiliates*/Withholding tax is applied as a final tax on the recipient for payments of royalties, interest and service fees to foreign nonresident companies. Excessive and nonarm's-length payments to related parties will be disallowed as deductions. The tax law denies a deduction for all payments from a branch to its head office for royalties, interest, and services provided by the head office (exceptions apply to loans between bank branches and their head offices).

*Taxes*/Land and building tax and regional taxes may be deducted from taxable income. Except in certain cases, noncreditable input VAT is also deductible against taxable income.

## Nondeductible items

*Benefits-in-kind*/Benefits received in kind by employees, such as free housing, are not tax deductible to the entity providing the benefit. Until recently, the only exceptions are meal and transportation made available to all staff. Starting April 2002, 50% of the costs of the free use of company cars and cellular telephones, including depreciation, can be claimed as a deductible expense. Apart from these, benefits-in-kind such as housing provided in remote areas as designated by the Minister of Finance and Integrated Economic Development Areas as designated by Presidential Decree can also be claimed as tax-deductible expenses.

*Other significant items*/The Minister of Finance is authorized to make a determination on the ratio of debt to equity. Debt may be considered equity, thus giving rise to the disallowance of related costs as a tax deduction. However, the Minister of Finance has not yet issued any ruling on this matter.

## Group taxation

Consolidated returns are not allowed.

## Tax incentives

*Inward investment*/Corporations making new or expansion investment in priority sectors, especially in export-oriented industries, including hard-crop plantation, mining or other businesses as stipulated by Presidential Decrees and/or in remote areas are entitled to the following tax incentives.

1. Reduction of taxable income up to 30% of the investment.
2. Accelerated depreciation.
3. Extension of period for loss carryforward up to a maximum of ten years.
4. Reduction of branch profits tax.

Additional incentives are provided if the investment or expansion is made in eastern Indonesia designated as the Integrated Economic Development Area (KAPET). These include:

- Exemption of certain transactions from VAT and sales tax on luxury goods.
- Exemption from prepaid income tax on the importation of capital goods and materials for further processing.
- Deferment or exemption of import duties on the importation of cap goods, materials, and spare parts.

Permanent establishments that reinvest their after-tax profits in Indonesia within the same year, or in the following year at the latest, are exempt from income tax on these profits. The permanent establishments should invest in the form of capital participation as founder shareholders for at least two years after the invested company starts its commercial production.

*Other incentives*/Income earned by venture capital companies in the form of profit sharing from their investments in Indonesia is exempt from tax, provided that the following conditions apply.

1. Entities are small and medium-scale businesses in one of the sectors designated by the Indonesian government; and
2. Investments are not listed on the Indonesian stock exchanges.

Subject to the approval of the Director General of Tax, tax-neutral mergers can be conducted between companies in which assets are transferred at their book value.

In the case of a business split resulting in the creation of a new company, transferring assets at their book value is only allowed if the business split constitutes part of the plan of going public.

# Indonesia

## Withholding taxes

Withholding tax is levied on a variety of payments to corporations and individuals, resident and nonresident, at the following rates.

| | Dividends | | | | |
| | Portfolio (1) | Substantial holdings (1, 2) | Interest (3) | Royalties (4) | Branch profits (5) |
|---|---|---|---|---|---|
| | % | % | % | % | % |
| Resident corporations .............. | Nil | Nil | 15 | 15 | N/A |
| Resident individuals ................. | 15 | 15 | 15 | 15 | N/A |
| Nonresident corporations and individuals: | | | | | |
| Nontreaty ................................. | 20 | 20 | 20 | 20 | 20/0 (6) |
| Treaty (7): | | | | | |
| Australia .............................. | 15 | 15 | 10/0 | 15/10 | 15 |
| Austria ................................ | 15 | 10 | 10/0 | 10 | 12 |
| Belgium (2) ......................... | 15 | 10 | 10/0 | 10 | 10 |
| Brunei (3) ............................ | 15 | 15 | 15/0 | 15 | 10 |
| Bulgaria .............................. | 15 | 15 | 10/0 | 10 | 15 |
| Canada ............................... | 15 | 10 | 10/0 | 10 | 15 |
| Czech Republic ................... | 15 | 10 | 12.5/0 | 12.5 | 12.5 |
| Denmark ............................. | 20 | 10 | 10/0 | 15 | 15 |
| Egypt (3) ............................. | 15 | 15 | 15/0 | 15 | 15 |
| Finland ................................ | 15 | 10 | 10/0 | 15/10 | 15 |
| France ................................. | 15 | 10 | 15/10/0 | 10 | 10 |
| Germany ............................. | 15 | 10 | 10/0 | 15/10 (4) | 10 |
| Hungary .............................. | 15 | 15 | 15/0 | 15 | 20 (5)(6) |
| India ................................... | 15 | 10 | 10/0 | 15 | 10 |
| Italy .................................... | 15 | 10 | 10/0 | 15/10 | 12 |
| Japan .................................. | 15 | 10 | 10/0 | 10 | 10 |
| Jordan ................................. | 10 | 10 | 10/0 | 10 | 20(5) |
| Korea (South) ...................... | 15 | 10 | 10/0 | 15 | 10 |
| Kuwait ................................. | 10 | 10 | 5/0 | 20 | 10/0 (7) |
| Luxembourg ........................ | 15 | 10 | 10/0 | 12.5 (3) | 10 |
| Malaysia .............................. | 15 | 15 | 15/0 | 15 | 12.5 |
| Mauritius ............................. | 10 | 5 | 10/0 | 10 | 10 |
| Mongolia ............................. | 10 | 10 | 10/0 | 10 | 10 |
| Netherlands ......................... | 15 | 10 | 10/0 | 10 | 9 |
| New Zealand ....................... | 15 | 15 | 10/0 | 15 | 20 (5) |
| Norway ................................ | 15 | 15 | 10/0 | 15/10 | 15 |
| Pakistan .............................. | 15 | 10 | 15/0 | 15 (3) | 10 |
| Philippines .......................... | 20 | 15 | 15/10/0 | 15 | 20 |
| Poland ................................. | 15 | 10 | 10/0 | 15 | 10 |
| Romania (8) ......................... | 15 | 12.5 | 12.5 | 15/12.5 | 10 |
| Seychelles .......................... | 10 | 10 | 10/0 | 10 | 20 (5) |
| Singapore ........................... | 15 | 10 | 10/0 | 15 | 15 |
| Spain .................................. | 15 | 10 | 10/0 | 10 | 10 |
| South Africa ........................ | 15 | 10 | 10/0 | 10 | 20 (4)(5) |
| Sri Lanka ............................. | 15 | 15 | 15/0 | 15 | 20 (5) |
| Sudan ................................. | 10 | 10 | 15/0 | 10 | 10 |

| | Dividends | | | | Branch |
| | Portfolio (1) | Substantial holdings (1, 2) | Interest (3) | Royalties (4) | profits (5) |
|---|---|---|---|---|---|
| | % | % | % | % | % |
| Sweden | 15 | 10 | 10/0 | 15/10 | 15 |
| Switzerland | 15 | 10 | 10/0 | 12.5 (3) | 10 |
| Syria | 10 | 10 | 10 | 20/15 | 10 |
| Taiwan | 10 | 10 | 10/0 | 10 | 5 |
| Thailand | 15 | 15 | 15/0 | 15/10 | 20 |
| Tunisia | 12 | 12 | 12/0 | 15 | 12 |
| Turkey | 10 | 10 | 10/0 | 10 | 10 |
| Ukraine | 15 | 10 | 10/0 | 10 | 10 |
| United Arab Emirates | 10 | 10 | 5/0 | 5 | 5 |
| United Kingdom | 15 | 10 | 10/0 | 15/10 | 10 |
| United States | 15 | 10 | 10/0 | 10 | 10 |
| Uzbekistan | 10 | 10 | 10/0 | 10 | 10 |
| Venezuela (2) | 15 | 10 | 10/0 | 20/10 | 10 |
| Vietnam | 15 | 15 | 15/0 | 15 | 10 |

Notes:

1. The withholding tax rates quoted above relate to the treaty presently in force unless indicated otherwise.
2. The amended treaty has been ratified but is not yet effective for tax purposes.
3. The treaty has been ratified but is not yet effective for tax purposes.
4. Fees for services are subject to withholding tax at the rates of 5%, 7.5%, 10%, and 15% for Switzerland, Germany, Luxembourg, and Pakistan, respectively.
5. The treaty provisions are silent on the rate. The Indonesian Tax Office interprets this to mean that the rate as regulated by Indonesian Tax Law (20%) should apply.
6. Tax only applies if profits are actually remitted.
7. Tax is only applicable if profits are remitted to a head office within the 12-month period after the profits accrue.
8. Includes a 10% withholding tax on commissions.

In addition to the above treaties, there are agreements with Saudi Arabia, Morocco, Bangladesh, Croatia, South Africa, and Laos for the reciprocal exemption of taxes and customs duties on the activities of the two countries' air transport enterprises.

## Tax administration

**Returns**/Corporate taxpayers are required to file annual tax returns within three months of the end of the tax year. The tax year-end will coincide with the company's book year-end, that is, it does not have to be a calendar year-end. The system is basically one of self-assessment. (See Note 1a under "Corporation tax calculation.")

**Payment of tax**/Corporate tax installments may be paid by third parties in specified situations and by the company in monthly installments. Refer to Note 1 under "Corporation tax calculation."

# Indonesia

## *CORPORATION TAX CALCULATION*

Year ending December 31, 2002

|  | | (In millions of rupiah) |
|---|---:|---:|
| Net profit before taxation shown by the accounts | | 1,000 |
| Add: | | |
| Depreciation charged in the accounts | 30 | |
| Dividends received from Indonesian companies | 15 | |
| Income subject to final tax | 5 | |
| Increase in provisions not deductible for tax | 10 | |
| Donations not deductible for tax | 5 | |
| Cost of employee housing not deductible for tax | 40 | 105 |
| | | 1,105 |
| Deduct: | | |
| Depreciation allowed for tax purposes | 60 | |
| Expenses relating to income subject to final tax | 20 | |
| Losses carried over from previous years | 45 | 125 |
| Taxable income | | 980 |
| Tax thereon: | | |
| First 50 million at 10% | 5.00 | |
| Next 50 million at 15% | 7.50 | |
| Balance of 880 million at 30% | 264.00 | 276.50 |
| *Less*—Tax paid during the year: | | |
| Monthly corporate tax installments (1 a) | 200.00 | |
| Withholding tax collected (1 b, c) | 50.00 | (250.00) |
| Balance payable/(refundable) (1 d) | | Rp 26.50 |

Notes:

1. Payment of corporation income tax:
   a. Income tax (self-assessment of corporation tax)—Companies and branches are required to calculate and pay corporation tax monthly. The monthly payment is equal to the tax due for the preceding tax year reduced by the amount of tax withheld by other parties and the credit for tax paid abroad, divided by 12. The monthly payment for the period before the final tax due in the preceding year is known is equal to the previous year's monthly payment. Special rules apply if the company is entitled to a tax refund or has received Tax Assessment Letters from the Tax Office.
   b. Indonesian income tax on certain income is collected by withholding (collection of income tax by others). These taxes are considered a prepayment of the recipient's corporate tax liability. Examples include the following.

| Estimated net income (ENI) | ENI % | Actual withholding (% of gross amounts) |
|---|---|---|
| Rentals other than land and/or buildings | | |
| • rental of land transportation vehicles ............... | 20 | 3 |
| • others (payments under finance leases are not subject to withholding tax)................. | 40 | 6 |
| Fees for services: | | |
| • professional services, including legal, tax and other consulting services ................... | 50 | 7.5 |
| • construction contracting services...................... | 13.33 | 2 |
| • construction planning services.......................... | 26.67 | 4 |
| • construction supervision services ..................... | 26.67 | 4 |
| • technical and management services ................ | 40 | 6 |
| • design services including interior, landscape, machine, equipment, vehicles, transportation equipment, advertising/logo and packaging design services ...................... | 40 | 6 |
| • accounting and bookkeeping services.............. | 40 | 6 |
| • installation services .......................................... | 40 | 6 |
| • maintenance/repair services ............................ | 40 | 6 |
| • custodial/storage/consignment services (excluding storage rental which is already subject to final tax)........................................ | 40 | 6 |
| • securities trading services ............................... | 40 | 6 |
| • technology information services, including internet services............................................. | 40 | 6 |
| • telecommunication services not for public purposes......................................................... | 40 | 6 |
| • waste treatment and disposal .......................... | 40 | 6 |
| • forest felling services, including land clearing ........................................................... | 40 | 6 |
| • drilling and support services in mining (excluding drilling services in oil/gas provided by permanent establishments (PEs)) .................................... | 40 | 6 |
| • mining and support services in non-oil/gas mining industry ........................... | 40 | 6 |
| • intermediary services........................................ | 40 | 6 |
| • appraisal services............................................. | 40 | 6 |
| • actuarial services.............................................. | 40 | 6 |
| • film dubbing/mixing services ............................ | 40 | 6 |
| • contract manufacturing (*maklon*)...................... | 40 | 6 |
| • recruitment/manpower supply........................... | 40 | 6 |
| • computer software services ............................. | 40 | 6 |
| • pest control and cleaning services .................. | 10 | 1.5 |
| • services other than the above for which payments are borne by government budgets .......................................................... | 10 | 1.5 |

   c. Fiscal exit taxes (Rp1,000,000 per exit from Indonesia by plane, Rp500,000 by ship or Rp200,000 by land) borne by a company for its employees' business trips are considered prepayment of the company's income tax liability.

   d. Within three months after the end of the financial year, a company is required to calculate the corporation tax due. If, after deduction of the prepaid income tax and withholding tax as aforementioned, an amount is still due, then the balance should be paid. This is called the Final Payment, which should be made by the 25th of the third month after the end of the financial year. Should prepaid taxes exceed the final calculation of corporate taxes, the excess tax paid must be refunded or offset against other tax liabilities.

2. Exchange rate of the rupiah at December 31, 2002: US$1 = Rp8,940.

The exchange rate has varied significantly in recent times. The official rates published weekly by the tax office are used in computing taxable income.

## PwC contact

For additional information on taxation in Iran, contact:

Abbas Hoshi
Hoshiyar/Behmand & Co.*
130, Ghaemmagham Farahani Avenue
(P.O. Box 15815-1619)
Tehran, Iran
Telephone: (98) (21) 8305391 – 3/8843708/10
Fax: (98) (21) 8844685
e-mail: hb-ir-pwc@dpi.net.ir (Fax is also recommended)
        a.hoshi@behmandhoshi.com
Web site: *www.behmandhoshi.com*

* Cooperating firm PricewaterhouseCoopers.

## General note

This entry is repeated from the 2003/2004 edition. For more up-to-date information consult the contact listed above or Jacqueline Collette at jacqueline.collete@us.pwc.com.

The new tax law was approved in February 2002. This tax law provides a low tax rate, which may attract new investment. This tax law is effective from March 20, 2002. Up to year 1979 there were tax treaties with Germany and France, and during the last two years further tax treaties have been signed with South Africa and a few of the new republics in Central Asia.

## Development

During the last two years there have been significant investments in the sectors of oil, gas, petroleum, and mining, mainly based on buy-back contracts. Investments in power plants through BOOT (build own operate transfer) and BOT (build operate transfer) contracts are also a new development in the energy sector.

## Taxes on corporate income

Registered business entities in Iran are taxed at different rates, depending on the type of entity. The types of entity are as follows.

1. Corporation (public or private) (i.e., joint stock company, limited liability company).
2. Partnership.
3. Branch of foreign corporation.

In accordance with the Constitution Law, foreign investment in Iran is not allowed unless permission is given by the parliament. Parliament has already approved the law governing registration of foreign companies. Branch offices in Iran (except for banking and insurance companies) do not need pre-approval by the authorities.

The new law "Encouragement and Protection of Foreign Investment in Iran" governing foreign investment in Iran was approved in July 2002 (as amendment to the previous law of year 1958). The new law contains provisions affecting. (1) investment in different sectors and also through different procedures including direct investment, buy-back and BOT contracts; (2) repatriation of profit; and (3) investments supported by the government.

Foreign companies can register a branch in Iran (permission is needed for banks and insurance activities only). Registration of branch office of all activities in Free Zone Areas is allowed.

Foreign companies that are not registered in Iran are taxed on their income earned from Iran (such as royalties and sale of rights).

***Free Zone Areas/***There are certain Free Zone Areas (Kish Island, Queshm, Chahbahar) in which 15 years' tax exemption and other advantages are available. The new "Special Industrial Zone" has also been introduced in different parts of the country in which special facilities are available (such as lower customs tariffs, etc.).

***Corporation and partnership taxes/***The net income of a corporation is taxed as follows.

1. The taxable income of a company (private or government-owned) is subject to only  a 25% corporate tax and there is no more tax to be claimed as shareholders' tax.
2. Stock dividends (bonus shares) are possible if issued against a general reserve. They are also exempt from income tax if the general reserve has been an exempt source (or net of tax).

***Branch of a foreign corporation/***Iranian branches of foreign corporations are taxed on their total income earned in Iran, including income derived from their investments in Iran, income from activities carried out in Iran either directly or through agencies, and income earned in Iran through the assignment of contracting, industrial rights or royalties or by providing technical assistance or training. Branch income is taxed on the basis of a 25% tax on net profit only.

***Special industries—contractors/***For tax purposes, contractors are defined as legal or natural persons that contract for any type of construction work, technical and capital installations, designing and planning of buildings and installations, drawings or topographical surveys, or supervision of various technical calculations. Contractors, whether they perform their work as individuals, domestic corporations, or branches, are usually taxed on net reported profit and deemed profit, respectively. The detailed procedure is explained below.

1. Entities for which the construction work is being performed are required to withhold 5% of every payment made to a contractor. They must pay over the amounts withheld to the Ministry of Economic Affairs and Finance within 30 days from the date of payment to the contractor.
2. At the end of each fiscal year the contractor will file a tax return. The net profit resulting from its activity will be subject to income tax. The 5% tax withheld (as explained in the preceding paragraph) will be a credit against income tax calculated on this profit. As far as foreign contracting companies performing their work in Iran through a registered branch (or without a branch) are concerned, the taxable income is a deemed profit of 12% of the gross amount of invoices cashed during each financial year.
3. Where the contractor is a foreign company (with registered branch in Iran) taxable income is a deemed taxable income equal to 12% of the gross amount of invoices cashed during the year; corporate tax at the 25% rate is imposed on the deemed taxable income. In such cases the withholding tax is 3% of the invoices cashed.
4. The contractor is given credit for 5% tax withheld on the gross receipts (see "Corporation tax calculation" below).

5. In the case of a foreign company with a contract with a governmental office in which the supply portion of the contract is imported in the name of the client, and also where part of the local supply is subcontracted to a local manufacturer, such portion of the contract is exempted from income tax.

6. On all contracts with foreign companies signed after March 21, 2003, the branch should report net operating profit, which will be the base of taxable income (rather than the deemed 12% profit on the receipts).

7. Under the Social Security Act, contract work is subject to a social security premium at a fixed rate, which is equal to 7% of the amount of the contract when the supply portion of the contract is with the contractor and 15% when it is with the client. In addition, unemployment charges are payable by the contractor at one-ninth of the social security fixed charges. (This one-ninth charge is in lieu of the government levy for unemployment charges of 3% of salary cost of all companies.) Consequently, the effective fixed charge rate is 7.77% of the contract amount (in the case of full service contracts such fixed rate is 16.67% of the contract amount). It should be noted that the imported supply portion (through letter of credit) is also exempted from such fixed charges. Contracts signed before April 1991 are subject to different rates. The fixed charges, after deduction of social security premium amounts paid on actual salary cost, should be paid to the Social Security Office in order to obtain a clearance letter. Under the prevailing regulation there is a 5% withholding deposit from each invoice. Such amounts, together with the last invoice, are payable to the contractor upon providing the social security clearance letter. It should be noted that this procedure is applicable to foreign companies. Iranian companies that are involved in development projects pay 1.6% of the total contract amount as a fixed charge for the social security premium.

*Corporation tax rates*/The corporation tax rate is 25% of net profit (or taxable income).

## Other taxes

Sale of property is subject to a 5% tax on the deemed sale amount to be determined by the authorities (such deemed governmental sale amount is very low compared with the actual sale amount).

*Municipality tax*/Each province is allowed to determine local municipality charges, as approved by the city council of each city.

*Expatriate's salary levy*/In accordance with parliamentary approval, a corporation or a branch is responsible for paying 30% of an expatriate's salary (to be determined on a deemed basis) plus 3% of the maximum salary subject to social security premiums on an employment charge to the Ministry of Labor.

*Value-added tax*/The value-added (VAT) tax law was prepared in 1990 and its final version is now under review by the government. It is expected to be in use from year 2003/2004 provided that parliament approves it. Different sales taxes are collected under the annual budget law and a special law. The most important, which are to be added on in the invoices for sales of goods and services, are as follows.

1. A rate of 2.00% — To be paid to the bank account of the Ministry of Education.

2. A rate of 1.00% — To be paid to the bank account of the municipality.

3. A rate of 0.05%—Municipality charges for contract work of a development project.
4. A rate of 0.02%—Training fund, to be deducted from the invoices of the contracting operations.

Note: A special law imposing a single rate for all levies (including preliminary steps for VAT law) is under preapproval process by the parliament. It is expected that such law will be in force from March 2003.

**Room charges**/A holder of commercial cards (for the importation of goods) is subject to special levies, the so-called chamber of commerce room charges, equal to 0.3% of taxable income.

## Withholding

The following withholding taxes must be followed by the legal entity (private and governmental sector).

| | |
|---|---|
| Salary income | Actual tax as per salary tax regulation. |
| Fee, contract income | A rate of 5% (3% for foreign contractors). |
| Dividend | Nil. |
| Royalties and sale of rights | Taxable income is 20% to 40% of gross receipts. Detailed taxable income rates for different entities (governmental office and private sector) will be announced by the tax office. |
| Guaranteed profit (interest) | Loans granted to a governmental office or Iranian. Bank by a foreign entity (bank or financial institution) without presence in Iran (branch or other sort of establishment) are exempted from taxes; in other cases, the matter is still under review. Such interest, payable by the private sector to a foreign bank or financial institution, may be subject to tax, the rate of which will be determined by the tax office, although this matter is still uncertain. |

## CORPORATION TAX CALCULATION

The taxation of two different activities is shown in the following table. Those activities are (1) contract work by a foreign company through its registered branch in Iran under note A to Article 107 of the Taxation Act, and (2) other activities (such as manufacturing, service, agency, or contract work by an Iranian company) where net profit is subject to tax.

| | Branch as contractor | Company/Branch other activities |
|---|---|---|
| | Rls | Rls |
| Gross income (invoice amounts subject to tax) for fiscal year | 10,000,000,000 | 20,000,000,000 |
| Less cost and expenses | — | 17,000,000,000 |
| Net profit | — | 3,000,000,000 |
| Disallowed expenses | — | — |
| Taxable profit | — | 3,000,000,000 |
| Deemed taxable profits (12% of gross income) | 1,200,000,000 | |
| Corporate tax on deemed taxable profits, rate (Article 105) | 25% | 25% |
| Corporate tax | 300,000,000 | 750,000,000 |

Effective rates of tax: for contract work, 3% of gross income; for other activities, 3.75% of gross income.

Notes:

1. The regulation governing disallowed expenses is also in use in Iranian tax practice. There are limits for certain expenses. Also, if expenses are not fully supported by acceptable documents, they are disallowed.

2. Chamber of commerce room charges (if above contractor holds a commercial card) are 0.3% of taxable income.

| | Rls | Rls |
|---|---|---|
| Chamber of commerce room tax | 3,600,000 | 9,000,000 |
| Total taxes | 303,600,000 | 759,000,000 |

3. In the case of contract practice, a 5% tax withheld will be deducted from tax due (for foreign contractors, withheld tax is 3%).

## Exchange rate

From March 21, 2002, one unique exchange rate (so-called market rate) is in use. The exchange rate as of December 31, 2002, is Rls7,950 to Rls7,980 = US$1.

# Ireland, Republic of

## PwC contact

For additional information on taxation in Ireland, contact:

Colm Kelly
PricewaterhouseCoopers
Wilton Place
Dublin 2, Ireland
Telephone: (353) (1) 6789999
Fax: (353) (1) 7048740
e-mail: colm.r.kelly@ie.pwc.com

## General note

The information in this entry is current as of February 2004 and incorporates
the provisions of the Finance Bill 2004. For subsequent developments consult the
contact listed above.

## Taxes on corporate income

*Corporation tax*/Corporation tax is chargeable as follows on income.

|  | %<br>Trading income<br>"standard rate" | %<br>Nontrading income<br>"passive rate" |
|---|---|---|
| January 1, 2002 to December 31, 2002 | 16 (1) | 25 |
| Profits arising after January 1, 2003 | 12.5 | 25 |

Note:

The rate is 12.5% where trading profits for the year are less than or equal
to €254,000.

Nontrading ("passive") income includes rental income, interest income, royalty
income, and dividends from foreign companies.

A rate of 10% applies on certain manufacturing activities (see "Tax incentives"
below).

Closely held companies are liable to a 20% surcharge on after-tax investment and
rental income that is not distributed within 18 months of the end of the accounting
period.

Close service companies are subject to a surcharge on the lesser of 15% of half
of their undistributed trading income and 100% of their undistributed after-tax
investment and rental income, or 20% of their after-tax undistributed investment
and rental income, whichever is the lesser.

Corporation tax at the rate of 25% is levied in respect of profits from certain
petroleum activities, working minerals, and dealing in and developing land.

*Dividend withholding tax*/An Irish resident company that makes a distribution
is required to withhold tax equal to the standard income tax rate (currently 20%),
unless the recipient of the distribution is a company resident in the state having
a 51% shareholding.

Certain exemptions from withholding tax exist where the recipient of the distribution
falls into one of the categories listed below, and provides the relevant declaration to
the payor of the distribution in advance of the distribution being made.

- Irish tax resident companies which hold less than a 51% shareholding of the company.
- Companies which are resident in the EU, or a country with which Ireland has a tax treaty, where the company is not ultimately controlled by Irish residents.
- Nonresident companies which are ultimately controlled by residents of the EU or tax treaty country.
- Companies whose shares are registered and regularly traded on an EU or treaty country stock exchange, or a company ultimately controlled by a company whose shares are registered on an EU or treaty country stock exchange, or a company controlled jointly by two companies whose shares are registered on an EU or tax treaty country stock exchange.
- Individuals who are resident in an EU or tax treaty country.
- Certain pension funds, retirement funds, sports bodies, collective investment funds, employee share ownership trusts.

Companies that make a distribution are required, within 14 days of the end of the month in which the distribution is made, to make a return to Revenue, and to pay over any tax withheld.

## Corporate residence

A company which is incorporated, or has its place of management and control, in Ireland, will be regarded as resident in Ireland for the purposes of corporation tax and capital gains tax. This is subject to certain exceptions where the company is resident in Ireland due only to its place of incorporation being Ireland. These exceptions apply where the company is resident in another tax treaty country, or, if not so resident, is controlled by persons resident in a treaty country where the company can show an economic link with another Irish resident trading company. Alternatively, the incorporation test will not apply where the shares of the company, or a related company, are traded on a recognized stock exchange.

## Other taxes

*Value-added tax*/The rates and the main categories to which they apply are as follows.

|  | % |
|---|---|
| Exported goods, fertilizers, books, food, and oral medicine, children's clothing and children's footwear | 0.0 |
| Livestock (including horses) and greyhounds (Until December 31, 2003) | 4.3 |
| (From January 1, 2004) | 4.4 |
| Supply of electricity; fuels (other than motor fuels); supply of developed property, newspapers, certain building materials, hotel accommodation, and certain tourist-related services; meals supplied in hotels, restaurants and similar establishments; admission to cinema and certain theatrical and musical performances; services supplied by veterinary surgeons; certain agricultural services; admissions to art exhibitions; waste disposal; repair and maintenance of movable goods, photographic and similar services; driving instruction (Until December 31, 2002) | 12.5 |
| (From January 1, 2003) | 13.5 |
| Goods and services not subject to one of the other rates (Note the above lists are not exhaustive) [from March 1, 2002] | 21.0 |

Exemptions include the following.

1. Specified financial services and insurance.
2. Short-term letting of property, with certain exceptions.
3. Transport of passengers.
4. Funeral undertaking.
5. Medical, hospital, and most educational services.
6. Admission to certain theatrical performances.

*Local taxes*/Rates are imposed on the owners or occupiers of certain land and buildings. They are based on the square meter area of buildings. Rates are an allowable deduction for corporation tax purposes. Local authorities are also empowered to levy charges on all occupiers for specific services, for example, water supply. These charges are also deductible for corporation tax purposes.

*Stamp duty*/Stamp duty is a tax on instruments. It is payable on the issue of share capital in a limited company, on transfers of land and certain other assets that cannot pass by delivery. It is also chargeable on all instruments wherever executed, provided the instruments relate to Irish property or activities in the state. The transfer of assets between certain associated companies is not liable to stamp duty, provided certain conditions are met.

*Stamp duty on intellectual property*/Finance Bill 2004 eliminates Irish stamp duty on the transfer of intellectual property such as patents, trademarks and copyrights. Previously such transfers could attract stamp duty at rates of up to 9%. The implementation of this provision is subject to EU approval from a State Aid perspective.

*Capital taxes*/Ireland does not levy a special tax on the net worth of companies.

*Social security*/Employed persons are compulsorily insured under a state-administered scheme of Pay-Related Social Insurance (PRSI). Contributions are made by both the employer and the employee. Contributions by the employer are an allowable deduction for corporation tax purposes.

## Branch income

Irish branches are subject to corporation tax. No tax is withheld on repatriation of branch profits.

## Income determination

*Inventory valuation*/Each item of inventory is valued for tax purposes at cost or market value, whichever is lower, and this will normally accord with accounting treatment. The method used in arriving at cost or market value of inventory must generally be consistent and must not be in conflict with tax law. The FIFO method is an acceptable method of calculation. The base-stock method has been held to be an inappropriate method for tax purposes, as has the LIFO method.

*Capital gains*/In general, gains on capital assets are liable to taxation calculated by reference to capital gains tax rules. A capital gains tax rate of 20% applies to all capital gains other than certain interests in offshore funds and foreign life assurance policies (where a tax rate of 23% applies). The base cost in computing capital gains is indexed for inflation (subject to certain restrictions in the case of development land) up to December 31, 2002. Indexation relief no longer applies in computing capital gains tax as of January 1, 2003. Capital losses can only be set against capital gains arising in the same year or carried forward indefinitely; there is no carryback. There are special provisions dealing with gains (and losses) from development land.

*Intercompany dividends*/Dividends from Irish resident companies are not liable to further tax, other than a surcharge on closely held companies if the dividend is not redistributed.

*Foreign income*/Resident companies are liable to Irish tax on worldwide income. Accordingly, in the case of an Irish resident company, foreign income and capital gains are, broadly speaking, subject in full to corporation tax. This applies to income of a foreign branch of an Irish company as well as to dividend income arising abroad.

In general, income of foreign subsidiaries of Irish companies is not taxed until remitted to Ireland.

Where income is received from a foreign country with which the state has a tax treaty, a credit is usually given for the tax paid in the foreign country against Irish taxes on the foreign income. The taxes that qualify for the foreign tax credit depend on the terms of the individual treaties.

Unilateral credit relief is also available where dividends are sourced from nontreaty countries and from second- or lower-tier subsidiaries resident in nontreaty countries, provided the dividends are received from 5% (previously 25%) subsidiaries.

*Repatriation of dividends*/Measures are also to be introduced in 2004 to amend favourably Ireland's double tax provisions relating to dividends received by Irish parents from their foreign subsidiaries. These measures focus on the "onshore pooling" of tax credits on dividends received from foreign subsidiaries. The amendments are subject to Ministerial Order and EU approval.

Although no special rules exist for the taxation of undistributed income of foreign subsidiaries, there are special rules that seek to tax the undistributed capital gains of certain closely controlled nonresident companies.

*Stock dividends*/Stock dividends are taxed on the shareholder on an equivalent amount which would have been assessable if the option to take stock dividends had not been exercised. If the recipient is an Irish resident company and it receives the dividend from a quoted Irish company, this will not be liable to tax. Where the stock dividend arises on a distribution from an Irish quoted company, dividend withholding tax with the appropriate exemptions and exclusions applies.

## Deductions

*Depreciation and depletion*/Book depreciation is not deductible for tax purposes. Instead, tax depreciation (known as capital allowances) is given in respect of expenditure incurred on assets which have been put into use by the company. The rates applying are set out below.

# Ireland, Republic of

| Asset type | Post December 31, 2000 expenditure | Post December 4, 2002 expenditure |
|---|---|---|
| Plant and machinery (new or secondhand) | 20% on a straight-line basis for five years. | 12.5% on a straight-line basis for eight years. |
| Industrial buildings used for manufacturing | 4% on a straight-line basis for 25 years. | 4% on a straight-line basis for 25 years. |
| Motor vehicles | 20% on a straight-line basis over five years. | 12.5% on a straight-line basis over eight years. |

The allowances are calculated on the cost after deduction of grants, except for plant and machinery used in the course of the manufacture of processed food for human consumption. In this case, the allowances are calculated on the gross cost.

*Accelerated capital allowances*/Accelerated capital allowances are available in respect of special buildings incentives in designated Renewal Areas.

Special accelerated allowances of up to 120% of expenditure are available for mining exploration.

*Net trading losses*/The availability of trading losses against income is a complex area. Trading losses of a company may be off-set against the "relevant trading income" of the company in the same accounting period, or the immediately preceding accounting period of equal length, on a gross basis or may be carried forward indefinitely against income from the trade in future accounting periods. To the extent that a company has unutilized trade losses following a claim against "relevant trading income" in the current or immediately preceding accounting period(s), any unutilized portion of the trade loss may be claimed on a "value basis" against the company's corporation tax liability on other chargeable income or gains of the current accounting period and if the loss is not fully utilized, against the corporation tax payable of the immediately preceding accounting period(s) of equal length. Trading losses arising from a trade qualifying for 10% manufacturing relief may be used to offset tax adjusted profits from the manufacturing trade itself, or used against the company's corporation tax liability on a "value basis." Any unutilized manufacturing trade losses, not utilized as outlined above, may be carried forward for offset against future trading profits from the same trade. Certain changes in ownership may prevent the carry forward of losses to future periods. Terminal losses may be carried back three years.

*Payments to foreign affiliates*/In general, there are no prohibitive rules on payments, other than certain interest, to foreign affiliates, provided the amounts are reasonable and computed on an arm's length basis.

*Taxes*/Taxes that are deductible in computing profits for corporation tax include value-added tax (VAT) not recovered, the employer's share of PRSI contributions, and local taxes, that is, rates levied on commercial property and local authority charges.

*Other significant items*/Interest is allowed only to the extent that borrowings are used for the purpose of a trade or other limited purposes. Expenditure on scientific research and development and payments for the acquisition of know-how in general are allowable deductions, as are the costs of obtaining or extending patents and obtaining and renewing trademarks. Contributions to certain employee pension schemes and the cost of setting up such schemes are also deductible.

***R&D credit*/**As a result of changes introduced in Finance Bill 2004, incremental R&D expenditure will qualify for a tax credit of 20% in addition to a tax deduction at 10% to 12.5%. The credit cannot be used to generate a tax refund, but it can be carried forward indefinitely against a company's Irish corporate tax bill. The credit is available for incremental expenditure incurred in all EU countries, not just expenditure in Ireland. However, there are restrictions on the deductibility of non-Irish expenditure where a tax deduction is available in another jurisdiction. The implementation of this provision is subject to EU approval from a State Aid perspective.

***Substantial shareholdings relief*/**Finance Bill 2004 introduces an exemption from capital gains tax for Irish resident companies who dispose of substantial shareholdings in their trading subsidiaries, where the trading subsidiary is tax resident in an EU or tax treaty country. The availability of the relief is dependant on the percentage shareholding and the value of the shareholding. The implementation of this provision is subject to EU approval from a State Aid perspective.

## Group taxation

Members of a corporation tax group may group their operating losses against profits of corresponding accounting periods. However, in companies qualifying for the 10% rate of corporation tax, losses can be set off against profits of other group companies from the sale of manufactured goods to which the 10% rate of corporation tax applies, or against income taxable at other rates on a value basis.

Assets may be transferred between members of a capital gains tax group without liability for capital gains tax. While a group may be formed by including an EU resident company as part of the group, the relief is only available to Irish resident members of the group or on Irish trade assets. From February 15, 2001, a capital gains tax group has been extended to include an Irish branch of an EU resident company which is a member of the group.

## Tax incentives

***Inward investment*/**Companies carrying on manufacturing operations in Ireland are liable to a reduced rate of corporation tax of 10% on profits from manufacturing operations. For the purposes of the relief, certain services are deemed to be manufacturing activities, including the following: financial services for nonresidents within the IFSC, repairs to ships, certain activities conducted at Shannon Airport, certain design and planning services for particular foreign construction projects, fish farming and processing, computer services, the remanufacture or repair of computer equipment by the original manufacturer, data processing, shared services, call centers, plant micropropagation, repair or maintenance of aircraft, commercial production of films within the state, and meat processing. Where the qualifying activity began before July 23, 1998, or where an existing activity is expanded after this date, the activity will qualify for the 10% rate of corporation tax until December 31, 2010, afterwards being taxed at the standard rate of 12.5%. Where the qualifying activity began on or after July 23, 1998 the qualification for the 10% rate finished on December 31, 2002, with the activity being subject to corporation tax at the standard (12.5%) rate thereafter.

In the case of qualifying activities carried on in the Customs House Docks Area (IFSC) and Shannon Airport, the expiry date for the 10% rate of tax is December

# Ireland, Republic of

31, 2005. Quota restrictions agreed with the EU Commission have limited the number of new financial services companies and Shannon based companies that qualify for the 10% rate. In the case of IFSC projects approved after August 1, 1998 and Shannon projects approved after May 1, 1998, the 10% rate expired on December 31, 2002. After expiration of the 10% rate, these activities are subject to the 12.5% rate of corporation tax.

*Grants*/Cash grants may be available for capital expenditure on machinery and equipment and industrial premises, training of employees, creation of employment, rent subsidies, research and development, and so on. The level of grant aid depends on a number of factors and is specific to each project. Rates depend on the location of the new industry.

## Withholding taxes

Irish resident companies are required to withhold tax on certain types of payments as set out below.

| Recipient | Dividends | Interest | Patents, royalties |
|---|---|---|---|
| | % | % | % |
| Resident companies ............... | Nil | 20 | 20 |
| Resident individuals................ | 20 | 20 | 20 |
| Nonresident companies and individuals: | | | |
| Nontreaty countries ................ | 20 | 20 | 20 |

| Treaty countries: | Dividends (1) | Interest (2) | Patents, royalties |
|---|---|---|---|
| | % | % | % |
| Australia............................. | 15 | 10 | 10 |
| Austria ............................... | Nil (3)/15 | Nil | Nil/10(4) |
| Belgium ............................. | Nil (3)/15 | 15 | Nil |
| Bulgaria ............................. | 5(5)/10 | Nil (6)/5 | 10 |
| Canada***......................... | Nil (7)/15 | 15(8) | Nil (9) |
| China, P.R......................... | 5(5)/10 | Nil (6)/10 | 10(10)/10(11) |
| Croatia............................... | 5(17)/10 | Nil | 10 |
| Cyprus*............................. | Nil | Nil | Nil/5(12) |
| Czech Republic.................. | 5(5)/15 | Nil | 10 |
| Denmark............................ | Nil (3)(5)/15 | Nil | Nil |
| Estonia ............................. | 5(5)/15 | 10 | 5(11)/10 |
| Finland.............................. | Nil (3)(13)/15 | Nil | Nil |
| France*............................. | Nil (3)/10(14)/15 | Nil | Nil (15) |
| Germany............................ | Nil (3)/15(16) | Nil | Nil |
| Hungary............................. | 5(17)/15 | Nil | Nil |
| India.................................. | 10 | Nil (6)/10 | 10 |
| Israel................................. | 10 | 5(18)/10 | 10 |
| Italy................................... | Nil (3)/15 | 10 | Nil |
| Japan................................ | 10(5)/15 | 10 | 10 |
| Korea, Rep. of................... | 10(13)/15 | Nil | Nil |
| Latvia................................ | 5(5)/15 | 10 | 5(11)/10 |
| Lithuania........................... | 5(5)/15 | 10 | 5(11)/10 |

| Treaty countries: | Dividends (1) | Interest (2) | Patents, royalties |
|---|---|---|---|
| | % | % | % |
| Luxembourg.......................... | Nil (3)/5(5)/15 | Nil | Nil |
| Malaysia ............................. | 10 | Nil (6)/10 | 8 |
| Mexico ............................... | 5(13)/10 | Nil (6)/5(19)/10 | 10 |
| Netherlands ........................ | Nil (3)(5)/15 | Nil | Nil |
| New Zealand........................ | 15 | 10 | 10 |
| Norway ............................... | 5(13)/15/ Nil (19) | Nil | Nil |
| Pakistan.............................. | 15/ Nil – 35(20) | No Limit | Nil |
| Poland ................................ | Nil (5)/15 | Nil (18)/10 | 10 |
| Portugal .............................. | Nil (3)/15 | Nil (6)/15 | 10 |
| Romania ............................. | 3 | Nil (18)/3 | 3 |
| Russia ................................ | 10 | Nil | Nil |
| Slovak Republic .................. | Nil (5)/10 | Nil | Nil/10(10) |
| Slovenia.............................. | 5(5)/15 | Nil (6)/5 | 5 |
| South Africa........................ | Nil | Nil | Nil |
| Spain .................................. | Nil (3)(5)/15 | Nil | 5(21)/8(22)/10 |
| Sweden............................... | Nil (3)/5(13)/15 | Nil | Nil |
| Switzerland ......................... | 5(5)/15 | Nil | Nil |
| United Kingdom .................. | Nil (3)/5(13)/15 | Nil | Nil |
| United States ...................... | 5(13)/15 | Nil | Nil |
| Zambia ............................... | Nil | Nil | Nil |

Ireland is currently negotiating treaties with the following countries.

| Argentina | Egypt** | Greece*** |
|---|---|---|
| Iceland*** | Malta** | Singapore** |
| Turkey | Ukraine | |

*These treaties are currently under renegotiation.

**These treaties are due to be signed in 2004.

***These treaties have been signed but are not yet in force.

The numbers in parentheses refer to the following numbered Notes.

Notes:

1. Ireland imposes withholding tax on distributions since April 6, 1999. As discussed earlier, companies resident in countries with which Ireland has a tax treaty may be able to qualify for exemption from withholding tax.

2. Certain financial institutions are obliged to withhold tax (Deposit Interest Retention Tax (DIRT)) at the standard rate of Irish tax (currently 20%) out of interest paid or credited on deposit accounts in the beneficial ownership of companies resident in the state, unless the financial institution is authorized to pay the interest gross. There is no DIRT on interest paid to nonresidents where a written declaration of nonresidence is completed. Certain annual interest payments are subject to withholding tax at 20%. No withholding tax applies to interest paid by an IFSC or Shannon 10% company, where the interest is paid in the course of trading operations.

3. Per EU Parent-Subsidiary Directive (5% holding).

4. Where the Irish resident recipient holds more than 50% of the share capital of the payer company.

5. Where the beneficial owner of the dividends is a resident of Ireland, the tax so charged shall not exceed this amount, if the beneficial owner is a company

which holds directly at least 25% of the capital of the company paying the dividends.

6. Certain government loans, and in the case of Mexico, certain pension funds.

7. Intercompany rate—100% holding (see Canada/Ireland treaty for other conditions).

8. From Ireland—domestic standard rate applies.

9. Copyright royalties and other like payments made in respect of the production or reproduction of any literary, dramatic, musical, or artistic work (but not including rents or royalties in respect of motion picture films and films or videotapes for use in connection with television)—otherwise domestic rate will apply.

10. For technical royalties or for information concerning industrial, commercial, or scientific experience.

11. For use of industrial, scientific, or commercial equipment. In the case of China, the rate is 10% of the adjusted amount of the royalties—adjusted amount means 60% of the gross amount of the royalties.

12. For films (not TV).

13. Where the beneficial owner of the dividends is a resident of Ireland, the tax so charged shall not exceed this amount, if the beneficial owner is a company which controls directly or indirectly 10% or more of the voting power in the company paying the dividends.

14. Where the beneficial owner of the dividends is a resident of Ireland the tax so charged shall not exceed this amount, if the beneficial owner is a company which has held for a year in its own name shares or *parts d'interet* representing 50% of the capital of the company paying the dividends.

15. Excluding films—domestic rate applies (see France/Ireland double taxation treaty).

16. Subject to variation (see Germany/Ireland double taxation treaty).

17. Where the recipient of the dividends is a beneficial owner of the dividends the tax so charged shall not exceed this percentage of the gross dividends if the beneficial owner holds directly at least 10% of the capital or voting power of the company paying the dividends.

18. Certain credit sales and bank interest and in the case of Romania any loan of whatever kind made for two years or more and any debt-claim guaranteed, insured or financed by the government of either contracting state.

19. For loans from banks and in the case of Norway, certain government funds.

20. For an Irish individual recipient (not engaged in trade or business through a permanent establishment) the withholding tax rate is the Pakistani tax rate (currently graduated scale to a top rate of 35%) which would have applied if the person were a Pakistani resident subject to tax on the person's world income.

21. Literary, dramatic, musical or artistic copyrights.

22. Films, tapes, and lease payments.

The above details are in general subject to any special relationship that may exist between the payer and the recipient, and it is assumed that the recipient does not have a permanent establishment (taxable presence) in Ireland.

## Tax administration

*Returns*/Corporation tax returns must be submitted within nine months* of the end of the accounting period for tax purposes in order to avoid a surcharge (maximum of €63,485) or a restriction of 50% of losses claimed, to a maximum of €158,715. The tax accounting period normally coincides with a company's financial accounting period, except where the latter period exceeds 12 months.

A system of self-assessment and revenue audits has been in operation since 1990.

For accounting periods ending in 2002 and onward, a current year tax payment regime has been introduced. This current year regime is being phased in over five years. Under the new system the first preliminary tax installment is payable one month* before the end of the company's accounting period. The second installment of preliminary tax is payable six months* after the end of the accounting period. Both installments must total 90% of the total tax due. For accounting periods ending on or after January 1, 2003 the final balance of tax is due nine months* after the end of the accounting period under the new "pay and file" system.

*From June 2002, all corporation tax installments must be paid by the 21st day of the month, where it would otherwise be due on a day later than the 21st in that month.

## *CORPORATION TAX CALCULATION*

### Distribution Company

Accounts for the year ending December 31, 2004

| | | |
|---|---:|---:|
| Profits before tax as shown in the accounts.............................................. | | € 1,000,000 |
| Add: | | |
| Depreciation ........................................................................ | 130,000 | |
| Other disallowable items ...................................................... | 10,000 | 140,000 |
| | | 1,140,000 |
| Less: | | |
| Capital gains........................................................................ | 45,000 | |
| Dividends received from Irish companies (1)........................ | 20,000 | 65,000 |
| | | 1,075,000 |
| Less: | | |
| Capital allowances .............................................................. | | 120,000 |
| Adjusted trading profit ............................................................... | | 955,000 |
| Capital gain (2, 3) | | |
| (28,500 x 20% x 100/12.5) ................................................... | | 45,600 |
| Total profits liable to corporate tax............................................. | | 1,000,600 |
| Corporation tax liability: | | |
| 1,000,600 at 12.5% ............................................................. | | 125,075 |
| Payable—Nov 21, 2003 (54%)................................................. | € | 67,541 |
| Payable—June 21, 2004 (36%)................................................ | € | 45,027 |
| Payable—September 21, 2004 (10% Balance) ......................... | € | 12,507 |

Notes:

1.  Corporation tax is not charged on dividend income received by an Irish resident company from another Irish resident company. Such income is exempt.
2.  The gain is calculated under capital gains tax rules.
3.  The capital gains tax rate is 20%. The gain of €28,500 must be adjusted to give an effective rate of 20% when the gain is taxed at the corporation tax rate of 12.5%.
4.  It is assumed that the above company is not a close company.
5.  The fixed exchange rate of the Euro at January 1, 2004: US$1 = € 0.793903.

## PwC contact

For additional information on taxation in the Isle of Man, contact:

David Churcher
PricewaterhouseCoopers
Sixty Circular Road
Douglas, Isle of Man
Telephone: (44) (1624) 689689
Fax: (44) (1624) 689690
e-mail: david.churcher@iom.pwc.com

## Significant developments

The Isle of Man government has previously stated its intention to reduce the rate of corporate tax to 0% for all companies by December 31, 2005. The exception to this will be that profits from banking activities will be taxed at 10%. The profits of certain insurance, shipping, fund management and administration, and aircraft operations are already taxed at 0%. In February 2004 the Isle of Man government extended the zero rating to approved activities in the space and satellite industry.

## Taxes on corporate income

*General rate*/Corporations pay income tax at the prevailing higher rate of 18%, although trading companies are taxed at 10% on the first £100 million of trading profits, and 15% thereafter. There is no corporation tax separate from income tax.

*Exempt companies*/If registered under the Isle of Man Companies Act, a company, regardless of whether or not incorporated in the Isle of Man, may claim exemption from Isle of Man income tax if it meets the following conditions.

1. It has at least one resident director and a resident and qualified company secretary.
2. It is owned by nonresidents.
3. It derives its income from business activities outside the Island, apart from money invested with the Isle of Man government and licensed banks.

The company cannot be the holder of a banking license under the Banking Act 1998, or be an insurance company within the meaning of the Exempt Insurance Company Act 1981. Regulations also prescribe that exempt companies cannot undertake certain activities such as manufacturing, retail or wholesale activities, exploration of natural resources, distribution and transportation in the Island, and the provision of trustee, custodian, corporate, and legal and professional services.

Application for exemption should be made before June 30 in the year of assessment, or within 30 days of the commencement of business for a new business. The fee is £450 per annum.

Exempt companies are excluded from obtaining relief under the provisions of the Isle of Man–United Kingdom tax treaty.

*International business companies*/A company registered under the Isle of Man Companies Act, whether it is incorporated in the Isle of Man or outside, may claim to pay Manx income tax at a negotiated rate (not exceeding 35%), subject to a minimum tax charge of £1,200 (£2,000 in respect of an insurance company), provided it meets the following conditions.

1. The company has at least one resident director and a resident and qualified secretary.
2. The company is owned by nonresidents.
3. The company derives its income from business activities outside the Island or from dealings with other international companies, apart from monies invested with the Isle of Man government and licensed banks.

The company cannot be a holder of a banking license or an investment business license.

*International limited liability companies*/A member of an international limited liability company (ILLC) is not subject to income tax in respect of income arising from that company, provided it meets the following conditions.

1. No member may be resident on the Island.
2. With limited exceptions, no resident on the Island may have an interest in the company.
3. Income must arise outside the Island from activities carried on outside the Island.
4. A registered office must be maintained on the Island.
5. A registered and qualified agent must be maintained on the Island.

Applications must be made annually, and a fee of £450 is payable with each application.

*International limited partnerships*/A limited partner in an international limited partnership is not subject to income tax in respect of income received from that partnership as long as the partnership has been granted a "certificate of status" as an international limited partnership. Applications must be made annually and a fee of £450 is payable with each application.

*Insurance companies*/Profits are taxed at 0%.

*Shipping and aircraft operators*/Profits are taxed at 0%.

*Managed banks*/Tax exemptions are available for certain managed banks. Exemption is granted on application to the Treasury through the Financial Supervision Commission. The Treasury must be satisfied that the managed bank does not transact any banking business with any person resident in the Isle of Man other than another bank. The bank must hold a banking license under the Banking Act 1998, and be managed by a licensed domestic bank in the Isle of Man. Offshore banking (managed bank) licenses are either restricted or unrestricted, depending on the proposed nature of the business of the bank. Fees for tax exemption through an unrestricted license are £37,500 per annum, with an initial fee of £5,000. For a restricted license the fee is £25,000 per annum, with an initial fee of £3,500.

*Space and satellite industry*/Profits of approved activities are taxed at 0%.

*Fund managers and fund administrators*/Administration and management of certain collective investment scheme profits are taxed at 0%.

*International loan business*/A special deduction of up to 80% of taxable income is available by concession for international loan business undertaken by banks in the Isle of Man. The deduction is available to subsidiaries or branches of nonresident parent companies.

*Nonresident companies*/Since April 1999, it has not been possible to make new nonresident declarations. Existing nonresident companies are likely to be phased out, but until then an annual duty of £1,000 is payable to the Registrar of Companies.

## Corporate residence

A company is considered to be resident in the place where "central management and control actually abides." This is generally interpreted as being the place where the board of directors meets. Unless a nonresident declaration was made before April 1999, all companies incorporated in the Isle of Man are deemed to be resident.

## Other taxes

There are no other corporate taxes.

VAT and customs and excise duties are levied and are similar to those in the United Kingdom.

## Branch income

The trading profits of branches are taxed in the same way as other corporate income at a rate of 10%. No further tax is withheld on the transfer of profits abroad.

## Income determination

*Inventory valuation*/Inventories are generally stated at the lower of cost or market value. Any method of valuation that is in accord with sound commercial principles is acceptable for tax purposes, provided it is adopted consistently at the beginning and end of the accounting period and does not conflict with tax law. In practice, inventories are normally valued for tax purposes at the lower of cost or net realizable value. A FIFO basis of determining cost where items cannot be identified is acceptable, but not the base stock method or the LIFO method.

In general, the book and tax methods of inventory valuation will conform.

*Capital gains*/Capital gains are exempt from tax.

*Intercompany dividends*/Dividends received by one Isle of Man company from another, whether subsidiary or not, are taxable in the recipient's hands. Dividends are paid gross to recipients within the Island and are deductible from the payer's taxable profits.

*Foreign income*/Resident corporations are liable to tax on their worldwide income. United Kingdom tax is relieved under the treaty with the United Kingdom by way of tax credits. However, the treaty does not cover dividends or debenture interest. The Isle of Man grants unilateral relief from double taxation in respect of all foreign-source income arising outside the United Kingdom by way of tax credit.

*Stock dividends*/Stock dividends are permitted and are usually treated as income of the recipient.

*Other significant items*/None.

# Isle of Man

## Deductions

*Depreciation and depletion*/Depreciation is generally calculated by the reducing-balance method. Plant and machinery, tourist premises, industrial buildings, commercial buildings within a designated area, fish processing buildings, and agricultural buildings and works have an initial allowance of 100%.

An additional special allowance is available for approved capital expenditure incurred on tourist premises. It is equal to 250% of the allowable capital expenditure and is given over four years.

Plant and machinery can have an initial allowance of 100% if the taxpayer so wishes. If a smaller initial percentage is taken, 25% of the written-down value is allowed for subsequent years. There are restrictions on allowances for expensive motorcars.

Isle of Man government grants are not taken into account in determining the amount of expenditure on which allowances may be given.

Tax depreciation is not required to conform with book depreciation.

Upon disposal, allowances will be reclaimed on the resale value.

*Net operating losses*/A claim is necessary for losses to be relieved against other income assessable in the year of the loss and/or the subsequent year. Losses can be carried forward indefinitely against further profits from the trade.

A trading loss incurred in the first four years of assessment of the trade may be carried back to the preceding three years against the claimant's other income, earlier years first. Terminal losses in the last year of trade can be carried back against profits for the previous three years of trading.

*Payments to foreign affiliates*/The Manx authorities can require deduction of income tax from any payments of taxable income to persons resident overseas.

*Taxes*/No taxes are deductible, other than the nonresident company duty (see above).

*Other significant items*/By extra statutory concession, management expenses of a public investment company resident in the Island are deductible. Any excess of expenses may be carried forward.

Corporations resident in the Isle of Man are not subject to income tax on so much of their income as is distributed to shareholders by way of dividend, bonus, interest, or share in profits.

## Group taxation

Trading losses, excess capital allowances and distributions exceeding profits can be offset (subject to certain restrictions) between 75% affiliates resident in the Isle of Man. Similar concessions are available to members of a consortium, but only a fraction of the loss or excess may be set off, that fraction being equal to the members' share in the consortium in the relevant year of assessment.

## Tax incentives

*Inward investment*/It is the policy of the Manx government to promote the continuing growth and diversification of the industrial sector and those export businesses in the service sector. To this end, both established and new companies may apply for the granting of a tax-free period for a maximum of five years. This may include an exemption in respect of distribution of income and profit to shareholders resident outside the Island from liability to Manx income tax. Grants are available for certain operating costs, including training and marketing.

*Film industry*/The Isle of Man government has created the Isle of Man Film Commission with the stated objective of creating a film industry on the Island. Incentives have been offered to make it attractive to invest in film productions carried out in the Isle of Man. The incentive offers up to 25% of the budget as a direct equity investment, with no upper or lower limits. Additionally, projects may qualify for production/credit grants of up to US$350,000 subject to approval on a purely discretionary basis.

*Capital investment*/See "Depreciation and depletion" for tax incentives. Capital grants of up to 40% of costs of new buildings, building improvements, and new plant and machinery are also available from the Manx government.

*Other incentives*/See "Exempt companies," "International business companies," "Managed banks," "Fund managers and fund administrators," and "International loan business."

There is no withholding tax on dividends paid to Manx residents. Tax is withheld at the prevailing higher rate (18%) on payments to nonresidents, whether corporate or individual recipients. In the cases of an exempt company, an international business company, a nonresident company, or a company which pays tax at 0% there is no withholding tax for nonresidents.

Payments of an income nature, other than dividends, made to nonresident individuals or corporations may be subject to income tax at the prevailing higher rate (18%) at the direction of the Assessor of Income Tax.

*Tax treaties*/No withholding rates are specified in the tax treaty with the United Kingdom (see above for current rates). The Isle of Man has entered into no other treaties apart from an arrangement with the United States regarding the international operation of ships, and it does not participate in the U.K. treaty network by convention. The Isle of Man entered into a tax exchange of information agreement with the United States in 2002, and is expected to enter into further agreements in due course.

## Tax administration

*Returns*/The tax year runs from April 6 to April 5. A return is made to the tax authorities, who then issue an assessment.

*Payment*/Payment is due on or before January 1 for income arising in the preceding financial year.

# Isle of Man

## *CORPORATE TAX CALCULATION*

Tax year 2004–2005

| | | |
|---|---:|---:|
| Net profit per profit and loss account for the year before tax and appropriations of profit ........................................... | | £ 1,000,000 |
| Add—Capital and other expenditure debited in the profit and loss account not allowable for income tax purposes: | | |
|     Depreciation of fixed assets ............................................... | 200,000 | |
|     Loss on sale of fixed assets ............................................... | 90,000 | |
|     Legal or professional fees re: acquisition/disposal of fixed assets ................................................................ | 5,000 | |
|     Provision for bad debts (general) ...................................... | 15,000 | 310,000 |
| | | 1,310,000 |
| Less—Capital receipts and other items credited in the profit and loss account not liable to income tax: | | |
|     Profit on sale of fixed assets ............................................. | 50,000 | |
|     Reserves written back....................................................... | 12,000 | |
|     Provisions written back ..................................................... | 13,000 | 75,000 |
| | | 1,235,000 |
| Add—Income received (or receivable) not credited in the profit and loss account: | | |
|     Loan interest received credited in the appropriation account ................................................... | | 15,000 |
| | | 1,250,000 |
| Less—Charges or allowances not debited in the profit and loss account: | | |
|     Bad debts written off to provision (general)........................ | | 10,000 |
| Assessable trading profit ........................................................ | | £ 1,240,000 |
| Taxable income and income tax liability are calculated as follows: | | |
|     Assessable trading profit ..................................................... | | £ 1,240,000 |
|     Less—Capital allowances..................................................... | | 340,000 |
|     Total income ........................................................................ | | 900,000 |
|     Less—Dividends paid and proposed..................................... | | 250,000 |
| Taxable income .................................................................... | | £   650,000 |
| Tax payable—650,000 at 10% ................................................ | | £    65,000 |
| Total tax payable .................................................................. | | £    65,000 |

Note:

Exchange rate of the pound sterling at January 1, 2004: US$1 = £0.5602.

## PwC contacts

For additional information on taxation in Israel, contact:

Gerry Seligman
Shlomi Zehavi
Vered Kirshner
PricewaterhouseCoopers
Kesselman & Kesselman
Trade Tower, 25 Hamered Street
Tel-Aviv 68125 Israel
Mail address: P.O. Box 452
                    Tel-Aviv 61003 Israel
Telephone: (972) (3) 795 45 55
Fax: (972) (3) 795 45 56
e-mail: gerry.seligman@il.pwc.com
         shlomi.zehavi@il.pwc.com
         vered.kirshner@il.pwc.com

## Significant developments

The Israeli Tax Reform legislation, with effect from January 1, 2003, now incorporates into the Income Tax Ordinance (ITO) transfer pricing provisions, and includes the arm's length principle which applies to any international transaction in which there is a special relationship between the parties of the transaction, and a price was settled on for property, a right, a service, or credit.

The transfer pricing provisions of the legislation are subject to the formulation of rules and regulations that are yet to be formally issued by the Ministry of Finance. It is anticipated that these regulations will be issued during 2004, and will be based upon internationally recognized transfer pricing principles. Companies with international transactions will need to carefully monitor this developing subject matter.

Effective March 1, 2004, the standard rate of value-added tax (VAT) has been reduced from 18% to 17% (which had been the effective rate prior to June 15, 2002).

## Taxes on corporate income

Company tax of 36% is levied on corporations. Approved enterprises (see below) are subject to reduced rates of tax according to the level of foreign ownership. As of January 1, 2003, Israeli corporations are subject to tax on their worldwide income. Foreign corporations are subject to Israeli tax to the extent of their income from Israeli sources. Income sourcing rules determine when income is to be considered from an Israeli source.

There are no local taxes on corporate income.

## Corporate residence

The following are considered to be resident in Israel.
1. A company incorporated in Israel.
2. A company whose business is controlled and managed from Israel.

# Israel

There are no published guidelines from the tax authorities that describe the type of activities of a preparatory or auxiliary nature that generally would qualify as being those of a representative office, and that would consequently be exempt from Israeli taxation. Such exemption may be available under an applicable tax treaty.

As of January 1, 2003, a "foreign vocation" company may be deemed to be managed and controlled in Israel to the extent of its income from a "special vocation." A "foreign vocation" company is an entity controlled (75% or more) directly or indirectly by Israeli resident individuals, most of the income of which is generated from the conduct of a special vocation conducted by the Israeli resident shareholders. A "special vocation" has been defined in regulations, and includes an extensive variety of vocations, such as law, accountancy, business management, telecommunications, scientific research, engineering, and so on.

## Other taxes

*Value-added tax*/The rate of VAT was reduced effective March 1, 2004 from 18% to 17%. Exports of goods and certain services and various other transactions are zero-rated, and certain transactions are exempt. Banks and other financial institutions pay VAT-equivalent taxes at the rate of 17%, based on their total payroll and on profits. Not-for-profit organizations pay VAT (wage tax) at the rate of 8.5% of their total payroll.

*Land appreciation tax*/Capital gains on real estate are subject to the Land Appreciation Tax Law. The law relates to any real estate in Israel, including houses, buildings and anything permanently fixed to land, real estate rights, and leases for 25 years or more. Tax calculations closely follow the calculation of company tax on capital gains (see below). The tax rate on the real gain is reduced from 36% to 25% on assets purchased after November 7, 2001. Regarding assets purchased prior to November 7, 2001, the reduced tax rate will be applicable only to the gain accumulated after November 7, 2001. The gain will be attributed to the period commencing on November 7, 2001 according to the ratio of the holding period after this date to the entire holding period. Other beneficial provisions apply to the sale of real estate between November 7, 2001 and December 31, 2003.

*Acquisition tax*/The purchaser of real estate is subject to acquisition tax at rates of 0.5% up to a maximum of 5%.

*Sales tax*/Sales tax at the rate of 2.5% is applicable to the sale of most real estate rights. The sales tax does not apply to certain types of apartments, which are classified as inventory. Sales tax will not apply to sales of real estate purchased after November 7, 2001. Certain other exemptions will be available.

## Branch income

Tax rates on branch profits are the same as on corporate profits. No tax is withheld on transfers of profits to the foreign head office unless the branch is an approved enterprise (see below). A branch is liable to tax at the standard corporate rate on Israel-source income and capital gains.

## Income determination

*Inventory valuation*/Inventories are generally valued at lower of cost or market value (net realizable value). Conformity is required between book and tax reporting of inventory.

A FIFO or weighted-average basis of valuation is acceptable; LIFO is not.

*Capital gains*/Capital gains tax is generally payable on capital gains by residents of Israel on the sale of assets (irrespective of the location of the assets) and by nonresidents on the sale of the following.

- Assets located in Israel.
- Assets located abroad that are essentially a direct or indirect right to an asset, or to inventory or that are an indirect right to a real estate right or to an asset in a real estate association located in Israel. Taxation will apply only in respect of that part of the consideration that stems from the above property located in Israel.
- Assets that are a share or the right to a share in an Israeli entity.
- Assets that are a right in a foreign resident entity, which is essentially a direct or indirect right to property located in Israel. Taxation will apply only with respect to that part of the consideration that stems from the property located in Israel.

Capital gains realized by a nonresident from the sale of assets may qualify for treaty exemption depending upon the particular circumstances and the provisions of the applicable treaty. When assets are attributable to an Israeli permanent establishment or are real estate rights, treaty exemption will generally not be available.

Company tax on capital gains is imposed on the disposal of fixed and intangible assets where the disposal price is in excess of the depreciated cost.

For tax purposes, the capital gain is generally calculated in local currency, and there are provisions for segregating the taxable gain into its real and inflationary components. The inflationary amount is the original cost of the asset less depreciation (where applicable), multiplied by the percentage increase in the Israeli consumer price index (CPI) from the date of acquisition of the asset to the date of its sale. This inflationary amount component is exempt to the extent it accrued after January 1, 1994 and is generally subject to tax at the rate of 10% if it accrued before then. A nonresident that invests in taxable assets with foreign currency may elect to calculate the inflationary amount in that foreign currency. Under this option, in the event of a sale of shares in an Israeli company the inflationary amount attributable to exchange differences on the investment is always exempt from Israeli tax.

The "real gain," if any, accrued at the sale of an asset purchased on or after January 1, 2003 is generally taxed at a rate of 25%, as opposed to the previous 36% rate applicable to corporations with respect to sales transactions effected prior to January 1, 2003. Real gains derived from the disposal after January 1, 2003 of an asset purchased prior to this date will be subject to capital gains tax at a blended rate. The previous capital gains tax rate (36%) will be applied to the gain amount which bears the same ratio to the total gain realized as the ratio which the holding period commencing at the acquisition date and terminating on January 1, 2003 bears to the total holding period. The remainder of the gain realized will be subject to capital gains tax at the 25% rate.

Special rates apply to assets purchased prior to April 1, 1961. With effect from the beginning of 2005, these special tax rates will be increased by 1% in each tax year until the tax rate on the real gain reaches the new statutory rate of 25%.

In the case of a disposal of nontraded shares and of shares by corporations that are not subject to Section 6 of the Income Tax Law (Inflationary Adjustments) (see below), special provisions would apply to such part of the "real gain" which is attributed to the seller's share of retained profits. Generally, the seller's proportionate part of retained profits will be taxed as if this amount had been received as dividends immediately before the sale (i.e., at a general rate of 0%, similar to a dividend from an Israeli corporation which arises from Israeli-sourced income which is not subject to tax in the hands of an Israeli recipient corporation). However, the proportionate part of the retained profits that is attributable to the period up to December 31, 2002 will be subject to tax at the rate of 10%. The share of retained profits is the amount of gain equal to the proportional part of the retained profits of the company that the seller of the shares would have rights to by virtue of those shares. Profits for this purpose are generally defined as financial statement profits available for distribution that accumulated over the period from the end of the tax year prior to the year of acquisition of the shares to the end of the tax year prior to the year of sale on condition that such profits that accrued prior to January 1, 1996 shall not be taken into account for these purposes. An increase within the two years preceding the sale of the part of the seller's right to such profits shall similarly not be taken into account. The amount of the profits is not to exceed the amount of income taxed in the above-mentioned period, less the taxes thereon, any dividend distributed therefrom and losses that have accumulated in the company that have not been offset, with the addition of tax-exempt income.

Under an amendment to the Income Tax Law (Inflationary Adjustments), effective January 1, 1999, corporate investors that hold securities (other than corporations owned only by individuals that did not deduct interest expenses) are generally subject to the provisions of the Income Tax Law (Inflationary Adjustments) and are liable to tax at the rate of 36% on the sale of quoted securities. There is a comprehensive set of rules for determining the gains and losses from the sale of listed securities.

As of January 1, 2003, individuals and corporations that are not subject to Section 6 of the Income Tax Law (Inflationary Adjustments) are taxed on capital gains from the sale of securities traded on a stock exchange, including the Tel-Aviv Stock Exchange (TASE). The tax rate will generally be 15% provided the corporation has not claimed a deduction of interest expenses with regard to the securities in question. However, gains generated from the sale of "foreign securities" (most securities of non-Israeli corporations unless traded on the TASE) between January 1, 2003 and December 31, 2006 will be taxed at the rate of 35%.

An Israeli capital gains tax exemption is available to foreign residents, irrespective of whether or not the foreign resident is a resident of a country with which Israel has concluded a treaty for the avoidance of double taxation upon the disposal of an interest in a "research and development (R&D) intensive company" (as defined by Israeli tax regulations) where such interest was acquired through an allotment of shares as from 2003. Where the investment by a nonresident took the form of a stock purchase in an R&D intensive company (or in a regular company) the availability of a capital gains tax exemption would be determined under the provisions of an applicable tax treaty.

Non-Israeli residents are generally exempt from capital gains tax on the sale of shares traded on an Israeli stock exchange, as well as on the sale of stock of Israeli corporations traded on stock exchanges outside of Israel, under certain circumstances, unless the gain is attributable to a permanent establishment of the nonresident in Israel.

The cashless transfer of rights and assets arising from certain mergers, spin-offs, and asset transfers may be exempt from tax upon meeting various requirements.

*Exit tax*/Under the new exit tax provisions introduced by the tax reform legislation, both individuals and companies that cease to be Israeli tax residents are deemed to have disposed of all of their capital assets on the day immediately preceding their exit date, and are consequently subject to capital gains tax. This is primarily applicable to individuals, but might also apply to corporations incorporated outside of Israel whose management and control is transferred from Israel to another jurisdiction at a particular time. The taxation is generally deferred until the actual sale of the assets. Exemptions from the exit tax provisions are available for certain capital assets under the provisions of the law.

*Intercompany dividends*/Dividends received by an Israel-resident company from another Israeli-resident company which originate from income accrued or derived in Israel are exempt from company tax, except for dividends paid from income of an approved enterprise (see "Tax incentives"). Dividends received from an Israeli company which arise from foreign source income of the distributing company as well as dividends received by an Israeli company from a nonresident company are generally taxable to the receiving company at the rate of 25%. Under certain circumstances the receiving company may elect to be taxed on such dividends at the rate of 36% in which case it would also be entitled to a foreign tax credit with respect to corporate taxes paid by the company distributing the dividend, that is, an "underlying" tax credit.

*Foreign income*/As of January 1, 2003, an Israeli-resident company is liable to tax on its worldwide income. Double taxation is avoided by way of a foreign tax credit mechanism that applies unilaterally in the absence of an applicable double taxation treaty. The foreign tax credit is limited to the Israeli corporate tax payable with respect to the same income. Foreign sourced income is divided into categories ("baskets") on the basis of the income source, for example, dividends, business income, and so on, and a particular credit limitation applies to each basket. Excess uncredited foreign income can be carried forward for the subsequent five tax years.

Dividends are generally taxed when received. However, under the controlled foreign corporation (CFC) regime introduced by the tax reform legislation, an Israeli company or individual may be taxed on a proportion of the undistributed profits of certain Israeli-controlled nonresident companies in which the Israeli shareholder has a controlling interest (10% or more of any of the CFC's "means of control"). A CFC is a company to which a number of cumulative conditions apply. These include the fact that most of its income or profits in the tax year derive from passive sources and such passive income has been subject to an effective tax rate that does not exceed 20%.

*Stock dividends*/Stock dividends (bonus shares) do not give rise to any tax liability.

## Deductions

*Depreciation and depletion*/Rates of depreciation are determined by statute. Allowances are not permitted on land. Under recently enacted regulations, the depreciation of goodwill purchased after July 1, 2003 is allowed. Industrial enterprises are entitled to higher rates of depreciation. Higher rates of depreciation are permitted for equipment utilized on more than one shift. Depreciation for tax purposes is generally calculated on a straight-line basis, although the declining-balance method is allowed for certain industrial equipment.

Accelerated depreciation has been allowed in certain circumstances. Gains on the sale of fixed assets are subject to capital gains tax.

*Net operating losses*/Business losses can be set off against income from any source in the same year. Loss carrybacks are not allowed. Losses may be carried forward (generally linked to the CPI) and set off without time limit against income from any trade or business or capital gains arising in the business, but not against income from any other source.

Capital losses may offset capital gains realized by the taxpayer in the current year. Capital losses generated in 1996 and onward can be carried forward indefinitely. In a sale of shares by a corporation, the capital losses from the sale of shares are generally reduced by any dividends received by the selling corporation during the 24 months preceding the sale. Special rules have been introduced with respect to the offset of foreign sourced losses. Generally, foreign source losses can be offset against foreign sourced income from the same sources. Foreign sourced capital losses must first be offset against foreign sourced capital gains and may thereafter be offset against Israeli sourced capital gains.

*Payments to foreign affiliates*/Payments of interest, royalties, and management fees to foreign affiliates are deductible if based on normal commercial terms and practices, and preferably evidenced by an intercompany agreement. Where such payments attract withholding tax, the deduction will only be allowed where such tax has been withheld and paid in accordance with certain requirements. Transfer pricing provisions have been introduced and will become effective pending the publication of applicable regulations. Under the newly introduced legislative provisions, all cross border payments to foreign affiliates for goods and services have to comply with arm's length pricing standards.

*Other taxes*/Profits tax and payroll tax (under the Value-Added Tax Law) paid by banks and other financial institutions are allowable as a deductible expense.

*Other significant items*/Tax law includes provisions to neutralize the erosion of capital invested in a business, and conversely to prevent benefits emanating from the deduction of inflationary financial expenses for tax purposes. This is achieved by applying a supplementary set of inflationary adjustments to the normal taxable profit computed under regular historical cost principles.

The Income Tax Law (Inflationary Adjustments) 1985 introduced a special tax adjustment for the preservation of equity based on changes in the consumer price index (CPI), whereby certain corporate assets are classified broadly into fixed (inflation-resistant) assets and nonfixed assets. Where the shareholders' equity exceeds the depreciated cost of fixed assets, a tax deduction that takes into account the effect of the annual rate of inflation on such excess is allowed (up to a ceiling of 70% of the taxable income for companies in any single year, with the unused portion carried forward to the subsequent tax year on a linked basis without limit). If the depreciated cost of such fixed assets exceeds shareholders' equity, then the excess, multiplied by the annual inflation rate, is added to taxable income. In addition, subject to certain limitations, depreciation of fixed assets and losses carried forward are adjusted for inflation on the basis of changes in the CPI.

The provisions of the law apply mainly to corporate entities and to individuals who are required to maintain their books and records in accordance with the double-entry method. For other taxpayers a simplified method is available. Some companies that fulfill certain conditions of the law are entitled to submit Israeli tax returns based on books of accounts maintained in U.S. dollars, or to adjust their taxable income on the basis of changes in the exchange rate of the U.S. dollar vis-à-vis the shekel. Such election is binding for three years.

## Group taxation

*Consolidated tax returns*/As a general rule, a parent company and its subsidiaries may not submit consolidated tax returns. Only groups of industrial companies in the same line of business, as well as parent companies that control industrial companies in the same line of business and have at least 80% of their assets invested in industrial companies, are eligible to file consolidated tax returns.

## Transparent corporations

*Transparent corporations*/The tax reform legislation has introduced a new type of "hybrid" corporation known as a "transparent company." A transparent company constitutes a corporation for corporate law purposes, whereas it is transparent for tax purposes. This company must be an Israeli corporation that is wholly owned by up to a maximum of 50 Israeli resident individual shareholders.

The transparent company provisions will become effective upon introduction of relevant regulations.

## Tax incentives

*Inward investment*/"Approved enterprise" status, which provides for cash and tax benefits, may be granted to enterprises that increase the productive capacity of the economy, improve the balance of payments or provide new employment opportunities. The status is granted mainly to manufacturing and tourism enterprises. Approved enterprises with significant foreign investment are entitled to increased benefits (see "Capital investment").

A general condition for approval is that a minimum of 30% of the investment in fixed assets must be equity financed.

*Capital investment*/Approved enterprises are entitled to cash grants of up to 24% of the amount of the investment for purchases of fixed assets in specified areas of the country.

## Reduced tax rates

*General*/Companies enjoy reduced tax rates on income derived from an approved enterprise. The reduced tax rates are generally applicable for a seven-year benefit period (or a ten-year period in the case of a foreign investors company; see below), commencing with the year in which the approved enterprise first generates taxable income. Generally this period of benefits cannot extend beyond 12 years from the year the enterprise commenced its operations, or 14 years from the year in which the approval of its status as an approved enterprise was granted, whichever is earlier. These limits may be extended in special cases.

*Locally owned companies*/Income derived by a company from an approved enterprise during the seven-year period of benefits is generally subject to company

# Israel

tax at a rate of 25%. Lower rates may be applicable to a "foreign investors' company," as discussed below. An approved enterprise located in Development Area A is entitled to a tax holiday from company tax regarding its undistributed income derived in the initial two years (for enterprises approved after January 1, 1997).

A reduced withholding tax rate of 15% applies to dividends paid by an Israeli company from profits of an approved enterprise earned during the benefits period noted above if distributed either during the benefits period or during the 12 following years.

Consequently, the effective overall rate of Israeli tax on profits earned by an approved enterprise during the period of benefits will generally be 25% if retained by the company, or 36.25% if distributed to a shareholder. Foreign shareholders resident in certain tax-treaty countries may sometimes, depending on the treaty provisions, enjoy a lower withholding tax rate on dividends.

Special rules govern the allocation of taxable income of "mixed enterprises." These are essentially entities that derive only part of their income from an approved enterprise or that operate under a number of approvals relating to separate investment projects. The company tax payable in respect of income from each part of a mixed enterprise is separately computed, and a composite withholding tax rate is applicable to dividends distributed by a mixed enterprise.

***Foreign investors' companies—Israeli incorporated company***/An Israeli incorporated company that qualifies as a foreign investors' company (FIC) is entitled to enhanced tax benefits on approved enterprise income. In general, a FIC is a company, of which more than 25% of its share capital (in terms of rights to shares, profits, voting, and the appointment of directors) and combined share capital and investor loan capital are owned by foreign residents. A FIC benefits from reduced company tax on the profits of an approved enterprise for a period of ten years (instead of seven), commencing with the first year in which taxable income is generated. The total period of benefits continues to be restricted, so that it cannot extend beyond 12 years from the year in which operations commence or 14 years from the year in which the approval was granted, whichever is earlier. In addition, a FIC enjoys reduced company tax rates applicable to its approved enterprise income, as shown below.

| Percentage of foreign ownership | Company tax rate* |
|---|---|
| | % |
| Over 25% but less than 49% | 25 |
| 49% or more but less than 74% | 20 |
| 74% or more but less than 90% | 15 |
| 90% or more | 10 |

*An approved enterprise located in Development Area A is entitled to a tax holiday from company tax regarding its undistributed income derived in the initial two years of the period of benefits (for enterprises approved after January 1, 1997).

Dividends paid by an FIC out of profits of its approved enterprise are taxed in the hands of the recipient at the rate of 15%, without limitation as to their distribution date, provided the dividends are distributed out of approved enterprise profits derived during the benefits period. With respect to dividends paid from tax-exempt income, see below.

***Foreign investors' companies—Foreign incorporated company***/When a
foreign company owns an approved enterprise in Israel, the enterprise's profits
may, in principle, be subject to the reduced company tax rate of 10%, that is,
the rate at which a 90%-or-more-owned FIC would be taxed with respect to its
approved enterprise income.

In addition, a foreign resident company that owns an approved enterprise may be
subject to a branch tax at the rate of 15% of the profit after company tax. The
Income Tax Commissioner may allow payment of the branch tax to be deferred, so
long as it can be proved that the relevant income has not been remitted abroad.

***Alternative system of tax benefits for approved enterprises (tax holiday)***/
Companies with new or expanding approved enterprises may elect to forgo all
government cash grants (see above), and to receive instead a total exemption (i.e.,
a tax holiday) from company tax on undistributed profits of the approved enterprise
for ten years in Development Area A, for six years in Development Area B, and for
two years elsewhere in Israel.

After the tax holiday period, for the remaining period of benefits, the company's
income will be subject to the reduced tax rates that would have been applicable if
the tax holiday had not been elected.

The tax holiday provides an Israeli tax exemption as long as the approved
enterprise profits generated in the exempt period are retained within the company.
If those profits are subsequently distributed, company tax and dividend withholding
tax will be imposed on the income distributed, at the rates that would have been
applicable if the tax holiday had not been elected. Under certain antiavoidance
provisions applicable to tax holidays, amounts paid or credited directly or indirectly
by an approved enterprise to a relative, a major shareholder or a related entity
controlled by either a relative or a major shareholder may be treated as a taxable
distribution of profits by the approved enterprise unless those amounts are
otherwise taxed in the hands of the recipients.

***Other incentives***/Ports in Haifa, Ashdod, and Eilat have been declared free-port
zones, and investors in authorized enterprises in these ports may receive direct
and indirect tax benefits. Further, Israel has concluded free-trade agreements with
the United States, the European Union, and the European Free Trade Association
(EFTA).

## Withholding taxes

| Recipient | Dividends | Interest | Royalties |
|---|---|---|---|
| | % | % | % |
| Resident corporations ........................... | 0/25 | 0 to 45 | 0 to 20 |
| Resident individuals ............................. | 25 | 0 to 45 | 0 to 30 |
| Nonresident corporations: | | | |
| Nontreaty ........................................... | 25 | 25 | 25 |
| Treaty: | | | |
| Austria.............................................. | 25 | 15 | 10 |
| Belgium ............................................. | 15 | 15 | 10/0 |
| Belarus ............................................. | 10 | 0/5/10 | 5/10 |
| Bulgaria............................................. | 12.5/10 | 10/5 | 12.5 |
| Brazil................................................. | 10/15 | 0/15 | 10/15 |
| Bulgaria ............................................ | 10/12.5 | 5/10 | 12.5 |

# Israel

| Recipient | Dividends | Interest | Royalties |
|-----------|:---------:|:--------:|:---------:|
| | % | % | % |
| Canada............................................ | 15 | 15 | 0/15 |
| China, P.R. ..................................... | 10 | 10/7 | 10 |
| Czech Republic ............................... | 5/15 | 10/0 | 5 |
| Denmark.......................................... | 25 | 25 | 10 |
| Finland ............................................ | 5/10/15 | 0/10 | 10 |
| France ............................................ | 5/15 | 0/5/10 | 10/0 |
| Germany ......................................... | 25 | 0/15 | 5 /0 |
| Greece ............................................ | 25 | 10 | 10 |
| Hungary .......................................... | 15/5 | 0 | 0 |
| India ............................................... | 10 | 10/0 | 10 |
| Ireland, Rep. of............................... | 10 | 5/10 | 10 |
| Italy ................................................ | 10/15 | 0 | 0/10 |
| Jamaica........................................... | 22.5/15 | 15/0 | 10 |
| Japan .............................................. | 15/5 | 10 | 10 |
| Korea, Rep. of................................. | 5/10/15 | 10/7.5 | 2/5 |
| Mexico............................................. | 5/10 | 10 | 10 |
| Netherlands..................................... | 15/5 | 15/10 | 5 |
| Norway ............................................ | 25 | 25 | 10 |
| Philippines....................................... | 10/15 | 10 | 15 |
| Poland ............................................ | 10/5 | 5 | 10 |
| Romania.......................................... | 15 | 10/5 | 10 |
| Russia ............................................. | 10 | 0/10 | 10 |
| Singapore........................................ | 0 | 15 | 0 |
| Slovakia.......................................... | 5/10 | 2/5/10 | 5 |
| South Africa..................................... | 25 | 25 | 0 |
| Spain............................................... | 10 | 0/5/10 | 5/7 |
| Sweden ........................................... | 0 | 25 | 0 |
| Switzerland ..................................... | 5/10/15 | 5/10 | 5 |
| Thailand .......................................... | 10/15 | 15/10 | 15 |
| Turkey............................................. | 10 | 10 | 10 |
| United Kingdom............................... | 15 | 15 | 0 |
| United States................................... | 25/12.5 | 17.5 | 15 |
| Uzbekistan ...................................... | 10 | 10 | 5/10 |

## Tax administration

*Returns*/The tax year is generally the 12 months ending December 31 in each year. Certain entities may apply to have their tax year end on different dates, specifically, mutual funds, government companies, quoted companies, and subsidiaries of foreign quoted companies.

The Israeli system is based on a combined form of assessment and self-assessment.

*Payment of tax*/Generally, 12 monthly advance payments are levied at a fixed ratio of the company's turnover. Alternatively, a company may be required to make ten monthly payments beginning in the second month of its tax year, each payment being a fixed percentage of the previous year's tax assessment. Penalties are imposed on overdue advance payments and on delays in the submission of tax returns. The balance of any taxes due is payable from the beginning of the following tax year and is linked to the CPI. It bears interest of 4% until paid.

## CORPORATION TAX CALCULATION

Fiscal year ending December 31, 2003

|  |  | (In NIS thousands) |
|---|---:|---:|
| Net income before taxes per income statement | | 20,000 |
| Add—Nondeductible items: | | |
| Book depreciation | 1,000 | |
| Refreshments and local entertainment | 200 | |
| Motor expenses | 300 | |
| Foreign travel | 50 | |
| Increase in reserve for vacation | 1,000 | |
| Increase in reserve for severance pay | 2,000 | |
| Increase in reserve for doubtful debts | 200 | |
| Interest and fines to income tax authorities | 100 | 4,850 |
| | | 24,850 |
| Less: | | |
| Tax depreciation | 800 | |
| Tax-exempt income | 700 | |
| Interest from income tax authorities | 50 | 1,550 |
| Adjusted income before application of | | |
| Income Tax Law (Inflationary Adjustments) 1985 | | 23,300 |
| Adjustments according to | | |
| Income Tax Law (Inflationary Adjustments) 1985: | | |
| Inflationary deduction | 3,000 | |
| Additional depreciation | 200 | 3,200 |
| Taxable income | | 20,100 |
| Company tax at 36% | | 7,236 |
| *Less:* | | |
| Advance payments, including payments | | |
| in respect of excess expenses (1) | | (5,315) |
| Balance due | | 1,921 |

Notes:

1. A proportion of motor expenses and foreign travel is allowable in accordance with detailed rules. Certain disallowable amounts, known as excess expenses, attract advance tax payments during the year of 45% of the expense. Advance payments in respect of excess expenses can be deducted from regular advance payments.

2. Exchange rate of the new shekel at January 1, 2004: US$1 = NIS4.39.

# Italy

## PwC contact

For additional information on taxation in Italy, contact:

Massimo Cremona
Studio Pirola Pennuto Zei ed Associati
Via Vittor Pisani 16
20124 Milano, Italy
Telephone: (39) (02) 669951
Fax: (39) (02) 6691800
e-mail: massimo.cremona@studiopirola.com

## Significant developments

***EC Law 2003***/The Italian Parliament has approved EC Law 2003 that has incorporated 50 EC Directives into Italian legislation. One of the most interesting issues governed by EC Law 2003 is the application of the European accounting standards to the preparation of financial statements, including consolidated financial statements, of listed companies, banks and financial intermediaries.

Directive 2003/49/EC of June 3, 2003, concerning the common taxation regime applicable to interest and royalty payments between associated companies of different member States, has also been incorporated into Italian legislation. According to this Directive, interest and royalty payments made between European Union (EU) associated companies are exempt from tax, whether collected by deduction at source or by assessment. The date of application of the Directive is still uncertain.

***Italian tax reform***/The Italian government has reformed the current tax system through the enactment of Legislative Decree of December 12, 2003, n. 344. The new legislation, which entered into force on January 1, 2004, reduced the corporate income tax rate from 34% to 33%, and changed the name of corporation tax from IRPEG (*imposta sul reddito delle persone giuridiche*) to IRES (*imposta sul reddito delle società*).

The most significant measures include the following.
* Repeal of the 19% substitute tax on reorganizations from January 1, 2004.
* Repeal of the dual income tax (DIT) system.
* Introduction of an option to file a consolidated tax return for all Italian group entities (domestic tax consolidation) and of an option to file a worldwide consolidated tax return to include all foreign subsidiaries (worldwide tax consolidation).
* Thin capitalization provisions—according to this new regime, there are limits to the deductibility of intercompany financial costs.
* Introduction of a domestic notion of permanent establishment based on the definition given by the Organization for Economic Cooperation and Development (OECD) Model Tax Convention against double taxation.
* Participation exemption regime.
* Equity pro-rata and economical ratio.
* Revision and extension of controlled foreign companies (CFC) rules.
* Foreign tax credit rules.
* Consortium relief.

*International ruling*/Companies carrying on business in several countries may have access to international standard ruling procedures regarding transfer pricing regime, interest, dividends, and royalties.

*Tremonti incentive*/In order to foster innovation and research in the manufacturing industry, all companies operating at October 2, 2003, in addition to the ordinary cost deductions, may obtain a further deduction from business income.

*Step-up of corporate assets*/The Finance Act 2004 has re-introduced the possibility to step up business assets recorded in the financial statements at December 31, 2002 for both statutory and tax purposes. The substitute tax applies at a rate of 19% of the step-up for depreciable assets, and 15% of the step-up for non-depreciable assets.

*Tax amnesty for fiscal year 2002*/The possibility to apply for the tax amnesties has been extended to the fiscal year current at December 31, 2002, the tax returns for which were filed by October 31, 2003. Tax amnesty is possible only for entities whose fiscal year coincides with the calendar year.

*Digital storage of documents*/The new rules provide that electronic documents must be issued in such a way as to ensure their authenticity, integrity, and inalterability over time.

*Special VAT scheme for e-commerce*/A new special VAT scheme applicable to non-EU suppliers rendering services by electronic means to Italian or EU nontaxable persons has been in force in Italy since October 10, 2003.

*Participation exemption regime*/Capital gains realized by Italian holding or sub-holding companies on sales of shares will be exempt. Capital losses, or expenses arising on the sale of a shareholding, and write-downs, will not be deductible. Capital gains derived by corporate entities from sales of shareholdings, will not be subject to tax if the following applies.

- The shareholding is held uninterruptedly for at least 12 months.
- The shareholding is treated as a financial fixed asset in the first financial statement closed after the shareholding was acquired.
- The subsidiary is resident in a country not included in the blacklist attached to Italy's CFC legislation.
- The subsidiary carries on a business activity.

The dividends distributed under whatever form to Italian corporate entities by resident or nonresident companies having legal personality are 95% exempt.

*Thin capitalization rules*/Before the reform, there were no limits to the deductibility of intercompany financial costs; the new regime introduced a thin capitalization rule. Financing expenses on loans granted or guaranteed by qualified shareholders or their related parties will be deductible on the basis of a debt/equity ratio which has been determined at 5 to 1 for the first period of application, and 4 to 1 for the following fiscal years. The debt to be considered for purposes of the debt/equity ratio will consist of loans granted or guaranteed by a shareholder who holds, directly or indirectly, a significant shareholding in the paying company, or by a related party. Related party means the companies controlled by and affiliated with the shareholder.

If the debt/equity ratio is exceeded, the excess portion of the intercompany debt will be reclassified as equity, and the interest paid will be considered as a nondeductible dividend distribution. The thin capitalization rules at issue do not apply if, for example, the borrowing company proves that the loans granted exclusively derive from its own borrowing capacity.

*Equity pro-rata and economical ratio*/A further limit will apply to the deductibility of interest expense when the financed company holds shareholdings qualifying for the participation exemption. If the book value of the exempt shareholding exceeds the accounting net equity of the financed company, interest will only be deductible, after applying the thin capitalization rules, in proportion to the ratio of the excess to the liabilities of the financed company. The deductibility of the remaining interest could be limited by the Economical ratio between exempt income and total income of the company.

*Domestic tax consolidation*/All companies, whether parent companies or subsidiary companies belonging to a group, with the exception of foreign subsidiaries and foreign parent companies without a branch in Italy, can opt for tax consolidation. Such an option will be irrevocable for at least three years, unless the control requirement no longer applies. Group affiliation will solely depend on the control requirement, whether direct or indirect. Notwithstanding the percentage of ownership in the subsidiaries, in determining the consolidated taxable income to be included in the parent company's income tax return, the parent company will have to consider the total taxable income of each subsidiary. The dividends distributed by the companies included in the tax consolidation will be exempt.

The proportional limitation of deductibility of financing costs does not apply in the event of ownership of shares in companies belonging to the consolidated tax system; in case of interruption of tax consolidation, recapture rules apply with effect from the beginning of the fiscal period in which the option was exercised.

*International tax consolidation*/Resident controlling joint-stock companies and commercial entities subject to IRES, which are the ultimate holding companies of their group, may opt for international tax consolidation. If the controlling company opts for tax consolidation, all the nonresident controlled undertakings will be included in the consolidation area ("all in, all out" principle). All the income and losses produced by all the nonresident controlled undertakings, regardless of their distribution, may be allocated with proportion to the profit sharing percentage held by the controlling company.

The aggregate income of the controlled undertakings must be re-determined by the resident controlling company; any losses incurred by the nonresident controlled undertakings before the start of consolidation are not relevant.

The option cannot be revoked until the end of the controlling company's fifth fiscal year. Any renewals apply for at least three fiscal years, and are subject to the condition that the financial statements of the companies involved are certified by a qualified auditor.

There are a number of conditions, as follows.

- All companies in the same group must have the same year-end, except where local legislation makes this impossible.
- The Italian resident parent company and all consolidated subsidiaries must be subject to external audit.
- The subsidiaries must undertake to furnish the necessary information to the parent company in order for it to fulfill its fiscal obligations in a timely manner.

- A ruling procedure is to be initiated to obtain the authorities' approval of the validity of the option for group taxation.

**Revision and extension of CFC rules**/The rules governing CFC will also apply in the event that the Italian resident company, entity or individual concerned holds directly or indirectly, including through fiduciary companies or third parties, a share in the profits of companies or other entities resident or located in low tax jurisdictions.

This shareholding cannot be lower than 10% in companies listed on a stock exchange and 20% in any other companies. After January 1, 2004, the scope of application of the CFC rules is extended to affiliated foreign companies resident in low tax jurisdictions. (See below).

**Foreign tax credit rules**/If income earned abroad is included in the computation of aggregate income, any taxes definitively paid abroad upon such income shall be creditable against net tax in an amount equal to that part of the Italian tax which is proportional to the ratio of foreign source income to aggregate income, net of any losses of prior tax periods carried forward. If income is earned abroad through permanent establishments or controlled undertakings participating in an international tax consolidation, the credit due on the taxes definitively paid abroad and exceeding the relevant part of the Italian tax can be carried back or forward; when only a portion of the income earned abroad is included in the aggregate income, the foreign tax must be reduced accordingly.

**Domestic definition of PE**/The Italian notion of permanent establishment (PE) is largely based on the definition given by article 5 of the OECD Model Tax Convention against double taxation. For the purposes of income taxes and of the regional production tax, the term permanent establishment means a fixed place of business in which the business of a nonresident enterprise is wholly or partly carried on in the Italian territory.

Contrary to the definition given by article 5 of the OECD Model Tax Convention and OECD guidelines, the following applies.

- A building, erection or installation site, or supervision performed in connection with such site is considered to be a permanent establishment only if the site exists or the activity is carried out for more than three months.
- An internet service provider making a server available to a nonresident company is not per se an Italian permanent establishment of the latter.
- A resident or nonresident person who habitually concludes in the territory of the State contracts other than contracts for the purchase of goods in the name of the enterprise shall be deemed to be a permanent establishment of the enterprise.

The existence of a control relationship between a nonresident company and a resident company does not per se constitute either company a permanent establishment of the other.

**Consortium relief**/Companies with share capital may opt for the tax transparency ("flow-through") system, already in force for partnerships, under which the income of a company is not taxed in the hands of the company itself, but the profits or losses are entered in the name of each shareholder proportionally to its percentage of ownership, regardless of whether or not profits are distributed.

The conditions required are as follows.
- The percentage of ownership of each shareholder is not less than 10% and not more than 50%.
- The shareholders are in turn resident companies with share capital.
- The shareholders are nonresident companies with share capital and the profits distributed to them are not subject to tax.

The option is irrevocable for three accounting periods of the subsidiary, and it must be exercised by all the companies and communicated to the tax authorities. The income of each shareholder is entered in the accounting period current at the subsidiary's year-end.

***Repeal of 19% tax on reorganizations (mergers, demergers)/***The substitute tax regime has been abolished starting from January 1, 2004. Company reorganizations that were previously subject to tax at a special 19% rate are now neutral for tax purposes. The transactions qualifying for the 19% substitute tax were contributions, exchanges of shares, mergers, demergers, and so forth.

## Taxes on corporate income

***Corporate income tax/***Effective January 1, 2004, the legislation reduces the corporate income tax rate, IRES (*Imposta sul reddito delle società*), from 34% to 33%. IRES is levied on the total net income of any type, excluding income that is exempt or subject to definitive withholding tax. The tax is levied on the income of bodies corporate (as defined).

***IRAP/***The local tax on productive activities IRAP (*Imposta regionale sulle attività produttive*), became effective starting from January 1, 1998. The taxable base of IRAP is different from that determined for corporate income tax purposes. IRAP is computed not on taxable income but on the gross margin, as shown in the statutory financial statements. Moreover, any cost associated with labor, interest, and accruals for risk will be neutral (i.e., not deductible) for IRAP purposes. Starting from the fiscal year 2000, proportional deductions from taxable income have been introduced.

The ordinary IRAP rate is 4.25%. The local tax on productive activities (IRAP) is considered by unilateral domestic provisions as a tax covered by the conventions against double taxation entered into between Italy and other countries (e.g., Italy-United States). The IRAP due is not deductible in the calculation of corporate taxable income (IRES).

## Corporate residence

Joint-stock companies, partnerships with liability limited by shares, limited liability companies, co-operatives, and mutual insurance companies having their legal or administrative headquarters or their principal business purpose within the territory of the state, are taxable in Italy on their worldwide income. Partnerships, companies and any other entities (with or without legal personality) that do not have their legal or administrative headquarters or their principal purpose within the territory of the state are subject to Italian income tax only on their Italian-source income.

## Other taxes

*Value-added tax*/VAT (Imposta sul valore aggiunto) is levied on most goods and services at the standard rate of 20%, with other rates applying as follows.

|  | % |
|---|---|
| Export sales | Tax exempt |
| Food | 4 or 10 |
| Mass consumption goods, utilities | 10 or 20 |

During the year 2002, new rules were issued to incorporate the EU Directives regarding reverse charge mechanism for services supplies in the financial sector, and direct registration procedure for nonresident entities.

*Special VAT scheme for e-commerce*/According to Legislative Decree of August 1, 2003, no. 273, the statement of identification for VAT purposes in Italy and the subsequent notifications of change of particulars, the notifications of cessation of business and the returns summarizing all the transactions effected in each calendar quarter must be filed with the tax authorities' *Centro Operativo* in Pescara.

The ICI tax rate, a percentage established each year by the local authorities, can range from 0.4% to 0.7% and is applied on the estimated value of the property. It is due on a yearly basis.

## Branch income

A branch is taxed as a corporation, paying corporate income tax (IRES) and local tax on productive activities (IRAP). For rates, see above.

## Income determination

*Inventory valuation*/The tax code lays down a system of pricing of inventories, which is basically a LIFO method. However, other methods (such as average and FIFO) are also applicable.

Expenditure and charges, other than those specifically provided for by the law, incurred in the production of income, are deductible if the charges appear in the income statement.

There are no territorial limits on business expenses of a corporation.

*Capital gains*/Capital gains are normally taxable in the tax period in which they are realized or reported in the books of the company.
1. Fixed assets: The gain realized on the sale of fixed assets may be declared as taxable income in equal installments over a period not exceeding five years. The option to take gains to income in five equal installments is possible only if the company has owned fixed assets for more than three years.
2. Investments: (see "Participation exemption regime" above)
   a. In case of assets qualifying for the participation exemption regime, capital gains are exempt.
   b. In case of assets not qualifying for the participation exemption regime, capital gains are subject to 33% corporate income tax. The substitute tax regime on capital gains has been abolished.

*Dividends*/The tax reform has abolished the imputation system (tax credit baskets A and B) replacing it with a 95% dividend exemption for dividends distributed under whatever form, including those paid during the liquidation or winding up of the company, to Italian corporate entities by resident or nonresident companies with legal personality. The 95% exemption does not apply to dividends distributed by companies resident in tax havens, as per the blacklist issued by the Ministry of Finance. Alternatively, the taxpayer must prove that the shareholding in the foreign entity resident or located in the tax haven jurisdiction does not lead to the localization of income in tax haven countries or territories and obtained a favorable ruling.

A European Directive on dividend taxation entered into in force effective January 1, 1992 and applies to companies located in a European country. Dividends received by an Italian company from a European associated company (engaged to hold at least 25% for more than 12 months) should not be included in taxable income to the extent of 95% of the total. According to the new Directive, the minimum percentage of shareholding in the subsidiary's share capital will be gradually reduced to 10% with effect from January 1, 2009. Dividends paid by an Italian company to a European associated company (which controls the Italian company under the same conditions mentioned above) are not subject to withholding taxes. Both companies must be subject to corporate taxation in their respective home countries.

**CFC rules**/If an Italian resident, company or individual, holds control of a company resident or located in a country or territory qualifying for a privileged tax regime, at the end of the financial year or management period of the foreign controlled company, the income of the foreign entity is attributed to the resident entities in proportion to their stake therein. Control must be exercised at the end of the accounting period of the CFC company.

Consistently with the enforcement of the CFC legislation, Italian authorities released a new blacklist of low tax jurisdictions.

The CFC rules do not apply under the following.

1. An Italian resident proves that a company located in a jurisdiction considered to have a privileged tax regime carries out principally an industrial or commercial activity in the country where it has its registered office (this condition would be satisfied if there is an organized structure, such as offices, staff and organization, to carry out the activity).
2. The income realized by the CFC, at least 75% of which arises from other non-CFC countries, has been subject to ordinary tax in those jurisdictions.

For the CFC rules not to apply in the situations described above, an Italian resident must apply for a tax ruling (*diritto d'interpello*) and obtain approval from the local Italian tax authority (*Direzione centrale per la normativa e il contenzioso*).

The income from the foreign entity attributed to the resident person is subject to separate taxation at the average rate applied on the aggregate income of the resident person. In any case, the rate cannot be lower than 27%, and a tax credit for any taxes paid abroad on a definitive basis is granted. Profits distributed under whatever form by the nonresident persons referred to hereunder are not included in the resident entity's taxable income, up to the amount of the income already subjected to tax, as a consequence of the application of the CFC rules, in the same or in prior years. Taxes paid abroad on the income not included in the resident entity's income as above are creditable up to the amount of Italian taxes charged as above reduced by any tax credit for foreign taxes.

**Foreign affiliates**/Starting January 1, 2004, the scope of application of the CFC rules has been extended to affiliated foreign companies resident in low tax jurisdictions. Income produced by the affiliated foreign company is determined as the higher of the following,

- Profits realized before taxes shown in the financial statements drawn up by the affiliated foreign company, even if not required by any rule.
- Income inductively determined on the basis of coefficients applied to the assets (1%, 4%, and 15%).

Effective from January 1, 2002, costs and other negative components arising from transactions between resident companies and companies, all third parties, domiciled in a country outside the EU benefiting from a privileged tax regime, are not deductible from the taxable income of the Italian company. The Italian authorities released a new blacklist of privileged tax regimes with regard to their level of taxation, their lack of an adequate system for the exchange of information, and similar criteria. This rule also applies to companies whose activities are carried out in the listed countries. However, this provision does not apply when an enterprise resident in Italy provides proof that the foreign companies engage primarily in a real commercial activity or that the transactions effected correspond to a real economic interest and were executed correctly.

***Foreign income*/**An Italian domestic corporation is taxable on all income whether produced in Italy or abroad. There are no special rules for the taxation of the unremitted income of a subsidiary resident or located in countries or territories not qualifying for a privileged tax regime (as defined by domestic law). Double taxation may be avoided by way of a Treaty or by way of a foreign tax credit. Under the tax reform, the foreign tax credit may be used in the reference period, including when the taxes are paid, definitively or not, by the deadline for filing the income tax return.

***Stock dividends*/**In the case of any increase in the stock capital utilizing free reserves or retained earnings, the new shares issued or the increase in the par value of the existing shares does not constitute taxable income and does not give rise to the application of withholding tax on dividends. However, if subsequently a reimbursement of capital is made to shareholders, the decrease will be considered as a distribution of profits, subject to tax, up to the amount of the reserves capitalized.

***Step-up of corporate assets*/**The Finance Act 2004 has re-introduced the possibility to step up business assets recorded in the financial statements at December 31, 2002 for both statutory and tax purposes. The step-up can be made by resident or nonresident joint-stock companies and partnerships, and by nonresident individuals carrying out a commercial activity in Italy by means of a permanent establishment. All tangible and intangible assets can be stepped up, excluding those assets the production or exchange of which is the subject of the company's activity, and shareholdings in controlled or affiliated companies. With some exceptions, the assets to be stepped up must belong to the same homogeneous category. The step-up will have to be recorded in the relevant inventory and in the notes to the financial statements. The aim of the step-up is to take advantage of the differential between the corporate tax rate with the payment of a substitute tax at a rate of 19% of the step-up for depreciable assets and 15% of the step-up for nondepreciable assets. The substitute tax must be paid in three annual installments, by the deadline for the payment of the balance of income taxes.

# Italy

## Deductions

*Depreciation and depletion*/All fixed assets, except land, are depreciable for tax purposes. Assets with a unit cost of less than €500 may be written off in the year in which acquired. Depreciation is deductible on a straight-line basis, starting from the first tax period in which the asset concerned was used. In the first period, the assets must be depreciated at a rate that does not exceed one-half of normal rates. The depreciation and amortization charge is calculated on the cost of the asset. Depreciation rates of fixed assets are determined in accordance with a ministerial Decree. The rates of amortization of intangible assets should conform to the period of utilization of the assets as laid down by contract; in their absence, the rate used cannot exceed 33% per annum. Goodwill (if recorded in the books) can be amortized at a maximum rate of 10% per annum.

Rates lower than those referred to above can be used for depreciation and amortization. If depreciation rates are lower than 50% of those specified above, then the difference between 50% of the prescribed rate and the actual rates generally adopted cannot be charged in future years. However, if rates lower than 50% of the prescribed rates have been used because the utilization of the asset is lower than normal, further depreciation may be provided in future years.

In addition to normal depreciation, accelerated depreciation may be charged at a rate not exceeding 100% of normal rates for the first three years. Accelerated depreciation, within the above limits, can be claimed in the tax return even if not shown in the income statements.

To exploit natural resources a company would require a government concession. The annual cost of such a concession could be written off against income produced.

*Net operating losses*/A five-year loss carryover period is applicable for corporate income tax (IRES) but not for local tax on productive activities. Loss carryback is not allowed.

Fiscal losses produced in the first three years of activity are available to be carried forward indefinitely.

*Payments to foreign affiliates*/Transactions with foreign affiliated companies are closely scrutinized in order to determine whether the arm's length principle has been satisfied and whether the transfer price may be considered a "fair market value." Ministerial guidelines relating to the transfer pricing regime are in line with OECD recommendations.

*International ruling*/As provided for by the tax authorities, under Law Decree of September 30, 2003, no. 269, companies carrying on business in several countries may have access to international standard ruling procedures regarding transfer pricing regime, interest, dividends, and royalties. This procedure applies from the fiscal year subsequent to that current at October 2, 2003 by means of an agreement executed between the Revenue Office and the taxpayer, and is binding for the fiscal year during which the agreement is executed and for the two following fiscal years, unless there are changes in the circumstances of fact or of law relevant for the conclusion of the agreement executed by the taxpayer. A copy of the agreement must be sent by the tax authorities to the competent tax authorities of the state of residence or establishment of the companies with which the taxpayers put in place the relevant transactions. The ruling request must be filed with the competent Revenue Office of Milan or Rome. The international ruling procedure is binding only upon the Italian tax authorities, and not on the authorities of foreign countries.

*Taxes*/The local tax on productive activities is not deductible for purposes of computing corporate income tax (IRES). ICI (*Imposta comunale sugli immobili*) (local tax on real estate) is deductible for purposes of local tax on productive activities.

*Other significant items*/Expenses relating to study and research are deductible in the period in which incurred, or they may be capitalized and written off in a maximum of five equal installments commencing in the year in which incurred.

Advertising expenses are deductible either entirely in the tax period in which incurred or in equal installments in the period and the four subsequent periods.

Gift and entertainment expenses are deductible to the extent of 33% over five years (6.6% each year).

*Write-down of shareholdings*/Subject to certain conditions, investments in subsidiaries could be written down for tax purposes considering the term of reference and the decrease of the accounting net equity of the subsidiary. New limitations to the above rule were introduced during 2002 mainly to prevent abuse of the law in the case of a decrease of the net equity through dividend distribution.

## Tax incentives

*Inward investment and capital investment*/In order to attract new industrial enterprises to southern Italy and certain depressed mountain regions in central and northern Italy, non tax incentives take the forms of tax credits on new investments (until December 31, 2006), loans at low rates of interest, and outright grants toward capital investments. The benefits are available for all qualifying investors, foreign or Italian.

Tax incentives in southern Italy include, for manufacturing companies established between March 29, 1986 and December 31, 1993, an exemption from corporate income tax (IRES, normally 33%) for ten years from the year of incorporation.

As of January 1, 1998, exemptions from local income tax will be granted for IRAP purposes as described below.

## Tremonti incentive (TI)

In order to foster innovation and research in the manufacturing industry, all companies operating at October 2, 2003, in addition to the ordinary cost deductions, may obtain a further deduction from business income as follows

- A total of 10% of the costs borne in respect of research and development and digital technology.
- Expenses directly borne for participating in trade fairs held abroad;
- Expenses borne in respect of admission to quotation on a regulated market.

The incentive will apply to the expenses borne from January 1, 2004 by entities whose fiscal year coincides with the calendar year. In order to benefit from this incentive, the following applies.

- Details of the qualifying expenses must be reported in a special statement and filed with the Revenue Office.

# Italy

- A certificate attesting that the expenses have been actually borne will have to be issued by the president of the Board of Statutory Auditors.

The *Tremonti incentive* (TI) has been extended to the second tax period following the one current at October 25, 2001, with reference to investments realized until July 31, 2003. The 2001 *Tremonti incentive* aims to boost new investments in the form of new tangible and intangible assets. All business activities (for example, trading, manufacturing, new economy, banks, insurance) are entitled to the TI benefit. Most capital expenditures (such as the purchase or construction of new plants, purchase of new fixed assets) will be entitled to extraordinary tax deductions; it is not a mere acceleration of asset depreciation, but a permanent tax benefit. The qualified expenditure is not all of the capital expenditure for the year; it is only the expenditure for the year that is in excess of the average capital expenses of the prior fiscal years.

Four of the previous fiscal years are to be considered under the averaging mechanism. The benefit will be granted based on the date of purchase.

## Withholding taxes

Domestic corporations paying certain types of income are required to withhold as follows.

| Recipient | Dividends (1) | Interest (2) | Royalties (3) |
|---|---|---|---|
| | % | % | % |
| Resident corporations | Nil | 0, 12.5, 27 | Nil |
| Resident individuals | 12.5 | 12.5, 27 | 20 (4) |
| Nonresident corporations and individuals: | | | |
| Nontreaty | 27 (5) | 12.5, 27 (6) | 30 (4) |
| Treaty: | | | |
| Albania | Nil, 10 | Nil, 5 | Nil, 5 |
| Algeria | 15 | 15 | 5, 15 (7) |
| Argentina | 15 | Nil, 20 | 10, 18 (8) |
| Australia | 15 | Nil, 10 | Nil, 10 |
| Austria | 15 | Nil, 10 | Nil, 10 (9) |
| Bangladesh | 10, 15 | 10, 15 | 10 |
| Belarus | 15 | Nil | Nil |
| Belgium | 15 | 15 | 5 |
| Brazil | Nil, 15 | Nil, 15 | 15, 25 (9) |
| Bulgaria | 10 | Nil | 5 |
| Canada* | 15 | Nil, 15 | Nil, 10 (9) |
| China, P.R. | 10 | Nil, 10 | 10 |
| Cyprus | 15 | 10 | Nil |
| Czechoslovakia (former) | 15 | Nil | Nil, 5 |
| Denmark** | Nil, 15 | 10 | Nil, 5 |
| Ecuador | 15 | Nil, 10 | 5 |
| Egypt | 27 | Nil, 25 | 15 |
| Estonia | 5, 15 | 10 | 5, 10 (10) |
| Ethiopia | 10 | 10 | 20 |
| Finland | 10, 15 | Nil, 15 | Nil, 5 |
| France | 5, 15 (11) | Nil, 10 | Nil, 5 |
| Georgia | 5, 10 | Nil | Nil |

| Recipient | Dividends (1) | Interest (2) | Royalties (3) |
|---|---|---|---|
| | % | % | % |
| Germany..................................... | 15 | Nil, 10 | Nil, 5 (9) |
| Greece........................................ | 15 | Nil, 10 | Nil, 5 |
| Hungary...................................... | 10 | Nil | Nil |
| India ........................................... | 15, 25 | 15 | 20 |
| Indonesia.................................... | 10, 15 (12) | Nil, 10 | 10, 15 (9) |
| Ireland, Rep. of ........................... | 15 | 10 | Nil |
| Israel ......................................... | 10, 15 | 10 | 10 |
| Ivory Coast (Côte d'Ivoire) .......... | 15, 18 | Nil, 15 | 10 |
| Japan.......................................... | 10, 15 (13) | 10 | 10 |
| Kazakhstan.................................. | 5, 15 | Nil, 10 | 10 |
| Kenya ......................................... | 10 | 12.5 | Nil |
| Korea, Rep. of............................. | 10, 15 (13) | Nil, 10 | 10 |
| Kuwait......................................... | 5 (14) | Nil | 10 |
| Lithuania..................................... | 5, 15 | Nil, 10 | 5, 10 |
| Luxembourg (15) ........................ | 15 | 10 | 10 |
| Macedonia................................... | 5, 15 | Nil, 10 | Nil |
| Malaysia ..................................... | 10 | Nil, 15 | 15 |
| Malta .......................................... | 15 | Nil, 10 | Nil, 10 (9) |
| Mauritius..................................... | 5, 15 | Nil, 12.5, 27 | 15 |
| Mexico ........................................ | 15 | Nil, 15 | Nil, 15 |
| Morocco....................................... | 10, 15 (13) | Nil, 10 | 5, 10 (9) |
| Mozambique ............................... | 15 | 10 | 10 |
| Netherlands ................................ | 5, 10, 15 | Nil, 10 | 5 |
| New Zealand................................ | 15 | Nil, 10 | 10 |
| Norway ....................................... | 15 | Nil, 15 | 5 |
| Oman .......................................... | 5, 10 | 5 | 10 |
| Pakistan...................................... | 15, 25 (16) | Nil, 30 | 30 |
| Philippines .................................. | 15 | Nil, 10, 15 (17) | 15, 25 |
| Poland ........................................ | 10 | Nil, 10 | 10 |
| Portugal ...................................... | 15 | Nil, 15 | 12 |
| Romania ...................................... | 10 | Nil, 10 | 10 |
| Russia ........................................ | 5, 10 | 10 | Nil |
| Senegal ...................................... | 15 | 15 | 15 |
| Singapore ................................... | 10 | 12.5 | 15, 20 (9) |
| South Africa................................ | 5, 15 | Nil, 10 | 6 |
| Spain ......................................... | 15 | 12 | 4, 8 (9) |
| Sri Lanka .................................... | 15 Nil, 10 | 10, 15 (9) | |
| Sweden ...................................... | 10, 15 (18) Nil, 15 | 5 | |
| Switzerland.................................. | 15 | 12.5 | 5 |
| Tanzania ..................................... | 10 | 15 | 15 |
| Thailand...................................... | 15, 20 | Nil, 10 | 5, 15 (9) |
| Trinidad and Tobago..................... | 10, 20 (19) | 10 | Nil, 5 (9) |
| Tunisia ....................................... | 15 | Nil, 12 | 5, 12, 16 (9) |
| Turkey ........................................ | 15 | 15 | 10 |
| Ukraine....................................... | 5, 15 | 10 | 7 |
| United Arab Emirates................... | 5, 15 | Nil | 10 |
| United Kingdom .......................... | 5, 15 (11) | Nil, 10 | 8 |
| United States .............................. | 5, 10, 15 (20) | Nil, 15 | 5, 8, 10 (21) |

# Italy

| Recipient | Dividends (1) | Interest (2) | Royalties (3) |
|---|---|---|---|
| | % | % | % |
| Uzbekistan ................................ | 10 | 5 | 5 |
| Venezuela.................................. | 10 | Nil, 10 | 7, 10 (9) |
| Vietnam ..................................... | 5, 10, 15 | Nil, 10 | 7.5, 10 |
| Yugoslavia*** ............................ | 10 | 10 | 10 |
| Zambia ...................................... | 5, 15 (12) | 10 | 10 |

\* The Income Tax Convention signed between Italy and Canada on June 3, 2002, once effective, will replace the 1977 Treaty concluded by Italy and Canada.

\*\* The Income Tax Convention signed between Italy and Denmark on May 5, 1999 entered into force on January 27, 2003. The treaty replaces the Income and Capital Tax Convention concluded in 1980. Its provisions generally apply from January 1, 2004.

\*\*\* The Income and Capital Tax Convention signed between Italy and Slovenia on September 11, 2001, once in force, will replace the tax treaty concluded between Italy and Yugoslavia in Belgrade on February 24, 1982.

Notes:

The numbers in parentheses refer to the following numbered Notes.

1. The relevant treaty should be consulted to see whether a reduced rate for dividends is applicable in the case of payments to corporations having requisite control.

2. Different rates on interest apply depending on the source.

3. The rates apply on 75% of the gross amount of the royalties paid, unless otherwise noted.

4. The rate applies on 75% of the gross amount of the royalties paid.

5. Nonresidents have the right to be reimbursed up to four-ninths of the withholding levied, upon proving by certificate issued by the appropriate foreign tax office, that they have definitely paid abroad a tax on the same profits.

6. Rates depend on the nature of the interest and/or the recipient. Mainly, the rates on bond issues depend on the redemption period, in particular: 12.5% if the term of the bond issue is more than 18 months; 27% if the term is less. There is no withholding tax, provided that the recipient's state of residence has a tax treaty that covers the following:

   a. Interest on state bonds.

   b. Interest on bonds issued by banks and listed companies.

   c. Interest on bank accounts.

7. The 5% rate applies to royalties arising from the use of any copyright from literary, artistic, or scientific work.

8. The 10% rate applies to royalties arising from the use of any copyright of literary, artistic, or scientific work. The 18% rate applies in all other cases.

9. Rates depend on the nature of the royalty.

10. The 5% rate applies to royalties arising from scientific or industrial equipment.

11. Nonresident shareholder companies with more (less) than 10% of the voting shares are subject to 5% (15%) withholding tax.

12. Withholding tax is 10% if the foreign company holds at least 25% of the entire voting rights in the Italian company; otherwise, it is 15%.

13. Withholding tax is 10% if the foreign company holds at least 25% of the entire voting rights in the Italian company; otherwise it is 15%.

14. Withholding cannot exceed 5% if the recipient holds at least 75% of the entire voting rights in the Italian company.

15. Applicable only to companies that are not considered holding companies in Luxembourg.

16. Withholding tax is 15% if the foreign company holds at least 25% of the voting rights in the Italian company; otherwise, it is 25%.

17. Withholding cannot exceed 10% if the interest is in connection with a state bond issue.

18. Withholding cannot exceed 10% if the Swedish company holds at least 51% of the entire voting rights in the Italian company.

19. Withholding tax is 10% if the company in Trinidad and Tobago holds at least 25% of the entire voting rights in the Italian company; otherwise, it is 20%.

20. Under the terms of the double taxation agreement with the United States, if the recipient of a dividend is a U.S. corporation that controls more than 50% of the voting power of the Italian company declaring the dividend and provided certain other conditions are met, the rate of withholding is reduced to 5%. If the U.S. corporation controls more than 10%, the withholding is reduced to 10%. In all other cases the withholding tax is 15%.

21. The withholding is 5% when the royalty derives from artistic, scientific or literary work, 8% when the royalty derives from movies or films, and 10% in all other cases.

The Italian Parliament is expected to ratify soon pending income tax treaties with Armenia, Croatia, Iceland, San Marino, Syria, and Uganda.

## Tax administration

*Returns*/Tax returns must be prepared on the basis of the financial statements related to the fiscal year to which the returns refer. Corporate tax returns must be filed within one month from the shareholders' meeting approving the financial statements.

*Payment of tax*/An advance payment equal to 99% of the taxes paid in the prior year must be made in two installments, 40% when the prior year's tax return is filed, and 60% in the eleventh month of the company's financial year. The balance is due when the annual tax return is filed.

*Tax amnesty for fiscal year 2002*/The possibility to apply for the tax amnesties provided for by arts. seven (settlement of prior years), eight (simple supplementary return), and nine (definitive tax amnesty) of Finance Act 2003 has been extended to the fiscal year current at December 31, 2002, the tax returns for which were filed by October 31, 2003. The deadline for the payment is April 16, 2004, unless payment by installments is elected. The two-year extension of the deadline for the assessment of unaudited fiscal years for taxpayers who decide not to opt for such tax amnesties still applies.

# Italy

### *CORPORATION TAX CALCULATION*

Fiscal year ended December 31, 2003

## Corporate income tax (IRES)

| | (In thousands of euros) |
|---|---:|
| Profit shown in the Income Statement (A) | 1,000,000 |
| Adjustments increasing the taxable income: | |
|     Equal installments of capital gains | 40,000 |
|     Nondeductible interest expense | 30,000 |
|     Nondeductible or unpaid taxes | 30,000 |
| Total adjustments increasing the taxable income (B) | 100,000 |
| Adjustments decreasing the taxable income: | |
|     Equal installments of write-down of accounts receivable | 20,000 |
|     Exempt income subject to withholding at source | 20,000 |
|     Expenses in respect of transaction with Black list entities | 10,000 |
| Total adjustments decreasing the taxable income (C) | 50,000 |
| Taxable income for IRES (A + B − C) | 1,050,000 |
| IRES (33%) | 346,500 |

## Local income tax on productive activities (IRAP)

| | | (In thousands of euros) |
|---|---:|---:|
| Gross income from sales and services | | 600,000 |
| Add: | | |
|     Variations in stocks and work in progress (1) | | 10,000 |
|     Nonfinancial income | | 10,000 |
| *Less*—Cost of goods and utilities | | 200,000 |
| Gross profit | | 420,000 |
| Add: | | |
|     Cost of personnel | 220,000 | |
|     Accruals for risks | 10,000 | 230,000 |
| | | 650,000 |
| *Less*—Financial costs | | 20,000 |
|     Depreciation of tangible and intangible assets | | 30,000 |
| Earnings before tax | | 600,000 |
| Taxable income for IRAP | | 600,000 |
| Tax at 4.25% | | 25,500 |

Notes:

1. The variations in stocks and work in progress can be positive or negative.
2. Exchange rate of the Euro at January 1, 2004: US\$1 = €0.793903.

## PwC contact

For additional information on taxation in Côte d'Ivoire, contact:

Dominique Taty, Associate Partner
Fidafrica (member of PricewaterhouseCoopers)
Immeuble Colina, 2nd Floor, Bd Roume Plateau
01 BP 3173
Abidjan 01, Côte d'Ivoire
Telephone: (225) 20 22 25 88
Fax: (225) 20 22 23 75
e-mail: d.taty@ci.pwc.com

## General note

This entry is repeated from the 2003/2004 edition. For more up-to-date information consult the contact listed above or Jacqueline Collette at jacqueline.collete@us.pwc.com.

## Significant developments

There have been no significant tax or regulatory developments regarding corporate taxation in the past year.

## Taxes on corporate income

Tax on industrial and commercial profits in Côte d'Ivoire is levied at 35%, subject to a minimum tax. The minimum tax is based on total turnover and is calculated at the rate of 0.5% (banking activities, 0.15%; oil companies, 0.10%), with a minimum of CFAF2 million and a maximum of CFAF30 million.

## Corporate residence

Companies are considered resident in tax jurisdictions where they have a registered fixed establishment.

## Other taxes

*Value-added tax (TVA)/*TVA is a noncumulative tax levied on the sales of goods and services at the rate of 20%. Subject to certain restrictions, TVA is recoverable.

*Service tax (TPS)/*A cumulative tax of 10% is levied on bank services rendered.

*Special tax for equipment/*A tax of 0.08% is calculated on the total turnover and is paid monthly.

*Business franchise tax/*The business franchise tax includes a "turnover tax" and a proportional tax. The "turnover tax" is calculated on the turnover at the rate of 0.5% with a maximum of CFAF3,000,000 and a minimum of CFAF300,000. The proportional tax is based on the rental value of the professional office location (based on general office rents). The rate is 18.5%.

*Real estate tax/*A real estate tax is imposed at the rate of 15% on the rental value of the property. The rate is reduced to 4% for unoccupied buildings.

*Advance payment of property tax/*Property owners are required to withhold 15% of rentals, payable the 15th of every month to the tax authorities. This is an advance payment on annual real estate tax.

# Ivory Coast (Côte d'Ivoire)

**Payroll tax**/Taxes are levied at the rates of 2.8% for local employees and 12% for expatriate employees on the total taxable remuneration, including salaries, benefits, and benefits-in-kind.

**Registration taxes**/Registration of capital contributions is taxed, whether the capital or increase in capital is made in cash or in kind. The rate is 0.6% for contributions up to CFAF5 billion and 0.2% for contributions over CFAF5 billion. Increases in capital by incorporation of reserves are taxed at 6%.

In the event of a capital increase through a merger, the increase in the share capital of the acquiring company is taxed at half the above rate—0.3% for amounts up to CFAF5 billion and 0.1% for amounts over CFAF5 billion. Additionally, a tax of 6% is due on the amount by which the net assets exceed the called-up capital of the acquired company.

For capital increases resulting from a transfer of property, taxes are assessed at the rates of 2.5% for the transfer of rental buildings, 10% for lease transfers, 10% or 7.5% for the sale of real estate, and 10% for the sale of businesses.

**Stamp duty**/A direct tax is paid for any document subject to a registration procedure, for an acknowledgment of a cash payment, and for bills of exchange.

**Tax on insurance premiums**/Insurance premiums are subject to tax as follows.

|  | % |
|---|---|
| Marine policies | 7.0 |
| Life policies | 4.0 |
| Fire policies | 25.0 |
| Export credit insurance | 0.1 |
| Other (e.g., personal liability, transportation) | 14.5 |

Premiums paid under commercial shipping insurance policies for maritime risks are exempt. The tax may be paid by the insurance company, its agent, or the subscriber, when the subscriber pays the premiums directly abroad.

**Social security contributions**/Employers must contribute to the social security system (CNPS) at the following rates.

|  | % | Monthly ceiling CFAF |
|---|---|---|
| Family allowance | 5.75 | 70,000 |
| Work injury | 2.0–5.0 | 70,000 |
| Retirement pension | 4.8 | 1,647,315 |

**Withholding tax on public contracts**/Any payment made by the state or a public institution on a contract for goods or services is subject to a 10% withholding tax. The tax is recoverable and may be applied to TVA and to income taxes due and withheld by employers. Contractors who do not have a permanent establishment in Côte d'Ivoire are not subject to this tax. Surplus tax payments and tax credits are refundable.

## Branch income

The tax rate for branch income is the same as that for corporate income. After-tax branch earnings are subject to a 12% tax (IRVM) calculated on 50% of the taxable profit. This is analogous to the withholding tax on dividends.

## Income determination

*Inventory valuation*/Inventory is generally stated at the lower of cost or market value. Last in, first out (LIFO) and first in, first out (FIFO) are permitted. Book and tax conformity is required.

*Capital gains*/Capital gains are normally taxed at full corporate rates. However, the tax on capital gain, exclusive of recaptured depreciation, can be deferred if the gain is reinvested within three years.

*Intercompany dividends*/Intercompany dividends are included in taxable income at 50% of the net amount received (after 12% withholding tax). The exemption is increased to 95% for dividends received from a subsidiary if a parent company domiciled in Côte d'Ivoire owns 10% of the subsidiary.

*Foreign income*/Resident corporations are taxed on their worldwide income, except for profits derived from business conducted through a permanent establishment outside Côte d'Ivoire. Since income derived from business conducted outside Côte d'Ivoire is not taxable, no tax credit is allowed. Interest and dividends from foreign sources are entitled to certain deductions (see "Other significant items") to alleviate instances of double taxation. Subject to provisions of tax treaties, no deductions or tax credits are allowed for revenue from royalties and services.

*Stock dividends*/Stock dividends are unusual, but in the event they are declared, they are not taxable to the recipient.

*Other significant items*/Interest from loans and dividends is brought into taxable income at 50% of the net amount earned by the company. Dividends derived from subsidiaries are brought into taxable income at 5% of the net income earned.

## Deductions

*Depreciation and depletion*/Depreciation is generally computed on a straight-line basis over the useful life of the asset (buildings—20 years; automobiles—3 years); accelerated depreciation is sometimes permitted for machinery. The following depreciation rates are generally accepted for tax purposes.

|                       | %        |
|-----------------------|----------|
| Buildings             | 5        |
| Machinery, equipment  | 20, 10, 8 |
| Office furniture       | 10       |
| Office equipment       | 20       |
| Vehicles               | 33 1/3   |

A time coefficient is applied to the rate of depreciation to obtain the declining balance. Depreciation rates may be amended, but only after agreement with the tax authorities.

New plant and equipment may be depreciated at twice the normal rate in the first year of use, provided they are depreciated over at least six years. Under certain circumstances, buildings used for staff housing may be depreciated at 40% of cost in the first year. Annual depreciation must be booked to preserve tax deductibility. The whole or any part of the annual charge can then be deferred in annual accounts for fiscal years showing a tax loss. Recaptured depreciation is taxed at full rates. Tax and book conformity is obligatory.

Depletion allowances as such do not exist, but tax incentives are available for exploration to replace depleted natural reserves.

# Ivory Coast (Côte d'Ivoire)

***Net operating losses***/Losses may be carried forward five years. Losses derived from depreciation can be carried forward indefinitely.

***Payments to foreign affiliates***/Royalties, interest, and management and service fees paid to foreign parent companies are tax deductible under a cumulative limit of 5% of the turnover and 20% of the company overhead expenses; moreover, the onus is on the taxpayer to prove that expenses are justified and reflect real transactions.

### Other significant items

1. Legal reserve: 10% of net profit must be transferred to a reserve for legal fees until the reserve equals 5% of the paid-up share capital.
2. To be tax deductible, provisions must relate to existing liability or loss. General reserves are not deductible.
3. Interest paid to shareholders may be deducted. However, deductions are limited in that the total outstanding loans granted by shareholders or a parent company to an Ivorian company may not exceed the share capital. Interest paid on the portion of a loan that exceeds this limitation is not tax deductible. The maximum interest rate allowed is related to the BCEAO (*Banque Central des Etats de l'Afrique de l'Ouest*) rate plus three points. These deductions are cumulative.

## Group taxation

Group taxation is not permitted.

## Tax incentives

***Inward investment***/Investment Law No. 95-620 of August 3, 1995 divides the country into two investment zones, offering incentives for up to five or eight years in each area. The Investment Code provides for 100% tax exemption during the first three or six years (depending on the nature of the activity and the zone), then 50% and 25% progressively for the last two years of exemption. Exemption periods may be extended to complete a scheduled investment program.

Incentives are divided into two programs, which are "Prior Declaration" for investments of less than CFAF500 million that create new activity and "Prior Agreement" for investments of CFAF500 million or more that create new activity or develop an existing activity. Both programs are handled by the *Centre de Promotion des Investissements en Côte d'Ivoire* (CEPICI) and are open to all sectors except trade, public works, building construction, transportation, banking, and insurance.

Prior Declaration investments may be exempt from tax on corporate income and the business franchise tax. Prior Agreement investments benefit from exemptions varying with the size and nature of the project, as follows.

1. Creating a new enterprise or a new activity in an existing enterprise: Investments of CFAF500 million to CFAF2 billion may be exempt from tax on corporate income; business franchise tax; import duties and taxes (with the exception of a 5% tax on machinery, equipment, and spare parts).

   Investments of more than CFAF2 billion may be exempt from property tax, in addition to the above.

2. Developing an existing activity: Investments of at least CFAF500 million may be exempt from import duties and taxes (with the exception of a 5% tax on machinery, equipment, and spare parts).

These incentives may not be combined with sector-specific investment programs, such as for mining and hydrocarbons.

*Capital investment*/With prior approval of the tax authorities and varying with geographical location, 25% to 30% of the total investment in fixed assets related to commercial, industrial, or agricultural activity may be deducted from taxable income. The deduction is limited to 50% of taxable profits. The balance of deduction of the first year may be carried forward over the three following years.

*Export incentives*/No TVA is levied on export sales.

*Mining industry incentives*/During the exploration phase, investments may be exempt from payroll tax; TVA on goods and services; additional tax (on the sale of goods) on imports and purchases; all import taxes and duties including TVA on materials, machines, and equipment used in research activities; and half of the registration duties applicable to in-kind or cash share-capital contributions.

During the production phase, mining activities may have a five-year exemption from corporate income tax and relief from all import duties, including TVA on recovered investments required for exploitation, and they may be granted temporary admission of machines and equipment that facilitate research and exploitation. A tax on profit is levied as soon as investment funds are recovered. Mining enterprises may not combine these incentives with those of the Investment Code.

*Petroleum service contractors*/A special and optional tax treatment applies to petroleum service contractors that meet established criteria. Corporate tax, distribution tax, payroll tax, income tax on salaries, and the tax on insurance premiums are calculated on the turnover of the contractor. The total taxes represent 6.736% of turnover. Standard rates apply for business franchise tax and social security contributions for local personnel. The exemption from customs duties and VAT for oil companies is extended to petroleum service contractors.

## Withholding taxes

Withholding taxes are levied as follows.

1. IRVM (*impot sur le revenu des valeurs mobilieres*)—12% or 18% on dividends and directors' fees.
2. IRC—18% on interest payments, reduced to 13.5% (individuals) and 16.5% (businesses) on bank deposit interest. Foreign banks are subject to 18% tax on loan interest or 9% on equipment loans with minimum three-year terms.
3. BNC—25% of 80% of revenues on royalties, license fees, and management and service fees paid by Ivorian companies to foreign companies (effective rate—25% of net amount paid). Treaties with Belgium, Canada, France, Germany, Italy, Norway, Switzerland, and the United Kingdom provide a maximum BNC rate of 10%.
4. Interest on certificates of deposit (*bons de caisse*)—25%.

## Tax administration

*Returns*/Companies are required by law to have a December 31 fiscal year-end. The corporate tax return must be submitted by April 30 of the following year.

# Ivory Coast (Côte d'Ivoire)

***Payment of tax***/Tax withheld must be rendered to the tax authorities by the 15th of each month. Other taxes are rendered on varying dates.

## *CORPORATION TAX CALCULATION*

For year ended December 31, 2002

| | | |
|---|---:|---:|
| Net income before taxes | | CFAF 250,000,000 |
| Add back: | | |
| Charitable contributions | 50,000 | |
| Fines | 50,000 | |
| Nondeductible provisions at 12/31/2002 | 11,000,000 | 11,100,000 |
| | | 261,100,000 |
| Deduct: | | |
| Capital gains deferred | 2,000,000 | |
| Nondeductible provisions at 12/31/2001 | 9,900,000 | |
| 50% of dividends | 1,000,000 | |
| Loss carryforward—1997 | 5,000,000 | 17,900,000 |
| Difference | | CFAF 243,200,000 |
| 25% of approved investment | | 100,000,000 |
| Taxable income | | 143,200,000 |
| Tax thereon at 35% | | CFAF 50,120,000 |

Note:

Exchange rate of the CFA franc at December 31, 2002: US$1 = CFAF625.50.

Parity remains fixed between the CFA franc, used in 14 French-speaking African countries, and the Euro. The rate is €1 = CFAF655.957. The convertibility of the CFA franc continues to be assured as long as transfers are made through banking channels.

## PwC contact

For additional information on taxation in Jamaica, contact:

Eric A. Crawford
PricewaterhouseCoopers
Scotiabank Centre
Duke Street
Kingston, Jamaica
Telephone: (1) (876) 922-6230
Fax: (1) (876) 967 1949
e-mail: eric.crawford@jm.pwc.com

## Significant developments

The General Consumption Tax (GCT) base was widened. Certain goods and services, which were exempt or zero-rated, were recategorized to attract GCT at 15%.

A 4% cess on all imports was introduced for the month of May 2003. A 2% user fee on imports, effective June 1, 2003, then replaced this cess. Certain groups are exempted from this 2% charge.

Removal of the tax credit for bonus share issue as of June 1, 2003.

An environmental levy of $2.00 per kilogram has been imposed on containers imported, manufactured and/or distributed in Jamaica. Containers to which the levy will apply include plastic packaging material as used to package soft drinks and detergents, trash bags, plastic bottles, and fast food packaging (Styrofoam).

## Taxes on corporate income

Income tax at a basic rate of 33 1/3% is payable by most corporations, including Jamaican branches of foreign corporations.

Life insurance companies are taxed at 7.5% on their investment income less management expenses. This, however, is expected to change after the tabling of the 2004/2005 budget. Building societies (similar to savings and loans) are taxed at the rate of 30% on their profits.

There are no other local taxes on corporate income.

## Corporate residence

A corporation, wherever incorporated, is resident in Jamaica if the central management and control of its business are exercised there. Normally, this is the case if meetings of directors and shareholders are held in Jamaica and major policy decisions of the corporation are made there.

## Other taxes

*Annual fee*/A fee ranging from J$1000 to J$35,000 is payable, depending on the aggregate value of the company's assets. The maximum fee is payable where the aggregate asset value exceeds J$100 million.

*Life insurance premium tax*/This tax is payable by regionalized companies at 1.5% of premium income. For others the rate is 2% of premium income.

# Jamaica

**Consumption taxes, customs duties**/There is a value-added tax (VAT), called the General Consumption Tax (GCT). The standard rate is 15%. Higher rates are applicable to some goods (tobacco products, liquor, motor vehicles, and fuels), and there is a special regime for tourism activities. The list of items and services exempt from GCT includes a wide range of grocery and household items. Certain specified drugs, as well as other items and services, are zero-rated. GCT on telephone charges was increased to 20%. GCT is now charged on imported services, hence where a taxable activity consists of imported services by a person who is not resident in Jamaica, the recipient of those services shall be deemed to be the registered taxpayer, and shall pay the tax chargeable in respect of the supply.

The 2% user fee was imposed on all imports. Government departments, diplomats, international organizations, new manufacturers, 807 companies, and Food for the Poor are exempt from this 2% charge.

The government has amended the Customs Act to replace the existing definition of value for customs duty purposes with a system of valuation based on the World Trade Organization (WTO) Agreement on Customs Valuation, in fulfillment of Jamaica's obligations to the WTO and the Caribbean Community.

## Branch income

Branch income is taxed at the same rate as that of local corporations and on a similar basis. The transfer of profits to head office is subject to a withholding tax of 33 1/3% or at a lower treaty rate where applicable.

## Income determination

**Inventory valuation**/Inventories are valued at the lower of cost or market value. The Commissioner of Income Tax has made no pronouncement, but LIFO is generally not permitted. Book and tax methods of inventory valuation will generally conform.

Any method of valuation that accords with standard accounting practice is acceptable for tax purposes, provided it is consistently applied at the beginning and end of the accounting period and is not in contravention of the Income Tax Act.

**Capital gains**/There is no tax on capital gains. There is, however, a transfer tax of 7.5% of sales proceeds (limited to 37.5% of the capital gain) payable on the transfer of land, buildings, securities, and shares. There is also stamp duty of 1% payable on the transfer/disposal of shares, and 5.5% for real property sold/transferred. Transactions on the Jamaica Stock Exchange are exempt.

**Dividends**/Income tax on dividends is withheld at source. Between June 1, 2000 and March 31, 2001, dividends paid by a Jamaican corporation whose shares are quoted on the Jamaican Stock Exchange were taxed at the rate of 20% (down from 33 1/3 % when paid to corporations, or 25% when paid to individual shareholders). This rate was reduced to 10% in April 2001, and was reduced to 0% in April 2002. Dividends paid by unlisted companies are taxed at the rate of 33 1/3% and 25% if paid to corporations and individuals respectively. These rates may be varied by treaty.

The term "franked income" refers to dividends received by a corporation subject to income tax, resident in the island, from which tax has been deducted at source. Where such dividends are received by a Jamaican resident company, they may be paid to that company's shareholders and all the way up a chain of companies without further deduction of tax, since the very first deduction of tax settles the tax liabilities of all subsequent recipients of the dividend.

However, the revenue authorities do not issue refunds or recognize a credit in respect of the underlying tax attributable to franked income.

*Foreign income*/A resident corporation is taxable on its worldwide income. Avoidance of double taxation is achieved by credits under tax treaties or, in the case of most Commonwealth countries, under the general Income Tax Act itself. Where recourse cannot be had to either of these, partial relief is granted by a deduction against income for the foreign tax.

*Capital distributions*/Dividends paid out of income derived from nontrading sources (e.g., disposal of fixed assets) are termed capital distributions. Such dividends are subject to transfer tax (see "Capital gains") at the rate of 7.5%.

## Deductions

*Depreciation*/Depreciation is generally computed on the reducing-balance basis over the useful life of the asset at specified rates. An election may be made for machinery and equipment to be depreciated at higher rates on the straight-line basis. Provision also exists for increased depreciation on machinery and equipment used for more than one shift in certain qualifying industries. Capital gain on depreciable property is not taxed. However, a recharge limited to the extent of the depreciation allowed (balancing charge) is taxable. Machinery and plant acquired by a "qualifying business" may be depreciated over two years instead of the estimated useful life of the asset. A qualifying business is one so designated by the Ministry of Industry.

Tax depreciation is not required to conform with book depreciation.

*Net operating losses*/Losses incurred may be carried forward indefinitely until fully utilized. There are provisions designed to disallow the deduction of such losses where the company that has accumulated them is sold under certain circumstances.

*Payments to foreign affiliates*/Royalties, management service fees and interest charges paid to foreign affiliates are deductible to the extent that these payments are made at arm's length rates. Withholding tax should be paid in respect of all service payments unless exempt under a treaty.

*Taxes*/Taxes on real estate from which income is derived are deductible.

*Other significant items*/Approved donations not exceeding 5% of taxable income to certain qualified charities and educational institutions are deductible.

## Group taxation

Group taxation is not permitted.

## Tax incentives

*Inward investment*/A number of incentive laws grant certain approved industries relief from taxation for a specified number of years. The capital may be derived from either local or foreign sources. Tax relief is given to resident shareholders on dividends paid out of tax-free profits. Relief to nonresident shareholders is generally limited to the applicable foreign tax rate. Nonresidents who place deposits with Jamaican banks may earn interest free of Jamaican tax. The deposits may be designated in hard currency or Jamaican dollars.

*Capital investment*/Certain qualifying industries are able to write off, over a period of time, 120% of the cost of machinery and equipment, excluding private motor vehicles. Alternatively, a "qualifying business" that has been certified can get a special capital allowance permitting a write-off over two years for capital expenditure on new machinery.

*Other incentives*/The government introduced the Urban Renewal (Tax Relief) Act 1995 in an attempt to promote the improvement and restoration of areas suffering from blight or urban decay. Approved developers or organizations may obtain tax relief in connection with carrying out programs of development in specified areas declared by the Minister of Finance to be special development areas, with a view to restoring these areas. Relief is available from income tax for interest paid to an investor in respect of an urban renewal bond, interest earned on loans issued by an approved organization, capital expenditure by a developer in relation to a National Monument, and rental income paid to an approved developer in respect of the lease or rent of the improved property. In addition, a tax credit of 25% of capital expenditure incurred is available to a developer. Urban renewal bonds are exempt from stamp duty.

Certain tax benefits accrue to employees and employers in respect of contributions made to an approved Employee Share Ownership Plan (ESOP) as well as the allocation of shares from such plans.

*Long-term savings accounts*/Certain categories of interest income earned on long-term savings accounts (LSAs) are tax exempt. Interest paid or credited in respect of investments or deposits made by individuals with prescribed persons under the following circumstances.

1. If the deposit or investment remains for a minimum of five years without any withdrawal from the principal sum invested.
2. If the deposit or investment does not exceed J$1 million in any year.
3. If the account is not transferable, except on the death or bankruptcy of the depositor or investor.
4. If not more than 75% of the interest accrued in any year is withdrawn.
5. If at least 80% of the amount deposited in the account is invested in specified instruments, that is, Government of Jamaica securities or others approved by the Minister of Finance.
6. If the account is registered with the Minister of Finance.
7. If the amount deposited or invested is neither transferable (except on the death or bankruptcy of the depositor or investor), assignable nor available for use as collateral.

Tax exemption is also afforded to investments in life insurance contracts and unit trusts. There are separate criteria to be met in each case in order to qualify for tax exemption.

## Withholding taxes

The Jamaican Income Tax Act refers to deduction at source and not to withholding, and the references below are to deduction at source. If it is proved that this exceeds the tax actually payable, refunds are made.

Effective May 1, 2000, "prescribed persons" are required to withhold tax at source at a rate of 25% on interest income earned on investment instruments (subject to any lower rate as prescribed in a double taxation treaty). The Income Tax Act has been amended to provide a wider definition for the term "interest." "Prescribed persons" are entities defined as such. They include the Accountant General; banks operating under the Banking Act or the Bank of Jamaica Act; institutions operating under the Financial Institutions Act; building societies, societies registered under the Cooperative Societies Act; licensed securities dealers; a society registered under the Industrial and Provident Societies Act, unless certain conditions are met; the Ministry of Finance; life insurance companies; companies registered under the Companies Act in which the government or an agency of the government holds more than 50% of the ordinary shares and which issues interest-bearing securities; issuers of commercial paper; unit trust management companies; and any person who is connected with any of the persons mentioned above (with the exception of the Accountant General).

| | Dividends (1) | | | |
|---|---|---|---|---|
| **Recipient** | **Portfolio** | **Substantial holdings** | **Interest (2)** | **Royalties** |
| | % | % | % | % |
| Resident corporations............ | 33 1/3 (3) | 33 1/3 (3) | 25 (4) | Nil |
| Resident individuals .............. | 25.0 (3) | 25.0 (3) | 25.0 (4) | Nil |
| Nontreaty:.............................. | | | | |
| Nonresident corporations ...... | 33 1/3 | 33 1/3 | 33 1/3 | 33 1/3 |
| Nonresident individuals ......... | 25.0 | 25.0 | 25.0 | 25.0 |
| Treaty: | | | | |
| Canada............................ | 15.0 | 22.5 | 15.0 | 10.0 |
| CARICOM countries .......... | 0.0 (5) | 0.0 (5) | 15.0 (5) | 15.0 (5) |
| China, P.R. ...................... | 5.0 (6) | 5.0 (6) | 7.5 (6) | 10.0 |
| Denmark........................... | 15.0 | 10.0 (7) | 12.5 | 10.0 |
| France ............................. | 15.0 | 10.0 (7) | 10.0 | 10.0 |
| Germany........................... | 15.0 | 10.0 (7) | 12.5 (8) | 10.0 |
| Israel ............................... | 22.5 (9) | 15.0 | 15.0 | 10.0 |
| Norway ............................ | 15 (6) | 15 (6) | 12.5 | 10.0 |
| Sweden ........................... | 22.5 (6, 9) | 10.0 (6) | 12.5 | 10.0 |
| Switzerland....................... | 15.0 (6, 7) | 10.0 (6) | 10.0 | 10.0 |
| United Kingdom................. | 15.0 (6, 7) | 22.5 (6) | 12.5 | 10.0 |
| United States.................... | 15.0 (6, 7) | 10.0 (6) | 12.5 | 10.0 |

The numbers in parentheses refer to the following numbered Notes.

Notes:

1.  No tax is deducted where the dividends are paid out of franked income.

2.  No withholding tax is applicable where the interest is paid by a local bank or financial institution to an approved overseas organization, that is, a foreign bank or financial institution approved by the Minister of Finance.

3.  Tax is withheld at the rate of 0% as of April 1, 2002 where the dividend is paid by a listed company.

4.  Tax is deducted from interest paid to Jamaican residents if payment is made by a "prescribed person."

5.  Rates apply only to specified member states.

6. The lower treaty rates do not apply if the recipient has a permanent establishment in the other territory that is "effectively connected" with the company paying the dividend.
7. A rate of 15% applies to an individual regardless of shareholding.
8. Reduced to 10% if received by a bank recognized as a banking institution under the laws of that state.
9. A rate of 22.5% applies to an individual regardless of shareholding.

## Tax administration

Five taxation departments have been established, as follows.

1. The Tax Administration Services Department (TASD), which deals with administrative issues.
2. The Taxpayer Audit and Assessment Department (TAAD), which deals with the audit and assessment functions of income tax, general consumption tax (GCT/VAT), stamp duty, and transfer tax.
3. The Taxpayer Appeals Department (TAD), which processes appeals to decisions made by Tax Commissioners.
4. The Revenue Protection Department (RPD), which investigates customs breaches and fraudulent acts in respect of the various tax acts.
5. The Inland Revenue Department, which deals with all compliance and tax collection functions.

The Customs has been retained, substantially in its original form.

*Returns*/A corporation is subject to tax on its income for a calendar year. Where, however, the Commissioner of Income Tax is satisfied that a corporation normally prepares financial statements to a date other than December 31, the company may be permitted to use the profits of its own financial year rather than the calendar year as the basis of assessment.

Corporate taxpayers file annual self-assessed returns with the tax authorities.

*Payment of tax*/The balance of income tax payable for a taxation year, after deduction of the installments of estimated tax, is due on March 15 of the following year. It is the corporation's responsibility to determine the liability and settle it with the tax authorities. Quarterly installments of a corporation's income tax liability are required during the particular year of assessment. The installments are based on an estimate of that year's liability or the actual tax payable for the previous year. Income tax returns are due for filing by March 15 in the year following the year of assessment.

# Jamaica

## *CORPORATION TAX CALCULATION*

Calendar year 2003

| | | |
|---|---:|---:|
| Net profit before taxation | | J$ 1,000,000 |
| Add: | | |
| Depreciation charged in the financial statements | 45,000 | |
| Interest payable 2003—Accrued | 42,000 | |
| Interest receivable 2002—Accrued | 15,000 | |
| Donations not approved | 8,000 | |
| Legal expenses re: bonus share issue | 11,500 | |
| General provision for bad debts (1) | 15,000 | |
| Capital element of finance lease repayment | 50,000 | |
| Balancing charge (2) | 12,500 | 199,000 |
| | | 1,199,000 |
| Less: | | |
| Franked income received | 25,000 | |
| Interest earned on urban renewal bond | 20,000 | |
| Gain on disposal of fixed assets | 5,000 | |
| Interest receivable 2003—Accrued | 10,000 | |
| Capital allowances (3) annual and initial | 45,000 | |
| Balancing allowance (2) | 7,500 | |
| Special capital allowance (4) | 75,000 | 187,500 |
| Taxable income | | 1,011,500 |
| Tax payable at 33 1/3% | | 337,167 |
| Less: | | |
| Credit for tax deducted from foreign income | 1,000 | |
| Credit for bonus issue of shares (5) | 50,000 | |
| Credit for tax deducted from local bank interest | 12,250 | 63,250 |
| Net tax payable | | J$ 273,917 |

Notes:

1. Specific bad debts are allowed.
2. Tax-deductible allowance/taxable recharge arising on the disposal of an asset.
3. Tax depreciation granted in lieu of book depreciation.
4. Cost of new machinery purchased in 2003 is J$150,000. Amount available in 2003 is J$75,000 (assuming the company is a "qualifying business").
5. Tax credit is 25% of nominal value of bonus shares. Maximum qualifying amount of bonus shares is 50% of after-tax accounting profits.

   After-tax profit (1,000,000 − 337,167) x 50% therefore
   qualifying distribution limited to ................................................. 331,416

   Nominal value of bonus shares issued = J$200,000
   25% thereof .............................................................................. J$50,000
6. Exchange rate of the Jamaican dollar at January 1, 2004: US$1 = J$59.95.

# Japan

## PwC contact

For additional information on taxation in Japan, contact:

Hiroyuki Suzuki
PricewaterhouseCoopers
Kasumigaseki Building, 15F
2-5, Kasumigaseki 3-chome
Chiyoda-ku
Tokyo 100-6015, Japan
Telephone: (81) (3) 5251 2400
Fax: (81) (3) 5251 2424
e-mail: hiroyuki.suzuki@jp.pwc.com

## Significant developments

The 2003 tax reform includes several tax incentives that are intended to revitalize the sluggish condition in the Japanese economy and to strengthen the global competitiveness of Japanese business. The major elements of the reform are R&D credit, IT investment incentives and certain measures in relation to the industrial revitalization law. In order to compensate for the tax revenue loss as a consequence of the legislation of new incentives, several tax incentives were repealed. Further, as a part of the 2003 tax reform, it was decided that a new local tax regime would be introduced from the fiscal year beginning on or after April 1, 2004 in order to sustain the local tax revenue.

According to the Ministry of Finance, the tax reform measures are budgeted to cost ¥1.5 trillion (about US$14 billion) in lost tax revenues at the national level, rising to ¥1.8 trillion when local taxes are included. In particular, the R&D and IT investment incentives are expected to cost about ¥1 trillion, which is approximately 70% of the tax deduction effect at national level. This clearly demonstrates that R&D and IT incentives are the main measures in the 2003 tax reform.

## Taxes on corporate income

*Corporation tax*/The rates are as follows.

|  | % |
| --- | --- |
| Paid-in capital of over ¥100 million | 30.0 |
| Paid-in capital of ¥100 million or less: | |
| First ¥8,000,000 per annum | 22.0 |
| Over ¥8,000,000 per annum | 30.0 |

*Inhabitants tax*/A local tax consisting of prefectural and municipal taxes is computed as a percentage of the corporation tax. (Allocation to each local jurisdiction is based on the number of employees.) Each prefecture and municipality may elect an inhabitants tax rate within the range shown below.

|  | % |
| --- | --- |
| Prefecture | 5 to 6 |
| Municipality | 12.3 to 14.7 |
| Tokyo metropolitan (combined) | 17.3 to 20.7 |

In addition, each local government levies equalization per capita tax on each corporation that has an office or business place in its jurisdiction. This tax varies from ¥70,000 to ¥4,600,000, depending on the sum of paid-in capital plus capital surplus and number of employees.

*Enterprise tax*/This tax is imposed on the corporation's income allocated to each prefecture. (Allocation is generally made on the basis of the number of employees.) The enterprise tax rate is within the range shown below.

|  | % |
| --- | --- |
| First ¥4,000,000 per annum | 5.0 to 5.25 |
| Next ¥4,000,000 per annum | 7.3 to 7.665 |
| Over ¥8,000,000 per annum | 9.6 to 10.08 |

If the paid-in capital of a corporation is ¥10 million or more, and the corporation has places of business in more than two prefectures, the benefits from graduated rates are eliminated. The enterprise tax for utility corporations and insurance companies is 1.3% to 1.365% of net utility charges (as defined) and net insurance premiums (as defined), respectively.

Enterprise tax paid during the current period is deductible in arriving at taxable income for corporate tax purposes.

The Tokyo Metropolitan Government introduced a temporary enterprise tax applicable to all banks with liquid assets of ¥5 trillion or more. The tax, which is a 0.9% tax on gross profits, applies for fiscal years beginning between April 1, 2000 and March 31, 2004. The Osaka Prefectural Government also adopted a similar scheme applicable for fiscal year beginning between April 1, 2003 and March 31, 2004 with the applicable rate of 0.92% instead of the statutory 3% if approved in the Osaka Parliament.

From the fiscal year beginning on or after April 1, 2004, a new "size-based" tax (*Gaikei Hyojun Kazei*) is applied to the company whose paid-in capital is more than ¥100 million. Under the new tax system, factors such as the size of a corporation's personnel costs and its capital will determine the amount of tax payable whereas the existing profit-based enterprise tax will also continue to apply, although with the reduced tax rate. Thus, a loss company will be required to pay tax. The applicable rate is shown below.

|  | % |
| --- | --- |
| Profit-based tax: |  |
| First ¥4,000,000 per annum | 3.8 to 4.56 |
| Next ¥4,000,000 per annum | 5.5 to 6.6 |
| Over ¥8,000,000 per annum | 7.2 to 8.64 |
| Additional value-based tax: | 0.48 to 0.576 |
| Capital-based tax: | 0.2 to 0.24 |

## Corporate residence

A company incorporated under the laws of Japan is a domestic corporation. The nationality of its shareholders or place of central management is not pertinent. A corporation other than a domestic corporation is regarded as a foreign corporation.

## Other taxes

*Family holding company tax*/A family holding company is liable for an additional tax at the rates shown below on earnings retained in excess of specified limits.

# Japan

| Corporate tax: | % |
|---|---|
| First ¥30,000,000 per annum ........................................................... | 10 |
| Next ¥70,000,000 per annum ........................................................... | 15 |
| Over ¥100,000,000 per annum......................................................... | 20 |
| Inhabitants tax ................................................................................. | Corresponding increase at rates previously shown |

However, the above scheme is not applicable for certain small- and medium-sized companies during the taxable years starting on or after April 1, 2000 through March 31, 2004.

If any three or fewer individual shareholders, together with their relatives, own, either directly or indirectly, 50% or more of the total issued shares of a Japanese corporation, that corporation is subject to the additional tax.

*Consumption tax*/Consumption tax (value-added tax) is imposed at 5% on goods sold and services rendered in Japan. Exports and certain specific services invoiced to nonresidents are zero-rated.

*Business premises tax*/A company that uses business premises in excess of 1,000 square meters and/or has more than 100 employees in designated cities is liable to tax based on space and gross payroll. Newly constructed business office is no longer subject to the business premises tax on or after April 1, 2003.

*Fixed assets tax*/Real property and tangible depreciable fixed assets are subject to fixed assets tax at the rate of 1.4%.

## Branch income of a foreign corporation

The same rates apply as for corporate profits, although the family-holding additional tax does not apply to a branch of a foreign corporation. No tax is withheld on the repatriation of branch profits to the home office.

## Income determination

*Inventory valuation*/Inventory valuation methods allowable upon election by the taxpayer include actual individual cost, FIFO, LIFO, weighted average, moving average, straight average, most recent purchase, retail, and lower of cost or market. Conformity between statutory accounting and tax reporting is required.

*Capital gains*/Capital gains and losses are classified as ordinary income and losses respectively. If the proceeds from the sale of real property are reinvested in specified fixed assets, taxes generally levied on capital gains may be deferred under certain limited conditions. A special allowance is available in the case of expropriation of real property by either the national or local government.

Additional taxes on capital gains arising from the transfer of land are suspended for sales or transfers made during the period from January 1, 1998 to December 31, 2008.

*Intercompany dividends*/Dividends received from a Japanese corporation are excluded from taxable income for corporate income tax purposes, provided the taxpayer owns 25% or more of the shares in the dividend-paying corporation. If a corporation owns less than 25% of the shares in the dividend-paying corporation, dividends received from the dividend-paying corporation are excluded for 50% from taxable income. Interest allocable to the investment cost of the shares that generate the dividend income effectively reduces the amount of nontaxable dividend income. The tax withheld, at the applicable rate of 7% or 20%, depending on the type of stock, on dividends received is available as a tax credit.

*Foreign income*/A Japanese corporation is subject to Japanese corporate income taxes on its worldwide income as earned. However, Japanese corporations are allowed to claim a tax credit against corporation and inhabitants taxes for foreign income taxes paid. The foreign income taxes on dividend income from a foreign subsidiary include the foreign corporate income tax paid by the subsidiary (including certain second-tier subsidiaries), provided the Japanese corporation owns 25% or more continuously for six months or more, and fulfills certain other conditions. A foreign tax credit is not available for enterprise tax purposes, while foreign branch income attributable to business executed outside Japan is exempt from the enterprise tax.

Undistributed profit of a foreign subsidiary located in a tax haven is included in its Japanese parent company's taxable income under certain conditions, although a foreign tax credit is available. Tax havens are defined as certain countries or territories that do not impose corporate income tax or that tax the income of a foreign subsidiary at a rate of 25% or less.

*Stock dividends*/A Japanese corporation may not distribute retained earnings in the form of stock dividends. However, a Japanese corporation may increase paid-in capital by transferring retained earnings to paid-in capital. The Japanese corporation can then split its issued and outstanding shares to the extent of the increased paid-in capital. These transactions have the same economic effect as a stock dividend. Shares issued in this manner are not taxable to the recipient.

## Deductions

*Depreciation and depletion*/Depreciation of tangible fixed assets is computed by using either the straight-line or the declining-balance method at the taxpayer's election. The declining-balance method does not apply to buildings acquired on or after April 1, 1998 or to intangible fixed assets. The law provides useful lives for various categories of fixed assets and the rates of annual depreciation for both straight-line and declining-balance methods.

The following is a sample of useful lives and annual depreciation rates. Goodwill acquired on or after April 1, 1998 shall be amortized by 20% or less of the acquisition costs per year.

|  | | Rate | |
|---|---|---|---|
|  | Useful life | Straight linc (1) | Declining balance (2) |
|  | (Years) | | |
| Reinforced concrete buildings for offices......... | 50 | 0.020 | N/A |
| General passenger automobile ...................... | 6 | 0.166 | 0.319 |
| Electric computer (3)..................................... | 4/5 | 0.250/0.200 | 0.438/0.369 |
| Desk, chairs, or cabinets made of wood.......... | 8 | 0.125 | 0.250 |
| Machinery for automobile manufacturing plants................................... | 10 | 0.100 | 0.206 |
| Machinery for iron and steel manufacturing plants................................... | 14 | 0.071 | 0.152 |

# Japan

Notes:

1. Applicable to 90% of acquisition cost.
2. Applicable to net book value.
3. Four-year life is applied to personal computers (other than the ones used as computer servers), and five-year for other computers.

Special accelerated depreciation, in addition to normal depreciation, may be allowed in the year of acquisition, depending on the industry and type of asset. Differences between book depreciation and tax depreciation must be adjusted in the tax return. Depreciation is limited to the extent of book depreciation.

The production-percentage-depletion method, if elected, may be applied for properties used for mining.

*Net operating losses*/For corporate income tax purposes and enterprise tax purposes (and indirectly, inhabitants tax purposes), tax loss can be carried forward for offsetting future income for a five-year period (a seven- or ten-year period under specified conditions). Carryback of tax loss can be made for one year only for national corporation tax purposes, but currently is generally suspended. No carryback of losses is allowed for either enterprise or inhabitants tax purposes.

*Payments to foreign affiliates*/Royalties paid by a Japanese corporation to foreign affiliates are tax deductible, provided such amounts do not exceed those normally derived from an arm's length transaction.

In the case of thinly capitalized companies, the deductibility of interest paid on foreign related-party debt of a Japanese corporation is restricted. The amount of interest paid to foreign related parties that is disallowed as a deduction is determined by a formula. The disallowance rules apply to interest-bearing debt to foreign related parties if both of the following ratios are more than 3:1 - interest-bearing debt to net equity and interest-bearing debt to foreign related parties to the net equity investment by these parties. A taxpayer may avoid the application of these rules in cases in which its debt-to-equity ratio is greater than 3:1 by showing that an independent third party engaged in a similar business of similar size has a higher borrowing ratio than the taxpayer.

A management fee to a foreign affiliate may be deductible to the extent considered reasonable for specific benefits received by the Japanese corporation.

*Taxes*/As mentioned earlier, enterprise tax is deductible in arriving at taxable income for corporation tax purposes and enterprise tax purposes (except for utility corporations and insurance companies) at the time when it is paid. Corporation tax and inhabitants tax are not deductible. Business premises tax, fixed assets tax, and other taxes that are not income taxes are deductible in arriving at taxable income for corporate income tax purposes. Foreign income taxes may also be deductible if a Japanese corporation does not elect to claim a foreign tax credit.

*Other significant items*/Other deductions include the following.

1. Entertainment expenses—Entertainment expenses are not deductible for tax purposes. There is an exception for corporations whose paid-in capital does not exceed ¥100 million. Such corporations may take a tax deduction to the extent of 90% of the actual disbursement for the entertainment expense or ¥3.6 million (90% of ¥4 million), whichever is smaller for the fiscal year beginning between April 1, 2003 and March 31, 2006.

2. Charitable contributions—Except for certain designated donations, the tax deduction for charitable contributions is limited to the sum of 1.25% of certain taxable income and 0.125% of paid-in capital and capital surplus. However, donations to foreign affiliates are not deductible at all.

3. Director's remuneration—Except for bonuses, remuneration to a director is deductible, provided the amount is reasonable and does not exceed the amount, if any, approved by shareholders or provided for in the articles of incorporation.

4. Employee remuneration—Remuneration to employees is generally deductible. However, excessive salaries and retirement allowances paid to employees in a special relationship (as defined) with directors are treated as not tax deductible.

5. Reserves—Only those reserves for doubtful receivables and returned unsold goods may be deductible if the reserves are recorded in the books of account but subject to certain limitations. The reserves for seasonal bonuses and warranties are no longer deductible for fiscal years beginning on or after April 1, 2003. Further, the reserves for employee's severance indemnities and the reserves for extraordinary repairs are no longer deductible, and are to be reduced over a period of four years from fiscal year beginning on or after April 1, 2003.

6. Expenditures for payees whose names, addresses, and so on, are not disclosed to the tax authorities are not deductible. Such expenditures made before March 31, 2006 are subject to special taxation at 48.28% (at maximum) in addition to the ordinary corporation and inhabitants taxes.

## Group taxation

Under the consolidated tax regime, a consolidated group can report and pay national corporate income tax as one unit. For these purposes a consolidated group means a Japanese parent company and its 100% directly or indirectly owned Japanese subsidiaries. An application for consolidated filing is at the taxpayers' choice, but if made, must include all of the parent's eligible subsidiaries. Once started, consolidated filing should in principle continue indefinitely, unless a specific event (such as change of ownership) causes the qualifying conditions for consolidated filing to fail to be met, or an application to discontinue is approved by the Commissioner of the National Tax Administrative Agency (NTA). The consolidated group's national corporate income tax liability will be computed on a consolidated basis by aggregating the separate taxable income or loss of the member companies, and then making various consolidation adjustments. A profit arising from intra-group transactions is not excluded from the aggregate taxable income, in general. The consolidated national corporate income tax liability will then be determined by applying the normal corporate income tax rate to the consolidated taxable income, adjusted for consolidated tax credits. The total liabilities will then be allocated among the members. The parent company will file the consolidated return and pay the national corporate income tax on behalf of the group, although the member companies remain jointly and severally liable for the consolidated group's total national corporate income tax liability. Local corporate income taxes levied on member companies will continue to be paid on an individual basis although the amounts payable will be affected by the existence of the consolidation. The 2% surtax only applies in the fiscal years for 2002 and 2003.

# Japan

## Tax incentives

*R&D tax credit*/Under the amended R&D credit, taxpayers are able to opt either for the existing regime or a new regime, under which tax credit equal to 10% to 15% of total qualifying R&D spending are available, over and above any ordinary tax deduction against taxable profit. Under the new regime, a 10% to 15% (15% is only applicable for a small- or medium-sized corporation) tax credit is available based on the "R&D Ratio" subject to a limit of 20% of the taxpayer's corporation tax liability. Under the existing R&D tax credit regime, the R&D tax credit is allowed for 15% (should not exceed 12% of the taxpayer's corporation tax liability) of the amount exceeding the amount of the comparable R&D spending provided that the current R&D spending is over the respective amount of last two accounting years as well as the amount of the comparable R&D spending. The new regime applies for the fiscal year beginning on or after January 1, 2003 and the existing regime is extended to fiscal years beginning before April 1, 2006.

*IT Investment incentives*/In the case that IT related facilities are acquired and offered for business use during the period between January 1, 2003 and March 31, 2006, accelerated depreciation of 50% of the acquisition cost or the tax credit of 10% of the acquisition cost may be available. IT related facilities include both hardware and software. The tax credit for the leased properties satisfying certain requirements is available for corporations with capital of ¥300 million or less.

*Capital investment*/A 30% special depreciation rate may be used (or at an option, a tax credit (7% of the acquisition cost, but limited to 20% of the corporation tax liability) is available for small or medium-sized corporation) of certain designated machinery and equipment that save energy if acquired and offered for business use on or before March 31, 2006.

*Investment promotion*/A 30% special depreciation rate may be used or 7% tax credit (up to 20% of the corporation tax liability) may be applied for certain machinery, equipment, furniture, fixtures, trucks, and coasting vessels in a manufacturing business that are acquired by specific small and medium-sized companies if acquired and offered for business use through March 31, 2006. The 7% tax credit may also be applicable to certain leased assets.

*Cross-border investment incentives*/The following are available.

1. Overseas investment—A Japanese corporation making a qualified investment in a designated business to promote the production of certain designated natural resources may establish a tax-deductible reserve to the extent of 30% or 100% of the invested amount in the fiscal year beginning on or before March 31, 2006. The reserve must be restored to income from the sixth to the tenth year after a five-year grace period.

2. Inward investment—For certain designated inward investment enterprises, special rules for tax-loss carryforwards are provided. Losses incurred during the initial five-year period following the establishment (or foundation) of the designated inward investment business may be carried forward for a period of seven years rather than the standard carryforward period of five years when certain requirements are met. The special rules for tax-loss carry-forwards apply to blue-form tax return filing corporations that are qualified as designated inward investment enterprises from their incorporation through the ending date of the fiscal year that begins on or before March 31, 2006.

3. Inward import incentive and export incentive (for certain technical services) was repealed

**Special Measures Law for Industry Revitalization**/With the extension of the effective date of the Special Measures Law for Industry Revitalization, preferential tax treatments were provided for those companies who plan to restructure their business or reorganize their company. Such preferential treatments including the following.

1. Deferral of capital gain taxation arising on a contribution in kind to establish a joint venture company.

2. The extension of the carryforward of losses (from the closure of the business) from the normal five to seven years, and the one-year loss carry back.

3. Special accelerated depreciation, ranging from 24% to 40%, is allowed for investment in "innovative machines and equipment" (i.e., new equipment, required for a qualified plan, and using new technology developed by the corporation).

## Withholding taxes

Companies making certain payments are required to withhold as follows. (Note: The applicable treaty rates are effective as of May 31, 2002.)

| Recipient | Dividends | | Interest | Royalties (2) |
| | Portfolio (3) | Substantial holdings (1) | | |
|---|---|---|---|---|
| | % | % | % | % |
| Japanese corporations ...... | 7 or 20 (3) | 20 | Nil or 20 (4) | Nil |
| Resident individuals........... | 10 or 20 (3) | 20 | Nil or 20 (4) | Nil |
| Foreign corporations, nonresident individuals: | | | | |
| Non-treaty (5) ................... | 20 | 20 | Nil, 15 or 20 | 20 |
| Treaty (6): | | | | |
| Australia ......................... | 15 | 15 | 10 | 10 |
| Austria ........................... | 20 | 10 | 10 | 10 |
| Bangladesh.................... | 15 | 10 | 10 | 10 |
| Belgium ......................... | 15 | 10 | 10 | 10 |
| Brazil ............................. | 12.5 | 12.5 | 12.5 | 12.5, 15 or 20 (7) |
| Bulgaria ......................... | 15 | 10 | 10 | 10 |
| Canada.......................... | 15 | 5 | 10 | 10 |
| China, P.R. ................... | 10 | 10 | 10 | 10 |
| Czechoslovakia (former) (26) .............. | 15 | 10 | 10 | Nil or 10 (8) |
| Denmark........................ | 15 | 10 | 10 | 10 |
| Egypt (5)........................ | 15 | 15 | Nil, 15 or 20 | 15 or 20 (9) |
| Finland........................... | 15 | 10 | 10 | 10 |
| France ........................... | 15 | 5 (10) | 10 | 10 |
| Germany........................ | 15 | 10 | 10 | 10 |
| Hungary......................... | 10 | 10 | 10 | Nil or 10 (11) |
| India ............................. | 15 | 15 | 10 or 15 (12) | 20 |
| Indonesia...................... | 15 | 10 | 10 | 10 |
| Ireland, Rep. of ............. | 15 | 10 | 10 | 10 |

# Japan

| Recipient | Dividends | | Interest | Royalties (2) |
|---|---|---|---|---|
| | Portfolio (3) | Substantial holdings (1) | | |
| | % | % | % | % |
| Israel ........................... | 15 | 5 | 10 | 10 |
| Italy............................... | 15 | 10 | 10 | 10 |
| Korea, Rep. of (13) ........ | 15 | 5 (13) | 10 | 10 |
| Luxembourg................... | 15 | 5 | 10 | 10 |
| Malaysia (14)................. | 15 | 5 | 10 | 10 |
| Mexico .......................... | 15 | Nil or 5 (15) | 10 or 15 | 10 |
| Netherlands ................... | 15 | 5 | 10 | 10 |
| New Zealand (5) ............ | 15 | 15 | Nil, 15 or 20 | 20 |
| Norway .......................... | 15 | 5 | 10 | 10 |
| Pakistan......................... | 20 | 15 | Nil, 15 | Nil or 20 (16) |
| Philippines (17).............. | 20 | 10 | 10 or 15 | 15 or 20 |
| Poland ........................... | 10 | 10 | 10 | Nil or 10 (18) |
| Romania ........................ | 10 | 10 | 10 | 10 or 15 (19) |
| Singapore ...................... | 15 | 5 | 10 | 10 |
| South Africa  ............... | 15 | 5 | 10 | 10 |
| Spain ............................. | 15 | 10 | 10 | 10 |
| Sri Lanka ....................... | 20 | 20 | Nil, 15 or 20 (20) | Nil or 10 (20) |
| Sweden ......................... | 15 | Nil or 5 (21) | 10 | 10 |
| Switzerland.................... | 15 | 10 | 10 | 10 |
| Thailand......................... | 20 | 15 or 20 (22) | 10, or 20 (22) | 15 |
| Turkey............................ | 15 | 10 | 15 or 10 (23) | 10 |
| USSR (former) (24)........ | 15 | 15 | 10 | Nil or 10 (24) |
| United Kingdom (25) ..... | 15 | 10 | 10 | 10 |
| United States................. | 15 | 10 | 10 | 10 |
| Vietnam ......................... | 10 | 10 | 10 | 10 |
| Zambia .......................... | Nil | Nil | 10 | 10 |

The numbers in parentheses refer to the following numbered Notes.

Notes:

1. The tax treaty rates apply only to corporate shareholders. The applicable treaty should be checked for conditions required to claim the reduced rate.

2. The applicable treaty should be reviewed, because certain tax treaties exclude, for example, film royalties and/or gain from copyright transfer from taxable income.

3. For certain dividend received from January 1, 2004 through March 31, 2008, the reduced rate of 7% (for resident individuals, additional 3% will be levied) is applied instead of 20%. Thus, the withholding rate for resident individuals is either 10% or 20% whereas the rate for resident corporations or residents in nontreaty country is 7% or 20%. For residents in treaty countries, 7% or treaty rate will be applied.

4. Interest on bank deposits and/or certain designated financial instruments is subject to a 15% national withholding tax and a 5% local inhabitants withholding tax (20% combined). Taxation of such interest is fully realized by tax withholding, so resident individuals are not required to aggregate such interest income with other income. Interest on loans made by resident

individuals is not subject to withholding tax; instead, it is taxed in the aggregate with other income.

5. Dividends, interest, and royalties earned by nonresident individuals and/or foreign corporations are subject to a 20% national withholding tax under Japanese domestic tax laws. An exceptional rate of 15% is applied to interest on bank deposits and certain designated financial instruments. Interest on loans, however, is taxed at a 20% rate. A special exemption from withholding tax applies to certain long-term corporate bonds issued to nonresidents in foreign countries.

6. Tax treaties with many countries provide reduced tax rates, as indicated. Some treaties, however, provide higher tax rates (e.g., Pakistan and Thailand) or do not provide rates (e.g., Egypt, New Zealand). In these instances, rates specified under Japanese domestic tax laws apply. Each treaty should be consulted to see if a reduced rate for dividends (in the case of substantial holdings) is applicable.

7. Brazil—The tax treaty with Brazil provides a 25% tax rate for certain royalties. However, the withholding tax rate cannot exceed 20% on any royalties to be received by a nonresident taxpayer of Japan under Japanese income tax law. Film royalties and trademark royalties are taxed at 15% and 20%, respectively. Other royalties are taxed at 12.5%.

8. Czechoslovakia (former)—The treaty with the former Czechoslovakia is applied to the Czech Republic and the Slovak Republic. It stipulates that cultural royalties are tax exempt.

9. Egypt—Film royalties are taxed at 20%.

10. France—Dividends received by parent companies that are "qualified residents" are exempt from withholding taxes.

11. Hungary—Cultural royalties are tax exempt.

12. India—The rate of 10% applies if the recipient of the interest is a bank.

13. Korea, Rep. of—A reduced 10% rate of withholding tax on dividends from a substantial holding is applicable up to the end of 2003, after which time the rate will be 5%. Tax sparing credit will not be applicable to the income earned by the Japanese resident in the fiscal years beginning after December 31, 2003.

14. Malaysia—Tax sparing credit will not be applicable to the income earned by the Japanese resident in the fiscal years beginning after December 31, 2006.

15. Mexico—Dividends received from their subsidiaries by parent companies that have met certain conditions are exempt from withholding taxes.

16. Pakistan—Interest on industrial bonds and loans is tax exempt

17. Philippines—The tax treaty with the Philippines provides a 25% tax rate for certain dividends and royalties. However, the withholding tax rate cannot exceed 20% on any dividends and/or royalties to be received by a nonresident taxpayer of Japan under Japanese income tax law. Interest on government bonds and/or corporate debentures is taxed at 10%. Film royalties are taxed at 15%, and the withholding tax rate on royalties paid to designated pioneer companies cannot exceed 10%.

18. Poland—Cultural royalties are tax exempt.

19. Romania—The withholding tax rate on cultural royalties cannot exceed 10%.

20. Sri Lanka—Interest to financial institutions is tax exempt, as are film and copyright royalties.
21. Sweden—If certain conditions for beneficial owners are met, dividends are taxable only in the contracting state of which the beneficial owner is a resident.
22. Thailand—Dividends paid by a corporation that is engaged in industrial undertakings are taxed at 15%. Interest to financial institutions is taxed at 10%.
23. Turkey—Interest to financial institutions is taxed at 10%.
24. The treaty with the former USSR is applied to Armenia, Belarus, Georgia, Kyrgyzstan, Moldova, Russia, Tajikistan, Turkmenistan, Ukraine, and Uzbekistan; it stipulates that cultural royalties are tax exempt.
25. The existing Japan-U.K. double taxation treaty was signed on February 10, 1969 and became effective in 1970. A previous Japan-U.K. treaty, signed in 1962 and effective as of April 1963, is still applicable to Fiji, with whom the reduced rate is only applicable to royalties.
26. The treaty with the former Czechoslovakia is applied to the Czech Republic and Slovakia.

## Tax administration

*Returns*/Corporate income tax returns (i.e., the national corporation tax return, enterprise tax return and local inhabitants tax return) are self-assessment returns. The tax year is the corporation's annual accounting period specified in its articles of incorporation. The Japanese branch of a foreign corporation must use the same accounting period that is adopted by the corporation in its home country.

*Payment of tax*/Income taxes payable with the final corporate income tax return should be paid on or before the filing due date of the final returns (usually two months after the end of an accounting period). If an extension of time for filing is granted, the taxes may be paid on or before the extended due date, with interest at a rate of 4.1% per annum for the period from the day following the original due date (i.e., two months after the end of an accounting period) to the date of the actual payments. Provisional tax payments are required for a corporation that has a fiscal period longer than six months. Provisional taxes are generally computed as one-half of the tax liabilities for the previous year, but they may be reduced by the filing of interim tax returns that reflect semiannual results of operations.

## *CORPORATION TAX CALCULATION*

Fiscal year ended March 31, 2004

### Assumptions

1. The company's paid-in capital is ¥600 million.
2. The company does not have any offices other than in Tokyo.

### Computation of tax

|  | | (In millions of yen) |
| --- | --- | --- |
| Net income before taxes on income, per books | | 1,000 |
| | | |
| Add back: | | |
| Provisions and reserves over tax limit | 110 | |
| Entertainment expenses over tax limit | 60 | |
| Excess charitable donations | 10 | |
| Bonuses to directors | 30 | 210 |
| | | 1,210 |
| Deduct: | | |
| Enterprise tax paid: | | |
| Final payment for the previous accounting period | 50 | |
| Provisional payment for the current accounting period | 60 | 110 |
| Dividends from other Japanese corporations after deduction of attributable interest expense | | 100 |
| Taxable basis for enterprise tax and corporation tax | | 1,000 |
| Corporation tax: | | |
| Regular corporation tax at 30.0% | 300 | |
| *Less*—Tax credit on research and experimental expenses (maximum) | (42) | 258 |
| Inhabitants tax—300 at 20.7% | | 62 |
| Enterprise tax—1,000 at various rates (1) | | 100 |
| | ¥ | 420 |

Notes:

1. Enterprise tax in Tokyo is determined as follows.

|  | ¥ millions | At % | ¥ millions |
| --- | --- | --- | --- |
| First | 4 | 5.25 | 0.2 |
| Next | 4 | 7.665 | 0.3 |
| Remainder | 992 | 10.08 | 100.0 |
| | 1,000 | | 100.5 |

2. Exchange rate of the yen at January 1, 2004: US$1 = ¥107.247 (TTM).

# Kazakhstan

## PwC contacts

For more information on taxation in Kazakhstan, contact:

Richard Land
Courtney Fowler
Scott Walker
Natalya Revenko
Almas Nakipov
Robert Jurik
Michael Wagner
PricewaterhouseCoopers
29/6 Satpaev Avenue, 3rd Floor
Almaty 480070, Kazakhstan
Telephone: (7) (3272) 980448
Fax: (7) (3272) 980252
e-mail: richard.land@kz.pwc.com
       courtney.fowler@kz.pwc.com
       scott.walker@kz.pwc.com
       natalya.revenko@kz.pwc.com
       almas.nakipov@kz.pwc.com
       bob.jurik@kz.pwc.com
       michael.wagner@kz.pwc.com

## Significant developments

Many changes were introduced to the Kazakhstan Tax Code (the Tax Code "On Taxes and Other Mandatory Payments to the Budget" No. 209-II dated June 12, 2001) with effect from January 1, 2004. The amendments include the following significant changes with respect to the taxation of corporations.

- Introduction of a thin capitalization rule for highly leveraged entities (based on a 4:1 debt to equity ratio for most companies), which limits the deductibility of interest on loans received in foreign currency from nonresidents.

- Change in the definition of taxable "foreign currency exchange rate difference," which currently includes any difference resulted from transactions in foreign currency.

- Introduction of automatic procedures for applying an income tax exemption under a double tax treaty for services provided exclusively outside of Kazakhstan. The nonresident service provider should provide a certificate of residence confirming its rights to treaty benefits. The automatic application procedure relating to passive income (royalty, interest, dividends) remains intact (based on a certificate of residence).

- Amendments have been introduced to the list of services entailing Kazakhstan source income regardless of the place of their provision. The list now includes management, financial (with the exception of services involving the insurance and/or reinsurance of risks), consulting, auditing, legal (with the exception of attorneys services), and software maintenance and support services. Marketing, agency, and information services have been excluded from the list.

As in recent years, Kazakhstan withholding tax is triggered by the payment of Kazakhstan source income. Where a payment is not physically made, but the amount is taken as a corporate income tax deduction, withholding tax is required to be transferred to the tax authorities within ten days from the date of submission of the corporate income tax declaration. The deadline for submission of corporate income tax declarations is March 31 of the year following a reporting year.

## Taxes on corporate income

The tax rate for corporations continues to be 30%. All Kazakhstan legal entities and branches of foreign legal entities are subject to corporate income tax. Net income of branches of foreign legal entities is also subject to the branch net profits tax of 15% (potentially reducible to 5% to 10% under a relevant tax treaty). The tax year is the calendar year.

## Other taxes

*Value-added tax*/Starting January 1, 2004, the statutory VAT rate is 15% (reduced from previously effected 16%), with a few specific exemptions. This tax is applicable to the sales value of products and services and to imports. Export of goods is taxed at a zero rate. There is a list of goods, works, and services that are exempt from VAT.

VAT refunds are not generally available unless the entity is making zero-rated supplies. Excess input VAT may be carried forward for offset against output VAT of future periods, or in the absence of taxable turnover, offset against other tax liabilities.

The importation of goods is generally subject to import VAT at 15% (reduced from 16% starting January 1, 2004) assessed on the customs value of the imported goods which includes import customs duties (varying from 5% to 20%) and excise tax (where applicable).

Under a "temporary import regime," import VAT and customs duties are payable on an installment basis at 3% of the amount of import VAT and customs duties that would have been paid had the products been imported under the customs regime for "free circulation" (i.e., normal import). Additionally, importers may enjoy a temporary exemption from the payment of import VAT and customs duties for goods imported under a "financial lease" arrangement. Such exemption is available for the period of the financial lease. Upon expiry of the financial lease, customs duties and import VAT will be payable unless the imported products are exported.

## Other costs of doing business

*Royalty rates*/Royalty rates, applicable to subsurface users, have been subject to negotiation by project. Based on the recent amendments to the Tax Code, royalty rates vary from 2% to 6% depending on the accumulated production volume for the calendar year.

*Customs fees*/The customs processing fee (previously 0.2% to 0.4% of the customs fee) has changed, and is now €50 for the main page of a customs declaration, and €20 for each supplemental page of a customs declaration.

*Excise taxes*/Excise duties apply to the sale and import of crude oil (including natural gas liquids), petrol/gasoline (excluding aviation fuel), diesel fuel, electric energy, spirits or alcoholic beverages, caviar, tobacco, jewels, cars and firearms, as well as to excisable businesses (provision of gambling and lottery services).

# Kazakhstan

The Kazakhstan tax code provides for ad valorem and fixed excise rates. Taxable base for ad valorem rates is the selling price (excluding excise and VAT), whereas fixed rates apply to the natural per unit value. In the case of import, ad valorem rates apply to the customs value. Excise duty rates vary and historically are subject to frequent changes.

## Tax incentives

Tax incentives are available through individually negotiated foreign investment contracts.

Investment privileges may include the right for additional tax deductions for creation and expanding production, and exemption from property tax. Under the new Investment Law, investment privileges appear to be available only to companies registered as Kazakhstan legal entities and investing in formally approved priority sectors.

## Withholding taxes

Kazakhstan source income earned by nonregistered foreign legal entities is subject to Kazakhstan withholding tax, unless tax relief is available under the relevant double tax treaty.

Currently Kazakhstan has double tax treaties with 35 countries.

Below is the list of double tax treaties effective as of January 1, 2004.

| Recipient | Dividends | Interest | Royalties |
|-----------|-----------|----------|-----------|
|           | %         | %        | %         |
| Nontreaty | 15        | 15       | 20        |
| Treaty:   |           |          |           |
| Azerbaijan | 10       | 10       | 10        |
| Belarus   | 15        | 10       | 15        |
| Belgium   | 5/15 (4)  | 10       | 10        |
| Bulgaria  | 10        | 10       | 10        |
| Canada    | 5/15 (1)  | 10       | 10        |
| China*    | 10        | 10       | 10        |
| Czech Republic | 10   | 10       | 10        |
| Estonia   | 5/15 (2)  | 10       | 15        |
| France    | 5/15 (4)  | 10       | 10        |
| Germany   | 5/15 (2)  | 10       | 10        |
| Georgia   | 15        | 10       | 10        |
| Hungary   | 5/15 (2)  | 10       | 10        |
| India     | 10        | 10       | 10        |
| Iran      | 5/15 (5)  | 10       | 10        |
| Italy     | 5/15 (4)  | 10       | 10        |
| Korea     | 5/15 (4)  | 10       | 10        |
| Kyrgyzstan | 10       | 10       | 10        |
| Latvia*   | 5/15 (2)  | 10       | 10        |
| Lithuania | 5/15 (2)  | 10       | 10        |
| Moldova*  | 10/15 (2) | 10       | 10        |
| Mongolia  | 10        | 10       | 10        |
| Netherlands | 5/15 (1)| 10       | 10        |
| Pakistan  | 12.5/15 (1) | 12.5   | 15        |

| Recipient | Dividends | Interest | Royalties |
|---|---|---|---|
| | % | % | % |
| Poland | 10/15 (3) | 10 | 10 |
| Romania | 10 | 10 | 10 |
| Russia | 10 | 10 | 10 |
| Sweden | 5/15 (1) | 10 | 10 |
| Switzerland | 5/15 (4) | 10 | 10 |
| Tajikistan | 10/15 (6) | 10 | 10 |
| Turkey | 10 | 10 | 10 |
| Turkmenistan | 10 | 10 | 10 |
| Ukraine | 5/15 (2) | 10 | 10 |
| United Kingdom | 5/15 (1) | 10 | 10 |
| United States | 5/15 (1) | 10 | 10 |
| Uzbekistan | 10 | 10 | 10 |

*Added in 2003: China, Latvia, and Moldova.

The numbers in parentheses refer to the following numbered Notes.

Notes:

1. A rate of 5% (or 12.5% in case of Pakistan) if the recipient is a company controlling, directly or indirectly, at least 10% of the voting power of the company paying the dividends.
2. A rate of 5% (10% in case of Moldova) if the beneficial owner is a company that directly holds at least 25% of the capital of the paying company.
3. A rate of 10% if the recipient is a company holding at least 20% of the capital of the paying company.
4. A rate of 5% if the actual owner is a company (other than partnership), which owns not less than 10% of the capital of paying company.
5. A rate of 5% if the recipient is a company (other than partnership), which directly owns not less than 20% of the capital of paying company.
6. A rate of 10% if the actual owner is a legal entity, which owns not less than 30% of the authorized capital of the legal entity paying the dividends.

## Calculation of taxable income

There are very few book/tax differences for the purposes of calculating taxable income. All taxpayers must use the accrual method. Depreciation is calculated by pooling assets into groups. For calculation of deductible depreciation tax depreciation rates apply to the pooled asset group value. Depreciation is calculated using the declining-balance method.

Net operating losses may generally be carried forward for up to three years. Losses pertaining to activities carried out under subsurface use contracts may be carried forward for up to seven years. Capital gains are subject to ordinary income tax rates. Branches of foreign legal entities are subject to the same tax regime as Kazakhstan legal entities, subject to some modifications.

The applicable tax rate, 30%, is applied to net taxable income. Deductions for most taxes are allowed. The branch profits tax of 15% (potentially reducible to 5% to 10% under the majority of double tax treaties) is applied to earnings after corporate income tax.

# Kazakhstan

## Notes

All Kazakhstan legal entities must transact in tenge within the territory of Kazakhstan. Branches and representative offices of foreign legal entities may operate in hard currency, but are required to keep books and records in accordance with Kazakhstan Accounting Standards. Likewise, Kazakhstan legal entities, branches and representative offices are required to keep accounts in Kazakhstan national currency, tenge. Transactions in foreign currency are converted in tenge applying market exchange rate.

Loan and export-import transactions between residents and nonresidents for periods of more than 180 days and in amounts exceeding US$100,000 are subject to obligatory registration with the National Bank of Kazakhstan.

The Kazakhstan tax environment is very fluid. Therefore, current information regarding Kazakhstan taxes should be obtained before commencing any operations in the country.

Exchange rate of the tenge at January 1, 2004: US$1 = KZT 147.11.

## PwC contacts

For additional information on taxation in Kenya, contact:

Shaira Adamali, Gavin McEwen
PricewaterhouseCoopers
Rahimtulla Tower
Upper Hill Road
Nairobi, Kenya
Telephone: (254) (20) 2855000
Fax: (254) (20) 2855001
e-mail: shaira.adamali@ke.pwc.com
   gavin.t.mcewen@ke.pwc.com

## Significant developments

Significant changes over the past year include the following.

1. Withholding tax rates on payments to resident persons were changed from 10% to 5% for consultancy and agency fees, and from 5% to 3% for contractual fees.
2. A generous tax incentive scheme was introduced for remission of import duty and value-added tax (VAT) on application to the Minister of Finance on capital goods imported for business purposes.
3. VAT rates were reduced from 18% to 16% for the standard rate, and from 16% to 14% for the lower rate. VAT registered persons required to refund input tax deducted in respect of business premises used for making taxable supplies, where such premises are disposed off or converted for making exempt supplies before expiry of five years from the date of construction.
4. Investment deduction allowance on equipment, machinery and industrial buildings has now been increased from 70% to 100% for years of income beginning January 1, 2004.

## Taxes on corporate income

Corporations are taxed at the following rates.

|  | % |
| --- | --- |
| Locally incorporated companies | 30.0 |
| Branches of foreign companies | 37.5 |
| Export Processing Zone enterprises: | |
|  First ten years | 0.0 |
|  Next ten years | 25.0 |
|  Thereafter | 30.0 |
| Newly listed companies approved under Capital Market Act - first five years | 25.0 |

## Corporate residence

A company is considered resident in Kenya if it is incorporated under Kenyan laws, if the management and control of company affairs are exercised in Kenya, or if the company has been declared by the Minister, by announcement in the gazette, to be resident in Kenya for any year of income.

# Kenya

## Other taxes

*Value-added tax*/VAT is levied on the manufacture and supply of certain goods, the provision of taxable supplies in Kenya, and the importation of taxable goods and services, as specified in the VAT Act of 1989. The following rates apply.

|  | % |
| --- | --- |
| Standard rate | 16 |
| Pharmaceuticals, coffee for export, and certain other products | 0 |
| Restaurants | 14 |

Food items are exempt at the retail level only. They remain taxable at the ex-factory level.

Zero rating applies to the export of goods or services, to the supply of goods to certain designated persons, principally the government, and to the supply of goods or services to designated development projects.

Only specific persons can register for VAT, and only registered persons can claim a credit for input tax. Registration for VAT purpose is threefold; mandatory for any business whose taxable supplies exceed KShs 3 million annually, any business that make designated supplies; and voluntary for any other business. The input tax claim must be entered within 12 months. Input tax credit is not available for a number of items.

*Excise duty*/Excise tax is imposed on the manufacture of some commodities, principally aerated waters, cigarettes, alcohol, sports vehicles, perfumes, matches, and passenger cars.

*Import duty*/Imports of goods are generally subject to import duty at rates ranging from nil to 35%. Enterprises established in Export Processing Zones may be exempt from customs duty on machinery and inputs for exported products. Under an import duty exemption scheme, import duty may be remitted for raw materials used to manufacture goods for export. For investments that meet criteria and where prior approval has been obtained, import duty on machinery and equipment can be offset against income tax payable on the company's taxable profit. This import duty may now be refunded in cash if certain conditions hold.

*Stamp duty*/Stamp tax (duty) applies to transfer documents that must be stamped in order for the transfer to be registrable and admissible in a court of law. It is payable at the rate of 1% on authorized share capital and the transfer of securities listed on a stock exchange.

Most stamp taxes are chargeable with reference to the nature of the property being transferred. The highest rate is 4%, which applies to the transfer of immovable property within a municipality. Stamp duty is also payable on the registration of debentures or mortgages and leases.

*Compensating tax*/Where a company pays dividends out of profits that have not been subject to the full rate of corporate tax, it will be liable to a compensating tax at the corporate rate. This effectively ensures that all distributions have been subject to the effective corporate tax rate prior to distribution.

*Advance tax*/Advance tax is payable on the purchase of all commercial motor vehicles at various specified rates.

*Fringe benefit tax*/Where the employer provides loans to an employee at low or no interest, the employer is taxed at the resident corporation rate of tax of 30% on the difference between interest at the 90-day Treasury bill rate and the interest actually paid on the loan. This fringe benefit tax is payable monthly.

## Branch income

Branch income is taxed at 37.5%. Nonresident oil service subcontractors are taxed on 15% of gross income at the branch rate.

## Income determination

*Inventory valuation*/Inventories are generally stated at the lower of cost or market value. Any change in basis at year-end must be accompanied by a corresponding change in basis to the opening valuation.

*Capital gains*/There is no tax on capital gains.

*Intercompany dividends*/Domestic corporations may exclude dividends from domestic subsidiaries and corporations where ownership exceeds 12.5% of voting power. Financial institutions are also exempt from tax on dividends. Where the investing corporation owns less than 12.5%, a withholding tax of 5% is applicable as the final tax. Foreign dividends are outside the scope of Kenyan income tax.

*Foreign income*/A domestic corporation is taxed on its worldwide income, including foreign-branch income as earned. Credit is available for tax paid on income received from countries with which Kenya has a treaty. In other cases, a deduction is available. Foreign source investment income is outside the scope of Kenyan income tax except for banks.

*Stock dividends*/Stock dividends are treated in the same way as other dividends.

*Exclusions from taxable income*/While in general all income received by a resident company is subject to tax, some organizations, for example, charitable institutions, may be exempt because of the nature of their activities. Withholding tax is a final tax for dividend income.

The only other forms of income not subject to tax in the hands of a company are interest on tax reserve certificates and ordinary savings accounts with the post office and income from various government securities specified in the Tax Act.

*Insurance companies*/Insurance companies carrying on life insurance business must determine taxable income as the higher of income per the normal tax computation and the amount reported in the profit and loss account. If the latter basis is used, it cannot be reduced by losses brought forward.

## Deductions

*Depreciation and depletion*/Capital allowances are categorized and are calculated on a reducing-balance basis. Certain restrictions apply in the case of private motor vehicles. For private motor vehicles purchased on or after January 1, 1998, the maximum allowable value subject to the allowance is KShs1 million (approximately US$12,820).

|  | % |
|---|---|
| Heavy, self-propelled machinery, including tractors, harvesters, and earth-moving equipment | 37.5 |
| Computers and related equipment, calculators, copiers, and duplicating machines | 30.0 |
| Other self-propelled vehicles, including aircraft | 25.0 |
| All other machinery, including ships | 12.5 |

Fixed assets are organized in groups. Sale proceeds of an asset are deducted from the reduced balance of other items in its group. Where the value of the asset being sold was restricted, the sale proceeds will be proportionately restricted.

Upon disposal of all of the assets in a group, any remaining balance is a deductible expense in the tax year of final disposal. Where the sale proceeds exceed the tax written-down values, the excess is taxed as a balancing charge.

Capital allowances on industrial buildings and on hotels are calculated on a straight-line basis at the following rates, based on original cost only.

|  | % |
|---|---|
| Industrial buildings | 2.5 |
| Hotels | 4.0 |

No capital allowances are available for office buildings or other real estate. There are special allowances for farming and mining concerns, and for buildings and machinery used for manufacturing purposes.

*Taxes*/Taxes, including compensating tax, are not deductible expenses. However, tax paid in a country other than Kenya on income deemed to have accrued in or derived from Kenya is deductible where it is not eligible for a tax credit.

*Exchange differences*/The treatment of exchange differences is as follows.

1. Exchange losses realized on both trading and capital transactions (e.g., long-term loans) are deductible; similarly, exchange gains realized are taxable. Where the company is foreign-controlled, it is "thinly capitalized", and the loan is from a shareholder, relief for realized losses is deferred until such time as thin-capitalization no longer applies.

2. Exchange loss relief generally is restricted to the extent of notional exchange gains that would result if all foreign currency assets and liabilities were disposed of or satisfied on the last day of the year of income. Any unrealized portion is deemed realized in the succeeding year. Any unrealized portion arising from loans is deferred until realized before it can be deductible/taxable.

No relief is available for exchange losses incurred as a result of branch transactions with the head office; exchange gains of this nature are not taxable.

*Interest*/Interest is deductible when money is borrowed wholly and exclusively for the production of income. However, interest on loans effected for the production of investment income is deductible only to the extent of investment income chargeable each year. Any unrelieved interest is carried forward for deduction from succeeding years' chargeable investment income.

Where thin capitalization applies and the company is foreign controlled, relief on interest paid is restricted to the extent that the highest amount of loans outstanding during the year exceeds the greater of three times the paid-up capital and revenue reserves or the sum of all pre–June 16, 1988, loans still outstanding in the year. These rules do not apply to banks and financial institutions. Loans are defined as "loans, overdrafts, ordinary trade debts, overdrawn current accounts or any other form of indebtedness for which the company is paying a financial charge, interest, discount or premium."

*Leasing*/Lease payments on contracts are generally allowable, except for those for noncommercial vehicles.

*Net operating losses*/Income is divided into sources: trading, rental, farming, interest, and capital gains. Losses from one source may be carried forward and offset against future profits only from the same source; there is no time limit. Carryback of losses is not permitted.

*Payments to foreign affiliates*/Interest, royalties, and management or professional fees paid by the Kenya branch of a nonresident company to its head office are not deductible.

*Special deductions*/Expenditure on scientific research is deductible in full when incurred.

*Other significant items*/Required reserves are as follows.

1. Insurance companies are required to make specific reserves for unexpired risks.
2. All banks and financial institutions are required to contribute 0.15% of their average deposit liabilities to a Deposit Protection Fund maintained by the Central Bank. The Fund guarantees deposits up to KShs100,000. This payment is deductible for income tax purposes.
3. Adjustments to reserves for specific deductible items (e.g., bad debts and obsolescence).

## Group taxation

Group taxation is not permitted.

## Tax incentives

*Inward investment*/Enterprises carrying on business within Export Processing Zones (EPZs) are entitled to the following privileges.

1. Complete exemption from corporation tax for the first ten years of operation.
2. A reduced corporation tax rate of 25% for the next ten years.
3. Zero rating for VAT on the purchase of goods and services.
4. No withholding tax on payments of management fees or dividends to nonresidents.

*Capital investment*/The following capital allowance is available. An investment deduction of 100% (up from 70%) is available on new industrial buildings and on machinery installed therein and on hotels for periods commencing January 1, 2004.

The investment deduction can also be claimed on the purchase of machinery, new or secondhand, used for the purposes of manufacture, including workshop machinery used in maintaining machinery used in the process of manufacture.

A new generous scheme for remission of import duty and VAT on capital goods, plant and machinery imported for business use was introduced on June 12, 2003. In effect, this scheme allows an investor to import capital goods tax-free. An application for remission of the import taxes has to be made to the Minister of Finance prior to importation and certain goods such as motor vehicles and carpets are ineligible for the scheme.

This new scheme will run alongside the old scheme where a project that invests more than US$70,000 in capital equipment (excluding motor vehicles) over two years can claim a credit equivalent to the import duty payable on this equipment against the income tax liability. There are, however, certain qualifications under this latter scheme, as follows.

1. The Minister of Finance must be satisfied that there will be "net income benefits" to Kenya and approve the investment before the importation of the qualifying capital equipment.
2. This relief is not available to aid or government-funded projects.
3. The duty credit claimed must be deducted from the cost of the equipment for calculating wear and tear and any other capital allowances.
4. The import duty set-off is ordinarily not refundable in cash, but the credit can be carried forward indefinitely. However, from January 1, 2001, the import duty can be refunded in cash if certain conditions apply.

## Withholding taxes

*Payments to residents*/When a resident corporation pays dividends to other resident corporations and to individuals, a 5% final withholding tax is deducted. (If the recipient controls more than 12.5% of the voting power of the payer, there is no withholding tax.) The withholding tax on dividends is the final tax.

When a corporation or individual pays interest on a loan to a resident corporation or an individual, 15% withholding tax is applicable unless the payer or recipient is a financial institution or otherwise exempt from tax. The withholding tax rate for bearer deposits is 25%.

A withholding tax of 5% is applicable when royalty payments are made to Kenyan resident companies or individuals. This counts as a credit against the recipient's tax liability.

Withholding tax rates for commissions or fees paid by an insurance company are 5% for brokers and 10% for others.

Withholding tax rates have changed from 2% to 10% for consultancy and agency fees and 5% for contractual fees.

There is no withholding tax on rents paid to residents.

*Payments to nonresidents*/Tax is withheld from payments to nonresidents as follows.

| Recipient | Dividends | Interest | Royalties | Management and professional fees |
|---|---|---|---|---|
| | % | % | % | % |
| Foreign corporations and nonresident individuals (1): | | | | |
| Nontreaty | 10 | 15 | 20 | 20.0 |
| Oil industry | Nil | 10 | 20 | 12.5 |
| Treaty: | | | | |
| Canada | 10 | 15 | 15 | 15.0 |
| Denmark | 10 | 15 | 20 | 20.0 |

| Recipient | Dividends | Interest | Royalties | Management and professional fees |
|---|---|---|---|---|
| | % | % | % | % |
| Germany | 10 | 15 | 15 | 15.0 |
| India | 10 | 15 | 20 | 17.5 |
| Norway | 10 | 15 | 20 | 20.0 |
| Sweden | 10 | 15 | 20 | 20.0 |
| United Kingdom | 10 | 15 | 15 | 12.5 |
| Zambia | 10 | 15 | 20 | 20.0 |

Note:

The withholding tax rate on rents paid to foreign corporations and nonresident individuals is 30% for immovable property, and 15% for other property.

## Tax administration

*Returns*/The tax year of a company is the financial period that it adopts for accounting purposes. Once this period has been selected, it may not be changed without prior approval of the Income Tax Department. With effect from January 1, 1993, a self-assessment regime is applicable. All taxpayers in business are required to lodge a self-assessment return and audited accounts within six months of the tax year-end.

*Payment of tax*/Taxpayers in businesses other than the agricultural business are required to pay tax in four installments. These are due on the 20th day of the 4th, 6th, 9th, and 12th months, respectively. The tax due in each installment is the lesser of 27.5% of the tax assessed in the preceding year, and 25% of the taxpayer's estimate of the tax liability for the current year.

Taxpayers in the agricultural sector must pay tax in two installments. These installments are 75% and 25% of the lesser of 110% of the tax assessed for the preceding year and 100% of the estimated tax for the current year. Payments are due on the 20th day of the 9th and 12th months.

Any balance of tax due for all taxpayers, including those in the agricultural sector, is payable on the last day of the fourth month after the end of the year of income.

# Kenya

## *CORPORATION TAX CALCULATION*

For fiscal year ending December 31, 2003

| | | |
|---|---:|---:|
| Net income before taxes ................................................................... | | KShs 2,000,000 |
| Add: | | |
|    Depreciation................................................................. | 300,000 | |
|    Charitable donations .................................................... | 15,000 | |
|    Pension contributions .................................................... | 35,000 | |
|    Legal fees and stamp tax on property purchase ............ | 30,000 | |
|    Leave passages provision ............................................. | 40,000 | |
|    Increase in general bad debts reserve.......................... | 15,000 | |
|    Rental expenses (see below) ........................................ | 60,000 | |
|    Realized exchange losses (deferred)............................ | 30,000 | |
|    Unrealized exchange losses on loan account................ | 5,000 | 530,000 |
| | | 2,530,000 |
| Less: | | |
|    Capital allowances: | | |
|       Wear and tear........................................................... | 150,000 | |
|       Industrial building ..................................................... | 55,000 | |
|    Investment deduction (assumed to be 70% | | |
|       of qualifying cost) ..................................................... | 65,000 | |
|    Leave passages paid.................................................... | 55,000 | |
|    Rental income (see below) ........................................... | 40,000 | |
|    Capital profit................................................................ | 165,000 | 530,000 |
| Trading income ............................................................................... | | KShs 2,000,000 |
| Tax thereon at 30%.......................................................................... | | KShs  600,000 |
| Rental income: | | |
|    Income (see above) ...................................................... | | KShs  40,000 |
|    Expenses (see above) ................................................. | | (60,000) |
| Loss carried forward against future rental profit ................................ | | KShs  (20,000) |

Note:

Exchange rate of the Kenya shilling at March 19, 2004: US$1 = KShs76.8501.

## PwC contact

For additional information on taxation in Korea, contact:

Ando Yun/Hongkyu Park
Samil Accounting Corporation
Kukje Center Building, 21F
No. 191, 2-ka
Han-Kang-Ro, Yong-San-ku
Seoul 140-702, Korea
Telephone: (82) (2) 709 0551/ 709 0895
Fax: (82) (2) 796 7027, 790 1507
e-mail: andoyun@kr.pwc.com

## General note

This entry is repeated from the 2003/2004 edition. For more up-to-date information consult the contact listed above or Jacqueline Collette at jacqueline.collete@us.pwc.com.

## Taxes on corporate income

*Corporation tax/* The basic Korean corporate tax rates (effective for a fiscal year starting from January 1, 2002 or thereafter) are 15% on the first W100 million of taxable profit, and 27% on taxable profit over W100 million.

*Resident tax surcharges/* In addition to the basic tax rate, there is a resident tax surcharge of 10% on income tax liability.

## Corporate residence

A corporation having its head office or its principal office in Korea is a domestic corporation. A domestic corporation is a resident corporation. A nonresident corporation will generally be deemed to have a tax presence (i.e., permanent establishment) in Korea if one of the following applies.

1. It has any fixed place of business in Korea where the business of the entity is wholly or partly carried on.
2. It is represented by a dependent agent in Korea who has the authority to conclude contracts on its behalf.
3. Its employee provides services in Korea for more than 6 months within 12 consecutive months.
4. Its employee continuously or repeatedly renders similar services in Korea over 2 or more years, if each service is provided for less than 6 months within 12 consecutive months.

Exceptions include fixed places used only for purchasing, storage of property not for sale, advertising, publicity, collecting or furnishing of information, or other activities that are preparatory or auxiliary to the conduct of business.

Nonresident foreign corporations without domestic places of business in Korea are generally taxed (through withholding) at flat rates on gross receipts from Korean sources. Foreign construction and related companies that have a deemed permanent establishment in Korea but are not registered with the Korean tax authorities will be subject to Korean tax withholding on payments from Korean customers.

# Korea, Republic of

The International Tax Coordination Law (ITCL) was enacted effective January 1, 1996. This law provides the legal bases for taxation of all kinds of international transactions, focusing especially on new transfer-pricing rules, advance pricing arrangements (APAs), and mutual agreement procedures. For APAs the law is effective from January 1, 1997.

## Other taxes

*Value-added tax*/VAT is levied at a rate of 10% on sales and transfers of most goods and services, except exports.

*Excess retained earnings tax*/Abolished for the fiscal period starting from January 1, 2002 or thereafter.

*Minimum tax*/Corporate taxpayers should pay the minimum tax, which is defined as the greater of either 15% (12% for small and medium-size companies) of the taxable income before various deductions and exemptions or actual tax after various deductions and exemptions. The minimum tax applies to the corporate tax exemption pursuant to the Special Tax Treatment Control Law with exceptions (e.g., exemption for high-technology foreign investment).

## Branch income

Branches are taxed in the same manner as locally incorporated companies. Foreign exchange for remittance of retained earnings from the branch to its head office is subject to reporting to a designated foreign exchange bank in Korea under the Foreign Exchange Transaction Law.

Furthermore, if the tax treaty between Korea and the country of which the foreign corporation is a resident allows imposition of a branch profits tax, the tax is imposed on the adjusted taxable income of the Korean branch of the foreign corporation.

The branch profit tax is levied in addition to the regular corporation tax under the Corporation Tax Law. It is imposed at 25% (or at a reduced rate as provided in a treaty) of the adjusted taxable income of a foreign corporation effective from the taxable year beginning on or after January 1, 1996.

## Income determination

*Inventory valuation*/Inventories are generally stated at the lower of cost or market (LCM). Any one of seven inventory valuation methods, including LCM, specific identification, FIFO, LIFO, weighted-average, moving average, and retail method can be elected for tax purposes. Inventory valuation methods must be consistent for book and tax purposes.

*Capital gains*/Capital gains are included in taxable income. Gains from the sale of land or buildings will not be subject to additional tax effective from January 1, 2002. However, gain derived from the disposal of land and buildings located in designated area (under the Presidential Decree), with certain exceptions, will be subject to capital gain tax effective from January 1, 2002.

Capital losses are deductible from taxable income (whatever the source). The Korean tax system makes no distinction between short- and long-term gains.

*Intercompany dividends*/Korean corporations are taxed on dividends received from domestic subsidiaries with 50% or 30% exclusion of the dividends from taxable income, depending on ownership ratio in the subsidiaries. A holding company that qualifies under the Anti-Monopoly & Fair Trade Act can exclude 60%, 90%, or 100% of dividends received from domestic subsidiaries, based on the ownership ratio. A total of 90% of the dividends received by institutional investors from companies listed on the Korean Stock Exchange are not subject to corporation tax.

*Foreign income*/Domestic corporations are taxed on worldwide income, whereas foreign corporations are taxed in Korea on Korean-source income. A Korean corporation is taxed on its foreign-source income as earned at normal corporation tax rates. Double taxation is avoided by means of foreign tax credits. The foreign tax credits can be carried forward for five years.

*Stock dividends*/Companies are limited to 50% of a dividend declaration from retained earning whether they are listed or not. All distributions to shareholders are taxed as dividend income whether paid in cash or in stock, except for stock issued by transferring the capital reserves and the revaluation reserves of listed companies into capital.

## Deductions

*Depreciation*/With the exception of land, depreciation of all property, plant and equipment (including buildings; PP&E) used to generate income is allowed as a tax deduction. Generally, interest incurred on debt acquired to purchase, manufacture or construct PP&E must be capitalized until the PP&E is operational. This does not apply to interest associated with expansion or improvement of existing PP&E. For the depreciation expense recorded in the statutory books of accounts to be properly claimed, a detailed list of fixed assets, gross values (including capitalized interest), the useful lives of the assets, and the current year's depreciation charge must be submitted to the tax authorities along with the tax return. If any asset is not included in the listing, the related depreciation may not be allowed as a deduction.

The tax law allows the following methods for calculating depreciation:
1. Straight-line or declining-balance method for tangible fixed assets other than plant and buildings.
2. Straight-line method for plant, buildings and intangible assets.
3. Service-output or straight-line method for mining rights.
4. Service-output, declining-balance, or straight-line method for fixed assets used in mining.

In the acquisition year, an asset is depreciated over the period from the acquisition date to a fiscal year end (effective for assets acquired on or after January 1, 2002).

For fixed assets acquired after December 31, 1994 the salvage value is zero (10% salvage value was required for assets acquired before 1995). However, where the declining-balance method is used, 5% salvage value is required, and that amount is added to the allowed depreciation amount in the fiscal year when the undepreciated balance is less than 5% of the first acquisition cost.

The tax authorities must approve in advance any changes in the depreciation method and such approval can be obtained in exceptional cases (i.e., merger between two corporations having different depreciation methods).

The tax law specifies the basic service lives of assets. For assets acquired after December 31, 1994 the tax useful life and the depreciation rate of a fixed asset can be increased or decreased by 25% of its basic useful life at the taxpayer's option. The basic tax lives are also acceptable as the financial accounting service life under Korean generally accepted accounting principles. There are no specific rules on recapture of depreciation. Book and tax depreciation must be consistently applied.

*Net operating losses*/Loss carryover for five years is permitted. According to the Corporate Tax Law, small and medium-sized companies that have a net operating loss can carry it back a year. However, under the Special Tax Treatment Control Law, they are allowed to carry back a net operating loss two years in a fiscal year ended December 31, 2002 or before and receive a refund to the extent that corporate taxes calculated were paid in the prior year.

*Payments to foreign affiliates*/Interest, royalty, and management-fee payments to foreign affiliates are deductible for income tax purposes with sufficient back-up documentation.

*Taxes*/Certain local taxes, such as property tax and automobile tax, are deductible.

## Group taxation

Group taxation is not permitted.

## Tax incentives

*Inward investment*/The Korean government grants various privileges, incentives, and guarantees to certain foreign investors under the Foreign Investment Promotion Law, as follows.

1. Foreign-invested companies that engage in certain high-technology businesses, as designated by the government, or that settle into a foreign investment area designated under the Foreign Investment Promotion Law, can apply for 100% exemption from corporation tax for seven years, beginning from the earlier of the first year of profitable operations or the fifth year if no profits are generated by that time, and a 50% reduction for three years thereafter in proportion to the ratio of foreign investment. An exemption from withholding tax on dividends is eligible for foreign investors in the same manner as above during the same grace period. In addition, they can apply for 100% exemption from acquisition tax, registration tax, property tax, and aggregate land tax regarding assets acquired for their business for five years after business commencement date and 50% exemption for the following three years.

2. When advance approval is obtained, royalties paid under a high-technology inducement contract are totally exempt from withholding taxes for the first five years starting from the date of the first payment.

3. The Special Tax Treatment Control Law provides various tax incentives to stimulate exports. These include zero rated VAT of export goods and refunds of customs duties paid for imported raw materials used to manufacture export goods.

*Capital investment*/Tax credits are generally available for qualifying investments in energy saving, pollution control, vocational training facilities, investment in facilities for productivity enhancement, technology and human resources development, temporary investment, and so on.

*Other incentives*/Gains on the transfer of stock by a domestic person to a holding company established under the Anti-Monopoly & Fair Trade Act are not taxed until the domestic person sells the stock of the holding company acquired at the stock transfer.

## Withholding taxes

| Recipient | Dividends | Interest | Royalties |
|---|---|---|---|
| | % | % | % |
| Resident corporations (1).................... | Nil | 15 or 25 | Nil |
| Resident individuals (1)...................... | 15 | 15, 25, or 30 | Nil |
| Nonresident corporations and individuals: | | | |
| Treaty: | | | |
| Australia......................................... | 5 or 15%(2) | 15 | 15 |
| Austria............................................ | 10 or 15 (3) | 10 | 10 |
| Bangladesh .................................... | 10 or 15 (3) | 10 | 10 |
| Belgium.......................................... | 15 | 10 | 10 or 15 (4) |
| Brazil.............................................. | 15 | 10 or 15 (5) | 15 or 25 (6) |
| Bulgaria ......................................... | 5 or 10 (7) | 10 | 5 |
| Canada (8)...................................... | 15 | 15 | 15 |
| China, P.R. ..................................... | 5 or 10 (2) | 10 | 10 |
| Czech Republic .............................. | 5 or 10 (2) | 10 | 10 |
| Denmark ........................................ | 15 | 15 | 10 or 15 (4) |
| Egypt ............................................. | 10 or 15 (2) | 10 or 15 (9) | 15 |
| Fiji.................................................. | 10 or 15 (2) | 10 | 10 |
| Finland ........................................... | 10 or 15 (2) | 10 | 10 |
| France............................................ | 10 or 15 (3) | 10 | 10 |
| Germany ........................................ | 5 or 15 (2) | 10 | 2 or 10 (10) |
| Greece............................................ | 5 or 15 (2) | 8 | 10 |
| Hungary ......................................... | 5 or 10 (2) | 0 | 0 |
| India............................................... | 15 or 20 (11) | 10 or 15 (12) | 15 |
| Indonesia ....................................... | 10 or 15 (2) | 10 | 15 |
| Ireland, Rep. of............................... | 10 or 15 (3) | 0 | 0 |
| Israel.............................................. | 5, 10,15 (13) | 7.5 or 10 (14) | 2 or 5 (15) |
| Italy................................................ | 10 or 15 (2) | 10 | 10 |
| Japan.............................................. | 5 or 15 (2) | 10 | 10 |
| Kazakhstan .................................... | 5 or 15 (3) | 10 | 10 |
| Kuwait ............................................ | 10 | 10 | 15 |
| Luxembourg ................................... | 10 or 15 (2) | 10 | 10 or 15 (10) |
| Malaysia......................................... | 10 or 15 (2) | 15 | 10 or 15 (16) |
| Malta.............................................. | 5 or 15 (2) | 10 | 0 |
| Mexico ........................................... | 0 or 15 (17) | 5 or 15 (12) | 10 |
| Mongolia ........................................ | 5 | 5 | 10 |
| Morocco.......................................... | 5 or 10 (2) | 10 | 5 or 10 (18) |
| Netherlands ................................... | 10 or 15 (2) | 10 or 15 (19) | 10 or 15 (20) |
| New Zealand ................................... | 15 | 10 | 10 |
| Norway............................................ | 15 | 15 | 10 or 15 (20) |
| Pakistan ......................................... | 10 or 12.5 (11) | 12.5 | 10 |
| Philippines (2) ............................... | 10 or 15 (21) | 10 or 15 (22) | 10 or 15 (23) |
| Poland............................................ | 5 or 10 (3) | 10 | 10 |
| Portugal ......................................... | 10 or 15 (2) | 15 | 10 |

# Korea, Republic of

| Recipient | Dividends | Interest | Royalties |
|---|---|---|---|
| | % | % | % |
| Romania | 7 or 10 (2) | 10 | 7 or 10 (20) |
| Russia | 5 or 10 (24) | 0 | 5 |
| South Africa | 5 or 15 (2) | 10 | 10 |
| Singapore | 10 or 15 (2) | 10 | 15 |
| Spain | 10 or 15 (2) | 10 | 10 |
| Sri Lanka | 10 or 15 (2) | 10 | 10 |
| Sweden | 10 or 15 (2) | 10 or 15 (25) | 10 or 15 (20) |
| Switzerland | 10 or 15 (2) | 10 | 10 |
| Thailand (2) | 15 or 20 (26) | 10 | 15 |
| Tunisia | 15 | 12 | 15 |
| Turkey | 15 or 20 (2) | 10 or 15 (27) | 10 |
| United Kingdom | 5 or 15 (2) | 10 | 2 or 10 (15) |
| United States (2) | 10 or 15 (28) | 12 | 10 or 15 (29) |
| Uzbekistan | 5 or 15 (2) | 5 | 2 or 5 (15) |
| Vietnam | 10 | 10 | 5 or 15 (20) |

The numbers in parentheses refer to the following numbered Notes.

Notes:

1. Dividends paid to resident individuals by corporations are subject to a 15% withholding rate. In addition, tax withholding would include a residence surtax of 10% of the basic income tax liability. The basic withholding rate on interest is normally 15%. In addition, tax withholding would include a residence surtax (for individuals only) of 10% of the basis income tax amount.

2. Lower rate applies when a recipient holds 25% or more of equity interest.

3. Lower rate applies in case of equity ownership of 10% or more.

4. A 10% rate applies to royalties paid for the use of or the right associated with industrial activities. Otherwise, 15% rate applies.

5. Lower rate applies if the loan period extends to seven years or more, the recipient is a financial institution and the loan is used for certain designated purposes.

6. Higher rate applies to royalties associated with the use of trademarks or trademark rights.

7. A 5% rate applies in case of equity ownership of 15% or more. Otherwise, 10% rate applies.

8. In addition to the indicated tax rate, a residence tax surcharge is assessed at a rate of 10% of the respective tax rate.

9. Lower rate applies in case of a loan period of longer than three years.

10. Lower rate applies if it is for the use of or right to use industrial, commercial, and scientific equipment or information.

11. Lower rate applies in case of equity ownership of 20% or more.

12. Lower rate applies if recipient is a bank.

13. A 5% rate applies if a recipient holds 10% or more ownership in a paying corporation but, even in case of 10% or more ownership, 10% rate applies if the dividends are paid out of profits subject to tax at a lower rate than the normal corporate tax rate of a country where a payer resides. In other cases, 15% applies.

14. A 7.5% rate applies when a recipient of interest income is a bank or a financial institution; otherwise, 10% rate applies.

15. A 2% rate applies to royalties paid for use of or right to use industrial, commercial, and scientific equipment.

16. A 15% rate applies if royalties are for use of or right to use cinematography films or tapes for radio or television broadcasting or any copyright of literary or artistic work.

17. A 0% rate applies in case of equity ownership of 10% or more. Otherwise, 15% rate applies.

18. A 5% rate applies to royalties for use of copyrighted literature, music. Otherwise 10% applies.

19. Lower rate applies if the term of the loans exceeds seven years.

20. Lower rate applies if it is for the use of or right to use patent, trademark, design, or secret formula, or industrial, commercial, and scientific equipment or information.

21. A 10% rate applies in cases of equity ownership of 25% or more, or dividend paid by a resident company engaged in a preferred pioneer area and registered with Board of Investment. Otherwise, 15% rate applies.

22. A 10% rate applies in cases where the interest is paid in respect of public issues of bonds, debentures, or similar obligations or interest paid by a company that is a resident of the Philippines, registered with the Board of Investment and engaged in preferred pioneer areas of investment under the investment incentive laws. Otherwise, 15% rate applies.

23. A 10% rate applies in case of royalties paid by a company that is a resident of the Philippines, registered with the Board of Investment and engaged in preferred pioneer areas of investment under the investment incentives laws. Otherwise, 15% rate applies.

24. A 5% rate applies if a recipient holds 30% or more of equity interest in the amount of at least US$100,000.

25. A 10% rate applies when a recipient of interest income is a bank and income is connected with a loan with a term in excess of seven years. Otherwise, 15% rate applies.

26. A 15% rate applies if a recipient owns at least 10% of the voting stock and the payer engages in an industrial undertaking. 20% rate applies if a recipient owns at least 25% of the voting stock or the payer engages in an industrial undertaking

27. Lower rate applies if the term of the loan exceeds two years.

28. A 10% rate applies if equity ownership is 10% or more and not more than 25% of the gross income of a paying corporation for a preceding tax year consists of interest or dividends.

29. A 10% rate applies to royalties for use of copyrighted literature, music, films, and television or radio broadcasts. Otherwise, 15% rate applies.

## Tax administration

*Returns*/The taxable year is on a fiscal-year basis as elected by companies. However, it cannot exceed 12 months. The corporate tax return must be filed within three months from the end of a fiscal year. The tax amount is self-assessed.

However, the government can exercise the right to reassess the tax amount, if necessary, within five years of the filing date of the return.

***Payment of tax***/A corporation must file an interim tax return and pay an interim tax for the first six months within two months after the end of the six-month period. The interim tax liability is calculated based on the 50% of the corporate tax paid for the previous fiscal year or calculated by closing the books of accounts for the interim period (the first six-month period). The remaining tax is due with the final return for a fiscal year.

## *CORPORATION TAX CALCULATION*

Based on the law and tax rates in effect for the fiscal year ending December 31, 2002

Year ending December 31, 2002

| | | |
|---|---:|---:|
| Net income before taxes | | W 100,000,000 |
| Add: | | |
| Nondeductible expenses: | | |
| Depreciation in excess of limitation | 10,000,000 | |
| Bad debt without designated evidence | 3,000,000 | |
| Entertainment expenses in excess of limitation | 5,000,000 | |
| Provision for severance indemnities in excess of limitation | 6,000,000 | |
| Expensed supplies on hand at year-end | 2,000,000 | |
| Income that should be included: | | |
| Deemed rental income on shareholder officers' housing | 3,000,000 | |
| Deemed interest income on the company's advances to employees and shareholders | 1,000,000 | 30,000,000 |
| | | 130,000,000 |
| Less: | | |
| Expensed supplies on hand at prior year-end | 3,000,000 | 3,000,000 |
| Taxable income | | W 127,000,000 |
| Loss of the preceding five years brought forward | | (5,000,000) |
| Tax base | | W 122,000,000 |
| Tax calculated thereon: | | |
| First 100,000,000 at 15% | | W 15,000,000 |
| Balance—22,000,000 at 27% | | 5,940,000 |
| Corporation tax for the year (1) | | 20,940,000 |
| *Less*—Tax credit: | | |
| Interim payment | 15,000,000 | |
| Withholding tax paid at source | 5,000,000 | (20,000,000) |
| Tax payable | | W 940,000 |

Notes:

1. In addition, a resident tax surcharge of 10% of the corporation tax liability must be paid.
2. Exchange rate (base rate) of the won at December 31, 2002: US$1=W1200.4.

## PwC contacts

For additional information on taxation in Latvia, contact:

Helen Barker
PricewaterhouseCoopers SIA
Kr. Valdemara 19
LV–1010 Riga, Latvia
Telephone: (371) 709 44 21
Fax: (371) 783 00 55
e-mail: helen.barker@lv.pwc.com

or Zlata Elksniṇa-Zaščirinska
PricewaterhouseCoopers SIA
Kr. Valdemara 19
LV-1010 Riga, Latvia
Telephone: (371) 709 45 15
Fax: (371) 783 00 55
e-mail: zlata.elksnina@lv.pwc.com

## Significant developments

Several changes in the current tax legislation were made during 2003. The final step in the gradual drop in corporate income tax rate has been achieved, and the rate for the year 2004 will be just 15%. Several amendments to the corporate tax legislation during 2003 appear to be directly influenced by EC requirements. These include new rules to be followed during reorganizations and exemptions from withholding tax on certain dividend payments to EU resident companies. In addition, the thin capitalization rules in Latvia have become slightly more lenient.

The new VAT rate of 9% introduced last year has been reduced to 5%, and will be effective from May 1, 2004, when Latvia joins the EU. In addition, certain supplies that were previously VAT exempt will become subject to VAT at this lower rate of 5%. Several draft amendments to the VAT Act are at their final stages of review as Latvia prepares itself to deal with the new concept of an "intra-community" transaction.

The Latvian parliament has continued its deferral of a reduction of the real estate tax rate. This deferral is now thought to apply until December 31, 2006. The current tax rate of 1.5% will apply to the average net book value of buildings and structures and to the cadastral value of land.

From January 1, 2003, seven new double taxation treaties have come into effect, with Kazakhstan, Romania, Slovenia, and Switzerland from January 1, 2003, and with Belgium, Portugal, and Turkey from January 1, 2004.

## Taxes on corporate income

The current corporate tax rate is 15%. The corporate tax rate for 2003 was 19%.

There are no local taxes on corporate income.

## Corporate residence

A company is resident in Latvia if it is incorporated there. Branches of foreign companies are resident in Latvia if incorporated in Latvia, or if they should have been incorporated in Latvia (e.g., permanent establishments).

## Other taxes and duties

*Value-added tax*/Sales of most goods and services and imported goods are subject to VAT at the rate of 18%. Exports of goods and services are zero-rated. Some supplies are exempt, such as medical services, banking and insurance, theater, cinema (except videos), concerts, museums, exhibitions, and rents paid by individuals for apartments. Certain services supplied by nonresidents to Latvian companies are subject to 18% VAT, which is recoverable by the Latvian recipient. As from May 1, 2004, several types of supplies, which were previously exempt, for example, medicine, medical equipment, and scientific and school literature, are subject to VAT at a rate of 5%. Other supplies, previously subject to VAT at 9% or 18%, for example, veterinary equipment, books, mass media, hotel accommodation, water and sewerage services are subject to VAT at a rate of 5%.

*Excise tax*/Excise tax is levied on the import and production of certain products. As a general rule, the value used is the sales price of the goods when produced in Latvia or customs value of goods when imported. For some types of goods the tax is applied based on quantity. The rates are as follows.

| | LVL |
|---|---|
| Wine and other fermented beverages ...................... | 0.30/liter |
| Beer with alcohol content between 0.5% and 2.8%.. | 0.033/liter |
| Beer with alcohol content between 2.8% and 4%..... | 0.047/liter |
| Beer with alcohol content between 4% and 5.5%..... | 0.064/liter |
| Beer with alcohol content between 5.5% and 7%..... | 0.081/liter |
| Beer with alcohol content above 7% ....................... | 0.42/liter |
| Sub product with alcoholic content to 15%.............. | 0.42/liter |
| Sub product with alcoholic content between 15% and 22% ..................................................... | 0.70/liter |
| Spirits and other alcoholic beverages...................... | 5.5/liter of pure spirit |
| Cigarettes up to 90mm............................................ | 0.00631/unit plus 6.1% max retail price |
| Cigarettes from 90mm to 180 mm........................... | As for above x 2 |
| Cigarettes from 180 mm to 270 mm........................ | As for above x 3 |
| Cigarillos, cigars ..................................................... | 0.011/unit |
| Fine cut tobacco for cigarettes ............................... | 0.0166/unit |
| Other smoking tobacco ............................................ | 0.114/unit |
| Leaded gasoline ...................................................... | 0.21/litre |
| Unleaded gasoline ................................................... | 0.16/litre |
| Diesel fuel and its components .............................. | 0.1/litre |
| Petroleum and its components................................. | 0.1/litre |
| Fuel oil and its components .................................... | 0.007/litre |
| Oil gas and other hydrocarbons ............................. | 0.05/litre |
| Soft beverages........................................................ | 0.02/liter |
| Coffee..................................................................... | 0.5/kg |
| Passenger cars/motorcycles (year of assembly) ...... | 250 to 75 Ls/unit (for motorcycles 25% of tax applicable) |

*Customs tax (tariffs)*/Customs tax is applied on most goods and commodities crossing the border into Latvia. Exports are generally free of customs tax. The rate for customs tariffs depends on the type of goods, the origin of the goods and the status of the country trading with Latvia. From May 1, 2004, goods and commodities crossing the border into Latvia from other member states will not be treated as imported into Latvia if already in free circulation in the member state from whence they came. All trade agreements that Latvia has with other countries will come to an end, as Latvia joins the EU. Latvia is a member of the World Trade Organization.

*Real estate tax*/Buildings and structures are subject to real estate tax at a rate of 1.5% of their average net book value, while land is taxed at an annual rate of 1.5% of its registered value. Certain reliefs and exemptions determined by municipalities are available in respect of land and dwellings, as well as qualifying business assets. Qualifying business assets are buildings that have been constructed or reconstructed after January 1, 2001.

*Tax on natural resource products*/Production and import of environmental-impact products, such as car tires; mineral oils; car batteries; disposable plastic plates and table accessories; and products in glass, metal, wood, plastic, or cardboard packaging, are subject to tax. There is also a tax on the use of natural resources and on activities that pollute the environment. The particular tax rates differ and are stated either as a percentage of sales price or as a fixed amount per unit. When packaged products are imported the packaging material is subject to the natural resource tax at the time of importation.

*Stamp taxes*/Stamp taxes are levied for certain legal and other kinds of services, such as court trials, company formation and registration, licenses for certain types of business activities, provision of information, notary services, operation of bills of exchange, and registration of real estate at the Land Title Register.

*Local duties*/Certain activities are subject to local duties (e.g., construction permits).

## Branch income

As a general rule, branches are taxed in a similar way to companies, with certain adjustments made for payments made to the head office. The corporate income tax rate is also applicable to branches and will be 15% for 2004.

## Income determination

Taxable income is based on accounting profit with some adjustments to reflect specific tax legislation.

*Inventory valuation*/Inventory is valued at the lower of cost or market value. Cost can be computed on a FIFO or a weighted-average basis. Cost can mean purchase price or production cost.

*Capital gains*/Capital gain on the disposal of all assets is calculated as the difference between sale proceeds and net book value. This gain is taxed as ordinary income at the relevant corporate income tax rate. However, gains or losses from trading publicly quoted securities are not subject to tax. Capital losses on the sale of other securities may be carried forward for five years and offset only against capital gains on the sale of such securities.

*Intercompany dividends*/Dividends paid by companies registered in Latvia are tax exempt, provided they are paid out of income net of corporate income tax. If the payor of dividends is not subject to income tax, dividends received will be included in the recipient's taxable income.

# Latvia

Dividends paid by nonresident companies and Latvian companies currently enjoying a tax holiday in Latvia are included in the taxable income of the company receiving the dividend.

Dividends received by a Latvian company from a nonresident company are exempt from corporate income tax provided the Latvian company has at least a 25% shareholding with voting rights. There are some exceptions with respect to companies registered in statutorily black listed low tax zones or tax havens.

*Foreign income*/Resident corporations are taxed on their worldwide income. Tax paid abroad on income included in the taxable base is allowed as a credit against corporate income tax. However, the credit may not exceed the Latvian tax attributable to the income taxed abroad.

*Stock dividends*/The distribution of a company's shares to its shareholders in proportion to the shares already owned by them (after an increase of the share capital through conversion of accrued capital) is not a taxable event for the shareholders.

## Deductions

*Depreciation*/Fixed assets may be depreciated for tax purposes according to the reducing-balance method by applying the following rates.

|  | % |
|---|---|
| Buildings, constructions, and long-term plant | 10 |
| Technology and energy installations, fleet, railway | 20 |
| Computer hardware and software, information systems, electronic equipment | 70 |
| Other fixed assets | 40 |
| Oil rigs, oil exploration, and extraction ships | 15 |

Intangible assets obtained after January 1, 1995 can be amortized on the following terms.

|  | Years |
|---|---|
| Concessions | 10 |
| Patents, licenses, and trademarks | 5 |
| Expenses for research and development | 1 |

The intangible assets listed above may only be amortized if they were paid for. Any intangible assets not fitting into the categories described above cannot be depreciated for tax purposes.

*Net operating losses*/Losses can be carried forward for up to five years. A company, more than 50% of whose shares (control) have changed hands, can utilize its tax losses only if it continues for five years the same business it carried on during the two years before the change of control. When companies are reorganized by merger or spin-off, it may be possible to utilize losses accrued after January 1, 2001.

*Payments to foreign affiliates*/Generally, a Latvian corporation can deduct the full amount of royalties, service fees, and interest (subject to limits) made to related parties, provided such payments are at arm's length. Such payments may be subject to withholding tax (see below).

*Taxes*/Excise tax, National Social Insurance contributions, the tax on environmental pollution and natural resources, customs tariffs, and real estate tax are deductible to the extent they form a part of the company's expenses for financial accounting purposes.

*Other significant items*/Interest paid to credit institutions is fully deductible. Interest paid to other entities is deductible up to limits based on a debt: equity ratio of approximately 4:1 at the end of the financial year, and an interest rate of 1.2 times the short-term interest rate of Latvian banks fixed by the Central Statistics Bureau. The interest rate for short-term loans in December 2003 was 5.8%.

## Group taxation

From January 1, 1997, loss-making companies within a group are able to surrender their tax losses in a given period to profitable companies within the same group. A group is defined as Latvian-resident companies whose parent must own, directly or indirectly, 90%. The parent itself may be resident in Latvia or a country with which Latvia has a double taxation agreement.

## Tax incentives

*Tax holidays*/The main tax incentives are eliminated for any companies that failed to meet the necessary criteria by April 1, 1995. However, companies already qualifying for the special tax holidays will be able to use them until end of year 2005, provided they continue to meet the criteria throughout the period of the tax holiday.

*Other incentives*/The main benefits for special types of companies are as follows.

1. Corporate income tax liability can be reduced by 85% or by 90% of the amount paid to Latvian charitable organizations, provided such a reduction does not exceed 20% of the total amount of corporate income tax.
2. Companies investing more than LVL10 million over a period not exceeding three years can apply for tax relief equal to 40% of the investment.
3. Companies operating in special economic zones are entitled to significant tax reliefs, although these are gradually being reduced as a result of pressure from the EU.

## Withholding taxes

Domestic corporations paying certain types of income are required to withhold as follows.

| Recipient | Dividends (1) | Interest (2) | Royalties (3) |
|---|---|---|---|
| | % | % | % |
| Resident corporations (4) | 0 | 0 | 0 |
| Nontreaty | 10 | 0/5/10 | 15/5 [5] |
| Treaty: | | | |
| Armenia | 10 [5] | 0/5/10 | 10 [5] |
| Belarus | 10 | 0/5/10 | 10 [5] |
| Belgium | 10 [5] | 0/5/10 | 10 |
| Canada | 10 | 0/5/10 | 10 [5] |
| China, P.R. | 10 [5] | 0/5/10 | 10 [5] |
| Croatia | 10 [5] | 0/5/10 | 10 [5] |
| Czech Republic | 10 [5] | 0/5/10 | 10 [5] |
| Denmark | 10 [5] | 0/5/10 | 10 [5] |

# Latvia

| Recipient | Dividends (1) | Interest (2) | Royalties (3) |
|---|---|---|---|
| | % | % | % |
| Estonia | 10 [5] | 0/5/10 | 10 [5] |
| Finland | 10 [5] | 0/5/10 | 10 [5] |
| France | 10 [5] | 0/5/10 | 10 [5] |
| Germany | 10 [5] | 0/5/10 | 10 [5] |
| Greece | 10 [5] | 0/5/10 | 10 [5] |
| Iceland | 10 [5] | 0/5/10 | 10 [5] |
| Ireland, Rep. of | 10 [5] | 0/5/10 | 10 [5] |
| Kazakhstan | 10 [5] | 0/5/10 | 10 [5] |
| Lithuania | 10 [0] | 0 | 0 |
| Malta | 10 [5] | 0/5/10 | 10 [5] |
| Moldova | 10 | 0/5/10 | 10 [5] |
| Netherlands | 10 [5] | 0/5/10 | 10 [5] |
| Norway | 10 [5] | 0/5/10 | 10 [5] |
| Poland | 10 [5] | 0/5/10 | 10 [5] |
| Portugal | 10 | 0/5/10 | 10 [5] |
| Romania | 10 [5] | 0/5/10 | 10 [5] |
| Singapore | 10 [5] | 0/5/10 | 7.5 [5] |
| Slovak Republic | 10 | 0/5/10 | 10 [5] |
| Slovenia | 10 [5] | 0/5/10 | 10 [5] |
| Sweden | 10 [5] | 0/5/10 | 10 [5] |
| Switzerland | 10 [5] | 0/5/10 | 10 [5] |
| Turkey | 10 | 0/5/10 | 10 [5] |
| Ukraine | 10 [5] | 0/5/10 | 10 [5] |
| United States | 10 [5] | 0/5/10 | 10 [5] |
| United Kingdom | 10 [5] | 0/5/10 | 10 [5] |
| Uzbekistan | 10 | 0/5/10 | 10 [5] |

Notes:

1. Amounts in brackets indicate the rates that apply when the beneficial owner is a company that holds directly at least 25% of the shares (10% for United States and France). According to the majority of the double taxation treaties the 25% requirement is fulfilled if the shareholder has 25% of the capital. The treaties with Estonia and Lithuania prescribe a 25% holding of the capital and votes, and the treaty with Canada 25% of the votes. Although some treaties provide a withholding tax rate of 15% on dividends, Latvian legislation applies a maximum rate of 10%, which is the highest applicable rate for dividends paid to all countries.

2. Only interest payments to associated parties are subject to withholding tax. The tax is 10% unless payment is made by commercial banks registered in Latvia to an associated party, when the withholding tax is 5%. If interest payments are made to a designated government credit institution, some treaties exempt the payments from withholding tax.

3. Royalty payments or payments for the right to use copyright of literary or artistic works, including movies, videos and recordings, are subject to 15%, 7.5%, or 10% withholding tax. Amounts in brackets indicate rates that apply when the royalty is paid for the use of commercial or scientific equipment. Payments in respect of other types of intellectual property are subject to 5% withholding tax.

4. If dividends are paid out net of corporate tax.

5. In addition to the above, the following payments made to nonresidents located in nontreaty countries are subject to withholding tax.

|  | % |
|---|---|
| Payments for the provision of management and consulting services | 10 |
| Rental income from property located in Latvia | 5 |
| Gains from the sale of real estate in Latvia | 2 |

## Tax administration

*Returns*/The fiscal year is normally based on the calendar year, although companies may opt for different dates for commencing and ending their fiscal year, which may not exceed 12 months, except for the first year of operation, which may last up to 18 months. Tax returns are filed annually, together with the annual reports.

*Payment of tax*/In most cases taxes are paid in quarterly or monthly installments, with a final settlement when the assessment is issued. The quarterly installments are based on the estimated ultimate liability, which is generally the final tax liability of the previous year.

### *CORPORATION TAX CALCULATION*

Calendar year ending December 31, 2003

| | | | |
|---|---|---|---|
| Net profit before taxes | | LVL | 1,000,000 |
| Add—Depreciation | 20,000 | | |
| Less—Adjustments to profit: | | | |
|    Capital allowances | 35,000 | | |
|    40% of representation expenses | 12,000 | | |
|    Real estate tax | 15,000 | | |
|    Losses carried forward from previous years | 30,000 | | (72,000) |
| Total taxable incomeTotal taxable income | | LVL | 928,000 |
| Corporate income tax at 19% | | LVL | 176,320 |
| Less—Charity reliefs (payment of 15,000 at 85%) | | | (12,750) |
| Corporate tax payable | | LVL | 163,570 |

Note:

Exchange rate of the lats at January 1, 2004: US$1 = LVL0.53397.

# Liechtenstein

## PwC contacts

For additional information on taxation in Liechtenstein, contact:

Werner Schmid, Tax Partner
Victor Meyer, Tax Partner
PricewaterhouseCoopers AG
Stampfenbachstrasse 73
8035 Zurich, Switzerland
Telephone: (41) (1) 630 11 11
Fax: (41) (1) 630 41 15
e-mail: werner.schmid@ch.pwc.com
        victor.meyer@ch.pwc.com

## Significant developments

There have been no significant tax or regulatory developments in the past year.

## Taxes on corporate income

Taxable income is taxed at basic rates ranging from a minimum of 7.5% to a maximum of 15%. The applicable rate is determined by the ratio of profit to capital and reserves, based on the following formula.

$$\text{(Taxable income} \times 100) \div \text{(Taxable capital} \times 2) = X\%$$

If the dividend distribution exceeds 8% of taxable capital, a surcharge of one to five percentage points is added to the basic income tax rate applicable for the year in which the dividend is declared, on the basis of the following table.

| Dividend in excess of percentage of taxable capital | Increase of tax rate in percentage points |
|---|---|
| 8 | 1.0 |
| 10 | 1.5 |
| 12 | 2.0 |
| 14 | 2.5 |
| 16 | 3.0 |
| 18 | 3.5 |
| 20 | 4.0 |
| 22 | 4.5 |
| 24 | 5.0 |

Consequently, the maximum rate applicable is 20%.

There are two categories of companies in Liechtenstein for income tax purposes, ordinary taxed companies and privileged companies. Ordinary taxed companies are subject to income tax and capital gains tax on equity, whereas privileged companies are not taxed on income and have reduced capital taxes. Privileged companies include trusts, establishments, captive insurance companies, foreign investment companies, investment companies, foreign insurance companies carrying on business in Liechtenstein (i.e., collecting premiums within Liechtenstein), domiciliary and holding companies.

For details on the taxation of domiciliary and holding companies see "Tax incentives."

## Corporate residence

A company is considered to be resident in Liechtenstein, and thus subject to unlimited tax liability, if its registered seat (address) or place of effective management is within Liechtenstein.

## Other taxes

*Capital taxes*/An annual capital tax of 0.2% is levied on taxable capital. Capital tax is subject to participation relief and, consequently, is reduced in proportion to substantial participation/total assets ratio, provided that the respective conditions are met ("participation relief" see below). For investment trusts and investment companies, capital tax on that part of the capital exceeding CHF2 million is 0.04% (below this amount, the rate is 0.01%). Captive insurance companies pay an annual capital tax of 0.1% on taxable capital up to CHF50 million. Between CHF50 million and CHF100 million the applicable tax rate is 0.075%. Taxable capital exceeding CHF100 million is taxed at a rate of 0.05%. A foreign insurance company collecting premiums within Liechtenstein pays a tax of 1% of the premium income from life and social pension insurance and a tax of 2% of all other premium income.

*Value-added tax*/As from January 1, 1995 the delivery of goods and the supply of services rendered within the Liechtenstein and Swiss territory, and the acquisition of services rendered from abroad by Liechtenstein and Swiss companies, are subject to value-added tax (VAT) at the standard rate of 7.6%. Certain goods, such as food, pharmaceuticals and books, are taxed at a reduced rate of 2.4%. The reduced rate for lodging is 3.6%. The range of tax-exempt services includes healthcare, education, culture, and most of the banking services. Exports are in general zero-rated.

## Branch income

The same principles apply as for corporations, provided transactions with the head office or other branches are on an arm's length basis. Liechtenstein taxation is imposed on the profit attributable to the branch and on the capital invested in the branch.

There is no withholding tax on profit transfers to the head office.

## Income determination

*Inventory valuation*/Inventories must be stated at the lower of cost or market. The tax authorities will permit a general reserve against stock contingencies of up to one-third of the inventory cost or market value at the balance sheet date without inquiry into its justification, provided a detailed record of inventory is available for review by the tax authorities. The need for a reserve in excess of this amount (e.g., for obsolescence, slow-moving stocks) must be substantiated to the satisfaction of the tax authorities.

*Capital gains*/Capital gains, other than those arising on the sale of real estate, are classified as normal business income, and are subject to tax at the regular corporate tax rates.

# Liechtenstein

Capital gains from the sale of real estate are subject to a separately assessed real estate profits tax. The taxable gain is basically the difference between proceeds of the sale and the original purchase price of the property, plus any capital expenditure incurred. The basic tax rate is at present 1.08%, subject to various surcharges, depending, *inter alia*, on how long the vendor has owned the property concerned, and the amount of taxable profit. The maximum rate of real estate profits tax is at present 34.02%.

*Intercompany dividends*/Dividends net of foreign taxes assessed are subject to ordinary corporate taxes, unless the company has holding or domiciliary status (see "Tax incentives"). For foreign and domestic dividends, participation relief is available. Participation relief is granted only in connection with substantial participations in an ordinary taxed corporation (i.e., participation of at least 20%, or market value exceeding CHF2 million) after a holding period of at least 12 months.

*Foreign income*/Resident corporations operating locally are basically taxed on their worldwide income, with the exception of income from real estate and permanent establishments situated abroad.

Profits of a domestic corporation's foreign branch are usually exempt from Liechtenstein corporate income tax. However, the progression proviso (i.e., exempt foreign-branch income is nevertheless included for the determination of the tax rate applicable) is applied, and the treatment of these profits depends on the method of allocation.

The income of a foreign subsidiary is taxable only when repatriated to the Liechtenstein parent company in the form of dividends, interest, and so on.

The proceeds from the sale of a subsidiary in excess of the carrying value of the investment are taxable as ordinary income, unless the company is a privileged company in which case the proceeds are free of tax.

*Stock dividends*/A company may increase its share capital by capitalizing reserves or undistributed profits. Provided the shareholder's investment at book value remains unchanged, the stock dividend does not represent taxable income. An upward adjustment of the investment book value will constitute taxable income subject to ordinary income tax.

Dividends-in-kind are estimated at fair market value, and represent taxable income at the shareholder's level, which might be subject to the participation relief.

## Deductions

*Depreciation and depletion*/Depreciation of intangible and tangible fixed assets is allowed to the extent it is "commercially justified." For tax purposes, either the straight-line or the declining-balance method may be used. Depreciation and amortization not recorded in the statutory accounts are not deductible for tax purposes.

| | Rate per annum | |
|---|---|---|
| | **On cost** | **On net book value** |
| | % | % |
| **Immovable assets** | | |
| Vacant plots, land without structures ............................................ | Nil | Nil |
| Dwelling houses, offices, shops, or cinema buildings ................... | 1.0 | 2.0 |
| Buildings of the restaurant and hotel trade ................................... | 1.5 | 3.0 |
| Factories, warehouses, and industrial buildings ........................... | 2.5 | 5.0 |
| Water mains for industrial purposes, storage tanks, cold storage and air-conditioning plant, telephone equipment, etc. ....................................................... | 7.5 | 15.0 |
| **Movable assets** | | |
| Office furniture and machines, workshop and storeroom equipment ............................................................... | 10.0 | 20.0 |
| Furniture of the hotel and restaurant trade .................................... | 12.5 | 25.0 |
| IT equipment and capitalized software, machinery, Equipment, and vehicles (excluding motorcars) ........................... | 15.0 | 30.0 |
| Motorcars, machinery, and equipment used in more than one shift or used under heavy conditions, larger machine tools ......................................................................... | 17.5 | 35.0 |
| Machine tools, larger hand tools; hotel and restaurant crockery, cutlery, and linen ....................................................... | 25.0 | 50.0 |
| Officially approved installations and equipment against water pollution, energy-saving equipment and installations using solar energy, etc. .................................. | 25.0 | 50.0 |
| **Intangible assets** | | |
| Goodwill, patent-license and other rights of use ........................... | 12.5 | 25.0 |

Upon the sale or scrapping of an asset, the difference between the sales proceeds and the tax written-down value is treated as ordinary income or expense.

*Net operating losses*/A loss may be carried forward and offset against the profits for future years for up to a maximum of five years. Losses may not be carried back.

*Payments to foreign affiliates*/Interest, royalties, and license and other fees to foreign affiliates are allowable as deductions to the extent that they meet the arm's length test, for example, are equivalent to charges that would be made by an unrelated third party.

*Taxes*/All taxes paid, including corporate income tax, are deductible from income in the accounting period in which they are paid.

## Group taxation

Each corporation is taxed as a separate entity, for example, a parent company and its local subsidiaries are taxed separately. Accordingly, there is no possibility of offsetting the losses of one group company against the profits of another.

# Liechtenstein

## Tax incentives

Liechtenstein is well known for its domiciliary and holding companies. A domiciliary company is a legal entity incorporated in any of the legal forms governed by the Persons and Companies Code that has its registered seat in Liechtenstein, but carries out no commercial activities within the country.

A holding company is a corporate body with its registered seat in Liechtenstein whose purpose consists entirely or mainly of the administration or management of assets or investments.

The status for qualification as a domiciliary or holding company is, therefore, merely a question of the company's purpose. The legal form of the company (e.g., corporation, establishment (*Anstalt*) may be that most suitable to the shareholders or the activities to be performed.

Business entities having the status of a domiciliary or holding company are exempt from any income tax. The benefit of this income tax exemption must, however, be considered together with the absence of any significant double taxation treaty. For instance, the double taxation treaty with Austria expressly precludes foreign-owned domiciliary and holding companies from taking advantage of the treaty. Any foreign taxes levied on the company's income are therefore final.

A capital tax of 0.1% is, however, levied on the domiciliary or holding company's net equity, that is, on paid-in capital, all reserves and retained earnings. The capital tax is payable annually in advance; the minimum tax is CHF1,000.

Dividend distributions of domiciliary or holding companies whose capital is divided into shares are subject to a 4% coupon (withholding) tax with the exception of captive insurance companies and trusts.

Captive insurance companies (including holding companies) are exempt from any income tax on that part of their income derived from the captive insurance business, whereas income from third-party insurance is subject to ordinary income tax. Captive insurance companies pay a capital tax of 0.1% on net equity. For the part of net equity exceeding CHF50 million there is a reduced tax rate of 0.075%. For net equity in excess of CHF100 million the rate is further reduced to 0.05%. Captive insurance companies can apply to be subject to ordinary income and capital taxes.

## Withholding taxes

| Recipient | Dividends* | Interest* | Royalties |
|---|---|---|---|
| | % | % | % |
| Resident corporations and individuals ........................ | 4 | 0 | Nil |
| Nonresident corporations and individuals: | | | |
| Nontreaty................................................................. | 4 | 0 | Nil |
| Treaty: | | | |
| Austria ................................................................. | 4 | 0 | Nil |

*A withholding (coupon) tax of 4% is levied on dividends of corporations and establishments whose capital is divided into shares (with the exception of captive insurance companies and trusts), as well as on interest from bonds and similar loans, on time deposits with domestic banks with a term in excess of 12 months and on loans in excess of CHF50,000 with a minimum term in excess of two years, but not on interest of normal intercompany loans. The taxpayer is always the Liechtenstein company, which, however, is legally obliged to charge the coupon tax to the recipient

*Tax treaties*/A comprehensive double taxation treaty on income is in effect with Austria. No other treaties are signed or under negotiation.

## Tax administration

*Returns*/Companies other than holding and domiciliary companies must file a tax return within six weeks after the adoption of the financial statements by the shareholders' meeting, but no later than July 1 of the calendar year following the fiscal year-end.

The tax assessment issued by the tax administration is based on the company's tax return, including the attachments and the financial statements filed.

Holding and domiciliary companies do not file a tax return. Rather, these companies simply furnish audited financial statements to the tax authorities or, if appropriate, a declaration of the noncommercial nature of operations to the Registry of Commerce within six months after the company's fiscal year-end.

Foreign insurance company collecting premiums within Liechtenstein furnish a statement on their collected premiums, divided into premium income from life and social pension insurance and other premium income

*Payment of tax*/Companies other than holding and domiciliary companies must pay the tax within 30 days of receipt of the assessment, which is generally in the fall of each year. Payment may be made in installments if approved by the tax administration. The taxes for holding and domiciliary companies are regularly payable in advance.

# Liechtenstein

*CORPORATION TAX CALCULATION*

## Calculation of taxable income for tax year 2003

### *Assessable profit*

(Profit for year ended December 31, 2003)

| | | |
|---|---:|---:|
| Reported profit after tax (including foreign and domestic dividends and capital gains on movable property) | | CHF 1,000,000 |
| Add back: | | |
| Recorded increase of excess inventory reserve | 350,000 | 350,000 |
| | | 1,350,000 |
| Less: | | |
| Recorded decrease of excess depreciation reserve | 250,000 | |
| Contributions to a tax-exempt pension fund (if any) | — | 250,000 |
| | | 1,100,000 |
| Deduct loss carryforward (if any) | | — |
| Taxable income | | CHF 1,100,000 |

### *Assessable capital*

(Position at December 31, 2003)

| | | |
|---|---:|---:|
| Paid-in capital, registered in the Register of Commerce | | CHF 4,000,000 |
| Legal reserve | | 300,000 |
| Other disclosed reserves | | 600,000 |
| Provision for income and capital taxes (1) | | 150,000 |
| Excess inventory reserves (1) | | 50,000 |
| Excess depreciation reserves (and other undisclosed reserves, if any) (1) | | 50,000 |
| Retained earnings brought forward (2) | | 250,000 |
| | | 5,400,000 |
| Deductions: | | |
| Net loss of current year | — | |
| Net deficit brought forward | — | |
| Capital increase during the year | 500,000 | |
| Dividends in excess of current year's net income (3) | 200,000 | 700,000 |
| Taxable capital | | CHF 4,700,000 |

Notes:

1. Provisions and reserves disallowed for tax purposes and consequently taxed as income.
2. Income of current year is not subject to capital tax.
3. Calculated as follows:

| | CHF |
|---|---:|
| Net income for the year | 1,000,000 |
| Dividend resolved/distributed based on results of business year 2003 | 1,200,000 |
| Dividend in excess of net income | 200,000 |

## Corporate tax calculations for tax year 2003

|  | CHF |
|---|---|
| Taxable income | 1,100,000 |
| Taxable capital | 4,700,000 |
| Dividend resolved or distributed | 1,200,000 |

Calculation of basic income tax rate

$$\text{(Taxable income} \times 100) \div (\text{Taxable capital} \times 2) = x\%$$

$$(1,100,000 \times 100) \div (4,700,000 \times 2) = 11.70\%$$

Basic income tax rate after rounding up to the next 0.5% = 12.0%.

Determination of surcharge based on dividend distribution

$$\text{(Dividend} \times 100) \div (\text{Taxable capital}) = x\%$$

$$(1,200,000 \times 100) \div (4,700,000) = 25.53\%$$

Surcharge according to table = 5%

Determination of effective income tax rate

|  | % |
|---|---|
| Basic income tax rate | 12.0 |
| Surcharge | 5.0 |
| Effective income tax rate | 17.0 |

Calculation of taxes payable

|  |  |
|---|---|
| Income tax—17.0% of 1,100,000 | CHF 187,000 |
| Capital tax—0.2% of 4,700,000 | 9,400 |
| Taxes payable | CHF 196,400 |

Note:

Exchange rate of the Swiss franc at January 1, 2004: US$1 = CHF1.2372.

# Lithuania

## PwC contact

For additional information on taxation in Lithuania, contact:

Diana Dominiene or Gintaras Balcius
PricewaterhouseCoopers UAB
T. Sevcenkos 21
LT–2009 Vilnius, Lithuania
Telephone: (370) (2) 39 2300
Fax: (370) 5 239 2301
e-mail: diana.dominiene@lt.pwc.com or gintaras.balcius@lt.pwc.com

A copy of all documents/enquiries should be sent to:

Cameron G. Greaves
TLS Baltic States Leader
PricewaterhouseCoopers UAB
T. Sevcenkos 21
LT-2009 Vilnius, Lithuania
Telephone: (370) 5 239 2300
Fax: (370) 5 239 2301
e-mail: cameron.greaves@lt.pwc.com

## General note

This entry is repeated from the 2003/2004 edition. For more up-to-date information consult the contact listed above or Jacqueline Collette at jacqueline.collete@us.pwc.com.

## Significant developments

A new Profit Tax Law was passed on January 1, 2002. The law stipulates a reduced profit tax rate and abolishes capital investment incentives.

## Taxes on corporate profit

The corporate profit tax rate is 15%. Incentives for capital reinvestment were abolished from January 1, 2002.

*Exemptions*/The following types of income are exempt from corporate profit tax.

1. Sponsorship received according to the procedure established by the Law of the Republic of Lithuania on Charity and Sponsorship.
2. Insurance indemnity not in excess of the value of lost property or other losses or damages; the refunded part of insurance premiums in excess of the premiums deducted from income in accordance with the procedure established; the part of insurance indemnity in excess of the premiums deducted from income in accordance with the procedure established.
3. Proceeds of a bankrupt company received from sale of its property.
4. Balance of insurance company's formation fund as prescribed by the Law on Insurance.
5. Pension contributions made to personal accounts of the participants in pension programs held by pension funds which operate under the Law on pension funds and investment income received by such funds; life insurance premiums received by investment companies with variable capital and private (closed) investment funds operating under the Law on Investment Funds;

income from investment and pension insurance premiums received by insurance companies when the duration of the insurance policy is at least 10 years as well as insurance investment income gained by insurance companies.

6. Income derived by health care institutions for services financed from the funds of the Compulsory Health Insurance Fund.
7. Income derived from revaluation of fixed assets and securities as established by laws and regulations.
8. Default interest except for that received from foreign companies registered or otherwise organized in tax haven territories or residents of such territories.
9. All or part of the profit gained from legal entities of unlimited civil liability who are payers of the tax and whose income is subject to the profits tax under this Law or to a similar tax under respective statutes of foreign countries with certain exceptions.
10. Fees collected by seaports and airports, charges for air traffic navigation services and funds collected from the lease of seaport-owned land.
11. Results arising from adjustments made in the previous tax periods as prescribed by the Law on Accounting.
12. Indemnification for damages received by the company with certain exceptions.

*Local taxes*/There are no local taxes on corporate profit.

## Corporate residence

A company is resident in Lithuania if it is incorporated there. A foreign company is deemed to have a permanent establishment (PE) in Lithuania in cases where the following applies.

1. It carries out commercial activities in Lithuania in whole or in part, continually.
2. It carries out its activity through an authorized individual (agent).
3. It uses a construction site or construction, assembly or equipment objects.
4. It uses equipment, including drilling installations and ships, for exploration for or extraction of natural resources.

A PE must register as a taxpayer with the State Tax Inspectorate in the territory where its activities are carried out. Its profits are subject to the corporate profit tax rate of 15%.

According to domestic law, where there is a double taxation treaty, the provisions of the treaty shall govern.

## Other taxes

*Value-added tax*/VAT is charged at the rate of 0% on exported goods and on services provided to entities outside the Republic of Lithuania. The temporary export of goods and temporary export of goods for recasting are not considered as exports for the purposes of VAT. The following services are charged at a rate of 0%.

- Services of real estate agents, valuers, contractors, projectors, architects, construction supervision, and other services, related to real estate that is or will be built abroad.
- Services of art, culture, sports, science, teaching, education and entertainment, valuation, and servicing of movable property—when the mentioned services are physically rendered abroad.

- Transfer of copyright, neighboring rights and rights to use the patent on an invention, industrial design, semiconductor's topography, trademark, company name, secret formula or technique, and franchise or granting the right to use them.
- Consulting, legal, auditing, accounting, advertising, market research, public opinion survey services, telecommunications services, development of software, data processing, transmission of information, transfer of sportsmen, and intermediary activities in the provision of the above services to foreign legal entities.
- Lease and finance lease of movable property to foreign legal entities, provided the lessor produces documents supporting the fact that the leased assets will be used outside Lithuania.
- Services for permanent residents of Lithuania provided outside Lithuania are treated as exported services. Transportation services are treated as provided beyond the boundaries of Lithuania when the beginning of the route is outside Lithuanian boundaries, or when the route begins and ends outside Lithuania but crosses Lithuanian boundaries.

VAT is charged at the rate of 18% on the import of goods and on the supply of goods and services in Lithuania, except for those referred to as exempt in the Law on VAT. The following goods and services are exempt: medical goods and services; social services; education; certain postal services; insurance and banking services; turnover of securities and raffles; funeral goods and services; publishing; services and works for which taxes are reckoned into the budget; state property under privatization; works and services paid for with donated funds; rent for dwelling houses and apartments being leased for more than two months; land rent; articles of traditional art; and other goods and services enumerated in the Law on VAT.

*State dues*/State dues are payable on activities of state institutions (except courts), such as the issuance of documents having legal force and other deeds.

*Land tax*/A 1.5% tax is levied annually on the value of private land. Tax is paid by the owner.

*Land lease tax*/State-owned land is subject to a 6% tax on the value of the land. Tax is paid by the lessee.

*Road tax*/Corporations and banks are subject to road tax. The tax rate and basis vary with the activity of the enterprise, as follows.

|  | Maximum rate | Basis |
|---|---|---|
|  | % |  |
| All entities except banks, trade and gas companies | 0.48 | Revenues |
| Trade companies | 0.3 | Revenues |
| Gas companies | 0.1 | Revenues |
| Banks | 1.0 | Income from services |

*Real estate tax*/Any company owning real estate must pay this tax. The annual rate is 1% of the taxable value of the real estate. Taxable value is replacement value calculated by taking into account locality coefficients.

*Excise taxes*/Excise duty is levied on unrefined ethyl alcohol, beer, wine, spirits, tobacco, petroleum products, fuel, oil, orimulsion, coffee, chocolate, foodstuffs containing cacao, electricity, erotic publications, luxury cars, sugar and products containing sugar, and perfume. The taxable value of goods made in Lithuania is the selling price of the goods, excluding excise tax and VAT. That of imported goods is customs value, including customs duty.

*Customs duties*/Customs duties are applied to goods and commodities exported from or imported into Lithuania, except for certain items that are exempt.

*Tax on pollution*/A company that creates chemical or biological pollution is taxed on the basis of the quantity of pollutant discharged into the atmosphere or water sources.

*Tax on natural resources*/A tax is payable on the value of extracted natural resources.

## Branch income

A branch of a foreign company is defined as a structural subunit of a foreign company, which has an establishment in Lithuania and which is entitled to engage in commercial activities in Lithuania, conclude contracts and undertake obligations according to the power of attorney issued to the branch by its founder. A branch does not have a status of a legal person. It is taxed in the same manner as a PE.

Lithuanian tax legislation legitimizes the concept of a PE as a dependent structural unit (including a branch) of a foreign company. According to the new PE taxation rules, a PE is taxed according to the same rules as Lithuanian companies. Revenues and expenses are calculated in the same manner. In addition, a PE is allowed to add to its expenses administrative expenses of the foreign company related to the PE's activities. Nevertheless, the rules are very general and there is no established practice as to how they should be applied.

## Income determination

*Inventory valuation*/Under domestic accounting legislation, basic raw materials and complete plant that are used in the production and included in the cost of produced stocks (products) are valued in the financial statements by the FIFO method. If stocks of a certain kind move differently through the enterprise, the value may be estimated and reflected in the financial statements by the LIFO, weighted-average, progressive-average, actual-price, or other method that corresponds to the stocks' movement. The method used must be disclosed in the notes to the annual accounts, and, among other things, the note must report the profit that would have been calculated if the FIFO method of valuation had been used.

*Capital gains*/Capital gains are taxed as part of the corporate profit of the enterprise.

*Intercompany dividends*/Dividends received from Lithuanian companies after withholding tax has been applied, and dividends from foreign companies after corporate profits tax has been applied, are not included in taxable income.

*Foreign income*/If a Lithuanian legal person derives profit subject to taxation abroad, and no treaty on the avoidance of double taxation is concluded with the appropriate country, the tax paid abroad may be deducted from the calculated corporate profit tax. In accordance with the regulations, the sum deducted from corporate profit tax may not exceed that part of the tax calculated in Lithuania that is attributed to the profit received in the foreign state.

*Stock dividends*/Dividends paid out to Lithuanian and foreign entities are subject to 29% tax rate. Dividend tax can be set off against profit tax but only up to the amount of the profit tax paid. Dividend tax exceeding profit tax may be carried forward to the next year for 5 years and set off against the next year's profit tax payable. No setoff or carryforward is allowed when dividends are paid out to foreign entities.

## Deductions

*Depreciation*/Intangible and tangible assets may be depreciated on a straight-line basis or by using the diminishing-value method. Depreciation may not exceed maximum rates established by law.

*Net operating losses*/Losses may be carried forward for five years after the end of the year in which losses arose except for losses incurred due to the transfer of securities and/or derivative financial instruments. Losses incurred due to the transfer of securities and/or derivative financial instruments shall be carried forward to the next tax year for three years but may be covered only with operational income generated by transfers of securities and/or derivative financial instruments.

*Taxes*/Taxes, dues, and other compulsory payments established by laws and decrees of the government (except VAT paid into the budget, interest on state use of capital, fines and other sanctions) are deductible for corporate tax purposes.

*Other significant items*/According to recent statutory amendments, allowable deductions are all expenses actually incurred in the usual course of business of an entity necessary to earn its income or achieve economic benefit unless the Profit Tax Law provides otherwise.

Allowable limited deductions are as follows.
1. Depreciation or amortization costs of fixed assets.
2. Maintenance, repair, and reconstruction costs of fixed tangible assets.
3. Business travel costs.
4. Advertising and representation costs.
5. Natural losses.
6. Taxes.
7. Bad debts.
8. Contributions for the benefit of employees.
9. Special provisions of credit institutions and insurance companies.
10. Sponsorship.
11. Membership fees, contributions and payments.
12. Losses within tax period.

## Group taxation

Each company is taxed individually. Losses cannot be transferred from one group company to another.

## Tax incentives

Under the Law on Foreign Companies, for a company established or in which foreign capital was invested before December 31, 1993, corporate profit tax levied on the share of profits attributable to the foreign investment, not used for salary payment and reinvested in the company is to be reduced by 70% for a five-year period from the date the profit is derived. On the expiration of this term, profit tax levied on the share of profits attributable to foreign investment is to be reduced by 50% for three years. For companies established or in which foreign capital was invested between January 1, 1994 and August 1, 1995, profit tax levied on the share of profits attributable to foreign investment is to be reduced by 50% for a six-year period.

From August 1, 1996, if the foreign investment has reached US$2 million in a Lithuanian company, the company concerned is exempt from payment of profit tax for a period of three years from the beginning of the accounting quarter in which the profit is derived. Such a company pays 50% less profit tax for the subsequent three years. However, this tax relief is not applicable to companies involved in wholesale or retail trade in oil products if the income generated from such trade exceeds 30% of total sales revenue.

These tax reliefs for foreign investors are effective if the investment was made or the company was registered before April 1, 1997. However, they are no longer available for investments made or companies registered on or after that date.

In addition, if as much as LTL200 million (US$50 million) is invested in a Lithuanian-registered company in the course of three years after October 1, 1998, the company is entitled to a guarantee that the rates of direct taxes effective at the time of investment and paid by the company will not be increased for a period of five years from the date of investment. At the request of the investor(s) the government should conclude an agreement to this effect. For strategic investors the period of static tax burden may be extended up to ten years.

Taxable profit of companies wherein an average number of employees listed on the payroll is no more than 10 and income within a tax period is not above LTL500,000 shall be subject to a tax rate of 13% except for cases specified in the law.

In addition to the tax incentives provided to foreign investors, there are tax reductions for businesses employing handicapped persons. Companies registered in free economic zones are subject to 80% reduction of corporate profit tax for five years from the date of registration. On the expiration of this term, corporate profit tax is to be reduced by 50% for five years. If the foreign investor owns not less than 30% of the authorized (own) capital of the company registered in a free economic zone and has invested no less than US$1 million of capital of foreign origin, the company is exempt from corporate profit tax for a period of five years from the date of its registration. Such a company pays 50% less corporate profit tax for the next ten years.

## Withholding taxes

***Domestic legislation****/*Income (earnings) the source of which is in Lithuania received by a foreign entity in Lithuania otherwise than through its permanent establishments is as follows.

1. Income generated by interest on any debt obligations including securities (except for Government securities issued on international financial markets), bonds, premiums and bonuses relating to such debt obligations, except for the income from interest on deposits and subordinated loans that meet the criteria established by legal acts issued by the Bank of Lithuania.
2. Income from distributed profit.

3. Royalties, including fees received for neighboring rights.

4. Income received for the transfer or assignment under the licensing contract of a right to use an object of industrial property, a franchise.

5. Income received in consideration for information provided about industrial, commercial, or scientific know-how.

6. Proceeds from the sale, transfer (with a title), or lease of an inherently immovable object located in Lithuania.

7. Indemnities received for infringement upon copyrights or related rights.

Withholding tax is levied on the above income at a rate of 10%.

Tax-haven companies

Tax rules for payments by Lithuanian entities to foreign corporations registered or resident in states and territories that have been designated by the Lithuanian government as tax havens, including payments to branches of such foreign corporations, changed from January 1, 2002. Tax haven means a foreign country or area (zone) put on the list of tax havens established by the Minister of Finance and satisfying at least two of the following criteria.

1. The tax rate for a similar tax in such territory is below 75% of that set in the Profit Tax Law.

2. In such territory different rules of levying a similar tax are applied depending on the country where the parent company is registered or otherwise organized.

3. In such territory different rules of levying a similar tax are applied depending on the country where the business is carried out.

4. The company has entered into a contract for a tax rate or tax base with the tax administrator of that country.

5. There is no effective exchange of information in such territory.

6. There is no financial and administrative transparency in such territory: tax administration rules are not quite clear and the application of them is not communicated to tax administrators of other countries.

A list of 60 such states and territories has been published.

With certain exceptions specified in the law, all payments to tax-haven companies or their branches for any kind of works or services, commodities, interest on funding, insurance premiums, guarantees, and so on, are nondeductible for profit tax purposes unless the Lithuanian entity provides evidence to the State Tax Authorities that the following applies.

1. The payments are related to usual activities of the paying and the receiving business entities.

2. The receiving foreign business entity manages the property necessary to carry out such usual activities, and there is a connection between the payment and an economically grounded business operation.

*Tax treaties*/Where a treaty for the avoidance of double taxation and prevention of fiscal evasion with the country in question contradicts domestic regulations, the treaty provisions prevail. At present Lithuania is a party to such treaties with 24 countries (see the table below).

Reduction of or exemption from withholding taxes under a double taxation treaty may be obtained if a special residence certificate (request for reduction or exemption from the Lithuanian anticipatory (withholding) tax withheld at source (Form DAS–1)) is completed and approved by the tax authorities before a taxable payment is transferred. If a payment that would have been subject to a tax treaty has already been made and withholding tax at the domestic rate was withheld, it is possible to obtain an appropriate refund (reduction) by completing a special claim for a refund of the Lithuanian tax withheld at source (Form DAS–2) and getting the approval of the tax authorities.

In addition, the tax authorities may require completion of a special certificate giving information about income received and taxes paid in Lithuania (Form DAS–3).

**Dividends, interest, royalties**/Foreign corporations are subject to withholding tax on loan interest generated from Lithuanian companies and PEs of foreign corporations at a rate of 10%. Withholding tax is not levied on loan interest generated by foreign banks and international financial institutions.

Lithuanian legal persons and foreign corporations are subject to withholding tax on dividends generated from Lithuanian corporations at a rate of 29%.

Lithuania's double taxation treaties include provisions for withholding taxes on dividends, interest, and royalties as shown below.

| Recipient | Cash dividends (1, 2) | Interest | Royalties (3) |
|---|---|---|---|
| | % | % | % |
| Resident corporations | 29 | Nil | Nil |
| Resident individuals | 29 | Nil | Nil |
| Nonresident corporations and individuals: | | | |
| Nontreaty | 29 | 10 | 10 |
| | | (4) | (4) |
| Treaty: | | | |
| Armenia | 15 (5) | 10 | 10 |
| Belarus | 10 | 10 | 10 |
| Canada | 15 (5) | 10 | 10 |
| China, P.R. | 15 (5) | 10 | 10 |
| Croatia | 15 (5) | 10 | 10 |
| Czech Republic | 15 (5) | 10 | 10 |
| Denmark | 15 (5) | 10 | 10 (5) |
| Estonia | 15 (0) | Nil | Nil |
| France | 15 (5) | 10 | 10 (5) |
| Finland | 15 (5) | 10 | 10 (5) |
| Germany | 15 (5) | 10 | 10 (5) |
| Iceland | 15 (5) | 10 | 10 (5) |
| Ireland, Rep. of | 15 (5) | 10 | 10 (5) |
| Italy | 15 (5) | 10 | 10 (5) |
| Kazakhstan | 15 (5) | 10 | 10 |
| Latvia | 15 (0) | Nil | Nil |
| Moldova | 10 | 10 | 10 |
| Netherlands | 15 (5) | 10 | 10 (5) |
| Norway | 15 (5) | 10 | 10 (5) |
| Poland | 15 (5) | 10 | 10 |
| Sweden | 15 (5) | 10 | 10 (5) |
| Turkey | 10 | 10 | 10 (5) |

# Lithuania

| Recipient | Cash dividends (1, 2) | Interest | Royalties (3) |
|---|---|---|---|
| | % | % | % |
| Ukraine .............................................. | 15 (5) | 10 | 10 |
| United States .................................... | 15 (5) | 10 | 10 (5) |

Notes:

1. The particular treaty should be consulted as to whether the reduced rate for dividends (shown in parentheses) is applicable in the case of payments to corporations that have the requisite control.

2. The rates in parentheses indicate the rates that apply when the beneficial owner is a company directly holding at least 25% of the capital of the company paying the dividend.

3. The rates in parentheses are the special rates applicable for royalties acquired for the use of industrial, commercial or scientific equipment.

4. Withholding tax is not levied on interest on deposits and subordinated loans that meet the criteria established by the Bank of Lithuania.

## Tax administration

### Returns

1. Corporate profit tax: The advance corporate profit tax return for the first nine months of the tax period is to be submitted by the last day of the first month (usually January) of the tax period. The return for the remaining months of the tax period is to be submitted by the last day of the tenth month (usually October) of the tax period. If the taxpayer has chosen to pay the advance amount on the basis of the amount of corporate profit tax calculated for each month of the current year, the return must be submitted quarterly and no later than the last day of the first month of the quarter.

   Following the end of the calendar year (or other tax period), corporate tax returns and financial statements must be submitted by the first day of the tenth month of the following tax period (October 1 for companies using the calendar year). The above provisions are applicable to profit tax returns submitted in the tax period starting in 2003.

2. Withholding tax on payments other than dividends: A tax-withholding entity must submit to the tax authorities a special certificate reporting sums paid and taxes withheld during the calendar month no later than 15 days after the end of the month in which the sums were paid.

3. Withholding tax on dividends: A tax-withholding entity must submit to the tax authorities a special certificate reporting dividends paid and tax withheld within 10 calendar days after the end of the month of dividend payment.

### Payment of tax

1. Corporate profit tax: The advance amount of corporate profit tax for the first nine months of the tax period is calculated on the basis of two-thirds of the actual profit tax for the preceding tax period. For example, the corporate profit tax for the first nine months of 2003 would be calculated on the basis of the appropriate portion of the actual amount of profit tax for 2001. The advance amount for the remainder of the tax period is based on one-third of the actual amount of profit tax for the previous period, for example, tax for the last three

months of 2003 would be based on the appropriate portion of the actual amount of profit tax for 2002.

The taxpayer may choose to pay the advance amount based on the tax calculated for each month of the current year. The advance tax (1/4 of the advance corporate profit tax) must be paid no later than the last day of the quarter; and for the last quarter, by the 25th day of the last month of the quarter.

If the amount of tax indicated in the return exceeds the amount actually paid during the tax period, the taxpayer is obliged to transfer the additional amount by the working day following the deadline for submission of the return. Overpaid tax is refunded in accordance with the Law on Tax Administration.

2. Withholding tax on payments other than dividends: Withholding tax is to be calculated, withheld and remitted by a Lithuanian company or a permanent establishment of a foreign corporation no later than the return submission deadline.

3. Withholding tax on dividends: Withholding tax is to be calculated, withheld and remitted by a Lithuanian company that pays dividends within ten calendar days after the end of the month of the payment.

## CORPORATION TAX CALCULATION

Calendar year ended December 31, 2002

| | | |
|---|---:|---:|
| Net profit before taxes and after possible deductions | | LTL 1,000,000 |
| Add—Expenses increasing taxable profit: | | |
| Nondeductible expenses | | 50,000 |
| | | 1,050,000 |
| Less: | | |
| Expenses reducing taxable profit | 30,000 | |
| Nontaxable income | 10,000 | 40,000 |
| Taxable profit | | LTL 1,010,000 |
| Corporate profit tax at 15% | | LTL 151,500 |

Note:

Exchange rate of the litas at February 2, 2003: €1 = LTL3.4528.

# Luxembourg

## PwC contact

For additional information on taxation in Luxembourg, contact:

René Beltjens
PricewaterhouseCoopers S.à.r.l. BP 1443
400, Route d'Esch
L–1014 Luxembourg
Telephone: (352) 49 48 48 1
Fax: (352) 49 48 48 2900
e-mail: rene.beltjens@lu.pwc.com

## Significant developments

On December 21, 2001, the Luxembourg government enacted a significant tax reform, which over 2002 enhanced the use of Luxembourg holding and/or operational companies for tax planning purposes. This reform includes a reduction of the corporate income tax rate, a broadening of the participation exemption, and simplification of the conditions for tax consolidation. The tax reform also includes provisions providing for flexible tax-free corporate reorganizations and enhanced tax credits for inward investments. Generally, the tax reform should apply to tax years ending after January 1, 2002 (i.e., to companies closing their accounts after January 1, 2002).

## Operational currency

On January 1, 2002, the euro (€) effectively replaced the Luxembourg franc (LF) as legal tender in Luxembourg. Generally, the exchange rate is LF 40.3399 = €1. However, Luxembourg companies may choose any Organization for Economic Cooperation and Development (OECD) currency as their operational currency.

Generally, foreign-currency balance sheets must be translated into euros for the determination of taxable income. However, banks, insurance and reinsurance companies, and certain financial companies may set up a provision for the neutralization of unrealized exchange gains. In the case of cessation of trade, they may also permanently exempt their conversion gains on exchange up to the surplus of the revalued total of equity over its former historical value.

## Taxes on corporate income

*Corporate income tax*/The corporate income tax rate is 22% for companies with an income in excess of €15,000. Additionally, a 4% solidarity tax is imposed on the corporate income tax amount. Businesses with income lower than €15,000 are subject to a lower rate. Taking into account the 4% solidarity tax, the effective corporate tax rate is reduced from 31.2% to 22.88% for tax years ending after January 1, 2002.

The corporate income tax does not apply to tax exempt entities (e.g., 1929 holding companies, see "Other Incentives"), or to tax transparent entities (e.g., general or limited partnerships or European Economic Interest Groupings).

*Municipal business tax on income*/Municipal business tax is levied by the communes and so varies from region to region. The tax reform of 2002 has reduced the municipal business tax (for Luxembourg City) from 9.09% to 7.5% for tax years ending after January 1, 2002.

*Aggregate rate*/As a result of the 2002 tax reform, the effective combined income tax rate for Luxembourg City (i.e., both corporate income tax and municipal business tax) is reduced from 37.45% to 30.38% for tax years ending after January 1, 2002.

## Corporate residence

Without regard to double tax treaty provisions, a company is considered to be resident if either its registered office or principal place of management is located in Luxembourg. The registered office is designated as such in the company's articles of incorporation. The principal place of management is generally defined as the center from which the company's activities are directed.

## Branch income

Branch income is generally taxed at corporate income tax rates. However, the municipal business tax generally only applies if the branch is carrying on commercial activity within Luxembourg.

## Other taxes

*Net wealth tax*/Both resident companies and branches of foreign companies are generally subject to net wealth tax levied at a rate of 0.5% on their net wealth, based on prescribed valuation methods. In general, assets are taken into account at market value (except for real estate, subject to a special regime). Shareholdings qualifying for the participation exemption (see below under "Income determination") are generally exempt from net wealth tax.

Due to the 2001 tax reform, resident companies and branches of foreign companies may claim a reduction of their net wealth tax liability by making an allocation to a special reserve before the closing of the tax year following the net wealth tax reduction. An amount corresponding to five times the net wealth tax to be reduced must be kept in this reserve for the five years following the tax year in which it was allocated. However, the reduction may not be higher than the corporate tax liability, before tax credit, of the taxpayer for that same year.

*Capital tax*/Capital contributed to a Luxembourg company or branch is generally subject to a 1% capital tax on the net value of the property contributed. However, investment funds pay a flat registration duty of €1,250 when they are established. For contributions to other types of business entities, there may be an exemption under the following circumstances (subject to certain conditions).

1. Share-for-share contribution.
2. All assets and liabilities contribution.
3. Conversion of retained earnings or reserves into share capital.
4. Migration of capital within the EU.

*Value-added tax*/Proceeds of sales and services rendered in Luxembourg are subject to value-added tax (VAT) at the standard rate of 15% or, on certain transactions, at 12%, 6%, or 3%. Taxpayers are entitled to offset against their VAT payable the amount of such tax charged to them by their suppliers or assessed on imports. Typical banking, insurance, reinsurance, and holding operations are generally exempt. VAT paid on expenses related to exempt non-EU banking, insurance, and reinsurance operations is recoverable.

# Luxembourg

*Subscription tax*/Certain holding companies and investment funds are subject to subscription tax (at various rates) on their market or net asset values. The 1929 holding companies are subject to a 0.2% subscription tax on the value of the shares issued, with a minimum amount of €48. For investment funds, the subscription tax is applied to the total net assets evaluated at the last day of each quarter. As a principle, the subscription tax rate is of 0.05%. Institutional funds and money market funds are subject to a reduced annual rate of 0.01%. Funds of funds are exempted from subscription tax.

*General registration taxes*/General registration taxes (inclusive of the transcription tax) are levied at 7% on the market value of real estate purchased or transferred (10% in the commune of Luxembourg City for commercial property) and 1% on mortgages on real estate. The taxes are deductible for income tax purposes.

*Special income tax*/"Billionaire" and "financial" holding companies are subject to a special income tax applied at varying percentage rates to interest expenses on bonds, payments to nonresident directors, and dividends distributed to shareholders. The minimum annual tax is €48,000 (see "Other incentives/holding companies" below for further information).

*Commune real estate tax*/Communes levy a real estate tax, the basis of which is the unitary value of real estate, which represents its estimated value in 1941. The basic rate varies from 0.7% to 1% of the unitary value, according to the category of property, and is multiplied by a coefficient, which varies with communes and different types of property. For commercial properties, the coefficient in Luxembourg City is 750%, which should be applied to 1% of the unitary value. The tax is deductible for income tax purposes.

## Income determination

*Inventory valuation*/Inventories are generally valued at the lower of actual or market cost. In general, both the FIFO and the LIFO methods of inventory valuation are acceptable for income tax purposes, provided the method accords with the facts.

*Intercompany dividends*/The tax reform of 2002 broadened the participation exemption regime to shareholdings held through Luxembourg tax transparent entities (e.g., general and limited partnerships), and brought a relaxation of the rules on distributions of preacquisition earnings and a partial exemption for nonqualifying shares of EU companies. Generally, the participation exemption applies if the following conditions are satisfied.

1. The distributing company is either a Luxembourg tax resident, EU tax resident, or a nonresident limited liability company subject to a corresponding tax rate (minimum 11% tax rate).
2. The beneficiary company is a Luxembourg tax resident or a permanent establishment (PE) of a company tax resident in either the European Union or a double tax treaty country.
3. The beneficiary company has held or undertakes to hold at least 10% of the shares of the distributing company, or of an acquisition price of at least €1.2 million, for an uninterrupted period of at least 12 months. The participation exemption may apply to cash dividends, dividends-in-kind, hidden profit distributions, and liquidation distributions.

*Capital gains*/Capital gains (and losses) are generally taxed as ordinary income (or losses). It is possible to postpone the taxation on gains on certain fixed assets where the gain is used to acquire replacement items. Under certain conditions, exempt capital gains and hidden reserves may be continued within a merger or other form of reorganization of resident companies or other EU companies.

The tax reform of 2002 has relaxed the requirements to qualify for the participation exemption on capital gains, which now also applies to shareholdings held through Luxembourg tax transparent entities (e.g., general partnerships, limited partnerships). In general, capital gains on the disposal of qualifying shareholdings held by either a Luxembourg company or a Luxembourg PE of a company resident either in the European Union or a double tax treaty country are exempt from Luxembourg corporate income taxes, provided the total shareholding constitutes at least 10% of total ownership or an acquisition price of €6 million, the disposing company has held or intends to hold the qualifying shareholding for at least 12 months.

*Foreign income*/A Luxembourg tax resident company is subject to corporate income tax on its worldwide income, whether derived from Luxembourg or from foreign sources. Dividends from foreign subsidiaries are taxed when received, except where exempt as mentioned above. Profits of a foreign branch of a Luxembourg company, which are not exempt through a double taxation treaty, may be granted a foreign tax credit. Any taxes paid in excess of the tax credit are deductible as expenses. Losses of foreign branches in non-treaty countries may be used to offset only future profits of the branch or other income arising in that country. If a double taxation treaty applies, the branch's losses are generally not deductible.

Securitization companies, which are incorporated under the law of March 9, 2004, are subject to normal corporate taxation. The remuneration of the securities they issue (both debt and capital) qualifies as tax deductible interest.

## Deductions

*Depreciation*/Rates must be consistent with economic reality. The depreciation must be calculated on the total acquisition cost, bearing in mind the normal life of the asset and the estimated residual value. Depreciation is normally calculated using the straight-line method. However, the declining-balance method is permitted for fixed assets other than buildings and intangible assets. The depreciation rate may not, however, exceed three times the rate applicable according to the straight-line method, or 30% (in the case of assets used exclusively for scientific and technical research, four times the applicable rate, or 40%). It is permissible to change from the declining-balance method to the straight-line method, but the converse is not allowed. Tax depreciation must be reflected in the accounts prepared for commercial purposes.

In the event of a sale of a depreciated asset, the net book value at the moment of the disposal must be compared with the sale price of that asset. If this comparison indicates a profit, corresponding income tax may be due unless the profit is reinvested. Capital losses are deductible.

# Luxembourg

Fixed assets with a value of less than €870 or a life that is not in excess of one year can be fully depreciated in the year of acquisition. Special accelerated depreciation on 60% of the cost of immovable assets that protect the national environment, save energy in Luxembourg, or permit the development of workplaces for handicapped workers is granted under certain conditions.

*Shareholdings*/Expenses linked to a shareholding qualifying for the participation exemption, including write-downs in the value of the shareholding booked as a consequence of a dividend distribution, are fully deductible but the participation exemption on dividends will not apply up to the amount of deductible expenses/ write-downs linked to the shareholding and incurred the year during which the dividend was received. Recapture rules may apply in the event of disposal of the shareholding. The book value of the qualifying shareholding can be deducted from the business assets for the determination of the taxable basis for net wealth tax. The excess portion of a debt linked to the qualifying shareholding is deductible from the taxable basis. (See "Intercompany dividends" above for a discussion on which shareholdings qualify for the participation exemption.)

*Net operating losses*/Losses can be carried forward for an unlimited period, but cannot be carried back.

*Payments to foreign affiliates*/Royalties, management service fees, and interest charges paid to foreign affiliates by a Luxembourg company are deductible items, provided they are equal to what the company would pay an unrelated entity for comparable services.

*Taxes*/Several taxes are deductible in determining income subject to corporate income tax including the capital tax, general registration taxes, and real estate tax. Also, certain taxes are deducted from the computed amount of income tax owed, including taxes withheld from Luxembourg dividend income, tax withheld abroad from dividend and interest income received by a Luxembourg corporation (subject to limitations), and investment tax credits (see "Tax incentives" below).

## Group taxation

The tax reform of 2002 has simplified the procedure and requirements to qualify for tax unity (consolidation). Generally, the conditions to qualify for tax unity include the following.

1. Each company is tax resident in Luxembourg.
2. At least 95% (99% for tax years ending before 2002) of each subsidiary's capital is directly or indirectly (i.e., through Luxembourg tax resident companies) held by the parent company.
3. Each company's fiscal year ends on the same date.
4. Tax unity is elected by the group.

The tax unity lasts for a five-year period, and is computed on the consolidated result. Tax losses that occurred before the consolidation period may be set off only against tax profits of the company that incurred the loss. Tax losses that are sustained by some group members during the consolidation period are compensated with the tax profits of the other group members. Tax losses arising during the consolidation period that exist after the consolidation period are attributed to the parent company. In the case of a European Economic Interest Group, income is taxable in the hands of the individual venturers.

## Tax incentives

*Inward and capital investment*/The various incentives include the following.

1. Investment tax credits: Luxembourg tax law provides for two types of investment tax credits. The complementary investment tax credit provides a credit of 10% of the complementary acquisition value of investments made during the tax year. The global investment tax credit provides for a credit of 6% of the acquisition value of investments made during the year, subject to a ceiling of €150,000 and 2% on the balance. In case of investments in fixed assets of an ecological nature, the rates can be raised to 8% and 4%, respectively. Certain investments are excluded from the credit calculation, including investments in real property, intangible assets, and vehicles (unless qualifying as an investment of net assets).

2. New businesses tax credit: A 25% exemption on both corporate income tax and municipal business tax for up to eight years on profits arising from the implementation of new businesses, manufacturing processes, and new high-technology services.

3. Audiovisual certificates: The government grants investment certificates which grant up to a 30% tax credit on taxable income derived by a Luxembourg tax resident company which produces qualifying audiovisual works of fiction in Luxembourg.

4. Venture capital investment certificates: The government grants venture capital certificates which can provide for up to a 30% exemption on profits derived from qualifying new enterprises, new production facilities or technologies suited for the development of the Luxembourg economy.

5. Small business incentives: Small- and medium-sized firms may benefit from the incentives for up to 10% of the cost incurred on investment and reorganization operations.

6. Regional and national incentives: To attract investment and reorganization in certain regions, incentives varying between 17.5% and 25% of the cost may be granted. Also, under certain conditions and limitations, incentives may also be granted to other firms situated in the national territory that are undertaking investment and reorganization operations.

7. Research and development incentives: To promote research and development, the government may grant incentives between 25% and 100% of related costs.

8. Environmental incentives: Under a new legislation, investments favoring the protection of the environment and the rational use of energy may benefit from incentives of up to 40% of related costs.

9. Organizations: The National Credit and Investment Corporation (*Société Nationale de Crédit et d'Investissement,* or SNCI) promotes the creation, expansion, reorientation, and rationalization of industrial and service organizations. The Committee for the Promotion of Luxembourg Exports (*Comité pour la Promotion des Exportations Luxembourgeoises,* or COPEL) grants interest rebates on loans financing the export of goods. The Ducroire Office gives guarantees against export risks, especially those relating to credit.

*Other incentives*/Other incentives include the following.

1. Holding companies: Holding companies set up under the law of July 31, 1929 (so-called 1929 holding companies) are generally exempt from income taxes (corporate income tax, municipal business tax) and withholding tax on

dividends paid, and are only subject to the previously described annual subscription tax and the capital tax. Luxembourg generally provides for three types of 1929 holding companies: ordinary (as described above); billionaire holdings, which require minimum capitalization of €24 million and provide for further tax exemptions; and financial holdings which provide for greater flexibility for intragroup financing. The latter regimes are subject to debate within EU and OECD. Expectations are, however, that they should remain applicable until 2010. Moreover, the Luxembourg authorities are contemplating amending the regulatory framework so that holding companies comply with EU and OECD requirements.

2. Investment funds: Investment funds resident in Luxembourg are generally exempt from corporate income tax, municipal business tax, and withholding tax on dividends, and are only subject to the previously described subscription tax and capital tax.

3. Financial participation companies (so-called SOPARFI): A SOPARFI (*Société de Participation Financière*) is not a specific type of company. Their tax regime results from the application of the common tax rules on participation exemption. Unlike the 1929 holding company regime, a SOPARFI is not tax exempt and benefits from Luxembourg's double tax treaties, EU Directives (e.g., Parent-Subsidiary Directive), and the participation exemption on dividends received (as discussed above).

4. Financial services companies: Banks, securities depositaries, insurance and reinsurance companies, as well as other financial service companies may benefit from preferential regulations when establishing their taxable basis for corporate income tax (e.g., provision for the neutralization of unrealized exchange gains; provision for future loan losses; provision for guarantee of deposits; mathematical reserves; and/or catastrophe reserves).

5. Shipping companies: Luxembourg-resident shipping companies are not subject to municipal business tax, and can benefit from investment tax credits and accelerated depreciation.

6. Nontax incentives: Several other available incentives are not given in the form of tax incentives, but rather as financial incentives, including the following.

   a. Loans at reduced interest rates.

   b. Government guarantees on loans.

   c. Real estate development assistance in certain industrial sites and buildings.

   d. Cash grants for the following business activities, if located in Luxembourg: high-technology investments; reorganizations of economically justified sectors; research and development of new products, services, or manufacturing processes. The lessee benefits from the cash grant if the investments are financed by leasing.

   e. Financial incentives for audiovisual productions carried out in Luxembourg.

## Withholding taxes

The following taxes are withheld on payments made.

| Recipient | Dividends | | Interest (4) | Royalties |
|---|---|---|---|---|
| | Portfolio (1, 2) | Substantial Holdings (3) | | |
| | % | % | % | % |
| Resident corporations | 20 | 0 (5) | — | — |
| Resident individuals | 20 | 20 | — | — |
| Nonresident corporations and individuals: | | | | |
| Nontreaty | 20 | 20/0 (3) | — | 10 (6) |
| Treaty (7): | | | | |
| Austria | 15 | 0/5 (3, 8) | — | — (9) |
| Belgium | 15 | 0/10 (3, 10) | — | — |
| Brazil (11) | 25 | 15 (12) | — | 25/15(6) |
| Bulgaria (11) | 15 | 5 (8) | — | 5 |
| Canada | 15 | 5 (12) | — | 0/10 (13) |
| China, P.R. | 10 | 5 (8) | — | 10/6 (14) |
| Czech Republic | 15 | 5 (8) | — | 0/10 (15) |
| Denmark | 15 | 5/0 (3, 8) | — | — |
| Finland | 15 | 5/0 (3, 16) | — | 0/5 (17) |
| France | 15 | 5/0 (3, 16) | — | — |
| Germany | 15 | 10/0 (3, 8) | — | 5 |
| Greece | 7.5 | 7.5/0 (3) | — | 5/7 (18) |
| Hungary | 15 | 5 (8) | — | — |
| Iceland | 15 | 5 (8) | — | — |
| Indonesia | 15 | 10 (8) | — | 12.5/10 (6) |
| Ireland, Rep. of | 15 | 5/0 (3, 8) | — | — |
| Italy | 15 | 15/0 (3) | — | 10 |
| Japan | 15 | 5 (19) | — | 10 |
| Korea, Rep. of | 15 | 10 (8) | — | 10/15 (6, 20) |
| Malta | 15 | 5 (8) | — | 10 |
| Mauritius | 10 | 5 (12) | — | — |
| Mexico | 15 | 5 | — | 10 |
| Mongolia | 15 | 5 (12) | — | 5 |
| Morocco | 15 | 10 (8) | — | 10 |
| Netherlands | 15 | 2.5/0 (3, 8) | — | — |
| Norway | 15 | 5 (8) | — | — |
| Poland | 15 | 5 (8) | — | 10 |
| Portugal | 15 | — (3) | — | 10 (21) |
| Romania | 15 | 5 (8) | — | 10 |
| Russia | 15 | 10 (22) | — | — |
| Singapore | 10 | 5 (23) | — | 10 |
| Slovak Republic | 15 | 5 (8) | — | 0/10 (17) |
| Slovenia | 15 | 5 (24) | — | 5 |
| South Africa | 15 | 5 (8) | — | — |
| Spain | 15 | 5/0 (3, 25) | — | 10 |
| Sweden | 15 | 5/0 (3, 8) | — | — |
| Switzerland | 15 | 5/0 (8) | — | — |
| Thailand | 15 | 5 (17) | — | 15 (6) |

# Luxembourg

| Recipient | Dividends | | Interest (4) | Royalties |
|---|---|---|---|---|
| | Portfolio (1, 2) | Substantial Holdings (3) | | |
| | % | % | % | % |
| Trinidad and Tobago ............... | 10 | 5 (12) | — | 10 |
| Tunisia.................................... | 10 | 10 | — | 12(6) |
| Ukraine ................................. | 15 | 5 (29) | — | 5/10 (30, 31) |
| United Kingdom...................... | 15 | 5/0 (3, 16) | — | 5 (26) |
| United States ......................... | 15 | 5/0 (27) | — | — |
| Uzbekistan ............................ | 15 | 5 (8) | — | 5 |
| Vietnam.................................. | 15 | 10/5 (28) | — | 10 |

The numbers in parentheses refer to the following numbered Notes.

Notes:

1. Dividends paid by Luxembourg 1929 holding companies or investment funds are exempt from withholding taxes.

2. No income tax is withheld on dividends paid, provided the distributing company is a fully taxable Luxembourg company and the receiving company is either tax resident in Luxembourg, in the EU, or a permanent establishment of a company that is tax resident in either Luxembourg, the EU, or in a double tax treaty country.

3. No withholding tax is levied on dividend distributions paid by a Luxembourg subsidiary to an EU parent company that has held or commits to hold 10% of its affiliate's capital or at least €1.2 million for a minimum of 12 months.

4. Interest paid to nonresidents is generally not subject to withholding tax in Luxembourg. However, interest that represents a right to profit participation on a bond may be classified as a dividend and subject to withholding tax as such. Under double taxation avoidance treaties, these profit participation bonds will be subject to a withholding tax when the holder is resident in the following countries: Belgium, Brazil, and Thailand—15%; Bulgaria, Canada, the People's Republic of China, France, Indonesia, Italy, Japan, the Republic of Korea, Mexico, Morocco, Poland, Romania, Singapore, Spain, Switzerland, Thailand, Uzbekistan, and Vietnam—10%; Portugal—10% or 15%; Greece—8%; Tunisia—7.5% or 10%.

5. A resident parent company fully liable to income tax, or a Luxembourg branch of an EU-resident company or of a company resident in a double taxation treaty country, has a substantial holding when the direct shareholding in a qualifying resident or nonresident subsidiary amounts to at least 10% or to a purchase price of €1.2 million (see "Intercompany dividends," above). However, dividends paid to a Luxembourg 1929 holding company or to an investment fund do not benefit from this exemption.

6. Luxembourg domestic law provides for a general withholding tax on royalties of 10%. However, royalties are taxed at 11.11% when the debtor has paid the tax to be levied

7. Double tax treaties have been concluded with Malaysia, Turkey, and the Ukraine, but are not yet in force. Double taxation treaties are under negotiation with Argentina, Australia, Azerbaijan, India, Israel, the Baltic States, Venezuela, and Yugoslavia.

8. The recipient company holds at least 25% of the Luxembourg company's shares or voting power. In some cases, a holding period requirement may have to be met as well.

9. Royalties paid to Austria are taxable at 10% if the Austrian company owns more than 50% of the Luxembourg company.

10. The recipient company owns a 25% investment or the equivalent of an acquisition price of €6,197,300. The investments may be held by several Belgian companies, provided one owns at least 50% of the shares of each of the others.

11. The reduced withholding tax rate applies only when the beneficiary has no permanent establishment in Luxembourg.

12. The recipient company holds at least 10% of the Luxembourg company's shares.

13. Royalties linked to the production and reproduction of literary, dramatic, musical, and artistic work (except for royalties related to cinema and television films) and royalties for the use of computer software or any patent or for information concerning industrial, commercial, or scientific experience are taxable only in Canada.

14. Royalties on industrial, commercial, or scientific equipment are taxed at the reduced rate of 6%. Hong Kong is not covered by the Luxembourg–P.R. China double taxation treaty.

15. Royalties from literary, artistic, and scientific rights, including royalties on films and radio programs, are exempt in Luxembourg.

16. The recipient company owns a 25% investment. The investment may be held by several treaty resident companies located in the same country (i.e., Finnish, French, British) provided one owns more than 50% of the shares of each of the others.

17. The rate of 5% applies only when the paying company is tax resident in Luxembourg, and holds directly at least 25% of the shareholding of the parent company.

18. Royalties from literary, artistic, and scientific rights, including royalties on films and radio programs, are taxed at 5%. Royalties from other sources are taxed at 7%.

19. The recipient company holds at least 25% of the Luxembourg company's voting power during the period of six months immediately before the end of the accounting period in which the distribution of profits takes place.

20. Royalties paid for the use of or the right to use Industrial, commercial, or scientific equipment or for information concerning industrial, commercial, or scientific experience are taxable at 10%.

21. Royalties include payments for technical assistance.

22. The recipient company holds at least 30% of the parent companies and the acquisition price reaches at least €75,000 (or equivalent).

23. The recipient company holds at least 25% of the Luxembourg company's shares. Dividends paid to the government of Singapore are exempt.

24. The dividends are taxable at a rate of 5% if the beneficial owner is a company that holds directly at least 25% of the capital of the company paying the dividends.

25. The recipient company holds directly at least 25% of the Luxembourg company's shares during a one-year period before the date of distribution of the dividend.

26. Royalties on films are treated as business income.

27. The substantial holding is taxable at 5% where the recipient U.S company owns at least 10% of the voting stock of the paying company. No withholding tax is levied when the U.S company has held during an uninterrupted period of two years a direct shareholding of at least 25% of the voting power of the paying company and certain conditions regarding the nature of activities performed by the distributing company are met.

28. The rate of 5% of withholding tax on the gross amount of the dividends applies where the effective recipient company owns directly or indirectly at least 50% of the share capital of the paying company or has invested more than US$10 million or the equivalent in Luxembourg or Vietnamese currency, in the capital of the company paying the dividends; the rate of 10% of withholding tax on the gross amount of the dividends applies where the beneficial owner is a company which holds directly or indirectly at least 25% but less than 50% of the capital of the company paying the dividends and has invested not more than US$10 million, or the equivalent in Luxembourg or Vietnamese currency, in the capital of the company paying the dividends.

29. The recipient company holds at least 20% of the Luxembourg company's shares.

30. For payments of any kind made as a consideration for the use of, or the right to use, any patent, trade mark, design or model, plan, secret formula or process, or for the use of, or the right to use information concerning industrial, commercial or, scientific experience.

31. For payments of any kind made as a consideration for the use of, or the right to use of literary, artistic, or scientific rights (including motion picture films and works on film or videotape for use in connection with television or radio broadcasting)

## Tax administration

*Returns*/Companies must file their tax returns at the latest on May 31 of each year following the calendar year during which the income was earned.

Assessments are issued after the end of the tax year and can normally be finalized within five years, although the deadline may be extended to ten years if the tax return is found to be incomplete or inexact, with or without fraudulent intent.

*Payment of tax*/Quarterly tax advances must be paid; these payments are fixed by the tax authorities on the basis of the tax assessed for the preceding year, or on the basis of the estimate for the first year. This estimate is given by the company pursuant to the request of the Luxembourg tax authorities.

## *CORPORATION TAX CALCULATION*

Calendar year 2003 (excluding business entities subject to special tax regimes)

### Assumptions

1. The entity's income after charging all expenditures and all taxes, except corporate income tax (CIT) and municipal business tax on income (MBTI), is €18,000,000.
2. The net wealth tax charge is €1,000,000 and is nondeductible for both MBTI and CIT purposes.
3. The company has received a dividend in the amount of €4,000,000 which qualifies for the participation exemption regime.
4. The above dividend arises from a shareholding that is partly financed by debt, of which an amount of €1,000,000 has been paid during the year as interest on the debt.
5. For the determination of the municipal business tax on income rate, a rate of 7.5% is used (i.e., rate for Luxembourg City).
6. The investment tax credit, which is deductible from corporate income tax, amounts to €10,000.
7. The entity benefits from a standard allowance of €17,500 against the MBTI.

### Municipal business tax on income (MBTI)

| | |
|---|---:|
| Commercial profit before income taxes | € 18,000,000 |
| Add: | |
| Net Wealth Tax | 1,000,000 |
| | 19,000,000 |
| Deduct: | |
| Exempt dividend | 3,000,000 |
| Subtotal | 16,000,000 |
| Less—Allowance | 17,500 |
| Taxable base | 15,982,500 |
| Municipal business tax on income (rounded)—15,982,500 x 7.5% | € 1,198,688 |

# Luxembourg

## Corporate income tax (CIT)

| | | |
|---|---|---:|
| Commercial profit before taxes | € | 18,000,000 |
| Add: | | |
| Net Wealth Tax (1) | | 1,000,000 |
| | | 19,000,000 |
| Deduct: | | |
| Exempt dividend | | 3,000,000 |
| Taxable base | | 16,000,000 |
| | | |
| Corporate income tax (rounded)—16,000,000 x 22% | | 3,520,000 |
| Solidarity fund supplement (rounded)—3,520,000 x 4% | | 140,800 |
| Total of corporate income tax and supplement | | 3,660,800 |
| Less—Investment tax credit | | (10,000) |
| Final corporate income tax | € | 3,650,800 |

Notes:

1. This net wealth tax liability may be reduced provided certain requirements are met (see "Other taxes").
2. Exchange rate of the euro at March 16, 2004: €1 = US$1.23290.

## PwC contact

For additional information on taxation in Macau, contact:

Christina Lam
Lowe Bingham & Matthews—PricewaterhouseCoopers
Sociedade de Auditores
Avenida Doutor Mario Soares
Bank of China Building
28/F, Unit C, Macau
Hong Kong
Telephone: (852) 2289 8888
Fax: (852) 2810 9888
Macau
Telephone: (853) 7995 111
Fax: (853) 7995 222
e-mail: christina.wc.lam@hk.pwc.com

## Significant developments

A person receiving both income from commercial activities and income from employment will no longer be required to combine the two income sources for the calculation for complementary tax purposes. Income derived from commercial activities and income derived from employment will be taxed separately under complementary tax regulations and professional tax regulations respectively.

Certain nontaxable allowances in the hands of a person in deriving the taxable income from commercial activities have been abolished.

The Macau-China avoidance of double taxation agreement was signed in December 2003 (see below).

## Taxes on corporate income

Complementary income (corporate) tax is imposed on the total income earned by individual or corporations irrespective of where their residence or headquarters are situated, excluding rental income from buildings located in Macau, which is taxed separately under property tax.

Complementary tax rates range from 2% to 15% if income is below MOP300,000. If income exceeds MOP300,000, the tax is 15%. (Tax rates from 2% to 15% are applied with complicated adjustments.)

A surcharge (stamp duty) of 5% on the complementary tax payable is also levied.

## Corporate residence

Corporate residence is determined on the basis of the place of incorporation.

## Branch income

Branch income is subject to tax at the same rate as that for corporations.
The taxable income is ascertained based on branch accounts.

## Other taxes

*Property tax*/Property tax is imposed on the owner of buildings situated in Macau. This is first payable four or six year after acquiring the property, depending on the location of the property. Additional exemption periods may apply in special cases. Rental income is the actual rental or the official ratable value established by the appointed committee of the Macau Tax Bureau. Rental income is not aggregated with earnings arising from other activities for other tax purposes. Rental income derived from real estate is not subject to complementary tax, and therefore related expenses are not deductible.

The tax is charged at 16% on the actual rental income or 10% on the official ratable value if not rented.

A deduction of up to 10% of the rental income shall be allowed upon request made to the Macau Tax Bureau to cover the cost of repairs and maintenance incurred by the taxpayer.

*Annual business tax*/All commercial or industrial operations carried out in Macau are subject to business tax at the beginning of each year. The amount taxed depends on the nature of the business. For example, the tax amounts applicable to various operations are shown below.

| | |
|---|---:|
| Offshore bank units | MOP 180,000 |
| Commercial banks | 80,000 |
| Construction companies | 500 |
| Hotels | 500 |
| Insurance companies | 500 |
| Textile companies | 300 |

*Consumer tax (excise duty)*/For Macau taxation purposes, excise duty is imposed only on goods entering into Macau. Excise duty is only imposed on certain items, as follows.

1. Tobacco
2. Spirits
3. Petrol/flammable oil
4. Lubricants and related chemical oil
5. Motor vehicles

There are two methods in determining the amount of excise duty payable, by quantity or value. The former basis calculates excise tax according to the weight of volume of goods and the latter is calculated based on the price of the goods imported into Macau. The rate of excise duty imposed on each item mentioned varies depending on the category within each item.

*Stamp duty*/Stamp duty is payable on certain types of documents and transactions at a small fixed amount, or at rates ranging from 0.1% to 10% on the value represented by the documents and transactions. The charge to stamp duty has been extended to property transfers and irrevocable transfer of certain assets. A 3% stamp duty is payable for property transfers, and 5% for irrevocable transfer of certain assets.

## Income determination

*Inventory valuation*/Inventory should be stated at actual cost, and conformity between book and tax reporting is required. Market selling price or replacement cost are allowed only in special circumstances. The write-down of inventory values is not permitted. Inventory valuation methods other than actual cost require the prior approval of the Director of the Macau Tax Bureau.

*Capital gains*/Gains or losses from the realization of capital assets of corporation are treated as current revenue or expense items for complementary tax purposes.

*Intercompany dividends*/Dividends from all sources are subject to complementary tax in the hands of a recipient incorporated in Macau. No deduction is allowed for dividends paid to overseas shareholders. However, where dividend to shareholders is paid out from taxed profit, no complementary tax is charged to the shareholders.

*Foreign income*/Companies incorporated in Macau are subject to complementary tax on all income, wherever received or credited. Currently, double taxation relief is available between Macau and Portugal, and most recently, Macau and the People's Republic of China (further explanation is provided below).

*Stock dividends*/Macau corporate laws do not recognize stock dividends.

## Deductions

*Depreciation and depletion*/An Initial allowance of 20% are granted on buildings.

The rates of tax depreciation are detailed in Decree-Law No.4/90/M, dated March 5, 1990. The Decree-Law prescribes the maximum annual tax depreciation rates (straight-line method) and maximum number of years (as a result of adopting one-half of the maximum rates) for different asset classes. For illustration, the maximum rates and maximum periods currently applicable to the general types of assets are set out below.

| | Maximum annual percentage rate | Maximum number of years |
|---|---|---|
| Tangible assets | | |
| Industrial buildings | 4 | 50 |
| Office and residential buildings | 2 | 100 |
| Machinery and installations, air conditioning, elevators, equipment | 10-20 | 20-10 |
| Tools | 20-33.3 | 10-6 |
| Laboratory, telex and interior telephone equipment, furniture, filing systems, typewriters and accounting machines | 16.66-25 | 12-8 |
| Computer hardware | 25 | 8 |
| Office installations | 14.29 | 14 |
| Trucks | 14.29 | 14 |
| Automobiles | 20 | 10 |
| Intangible assets preoperating expenses incurred prior to commencement of business | 33.33 | 6 |
| Deferred expenses arising in connection with increases in share capital; changes in form of business enterprises; issuance of debentures; marketing and other studies; financial expenses incurred for the acquisition or own production of fixed assets prior for completion | 33.33 | 6 |
| Patents | 10 | 20 |

# Macau

| | Maximum annual percentage rate | Maximum number of years |
|---|---|---|
| Manufacturing licenses, concessionary Agreements, and similar rights ................... | * | * |
| Trademark or premium on taking over leases of real estate ................................ | * | * |

*At the discretion of the authorities.

In the case of commercial and industrial buildings, the value attributable to the cost of the freehold land is not subject to depreciation. Where the value of the freehold land cannot be determined from the total cost of land and buildings, a portion equal to 20% is deemed to be attributable to the land value for the purpose of determining the value of buildings to be depreciated.

Depreciation rates charged in the accounts that exceed the prescribed tax depreciation rates can be claimed within three years, provided adequate adjustments in the underlying books and records have been made. Depreciation can be claimed on a monthly basis at the prescribed annual rates for assets not acquired at the beginning of the financial year.

The cost of repairs and maintenance exceeding 10% of the acquisition cost of the asset in a given year is deemed to be expenses of a capital nature, and should be capitalized and depreciated over the remaining life of the asset.

**Net operating losses**/Agreed tax losses can be carried forward for three years.

**Payments to foreign affiliates/foreign firms**/The regulations make no specific mention of royalties, interest and service fees paid to foreign affiliates. The Macau Tax Bureau is particularly sensitive to such payments, and their deductibility is closely monitored in each case. Payment for consulting services to foreign consultants may cause deductibility problem if such consulting contracts are not properly registered in Macau.

**Other significant items**/Other significant items are as follows.

1. The amount provided against doubtful trade receivables is an allowable tax deduction, but the provision cannot exceed 2% of the total receivables except in the case of banks, where the minimum provisions required under the local banking regulations are fully tax allowable.
2. Debts considered uncollectable may be written off only when adequate proof can be shown, usually by way of court proceedings of bankruptcy.
3. An amount provided against stock obsolescence of up to 3% of the total stock value at year-end is allowed as a tax deduction.
4. A deduction of up to 0.2% of the company's turnover is allowable for donations to charities recognized by the tax authorities.
5. Staff social welfare expenses paid for the benefit of employees and their families, for example, nurseries, kindergartens, canteens, libraries, and schools, are fully tax allowable.
6. The employer's contribution to the staff provident fund legally registered in Macau is fully tax deductible up to 15% of the employees' basic salary.
7. Tax fines are not deductible.
8. Losses arising from insurable risks are not allowable as a tax deduction.

In addition to the above, the assessor is empowered to disallow any business expenses, for example, entertainment, traveling, advertising, and commissions, where the amount incurred is considered to be excessive.

## Group taxation

There are no provisions for group taxation in Macau.

## Tax incentives

*Capital investment*/A 50% reduction on complementary tax, real estate tax and stamp duty, as well as exemptions from property tax and annual business tax, are allowable for investments aimed at contributing to the increase in exports of nonquota-restricted goods and installing high technology and new industries, and for investments that set up operations in areas that are traditionally nonindustrial, thereby contributing to the development of these areas.

Where profits are retained in reserves and reinvested in the same company on new installations of equipment within the following three financial years, if the investment is considered to be beneficial for the economic development of Macau, such profits can be deducted from taxable profits in the following three financial years, provided that they are earned from normal business operations.

*Offshore services business*/Profits derived by approved offshore institutions from prescribed offshore activities are exempt from all forms of taxes, such as corporate tax, annual business tax, real estate tax, and stamp duties.

## Withholding taxes

There are no provisions in the tax regulations to withhold taxes for any payments made by domestic corporations to overseas companies.

## Tax treaties

Arrangements have been entered into between Portugal and Macau, and the People's Republic of China and Macau for the avoidance of double taxation.

A comprehensive avoidance of double taxation agreement (DTA) was entered into between the Macau Special Administrative Region (SAR) and the PRC government on December 27, 2003. The following are some of the features of the DTA.

- Withholding tax rate on dividends, interest and royalties is 10%. There is also a reduced withholding tax rate of 7% on interest to banks and financial institutions.
- Gains arising from the alienation of shares representing a participation of not more than 25% of the shares in a nonreal property company which is a resident of one contracting side will only be taxable in the side in which the alienator is a resident. In other words, there is an exemption in the investee country for gains arising from the sale of portfolio investments situated in that country.
- There is no "limitation of benefits" article in the DTA.
- The DTA also covers business profits, income from dependent and independent personal services, income of artists or athletes, teachers, researchers, students, and apprentices, as well as income for government services.

The Macau SAR has also entered into a Closer Economic Partnership Arrangement (CEPA) with the PRC government on October 17, 2003, which came into effect on January 1, 2004. The content of the Macau SAR/PRC CEPA

# Macau

is similar to the CEPA between the Hong Kong SAR and the PRC government, except that certain zero-tariff items under Macau CEPA are not covered under Hong Kong CEPA. A list of 273 items of products that meet the Macau country of origin qualification enjoy zero tariffs on importation into the PRC.

## Tax administration

*Returns*/Assessments are made by the Macau Tax Bureau upon review of the tax returns, which must be lodged before June 30 of each year. The Macau tax year is on a calendar-year basis.

*Payment of tax*/Payment of tax is made in two equal installments in September and November. However, if the amount is not greater than MOP3,000, payment should be made in one lump sum in September.

### CORPORATION TAX CALCULATION

Year ended December 31, 2003 (calendar-year basis)

| | | |
|---|---:|---:|
| Net income before taxes | | MOP 1,000,000 |
| Add: | | |
| Donations to non-approved charities | 6,000 | |
| Social welfare expenses | 4,000 | |
| Tax fines | 1,000 | |
| Stock, cash or fixed asset losses resulting from fire (portion not covered by insurance) | 12,000 | |
| Provisions for doubtful trade receivables in excess of allowable limit | 20,000 | |
| Depreciation of fixed assets in excess of prescribed rates | 6,000 | 49,000 |
| | | 1,049,000 |
| Deduct—Rental income from properties net of related expenses | | 40,000 |
| Taxable income | | MOP 1,009,000 |
| Tax thereon: | | |
| Complementary tax at 15% | | MOP 151,350 |
| Surcharge (stamp duty) at 5%, payable on 151,350 | 7,568 | |
| | | MOP 158,918 |

Note:

Exchange rate of the Macau patacas at January 1, 2004: US$1= MOP8.2156.

## PwC contacts

For additional information on taxation in Malaysia, contact:

Chuan Keat Khoo
Peter K. S. Chow
PricewaterhouseCoopers
Wisma Sime Darby, 11th Floor
Jalan Raja Laut
50350 Kuala Lumpur, Malaysia
Telephone: (60) (3) 2693 1077
Fax: (60) (3) 2693 0997
e-mail: chuan.keat.khoo@my.pwc.com
        peter.chow@my.pwc.com

## Significant developments

Small- and medium-scale companies with paid-up capital of RM2.5 million or less are subject to corporate tax of 20% on chargeable income of up to RM100,000. With effect from tax year 2004, the threshold of chargeable income has been increased to RM500,000. The remaining chargeable income is taxed at 28%.

## Taxes on corporate income

*Income tax*/Income tax for resident and nonresident companies is imposed on income accruing in or derived from Malaysia at the flat rate of 28%. However, for resident companies with paid-up capital from ordinary shares of RM2.5 million or less, the rate of tax is 20% on the first RM500,000 of chargeable income, and 28% on any income in excess of RM500,000. A company is taxed on income from all sources (whether business or nonbusiness) arising in its financial year ending in the calendar year which coincides with that particular year of assessment. For example, a company that closes its accounts on June 30, 2004 is taxed on income earned during the financial year ending on June 30, 2004 for the year of assessment (YA) 2004.

Self-assessment for companies was implemented from the year 2001. Under the self-assessment system, companies are required to submit a return of income within seven months from the date of closing of accounts. Particulars required to be specified in the return include the amount of chargeable income and tax payable by the company. An assessment is deemed to have been made on the company on submission of the return. The return is deemed to be a notice of assessment that is deemed to be served on the company on the date the return is submitted.

*Petroleum income tax*/Petroleum income tax is imposed at the rate of 38% on profits from petroleum operations in Malaysia. No other taxes are imposed on income from petroleum operations.

## Corporate residence

A company is tax resident in Malaysia in a basis year if at any time during the basis year, the management and control of its affairs are exercised in Malaysia. Generally, management and control of a business is exercised at the place where the company's board meetings are held. Therefore, a single board meeting held in Malaysia at which significant decisions are made is sufficient cause for a company to be regarded as tax resident in Malaysia.

## Other taxes

*Real property gains tax*/Real property gains tax (RPGT) is imposed at scale rates from 5% to 30% on gains arising from the disposal of real property (which includes the disposal of shares in a real property company) situated in Malaysia (see "Capital gains").

*Sales tax*/A single-stage ad valorem tax at rates ranging from 5% to 25% is imposed on all goods imported into or manufactured in Malaysia, unless specifically exempted.

*Service tax*/Service tax is imposed at the rate of 5% on the value of taxable services sold or provided by taxable persons. A list of "taxable persons" and "taxable goods" is found in the Service Tax Regulations, 1975.

*Windfall profit levy*/A levy is imposed on crude palm oil and crude palm kernel oil at a maximum of RM50 per ton where the price exceeds RM2,000 per ton.

*Contract levy*/A levy of 0.25% on contract works having a contract sum above RM500,000 is imposed on every registered contractor by the Construction Industry Development Board (CIDB).

## Branch income

Tax rates on branch profits are the same as those on corporate profits. No tax is withheld on transfer of profits to a foreign head office.

## Income determination

*Inventory valuation*/Inventories are generally stated at the lower of cost or net realizable value. Cost for this purpose may be determined by using one of several possible bases, such as unit cost, average cost or FIFO, as long as the basis used is consistent from one year to another. LIFO may be used for accounting purposes but not for tax reporting.

*Capital gains*/Generally, gains on capital assets are not subject to tax. However, capital gains on the disposal of real property (which includes shares in a real property company (RPC)) situated in Malaysia are subject to real property gains tax. The tax is levied at rates ranging from a maximum rate of 30% (for assets held for less than two years) to a minimum of 5% (for assets held for five or more years). Capital losses on the sale of real property (other than losses on the disposal of RPC shares) are available for computation of relief, which is allowed as a deduction against total tax assessed on taxable gains arising on the sale of real property in the same year. A real property company is a controlled company that owns real property or RPC shares with a defined value of not less than 75% of its total tangible assets. Gains from the disposal of properties which are disposed of between June 1, 2003 and May 31, 2004, are exempted from RPGT. In addition, with effect from September 13, 2003, disposals to real estate investment trusts (REIT) and property trust funds (PTF) are exempted from real property gain tax.

*Intercompany dividends*/Dividends received from Malaysian companies are taxable on the recipient corporation, but the income tax deducted or deemed deducted from the dividends is available as a credit against the corporate income tax paid by that corporation. If a dividend is paid by a company which was subjected to tax at the rate of 20% (see "Taxes on corporate income"), tax deducted or deemed to be deducted from the dividend is deemed to be at the rate of 28%.

*Foreign income*/A Malaysian tax-resident corporation and a unit trust are not taxed on their foreign-source income, regardless of whether such income is received in Malaysia. However, income from the businesses of banking, insurance and air or sea transport is assessable on a global basis. Relief from double taxation is available by means of a bilateral credit if there is a tax treaty, or unilateral relief where there is no tax treaty. The relief is restricted to the lower of Malaysian tax payable or foreign tax paid if there is a treaty, or to one-half of the foreign tax paid if there is no treaty.

Undistributed income of foreign subsidiaries is not taxable.

*Stock dividends*/A Malaysian corporation may distribute bonus shares tax free to shareholders.

## Deductions

*Depreciation and depletion*/Tax depreciation on machinery, equipment, and industrial buildings is available at specific rates for all types of businesses. Locally acquired machinery and equipment qualify for an initial allowance of 20%, while imported heavy machinery (used in building and construction, mines, plantation and timber industries) qualifies for 10% when the expenditure is incurred and the asset is in use. An annual allowance ranging from 10% to 20% is calculated on cost for every year during which the asset is in use for the purposes of the business. An accelerated depreciation allowance is available for computers, information technology equipment, environmental protection equipment and waste recycling equipment.

Depreciation recapture on the sale of plant is taxable as ordinary income. Tax depreciation is not required to conform to book depreciation.

A depletion allowance is available on natural resource properties.

*Net operating losses*/The carryforward of business losses and tax depreciation is unlimited in time. Current-year business losses may be utilized against all sources of income. Any unutilized business losses are available for carryforward, but setoff is restricted to income from business sources only. Utilization of tax depreciation is also restricted to income from the same underlying business source. There is no provision for loss or tax depreciation carryback to previous tax years.

*Payments to foreign affiliates*/A Malaysian corporation can claim a deduction for royalties, management service fees and interest charges paid to affiliates, provided that these are made at arm's length (i.e , the amounts it would pay to an unrelated entity).

*Taxes*/Taxes on income are generally not deductible, whereas indirect taxes, such as sales tax and service tax, are deductible.

## Group taxation

Generally, there is no group taxation in Malaysia, except that a holding company that has invested in a 100%-owned subsidiary producing approved food products or engaged in deep sea fishing can opt for group relief for losses incurred by the subsidiary during the period before the subsidiary makes any profit. Application for approval should be made before December 31, 2005. A proposal was made in the "Economic Stimulus Package" announced in 2003, that group relief be extended under a prepackaged scheme to forest plantation and selected products in the manufacturing sector.

## Tax incentives

*Inward investment*/Incentives for inward investment are as follows.

1. **Pioneer status (PS):** Corporations in the manufacturing, agricultural, hotel, and tourist sectors or any other industrial or commercial sector that partici-pate in a promoted activity or produce a promoted product may be eligible for pioneer status. This incentive is given by way of an abatement of 70% of the annual profits for five years. The remaining 30% of the profits is taxed at the prevailing corporate income tax rate. The profits abated are exempt from tax and will be available for distribution as tax-free dividends.

   In the following cases the general rule of tax abatement and period of incentive is varied.

   a. Corporations undertaking a project of national and strategic importance involving heavy capital investment and high technology will be granted full exemption on its profits. The tax-relief period may be extended for a further five years. Projects recognized as of national and strategic importance include forest plantation activities, projects with Multimedia Super Corridor status and production of electronic wafers.

   b. High-technology companies engaging in a promoted activity or in the production of a promoted product in areas of new and emerging technologies, as well as companies participating in an industrial linkage program, may be granted pioneer status, which entitles them to full exemption on profits for a period of five years.

   c. Corporations with projects eligible for pioneer status that are located in the eastern corridor states of Peninsular Malaysia, Sabah, and Sarawak will be granted an abatement of 85% of their profits for five years. However, for applications made on or after September 13, 2003, the incentive is enhanced to an abatement of 100% for a period of five years. An existing pioneer or ex-pioneer corporation that undertakes an expansion program through a subsidiary or controlled company in the eastern corridor states of Peninular Malaysia, Sabah, or Sarawak that involves the same promoted activities or promoted products is eligible for a second round of pioneer status or investment tax allowances if certain conditions are satisfied. The eastern corridor states include Kelantan, Trengganu, and certain designated areas in the states of Pahang and Johor.

   d. Companies granted "strategic knowledge-based company" status are eligible for full exemption on their profits under the pioneer status or investment tax allowance (see section "Capital investment") incentive for a period of five years.

   e. Under various proposals made in 2003, the following enhanced relief is available.

      • Existing locally owned companies reinvesting in production of heavy machinery, machinery and equipment to be granted abatement of 70% on the increased statutory income arising from reinvestment for five years.

- New and existing companies utilizing oil palm biomass and reinvesting to produce value added products to be entitled to full exemption on profits for a period of ten years.
- Small companies that meet with specified conditions to be entitled to full exemption on profits for a period of five years.
- Second round of pioneer status is available for hotel and tourism companies which invest in expansion, modernizing and renovation, as well as for companies providing cold chain facilities and services for perishable agricultural produce.

A company granted PS which intends to reinvest before the expiry of its PS is eligible for reinvestment allowance provided that it surrenders its pioneer status (see item 3 under "Capital investment").

2. **Deduction for export expenses:** Resident corporations in the manufacturing, hotel, tourism, and service sectors are entitled to double deduction for expenditure incurred on the promotion of exports, such as overseas advertising, free samples, export market research, participation in trade exhibitions, preparation of tenders, travel, participation in virtual trade show, participation in trade portals for promotion of local products, maintenance of overseas sales offices and warehouses. For promotion of export of services, expenses such as feasibility studies for overseas tender projects, participation in a trade or industrial exhibition in Malaysia or overseas, airfares, and sustenance are entitled to double deduction. Expenses incurred by pioneer companies are aggregated and set off against post-pioneer (taxable) profits.

*Capital investment*/Incentives for capital investment are as follows.

1. **Investment tax allowance:** A corporation may be granted an investment tax allowance (ITA) of 60% of capital expenditure incurred on a factory or plant and machinery used for the purposes of an approved manufacturing, agricultural, hotel, tourist, knowledge intensive or other industrial or commercial activity (other than one granted pioneer status). ITA is granted on capital expenditure incurred for a period of five years. For an integrated agricultural activity, ITA may be granted to both the agricultural and the processing activities for five years each.

   The amount of investment tax allowance to be utilized for each year of assessment will be restricted to a maximum of 70% of the profits, while the balance of 30% of the profits will be taxed at the prevailing corporate income tax rate. Unutilized allowances may be carried forward indefinitely for setoff against future profits of the business. Dividends paid out of exempt profits are not liable to tax in the hands of shareholders.

   The ITA incentive is enhanced for the following types of projects.

   a. A corporation undertaking a project of national and strategic importance may be granted ITA at a rate of 100% and would be able to utilize the amount of ITA granted for setoff against the whole of its profits each year without restriction.

   b. A high-technology company or a company participating in a promoted activity or producing a promoted product in an industrial linkage program may be granted ITA at the rate of 60%, and the amount of ITA would be available for setoff against its profits without restriction. This incentive is an alternative to pioneer status. (See 1(b) under "Inward investment.").

   c. A company granted ITA in respect of a project located in the eastern corridor states of Peninsular Malaysia, Sabah, or Sarawak would be granted ITA at a rate of 80%, and the amount of ITA that could be utilized for each year would be restricted to a maximum of 85% of the profits. However, for applications made on or after September 13, 2003, the incentive is enhance to a rate of 100%, and the amount of allowance can be setoff against 100% of its profits for each year. An existing ITA or ex-ITA company that undertakes an expansion program through a subsidiary or controlled company in the eastern corridor states of Peninsular Malaysia, Sabah, or Sarawak involving the same promoted activities or promoted products is eligible for a second round of ITA or pioneer status if certain conditions are satisfied.

   d. A company that provides technical and vocational training in Malaysia may be granted ITA of 100% of qualifying capital expenditure incurred within a period of ten years, and the maximum amount of ITA that could be utilized each year would be restricted to 70% of profits.

   e. The following enhancement of the ITA incentive was proposed in 2004 Budget.

      • Existing locally owned companies reinvesting in production of heavy machinery, machinery and equipment to be granted ITA at the rate of 60% on additional qualifying expenditure incurred for a period of five years.

      • New and existing companies utilizing oil palm biomass to produce value added products that reinvest will be granted ITA at a rate of 100% and would be able to utilize the amount of ITA granted for setoff against whole of its profits each year without restriction.

      • A second round of ITA is available for hostel and tourism companies which invest in expansion, modernizing and renovation, as well as companies providing cold chain facilities and services for perishable agricultural produce.

2. **Industrial adjustment allowance:** A manufacturing corporation that undertakes an approved industrial adjustment program may be granted an industrial adjustment allowance (IAA) of up to 100% of capital expenditure on factory, plant and machinery incurred within a period of five years.

Industrial adjustment means any activity undertaken to restructure by reorganization, reconstruction or amalgamation with a view to strengthening industrial self-sufficiency, improving industrial technology, increasing productivity, and enhancing the efficient use of natural resources and the efficient management of manpower.

Corporations in operation before December 31, 1990 and engaged in certain subsectors of the wood-based, textile, or machinery and engineering industries are currently eligible for IAA. The IAA rates vary from 60% to 100%, depending on the activity and type of industry undertaken by such corporations.

The amount of profits equal to the IAA is exempt from tax and may be distributed to shareholders as tax-exempt dividends.

3. **Reinvestment allowance:** A corporation that embarks on a program to expand, modernize, automate, or diversify its existing manufacturing or processing business is entitled to a reinvestment allowance. The amount

of reinvestment allowance is 60% of qualifying capital expenditure incurred within a period of 15 years on a factory or plant and used for the expansion, modernization, automation, or diversification activity. The reinvestment allowance will be withdrawn if the asset for which the reinvestment allowance is granted is disposed of within two years. The amount of reinvestment allowance that can be utilized each year is limited to 70% of profits after deduction of tax depreciation allowances. The remaining 30% are taxed at the normal corporate income tax rate. Unutilized reinvestment allowances may be carried forward indefinitely for setoff against future profits of the business. The 70% restriction will not apply to projects that achieved the level of productivity as prescribed by the Minister of Finance and projects located in the eastern corridor states of Peninsular Malaysia, Sabah, and Sarawak. A reinvestment allowance is also extended to the following.

a. A tax-resident company undertaking an approved agricultural project that incurs qualifying capital expenditure for the purposes of expanding, modernizing or diversifying its cultivation and farm businesses.

b. Rearers of chickens and ducks, who reinvest for the purpose of modernizing their rearing system

Dividends paid out of exempt profits are not taxable in the hands of shareholders.

4. **Venture capital company:** A company investing in approved venture companies in the form of start-up or seed capital is given a deduction equivalent to the value of the investment. To qualify for the deduction the investment must not be in a company that is listed on a stock exchange, and it should not be in a company related to the investing company at the point of first investment. Alternatively tax exemption for ten years is available if at least 70% of its funds are invested in venture companies.

*Other incentives*/There are a number of other incentives, summarized as follows.

1. **Operational headquarters company:** An operational headquarters (OHQ) company that provides qualifying services to its offices and related companies may be granted approved OHQ status.

   The income (business income, interest and royalties) derived by an approved OHQ from the provision of qualifying services is exempt from income tax for a period of ten years. This includes income from services provided to related companies in Malaysia, provided such income does not exceed 20% of the OHQ income. Dividends distributed from exempt income are exempt in the hands of shareholders. Expatriates working in an OHQ are only taxed on the portion of chargeable income attributable to the number of days they are in Malaysia. An OHQ is also granted special facilities including the following.

   a. Approvals for expatriate posts are based on the requirements of the OHQ.

   b. Credit facilities in foreign currency can be obtained form licensed commercial banks in Malaysia without approval of the Central Bank of Malaysia.

   c. No restriction on investments in foreign securities and lending to related companies outside Malaysia.

   d. Allowed to open a single or foreign currency account with licensed commercial banks in Malaysia or offshore banks in Labuan.

2. **International procurement centers:** An international procurement center (IPC) is a company incorporated in Malaysia, whether local or foreign-owned, that carries on a business in Malaysia of procurement and sale of raw materials, components and finished products to its group companies in Malaysia or abroad.

Tax incentives include the following.

a. Full exemption for ten years, on profits after deduction of tax depreciation allowance for ten years.

b. Dividends paid from the exempt income are exempt from tax in the hands of shareholders.

c. Exemption from customs duties on goods brought into free zones, bonded warehouses, or licensed manufacturing warehouses for repackaging or cargo consolidation and integration before distribution to final consumers.

To qualify, an IPC must serve as a collection and consolidation center for finished goods, components and spare parts from overseas or within the country to be distributed to the dealer, importer or its subsidiary or associated company within or outside the country.

In addition, other available nontax incentives include the following.

a. Approval for expatriate posts based on the requirements of the IPC.

b. Ability to maintain more than one foreign currency account for the retention of export proceeds with any licensed commercial bank and without any limit on the balance in the accounts.

c. Permission to enter into foreign exchange forward contracts with a licensed commercial bank to sell forward export proceeds based on projected sales.

d. Exemption from foreign equity ownership restrictions.

3. **International trading companies:** Companies that obtained approval as "international trading companies" are exempt for five years on income equivalent to 20% of increased export value up to a maximum of 70% of statutory income. To qualify for the incentive the following conditions have to be met.

a. The company must be incorporated in Malaysia, with 60% Malaysian ownership.

b. Achieve minimum annual sales of RM10 million and not more than 20% of the company's annual sales may be derived from the trading of commodities.

c. Use local services (banking, finance and insurance) and infrastructure (local ports and airports) in its operations.

4. **Regional distribution center:** A regional distribution center (RDC) is a collection and consolidation center for finished goods, components and spare parts from overseas or within the country to be distributed to the dealer, importer or its subsidiary or associated company within or outside the country. Among the activities involved are bulk breaking, repackaging and labeling. Incentives accorded to an RDC include the following.

a. Full exemption on profits after deduction of tax depreciation allowance for ten years.

b. Dividends paid from the exempt income is exempt from tax in the hands of shareholders.

c. Import duty and sales tax exemption on goods for distribution.

Other nontax incentives include the following.

a. 100% equity holding by the promoter is allowed.

b. Approval for expatriate posts based on requirement of the RDC.

c. Eligibility to open one or more foreign currency accounts with any licensed commercial bank to retain their export proceeds, without any limit imposed.

d. Permission to enter into foreign exchange forward contracts with any licensed commercial bank to sell forward export proceeds, based on projected sales.

5. **Incentives for high-technology industries:** The government has embarked on the development of a Multimedia Super Corridor (MSC), which is designed to be the research and development (R&D) center of industries based on information technology (IT). The MSC spans a greenfield site 15 by 50 kilometers, extending from the Kuala Lumpur City Centre in the north to the Kuala Lumpur International Airport in Sepang to the south. Describing it as "an island with its own laws, policies and practices to ensure it has the best environment in Asia," the government has also pledged to provide the MSC with a world-class physical and information infrastructure. Eight special areas will be promoted, including telemedicine, smart schools, R&D clusters, multipurpose cards, and electronic government.

In order to ensure that MSC companies have the best environment in Asia for harnessing multimedia services, the Multimedia Development Corporation (MDC) was established to develop and manage the MSC. The MDC is a fully empowered "one-stop shop" that acts as approving authority for companies applying for MSC company status.

Companies, institutions of higher learning and faculties awarded MSC status are eligible for both financial and nonfinancial incentives in three categories, depending on location. They are designated cybercities, outside cybercities but within the MSC, and outside the MSC and designated cybercities. The designated cybercities are Cyberjaya, Technology Park, Kuala Lumpur City Centre, and Lembah Silikon (*Universiti Putra Malaysia*). All categories will qualify for the following fiscal and nonfiscal incentives.

a. Pioneer status for ten years or investment tax allowance for five years of 100% for five years for a new company or an existing company on its additional income.

b. Eligible for R&D grants (for majority Malaysian-own, MSC-status companies).

c. Exemption from indirect taxes on multimedia equipment.

d. Unrestricted employment of local and foreign knowledge workers.

e. Freedom to source funds globally for investments.

f. Protection of intellectual property and cyberlaws.

g. No censorship of the internet.

h. Services of MDC as "one-stop shop."

Those in the first and second categories will also enjoy a world-class physical and information infrastructure and global competitive telecommunication tariffs. In addition, the first category would be eligible to tender for key MSC infrastructure projects for companies willing to use the MSC as a regional hub.

6. **Unit trusts:** Gains from the realization of investments are not regarded as taxable income of a unit trust. Interest received by unit trusts from certain bonds and securities, as well as interest credited by banks and other financial institutions licensed under the Banking and Financial Institutions Act 1989 or the Islamic Banking Act 1983, are exempt from tax. Distributions from such gains are tax exempt to the unit holders.

   Capital allowance in respect of plant and machinery used for the purpose of the letting of properties is allowed at the rate of 10% per annum against the rental income of a property unit trust.

7. **Research and development:** Companies that provide R&D services to third parties are eligible for pioneer status with full exemption of their profits for a period of five years. A second round of pioneer status incentive for another five years is available. As an alternative, such companies may be granted ITA at the rate of 100% of qualifying capital expenditure incurred within a period of ten years and a further ten years for a second round of ITA. The ITA incentive may also be granted to companies undertaking R&D for their group companies.

   Companies undertaking in-house R&D projects are eligible for ITA at the rate of 50% of the qualifying capital expenditure incurred within a period of ten years.

   Double deduction is granted for expenses incurred on approved research and development projects, as well as for payments made to defined R&D companies. Local universities will be recognized as approved research institutes for the purposes of claims for the double-deduction incentive by companies making cash contributions or payments for the use of the services of such universities for R&D activities.

   Buildings used for approved R&D activities qualify for the industrial building allowance at the normal rate.

8. **Training:** There is a double deduction for approved training expenditure incurred in the training of employees under an approved training program. Manufacturing corporations with 50 or more Malaysian employees registered with the Human Resources Development Fund will not be eligible for this incentive. These corporations are, however, eligible to seek financial assistance from the Fund for the training of their employees.

   Preoperating training expenses are also available as a double deduction to small- and medium-scale manufacturing companies that are not registered with the Human Resources Development Fund. The normal deduction for preoperating training expenses may also be available to certain resident companies.

9. **Approved service projects:** A resident company undertaking a project in the service sector in relation to transport, communications, utilities, or other approved subsectors may elect to apply for either an investment allowance or income tax exemption for a period of five years. The mechanisms for tax exemption and investment allowance are similar to those for pioneer status and investment tax allowance respectively.

   For projects located in Sabah, Sarawak, and the eastern corridor states of Peninsular Malaysia the rate of tax exemption is increased to 85%, and the rate of investment allowance is increased to 80%. Service projects of national and strategic importance will qualify for tax exemption of 100% for a period of ten years or investment allowance of 100%.

As in the case of companies enjoying pioneer status and investment tax allowance, dividends paid out of exempt profits are exempt in the hands of shareholders.

Buildings used solely for the purposes of approved service projects qualify for an industrial building allowance.

10. **Foreign fund management company:** A foreign fund management company providing fund management services to foreign clients will be taxed at a concessionary rate of 10% in respect of its income derived from the management of foreign funds while income arising from services rendered to clients in Malaysia will be taxed at the prevailing corporate tax rate. Its income after deduction of tax at 10% may be distributed as tax-exempt dividends to its shareholders.

A foreign fund management company is a Malaysian incorporated company licensed under the Securities Industry Act 1983. Its activities are regulated by the Securities Commission.

11. **Shipping:** Tax-resident corporations and individuals carrying on shipping business are exempt from tax on income derived from the operation of Malaysian ships. Dividends distributed by a company qualifying for this incentive are exempt from tax in the hands of the shareholders.

12. **Export incentives:** Partial tax exemption is granted at various rates for export-oriented companies. Manufacturing companies are eligible for exemption on profits after deduction of tax depreciation allowances on 10% (or 15%) of the value of the increase in the company's exports, provided it attains at least 30% (or 50%) value added. Companies exporting fruits and cut flowers, or exporting selected services, also enjoy an exemption on profits, after deduction of tax depreciation allowances, equivalent to 10% of the value of the increase in exports. Companies engaged in export of selected services are eligible for exemption on profits on 50% of the value of increased exports.

The 2003 Budget contained a proposal for a Malaysian-owned manufacturing company to be granted exemption on profits after deduction of tax depreciation allowance of an amount equal to 30% of the value of increased export value, provided it achieves a significant increase in exports. The rate is increased to 50% of the value of increased export for a company that succeeds in penetrating new markets. Full exemption on increased export value is granted if the company achieves the highest increase in export.

13. **Resource-based industries:** Malaysian companies that are engaged in the manufacture of rubber, oil palm and wood based products that are of export potential may be granted the following tax incentives when they incur capital expenditure for the purpose of any expansion.

   a. Companies located outside promoted areas, either of the following.
   - Pioneer status for five years (exemption is restricted to 70% of statutory income).
   - Investment tax allowance (ITA) of 60% of qualifying capital expenditure incurred within five years (ITA is restricted to 70% of statutory income).

   b. Companies located within promoted areas, either of the following.

- Pioneer status for five years (exemption is restricted to 85% of statutory income).
- ITA for five years (ITA is restricted to 85% of statutory income).

14. **Manufacturing related services:** Companies providing integrated logistic, marketing support and utility services to be given the following incentives.

    a. Income tax exemption of 70% of statutory income for five years. The rate of exemption is enhanced to 85% of statutory income for projects located in areas designated as the "Eastern Corridor of Peninsula Malaysia, Sabah, and Sarawak."

    b. Exemption from import duty and sales tax on equipment in the related projects.

15. **Offshore trading through websites in Malaysia:** Income received by companies undertaking offshore trading (comprised of the buying and selling of foreign goods to nonresidents) via websites in Malaysia, is to be taxed at a reduced rate of 10% for a period of five years. The approval of the Minister of Finance must be obtained.

*Labuan—An international offshore financial center*/Labuan, which is a federal territory of Malaysia, was established in October 1990 as an international offshore financial center (IOFC) to provide for the development of offshore activities in the areas of offshore banking and insurance, trust and fund management, offshore investment holding and licensing companies, offshore limited partnerships, offshore leasing, offshore money brokering, and other offshore activities carried on by multinational companies. Certain types of shipping operations are not included in the list of promoted activities. These involve transportation of passengers or cargo by sea and the letting of ships on a voyage or time charter basis.

The following are highlights of what Labuan offers to encourage offshore activities.

1. Income from offshore trading activities is taxed at the rate of 3% of net profits, as reflected in the audited accounts, or, upon election, a fixed sum of RM20,000. A tax rebate on zakat (obligatory charity for Muslims) payments made is available, subject to a maximum of the amount of tax charged for that year. The scope of offshore activity has been extended to allow an offshore company with non-Malaysian shareholders to invest in Malaysian incorporated companies through portfolio and collective investment schemes.

2. Income from offshore nontrading activities is exempt from tax.

3. Offshore insurance business carried on through a branch of a Malaysia-incorporated insurance company and nonoffshore activities carried on by an offshore company are subject to normal Malaysian income tax and are not eligible for the tax concessions. However, income attributable to offshore banking activities carried on by a branch of a Malaysia-incorporated bank will be subject to tax at the preferential tax rates accorded to Labuan offshore companies (see item 1 above).

4. Tax exemption of 50% of the employment income derived by an expatriate from the exercise of an employment in Labuan in a managerial capacity with an offshore company is available. This incentive is due to expire in the tax year 2004. In addition, director's fees received by a director of a Labuan offshore company, who is a non-Malaysian citizen, is exempt for the years of assessment 2002 to 2006.

5. Offshore companies are not subject to stamp duty in respect of instruments negotiated in connection with their offshore business activities.

6. Trust companies providing legal, accounting, financial, or secretarial services are eligible for a 65% exemption of income. The incentive is due to expire in the tax year 2004.

## Withholding taxes

Corporations paying certain types of income are required to withhold tax as follows.

| Recipient | Dividends (1) | Interest (2) | Royalties and certain rentals (3, 4, 5) |
|---|---|---|---|
| | % | % | % |
| Resident corporations .................. | Nil | Nil | Nil |
| Resident individuals ...................... | Nil | Nil or 5 | Nil |
| Nonresident corporations and individuals: | | | |
| Nontreaty ..................................... | Nil | Nil or 15 | 10 |
| Treaty: | | | |
| Albania* ................................... | Nil | Nil or 10 | 10 |
| Australia.................................... | Nil | Nil or 15 | 10 |
| Austria...................................... | Nil | Nil or 15 | 10 |
| Bahrain .................................... | Nil | Nil or 5 | 8 |
| Bangladesh .............................. | Nil | Nil or 15 | Nil or 10 |
| Belgium..................................... | Nil | Nil or 10 | 10 |
| Canada ..................................... | Nil | Nil or 15 | Nil or 10 (6) |
| China, P.R. ............................... | Nil | Nil or 10 | 10 |
| Croatia*.................................... | Nil | Nil or 10 | 10 |
| Czech Republic ......................... | Nil | Nil or 12 | 10 |
| Denmark ................................... | Nil | Nil or 15 | Nil or 10 |
| Egypt* ...................................... | Nil | Nil or 15 | 10 |
| Fiji............................................ | Nil | Nil or 15 | 10 |
| Finland ..................................... | Nil | Nil or 15 | Nil or 10 |
| France....................................... | Nil | Nil or 15 | Nil or 10 |
| Germany ................................... | Nil | Nil or 15 | Nil or 10 |
| Hungary .................................... | Nil | Nil or 15 | 10 |
| India (old agreement) ............... | Nil | Nil or 15 | Nil or 10 |
| India (new agreement)* ............. | Nil | Nil or 10 (7) | 10 (7) |
| Indonesia .................................. | Nil | Nil or 15 | 10 |
| Iran*......................................... | Nil | Nil or 15 | 10 |
| Ireland, Rep. of......................... | Nil | Nil or 10 | 8 |
| Italy.......................................... | Nil | Nil or 15 | Nil or 10 (6) |
| Japan........................................ | Nil | Nil or 10 | 10 (6) |
| Jordan....................................... | Nil | Nil or 15 | 10 |
| Korea, Rep. of .......................... | Nil | Nil or 15 | Nil or 10 |
| Kyrgyzstan*............................... | Nil | Nil or 10 | 10 |
| Lebanon*................................... | Nil | Nil or 10 | 8 |
| Luxembourg*............................. | Nil | Nil or 10 | 8 |
| Malta......................................... | Nil | Nil or 15 | 10 |
| Mauritius .................................. | Nil | Nil or 15 | 10 |

# Malaysia

| Recipient | Dividends (1) | Interest (2) | Royalties and certain rentals (3, 4, 5) |
|---|---|---|---|
| | % | % | % |
| Mongolia | Nil | Nil or 10 | 10 |
| Morocco* | Nil | Nil or 10 | 10 |
| Myanmar* | Nil | Nil or 10 | 10 |
| Namibia* | Nil | Nil or 10 | 5 |
| Netherlands | Nil | Nil or 10 | Nil or 8 |
| New Zealand | Nil | Nil or 15 | Nil or 10 |
| Norway | Nil | Nil or 15 | Nil or 10 (6) |
| Pakistan | Nil | Nil or 15 | Nil or 10 |
| Papua New Guinea | Nil | Nil or 15 | 10 |
| Philippines | Nil | Nil or 15 | Nil or 10 |
| Poland | Nil | Nil or 15 | Nil or 10 |
| Romania | Nil | Nil or 15 | Nil or 10 |
| Russian Federation | Nil | Nil or 15 | 10 |
| Singapore | Nil | 15 | 10 (6) |
| Sri Lanka | Nil | Nil or 10 | 10 |
| Sudan* | Nil | Nil or 10 | 10 |
| Sweden (old agreement) | Nil | Nil or 15 | Nil or 10 (6) |
| Sweden (new agreement)* | Nil | Nil or 10 (7) | 8 (7) |
| Switzerland | Nil | Nil or 10 | Nil or 10 |
| Thailand | Nil | Nil or 15 | Nil or 10 (6) |
| Turkey | Nil | Nil or 15 | 10 |
| United Arab Emirates | Nil | Nil or 5 | 10 |
| United Kingdom | Nil | Nil or 10 | 8 |
| Uzbekistan | Nil | Nil or 10 | 10 |
| Vietnam | Nil | Nil or 10 | 10 |
| Zimbabwe* | Nil | Nil or 10 | 10 |

*Treaties pending ratification

The numbers in parentheses refer to the following numbered Notes.

Notes:

Restricted tax treaties dealing with taxation of specific transport operations in international traffic have also been signed with Argentina, Saudi Arabia, and the United States.

1. Dividends are franked with (deemed to be paid net of) the tax paid by corporations. If any dividend-paying corporation has not paid sufficient tax to cover the total tax deemed deducted from dividends, it must pay the balance of the tax to the tax authorities.

   Malaysia at present has no withholding tax on dividends in addition to tax on the profits out of which the dividends are declared. Some treaties provide for a maximum withholding tax on dividends should Malaysia impose such a withholding tax in the future.

   Because of its proximity, many Malaysian corporations also trade in Singapore and are taxed there. The double taxation agreement between the two countries has special provisions for the allocation and franking of dividends in such cases.

2. Interest on loans given to or guaranteed by the Malaysian government is exempt from tax. Interest paid to a nonresident by a commercial or merchant bank operating in Malaysia is also exempt from tax.

3. Approved royalty payments under certain treaty provisions are exempt from withholding tax.

4. Other income:

   a. With effect from September 21, 2002, contract payments made by a person (including a partnership) to nonresident contractors (including professionals) in respect of services under a contract project are subject to a 13% deduction of tax (10% on account of the contractors' tax liability and 3% on account of their employees' tax liability). This deduction of tax at source does not represent a final tax, which is determined upon the filing of the tax return.

   b. Payments made to nonresidents in respect of the provision of technical services performed in Malaysia and rental of movable properties are subject to a 10% withholding tax.

5. Royalty income received by nonresident franchisors under franchised education scheme programs approved by the Ministry of Education is exempted from tax.

6. Royalty income does not include artistic work and/or cinematographic films and tapes for television or broadcasting.

7. New agreements signed with India and Sweden are still pending ratification. Meanwhile the old rates still apply.

## Tax administration

***Returns***/Returns of income for the year 2004 will be issued to companies as follows.

| Accounting year-end in | Return form issued in |
| --- | --- |
| January, February, March 2004 | April 2004 |
| April, May, June 2004 | July 2004 |
| July, August, September 2004 | October 2004 |
| October, November, December 2004 | January 2005 |

Returns are to be submitted within seven months after the closing of accounts.

***Payment of tax***/Tax payable under an assessment upon submission of a return is due and payable by the "due date". The "due date" is defined as the last day on expiry of seven months from the date on which the accounts are closed.

Companies are required to furnish estimates of their tax payable for a year of assessment not later than 30 days before the beginning of the basis period A revised estimate can be submitted in the sixth and ninth months of the basis period for a year of assessment.

Companies are then required to pay tax by monthly installments (based on the estimates submitted) commencing from the second month of the company's basis period (financial year).

## *CORPORATION TAX CALCULATION*

Year of assessment (tax year) 2004

Public or private corporation resident in Malaysia

| | | |
|---|---:|---:|
| Net profit before taxes for year ended December 31, 2004 .................... | | RM 2,000,000 |
| Add: | | |
|     Depreciation charged in accounts ..................................... | 150,000 | |
|     Amounts transferred to provisions..................................... | 110,000 | |
|     Donations........................................................................ | 10,000 | |
|     Legal fees (capital nature)................................................ | 3,000 | |
|     Entertainment (not allowed as deduction) ........................ | 40,000 | 313,000 |
| | | 2,313,000 |
| Less: | | |
|     Interest income ............................................................... | 500,000 | |
|     Dividend income .............................................................. | 360,000 | |
|     Profit on sale of fixed assets ........................................... | 13,000 | |
|     Expenditure charged against provisions........................... | 380,000 | 1,253,000 |
| Adjusted income ................................................................... | | 1,060,000 |
| Add—Balancing charge on sale of fixed assets.................................... | | 12,000 |
| | | 1,072,000 |
| Less—Capital allowances ................................................................. | | 37,000 |
| Statutory income ........................................................................... | | 1,035,000 |
| Add: | | |
|     Interest income ............................................................... | 500,000 | |
|     Malaysian dividends (regrossed)...................................... | 500,000 | 1,000,000 |
| | | 2,035,000 |
| Less—Approved donations ................................................................. | | 6,000 |
| Chargeable income........................................................................... | | RM 2,029,000 |
| Tax thereon at 28%........................................................................... | | RM   568,120 |
| *Less*—Tax deducted at source on dividends | | |
|     (28% of 500,000) ............................................................. | | (140,000) |
| Tax payable ..................................................................................... | | RM   428,120 |

Note:

Exchange rate of the ringgit has been fixed at US$1 = RM3.80 since September 1, 1998.

## PwC contacts

For additional information on taxation in Malta, contact:

Dr. Antoine Fiott
Dr. Neville Gatt
PricewaterhouseCoopers
167 Merchants Street
Valletta VLT03, Malta
Telephone: (356) 21 247000
Fax: (356) 21 244768
e-mail: antoine.fiott@mt.pwc.com
        neville.gatt@mt.pwc.com

## Significant developments

1. The amendments to align Maltese VAT law with European Union VAT legislation have been published and will come into force on May 1, 2004. Furthermore the standard VAT rate was increased by 3% to 18% as from January 1, 2004.

2. Certain procedural amendments have been introduced for income tax purposes in respect of transfers of immovable property between companies within the same group (such transfers currently benefit from an income tax exemption), but the details of the new procedures are still to be prescribed.

3. The Minister of Finance has been empowered to issue rules in order to regulate the circumstances and the manner in which the current income tax exemption should apply on an exchange of shares on the restructuring of holdings upon mergers, demergers, divisions, amalgamations and reorganizations. In respect of stamp duty, certain restrictions have been introduced on the exemption which applied so far on divisions/mergers of companies. Also the manner of calculating the amount on which the stamp duty is payable on a transfer/exchange of shares in companies holding immovable property is now subject to certain conditions.

4. A new provision enables the Finance Minister to make rules for the implementation of any Directive of the European Union relating to any matter which affects the operation of the income tax acts.

5. The beneficial tax regime which applied for investment services companies/ insurance managers and their expatriate employees will no longer apply for companies obtaining their investment services license under the Investment Services Act after October 1, 2003. In respect of companies which held an investment services license before this date, the tax benefits would continue to apply (both in respect of the company and the expatriates) up to a date that has as yet to be determined.

6. Certain amendments on the taxation of collective investment schemes and distributions from such schemes have been introduced.

7. Protective levies mainly on agricultural and meat products still apply, but these should be fully phased out by May 1, 2004.

8. Consistent with previous years, a further liberalization of exchange controls has been effected.

# Malta

## Taxes on corporate income

*Income tax*/Companies are subject to tax at a flat rate of 35%. There is no corporation tax structure separate from income tax.

*Petroleum profits tax*/Petroleum profits tax is levied as income tax, but the taxable profits are computed in a special way, including a production-sharing basis. Profits in respect of production-sharing contracts signed after January 1, 1996 are taxed at 35%. Other petroleum profits are taxed at 50%.

*Insurance profits tax*/Insurance profits tax is levied as income tax, and imposed at the same rate as other corporate profits, but it is computed in a special way. In the case of nonresident companies the computation is applied with reference only to business carried on in or from Malta.

## Corporate residence

All companies incorporated in Malta are considered to be both domiciled and resident in Malta. Other bodies of persons (including companies incorporated overseas) are considered to be resident in Malta when the control and management of their business are exercised in the country.

## Other taxes

There are no other corporate taxes.

*Value-added tax*/Supplies of goods and services in Malta are subject to VAT at the standard rate of 18% (5% on hotel and holiday accommodation, alternative energy equipment, and supply of electricity). Exports, food, and certain other goods and services are exempt with credit.

*Customs and excise duties*/Goods imported from outside the European Union (EU) are subject to customs duties at a rate which in most cases is set at 8.1%. A customs code provides for customs procedures and concepts which are based on European Community requirements. Excise duties are chargeable on certain petroleum oils and gases, alcoholic drinks, and tobacco products. All of the protective levies have been phased out, except for levies mainly on agricultural and meat products, which are due to be removed by May 1, 2004.

*Employer's social security contributions*/Employers are obliged to pay social security contributions at the rate of 10% of the individual employee's salary, and at fixed rates of Lm12.98 per week for annual salaries exceeding Lm6,748.

*Stamp duty*/Stamp duty is charged on, *inter alia,* transfers of immovable property (5% for both residents and nonresidents) and marketable securities (2%, but 5% in the case of transfers of shares in property companies).

## Branch income

The tax rate on branch income is the same as that for resident companies. Other than the tax charged on a branch's income, no tax is withheld on transfers of profits to head office.

## Income determination

*Inventory valuation*/Stock valuations are generally made at the lower of cost or market value. LIFO is not accepted for taxation purposes. In general, the book and tax methods of inventory valuation will conform. Obsolescence is accepted where proved, but there are no provisions to take account of monetary inflation on the inventory valuation.

*Capital gains*/Tax is chargeable on capital gains realized on the transfer of immovable property (real estate), shares and other securities, business, goodwill, copyrights, patents, trade names, and trademarks. No tax is levied on investments that yield a fixed rate of return, and on shares in a company listed on a recognized stock exchange other than shares held in certain collective investment schemes. If the asset is transferred between group companies, no loss or gain is deemed to arise from the transfer (subject to certain new procedural amendments which still have to be defined). Gains realized from the transfer of other assets fall outside the scope of the tax. Gains arising outside Malta and derived by a company that is either not domiciled or not ordinarily resident in Malta are not subject to tax. There are also a number of exemptions provided in the law. Capital gains realized by nonresidents on disposals of units in collective investment schemes, similar investments relating to linked long-term insurance business and shares or securities in companies (except companies whose assets consist solely or mainly of Maltese immovable property) are exempt from tax.

*Rollover relief*/Group relief and reorganization relief are granted.

*Intercompany dividends*/Dividends received by one company from another, whether or not a subsidiary, are taxable on the gross amount in the recipient's hands. If the distributed profits have been taxed, no further tax should be chargeable to the recipient company. However, for resident shareholders, if the corporate rate of tax in the year in which the profits are earned is lower than that in the year in which they are distributed, an amount equivalent to the difference in rates (topping up) is payable. If the distribution is made from untaxed income, the dividend would be tax-free in the hands of the recipient company.

*Foreign income*/A company is taxable on its worldwide income when it is ordinarily resident and domiciled in Malta. A company that is either not ordinarily resident or not domiciled in Malta is taxable on its foreign income only insofar as such income is remitted to Malta. Foreign tax is relieved by way of tax credits. This may occur under the terms of a double taxation treaty. Where no treaty exists, the foreign tax can be relieved through a system of unilateral relief. Relief for underlying tax is also granted, either in terms of a double taxation treaty or as unilateral relief in the case of a Maltese company. Such reliefs may be available if, inter alia, evidence of tax paid abroad is produced.

Profits of Malta-resident companies are subdivided for tax purposes into three accounts, the Maltese Taxed Account, the Untaxed Account and the Foreign Income Account. The last of these includes, among other things, taxable profits of Maltese-resident companies resulting from foreign investments, profits of a foreign permanent establishment, and profits resulting from foreign investments, assets or liabilities of an onshore bank licensed in Malta. Income allocated to the Foreign Income Account for which no evidence of tax paid abroad is required can qualify for a flat-rate foreign tax credit of 25%. Depending on the nature of the income distributed by the company, nonresidents receiving distributions from the Foreign Income Account will be entitled to a two-thirds or full refund of tax paid on such profits by the distributing company.

*Stock dividends*/A Maltese company can distribute bonus shares from profits, whether of an income or of a capital nature, and from share premium and capital redemption reserves. When bonus shares represent a capitalization of profits, they are deemed to be dividends for tax purposes. Such bonus shares are subject to tax in the recipients' hands, gross of any tax paid at the corporate level on the relative profits, but tax credits equivalent to the grossing-up made are then available to stockholders.

## Deductions

*Income tax deductions*/The basic condition for deductibility of expenses is that deductions are only allowable with respect to expenditures wholly and exclusively incurred in the production of the income.

The Income Tax (Deductions) Rules, 2001 provide for specific conditions on deductions with respect to the use of cars and the payment of emoluments. The cost on which capital allowances on certain motor vehicles may be claimed is restricted to Lm3,000. Deductions for lease payments on cars are restricted in a manner that corresponds to the said restriction of Lm3,000 that applies to capital allowances on owned cars. In respect of payment of emoluments, the Deduction Rules require that in order for emoluments to be allowed for tax purposes in the hands of the employing company, they must have been duly accounted for, in particular, the emoluments must have been reported on the appropriate forms and within the statutory time limit to the Office of Inland Revenue. The rules also provide for restrictions on deductibility of emoluments in respect of the payment of certain fringe benefits to employees.

*Depreciation and depletion*/Tax depreciation is computed by the straight-line method. The rate of depreciation on plant and machinery varies according to the category of the plant and machinery in question. The wear and tear rate on industrial buildings and structures (including hotels) cannot exceed 2% per annum. New acquisitions of industrial buildings and structures are entitled to a concurrent extra 10% allowance in the year of acquisition. Tax depreciation is not required to conform to book depreciation.

The total allowances over the asset's useful life cannot exceed 100% of its cost. If on disposal of a tax-depreciated asset a surplus arises, it is either added to the year's income or utilized to reduce the cost of any replacement. If the asset has been underdepreciated, a balancing allowance is granted.

No deduction is available for the depletion of natural resources.

The rules on tax deductions for wear and tear of plant and machinery provide for certain specific treatment in particular situations including, *inter alia*, the following.

1. To establish the cost of an asset when it is transferred between related companies, one should take the lower of the actual cost of the asset or the tax written-down value adjusted by any balancing charge or allowance incurred by the transferring company.
2. Deductions for wear and tear are only allowed where proper records and documentation have been kept of the cost of the respective assets.
3. A proportional deduction is allowed where an asset is used partly in the production of income and partly for other purposes.

*Net operating losses*/Net operating losses can be carried forward indefinitely until absorbed. There is no carryback of losses, not even in terminal years. Unabsorbed capital allowances can be carried forward only against the same underlying source of income. Where the source ceases to exist, any remaining balance is lost.

*Payments to foreign affiliates*/There are no restrictions on the deductibility of royalties, interest, and service fees paid to foreign affiliates, provided the transactions are carried out at arm's length. Interest, discount, premium, or royalties derived by nonresidents are exempt from tax, subject to the applicable statutory requirements.

*Taxes*/Taxes of an income tax nature are not deductible (though a credit against the Maltese tax charge may be obtained, see "Income determination, Foreign income" above). Other taxes form part of expenses and are deductible in full.

*Other significant items*/Capital expenditure on scientific research, patents, and intellectual property rights is written off over a number of years. In the case of scientific research carried on in Malta as from January 1, 2003, a deduction is granted at 150% of the expenditure. Certain pretrading expenses are allowed as a deduction.

## Group taxation

Two companies that, for tax purposes, are resident exclusively in Malta, where one is a 51% subsidiary of the other, or both are 51% subsidiaries of a third Malta-resident company, qualify as members of a group of companies. Allowable losses may be surrendered by a company to another company within the group where both companies have concurrent accounting periods, and form part of such group throughout the entire basis year for which this relief is claimed. Each company makes a separate tax return, and no combined grouping or consolidated returns are possible.

## Tax incentives

*Inward investment*/Investments by foreigners may be readily repatriated together with profits.

The Business Promotion Act, and the regulations issued in terms of the Act, provide a comprehensive package of incentives. The most attractive incentives are reserved for enterprises carrying on activities in Malta which are included among the list of target activities. The accent is on high-value-added activities. Approval of a project's eligibility for benefits by the Malta enterprise is required. In general, eligibility does not depend on whether the company produces for the local or for export markets. The main tax incentives include the following.

1. New enterprises engaged in a trade consisting solely of target activities in Malta are entitled to reduced tax rates of 5% for the first seven years, 10% for the next six consecutive years, and 15% for the next consecutive five years. Qualifying companies registered in Malta before November 1, 2000 can only qualify for the tax rate of 10% for six years, and 15% for the following five years. The income qualifying for the reduced tax rates is subject to certain maximum amounts based on the number of employees of the company and the applicable reduced tax rate. This benefit will cease to apply after basis tax year 2008.

2. Enterprises qualifying for the reduced tax rates would also qualify for investment tax credits, whereby a percentage of up to 50% (65% in the case of small and medium-sized enterprises) of qualifying expenditure is set off against the tax charge (not against taxable income). Any unutilized credits are carried forward and added to the credits for subsequent years. The amount carried forward is increased by 7%.

3. Enterprises that do not carry on target activities, but carry on a trade consisting solely of manufacturing, assembly, processing and similar activities, or analogous services of an industrial nature, may qualify for the operation of the value-added incentive scheme which basically grants reduced rates on a part of the trading profits. The same rates applicable in Item 1 above apply, but the difference here is that the reduced rates only apply to a multiple/factor (based on increased value added) of the increased chargeable income. This benefit will cease to apply after basis tax year 2008.

4. New tax credits and special incentives may be availed of, subject to certain conditions, as from basis tax year 2003. These new tax credits are calculated on the basis of specific expenditure incurred by a company, while the special incentives afford, in certain instances, tax exemptions on all or part of the chargeable income.

5. Investment allowances are granted over and above tax depreciation in the year of acquisition of plant and machinery or industrial buildings/structures.

6. No further tax is charged on distributions out of profits that had been taxed at a reduced rate. This benefit is also extended to amounts that had not suffered any tax on account of the investment allowance, investment tax credits and the specific tax credits/special incentives provided by the Business Promotion Regulations.

7. The tax rate applicable to profits reinvested in the enterprise pursuant to a project approved by the Malta enterprise is set at 15.75%.

8. The combination of certain tax treaties and Maltese domestic law lowers the Maltese tax rate on certain companies receiving certain industrial assistance to 15%.

*Capital investment*/In the case of companies qualifying for benefits under the Business Promotion Act, an investment allowance of 50% on plant and machinery, and of 20% on industrial buildings and structures is available, bringing the total allowances granted during the lifetime of the assets up to 150% and 120%, respectively. Accelerated depreciation of 25% and of 4% per annum (calculated by the straight-line method) is granted on plant and machinery and on industrial buildings and structures respectively.

*Shipping profits*/Under the Merchant Shipping Act, ships can be registered with the Minister of Finance to obtain exemption for shipping profits. These profits can be distributed tax free. The related company shares are exempt from the provisions of the Duty on Documents and Transfers Act (stamp duties).

*International business profits*/Tax benefits are given to shareholders in onshore companies, as regards distributions by such companies of specified types of income. Some tax incentives are also granted as regards collective investment schemes.

Trusts registered with the Malta Financial Services Authority are taxed at a fixed annual rate of Lm200. Substantial changes to Maltese trust law are in the pipeline, and such changes are aimed, *inter alia,* at ensuring that trusts are as transparent as possible for local tax purposes, and that any income is taxed as if it were received by the beneficiaries.

## Withholding taxes

Domestic corporations paying certain types of income are required to deduct tax as follows.

| Recipient | Dividends (1) | Interest | Royalties |
|---|---|---|---|
| | % | % | % |
| Resident corporations | 35 | 35 (2) | Nil |
| Resident individuals | 35 | 25 (2) | Nil |
| Nonresident corporations: | | | |
| Nontreaty | 35 | Nil (3) | Nil (3) |
| Nonresident individuals: | | | |
| Nontreaty | 35 | Nil (3) | Nil (3) |
| Nonresident corporations and individuals: | | | |
| Treaty | (4) | Nil (3) | Nil (3) |
| Albania | 35 | | |
| Australia | 35 | | |
| Austria | 32.5 | | |
| Barbados | 35 | | |
| Belgium | 35 | | |
| Bulgaria | 30 | | |
| Canada | 35 | | |
| China, P.R. | 35 | | |
| Croatia | 35 | | |
| Cyprus | 35 | | |
| Czech Republic | 35 | | |
| Denmark | 35 | | |
| Egypt | 35 | | |
| Estonia | 35 | | |
| Finland | 35 | | |
| France | 35 | | |
| Germany | 35 | | |
| Hungary | 35 | | |
| India | 35 | | |
| Italy | 35 | | |
| Korea, Rep. of | 35 | | |
| Latvia | 35 | | |
| Lebanon | 35 | | |
| Libya | 15 | | |
| Luxembourg | 35 | | |
| Malaysia | 35 | | |
| Netherlands | 35 | | |
| Norway | 35 | | |
| Pakistan | 35 | | |
| Poland | 35 | | |
| Portugal | 35 | | |
| Romania | 30 | | |
| Slovakia | 35 | | |
| Slovenia | 35 | | |
| South Africa | 35 | | |
| Sweden | 35 | | |
| Syria | 35 | | |

# Malta

| Recipient | Dividends (1) | Interest | Royalties |
|---|---|---|---|
| | % | % | % |
| Tunisia ................................................................... | 35 | | |
| United Kingdom ................................................... | 35 | | |

Treaties relating to international air and shipping traffic are in force with Switzerland and the United States.

Notes:

The numbers in parentheses refer to the following numbered Notes.

1. Malta makes no distinction between portfolio and substantial holdings. The tax at source is not actually a withholding tax, because no additional tax is imposed on distributions other than the tax charged on the company in respect of distributed profits. Under Malta's full-imputation system of taxation of dividends, the corporate tax is assimilated with the personal income tax of the shareholder in respect of the dividend. In the shareholder's hands the dividend is charged to gross tax, and the relevant amount of corporate tax is set off against the shareholder's tax liability on income from all taxable sources. Special provisions exist for taxation of distributions from income that would not have suffered tax at corporate level.

2. Deduction is required only where the interest is debenture interest, or interest on any other loan advanced to a corporation for capital purposes. Tax deductions are in effect prepayments of the recipient's final liability, because a reassessment on income is made upon the submission of returns. Any resulting overpayment is refunded.

3. Interest and royalty income derived by nonresidents is exempt from tax in Malta, as long as certain conditions are complied with (e.g., they are not effectively connected to a permanent establishment of the recipient situated in Malta).

4. Under its treaties Malta retains the right to tax dividends at a rate not exceeding that paid by the company in question on the profits out of which the dividends are distributed. This rate is currently 35% (in the treaties with Austria, Bulgaria, Libya, and Romania, the tax rate is set at a lower rate). In a number of treaties the rate of deduction and of tax is reduced to 15% in the case of companies enjoying certain tax incentives. See also Note 1 with regard to Malta's full-imputation system of taxation of dividends.

## Tax administration

*Returns*/A return of the income earned during the previous year must be filed for every year of assessment. The year of assessment is a calendar year, but the accounts during the basis year may, with Inland Revenue permission, be made up to a day prior to December 31. Companies pay tax in the currency in which their share capital is denominated. The tax return for a company must be submitted at the later of nine months following the end of the financial year or on March 31 of the year of assessment. Penalties are incurred on late filing of returns. The tax return submitted by the company is a self-assessment, and the Commissioner of Inland Revenue will not raise an assessment unless the Commissioner does not agree with the self-assessment.

***Payment of tax***/During the basis tax year, a company is required to make provisional tax (PT) payments every four months. The PT payments are based on the last self-assessment filed by the company, and payments are divided into three installments of 20%, 30%, and 50%, respectively. Any tax liability that is still due at the tax return date after deducting all tax credits must be settled immediately with the submission of the return. Interest at 1% per month is charged on any unpaid tax.

Tax on profits allocated to the Foreign Income Account becomes payable at the earlier of the date of distribution of those profits, and eighteen months after the end of the relative accounting period.

The employer is required to deduct income tax and social security contributions from the employees' salaries, and pass on such tax/contributions to the Office of Inland Revenue. This system of withholding tax at source is referred to as the Final Settlement System (FSS), and the employer is legally required to operate this system. The salary from which the deduction is to be effected should also include the value of any taxable fringe benefits. There are three main categories of fringe benefits, and these are (1) use of motor vehicles, (2) use of other assets including accommodation, and (3) other benefits. The method of valuation in each case varies, and the employer is required to refer to the Fringe Benefits Regulations (and also to the fringe benefits guidelines) so as to calculate the correct value of any fringe benefits being provided to the employees, and to deduct the right amount of tax accordingly.

# Malta

## CORPORATION TAX CALCULATION

| | Local income | | Foreign income | |
|---|---|---|---|---|
| | Lm | Lm | Lm | Lm |
| Net profit before tax as shown in the accounts for fiscal year 2004..................... | | 800,000 | | 200,000 |
| Add back amounts not allowable for tax purposes or that require adjustments: | | | | |
| Depreciation ........................................... | 200,000 | | 10,000 | |
| Donations ............................................... | 5,000 | | — | |
| Increase in provision for bad or doubtful debts...................................... | 5,000 | | — | |
| Structural alterations of a capital nature ......................................... | 65,000 | | — | |
| Contributions to unapproved pension scheme................................... | 5,000 | 280,000 | — | 10,000 |
| | | 1,080,000 | | 210,000 |
| Less: | | | | |
| Initial allowances on industrial buildings ............................... | 125,000 | | — | |
| Wear-and-tear allowance .......................... | 118,000 | | 20,000 | |
| Balancing allowance ................................ | 2,000 | 245,000 | — | 20,000 |
| | | 835,000 | | 190,000 |
| Add—Flat-rate foreign tax credit (25% of 30,000) ......................................... | | — | | 7,500 |
| Taxable income............................................ | | 835,000 | | 197,500 |
| Tax thereon at 35%...................................... | | 292,250 | | 69,125 |
| Less: | | | | |
| Double taxation treaty relief (1) ................. | — | | 12,000 | |
| Unilateral tax relief (2)............................... | — | | 10,000 | |
| Flat-rate foreign tax credit (25%) (3) ......... | — | | 7,500 | |
| Tax deducted at source from dividend received (4)......................................... | 35,000 | (35,000) | — | (29,500) |
| Net tax payable (5)....................................... | | 257,250 | | 39,625 |

Notes:

1. Double taxation treaty relief is in respect of gross royalty income of Lm120,000 taxed at 10% in a foreign country.

2. Unilateral tax relief is in respect of income of Lm40,000 taxed abroad at 25%.

3. The flat-rate foreign tax credit is computed on income before payments or other deductions of Lm30,000 allocated to the Foreign Income Account, in respect of which double taxation treaty relief and unilateral tax relief are not claimed.

4. Tax has been deducted at source at 35% from dividends included gross at Lm100,000 in the net profits.

5. The net tax payable is Lm296,875, being the total of the tax payable on local income and the tax payable on foreign income.

6. Exchange rate for the Maltese lira at January 1, 2004: US$1 = Lm0.40818.

## PwC contact

For additional information on taxation in Mauritius, contact:

N. M. Robert Bigaignon
PricewaterhouseCoopers
Cerné House, 6th Floor
Chaussée
Port Louis, Mauritius
Telephone: (230) 212 5011
Fax: (230) 208 8037
e-mail: robert.bigaignon@mu.pwc.com

## Significant developments

In recent years the focus has been on regional development and development of the information and communication technology sector. Various tax incentives have been introduced.

Companies investing in countries that are members of regional blocs such as the Southern Africa Development Community (SADC) and Common Market for Eastern and Southern Africa (COMESA), of which Mauritius is also a member, are subject to tax at a reduced rate of 15%, and dividends received by them from outside Mauritius are free of tax. Further, an investment made through such a company that is approved by the authorities is treated as a capital expenditure qualifying for capital allowance and investment allowance.

Companies under the Regional Headquarters Scheme are exempt from tax for a period of ten years from the year they start operations. They are thereafter taxed at 15%.

Information and communication technology (ICT) companies are generally taxed at 15%. However, under the ICT scheme, specified pioneering high-skills operators are exempt till 2008 and companies engaged in business process outsourcing/back office operations, call centers or contact centers may by irrevocable notice elect to pay tax at 5%.

Dividends payable by the companies are exempt.

## Taxes on corporate income

Income tax is payable on total net income before distribution at the following rates.

|  | % |
|---|---|
| Companies holding a Class B Banking License or a Category 1 Global Business License (previously offshore companies) and offshore trusts (see below) | 15 |
| Companies licensed to carry out activities in a free-port zone:- | |
| Private free port developers and operators carrying activities other than processing | Exempt |
| Third party free port developers and operators carrying processing activities ... | 15 |
| Tax incentive companies | 15 |
| All other companies | 25 |

Tax incentive companies include unit trusts, authorized mutual funds, venture capital funds, manufacturing companies, companies operating in other priority sectors, such as agriculture, housing, hotel and tourism, health, education, export information and communication technology, small- and medium-size industries and companies holding Investment Certificates under the Investment Promotion Act.

Category 2 Global Business Companies (previously International Companies) incorporated under the laws of Mauritius are exempt from income tax.

Under the local tax law, credit for foreign tax on foreign-source income is allowed against Mauritius tax computed by reference to that income. Such credit is also allowed under tax treaties. In any case the credit should not exceed Mauritius tax computed by reference to the foreign source income. A Category 1 Global Business Company may, in the absence of evidence of payment of foreign tax, claim as tax credit an amount equal to 80% of Mauritius tax chargeable on the foreign-source income.

In the case of dividends received from abroad a tax credit in respect of underlying tax is also available, provided that the Mauritian shareholder holds at least 5% of the share capital of the company paying the dividend. Mauritius also allows a tax-sparing credit under its local tax legislation.

## Corporate residence

A company incorporated in Mauritius is resident in Mauritius for tax purposes. A company not incorporated in Mauritius is resident in Mauritius only if it has its central management and control there. A Category 2 Global Business company is not considered as resident in Mauritius for the purposes of double taxation treaties.

## Other taxes

*Local income taxes*/Local income taxes leviable by local administration, such as urban councils, do not exist in Mauritius.

*Morcellement tax*/A capital gains (*morcellement*) tax is payable by every landowner that makes a parceling of land. The tax is calculated on the excess, if any, of the sale price over the aggregate of the amounts of purchase price and the cost of infrastructure works.

*Land development tax*/Land development tax is payable by every person that makes a parceling of land.

*Value-added tax*/Value-added tax (VAT) was introduced on September 7, 1998 to replace the sales tax. VAT is charged by VAT-registered entities at the standard rate of 15% on all goods and services supplied by them, other than exempt supplies. A VAT-registered entity is one whose turnover of taxable supplies exceeds Rs3 million a year.

## Branch income

Tax rates on branch income are the same as on corporate profits. No tax is withheld on the remittance of profits to a head office.

## Income determination

*Inventory valuation*/Inventories should be valued at the lower of historical cost or net realizable value, in accordance with Mauritius Accounting Standard 5 (MAS 5). The LIFO basis of valuation is not allowed for tax purposes.

Conformity is required between book and tax reporting. Where the Revenue is not satisfied that the basis of valuation is acceptable, for example, where the LIFO basis has been applied, it will make such adjustment as it believes is appropriate to determine the profits arising from the business carried on.

*Capital gains*/There is no tax on capital gains. Gains realized from the sale of any property or interest in property acquired in the course of a business the main purpose of which is the acquisition and sale of property as part of a profit-making undertaking or scheme are taxable as ordinary income. Where a transaction is in the nature of trade, the Revenue may take the view that it is an ordinary trading transaction and assess the gains derived as income. Any profit from dealings in units and securities, however, are exempt from tax.

*Intercompany dividends*/Companies, whether resident or not, are exempt from tax on dividends received from resident companies.

*Foreign income*/Resident corporations are taxed on their worldwide income with the following qualifications.

1. Generally, double taxation is avoided by means of a unilateral credit relief for foreign tax paid. The net amount of foreign income that has borne tax is grossed up at the foreign rate of tax, and the foreign tax paid is allowed as a credit against the Mauritius tax payable. However, the tax credit cannot exceed the Mauritius tax referable to the relevant foreign income. Unused credit is not refunded. In the case of foreign dividends, the tax credit includes foreign tax imposed on the profits out of which the dividends are paid (underlying tax), provided that the shareholding in the foreign company is at least 5%.

2. As regards foreign income derived from countries with which Mauritius has treaties for the avoidance of double taxation, tax credit is given for foreign tax in accordance with the treaties. There are clauses in the double taxation conventions that provide that income arising from certain specified foreign sources is to be exempt from Mauritius tax. Mauritius has signed double taxation conventions with Belgium, Botswana, People's Republic of China, Croatia, Cyprus, France, Germany, India, Indonesia, Italy, Kuwait, Luxembourg, Madagascar, Malaysia, Mozambique, Namibia, Nepal, Oman, Pakistan, Rwanda, Singapore, South Africa, Sri Lanka, Swaziland, Sweden, Thailand, United Kingdom, and Zimbabwe. Double taxation treaties with Lesotho, Russia, Senegal, and Uganda have been signed and are awaiting ratification. Treaties with Bangladesh, Barbados, Malawi, Nigeria, Tunisia, Vietnam, and Zambia have been negotiated but have not been signed yet. Treaties with Canada, Czech Republic, Greece, Portugal, and Seychelles are under negotiation.

Undistributed income of foreign subsidiaries is not subject to any special taxation. The income of the foreign subsidiary before distribution must not be included in the accounts of the local parent company. Dividends paid by the foreign subsidiary to the local parent company will, however, be taxable to the latter whether or not such dividends are actually received in Mauritius. However, dividends received from outside Mauritius by a company holding a regional development certificate are tax exempt.

*Stock dividends*/A resident company can distribute stock dividends (bonus shares) proportionately to all its shareholders. Stock dividends per se or convertible into cash are not taxable in the hands of the recipient. Dividends in kind are treated as taxable benefits.

*Other significant items*/The income derived by sugar companies from the production of the first 60 tons of sugar in any income year is exempt from tax.

Income derived by a nonresident company from the provision in Mauritius of consultancy services or training is tax exempt, provided the period of the services or training does not in the aggregate exceed 183 days in an income year.

A corporate owner of a foreign vessel registered in Mauritius or of a local vessel registered in Mauritius is exempt from tax on its income derived from the operation of such vessel. In the case of a local vessel, the exemption is limited to income derived from deep-sea international trade, with fishing excluded.

## Deductions

*Depreciation and depletion*/Depreciation is generally computed on the straight-line basis at specified rates. Two types of allowance are available.

1. Investment allowance—At the uniform rate of 25% on the construction of industrial buildings and hotel buildings to be used for the production of gross income, and on the acquisition of new plant and machinery and equipment (other than road vehicles) to be used for the production of gross income. Computer software also qualifies for the investment allowance. This investment allowance is not deducted in computing written-down or residual values. An additional investment allowance of 25% is available to a manufacturing company on the acquisition of state-of-the-art technological equipment other than road vehicles, provided that the expenditure is incurred before July 1, 2004. The additional investment allowance is also available to an ITC company on the acquisition of new plant and machinery or computer software.

2. Annual allowance—At rates varying between 5% and 33.33%, as follows.
   a. A rate of 5% on industrial buildings and buildings used for education and training.
   b. A rate of 10% on ships and aircraft, furniture, and fittings.
   c. A rate of 20% on plant or machinery generally, motor vehicles, hotel buildings, agricultural improvements, and scientific research.
   d. A rate of 33.33% on electronic and high-precision machinery, computer hardware and peripherals, and computer software.
   e. A rate of 100% on aircraft leased by a company engaged in aircraft leasing.

A rate of 100% depreciation is allowed in respect of plant or machinery costing Rs10,000 or less.

An approved investment in a company that holds a regional development certificate also qualifies for capital allowance and investment allowance.

Tax depreciation need not conform to book depreciation. Depreciation is generally recaptured on disposal or sale when balancing charges or allowances are computed.

No depreciation is allowed on commercial buildings.

*Net operating losses*/Losses made in an accounting year are carried forward indefinitely until absorbed by future profits, provided the corporation can demonstrate a 50% continuity of shareholding between the year of loss and the year of claim. Loss carrybacks are not permitted.

A wholly owned subsidiary incorporated on or after July 1, 1993 that is a tax incentive company may transfer its unrelieved loss to its holding company in the income year in which such loss is incurred. Similarly, a subsidiary operating a business in the Island of Rodrigues may transfer its unrelieved loss to its holding company in Mauritius.

Starting from the year of assessment 1994/1995, where a sugar factory operator that is not also a sugar cane planter incurs a loss, such loss to the extent it is unrelieved may be transferred in the income year in which it is incurred to a planter related to the operator. Where a company takes over another company engaged in manufacturing activities, any unrelieved loss of the acquiree may be transferred to the acquirer in the income year in which the takeover takes place, on such conditions relating to safeguard of employment as may be approved by the Minister of Finance.

***Payments to foreign affiliates***/Royalties, interest, and service fees payable to foreign affiliates are allowed as expenses, provided they correspond to actual expenses incurred, are reasonable and do not exceed what would be paid under an arm's length agreement. There are certain limitations if the recipient of the interest is not liable to Mauritius tax. Royalties paid by Category 1 Global Business companies, companies holding a Class B Banking License, and trusts to nonresidents are tax-exempt.

***Taxes***/Taxes paid are not normally deductible. However, municipal taxes relating to buildings that are let are deductible.

***Other significant items***/Donations to approved charitable institutions are deductible, subject to a maximum of Rs200,000 per annum.

Effective July 1, 1999, contributions made to an employees' share scheme are allowed as a deduction.

Preoperational expenses incurred by a tax incentive company incorporated on or after July 1, 1993 are allowed as a deduction from its gross income.

A bank or an approved financial institution may claim as deductions any irrecoverable loans due by a company in liquidation in respect of which winding-up procedures have started or by a company in receivership. It may also claim a deduction in respect of specific loans due from tax incentive companies that are considered to be irrecoverable, subject to an amount not exceeding 2% of the total loans due.

A company investing in the share capital of a start-up company within 24 months of the incorporation of the latter is entitled to a deduction of 33-1/3% of such investment in each of the first three years. A start-up company is a company engaged in information technology (IT), telecommunications and multimedia development and controlled by individuals. This deduction and the 30% credit mentioned under "Tax incentives" below cannot be claimed in respect of the same investment.

A deduction is available in respect of any expenditure incurred for the setting up of approved social security infrastructure as well as for any contribution made towards the provision of national ambulance services.

A company engaged in tourism or export activities may claim a double deduction for any expenditure incurred on overseas marketing and advertising, export promotion or the preparation of tenders for the export of goods or services. A double deduction is also available in respect of emoluments paid to disabled persons and to employees working in the Island of Rodrigues.

A company is entitled to a deduction not exceeding Rs1 million in respect of contributions to any sports club, sport federation, multisport federation, or sports training center set up by the government.

## Group taxation

There are no group provisions in the Mauritius tax legislation other than the transfer of losses by tax incentive companies, sugar factory operators and subsidiaries located in the Island of Rodrigues (see "Net operating losses").

## Tax incentives

*Inward investment/*The following incentives are available.

1. A reduced rate of corporation tax of 15% applies to all companies qualifying as tax incentive companies. Companies under the Regional Headquarters Scheme are, however, exempt for a period of ten years. Companies engaged in spinning are also exempt for a period ten income years provided they start operations by June 30, 2006.

   Moreover, the following incentives are available in respect of ICT projects.

   - A 15% corporate tax rate for operators in the sector.
   - Availability of a tax holiday up to 2008 for specified pioneering high-skills ICT operators.
   - Companies engaged in business process outsourcing/back office operations, call centers or contact centers may by irrevocable notice elect to pay tax at 5%.
   - Full depreciation of ICT equipment over three years, together with a first year's allowance of 50%.
   - A 50% relief on personal income tax for a specified number of foreign IT specialists per company.

   The income of certain companies operating in the Freeport Zone is exempt from tax.

2. A company (other than a tax incentive company) that subscribes to the share capital issued by a tax incentive company, or a company listed on the stock exchange, or an equity fund, is entitled to deduct from the tax payable 30% of the cash paid up as share capital spread equally over three years. The tax credit is limited to Rs300,000 in any one income year. Investment in units of a unit trust scheme also qualifies for this relief.

3. A company (other than a tax incentive company) engaged in the export of goods manufactured or produced locally, or in the provision of services overseas, pays income tax at the rate of 25%, but is entitled to a tax credit (deduction from tax) at the following rates.

   - A rate of 15% of tax where export sales range between 10% and 30% of total turnover.
   - A rate of 25% of tax where export sales range between 30% and 50% of total turnover.
   - A rate of 40% of tax where export sales exceed 50% of total turnover.

The incentives under (2) and (3) above are conditional on the effective tax rate of the beneficiary company not falling below 15%.

*Capital investment*/The following capital investment incentives are available.

1. Investment allowance and annual allowance—See "Deductions."

2. Where a company (other than a tax incentive company) that is the holder of an investment certificate in respect of a modernization and expansion has incurred capital expenditure of not less than Rs10 million within two years from the date of the issue of the certificate on new plant and equipment and modernization and expansion technology, it will be allowed a special deduction from income tax otherwise payable of an amount equal to 10% of the capital expenditure incurred. The relief may at the option of the company be spread over a period of three years from the year in which the expenditure is incurred. The deduction is allowed in addition to any investment allowance, additional investment allowance and annual allowance on such expenditure. The effective tax rate of the company should, however, not fall below 15% after taking the credit.

3. Where a company has subscribed in an income year to the stated capital of a spinning company of an amount exceeding Rs60 million, or at least 20% of the stated capital, whichever is the higher, it shall be allowed a tax credit by way of deduction from its income tax otherwise payable for the income year immediately preceding the income year in which the shares were acquired and at the option of the company.

   • For each of the three subsequent income years, of an amount equal to 15% of the amount actually paid in cash.

   • For each of the five subsequent income years, of an amount equal to 10% of the amount actually paid in cash.

*Other incentives*/As follows.

1. No special incentives are granted to holding and investment companies, other than those mentioned under "Capital gains," "Intercompany dividends" and "Inward investment."

2. Owners of foreign vessels registered in Mauritius are exempt from income tax on income derived from such vessels. Owners of local vessels registered in Mauritius are also exempt to the extent that the income is derived from deep-sea international trade, with fishing excluded.

## Withholding taxes

There is no withholding tax in Mauritius. A nonresident company receiving service fees or interest from Mauritius is subject to tax thereon at the corporate rate of 25% through a self-assessment system. Interest is either exempt from tax or taxed at reduced rates under certain tax treaties. For dividends, see "Intercompany dividends" above.

## Tax administration

*Returns*/Companies are assessed for a year of assessment that begins on July 1 and ends on June 30 on their income, for the preceding year ended June 30. Where their accounting year straddles June 30, the income is apportioned between the two basis years on a time basis. Where a company closes its accounts at a date other than June 30, it may make an election to adopt as its basis year the accounting year ending in the period of 12 months preceding the year of assessment.

Every company, whether or not a taxpayer, must file a return of its income on the basis of the income year preceding the year of assessment. Where the accounting (basis) year ends on June 30, the return must be filed not later than January 31 next following. Otherwise, the due date for filing a return is September 30 in the year of assessment.

*Payment of tax*/If the accounts are closed at June 30, the tax is payable in full no later than January 31 in the year of assessment. If the accounts are closed at a date other than June 30, the whole tax liability is payable in one lump sum on September 30 in the year of assessment.

If timely payment is not made, a penalty representing 2% of the tax unpaid for each month or part of a month is payable until the tax is paid, the maximum penalty being 100%. A penalty of Rs5,000 for each month or part of a month is also prescribed for failure to file a return, subject to a maximum of Rs50,000.

## *CORPORATION TAX CALCULATION*

Year of assessment ending June 30, 2004 based on financial year ending June 30, 2003.

| | | |
|---|---:|---:|
| Net profit before distribution of dividends and before taxation as shown in accounts for year ending June 30, 2003 | | Rs 10,000,000 |
| Add: | | |
| Depreciation charged in accounts | 2,000,000 | |
| Net loss on disposal of assets debited to profit and loss | 50,000 | |
| Entertainment expenses | 30,000 | |
| Gifts and donations | 20,000 | |
| Legal fees incurred in connection with purchase of building | 10,000 | |
| Survey fees for revaluation of assets | 20,000 | |
| Goodwill written off | 150,000 | |
| Provision for doubtful debts | 25,000 | |
| Alterations and improvements to buildings | 140,000 | |
| Bad debts recovered (previously written off) | 12,000 | |
| Fines | 3,000 | 2,460,000 |
| | | 12,460,000 |
| Deduct: | | |
| Capital profit on sale of shares credited to profit and loss account | 200,000 | |
| Donations to approved charitable institutions | 4,500 | |
| Dividends received from other resident companies (1) | 550,000 | 754,500 |
| | | 11,705,500 |
| Deduct—Capital allowances: | | |
| Investment allowance | 300,000 | |
| Annual allowance | 400,000 | |
| | 700,000 | |
| *Less*—Balancing charge | (10,000) | (690,000) |
| Deduct—Loss brought forward from preceding year | | (600,000) |
| Chargeable income | | Rs 10,415,500 |
| Income tax at 25% | | Rs 2,603,875 |
| *Less*—Investment tax credit for shares acquired in tax incentive company | | (40,125) |
| Net tax payable in one lump sum on or before January 31, 2004 | | Rs 2,563,750 |

Notes:

1. Expenses incurred in earning the dividends will not be deductible.
2. Exchange rate of the Mauritian rupee at January 1, 2004: US$1 = Rs26.50.

# Mexico

## PwC contact

For additional information on taxation in Mexico, contact:

Roberto del Toro
PricewaterhouseCoopers
Mariano Escobedo No. 573
Col. Rincón del Bosque
11580 México, D.F.
Telephone: (52) (5) 263 6059
Fax: (52) (5) 263 6010
e-mail: roberto.del.toro@mx.pwc.com

## Significant developments

A new income tax law was approved as from January 1, 2002. As from that date, the 5% withholding on dividends (on a grossed-up basis) paid to Mexican individuals and residents abroad was eliminated. During 2003, there were several amendments to correct certain provisions included in the 2002 Tax Reform resulting in some degree of legal certainty to the taxpayers. One of the most important changes was the elimination of the tax on luxury goods and on certain transactions with the general public that was enacted in 2002.

While the 2004 Tax Reform does not contain significant amendments to the income tax law, it does contain amendments to the federal tax code. These changes are mainly related to residency rules, rules for tax-free split-ups and mergers, rules concerning derivative transactions, joint venture agreements and ruling requests. Also, it is intended that as from the second half of 2004, overpayments of taxes can be compensated against any federal tax liability. It is important to note that as a part of this 2004 Tax Reform, the substitute tax on salary credits (*Impuesto Sustitutivo del Credito al Salario,* or ISCAS), which was in force as from January 1, 2002, was eliminated.

The information contained in this chapter is based on provisions in force at January 1, 2004, unless otherwise indicated.

## Taxes on corporate income

*Federal income tax*/The federal corporate income tax rate for 2004 is 33%. This rate will decrease one percentage point in 2005, to 32%.

There is a 50% income tax rate reduction (i.e., to 16.5% in 2004, and 16% in 2005 and thereafter) available to taxpayers engaged exclusively in agriculture, animal husbandry, fishing, or forestry. The reduced rate available to taxpayers engaged exclusively in book publishing in 2004 is 26.4%, and 28.8% in 2005. If said taxpayers are also engaged in other activities, the reduced rate applies only to the income arising from publishing operations.

Provisions designed to recognize the effects of inflation for tax purposes in the areas of monetary assets and liabilities (annual monetary adjustment), inventories (deduction upon purchase) and depreciable assets are provided for in the law because of the economic effects of inflation, although the rate thereof has been decreasing. Once a corporation has paid its income tax, after-tax earnings (i.e., earnings arising from the after-tax earnings account, *Cuenta de utilidad fiscal neta,* or CUFIN) may be distributed to the shareholders with no tax liability at the corporate level.

Additionally, if a corporation makes a distribution out of earnings that for any reason have not been subject to corporate income tax, such as book earnings not yet recognized for tax purposes, it will have to pay a corporate tax at the general corporate income tax rate on distributed earnings (grossed-up by a factor of 1.4925 in 2004, and 1.4706 in 2005). The tax paid on dividends distributed in the excess of the CUFIN can be credited against the corporate income tax of the distributing company in the same tax year in which it was paid, or in the following two tax years. The CUFIN of the tax years in which that credit is applied will be reduced by an amount equal to the grossed-up dividend distribution. All corporate entities, including associations of a civil nature branches, and so on, unless specifically excepted as nonprofit organizations, are subject to the rules applicable to corporations.

*Financial system*/The financial system is subject to certain reporting requirements to the tax authorities. As from the second half of 2002, the financial system must comply with additional reporting requirements regarding payments made to individual residents for investments, investor identity information and the amount of interest paid.

*Shares sold through the stock market*/The sale of shares is exempt from income tax when sold by individuals and residents abroad through authorized stock markets, provided certain rules are satisfied.

*Interest*/Income tax withholding on interest paid by financial institutions to Mexican resident investors is set in general terms at 0.5% (annual rate) of the invested capital.

*Minimum tax*/A minimum tax, also known as the asset tax, is payable at the rate of 1.8% of the value of the assets of the following taxpayers: corporations, unincorporated businesses, organizations of a civil nature not specifically exempted, branches or other permanent establishments of foreign parties, and foreign residents who maintain assets used or to be transformed in Mexico. The tax supplements the federal income tax, that is, it is payable and increases the overall tax burden only if it exceeds regular income tax. This feature is achieved by allowing an amount equal to the taxpayer's regular income tax as a credit against its minimum 1.8% tax liability for the current year.

In addition to the above credit, the excess of annual income tax due over the minimum tax due in each of the last three tax years may be credited against minimum tax for the year. This excess is restated for inflation.

During the first four years of a company's operations, minimum tax is generally not payable.

The asset tax paid in the previous ten years (restated for inflation) may be recovered in the year in which the income tax exceeds the asset tax for the current year, in an amount equivalent to that excess.

There is an option that allows taxpayers to determine asset tax for the year based on the tax due in the fourth preceding period (restated for inflation). Once the election is made, taxpayers are required to continue determining asset tax under that option.

As for 2004 and until 2007, foreign residents who maintain inventories in Mexico under *maquila* (in-bond) programs could consider their value, for purposes of calculating the minimum tax, only for the part involved in the production of merchandise for domestic sales.

*State taxes*/There are no state taxes on corporate net income.

## Corporate residence

The federal tax code provides that corporations are deemed to be residents of Mexico if they are incorporated under the provisions of Mexican corporate law, or if the principal center of administration or the effective place of management is located in Mexico. Under the Mexican income tax law, permanent establishments (PEs) of nonresidents are generally treated under the same rules as resident entities with respect to income attributed to said PEs. A definition of "permanent establishment" in a tax treaty overrides domestic law definitions if the taxpayer is willing to apply the treaty. See "branch income" below.

When a Mexican resident company ceases to be a Mexican resident in terms of the Mexican federal tax code, it is deemed to be liquidated for tax purposes. In such cases, as from 2004, a notice must be filed before the Mexican tax authorities within 15 working days following the date in which the change of tax residency takes place, and a short period return is due within three months of the residency change.

## Other taxes

*Value-added tax*/VAT at the general rate of 15% is payable on sales of goods and services, as well as on lease payments and the importation of goods and services, except in the border zones, where the 10% VAT rate generally applies. The sale of medicines, as well as the sale of most food products, is zero-rated. The principal VAT-exempt transactions are the sale of land, credit instruments (including equity shares), residential construction, interest paid by banks, medical services, education, salaries and wages, and rentals of residential property.

The sale in Mexico of temporarily imported goods, by nonresidents to other nonresidents, to a company with a PITEX program (*Programa de Importación para Producir Artículos de Exportación*), to a company with a *maquila* program, or to companies belonging to the automotive industry, is also VAT-exempt under certain circumstances.

The 0% VAT rate, which in general terms means that no VAT is payable, is applicable to a substantial number of transactions, including the sale of books, magazines and newspapers published by the taxpayer; the exportation of goods and certain services (including the *maquila* and sub-*maquila* of goods intended for exportation); the sale of certain basic foodstuffs, agricultural goods and services; sales and rentals of farm machinery and equipment; and other trans-actions of lesser importance.

Taxes paid by business enterprises on their purchases and expenses related to VAT taxable activities, or subject to the 0% VAT rate, may usually be credited against their liability for tax they collect from customers on their own sales, services rendered, and so on. The input VAT credit on goods or services of a general nature, or those not specially identified with either taxable or exempt activities for VAT purposes, is determined based on the prior year's ratio of taxable to total activities. Creditable VAT paid on purchases and expenses in excess of

VAT collected from customers is recoverable (i.e., can be refunded or credited against subsequent VAT liabilities).

VAT is a "cash basis" tax, with few exceptions (e.g., VAT derived from certain interest must be paid on an accrued basis), that is, only the receipt of payment for goods or services triggers the output VAT liability, and an input VAT credit may be claimed when the taxpayer pays VAT to its providers of goods and services. VAT is calculated for each calendar month. VAT so determined is a final tax.

VAT must generally be withheld by Mexican individuals or entities acquiring tangible assets in Mexico from residents abroad, or leasing tangible goods from residents abroad, if such foreign residents do not have a permanent establishment in the country to which income is attributed. Mexican business entities are required to withhold VAT on payments to individuals or entities for services consisting of ground transportation of goods. Mexican corporations must also withhold VAT on commissions paid to individuals, as well as on independent services rendered by Mexican individuals, and on tangible goods leased from individuals. Also, as from 2003, PITEX companies, *maquiladoras* (in-bond companies) and bonded warehouse transactions effected by the automotive and auto-parts industries are obligated to withhold VAT from their domestic suppliers.

***Compulsory profit sharing***/Although profit sharing is not a tax, it is important to consider that every business concern with employees is required to distribute a portion of its annual profits among all employees, except directors and the general manager, irrespective of its form of organization. The amount distributable to the employees in most cases is 10% of taxable income, adjusted to eliminate income or deductions that relate to the recognition of inflation, and increased by dividend income, which is not included in taxable income of Mexican corporations. Special rules apply to a limited number of specific businesses.

No profit sharing is paid during the first year of operations.

Profit sharing paid in 2004 will be deductible at 40%, based on the difference between the profit sharing paid and the related employer-deductible expenses that are not taxable income for the employees. In 2005, profit sharing paid will be deductible at 80% on the same basis.

***Excise tax***/The excise tax law *(Impuesto Especial Sobre Producción y Servicios,* or IEPS) levies substantial federal excise rates on the importation and/or sale of certain items, such as gasoline, beer, wine, spirits, cigarettes and other tobacco products, and on certain services related to these activities, such as commission, mediation and distribution

As a result of the tax amendments for 2004, IEPS on the sale of mineralized water and on telecommunication services was eliminated.

In general terms, goods are exempt from the IEPS when exported. However, since the IEPS paid by exporters is not creditable, that tax becomes an additional cost.

A 20% tax is imposed on the importation and/or sale of carbonated beverages, concentrates, powders, syrups, and flavored extracts. IEPS is payable (output tax) and creditable (input tax) on a cash basis. It is payable at the date on which the invoice is collected from the client and can be credited when the invoice is paid to the supplier. On importations, IEPS is creditable when paid at the customs offices.

An important amendment for 2004 is that the IESP Law allows taxpayers who are not subject to this tax to credit IESP paid on the acquisition, and/or the importation of certain goods, such as alcohol and semi-processed and fluid syrups (as a raw material) against income tax payable.

*Vehicle taxes*/Taxes are also levied on the ownership of motor vehicles, as well as on the acquisition of new vehicles.

## Branch income

Mexican branches of foreign corporations (i.e., PEs) are generally subject to the same tax rules as Mexican corporations, with certain exceptions. For example, branches may deduct pro rata allocations of home office expenses, provided certain requirements are complied with (such as the existence of an applicable tax treaty and a comprehensive agreement for the exchange of tax information with Mexico), but may not deduct remittances to their home offices, even when they are classified as royalties, fees, commissions, services, or interest.

In general terms, on other remittances from branches or other PEs (including earnings, except, of course, remittances representing a return to the home office of capital invested in the branch), the general corporate tax rate applies, on a grossed-up basis, unless the remittance arises from the CUFIN account balance.

The income tax law considers a PE to be any place in Mexico where business activities or services are carried out or rendered by nonresidents, such as agencies, offices, mining exploration sites, or any other place of exploration, extraction or exploitation of natural resources, regardless of the length of time involved. A foreign insurance company could also be considered as having a PE when it engages in activities consisting of insuring risk or collecting premiums in Mexico through a party other than an independent agent, with the exception of reinsurance activities. Except in the cases of sites used for the maintenance of display, storage or purchasing facilities or inventories imported in-bond to be processed by a third party, short-term construction services, and offices to carry out auxiliary or preliminary information gathering or scientific research, a PE is generally deemed to exist and is taxed as a branch. Nonresidents may also keep merchandise in bonded warehouses (including merchandise delivered for importation into Mexico) without being considered to have a PE.

A nonresident is not considered to have a PE in Mexico derived from the legal or economic relationships maintained with companies carrying out *maquila* operations (*maquiladoras*) which normally process goods or merchandise maintained in Mexico by the nonresident by using assets provided by the nonresident or any related party, as long as certain requirements are met, such as the nonresident being a resident of a country with which Mexico has a tax treaty in force and the *maquiladora* complying with the transfer pricing provisions for related-party transactions established in the law.

Additionally, as from 2004 to 2007, *maquiladoras* under shelter programs could be considered to not be a PE in Mexico, when assets of foreign residents are involved.

The definitions of PE under tax treaties with other countries may differ from domestic law definitions. Accordingly, each case should be carefully analyzed.

## Income determination

*Recognition of income*/Income is generally recognized on the accrual basis. However, the service revenues of civil entities that render professional services (e.g., law and accounting firms) are reflected as per the cash basis method.

*Inventory valuation*/Inventories are recorded for asset tax purposes, even though all purchases and costs of production of merchandise and related costs are treated as deductible expenses for income tax purposes when incurred. For asset tax purposes, inventories must be restated under Mexican GAAP, or by otherwise applying one of the methods provided in the asset tax law, that is, valuation of inventory in accordance with the price of the latest purchase or at replacement value.

*Capital gains*/Capital gains are taxed as follows.

1. Securities: Gains are includable in regular taxable income. There are two different procedures for computing the tax basis of a Mexican company's shares, depending on the period for which the shares are held (i.e., less or more than 12 months).

   The tax basis of shares of Mexican corporations sold may be increased by the inflation adjustment factor for the holding period.

   In the case of shares with a holding period of more than 12 months, there are certain items to be considered when computing the tax basis, such as the change in the CUFIN account of the issuing corporation (including the possible negative CUFIN effects), as adjusted for inflation, during the period the shares were held (considering for this purpose the CUFIN balance after January 1, 1975, if the shares were acquired before that date), the unamortized prior years' tax losses at the date of the sale, as well as tax losses arising prior to the date on which those shares were acquired and amortized during the holding period, and any capital reductions of the issuing company.

   When the sum of the CUFIN balance at the date of the acquisition of the shares, the unamortized prior years' tax losses at the date of the sale, and the negative CUFIN balance of the issuing corporation is higher than the sum of the CUFIN balance at the date of the sale and tax losses arising prior to the date on which those shares were acquired and amortized during the shares' holding period, the difference must be subtracted from the tax basis of the shares to be sold (potentially resulting in the tax basis of the shares being equal to zero). When said difference exceeds the tax basis of the shares sold, said excess (restated for inflation) must be subtracted from the tax basis of the shares in any subsequent share sale by the same taxpayer, even if the shares are issued by a different company.

   The above-mentioned procedure allows determination of an average cost (tax basis) of the shares, which is updated and considered as the acquisition cost for future sales.

   A different but simpler procedure applies for computing the tax basis of shares held during a period of 12 months or less.

   Deduction of losses arising in the sale of shares is limited to the amount of gains from similar transactions in the same or the following five fiscal years. Losses may not be deducted by nonresidents selling shares.

   In general terms, the sale by nonresidents of shares issued by a Mexican company is subject to a 25% withholding tax applicable on the gross amount of the transaction.

   Alternatively, gains realized by nonresidents on the sale of shares issued by a Mexican company may be taxed by applying the statutory 33% rate to the net gain (i.e., value of the transfer less the tax basis of the shares). This election is available only if the foreign shareholder is a resident of a country that is not considered to qualify as a "preferred tax regime jurisdiction" (tax haven) or a country with a territorial tax system. The selling resident abroad must have previously appointed a representative in Mexico, and have a public accountant issue a statutory tax audit report on the transfer of shares. The public accountant issuing the respective report must specify the accounting value of the shares sold, and explain the factors used in determining the sales price, at market value, of the shares, when shares are sold between related parties.

As a result of the reforms made to the regulations of the Mexican income tax law in 2003, additional requirements have to be satisfied when a sale of shares is carried out as part of a reorganization.

The representative is jointly liable for the tax on the sale of shares, even when the statutory report is issued by the public accountant.

The domestic law no longer provides for tax-free reorganizations when non-Mexican entities are involved. However, the tax authorities may authorize the deferral of taxes that would otherwise be triggered by the transfer of shares through a reorganization of companies belonging to the same group (the authorization must be obtained prior to the share transfer). The tax deferred is determined considering an arm's length price. This tax, adjusted for inflation, is due upon the sale of the originally transferred shares outside the same economic group. An economic group consists of 51% common ownership by vote.

In principle, such authorizations for deferral are not granted if the party acquiring or selling the shares is a resident of a tax haven, or of a country that has not signed a broad exchange of information agreement with Mexico. However, in the latter case, an authorization may still be granted if the taxpayer provides documentation to the Mexican tax authorities stating that the taxpayer has authorized the foreign tax authorities to provide information to the Mexican authorities regarding the operation for tax purposes.

If the sale of shares qualifies as an exempt reorganization under tax treaty rules, the nonresident must appoint, prior to the sale, a legal representative in Mexico, and file a notice before the Mexican tax authorities informing them of such appointment and the details of the reorganization process intended to be effected. Additionally, certain formal requirements have been established in the regulations of the Mexican income tax law that must be complied with when carrying out this type of transactions.

Tax treaty rules (optional) override domestic law rules when the seller resides in a tax treaty country.

2. Real estate: In determining the taxable gain, the cost basis of the land and buildings may be adjusted (i.e., increased) for tax purposes on the basis of the time the assets have been held. This is done by applying inflation adjustment factors to the net undepreciated balance. Similar rules apply to nonresidents electing to pay 33% tax on net income by appointing a legal representative in Mexico. Otherwise, the 25% final withholding tax on gross income applies to nonresidents.

3. Machinery and equipment: Gains or losses from the disposition of machinery, equipment and other fixed assets are also calculated after adjusting the basis in these assets, by applying inflation factors to the net undepreciated balance.

**Inflationary gain or loss**/Taxpayers are required to calculate an adjustment due to inflation (i.e., additional taxable income) on an annual basis by applying the percentage increases in the National Consumer Price Index (NCPI) to essentially all liabilities reduced by their monetary assets, including bank balances, investments (except in shares) and some notes and accounts receivable. Contrarily, taxpayers may calculate a monetary inflationary loss (i.e., additional deduction) on their monetary assets, including bank balances, investments (except shares) and some notes and accounts receivable.

*Intercompany dividends*/Dividends received by Mexican corporations from other Mexican corporations need not be included in gross income. However, dividend income is subject to 10% compulsory profit sharing, and must form part of the recipient corporation's CUFIN account.

No further taxes apply on dividends distributed out of the paying corporation's net after taxed income. On other corporate distributions that for any reason represent income that has not been subject to the corporate income tax of the distributing corporation, a corporate tax at the general corporate income tax rate is imposed (on a grossed-up basis) on the corporation, as discussed above.

*Foreign income*/A Mexican corporation is taxed on foreign source income when earned. Double taxation is reduced, or possibly avoided, by means of foreign tax credits. However, the undistributed profits of a foreign subsidiary are not subject to Mexican tax until dividends are paid, with the exception of companies with investments in entities located in a tax haven ("preferred tax regime jurisdiction"), in which case income is generally taxable even if no distributions are received.

*Investments in tax havens ("preferred tax regime jurisdictions")*/Investments in tax havens include those made directly or indirectly in entities, branches, real property, shares, bank accounts or investment accounts, and any kind of participation in entities, trusts, joint ventures or investment funds, as well as in any other similar legal entities created or incorporated in accordance with foreign law and located in a tax haven, including those that are carried out through an intermediary.

A business, entity, trust or joint venture is considered to be located in a tax haven when it has a physical presence, an address, a post office box or effective management in a tax haven, or when banking accounts are held in financing entities located in a tax haven.

Income and profits arising from investments in tax havens are taxed separately. This income cannot be combined with other taxable income or losses, and is not considered for the purpose of making advance income tax payments. Tax applicable to this type of income is payable together with the corporate annual tax return.

In general, the annual inflationary adjustment on liabilities of the investment in the tax haven and interest income are included in taxable income without subtracting the annual inflationary adjustment on receivables. However, the annual inflationary adjustment on receivables may be subtracted from interest income earned, provided an information return is filed.

Tax on investments in tax havens is determined by applying the general corporate income tax rate to taxable income. Additionally, net operating loss carryforwards associated with an investment in a tax haven may be amortized against the tax profit of the following tax years arising from investments in tax havens, and tax deductions related to said investment may be applied, as long as accounting records pertaining to said investments are available and the annual information return on said investments is filed on time.

Undistributed income from investments in companies or other entities located in tax havens need not be immediately included in taxable income under the above provisions in certain particular cases (e.g., when they arise from activities that qualify as business activities in terms of the applicable provisions, and in the case of indirect investments in a tax haven when certain conditions are met).

**Maquiladoras *(In-bond processing companies)*/**Related foreign companies of *maquiladoras* are considered to not have a PE in Mexico to the extent they are residents of a country that has a tax treaty in force with Mexico, that all the terms and requirements of the treaty are complied with, and the mutual agreements of Mexico and its treaty partner are satisfied. This relief applies only if the *maquiladora* complies with any of the following options stated by the domestic law.

1. Maintain documentation on transfer pricing in accordance with applicable provisions, adding to the *maquila* fee 1% of the net book value of the machinery and equipment owned by the foreign related company and used by the *maquiladora* in its activities.
2. Report taxable income of at least the higher of the following values.
   a. A rate of 6.9% of assets used in the *maquila* activity (including the inventories and fixed assets owned by the foreign related party).
   b. A rate of 6.5% of the operating costs and expenses of the *maquiladora*.
3. Maintain documentation on transfer pricing using the transactional net margin method (TNMM) and considering a return on the net book value of machinery and equipment owned by the foreign related company used by the *maquiladora* in its activities, adjusted by financing terms.

*Maquiladoras* that apply option 1 or 3 may request an advanced price agreement (APA) from the Mexican tax authorities. However, this APA is not mandatory to obtain the PE relief.

*Maquiladoras* that apply any of the three options above are not required to file the annual information return on transactions with foreign related parties. This exemption is only available for the *maquila* activity.

These provisions also provide relief for asset tax payable by foreign residents on inventories and machinery and equipment owned by them and used in Mexico, in the proportion that the *maquiladora's* production for export represents of total production.

If the *maquiladora* renders services other than exported *maquila* services (i.e., domestic sales), specific transfer pricing requirements apply, and potential PE issues must be evaluated.

In October 2003, a Presidential Decree was enacted granting a reduction in the corporate income tax rates to *maquiladoras.*

**Mexico's tax treaties/**Tax treaties with Australia, Belgium, Canada, Chile, the Czech Republic, Denmark, Ecuador, Finland, France, Germany, Ireland, Israel, Italy, Japan, the Republic of Korea, Luxembourg, the Netherlands, Norway, Poland, Portugal, Romania, Singapore, Spain, Sweden, Switzerland, the United Kingdom, and the United States have been published in the Official Gazette, and are ratified and in force.

As of April 2004, the following treaties must still be ratified by the respective governments to become effective, or are being negotiated: Austria, Brazil, China, Greece, Hungary, India, Indonesia, Malaysia, Nicaragua, Slovakia, Russia, Thailand, and Venezuela.

***Stock dividends***/Dividend distributions are generally taxable at the corporate level as mentioned above, whether they are paid in cash or in-kind when paid out of untaxed earnings. However, when these taxable dividends are reinvested in the same company within 30 calendar days following their distribution, they are not taxed until they are distributed as a taxable capital reduction (including capital reimbursement in the company's liquidation).

## Deductions

***General rule***/The applicable deduction requirements must be complied with no later than the last day of the tax year to which the deduction applies, although the invoice supporting the expense may be provided up to the date on which the tax return for the period in question is filed (or comes due). An expense invoice must contain a date within the year for which the deduction is claimed.

***Depreciation, amortization, and depletion***/Straight-line depreciation is allowed at the rates specified in the law, and the deduction may be increased by the application of the percentage increases in the NCPI as from the month of acquisition of the asset. When an asset is disposed of or becomes useless, the remaining undepreciated historical cost may also be deducted, after application of the appropriate inflation adjustment factor.

Mining exploration and development expenses incurred prior to the commencement of operations and the cost of mining claims may be amortized at 10% per year, after applying inflation adjustment factors, unless the taxpayer elects to deduct these costs as incurred.

Intangible assets for the exploitation of goods that are of the public domain, or for the rendering of a public service under concession, are considered deferred assets (i.e., not deducted as incurred). Therefore, these assets are subject to amortization for income tax purposes, and must be included in the asset tax base.

Specific annual depreciation rates are established for goods used in certain industries.

***Net operating losses***/Subject to certain limitations, losses incurred in prior years by business enterprises may be carried forward and deducted from income of the ten subsequent years.

Losses carried forward may be increased by the percentage increase in the NCPI between the seventh and twelfth months of the fiscal year in which they are incurred, and thereafter up to the sixth month of the fiscal year in which they are applied.

Tax loss carryforwards are a right of the specific taxpayer, and cannot be transferred to another entity, even in the case of a merger. In the case of a spin-off, tax loss carryforwards can be divided between the surviving entity and the spun-off entity(ies) in proportion to the following.

1. The inventories and accounts receivable transferred in the case of commercial entities.
2. The fixed assets transferred, in all other cases.

***Payments to foreign affiliates***/Payments of a prorated portion of expenses of nonresidents (i.e., allocations) are not deductible by Mexican corporations. Additionally, taxable income and authorized deductions must be determined on the basis of the prices that would be agreed with independent parties in comparable transactions (arm's length values).

For this purpose, taxpayers must secure and maintain contemporaneous documentation supporting transactions with related parties residing abroad, provided that income and deductions are based on market values. This documentation must be prepared per type of operation, and must include all operations carried out with related parties.

Domestic transactions must also be supported by the application of a recognized transfer pricing method.

Payments made to residents of tax havens are considered nondeductible, unless it can be demonstrated that the price of the transaction is the same as would be set between or among unrelated parties in comparable transactions. Unless the contrary is demonstrated, it is assumed that operations with companies, entities or trusts resident in tax havens are carried out between or among related parties, and that prices are not set as they would be in comparable operations between or among independent parties.

The sales price of shares (other than publicly traded shares) sold to a related party must be set at market value and the transaction must be supported by the corresponding contemporaneous transfer pricing documentation.

In order to be deductible, payments of technical assistance fees and for the transfer of technology or royalties must be made directly to companies having the required technical capabilities, and should correspond to services actually received.

***Taxes***/In general, all federal, state, and local taxes levied on a company (not including those required to be withheld from other parties) represent income tax deductible expenses, with the following exceptions.

1. Federal income tax.
2. Federal minimum tax on assets.
3. Federal VAT and excise tax when the company is entitled to credit the tax.
4. Taxes on acquisitions of fixed assets and real estate, which must be capitalized and deducted as part of the total cost of such assets to be depreciated.

## Group taxation

The income tax law contains a chapter that allows certain holding companies to file a consolidated income tax return with their majority-owned subsidiaries. Tax consolidation is applicable for income tax and asset tax purposes, but not for other taxes (e.g., VAT) or compulsory profit sharing.

In general terms, the consolidation regime allows certain benefits, such as offsetting losses incurred by one company against the profits of another controlled company. However, as from 1999, only 60% of the controlling company's interest in the controlled companies may now be consolidated for income tax purposes. All holding companies are also allowed to consolidate only 60% of their results. For the remaining 40% interest, holding, and controlled companies must determine their tax result on a nonconsolidated basis and are subject to formal filing and compliance requirements.

For asset tax purposes, consolidating companies may opt to calculate the tax considering 60% of the controlling company's interest in the controlled companies. Otherwise, they must consolidate asset tax on the ownership percentage of the holding company in the controlled companies. However, in this latter case, certain restrictions may apply to some benefits, such as the refund of asset tax paid in previous years.

The principal advantages of filing a consolidated return are the following.

1. The possibility of deducting (at the consolidated level) the portion of the tax losses incurred by the subsidiaries corresponding to 60% of the portion of shares owned by the holding company. In the case of tax losses incurred before the consolidation, the deduction may be applied only up to the amount of the controlling or controlled company's individual taxable profit in the period in question.

2. The filing of a consolidated asset tax return for the entire group, thus optimizing the determination of the respective tax liabilities by allowing excess income tax credits of one company to be offset against the net 1.8% tax liabilities of other companies within the group.

   As previously mentioned, taxpayers are generally exempt from asset tax during their first four years of operation. However, this exemption is not applicable in the case of the controlling and controlled companies (except in the proportion in which the holding company has no direct or indirect participation in the capital stock of said controlled companies) with the exception of assets acquired by the controlled companies incorporated into the consolidation regime, when they are new or used for the first time in Mexico.

3. Tax-deferred flow of dividends in excess of the net previously taxed income, (individual CUFIN), to the extent that the dividend flow remains within the consolidation group.

The principal requirement for a company to qualify as a holding company for this purpose is that it must be a Mexican tax resident, and no more than 50% of the holding company's shares are held by other companies, regardless of their country of residence, although shares that qualify as placed among the general investing public and nonvoting shares are not regarded as company-owned for this purpose. Unfortunately, this rule precludes the possibility of filing a consolidated return for a Mexican group of companies that would otherwise qualify if more than 50% of the holding company's shares is held by a foreign corporation, unless the foreign corporation is a resident in a country that has executed a comprehensive agreement for the exchange of tax information with Mexico. At present, Belgium, Canada, Chile, the Czech Republic, Ecuador, Finland, France, Israel, Italy, the Republic of Korea, the Netherlands, Norway, Romania, Singapore, Spain, Sweden, and the United States have agreements of this nature with Mexico, and other agreements or tax treaties that might contain such an agreement are awaiting ratification or being negotiated.

## Tax incentives

*Inward investment*/Tax incentives for inward investment are as follows.

# Mexico

1. Duty-free imports: Nonpayment of customs duties under specific conditions and programs is also authorized for materials to be re-exported, and for materials for the production of exports or materials to be converted into exported end products. Duty-free imports are widely used by, among others, *maquila* (in-bond) companies and by manufacturers of a wide variety of items.

   These companies may be 100% foreign-owned. Beginning in 2001, in principle, non-North American Free Trade Agreement (NAFTA) originating raw materials and components must pay import customs duties when they are incorporated into finished goods bound for NAFTA countries. Companies must pay customs duties (if any) on equipment when entering Mexico, regardless of its origin.

   Competitive supply conditions are established through Sectorial Relief Programs, which allow reduction of customs duties for certain manufacturing industries. These programs were created by the federal government in order to establish competitive tariff conditions for Mexican manufacturers needing to import raw materials and fixed assets from non-NAFTA countries due to the changes made in 2001, where nonoriginating merchandise must pay duties.

2. Investments in certain new fixed assets outside of Mexico City, Guadalajara, and Monterrey are entitled to an accelerated depreciation deduction considering a present value discounted rate of the future stream of depreciation. Taxpayers may benefit from this deduction in the above-mentioned cities if they can show that their business operations are labor intensive, do not contribute to pollution, and do not require the intensive use of water, under certain rules.

3. An income tax incentive may be available to taxpayers involved in certain technological research and development projects carried out during the year. Said incentive consists of applying a 30% tax credit to corporate income tax for the same year in which said credit is determined in relation to the expenses and investments in technological research and development.

4. A new incentive offers a credit equivalent to 20% of the salary paid to workers/employees with certain types of disabilities.

*Capital investment*/There are no incentives to encourage capital investment. However, investing through equity instead of debt reduces or eliminates the need to include the "inflationary gain" mentioned above in taxable income.

*Other incentives*/Certain other specific and limited tax incentives may be applied for taxpayers engaged in certain activities (e.g., those engaged in air or sea transportation of goods or passengers with respect to aircraft and ships with a federal government commercial concession or permit; in the agricultural and forestry sectors; in bond warehouses with respect to owned real property used for the storage, safeguarding or conservation of goods or merchandise, business trusts related to the construction, acquisition, leasing, or alienation of real estate, etc).

## Withholding taxes

*Payments to Mexican residents*/Payments to resident corporations and permanent establishments in Mexico are generally not subject to withholding taxes.

Payments by resident corporations to resident individuals are subject to withholding tax as follows.

| | Percentage of income tax to be withheld |
|---|---|
| Wages, salaries and other remuneration (1) | 0–33 |
| Fees: | |
|     Members of boards of directors and advisory boards | 33 |
|     Other professional fees | 10 |
| Lease payments on real property | 10 |
| Interest on securities (2) | 0.5 |
| Interest on nonqualified securities | 20 |
| Dividends | Nil |
| Miscellaneous types of income of individuals, | |
|     usually sporadic payments | 20 |

Notes:

1. At a rate of 33% in 2004, to be reduced to 32% in 2005.
2. This withholding tax is calculated on the total amount of the capital invested.

***Payments to nonresidents***/Income tax must be usually withheld from payments to nonresident corporations and individuals. In the case of nontreaty countries, the statutory withholding rates are as noted below.

Income tax of 40%, with no deductions, must be withheld on most payments made to foreign parties located in tax havens, in lieu of the tax provided in the domestic law for nontax-haven residents. This is not applicable in certain cases, such as on income not subject to Mexican taxation in accordance with the regular provisions for income of nonresidents from a source of wealth located in Mexico, income from dividends, gains distributed by legal entities, and certain types of interest, including interest payments made to foreign banks. In these cases, the regular provisions of the domestic law should be applied to determine the income tax withholding.

Additionally, revenues for intermediation services, including commissions for brokerage, agency, distribution, assignment or estimates and generally all income from the negotiation of third party interests, when paid to tax haven residents, are also subject to 40% withholding tax.

Nonresidents' wages and salaries are taxed on the basis of 12-month period earnings as follows.

| Taxable income (A) | | % |
|---|---|---|
| **From** | **To** | |
| 0 | Ps 125,900 | Nil |
| Ps 125,901 | 1,000,000 | 15 |
| 1,000,001 | | 30 |

(A) Limits in force at January 1, 2004.

The above mentioned rates are also applicable to retirement fund deliveries.

However, no tax is imposed when the compensation (wages, salaries, or fees other than board fees) is paid by a nonresident of Mexico with no establishment in Mexico (even if not subject to tax) to which the services relate, provided the individual remains in Mexico for fewer than 183 days (consecutive or not) in any 12-month period.

# Mexico

The tax, when applicable, is withheld if the income is paid by a resident (or a nonresident with a permanent establishment in Mexico). Otherwise, the tax is generally payable during the 15 following working days, by the party earning the Mexican-source income.

|  | % |
|---|---|
| Professional fees for services rendered in Mexico | 25 |
| Lease payments: | |
| Lease of real property | 25 |
| Lease of containers, airplanes, and ships authorized by the Mexican Government to be commercially exploited in the transportation of goods or persons | 5 |
| Lease of personal property | 25 |
| Time-sharing services (1) | 25 |
| Charter agreements | 10 |
| Sales: | |
| Real property located in Mexico (1) | 25 |
| Shares of Mexican companies (1, 2) | 25 |
| Transfers of ownership of Mexican public debt by other than the original creditors (intended to cover debt-for-equity swaps) (1) | 25 |
| Derivative transactions: | |
| On capital (1) | 25 |
| On debt (3) | Same rates applicable to interest |
| Interest (4): | |
| Paid to foreign government financing entities, to duly registered foreign banks and other entities that provide financing with funds obtained by issuing publicly traded debt instruments abroad, registered with the Ministry of Finance (5) | 10 |
| Interest on debt instruments placed abroad (6) | 4.9 |
| Other interest payments to foreign financial institutions (7) | 4.9 |
| Paid by Mexican financial institutions to residents abroad, other than those on which the above mentioned lower rates may apply | 21 |
| Paid to foreign suppliers of machinery and equipment, to others to finance purchases of such assets or inventory or working capital loans, if the lender is duly registered | 21 |
| Paid to reinsurance entities | 15 |
| Other interest payments (8) | 33 |
| Financial leases (on the portion deemed to qualify as interest or finance charge) | 15 |
| Dividends | Nil |
| Royalties (9): | |
| For the use of railroad cars | 5 |
| For the use of copyrights on scientific, literary or art works, including motion pictures and radio and television recordings, as well as software and payments for the transmission of video and audio signals via satellite, cable, optic fiber and similar media (10) | 25 |
| On patents, invention or improvement certificates, trademarks, brand names, and advertising (8, 10) | 33 |
| For the use of drawings or models, plans, formulas or procedures, and of scientific, commercial and industrial equipment; on amounts paid for information regarding scientific, commercial and industrial experience; for technical assistance (10) | 25 |

|  | % |
|---|---|
| Short-term construction, and the respective installation, maintenance, technical direction or supervision (11) | 25 |
| Reinsurance premiums | 2 |
| Income obtained by athletes and artists (1) | 25 |
| Other income (forgiven debts, indemnifications, rights to participate in business, investments, etc) (8) | 33 |

Notes:

1. The nonresident may elect to pay a tax of 33% in the case of time-sharing services, sale of shares, sale of real property, activities of sportsmen and artists, and derivative stock and debt transactions; and 40% in the case of the transfer of public debt), on the net tax profit, if certain requirements are complied with and the nonresident has a resident legal representative (who/which, in the case of time-sharing services, must keep the audited financial statements of the taxpayer available for inspection by the tax authorities). No legal representative is required for sales of real property by public deed. A tax opinion issued by a registered public accountant is also required under this option in the case of the sale of shares. In the case of shares and debt-for-equity swap transactions, this election is available only if the foreign taxpayer is not a resident of a country classified as a tax haven or a country with a territorial tax system. In addition, there is an option to defer Mexican income tax arising from the sale of shares due to a corporate reorganization within the same group, provided certain conditions are met.

2. The sale of shares through the Mexican Stock Exchange considered as available to the general investing public and government securities are exempt from tax withholding, provided certain rules are complied with.

3. This withholding rate is applicable on a net basis, that is, on the gain arising from the transaction. If the transaction were payable in kind, the applicable withholding rate would be 10%.

4. Interest payments to nonresidents are exempt from Mexican income tax when they are paid on the following.

   a. Loans to the federal government or to the Bank of Mexico (Central Bank); also on bonds issued by said entities, to be acquired and paid abroad.

   b. Loans for three or more years granted or guaranteed by duly registered financial entities that promote exports through special financing.

   c. Preferential loans granted or guaranteed by foreign financial entities to institutions authorized to receive tax-deductible donations in Mexico, provided these institutions are properly registered and use the funds for purposes consistent with their status.

5. In 2004, 4.9% may be applied when the interest is paid to registered banks resident in countries with which Mexico has signed a tax treaty.

6. The 4.9% withholding rate applies provided the placement is handled through banks or brokerage firms resident in a country with which Mexico has signed a tax treaty, and if there is compliance with the information requirements established in the general rules issued by the Ministry of Finance. If there is failure to comply with these requirements, the 10% withholding rate applies.

   The 4.9% and 10% withholding rates mentioned in the preceding paragraphs do not apply, and instead a 33% withholding is applicable to interest, when the direct or indirect beneficiaries of the interest, either individually or jointly with related parties, receive more than 5% of the interest arising from the instrument in question, and are either (a) holders of more than 10% of the voting shares of the issuing company, either directly or indirectly, either individually or jointly with related parties, or (b) business entities holding more than 20% of their shares, either directly or indirectly, either individually or jointly with parties related to the issuer.

7. The 4.9% tax withholding rate is applicable to interest payments made to foreign financial institutions in which the Mexican federal government or the Mexican Central Bank has a capital participation.

8. The tax rate is reduced to 32% in 2005.

9. Proceeds from the sale of most intangible property, even when the gains from the sale are not subject to productivity, use or disposition, are treated as royalties, subject to Mexican income tax withholding.

10. When the agreements involve a patent or an invention or improvement certificate (subject to tax withholding at the general corporate rate) and other items qualifying as royalties (or technical assistance) subject to the 25% withholding rate, the tax must be calculated by applying the rates applicable to the gross amount of the payment.

11. The nonresident taxpayer may elect to pay 33% tax on the net profit, if the taxpayer has a resident legal representative and so advises the customer, who then makes no withholding. When the job lasts more than 183 days, the foreign taxpayer is deemed to have a permanent establishment for tax purposes and is taxed in the same manner as a local resident corporation.

The statutory withholding rates mentioned above may be reduced by applying tax treaty provisions. During the last decade, Mexico has embarked on a policy of negotiating a network of tax treaties with its principal trading and investment partners.

The tax rates specified in the treaties published in the Official Gazette as of March 1, 2004 currently in force are as follows.

| | Dividends | | | |
|---|---|---|---|---|
| | **Portfolio** | **Substantial holdings** | **Interest** | **Royalties** |
| | % | % | % | % |
| Australia | 15 | 0 (14) | 10, 15 (19) | 10 |
| Belgium | 15 | 5 (1) | 10, 15 (2) | 10 |
| Canada | 15 | 10 (3) | 10 (4) | 10 (4) |
| Chile | 10 | 5 (5) | 15 (6) | 15 (6) |
| Czech Republic | 10 (9) | 10 (9) | 10 | 10 |
| Denmark | 15 | 0 (7) | 5, 15 (8) | 10 |
| Ecuador | 5 (9) | 5 (9) | 10,15 (10) | 10 |
| Finland | Nil | Nil | 10, 15 (11) | 10 |
| France | 0, 5 (9, 12) | 0, 5 (9, 12) | 5, 10 (4, 13) | 10 (4) |
| Germany | 15 | 5 (14) | 10, 15 (15) | 10 |
| Ireland, Rep. of | 10 | 5 (16) | 5, 10, (8) | 10 |
| Israel | 10 | 5 (17) | 10 | 10 |
| Italy | 15 (9) | 15 (9) | 10 (4) | 15 |
| Japan | 15 | 0, 5 (18) | 10, 15 (19) | 10 |
| Korea, Rep. of | 15 | 0 (14) | 5, 15 (8) | 10 |

| | Dividends | | | |
|---|---|---|---|---|
| | Portfolio | Substantial holdings | Interest | Royalties |
| | % | % | % | % |
| Luxembourg.................... | 15 | 8 (20) | 10 (21) | 10 |
| Netherlands.................... | 15 | Nil (22) | 5, 10, 15 (13, 23) | 10 (24) |
| Norway .......................... | 15 | Nil (7) | 10, 15 (2) | 10 |
| Poland ........................... | 15 | 5 (7) | 10, 15 (25) | 10 |
| Portugal......................... | 10 (9) | 10 (9) | 10 | 10 |
| Romania......................... | 10 (9) | 10 (9) | 15 | 15 |
| Singapore....................... | Nil | Nil | 5, 15 (8) | 10 |
| Spain............................. | 15 | 5 (7) | 5, 10, 15 (4, 8, 26) | 10 |
| Sweden ......................... | 15 | 5 (27) | 10, 15 (2) | 10 |
| Switzerland..................... | 15 | 5 (7) | 10, 15 (22) | 10 |
| United Kingdom.............. | Nil | Nil | 5, 10, 15 (13, 23) | 10 |
| United States.................. | 10 | 5 (16) | 4.9, 10, 15 (23, 28) | 10 |

Notes:

The numbers in parentheses refer to the following numbered Notes. The applicable tax rates on interest paid abroad in accordance with the tax treaties executed by Mexico are detailed below; however, as previously mentioned, beginning in 2002, dividends paid to parties resident abroad are no longer subject to withholding tax in Mexico under domestic law.

There are certain specific cases of interest paid to parties resident abroad that might be exempted in terms of certain tax treaties (e.g., interest paid to a pension fund or paid by a bank, interest paid on certain loans granted or guaranteed by certain entities for exports under preferable conditions, etc.), which are not detailed in the information below.

Note that some of the tax treaties signed by Mexico contain a transitory tax rate on interest to be applied during a certain period as from the date on which the tax treaty in question goes into effect. For the purpose of the following information, only the tax rates on interest currently in force are mentioned, and the transitory tax rates are only mentioned when the transitory period has not yet elapsed.

1. This rate applies where the company that is the effective beneficiary of the dividends directly or indirectly owns at least 25% of the capital of the distributing company.
2. The 10% rate applies to loans from banks.
3. This rate applies where a company that is the effective beneficiary of the dividends directly or indirectly owns at least 25% of the voting shares of the payer.
4. Reduced withholding rate resulting from the application of the most favored nation clause.
5. This rate applies where a company that is the effective beneficiary of the dividends owns at least 20% of the voting shares of the company paying the dividends.
6. The protocol of the Mexico/Chile tax treaty provides that if subsequent to the signature of that treaty, Chile concludes an Agreement or Convention with another country whereby Chile agrees to a tax rate that is lower or preferential to the rate specified in the Mexico/Chile treaty with respect to such income,

said lower or preferential rate (that cannot be below 5% on interest on loans from banks and 10% in any other case; 10% in the case of royalties) automatically applies.

7. This rate applies where the company that is the effective beneficiary of the dividends (except for civil partnerships) directly owns at least 25% of the capital of the company distributing dividends. In the case of Norway, the taxation is limited to the country of residence of the party receiving the dividends, provided the above-mentioned substantial holding rule is complied with.

8. The 5% withholding tax rate is applicable to interest paid to banks.

9. This is the maximum withholding rate for dividends, with no distinction for substantial holdings. In the case of Ecuador, the tax payable on dividends paid to residents in Mexico must not exceed a limit established in the treaty

10. During the first five years of the Mexico/Ecuador treaty currently in effect, the 15% rate will be applied to all types of interest. The 10% reduced rate will apply to interest on loans from banks as from December 13, 2005.

11. The 10% rate applies to interest on loans from banks and to interest derived from bonds or securities that are regularly and substantially traded on a recognized securities market, as well as to interest paid by the purchaser of machinery and equipment to a beneficial owner that is the seller of the machinery and equipment in a sale on credit.

12. No withholding applies when more than 50% of the shares of the recipient corporation are owned by residents of France or Mexico or when the effective beneficiary of the dividend is a resident individual. Accordingly, withholding tax applies to dividends when more than 50% of the recipient corporation's shares are owned by residents of other countries. However, the tax withholding must not exceed 5% when the party receiving the dividend is the effective beneficiary of said dividend.

    Dividends paid by a company resident in France to a resident of Mexico, other than a company which directly or indirectly holds at least 10 percent of the capital stock of the first-mentioned company, may also be taxed in France, in accordance with the law of France, but if the recipient of the dividends is the beneficial owner, the tax thus charged must not exceed 15 percent of the gross amount of the dividends.

13. The 5% rate applies to interest on loans from banks and insurance companies and to interest on securities regularly and substantially traded on a recognized national stock exchange.

14. This rate applies when the recipient corporation that is the effective beneficiary of the dividend (except for civil partnerships) directly owns at least 10% of the capital of the distributing corporation.

15. The 10% rate applies to interest on loans from banks, insurance companies, and retirement and pension plans.

16. This rate applies where the recipient corporation that is the effective beneficiary of the dividend owns at least 10% of the voting shares of the paying corporation. The Mexico/U.S. tax treaty contains a most favored nation clause.

17. The 5% rate applies where a company that is the effective beneficiary of dividends directly or indirectly owns at least 10% of the capital of the company distributing the dividends. There is a 10% tax rate that applies when these

same ownership requirements are complied with, but the company paying dividends is a resident of Israel (provided dividends are paid from earnings taxed in Israel at a tax rate lower than the regular corporate tax in Israel).

18. The 5% rate applies when a company that is the effective beneficiary of the dividends owns at least 25% of the voting shares of the company paying dividends during the six months prior to the end of the tax period in which dividends are paid. Under certain particular rules and provided this ownership requirement is complied with, dividend payments are only subject to tax in the country of residence of the recipient of said dividends.

19. The 10% rate applies to interest on loans from banks and insurance companies, to interest on securities regularly and substantially traded on a recognized national stock exchange, to interest paid to the original seller of machinery and equipment, and to interest paid by banks.

20. The applicable tax rate on the gross amount of the dividends when the recipient company (effective beneficiary) (except for civil partnerships) directly holds at least 10% of the capital of the corporation paying the dividend must not exceed 5% in the case of Luxembourg, and 8% in the case of Mexico.

21. The protocol of the Mexico-Luxembourg tax treaty states that this rate might be reviewed in the future by the contracting states if withholding tax is not fully creditable, and can be adjusted under the principle of avoiding double taxation, provided the adjusted withholding rate is not lower than 5%.

22. Dividends paid by a company resident in Mexico to a company resident in the Netherlands (which is the actual beneficiary of said dividends) are subject to a maximum tax of 5% on the gross amount of the dividends, if the beneficial owner is a company that directly or indirectly owns at least 10% of the capital of the company paying said dividends.

    However, as long as a company resident in the Netherlands is not subject to Dutch income tax on dividends received from a company resident in Mexico in the terms of the Dutch income tax law and any future amendments thereto, the dividends mentioned in the preceding paragraph may only be taxed in the Netherlands (not in Mexico).

23. The 10% rate on interest applies in the case of interest paid to the original seller of machinery and equipment and interest paid by banks.

24. The original rate is 15%, but has been reduced to 10%, as long as the Netherlands does not impose a withholding tax.

25. The 10% rate applies to interest on loans from banks, insurance companies, and securities regularly and substantially traded on a recognized national stock exchange.

26. The 10% rate applies on securities regularly and substantially traded on a recognized national stock exchange and on interest paid to the original seller of machinery and equipment.

27. This rate applies where a company that is the effective beneficiary of the dividends (except for civil partnerships, although limited liability partnerships are included) directly owns at least 10% of the voting shares of the company distributing the dividends.

28. The 4.9% rate applies to interest on loans from banks and insurance companies and to interest on securities regularly and substantially traded on a recognized national stock exchange.

# Mexico

## Tax administration

*Returns*/Corporate taxpayers are required to file annual income tax returns and asset tax returns for the preceding calendar year by March 31, and/or to pay any balance of tax shown as due at that time. Controlling (holding) companies in the tax consolidation regime are required to file the annual consolidated tax return within four months following the end of the preceding tax period (i.e., usually by April 30). Thereafter, the taxpayers are generally required to obtain the certification of this tax compliance by an independent auditor and to file the related tax compliance opinion by the end of June. This certification process covers all federal taxes other than custom duties.

Employees' profit sharing is due by May 31 of the following year.

*Payment of tax*/Corporate taxpayers are required to make estimated payments of income tax on the 17th of each month on the basis of their estimated taxable income at the end of the previous month, calculated principally by applying the profit factor to the current monthly gross income (the profit factor is determined by dividing the taxable profit by gross income shown in the annual return for the preceding year, or, if no profit factor is to be found in that annual return, the factor appearing in the year preceding that must be used, and so on, up to five years, with certain adjustments). For this purpose, gross income includes nominal income, excluding inflationary effects.

Definitive monthly VAT payments are required on the 17th of the immediately following month.

Special procedures are provided for computing advance income tax payments, and obtaining authorization to reduce the amounts of monthly advances after the sixth month of the year. No advance payments or adjustments thereto are required in the first year of operations.

Corporations and unincorporated businesses or individuals must also make monthly estimated tax payments during their taxable year on account of the 1.8% minimum tax on assets. Estimated advance payments are computed based on asset tax due in the preceding annual tax period. Estimated income tax payments made as discussed above are creditable against the estimated tax payments required on account of the 1.8% minimum tax on assets. No 1.8% minimum tax is generally payable during the pre-operating period or the first four years of operations.

Information returns must be filed no latter than February 15 of each year, reporting on, among others, the following activities conduced in the immediately preceding year.

1. Payments made to parties resident abroad.
2. Loans received from or guaranteed by nonresidents.
3. Transactions conducted through a business trust.
4. Parties from which the taxpayer withholds income tax.
5. Parties to which the taxpayer has made donations.
6. Parties to which the taxpayer has paid dividends, and the amount of said payments.

Taxpayers making salary payments are also required to file information returns no later than February 15 of each year reporting on salaries paid and on the salary credit paid in the immediately preceding calendar year.

In addition, an annual information tax return must be filed on investments made or held in a tax haven. This must be done in February of the immediately following year.

An information return on transactions carried out with nonresident related parties must be filed together with the corporate annual tax return (no later than March of the following year).

*Statute of limitations*/In general, the right of the tax authorities to collect taxes, review tax returns or claim additional tax expires five years after the date the respective return is filed. However, in cases where the taxpayer has not secured a federal tax registration number, has no accounting records, has failed to keep them for the required ten-year period, or has not filed a tax return, the statute of limitations expires in ten years. Similarly, the period for claiming a refund of overpaid tax expires after five years.

# Mexico

## CORPORATE TAX CALCULATION

Calendar year 2004

## Corporate income tax and employee profit-sharing calculation

| | Taxable income | Profit-sharing base |
|---|---|---|
| Net book income before taxes and profit sharing.......................................................... | Ps 10,000,000 | Ps 10,000,000 |
| Add—Nondeductible expenses: | | |
| Excess provision for bad debts over specific deductible losses.................................... | 180,000* | 180,000* |
| Entertainment and other miscellaneous nondeductible expenses (1) ............................... | 920,000* | 920,000* |
| | 11,100,000 | 11,100,000 |
| Deductions: | | |
| Adjustment to tax cost of fixed assets sold.............. | 100,000** | |
| Depreciation of fixed assets, adjusted for inflation, in excess of book depreciation............................................ | 300,000** | |
| Annual inflationary loss adjustment (2) ................... | 450,000** | |
| Inventory purchases in excess of cost of sales, as per books ......................................... | 1,000,000 | 1,000,000 |
| | Ps 9,250,000 | Ps 10,100,000 |
| Corporate income tax (33% (3) of 9,250,000) rounded out .......................................................... | Ps 3,052,500 | |
| Employee profit sharing (10% of 10,100,000) ............. | | Ps 1,010,000 |

\* Nondeductible items for income tax and profit-sharing purposes.

\*\* Items related to the recognition of inflation for tax purposes, not taken into account in determining the profit-sharing base.

Notes:

1. Includes nondeductible travel expenses, expenses that do not meet all deductibility requirements, and so forth.
2. The annual inflationary gain or loss adjustment is calculated by applying the percentage increase in the National Consumer Price Index to average liabilities and to some credits outstanding, respectively.
3. The corporate income tax rate for 2004, which will be reduced to 32% in 2005.
4. Exchange rate of the peso at March 1, 2004: US$1 = Ps11.0715.

## PwC contact

For additional information on taxation in Mozambique, contact:

M. Isabel Fernandes
PricewaterhouseCoopers
Rovuma Carlton Hotel
Centro de Escritórios, 3º andar, 1
Maputo - Mozambique
Telephone: (258 1) 307620
Fax: (258 1) 307621
e-mail: maria.isabel.fernandes@mz.pwc.com

## Significant developments

Mozambique has been going through a major tax reform as from the beginning of 2003, which has consisted of the replacement of the existing corporate income tax, and the strengthening of the Tax Administration by improving collection procedures and increasing enforcement capacity. Effective January 1, 2003, a new Code on Corporate Income Tax (*CIRPC—Código do Imposto Sobre o Rendimento das Pessoas Colectivas*) came into force.

Mozambique has also introduced, with effect from July 1, 2002, a new Code of Fiscal Benefits, replacing the general tax benefits conceded under the previous Code as well as sectorial incentives granted under specific legal Diplomas.

## Taxes on corporate income

Corporate tax is payable on corporate income at the rate of 32%, except for income arising from agriculture and cattle breeding activities, which is subject to a reduced rate of 10% until 2010. Special rates apply to income generated in Mozambique that is attributable to nonresidents, as described below under "Withholding taxes." Confidential and inadequately documented expenses are not only costs not deductible for tax purposes, but are also taxed separately at the rate of 35%.

## Corporate residence

Corporate tax is assessed on the worldwide income of business entities that have their head office or effective management in Mozambique. Corporate tax is also applicable to the income of nonresident companies deemed to have a permanent establishment in Mozambique.

## Other taxes

*Value-added tax*/VAT is chargeable on the sale of most goods and services, as well on their importation. The standard rate is 17%. Usually, VAT is always recoverable by corporate entities, except for those engaged in special business activities (e.g., financial and insurance operations, leasing (exemption with restrictions), sale of immovable property, etc.).

*Property transfer tax*/In Mozambique, property transfer tax is charged on transfers of real estate, excluding the land, which is owned by the state. The rate of tax is 5% of the selling price for the first transfer, and 10% for any subsequent sales.

# Mozambique

*Property tax on buildings*/The rate of tax is 12% of the annual rental value of buildings, reduced by 10% for maintenance.

*Gifts and inheritance tax*/This tax is payable on transfers of all movable and immovable property by way of gift or bequest to persons resident in Mozambique, or in respect of possessions situated in Mozambique. The tax is payable by the beneficiary, and the rates vary from 0% to 15%, depending upon the degree of relationship between the donor and donee, and upon the value of goods or rights transferred.

*Stamp tax and service charges*/Various documents require the payment of stamp duties. Service charges are payable for the performance of certain services for official purposes, such as those rendered by the Public Notaries. These duties have been recently increased by 500%, that is, multiplied by five times their former rates.

*Municipality taxes*/Municipality taxes that should be considered for corporate purposes include the following.

1.  Municipality tax on real estate—This tax replaces the Property Tax on Buildings on immovable property situated within the municipality. It is levied on the value of immovable assets owned or possessed by corporate entities. Effective tax rates vary from 0.2% to 1% of the value, depending upon the decision of each municipality.
2.  Municipality tax on economic activities—Levied on commercial or industrial activities carried within the municipal territory. Tax rates are to be established annually by each municipality.
3.  Municipal surtax—This local surtax (called *Derrama*) may be imposed by municipalities at a rate up to 15% of the following taxes.
    a.  Corporate tax.
    b.  Tax on real estate.

The local surtax is levied in relation to profits derived from activities carried out in the territory of each municipality.

When the municipalities decide to impose the surtax, the final corporate taxation will be increased by adding the surtax (rated up to a maximum of 15%) to the corporate tax. For example, normal corporate tax (32%) + municipal surtax (15%) = 32% + 4.8% = 36.8%, which is the final corporate tax rate.

## Branch income

From a tax perspective, branches are subject to Mozambican corporate tax as a separate entity and, therefore, the regime is the same that would apply to a Mozambican company. However, on the grounds that branches do not distribute dividends, no withholding tax would apply to the after-tax profits arising in Mozambique.

## Income determination

*Inventory valuation*/Inventories are stated at cost. The FIFO and average-cost methods of valuation are accepted. LIFO is expressly permitted for statutory accounting and is normally accepted by the tax authorities.

It is possible to reduce cost to market value if the latter is lower. This provision can be used only when the loss is realized.

*Capital gains*/Capital gains, less capital losses, derived from tangible fixed assets, including insurance indemnities received in case of accident, are taxed as part of normal income. If the taxpayer reinvests the sale proceeds within the three tax years following the year of sale, the gain is deferred up to the end of the third year. A four-year reinvestment period should be accepted provided a prior application is submitted to the Planning and Finance Minister. However, if the taxpayer does not realize the reinvestment, the corporate tax that was not assessed during the three-year period should be assessed, along with compensatory interest.

*Intercompany dividends*/In the case of resident companies, income arising from dividends are excluded from taxable income, provided that the shares represent at least 25% of the total capital, and that they are held for at least two consecutive years (or with an undertaking to hold them for this period). The same applies to income from risk capital companies and holding companies (*Sociedade Gestora de Participacoes Sociais* (SGPSs)) and income from subsidiaries resulting from the application of technical reserves in insurance companies.

If the shareholding falls outside the parameters indicated above, the tax withheld (20%) constitutes a payment on account. A tax credit corresponding to 60% of the corporate tax is attributable to the gross-up dividend.

*Foreign income*/Mozambican companies are taxed on the totality of income earned on a worldwide basis. Double taxation treaties allow tax paid abroad to be set off against the Mozambican corporate tax. Mozambique has three double tax treaties in force, with Italy (not yet ratified), Portugal, and Mauritius.

*Stock dividends*/Dividends of corporate shares listed in the Mozambican stock exchange are taxed under the withholding regime (20%).

*Other significant items*/Companies in general may create specific provisions for doubtful or bad debts, which are allowed as a tax-deductible cost.

## Deductions

*Depreciation and depletion*/Depreciation is considered as a deductible cost for corporate tax purposes, according to the regulations of the Decree No. 21/2002 of July 30, 2002, although subject to restrictive and specific rules. Depreciation rules are contained in a specific legal diploma, which is *Portaria* No. 20 817, of January 27, 1968. This legal diploma establishes the rates and limits legally allowed for depreciation purposes.

The main legal principles regarding depreciation are as follows.

- The establishment of the applicable rates falls under the competence of the Ministry of Planning and Finance.
- The calculation is carried out on a straight-line basis in accordance with the rates applicable.
- Depreciation can only be deducted from the profits of a financial year when they are duly registered as costs within the same financial year.

# Mozambique

The main depreciation rates are as follows.

## Tangible assets

|  | % |
|---|---|
| Industrial buildings | 4 |
| Office and residential buildings | 2 |
| Machinery and installations, air conditioning, and telephone equipment | 10 |
| Lifts | 8.33 |
| Tools | 25 |
| Laboratory equipment | 12.5 |
| Telex and interior equipment | 10 |
| Furniture and filling systems | 10 |
| Typewriters and accounting machines | 14.28 |
| Computer hardware | 16.66 |
| Warehouse and filing installations: | |
| Of concrete | 5 |
| Of wood | 6.66 |
| Of steel | 8.33 |
| Trucks | 20 |
| Automobiles | 25 |

## Intangible assets

|  | % |
|---|---|
| Preoperating expenses incurred prior to the commencement of business | 33.33 |
| Deferred expenses arising in connection with increases in share capital, changes in form of business enterprises; issuance of debentures; marketing and other studies; financial expenses incurred for the acquisition or own production of fixed assets prior to completion | 33.33 |
| Patents | 10 |
| Manufacturing licenses, concessionaire agreements and similar rights | 5 (1) |
| Trademark or premium of taking over leases of real estate (2) | |

Notes:

1.  Subject to certain conditions set forth by the tax authorities.
2.  Depreciation allowed in cases of effective reduction of value within the limits regarded as reasonable by the tax authorities.

***Net operating losses***/The carryback of losses is not allowed in Mozambique. However, losses can be carried forward for a period of five years.

***Payments to foreign affiliates/related companies***/Any payments to non-Mozambican residents will be allowed as deductible expenses, provided that the amount does not exceed the normal rates, and that the taxpayer is able to prove that a business transaction was in fact carried out with the nonresident company. The Tax Administration may re-determine taxable income if, due to a special relation between the Mozambican and the nonresident company, special conditions existed which allowed a calculation of profit diverse from the profit that would have been calculated without the existence of the special relation.

Where loans from related foreign corporations exceed twice the corresponding equity in the borrowing Mozambican corporation, the interest on the excess borrowing is not tax deductible.

***Taxes***/Taxes paid in relation to the activity of the company are tax deductible, excluding the corporate tax itself.

## Other significant items

The following costs not deductible for tax purposes.

1. *Per diem* and travel of employee in own vehicle: 50% of expenses related to *per diem* and travel of employee in own vehicle are deductible.
2. Entertainment expenses: 80% of entertainment expenses are not deductible.
3. Doubtful debts: The provision for doubtful debts set up in any tax year may not exceed 1.5% per year up to the limit, in aggregate, of 6% of the credits resulting from the normal activity of the company existing at the year-end.
4. Charitable: Donations for social and cultural activities are considered as costs up to 5% of the taxable income of the previous year. Donations to the state are considered as costs in the whole amount.
5. Expenses and costs incurred with passenger cars, including leases or rents, maintenance, repairs, and fuel: 50% is not deductible.
6. Tax paid by the company but legally due from third parties.
7. Fines and other penalties due to any infringement, which do not have a contractual nature, including interests.
8. Compensation paid when the respective risk can be insured.
9. Confidential and not adequately documented expenses.

**Group taxation**/There are no group taxation provisions available in Mozambique. Each member of a group of companies preparing consolidated accounts for accounting purposes must file separate tax returns in order to be taxed on its profits on a stand-alone basis.

## Tax incentives

**Inward investments**/In addition to the guarantees of ownership and remittance abroad of funds, the Mozambican government also guarantees the concession of tax and customs incentives.

**Exemption of import duties**/An exemption from customs duties applies upon the importation of capital equipment, listed in Section K of the Customs Tariff Schedule.

**Tax credit for investment**/Investment in new, fixed tangible assets used in the operations of the enterprise within the Mozambican territory may benefit from an Investment Tax Credit equal to 5% of the total investment realized, for a period of five years. This Investment Tax Credit shall be deductible from the amount of the assessment of the corporate income tax up to the total amount of the tax assessment. This incentive shall not apply when the investment in tangible fixed assets is in respect of the construction, acquisition, restoration or extension of buildings, passenger vehicles, furnishings and articles of comfort and decoration, leisure equipment, advanced technology and other assets not directly associated with the production activity carried out by the enterprise.

**Accelerated depreciation**/New immovable assets, used in the furtherance of the undertakings, may be depreciated at twice the normal rate. This benefit is also granted to rehabilitated immovable assets, machinery, and equipment used in agro-industrial activities.

**Deduction from taxable income**/The amount invested in specialized equipment considered as advanced technology shall, during the first five years from the date of commencement of activity, benefit from a deduction from taxable income for purposes of calculating the corporate income tax up to a maximum of 15% of taxable income. Also, investment expenditure for professional training of Mozambican workers shall, up to a maximum amount of 5% of the taxable income, be deductible from taxable income for the purposes of calculating the corporate income tax during the first five years from the date of commencement of activity.

*Tax deductible expenditure (tax cost)*/During a period of ten years counting from the date of production, the following expenditure may be treated as deductible expenditure for purposes of calculating the corporate income tax.

- In case of undertakings carried out in the city of Maputo, 120% of the value of expenditure in the construction and rehabilitation of roads, railways, airports, telecommunications, water supply, electric energy and other works of public utility.
- In case of the rest of the provinces, an amount equal to 150% of the expenditure referred to in the paragraph above.
- In case of expenditure for the acquisition for personal ownership of works of art and other objects that are representative of the Mozambican culture, as well as activities that contribute to the development of such works, 50% of the expenditure.

## Other generic benefits

- Exemption from stamp tax for the acts of incorporation of companies, including the alteration of the share capital and the articles of association, during the first five years counting from the date of commencement of the investment or the date of commencement of operations.
- A 50% reduction in the rate of the real property transfer tax for the acquisition of immovable property used in industry, agro-industry and hotel industry, provided that the property is acquired within the first three years counting from the date of the authorization of the investment.

*Special additional tax incentives*/Besides the normal regime described above, the current Mozambican Code of Fiscal Benefits also has a specific tax regime established for investments on the following areas.

- Agriculture—An 80% reduction in the tax rate applicable to profits from agricultural ventures, until the year 2012.
- Hotel and tourism—Investment Tax Credit equal to 8% of the total investment realized, for a period of five tax years, and accelerated depreciation, up to three times the normal rate, for new immovable assets, automotive vehicles and other tangible fixed equipment assets when used in hotel and tourism activities.
- Large scale projects—Undertakings having investment that exceed the equivalent to US$500 million, as well as investments in public domain infrastructure carried out under the regime of a concession, may benefit from Investment Tax Credit ranging between 5% and 10% of the total investment realized, and other benefits on import duties, real property transfer tax and stamp duty.
- Rapid development zones—Investment carried out in the Zambezi Valley, Niassa Province, Nacala District, Moçambique Island, and Ibo Island shall benefit from the following.

- Besides the exemption from import duties on the importation of goods included in class K of the Customs Tariff Schedule, also the exemption on the importation of goods included in class "I" of the said Schedule.
- Investment Tax Credit equal to 20% the total investment realized, during the first five tax years.
- Exemption from real property transfer tax, provided that the property is an infrastructure to be used on the development of economic activities.
- Industrial free zones
  - Exemption from customs duties on the importation of construction materials, machinery, equipment, accessories, accompanying spare parts and other goods destined to the exercise of the activity licensed as an Industrial Free Zone.
  - A 60% reduction in the rate of corporate income tax on the profits derived from the exercise of the activities, for a period of ten years.
  - Exemption from real property transfer tax payable on the acquisition and use of immovable assets.
- Mining activity
  - Exemption from customs duties on the importation of equipments, apparatus, materials, and spare parts for prospecting and exploration, mineral production and the exportation of mineral resources.
  - The imports referred to in the paragraph above shall also benefit from an exemption on VAT and Specific Consumption Tax.
  - A 25% reduction in the rate of the corporate income tax for investments that exceed US$500,000, during the first five years from the date of commencement of production, and until the year 2010.
- Petroleum activity
  - Exemption from customs duties with regard to the importation of goods destined to be used in petroleum operations, vehicles and other imported supplies, excluding passenger vehicles.
  - Temporary importation with suspension of payment of duties and other customs and fiscal charges on goods destined for use on petroleum operations.
  - Exemption from customs duties on the exportation of the goods referred to in the paragraph above, once such goods are no longer needed for the petroleum operations.
  - Exemption of customs duties and customs charges with regards to the exportation of petroleum produced in Mozambique.
  - The imports and exports referred to in the preceding paragraphs shall also benefit from an exemption on the VAT.
  - A 25% reduction in the rate of the corporate income tax, during the first eight years from the date of commencement of production, and until the year 2010.

## Petroleum Production Tax

Petroleum Production Tax shall be paid on all petroleum produced in Mozambique, being the producer thereof subject to this tax obligation.

Petroleum Production Tax shall be paid each month on the quantities of petroleum produced in the previous month.

The rates of this tax vary from 8% to 12.5% for crude petroleum.

When exploration takes place in deep waters, the rates are as follows.
- A rate of 8% up to 250m depth.
- A rate of 6% between 250m and 500m depth.
- A rate of 4% between 500m and 1000m depth.
- A rate of 2% over 1000m depth.

The payment of the Petroleum Production Tax may be in-kind, or in cash, at the option of the government.

Payment will be in kind unless the government notifies the taxpayer to the contrary, by giving notice at least 190 days prior to the first day of the month to which the tax refers.

Whenever the government establishes the payment in kind, the Petroleum Production Tax shall be paid by the end of each month by delivering to the government, or other duly authorized entity, 15% of the quantity of petroleum produced during the previous month.

Whenever the government establishes the payment in cash, the Petroleum Production Tax due at the end of each month shall be calculated by the application of the above mentioned tax rates to the petroleum produced during the previous month.

## Mining tax regime

According to the mining tax regime in force in Mozambique, the mining activity is subject to Production Tax, levied upon the mineral product arising out of the mining activity, which rates are established by the Minister's Council, and vary form 10% to 12% for diamonds, and 3% to 8% for the remaining mining products.

The mining activity is also subject to Land Tax, which rate has not been established yet.

## Withholding taxes

Any non-Mozambican resident entity carrying out an economic activity in Mozambique, without being registered as a taxpayer, is subject to a final 20% withholding tax, applied on the net income proceeding from the following.
- Intellectual or industrial property.
- Information related to an industrial, commercial or scientific experience.
- Using of agricultural, industrial, commercial, or scientific equipment.
- Investment of capital.
- Income from real estate.
- Remunerations of statutory bodies of companies.
- Prizes from gambling, lottery and contests.
- Shows and sports professional activities.
- Intermediation of contracts and rendering of services.

*Tax Treaties*/Mozambique has three double tax treaties (DTT) in force, with Italy (not yet ratified), Portugal, and Mauritius.

In accordance with these double tax treaties, the following tax rates will be applicable to dividends, royalties and interest.

| Double Tax Treaties | Tax rate % on net dividends | | |
|---|---|---|---|
| | Italy | Portugal | Mauritius |
| Dividends | 15% | 15% | 8%—If the recipient of the dividends is a company which has more than 25% of the share capital in the company that distributes the dividends. 10%—If the recipient is a company, which has less than 25% of the share capital in the company that distributes the dividends. 15%—In all other cases. |
| Interest | 10% | 10% | 8% |
| Royalties | 10% | 10% | 5% |

## Tax administration

*Returns*/The tax year is, as a general rule, the calendar year. A different tax year may be applied for in case of companies that carry out activities that justify a different year, or in case of nonresident companies with permanent establishment in Mozambique.

Corporate tax assessment must be prepared by the companies on annual returns, based on the accounting records.

The presentation of the accounts is due by the last working day of May, for companies using the calendar year as their tax year. In case of companies with a tax year not coincident with the calendar year, the presentation of accounts is due by the last day of the fifth month subsequent to the respective year-end.

*Payments*/Mozambican companies and nonresident companies with permanent establishment in Mozambique shall pay corporate tax in the following manner.

- In three advance on account payments, due in May, July, and September of the respective tax year; or if the tax year chosen is not coincident with the calendar year, on the fifth, seventh, and ninth months of the respective tax year.
- The difference between the total amount reflected on the accounts and the on account payments, by the last working day of May, or if the tax year chosen is not coincident with the calendar year, by the last day of the fifth month subsequent to the respective year-end.

# Mozambique

## *CORPORATION TAX CALCULATION*

Fiscal year ending December 31, 2003 (calendar-year basis)

| | |
|---|---|
| Pretax profit as stated in the statutory account........................ | MZM 60,000,000,000 |

Includes

| | |
|---|---|
| Gross dividend received from a company (20% equity)........ | 600,000,000 |
| Gross dividend received (40% equity held for three years) .................................................................... | 550,000,000 |
| Gross interest received on term deposits account ............... | 10,000,000 |

Adjustments to book income

Add (deduct)

| | |
|---|---|
| Gross dividend received (40% equity held for three years) .................................................................... | (550,000,000) |
| 60% of corporate tax paid on dividends received from (20% equity) ................................................................ | 169,411,765(*) |
| Depreciation in excess of tax rates ...................................... | 35,000,000 |
| Assessable income ................................................................ | MZM 59,654,411,765 |

Computation of tax

| | |
|---|---|
| Corporate tax at 32%.............................................................. | MZM 19,089,411,765 |

Less:

| | |
|---|---|
| 60% of corporate tax paid on dividends received from (20% equity) ................................................................ | 169,411,765(*) |
| Corporate tax withheld on account: | |
| Dividends paid (20% equity) ................................................. | 120,000,000 |
| Interest ................................................................................. | 2,000,000 |
| Tax payable ........................................................................... | MZM 18,798,000,000 |

Note:

(*) (600,000,000/(1-0.32)) x 0.32 x 0.60 = 169,411,765

Exchange rate at January 1, 2004: USD$1 = MZM23,215 (Metical).

## PwC contact

For additional information on taxation in Namibia, contact:

Albe Botha
PricewaterhouseCoopers
Windhoek, Namibia
Telephone: (264) (61) 284 1000
Fax: (264) (61) 284 1260
e-mail: albe.botha@na.pwc.com

## Significant developments

We expect major developments and improvements to the income tax system are expected in the fields of capital gain tax, estate duty, and transfer pricing. No draft legislation has been issued to date, but it is expected in due course.

## Taxes on corporate income

Taxes on corporate income are levied at the following rates.

|  | % |
| --- | --- |
| On distributed or undistributed profits of local corporations and branches | 35.0 |
| For diamond mining corporations and branches: | |
| On distributed and undistributed profits | 55.0 |
| For other mining corporations and branches: | |
| On distributed and undistributed profits | 37.5 |
| For life insurance companies: | |
| On investment income only | 14.0 |

## Corporate residence

Corporate residence is determined by whether the company is deemed to have permanent establishment in the country. For tax purposes, permanent establishment is the fixed place in which a foreign company undertakes all, or part, of its activities.

## Other taxes

*Value-added tax*/This tax is levied at the rates of either 15% or 0% whenever ownership of goods changes, goods are imported, and services are rendered. Most goods and services are taxed at a rate of 15%. Certain goods and services, which are explicitly listed in the law, are subject to the 0% rate. VAT paid or accrued on the purchase of goods is compensated by taxes paid or accrued in their selling; differences are payable or carried forward as tax credits. When goods are imported there is also a surcharge of 10% payable, which results in import VAT amounting to 16.5% instead of 15%.

## Branch income

Distributed or retained branch profits are taxed at the aforementioned 35% rate. No further taxes are payable when profits are remitted to headquarters in countries with which Namibia has a double taxation agreement.

# Namibia, Republic of

## Income determination

*Inventory valuation*/The valuation of inventories is based on the FIFO basis.

*Intercompany dividends*/Dividends received by a company from other domestic companies are exempt from income taxes. The same treatment applies to dividends received by a branch of a foreign company from a local company.

*Foreign income*/Namibian income tax is based on the source principals. Foreign income may in certain limited cases be deemed to be from a source in Namibia.

## Deductions

*Depreciation and depletion*/The rates used in the calculation of depreciation for income tax purposes (called wear and tear) are set as follows.

|  | % |
|---|---|
| Newly erected buildings (excluding land) | |
|     Initial allowance in the year of erection completion | 20 |
|     Annual allowance for 20 years after year of erection completion | 4 |
| All furniture, equipment, motor vehicles, and computers | 33 |
| Intangible assets | Useful life |

Depreciation rates apply to the cost of assets.

*Net operating losses*/The carrying forward of tax losses is allowed.

*Payments to foreign affiliates*/In most cases, payments made abroad are deductible, as long as withholding of income taxes has been performed. Payments for goods imported are not subject to withholding of income taxes.

*Taxes*/Taxes, rates, levies, and contributions on activities that help generate taxable income are deductible. Interest and fines paid as penalties caused by delay of payment of due tax obligations or social security obligations are not deductible. Nor are income taxes deductible.

## Tax incentives

*Registered manufacturers*/Special tax incentives are available to registered manufacturers approved by the Ministry of Trade and Industry and Ministry of Finance. To qualify for registration such manufacturing enterprises must be beneficial to the economic development of Namibia or the economic advancement of it inhabitants by meeting the requirements of the income tax act. The incentives available include the following.

- Special deduction rates for erection of buildings.
- Special allowance on training expenses incurred.
- Special allowance on manufacturing staff expenses.
- Special allowance on export expenses incurred in a foreign country.
- Special allowance on transport costs incurred.
- A special income tax rate on distributed and undistributed profits of 18%.

*Export processing zone*/New enterprises that export to countries outside the South African Customs Union (SACU) can qualify for export processing zone (EPZ) status. The benefits of an EPZ enterprise are as follows.

- Relief from corporate income tax, import duties and stamp duties, but excluding tax on employees' income and withholding tax on dividends.

- Training grants of 75% of training costs.
- Foreign currency bank accounts, free of exchange control.
- Relief from certain Labor Act provisions.

## Withholding taxes

*Nonresident shareholders tax*/This tax is levied on dividends paid to foreign shareholders at 10% of the dividend payable to the foreign shareholder. Double tax agreements with certain countries state other rates to be used in the calculation of Nonresident Shareholders Tax.

*Withholding tax on royalties*/A withholding tax is payable on royalties paid to foreign sources at 10.5% of the royalty. Double tax agreements with certain countries state other rates to be used in the calculation of withholding tax.

*Tax treaties*/Namibia currently has tax treaties with France, Germany, India, Mauritius, Romania, Russian Federation, South Africa, Sweden, and the United Kingdom.

## Tax administration

*Returns*/A fiscal year goes from March 1 to February 28/29. The tax system operates on the basis of self-assessment, with subsequent inspection by the tax authorities.

*Tax payment*/Businesses must file their corporate income tax returns within seven months after year end.

Corporations are required to pay tax advances in two payments (the first six months after the start of a financial year, the second at year-end). The amount of the advances to be paid is determined based on an estimated taxable income calculation.

## CORPORATION TAX CALCULATION

Fiscal year 2003*

| | | |
|---|---:|---:|
| Income (including $800 cash dividend and $3,200 of interest and capital gains received) | | $ 40,000 |
| Deduct: | | |
|   Cash dividend received | 800 | |
|   Capital gain received | 3,200 | 4,000 |
| Taxable profits | | 36,000 |
| Tax payable (at 35%) | | 12,600 |
| Less: | | |
|   Advanced payments | 11,400 | (11,400) |
| Net tax payable | | $ 1,200 |

Note:
*All transactions are presently made and accounted for in US$.

# The Netherlands

## PwC contacts

For additional information on taxation in the Netherlands, contact:

George de Soeten
PricewaterhouseCoopers N.V.
Marten Meesweg 25
3068 AV Rotterdam
The Netherlands
Telephone: (31) (10) 4075 500
Fax: (31) (10) 4564 333
LN address: George de Soeten/NL/TLS/PwC
e-mail: george.de.soeten@nl.pwc.com

Mail address:
P.O. Box 8800
3009 AV Rotterdam
The Netherlands

Knowledge managers
Ingrid Berger
e-mail: ingrid.berger@nl.pwc.com
Bart Jansen
e-mail: bart.jansen@nl.pwc.com

## Significant developments

On September 18, 2003, the European Court of Justice ruled on the so-called Bosal case. The provision in the Dutch Corporate Income Tax Act that determines that (financing) costs, attributable to shareholdings in foreign companies qualifying for the participation exemption are not deductible, is in breach of EU law, according to the Court. The Dutch legislator responded to this ruling of the court with new legislation. Based on this legislation, costs relating to qualifying participations are deductible, regardless whether they are foreign or Dutch. To set off the resulting decrease in tax revenue, thin capitalization rules were introduced as per January 1, 2004 (see below). Furthermore, limitations on loss utilization for holding/finance companies were introduced (see below).

## Taxes on corporate income

Corporate income is taxed in accordance with the Dutch Corporate Income Tax Act of 1969, at a rate of 34.5%. The first €22,689, however, are taxed at a rate of 29%. There are no provincial or municipal corporate income taxes.

## Corporate residence

The corporate residence is determined by each corporation's circumstances. Management and control are important factors in this respect. Companies incorporated under Dutch law are deemed to be residents of the Netherlands (although, not in respect to certain provisions, e.g., participation exemption).

## Branch income

Rates for branch profits are the same as for other corporate profits, but no tax is withheld on transfers of profits to the head office.

## Other taxes

*Value-added tax*/Known in Dutch as BTW (*Belasting over de Toegevoegde Waarde*), VAT is payable on sales of goods and on services rendered in the

Netherlands, as well as on the importation of goods and on the "intra-European" acquisition of goods. There are three tax rates, as shown below.

|  | % |
| --- | --- |
| Main tariff | 19 |
| Reduced tariff on certain prime necessities | 6.0 |
| Special tariff, applicable mainly to intra-European Union supplies; exports, imports stored in bonded warehouses; services rendered in connection with the above; and certain other services | 0.0 |

The following are exempt from tax.

1. The supply of immovable property two years after putting it into use and lease. However, if the lessee's use of the immovable property is 90% or more for input VAT-deductible purposes, the lessor and lessee may opt to be subject to VAT on rent, in which case the lessor may deduct the VAT charged in respect of the property.

2. Medical, cultural, social, and educational services.

3. Services provided by banks and other financial institutions in connection with payment transactions and the granting of credit facilities.

4. Insurance transactions.

5. Transactions in shares.

***Transfer tax on immovable property***/Acquisition of economic or legal ownership of immovable property in the Netherlands is subject to 6% transfer tax on market value; some exemptions are available.

***Capital tax***/Capital tax is payable once only on each contribution to the capital of a Dutch company. The tax is levied at the rate of 0.55% of the par value of shares issued or the actual value of the contribution, whichever is higher. So-called informal contributions to capital (e.g., contributions to capital for which no shares are issued) are also subject to capital tax. There are several exemption possibilities.

***Additional corporate income tax***/Subject to certain conditions, a 20% additional corporate income tax will have to be paid by an entity distributing so-called excessive profit distributions. The 20% surtax could be due on excessive dividends paid in the years 2001 up to and including 2005 ("distribution levy"). The levy is not due to the extent that shareholders have owned 5% or more of the shares in the Dutch company concerned for a period of three years or more.

***Other indirect taxes***/Insurance tax of 7% is payable on insurance premiums if the party taking out the policy is a resident of the Netherlands or if the insured object is in the Netherlands. (Several exemptions are available.)

Municipalities impose immovable property tax on both the owners and the users of the immovable property. The rates depend on the municipality. The taxable basis is the market value of the immovable property.

Excise tax is levied on certain consumer goods (e.g., cigarettes, cigars, mineral oils, alcoholic products, etc.). If the goods are used solely as raw materials, no excise tax is levied. Excise tax is refundable if an article is exported.

# The Netherlands

## Income determination

*Inventory valuation*/In general, inventories are stated at the lower of cost or market value. Cost may be determined on the basis of FIFO, LIFO, base stock, or average cost. The LIFO system can be used for commercial and tax purposes, but there is no requirement of conformity between commercial and tax reporting.

*Capital gains*/Capital gains are taxed as ordinary income. However, capital gains realized on disposal of a shareholding qualifying for the participation exemption, are tax exempt (discussed under "Intercompany dividends" below). The gain on disposal of depreciable assets may be carried over to a special tax deferral reinvestment reserve, but must then be deducted from the acquisition cost of the later acquired assets. Except in special circumstances, the reserve cannot be maintained for more than three consecutive years. If the reserve has not been fully applied after three years, the remainder will be liable to taxation. Capital losses are deductible unless attributable to the disposal of a shareholding qualifying for the participation exemption.

Shareholdings of at least 25% qualifying for the participation exemption may be depreciated within five years from the date of their acquisition if their market value falls below the acquisition price. The consequent loss is deductible but must be recovered within a period of, at most, ten years as from the acquisition.

*Intercompany dividends*/Subject to fulfillment of the conditions for the participation exemption, a Dutch company or branch of a foreign company is exempt from Dutch tax on all "benefits" connected with a qualifying shareholding, including cash dividends, dividends-in-kind, bonus shares, hidden profit distributions, and capital gains.

In general, the participation exemption will apply to a shareholding in a Dutch company if the holding is at least 5% of the investee's capital and the shares are not held as inventory.

Two additional conditions apply to participations in non-Dutch companies.

1. The shareholding is a nonportfolio investment.
2. The investee company is subject to a central-government-level profits tax in the state of residence.

Foreign intragroup financing participations are deemed to be held as portfolio investments, unless credible evidence can be given that the foreign participation is actively engaged in intragroup financing activities. In that case the participation exemption will apply.

The portfolio test for the participation exemption is relaxed where the participation is held in a company resident in another European Union (EU) member state, provided the investment qualifies under the EU Parent/Subsidiary Directive and the investee company does not benefit from a special tax regime. However, as from January 1, 2003, the participation exemption does not apply to such an EU subsidiary, if the possessions of that company mainly consist, directly or indirectly, of the following.

Participations in companies that, if they were held directly, would not qualify for the participation exemption. Compared to the current regulation it will no longer make any difference where the latter mentioned subsidiaries are situated (i.e., EU or outside EU).

Assets in a third country which, if they were held by the taxpayer directly, based on a regulation for avoidance of double taxation (tax treaties) would not result in an exemption for corporate income tax for the profits derived from them.

Counterproof is possible if the interposition of the EU company is in leading degree administered by other grounds than tax avoidance.

Dividends not qualifying under the participation exemption are taxable in full at the ordinary corporate income tax rate.

*Foreign income*/A Dutch resident company is subject to corporate tax on its total worldwide income. Double taxation of certain foreign-source income, including foreign branch income, is avoided by reducing Dutch tax by the ratio of foreign income (subject to a foreign income tax and/or covered by certain tax treaty provisions) to total income, the so-called exemption method. (Currency exchange profits or losses on the head office's investment in its foreign branch are not considered "foreign income" for the purposes of these relief provisions.) Unilateral relief from double taxation for income from foreign financing branches is provided by means of a credit of 17.5% of the passive financing income for foreign taxes deemed paid or the foreign tax actually paid. Nevertheless, the exemption method will apply if the taxpayer can demonstrate that the foreign branch is actively engaged in intragroup financing activities.

Double taxation of foreign dividends, interest and royalties is relieved by a tax credit provided by Dutch tax treaties or unilaterally if the payer of the income streams is a resident of a designated developing country. If no treaty or unilateral relief applies, a deduction of the foreign tax paid is allowed in computing net taxable income. However, relief by exemption is given for dividends from foreign investments qualifying for the participation exemption (see above). In that case, there is no Dutch tax to credit against taxes withheld in the subsidiary's country of residence.

In most circumstances, the foreign dividend is exempt for Dutch corporate tax under the participation exemption. As a consequence, foreign withholding taxes cannot be credited, and they constitute a real cost for the companies concerned. A credit of the foreign withholding tax is granted against Dutch dividend withholding tax due on the distribution to foreign parents of the Dutch company. The credit amounts to a maximum of 3% of the gross dividend paid, to the extent that it can be paid out of foreign-source dividends received that have suffered at least 5% withholding tax and the foreign company is liable to corporate tax. This tax credit does not form taxable income for corporate income tax purposes.

*Stock dividends*/Stock dividends are taxed as dividend income to the extent that they are paid out of earned surplus. They are not taxable if paid out of share premium (so-called agio), provided the share premium account was not created pursuant to a share-for-share merger in which only Dutch companies were involved. In the case of a share-for-share merger, in which shares in foreign subsidiaries were contributed to a Dutch company, the Dutch company can distribute the difference between the fair market value and the paid-in capital of the subsidiaries being contributed as a stock dividend without triggering Dutch dividend withholding tax (step-up in basis), provided certain requirements are met.

# The Netherlands

## Deductions

***Depreciation and depletion*** /Depreciation may be computed by a straight-line or a reducing-balance method or, in accordance with any other sound business practice on the basis of historical cost. Depreciation is applied from the date the asset comes into use. Dutch tax law does not prescribe specific depreciation rates and does not require that commercial and tax depreciation coincide, although in practice they will often be similar. Depreciation of land is not permitted.

The sale of depreciated assets triggers tax on the difference between the sale price and the depreciated book value unless a reinvestment reserve is set up (discussed under "Capital gains").

The law provides for accelerated depreciation of specific assets (see "Tax incentives").

A depletion allowance for natural resources may be granted for tax purposes when it conforms to sound business practice and is appropriate for accounting purposes.

***Net operating losses*** /Losses may be carried forward indefinitely. Loss carryback is permitted for three years.

Complex rules may prohibit the utilization of net operating losses after a change of 30% or more of the ultimate control in a company. Furthermore, as per January 1, 2004, new limitations on the possibilities for loss utilization for holding/finance companies were introduced. Based on these new rules, losses incurred by a pure holding or group finance company can be offset only against holding or finance income in preceding and following years, provided that certain strict conditions are met. These conditions are meant to counter tax planning whereby the Dutch company concerned acquires (e.g., by way of equity contribution or exchange) other assets that enhance its income streams and therefore its capacity to make use of the losses. Companies carrying out significant other activities (with 25 or more employees) are in principle unaffected by these loss relief restrictions. These new rules apply to all loss carryforwards available at January 1, 2004 as well as future losses to be incurred.

***Payments to foreign affiliates*** /A Dutch corporation can generally claim a deduction for royalties, management service fees, and interest charges paid to foreign affiliates, to the extent that the amounts are not in excess of what it would pay an unrelated entity (i.e., arm's length principle). Dutch companies are obliged to produce transfer pricing documentation describing the calculation of the transfer price and the comparability of the transfer price with third party prices.

***Interest on intragroup debts*** /Interest paid on intragroup debts relating to certain transactions is excluded from deduction, unless the taxpayer gives credible evidence of overriding commercial reasons for the transaction as well as the l oan, or of effective taxation of the interest in the hands of the recipient that is comparable to Dutch taxation as far as the base and rate of taxation are concerned. Furthermore, interest on certain profit depending or participating loans will be qualified as dividend and will thus not be tax deductible. Interest paid upon these loans might fall under the participation exemption, if the creditor also holds a qualifying participation in the debtor. Intragroup conduits may be denied a credit of foreign withholding tax with respect to royalties or interest received, if no economical risk is deployed.

As of January 1, 2004, new limitations on the deductibility on interest paid on intragroup debts were introduced in the form of thin capitalization rules. These rules apply to all Dutch companies that are part of a domestic or international group of companies. The allowed debt-to-equity ratio is 3:1, based on the average of the tax equity at the beginning and at the end of the year. A higher ratio may apply at the request of the taxpayer if the group to which the Dutch company belongs has, according to the financial statements, a higher, worldwide debt-to-equity ratio. Interest paid on loans exceeding the 3:1 ratio, are disallowed only to the extent it exceeds intercompany interest received. The deduction of interest paid on genuine third party loans is not limited by the thin capitalization rules.

***Taxes***/Certain taxes are deductible. They may include capital tax and tax paid on insurance transactions. Tax paid on the transfer of immovable property must be included in the cost price and taken into account in the course of normal depreciation.

***Other deductions***/Deduction of certain expenses (e.g., especially costs for food, drink, and entertainment) paid by employers for employees is limited to 90% of the expenses (so-called Oort expenses). The limitation applies only if one or more employees own at least 5% of the shares (a substantial interest) in the employer's company. Alternatively, employers can opt for a 100% cost deduction taking into account a threshold of nondeductible expenses of €1,500 per employee with a substantial interest.

## Group taxation

A parent company and its Dutch-resident subsidiaries (if the parent owns at least 95% of the shares) may, under certain conditions, file a tax return as one entity ("fiscal unity"). Group taxation is available for companies having their place of effective management in the Netherlands, both for Dutch tax and treaty purposes. Interest on intragroup debts relating to takeovers, where the acquiring company enters into a fiscal unity with the target company, is deductible only from the profits the parent company would have realized without the fiscal unity during the first eight years after the takeover.

## Tax incentives

***Small investments***/A system of allowances for small investments is in place. To calculate this annual allowance, investments of more than €450 each are totaled to determine the percentage of the allowance. Under the system a deduction from corporate income of 25% of the value of the total investments is granted on investments ranging from €2,000 to €33,000, with the percentage declining along a sliding scale to 3% if the investments amount to between €254,000 and €286,000. For total investments in a year of more than €286,000, no allowance is given.

***Investments in energy-efficient assets***/For investments in energy-efficient assets, there is a deduction from corporate income tax of 55% of the value of the total annual investments from €2,000 to €106,000,000.

***Investments in environmental investments***/For investments in certain new environmental assets exceeding €2,000 per calendar year, there is a deduction of corporate income tax of 40%, 30%, or 15%, respectively, depending on the ministerial classification of the assets.

*Investments in co-participations in film companies*/For investments in co-participations in film companies producing designated films mainly for the Dutch market an investment deduction of 47% can be made, for investments ranging between €2,000 and €25,000.

*New technology*/Research into and development of applied new technology are subsidized by a reduction of wage tax to be paid on wages of employees engaged in research into or development of technologically new products. The subsidy accrues to the employer; the employee is credited for the normal (unreduced) amount of wage tax. The benefit for each employer (or group of companies) may not exceed €7,941,154 per year.

To obtain the relief under the research and development (R&D) incentive program, taxpayers must file an application with the Ministry of Economic Affairs. The budget for this subsidy is fixed, so the amount of the subsidy is dependent on the budget still available.

*Discretionary depreciation*/Accelerated depreciation of up to 100% is allowed for investments in the following assets.

1. Assets at least 30% of whose environment-improving results accrue to the Netherlands and that appear on the so-called VAMIL (*Vervroegde Afschrijving Milieu Investeringen*) list.
2. Assets that improve working conditions.
3. Production costs of qualifying Dutch films.

Accelerated depreciation is also possible for certain other designated assets, for example, investments of starting entrepreneurs.

Investment costs minus residual value of sea-vessels that are operated mainly from the Netherlands may be depreciated linearly over five years. Instead of accelerated depreciation, the taxpayer may choose lump-sum taxation.

Further, reductions of wage tax to be paid on wages of employees are, for example, available for companies incurring costs for, daycare facilities or paid parental leave.

## Withholding taxes

Domestic corporations are required to withhold taxes as follows.

| Recipient | Dividends (stock/cash) | Interest (1) | Royalties and certain rentals (1) | Personal services (1) |
|---|---|---|---|---|
| | % | % | % | % |
| Resident corporations ........ | Nil or 25 | Nil | Nil | Nil |
| Resident individuals ........... | 25 | Nil | Nil | Nil |
| Nonresident corporations and individuals: | | | | |
| Nontreaty........................... | 25 | Nil | Nil | Nil |
| Treaty: | | | | |
| Argentina........................ | 15 or 10 (2) | | | |
| Armenia.......................... | 15 or 0–5 (3, 4) | | | |
| Australia ........................ | 15 (5) | | | |
| Austria........................... | Nil (6)/15 or 5 (3,7) | | | |
| Bangladesh .................... | 15 or 10 (8) | | | |

| Recipient | Dividends (stock/cash) | Interest (1) | Royalties and certain rentals (1) | Personal services (1) |
|---|---|---|---|---|
| | % | % | % | % |
| Belarus | Nil, 15 or 0−5 (2, 9) | | | |
| Belgium | Nil (6)/15 or 5 (2) | | | |
| Brazil | 15 | | | |
| Bulgaria | 15 or 5 (2) | | | |
| Canada | 15 or 5 (10) | | | |
| China, P.R. | 10 (5,11) | | | |
| Croatia | 15 or 0 (8) | | | |
| Czech Republic | 10 or Nil (2) | | | |
| Denmark | Nil (6)/15 or Nil (5, 8) | | | |
| Egypt | Nil/15 | | | |
| Estonia | 15/5 (2) | | | |
| Finland | Nil (6)/15 or Nil (8) | | | |
| France | Nil (6)/15 or 5 (2, 5) | | | |
| Germany | Nil (6)/15 or 10 (5, 12) | | | |
| Greece | Nil (6)/15 or 5 (2, 5) | | | |
| Hungary | 15 or 5 (2) | | | |
| Iceland | 15 or Nil (8) | | | |
| India | 15 (5) | | | |
| Indonesia | 15/10 (2, 5, 13) | | | |
| Ireland, Rep. of | Nil (6)/15 or Nil (5, 14) | | | |
| Israel | 15 or 5 (2) | | | |
| Italy | Nil (6)/15, 10 or 5 (15) | | | |
| Japan | 15 or 5 (5, 16) | | | |
| Kazakhstan | 15, 5 (17, 18) | | | |
| Korea, Rep. of | 15 or 10 (2) | | | |
| Kuwait | 10 or 0 (8) | | | |
| Latvia | 15 or 5 (2) | | | |
| Lithuania | 15 or 5 | | | |
| Luxembourg | Nil (6, 19)/15 or 2.5 (2, 19) | | | |
| Macedonia | 15 or 0 (8) | | | |
| Malawi | 25 (20) | | | |
| Malaysia | 15 or Nil (7) | | | |
| Malta | 15 or 5 (2) | | | |
| Mexico | 15 or 5 (17) | | | |
| Moldavia | 15, 5 or Nil (21, 22, 23) | | | |

# The Netherlands

| Recipient | Dividends (stock/cash) | Interest (1) | Royalties and certain rentals (1) | Personal services (1) |
|---|---|---|---|---|
| | % | % | % | % |
| Morocco | 25 or 10 (2) | | | |
| Netherlands Antilles | 15, 5–7 or 2-8,3 (24) | | | |
| New Zealand | 15 | | | |
| Nigeria | 15 or 12.5 (8) | | | |
| Norway | 15 or 0 (2) | | | |
| Pakistan | 20 or 10 (2) | | | |
| Philippines | 15 or 10 (8) | | | |
| Poland | 15 or Nil (2) | | | |
| Portugal | Nil (6)/10 | | | |
| Romania | 15 or 0–5 (25) | | | |
| Russian Federation | 15 or 5 (26) | | | |
| Serbia-Montenegro | 15 or 5 (2) | | | |
| Singapore | 15 or Nil (7) | | | |
| Slovak Republic | 10 or Nil (2) | | | |
| Slovenia | 15 or 5 (2, 5) | | | |
| South Africa | 15 or 5 (5, 14) | | | |
| Soviet Union | 15 (27) | | | |
| Spain | Nil (6)/15 or 5 (5, 28) | | | |
| Sri Lanka | 15 or 10 (2) | | | |
| Suriname | 20, 15 or 7.5 (2) | | | |
| Sweden | Nil (6)/15 or Nil (2) | | | |
| Switzerland | 15 or Nil (2, 5) | | | |
| Taiwan | 10 | | | |
| Thailand | 25 or 5 (2) | | | |
| Tunisia | 20 or 0 (8) | | | |
| Turkey | 20 or 5-15 (2) | | | |
| Ukraine | 15, 10 or Nil (29, 30) | | | |
| United Kingdom | Nil (6)/15 or 5 (5, 14) | | | |
| United States | 15 or 5 (31) (32) | | | |
| Uzbekistan | Nil, 5 or 15 (33) | | | |
| Venezuela | 10 or Nil (2) | | | |
| Vietnam | 15, 7 or 5 (34) | | | |
| Zambia | 15 or 5 (2) | | | |
| Zimbabwe | 20 or 10 (2) | | | |

Notes:

1. A nil withholding tax rate applies to payments to a resident corporation when its shareholding qualifies for the participation exemption and the shares form part of a company whose activities are carried on in the Netherlands. However, dividend withholding tax may be levied on certain profit participating loans.
2. The lower rate applies if the foreign company owns directly at least 25% of the capital of the Dutch company.

3. The 5% rate is applicable if the foreign company directly owns 10% of capital of the Dutch company. The 0% rate is applicable if the dividend originates from ordinary taxed profits and the dividend is tax exempt in the hands of the recipient.

4. The treaty has been negotiated, but is not effective yet.

5. Revisions of protocol are currently being negotiated with the following countries: Australia, Austria, the People's Republic of China, Denmark, Greece, Japan, Poland, and the United Kingdom. The treaties with France, Germany, India, Indonesia, the Republic of Ireland, Luxembourg, Spain, and Switzerland are being renegotiated. Tax treaties are currently under negotiation with Albania, Azerbaijan, Bolivia, Chile, Croatia, Cuba, Cyprus, Ecuador, Georgia, Iran, Jordan, Kyrgyzstan, Kuwait, Mongolia, Peru, Saudi Arabia, Slovenia, Small Yugoslavia, Turkmenistan, Uganda, and the United Arab Emirates.

6. Indicates member state of the European Union. The EU Parent/Subsidiary Directive applies from January 1, 1992. According to the Directive, dividends paid by a Dutch company (BV or NV (*naamloze vennootschap*)) to a qualifying parent company resident in another EU member state must be exempt from Dutch withholding tax, provided certain conditions are met. Among other things, the EU parent company must hold at least 25% of the Dutch dividend-paying company's capital (or, in certain cases, voting rights) for a continuous period of at least one year. A provisional exemption from dividend withholding tax will apply from the start of the one-year holding period. The exemption will be cancelled retroactively if, following the dividend distribution, the one-year holding requirement is not actually met. The Dutch dividend-distributing company must provide to the Dutch tax authorities a satisfactory guarantee for the payment of dividend withholding taxes that, but for the provisional exemption, would be due. The exemption is also applicable if the parent company is a resident of a EU member state and owns at least 10% of the (voting) shares in the Dutch company but only on the basis of reciprocity (Finland, Germany, Greece, Luxembourg, Spain, and United Kingdom). Should the withholding tax exemption not be available under the EU Parent/Subsidiary Directive the treaty rate(s) set out in the right-hand side of the same column (following "/") will apply.

7. The lower rate applies if the foreign company owns, directly or indirectly, at least 25% of the capital of the Dutch company.

8. The lower rate applies if the foreign company directly owns at least 10% of the capital of the Dutch company.

9. The nil rate applies if the foreign company directly owns at least 50% of the capital of the Dutch company, or invested more than €250,000 in the Dutch company or owns directly 25% of the capital of the Dutch company and has a statement indicating that the investment in Dutch capital is, directly or indirectly, guaranteed by the government of Belarus.

10. The 5% rate applies if the foreign company owns, directly or indirectly, at least 25% of the capital or at least 10% of the voting rights in the Dutch company.

11. The treaty is not applicable for Hong Kong and Taiwan.

12. The lower rate applies if the foreign company owns at least 25% of the voting shares of the Dutch company.

13. The treaty with Indonesia is cancelled. Parties, however, agreed to apply the old treaty until a new treaty is effective.
14. The lower rate applies if the foreign company owns at least 25% of the voting rights in the Dutch company.
15. The 5% rate is applicable if the Italian company owns at least 50% of the voting shares in the Dutch company for a continuous period of at least 12 months prior to the date chosen for distribution of a dividend. The 10% rate is applicable if the Italian company owns at least 10% of the voting shares in the Dutch company for the continuous period mentioned above. In other cases, the dividend withholding tax rate is 15%.
16. The lower rate applies if the foreign company owns at least 25% of the voting shares of the Dutch company for a continuous period of at least six months immediately before the end of the book year to which the dividend distribution relates.
17. The lower rate applies if the foreign company owns, directly or indirectly, at least 10% of the capital of the Dutch company.
18. The 5% rate is applicable if the foreign company owns, directly or indirectly, at least 50% of the capital of the Dutch company or if it has invested more than US$1 million in the Dutch company, insofar as the government of Kazakhstan has guaranteed the investment.
19. These rates do not apply to dividend payments to Luxembourg "1929" holding companies.
20. The dividend article of the treaty is not applicable anymore. The national withholding tax rate is applicable.
21. The nil rate is applicable if the foreign company owns, directly or indirectly, at least 50% of the capital of the Dutch company and invested more than US$300,000 in the Dutch company.
22. The 5% rate is applicable if the foreign company owns directly 25% or more of the capital of the Dutch company.
23. The 15% rate is applicable on portfolio investments.
24. The rate is 15% unless the dividend is paid to an Antillean company holding at least 25% of the paid-up capital in the Dutch company. In this latter case, the withholding tax rate will be reduced to the following.
    a. A rate of 5% if the dividends received are subject to Antillean profits tax of at least 5.5% on the dividend.
    b. A rate of 7.5% if the profits tax is less than 5.5%. The combined Netherlands Antilles corporate income tax and Dutch dividend withholding for participation of at least 25% tax must not exceed 8.3%. Depending on the tax percentage levied in the Netherlands Antilles, the Dutch dividend withholding tax will be restituted accordingly.
25. The 5% rate is applicable if the recipient of the dividend is the beneficial owner and directly owns 10% of the capital of the Dutch company. The 5% rate is applicable if the recipient of the dividend is the beneficial owner and directly owns at least 25% of the capital of the Dutch company.
26. The 5% rate is applicable if the recipient of the dividend is the beneficial owner and directly owns at least 25% in the capital of the Dutch company with a minimum investment of at least €75,000.

27. The Netherlands applies the treaty with the former Soviet Union unilaterally to Azerbaijan, Kyrgyzstan, Tajikistan, Turkmenistan, and Uzbekistan.

28. The lower treaty rate applies if the Spanish company owns 50% or more of the capital of the Dutch company, or if the Spanish company owns 25% or more of the capital of the Dutch company and another Spanish company also owns 25% or more of that capital.

29. The nil rate is applicable if the foreign company owns, directly or indirectly, at least 50% of the capital of the Dutch company or invested more than US$300,000 in the Dutch company.

30. The 5% rate is applicable if the foreign company owns directly 20% or more of the capital of the Dutch company.

31. The lower rate applies if the foreign company owns directly at least 10% of the voting rights in the Dutch company.

32. On March 8, 2004, the Netherlands and the United States signed a protocol amending the applicable tax treaty. Based on this protocol, the withholding tax on dividends will be reduced to 0% if the receiving company owns 80% or more of the voting power of the distributing company, provided that certain other conditions are also met. This reduction of the dividend withholding tax will take effect on the first day of the second month after the completion of the approval procedure.

33. The 5% rate is applicable if the foreign company owns directly 25% or more of the capital of the Dutch company. The nil rate is applicable if the dividend for that company qualifies for the participation exemption in the Netherlands. The 15% rate is applicable to portfolio dividends.

34. The 5% rate is applicable if the foreign company owns, directly or indirectly, at least 50% of the capital of the Dutch company or invested more than US$10 million in the Dutch company. The 7% rate applies to the foreign company owning, directly or indirectly, at least 25% of the capital of the Dutch company.

## Tax administration

*Returns*/Tax returns must be filed either every calendar year or every financial year. The Dutch tax authorities generally make a provisional assessment before issuing the final assessment after a full examination of the return.

*Payment of tax*/The corporate tax assessed must be paid within two months of the date of the assessment. In addition, provisional assessments are issued for the current tax year on the basis of the prior year's taxable income.

## *CORPORATION TAX CALCULATION*

Calendar year 2003

| | | |
|---|---:|---:|
| Fiscal business capital at end of fiscal year<br>Ending December 31, 2003 ..................................................... | | € 9,000,000 |
| Add: | | |
| Repayments of capital during 2003................................. | 50,000 | |
| Distribution of profits....................................................... | 200,000 | 250,000 |
| | | 9,250,000 |
| Deduct: | | |
| Fiscal business capital at beginning of fiscal year<br>(January 1, 2003)...................................................... | 8,000,000 | |
| Capital paid in during 2003 ............................................ | 250,000 | 8,250,000 |
| Posttax commercial income ................................................. | | 1,000,000 |
| Add: | | |
| Corporate income tax expense ....................................... | 100,000 | |
| Dividend distributions, including deemed<br>reimbursements of capital contributions<br>to founders, shareholders, etc...................................... | 25,000 | 125,000 |
| | | 1,125,000 |
| Deduct—Dividends received from participations<br>covered by the participation exemption ............................................. | | 100,000 |
| | | 1,025,000 |
| Add: | | |
| Expenses related to tax-exempt foreign<br>participations .................................................................................. | | 50,000 |
| Taxable profit ........................................................................... | | 1,075,000 |
| Deduct—Accumulated losses.................................................... | | 50,000 |
| Taxable amount ....................................................................... | | € 1,025,000 |
| Tax on 1,025,000 (29% x 50,000 + 34.5% x 975,000)............................. | | €   350,875 |
| *Deduct:* | | |
| Foreign tax credit............................................................. | 15,000 | |
| Taxes paid previously on provisional assessment ............ | 125,000 | (140,000) |
| Remaining corporate tax to be paid ....................................... | | €   210,875 |

Note:

Exchange rate of the Euro at March 16, 2004: US$1 = €0.819209.

## PwC contacts

For additional information on taxation in the Netherlands Antilles, contact:

Peter Bolwerk/Steve Vanenburg
PricewaterhouseCoopers N.A.
Julianaplein 38
Curaçao, Netherlands Antilles
Telephone: (599) (9) 4300000
Fax: (599) (9) 4611119
LN domain: Peter J. Bolwerk/Willemstad/C&L/AN@Americas-Carib
              Steve R. Vanenburg/Willemstad/C&L/AN@Americas-Carib
e-mail: peter.j.bolwerk@an.pwc.com
         steve.r.vanenburg@an.pwc.com

## Significant developments

*New Fiscal Framework*/On December 29, 1999, the Netherlands Antilles has approved three tax bills, which are known as the New Fiscal Framework (NFF), published under P.B. 244, 245 and 246. Because of recent developments the NFF was updated by two tax bills published under P.B. 2001, no. 144 and 145. The NFF came into force retroactively to January 1, 2001, as published in P.B. 2001, no. 146. The NFF is complimentary to an amendment of the TAK (Tax Agreement of the Kingdom) which has taken effect on January 1, 2002.

The principal reasons for the enactment of the NFF are as follows.

The objective of the government of the Netherlands Antilles is to part from its tax haven image and to revitalize its financial services industry. In order to part from its tax-haven image, the offshore legislation which is laid down in the articles 8A, 8B, 14 and 14A of the Profit Tax Ordinance 1940 (PTO 1940) and the 1979 and 1993 Guarantee Ordinance on Profit Tax (GOPT) needed to be retired.

The most important features of the NFF are as follows.

*Abolition of the offshore regime*/The distinction between offshore taxpayers and onshore taxpayers was in principle abolished as of January 1, 2001. The NFF provides for a 34.5% flat rate (consisting of a 30%, profit tax rate and 15% island surtax), which is applicable to all taxpayers. This flat rate is applicable from January 1, 2000.

*Transitional legislation*/The NFF provides for a transitional legislation granting the advantages of the present offshore regime to qualifying offshore companies incorporated before January 1, 2002, provided certain conditions are met. These companies can benefit from the present offshore regime until the year 2019.

The elements of the NFF are as follows.

1.  In the Profit Tax Ordinance:
    *   Introduction of a tax exempt company (*Nederlands Antilliaanse Besloten Vennootschap,* or NABV) i.e., a company that is exempt from both the corporate income tax and the new dividend withholding tax.
    *   Introduction of a participation exemption.
    *   Extension of the period for loss carryforwards.
    *   Introduction of merger provisions.
    *   Introduction of a fiscal unity treatment (consolidated tax group).

2. Introduction of a dividend withholding tax. This tax will only take effect on a date that will be announced in a separate ordinance, but that is not expected to happen in the near future.

***E-zone legislation***/As of March 1, 2001 the e-zone legislation entered into force. The main purpose of the e-zone legislation is to expand and strengthen the economic position of the Netherlands Antilles. The e-zone legislation provides potential e-commerce investors a variety of tax saving opportunities. The e-zone legislation is not only aimed at e-commerce, it is also a continuation of the former free zone legislation.

## Taxes on corporate income

***General***/Resident corporations are taxed on worldwide income. Nonresident companies are taxed on the following Antillean-source income.

1. Income attributable to a permanent establishment.
2. Income from real property situated in the Netherlands Antilles.
3. Interest on loans secured by a mortgage on property situated in the Netherlands Antilles.

Companies are generally taxed at a flat tax rate of 34.5% (consisting of a 30% profit tax rate and a 15% municipal surtax) as per January 1, 2000.

Special rates apply to the taxable income of certain companies.

|  | % |
|---|---|
| E-zone companies | 2 |
| Shipping and aviation companies: | |
| Option 1: | |
| First NAf100,000 | 7.73 |
| Over NAf100,000 | 9.66 |
| Option 2: | |
| Tonnage: NAf0.40 per registered gross ton; maximum of NAf1,000 per vessel | |
| New industries and hotels | 2 |
| Land development companies | 2 |

Capital gains are not differentiated from operating income and are subject to the same applicable rates.

Corporations are taxed on their income as reflected in the profit and loss account, less certain deductible items.

***Companies under transitional offshore rules***/The transitional rules distinguish between three types of offshore companies.

1. Offshore companies that on the last day of the financial year that ended before January 1, 2002, exclusively or almost exclusively had investments in and revenues from investments as mentioned in article 8A, 8B, 14 or 14A (in principle the income is restricted to income from portfolio investment, royalty, holding, financing and technical support) will be grand fathered through the last day of the financial year of the company that starts before July 1, 2019 ultimately.
2. Offshore companies of which on the last day of the financial year that ended before January 1, 2002, the entire or nearly the entire profit is subject to the tax rates of the GOPT 1993 (i.e., 15%, 24% to 30% and 2.4% to 3%) and

which have a valid ruling with the tax inspector (e.g., trading companies, banks, captives commissions, and fee-earning companies) on aforementioned date or for which a request for (extension of) such a ruling has been filed on that date. For profit tax purposes these companies will be grandfathered through the last day of the financial year of the company that starts before July 1, 2019 ultimately.

3. Companies that on the last day of the financial year that ended before January 1, 2002, had invested entirely or nearly entirely in real estate property or rights connected thereto, located outside the Netherlands Antilles (so called article 12 PTO 1940 companies). For profit tax purposes these companies will be grand fathered through the last day of the financial year of the company that starts before July 1, 2019.

Specific rules are applicable to companies that have been incorporated after June 30, 1999 but before December 31, 2001. These companies may also qualify for the aforementioned transitional rules provided that these companies will unfold essential own activities. In principle a company will not be considered to have unfolded essential own activities if the assets of the companies consist predominantly of deposits or receivables on shareholders or affiliated parties.

The grandfathering period continues until the year 2019. However, taking into account the level one commitment of the Netherlands Antilles Minister of Finance to the Organization for Economic Cooperation and Development (OECD) with respect to the abolishment of harmful tax regimes in the Netherlands Antilles, the grandfathering period may be shortened.

## Corporate residence

Corporate residence is, in principle, determined by the place of incorporation. However, circumstances may also determine residence. For example, a foreign company with effective management in the Netherlands Antilles is considered a resident. On the basis of the NFF, a Netherlands Antilles company will always be considered a resident of the Netherlands Antilles.

Offshore entities in the Netherlands Antilles must have a local managing director. This function is easily provided by one of the many trust companies established in the Netherlands Antilles.

*Transfer of legal seat*/Legislation has been enacted under which a Netherlands Antilles company is allowed to transfer its legal seat to another jurisdiction (if permitted under the laws of the other country), and a foreign company may migrate to the Netherlands Antilles.

## Other taxes

There are no other corporate taxes.

## Branch income

The NFF includes a definition of a branch (permanent establishment/permanent representatives that is in line with the definition in the OECD Model Double Taxation Convention on Income and Capital.

An exemption from profit tax is granted for 95% of the result that is realized through a permanent establishment that is located in another country. The remaining 5% is

# Netherlands Antilles

subject to tax against the standard tax rate (34.5%) or, is in case of loss, deductible.

## Income determination

*Inventory valuation*/Both LIFO and FIFO are permitted provided the system chosen is in conformity with sound commercial practice. Conformity of book and tax reporting is not required. However, occasions for differences are very rare.

*Capital gains*/For onshore companies, capital gains or losses are in principal considered ordinary income and subject to standard corporate rates. The NFF grants an exemption from profit tax for advantages (dividends and capital gains) from a qualifying participation (see "Intercompany dividends"). Under the transitional regime for offshore companies (investment, holding, finance, and patent holding companies), capital gains and losses are tax exempt.

### Intercompany dividends

1. Participation exemption—The NFF grants an exemption from profit tax for advantages (dividends and capital gains) from a qualifying participation. Expenses incurred in connection with a qualifying participation (including capital losses) are not deductible, unless it can be demonstrated that these are indirectly incurred to realize profit that is subject to tax in the Netherlands Antilles.

   With regard to the scope of the exemption, a distinction should be made between a foreign qualifying participation and a domestic qualifying participation.

2. Participation in resident company—A full exemption from profit tax is applicable for advantage received/realized in connection with a domestic participation.

3. Participation in nonresident company—If the advantage is received/realized in connection with a foreign participation, the exemption from profit tax is limited to 95% of the advantage. The remaining 5% is subject to tax against the standard tax rate (34.5%). A participation in an NABV is treated as an interest in a nonresident company.

4. Participation defined—A qualifying participation is, among others, an interest of 5% of the paid in share capital (or voting rights or profit certificates) of a company. An interest which does not meet this criterion may nevertheless be considered a qualifying participation if the acquisition price of interest amounts to at least NAf1,000,000.

The NFF does not require that the nonresident company is subject to profit tax or corporate income tax in its country of residence, nor that the participation should be held for a certain period before claiming the benefits of the exemption nor that the foreign company should be an active company.

*Foreign income*/A Netherlands Antilles corporation is taxed on foreign interest and other income as earned, and on foreign dividends when received. Except as provided in treaty arrangements, there is no general provision in the tax law allowing credits for foreign taxes paid. Undistributed income of foreign subsidiaries is not taxable.

However, a Netherlands Antilles corporation with a permanent establishment outside the Kingdom of the Netherlands (the Netherlands, the Netherlands Antilles, and Aruba) is taxed on its income realized through the permanent establishment, after deduction of foreign taxes. Under the NFF, 95% of the advantage is exempt from profit tax. The remaining 5% is subject to tax against the standard tax rate (34.5%).

Foreign taxes withheld on dividends, interest, and royalties derived outside the Netherlands Antilles may be deducted.

**Stock dividends**/Stock dividends are allowed and treated as regular dividend income.

## Deductions

**Depreciation and depletion**/Depreciation of tangible fixed assets, excluding land, is taken over the estimated useful life of the asset. The depreciable base includes purchase price, customs duties, shipping costs, and installation costs, less residual value, if any. The straight-line method is customary, but the declining-balance method is also acceptable. In addition, an accelerated deduction of one-third of the assets' depreciable basis may be taken. The assets' remaining cost basis (two-thirds) is depreciated using the normal method.

The cost basis of certain intangible assets such as patents, trademarks, and copyrights can be amortized over their expected useful lives. Goodwill and other intangibles resulting from the excess of purchase price over the cost basis of assets purchased are amortized over three to five years.

**Net operating losses**/Losses may be carried forward for a period of ten years. Losses, which have arisen prior to the year 1996, may only be carried forward five years. Start-up losses during the first four years for companies having tax holidays may be carried forward indefinitely. Carrybacks are not permitted.

**Payments to foreign affiliates**/The NFF introduces specific limitations for deduction of interest in certain cases of restructuring and refinancing involving the creation of artificial flows of interest payments to persons who are tax exempt or low taxed in their jurisdiction.

**Taxes**/Taxes, other than the corporate tax itself, incurred in the course of doing business are deductible.

**Other significant items**/Charitable donations to qualifying entities within the Kingdom of the Netherlands may be deducted to the extent that they exceed 1% of net income and NAf100 after utilization of tax loss carryforwards. The maximum deduction is 3% of net income.

## Group taxation

**Fiscal unity**/The NFF bill introduces a fiscal unity treatment for corporate income tax purposes. Resident companies with wholly owned resident subsidiaries could qualify for this regime. The parent company will be entitled to submit one consolidated income tax return on behalf of the whole fiscal unity group. As a result, only the parent company is assessed.

Within certain limitations, losses of one company can be offset against the profits made by another company in the fiscal unity. No profits need to be recognized on intercompany transactions, as these are disregarded for tax purposes. The fiscal unity applies for profit tax purposes only; the participating entities remain separate and identifiable under civil law.

# Netherlands Antilles

Fiscal unity relief is confined to companies organized under the laws of the Netherlands Antilles, the Netherlands, or Aruba. The companies, which invoke this relief, must have their place of management in the Netherlands Antilles.

On the basis of the nondiscrimination provision of a relevant tax treaty, entities established under the laws of a tax treaty party may also be admitted to the fiscal unity regime provided that they are resident in the Netherlands Antilles.

*Mergers*/The NFF introduces a tax facility for business mergers. In a business merger, a company acquires all or a substantial part of the trade or business of another company with a view toward combining the business operations of the two companies into a permanent financial, organizational, and economic organization. If the business is transferred as part of a business merger, the gains realized by the transferor will not be subject to profit tax if certain conditions are met.

## Tax incentives

*Inward investment and capital investment*/There are tax incentives or holidays for the establishment of new economic enterprises and hotels with a predetermined minimum employment and capital investment. Special provisions relate to the taxation of insurance companies.

*Investment allowance*/For a minimum investment of NAf5,000, an 8% investment allowance on acquisitions and improvements (for new buildings, 12%) is permitted as a deduction from taxable profit in the year of investment, and in the subsequent year, for businesses operating within the Netherlands Antilles.

*Accelerated depreciation and tax rollover reserve*/For up to one-third of capital cost, depreciation may be accelerated. If a profit results at the time of sale of capital assets with the intention to replace that asset, the profit may be placed in a tax rollover account.

## Other incentives

1. Ocean shipping and aviation companies—These companies are taxed at special rates of 9.66% including surtax. Shipping companies can also elect to pay tax at the rate of NAf0.40 per gross registered ton (minimum tax of NAf1,000 per vessel) in lieu of being taxed on net income.

2. E-zone companies—E-zone companies are subject to 2% corporation tax until January 1, 2026, and will be granted special facilities regarding turnover tax and pay no import or export duties. The e-zone area also includes a full free processing zone and an international service center (e.g., repair and maintenance of machinery situated outside the Netherlands Antilles and other export services are now allowed).

3. New industries and hotels—These are granted partial exemption from profit tax and a minimum 2% tax rate for a period of 5 to 11 years. There is exemption from import duties on materials and goods necessary for construction and initial equipment, and from land and occupancy tax for a period of ten years. A minimum investment is required. Losses incurred during the first four years of operations may be offset against taxable income indefinitely.

4. Land development companies—Land development companies are granted a tax holiday and exemption from import duties on materials and goods used in development/construction activities. They are exempt from tax on profits realized on the sale of the developed land. A minimum investment of NAf1

million is required. Activities should be expected to enhance the economic development of the Netherlands Antilles.

5. Private foundations—As of November 1, 1998, the Netherlands Antilles has introduced the "private" foundation as a variant of the long-existing "common" foundation. The most important difference is that the purposes of a common foundation may not include making distributions (other than distributions of an idealistic or social nature). This restriction does not apply to private foundations, whose purposes may include making distributions to incorporators and others. A private foundation may not run a business or enterprise for profit. Acting as a holding company or investment company is not considered running a business. It is exempt from Netherlands Antilles profit tax, and its distributions are exempt from Netherlands Antilles gift tax, as are contributions of assets to the foundation by a nonresident. Gift tax in the contributor's country may be applicable. The private foundation is intended to be an alternative to the Anglo-Saxon trust, especially in civil law jurisdictions.

6. The tax exempt NABV—The NFF provides for a company that is exempt from profit tax. To qualify for the exemption, a number of conditions must be met, including the disclosure of beneficiaries, the management, the financials and the activities (in principle only investment, and financing) of a company. For profit tax purposes (i.e., for the application of the participation exemption, the tax exempt NABV is considered a foreign participation.

7. Mergers—The NFF introduces a relief for business mergers.

8. Fiscal unity treatment—The NFF introduces fiscal unity treatment for corporate income tax purposes.

*Exchange controls*/In general, exchange control regulations are very liberal for offshore companies. Offshore companies established in the Netherlands Antilles can obtain nonresident status for exchange control purposes, which basically provides for total exemption from exchange controls. Onshore companies are subject to slightly stricter rules. These companies are subject to a license fee of 1%.

## Withholding taxes

For the time being, the Netherlands Antilles 10% dividend withholding tax will not enter into force.

*Tax treaties*/The Netherlands Antilles currently has tax treaties in effect with the Netherlands and Norway.

## Tax treaties

The Netherlands Antilles currently has tax treaties in effect with the Netherlands, Aruba, and Norway.

*Tax Arrangement for the Kingdom of the Netherlands Antilles (TAK)*/As part of the Kingdom of the Netherlands, the Netherlands Antilles is party to a federal tax agreement with the Netherlands and Aruba (TAK). Subject to this treaty, dividends, interest, and royalties paid out to the Antilles company may qualify for reduced rates of withholding taxes in the subject countries.

Dutch dividend withholding taxes are reduced from 25% to 15%, if the Antilles company owns less than 25% of the Dutch company. In the Netherlands Antilles, only 5% of these dividends will be taxed, at a rate of 34.5%, which results in an effective profit tax rate of 1.725%.

Since the amendment of the TAK that came into force on January 1, 2002, in case the Antilles company's interest is 25% or more, Dutch withholding tax can be reduced to 8.3%. This tax will then under a special procedure be paid to the Netherlands Antilles tax authorities. These dividends will be fully exempt from profit tax in the Netherlands Antilles.

Capital gains derived from shareholdings in Netherlands corporations will be fully exempted from profit tax in the Netherlands Antilles provided that the shareholding amounts to at least 25%. If the shareholding amounts to less than 25%, the capital gain will be tax exempt for 95%.

The new withholding tax regime in the TAK also applies to Netherlands Antilles offshore companies.

## Tax administration

*Returns*/Profit tax is levied by way of a self-assessment system. Returns are to be filed on a calendar-year basis.

*Payment of tax*/Payment is to be made at the time of filing and in a lump sum on the basis of the self-assessment.

### *CORPORATION TAX CALCULATION*

Fiscal year ended December 31, 2003

### Operating company

| | | |
|---|---|---:|
| Net income before taxes | NAf | 1,780,000 |
| Participation exemption—Dividend from wholly owned Netherlands Antilles subsidiary | | 500,000 |
| Taxable income | NAf | 1,280,000 |
| Tax calculation: 1,280,000 at 34.5% | | |
| Tax payable | NAf | 441,600 |

### A qualifying offshore investment company under the transitional legislation

| | | |
|---|---|---:|
| Net income from securities before taxes | NAf | 1,780,000 |
| Tax calculation: | | |
| First 100,000 at 2.4% | NAf | 2,400 |
| Next 1,680,000 at 3.0% | | 50,400 |
| Tax payable (1) | NAf | 52,800 |

Notes:

1. No surtax is applicable to investment and holding companies.
2. Exchange rate of the Netherlands Antilles guilder at January 1, 2004: US$1 = NAf1.7686.

## PwC contact

For additional information on taxation in New Caledonia, contact:

Jeanroger Vallé
PricewaterhouseCoopers
10 rue Jules Garnier
Nouméa, New Caledonia
Mail address: B.P. 4213
                98847 Nouméa Cedex
                New Caledonia
Telephone: (687) 28 66 67
Fax: (687) 28 53 21
e-mail: nccontacts@nc.pwc.com
        Att: Jeanroger Vallé

## General note

This entry is repeated from the 2003/2004 edition. For more up-to-date information consult the contact listed above or Jacqueline Collette at jacqueline.collete@us.pwc.com.

## Significant developments

There have been significant tax or regulatory developments in the past year regarding tax incentives.

## Taxes on corporate income

All corporations, whether public or private, pay tax at the rate of 30% on New Caledonia–source income only.

For tax periods opened as of January 2003, corporations whose annual turnover does not exceed XPF200,000,000 and at least 75% of whose capital is owned by individuals will pay tax at the rate of 20% on their taxable income up to XPF 4,500,000 and 30% on the balance.

Nickel-related industries are taxable at the rate of 35%. Corporations created in development zones between January 1, 1998 and December 31, 2001 are eligible for a tax holiday for eight years.

Under certain conditions, metallurgical companies may be entitled to tax benefits during the construction and operation of the plant.

Taxable income is defined as the difference between the net book values of the company at the beginning and at the end of the financial period, loss share capital contributions plus distributions. Other specific adjustments are made to taxable income. Net book value includes intangible assets.

Dividend income received from nonresident companies is subject to tax as normal company income, for its gross amount, the withholding levied in the state of source being considered a tax credit.

Dividend income received from resident companies is exempt from tax.

## Corporate residence

The place of effective central management determines corporate residence. However, the revenue taxed locally is restricted to the revenue resulting from local operations. There is no provision in the code for worldwide income taxation. Permanent establishments of foreign corporations are taxed locally.

## Other taxes

There is no sales tax or value-added tax (VAT) in New Caledonia, but there is a tax on services imposed at the rate of 4%. This tax applies to services generally, but certain exceptions apply (e.g., medical services and teaching).

*Business license fee (patente)*/This tax, to which all businesses, whether commercial or professional, are subject, is divided into fixed and variable components. The fixed component is calculated by various formulas, the elements of which include the space utilized and the number of vehicles. The variable component is 1.2% of the cost, insurance, freight (CIF) value of imports increased by a surtax.

*Import duties*/Rates and definitions of import duties vary widely and are significant in the budget of the Territory. Consultation with a specialist is recommended.

**Impôt sur le revenu des créances, dépôts et cautionnements (*IRCDC*)**/This tax is applicable to interest or other revenue received by New Caledonian resident companies (including permanent establishments) on their deposits of all types, intragroup loans, and current accounts and guarantees. The IRCDC rate is 8% of gross revenue. Notable exclusions are bank savings and current accounts financing real estate operations. Interest charged on loans to a subsidiary or branch of a nonresident entity is not subject to the tax.

*Capital gains tax*/Capital gains may be taxed as revenue, depending on the source.

*Capital taxes*/There are no taxes on capital.

*Stamp duty*/The Territory imposes duties on documents that effectively transfer title in real property and private companies at the rates of 13% and 3%, respectively. Certain other documents must also be registered and are subject to duty at a nominal rate.

*Taxes on natural resources*/The Territory imposes a tax in the form of a rental or royalty on mineral and oil holdings, whether for exploration purposes or for development and extraction.

*Local taxes*/Only the Territory levies income taxes. Communes and Provinces levy rates that are not assessed on income.

## Branch income

A branch of a foreign corporation is taxed on the accounting net income of the branch as though it were a resident corporation. The accounting net income is deemed to be automatically distributed and subject to 13.25% withholding tax, including all local taxes (see "Withholding taxes").

## Income determination

Taxable income is defined as the difference between net book values of the company at the beginning and the end of the financial period, less share capital contributions plus distributions. Other specific adjustments are made to taxable income. Net book value includes intangible assets.

*Inventory valuation*/FIFO and weighted-average costs are the only recognized valuation methods. LIFO is not permitted. Inventory valuation methods must be consistent for book and tax purposes. Provisions may be set up to cover price increases for stock items. See "Deductions" below.

*Capital gains*/Gains on fixed assets are divided into short-term and long-term gains. Short-term gains are included in taxable income and taxed at 30%, with an option to spread them equally over three years. Long-term gains (those on sales of assets held for at least two years) are taxed at reduced rates, which are: (1) at a 15% standard rate and (2) at 25% for gains from construction property or shares of companies whose main assets are construction property.

Corporations subject to corporate income tax can benefit from these reduced rates for long-term capital gains only if the net balance, that is, 85% and 75%, respectively, is allocated to a "special long-term gain reserve." Distributions offsetting this reserve are partly added back to the tax result in order to bring the total burden on the gain from the reduced rate back up to 30%.

Short-term gains are those on fixed assets held for less than two years and that part of the gain on depreciable fixed assets held for at least two years that corresponds to depreciation charged on those assets.

Long-term losses are those on the disposal of nondepreciable assets held for more than two years. Short-term losses are losses on the disposal of any other fixed assets. Long-term losses can offset only the long-term gains from the following ten tax periods. Short-term losses are deductible from the current taxable profit.

*Intercompany dividends*/Dividend income received from resident companies is exempt from tax.

*Foreign income*/Dividend income received from nonresident companies is subject to tax as normal company income on the gross amount, withholding tax levied in the state of source being considered as a tax credit. Other than dividends, interest and royalties received from abroad, only income from local sources is taxed.

*Stock dividends*/Stock dividends are subject to IRVM withholding tax (as are cash dividends) and, like cash dividends, are excluded from the income tax base of the recipient New Caledonian company.

## Deductions

*Depreciation and depletion*/Depreciation is computed by the straight-line or the reducing-balance method, at the option of the taxpayer. Reducing balance rates are automatically 50% higher than straight-line rates.

*Net operating losses*/There is a five-year loss carryforward (no carryback), except for that part of the loss representing depreciation, which can be carried forward without time limit.

*Payments to foreign affiliates*/There are no special provisions for transactions of this nature.

*Taxes*/In computing the liability for income tax, a deduction is available for amounts paid for social security taxes and land and property taxes. Stamp duty may be deductible through depreciation or as part of the cost of inventory, or if it is part of borrowing expense (deductible over five years). Tax fines are not deductible.

*Provisions for price increases*/Business entities may calculate a tax deductible provision for increases in the price of items in stock. This is done by identifying unit price increases of more than 10% over a maximum of two years and multiplying the excess of 10% by the quantity of that article in stock. Charges to this provision must be added back to taxable income at the end of the sixth year following that in which the provision was set up.

## Group taxation

There is no provision for group consolidation of income for tax purposes.

## Tax incentives

Some investments by companies in the sectors of tourism, hotels, industry, transport, fisheries, new energy sources, agriculture, construction, and public works are 100% tax deductible (until December 2002) or (as of 2002 until 2006) give rise to a tax credit of 15%. As of January 1, 1991, subject to prior agreement, profit realized by a corporation in the sector of hostelry and tourism is exempt from income tax for 15 to 20 years. There are further incentives in the form of subsidies obtained by application to the Investment Code Authority. In certain cases these may amount to as much as 40% of the total funds required.

Nonresident investment in a New Caledonia company or the establishment of a new company in New Caledonia are free but must be declared (administrative declaration) to the Province where the company is located (South, North, or Islands).

## Withholding taxes

**Impôt sur le revenu des valeurs mobilières (*IRVM*)**/IRVM is a withholding tax that is applicable to dividends, debenture interest, director's fees, and branch net income that is deemed distributed. The IRVM rate is 13.25%, including all local taxes. The definition of dividends includes all forms of distribution of unappropriated profits.

*Tax treaties*/The only tax treaty is with Metropolitan France, of which New Caledonia is a *Territoire*. Under this treaty dividends are taxable at source at the maximum rates of 5% and 15%, depending on whether the recipient is a corporation (not a partnership) or an individual, respectively. Royalties are taxed at up to 10% (no withholding tax in New Caledonia on royalties). Interest is not subject to withholding in the state of source.

## Tax administration

*Returns*/The taxable year is the fiscal year, as elected by the company. This is generally the calendar year. Corporate tax returns must be filed within four months from the end of the fiscal year. The tax amount is self-assessed.

*Payment of tax*/Companies are required to pay tax in three installments. The first two installments are payable by the end of the seventh and eleventh months during the financial year, and are calculated on the basis of one-third of the tax paid for the previous year. The balance is payable four months after the balance sheet date.

## *CORPORATION TAX CALCULATION*

Based on the law and tax rates in effect at January 1, 2002

| | | |
|---|---:|---:|
| Net income before taxes | | XPF 1,000,000 |
| Add: | | |
| Nondeductible expenses: | | |
| Excess depreciation on a company car with a cost of more than 3,000,000 | 10,000 | |
| Penalties | 5,000 | |
| Excess interest on shareholders' loans | 2,000 | |
| Withholding tax on interest revenues | 7,000 | |
| Provision for bad debts without designated evidence | 6,000 | |
| Income that should be included: | | |
| Share of profit in partnership investments | 20,000 | 50,000 |
| | | 1,050,000 |
| Less: | | |
| Net dividends received from New Caledonian companies | 50,000 | |
| Investments in priority development sectors | 100,000 | |
| Losses brought forward | 300,000 | 450,000 |
| Taxable income | | XPF 600,000 |
| Tax thereon at 30% | | XPF 180,000 |
| *Less*—Tax credit: | | |
| Withholding tax on interest revenue | | (7,000) |
| Corporation tax for the year | | XPF 173,000 |

Notes:

1. Exchange rate (selling) of the Pacific franc at February 28, 2002: US$1 = XPF110.989.

2. The Pacific franc is pegged to the EURO at 1 € = XPF119.33.

# New Zealand

## PwC contact

For additional information on taxation in New Zealand, contact:

Julia C. Hoare
PricewaterhouseCoopers
Private Bag 92162
Auckland, New Zealand
Telephone: (64) (9) 355 8000
Fax: (64) (9) 355 8001
e-mail: julia.hoare@nz.pwc.com

## Significant developments

In 2003 the New Zealand and Australian governments introduced new elective rules that allow trans Tasman groups of companies to attach both imputation credits (representing New Zealand tax paid) and franking credits (representing Australian tax paid) to dividends paid to shareholders.

In 2003 the New Zealand government passed legislation that introduced progressive tax rates for employer contributions to superannuation funds and a new deferred deduction rule targeting arrangements that offer investors tax deductions greater than the amounts they have invested.

In an effort to reduce the tax-related costs to New Zealand businesses of recruiting internationally mobile labor, the government is proposing to exempt from New Zealand tax particular types of foreign sourced income derived by migrants and returning expatriate New Zealanders for a period after their arrival in New Zealand. The proposals, as currently drafted, are targeted at employees, although the scope may be extended to include other migrants. Legislation is unlikely to be introduced until late 2004.

In 2003 the government proposed a new tax payment regime, which, if implemented, will change the frequency and timing of provisional tax payments. One of the proposals, a 6.7% discount on tax payable on a new business's first year income, is likely to be introduced in April 2004. The other proposals may be included in legislation to be introduced in late 2004.

## Taxes on corporate income

*Income tax*/Resident and nonresident companies (including branches) are subject to income tax at a flat rate of 33%.

*State and municipal taxes*/Nil.

## Corporate residence

Residence is determined by place of incorporation, location of head office or center of management or by directors' exercising in New Zealand control of the company.

## Other taxes

*Accident compensation levy*/Levied on the employer annually, on the basis of payroll and industry type.

*Excise duty*/Excise duty is levied on petroleum products, tobacco, and alcohol.

*Goods and services tax*/Goods and services tax (GST) is a form of value-added tax (VAT). It applies to most supplies of goods and services. The narrow category of exempt supplies includes financial services. The rate applied to taxable supplies is 12.5% or 0%. The 0% rate applies to only a few supplies, including exports. Two significant changes were introduced in 2003—a "reverse charge" mechanism that requires the self assessment of GST on the value of services imported by GST registered persons and the zero rating of financial services supplied to other registered businesses.

*Fringe benefit tax*/Employers are subject to a tax deductible fringe benefit tax (FBT) on the value of noncash fringe benefits provided to their employees. Employers can elect to pay FBT at flat rates (64% on attributed benefits, 49% on pool benefits, i.e., those benefits which cannot be attributed to a particular employee) applied against the value of the benefit, or can attribute fringe benefits to individual employees and pay FBT based on each employee's marginal tax rate. Under the attribution option, the applicable FBT rate depends on the net remuneration (including fringe benefits) paid to the employee. The attribution calculation treats the fringe benefit as if it was paid in cash and calculates FBT as the notional increase in income that otherwise would have arisen. The multirates are as follows.

| Net remuneration | FBT rate % |
| --- | --- |
| 8,075 or less | 17.65 |
| 8,076 – 30,590 | 26.58 |
| 30,591 – 45,330 | 49.25 |
| > 45,330 | 63.93 |

Fringe benefits include cars available for private use, loans at less than prescribed interest rates, and contributions to medical insurance funds and to foreign superannuation schemes. Employers' contributions to approved superannuation schemes (excludes foreign schemes) are subject to 33% withholding tax. Fringe benefit tax is also applicable to benefits received by an employee from a third party where there is an arrangement between the employer and the third party, and where the benefit would be subject to fringe benefit tax if it had been provided by the employer.

The government has undertaken a review of FBT and proposed significant changes in relation to motor vehicles and car parks. Any changes are expected to be introduced in 2005.

*Superannuation fund withdrawal tax*/An effective tax of 5% applies to amounts withdrawn from superannuation funds, to the extent the withdrawals include the return of superannuation contributions made by an employer on an employee's behalf after April 1, 2000. The tax also applies to withdrawals of earnings derived after April 1, 2000 on employer contributions.

## Income determination

*Inventory valuation*/Inventory must be valued by a cost valuation method or, where market selling value is lower than cost, may be valued at market selling value. If the inventory is shares, it must be valued at cost. Cost is determined under generally accepted accounting principles. Acceptable cost flow methods are FIFO or weighted average cost. Some valuation concessions are available to small taxpayers.

# New Zealand

*Capital gains*/There is no capital gains tax. However, the income tax legislation specifically includes various forms of gain that would otherwise be considered a capital gain within the definition of "income." Taxable income includes gains on sale of real estate in certain circumstances and on personal property where the taxpayer acquired the property for resale or deals in such property or where a profit-making purpose or scheme can be deemed or imputed.

*Intercompany dividends*/Dividends derived from resident companies are exempt where there is 100% common ownership and the same balance date.

Dividends paid by nonresident companies are exempt from income tax, but are subject to a dividend withholding payment (DWP) at the corporate tax rate. The dividend, grossed up by foreign withholding tax and income tax (or deemed income tax) on the dividend payer's income, is multiplied by the corporate tax rate. Credit is then given for the foreign withholding tax and underlying income tax or deemed income tax.

Resident companies may also keep a memorandum account called a withholding payment account (WPA), which is credited with an amount equal to DWP paid. Withholding payment credits may be attached to dividends distributed.

The foreign investor tax credit (FITC) regime effectively eliminates nonresident withholding tax (NRWT) on fully imputed dividends. The FITC regime provides that total New Zealand tax paid on a nonresident investor's earnings through a New Zealand company can be limited to 33%. It does not operate by exemption from NRWT. Rather, where a dividend is imputed, the paying company qualifies for a reduction in its income tax if it pays a supplementary dividend. The amount of reduced company income tax is equal to the supplementary dividend. The combination of reduced income tax plus NRWT on both dividends can result in total New Zealand tax on the earnings of only 33%.

Deemed dividends may arise from transactions between related companies where the transactions are not at market value.

*Foreign income*/A New Zealand corporation is taxed on foreign branch income as earned. Double taxation with respect to all types of taxable income, including interest, rents, and royalties, is avoided by foreign tax credits. Foreign dividends received are exempt from income tax but are subject to the foreign dividend withholding payment.

New Zealand residents are taxed on deemed income derived from an interest in a nonresident company, foreign investment fund or foreign trust. New Zealand tax is imposed on residents with income interests of 10% or more in certain controlled foreign corporations (CFCs) on the notional share of income attributable to their interest in the CFC. The regime applies to all types of income but does not apply to CFCs resident in "grey list" countries, except where the CFC derives exempt income from carrying on a business outside its country of residence. Grey list countries are Australia, Canada, Germany, Japan, Norway, the United Kingdom, and the United States.

The conduit tax relief (CTR) regime provides relief for nonresident investors who invest in non-New Zealand companies through a New Zealand subsidiary (the "conduit" company). The regime is complex, but effectively defers New Zealand tax on the nonresident shareholder's share of the New Zealand company's conduit income that is not distributed by the New Zealand company. NRWT (generally at 15%) is imposed on dividend income distributed by the New Zealand company to the nonresident shareholder.

*Stock dividends*/Bonus issues can be taxable or nontaxable. With a taxable bonus issue, the amount capitalized becomes available for tax-free distribution upon a subsequent share cancellation. With a nontaxable bonus issue, the amount capitalized is not available for tax-free distribution upon a subsequent share cancellation.

*Other significant items—financial instruments*/Income or expenditure (including foreign exchange gains and losses) from financial arrangements must be recognized on an accrual basis (generally, yield to maturity or other commercially acceptable method). These rules do not apply to the income or expenditure of a nonresident if the financial arrangement does not relate to a business carried on in New Zealand.

## Deductions

*Depreciation and depletion*/For tax purposes, depreciation of property can be computed either under the diminishing value method, the straight-line method, or a pooling method. The rates of depreciation depend on the following factors.

1. Type of asset.
2. Whether the asset is acquired new or secondhand.

Taxpayers must use the economic depreciation rates prescribed by the Inland Revenue Department (IRD), together with a 20% uplift in the case of new assets (other than buildings and imported motor vehicles). Fixed life intangible property (including the right to use land and resource consents) is depreciable on a straight-line basis over its legal life. Any depreciation recovered on the sale of an asset (up to its original cost) is taxable in the year of sale.

*Entertainment expenditure*/Entertainment expenditure is generally only 50% deductible. However, entertainment expenditure incurred overseas is fully deductible.

*Interest*/Interest incurred by most companies will be deductible, subject to existing thin capitalization and conduit interest allocation rules.

*Net operating losses*/Losses may be carried forward indefinitely for offset against future profits, subject to the company maintaining 49% continuity of ownership. There is no loss carryback. A legislative amendment in 2002 ensures that losses of a subsidiary are preserved on a spinout, that is, when shares in the subsidiary are transferred to shareholders of its parent company.

*Payments to foreign affiliates*/A New Zealand corporation can claim a deduction for royalties, management service fees and interest charges paid to nonresident associates, provided the charges satisfy the "arm's length principle" which forms the basis of New Zealand's transfer pricing regime.

*Research and development*/Research and development costs which are expensed under New Zealand's Financial Reporting Standard–13: Accounting for research and development activities, are tax deductible. Expenses written off as immaterial and not tested against the asset-recognition criteria in FRS–13 are not automatically deductible for tax purposes.

*Taxes*/Fringe benefit tax is deductible, as is goods and services tax payable on the value of a fringe benefit.

## Group taxation

Companies that are commonly owned to the extent of 66% or more constitute a "group." Group companies are able to offset losses by election as well as by subvention payment. A subvention payment is a payment made by the profit company to the loss company and is equal to the amount of losses to be offset. The payment is deductible to the profit company and assessable to the loss company. Certain companies subject to special bases of assessment (e.g., mining companies other than petroleum extraction companies) are excluded from the grouping provisions. Branches of nonresident companies may be included, provided they continue to carry on business in New Zealand through a fixed establishment.

Groups of resident companies that have 100% common ownership may elect to be subject to the consolidated group regime. The group is effectively treated as a single company and transfers of assets, dividends, interest, and management fees will generally be disregarded for tax purposes. The group files a single return and is issued a single assessment. Group members are jointly and severally liable for tax purposes.

Losses incurred by a dual resident company are not available for offset by election or subvention payment.

## Tax incentives

*Inward investment*/There are no specific tax incentives designed to encourage the flow of investment funds into New Zealand. However, investment is made more attractive by the FITC regime and the CTR regime (see "Foreign income" above).

*Capital investment*/Investment allowances on fixed assets are not available.

## Withholding taxes

Resident corporations paying certain types of income are required to withhold tax on gross income, as shown in the table below.

| Recipient | Dividends % | Interest % | Royalties % |
|---|---|---|---|
| Resident corporations | 33 (1) | 33 (1) | Nil |
| Resident individuals | 33 (1) | 33 (1) | Nil |
| Nonresident corporations and individuals | (2) | (3) | |
| Nontreaty | 30 (4) | 15 (5) | 15 |
| Treaty: | | | |
| Australia | 15 | 10 | 10 |
| Belgium | 15 | 10 | 10 |
| Canada | 15 | 15 | 15 |
| Chile | 15 | 10 (13) | 10 (14) |
| China, P.R. | 15 | 10 | 10 |
| Denmark | 15 | 10 | 10 |
| Fiji | 15 | 10 (5) | 15 |
| Finland | 15 | 10 | 10 |
| France | 15 | 10 | 10 |
| Germany | 15 | 10 | 10 |
| India | 15 | 10 | 10 |
| Indonesia | 15 | 10 | 15 |
| Ireland, Rep. of | 15 | 10 | 10 |
| Italy | 15 | 10 | 10 |
| Japan | 15 | 15 (5) | 15 (6) |
| Korea, Rep. of | 15 | 10 | 10 |
| Malaysia | 15 | 15 (5) | 15 |
| Netherlands | 15 | 10 | 10 |
| Norway | 15 | 10 | 10 |
| Philippines | 15 (7) | 15 | 15 (8) |
| Russian Federation | 15 | 10 | 10 (9) |
| Singapore | 15 | 15 (5) | 15 |
| South Africa | 15 | 10 | 10 (10) |
| Sweden | 15 | 10 | 10 |
| Switzerland | 15 | 10 | 10 |
| Taiwan | 15 | 10 | 10 |
| Thailand | 15 | 10 (11) | 10 (12) |
| United Arab Emirates | 15 | 10 | 10 (15) |
| United Kingdom | 15 | 10 | 10 |
| United States | 15 | 10 | 10 |

Notes:

The numbers in parentheses refer to the following numbered Notes.

1. Resident withholding taxes apply to both interest and dividends. Unless the recipient corporation holds an exemption certificate, and if the recipient provides a tax file number, the default rate of the interest withholding tax is 33%. Recipients can elect for the rate of interest withholding to be 39%. For corporates the rate of interest withholding will be 39% where the recipient does not provide a tax file number. The rate of withholding tax on dividends

paid is 33%, but the tax is reduced by the aggregate imputation and withholding payment credits attached to the dividend or taxable bonus share. Interest and dividends paid between group companies and in certain other limited circumstances are exempt from the withholding tax.

2. Nonresident investors—The FITC and CTR regimes provide relief to companies paying dividends to nonresident investors.

3. Resident corporations paying interest to nonassociated nonresident corporations and individuals need not withhold tax if they have approved-issuer status and the security under which interest is payable is registered with the IRD (Inland Revenue Department). In this case, the resident corporation pays a 2% levy (tax deductible) on the interest payments instead of the withholding tax otherwise applicable.

4. The rate of withholding tax on all fully imputed dividends is 15%, whether they are paid to investors in treaty or in nontreaty countries.

5. Net interest income is subject to reassessment at the company tax rate where the payer and the recipient are "associated persons," but withholding tax is the minimum liability. Nonresident withholding tax is not imposed where the recipient of the interest has a fixed establishment in New Zealand.

6. Net income from industrial royalties is subject to reassessment at the company tax rate, but withholding tax is the minimum liability.

7. A rate of 15% if the beneficial owner is a company; 25% in all other cases.

8. Royalties arising in New Zealand, 15%. Royalties arising in the Philippines, 15% if the enterprise is registered with the Philippine Board of Investments and engaged in preferred areas of activity; in all other cases, 25%.

9. The Russian Federation DTA is effective in New Zealand from January 1, 2004 for withholding taxes, and from April 1, 2004 for all other taxes.

10. The South African DTA has been signed but is not yet in force.

11. A rate of 10% if the interest is received by a financial institution or relates to indebtedness arising from a credit sale between non-associated persons. In all other cases, the rate is 15%.

12. A rate of 10% or 15%, depending on the type of royalty.

13. A rate of 10% if the interest received is derived from loans granted by banks or insurance companies. In all other cases, the rate is 15%.

14. The Chilean DTA has been signed but is not yet in force.

15. The United Arab Emirates DTA has been signed but is not yet in force.

16. There is an explicit provision in most treaties for tax at the company rate to be applied on the amounts of interest and royalties in excess of fair market values in nonarm's length circumstances.

17. Withholding tax is not imposed where the recipient of the interest has a fixed establishment in New Zealand, but the net interest will generally be subject to assessment at the company tax rate.

18. Withholding tax of 15% is also deducted from payments for certain contract work performed in New Zealand by a nonresident corporation or individual. This is neither a minimum nor a final liability. Exemption or lower-tax-rate certificates can be obtained upon application in certain circumstances, for example, when there is no permanent establishment.

Nonresident withholding tax is required to be deducted from payments to nonresident contractors, including companies that do not hold valid certificates of exemption. The tax withheld is an interim tax credited against the taxpayer's ultimate income tax liability. Nonresident contractors (including companies) present in New Zealand for less than 92 days in any 12-month period and eligible for total relief under a double taxation agreement (DTA) no longer have to apply for a certificate of exemption.

## Tax administration

*Returns*/Tax returns are based on the fiscal year ending March 31, although other fiscal year-ends are possible if permission is obtained. The system is one of self-assessment, under which the corporation files an income tax return each year. For those not linked to a tax agent, returns must be filed by July 7 for March balance dates, or by the seventh day of the fourth month following a substituted balance date. Those linked to a tax agent with a substituted balance date have extensions of time for filing their tax returns.

*Payment of tax*/Tax is paid in installments. Provisional tax paid on account of the current year's liability is payable in advance in three installments in the 4th, 8th, and 12th months of the taxpayer's income year. Terminal tax is generally payable on April 7, or on the 7th day of the 13th month of the income year following balance date, provided taxpayers are linked to a tax agent. Where provisional tax paid is less than the amount of income tax deemed due on that installment date, interest is imposed. If provisional tax is overpaid, interest is payable to the taxpayer. Interest is deductible for tax purposes by business taxpayers, and interest earned on overpaid provisional tax is gross income for tax purposes. Interest rates effective from November 8, 2001 are 11.93% on underpayments and 4.83% on overpayments.

New rules have been introduced that allow taxpayers to pool their provisional tax payments with those of other taxpayers through an arrangement with a commercial intermediary. Tax pooling allows underpayments to be offset by overpayments within the same pool and vice versa. The new rules apply from April 1, 2003.

# New Zealand

## *CORPORATION TAX CALCULATION*

Fiscal year ended March 31, 2004

### New Zealand resident company

| | | |
|---|---:|---:|
| Net income before taxes | | NZ$ 1,000,000 |
| Add: | | |
| Nondeductible legal fees | 5,000 | |
| Entertainment expenditure 50% nondeductible | 30,000 | |
| Increase in provision for doubtful debts | 25,000 | |
| Accrued holiday pay not taken within 63 days of balance date | 70,000 | |
| Depreciation charged in accounts in excess of amounts allowable for tax purposes | 20,000 | 150,000 |
| | | 1,150,000 |
| Deduct—Financial instrument (arrangement) adjustment | | 115,000 |
| | | 1,035,000 |
| Exempt income—Gross dividend income (Resident from wholly owned resident subsidiary or foreign) | | 100,000 |
| Taxable income | | NZ$ 935,000 |
| Tax thereon at 33% | | NZ$ 308,550 |

Note:

Exchange rate of the New Zealand dollar at January 1, 2004: US$1 = NZ$1.52486.

## PwC contact

For additional information on taxation in Norway, contact:

Eva E. Skancke
Advokatfirmaet PricewaterhouseCoopers DA
Karenslyst Allè 12
0245 Oslo, Norway
Telephone: (47) 23 16 06 72
Fax: (47) 23 16 13 72
LN address: Eva E. Skancke@Price Waterhouse-Europe
e-mail: eva.e.skancke@no.pwc.com

## General note

This entry is repeated from the 2003/2004 edition. For more up-to-date information consult the contact listed above or Jacqueline Collette at jacqueline.collete@us.pwc.com.

The tax rates and rules in effect at January 1, 2003 have been used. (Changes with respect to the income year 2003 are still possible.)

## Significant developments

There have been no significant tax or regulatory developments during the past year.

## Taxes on corporate income

*Income tax*/Corporate tax is assessed at a rate of 28%.

*Special oil tax*/Companies involved in the production or pipeline transport of oil and gas are liable to income tax at 28% plus a special oil tax at a rate of 50%. The special oil tax is calculated according to the provisions of the Petroleum Tax Act.

## Corporate residence

Companies incorporated in Norway in accordance with Norwegian law and registered in Norway are, as a general rule, regarded as resident in Norway. If management on board/directors level is carried out outside Norway, the residency in Norway for tax purposes may cease and the company will be subject to liquidation for tax purposes. Note that several factors should be considered in order to determine whether or not the residency has been moved.

Foreign corporations will be regarded as resident in Norway if the place of effective management is in Norway. The place of effective management will, for example, be deemed to be in Norway if the board of directors makes its decisions in Norway.

## Other taxes

*Value-added tax*/There is normally a VAT of 24%.

*Capital taxes*/Companies (ASs [aksjeselskap] and ASAs [allmen aksjeselskap]) are not subject to capital tax.

# Norway

## Branch income

Branch income is taxed at corporate rates. Branches of foreign limited liability companies are not subject to capital tax.

## Income determination

*Inventory valuation*/Inventory is valued at cost. Cost is normally FIFO. LIFO is not acceptable for tax purposes. Conformity between book and tax reporting is not required.

*Capital gains*/Capital gains realized in the course of a business activity are almost always regarded as taxable income. Sales gains in respect of real estate transactions are taxed, regardless of whether they are incurred in connection with business activity. Losses can be offset against the taxpayer's other income.

Gains realized on both business-related and nonbusiness-related securities (including shares) are, in principle, taxable. Realized losses will be eligible for corresponding deductions.

A safeguard against the double taxation of capital gains on shares has been introduced. This is the RISK (opening value adjustment) method, which takes into account tax paid on retained profits during the ownership period. The opening value of the share is to be adjusted according to changes in the company's retained earnings during the ownership period. Gains from the disposal of shares in foreign companies are to be taxed in full without allowing for opening value adjustments. The gain is taxed as ordinary income, that is, at the rate of 28%.

Dividends are taxed at the rate of 28%.

*Intercompany dividends*/The imputation system applies for the taxation of company profits and dividends in order to avoid the double taxation of companies and shareholders. Under the imputation system, companies pay tax on both retained and distributed profit. Norwegian shareholders will get full credit for the underlying corporate tax paid on distributed profits from a Norwegian company. For this tax credit to apply, the dividends must originate from a company with general tax liability in Norway, and the recipient shareholder must be fully taxable in Norway for dividends received.

A Norwegian parent company (at least 10% ownership) will be allowed a deduction (credit) from Norwegian taxes for underlying company tax paid on dividends received from a foreign subsidiary or subsubsidiary located in the same jurisdiction as the first-tier subsidiary. This deduction, together with any deduction for withholding taxes paid, may not exceed the Norwegian tax attributable to gross dividends. The same applies to a subsubsidiary located in the same country as the subsidiary. The parent company must then own at least 25% of the subsubsidiary to qualify for a deduction.

*Foreign income*/If double taxation is not avoided by a tax treaty with the country concerned, a Norwegian corporation is subject to Norwegian income tax on (1) foreign-branch income and (2) foreign dividends when received.

Deduction for foreign tax may be claimed as an expense or as a credit against Norwegian tax payable on that income.

*Stock dividends*/Stock dividends are not taxable on receipt, provided that the dividends have been distributed in accordance with the tax and joint stock company acts.

## Deductions

***Depreciation and depletion*/**For depreciation, the declining-balance method is mandatory. The depreciation rates given below are the maximum rates (2003):

|  | % |
|---|---|
| Office machines, etc. | 30 |
| Acquired goodwill/business value | 20 |
| Trucks, lorries, buses, taxicabs, vehicles for the disabled | 20 |
| Cars, tractors, other vehicular machinery, instruments, fixtures and furniture, etc. | 20 |
| Ships, vessels, offshore rigs, etc. | 14 |
| Aircraft, helicopters | 12 |
| Buildings and construction, hotels, hostels, inns, etc. | 4 |
| Office buildings | 2 |

Special depreciation rules apply to assets that are moved in and out of Norwegian jurisdiction.

Oil companies must apply straight-line depreciation over six years on offshore installations.

Depletion allowances do not exist. Where the special oil tax of 50% is calculated, a special deduction in addition to normal depreciation is allowed (uplift). The uplift is calculated as 5% of the cost of depreciable assets used in production or pipeline transport and is allowed for six years.

***Net operating losses*/**A loss carryover for up to 10 years is available (for entities liable to the special oil tax the carryover is unlimited). Losses incurred in the year of ceasing business may be carried back for a period of two years. If a loss is incurred in the next to last year, it may be carried back to the preceding year.

***Payments to foreign affiliates*/**Royalties and service fees are freely transferable to related companies abroad, provided calculation is based on arm's-length terms. There are no formal thin-capitalization rules in Norway. The terms of the loan should, however, be comparable to those that would have been agreed upon by unrelated parties. Interest on financing to the extent that this rule is not satisfied may be regarded as deemed dividends and thus nondeductible and, in addition, subject to Norwegian withholding tax.

***Taxes*/**Real estate tax, as well as foreign income and capital taxes paid by the taxpayer, is deductible in determining corporate income.

***Goodwill*/**Acquired goodwill may be depreciated by the declining-balance method at a maximum of 20% per annum. The revenue has, however, on several occasions recently questioned the allocation to goodwill and claimed that a part of the purchase price should be allocated to brand and firm names, etcetera (which may, as a rule, not be depreciated unless of a time-limited nature).

These rules do not apply to companies engaged in oil- and gas-producing activities subject to the Petroleum Tax Act.

## Group taxation

Income taxes are assessed on companies individually, not on a consolidated basis. This may be avoided through group contributions between Norwegian companies, provided common direct or indirect (including foreign) ownership is more than 90%.

Group contributions are not deductible for companies engaged in oil- and gas-producing activities subject to the Petroleum Tax Act.

Assets may be transferred tax free between group companies at tax book value for tax purposes and at market value for financial book purposes. Payment in this respect must equal market value of the assets transferred for tax and financial book purposes. The same applies to payment in shares. If the transferee at a later stage steps out of the tax group and is still the owner of the transferred assets, the transferor will be taxed for the difference between the tax book value and the market value of the assets.

## Tax incentives

Joint stock companies that own or lease ships or contracting vessels in traffic or drilling rigs can choose a special shipping company taxation so that their net income from their own and rented vessels will be exempt from taxation. The employees of the company will not be included in the scheme. Net financial income is taxed on a regular basis. In addition, there will be a tonnage duty payable according to the Law of June 19, 1964, number 20, section 7a, regarding measurement of vessels.

## Withholding taxes

Norway does not levy withholding taxes on payments of royalties and interest. Dividend payments are subject to withholding tax at the following rates:

| Recipient | Dividends | |
|---|---|---|
| | Regular rate | Parent/ subsidiary |
| | % | % |
| Nontreaty | 25 | 25 |
| Treaty: | | |
| Albania | 15 | 5 (1) |
| Argentina | 15 | 10 (1) |
| Australia | 15 | 15 |
| Austria | 15 | 5 (1) |
| Azerbaijan | 15 | 10 (2) |
| Barbados | 15 | 5 (1) |
| Belgium | 15 | 5 (1) |
| Benin | 20 | 20 |
| Brazil | 25 | 25 |
| Bulgaria | 15 | 15 |
| Canada | 15 | 5 (3) |
| China, P.R. | 15 | 15 |
| Croatia (4) | 15 | 15 |
| Cyprus | 5 | 0 (5) |
| Czech Republic (6) | 15 | 5 (1) |
| Denmark | 15 | 0 (3) |
| Egypt | 15 | 15 |
| Estonia | 15 | 5 (1) |
| Faroe Islands | 15 | 0 (3) |
| Finland | 15 | 0 (3) |
| France | 15 | 5 (3)/0 (1) |

| Recipient | Dividends | |
|---|---|---|
| | Regular rate | Parent/ subsidiary |
| | % | % |
| Gambia | 15 | 5 (1) |
| Germany | 15 | 0 (1) |
| Greece | 20 | 20 |
| Hungary | 10 | 10 |
| Iceland | 15 | 0 (3) |
| India | 25 | 15 (1) |
| Indonesia | 15 | 15 |
| Ireland, Rep. of | 10 | 0 (7) |
| Israel | 15 | 5 (5) |
| Italy | 15 | 15 |
| Ivory Coast (Côte d'Ivoire) | 15 | 15 |
| Jamaica | 15 | 15 |
| Japan | 15 | 5 (8) |
| Kenya | 25 | 15 (8) |
| Korea, Rep. of | 15 | 15 |
| Latvia | 15 | 5 (1) |
| Lithuania | 15 | 5 (1) |
| Luxembourg | 15 | 5 (1) |
| Malawi | 5 | 0 (5) |
| Malaysia | 0 | 0 |
| Malta | 15 | 15 |
| Mexico | 15 | 0 (1) |
| Morocco | 15 | 15 |
| Nepal | 15 | 5 (1)/10 (3) |
| Netherlands | 15 | 0 (1) |
| Netherlands Antilles | 15 | 5 (1) |
| New Zealand | 15 | 15 |
| Nordic Treaty | 15 | 0 (3) |
| Pakistan | 15 | 15 |
| Philippines | 25 | 15 (3) |
| Poland | 15 | 5 (1) |
| Portugal | 15 | 10 (1) |
| Romania | 10 | 10 |
| Russia (9) | 10 | 10 |
| Senegal | 16 | 16 |
| Siorra Leone | 5 | 0 (5) |
| Singapore | 15 | 5 (1) |
| Slovak Republic (6) | 15 | 5 (1) |
| Slovenia (4) | 15 | 15 |
| South Africa | 15 | 5 (1) |
| Spain | 15 | 10 (1) |
| Sri Lanka | 15 | 15 |
| Sweden | 15 | 0 (3) |
| Switzerland | 15 | 5 (1) |
| Tanzania | 20 | 20 |
| Thailand | 25 | 20 (8) |
| Trinidad and Tobago | 20 | 10 (8) |

# Norway

| Recipient | Dividends Regular rate | Parent/ subsidiary |
|---|---|---|
| | % | % |
| Tunisia | 20 | 20 |
| Turkey | 25 | 20 (1) |
| Uganda | 15 | 10 (1) |
| Ukraine | 15 | 5 (1) |
| United Kingdom | 15 | 5 (10) |
| United States | 15 | 15 |
| Venezuela | 10 | 5 (3) |
| Vietnam | 15 | 5/10 (11) |
| Yugoslavia (former) (4) | 15 | 15 |
| Zambia | 15 | 15 |
| Zimbabwe | 20 | 15 (1) |

Notes:

1. A total of 25% capital.
2. A total of 30% capital and an investment of no less than US$100,000.
3. A total of 10% capital.
4. According to the Foreign Ministry, the tax treaty with Yugoslavia of September 1, 1983, is, for the time being, suspended. In the meantime, notes have been exchanged. For Croatia, the treaty is applicable from March 6, 1996. For Slovenia, the treaty is applicable from the time of independence.
5. A total of 50% of voting rights.
6. The Czechoslovak treaty of June 27, 1979, is applicable for the Czech Republic and the Slovak Republic until further notice.
7. A total of 25% based on share capital when full voting rights.
8. A total of 25% of voting rights.
9. New agreement/rates as of March 1, 2003.
10. A total of 10% of voting rights.
11. A total of 5% for 70% capital; 10% for 25% to 70% capital.

## Tax administration

*Returns/*The income tax year normally runs from January 1 to December 31, with assessments being issued in the early fall of the following calendar year. Companies are liable for both advance payments and final settlements in the calendar year of assessment. Companies with a financial year other than the calendar year may, upon application, be granted permission to use their financial year for tax purposes as well.

Companies are required to file their tax returns by the end of February in the year following their financial year. The annual assessment is made by various local tax assessment offices and independent, locally elected boards, which notify the taxpayer if taxable income is determined to be different from that shown in the tax return.

*Payment of tax/*Companies are required to make advance payments of tax on February 15 and April 15 in the year following the income year. The two payments should together cover 2/3 of the expected total tax. The balance of 50% is paid in two installments within two months after assessments have been issued.

## *CORPORATION TAX CALCULATION*

Fiscal year ending December 31, 2002

### Income tax

| | | |
|---|---:|---:|
| Profit as shown in income statement, including dividends received (1) ....................................................... | | NOK 550,000 |
| Add—Nondeductible items: | | |
| Provision for income and capital taxes............................ | 600,000 | |
| Excess of book depreciation over allowances that can be claimed............................................................... | 30,000 | |
| Donations and subscriptions ......................................... | 5,000 | |
| Nondeductible entertainment expenses......................... | 10,000 | 645,000 |
| Taxable income .............................................................. | | NOK 1,195,000 |
| Corporate tax at 28% ...................................................... | | NOK 334,600 |

Notes:

1. A credit for tax on distributed dividends paid by a Norwegian company is available for application to the shareholder's tax on dividends received.

2. Exchange rate of the krone at December 31, 2002: US$1 = NOK6.9657.

# Oman

## PwC contact

For additional information on taxation in Oman, contact:

Jeffrey S. Todd
PricewaterhouseCoopers
Hatat House, Suites 205–210
P.O. Box 3075, PC112
Ruwi, Sultanate of Oman
Telephone: (968) 56 37 17
Fax: (968) 56 44 08
e-mail: jeff.todd@om.pwc.com

## Significant developments

There have been no significant tax developments in the past year.

## Taxes on corporate income

There are two categories of companies to which the following rates are applicable for the tax year 2001 and subsequent years.

1. Wholly owned Omani companies, companies in which foreign participation is 70% or less, investment funds established under the Capital Market Law, and public joint stock companies listed on the Muscat Securities Market (MSM). These companies are charged tax at the following rates.

| Net income | Rates |
|---|---|
|  | % |
| First RO30,000 | Nil |
| Over RO30,000 | 12 |

2. Companies with more than 70% foreign ownership. These companies are taxed according to the table below. Tax is computed (1) by applying the percentage relative to the bracket in which the taxable income falls or (2) by applying the percentage of the bracket for taxable income immediately below that in which the taxable income falls to the upper limit of that bracket and adding the excess of taxable income over that upper limit to the result. The lower amount is the tax payable.

| Taxable income | | Rate |
|---|---|---|
| Over | Not over | |
|  |  | % |
| 0 | RO 5,000 | Nil |
| RO 5,000 | 18,000 | 5 |
| 18,000 | 35,000 | 10 |
| 35,000 | 55,000 | 15 |
| 55,000 | 75,000 | 20 |
| 75,000 | 100,000 | 25 |
| 100,000 | And above | 30 |

Special provisions are applicable to the taxation of income derived from the sale of petroleum. The tax rate specified for such companies is 55%. However, in practice, the tax on such activities is governed by the individual Exploration and Production Sharing Agreement entered into between the government of Oman and the company engaged in the sale of petroleum.

## Corporate residence

The Oman Income Tax Decree of 1981 (the Law) seeks to tax income that has been realized or has arisen in Oman, regardless of the residence of the taxable entity. Consequently, corporate residence has not been specifically defined in the Law. "Company" has been defined to include partnership, limited partnership, joint stock company, and limited liability company and joint ventures incorporated under the Omani Commercial Companies Law or any other Law, and any establishment of a permanent nature supported by a foreign company.

The fundamental criterion used for deciding whether income has been realized or has arisen in Oman is whether it has been derived from having a permanent establishment in Oman. "Permanent establishment" has been defined in very broad terms and includes places of sale, places of management, branches, offices, factories, workshops, mines, quarries, and building sites for construction. However, the mere use of storage or display facilities does not constitute a permanent establishment.

Under this definition, while the export of goods into Oman will not be deemed to be a taxable activity, a contract for the supply and installation of equipment is likely to attract tax. By the same criterion, services rendered by personnel visiting Oman will be treated as taxable activities.

## Other taxes

No other taxes are levied on sales or profits other than the withholding taxes discussed below.

## Branch income

Branches are subject to the corporate tax rates applicable to companies with more than 70% foreign ownership.

## Income determination

*Inventory valuation*/Inventory should be valued using the method complying with International Accounting Standards.

*Capital gains*/There are no specific provisions relating to capital gains. Generally, capital gains are taxed as ordinary income. However, specific advice should be sought particularly regarding gains on investments.

*Intercompany dividends*/Dividends received from investments in shares or the share capital of another entity are not taxable from the tax year 2001.

*Foreign income*/The treatment of foreign income is not covered by the tax laws and specific advice should be sought in this area.

*Stock dividends*/The issuing of stock dividends has not been addressed by the Law.

# Oman

## Deductions

**Depreciation**/Depreciation is taken on a straight-line basis as follows.

|  | % |
|---|---|
| Buildings: |  |
|     Permanent | 4 |
|     Semipermanent | 15 |
| Vehicles, furnishings, and heavy equipment | 33.33 |
| Other equipment, aircraft, and ships | 15 |
| Hospital buildings, educational establishments, and equipment for scientific research | 100 |

The rate of depreciation allowed is doubled on buildings used for industrial purposes. Additional depreciation up to a maximum of 50% is allowed on tools and equipment used on a three-shift basis.

**Net operating losses**/Carryforward of losses is limited to five years, except in the case of companies that incurred losses during a mandatory tax-exempt period, where there is no time limit as to how far such losses can be carried forward for setoff against future profits.

**Restrictions on allowable expenses**/The Law has imposed restrictions on the deductibility of certain expenses. The principal items affected are the following.

1. Sponsorship fees paid to Omani sponsors are restricted to 5% of net taxable income before charging sponsorship fees. Net taxable income is determined after setting off any losses carried forward.

2. Charges or expenses allocated from the head office or other group companies are restricted to the lowest of the following.

    a. Expenses allocated to Oman operations.

    b. Average of such expenses approved for the Oman operations during the three years immediately preceding the previous taxable year subject to assessment.

    c. A total of 3% of the total income derived from Oman operations during the year subject to assessment. This percentage is increased to 5% in respect of branches of foreign banks and insurance companies, and to 10% in respect of operations of major industrial companies that use the latest and most advanced production techniques, pursue scientific research, provide technical assistance, or use patents that require exchange of information and technical assistance with their associates. The Minister of Finance has discretionary authority to increase this percentage above 10%, but such authority is exercised very rarely.

3. Commissions paid by insurance companies are restricted to 25% of net premiums collected.

4. Amounts charged to the profit and loss account for creating provisions in respect of bad debts, stock obsolescence, warranties, and similar types of contingencies are not tax deductible. Deduction is allowed only at the time of write-off. However, provisions created by licensed banks in respect of bad debts are allowable within the limits approved/required by the Central Bank of Oman.

Charitable donations are limited to specified institutions and organizations, and are subject to an overall limitation of 5% of total income.

Amounts paid as tax consultancy or advisory fees are disallowed.

## Tax incentives

Companies engaged principally in the following activities are exempt from tax.

1. Industry and mining.
2. Export of products manufactured or processed locally.
3. Promotion of tourism, including operating hotels and tourist villages other than under management contracts.
4. Agriculture and animal husbandry and the processing of agricultural produce.
5. Fishing and fish processing.
6. Implementation of public utilities projects other than under management or construction contracts.
7. University and higher education undertaken by private universities, colleges, and higher institutions.

The exemption is valid for a period of five years from the date of commencement of production or the practice of activities, and may be made subject to such conditions as the Minister of Commerce and industry may specify. The exemption is renewable for a period not exceeding five years, subject to approval by the Financial Affairs and Energy Resources Council.

Omani marine companies, whether wholly owned by Omanis or with foreign and Omani ownership and registered in Oman, are exempt from tax. Foreign marine companies conducting activities in Oman through an authorized agent are exempted from tax with effect from the date of commencement of activity, provided that reciprocal treatment is afforded by the country of a foreign company.

Foreign companies engaged in oil and gas exploration activities, while taxable under the Law, normally have their tax obligations discharged by the government under the terms of the Exploration and Production Sharing Agreement.

Foreign companies working for the government in projects deemed to be of national importance have been known to negotiate a tax protection clause whereby any tax paid by them is reimbursed by the government.

## Withholding taxes and tax treaties

Withholding tax was introduced under an amendment effective from November 2, 1996. Foreign companies that do not have a permanent establishment in Oman for tax purposes, and that derive income from Oman by way of royalties, management fees, rental of equipment or machinery or transfer of technical expertise or research and development are now subject to withholding tax at 10% of gross income from such sources. Such tax is required to be withheld by the Omani-based company, and paid to the tax department within 14 days of the end of the month in which tax is deducted or payments are due or made to the foreign company.

At present, Oman has comprehensive double taxation treaties with Algeria, the People's Republic of China, Egypt, France, India, Lebanon, Mauritius, Pakistan, Russia, South Africa, Tunisia, the United Kingdom, and Yemen . There are also agreements with various countries with which there are air links relating to air transport income. Tax credit is allowed by certain countries, for example, Germany, Italy, and the United States, in respect of tax paid by foreign business entities in Oman.

# Oman

## Tax administration

*Returns*/The tax year is the calendar year. Assessments can be made on the basis of a year-end other than December 31, provided permission is granted in advance by the Omani tax authorities and the company then adheres to the year-end on a consistent basis.

A provisional declaration of tax must be submitted in the prescribed form within three months from the end of the accounting period to which it relates. The final annual return of income should be submitted in the prescribed format within six months from the end of the accounting period to which it relates. Reasonable time extensions can be sought, and are normally provided for filing the provisional and annual returns of income, but these do not defer payment of tax, which will be subject to additional tax at 1% per month from the due date to the actual date of payment.

In the case of companies having a paid-up capital in excess of RO20,000, the annual return of income should be accompanied by audited accounts signed by an auditor registered in Oman. The Law requires accounts to be prepared in accordance with one of the generally accepted methods of commercial accounting consistently applied. It specifically provides for accrual accounting, unless prior permission of the Secretary General of Taxation (the Secretary General) has been obtained. The accounts must be submitted in local currency, unless prior approval of the Secretary General has been obtained for submitting them in foreign currency.

Failure to file the provisional or annual returns of income could result in an estimated profit assessment by the Secretary General. Failure to submit audited accounts as required under the Law is deemed to result in an incomplete annual return of income, and could attract an estimated profit assessment.

The Law confers wide powers on the Secretary General for calling up information. Experience has shown that, notwithstanding the presentation of audited accounts, the tax department requests very detailed information and supporting documentation relating to revenue and expenses. Failure to provide such information, or the provision of incorrect information, can result in an additional assessment by the Secretary General, and/or various penalties on the company and/or the officer responsible for providing the information.

*Payment of tax*/Any tax estimated to be payable in respect of an accounting period should be paid with the provisional assessment, and "topped up" for any additional amount computed as payable following submission of the annual return of income. Failure to pay taxes by the due date attracts interest at the rate of 1% per month from the date on which such tax was due to the date of payment.

The difference between the amount paid and the amount assessed, subject to filing of an objection, should be paid within one month from the date of the assessment. The additional amount assessed attracts interest at the rate of 1% per month from the date on which such tax was due to the date of payment.

Under the Law, the Secretary General has the authority, with the approval of the Minister and the Tax Committee, to sequester and sell the assets of a taxable entity to recover the taxes due.

If decisive proof is presented to the Secretary General that any person has paid tax for any year exceeding the tax due and payable for such tax year as finally settled, such person has the right to recover the tax. However, if any tax has become payable by such person in respect of another tax year, the excess amount will be adjusted against the future tax liability. Any request for recovery must be presented within five years from the end of the tax year to which it relates.

*Objections and appeals*/A company has a right to object to any assessment issued by the Secretary General. The objection document should be prepared in writing (in English and in Arabic) and filed with the office of the Secretary General for Taxation within 45 days from the date of assessment. The Secretary General is required to give a judgment within three months, extendable up to six months at his discretion of the date of receiving the objection. No additional tax is payable until the Secretary General issues the judgment.

The company has the right to file a petition against the judgment of the Secretary General for Taxation with the Tax Committee at the Ministry of Finance within 45 days of the date of the judgment. The petition should be in Arabic, and may include a request by the company to be granted dispensation from paying the additional tax demanded in the judgment. The Tax Committee may, when the company furnishes a bank guarantee, grant such dispensation. The Tax Committee is required to give its judgment within four months of receiving the petition.

The company has the right to appeal against the judgment given by the Tax Committee within 45 days of the date of the judgment. The appeal is to be filed with the Court of First Instance. The appeal should be in Arabic, and the company must be represented by an authorized lawyer. However, before filing the appeal, the company must pay the fee to the Secretariat of the Court. Lodging of this appeal will not absolve the company from paying the disputed tax. Nevertheless, the Court may, on the basis of a request by the company and upon the company's furnishing an unconditional bank guarantee in favor of the Ministry of Finance, order that the disputed tax is not to be paid.

The final judicial authority is the Appellate Court, and petitions can be filed with this court within 45 days of receiving a decision from the Court of First Instance. All proceedings in the above courts are in Arabic.

*Maintenance of records*/The Law requires accounting records and supporting documentation to be maintained for ten years after the end of the accounting period to which these records relate.

# Oman

*CORPORATION TAX CALCULATION*

## Calculation for a company fully owned by foreign shareholder

Year ended December 31, 2003

### Taxable income

| | | |
|---|---:|---:|
| Net profit per accounts | | RO 77,560 |
| Add: | | |
| General provision for doubtful debts | 8,000 | |
| Depreciation per accounts | 12,750 | |
| Sponsorship fees | 15,000 | |
| Head office/group charges | 30,000 | 65,750 |
| | | 144,310 |
| Less: | | |
| Depreciation of assets per tax law | 18,300 | |
| Debts written off | 4,150 | |
| Head office/group charges allowed per tax law | 14,000 | 36,450 |
| | | 107,860 |
| Sponsorship fee allowed per tax law | | 5,393 |
| Taxable income | | RO 102,467 |

### Computation of tax

1. First method of computation:

   Within the bracket RO100,001 and above at 30%

   |  | RO |
   |---|---:|
   | Total tax payable | 30,740 |

2. Second method of computation:

   Within the bracket immediately below that for the taxable income:

   |  | RO |
   |---|---:|
   | RO (75,000 – RO100,000 at 25%) | 25,000 |
   | Plus RO102,467 minus RO100,000 | 2,467 |
   | Total tax payable | 27,467 |

Since the lower amount is the tax payable, the tax is RO27,467 (method 2), payable within three months of the end of the accounting period.

Note:

Exchange rate of the Omani rial at March 10, 2004: US$1 = RO0.390786.

## PwC contact

For additional information on taxation in Pakistan, contact:

Syed Shabbar Zaidi
A.F. Ferguson & Co.
State Life Building 1-C
I.I. Chundrigar Road
Karachi 74000 Pakistan
Telephone: (92) (21) 242 6682-6, 2426711-5
Fax: (92) (21) 241 5007, 242 7938
e-mail: s.m.shabbar.zaidi@pk.pwc.com

## Note

A new tax law, "Income Tax Ordinance, 2001," has been promulgated in Pakistan, which is effective from July 1, 2002. The following information on taxation in Pakistan is according to that new law and is accurate as of January 31, 2004.

## Taxes on corporate income

*Federal taxes*/Federal tax on taxable income is assessed at the following rates for the tax years noted.

For the tax year ending after July 1, 2003 and prior to July 1, 2004 the rates are as follows.

Banking company.................................................................................................... 44%
Public company other than a banking company...................................................... 35%
Private company other than a banking company .................................................... 41%

The rate of taxation in the case of a banking company, and private company, other than a banking company, is due to decrease by 3% and 2% each year, respectively, until the rates become 35%.

The term "public company" implies a company listed on any stock exchange in Pakistan, or one in which not less than 50% of the shares are held by the federal or provincial government, in which shares are held by foreign government or a foreign company owned by foreign government, or a public trust.

In the case of a *modaraba* (see "Income Determination/Other significant items" below for a definition) except relating to trading activities, income is exempt from tax, provided that 90% of its profit is distributed to the certificate holders as cash dividend.

*Presumptive tax scheme*/For resident assessees, a presumptive tax scheme is in force. Under this scheme, taxes withheld at source on the sale of goods and the execution of contracts or that collected at the time of import (for other than industrial raw materials and plant, machinery and equipment for own use) is considered a final tax liability in respect of the income arising from the sale, contract or import.

In the case of exports, tax collected at the time of realization of foreign exchange proceeds is treated as final tax for that income.

The presumptive tax scheme is also applicable to nonresident taxpayers, at their option. It would then only apply to payments made on account of the execution of

# Pakistan

any contract, other than for supply of goods or one rendering royalty or fee for technical services.

*Minimum tax*/For resident companies, notwithstanding any other provision, a minimum tax equal to 0.5% of the gross turnover is payable. This provision is not applicable to a nonresident.

## Corporate residence

A company is resident in Pakistan if it is incorporated or formed by or under the law in force in Pakistan, or if the control and management of its affairs is situated wholly in Pakistan in that year. The term "company" includes a corporate body incorporated outside Pakistan as well as any foreign association, whether incorporated or not, which the Central Revenue authorities may declare to be a company.

## Other taxes

*Value-added tax*/VAT (locally termed as sales tax) is ordinarily levied at 15% on the value of goods, unless specifically exempt, after allowing related input credits. Excise tax is levied on certain types of manufacturing and import of goods and rendering of services. In the case of sale or transfer of immovable property, stamp duty is leviable (with varying rates on the basis of location of the property) on the value of the property.

## Branch income

In determining the Pakistan-source income of a nonresident, in addition to business income attributable to the permanent establishment (PE), like a branch in Pakistan, there shall also be considered sales in Pakistan of goods of same or similar kind as those sold through a PE in Pakistan, and other business activities carried on in Pakistan of same or similar kind as those effected through a PE in Pakistan.

A PE shall not be allowed deductions in respect of amounts paid or payable to the head office, other than reimbursement for third party services, for royalties, fees, management fees, and profit on debt except in connection with a banking business.

The rates of tax for a branch of a company incorporated outside Pakistan are the same as those applicable on Pakistan corporate income. No tax is withheld on the transfer of profits to the home office.

*Payments to a PE*/branch in Pakistan of a nonresident is subject to deduction of tax at source, on the same basis as a resident in case of sale of goods, rendering of professional services and execution of contracts. In other circumstances a reduced/nil withholding rate certificate can be obtained from the assessing officer.

## Income determination

*Inventory valuation*/Inventories are to be stated at the lower of cost or net realisable value. The FIFO and average methods are accepted. Conformity of methods used for book and tax reporting is desirable, and the method used should be consistently applied.

*Capital gains*/There is no capital gain on the sale of immovable property. Gain on disposal of shares of a resident company or a nonresident company whose assets wholly or principally consist of immovable property situated in Pakistan, or rights to explore/exploit natural resources in Pakistan, shall be Pakistan-source income. Capital gains on the sale of shares of public companies or *modaraba* (profit-sharing) certificates are exempt from tax up to assessment year ending on or before June 30, 2005. Capital gains, other than on statutorily depreciable assets, realized within one year of acquisition are fully taxed. After one year, 75% of such gains are taxed, and 25% are exempt.

Capital gains on statutorily depreciable assets (other than immovable property) are chargeable to tax as normal business income in the year of sale. They are measured as the difference between the sale proceeds and the tax written-down value of the relevant asset sold.

In case of an asset disposal transaction that is on non-arm's length basis, fair market value of the asset shall be taken to be the consideration received by the seller, as well as, the cost for the buyer.

Where assets are transferred outside Pakistan, the original cost is treated as sale price, which means that the entire depreciation is recaptured at the time of export.

No gain or loss shall be taken to arise on disposal of an asset by a resident company to another resident company, if certain conditions are met. The required conditions include, inter alia, that transferor is 100% owned by the transferee, or vice versa, or both of them are 100% owned by a third company, and the transferee must not be exempt in the year in which transfer takes place.

No gain or loss is taken to arise on disposal of assets to the shareholders upon liquidation of a company.

Capital losses can be offset only against capital gains. Unabsorbed capital losses can be carried forward for adjustment against capital gains of the succeeding six years.

*Intercompany dividends*/Income tax is payable on dividends declared by a resident or nonresident company and received by the following.

Public company or an insurance company ........................................................... 5%
All other cases ................................................................................................... 10%*

*Or lower treaty rate

The above deduction at source shall be full and final discharge of tax liability on dividend income.

*Foreign income*/A resident company is taxed on its worldwide income. It is taxed on its foreign income as earned. Double taxation of foreign income is avoided by means of foreign tax credits. This relief is allowed to the resident company on the doubly taxed income at the lower of the Pakistan or foreign tax rate. Undistributed income of a nonresident subsidiary is not subject to tax.

*Stock dividends*/Stock dividends are not considered as income.

*Other significant items*/Liabilities allowed as a tax deduction in a tax year and remaining unpaid for three subsequent years are deemed to be income in the first tax year subsequent to the said three years. Such items are subsequently allowed as a deduction in the year the liability is discharged.

Royalties received by nonresidents are deemed to accrue or arise in Pakistan and are taxable if paid by a resident in Pakistan or borne by a PE of a nonresident in Pakistan.

Income from "fees for technical services" (FTS) is deemed to accrue or arise in Pakistan if paid by a resident in Pakistan, or borne by a PE of a nonresident in Pakistan. FTS means any consideration for the rendering of any managerial, technical, or consultancy services (including the provision of the services of technical or other personnel), but does not include consideration for any construction, assembly or like project undertaken by the recipient, or consideration that would be income of the recipient chargeable under the head salary.

Withholding tax on payments of royalties and FTS, when royalties or FTS are not attributable to a PE in Pakistan, is 15% on gross fees. The tax withheld would be deemed to be the final tax liability of the nonresident. The rate of tax is, thus, 15% or a lower treaty rate. In case of a nonresident where royalties or FTS are attributable to a PE in Pakistan, the amount of royalties/FTS shall be chargeable to tax as normal income, and withholding on payments can be avoided subject to approval of the commissioner.

*Modaraba* (profit-sharing) is a financing vehicle which enables a management company to control and manage the business of a *modaraba* company with a minimum of 10% equity participation. The management company is entitled to remuneration based on an agreed percentage (but not exceeding 10%) of annual profits of the *modaraba* business. A *modaraba* can be for a specific purpose or many purposes, and for a limited or unlimited period. The income of a *modaraba* not relating to trading activity is free from tax if 90% of its profits are distributed as cash dividend.

Agricultural income is exempt from tax.

## Deductions

*Precommencement expenditure*/Expenditures incurred before the commencement of a business wholly and exclusively to derive income chargeable to tax is allowed to be deducted over a period of five years.

*Intangibles*/The cost incurred on acquisition of a patent, invention, design or model, secret formula or process, copyright, or other like property or right, and any expenditure that provides an advantage or benefit for a period of more than one year is allowed as deduction on a straight line basis over a period of ten years.

*Depreciation*/Normal depreciation is allowable at prescribed rates by the reducing-balance method.

| | % |
|---|---|
| Buildings: | |
| General rate | 5 |
| Factory/workshop | 10 |
| Furniture | 10 |
| Machinery and equipment: | |
| General rate | 10 |
| Special rate: | |
| Ships | 5 to 20 |
| Other | 20 to 30 |
| Below-ground installation in mineral oil concerns | 100 |

New plant and machinery placed into service in Pakistan for the first time in a tax year, and used wholly and exclusively in deriving income chargeable to tax, is entitled to initial allowance at the rate of 50% of the cost in that year.

Book depreciation need not confirm to tax depreciation. Unabsorbed tax depreciation not set off against the income of the year is carried forward, and added to depreciation of the assets of the same business in the following year. Tax depreciation can be carried forward without limit until fully absorbed.

*Thin capitalization*/In the case of a resident company that is 50% or more owned by a nonresident person (either alone or together with an associate or associates), the allowance of profit on debt in the case of foreign debt is subjected to certain restriction where debt due from associated companies is three times or more of the foreign equity of the nonresident.

*Net operating losses*/Operating losses may be carried forward and set off against the profits of the succeeding six years of the same business in which the loss was incurred. Unabsorbed depreciation can be carried forward indefinitely.

Losses of an entity carried forward cannot be utilized if there is a 50% or more change in its underlying ownership and business is changed after the ownership change, or new business is commenced with the objective of utilizing brought forward losses.

No carryback of losses is permitted.

*Taxes*/Taxes on income are not deductible. Sales tax and excise tax are tax deductible.

*Other significant items*/The deductibility of head office expenditure of a nonresident assessee is limited to the amount that it bears to the turnover of the assessee in Pakistan in the same proportion as its total head office expenditures bears to its world turnover. However, such domestic rules are overridden if the branch is a tax resident of country having an agreement for avoidance of double taxation (treaty), and that treaty provides a different basis for the allowance of such expenses.

Expenditures on scientific research incurred in Pakistan wholly and exclusively for the purpose of deriving income chargeable to tax are allowable expenditures.

Exchange gains and losses on foreign currency loans specifically obtained for acquiring an asset are adjusted against the depreciable cost of the asset.

Any lease rental incurred by a person in the tax year to a scheduled bank, financial institution, approved modaraba or approved leasing company shall be a deductible expense.

## Group taxation

Group taxation is not permitted.

## Tax incentives

Any tax relief from Pakistani income tax, which is not provided for in the Income Tax Ordinance, or by treaty, is not valid.

*Inward investment and capital investment*/Incentives are available as follows.

1. Profits and gains derived from an electric power generation project set up in Pakistan are exempt.

2. Profits and gains derived by a company from the export of computer software and its related services developed in Pakistan are exempt through June 30, 2016.
3. Profits and gains derived by a joint venture capital company registered under Venture Capital Companies and Funds Management Rules 2000, between July 1, 2000 and June 30, 2007, are exempt.
4. Profits and gains derived from running of any computer training institution, or computer training scheme, duly recognized by a board of education or university grant commission are exempt from tax for five years, beginning with the month in which such institution is set up. This provision is effective through June 30, 2005.

## Withholding taxes

Resident corporations paying certain types of income must withhold as follows.

| Recipient (1, 2, 3) | Dividends | Interest | Royalties |
|---|---|---|---|
| | % | % | % |
| Resident individuals | 10 | 10, 20 | N/A |
| Resident corporations | 10 | 10, 20 | Nil |
| Nonresident individuals: | | | |
| Nontreaty | 10 | 30 | 15 |
| Treaty | 10 | (4) | (4) |
| Nonresident corporations: | | | |
| Nontreaty | 10 | (5) | 15 |
| Treaty: | (6) | (7) | |
| Austria | 10 | (8) | 20 |
| Bangladesh | 10 | 15 | 15 |
| Belgium | 10 | 15 | 20, 15 |
| Canada | 10 | 25 | 20, 15 |
| Denmark | 10 | 15 | 15 |
| France | 10 | 30 | (9) |
| Germany | 10 | (8) | (9) |
| Hungary | 10 | 15 | 15 |
| Indonesia | 10 | 15 | 15 |
| Ireland, Rep. of | 10 | (8) | (9) |
| Italy | 10 | 30 | 30 |
| Japan | 3.75 | 0, 30 | (9) |
| Kazakhstan | 10 | 12.5 | 15 |
| Korea, Rep. of | 10 | 12.5 | 10 |
| Libya | (8) | (8) | (8) |
| Malaysia | 10 | 15 | 15 |
| Malta | 10 | 10 | 10 |
| Mauritius | 10 | 10 | 12.5 |
| Netherlands | 10 | 10, 15, 20 | 15, 5 |
| Nigeria | 10 | 15 | 15 |
| Norway | 10 | 10 | 12 |
| Philippines | 10 | 15 | 25 |
| Poland | 10 | (8) | 20, 15 |
| Qatar | 10 | 10 | 10 |
| Romania | 10 | 10 | 12.5 |
| Singapore | 10 | 12.5 | 10 |

| Recipient (1, 2, 3) | Dividends | Interest | Royalties |
|---|---|---|---|
| | % | % | % |
| Sri Lanka | 10 | 10 | 20 |
| Sweden | 10 | 15 | 10 |
| Switzerland | 10 | 30 | (9) |
| Thailand | 10 | 10, 25 | 10, 20 |
| Turkmenistan | 10 | 10 | 10 |
| Turkey | 10 | 10 | 10 |
| Tunisia | 10 | 13 | 10 |
| United Arab Emirates | 10 | 10 | 12 |
| United Kingdom | 10 | 15 | 12.5 |
| United States | 3.75 | (8) | (9) |
| Uzbekistan | 10 | 10 | 15 |

Notes:

The numbers in parentheses refer to the following Numbered notes.

1. This table is a summary only, and does not reproduce all the provisions that may be relevant in determining the application of withholding taxes in each tax treaty.
2. Resident and nonresident imply tax status.
3. Individuals and companies are required to render annual returns of income and pay tax at the applicable rates, and credit is given for withholding tax deducted.
4. Withholding rates for interest and royalties given for nonresident corporations (treaty countries) apply also to nonresident individuals.
5. Withholding rates for companies would be at the rate of 30%.
6. The following remarks on dividends should be noted.
   a. The intercorporate rate of tax on dividends received by a foreign corporation is 10%. Correspondingly, treaty withholding rates in excess of 10% have not been specified.
   b. The rates given in the table for treaty countries relate to recipient corporations. The maximum rate as stated above in respect of inter-corporate dividends is 10%. The lower rates are expressly provided in respect of dividends paid to a parent/associated corporation that has a certain minimum holding in a Pakistan industrial undertaking. The levels of holding are noted below.

   | | % |
   |---|---|
   | Japan | 33.33 |
   | United States | 50 |

7. Certain treaties provide for tax exemption of interest paid to the government or the central bank of the contracting state and on foreign loans specifically approved by the federal government.
8. No concession is provided under the treaty.
9. A fair and reasonable consideration for royalties is exempt from tax, provided the recipient does not have a permanent establishment in Pakistan.

# Pakistan

## Tax administration

*Returns and assessment*/All companies are required to file an income tax return each year by December 31 for the preceding financial year (July 1 through June 30), accounting for business income on accrual basis. Tax authorities are empowered to approve a special year-end. In case the special year ends on December 31, then the tax return is required to be filed by September 30 next following the year-end.

An across-the-board self-assessment scheme is in place, whereby assessment is taken to be finalized upon filing of the return. The commissioner, however, has powers to amend the assessment, if the commissioner is of the view that Ordinance has been incorrectly applied, or otherwise has definite information that assessment made is incorrect. These powers are to be exercised within a prescribed time frame. In case of transactions between the associates, the commissioner can substitute the transaction value with the fair market consideration. Further, in case of any assessee, the commissioner can determine tax liability according to the substance of the transaction, disregarding formal arrangement between the parties.

*Payment of tax*/Companies are required to pay advance tax on the basis of their turnover for that year in respect of their income (excluding capital gains and presumptive income). The advance tax to be paid is an amount which bears the same proportion to the turnover of that year as the tax assessed bears to the turnover assessed for the latest assessment year. The advance tax is to be paid after adjusting the taxes withheld at source (other than the tax withheld relating to presumptive tax).

Advance tax is required to be paid in four quarterly installments on or before October 7, January 7, April 7, and June 21 in each financial year. Credit for tax paid in a tax year shall be allowed against tax liability of that year.

The total tax liability is to be discharged at the time of filing the return of income. Advance taxes and taxes withheld are adjustable against the tax payable with the return of income.

## CORPORATION TAX CALCULATION

| | | |
|---|---:|---:|
| Accounting profit for the year ended June 30, 2003 | | PRs 1,000,000 |
| Add: | | |
| Accounting depreciation | | 100,000 |
| Accounting loss on disposal of fixed assets | | 5,000 |
| Provision for: | | |
| Bad and doubtful debts | 40,000 | |
| Gratuities | 30,000 | |
| Other contingencies | 30,000 | 100,000 |
| Excess perquisites (1) | | 60,000 |
| Trading liabilities (2) | | 25,000 |
| Donations: | | |
| Approved institutions (subject to rebate | | |
| of income tax) | 20,000 | |
| Other | 15,000 | 35,000 |
| | | 1,325,000 |
| *Less:* | | |
| Tax loss on disposal of fixed assets | 2,500 | |
| Bad debts written off | 100,000 | |
| Bad debts recovered (allowed in prior years) | (20,000) | |
| Dividend income (considered separately) | 20,000 | |
| Capital gain on sale of shares | | |
| (considered separately) | 50,000 | |
| Tax depreciation | 150,000 | 302,500 |
| Taxable income | | 1,022,500 |
| *Less:* | | |
| Unabsorbed depreciation | 29,600 | |
| Unabsorbed loss brought forward | 100,000 | (129,600) |
| | | 892,900 |
| Dividend income | | 20,000 |
| Capital gain | | 50,000 |
| Total income | | 962,900 |
| Tax thereon: | | |
| Business income of PRs892,900 x 41% | | 366,089 |
| *Less:* | | |
| Rebate (41% on approved donation of PRs20,000) | | (8,200) |
| | | 357,889 |
| Add: | | |
| Dividend income (20,000 x 10%) | | 2,000 |
| | | 359,889 |
| Capital gain (exempt from tax) (3) | | — |
| Total tax payable | | 359,889 |

# Pakistan

Notes:

1. Amount of allowance and taxable perquisites in excess of 50% of salary of an employee.
2. Trading liabilities remaining unpaid for more than three years.
3. Capital gain on sale of shares is exempt from tax.
4. Exchange rate of the rupee at April 8, 2004: US$1 = PRs59.374.

## PwC contact

For additional information on taxation in Panama, contact:

Antonio E. Latorraca
PricewaterhouseCoopers
Samuel Lewis Avenue & 55 East Street
Obarrio, Panama
Telephone: (507) 206 9200
Fax: (507) 264 5627
Mail address: PO Box 6-4493
Mail address: El Dorado, Panama
e-mail: antonio.latorraca@pa.pwc.com

## Taxes on corporate income

A flat 30% rate is applicable to all companies doing business in Panama, and to the net taxable income earned by Free Zone (Trade and Oil Products) companies on internal sales (i.e., sales within Panama). However, this rate will drop to 29% in 2005 and to 28% in 2007.

## Corporate residence

Corporate residence is determined by the articles of incorporation (statutory seat).

## Other taxes

*Annual company tax*/Domestic and foreign companies registered in the Public Registry are subject to an annual tax of B/. 250, regardless of whether or not they are doing business in Panama. The tax must be paid annually by the company's legal representative or resident agent, depending on the date that the articles of incorporation were recorded in the Public Registry. If the company's incorporation date is during the first six months of the year, then payment must be made before June 30 of each year. If the company's incorporation date is during the latter six months of the year, then payment must be carried out before December 31 of each year.

*Annual license tax*/All commercial and industrial enterprises doing business within the Republic of Panama, except those exempted by specific laws, are required to have a license to do business. The tax, payable annually in advance, Is 2% of a company's net worth, including amounts owed to the foreign home office or to the foreign parent company or affiliated companies. The tax is payable up to a maximum of B/. 40,000.

*Value-added tax*/Many consumer goods, excluding food and medicine, as well as most services, excluding those related to health care, transportation, education, exportation, securities exchanges, among others, are subject to a 5% VAT. The rate for cigarettes is 15%, and for alcoholic beverages is 10%.

*Selective consumer tax*/Special consumer goods such as automobiles and other noncommercial vehicles, vessels, and airships, jewelry, firearms, cable and satellite television, and mobile phones are subject to an additional 5% tax.

*Complementary tax*/Local corporations must pay a 4% complementary tax each year on behalf of their shareholders if no dividends are declared. This 4% will be credited against the dividend tax when dividends are declared.

# Panama

## Branch income

Branches of foreign corporations are subject to the same taxes and rates as Panamanian corporations.

## Income determination

*Inventory valuation*/The tax regulations permit the use of the specific-cost, LIFO, retail-inventory, or average-cost method, according to the normal course of operations. Other methods (including FIFO) are acceptable as long as the method is appropriate to the business, of constant application, and of easy examination by the authorities. The taxpayer may change its method only after using it for at least five years, with a written notification to the Income Tax Department authorities.

*Capital gains*/The rate of taxation of gains on the sale of real estate is determined by a formula. Losses on real estate sales offset only gains on real estate sales. A minimum transfer tax of 2% is based on the higher of the sales price or the registered value of the property in the Public Registry plus a surcharge of 5% for each 12-month period for which the property is held. The 2% tax paid can be applied only as a prepayment of any tax due on taxable income from sales of real estate.

The taxpayer can elect not to pay the transfer tax if income taxes are calculated at a rate of 5% on the resulting taxable base, using a 10% rather than a 5% surcharge. Income taxes calculated in such a manner must be paid in advance for the property to be registered in the Public Registry.

Income from the sale of securities is taxable as ordinary gross income. However, income from the sale of government securities and those issued by companies registered with the National Securities Commission is not taxable, if the following conditions are met.

1. Made through the Stock Exchange of Panama or other organized market.
2. Be a result of a public offer of values.
3. Be a result of the merger, consolidation, or corporate reorganization.

*Intercompany dividends*/Shareholders pay a dividend tax of 10% through a definitive withholding by the corporation that distributes the dividend. Dividends on bearer shares are subject to a 20% dividend tax. The tax is payable whenever dividends are declared (book entry) or when actual distribution is made (cash distribution). Dividends derived from exempt, nontaxable foreign and offshore income and from reexportation activities of Free Zone companies are not subject to dividend tax.

A complementary tax of 4% is paid each year with the income tax return if the company is not declaring dividends that year, or declaring less than 40% of its profits as dividends. This 4% is considered an advance payment of dividend tax and should be applied as a credit when the dividend tax is to be paid, upon filing the dividends distribution tax return.

Branches of foreign corporations must pay 10% of their after-tax income as a dividend tax each year with their income tax return.

*Foreign income*/Only income earned in Panama is subject to Panamanian income tax.

*Stock dividends*/Stock dividends on nominal shares are tax exempt (although credit for complementary tax paid on such profits will be lost). Exemption is subject to the taxpayer's agreeing not to reacquire its shares within five years from capitalization or to grant loans to its shareholders. Balances owed by shareholders at capitalization time must be repaid within six months. Banks and finance companies are exempt from this latter rule.

*Interest income*/Interest earned on Panamanian government securities or on savings and time deposits with banks established in Panama is not taxable. Interest earned on securities issued by companies registered with the National Securities Commission is also not taxable, provided the securities were acquired through a securities exchange duly established to operate in the Republic of Panama. Also, interest earned on loans granted to the agricultural and agroindustrial sectors is not taxable.

## Deductions

*Depreciation and depletion*/Depreciation is normally calculated according to the number of years of the economic useful life of assets, applying any of the following methods: straight-line method, sum-of-digits method, or declining-balance method. Economic useful life of assets will depend on the activity and the conditions under which the assets are used, normal shifts of activities, quality of maintenance, obsolescence, and depreciation charts of recognized technical value. In all cases, economic useful lives shorter than three years for movable and physical assets, and 30 years for real estate and buildings are not allowed.

Depletion of mines and other natural resources is based on units produced or extracted. Any other method requires the approval of the Income Tax Department.

*Net operating losses*/Tax legislation provides a general five-year loss carryforward. Losses incurred in any given year can be taken as a valid deduction over the next five years at a rate of 20% of the loss per year, provided this deduction does not reduce taxable income by more than 50%. The excess over this limitation for any given year, or any amounts not deductible in years where a loss results, will be lost.

*Payments to foreign affiliates*/Royalties and service fees paid to foreign affiliates are deductible expenses and are subject to withholding tax at the current tax rate on 100% of the remitted or accrued amount. Royalties paid by companies operating in Free Zones to nonresidents are not deductible. Royalties accrued by nonresidents from Free Zone companies are not taxable. Nonresident companies receiving taxable royalties or other taxable remittances are allowed to present a tax return in which the gross withholding tax will be allowed as a credit.

Interest, commissions, and other financial charges paid to or accrued in the name of foreign entities are subject to a 6% withholding tax on 100% of the amount paid or accrued.

## Group taxation

Group taxation is not permitted in Panama.

## Tax incentives

*Inward investment and capital investment*/Incentives are available as follows.

1. Corporations operating in the Colón Free Zone are not taxed on income derived from sales from the Free Zone to foreign countries, and to other companies within the Colón Free Zone.

Income derived from sales from the Free Zone to Panama is taxed at the normal rate for Panamanian corporations.

The 10% dividend tax is generally not applicable to companies operating in the Free Zone. However, dividends declared by Free Zone companies from income earned on sales in the Republic of Panama are subject to the 10% or 20% withholding tax. Royalties paid by companies operating in the Free Zone to foreign affiliates are not deductible and are not subject to withholding tax.

2. Other legislation is designed to encourage construction by exempting the cost of new houses and buildings (but not land value) from real estate taxes for a period of five to 25 years after completion.

## Other incentives

Manufacturing, assembling, high-technology, and specialized services companies established in special processing zones for exporting are granted the following incentives.

1. Exemption from 100% of import duties and the 5% value added tax on machinery, equipment, spare parts, and materials used directly in the construction and maintenance of the buildings of the Zone, except for office materials, furniture, and vehicles.

2. Exemption from 100% of the real estate tax.

3. Exemption from 100% of the tax on gains on the first sale of the real estate.

4. Exemption of the income tax at the following rate: 80% in year 1, 60% in year 2, 40% in year 3, and 20% in year 4.

5. Exemption of the income tax, at the same rate as above, on net earnings reinvested after the 21 years of the contract, provided the amount reinvested exceeds 20% of net taxable income during the respective fiscal year.

6. Exemption from 100% of capital or asset taxes, except for the license tax.

7. A three-year carryforward of losses, which may be deducted in any of the three years or prorated over the period.

*Incentives to encourage direct and indirect forest investments and reforestation activities*/Companies established for these purposes are granted the following incentives.

1. Exemption of the income tax on gains at the following rate: 80% in year 1, 60% in year 2, 40% in year 3, and 20% in year 4.

2. A total of 100% of the amounts of forest and indirect forest investments are considered as deductible expenses.

3. Exemption from 100% of import duties and the 5% VAT on machinery, equipment, seeds, and other essential materials for exclusive use in these activities.

Banks and finance and credit institutions that grant loans and/or credit lines to finance forest investments or reforestation activities are entitled to other incentives.

*Incentives for "small-business" companies*/Any company that qualifies as a "small-business" company will benefit from an individual/corporation combined tax rate as follows.

1. The individual tax rate is applicable for the first US$100,000 of the small-business company's gross income.
2. The corporate tax rate is applicable for the excess over US$100,000, but not over US$200,000.

Also, these companies are exempt from dividend and complementary taxes.

To qualify as a small-business company, a company must fulfill the following requirements.

1. The company should not be a related or affiliated company, one that is the result of the fractionalization of other corporations or one that is controlled by another company.
2. Its annual gross income should not exceed US$200,000.
3. Its stock must be divided into nominal shares, and its shareholders must be physical persons.

## Withholding taxes

*On payments to resident corporations and individuals*/Payments to resident corporations and individuals are not subject to withholding taxes, except for payments on dividends distributed from retained earnings arising from Panamanian-source income. In this case, the dividend is subject to a flat 10% dividend tax. However, dividends on bearer shares are subject to a 20% dividend tax.

*On payments to foreign corporations and nonresident aliens*/Dividends are subject to a 10% dividend tax, except when capitalized. Interest and commissions are subject to a 6% flat rate on the full amount paid or credited to the recipient. Interest earned on Panamanian government securities or on savings and time deposits with banks established in Panama is not taxable. Royalties, technical assistance, and professional service fees paid are subject to withholding tax at corporate or individual tax rates, depending on the recipient. In this case, the recipient of the taxable income is allowed to request a foreign taxpayer ID, and file an income tax return, in order to deduct the related expenses. The withheld tax will be credited on the income tax return, and the refund may be requested.

*Tax treaties*/Panama does not have any tax treaties.

## Tax administration

*Returns*/Tax returns are to be filed only by companies having taxable income and, in general, are filed on a calendar-year basis. However, permission for special fiscal years can be obtained from the Income Tax Department. Filing must be made within three months after the close of the fiscal year.

*Payment of tax*/Taxes due must be paid at the time of filing, except for estimated taxes for the following year (based on the current-year taxes), which are to be paid in three equal installments due 6, 9, and 12 months after the close of the fiscal year.

# Panama

## *CORPORATION TAX CALCULATION*

Fiscal year ending December 31, 2003

| | | |
|---|---:|---:|
| Gross income | | B/ 2,000,000 |
| Sales cost | 1,300,000 | |
| Gross profit | | 700,000 |
| General administrative expenses | 400,000 | |
| Net income before taxes | | 300,000 |
| Deduct: | | |
|    Nontaxable income | 200,000 | |
| Plus: | | |
|    Nondeductible expenses | | 125,000 |
| Taxable income | | 225,000 |
| Losses carryforward | 112,500 | |
| Net taxable income | | 112,500 |
| Income tax at 30% | | B/   33,750 |

Note:

Exchange rate of the balboa at January 1, 2004: US$1 = B/1.00.

# Paraguay

## PwC contacts

For additional information on taxation in Paraguay, contact:

Daniel O. Elicetche
E. Rubén Taboada
PricewaterhouseCoopers
General Díaz 521
6° Piso, Edificio Internacional Faro
Asunción, Paraguay
Telephone: (595) (21) 445 003
Fax: (595) (21) 444 893
LN address: Daniel O. Elicetche/PY/TLS/PwC
    Ruben Taboada/PY/ABAS/PwC
e-mail: daniel.o.elicetche@py.pwc.com
   ruben.taboada@py.pwc.com

## Significant developments

There have been no significant tax or regulatory developments in the past year. However, there is a project of law at the Paraguayan Congress that establishes some changes to the tax system for the future.

## Taxes on corporate income

The tax reform has three systems in accordance with the kinds of taxpayer (annual income), as follows.

1. For income from commercial, industrial, and service activities, the general income tax rate of 30% applies.
2. For income from agricultural and cattle activities, a rate of 25% applies.
3. For those whose annual income is less than PYG52,389,833 (approximately US$8,489 the amount for 2003), a single tax at a rate of 4% applies.

The systems noted in items (1) and (3) have been in force since January 1, 1992. Income tax on agricultural and cattle activities is applicable from January 1, 1995.

## Corporate residence

Corporate legal residence is the place of direction or central management if the corporation's charter does not state otherwise. A corporation with several branches has its residence at the location of such branches only for purposes of the execution of liabilities contracted by the corporation's branch agents.

## Other taxes

*Tax on acts and documents*/According to Law No. 125/91, the tax on acts and documents has been partially abolished since July 1, 1994. Still remaining in force is the tax on operations related to banking loans (at the rate of 1% to 1.74%).

*Value-added tax*/VAT applies to all corporations and to individuals or associations of individuals rendering personal services. VAT is a substitute for sales tax and tax on services.

*Capital tax*/The taxation on capital established by Law No. 70/68 was annulled by Law No. 125/91. The new system does not include any tax on capital except for real estate tax (see below).

*Real estate tax*/Real estate tax is levied annually at the rate of 1% of the fiscal valuation of the assessable property, which is generally less than actual value. If a rural property is smaller than five hectares and is used for agricultural and cattle activity, it is taxed at a 0.5% rate. In certain areas an additional tax is levied on the fiscal value of vacant and semivacant land when the built-up portion falls within certain determined percentage limits. Large tracts of land in rural areas are subject to an additional tax determined on a percentage basis and also to a proportional tax of 0.5% to 1% on the fiscal valuation of tracts from 10,000 to 60,000 hectares or more.

The 1992 Constitution of the Republic of Paraguay establishes that municipalities and departments are to be entitled to the full amount of taxes applicable directly to real estate. Collection of these taxes is to be the responsibility of municipal governments.

*Social security taxes*/Individual employees are subject to social security taxes only if they are under a dependent labor relationship with a local entity.

The employee will be taxed by social security taxes on all gains and profits from his employment at the rate of 9%, and the employer on the payments made to the employees in respect of their work, at the rate of 16.5%.

Social security taxes must be paid monthly.

## Branch income

Branches are taxed at the same rate as domestic corporations. Profits transferred or credited to the head office are subject to 5% withholding tax at the end of the fiscal period, whether or not remitted to the head office abroad.

## Income determination

*Inventory valuation*/The taxpayer may adopt any method of inventory valuation, provided it is technically acceptable; for example, FIFO, LIFO, average cost. It must be applied consistently and may be changed only with the prior approval of the Undersecretary of State for Taxation.

Damaged, deteriorated, and obsolete inventories may be written down to values fixed by the taxpayer. The tax administration can reject that valuation if it is not in accordance with reality.

**Capital gains**/Gains on all assets, tangible and intangible, are taxable as part of profits liable to income tax at a rate of 30%.

*Intercompany dividends*/Dividends are not taxable income except when the recipient is nonresident, in which case they are subject to a 5% withholding tax.

*Foreign income*/Foreign-source income is not taxable.

*Stock dividends*/Stock dividends are not taxable income.

## Deductions

*Depreciation and depletion*/The maximum depreciation rates allowed range from 2.5% for urban buildings to 25% for computer equipment. Depreciation is calculated by the straight-line method in accordance with the useful life of assets, as determined by the Undersecretary of State for Taxation. The Undersecretary may also authorize the use of other depreciation or depletion methods that are technically justified and generally accepted. Fixed assets must be revalued annually on the basis of the increase in the wholesalers' price index. Capital gains derived from the revaluation of fixed assets are not taxable income.

No conformity between book and tax depreciation is required, although it is common practice.

*Net operating losses*/Tax losses incurred in one year can be carried forward against future years' net taxable income for up to three years.

*Payments to foreign affiliates*/There are no limits on deductibility of payments to foreign affiliates for management fees, research and development, and general and administrative expenses. For the applicable withholding tax rates, see "Withholding taxes."

*Taxes*/In general, all taxes mentioned under "Other taxes" are deductible. Income tax and any fiscal surcharges or fines are not deductible.

Other significant items/Special rules apply for the deduction of donations, extraordinary losses, deferred expenses, taxes, bad debts, and executive remuneration. General provisions for expenses or other potential losses are not deductible.

Other special nondeductible items are as follows.

1. Interest on capital, on loans or on any other investment by the owner, a partner, or a shareholder in the business.
2. Personal expenses of the owner, a partner, or a shareholder and moneys drawn on account of future earnings.
3. Amortization of payments for goodwill.
4. Direct expenses incurred in the earning of nontaxable income.
5. Earnings in any fiscal period retained in the business as capital increases or reserve accounts.

## Group taxation

Group taxation is not permitted.

## Tax incentives

*Inward investment*/Law No. 60/90, which encourages foreign investment in Paraguay, establishes a system for economic development incentives, grants and specific benefits; permits the repatriation of capital and profits; and provides guarantees against inconvertibility.

Investment incentives included in Law No. 60/90 take the form of exemptions from certain taxes and reductions of other taxes.

A 95% income tax exemption for five years is available for income sourced in the investments made. There is also total tax exemption on the remittance of dividends, profits, royalties, and payments for rights to use trademarks and patents.

Contributors that do not have the benefits of Law No. 60/90, and consequently do not make use of the 95% income tax exemption may be able to benefit under Law No. 125/91. This law also established local reinvestment incentives for industrial and reforestation activities. They consist of a reduction of the income tax rate from 30% to 10%.

# Paraguay

*Other incentives*/Exports are exempt from certain customs duties and from VAT. A Capital Market Law (No. 1284/98) established incentives for companies listed on the Asunción Stock Exchange. Also, Law 536/95 established incentives for forestry activities.

## Withholding taxes

*On payments by a domestic corporation*/Withholding taxes are as shown below.

| Recipient | Dividends | | Interest | Royalties | Fees |
|---|---|---|---|---|---|
| | Portfolio | Substantial holdings | | | |
| | | | (1, 2) | (2, 3) | (2, 4, 5) |
| | % | % | % | % | % |
| Resident corporations and individuals ..................... | Nil | Nil | Nil | Nil | Nil |
| Nonresident corporations ......... | 5 | 5 | 35 | 35 | 35 |
| Nonresident individuals ............ | 5 | 5 | 35 | 35 | Nil |

The numbers in parentheses refer to the following numbered Notes.

Notes:

1. The withholding tax on interest is based on 100% of the amount paid when remitted to the head office abroad. In other cases it is based on 50% of the amount paid.
2. VAT is withheld on interest (except in the case of foreign banks), royalties and fees for financing and/or for services provided for nonresident corporations or individuals at a rate of 9.09%.
3. The withholding tax on royalties is based on 100% of the amount paid when remitted to the head office abroad. In other cases, it is based on 50% of the amount paid.
4. The withholding tax on fees is based on 100% of the amount paid when remitted to the head office abroad. In other cases, it is based on 50% of the amount paid.
5. Fees for personal services rendered by nonresident individuals are not subject to withholding income tax.

## Tax treaties

Paraguay has ratified treaties to avoid double taxation of income proceeding from the utilization of international transport with Argentina, Belgium, Chile, Germany, and Uruguay.

- Airlines: for all.
- Terrestrial: Chile, Argentina.
- Fluvial: Argentina.

## Tax administration

*Returns*/Returns are submitted on a fiscal-year basis as a self-assessment.

*Payment of tax*/Advance payments, equivalent to 25% of the previous year's tax, must be made in the first, third, fifth, and seventh months of the year following the date for the filing of tax returns (generally April of each year).

## *CORPORATION TAX CALCULATION*

Fiscal year ended December 31, 2003

| | | |
|---|---:|---:|
| Net income per financial statements (before income tax) .................................................................... | | PYG 100,000,000 |
| Add: | | |
| Difference on executive's remuneration.................... | 20,000,000 | |
| Excess foreign expenses ......................................... | 10,000,000 | |
| Provision for expense contingency........................... | 10,000,000 | |
| Surcharges and fines............................................... | 1,000,000 | 41,000,000 |
| | | 141,000,000 |
| Deduct: | | |
| Interest from savings accounts ............................... | 20,000,000 | |
| Dividends received from domestic companies.......... | 35,000,000 | 55,000,000 |
| Taxable income ............................................................. | | PYG 86,000,000 |
| Tax payable at 30% ....................................................... | | PYG 25,800,000 |

Notes:

1.  Charitable contributions to institutions in Paraguay that are registered as such are deductible up to 1% of the net income obtained by the company in a fiscal year. Expenses incurred outside the country that are related to import and export operations are deductible up to 1% of FOB import and export values. Other foreign expenses are deductible if they are needed in order to obtain income.

2.  The remuneration of partner/manager or president/director and managers can be deducted for corporate income tax purposes. The deduction is based on three scales that takes into account the financial year's net earned taxable income, the first one establishes a deduction of up to a monthly maximum of 12 minimum salaries, the second one, applicable only for partner/manager or president/director, if there is more than one, establishes a deduction of a maximum of nine minimum salaries, and the third scale applicable just for managers, establishes a deduction of a maximum of 10 minimum salaries. The scale will be reduced to 50% when the partner/director/manager is rendering services in two companies, and to 25% when is rendering services in more than two companies.

3.  Exchange rate of the guaraní at March 19, 2004: US$1 = PYG 6,077.71.

# Peru

## PwC contacts

For additional information on taxation in Peru, contact:

Rudolf Röder
Monica Nieva
Walter Aguirre
PricewaterhouseCoopers
Canaval y Moreyra 380, Floor 19
Lima 27, Peru
Telephone: (511) 2116500
Fax: (511) 4422073
e-mail: rudolf.roeder@pe.pwc.com
       monica.nieva@pe.pwc.com
       walter.aguirre@pe.pwc.com

## Significant developments

As of March 2004, a Financial Transactions Tax (*Impuesto a Transacciones Financieras*) is in force. In general terms, this tax assesses transactions through the Financial System at a rate of 0.15%. This new tax will be in force until December 2006.

## Taxes on corporate income

Corporate tax for domiciled entities is assessed by applying a rate of 30% on taxable income. Nondomiciled entities are assessed by applying a rate of 30% on taxable income.

## Corporate residence

For income tax purposes, the following entities, among others, are considered as domiciled entities in Peru.

1. Corporations duly incorporated in Peru.
2. Branches, agencies, and permanent establishments in Peru of nondomiciled individuals or entities.
3. Partnerships and limited liability companies.

## Other taxes

*Value-added tax*/The general rate of VAT is 19% and it is applicable to the following operations.

1. Sale of goods within the country.
2. Rendering or use of services within the country.
3. Construction contracts.
4. The first sale of real estate made by constructors.
5. Import of goods.

This tax is determined on a monthly basis by deducting from the VAT billed (gross tax) the VAT paid upon acquisitions of goods and services (fiscal credit). The difference is the VAT that must be paid to the tax administration within the first 12 working days of the following month, according to the schedule approved by the Tax Administration (*Superintendencia Nacional de Administracion Tributaria,* or SUNAT).

*Excise Tax*/Certain luxury goods are subject to an additional tax (i.e., excise tax) with rates between 10 and 100%. Likewise, fixed amounts are applied to oil and related products.

## Branch income

Corporate tax on branches is determined in the same manner as that on corporations. However, in case of net income, the 4.1% withholding on dividends will be automatically applied at year end.

## Income determination

*Inflation accounting*/As of 1996, taxation on corporations is determined by adjusting the balance accounts for inflation.

*Inventory valuation*/The FIFO, average, specific-identification, retail, and normal or base-stock methods are allowed. LIFO is not permitted.

*Capital gains*/Capital gains are taxed as ordinary income.

*Foreign income*/A Peruvian corporation is taxed on foreign income. Double taxation is avoided by means of foreign tax credits.

*Dividends*/Distributed dividends in favor of domiciled and nondomiciled individuals, as well as to nondomiciled entities, are subject to a 4.1% income tax rate.

## Deductions

*Depreciation and depletion*/Building's annual depreciation rate is 3%. Normally, assets are depreciated using the straight-line method over their useful life. Conformity between book and tax depreciation is required, but without exceeding the following maximum rates.

|  | % |
|---|---|
| Cattle (working) | 25 |
| Fishing nets | 25 |
| Vehicles for land transportation and furnaces (except trains) | 20 |
| Machinery and equipment for petroleum, construction, and mining activities | 20 |
| Data-processing equipment | 25 |
| Machinery and equipment acquired as from January 1, 1991 | 10 |
| Othor fixed assets (including machinery and equipment) | 10 |

Depletion allowances are not contemplated by current legislation.

*Net operating losses*/As of January 1, 2004, tax losses, adjusted for inflation, can be carried forward using one of the following systems.

1. Losses can be carried forward for four years as from the year in which they are incurred. Losses which are not offset after said four year period are lost.
2. Losses can be compensate, imputing it year by year until its amount is ran out of, up to 50% of the income obtained in the immediate following years.

Carryback of losses is not allowed.

*Payments to foreign affiliates*/Payment of royalties to nondomiciled affiliates is allowed and is deductible from gross income. Royalty contracts should be registered with the appropriate government authority, but lack of registration does not affect deductibility.

*Taxes*/Other taxes assessable on properties and activities generating taxable income are deductible for income tax purposes.

## Other significant items

*Labor profit sharing*/Companies must allocate a percentage between 5% and 10% of income before taxes to paid participation for workers. This is distributed to employees according to their effective working days during the year and their annual remuneration.

## Group taxation

Group taxation is not permitted.

## Tax incentives

*Inward investment and capital investment*/Industrial entities established in the jungle, frontier zones, the Free Zone of Tacna (ZOFRATACNA) and the Exportation, Industry and Service Centers (*Centro de Exportacion Transformacion Industria* (CETICOS)) are allowed certain tax benefits.

*Other incentives*/Exemption from VAT is provided for industrial entities established in jungle and frontier zones. Other tax benefits are available for mining, oil, agriculture, and tourism activities.

*Investment promotion in the Amazon*/Certain tax benefits with regard to VAT and income tax have been established for taxpayers located in the area designated by the law as the "Amazon Region" and that are engaged in the following activities.

1. Agriculture and livestock enterprises.
2. Aquaculture.
3. Fishing.
4. Tourism.
5. Manufacturing activities linked to the processing, transformation, and commercialization of primary products originating in the activities listed above and in forest transformation, provided these products are produced in the area.

These benefits will be in force for 50 years, from 1999.

## Withholding taxes

Domestic corporations are required to withhold income tax at the following rates.

|  | % |
|---|---|
| Credit interest | 4.99 |
| Interest from credits granted by foreign affiliates | 30 |
| Royalties | 30 |
| Services rendered in Peru | 30 |
| Technical assistance | 30 |
| Leasing of aircraft: Taxable income is 60% of gross income. Tax thereon is 10%, for an effective rate of | 6 |
| Leasing of ships: Taxable income is 80% of gross income. Tax thereon is 10%, for an effective rate of | 8 |
| Other income received by nondomiciled recipients | 30 |
| Dividends distributed | 4.1 |

*Tax treaties*/Peru has signed tax treaties with Canada, Chile, and Sweden, and, as a member of the Andean Community, is bound by the rules to avoid double taxation among member countries (Bolivia, Colombia, Ecuador, and Venezuela). Tax treaties are included within the scope of tax legislation.

## Tax administration

*Returns*/The filing deadline for the income tax return is generally the first week of April. According to law, the fiscal year must coincide with the calendar year. The system is one of self-assessment, but the tax return filed with the tax authorities is subject to review.

*Payment of taxes*/Income tax is paid in advance installments calculated based on monthly revenue, either by applying a 2% rate or by applying a factor equivalent to the effective tax rate on net revenue of the prior year. Income tax is paid in 13 installments. As noted, the first 12 must be paid on a monthly basis. The last one is due at the time of filing the annual tax return. The "additional payment in advance" must be considered in the installments from April through December. However, it must be noted that the corresponding amount can be used as credit against the advance installments and the regular annual tax return (13th installment).

Late payment of interim or final installments is subject to moratorium interest. Excess payments are subject to indexation up to the date of reimbursement or application to future taxes.

## CORPORATION TAX CALCULATION

Example for calendar year 2004

|  | Nuevos Soles S/ |  |
|---|---|---|
| Net sales | 10,000,000 | |
| Cost of sales | (8,530,000) | |
| Gross profit | | 1,470,000 |
| Operating expenses | (700,000) | |
| Administrative expenses | (1,300,000) | |
| Sales expenses | | (2,000,000) |
| Operating Profit (loss) | | (530,000) |
| Other revenues (expenses): | | |
| Interest from local bank deposits (1) | 900,000 | |
| Dividends from local companies (2) | 290,000 | |
| Dividends from foreign companies (2) | 200,000 | |
| Capital gains (3) | 250,000 | |
| Financial expenses: | | |
| Paid to Bank (4) | (780,000) | |
| Paid to Affiliates (5) | (865,000) | |
| Interest and fines (6) | (373,000) | |
| | | (378,000) |
| Result from exposure to inflation | | 306,000 |
| Profit (loss) before taxes and profit sharing | | (602,000) |
| Add: | | |
| Limited financial expenses (4) | | 780,000 |
| Excess depreciation (7) | | 540,000 |
| Financial expenses for financing of affiliates (5) | | 865,000 |
| Interest and fines (6) | | 373,000 |
| | | 2,558,000 |
| Deduct: | | |
| Interest from bank deposits (1) | | (900,000) |
| Dividends from local companies (2) | | (290,000) |
| Capital gains (3) | | (250,000) |
| | | (1,440,000) |
| Net income (loss) | | 516,000 |
| Profit sharing (10%) | | (51,600) |
| Net taxable income (loss carryforward) | | 464,400 |
| Income tax (30%) | | 139,320 |

Notes:

1. Interest from local bank deposits is tax exempt.
2. Dividends received by domiciled companies from other domiciled company are not considered within taxable income. However, foreign dividends must be considered in order to determine taxable income.
3. Capital gains from the sale of securities through negotiation mechanisms pursuant to the Securities Market Law are tax exempt (as long as the company does not qualify as a security trader).

4. Financial (interest) expenses not exceeding exempt interest income must be added back when determining taxable income.

5. Indebtedness with related parties is limited to three times the net equity of the debtor as of the close of the previous year. In this case the net equity is equivalent to 0 at said date.

6. Fines, moratorium interest, and penalties imposed by the national public sector are not tax deductible.

7. Depreciation calculated with percentages exceeding those envisaged in the tax law is not tax deductible.

8. Exchange rate of the nuevo sol at March 22, 2004: US$1 = S/ 3.45820.

# Philippines

## PwC contact

For additional information on taxation in the Philippines, contact:

Tammy H. Lipana
PricewaterhouseCoopers Philippines
29th Floor Philamlife Tower
8767 Paseo de Roxas
1226 Makati City, Philippines
Telephone: (63) (2) 845 27 28, (63) (2) 459 2001 (direct)
Fax: (63) (2) 845 28 06
e-mail: tammy.lipana@ph.pwc.com

## Significant developments

Various legislation and regulations aimed at stimulating economic activities, generating revenues for the government and improving tax administration were passed in 2003 and early 2004. Significant developments include the following.

*Use of U.S. Dollar or Japanese Yen in financial reporting for income tax purposes*/Where the U.S. dollar or the Japanese yen is the functional currency used by a company, the Bureau of Internal Revenue (BIR) allows the use of either currency in financial reporting under certain conditions. This means that the recording of transactions in its books of accounts and the preparation of financial statements in the functional currencies of the company are now permitted. The entity shall then compute its income tax based on the U.S. dollar/Japanese yen financial statements using the prescribed exchange rates and prepare its tax returns and pay the taxes due in Philippine pesos.

*VAT on financial services*/Banks and financial intermediaries became subject to VAT on their services from January 1, 2003. An act was passed, however, that exempts banks and financial intermediaries from VAT from January 1, 2004, and reinstates the gross receipts tax.

*Documentary stamp tax (DST)*/Effective from March 21, 2004, rates of DST have generally declined, and a more extensive list of exemptions has been enumerated. Sales of shares in listed companies will be exempt from DST for five years. DST on insurance premiums is now based on amount coverage.

*Tax treaties*/Tax treaties with Bahrain, Bangladesh, Czech Republic, and Vietnam came into effect January 1, 2004. A renegotiated convention with Sweden also came into effect on January 1, 2004.

## Taxes on corporate income

*Domestic corporations*/The following rates apply to domestic corporations.

|  | % |
|---|---|
| In general, on net income from all sources | 32 |
| Minimum corporate income tax (MCIT) on gross income, beginning in the fourth taxable year from the start of business operations | 2 |
| Proprietary educational institutions and nonprofit hospitals: | |
| On net taxable income if gross income from unrelated trade, business and other activities does not exceed 50% of the total gross income from all sources | 10 |
| On net taxable income if gross income from unrelated activities exceeds 50% of income | 32 |

|  | % |
|---|---|

Nonstock, nonprofit educational institutions (all assets and revenues used actually, directly and exclusively for educational purposes)................... Exempt

*Improperly accumulated earnings tax*/An improperly accumulated earnings tax of 10% is imposed on improperly accumulated taxable income. The tax applies to every corporation formed or used for the purpose of avoiding income tax with respect to its shareholders, or the shareholders of any other corporation, by permitting earnings and profits to accumulate instead of being divided or distributed. Exceptions are made for publicly held corporations, banks and nonbank financial intermediaries, and insurance companies.

*Resident foreign corporations*/Resident foreign corporations are taxed in the same manner as domestic corporations (except on capital gains on the sale of buildings not used in business, which are taxable as ordinary income), but only on Philippine-source income. International carriers are subject to an income tax of 2.5% on their gross Philippine billings. Where there is a tax treaty, the preferential rate provided in it applies.

Income of offshore banking units (OBUs) and foreign currency deposit units (FCDUs) from other OBUs or FCDUs, or from foreign currency transactions with other local commercial banks (including branches of foreign banks) authorized by the Bangko Sentral ng Pilipinas (central bank) to transact business with OBUs and FCDUs, as well as interest income from foreign currency loans granted to residents, are subject to a 10% final income tax.

*Nonresident foreign corporations*/In general, nonresident corporations are taxed on gross income received from sources within the Philippines at 32%, except for reinsurance premiums, which are exempt, and on interest on foreign loans, which is taxed at 20%. Dividends from domestic corporations are subject to a final withholding tax at the rate of 15% if the country in which the corporation is domiciled does not impose income tax on such dividends, or allows a tax deemed paid credit of 17%. If the recipient is a resident of a country with which the Philippines has a tax treaty, the treaty rate applies if lower. Otherwise, the normal corporate rates apply.

Rentals and charter fees payable to nonresident owners of vessels chartered by Philippine nationals on leases or charters approved by the Maritime Industry Authority are subject to a final tax of 4.5%. Rentals, charter fees, and other fees payable to nonresident lessors of aircraft, machinery and other equipment are subject to a final tax of 7.5%.

Regional or area headquarters of multinational corporations that do not earn or derive income from the Philippines, and that act as supervisory, communications and coordinating centers for their affiliates, subsidiaries or branches in the Asia-Pacific region and other foreign markets are not subject to tax.

Regional operating headquarters pay a tax of 10% of their taxable income. A regional operating headquarters is a branch established in the Philippines by a multinational company that is engaged in general administration and planning; business planning and coordination; sourcing and procurement of raw materials and components; corporate finance advisory services; marketing control and sales promotion; training and personnel management; logistic services; research and development services and product development; technical support and maintenance; data processing and communication; or business development.

# Philippines

Subcontractors (domestic or foreign) entering into a contract with a service contractor engaged in petroleum operations in the Philippines are subject to a final income tax equivalent to 8% of their gross income from the contract.

## Corporate residence

A corporation is considered resident if it is duly licensed to engage in trade or business within the Philippines.

## Other taxes

*Fringe benefits tax*/A final tax of 32%, payable by the employer, is imposed on the grossed-up monetary value of fringe benefits, for example, housing, expense accounts, vehicles of any kind, household personnel, interest on loans at lower than market rates (the current benchmark rate is 12%), membership dues for social and athletic clubs, foreign travel expenses, holiday and vacation expenses, educational assistance, insurance, and so on, furnished or granted to managerial or supervisory personnel by the employer, unless the fringe benefit is required by the nature of or necessary to the trade, business or profession of the employer, or when the fringe benefit is for the convenience or advantage of the employer.

The following fringe benefits are not subject to the tax.

1. Those authorized and exempted from tax under special laws.
2. Contributions of the employer for the benefit of the employee to retirement, insurance and hospitalization benefit plans.
3. Those granted to rank-and-file employees. (However, the employees may be subject to withholding tax on compensation.)
4. Those of relatively small value.

The fringe benefits tax is payable on the calendar quarter basis, and is an additional deductible expense for the employer. Fringe benefits already subjected to fringe benefits tax will no longer be included in the employee's taxable income.

The grossed-up monetary value of the fringe benefit is generally computed by dividing the actual monetary value of the benefit by 68%.

*Value-added tax*/VAT applies to practically all sales of services and imports and sales, barter, exchange, or lease of goods or properties (tangible or intangible). The tax is equivalent to a uniform rate of 10%, based on the gross selling price of goods or properties sold, or gross receipts from the sale of services. On importation of goods, the basis of the tax is the value used by the Bureau of Customs in determining tariff and customs duties plus customs duties; excise taxes, if any; and other charges. Where the valuation used by the Bureau of Customs is by volume or quantity, the VAT basis is the landed cost plus excise taxes, if any.

Certain transactions are zero-rated or exempt from VAT. For example, export sales by VAT-registered persons are zero-rated, while export sales by persons who are not VAT-registered are exempt from VAT. Certain sales of services exempt from VAT are subject to percentage taxes based on gross sales, receipts or income.

*Other national taxes*/Aside from income tax and VAT, other internal revenue taxes imposable include excise tax, documentary stamp tax, and percentage taxes.

*Local government taxes*/Local government units impose local (business) taxes and permit fees, which are generally based on the prior year's gross sales or gross receipts.

## Branch income

The income tax rate on branch profits is the same as on corporate profits. In general, profits remitted abroad by a branch office are subject to a 15% tax rate, based on the total profits applied or earmarked for remittance, without any deduction for the tax component thereof. A lower rate may apply under certain tax treaties. Profits remitted by a branch registered with the Philippine Economic Zone Authority (PEZA) are exempt.

## Income determination

*Inventory valuation*/Inventories are generally stated at cost or at the lower of cost or market. LIFO is not allowed for tax purposes. Generally, the inventory valuation method for tax purposes must conform to that used for book purposes.

*Capital gains*/Capital gains arise from the sale or exchange of "capital assets." Capital assets are property held by the taxpayer (whether or not connected with its trade) other than the following.

1. Inventories or property held primarily for sale to customers in the ordinary course of business.
2. Real property or depreciable property used in trade or business.
3. Property of a kind that would be included in the inventory of the taxpayer if on hand at the close of the taxable year.

Capital losses are deductible only to the extent of capital gains.

There are no holding period requirements for capital assets of corporations. A 6% final tax is imposed on the higher of the gross selling price or fair market value upon the sale, exchange or disposition of land or buildings not actually used in the business of a corporation, withheld at the time of sale. Net capital gains derived from the sale, exchange, transfer, or similar transactions of shares of stock and other securities not traded through a local stock exchange are taxed at 5% of gains not over PHP100,000, and 10% of gains over PHP100,000. Sales of shares of stock and other securities listed and traded on a local stock exchange are subject to a stock transaction tax of 0.5%, based on the gross selling price.

Capital gains from the sale of bonds, debentures or other certificates of indebtedness with a maturity of more than five years are exempt from tax.

A tax is levied on every sale, barter, exchange, or other disposition through an initial public offering (IPO) of shares of stock in closely held corporations. A "close corporation" is any corporation of which at least 50% in value of the total outstanding capital stock, or at least 50% of the total combined voting power of all classes of stock entitled to vote, is owned directly or indirectly by or for not more than 20 individuals. The tax rates provided hereunder are based on the proportion of the gross selling price, or gross value in money, of the shares of stock sold, bartered, exchanged, or otherwise disposed of to the total outstanding shares of stock after listing on the local stock exchange.

# Philippines

*Intercompany dividends*/Dividends received by a domestic or resident foreign corporation from another domestic corporation are not subject to tax. These dividends are excluded from the taxable income of the recipient.

Dividends received by a nonresident foreign corporation from a domestic corporation are subject to a final withholding tax at the rate of 15% if the country in which the corporation is domiciled either does not impose income tax on such dividends, or allows tax deemed paid credit of 17%. If the recipient is a resident of a country with which the Philippines has a tax treaty, the treaty rate applies if lower. Otherwise, the normal corporate income tax rate of 32% applies.

*Foreign income*/A Philippine (domestic) corporation is taxed on its worldwide income. A domestic corporation is taxed on income from foreign sources when earned or received, depending on the accounting method used by the taxpayer. Double taxation is generally relieved through a credit for foreign taxes. However, a taxpayer can take a deduction for foreign taxes instead, if that leads to a more favorable outcome.

*Stock dividends*/A Philippine corporation can distribute stock dividends tax free proportionately to all shareholders.

*Other significant items*/Interest on bank savings, time deposits, and money market placements, and royalties received by domestic or resident corporations from a domestic corporation, are subject to a final tax of 20%. Interest income of domestic or resident corporations from FCDU deposits is subject to a final tax of 7.5%. Such income is excluded from gross income reportable in corporate income tax returns. Interest on loans granted to residents by OBUs and FCDUs, and income from foreign currency transactions with local commercial banks (domestic), and branches of foreign banks and other FCDUs, are subject to a 10% final tax, while income derived from foreign currency transactions with nonresidents is exempt from tax.

Other nontaxable items include proceeds of life insurance policies; return of policy premium; gifts, bequests and devises; interest on certain government securities; income exempt under a treaty; gains from sale, exchange or retirement of bonds, debentures or other certificates of indebtedness with maturities of more than five years; and gains from redemption of shares of stock in mutual fund companies.

## Deductions

*Depreciation and depletion*/Depreciation is generally computed on a straight-line basis, although any reasonable method may be elected if the aggregate amount of depreciation, plus salvage value at the end of the useful life of the property, will equal the cost of the property. Gain on the sale of depreciated property is taxable as ordinary income. Generally, book depreciation should conform to tax depreciation, unless the latter includes incentives. Properties used in petroleum operations may be depreciated over a period of ten years using the straight-line or declining-balance method, at the option of the service contractor. Properties used in mining operations with expected life of more than ten years may be depreciated over any number of years between five years and their expected life.

A cost depletion allowance is available as follows.

1. For oil and gas wells—Based on actual reduction in flow and production ascertained not by flush flow, but by the settled production or regular flow.
2. For mines—An amount not to exceed the market value as used for purposes of imposing the mining ad valorem taxes on the products mined and sold during the year.

**Net operating losses**/A net operating loss for any taxable year immediately preceding the current taxable year, that had not been previously offset as a deduction from gross income, may be carried over as a deduction from gross income for the next three consecutive taxable years immediately following the year of this loss (except losses during the period when the taxpayer was tax exempt), provided there has been no substantial change in the ownership of the business or enterprise. For mines other than oil and gas wells, a net operating loss calculated without the benefit of incentives provided for under Executive Order (EO) No. 226, or the Omnibus Investments Code (OIC) of 1987, as amended, incurred in any of the first ten years of operation may be carried over as a deduction from taxable income for the next five years immediately following the year of such loss. Loss carrybacks are not allowed.

**Payments to foreign affiliates**/A Philippine corporation can claim a deduction for royalties, management service fees, and interest charges paid to foreign affiliates, provided such amounts are equal to what it would pay an unrelated entity, and the appropriate withholding taxes are withheld and remitted. The registration of licensing and management agreements, now known as technology transfer arrangements (TTAs), has been liberalized. Only TTAs not conforming to certain provisions of the Intellectual Property Code require approval by and registration with the Documentation, Information and Technology Transfer Bureau of the Intellectual Property Office (formerly Bureau of Patents, Trademarks and Technology Transfer) to render the contracts enforceable.

**Taxes**/Corporate taxpayers can claim a deduction for all taxes paid or accrued within the taxable year in connection with their trade or business, except for the following.

1. Philippine income tax.
2. Income taxes imposed by authority of any foreign country, unless the taxpayer elects to take a deduction in lieu of a foreign tax credit.
3. Estate and donor's taxes.
4. Taxes assessed against local benefits of a kind tending to increase the value of the property assessed.

In the case of a foreign corporation, deductions for taxes are allowed only if they are connected with income from sources within the Philippines.

**Special deductions**/A resident foreign corporation is allowed to claim allocated head office expenses as a deduction, subject to compliance with certain requirements.

**Other significant items**/The deduction for charitable contributions ordinarily may not exceed 5% of taxable income. However, contributions to certain institutions are 100% deductible, subject to certain conditions. Special deductions are allowed for certain businesses, for example, insurance, mining and petroleum. The allowable deduction for interest expense is reduced by an amount equal to 38% of interest income, subject to final tax. Entertainment, amusement, and recreation expenses should not exceed 0.50% of net sales for taxpayers engaged in sale of goods or properties, or 1.00% of net revenue for taxpayers engaged in sale of services, including professionals and lessors of properties.

## Group taxation

Group taxation is not permitted.

## Tax incentives

*Inward investment*/See "Capital investment" below.

*Capital investment*/Tax incentives available to export enterprises registered with the Board of Investments (BOI) are as follows.

1. Income tax holiday giving full exemption from corporate income tax for six years for pioneer firms and those locating in less-developed areas, and four years for nonpioneer firms from the date of commercial operation, or target date of operation, whichever is earlier. Expanding export-oriented firms are given three years. Subject to certain exceptions, new and expansion projects located in the National Capital Region (NCR) or Metro Manila are no longer entitled to the income tax holiday.

2. Tax and duty exemption on imported spare parts and supplies for export producers with a customs bonded manufacturing warehouse exporting at least 70% of production.

3. Full deduction of the cost of major infrastructure undertaken by enterprises in less-developed areas.

4. Additional deduction of 50% of the incremental labor expense if the prescribed ratio of capital assets to annual labor is met, and 100% of the incremental labor if located in less-developed areas within five years from date of registration. (This incentive cannot be availed of simultaneously with the income tax holiday.)

5. Ten-year exemption from taxes and duties on importation of breeding stock and genetic materials.

6. Tax credit on domestic breeding stocks and genetic materials (ten years).

7. Exemption from wharfage, any export tax, duty, impost, or fees.

8. Tax credits equivalent to taxes and duties paid on purchases of raw materials, supplies and semi-manufactured products forming part of the products for export.

*Other incentives*/Other incentives available are as follows.

Export and free-trade enterprises, information technology (IT) enterprises, and special economic zone developers/operators (including IT buildings located in Metro Manila and IT parks) registered with PEZA are entitled to an income tax holiday of six years for pioneer firms, and four years for nonpioneer firms. Foreign articles brought into the zones will be exempt from import duties and taxes. Local purchases of goods from VAT-registered suppliers outside the economic zones are zero-rated. After the lapse of the income tax holiday incentives, enterprises registered and operating within special economic zones/export processing zones will pay only 5% final tax on gross income earned, in lieu of paying all local and national taxes. A regional or area headquarters established in the country as a supervisory, communications and coordination center for a corporation's subsidiaries, affiliates and branches in the Asia–Pacific region, and which headquarters do not derive income from the Philippines, are not subject to any income tax, and are entitled to certain nontax incentives. Regional operating headquarters (ROHQ) which are allowed to derive income in the Philippines by performing qualifying business services to its affiliates, subsidiaries, or branches in the Philippines, in the Asia-Pacific Region and other foreign markets may avail itself of the following incentives.

1. Income tax at the preferential rate of 10% of its taxable income.
2. Exemption from all kinds of local taxes, fees, or charges imposed by a local government unit, except real property tax on land improvements and equipment.
3. Tax and duty-free importation of equipment and materials for training and conferences, which are needed and used solely for its functions as ROHQ and which are not locally available, subject to the prior approval of the BOI.
4. Importation of new motor vehicles, subject to the payment of corresponding duties and taxes.

## Withholding taxes

Corporations and individuals engaged in business and paying certain types of income to nonresidents are required to withhold the appropriate tax, which generally is 32% in the case of payments to nonresident foreign corporations, or 25% for nonresident aliens not engaged in trade or business. For withholding taxes on resident corporations, see the discussions under "Income determination" above.

***Tax treaty rates***/For countries with which the Philippines has concluded tax treaties, the taxes to be withheld are as follows.

At January 1, 2004

| Country | Dividends (1) | Interest (2) | Royalties |
|---|---|---|---|
| | % | % | % |
| Australia | 15/25 (3) | 10/15 (4) | 15/25 (5) |
| Austria | 10/25 (6) | 10/15 (4, 7) | 10/15 (5, 8) |
| Bahrain | 10/15 (6) | 10 | 10/15 (9) |
| Bangladesh | 10/15 (10) | 15 | 15 |
| Belgium | 10/15 (6) | 10 | 15 |
| Brazil | 15 | 10/15 (4) | 15/25 (11) |
| Canada | 15/25 (6) | 10/15 (4) | 25 (8) |
| China, P.R. | 10/15 (6) | 10 | 10/15 (12) |
| Czech Republic | 10/15 (6) | 10 | 10/15 (13) |
| Denmark | 10/15 (10) | 10 | 15 |
| Finland | 15/32 (6) | 10/15 (4) | 15/25 (14) |
| France | 10/15 (6) | 10/15 (4) | 15 |
| Germany | 10/15 (10) | 10/15 (4, 15, 16) | 10/15 (12) |
| Hungary | 15/20 (10) | 15 | 15 (8) |
| India | 15/20 (6) | 10/15 (4, 16) | 15/32 (5) |
| Indonesia | 15/20 (10) | 10/15 (4) | 15/25 (5) |
| Israel | 10/15 (6) | 10 | 15 (8) |
| Italy | 15 | 10/15 (4) | 15/25 (5, 8, 17) |
| Japan | 10/25 (10) | 10/15 (18) | 10/15/25 (5, 19) |
| Korea, Rep. of | 10/25 (10) | 10/15 (4) | 10/15 (5) |

# Philippines

| Country | Dividends (1) | Interest (2) | Royalties |
|---|---|---|---|
| | % | % | % |
| Malaysia | 15 | 15 | 15/25 (5) |
| Netherlands | 10/15 (6) | 10/15 (4, 15, 16) | 10/15 (5) |
| New Zealand | 15 | 10/15 (4) | 15/25 (5) |
| Norway | 15/25 (6) | 15 | 7.5/10/25 (8, 20) |
| Pakistan | 15/25 (10) | 10/15 (4) | 15/25 (5) |
| Romania | 10/15 (10) | 10/15 (4, 15, 16) | 10/15/25 (21) |
| Russia | 15 | 15 | 15 |
| Singapore | 5/25 (22) | 10/15 (4) | 15/25 (5, 17) |
| Spain | 10/15 (6) | 10/15 (4, 15) | 10/15/20 (23) |
| Sweden | 10/15 (10) | 10 | 15 |
| Switzerland | 10/15 (6) | 10 | 15 |
| Thailand | 15/20/32 (24) | 10/15 (4) | 15/25 (5, 17) |
| United Kingdom | 15/25 (6) | 10/15 (4) | 15/25 (5, 19) |
| United States | 20/25 (6) | 10/15 (4) | 15/25 (5, 8) |
| Vietnam | 10/15 (6) | 15 | 15 |

Notes:

1. The lower rate generally applies if the beneficial owner of the dividends is a company with a substantial ownership in the dividend paying company.
2. Interest derived by a foreign government or its agencies is typically exempt from Philippine tax. Many treaties also contain special rules for both Philippine and home country taxation of interest paid on instruments secured by a government agency of one of the countries. Such provisions have been excluded from the analysis.
3. Entitlement to the lower rate depends on how the dividend will be taxed in Australia.
4. The 10% rate applies to interest paid in respect of the public issues of bonds, debentures, or similar obligations.
5. The lower rate applies to royalties paid by an enterprise registered with the Philippine Board of Investments and engaged in preferred areas of activity.
6. The threshold for substantial ownership is 10%.
7. The 10% rate also applies to interest paid by a company registered with the Board of Investments and engaged in preferred pioneer areas of investment in the Philippines.
8. The treaty also contains a most-favored-nation rule, limiting the Philippine tax on royalties to the lowest rate of Philippine tax that may be imposed on royalties of the same kind paid in similar circumstances to a resident of a third state.
9. The 15% rate applies to royalties arising from the use of, or the right to use, any copyright of literary, artistic, or scientific work including cinematograph films or tapes for television or broadcasting.
10. The threshold for substantial ownership is 25%.
11. The 25% rate applies to royalties arising from the use or the right to use trademarks and cinematographic films, films or tapes for television or radio broadcasting. The 15% applies to any other royalties.
12. The 10% rate applies to the use of, or the right to use, any patent, trademark, design or model, plan, secret formula or process, or from the use of, or the

right to use, industrial, commercial, or scientific equipment, or for information concerning industrial, commercial, or scientific experience. However, application of the rate is generally at the discretion of the Philippine competent authorities, so it is unclear exactly when it will apply.

13. The 10% rate applies to royalties arising from the use of, or the right to use, any copyright of literary, artistic, or scientific work (other than copyright of cinematograph films), any patent, trademark, design or model, plan, secret formula or process, or from the use of, or the right to use, industrial, commercial, or scientific equipment, or for information concerning industrial, commercial, or scientific experience.

14. The 15% rate applies to royalties paid by an enterprise registered and engaged in preferred areas of activities, and to royalties in respect of cinematographic films or tapes for television or broadcasting, and for the use of, or the right to use, any copyright. The 25% rate applies to other royalties.

15. The 10% rate also applies to interest paid in connection with the sale on credit of any industrial, commercial, or scientific equipment.

16. The 10% rate also applies to interest paid on any loans granted by a bank.

17. The 15% rate also applies to royalties in respect of cinematographic films or tapes for television or broadcasting.

18. The 10% rate applies to interest paid on government securities, or bonds or debentures. The 15% rate applies to any other interest income.

19. The 15% rate applies to royalties paid for the use of or the right to use cinematographic films and films or tapes for radio or television broadcasting.

20. The 7.5% rate applies to the lease of containers. The 10% rate applies to royalties paid by an enterprise registered with the Board of Investments. The 25% rate applies to other royalties.

21. The 10% rate applies to royalties paid by an enterprise registered with the Board of Investments and engaged in preferred pioneer areas of activity. The 15% rate applies to rentals from cinematographic films and tapes for television or broadcasting. The 25% rate applies to all other royalties.

22. The threshold for substantial ownership is 15%.

23. The 10% rate applies to royalties paid by an enterprise registered with the Board of Investments and engaged in preferred pioneer areas of activity. The 20% rate applies to rentals from cinematographic films and tapes for television or broadcasting. The 15% rate applies to all other royalties.

24. The lower rates apply only if the Thai corporate shareholder holds owns more than 15% of the dividend paying company. The 15% rate applies if the Thai company is engaged In an industrial undertaking, and the 20% rate applies otherwise.

## Tax administration

**Returns**/Corporations should file their returns and compute their income on the basis of an accounting period of 12 months. This accounting period may be either a calendar year or a fiscal year. With prior approval of the Commissioner of Internal Revenue, corporations may change their accounting period from calendar year to fiscal year, or vice versa. Corporate taxpayers file self-assessing returns. Electronic filing and payment of taxes are available under the Electronic Filing and Payment System (EFPS) of the BIR.

# Philippines

**Payment of tax**/Every corporation files cumulative quarterly income tax returns for the first three quarters, and pays the tax due thereon within 60 days after each quarter. A final adjustment return covering the total net taxable income of the preceding taxable year must be filed on the fifteenth day of the fourth month following the close of the taxable year. The balance of the tax due after deducting the quarterly payments must be paid, while the excess may be claimed as refund or tax credit. Excess estimated quarterly income taxes paid may be carried over and credited against estimated quarterly income tax liabilities for succeeding taxable years. Once the option to carry over has been made, such option is irrevocable for that taxable period, and no cash refund or tax credit certificate (TCC) is allowed.

## CORPORATION TAX CALCULATION

Calendar year 2004

| | | |
|---|---:|---:|
| Net income before income taxes (1) | | PHP 1,000,000 |
| Add: | | |
| Provision to reserve accounts (bad debts, etc.) | 100,000 | |
| Charitable contributions in excess of limitation | 13,000 | |
| Unallowable interest expense (38% of 50,000) | 19,000 | |
| Unallowable entertainment, amusement and | | |
| recreation expenses | 87,000 | 219,000 |
| | | 1,219,000 |
| Deduct: | | |
| Dividends received from domestic corporation | 50,000 | |
| Charges against reserves (bad debts, etc.) | 50,000 | |
| Interest on government securities | 50,000 | |
| Net loss carryover | 80,735 | 230,735 |
| Taxable income | | PHP 988,265 |
| Tax thereon (32% on PHP988,265) | | PHP 316,245 |

Notes:

1. Includes interest income of PHP50,000 subject to 20% final tax and net of interest expense of PHP100,000.
2. Exchange rate of the Philippine peso at January 1, 2004: US$1 = PHP55.53.

## PwC contact

For additional information on taxation in Poland, contact:

Piotr Kowalski
PricewaterhouseCoopers Warsaw
Al. Armii Ludowej 14
00-638 Warsaw, Poland
Telephone: (48) (22) 523 4000
Fax: (48) (22) 523 4040
e-mail: piotr.kowalski@pl.pwc.com

## Significant developments

The year 2004 is a year of numerous important changes in the Polish tax law. Some of them have already come into force, and others will come into force on May 1, 2004, when Poland effectively joins the EU.

Starting from January 1, 2004, the corporate income tax rate has been decreased to 19% (from 27% in 2003). However, the withholding tax rate on dividends has been increased to 19% (from 15% in 2003). Furthermore, when Poland effectively joins the EU (which shall take place on May 1, 2004) the new withholding tax regime shall apply to dividends paid among Polish and EU companies (see "Withholding taxes" below).

Furthermore, on May 1, 2004 major changes in value-added tax (VAT) legislation will enter into force. The new VAT law, which will replace the old VAT Law of 1993, is aimed to adapt Polish VAT provisions to the EU requirements (in particular to the VI Directive). In spite of the extensive scope of the reform, the standard VAT rate will remain at the level of 22%.

The Polish Parliament has also enacted a new excise law, which came into force on March 1, 2004. However, most of the provisions included in this law will become effective on May 1, 2004.

Finally, accession to the EU will trigger a great change in the applicable customs regime.

## Taxes on corporate income

All legal entities and organizational entities without a corporate status (with the exception of partnerships) that conduct economic activity are obliged to pay corporate income tax at a rate of 19%.

Companies with foreign participation can be set up in Poland as either limited liability companies or joint stock companies. Limited liability companies and joint stock companies are legal entities whose income is taxed at the aforementioned rates of the company's derived tax base. There is no limitation on the percentage of foreign participation.

Foreign entrepreneurs are also allowed, under certain conditions, to establish their branch offices (exclusively within the scope of their "foreign" business activity) and representative offices (exclusively with regard to promotion and advertising) in Poland.

# Poland

## Corporate residence

A company is considered resident if it has its legal seat or management on the territory of the Republic of Poland. The territory of the Republic of Poland is defined as inclusive of the portion of the continental shelf beyond the territorial waters of the Republic of Poland over which the country, under domestic law and in compliance with international law, exercises rights relating to the exploration and exploitation of the seabed and of the natural resources therein.

## Other taxes

*Value-added tax*/Starting from May 1, 2004, a new VAT law will come into force. The aim of this law is to adapt Polish VAT legislation to the EU requirements, and in fact, most of the provisions are based on the VI Directive. Standard VAT rate applicable to sale of goods and services will remain at the level of 22%. Certain items will be subject to reduced rate of 7%, including, among others, pharmaceutical products and passenger transport services. Some supplies will be exempt from VAT, including (but not limited to) certain financial, insurance, and educational services. Certain activities will be zero-rated, for example, export of goods to countries outside the EU, as well as international transport of goods (i.e., transport to or from countries outside of the EU). Furthermore, numerous services, if rendered to a foreign customer will not be subject to the Polish VAT, while a Polish VAT taxpayer will be entitled to deduct input VAT paid in connection with rendering such services.

*Excise tax*/Starting from May 1, 2004, when the new excise law will entirely come into force (part of this law has come into force already), excise tax will be levied on production, sale, import and intra-community acquisition of excise goods, which include among others alcohol, cigarettes, petrol, passenger cars, and cosmetics.

*Property tax*/For purposes of the property tax, taxpayers are natural and legal persons that are owners or freeholders of property and dependent holders of property belonging to the state. Property that is subject to the tax includes buildings, constructions used for business, and land that is not subject to agricultural tax. The tax rates are determined by particular county councils, but cannot be higher than the following (for 2004) amounts.

1. For buildings used for business—PLN 17.42/square meter.
2. For land used for business—PLN 0.63/square meter.
3. Construction—2% of the value.

*Customs duty*/When Poland effectively becomes a EU member on May 1, 2004, it will be subject to the EU customs provisions. Consequently, trade between Poland and other EU countries will be customs-free. Furthermore, Poland will have to apply EU customs tariff, which will, generally, result in decrease of customs rates on imports from non-EU countries. It should also be noted that even before the accession date, nearly all industry products of EU origin imported from EU countries used to be subject to 0% customs rate.

## Branch income

Under the Business Activity Law, foreign entrepreneurs are allowed, under certain conditions, to establish their branch offices (exclusively within the scope of their "foreign" business activity) and representative offices (exclusively with regard to promotion and advertising) in Poland.

A branch office has nearly always a permanent establishment (PE) status in Poland. Consequently, it pays corporate income tax at the standard rate of 19% on the basis of income attributed to its operations in Poland. For this purpose, as well as for accounting purposes, a branch is obliged to keep accounting books that should include all data necessary to establish taxable base. With this respect, general income determination rules (see below) relevant to Polish companies apply to branches as well. In those few cases, where a branch can establish, on the basis of a tax treaty, that its business presence in Poland does not amount to a permanent establishment, its profits are not subject to Polish tax.

## Income determination

***Accounting books***/Taxable income is determined based on accounting books. Therefore, the books should include data necessary to establish the taxable base. However, due to numerous temporary or permanent differences between tax and accounting regulations, taxable income is a gross accounting profit after adjustments.

***Inventory***/No write-offs in value of inventory are recognized for tax purposes until inventory is sold or otherwise disposed of. When inventory is disposed of, tax-deductible cost should equal expenses incurred on purchasing or manufacturing the disposed inventory. The methods acceptable for inventory valuation for tax (and accounting) purposes are standard cost, average (weighted) cost, FIFO, and LIFO.

***Capital gains***/There is no separate capital gains tax. Capital gains or losses are aggregated with the entity's other taxable income or losses. Capital losses are tax deductible.

***Intercompany dividends***/Dividends received from Polish subsidiaries and other domestic corporations within Poland are not included in the taxable income of the recipient but are subject to withholding taxes (see "Withholding taxes").

***Foreign income***/Resident corporations are taxed on their worldwide income, unless an agreement between the Republic of Poland and the foreign state stipulates otherwise.

***Stock dividends***/The payment of stock dividends is treated as a distribution of dividends, which means that they are not included in taxable income of the recipient but are subject to withholding taxes (see "Withholding taxes").

## Deductions

***Depreciation and depletion***/Depreciation is treated as a tax-allowable cost, and can be calculated by using the straight-line method. Maximum straight-line rates are provided by the tax law. However, for certain categories of plant and machinery and motor vehicles (not including passenger cars) the reducing-balance method of depreciation may be applied so that depreciation can be charged at a higher rate. These rates are computed by multiplying the standard rate by a maximum factor of two or, in the case of regions threatened by high structural unemployment, a maximum factor of three. The basis of the calculation is the net value of fixed assets. The reducing-balance method is applied until the annual depreciation charge equals the depreciation charge that would have been produced under the straight-line method. In this way, during the initial period of using the fixed assets the owner receives the benefit of accelerated depreciation. Depreciation rate may also be increased to 30% in respect of certain "brand new" fixed assets in the first tax year when a given asset was entered in the records.

# Poland

The main categories of assets and their statutory annual tax depreciation rates are as follows.

|  | % |
| --- | --- |
| Various buildings and constructions | 1.5 to 10 |
| Machinery and equipment (general) | 7 to 20 |
| Machinery for road building and construction | 18 to 20 |
| Machinery for paper industry | 14 |
| Various rail vehicles, ships, and aircraft | 7 to 20 |
| Trucks | 20 |
| Office equipment | 14 |
| Computers | 30 |

Accelerated depreciation (within specified limits) is also available for assets used in deteriorated conditions and for second-hand assets.

*Tax losses*/A taxpayer has the right to carry forward a loss incurred in a tax year by deducting the loss against its taxable income generated in the following five years, provided that no more than 50% of the loss reported in a particular year can be deducted in one of the following five years.

*Payments to foreign affiliates*/Under current legislation, deductions can be claimed for royalties, management services, and interest charges paid to foreign affiliates (interest subject to thin-capitalization restrictions), provided exchange control regulations and transfer pricing restrictions are observed.

*Thin capitalization*/Part of the interest paid by a Polish company on a loan granted by a qualified lender (qualified shareholder or qualified sister company) will not be considered as tax-deductible cost, if the value of the Polish company's overall debt from the shareholders and other affiliates mentioned in the tax law exceeds three times the value of the Polish company's share capital (3:1 debt-to-equity ratio). A qualified shareholder is defined as a shareholder or group of shareholders owning 25% or more of the voting power of the Polish company.

*Taxes*/Taxes on income and, in most cases, VAT are not deductible. However, VAT is deductible for corporate income tax purposes if it cannot be offset against the company's output VAT. Other taxes that are part of expenses are, in general, deductible in full.

*Business expenses*/Businesses are entitled to deduct from their revenues costs borne in order to generate revenue related to the fiscal period for which the deductions are made. The law provides a list of items of expenditure that are not tax deductible. The list contains 65 items, including the following.

1. Expenses on assets subject to depreciation.
2. Written-off lapsed accounts receivable.
3. Expenditure borne on abandoned investments.
4. Unrealized foreign exchange losses.
5. Nonpublic advertising costs in excess of 0.25% of taxable revenue.
6. Accrued but unpaid interest.
7. Accounting and comparable provisions.
8. Tax penalties and penalty interest.

## Group taxation

Companies wanting to use group taxation must conclude an agreement in the form of a notarized deed forming a capital tax group for a period of at least three years. Only limited liability and joint stock companies having a seat in Poland may participate in the group. The dominant company must hold directly 95% of the shares of the dependent companies. There are some additional restrictions and requirements regarding shareholding among the companies, including the minimum share capital and the minimum group profitability of at least 6% (understood as the ratio of taxable income to taxable revenue). In general, rules applicable to tax capital groups are viewed as very difficult to meet and thus this form of taxation barely exists in practice.

## Tax incentives

Polish legislation provides for investment incentives related to business activities carried out in "special economic zones." The current number of such zones is 14. A business entity can benefit from tax incentives offered by a special economic zone provided that the entity obtains a permit to conduct business activities in such zone, and meets other requirements laid out in Polish law. The related permits are issued by the Minister of Economy. Based on the permits that are granted currently, most of special economic zones offer income tax exemption up to the amount of 50% of the investment expenditures. Furthermore, entities classified as small or medium can be granted the income tax exemption up to the amount of 65% of the investment expenditures. Consequently, in the case of significant investments, businesses conducting activities in special economic zones can enjoy total exemption from income tax for quite a long time.

## Withholding taxes

Dividend payments made by domestic payers to resident corporations are taxed at a 19% rate, but those corporations are eligible for a tax credit equal to the amount of the tax, provided they have sufficient taxable profit to utilize the credit. If it is not possible to utilize the tax credit in a fiscal period, it may be carried forward and utilized in the following fiscal periods. The net result is that resident corporations with taxable income are free of tax on dividends received from other resident corporations.

Polish corporations are required to withhold tax on payments of dividends, interest, and royalties. The table below provides information on general withholding tax rates provided for in Polish corporate income tax law, as well as the rates that are based on double tax treaties concluded with particular countries. Besides, it should be noted that starting from the date when Poland effectively joins the European Union (i.e., May 1, 2004), dividends paid to EU corporate residents will be exempted from withholding tax subject to certain conditions specified in the Polish corporate income tax (CIT) Law (including, among others, the requirement that foreign beneficiary holds at least 25% shares in Polish company for at least two years). The exemption will not concern income resulted from redemption of shares and liquidation of a company.

Apart from dividends, royalties, and interest, Polish companies are, in general, required to withhold 20% tax on payments made to nonresidents for specified intangible supplies including (but not limited to) advisory, accounting, market-research and advertising services. However, if remuneration for these services is paid to a country that has a double tax treaty with Poland, this particular withholding tax can be easily avoided.

# Poland

| Recipient | Dividends | Interest | Royalties |
|---|---|---|---|
| | % | % | % |
| Nontreaty | 19 | 20 | 20 |
| Treaty: | | | |
| Albania | 10 (1) | 10 | 5 |
| Australia | 15 | 10 | 10 |
| Austria | 10 | 0 | 0 |
| Bangladesh | 15 (2) | 10 (3) | 10 |
| Belarus | 15 (4) | 10 | 0 |
| Belgium | 10 | 10 (5) | 10 |
| Bulgaria | 10 | 10 (3) | 5 |
| Canada | 15 | 15 (3) | 10 (6) |
| Chile | 15 (8) | 15 | 15 (37) |
| China, P.R. | 10 | 10 (3) | 10 (7) |
| Croatia | 15 (1) | 10 (3) | 10 |
| Cyprus | 10 | 10 (3) | 5 |
| Czech Republic | 10 (8) | 10 (3) | 5 |
| Denmark | 15 (9, 10) | 5 (3, 11) | 5 |
| Egypt | 12 | 12 (2) | 12 |
| Estonia | 15 (1) | 10 (3) | 10 |
| Finland | 15 (1) | 0 | 0 (12) |
| France | 15 (13) | 0 | 10 (14) |
| Germany | 15 (1, 15) | 0 | 0 |
| Greece | 15 | 10 | 10 |
| Hungary | 10 | 10 (3) | 10 |
| Iceland | 15 (1) | 10 (3) | 10 |
| India | 15 | 15 (2, 16) | 22.5 |
| Indonesia | 15 (17) | 10 (18) | 15 |
| Ireland, Rep. of | 15 (19) | 10 (20) | 10 (21) |
| Israel | 10 (22) | 5 | 10 (23) |
| Italy | 10 | 10 (3) | 10 |
| Japan | 10 | 10 (3) | 10 (24) |
| Jordan | 10 | 10 (3) | 10 |
| Kazakhstan | 15 (17) | 10 | 10 |
| Korea, Rep. of | 10 (10) | 10 (16, 18, 25) | 10 |
| Kuwait | 5 (26) | 5 (3) | 15 |
| Latvia | 15 (1) | 10 (3) | 10 |
| Lithuania | 15 (1) | 10 (3) | 10 |
| Luxembourg | 15 (1) | 10 (27) | 10 |
| Macedonia | 15 (1) | 10 (3) | 10 |
| Malaysia | 0 | 15 (28) | 15 (28) |
| Malta | 15 (29, 30) | 10 (18) | 10 |
| Mexico | 15 (1) | 15 (31, 32) | 10 |
| Moldova | 15 (1) | 10 | 10 |
| Morocco | 15 (33) | 10 | 10 |
| Mongolia | 10 | 10 (15) | 5 |
| Netherlands | 15 (34, 35) | 5 (36) | 5 |
| Norway | 15 (1) | 0 | 10 (14) |
| Pakistan | 15 (39) | 20 (40) | 20 (41) |
| Philippines | 15 (42) | 10 (18) | 15 |
| Portugal | 15 (42) | 10 (18) | 10 |

| Recipient | Dividends | Interest | Royalties |
|---|---|---|---|
|  | % | % | % |
| Romania | 5 (1) | 10 (3) | 10 |
| Russia | 10 | 10 (18) | 10 |
| Singapore | 10 | 10 (18) | 10 |
| Slovak Republic | 10 (8) | 10 (3) | 5 |
| Slovenia | 15 (1) | 10 (18) | 10 |
| South Africa | 15 (1) | 10 (3) | 10 |
| Spain | 15 (43) | 0 | 10 (6) |
| Sri Lanka | 15 | 0 | 10 |
| Sweden | 15 (43) | 0 | 10 |
| Switzerland | 15 (1) | 10 | 10 (44) |
| Syria | 10 | 10 (38) | 18 |
| Thailand | 20 (45) | 20 (18, 46) | 15 (47) |
| Tunisia | 10 (1) | 12 | 12 |
| Turkey | 15 (42) | 10 (3) | 10 |
| Ukraine | 15 (1) | 10 | 10 |
| United Arab Emirates | 5 (48) | 5 (3) | 5 |
| United Kingdom | 15 (49) | 0 | 10 |
| United States | 15 (49) | 0 | 10 |
| Uzbekistan | 15 (8) | 10 (18) | 10 |
| Vietnam | 15 (42) | 10 | 15 (50) |
| Yugoslavia (former) | 15 (1) | 10 | 10 |
| Yugoslavia (Fed. Rep.) | 15 (1) | 10 | 10 |
| Zimbabwe | 15 (42) | 10 | 10 |

Notes:

1. A rate of 5% if the recipient company holds directly at least 25% of the share capital of the paying company.

2. A rate of 10% if the recipient company holds directly at least 10% of the share capital of the paying company.

3. A rate of 0% if interest is paid in respect of a loan made or guaranteed by the government of the other state, its local authorities, the central bank of the contracting state, or any financial institution controlled by the government of the contracting state.

4. A rate of 10% if the recipient company holds directly more than 30% of the share capital of the paying company.

5. A rate of 0% for interest on current accounts or registered loans between banks of the two states, cash deposits with banks and interest received by the state.

6. A rate of 0% on royalties from copyrights of literary, dramatic, musical, or artistic works (excluding royalties in respect of motion picture films and works on film or videotape for use in connection with television).

7. A rate of 10% of 70% of gross income arising from payments for the use of or the right to use any industrial, commercial, or scientific equipment.

8. A rate of 5% if the recipient company holds directly at least 20% of the capital of the company paying the dividends.

9. A rate of 0% if the beneficial owner is a company which holds directly at least 25% of the capital of the company paying dividends and if such holding is being possessed for an uninterrupted period of no less than one year.

10. A rate of 5% if the beneficial owner is a pension fund or other similar institution established and controlled in accordance with the law of the contracting state.

11. A rate of 0% if interest is paid in connection with the sale of any industrial, commercial, or scientific equipment, in respect of the obligation of the government of the contracting state, to the political subdivision or local authority thereof.

12. A rate of 10% of payments received as a consideration for the use of or the right to use any patent, trademark, design or model, plan, secret formula or process, or any industrial, commercial, or scientific equipment, or for information concerning industrial, commercial, or scientific experience.

13. A rate of 5% if the recipient company holds directly at least 10% of the payer's capital.

14. A rate of 0% on royalties from copyrights of literary, artistic, or scientific works.

15. A rate of 15% if the difference in tax rates on undistributed and distributed profits is 20% or more.

16. A rate of 0% on interest on certain trade loans or credits.

17. A rate of 10% if the recipient company holds directly at least 20% of the capital of the paying company.

18. As per note 3, but without the phrase "or guaranteed."

19. A rate of 0% if the recipient company holds directly at least 25% of the voting power of the payer.

20. A rate of 0% on interest paid in connection with the sale on credit of any industrial, commercial, or scientific equipment or of any merchandise by one enterprise to another or on any loan granted by a bank.

21. A rate of 0% on fees for technical services.

22. A rate of 5% if the recipient company holds directly at least 15% of the payer's capital.

23. A lower rate of 5% is applicable for the use of or the right to use industrial, commercial, or scientific equipment.

24. A rate of 0% on cultural royalties (payments for the use of or the right to use any copyright of literary, artistic, or scientific work, including cinematographic films and films or tapes for radio or television broadcasting) if the beneficial owner is resident in the other state.

25. A rate of 0% on interest paid in connection with the sale on credit of any industrial, commercial, or scientific equipment or of any merchandise by one enterprise to another enterprise.

26. A rate of 0% on dividends of which the beneficial owner is the government or any government agency or a company the capital of which is owned directly or indirectly at least 25% by the government or governmental institutions of either party.

27. A rate of 0% on interest paid in respect of bank credits or loans or on interest derived by a contracting state for its own account.

28. Interest on an approved loan or long-term loan and royalties paid to a resident of Poland are exempt from Malaysian tax, subject to approval by the competent authority of Malaysia.

29. Where the dividends are paid by a company resident in Malta to a resident of Poland that is the beneficial owner thereof, Malta tax on the gross amount of the dividends should not exceed that chargeable on the profits out of which the dividends are paid.

30. A rate of 5% if the recipient company being a resident of Malta holds directly at least 20% of the capital of the Poland-resident company paying the dividends.

31. A rate of 5% if the beneficial owner is a bank or an insurance office or if interest is derived from bonds and securities that are regularly traded on a recognized securities market.

32. A rate of 0% if the beneficial owner is: a contracting state, a political subdivision, local authority, pension or retirement fund, or if the interest is paid in respect of a loan guaranteed or insured by national banks for a period no less than three years.

33. A rate of 7% if the recipient company holds directly at least 25% of the share capital of the paying company.

34. A rate of 0% if the recipient company holds directly at least 25% of the share capital of the paying company.

35. A rate of 0% if the recipient company holds directly at least 25% of the share capital of the paying company; this rule shall be applicable until Poland and the Netherlands implement in full the 90/435/EEC Directive.

36. A rate of 0% rate is applicable under specific condition; furthermore 0% rate is applicable until December 31, 2004 to contracts concluded before February 13, 2002.

37. A rate of 5% rate is applicable to payments being a consideration for the use of or the right to use any industrial, commercial, or scientific equipment.

38. A rate of 0% if interest is related inter alia to debt claim or a loan issued, guaranteed or supported by a contracting state or other person acting on behalf of the contracting state.

39. The rate of 15% is also applicable if the beneficial owner controls at least one-third of the company's stock.

40. A rate of 0% on interest paid to a Polish company on loans approved by the Pakistan Ministry of Finance and interest derived by the Central Bank of Pakistan and Bank *Handlowy w Warszawie S.A.*

41. A lower rate of 15% applies to payments received as consideration for technical know-how or information concerning industrial, commercial, or scientific experience.

42. A rate of 10% if the recipient company holds directly at least 25% of the capital of the paying company.

43. A rate of 5% if the recipient company holds directly at least 25% of the voting power of the paying company.

44. A rate of 0% according to protocol, as long as Switzerland does not levy withholding tax on royalties paid to nonresidents.

45. A rate of 20% if the recipient company holds directly at least 25% of the share capital of the paying company.

46. A rate of 10% if the interest is received by a financial institution (including an insurance company).

47. The lower rate of 5% is applicable for copyright of literary, artistic, or scientific work, excluding cinematographic films or tapes for television or broadcasting.

48. A rate of 0% on dividends of which the beneficial owner is the government or its agency.

49. A rate of 5% if the recipient company is the beneficial owner, holding directly or indirectly at least 10% of the voting power of the paying company.

# Poland

50. A rate of 10% if payments are received as consideration for the use of any patent, trademark, design or model, plan, or secret formula or for information concerning industrial or scientific experience.

Poland is also a member of the Comecon multilateral double taxation treaty until Organization for Economic Cooperation and Development (OECD)-type treaties between the former Comecon members come into force.

## Tax administration

***Returns***/Generally, companies are required to file monthly corporate income tax returns for tax advances paid during the year. These should be filed by the 20th day of the month following the reported month. Under certain circumstances, taxpayers may file only one half-year return.

In addition, a company subject to tax is required to file an annual return with the tax office according to a specified format. The return should state the amount of income earned in the fiscal year, and should be filed by the end of the third month following the end of the taxpayer's fiscal year. In this period the company must pay the difference between the tax due on income stated in the return and the sum of monthly tax advances paid for the period from the beginning of the year.

***Payment of tax***/Generally, the taxpayer must pay monthly advances in amounts equal to the difference between the tax due on the income earned since the beginning of the year, and the sum of advances paid for preceding months. The monthly advances for the 1st to the 11th months of the taxpayer's fiscal year are payable no later than the 20th of the following month. By the 20th day of the 12th month the taxpayer must remit an amount equal to twice the tax due for the 11th month. This payment covers the tax advances due for both the 11th and 12th months. In other words, there is no tax advance due by the 20th of the first month of the next year.

Having met certain requirements, the taxpayer may also pay tax advances for all months of the fiscal year, one-twelfth of tax declared in a return, filed in the previous fiscal year (or a year earlier, when he did not declare income in that declaration).

The law requires all tax and related payments as well as payments made between business entities to be made through bank accounts. Information about bank accounts held must be given to the tax office.

## CORPORATION TAX CALCULATION

Calendar year ended December 31, 2004

(In PLN thousands)

| | |
|---|---|
| Net profit before taxes | 100,000 |
| Less: | |
| Loss brought forward | 8,300 |
| Taxable income | 91,700 |
| Corporate income tax payable at 19% | 17,423 |

Note:

Average exchange rate of the zloty at January 1, 2004: US$1 = PLN 3.7405.

## PwC contact

For additional information on taxation in Portugal, contact:

José Fonseca
PricewaterhouseCoopers
Edifício Caravelas
Rua Dr. Eduardo Neves, 9–6°
1069-053 Lisbon, Portugal
Telephone: (351) 21 791 40 50
Fax: (351) 21 791 40 60
e-mail: jose.fonseca@pt.pwc.global

## General note

The information in this entry is current as of January 2004. For subsequent developments consult the contact listed above.

From January 1, 2004 onward, the inheritance and gift tax has been abolished. From this date onward the gratuitous transfer of assets (e.g., gift or inheritance) is subject to stamp tax (exemptions are available for spouses and direct ascendants or descendants). For entities subject to corporate income tax, gratuitous acquisitions are aggregated to the year-end taxable profit being taxed at the general applicable rates.

The 2003 Property Tax Reform (enacted in November 2003) introduced considerable amendments to the previously existing local property tax (*Contribuição Autárquica*) and property transfer tax (Sisa). These are now respectively called *Imposto Municipal sobre Imóveis* (IMI) and *Imposto Municipal sobre a Transmissão Onerosa de Imóveis* (IMT).

## Taxes on corporate income

The corporate tax rate is 25%, increased to 27.5% in most cases by a municipal surcharge (*derrama*) of 10%. Special rates apply to income generated in Portugal that is attributable to nonresidents, as discussed below under "Withholding taxes."

## Corporate residence

Tax is assessed on the worldwide income of business entities with a head office or effective management in Portugal. Tax is also applicable to income attributable to a nonresident company deemed to have a permanent establishment in Portugal.

## Other taxes

*Surcharges*/The following surcharges, self-assessed with the corporate tax, are levied on (a) representation and entertainment expenses, at 6%, (b) company car costs, at 6%, (c) confidential and nondocumented payments, at 50%.

*Value-added tax*/VAT closely follows the European Union (EU) Sixth Directive, and is assessed at the normal rate of 19%, at an intermediate rate of 12%, and at a reduced rate of 5%. Restaurant services, basic canned foods, fruit jellies, fats, honey, coffee, natural water, fruit juices, decorative flowers, petroleum and diesel fuel for equipment for agricultural and fishing activities and certain ecological equipment, are subject to the 12% rate. Food, books, some pharmaceutical products, milk products, and certain services are assessed at 5%. Exports and intra-EU-transmissions of goods are zero-rated.

# Portugal

***Stamp tax***/Stamp tax is payable on a wide variety of transactions and documents, at rates at rates that may be set in specific amounts, or on a percentage basis. Important examples include the following.

|  | % |
| --- | --- |
| Loans (on the principal) | 0.5–0.6 |
| Guarantees | 0.5–0.6 |
| Bank interest and fees | 4 |
| Insurance premiums | 3–9 |
| Incorporation of companies (on the share capital) | 0.4 |
| Real estate purchases and sales | 0.8 |
| Transfer of a going-concern | 5 |
| Donations and inheritances | 10 |

***Local property tax (IMI)***/For local property tax, the main change was centered on the assessment of the taxable basis. This is now calculated by reference to a formula based on objective criteria, such as the construction cost per square meter, area, age, and construction quality and comfort indexes. The new evaluation rules will be implemented within the following ten years. However, a transfer of real estate after the new legislation came into force (December 1, 2004) will trigger a valuation procedure of the underlying asset.

The property tax is still in addition to corporate or individual tax assessed on actual income generated by real estate.

| Tax rates | % |
| --- | --- |
| Urban real estate | 0.4–0.8 |
| Urban real estate (valuated under the new rules) | 0.2–0.5 |
| Rural real estate | 0.8 |

The tax rate of municipal tax on immovable property for residential property owned by a nonresident located in a blacklisted low taxation territory is always 5% (increased from the previous 2%).

***Municipal property transfer tax (IMT)***/IMT is payable in Portugal on the onerous transfer of local real estate. The tax is due from the purchaser, and the taxable basis is calculated by reference to the IMI valuation, or the price agreed upon by the contracting parties, whichever is higher. Similar to the IMI rules, the transfer of real estate after January 1, 2004 (when the IMT changes came into force) will spur the revaluation of the taxable basis (under the IMI rules).

The main changes introduced related to the applicable tax rates (with an overall reduction), the calculation of the taxable basis (now undertaken by reference to objective criteria in addition to the contractual price) and the incidence rule (extended to operations that qualify as a transfer from a substance over form perspective).

The IMT rates are set at 5% for rural real estate, and 6.5% for urban real estate and land for construction. For nonresidents located in blacklisted off-shore jurisdictions, the rate is always 15%.

The transfer of residential property is subject to IMT at marginal and progressive tax rates from 2% up to 8%. An exemption is available for a taxable basis not higher than €80,000. Taxable basis higher that €500,000 is subject to a 6% flat rate.

## Branch income

Branch profits are taxed on the same basis as corporate profits. Income remitted by a branch is exempt from tax withheld at source.

## Income determination

Taxable income is based on the accounting income adjusted according, when applicable, to the specific provisions of the tax legislation.

*Inventory valuation*/Inventories are stated at cost. The FIFO, LIFO, and average-cost methods of valuation are accepted.

It is possible to reduce cost to market value if the latter is lower. This provision can be utilized only when a loss is realized, a concept interpreted restrictively by the authorities.

*Capital gains*/Capital gains arising on the sale of fixed assets (net of losses) and on the sale of shares (net of 50% of losses) are taxed as part of normal income. In certain circumstances, namely if the assets have been held for more than one year, only 50% of the net gains are taxed, provided the sales proceeds are reinvested. Capital losses regarding shares owned for less than three years when acquired from related companies, offshore companies or companies subject to a privileged taxation regime are not deductible. Capital losses are not tax deductible if the shares are transferred to related parties, offshore companies or entities subject to a privileged taxation regime.

Capital gains/losses realized by holding companies are not taxed/deductible, provided the underlying shares have been held for more than one year (or three years if the shares were acquired from related parties, off-shore companies or entities subject to a special tax regime).

The net book value of fixed assets is adjusted by official inflation indexes in the computation of taxable capital gains or losses of assets that have been held for at least two years.

*Intercompany dividends*/For Portuguese residents or EU residents (meeting the Parent/subsidiary Directive 90/435/CEE), 100% of the dividends is excluded from the taxable income if the shares represent at least 10% of total capital, or have an acquisition value not lower than €20 million, and have been held for at least one year (this minimum holding period should be met before or after distribution)). This also applies to regional development corporations (*sociedades de desenvolvimento regional*), investment companies, securities dealers and insurance companies (technical reserves) regardless of the proportion of capital or the period held. For holding companies (*Sociedade Gestora do Participações Sociais,* or SGPS) and venture capital companies, the deduction requires the fulfillment of the shareholding period.

If the above conditions are not met, Portuguese corporations are taxed only on 50% of the dividends distributed by a company resident in Portugal.

*Foreign income*/A Portuguese company is taxed on foreign income from a branch operation. In other cases, tax is assessed on the basis of income received. Tax paid abroad can be offset against corresponding Portuguese tax. International tax credits may be carried forward for the following five tax years.

*Stock dividends*/Stock dividends are not taxed.

# Portugal

*Other significant items*/Doubtful debts are deductible upon declared bankruptcy or a special company's recovery court action.

Provisions are made for deductions of debts overdue by the following amounts of time to the extent of the following percentages.

| | % |
|---|---|
| More than 6 and less than 12 months | 25 |
| More than 12 and less than 18 months | 50 |
| More than 18 and less than 24 months | 75 |
| More than 24 months | 100 |

No provision can be made if overdue amounts are guaranteed by insurance or mortgage or are due by government agencies or by related parties (10% or more of capital).

The aging of bills of exchange is calculated from the date that the respective payment is due, and not from the date of delivery of goods or services to which they relate.

## Deductions

*Depreciation and depletion*/Depreciation must be computed by using the straight-line method or the declining-balance method. The latter cannot be applied to buildings, passenger vehicles, furniture, social welfare equipment, and second-hand assets. Straight-line rates of depreciation are normally consistent with rates privately used by business and industry and are increased, for the purposes of applying the declining-balance method, by coefficients of 1.5 if assets have a useful life of less than five years, of 2 if useful life is five or six years, and of 2.5 for useful lives in excess of six years.

Rates can be reduced by 50% in any one year at the taxpayer's option. If the reduction is more than 50%, the difference will not be allowed for tax purposes at a later date. Any depreciation in excess of the maximum must be subsequently adjusted in the accounting records to be allowed for tax purposes in future years. A total of 60% of additional depreciation on revaluation of fixed assets, as permitted from time to time, is allowed for tax purposes.

Depreciation rates may be increased by 25% where more than one shift is worked. (for two shifts, 50%).

Depreciation of yachts and motor vehicles that are not essential for business activities, and depreciation on the excess of €30,000 each on passenger cars and certain other vehicles, is not allowed as a cost for tax purposes.

The qualifying cost of an asset for tax purposes is the acquisition or production cost (for fixed assets acquired up to December 2000, this is reduced by any capital gain deferred on the acquisition of the asset under former capital gains reinvestment provisions). Start-up and R&D expenses may be depreciated over three years. Patents, trademarks, licenses, and similar rights may be depreciated for tax purposes if acquired for a limited time-span. Goodwill cannot be depreciated (unless subject to an effective economic depreciation approved by the Portuguese tax authorities).

Some examples relating to the maximum straight-line depreciation rate are as follows.

| Type of asset | Rate % |
|---|---|
| Office building ............................................................................................. | 2 |
| Industrial building ....................................................................................... | 5 |
| Electronic equipments ................................................................................ | 20 |
| Computers .................................................................................................. | 25 |
| Ordinary tool & paintings............................................................................ | 25 |
| Engines & machine tools............................................................................ | 12.5 |
| Office equipment......................................................................................... | 12.5 |
| Software...................................................................................................... | 33.3 |
| Light passenger vehicles............................................................................ | 25 |

***Tax losses***/Tax losses can be carried forward for six years. Carryback of losses is not allowed.

***Payments to foreign affiliates***/A Portuguese corporation is allowed to deduct royalties and interest paid to foreign affiliates, provided the amounts do not exceed normal rates. Service fees paid are allowed if there is adequate proof that the service was rendered.

***Interest on loans provided by the shareholders***/Should the rate applicable to interest and other compensation regarding loans provided by the shareholders to the company be higher than the Euro Interbank Offered Rate (EURIBOR) 12-month rate rounded up with a spread of 1.5% (at the date of constitution of the loan), the excessive amount paid will not be tax deductible. This rule does not apply when the shareholder is resident of a tax treaty country, or when the interest rate is at arm's length under the transfer pricing provisions.

***Transfer pricing***/The tax authorities are entitled to adjust taxable income if the taxpayer and another individual or entity, due to their special relationship, have established particular conditions which diverge from the conditions normally agreed upon between independent persons and distort the results that would arise if those relations were at arm's length. For tax years starting on or after January 1, 2002, Portugal has implemented detailed transfer pricing legislation, which broadly follows the Organization for Economic Cooperation and Development (OECD) guidelines.

***Thin capitalization***/Where loans from nonresident related parties exceeds twice the parties' capital in the borrowing Portuguese entity, the interest on the excess borrowing is not tax deductible. This rule may not apply if the company proves, under a safeguard clause, that taking into account its type of activity, the sector in which operates, its dimensions and other relevant criteria, it would be possible to obtain the same loan on similar terms from an independent entity.

***Antiavoidance***/A general antiavoidance provision has been enacted, pursuant to which contracts and other acts are ineffective whenever it is demonstrated that they were tax-driven to reduce taxation that would be due under contracts bearing a similar economic effect in which case taxation would be based on the latter.

***Controlled foreign corporations***/Profits derived by an affiliate resident in a blacklisted offshore jurisdiction, or in a jurisdiction where it is subject to an effective tax rate equal to or lower than 60% of the Portuguese corporate tax rate, are imputed to the Portuguese shareholder, provided it holds, directly or indirectly, a minimum holding participation of 25% (10% if more than 50% of the capital is held by Portuguese shareholders). Upon distribution of the profits, a deduction is available for previously imputed income.

# Portugal

*Taxes*/All taxes other than corporate tax and municipal surcharge constitute a normal business expense.

*Vacation accrual*/Vacation pay and subsidy are tax deductible in the year when the benefit accrues, regardless of the year in which payment is made.

*Other significant items*/Pension, invalidity and health schemes are tax deductible up to 15% of annual staff expenses, provided they are available to all employees and the management and disposition of the benefits are outside the control of the taxpayer, such as under an insured scheme with vested benefits.

Uninsured losses, including indemnities to third parties, are disallowed unless the risk could not be insured. Donations to authorized cultural, scientific, and charitable institutions are allowable up to 0.8% of turnover. Donations to the state, municipalities, and foundations that are more than 50% owned by the state or municipalities are fully deductible, with the possibility of the cost to be raised up to 140%. Special application may be made to obtain full tax relief in other situations.

Confidential or nondocumented expenses are not tax deductible and are subject to a 50% tax surcharge for fully taxable entities.

## Group taxation

The taxation of group income can be obtained by presenting a special form to the tax authorities for companies with a head office and effective management in Portugal. Such income is provided one of the companies, directly or indirectly, holds 90% or more of the statutory capital of the others and a minimum of 50% of the voting rights. Tax grouping generally enables the group companies to offset losses incurred by one company against profits of another company. Tax losses obtained previous to the beginning of the tax grouping can be carried forward only against the particular company's taxable income.

In order to be taxed under this regime, the following conditions need to be met by the group companies.

1. They must be tax resident in Portugal.
2. They must be subject to the normal regime of taxation at the highest corporate tax rate.
3. A minimum holding participation of 90% is required.
4. Excluding newly incorporated companies, all companies should be held by the parent company for more than one year.
5. The parent company should not be controlled by any other Portuguese resident company that fulfils the requirements to be the group parent company.
6. They cannot be dormant for more than one year.
7. They cannot be dissolved or insolvent.
8. They cannot have tax losses in the three years prior to the regime application.
9. They cannot have a tax period different from the parent company's.

Tax grouping is granted for a renewable five-year period. When the regime comes to end or when one company ceases to qualify for this regime, the tax losses obtained during the regime cannot be carried forward and deducted against future individual taxable income of the companies.

## Tax incentives

Tax benefits and incentives can be summarized as follows.

### General tax benefits and incentives

1. Contractual tax incentives—Industrial investment projects up to 2010 (minimum € 4,987,978.97) that qualify of strategic economic interest are eligible for tax incentives. These are granted case-by-case under a government contract, and include a 5% to 20% investment tax credit and exemption from real estate taxes and stamp duty.

2. Dividends from privatized companies—50% are tax exempt when derived from shares acquired up to December 31, 2002, as a result of privatizations. The exemption applies since the tax year where the shares were purchased until five tax years following the termination of the privatization program.

3. Investment funds

   a. Other investment funds—Portfolio investment funds are taxable at the following final rates.

   | | % |
   |---|---|
   | Capital gains (net of capital losses) on shares held < 12 months | 10 |
   | Capital gains (net of capital losses) on shares held > 12 months | — |
   | Other income: | |
   | Earned in Portugal | 25 |
   | Earned abroad | 20/25 |

   b. Real estate investment funds are subject to corporate tax at the following rates.

   | | % |
   |---|---|
   | Rents (net of expenses) | 20 |
   | Real estate capital gains (net of capital losses) | 12.5 |
   | Capital gains (net of capital losses) on shares held < 12 months | 10 |
   | Capital gains (net of capital losses) on shares held > 12 months | — |
   | Other income: | |
   | See section a) above | |

   c. Funds of funds: Income and gains is exempt from corporate income tax

   Income paid by investment funds is exempt from withholding tax. Income received by individuals is not subject to further taxation. Income received by companies is taxed as normal income, qualifying taxes paid by the investment fund as payment on account against the final corporate tax due.

   In turn, 40% of the income derived by companies from units held in funds of funds must be aggregated to the respective world-wide taxable profit (underlying credit is not available).

4. Property investment and management companies (*Sociedade de Gestao e Investmento Imnobiliaro,* or SGIIs)—SGIIs, until December 31, 2005 are entitled to the following tax incentives: (a) profits are taxed at a reduced corporate tax rate of 25%; (b) acquisitions of real estate are exempt from real estate transfer tax; (c) urban houses that will be leased for private residences are exempt from municipal real estate tax.

5. Pension funds—Pension funds are exempt from corporate tax, real estate transfer tax, and gift and inheritance tax.

6. Contractors for NATO infrastructures—These contractors are exempt from corporate tax.

7. Net young employment creation—The annual salary and social security costs derived from the net job creation for employees up to 30 years, are increased by 50% for corporate income tax purposes, provided such increase does not exceed €5,118.4 per employee. This additional deduction is available for a maximum of five years.

8. Inland region investment—Inland region investment is entitled to a reduction of the corporate tax rate to 25% (20% for the initial five tax years following start-up) for companies resident in the inland regions defined by the Portuguese state, special credit line for the incorporation of micro-companies in those inland regions, deduction up to 130% of depreciation on investments on fixed assets (excluding soils and cars), exemption in the first three years of social security contributions (company responsibility) resulting from net employment creation.

9. Tax reserve for investment (for 2003 and 2004)—Tax reserves are entitled to a deduction corresponding to 20% of the year-end taxable income, provided this is invested within the following two tax years in the acquisition of fixed assets (some exclusions apply) and R&D. This benefit is applicable to entities operating in the mining, manufacturing and tourism sectors.

### Tax benefits and incentives for nonresident corporate entities

1. Capital gains—The gain on the sale of shares and quotas held in a Portuguese company by a nonresident company may be tax exempt. However, there are some important exceptions, such as where the nonresident shareholder is owned for more than 25%, directly or indirectly, by a Portuguese resident company; where the nonresident shareholder is located in a country that is included in a blacklist from the Ministry of Finance; and where the assets of the company sold consist mainly of immovable property.

2. Government bonds—Interest on government bonds is tax exempt (where held by entities not located in blacklisted off-shore jurisdictions) under certain conditions.

3. Loan interest and lease rentals on imported equipment that are paid by the state, regional authorities, and public services can qualify for partial or full exemption from tax upon an appropriate application.

4. Interest paid by resident credit institutions to nonresident financial companies as well as gains arising from swap transactions (not located in blacklisted off-shore jurisdictions).

5. Interest derived by nonresident credit institutions on term deposits held to resident authorized to receive such deposits.

### Madeira and Azores international business center

Qualifying industrial shipping, international services (e.g., holding and trusts) and financial entities licensed before December 31, 2000, to operate in the ambit are eligible for a corporate income tax exemption until December 31, 2011.

Azores and Madeira international business centre based companies generally benefit from Portugal's network of double tax agreements.

This regime has been approved by the European Commission. For companies licensed from January 1, 2003 onward, a new (more restrictive) regime will apply.

## Withholding taxes

### General withholding tax rates

| Payment | Residents | Nonresidents |
|---|---|---|
| | % (1) | % |
| Dividends | 15 (2) | 25 (2) |
| Interest: | | |
|     Bank deposits | 20 | 20 |
|     Other | 15 | 20 |
| Royalties | 15 | 15 |
| Income on real estate | 15 | 15 (1) |
| Service charges | — | 15 (3) |

The numbers in parentheses refer to the following numbered Notes.

Notes:

1. Tax withheld constitutes a payment on account of final corporate or individual income tax due.
2. Not subject in the case of holdings of 10% or more or if the parent/subsidiary directive is applicable.
3. Not subject if a tax treaty is applicable.

***Tax treaty rates/***Tax treaties reduce these rates as follows.

| Countries | Dividends | Interest | Royalties |
|---|---|---|---|
| | % | % | % |
| Austria (1, 2) | 15 | 10 | 10 (5) |
| Belgium (2) | 15 | 15 | 10 |
| Brazil (3) | 15 (10) | 15 | 15 |
| Bulgaria (3) | 15 (10) | 10 | 10 |
| Canada (3) | 15 (10) | 10 | 10 |
| Cape Verde | 10 | 10 | 10 |
| China, P.R. | 10 | 10 | 10 |
| Cuba (3, 4) | 10 (5) | 10 | 5 |
| Czech Republic (3) | 15 (10) | 10 | 10 |
| Denmark (2) | 10 | 10 | 10 |
| Finland (2, 3) | 15 (10) | 15 | 10 |
| France (2, 5) | 15 | 12 (10) | 5 |
| Germany (2, 6) | 15 | 15 (10) | 10 |
| Greece (2) | 15 | 15 | 10 |
| Hungary (3) | 15 (10) | 10 | 10 |
| India (3) | 15 (10) | 10 | 10 |
| Iceland (3) | 15 (10) | 10 | 10 |
| Ireland, Rep. of (2) | 15 | 15 | 10 |
| Italy (2) | 15 | 15 | 12 |
| Korea, Rep. of (3) | 15 (10) | 15 | 10 |
| Luxembourg (2, 7) | 15 | 15 (10) | 10 |
| Macau | 10 | 10 | 10 |
| Malta (3) | 15 (10) | 10 | 10 |
| Mexico | 10 | 10 | 10 |
| Mozambique | 15 | 10 | 10 |
| Morocco (3) | 15 (10) | 12 | 10 |
| Netherlands (2) | 10 | 10 | 10 |

# Portugal

| Countries | Dividends | Interest | Royalties |
|---|---|---|---|
| | % | % | % |
| Norway (3) | 15 (10) | 15 | 10 |
| Poland (3) | 15 (10) | 10 | 10 |
| Romania (3) | 15 (10) | 10 | 10 |
| Russia (3) | 15 (10) | 10 | 10 |
| Singapore | 10 | 10 | 10 |
| Spain (2, 3, 8) | 15 (10) | 15 | 5 |
| Switzerland (3) | 15 (10) | 10 | 5 |
| Tunisia | 15 | 15 | 10 |
| Ukraine (3) | 15 (10) | 10 | 10 |
| United Kingdom (2, 3) | 15 (10) | 10 | 5 |
| United States (3) | 15 (5) | 10 | 10 |
| Venezuela (9) | 10 | 10 | 12 (10) |

Notes:

1. The rate in parentheses applies to royalties when the beneficiary holds 50% or less of capital at source.
2. There is no tax rate for dividends if the EU Parent/Subsidiary Directive is applicable.
3. The rate in parentheses applies to dividends when the beneficiary directly holds 25% or more of share capital.
4. Already approved but not yet in force.
5. The rate in parentheses applies to interest on debentures raised in France after January 1, 1965 or on significant loans or debentures raised in Portugal or abroad under major development projects listed in the treaty annex.
6. The rate in parentheses applies to bank loans, but if interest is payable from Portugal, bank loans must qualify as being of economic or social interest or fall under an approved development plan.
7. The rate in parentheses apply to interest received by financial institutions.
8. The treaty's reduced rates are not applicable if the beneficial owner is not thoughted in a trading activity is held, directly or indirectly, in more than 50% by nonresident entities.
9. The rate in parentheses applies to technical assistance.

## Tax administration

*Returns*/The tax year is, as a general rule, the calendar year, and the annual corporate tax return must be submitted by May 31. A different tax year is allowed in the case of a permanent establishment of a nonresident entity, which can adopt the tax period of the nonresident company (if this option is taken, the new tax period must be compulsively maintained for a minimum of five years). Other entities may apply for a different tax period based on economic grounds.

The system is one of self-assessment.

*Payment of tax*/Tax is paid in four installments. The first three correspond to 85% of the previous year's corporate tax assessment (for taxpayers with a turnover above €498,798, 75% if below). The installments are paid in July, September, and December of the year in which taxable income arises. The fourth installment is paid (or received) through self-assessment upon filing the annual tax return in May of the following year.

If the tax year ends on a date other than December 31, interim payments take place in the 7th, 9th and 12th months of the tax year. Filing of the annual tax return together with the final payment is in the fifth month following the close of the tax year.

Payments on account are not required if the previous year's corporate tax assessment is less than €199.52, and may be suspended upon declaring that no further tax is due in respect of the current year. However, interest is assessed at a rate of 7% if this results in postponing more than 20% of the tax that would otherwise have been paid.

In special occasions, a special payment on account is due in a minimum of €1,250 up to €40,000, paid in March, or in March and October (3rd or 3rd and 10th month of the tax year if it ends on a date other than December 31).

The statute limitation period is four years, which may be extended to six years in cases where tax losses are used.

## CORPORATION TAX CALCULATION

Fiscal year ending in 2004

### Taxable income determination

| | €  |
|---|---:|
| Pretax profit as stated in the statutory accounts | 50,000 |

Includes:

| | | |
|---|---:|---:|
| Gross dividend received (10% equity held for one year) | 5,000 | |
| Gross dividend received from a company (Limitada) (5% equity) | 1,500 | |
| Gross interest received on term deposit account | 500 | |
| Gross real estate income on own property | 20,000 | |

Adjustments to book income:
Deductions:

| | |
|---|---:|
| 100% relief on gross dividend received | (5,000) |
| 50% relief on gross dividend received | (750) |

Add:

| | |
|---|---:|
| Depreciation in excess of tax rates | 1,750 |
| Taxable income | 46,000 |

### Computation of tax

| | |
|---|---:|
| Corporate tax at 25% | 11,500 |
| Municipal surcharge (10%) | 1,150 |
| Total tax charge for the year | 12,650 |

Less:
Corporate tax withheld on account:

| | | |
|---|---:|---:|
| Dividends paid by an Limitada (15%) | 225 | |
| Interest (20%) | 100 | |
| Real estate income (15%) | 3,000 | (3,325) |
| Tax payable | | 9,325 |

Note:
Exchange rate at January 1, 2004: US$1= €0.793903.

# Puerto Rico

## PwC contact

For additional information on taxation in Puerto Rico, contact:

Marta Acevedo
PricewaterhouseCoopers LLP
Banco Bilbao Vizcaya Tower, Suite 900
254 Muñoz Rivera Avenue
Hato Rey, Puerto Rico 00918
Telephone: (1) (787) 772 7929
Fax: (1) (787) 766 1094
E-mail: marta.acevedo@us.pwc.com

## Significant developments

In the last few years, the government of Puerto Rico has approved various tax laws to attract existing and new entities to do business in Puerto Rico. Businesses that meet certain requirements (basically, businesses that manufacture products new to the island or specially designated products and businesses within certain service and export industries and research and development) may qualify for a reduced flat income tax rate of 7% applicable to industrial development income, which in certain cases may be reduced to a 0% rate. Furthermore, qualifying businesses would have no tollgate tax liability on distributions from industrial development income. Different reduced tax rates may result, depending on the industrial incentives law under which specific qualifying business may be operating.

## Taxes on corporate income

*Corporation tax*/The corporate tax is comprised of normal tax and surtax. The normal tax is imposed at a rate of 20%, while the surtax is imposed on normal tax net income after a deduction of $25,000. The rates are as follows.

### Surtax net income

| Over | Not over | | Tax on Column 1 | Percentage on excess |
|---|---|---|---|---|
| (Column 1) | | | | |
| 0 | $ 75,000 | ................................................ | — | 5 |
| $ 75,000 | 125,000 | ................................................ | $ 3,750 | 15 |
| 125,000 | 175,000 | ................................................ | 11,250 | 16 |
| 175,000 | 225,000 | ................................................ | 19,250 | 17 |
| 225,000 | 275,000 | ................................................ | 27,750 | 18 |
| 275,000 | | ................................................ | 36,750 | 19 |

*Recovery of tax by differences in tax rates*/When a corporation's net income subject to tax exceeds $500,000 for any taxable year, for the purposes of recovering the tax not imposed by the difference in tax rates, a tax of 5% on net income subject to tax in excess of $500,000 is to be imposed. This computation should be performed to the extent that the total tax determined on net income subject to tax does not exceed 39%.

*Alternative minimum tax*/The law also imposes an alternative minimum tax (AMT) at a rate of 22% to ensure that most corporations pay a minimum amount of tax. The AMT is an entirely separate tax computation that the corporate tax-payer must compute each year in addition to the regular tax computation. This computation does not take into consideration certain tax preference items (i.e., flexible and/or accelerated depreciation) and includes other book income adjustments that are not considered in the regular tax computation. In addition, the AMT may be reduced by certain foreign tax credits and may be carried forward indefinitely as a credit against regular income tax, with certain limitations.

## Corporate residence

A corporation is considered to be resident in Puerto Rico if it is incorporated under the laws of Puerto Rico or, in the case of a foreign corporation, if it is engaged in trade or business in Puerto Rico.

## Other taxes

*Property and municipal taxes*/Property taxes are imposed (unless expressly exempted by law, as in the case of tax-exempt industries) on real and personal property owned on each January 1. The tax depends on the location (municipality) of the assets, and the maximum tax is 8.33% on real property, and 6.33% on personal property.

Municipal license taxes are imposed on the gross business volume (unless expressly exempted by law, as in the case of tax-exempt industries) during the tax year.

For fiscal years 2003/2004, for savings and loan associations and other financial businesses the maximum rate is 1.5%, and for other persons engaged in a taxable business, the maximum tax rate is 0.5%.

For corporations with existing tax incentive grants as of August 30, 1991, the maximum tax rate continues to be 1% for all financial businesses, and the maximum rate continues to be 0.3% for other persons engaged in taxable businesses.

## Branch income

A branch operating in Puerto Rico is taxed only on its Puerto Rico source income and income effectively connected with its local operations. Tax rates on branch income are the same as on corporate income. In addition, the law provides for the imposition of a branch profits tax (BPT) on foreign corporations and partnerships doing business in Puerto Rico to avoid tax-free repatriation of earnings generated in Puerto Rico.

The BPT is 10% for taxable years beginning after June 30, 1995, and is applied to amounts deemed to be repatriated from the branch in Puerto Rico. This deemed dividend will generally be triggered if the branch has earnings and profits generated in Puerto Rico that are not reinvested in Puerto Rico.

BPT is not applicable to those corporations or partnerships deriving at least 80% of their gross income from Puerto Rico sources. Also, it is not applicable to income considered exempt under tax-incentive legislation ("industrial development income").

## Income determination

*Inventory valuation*/Inventories are generally stated at the lower of cost or market. If LIFO is used for book purposes, it can be elected for tax purposes.

# Puerto Rico

*Capital gains*/Gains on capital assets held for more than six months are taxed at a maximum alternative tax rate of 25% (12.5% if the property sold is located in Puerto Rico). Gains on assets held for six months or less are taxed at ordinary income rates.

Capital losses are allowed only as an offset to capital gains. An excess of capital losses over capital gains in a taxable year may be carried forward five years.

*Intercompany dividends*/Corporations doing business in Puerto Rico can deduct 85% of dividends received from Puerto Rican corporations, and 100% of the dividends if received from a controlled corporation (owned at least 80%) also doing business in Puerto Rico.

*Foreign income*/Puerto Rican corporations are taxed on worldwide income, while resident foreign corporations are taxed only on its Puerto Rico source income, and certain foreign income effectively connected with their Puerto Rico operations. Double taxation is avoided by means of foreign tax credits. No provision is made for current taxation of undistributed income of foreign subsidiaries. However, any regular corporation or partnership organized for the purpose of preventing the imposition of tax at the shareholder level by means of improperly accumulating earnings or profits would be subject to an accumulated earnings tax. Certain exempt companies are required to prepay half of their dividend tax in the year the income is generated, irrespective of whether an actual dividend distribution is made.

*Stock dividends*/A Puerto Rican corporation can distribute tax free a dividend of common stock to all common stock shareholders inasmuch as the distribution is made to all shareholders in proportion to their respective stock holdings.

## Deductions

*Depreciation and depletion*/Depreciation is generally computed on a straight-line basis, although an accelerated method, flexible depreciation, may be used by qualifying taxpayers with respect to property acquired in taxable years commencing before June 30, 1995. Useful life is the usual basis. By using flexible depreciation, the taxpayer may depreciate all of the cost, part of the cost or none of the cost of qualifying depreciable property to the extent of 100% of the net income for the year (determined without such deduction) of the business or commercial activity in which the flexibly depreciated property is used. If an asset is sold before the end of its useful life, the excess of the accumulated flexible depreciation over the accumulated straight-line depreciation is taxed at ordinary (as opposed to capital gains) rates.

The Puerto Rican Internal Revenue Code of 1994, as amended, provides accelerated depreciation methods for property acquired during all taxable years beginning after June 30, 1995. The flexible depreciation method has been repealed with respect to property acquired during taxable years commenced after June 30, 1995. The method will range from a 200% double-declining balance for five- and ten-year property, to 150% declining balance for 15- and 20-year property. This method must be elected by the taxpayer with the alternative of switching to straight-line depreciation when it yields a higher deduction.

The basis that may be used for depreciating an automobile acquired after December 31, 1987 is generally limited to a maximum of $25,000. In addition, the depreciation must be generally computed using a useful life of not less than five years. A three-year recovery period is allowed if the automobile is used exclusively in sales-related activities.

A reasonable allowance for depletion of natural resources based on cost is deductible.

No conformity of book and tax treatment is required.

For goodwill purchased during taxable years commenced after June 30, 1995 a deduction for amortization of purchased goodwill is allowed, based on the 15-year straight-line method. Other intangibles may be amortized, as long as they are used in the trade or business and have a definite useful life.

*Net operating losses*/A seven-year carryforward is available, which must be adjusted for tax-exempt income. No carryback is allowable.

*Payments to foreign affiliates*/A Puerto Rican corporation can claim a deduction for royalties, management service fees, and interest charges paid to foreign affiliates, provided such amounts can be documented and justified under arm's length pricing rules. Payments of interest, royalties, and other fixed income could be subject to a 29% withholding at source.

*Taxes*/A deduction is available for taxes paid or accrued during the taxable year, such as property taxes, municipal license taxes, or excise taxes. In addition, a deduction for income taxes imposed by a foreign country is also available if the election to take them as a credit is not made.

*Other significant items*/Deductions for allowable charitable contributions may not exceed 5% of taxable income, computed without the benefit of the deduction. If a corporation makes contributions in excess of the 5% allowed, the corporation may carry the excess forward five taxable years. The deduction for charitable contributions under this subsection in each one of the five taxable years may not exceed 5% of the taxpayer's net income.

The corporate deduction for meals and entertainment is generally limited to 50% of the amounts incurred. The deduction cannot exceed 25% of the gross income of the corporation. Expenses incurred for conventions held outside Puerto Rico and the United States are generally disallowed unless certain conditions are met.

Insurance premiums may be deducted in full if paid to insurers authorized to contract insurance in Puerto Rico.

Deductions for eligible contributions to qualified employee stock ownership plans may not exceed 25% of total compensation paid to or otherwise accumulated for employees participating in such plans.

## Group taxation

There is no provision for consolidated tax returns.

## Tax incentives

*Inward investment*/To encourage industrialization in Puerto Rico, businesses that meet certain requirements (basically, businesses that manufacture products new to the island, or specially designated products and businesses within certain service and export industries and research and development) may qualify for a reduced flat income tax rate of 7% applicable to industrial development income, which in certain cases may be reduced to a 0% rate. Furthermore, qualifying businesses would have no tollgate tax liability on distributions from industrial development income. Different reduced tax rates may result, depending on the industrial incentives law under which specific qualifying business may be operating.

This exemption from taxes does not relieve these entities from the obligation to file an annual report with the Secretary of State and to file various returns, including those for income and property taxes.

*Capital investment*/To encourage high-risk investment a corporation, partnership or fund may be formed as a venture-capital organization (venture fund), drawing up to US$50 million from its investors. Licenses to operate are granted for a period of ten years. Under certain conditions the venture fund may enjoy 100% exemption from income and municipal license taxes. Investors may take a credit of up to 25% of their investment in an initial offering as a credit against their income tax liability, including the AMT, in the year in which they invest. The unused portion of the credit may be carried forward for the next five taxable years or sold, ceded or otherwise transferred.

Dividend distributions are normally subject to withholding taxes, but they are exempt from municipal license taxes. Gains and losses realized on the sale or other disposition of the investment also enjoy special tax treatment. Investments in these funds are exempt from personal property tax.

*Other incentives*/A foreign business entity may organize a Puerto Rico corporation or partnership, or simply a separate business unit, to operate as an international banking entity (IBE). An IBE may, for example, engage in banking business if its funds are invested outside Puerto Rico and it obtains the appropriate license.

Income derived by an IBE from eligible activities is exempt from income taxes, except in the case of any IBE which operates as part of a bank that is organized under de Puerto Rico Bank Act and that has a net income derived from qualified operations in excess of 20% of the total net income generated by the bank during a taxable year. The excess over the 20% of the total net income will be taxed at regular income tax rates.

However, there are some transitional rules, and for the years beginning after June 30, 2003 but before July 1, 2004, the tax will be imposed in the cases were the net income exceeds 40% of the bank total net income. For years beginning after June 30, 2004 and before July 1, 2005, the applicable percentage will be 30%.

An IBE is also exempt from property and municipal license taxes. Dividends paid by an IBE are not subject to local withholding taxes if paid to nonresident individuals, foreign corporations or foreign partnerships not doing business locally. Payments of interest and/or finance charges to these classes of investors are also exempt from local income taxes.

## Withholding taxes

***Dividend income***/The withholding tax rates applicable to dividend income are shown below (1).

|  | % |
|---|---|
| General rates: | |
| Resident corporate recipients | 10 |
| Nonresident corporate recipients (2) | 10 |
| Nonresident U.S. citizens (2) | 10 |
| Nonresident non-U.S. citizens (2) | 10 |
| Special rates: | |
| Distributions of income from nonexempt manufacturing, hotel and shipping activities to nonresident corporate recipients | 10 |
| Distributions from exempt industrial development income (3) | 0–10 |

Notes:

1. Every nonresident individual, either alien or U.S. citizen, is required to file an income tax return if income exceeds certain limits and if the tax liability was not fully satisfied at source. If the tax obligation is not fully satisfied, the taxpayer will be required to file a return and pay taxes determined at normal graduated rates.

2. Dividends paid to noncorporate recipients and nonresident corporate recipients by Puerto Rican corporations and by foreign corporations that have derived 80% or more of their gross income during the preceding three-year period from sources effectively connected or treated as effectively connected with the operation of a trade or business in Puerto Rico are generally subject to withholding tax at the rate applicable to that type of taxpayer.

3. The rate may vary, depending on the industrial incentive grant under which the company operates.

***Other income***/The withholding tax rates, applicable only to nonresident recipients, on all other fixed and determinable annual or periodic income from Puerto Rican sources, including interest, royalties, rents, and compensation for services performed locally, are as follows.

|  | % |
|---|---|
| General rate for corporate recipients | 29 |
| General rate for U.S. citizens | 20 |
| General rate for non-U.S. citizens | 29 |
| Special rate for non-U.S. citizens with respect to payments for real property or shares of stock | 29 |

Note:

For taxable years beginning after June 30, 1995 all interest payments to unrelated taxpayers are not subject to any withholding at source.

## Tax administration

***Returns***/Corporations must self-assess their income taxes on their yearly income tax return on the basis of their taxable year. This taxable year can be either a fiscal or a calendar year. Once the corporation has adopted a calendar or a fiscal year, it should use that year to compute taxable net income unless authorization for change is obtained from the Secretary of the Treasury.

# Puerto Rico

**Payment of tax**/Corporate taxes due after estimated tax payments, if any, are to be paid in full on or before the 15th day of the 4th month following the close of the taxable year (April 15 for calendar-year corporations).

## CORPORATION TAX CALCULATION

Year ending December 31, 2003

| | | |
|---|---:|---:|
| Net income before taxes | | $ 1,000,000 |
| Add: | | |
|    Charitable contributions (excess over limitation) | 50,000 | |
|    Nondeductible inventory reserve | 100,000 | 150,000 |
| | | 1,150,000 |
| Deduct: | | |
|    100% of dividend from wholly owned | | |
|       taxable domestic subsidiary | 75,000 | |
|    Loss carryforward | 75,000 | 150,000 |
| Taxable income | | $ 1,000,000 |
| Normal tax—20% | | $ 200,000 |
| Surtax (1)—Additional tax on taxable income less 25,000: | | |
|    On first 275,000 | | 36,750 |
|    On excess—700,000 (1,000,000 – 275,000 – 25,000) at 19% | | 133,000 |
| Regular tax | | 369,750 |
| Amount of recapture (2) | | 20,250 |
| Tax payable | | $ 390,000 |

Notes:

1. The Puerto Rican law provides for limiting the aggregate exemption for surtax of a controlled group of corporations to $25,000.

2. The amount determined for recapture is $25,000 (($1,000,000 – $500,000) at 5%). However, as noted under "Recovery of tax by differences in tax rates" above, this computation is to be performed to the extent that the total tax determined on net income subject to tax does not exceed 39%. Therefore, the amount of recapture is $20,250.

3. The monetary unit is the U.S. dollar.

## PwC contact

For additional information on taxation in Romania, contact:

Ron Barden, Partner
PricewaterhouseCoopers Auditors & Accountants SRL
Bucharest, Romania
Telephone: +40 (21) 202 8500
Fax: +40 (21) 202 8600
e-mail: ron.barden@ro.pwc.com

## Significant developments

The Fiscal Code entered into force on January 1, 2004, unifying and modifying legislation on the major areas of taxation in Romania (i.e., profit tax, withholding taxes, income tax, value-added tax, excise duties, and local taxes).

## Taxes on corporate income

The standard profit tax rate is 25%, for both Romanian companies and foreign companies operating through a permanent establishment in Romania.

Capital gains will be taxable at 10% as of January 1, 2006 for gains obtained from the sale of real estate property located in Romania, as well as from sales of shares held in a Romanian company, provided that certain conditions are fulfilled, as detailed further below.

The profit tax liability due from nightclubs and gambling operations cannot be less than 5% of the revenue obtained from such activities.

Micro-companies (turnover of up to €100,000 and between one and nine employees) are taxed at 1.5% of revenue earned, payable each quarter, by the 25th of the month following the quarter for which the tax is paid.

## Corporate residence

A company is considered resident in Romania if it was set up under Romanian law, or has its place of effective management in Romania.

## Other taxes

*Value-added tax*/The standard VAT rate is 19%, and is applied to all supplies of goods and services, including imports, not qualifying for an exemption (with or without credit) or for the VAT reduced rate.

The reduced VAT rate is of 9%, and is applicable starting January 1, 2004 to the following items, including admission fees at museums, historical monuments, architecture and archaeological monuments, zoos and botanical gardens, fairs and exhibitions, supply of school manuals, books, newspapers and periodicals, supply of prostheses and orthopedic products, medicine for human and veterinarian use, accommodation in hotels or in areas with a similar function.

Operations exempt with credit (deduction right) for input VAT include the export of goods, transport and related services, goods sold at duty-free shops, international transport of passengers, certain operations performed in free trade zones and free harbors, the supply of goods to bonded warehouses and related services, services provided in connection with goods placed under suspensive customs regimes, the supply of goods and services under grant-funded projects, and supplies to diplomatic missions, and so on.

VAT exemption without credit applies to a range of activities including banking, financial, insurance, lease of certain real estate properties, and to medical, veterinary, social assistance, and educational organizations if provided by the licensed entities.

Registered VAT payers can benefit from VAT payment exoneration, based on a VAT exoneration certificate issued by the tax authorities. This procedure applies to industrial machinery, technological equipment, installations, equipment, metering devices, automated equipment imported for investments, as well as farming machinery and vehicles and to some listed raw materials that are not produced in Romania or which are in short supply.

The rules for establishing the place of supply of goods and services (and therefore the place of VAT taxation) are similar to those stipulated in the European Union 6th VAT Directive.

Services provided by foreign entities to Romanian companies whose place of supply is in Romania under territoriality rules are subject to Romanian VAT under a reverse charge mechanism, if the nonresidents fail to appoint a fiscal representative. VAT reverse charge should not be physically paid, but only shown in the VAT return as both input and output tax. From January 1, 2004, VAT payers who are the beneficiaries of services provided by nonresidents are required to issue self-invoices for VAT purposes for these services.

***Customs duties***/The Romanian Customs Import Tariff is based on the Harmonized System for the denomination and classification of goods (2002 version), and is in line with the Combined Nomenclature adopted by European Union (EU) member states (eight-digit code).

Customs duties are expressed as a percentage of the customs value, that is, they are ad valorem taxes. The customs value is determined and declared by the importer in accordance with the World Trade Organization (WTO) Customs Valuation Agreement (i.e., the agreement pertaining to the implementation of Article VII of the GATT).

With the exception of agricultural and food products, which have a specific tariff regime, customs duty rates vary from 0% to 30%, depending on the type and description of the goods.

Preferential customs duty rates apply on goods originating from EU, EFTA (European Free Trade Association) and CEFTA (Central European Free Trade Association) countries, as well as from countries with which Romania has signed bilateral free trade agreements (Albania, Croatia, Israel, Lithuania, Macedonia, Moldova, and Turkey). With few exceptions, the customs duties for industrial products originating from these trade blocs or countries have been eliminated. Preferential customs duty rates also apply on certain goods originating in developing countries that are members of P16 and Global System of Trade Preferences among Developing Countries (GSTP). In order to benefit from preferential customs duties, the importers have to present valid proof of preferential origin at customs.

*Local tax*/A property tax of 0.5% to 1% is levied annually on the book value of buildings. The property tax on buildings obtained prior to January 1, 1998 and not re-valued since that date ranges from 5% to 10%. There is also a tax on land.

*Social security taxes*/Employers are subject to social security contributions, as follows.

- A 22%, 27%, or 32% social security fund contribution, depending on working conditions.
- A 7% health fund contribution.
- A 3% unemployment fund contribution.
- A 0.5% work accidents insurance fund contribution.
- Between 0.25% and 0.75% labor office commission.

## Branch income

*Branch*/A company with its head office outside Romanian may set up a branch. Profits derived by the branch are taxed at the standard profit tax rate of 25%. Branches can only operate in the same field of activity as their parent companies.

*Representative offices*/Representative offices are often established as a first step to operating in Romania. A representative office can only undertake auxiliary or preparatory activities, cannot trade in its own name and cannot engage in any contractual activity. A representative office can only perform a limited range of activities without being considered a permanent establishment for profit tax purposes.

Representative offices are subject to a yearly flat tax of €4,000 (payable in local currency ROL). If a representative office is set up or closed down during a year, the tax due for that year is pro-rated on the basis of the number of months the representative office operated in that fiscal year.

## Income determination

The taxable profit of a company is calculated as the difference between its revenue derived from all sources, and the related expenses incurred during a fiscal year, of which nontaxable revenues are deducted and nondeductible expenses are added.

*Inventory valuation*/The methods permitted for inventory valuation under Romanian law are standard cost, average (weighted) cost, FIFO, and LIFO.

Assets are generally valuated at their acquisition cost, production cost or market value. Fixed assets could be revalued as at December 31, 2003 based on the inflation rate communicated by the Romanian National Institute for Statistics. Also, the revaluation of the patrimony should be performed at the reorganization of a company (i.e., through a merger or spin-off).

*Capital gains*/Capital gains earned by a Romanian resident company are included in ordinary profits, and taxed at 25%. Profits related to income obtained by nonresidents (i.e., capital gains) from real estate property located in Romania or the sales of shares held in a Romanian company are also taxable in Romania at 25%. However, this 25% rate may be reduced by the provision of relevant double tax treaties.

# Romania

As of January 1, 2006, a 10% tax will be available for gains from sale of real estate property located in Romania as well as on the sale of shares held in a Romanian company provided the following conditions are fulfilled.

- The property/shares are acquired after December 31, 2003.
- The property/shares are held for more than two years.
- The buyer and seller are not related parties.

*Intercompany dividends*/Dividends received by a Romanian company from another Romanian company are nontaxable revenue.

Dividends received by a Romanian company from a foreign company are taxed at 25% in Romania. Credit is available for tax paid abroad.

After Romania's accession to the EU, dividends received from a company within the EU will be nontaxable revenues if the Romanian company holds for at least two years a minimum 25% of the capital of the company distributing the dividends.

*Foreign income*/Resident companies are taxed on all income, including from sources outside Romanian territory, unless a double tax treaty between Romania and the said state stipulates otherwise.

*Stock options*/The Romanian Fiscal Code does not specifically define the corporate tax treatment for granting stock options to employees. However, the Application Norms of the Fiscal Code stipulate that expenses incurred in assigning a company's own shares to employees shall be considered nondeductible.

## Deductions

Companies may deduct all expenses incurred in order to obtain taxable revenues.

The deductible expenses include the following.

- Legal reserve of 5% applied to the accounting profit before tax, from which nontaxable revenue is deducted and nondeductible expenses are added until the reserve reaches one-fifth of the subscribed and paid share capital.
- Depreciation, amortization and depletion up to the rates provided by law (see below).
- Registration fees, subscription fees, and contributions due to chambers of commerce and industry, trade unions, and employers associations.
- Expenses incurred for management, consultancy, and assistance when specific conditions are met regarding documentation and substance.
- Provisions for doubtful debts limited to 20% for 2004, 25% for 2005, 30% for 2006, and fully in 2007 if certain conditions are met.

Nonetheless, the deductibility of certain expenses is limited, and a number of expenses are specifically nondeductible, for example, as follows.

- Fines and penalties due to Romanian or foreign authorities, as well as to nonresidents based on commercial agreements.
- Expenses related to nontaxable revenues.
- Sponsorship and patronage expenses (but taxpayers are granted fiscal credit of up to 0.3%, of turnover and 20% of the profit tax due).
- Protocol expenses, over the limit of 2% applied on the difference between taxable revenues and deductible expenses, except the protocol expenses.

- Expenses registered for accounting purposes that are not substantiated with "justifying" documents.

Romania has rules limiting the deductibility of interest and foreign exchange expenses. Thus, interest on loans contracted with institutions other than banks, financial institutions and leasing companies (i.e., loans from a parent company) is deductible for profit tax purposes if it does not exceed the National Bank of Romania benchmark interest rate for loans denominated in ROL, or an annual rate of 9% (subject to annual review) for loans denominated in foreign currency. The deductibility of such expenses will be further subject to limitation under the thin capitalization rules, as detailed below.

***Thin capitalization rules***/If a company's equity is negative or its debt to equity ratio equal to or higher than 1:1 (3:1 as of 2006), the deductibility of interest expenses and net foreign exchange losses will be limited to interest revenue plus 10% of other revenue. Such nondeductible expenses can be carried forward for an unlimited period until full deductibility is reached.

***Depreciation and amortization***/Romanian law distinguishes between fiscal and accounting depreciation. From January 1, 2004, companies should maintain a separate record to reflect the separate computation of the fiscal and the accounting depreciation.

Assets are generally depreciated using the straight-line method. However, accelerated or digressive depreciation methods may be used to determine fiscal depreciation, while the accounting depreciation method may be different. Accelerated depreciation (50% deduction from the book value in the first year of operation) can be used for technological equipment and other tools, installations, computers and related peripherals. The useful life used to compute the accounting depreciation of certain assets is established by law (i.e., for buildings—50 years, for software—3 years, for computers—3 years, and for automobiles—5 years). Land is not considered a depreciable asset.

***Net operating losses***/The carrying forward of tax losses is allowed for up to a maximum of five years, on a FIFO basis. No adjustment for inflation is allowed. There is no tax loss carryback.

***Taxes***/Corporate income taxes are not deductible, nor are late payment interest and fines related to tax liabilities or social security obligations.

***Other significant items***/Other important rules under Romanian law relate to transactions between related parties, which should be performed at arm's length. Prices should be set at the level which any two third parties would have agreed to in the same or similar conditions. There are four methods for assessing the performance of transactions at arms' length, as follows.

- Comparable prices method.
- Cost plus method.
- Sales minus method.
- Any other method recognized by the Organization for Economic Cooperation and Development (OECD) Model Convention.

# Romania

## Group taxation

There is no system of group taxation in Romania. Members of a group must file separate returns and therefore are taxed separately. No provision exists for offsetting the losses of group members against the profits of other group members.

## Tax incentives

The Fiscal Code limits the applicability period for certain existent fiscal incentives, such as follows.

1. Free trade zones—Until December 31, 2004, companies may benefit from a reduced 5% profit tax rate for taxable profit related to revenues obtained from operating in a free trade zone under license.

2. Investments with significant economic impact (cash investments of over US$1 million)—Until December 31, 2006, a supplementary tax deduction of 20% of the value of investments is allowed in the month the investment is commissioned. A company may also use accelerated depreciation for such investments, except for buildings. A customs duty exemption is available for certain new tangible and intangible goods imported as part of the investment. A land tax exemption may be granted for a limited period.

3. Industrial parks—Until December 31, 2006, a supplementary tax deduction is allowed from the taxable profit, capped at 20% of the value of investments in construction or renovation, internal infrastructure and infrastructure for connection with public utility networks. Buildings and land in industrial parks are exempt from property tax.

4. Disadvantaged areas—If an investment certificate is obtained before July 1, 2002, tax exemption for profits from new investments will continue to apply as long as the disadvantaged area is categorized as such. Companies, which by July 1, 2002, had invested a minimum of US$1 million in fixed assets for use in the processing industry, are exempt from profit tax until June 30, 2007.

5. Oil and gas incentives—Concession titleholders and their subcontractors can benefit of exemption from customs duty on imported equipment.

## Withholding taxes

Based on the Romanian legislation, nonresidents are liable for the following withholding taxes.

1. A rate of 5% on interest for term deposits (interest for current deposits in Romanian banks).
2. A rate of 20% from gambling by nonresidents.
3. A rate of 15% on other revenue derived from Romania, such as the following.
   - Royalties.
   - Dividends.
   - Revenue from services if performed in Romania.
   - Revenue obtained from management, brokerage or consultancy services, irrespective of where the services are performed.
   - Commissions.
   - Income from international transport.
   - Interest, other than interest for term deposits, as above.

Double taxation treaties which Romania is party to will reduce the withholding tax rate on the payments listed above, based on a fiscal residence certificate made available by the nonresident beneficiary of income.

## Tax administration

In Romania, the fiscal year is the calendar year.

Companies applying accounting regulations harmonized with International Accounting Standards have to file their annual financial statements to the tax authorities within 120 days of year-end. Companies applying simplified accounting regulations harmonized with the European Directives have to file their annual financial statements within 90 days of year-end. Micro-companies have to file their annual financial statements within 60 days of year-end.

Annual profit tax returns should be submitted to the tax authorities with annual financial statements. There are certain returns that should be submitted monthly. The return on tax liabilities due to the consolidated general budget, the VAT return and social security contribution returns.

*Tax payment*/Payment of profit tax and most local taxes should be made quarterly while VAT, salary related contributions, and withholding tax should be paid monthly.

# Romania

## *CORPORATION TAX CALCULATION*

Calendar year ending December 31, 2004

|  | | (In ROL million) |
|---|---:|---:|
| Net profit before tax | | 100,000 |
| Less—Deductions: | | |
| Dividends received from Romanian company | 10,000 | |
| Deductible contribution to reserve fund (5% of profit) | 5,000 | 15,000 |
| | | 85,000 |
| Add—Nondeductible expenses: | | |
| Penalties | 2,500 | |
| Protocol expenses over the deductibility limit | 2,500 | |
| Sponsorship expenses | 1,500 | 6,500 |
| Taxable income before offset of losses brought forward | | 91,500 |
| Less—Loss brought forward | | 10,000 |
| Taxable income | | 81,500 |
| Tax on profit—25% | | 20,375 |
| *Less:* | | |
| Fiscal credit granted for sponsorship (assumed within legal limit) | 1,500 | |
| Tax on profit paid from the beginning of the year | 12,000 | (13,500) |
| Payable tax on profit | | 6,875 |

Note:

Official exchange rate of the lei at January 1, 2004: US$1 = ROL32,595.

## PwC contact

For additional information on taxation in the Russian Federation, contact:

Natalia Milchakova
PricewaterhouseCoopers
Kosmodamianskaya nab., 52, Building 5
115054 Moscow, Russia
Telephone: (7) (095) 967 6000
Fax: (7) (095) 967 6001
e-mail: natalia.milchakova@ru.pwc.com

## Significant developments

The corporate taxation structure has been in a constant state of change as new legislation has appeared since reforms began more than ten years ago. Taxpayers have experienced many inconsistencies in tax administration at both the federal and regional levels. To improve the situation, the government has launched development of a comprehensive tax code. Currently, almost all parts of the new code, including the general part, VAT, excises, personal income tax, unified social tax, profits tax from organizations, natural resources exploration tax, property tax from organizations, special taxation for production sharing arrangements, transport tax, gambling tax, as well as special taxation for small and medium businesses and agricultural products producers chapters, are already effective. State and customs duty, property tax from individuals, inheritance and gift tax, land tax and some other taxes are governed by separate legislative acts most of which will be incorporated in the tax code. Even though no significant changes are expected in so far as major components of tax code are concerned (with exception of Unified Social Tax), some changes will occur, and it is therefore recommended that confirmation regarding the latest position be sought from the above contact.

Sales tax charged on sales to individuals was eliminated with effect from January 1, 2004.

## Taxes on corporate income

*Profits tax*/Profits earned by enterprises are taxed at a rate not exceeding 24%, of which 5% is paid to the federal budget, 17% is paid to the regional budgets, and 2% is paid to the local budgets. Regional legislative authorities are allowed to reduce (for certain categories of taxpayers) the tax payable to their respective budgets by four percentage points, thus in some regions of Russia the regional portion of profits tax may amount to 13%.

## Corporate residence

The tax system in Russia distinguishes between Russian entities and foreign entities on the basis of their place of incorporation. Foreign entities are subject to Russian tax on profits earned from activities conducted through permanent establishments on the territory of the Russian Federation or on income from sources in Russia. Certain concessions apply under double taxation treaties.

All taxpayers are required to obtain a tax registration and will be assigned a taxpayer identification number, whether or not their activities are taxable.

# Russian Federation

## Other taxes

*Value added tax*/VAT was introduced in Russia with effect from 1992. The current legislation governing VAT is effective as of January 1, 2001. The VAT system, while not originally based on the EU model system, is gradually moving toward it. VAT applies to the value added by each element in the chain of production from producer to consumer. The standard rate is 18% (with a lower rate of 10% applying to certain basic foodstuffs, children's clothing, drugs and medical goods, and printed publications). The same VAT rates are applied for import of goods to the territory of Russia. Exports and related services are taxed at a zero-rate.

Taxpayers (except for taxpayers selling excisable goods) can be exempt from VAT if sales proceeds for the three preceding months do not exceed RUB 1 million (excluding VAT). The exemption is given for 12 consecutive months

The list of exempt goods and services includes basic banking and insurance services, educational services by certified establishments, sale of certain vitally important medical equipment, passenger transportation, and certain other socially important services. Most accredited representative offices of foreign legal entities (as well as accredited employees of these representative offices) are exempt from VAT on property rental payments. Most exemptions from VAT carry no right to input credit in Russia. Instead, input VAT is deducted for profits tax purposes.

Most taxpayers are on an EU-type input-output VAT system, whereby a VAT payer accounts for VAT on its full sales price, and deducts VAT incurred on costs of inventory and related expenses. VAT may be calculated on either the accrual or the cash basis.

While VAT incurred on acquired inventory and services can be reclaimed once paid, VAT on acquired fixed assets additionally requires that the asset is booked into the accounts, and VAT in relation to construction projects is reclaimable after commissioning of the building. There is, in addition, a self-charge to VAT on construction using one's own resources.

Exports of goods to destinations outside Russia, including to the CIS (Commonwealth of Independent States), (apart from oil and gas products), transportation and other services related to the export of goods from and import of goods into Russia, international passengers transportation, sales to diplomatic functions, and certain other transactions are zero-rated with a right to offset input VAT. To apply zero-rate and achieve input credit for exported goods, there must be proof of actual export. A significant volume of documents and a special tax return have to be submitted to the tax authorities. Advance payments for goods to be exported are generally subject to VAT. The VAT paid on these advance payments may be reclaimed as soon as it has been proved that the goods were actually exported.

The reverse-charge mechanism was introduced into the VAT legislation with effect from April 28, 1995. Under this mechanism, a Russian company must account for VAT on any payment it makes to a nontax-registered foreign company if the payment is connected to the sale of goods (services) in the territory of the Russian Federation. The VAT so withheld is eligible for normal input VAT credit by the Russian payer. The foreign supplier is allowed to offset VAT collected through the reverse-charge mechanism against Russian VAT paid at importation and on domestically acquired supplies only by registering for taxes in Russia. There is no special VAT registration.

An EU-type set of place-of-supply rules was introduced with effect from January 1, 1996, for determining where services are supplied for VAT purposes. These rules divide all services into different categories for determining where they are deemed to be supplied for VAT purposes. For example, certain services are deemed supplied where performed, some where the "buyer" of the services is located, and others where certain property is located.

Effective from January 1, 1997, uniform invoicing for VAT purposes applies to all Russian-registered taxpayers that are providers of goods and services. Invoices of a standard format are to be issued within five days of a supply of goods (services). The duplicate copy of the invoice is registered in a sales journal, and incoming invoices are to be recorded in a purchase book. As of January 1, 2001, compliance with new invoicing procedures is critical to the supplier's ability to recover input VAT.

VAT returns are due on a monthly basis, with payment due by the 20th of the following month.

Taxpayers with monthly revenues of less than RUB1 million may file VAT returns on a quarterly basis. With effect from January 1, 2001, individual entrepreneurs are VAT payers and are liable to VAT reporting requirements. Individual entrepreneurs and companies generating quarterly revenues of less than RUB 1 million are relieved from their VAT liabilities upon application to the tax authority.

*Import VAT*/A limited range of goods is granted exemption from import VAT. The list of such goods includes, for example, humanitarian aid, goods designated for diplomatic corps, and so on. Relief from import VAT is available on technological equipment, their components, and spare parts imported as contributions to the charter capital of enterprises.

*Import duties*/In addition to VAT, customs duties are levied on assets physically imported into the Russian Federation. The rate varies according to the tariff code of the goods imported, as well as according to the country of origin. There is special relief from customs duties for qualifying goods contributed to the charter capital of Russian companies with foreign investments.

*Excise duty*/Excise duty is levied on a limited range of goods, mainly luxury items, for example, alcohol, cigarettes, cars. Excisable goods do not qualify for duty relief on contributions to charter capital.

*Customs processing fee*/Goods that are moved across the Russian Federation customs border are subject to a customs processing fee. In the majority of cases, the rate of this fee is 0.15% of the customs value.

*Property tax*/Property tax was originally introduced in 1991, and has undergone several amendments. This tax is levied with respect to the average annual net book value of fixed assets of Russian legal entities and permanent establishments of foreign legal entities. Foreign legal entities without permanent establishments in Russia pay property tax with respect to immovable property located in Russia, the tax base for these purposes is determined as in accordance with information on the value of these properties from inventory bodies. The property tax is levied at the maximum rate of 2.2%.

*Transport tax*/Transport tax is imposed on cars, motorcycles, buses, vans, planes, helicopters, yachts, boats, ships, and other water, air and land transport registered in Russia. Fixed rates (per unit of horsepower, gross ton or unit of transport), which are differentiated, based on the engine capacity, gross tonnage, and type of transport are applied. The actual rates in the regions may be subject to the maximum five-fold increase/decrease by legislative bodies of Russian Federation constituents. Reporting and payment rules are established by the regional legislative authorities (e.g., in Moscow reporting and payment shall be made on an annual basis by January 20 following the reporting year).

## Branch income (permanent establishment)

The term "permanent establishment" (PE) is defined as a bureau, office, division, agency, or any other permanent place where regular business activity is carried on and/or is connected with exploiting natural resources, executing work under contract on the construction, installation, erection, assembly, adjustment, and maintenance of equipment; or supplying services or carrying out other work. Organizations and individuals in the territory of the Russian Federation authorized to represent foreign legal entities on the basis of a contract, acting on behalf of that foreign legal entity, and having authorization to conclude contracts in the name of that foreign legal entity or to negotiate significant terms of contracts are also considered to constitute a PE of a foreign legal entity. However, if a Russian legal entity or an individual acts as an agent in the course of ordinary business, this should not constitute a PE. The profit earned by a foreign legal entity through a PE in the Russian Federation is subject to profits tax.

The determination of branch income is broadly similar to determination of income by a Russian legal entity, except for in the case of a branch, only income related to activity in the Russian Federation is subject to tax. Profit earned from business activities in the Russian Federation through a permanent establishment is calculated according to the profits tax chapter of the tax code provisions based on tax accounting records using direct method. The use of "indirect" method is allowed only for preparatory and auxiliary activity in favor of third parties on a free of charge basis.

## Income determination

Taxable profit is the total income less allowable expenses/losses. Total income is considered as sales income (i.e., from realization of goods, works, services, property, and property rights) plus nonsales income (all other types of income). Foreign currency income is converted into rubles at the rate of exchange set by the Central Bank of the Russian Federation.

Starting from January 1, 2002 the accrual method by default shall be applied. However, there are special rules for income recognition for transfer of title, transfer of results of work or provision of services as well as for interest, royalty, and rents. Cash method can be used only if the last four average quarterly sales are less than RUB 1 million per quarter.

Free of charge receipts of property, cash, services, works, and property rights are subject to profits tax. Income should be recognized at market price, but no less than residual value (for depreciable property) and production (acquisition) costs (for goods). Costs related to free of charge transfers for a transferor are nondeductible. However, the receipt of property from a Russian or foreign share-holder (individual or legal entity) owning not less than 50% of recipient's capital shall not be subject to tax provided this property (other than cash) is not transferred to third parties within one year from receipt. This exemption applies only to Russian legal entities.

*Inventory valuation*/There are several methods of valuation of purchased goods (i.e., FIFO, LIFO, weighted-average, and historical value of a unit). Securities can be utilized at FIFO, LIFO, and historical value of a unit; no weighted-average method can be applied.

*Capital gains*/Profit from the sale of fixed assets and other property is calculated on the difference between the sale price and the historical cost of the asset or property (or net book value for fixed assets and intangible assets which are subject to depreciation). Losses on such sales reduce taxable income, and are deductible monthly by equal installments during the period, defined as the difference between the normative useful life of the assets and the actual time in use. Losses from sale/purchase of foreign currency are deductible.

*Interest and dividends*/Dividends distributed by Russian organizations are taxable at a 6% rate if the dividends are received by Russian residents. Dividends to nonresidents are subject to 15% tax subject to double tax treaties provisions. The tax shall be withheld by the paying entity. There is a special offset mechanism for dividends paid out by group companies to its shareholders.

Interest on state and municipal bonds is taxed at 15%. Interest on state and municipal bonds issued prior to January 20, 1997, as well as interest on certain hard currency denominated state bonds issued in 1999, are exempt. Other interest is taxed at 20%.

*Foreign income*/Enterprises and organizations that are legal entities under the law of the Russian Federation are taxable on their worldwide income. Foreign taxes paid by such enterprises on profits earned outside the Russian Federation can be offset against the profits tax payable in Russia in an amount not exceeding the profits tax payable in Russia on these profits.

*Exchange gains and losses*/Exchange gains and losses due to the obligatory revaluation of assets and liabilities stated in hard currency (this includes monetary assets and liabilities, payables, and receivables in hard currency) are posted in the profit and loss account and are accounted for when calculating profits tax.

## Deductions

*General*/Tax deduction is available if expenses are economically justified, supported by statutory documents, and relate to income-earning activity. Documentary support remains a key issue. Certain expenses must be capitalized or deferred (development of natural resource, R&D, losses on sale of fixed assets). Notwithstanding that there is an open list of expenses allowed for deduction, specific nondeductible expenses and statutory limits for deductibility of certain expenses are listed, such as business trip expenses, representative expenses, training of employees, compensation for use of private cars for business purposes, certain advertising costs, and so on.

*Loss carryforward*/A loss carryforward provision is available for total tax loss rather than operating loss. There is a ten-year carry forward period. The amount of loss carried forward cannot exceed 30% of current period profit. Loss carryback is not allowed. A surviving company may utilize the losses of a liquidated company in a reorganization.

# Russian Federation

*Interest*/Interest on business loans is deductible regardless of the source and use (current and investment). However, the following limitations apply.

- Deduction is allowed within the limits of an average interest rate for similar loans issued ±20% fluctuation.
- In the absence of similar loans, or at the taxpayer's choice, deduction is allowed in an amount not exceeding the Central Bank rate times 1.1 for rubles, and 15% for foreign currency.

Thin capitalization rules apply only to loans received from foreign owners (direct or indirect) who own more than 20% of share capital. If the ownership criteria are met, the maximum amount of deduction on such loans will be calculated based on the debt to equity ratio of 3:1.

*Doubtful debt reserve*/A doubtful debt reserve is created based on inventory of debtors performed at the end of reporting (tax) period. A doubtful debt is any debt if it is not repaid within the period set up by the agreement, and not collateralized or guaranteed (other than loans). For debts outstanding for more than 90 days, provision for the full amount is created. For debts outstanding for 45 to 90 days, provision for 50% of debts outstanding is created. For debts outstanding for less than 45 days, no provision is created. If a newly created reserve exceeds the balance of reserve of the preceding period, the difference should be recognized as expense of the current reporting period. Provision can not exceed 10% of revenue of reporting (tax) period. Companies (not banks) are not allowed to deduct provision for interest overdue.

*Insurance premiums*/There are no limits on deductibility of property insurance (subject to state tariffs limitation where established). Long-term life and pension insurance is deductible within 12% of the payroll fund. Voluntary medical insurance is deductible within 3% of the payroll fund. Accident and injury insurance of employees is not deductible unless occurring in relation to work (within RUB 10,000 per annum per employee).

*R&D expenses*/For R&D used in production/sales, 100% of costs are deductible evenly over three years upon completion. For R&D related to improvement of existing technology or the development of new technology, or the creation of new materials, which does not yield positive results, 70% of costs are deductible evenly over three years.

*Depreciation*/Two methods of depreciation for profits tax purposes (at the option of taxpayer) are established, that is, straight line (evenly over useful life of assets) and reducing balance method (cannot be used for buildings and equipment with useful life of more that 20 years). Accounting depreciation is not taken into account for profits tax purposes. Immediate write off of property with initial value less than RUB 10,000 is obligatory. No revaluation of fixed assets for tax depreciation purposes after January 1, 2002 exists. Depreciation is not allowed on assets purchased out of funds received from a foreign investor for capital investments, or for assets provided for use on gratuitous basis.

All depreciable property is classified into ten groups, depending on the asset's useful life. The useful life of fixed assets should be determined based on the statutory classification. Intangibles (intellectual property and exclusive rights to it, except goodwill) are amortized based on useful life, or ten years by default. In some cases a special coefficient can be applied to the general depreciation allowance, as follows.

- A coefficient of 0.5 for expensive light vehicles and minivans (initial acquisition cost greater than RUB 300,000 and RUB 400,000 accordingly).
- Up to 2 for fixed assets used in aggressive environment.
- Up to 3 for leased fixed assets (for lease of expensive cars, the coefficient 0.5 should apply).

*Payments to foreign affiliates*/There are no special tax provisions dealing with the deductibility of payments to foreign affiliates for services provided. Royalty payments (periodical payments for nonexclusive rights), provision of personnel, management service fees, information, consultancy, legal and similar fees, and lease payments are deducted in full, subject to potential transfer pricing rules application. Deductibility of nonstatutory audit fees (U.S. GAAP) is questionable. Charges with respect to general and administrative expenses incurred by foreign affiliates may be deductible, but care should be taken in regards to documentary support.

## Group taxation

In general, Russian tax law does not include provisions for consolidated reporting by affiliates or group relief. However, under special permission from the Ministry of Taxes and Levies, a foreign legal entity having several PEs in Russia which are carrying on activity within the "unified technology process," can consolidate computation and payment of profits tax.

## Tax concessions and reductions

Tax concessions and reductions are generally no longer available as of January 1, 2002. Concessions enjoyed by some companies under the grandfathering rules should have generally come to an end from January 1, 2004. Regional authorities may introduce tax concessions in the form of profits tax rate reduction for their part of profits tax, but the regional tax rate cannot be less than 12%. There are tax exemptions of income received for certain taxpayers (noncommercial organizations, organizations financed from the Russian budget, religious, and other qualifying organizations).

*Tax accounting*/Starting from January 1, 2002, tax accounting is mandatory. Tax accounting may be based on statutory accounting records or be separate. Over 20 articles in the tax code are devoted to tax accounting for profits tax purposes for separate categories of income, expenses, and calculation of taxable profit.

*Transition period tax base*/With introduction of the profits tax chapter of the tax code in 2002, special rules for the transitional period tax base were established, and tax with respect to transitional profits tax base is payable at 24% up to 2006, under the schedule set by the law. Some losses generated under the transitional rules are nondeductible.

## Withholding taxes

Under profits tax law, passive income (such as dividends, interest, royalties) and income from sale of immovable property and shares related to charter capital consisting of more than 50% of immovable property, lease income, freight, and international transportation received by foreign legal entities from sources in Russia is subject to profits tax withholding at source. Any other income received by foreign legal entities that do not have PEs in Russia is not subject to withholding

# Russian Federation

tax. Unless lower treaty rates apply, the domestic withholding rate for dividends is 15%, while income of a foreign legal entity from all other income including interest, intellectual property such as royalties, copyrights, licenses, rentals, and other types of income listed in the tax code (excluding freight, which is taxed at 10%) from sources in the territory of the Russian Federation is taxed at 20%. A foreign legal entity should provide to a Russian tax agent (a company paying income) a residence certificate from the tax (or other competent authority), in order to enjoy double tax treaty benefits.

The Russian tax authorities recognize the terms of the former USSR treaties until renegotiated by the Russian government. The tax treaty network is continuously being updated. This list is current as of January 1, 2004, and indicates the withholding tax rates stipulated in the treaties.

| | Treaty benefits available from | Dividends (%) | Interest (%) | Royalties (%) | Construction site duration (months) | Protocol (important aspects) |
|---|---|---|---|---|---|---|
| Albania/RF | January 1, 1998 | 10 | 10 | 10 | 12 | |
| Armenia/RF | January 1, 1999 | 5 (8) or 10 | 0 | 0 | 18 | |
| Australia/RF (7) | January 1, 2004 (1) | 5 (48) or 15 | 10 | 10 | 12 | |
| Austria/RF | January 1, 2003 | 5 (43) or 15 | 0 | 0 | 12 (41) | extension of a transition period for old construction sites (41) |
| Azerbaijan/RF | January 1, 1999 | 10 | 0 (10) or 10 | 10 | 12 | |
| Belarus/RF | January 1, 1998 | 15 | 0 (9) or 10 | 10 | 0 | |
| Belgium/RF | January 1, 2001 | 10 | 0 (67) or 10 | 0 | 12 | |
| Bulgaria/RF | January 1, 1996 | 15 | 0 (12) or 15 | 15 | 12 | |
| Canada/RF | January 1, 1998 | 10 (18) or 15 | 0 (17) or 10 | 0 (68) or 10 | 12 | |
| China, P. R./RF | January 1, 1998 | 10 | 0 (19) or 10 | 10 | 18 | |
| Croatia/RF | January 1, 1998 | 5 (34) or 10 | 10 | 10 | 12 | |
| Cyprus/RF | January 1, 2000 | 5 (69) or 10 | 0 | 0 | 12 | |
| Czech/RF | January 1, 1998 | 10 | 0 | 10 | 12 | |
| Denmark/RF | January 1, 1998 | 10 | 0 | 0 | 12 | |
| Egypt | January 1, 2001 | 10 | 0 (70) or 15 | 15 | 6 | |
| Finland/RF | January 1, 2003 | 5 (44) or 12 | 0 | 0 | 12 or 18 (42) | special duration periods for various construction sites (42) |
| France/RF | January 1, 2000 | 5 (71) or 10 or 15 | 0 | 0 | 12 | |
| Germany/RF | January 1, 1997 | 5 (30) or 15 | 0 | 0 | 12 | deductibility of certain items (11) |
| Hungary/RF | January 1, 1998 | 10 | 0 | 0 | 12 | |
| Iceland/RF | January 1, 2004 | 5 (53) or 15 | 0 | 0 | 12 | |
| India/RF | January 1, 1999 | 10 | 0 (14) or 10 | 10 | 12 | |
| Indonesia/RF | January 1, 2003 | 15 | 0 (89) or 15 | 15 | 3 | |
| Iran/RF | January 1, 2003 | 5 (54) or 10 | 0 (55) or 7.5 | 5 | 12 | |
| Ireland, Rep. of/RF | January 1, 1996 (2) | 10 | 0 | 0 | 12 | |

| | Treaty benefits available from | Dividends (%) | Interest (%) | Royalties (%) | Construction site duration (months) | Protocol (important aspects) |
|---|---|---|---|---|---|---|
| Israel/RF | January 1, 2001 | 10 | 0 (90) or 10 | 10 | 12 | |
| Italy/RF | January 1, 1999 | 5 (15) or 10 | 10 | 0 | 12 | |
| Japan/USSR | January 1, 1987 | 15 | 0 (36) or 10 | 0 (91) or 10 | 12 | |
| Kazakhstan/RF | January 1, 1998 | 10 | 0 (16) or 10 | 10 | 12 | |
| Korea, Democratic People's Republic of/RF | January 1, 2001 | 10 | 0 | 0 | 12 | |
| Korea, Rep. of/RF | January 1, 1996 | 5 (39) or 10 | 0 | 5 | 12 or 24 (40) | |
| Kuwait/RF | January 1, 2004 | 0 (46) or 5 | 0 | 10 | 6 | additional cases when 0% rate is applied to dividends (47) |
| Kyrgyzstan/RF | January 1, 2001 | 10 | 0 (92) or 10 | 10 | 12 | |
| Lebanon/RF | January 1, 2001 | 10 | 0 (93) or 5 | 5 | 12 | |
| Luxembourg/RF | January 1, 1998 | 10 (21) or 15 | 0 | 0 | 12 | |
| Macedonia/RF | January 1, 2001 | 10 | 10 | 10 | 12 | |
| Malaysia/USSR | January 1, 1989 | 0 or 15 (87) | 0 (22) or 15 | 10 (72) or 15 | 6 (88) or 12 | |
| Mali/RF | January 1, 2000 | 10 (73) or 15 | 0 (94) or 15 | 0 | 0 | |
| Moldova/RF | January 1, 1998 | 10 | 0 | 10 | 12 | |
| Mongolia/RF | January 1, 1998 | 10 | 0 (23) or 10 | rates in accordance with domestic law | 24 | |
| Morocco/RF | January 1, 2000 | 5 (74) or 10 | 0 (75) or 10 | 10 | 8 | |
| Namibia/RF | January 1, 2001 | 5 (76) or 10 | 0 (77) or 10 | 5 | 9 | |
| Netherlands/RF | January 1, 1999 | 5 (24) or 15 | 0 | 0 | 12 | additions to definition of dividends and criteria to apply 5% rate (25) |
| New Zealand/RF | January 1, 2004 | 15 | 10 | 10 | 12 | |
| Norway/RF | January 1, 2003 | 10 | 0 (60) or 10 | 0 | 12 | |
| Philippines/RF | January 1, 1998 | 15 | 0 (29) or 15 | 15 | 183 days | |
| Poland/RF | January 1, 1994 | 10 | 0 (78) or 10 | 10 | 12 or 24 (20) | |
| Portugal/RF | January 1, 2003 | 10 (62) or 15 | 0 (63) or 10 | 10 | 12 | |
| Qatar/RF | January 1, 2001 | 5 | 0 (79) or 5 | 0 | 6 | |
| Romania/RF | January 1, 1996 | 15 | 0 (26) or 15 | 10 | 12 | |
| Slovakia/RF | January 1, 1998 | 10 | 0 | 10 | 12 | |
| Slovenia/RF | January 1, 1998 | 10 | 10 | 10 | 12 | |
| South Africa/RF | September 1, 2000 (37) January 1, 2001 (38) | 10 (80) or 15 | 0 (95) or 10 | 0 | 12 | |
| Spain/RF | January 1, 2001 | 5 (81) or 10 or 15 | 0 (96) or 5 | 5 | 12 | dividends include liquidation proceeds |

# Russian Federation

| | Treaty benefits available from | Dividends (%) | Interest (%) | Royalties (%) | Construction site duration (months) | Protocol (important aspects) |
|---|---|---|---|---|---|---|
| Sri Lanka/RF | January 1, 2003 | 10 (45) or 15 | 0 (64) or 10 | 10 | 6 | |
| Sweden/RF | January 1, 1996 | 5 (33) or 15 | 0 | 0 | 12 | |
| Switzerland/RF | January 1, 1998 | 5 (32) or 15 | 0 or 5 or 10 (31) | 0 | 12 | |
| Syria/RF | January 1, 2004 | 15 | 0 (12) or 10 | 4.5 (82) or 13.5 or 18 | 6 | |
| Tajikistan/RF | January 1, 2004 | 5 (65) or 10 | 0 (66) or 10 | 0 | 24 | |
| Turkey/RF | January 1, 2000 | 10 | 0 (83) or 10 | 10 | 18 | |
| Turkmenistan/RF | January 1, 2000 | 10 | 5 | 5 | 12 | |
| Ukraine/RF | January 1, 2000 | 5 (84) or 15 | 0 (85) or 10 | 10 | 12 | |
| United Kingdom/RF | January 1, 1998 (3) | 10 | 0 | 0 | 12 | |
| United States/RF | January 1, 1994 (4) | 5 (27) or 10 | 0 | 0 | 18 | |
| Uzbekistan/RF | January 1, 1996 | 10 | 0 (28) or 10 | 0 | 12 | |
| Vietnam/RF | January 1, 1997 | 10 (13) or 15 | 10 | 15 | 6 | |
| Yugoslavia/RF | January 1, 1998 | 5 (35) or 15 | 10 | 10 | 18 | |
| **Signed but noneffective treaties** | | | | | | |
| Argentina/RF | Not effective | N/A (6) | N/A (6) | N/A (6) | | |
| Cuba/RF | Not effective | 5 (49) or 15 | 0 (50) or 10 | 5 | 12 | |
| Estonia/RF | Not effective | 5 (99) or 10 | 0 (100) or 10 | 10 | 9 | |
| Ethiopia/RF | Status unclear (5) | 5 | 0 (51) or 5 | 15 | 9 | |
| Georgia/RF | Not effective | 10 | 0 (98) or 10 | 5 | 9 | |
| Greece/RF | Not effective | 5 (52) or 10 | 7 | 7 | 9 | |
| Lithuania/RF | Not effective | 5 (56) or 10 | 0 (57) or 10 | 5 (86) or 10 | 9 | |
| Malta/RF | Not effective | 5 (58) or 10 | 0 | 0 | 6 | |
| Mauritius/RF | Status unclear (5) | 5 (59) or 10 | 0 | 0 | 12 | |
| Oman/RF | Not effective | 5 (61) or 10 | 0 | 5 | 9 | |
| Singapore/RF | Not effective | N/A (6) | N/A (6) | N/A (6) | | |
| Thailand/RF | Not effective | 15 | 0 (97) or 10 | 15 | 6 | |

Notes:

1. In Australia, tax reliefs are available from July 1, 2004.
2. In Ireland, tax reliefs are available from January 1, 1996 or April 6, 1996 (depending on the tax).
3. In the United Kingdom, tax reliefs are available from April 1, 1998 or April 6, 1998 (depending on the tax).
4. In the United States and Russian Federation, tax reliefs are available from January 1, 1994 or February 1, 1994 (depending on the tax).
5. There is no information on whether the treaty has been concluded (information awaited from the Russian Federation Ministry of Foreign Affairs).
6. Details of the treaty are not available (information awaited from the Russian Federation Ministry of Foreign Affairs).
7. The double tax treaty with Australia is effective in accordance with information bulletin of the Russian Federation Ministry of Finance of March 2, 2004 (see *www.minfin.ru/off_inf/723.htm*).

8. A rate of 5% on dividends payable to a resident of the other contracting state which invested at least US$40,000 in the charter capital of the company paying such dividends.

9. A rate of 0% on interest payable to the government or the national bank of the contracting state.

10. A rate of 0% on interest payable to the government or other authorized body of the contracting state.

11. For example, full deductibility of advertising expenses.

12. A rate of 0% on interest payable to the government of the other contracting state and its national bank.

13. A rate of 10% on dividends payable to a company which invested at least US$10 million in the charter capital of the company paying such dividends.

14. A rate 0% on interest receivable by the government, political unit or local authority, central bank, any other governmental authorities or financial institutions, which may be determined and approved through an exchange of notes between competent state bodies and agencies.

15. A rate of 5% on dividends payable to a company which directly holds at least 10% of the capital of the company paying such dividends, and the participation amounts to at least US$100,000.

16. A rate of 0% on interest payable to the contracting state, its administrative and territorial unit or local authority or any other agency of this state, its unit or local authority.

17. A rate of 0% on interest payable to the following.
    (a) To the central bank of the contracting state.
    (b) To a resident of the contracting state in respect of indebtedness of the other state or of its state authorities, including local authorities thereof.
    (c) In respect of a loan made, guaranteed or insured, or a credit extended, guaranteed or insured by an organization created and wholly owned by the government of a contracting state for the purpose of facilitating export, it is understood that, for the purposes of this provision, the Export Development Corporation created under the laws of Canada meets these requirements, and that any organization wholly owned by, and created under the laws by the government of the Russian Federation with similar mandate and functions shall, from the date mentioned in an exchange of letters between the competent authorities of the contracting states, also be considered to meet the requirements of this provision.

18. A rate of 10% on dividends payable to a company which holds at least 10% of voting shares (or in case of Russia if there is no such shares, not less than 10% of the charter capital) of the company paying such dividends.

19. A rate of 0% on interest receivable by the government, its local body of power, the central bank or any other financial institution fully owned by this government. This is applicable on the basis of reciprocity.

20. A total of 24 months in exceptional cases on the basis of an application submitted by the relevant persons and approved by a competent body of the contracting state.

21. A rate of 10% on dividends payable to a person which directly holds at least 30% of the capital of the company paying such dividends, and the participation in the charter capital amounts to at least €75,000.

22. A rate of 0% on interest payable to the government, central bank or with respect to loans provided thereby, supplied, guaranteed or insured by the government, a person with the permanent residence in the USSR (for these purposes, in the Russian Federation) if the loan or any other debt on this interest is paid out on an approved loan, as the legislation of Malaysia prescribes.

23. A rate of 0% on interest payable to the government of the contracting state, its central bank, or Bank for Trade and Development of Mongolia and the *Vneshtorgbank* of Russia.

24. A rate of 5% on dividends payable to a company (other than a partnership) owning directly at least 25% in the capital of the company paying such dividends and which invested at least €75,000 in the capital of the paying company.

25. Dividends include income from bonds with a right to participate in profits of a company; participation in the amount of €75,000 is calculated at the moment when the investment is made, and includes investments made at an earlier date and subsequently withdrawn.

26. A rate of 0% on interest payable to the following.

    (a) The government of Romania, its national bank, bank for foreign trade, or Eximbank.

    (b) The government of Russia, its central bank, or bank for foreign trade.

27. A rate of 5% on dividends payable to a company owning not less than 10% of voting shares (or in case of Russia if there is no such shares, 10% of the charter capital) of the company paying such dividends.

28. A rate of 0% on interest payable to the following.

    (a) To the contracting state, its constituents or local authorities, central bank, an organization for guaranteeing export loans or any other similar organizations, the list of which is subject to periodical revisions.

    (b) By the purchaser to the seller under commercial loans in the form of deferred payment for purchased goods, equipment, and rendered services.

29. A rate of 0% on interest payable by the contracting state to the government, its political subdivision, or local authority of the other contracting state.

30. A rate of 5% on dividends payable to a company which directly holds at least 10% of the charter capital of the company paying such dividends, and participation amounts to at least DM160,000.

31. A rate of 0% on interest payable in connection with credit sales by one enterprise to another of any type of industrial, commercial, or scientific equipment, and any other products. A rate of 5% applies on loans granted by a bank.

32. A rate of 5% on dividends payable to a company (other than a partnership) owning directly at least 20% in the capital of the company paying such dividends, and foreign capital invested amounts to at least SF200,000 on the date of dividend accrual.

33. A rate of 5% on dividends payable to a company (other than a partnership), which directly owns 100% of the capital of the company paying the dividends, or, in case of a joint venture, owns at least 30% of the capital of such joint venture, and in any of these cases the invested foreign capital amounts to at least US$100,000 as on the date of the actual dividend distribution.

34. A rate of 5% on dividends payable to a company which holds at least 25% of the capital of the company paying such dividends, and the participation amounts to at least US$100,000.

35. A rate of 5% on dividends payable to the company (other than a partnership) which owns directly at least 25% in the capital of the company paying such dividends and which invested at least US$100,000 in the capital of the paying company.

36. A rate of 0% on interest receivable by the government of the contracting state, its local authority, the central bank or any financial institution fully owned by the government of that state, or any person with a permanent residence in that state with respect to loans, guaranteed, insured or indirectly financed by the government of that state, its local authority, the central bank, or any financial institution fully owned by the government of that state.

37. This is with respect to taxes withheld at source from amounts paid or accrued starting from September 1, 2000.

38. This is with respect to other taxes to the tax periods starting from 2001.

39. A rate of 5% on dividends to a company (other than a partnership) which directly holds at least 30% of the capital of the company paying such dividends and which invested at least US$100,000 in the capital of the paying company.

40. A period of 24 months in exceptional cases on the basis of an application submitted by the relevant persons and approved by a competent body of the contracting state.

41. If a construction site existed as of the date when the Convention entered into force, the 12 months period will start on the date of entry into force. However, it will not exceed 24 months from the date when the construction site started to exist.

42. For a period of 18 months for a building site or construction, assembly or installation project or supervisory activity involving mainly the erection of factories, workshops, power stations, or any other industrial buildings or structures, 12 months for all other cases, including an installation or drilling rig or ship to explore for or exploit natural resources, and 36 months for construction sites which began before January 1, 2003.

43. A rate of 5% on dividends payable to a company (other than a partnership) which directly holds at least 10% of the capital of the company paying such dividends, and participation exceeds US$100,000.

44. A rate of 5% on dividends payable to a company (other than a partnership) which directly holds at least 30% of the capital of the company paying such dividends, and the participation exceeds US$100,000 at the moment when the dividends become due and payable.

45. A rate of 10% on dividends payable to a company (other than a partnership) owning directly at least 25% in the capital of the company paying such dividends.

46. A rate of 0% on dividends payable to the government, political subdivision or a local authority of the other contracting state, the central bank of the other contracting state, or other governmental agencies or financial institutions which may be designated and agreed upon by the competent authorities of contracting states through the exchange of notes.

47. A rate of 0% on dividends payable to any governmental institution, an entity established by the governments or governmental institutions of both contracting states, a company which is controlled by or at least 25% of the capital is directly or indirectly owned by the government (or other governmental institution mentioned thereof) of other contracting state.

48. A rate of 5% on dividends to the extent such dividends are paid from profits taxable at a normal tax rate, and if the following applies.

    (a) A company (other than a partnership) owns directly at least 10% in the charter capital of the paying company.

    (b) A recipient invested at least A$700,000 in the capital of the paying company.

    (c) Dividends paid by a resident of Russia are exempt from taxation in Australia.

49. A rate of 5% on dividends payable to a company (other than a partnership) which directly holds at least 25% of the capital of the company paying such dividends.

50. A rate of 0% on interest payable to the government of the other contracting state or to its political subdivisions or to local authority thereof, or to a body or financial banking organization which is fully owned or controlled by that contracting state or its political subdivisions or local government bodies, or to other bodies or organizations (including financial institutions) in connection with a loan made within the framework of agreements between the governments of the contracting states.

51. A rate of 0% on interest payable under the following circumstances.

    (a) By the government of the contracting state, its political subdivision or local authority thereof.

    (b) To the government of the other contracting state, its political subdivision, or local authority thereof, or any credit or financial agency or institution owned by that other contracting state, political subdivision, or local authority thereof.

    (c) To any person in connection with loans made under an agreement concluded between the governments of the contracting states, political subdivisions, or local authorities thereof.

52. A rate of 5% on dividends payable to a company (other than a partnership) which directly holds at least 25% of the capital of the company paying such dividends.

53. A rate of 5% on dividends payable to a company (other than a partnership) which directly holds at least 25% of the capital of the company paying such dividends, and the foreign capital invested exceeds US$100,000.

54. A rate of 5% on dividends payable to a company (other than a partnership) which directly holds at least 25% of the capital of the company paying such dividends.

55. A rate of 0% on interests payable to the other contracting state, a political subdivision or local authorities thereof, the central bank or bank for foreign trade or state agency for the security of export loans and other state-owned banks or any other state agency of the other contracting state.

56. A rate of 5% on dividends payable to a company (other than a partnership) which directly holds at least 25% of the company paying such dividends, the participation exceeds US$100,000.

57. A rate of 0% on interest payable to the government of the contracting state, including its political subdivisions and local bodies of power, or to the central bank, or on interest gained on the credits secured by the government of that state.

58. For dividends payable by a resident of Russia to a resident of Malta, the rates are as follows.

    (a) A rate of 5% on dividends payable to a company which directly holds at least 20% of the capital of the company paying such dividends (this share should be at least US$100,000).

    (b) A rate of 10% in all other cases.

    For dividends payable by a resident of Malta to a resident of Russia the Malta's tax shall not exceed tax on profits out of which the dividends are paid.

59. A rate of 5% on dividends payable to a person which invested directly at least US$500,000 in the charter capital of the company paying such dividends.

60. A rate of 0% on interest payable under the following circumstances.

    (a) To the contracting state, a regional or local authority thereof or by an instrumentality of that State which is not subject to tax therein.

    (b) - To the Central Bank of Norway, the Norwegian Guarantee Institute for Export Credits, A/S Eksportfinans.

    - To the Central Bank of Russia, Foreign Trade Bank (*Vneshtorgbank*) of Russia.

    - Or to any other institution similar to the above-mentioned institutions, as may be agreed from time to time between the competent authorities of the contracting states.

    (c) By a purchaser to a seller in connection with a commercial credit resulting from deferred payments for goods, merchandise, equipment, or services.

61. A rate of 5% on dividends payable to a person which invested directly at least US$500,000 in the capital of the company paying such dividends.

62. A rate of 10% on dividends payable to a company which has been owing directly at least 25% in the capital of the company paying the dividends for an uninterrupted period of two years prior to the payment of the dividend.

63. A rate of 0% on interest payable under the following circumstances.

    (a) By the contracting state, a political or administrative subdivision, or a local authority thereof.

    (b) To the other contracting state, a political or administrative subdivision, or a local authority thereof or any institution specified and agreed on by exchange of notes between the competent authorities of the contracting states in connection with any credit granted or guaranteed by them under an agreement between the governments of the contracting states.

64. A rate of 0% on interests payable to the following.

    (a) The government, a political subdivision, or a local authority of the other contracting state.

    (b) The central bank of the other contracting state.

    (c) Any other governmental agency or financial institution as may be specified and agreed by exchange of notes between the competent authorities of the contracting states.

65. A rate of 5% on dividends payable to a person owning directly at least 25% of the capital of the company paying such dividends.

66. A rate of 0% on interest payable under the following circumstances.

    (a) To the contracting state, the subjects and local authorities thereof.

    (b) To the central bank, organization engaged in guaranteeing export credits, or any other organizations, as may be agreed from time to time between the competent authorities of the contracting state.

    (c) By a purchaser to a seller in connection with a commercial credit resulting from deferred payments for goods, equipment, works or services.

67. A rate of 0% on the following types of interest.

    (a) Payable to the other contracting state, its political subdivisions, or to local government bodies.

    (b) Payable to a resident of the other contracting state on the basis of a loan or credit, which is guaranteed or secured by the other contracting state, its political and administrative units or local government bodies.

    (c) On loans (other than loans in bearer form) granted by the banks or credit institutions of the other contracting state.

68. A rate of 0% applied to the following.

    (a) Copyright royalties and other like payments in respect of the production or reproduction of any literary, dramatic, musical or other artistic work (but not including royalties in respect of motion picture films nor royalties in respect of works on film or videotape or other means of reproduction for use in connection with television broadcasting).

    (b) Royalties for the use of, or the right to use, computer software.

    (c) Where the payer and the beneficial owner of the royalties are not related persons, royalties for the use of, or the right to use, any patent or any information concerning industrial, commercial, or scientific experience (but not including any such information provided under a rental or franchise agreement), arising in a contracting state and paid to a resident of the other contracting state who is the beneficial owner thereof shall be taxable only in that other state.

69. A rate of 5% on dividends payable to a company which invested directly at least US$100,000 in the capital of the company paying such dividends.

70. A rate of 0% on interest payable under the following circumstances.

    (a) To the other contracting state, or to its political subdivisions, or local governmental bodies.

    (b) To the central bank, or any other bank, the capital of which by more than 51% is owned by the other contracting state.

71. A rate of 5% on dividends payable to a company which invested at least FF500,000 in the company paying such dividends, irrespective of the form or kind of the investment (the value of each investment is estimated as of the date when it was effected) and payable to a company subject to profit tax under the general regime established by the tax law of the contracting state of which it is a resident and which is exempt from this tax on the account of these dividends. A rate of 10% applies on dividends if only one of the above terms is observed.

72. A rate of 10% for the use, or granting of the right of using, any patent, trademark, drawing or model, plan, secret formula or process, or copyright in the author's work, or for the use or granting of the right of using industrial, commercial, or scientific equipment, or for information on industrial, commercial, or scientific experience, and 15% for the use, or granting of the right of using, motion pictures or magnetic tapes for radio broadcasting or television, any copyright in works of literature and art.

73. A rate of 10% on dividends payable to a person which invested at least FF1,000,000 in the company paying such dividends.

74. A rate of 5% on dividends payable to a person which participation in the capital of the company paying such dividends exceeds US$500,000.

75. A rate of 0% on loans granted to one of the contracting states or guaranteed by a contracting state, or on foreign currency deposits.

76. A rate of 5% on dividends to a company (other than partnership) which owns directly at least 25% in the charter capital of the company paying such dividends and which invested directly at least US$100,000 in the charter capital of the paying company.

77. A rate of 0% on interest payable to the government of the other contracting state, its political subdivision or local authority thereof, or an agency of the government of the other contracting state which may be agreed upon in writing between the competent authorities of both contracting states.

78. A rate of 0% on interest payable to the government, its regional or local authority, or the central bank of that state.

79. A rate of 0% on interest payable to the contracting state, a political subdivision or a local authority thereof, or any governmental institution of the contracting state created under national legislation of that contracting state.

80. A rate of 10% on dividends payable to persons owning at least 30% in the capital of the company paying such dividends and which invested directly at least US$100,000 in the capital of the paying company.

81. A rate of 5% on dividends payable to a company (other than a partnership) which invested at least e100,000 in the capital of the company paying such dividends, and which are exempt from tax in the other contracting state. A rate of 10% applies on dividends if only one of the above terms is observed.

82. A rate of 4.5% for cinematography films, programs and recordings for radio or television broadcasting, 13.5% for any copyright of literary, artistic, or scientific work, and 18% for any patent, trademark, design or model, plan, secret formula or process, any computer software program, or for information concerning industrial, commercial, or scientific experience.

83. A rate of 0% on interest payable to the government of Turkey, its central bank, or Eximbank of Turkey, the government of Russia, its central bank, or the Vneshtorgbank of Russia.

84. A rate of 5% on dividends payable to a person which invested at least US$50,000 in the charter capital of the company paying such dividends.

85. A rate of 0% on interest payable to the contracting state, its national bank, any other state body or a local authority thereof, or in connection with any credit guaranteed by the above institutions.

86. A rate of 5% on consideration for the use of industrial, commercial, or scientific equipment.

87. A rate of 0% on dividends payable by a resident of Malaysia to a juridical person resident of the USSR (for these purposes, the Russian Federation), and a rate of 15% on profits of a joint venture in the former USSR distributed to its participant who is a person with the permanent residency in Malaysia.

88. A period of six months for an assembly or erection project, and 12 months for a building site.

89. A period of 0% on interests payable to the government of the contracting state, including its local authorities, political units, or the central bank.

90. A rate of 0% on interest payable to the government of the contracting state, its local authorities, the central bank, a resident of the other contracting state on the basis of a debt guaranteed, secured or indirectly financed by the government of the other contracting state, its local government bodies of the central bank.

91. A rate of 0% for copyrights of literary, artistic, or scientific work, including cinematography films, recordings for radio or television broadcasting.

92. A rate of 0% on interest payable to the other contracting state, the central bank, a governmental agency, or any other designated financial institution determined by exchange of notes.

93. A rate of 0% on interest payable to the government of the other contracting state, its political unit or a local body of power.

94. A rate of 0% on interest payable by the government or its local authority, to the government, its local authority, or the central bank, or to other institutions including financial organizations on credits within the framework of agreements concluded between governments of the contracting states.

95. A rate of 0% on interests with respect to loans granted or guaranteed by the government, local authorities, or the central bank.

96. A rate of 0% on interest payable to the government, its political unit or local authorities, or payable on a long-term credit (seven years or more) granted by a bank or a credit institution.

97. A rate of 0% on interest payable to the government, its state body, the central bank or the export-import bank of Thailand, and a rate of 10% on interest payable to an organization which has a banking license (for Russia), or a financial organization, including insurance companies (for Thailand). In any other cases, interest is subject to the withholding tax in accordance with the local legislation.

98. A rate of 0% on interest payable to the contracting state.

99. A rate of 5% on dividends payable to a company (other than a partnership) which holds directly at least 25% of the capital of the company paying such dividends and which invested at least US$75,000 in the capital of the paying company.

100. A rate of 0% on interest payable to the government of the contracting state, including its political subdivisions and local authorities, or the central bank, or interest derived on loans guaranteed by the government of that other contracting state.

## Tax administration

***Returns and payments**/*In 2004, legal entities may choose between two profits tax payment systems, either quarterly assessments of tax (paying monthly advance payments) or monthly payment of tax on actual profit. Only quarterly assessment system should be applied by organizations with average quarterly revenue less than RUB 3 million (calculated for preceding four quarters), organizations financed from the Russian budget, PEs of foreign legal entities, and some other organizations. The method chosen should be applied consistently through the year.

*Filing*/An annual declaration must be filed by March 28 of the year following the end of the reporting year. Interim declarations (quarterly or monthly) must be filed within 28 days following the end of a reporting period. Profits tax is payable within the same dates. Foreign companies operating through a permanent establishment are required to submit a return by March 28 following the calendar year. Because of the regional tax basis, companies are required to file tax returns in each place in which they do business.

## Foreign currency regulation issues

*Existing system of currency legislation*/Until June 18, 2004, the day the main part of the new law "Concerning Currency Regulation and Currency Control" No. 173-ФЗ of December 10, 2003 (the "New Currency Law") comes into force, foreign investors or foreign entities that have a contractual relationship with a Russian resident must monitor Russian currency regulations established in accordance with the Law "Concerning Currency Regulation and Currency Control" No. 3615-1 of 9 October 1992 (the "Currency Law").

In accordance with Currency Law, there is a closed-ended list of foreign currency transactions that can be performed without obtaining authorization (permission, license) from the Central Bank of Russia (CBR). Certain transactions which broadly cover loans for periods of up to 180 days, as well as grants, payments relating to import-export operations with deferral of payment for no more than 90 days and nontrade transfers (an open-ended list of which has been introduced into the Currency Law), may be carried out without a CBR license. Loans granted to residents by nonresidents for periods exceeding 180 days do not require registration or licensing with the CBR, and may be effected on a notification basis. In contrast, however, loans granted to nonresidents by residents for periods exceeding 180 days require CBR authorization.

Foreign currency can be purchased for making prepayments on imported goods only if an amount equivalent to 20% of the ruble value of the currency purchased is deposited with the relevant Russian bank. A deposit may be avoided if a first class foreign bank guarantee is presented and in certain other cases. There is tight control over the receipt of foreign currency from export operations and for payments for the import of goods in foreign currency.

Purchases of foreign currency may be performed in the domestic currency market through an authorized bank provided that the foreign currency is to be used for an authorized purpose. Foreign currency purchased in Russia for rubles and not used for an authorized purpose within seven days should be sold back at the domestic currency market. Documentary support of the purpose of the transaction, in accordance with the prescribed rules, is essential. Compliance with the requirements is regulated by banks, which face significant penalties for incorrectly processed transactions.

Foreign legal entities are allowed to maintain foreign currency and certain types of ruble bank accounts. Each type of ruble account may be used for a specified number of transactions only. Generally, proceeds from sales in rubles can be converted into another currency and repatriated, or used to pay for local expenses. It is possible to receive rubles from sales proceeds in Russia without the necessity of opening a Russian bank account in the name of the company, through the mechanism of correspondent ruble bank accounts and having such proceeds converted into foreign currency and remitted abroad.

Russian legal entities, including companies with foreign participation, are required to sell 25% of their foreign currency export earnings for rubles through authorized banks in the domestic currency market, or directly to authorized banks, within seven days of the receipt of foreign currency proceeds. There are strict rules as to how and where such currency proceeds can be sold.

**New currency legislation**/The New Currency Law, the main part of which will come into force on June 18, 2004, will introduce a substantially new approach to regulation of currency transactions, as follows.

*Currency transactions between residents and nonresidents*

In accordance with the New Currency Law, currency transactions between residents and nonresidents may be freely conducted, with the exception of currency transactions for which the law establishes the possibility of restrictions. Examples of transactions that may be restricted, among others, include the following transactions.

- Transactions related to foreign trade activity, according to which residents provide nonresidents a deferment on payment (e.g., in exporting) or commercial credit as an advance payment (e.g., in importing) for a term of more than 180 days.
- Settlements related to a resident's acquisition of shares, holdings, or common shares in a legal entity from nonresidents.
- Transfers involving the granting or receipt of credit or a loan in foreign currency or Russian Federation currency.
- Transactions with "foreign" and domestic securities, including settlements related to the transfer of securities.

The New Currency Law allows only two kinds of restrictions to be established, as follows.

The requirement that a resident or nonresident reserve, in a separate account in an authorized bank, Russian Federation currency in an amount and for a term as determined by an authority of currency regulation in accordance with the law.

- The requirement that a resident or nonresident use a special account for the designated currency transaction.
- Depending on the type of currency transaction, the Russian Federation government, the Russian Federation government with the consent of the Bank of Russia, the Bank of Russia or the Bank of Russia with the consent of the Russian Federation government may establish such restrictions. If these authorities do not establish any restrictions, currency transactions may be freely conducted.

*Currency transactions between residents in the Russian Federation in foreign currency or with foreign securities*

Currency transactions between residents are prohibited, with the exception of several transactions specified by the New Currency Law. Specifically, the following types of currency transactions, among others, may be performed between residents without restriction.

- Transactions between commission agents (or agents) and commission principals (or principals) where the commission agents (or agents) render services involving the conclusion and performance of contracts with nonresidents for the transfer of goods, performance of works or services or the transfer of information or results of intellectual activity, including the exclusive rights to these items.
- Transactions involving the execution of mandatory payments (e.g., tax, fees and other such payments) in foreign currency, as required by Russian Federation law, to the federal budget, a budget of a Russian Federation subject or a local budget.
- Transactions between residents and authorized banks involving the receipt or return of credits or loans, or the payment of amounts of interest or penalties under respective contracts.
- Transactions involving a resident's acquisition of promissory notes from an authorized bank that are made by this or another authorized bank, the presentation of such notes for payment, the receipt of payment per such notes or the resident's alienation of such promissory notes to an authorized bank.

*Currency transactions of nonresidents in Russia*

Transactions between nonresidents in foreign currency are performed without any restriction. Nonresidents' currency transactions between themselves with domestic securities in the Russian Federation may be performed pursuant to the procedure established by the Bank of Russia, which may require the use of a special account for performing such transactions.

*Accounts of residents in banks located outside the Russian Federation*

Natural persons who are residents have the right to open accounts in foreign currency without restriction in banks located in foreign states that are members of the Organization for Economic Cooperation and Development (OECD) or the Financial Action Task Force on Money Laundering (FATF). Natural persons who are residents will be able to use money that is deposited in such accounts for performing any kind of currency transaction that does not involve the transfer of property or the performance of services in Russia.

In accordance with the New Currency Law, a resident legal entity will have the right to open accounts in foreign banks in countries that are members of OECD or FATF without restriction, and perform currency transactions with money deposited in such accounts (with the exception of foreign currency transactions with residents) from June 19, 2005.

A resident natural person or a resident legal entity (from June 19, 2005) may also open foreign accounts in countries that are not members of OECD or FATF in accordance with the procedure established by the Bank of Russia, which may require advance registration of the account.

Foreign investors or foreign entities that have a contractual relationship with a Russian resident must monitor Russian currency regulations very carefully since these rules change frequently.

In light of the high penalties for failing to observe the Currency Law (the New Currency Law), foreign investors should seek out up-to-date legal advice to ensure that they are in compliance with all Russian currency requirements.

# Russian Federation

## *CORPORATION TAX CALCULATION*

Fiscal year ending December 31, 2003

| | | |
|---|---|---|
| Gross profit (1) ............................................................................ | | RUB 80,000,000 |
| Reduction of profits: | | |
| Property (cash) received from more that | | |
|    50% owned subsidiary ..................................... | RUB 5,000,000 | |
| Dividends received from another | | |
|    Russian enterprise (2)..................................... | RUB 10,000,000 | |
| Interest on state securities (3)............................ | RUB 5,000,000 | (20,000,000) |
| | | RUB 60,000,000 |
| Tax concessions: | | |
| Loss carry forward (4) ......................................... | RUB 15,000,000 | (15,000,000) |
| Taxable profit ................................................................................ | | RUB 45,000,000 |
| Tax at 24%.................................................................................... | | RUB 10,800,000 |

Notes:

1. The amount of "gross profit" is calculated under tax accounting rules.
2. Dividends received from other Russian enterprises would have already been subjected to a 6% withholding tax at source.
3. Interest on state securities is taxable at source.
4. The amount of loss carried forward cannot exceed 30% of the taxable base calculated without taking into account this loss.
5. Exchange rate of the ruble at January 1, 2004: US$1 = RUB 29.24.

## PwC contact

For additional information on taxation in St. Lucia, contact:

Richard N.C. Peterkin
PricewaterhouseCoopers
Price Waterhouse Centre
Pointe Seraphine
(P.O. Box 195)
Castries, St. Lucia, W.I.
Telephone: (1) (758) 456 2600
Fax: (1) (758) 452 1061
LN: Richard.n.peterkin@lc.pwc.com

## Significant developments

There were no significant regulatory or tax developments in 2003.

## Taxes on corporate income

*Income tax*/Resident companies are subject to tax at a flat rate of 33% on chargeable income. Associations of underwriters are taxed at 33% on 10% of the gross premium arising in St. Lucia, and life insurance companies are taxed at 33% on 10% of the gross investment income arising in St. Lucia.

## Corporate residence

Companies are regarded as resident if they are incorporated or managed and controlled in St. Lucia.

## Other taxes

There are no other corporate taxes.

## Branch income

The tax rate on branch income is the same as that on resident companies. No tax is withheld on transfers of profits to the head office.

## Income determination

*Inventory valuation*/Stocks are generally valued at the lower of cost or market value. Obsolescence is permitted where it occurs, but there are no provisions to account for monetary inflation on the inventory valuation.

*Capital gains*/There is no tax on capital gains except in instances where such gains form part of the income-earning activities of the business; in this instance, the corporate rate applies.

*Intercompany dividends*/Intercompany dividends and dividends paid to individuals are not subject to tax. There is no withholding tax on dividends paid to nonresident individuals or corporations.

*Foreign income*/Resident companies are taxed in St. Lucia on income earned outside St. Lucia. Agreements exist with some countries for the avoidance of double taxation, with foreign tax allowed as a credit against tax charged in

# St. Lucia

St. Lucia. Within the Caribbean community there is an agreement among the governments of the member states for the avoidance of double taxation. Where no treaty exists, the foreign tax to be set off is the lesser of the foreign tax or the tax payable on that income in St. Lucia.

*Stock dividends*/A bonus issue of shares out of distributable earnings or out of a capital surplus on the sale of fixed assets of a company is not taxable. Upon the reconstruction or winding-up of a company, a distribution to shareholders in excess of the paid-up value of shares is not taxable.

## Deductions

*Depreciation and depletion*/The following capital allowances are available.
1. An initial allowance of 20% is granted on the acquisition of industrial and agricultural buildings; on plant and machinery, including motor vehicles and furniture; and on fixtures and equipment.
2. Thereafter, annual allowances for wear and tear, ranging from 10% to 33.33%, are granted on the reducing-balance method, except for industrial and agricultural buildings, which are restricted to 5%.

Gains on disposal are taxable as ordinary income to the extent of depreciation recovered, and any excess is tax free. If an asset has been underdepreciated, a balancing allowance is granted.

*Net operating losses*/Net operating losses may be carried forward for up to six years if they have not been fully absorbed earlier. Losses may not be carried back. In carrying losses forward the amount allowed cannot exceed one-half of the assessable income of the subsequent year or years.

*Payments to foreign affiliates*/There are no restrictions on the deductibility of interest paid to foreign affiliates if the transaction is carried out at arm's length. However, deductions for management charges and royalties are restricted to the lesser of the aggregate of those charges or 10% of all allowable business deductions, excluding cost of sales and capital allowances.

*Taxes*/Property taxes are deductible where the property is used in producing assessable income. Income and other taxes of that nature are not deductible.

*Other significant items*/Foreign exchange gains or losses arising from foreign exchange transactions on trading items are assessable/deductible as realized gains or losses if settled within normal credit terms. Gains or losses on other instruments, including intercompany loans, are recognized only when actually realized.

## Group taxation

Group taxation is not allowed in St. Lucia.

## Tax incentives

*Inward investment*/A comprehensive package of incentives is contained in the Fiscal Incentives Act of 1974. These and other incentives include the following.
1. Duty-free importation of raw materials, machinery, components, and spare parts.
2. Exemption from income tax as follows.

| Type of enterprise | Up to |
|---|---|
| | Years |
| Group I (local value added: 50%) | 15 |
| Group II (local value added: 25%–49%) | 12 |
| Group III | 10 |
| Enclave | 15 |

3.  Guaranteed repatriation of capital, dividends and interest.
4.  Carryforward of net losses incurred during the tax holiday in full for six years from the year the loss is incurred.
5.  Export allowances.

*Capital investment*/There is no investment allowance on fixed assets.

*Other incentives*/Hotel companies are granted a tax holiday of up to 15 years. Dividends out of earnings are also tax-free. The status of "development alien" may be obtained by a nonresident developer or financial institution, which status entitles the developer to exemption from, inter alia (among other things), aliens' landholding license fees. Other incentives are negotiable with the government and will depend primarily on the following.

1.  Economic impact of using labor and local resources and producing export oriented products; and
2.  Amount of the investment.

## Withholding taxes

Domestic corporations paying certain types of income are required to withhold tax on gross income as follows.

| Recipient | % |
|---|---|
| Resident corporations: | |
| Payments to contractors | 10 |
| Equipment hire | 10 |
| Nonresident corporations: | 10 |
| Royalties | 25 |
| Management fees | 25 |
| Commissions or fees (not by way of employment) | 25 |
| Income of a trust | 25 |
| Premiums, including insurance premiums | 25 |

Interest and dividends are exempt from withholding tax.

## Tax administration

*Returns*/Tax returns must be filed within three months after the year of income. Returns must cover a 12-month period, which may be changed only with the Comptroller's permission.

*Payment of tax*/Tax is payable in installments. Advance tax is payable on March 25, June 25, and September 25 in each year of income, based on the preceding year's income. Any remainder is payable within three months of the end of the financial year.

# St. Lucia

## CORPORATION TAX CALCULATION

Calendar year ending December 31, 2004

### St. Lucia resident company

| | | |
|---|---:|---:|
| Net income before taxes | | EC$ 3,000,000 |
| Add: | | |
| Depreciation | 75,000 | |
| General provision for bad debts | 50,000 | |
| Uncovenanted donations | 10,000 | |
| Legal fees—Acquiring buildings (1) | 30,000 | |
| Penalty—Late payment of corporation tax | 5,000 | 170,000 |
| Deduct: | | |
| Wear and tear allowances | 60,000 | |
| Exempt income—Gross dividend | 40,000 | |
| Capital gain on sale of nondepreciable | | |
| fixed assets (land and buildings) (1) | 200,000 | 300,000 |
| Chargeable income | | EC$ 2,870,000 |
| Income tax payable at 33% | | EC$ 947,100 |

Notes:

1. The company sold its business premises during the year and acquired a new property in its place.
2. Exchange rate of the Eastern Caribbean dollar at January 1, 2004: US$1 = EC$2.7000.

## PwC contact

For additional information on taxation in Saudi Arabia, contact:

Sami B. Al Sarraj
Al Juraid & Company
10th Floor, North Tower
King Faisal Foundation Building
PO Box 8282
Riyadh 11482, Saudi Arabia
Telephone: (966) (1) 465 4240
Fax: (966) (1) 465 1663
e-mail: salsarraj@aljuraid.com

## Significant developments

In April 2000, Saudi Arabia issued sweeping changes in relation to income taxation and foreign investment in Saudi Arabia. The changes included the following.

- Reduction of the maximum income tax rate from 45% to 30%.
- Allowing the unlimited carryforward of net operating losses for tax purposes.
- Eliminating the tax holidays previously afforded to certain foreign investors.
- Allowing foreign companies to now invest 100% in Saudi companies in certain approved sectors.

In October 2003, Saudi Arabia issued the following changes.

- Restricting the carryforward loss to 25% of the current year adjusted profit. The balance of the carryforward loss will be offset against the subsequent years' adjusted profit on the same basis for indefinite years.
- Imposing taxes on interest paid to foreign banks.
- Imposing taxes on reinsurance premiums paid to foreign parties.

In January 2004, Saudi Arabia issued new tax regulations which superseded the old regulations. Although these new regulations have been approved, they are not yet made available to the public. The new tax regulations will be effective 90 days after they are published in the official gazette. The major change in the new regulations relates to the reduction of the tax rate to be a flat rate of 20% of the taxable profit.

## Taxes on corporate income

*Income tax*/The scale of income tax rates on net income allocated to foreign shareholders is as follows.

| Taxable income | % |
| --- | --- |
| First SR100,000 | 25 |
| Next SR400,000 | 20 |
| Next SR500,000 | 25 |
| Thereafter | 30 |

As indicated above, these are old rates. However, they will continue to be applied awaiting the publication of the new tax regulations.

Only non-Saudi investors are liable for income tax in Saudi Arabia. Saudi citizen investors (and citizens of the Gulf Cooperative Council countries, who are considered to be Saudi citizens for Saudi tax purposes) are liable for *Zakat*, an Islamic assessment. Where a company is owned by both Saudi and non-Saudi interests, the portion of taxable income attributable to the non-Saudi interest is subject to income tax, and the Saudi share goes into the basis on which *Zakat* is assessed.

***Taxes on imputed profits for nonresident payments***/When payments are made to nonresident companies by companies registered in Saudi Arabia for work performed inside Saudi Arabia, the Saudi Arabian tax authorities generally hold the Saudi-based company responsible for taxes on such payments as agent of the recipient. This procedure applies to payments for plant and equipment rentals, insurance premiums, payments to subcontractors, professional services, management fees, royalties, and other payments.

Assessment of Saudi Arabian taxes on these payments is on an arbitrary basis, with the minimum profit imputed at 15% to 20% of the payments for services that are technical in nature. Higher imputed profit rates for services, royalties, licensing, and other similar items or other forms of income, particularly fees for management, are used. Royalties are generally regarded as 100% taxable to the recipient. The domestic company is liable for taxes relating to these foreign payments even if it enjoys a prior tax holiday on its own Saudi Arabian profits.

## Corporate residence

Residence is determined on the basis of the following criteria.

1. Place of incorporation of the company.
2. Place of the administration office, factory, and so on.
3. The presence of a person or persons in Saudi Arabia who are employed by the foreign enterprise, and who have the authority to negotiate and sign contracts on behalf of the enterprise.
4. The existence of equipment, machines, or other assets owned by the foreign enterprise and leased to companies or individuals in Saudi Arabia, although the lease may be arranged outside Saudi Arabia.

## Other taxes

There is no value-added tax (VAT) system in Saudi Arabia. Neither is there any form of stamp, transfer, excise, sales, turnover, production, real estate, or property taxation, except insofar as they may fall within the scope of *Zakat*, which is applicable only to Saudi companies and individuals.

## Branch income

Branches of foreign corporations are taxed as discussed under "Taxes on corporate income" above.

## Income determination

***Inventory valuation***/The average-cost method is used for valuing inventory under Saudi tax laws.

***Capital gains***/Gains on disposal of assets in Saudi Arabia are taxed as part of the normal profits of the business. That is, there are no special tax rates applicable to capital gains.

*Intercompany dividends*/There is no tax liability on dividends received from either domestic subsidiaries or unrelated domestic companies, provided the dividends were paid out of profits subject to Saudi tax. In addition, dividends and interest received from sources outside Saudi Arabia are not subject to taxation in Saudi Arabia. However, such dividends and interest should be included in the total revenue of the local entity and be subject to Saudi income tax/*Zakat*.

*Foreign income*/The gross income of any company carrying on its activities at the same time both inside and outside Saudi Arabia is considered to include all the income that the company receives locally from any source within Saudi Arabia, as well as the income that the company derives from any activities either inside or outside Saudi Arabia that are associated with its activity in Saudi Arabia.

*Stock dividends*/Stock dividends may be distributed tax free to the recipient shareholders.

*Other significant items—imports and supply contracts*/Saudi tax law provides that no profit will be considered to arise from a contract for the supply of goods to Saudi Arabia, provided delivery of the goods is either free on board (FOB) or cost, insurance, and freight (CIF) to a Saudi port. However, should the contract provide for the delivery and/or installation of materials at a point inside Saudi Arabia, the supplier may be considered to be carrying on business within Saudi Arabia, and, as a consequence, the contract may be subject to Saudi taxation as follows.

1. If the material cost was identified in the supply contract separately from the cost of work performed in the Kingdom, then taxes will be assessed on the work that will be performed in the Kingdom on a deemed-profit basis of 15% of the total value of such work.

2. If the supply contract indicates a total cost for the supply and other activities in the Kingdom, then the work performed in the Kingdom will be assigned a value equal to 10% of the total contract value for each type of activity, and a deemed profit of 15% of the estimated work will be computed, which will be subject to tax according to the Saudi tax authorities.

It is desirable in those cases where title cannot be passed at the Saudi port of entry for a separate contract to be entered into for any transportation or installation activities carried on in Saudi Arabia.

## Deductions

*Depreciation*/Useful asset lives are governed by guidelines established by the Saudi tax authorities, and the straight-line method is generally required. It is possible to negotiate shorter lives where there is exceptional wear and tear; however, the normal practice is to use the Saudi guidelines. Sample annual depreciation rates authorized by the Saudi tax authorities are shown below.

|  | % |
| --- | --- |
| Buildings | 3 |
| Heavy equipment | 7.5 |
| Construction equipment | 12.5 |
| Office furniture and equipment | 10–15 |
| Passenger vehicles | 25 |

The above depreciation rates are expected to be changed according to the new tax regulations.

# Saudi Arabia

*Net operating losses*/Net losses as adjusted by the tax authority are currently carried forward for indefinite periods in an amount equal to 25% of the current year adjusted profit.

*Payments to foreign affiliates*/Payments for services provided from outside Saudi Arabia that are directly attributable to the earning of profits in Saudi Arabia are deductible. However, payments for such services that arise from activities carried on in Saudi Arabia may be regarded as income to the recipient and consequently subject to taxation on an imputed-profit basis (see "Taxes on imputed profits for nonresident payments" above). Foreign administrative charges or allocations of head office expenses are generally not deductible.

*Taxes*/Income tax is not deductible.

*Other significant items*/Payroll taxes and insurance related to expatriate personnel paid to foreign countries are not deductible in Saudi Arabia. Contributions made by foreign corporations to recognized charitable organizations in Saudi Arabia are acceptable as deductible items, provided the taxpayer can supply support for such expenses.

## Group taxation

Group taxation is not permitted in Saudi Arabia. However, a foreign entity with more than one project and operating them under the same temporary commercial registration is required to consolidate its accounts, and subject the net income for all contracts to Saudi income tax/*Zakat*.

## Tax incentives

*Inward investment*/The Saudi Arabian government may grant the following incentives to qualifying companies.

1. No restrictions on repatriation of profits, fees, capital, salaries, or other monies.
2. Low-interest or interest-free loans for up to 80% of fixed costs for agricultural projects of less than SR3 million, and up to 40% for agricultural projects in excess of SR3 million.
3. Low-interest or interest-free loans for up to 50% of the fixed cost of any industrial project.
4. Sites for erection of plant and industrial buildings and living quarters for the workforce at nominal rents.
5. Exemption from customs duties on machinery and raw materials required for approved projects.
6. Tariff protection for local products.
7. Owning real estate.
8. Sponsoring its employees.

*Capital investment*/No specific incentives are available for capital investment other than those listed under "Inward investment" above.

## Withholding taxes

There are no formal withholding taxes as such in Saudi Arabia. However, a company making certain kinds of payments (see "Taxes on imputed profits for nonresident payments" above) is considered to be responsible for the tax liability of the recipient and, accordingly, is required to retain the tax at the corporate rate on the deemed-profit element. This retained tax is due and payable at the time the company's own tax is due, that is, two and one-half months after its year-end.

There is no requirement to withhold tax on payments of dividends.

*Tax treaties*/Except for the limited tax treaty with France, Saudi Arabia has no double taxation treaties with other countries.

## Tax administration

*Returns*/Tax filings are on a fiscal-year basis. Returns are due to be filed with the Department of *Zakat* and Income Tax (DZIT) by the 15th day of the third month following the end of the accounting year. Extensions for filing can be obtained for up to six months, but, even where these are granted, an estimate of profit and the appropriate tax payment must be submitted by the original due date with the filing of a provisional return. The system is one of self-assessment.

*Payment of tax*/Estimated tax payments are not required during the year. The full amount of the self-assessed tax liability is payable with the filing of the return. A penalty is due where this amount is understated by more than 10%.

# Saudi Arabia

### *CORPORATION TAX CALCULATION*

Calendar year 2003

## Company with non-Saudi participation

A company established in Saudi Arabia that is owned 60% by non-Saudi investors and 40% by Saudi interests.

| | | |
|---|---:|---:|
| Profit per accounts ................................................................ | | SR 10,000,000 |
| Add: | | |
|     Transfer to general provisions........................................ | 200,000 | |
|     Depreciation per accounts............................................. | 1,000,000 | |
|     Donations not allowed .................................................. | 10,000 | 1,210,000 |
| | | 11,210,000 |
| Less: | | |
|     Depreciation on tax basis ............................................. | 840,000 | |
|     Charges to provision for employee leave passages ....... | 20,000 | 860,000 |
| | | SR 10,350,000 |
| Subject to income tax (60%).............................................. | | SR 6,210,000 |
| Less: Carryforward loss of 25% of the taxable income ...... | | 1,552,500 |
| Adjusted taxable income ................................................... | | 4,657,500 |
| Income tax payable: | | |
|     On first 1,000,000......................................................... | | SR    230,000 |
|     On excess—3,657,500 at 30% ..................................... | | 1,097,250 |
| Income tax payable ......................................................... | | SR 1,327,250 |

For *Zakat* payable, see Note 1.

## *Zakat* calculation—Saudi company

| | | |
|---|---:|---:|
| Capital resources: | | |
|     Paid-up capital ............................................................. | | SR 1,000,000 |
|     Total reserves............................................................... | 500,000 | |
|     *Less*—Reserve for provident fund................................ | (100,000) | 400,000 |
|     Total revenue for the year ............................................ | 2,000,000 | |
|     *Less*—All costs for the year ........................................ | (1,800,000) | 200,000 |
| | | 1,600,000 |
| Less: | | |
|     Net book value of fixed assets...................................... | 1,200,000 | |
|     Accumulated deficit ..................................................... | 100,000 | 1,300,000 |
| Net assessable financial resources ..................................... | | SR   300,000 |
| *Zakat* payable at 2.5%.......................................................... | | SR     7,500 |

Notes:

1. If the company were 60% owned by non-Saudi investors and 40% by Saudi interests, the *Zakat* payable would be 2.5% x 40% x SR300,000 = SR3,000.
2. Exchange rate of the Saudi Riyal at March 15, 2004: US$1 = SR3.75005.

## PwC contact

For additional information on taxation in Singapore, contact:

David Sandison
PricewaterhouseCoopers Services Pte Ltd.
8 Cross Street #17-00
PWC Building
Singapore 048424
Telephone: (65) 6236 3388
Fax: (65) 6236 3715
e-mail: david.sandison@sg.pwc.com

## Significant developments

A reduction in the corporate tax rate to 20% was announced in the February 2004 Budget Speech. The new rate takes effect from the year of assessment 2005 (i.e., for income derived in accounting periods ending in 2004).

## Taxes on corporate income

Tax on corporate income is imposed at a flat rate of 20%, (22% for income year 2003) with an exemption for taxable income of up to S$52,500 out of the first S$100,000 of chargeable income. For qualifying start-up companies, a three-year tax exemption on the first S$100,000 of chargeable income (beginning from income year 2004 to 2008) will be available.

Prior to January 1, 2003, a full imputation system applied in relation to the payment of taxed corporate profits to shareholders by way of a dividend. This was changed to a one-tier taxation system with effect from January 1, 2003. Under this new tax system, all dividends are tax exempt in the shareholder's hands and carry no franking credit with them. However, for the period January 1, 2003 to December 31, 2007, companies with franking credits remaining as at December 31, 2002 can choose to continue under the imputation system, subject to some fairly restrictive conditions.

## Corporate residence

The tax residence of a corporation is determined by the place where the management and control of its business is exercised. This is generally taken to mean the place where the directors meet to exercise de facto control.

## Other taxes

*Goods and services tax*/Goods and services tax (GST) or value-added tax (VAT), is charged at 5% from January 1, 2004. There are few exemptions, the main ones being financial services, life insurance and the sale or rental of residential properties.

*Foreign workers levy*/In certain industries there is a levy not exceeding S$470 per month for each foreign employee.

*Property tax*/Property tax is levied at 10% on the annual value of all houses, land, buildings, or tenements. For commercial properties, a fixed rebate of up to S$2,000 and a further 10% rebate (30% for hotels) on the remaining tax payable is given.

*Stamp taxes*/Stamp taxes are levied only on written documents relating to stock, shares, and immovable property. The rates vary according to the nature of the document and the values referred to in the document. Stamp duty on contract notes on share transactions was abolished on June 30, 2000. For residential properties sold within three years of purchase, the seller's stamp duty (which was suspended in 1997) was formally abolished in 2003.

With effect from April 1, 2003, leases with annual rents not exceeding S$1,000 will be exempt from stamp duty.

## Branch income

Tax rates on branch profits are the same as on corporate profits. There is no branch profits remittance tax on the repatriation of profits to the head office.

## Income determination

*Inventory valuation*/There are no special rules as to which valuation basis should be adopted for inventories (stock-in-trade) in the case of a continuing business, as long as the basis is consistent from one year to another. However, the LIFO basis of valuation is not permitted for tax purposes. Generally, tax reporting conforms to book reporting.

*Capital gains*/There is no tax on capital gains. Where there is a series of transactions or where the holding period of an asset is relatively short, the tax authorities may take the view that a business is being carried on and attempt to assess the gains as trading profits of the corporation. The U.K. Badges of Trade are generally applied in determining this issue.

While capital gains are not taxed, as part of the antispeculation measures introduced by the Singapore government in May 1996, profits from real property sold within three years of purchase were taxable as income. The proportion taxable decreased by a third with each year that the asset was held. Besides real property, the tax also applied to short-term gains from the sale of shares in a private company that held 75% or more of its assets in the form of real property or in the form of shares in real property companies. The special rules applied only to properties located in Singapore. However, with effect from October 13, 2001 (i.e., for sales contracted on or after this date), these measures were abolished, and therefore such gains are no longer subject to income tax except those which are considered revenue in nature under the general tax principles outlined above.

*Intercompany dividends*/There are no special concessions on franked intercompany dividends, which are taxable in the hands of the recipient with credit for the imputed Singapore tax deducted therefrom. With effect from January 1, 2003, Singapore dividends will be exempt in the hands of the recipient if the company paying the dividend has moved on to the new one-tier taxation system, described above.

*Foreign income*/A corporation, whether resident in Singapore or not, is taxed on foreign income when it is received in Singapore. Legislative provisions govern the basis of treating foreign income as received in Singapore. There are no special rules for taxing the undistributed income of foreign subsidiaries. Where income is earned from treaty countries, double taxation is avoided by means of foreign tax credits granted under those treaties. For nontreaty countries, unilateral tax credits are given in respect of foreign tax on branch profits, dividends, royalties, salaries, and service fee income derived therefrom. With effect from June 1, 2003, foreign dividends, foreign branch profits, and foreign service fee income remitted to Singapore will be exempt from tax subject to certain conditions.

*Stock dividends*/Stock dividends are generally not taxable. However, certain distributions could be treated as deemed dividends in certain circumstances. See below for further details.

*Deemed dividends*/Certain distributions to shareholders under a capital-reduction scheme, a share buy-back or a share redemption exercise may be treated as dividends distributions. This issue will be of diminishing importance as companies move to the new one-tier system.

## Deductions

*Depreciation and depletion*/Tax depreciation is allowable on industrial buildings used for qualifying activities at specified rates, and on machinery and equipment on a straight-line basis over their specified working life for all types of business. In lieu of the straight-line basis, accelerated tax depreciation allowances can be claimed by all businesses on all machinery and equipment (except for motorcars, motorcycles, and light-goods vehicles) in equal installments over three consecutive years. A 100% depreciation allowance is available on capital expenditure incurred on computers, robots, standby generators, pollution control and energy-efficient equipment, certain diesel-driven vehicles and prescribed automation equipment. Gains on tax depreciable property are taxed as ordinary income to the extent that tax depreciation has been allowed, that is, any clawback of tax depreciation on the disposal of the asset is taxed.

*Net operating losses*/Loss carryover, including unutilized tax depreciation allowances, is unlimited, provided shareholdings in the loss-making corporation have not changed beyond 50% of the issued and paid-up capital. Additionally, for tax depreciation allowances, the same trade needs to be continued. Carrybacks of tax losses and unutilized tax depreciation are not permitted. The tax authorities may exercise discretion to allow carryover of tax losses and unutilized tax depreciation even when there has been a change in shareholdings beyond 50%, absent any tax avoidance motives.

*Payments to nonresidents, including foreign affiliates*/Such payments are deductible, provided they are fair and reasonable, are revenue in nature, and can be seen to be relevant to earning the payer's income. Unless a lower treaty rate applies, interest, royalties and rental of movable property are subject to withholding tax at 15%. From January 1, 2005, the withholding tax rate for royalty payment is reduced to 10%.

The tax so withheld represents a final tax, and applies only to nonresidents who are not carrying on any business in Singapore, or who have no permanent establishment in Singapore. Technical assistance and management fees are taxed at the prevailing corporate rate. However, this is not a final tax. Royalties, interest, rental of movable property, technical assistance, and management fees can be exempt from withholding tax in certain situations, usually under fiscal incentives.

Payments made to nonresident professionals who perform services in Singapore will also be subject to a final tax of 15% on the gross income unless the prevailing corporate rate of 20% on net income results in a lower amount. An election must be made by the nonresident professional if the 20% rate is preferred.

# Singapore

*Taxes*/Income taxes are not normally deductible in determining corporate income. However, irrecoverable goods and services taxes are deductible under certain circumstances. The foreign workers' levy and property taxes are deductible to the extent they are incurred wholly and exclusively in the production of income.

*Other significant items*/Private automobile expenses are not deductible.

The tax deduction for medical expenses is limited to 2% of total payroll. With effect from April 1, 2004, the amount deductible will be limited to 1% if the employer does not implement any of the new portable medical benefits introduced by the Singapore government. Where the company is exempt or taxed at a reduced rate, the expenses disallowed will be taxed at the prevailing corporate rate.

## Group taxation

A company is allowed to transfer the excess of the following items to another company within the same group if certain conditions are satisfied.

- Current year trade losses.
- Current year tax depreciation.
- Current year approved donations.

Broadly, to qualify for group relief, companies must meet the following requirements.

- The companies must be incorporated in Singapore.
- The companies must belong to the same "75%" group of companies, that is, there must be at least a 75% ownership relationship between claimant and transferor.
- The companies must have the same accounting year-end.

In addition, certain prescribed set-off and apportionment rules must be complied with.

## Tax incentives

There are various tax incentives. Where appropriate, exempt dividends may be paid to shareholders out of exempt profits. Under the imputation system, however, exempt dividends cannot be paid out of shares of a preferential nature. Under the one-tier system, there is no distinction.

*Inward investment*/The various incentives include the following.

1. Pioneer industries—Corporations manufacturing approved products with high technological content, providing qualifying services or engaging in counter-trade activities may apply for tax exemption for 5 to 15 years. Dividends paid out of exempt pioneer profits are not subject to tax in the hands of recipients, provided they are not in respect of shares of a preferential nature. Corporations may apply for their postpioneer profits to be taxed at a reduced rate under the Development and Expansion Incentive (see below).

2. High-value-added or expanding industries—Corporations engaging in new high-value-added projects, expanding or upgrading their operations, or undertaking incremental activities after their pioneer or post pioneer period may apply for their profits to be taxed at a reduced rate of not less than 5% for an initial period of up to ten years. The total tax relief period is subject to a maximum of 20 years (inclusive of the postpioneer relief period previously

granted, if applicable). This is known as the Development and Expansion Incentive.

3. Export of services—An approved enterprise providing selected services with respect to overseas projects is given tax exemption on 90% of the qualifying export income. The exemption is given for a period of five years, with provision for an extension.

*Capital investment*/The various incentives include the following.

1. Investment allowance—Tax exemption is granted on an amount of profits based on a specified percentage (up to 100%) of capital expenditure incurred for qualifying projects or activities within a period of up to five years.

2. Venture capital and technopreneur investment incentives—These incentives permit a deduction for investment losses (i.e., losses incurred on the sale of shares in a qualifying company or upon liquidation of the qualifying company) against the investor's other taxable income if they satisfy certain pre-set conditions. There is no loss relief if the qualifying shares are held for less than two years, or if they are sold after eight years from the date of allotment. The relief is not available to the transferee of such shares. Eligible investors will also be allowed a two-year tax deferral, interest-free, calculated by reference to the first three years' operating losses of the approved investments. As part of the 2004 Budget changes, the technopreneur investment incentive was renamed the enterprise investment incentive, and is no longer confined to high-tech businesses, as it has been expanded to all forms of start-up operations.

*Financial services*/The various incentives include the following.

1. Financial sector incentive (FSI) scheme—This scheme covers the approved bond intermediaries (ABIs), Asian currency units (ACUs), approved derivative traders (ADTs), approved fund managers (AFMs), equity capital market intermediaries (ECMIs), operational headquarters (OHQs), and syndicated offshore credit and underwriting facilities incentives that currently exist for the financial services industry. High growth, high value-added activities such as bond market, derivatives market, equity market (i.e., futures, securities trading which includes sale of stocks, shares, bonds and other securities and extends to brokerage, nominee, and custodian services in relation to securities trading), and credit facilities syndication will be exempt from tax or taxed at 5%, while other broader range financial activities will only qualify for a 10% tax rate. The tax incentive period may vary from five, seven, to ten years, subject to certain conditions being met.

2. Finance and treasury center (FTC)—Income derived by an FTC from approved finance and treasury center activities is taxed at a reduced rate of 10%. Approved activities include regional and international treasury and fund management activities, corporate finance and advisory services, economic and investment research and analysis, and credit control and administration.

3. Debt securities—A package of tax exemptions and reduced tax rates is available to various players in the Singapore bond market.

4. Offshore insurance—Approved insurance companies engaged in the business of insuring and reinsuring offshore risks are taxed at 10% on their qualifying income arising from their offshore risks business. Qualifying income from the writing of both onshore and offshore marine hull and liability risk insurance can be exempt from tax for up to ten years.

# Singapore

*Other incentives*/Other incentives include the following.

1. Enhanced headquarters (EHQ)—The Operational Headquarters (OHQ), Global Headquarters (GHQ), Business Headquarters (BHQ), and Manufacturing Headquarters (MHQ) incentives were streamlined early 2003 under the new EHQ scheme. Under this scheme, regional headquarters in Singapore can qualify for tax exemption for dividend income from regional network companies and also concessionary rates of tax at 5% or 10% on qualifying income earned from the provision of certain headquarters services which include sales/trading services, management and royalty income.

2. Incentives for shipping companies, investment holding companies, oil traders, international traders, general insurance companies, leasing companies, trust companies, cyber traders, international freight and logistics operators, exhibition organizers, and art and antique dealers include tax exemptions or concessionary tax rates of 10% for qualifying income. The concessionary tax rate for qualifying oil traders and international traders may be further reduced to 5%.

## Withholding taxes

Domestic corporations paying certain types of income are required to withhold tax, as shown below.

| Recipient | Dividends (1) | Interest (2) | Royalties (2) |
|---|---|---|---|
| | % | % | % |
| Resident individuals | Nil | Nil | Nil |
| Resident corporations | Nil | Nil | Nil |
| Nonresident corporations and individuals: | | | |
| Nontreaty | Nil | 15 | 15/10 (3d) |
| Treaty: | | | |
| Australia | Nil | 10 | 10 (3a) |
| Austria | Nil | 5 (4b, e) | 5 |
| Bahrain (5a) | Nil | 15 | 15/10 (3d) |
| Bangladesh | Nil | 10 | 10 (3a) |
| Belgium | Nil | 15 | Nil (3a) |
| Bulgaria | Nil | 5 (4b) | 5 |
| Canada | Nil | 15 | 15/10 (3d) |
| Chile (5b) | Nil | 15 | 15/10 (3d) |
| China, P.R. | Nil | 10/7 (4a, b) | 10 |
| Cyprus | Nil | 10/7 (4a, b) | 10 |
| Czech Republic | Nil | Nil | 10 |
| Denmark | Nil | 10 (4b) | 10 |
| Egypt | Nil | 15(4b) | 15/10 (3d) |
| Finland | Nil | 5(4b) | 5 |
| France | Nil | 10/Nil (4c) | Nil (3a) |
| Germany | Nil | 10 (4b) | Nil (3a) |
| Hungary | Nil | 5 (4b, e) | 5 |
| India | Nil | 15/10 (4a) | 15/10 (3b, d) |
| Indonesia | Nil | 10 (4b) | 15/10 (3d) |
| Israel | Nil | 15 | 15/10 (3d) |
| Italy | Nil | 12.5 | 15/10 (3d) |
| Japan | Nil | 10 (4b, c) | 10 |

| Recipient | Dividends (1) | Interest (2) | Royalties (2) |
|---|---|---|---|
| | % | % | % |
| Korea, Rep. of | Nil | 10 (4b) | 15/10 (3d) |
| Kuwait | Nil | 7 (4b) | 10 |
| Latvia | Nil | 10 (4b) | 7.5 |
| Luxembourg | Nil | 10 (4b) | 10 |
| Malaysia | Nil | 15 | 15/10 (3d) |
| Mauritius | Nil | 0 | 0 |
| Mexico | Nil | 15/5 (4a, b) | 10 |
| Myanmar | Nil | 10/8 (4a, b) | 15/10 (3c, d) |
| Netherlands | Nil | 10 (4b) | Nil (3a) |
| New Zealand | Nil | 15 | 15/10 (3d) |
| Norway | Nil | 7 (4b) | 7 |
| Oman (5a) | Nil | 15 | 15/10 (3d) |
| Pakistan | Nil | 12.5 (4b) | 10 (3a) |
| Papua New Guinea | Nil | 10 | 10 |
| Philippines | Nil | 15 | 15/10 (3d) |
| Poland | Nil | 10 (4b) | 10 |
| Portugal | Nil | 10 (4b, f) | 10 |
| Romania | Nil | 5 (4b) | 5 |
| Saudi Arabia (5a) | Nil | 15 | 15/10 (3d) |
| South Africa | Nil | Nil | 5 |
| Sri Lanka | Nil | 10/Nil (4a, b) | 15/10 (3d) |
| Sweden | Nil | 15/10 (4b, c) | Nil (3a) |
| Switzerland | Nil | 10 | 5 (3a) |
| Taiwan | Nil | 15 | 15/10 (3d) |
| Thailand | Nil | 15/10 (4a, b) | 15/10 (3d) |
| Turkey | Nil | 10/7.5 (4a, b) | 10 |
| United Arab Emirates | Nil | 7 (4b) | 5 |
| United Kingdom | Nil | 10 (4b, d) | 10 (3e) |
| United States (5c) | Nil | 15 | 15/10 (3d) |
| Vietnam | Nil | 10 (4b) | 15/5 (3c) |

Notes:

1. Dividends are franked with (deemed to be paid net of) the prevailing corporate tax rate. If any corporation has not paid sufficient tax to cover the total tax deemed deducted from dividends, it must pay the balance of the tax to the tax authorities. However, with effect from January 1, 2003, the franking system is no longer relevant if the company moves on to the one tier taxation system.

   Because of its proximity, many Singapore corporations also trade in Malaysia and are taxed there. The double taxation agreement between the two has special provisions for the allocation and franking of dividends in such cases.

   At present, Singapore has no withholding tax on dividends in addition to the tax on the profits out of which the dividends are declared and some of the treaties provide for a maximum withholding tax on dividends should Singapore impose such a withholding tax in the future.

2. The nontreaty rate of 15% (a final tax) applies only to nonresidents who do not carry on business in Singapore, or have a permanent establishment in Singapore. This rate may be further reduced by tax incentives. With effect from January 1, 2005, the rate for royalties is reduced to 10%.

3. Royalties:
   a. Royalties on literary or artistic copyrights, including film royalties, are taxed at the nontreaty rate of 15%. With effect from January 1, 2005, the rate is reduced to 10%.
   b. Lower rate for payments in respect of industrial, commercial, or scientific equipment.
   c. Lower rate for payments in connection with patents, designs, secret formulas/processes, or industrial, commercial, or scientific equipment/experience and the 15% rate for other payments are reduced to 10% with effect from January 1, 2005.
   d. Lower rate applies with effect from January 1, 2005.
   e. A rate of 15% prior to January 1, 2000.
4. Interest:
   a. Lower rate or exemption if received by a financial institution.
   b. Exempt if paid to the government.
   c. Lower rate or exemption if paid by an approved industrial undertaking (for Japan, exemption ceased to apply from January 1, 2001).
   d. A rate of 15% prior to January 1, 2000.
   e. Exempt if paid by a bank and received by a bank.
   f. Exempt if paid to bank but linked to government loan agreement or paid to specific financial institutions/banks.
5. Treaties:
   a. Treaties with Bahrain, Oman, and Saudi Arabia cover only international air transport.
   b. Treaty with Chile covers only international ship operations.
   c. Treaty with the United States covers only shipping and air transport activities.

## Tax administration

***Returns****/*Tax is computed for each tax year based on the income earned in the preceding year (the tax basis period). The tax basis period is the calendar year; however for business profits, the accounting year would generally be adopted. The corporation files a return of income, and the tax is assessed by the Comptroller of Income Tax. There is no fixed date for the issue of assessments.

***Payment of tax****/*Assessed tax is payable within one month after the service of the notice of assessment, whether or not a notice of objection to the assessment has been lodged with the tax authorities. Application may be made to the Comptroller to pay estimated tax liabilities on a monthly basis. However, the Comptroller is under no obligation to grant such an application.

## *CORPORATION TAX CALCULATION*

Fiscal year ended December 31, 2003 (year of assessment 2004)

| | | |
|---|---:|---:|
| Net income before taxes per profit and loss account (income statement) | | S$ 7,620,000 |
| Add: | | |
| Depreciation charged in accounts (1) | 835,000 | |
| Amounts transferred to general provisions | 130,000 | |
| Automobile expenses | 40,000 | |
| Donations | 1,500 | |
| Legal fees (capital nature) | 5,000 | |
| Fixed assets expensed | 21,000 | |
| Unrealized revenue exchange loss | 130,000 | 1,162,500 |
| | | 8,782,500 |
| Less: | | |
| Profit on sale of fixed assets | 15,000 | |
| Expenditure charged against general provisions | 150,000 | |
| Capital exchange gain | 145,000 | |
| Replacement assets capitalized | 20,000 | 330,000 |
| Adjusted profit | | 8,452,500 |
| Less: | | |
| Capital allowances (tax depreciation) (1) | 950,000 | |
| Less—Balancing charge on sale of fixed assets (2) | (25,000) | 925,000 |
| | | S$ 7,527,500 |
| Less: | | |
| Approved donations | | 500 |
| | | S$ 7,527,000 |
| Less: | | |
| Exempt amount (3, 4) | | 52,500 |
| Taxable income | | S$ 7,474,500 |
| Tax thereon at 22% | | S$ 1,644,390 |

Notes:

1. The rates of depreciation for book and tax purposes are often not the same, and adjustment for tax is therefore necessary.
2. Refers to gains on depreciable property that are taxable to the extent of tax depreciation previously allowed.
3. Computation of partial exempt amount:

| | |
|---|---:|
| On the first S$10,000 at 75% | S$ 7,500 |
| On the next S$90,000 at 50% | 45,000 |
| Total exempt amount | S$ 52,500 |

4. The exemption (of up to S$52,500 of chargeable income) does not apply to Singapore dividends, income subject to final withholding tax and tax at a concessionary rate.
5. The exchange rate of the Singapore dollar at February 16, 2004: US$1 = S$1.6757.

# Slovak Republic

## PwC contact

For additional information on taxation in the Slovak Republic, contact:

Joe Kerrane
PricewaterhouseCoopers
Hviezdoslavovo namestie 20
815 32 Bratislava
Slovak Republic
Telephone: (421) (2) 5441 41 01
Fax: (421) (2) 5441 41 02
e-mail: joe.kerrane@sk.pwc.com

## General note

This entry is repeated from the 2003/2004 edition. For more up-to-date information consult the contact listed above or Jacqueline Collette at jacqueline.collete@us.pwc.com.

The tax legislation in the Slovak Republic was amended on January 1, 2003. The legislation may be subject to frequent amendments and official interpretation as the market economy develops. Therefore, it is advisable to contact PwC Bratislava for up-to-date information.

## Taxes on corporate income

The rate of corporate income tax for 2003 is 25%.

A 15% rate applies to companies engaged in agriculture and an 18% rate to companies employing disabled people. Corporate income tax applies to the profits of all companies, including branches of foreign companies and permanent establishments. Corporate partners in general partnerships and corporate general partners in a limited partnership are subject to corporate income tax on their share of the profits in the partnership.

## Corporate residence

A company is resident in the Slovak Republic if it has its registered seat in the Slovak Republic. It is important to note that a foreign company may create a permanent establishment if its employees (or persons working for it) are present and providing services in the Slovak Republic for 183 days or more in any 12-month period.

## Other taxes

In addition to the corporate income tax, the following taxes may also apply.

*Value-added tax*/VAT is charged at 20% on the supply of goods and services within the Slovak Republic. Certain selected services and goods are taxed at a rate of 14%. Export of goods and some services is exempt with credit. Some supplies are exempt without credit, such as financial activities (including the transfer of equity and the purchase of monetary receivables), insurance services, radio and TV broadcasting, education, healthcare, and social welfare.

*Road tax*/Road tax is applied to vehicles (including private vehicles) used for commercial purposes. Foreign-registered vehicles are also liable to road tax while in the Slovak Republic. Rates depend on engine capacity and vehicle size.

*Real estate tax*/This tax is payable by users of land, buildings, or apartments. It is based on area, location, and usage.

*Transfer taxes*/Real estate transfer tax is levied on the transferor of real estate. Inheritance and gift taxes are levied on the recipient of other types of transferred property.

*Excise tax*/Excise tax is charged on the production or import of tobacco products, wines, spirits, beer, and mineral oils.

*Import surcharge*/There is no import surcharge in the Slovak Republic.

## Branch income

A foreign company can trade through a Slovak branch. The determination of taxable amounts is the same as for corporations. For nontrading branches, the branch must negotiate the method for determining its tax base with the tax authorities. A nontrading branch must pay 25% tax on its attributable profits. A trading branch is subject to tax in the same way as a company.

## Income determination

*Inventory valuation*/Stock (i.e., inventory) is valued at the lower of cost and net realizable value, using the FIFO or weighted-average method of valuation. LIFO is not acceptable. Currently, stock provisions are generally not tax deductible.

*Capital gains*/There is no special capital gains tax law. Capital gains are taxable under the income tax act. Capital losses on the sale of fixed assets are generally tax deductible (with the exemption of, e.g., motor vehicles, TVs, and radios) and on investments are generally not tax deductible.

*Intercompany dividends*/Dividends are liable to withholding tax at source. Dividends from domestic companies are not included in the recipient's taxable income. However, all inter-group transactions must be carried out at arm's length.

As the Slovak Republic is a member of the OECD, Slovak tax law lists various transfer-pricing methods for determining an appropriate arm's length price that are consistent with OECD guidelines.

*Foreign income*/Companies resident in the Slovak Republic are taxed on their worldwide income. A Slovak corporation is taxed on branch income when earned and on foreign dividends when received. The Slovak Republic does not make a distinction between income received from treaty and that received from nontreaty countries. Unless an individual treaty specifically provides otherwise, credit relief is available for foreign tax paid.

*Unrealized exchange gains and losses*/Based on an amendment of the Accounting Act, most unrealized exchange gains/losses should be charged to the profit and loss account and would in turn be treated taxable/tax deductible. However, this issue should be clarified by the Slovak Ministry of Finance.

*Statutory reserve fund*/When a joint-stock company incorporates, it must create a reserve fund of at least 10% of the share capital. The statutory reserve fund must be increased annually with an amount set out in the articles of association, but not less than 10% of net profit and up to the minimum amount set out in the articles of association or 20% of the share capital.

# Slovak Republic

A limited liability company must create a reserve fund no later than the first year in which the company reports a profit. The minimum contribution to the fund this first year is 5% of the net profit, but cannot be higher than 10% of the company's share capital. The fund must be increased annually by an amount set out in the memorandum of association. The minimum annual contribution must be 5% of net profit. The reserve fund cannot exceed 10% of the share capital. The branch of a foreign company is not required to set up a reserve fund.

## Deductions

**Depreciation and depletion/**Tax depreciation is calculated on an asset-by-asset basis on a straight-line or reducing-balance basis at statutory rates. A company may choose which method to apply to a new asset, but once made, the choice cannot be altered. All assets are classified into five groups, which determine the number of years over which the asset will be written off, as follows.

| Group and types of assets | Write-off period |
|---|---|
| | (Years) |
| 1—Cars, vans, hand tools, computers | 4 |
| 2—Fixtures and fittings, certain types of machinery, intangible assets (excluding patents) | 6 |
| 3—Plant and machinery, goodwill, patents | 12 |
| 4—Motors, fixed constructions (other than buildings) | 20 |
| 5—Buildings | 30 |

No tax depreciation is available for land.

The law sets out the straight-line depreciation rates, as well as a formula and coefficients for calculating reducing-balance depreciation.

For tangible assets, accounting depreciation may differ from tax depreciation. Accounting depreciation must take into account the tangible fixed asset's usage period and the relationship of its usage to revenues, among other things. Small fixed assets can be written off immediately. The difference between accounting and tax depreciation of tangible fixed assets is reflected in the tax return.

For intangible assets, tax and accounting depreciation methods shall be set according to accounting legislation and must be the same (i.e., there should be no differences).

Intangible assets shall be fully depreciated within five years from the date of acquisition thereof, in accordance with the accounting regulations.

**Travel expenses and meal allowances/**Payments for travel expenses and meal allowances to employees, which are in excess of statutory limits are tax nondeductible for corporate income tax purposes.

**Net operating losses/**A taxpayer can carry forward losses incurred in up to three tax periods before that in which the taxpayer declared the first tax base and tax liability. The loss can be carried forward and claimed proportionally against profits realized in the next five tax periods. The taxpayer must use an amount equal to the deducted tax loss to acquire tangible assets within three tax periods from the period when the tax loss was deducted.

**Payments to foreign related parties/**Generally, a taxpayer can claim deductions for royalties, as well as for management service and interest charges paid to foreign related parties, provided these amounts do not exceed that which would be paid to unrelated entities. Deducting interest is limited to cases where a related entity provides credits and loans and the recipient has a debt-to-equity ratio greater than 4:1 (6:1 for banks and insurance companies).

*Taxes*/Road tax, real estate tax, and most other taxes (with the exception of gift tax, inheritance tax, as well as personal and corporate income taxes) are tax deductible as are social security contributions an employer pays for its employees. If the employer pays income tax on behalf of its employees, it is not tax deductible for corporate income tax purposes.

*Other deductions*/Fees paid to directors and members of other statutory bodies of companies are not tax deductible. Certain charitable donations are tax deductible. The minimum deductible donation is SKK2,000, while the maximum is 2% of the tax base.

## Group taxation

There is currently no concept of group taxation in the Slovak Republic. Each company in a group is taxed individually.

## Tax incentives

There are currently four investment incentive regimes under which corporate income tax credits can be claimed for up to ten years. Under the earliest two regimes, a company that met the required conditions could claim corporate tax credits of 100% automatically. However, all taxpayers applying the tax credits for the first time in 2002 or later now have to have prior approval of the Slovak State Aid Office. Furthermore, the amount of incentives that will be granted may be less than 100% of the annual corporate tax charge.

Companies that meet the conditions for the tax credit investment incentives under the two new regimes may also be able to obtain grants for the creation of new jobs and the retraining of employees. The amounts available depend on the location of the business – those in areas of high unemployment can apply for higher grants. The maximum grants are SKK160,000 (around €3,600) for each new job created and SKK10,000 (around €225) for each retrained employee.

## Withholding taxes

Slovak companies must withhold tax on payments of dividends, interest and royalties, as follows·

| Recipient | Dividends | Interest | Royalties |
|---|---|---|---|
| | % | % | % |
| Resident corporations | 15/25 (1) | 15 | 0 |
| Resident individuals | 15/25 (1) | 5/15/20 (2) | 0 |
| Nonresident corporations, individuals: | | | |
| Nontreaty: | | | |
| Corporations | 15/25 (1) | 15/25 (3) | 1/25 (4) |
| Individuals | 15/25 (1) | 15/25 (3) | 1/25 (4) |
| Treaty: | | | |
| Australia | 15 (5) | 10 | 10 |
| Austria | 10 | 0 | 0/5 (6) |
| Belgium | 5/15 (7) | 0/10 (8) | 5 |

# Slovak Republic

| Recipient | Dividends | Interest | Royalties |
|---|---|---|---|
| | % | % | % |
| Belarus | 10/15 (5) | 10 | 5/10 (9) |
| Bulgaria | 10 | 10 | 10 (10) |
| Brazil | 15 | 10/15 (11) | 15/25 (12) |
| Canada | 5/15 (13) | 0/10 (14) | 0/10 (6) |
| China, P.R. | 10 | 10 | 10 |
| Croatia | 5/10 (5) | 10 | 10 |
| Cyprus | 10 | 0/10 (15) | 0/5 (6) |
| Czech Republic | 5/15 (5) | 0 | 5 |
| Denmark | 15 | 0 | 0/5 (6) |
| Estonia | In process | In process | In process |
| Finland | 5/15 (5) | 0 | 1/5/10 (16) |
| France | 10 | 0 | 0/5 (5) |
| Germany | 5/15 (5) | 0 | 5 |
| Greece | Local rates | 10 | 0/10 (6) |
| Hungary | 5/15 (7) | 0 | 10 |
| India | 15/25 (7) | 15 | 30 |
| Indonesia (17) | 10 | 0/10 (18) | 10/15 (6) |
| Ireland, Rep. of | 0/10 (7) | 0 | 0/10 (5) |
| Israel | 5/10 (19) | 2/5/10 (20) | 5 |
| Italy | 15 | 0 | 0/5 (6) |
| Japan | 10/15 (21) | 0/10 (22) | 0/10 (6) |
| Luxembourg | 5/15 (23) | 0 | 0/10 (6) |
| Latvia | 10 | 0/10 (18) | 10 |
| Lithuania | 10 | 10 (24) | 10 |
| Malta | LPT/5 (25) | 0 | 5 |
| Netherlands (26) | 0/10 (5) | 0 | 5 |
| Nigeria | 12.5/15 (19) | 0/15 (24) | 10 |
| Norway | 5/15 (5) | 0 | 0/5 (6) |
| Poland | 5/10 (27) | 10 | 5 |
| Romania | 10 | 0/10 (22) | 10/15 (28) |
| Russia | 10 | 0 | 10 |
| South Africa | 5/10 (5) | 0 | 10 |
| Spain | 5/15 (5) | 0 | 0/5 (6) |
| Sri Lanka | 15 | 0 | 0/10 (6) |
| Sweden | 0/10 (5) | 0 | 0/5 (6) |
| Switzerland | 5/15 (5) | 0/10 (29) | 0/10 (6) |
| Tunisia | 10/15 (7) | 12 | 5/15 (6) |
| Turkmenistan | 10 | 0/10 (30) | 10 |
| Turkey | 5/15 (5) | 0/10 (30) | 10 |
| Ukraine | 10 | 10 | 10 |
| United Kingdom and Northern Ireland | 5/15 (31) | 0 | 0/10 (6) |
| United States | 5/15 (12) | 0 | 0/10 (6) |
| Yugoslavia | 5/15 (5) | 10 | 10 |

Notes:

1. The higher rate applies to settlement payments and to a liquidation surplus.
2. The lowest rate applies to payment of interest from savings deposits and certificates with Slovak savings banks or similar savings accounts. The 20% rate is to be withheld by employers paying interest on deposits made by their employees.

3. The lower rate applies to the payment of interest from savings deposits and certificates with Slovak savings banks or similar savings accounts.
4. The lower rate applies to lease contracts under which the lessee has the right to purchase the leased asset at the end of the lease period, provided the lease is of a certain minimum duration. A 25% withholding tax is also applied to payments for management and consultancy agreements.
5. The lower rate applies if the recipient is a company (some treaties exclude partnerships) that owns at least 25% of the capital of the company paying the dividend directly.
6. The lower rate applies to cultural royalties.
7. The lower rate applies if the recipient is a company that has beneficial ownership of at least 25% of the capital of the company paying the dividends.
8. The zero rate applies to interest on trade receivables resulting from credits on goods or services, monetary deposits in banks and interests from bank accounts.
9. The lower rate applies to cultural royalties and the higher rate to payments in respect of the use of trademarks and vehicles.
10. This rate applies also to payment for services.
11. The lower rate applies to interest on loans and credits granted by a bank for at least ten years in connection with the selling of industrial equipment; with study, installation or furnishing of industrial or scientific units; or with public works.
12. The higher rate applies to payments for the use of trademarks.
13. The lower rate applies if the recipient is a company that owns at least 10% of the voting shares of the company paying the dividend.
14. The lower rate applies to interest paid in respect of debts of the other state government or a political subdivision/local authority thereof and in respect of a loan made/guaranteed by the other state government in respect of imports/exports.
15. The lower rate applies if the interest is received from the government or its instrumentalities.
16. The 1% rate applies to the financial lease of equipment, the 5% rate applies to the rental of equipment or software and to cultural royalties, and the 10% rate applies to payments for the use of trademarks.
17. The double tax treaty came into effect on January 1, 2002. The text has not yet been published in the Collection of Laws.
18. The zero rate applies if the interest is received by the government including local authorities thereof, a political subdivision, the central bank or any financial institution controlled by the government, from the government of another state.
19. The lower rate applies if the recipient is a company that owns at least 10% of the shares in the company paying the dividend.
20. The 2% rate applies to state bonds and obligations, and loans insured and guaranteed by the government; the 5% rate applies if received by a financial institution (in common business activities); the 10% rate applies in all other cases.

21. The lower rate applies if the recipient is a company that owns at least 25% of the voting shares of the company paying the dividend during the six months immediately preceding the date of payment of the dividend.
22. The lower rate applies if the interest is received by the government or its instrumentalities.
23. The lower rate applies if the recipient owns directly no less than 25% of the capital of the company paying the dividend.
24. The lower rate applies if the recipient and beneficial owner is the government or an institution established by the government for foreign trade financing (if the loans are approved by both governments).
25. Local profit tax (LPT) applies if the dividends are paid by a company with residence in Malta to a recipient with residence in the Slovak Republic; the 5% rate applies if the dividends are paid by a company with residence in the Slovak Republic to a recipient with residence in Malta.
26. As amended by the protocol number 199/1997 Z.z. (Col.).
27. The lower rate applies if the recipient is a company (not a partnership) that holds directly at least 20% of the capital of the company.
28. The rate of 10% applies to royalties for the use of trademarks, patents or know-how. The higher rate applies in all other cases.
29. Withholding tax reduced to nil on bank loans.
30. The zero rate (of local tax) applies if the interest is paid by the government or central bank of the state to the government or central bank of the other state.
31. The lower rate applies if the recipient is a company that controls at least 25% of the voting shares of the company paying the dividend.

## Tax administration

*Returns/*The fiscal year runs from January 1 to December 31. A combined tax and accounting return must be made by March 31 following the end of the calendar year. The deadline for filing the tax return is automatically extended to June 30 if a registered Slovak tax advisor will file the return and the respective Tax Office is aware of this by March 31. In other cases, a request can be made to extend the filing deadline, to September 30, for example, if the taxpayer has income from foreign sources. The request should be submitted no later than March 31. The tax authorities have 30 days to communicate their decision regarding extension of the filing deadline. Any outstanding tax must be paid by the same date as the tax return is filed.

Beginning January 1, 2004, the taxpayer may request the respective tax office for approval to use a different accounting and tax period, that is, different from the calendar year.

*Payment of tax/*Corporate tax must be paid monthly or quarterly in advance. Installments are based on the last known tax liability (for the preceding tax period). If the taxpayer is incorporated within the first nine months of the tax year, tax installments must be paid based on the expected tax. It is not necessary to pay tax advances if the last tax liability did not exceed SKK50,000. After the tax return is filed, the final tax liability is known, any outstanding tax is paid and a new schedule for paying advances for the current year is made.

## CORPORATION TAX CALCULATION

Calendar year ended December 31, 2002

(According to the laws in place at January 1, 2003)

| | | |
|---|---:|---:|
| Net profit before taxes shown by the accounts | | SKK 1,000,000 |
| Add: | | |
| Accounting depreciation | 300,000 | |
| Entertainment | 35,000 | |
| Excess travel expenses | 30,000 | 365,000 |
| | | 1,365,000 |
| Less: | | |
| Tax depreciation | 280,000 | |
| Slovak-source dividends | 10,000 | 290,000 |
| Total taxable income | | SKK 1,075,000 |
| Tax payable—at 25% | | SKK 268,750 |
| Foreign tax credits | | (10,000) |
| Total tax payable | | SKK 258,750 |

Note:

Exchange rate of the Slovak crown (koruna) as of December 31, 2002: US$1 = SKK40.036.

743

# Slovenia

## PwC contact

Nada Drobnic
PricewaterhouseCoopers
Parmova 53
1000 Ljubljana, Slovenia
Telephone: (386) (1) 475 01 00/01
Fax: (386) (1) 475 01 09
LN address: Nada Drobnic/SI/TLS/PwC@EMEA - SI
e-mail: nada.drobnic@si.pwc.com

## Significant developments

Amendments to the Corporate Income Tax Law are in effect from January 2003. Along with amendments of the law, rules on tax nondeductible expenses of a taxable person have been issued, effective from January 2003, where, to a certain extent, specification of tax nondeductible expenses has been provided.

## Taxes on corporate income

Corporate profit tax is generally levied at the rate of 25%, while average effective corporate income tax rate is only 11%, due to various allowances and incentives. Taxable entities are all legal entities, resident and nonresident, that obtain profit through the permanent execution of an activity in the territory of the Republic of Slovenia.

## Income determination

Taxable profit is net accounting profit adjusted for tax purposes.

*Intercompany transactions*/In transactions between associated persons, prices are limited to the level of average current prices for the specific kind of goods or services on the domestic or comparable foreign market.

*Foreign income*/Entities resident in Slovenia are liable for tax on worldwide income. Nonresidents, for example, branches of foreign businesses, are taxed only on income derived from activities in Slovenia. If a permanent establishment is regulated otherwise in an agreement for the avoidance of double taxation, the provisions of such agreement apply.

Dividends earned abroad and transferred to Slovenia are excluded from the tax base if tax has been paid abroad.

## Deductions

*Depreciation*/The Corporate Tax Law prescribes five depreciation groups, with maximum annual depreciation rates for each. Depreciation charges in excess of these rates are not deductible.

*Net operating losses*/Tax losses may be carried forward to reduce taxable income for five years. This relief may not exceed the amount of currently taxable profits. Losses from the earliest loss year are utilized first.

*Business-related expenses*/Salaries, bonuses arising from employment, long-term reservations, entertainment expenses, costs of the board of directors and supervisory board, and certain other expenses are deductible to the extent prescribed by the Corporate Tax Law and rules on tax nondeductible expenses.

*Related-party interest*/Companies can deduct interest expense on loans from their owners or other associated parties up to a maximum of the amount calculated by using the total average interbank annual interest rate at the time of loan approval.

## Group taxation

If a taxpayer owns more than 90% of another resident taxpayer's share capital, a consolidated tax return may be submitted to the tax authorities. Group taxation has to apply for a minimum of three years.

## Tax incentives

*Capital investment*/Up to 40% of the amount invested in tangible fixed assets (except for passenger cars) and intangible long-term assets can be deducted from the tax base, but only for investment taking place in Slovenia. A taxpayer that takes advantage of this deduction may not use the profit for dividend payments for a period of three years from the year in which the deduction was utilized. If any of the deducted amount is so used, that portion must be added back to taxable income for the year in which such dividends were paid (distributed). If the assets in question are sold within three years after the allowance has been granted, the tax base for the year of sale must be increased by the amount of the allowance granted.

Taxable profit may be reduced by allocating 10% to an investment reserve for the purpose of future investment in tangible and intangible fixed assets, and for investments in the same or other Slovenian entities. Such tax relief shall be recognized for a period of two years.

*Employment incentives*/An enterprise that employs, for an expected period of at least two years, trainees or previously unemployed persons, can decrease taxable profit by 30% of the gross wages of such employees for the first 12 months of their employment. Employment of the disabled can reduce taxable profit by 50% of the salaries of those employees. Employees classified as 100% disabled or deaf-mute can make the employer eligible for a deduction from taxable profit of 70% of their salaries or wages. Available deductions may not exceed the amount of profits otherwise taxable.

## Withholding taxes

Tax is withheld from dividends paid to Slovenian residents at the rate of 25%, and from dividends paid to nonresidents at the rate of 15%.

## Tax administration

The tax year is the calendar year. Tax is paid in monthly installments in advance on the basis of the previous year's assessment. Tax returns must be filed on forms prescribed by the Ministry of Finance. They are due by March 31 of the year following the tax year. The due date for group tax returns is April 15.

The difference between the total of advance payments and the tax payable according to the actual tax return must be settled within ten days from the date of submitting the return. If advance payments exceed the tax payable, a refund can be requested.

## Note

The exchange rate of Slovenian tolar at March 10, 2004: US$1 = SIT 192.541.

# Solomon Islands

## PwC contact

For additional information on taxation in the Solomon Islands, contact:

Wayne Morris
PricewaterhouseCoopers
P.O. Box 70
Honiara, Solomon Islands
Telephone: (677) 21851
Fax: (677) 23342
LN address: Wayne F Morris@C&L SB@C&L INT
e-mail: wayne.morris@sb.pwc.com

## Significant developments

There have been no changes to the Income Tax Act during the last year.

## Taxes on corporate income

The corporation tax rates are as follows.

|  | % |
| --- | --- |
| Resident corporations incorporated locally | 30 |
| Corporations incorporated overseas | 35 |

*Local income taxes*/None.

## Corporate residence

Corporations are classified for tax purposes as either resident or nonresident. Under the Companies Act there is a classification of private company, but for income tax purposes this distinction is not recognized. A resident corporation is incorporated in the Solomon Islands if either it has its central management and control in the Solomon Islands, or its voting power is controlled by shareholders resident in the Solomon Islands. The distinction between resident and nonresident corporations is important in that nonresident corporations are subject to tax only on their Solomon Islands income. The distinction also affects the rate of tax (see above). A company incorporated outside the Solomon Islands, even though it may be carrying on business only in the Solomon Islands, is also liable to tax at 35%. Corporations may be classified as prescribed companies under the Investment Act if the investment is likely to provide significant benefits to the Solomon Islands economy. Such companies are granted a tax holiday.

## Other taxes

*Turnover tax*/A turnover tax on loss companies and low-profit companies applies to income derived after January 1, 1991 and has the following features.

1. The tax is an income tax and is charged at the rate of 0.5% of income if gross income less allowable deductions (chargeable income) is nil or a loss; the normal corporate tax on chargeable income (35% resident, 50% nonresident) is the lesser of 0.5% of gross income or SBD$20,000.
2. The tax does not reduce the total of losses carried forward.
3. The tax is final and is not offset against normal corporate tax levied after losses are recouped.
4. The tax does not apply to companies receiving tax incentives, tax losses carried forward, or dividends paid.

*Value-Added Tax*/A comprehensive Sales Tax Act was introduced, effective August 1990. The Minister has the power to add to the schedule of taxable items. The tax rate is 10%. Taxable services include the following.

| | |
|---|---|
| Telephone services | Computer services |
| Restaurant services | Hire/lease of vessels and aircraft |
| Tickets for overseas travel | Hire/lease of plant machinery, equipment |
| Video and video tape rental | Electronic repairs and maintenance |
| Cinema tickets | Hairdressing services |
| Professional services | Contractors' fees |
| Vehicle hire and rental | Casino services |
| Real estate agency services | Laundry services |
| Provision of petroleum and diesel fuel | Tire services |

*Bonus issue tax*/Bonus issues are subject to tax when the amount capitalized is distributed. The rate of tax on such a distribution is 20%. The tax is separate and distinct and is credited against dividends paid upon wind up.

## Branch income

Nonresident corporations are subject to tax at 35% on Solomon Islands–source income, except where withholding tax is deemed to be final, as in the case of dividends, arm's length interest, royalties, professional services, insurance premiums paid to overseas insurers, film rentals, professional services, and payments to overseas contractors and fishermen, or where a treaty provides for such limitations.

The Minister has the power to amend, by order, the rate of tax to be deducted from nonresident income.

## Income determination

*Inventory valuation*/There is no provision for valuing inventories or determining inventory flows. Conformity between book and tax reporting is usually followed. Both LIFO and FIFO are permitted.

*Capital gains*/There is no capital gains tax in the Solomon Islands. However, the capital gain arising on the sale of any business assets on which depreciation (wear-and-tear deduction) has been allowed is subject to tax at normal rates. This applies to plant, machinery, vehicles, vessels, and business premises.

*Dividends*/Gross dividends are a deductible expense of the paying company when calculating assessable income. In some cases this tax is a final tax.

*Foreign tax relief*/Income derived by a resident corporation from sources outside the Solomon Islands is taxable on the same basis as if it had a Solomon Islands source only when the funds are received in the Solomon Islands. Foreign income is ascertained according to the income tax legislation of the country in which it was derived. A foreign tax credit is allowed, equal to the lesser of the foreign tax paid and the Solomon Islands tax payable on that income. The foreign tax credit must be utilized in the same fiscal period in which it is paid.

## Deductions

*Depreciation and depletion*/The Income Tax Act provides for a capital allowance (wear-and-tear) deduction in lieu of depreciation. The allowance is calculated at the following rates.

|  | % |
|---|---|
| Buildings, building fixtures and fittings, bridges, wharves, slipways, boilers, and oil storage tanks (declared value) | 5 |
| Assets used by a timber concessionaire for cutting, extracting and processing timber from a timber concession and low-cost housing for employees (declared value) | 35 |
| Cost of purchasing and planting coconuts, oil palms and cocoa; provision of yards, fences, and water supplies for livestock; prevention of soil erosion; experimentation, scientific or other research expenditure | 100 |
| Capital expenditure on mining (per annum) | 20 |
| Special development assets used by a business (deemed by the Minister as likely to benefit the national interest) | 100 |

Businesses prescribed under the Investment Act are also granted accelerated depreciation on new factory premises and extensions equal to 40% of the cost in the first year, and 5% thereafter.

*Net operating losses*/A deficit for any year may be set off against the profits of a future year if the shareholders are substantially the same (51%).

*Payments to foreign affiliates*/The deductibility of royalties, interest, and service fees paid to foreign affiliates is available only where withholding tax has been deducted and paid.

*Taxes*/No taxes are deductible.

*Other significant items*/Where an approved mining company has incurred expenditure in the construction of an approved infrastructure development scheme, such expenditure is allowed as a tax credit against income tax due and payable.

*Consolidation of income*/There is no provision for the filing of consolidated tax returns by related corporations or offsetting losses of one corporation against the profits of a related corporation.

## Incentives and grants

When the Investment Board approves an investment proposal, the following forms of government assistance are available.

1. Assistance with submission of proposal and securing land.
2. Tax relief.
3. Drawback of duty on reexports.
4. Import duty-free concession on capital goods used in the capital construction of new projects.
5. Assistance with training, employment, counseling, and staff selection.
6. Contracts to purchase output.

The legislation granting tax concessions is targeted at the following investments.

1. Manufacturing that has local value added of more than 25% of ex-factory sales of approved products (three- to six-year tax holiday, depending on percentage of local value added (LVA)).
2. Export-oriented manufacture with more than 25% LVA (three- to six-year tax holiday).
3. Investments over SBD$10 million (five- to ten-year holiday).

   Investments fostering tourism may alternatively apply for a five-year holiday plus a two-year write-off of depreciable assets constructed or purchased and a 150% deduction for approved overseas promotion costs.
4. Export businesses involved in agricultural produce, manufactured or processed goods, or fresh seafood may alternatively apply for a three- to six-year holiday, irrespective of LVA and the 150% tax deduction for export promotion.
5. Businesses involved in agricultural or export agricultural produce, dairy or goat farming, beef production, reforestation or fisheries, or offshore deep-sea fishing may apply alternatively for a tax holiday on the profits of such activities for five out of any ten years from commencement of commercial production.
6. Any business approved by the Investment Board can claim special addition incentives for write-off of new or expanded factories and training expenses and a 150% deduction for the interprovince transport of raw materials and qualifying products.

## Withholding taxes

**Nonresidents**/Certain gross income payments to nonresidents are liable to withholding tax in lieu of individual and corporation taxes. Effective July 1, 1997, the rates of deduction are as follows.

|                                                                     | %         |
|---------------------------------------------------------------------|-----------|
| Interest                                                            | 15.0      |
| Royalties                                                           | 15.0      |
| Income from contracting                                             | 7.5       |
| Outward income from ships and aircraft                              | 5.0       |
| Insurance premiums                                                  | 15.0      |
| Professional services                                               | 7.5       |
| Pole and line or longline fishermen                                 | 10.0      |
| Purse seiner fishermen                                              | 15.0      |
| Lease of equipment                                                  | 15.0      |
| Film rental                                                         | 5.0       |
| Interest paid by approved mining companies                          | As agreed |
| Payments to contractors/subcontractors by approved mining company   | 7.0       |
| Dividends paid by approved mining companies                         | Nil       |
| Management fees                                                     | 35.0      |
| Dividends                                                           | 35.0      |

# Solomon Islands

**Resident** /A resident withholding tax applies to gross payments made to persons (including corporations) as listed in the following table. The tax is a prepayment of tax assessed on lodgement of an annual income tax return, except for a body of persons other than a corporation (e.g., a village group) and resident individuals whose total income is less than SBD$10,000.

The payer is responsible for deduction of the tax and monthly remittance to the Tax Office. There are provisions for exemption certificates for "good taxpayers."

|  | % |
|---|---|
| Contracting and subcontracting | 7.5 |
| Royalties (timber and material resources removal/exploration) | 10.0 |
| Fishing operations | 10.0 |
| Leases of property (including subleasing) | 10.0 |
| Sales of copra | Nil |
| Sales of cocoa | Nil |
| Marine products (*bêche-de-mer*, shells, shark fin) | 10.0 |
| Stevedoring | 15.0 |
| Dividends | 20.0 |

The Minister has the power to vary the rates.

## Tax administration

**Returns**/December 31 is the standard year-end, but an alternative date may be adopted by business taxpayers.

**Payment of tax**/Corporations are required to pay tax in four installments during the year for which the tax liability will arise, and to settle any adjustment after the end of the year. Installments are payable in the 3rd, 6th, 9th, and 12th months of the calendar year, and any adjustment required is payable nine months after the end of the corporation's financial year. Payment of all installments is required even where an assessment has not been issued, unless prior approval is obtained from the Commissioner of Inland Revenue to amend or dispense with installments.

## *CORPORATION TAX CALCULATION*

For fiscal year ending December 31, 2003

| | | |
|---|---:|---:|
| Net income as per accounts ........................................................... | | SBD$ 4,895,000 |
| Add back: | | |
|    Accounting depreciation ............................................. | 650,000 | |
|    Increase in provisions................................................ | 150,000 | |
|    Profit on disposal of assets for tax............................. | — | |
|    Loss on disposal of assets for accounting ................. | — | 800,000 |
| | | 5,695,000 |
| Deduct: | | |
|    Losses brought forward ............................................. | 500,000 | |
|    Depreciation for tax .................................................. | 450,000 | |
|    Loss on disposal of assets for tax.............................. | — | |
|    Profit on disposal of assets for accounting.................. | 300,000 | |
|    Decrease in provisions .............................................. | 50,000 | |
|    Gross dividends paid.................................................. | 4,000,000 | |
|    Exempt income-interest............................................. | 5,000 | 5,305,000 |
| Taxable income........................................................................... | SBD$ | 390,000 |
| Tax payable at 30%..................................................................... | SBD$ | 117,000 |

Note:

Exchange rate of the Solomon Islands dollar at January 1, 2004:
US$1 = SBD$7.6161.

# South Africa

## PwC contact

For additional information on taxation in South Africa, contact:

Mark Badenhorst
PricewaterhouseCoopers
Private Bag X36
Sunninghill 2156
South Africa
Telephone: (27) (11) 797 4641
Fax: (27) (11) 209 4641
e-mail: mark.badenhorst@za.pwc.com

## Significant developments

The past year has, once again, seen a large volume of amendments to the tax legislation of South Africa (SA). Many of these changes were aimed at clarifying the uncertainties regarding the residence basis of taxation and the capital gains tax which were introduced during 2001. Other developments include the exemption of qualifying foreign dividends for years of assessment commencing on or after June 1, 2004.

## Taxes on corporate income

*Normal tax*/On taxable income earned by private and public companies other than those listed below, the tax rate for financial years ending between April 1, 2003 and March 31, 2004 is unchanged at 30%.

Gold mining companies are taxed on the basis of formulae that differ depending on whether the company elects to be subject to secondary tax on companies (see "Secondary tax on companies").

Close corporations are taxed at the same rate as public and private companies, and are subject to the same taxation rules.

Small business corporations (i.e., a company with only natural persons as members and with an annual turnover of not more than R5 million (R1 million for years ending before April 1, 2002 and R3 million for years ending before April 1, 2003)) are taxed at 15% on the first R150,000 (R100,000 for years ending before April 1, 2002) of taxable income, and at 30% on the excess.

An employment company, (i.e., a company that provides certain services that are performed by persons who have an interest in the company) is taxed at 35% of its taxable income. Similarly, a branch of a company with its place of effective management outside SA is taxed at 35%.

*Long-term insurance companies*/Life insurance companies are taxed as follows.

* Retirement funds—Exempt, except for an 18% (25% before March 1, 2003) tax on gross interest, foreign dividends and net rental income.
* Individual policyholder fund—30%.
* Untaxed policyholder fund—0%.
* Company policyholder fund—30%.
* Corporate fund—30%.

*Secondary tax on companies (STC)*/This tax is levied at a rate of 12.5% on net dividends declared by SA resident companies. The net dividend amount is calculated by deducting dividends accrued from dividends declared during the dividend cycle. The company declaring the dividend, not the recipient, is liable to pay the tax. Branches of foreign companies are exempt from STC.

## Corporate residence

Previously, SA taxed by reference to the source of income rather than the country in which a corporation is resident. For tax years commencing on or after January 1, 2001, a SA resident company is subject to tax on its worldwide income, irrespective of the source. Nonresidents will remain taxable on SA actual or deemed source income.

A company will be resident in SA if it is incorporated in SA, or has its place of effective management in SA, but (from February 26, 2003) excludes a company that is deemed to be exclusively resident in another country in terms of a tax treaty entered into between SA and that other country.

Royalties and know-how payments made to nonresidents for the use of or right to use intellectual property rights in SA are deemed to be from a SA source. The payer of the royalty or know-how payment is obliged to deduct a withholding tax of 12% of this payment, which is a final tax payable by the recipient of such income. The 12% withholding tax may be reduced in terms of a relevant tax treaty.

The income of foreign entities controlled by SA residents is, in certain circumstances, attributed to the SA residents controlling the entity.

Foreign dividends are taxed in SA from February 23, 2000. However, qualifying foreign dividends received or accrued during years of assessment commencing on or after June 1, 2004 will be exempt.

## Other taxes

*Donations tax*/Donations tax is payable by resident companies other than public companies at a flat rate of 20% from October 1, 2001 (previously 25%), subject to an exemption of R10,000 per annum for the aggregate of casual gifts if the donor is not a natural person.

*Provincial and city tax*/Regional services levies, comprising a payroll levy at the rate of 0.25% to 0.4% of remuneration paid to employees and a regional establishment levy at 0.10% to 0.20% of turnover (plus value-added tax (VAT) at 14%), apply to enterprises operating in areas for which regional services councils have been proclaimed.

*Skills Development Levy*/This levy provides for a compulsory levy to fund the education and training envisaged by the Skills Development Act. The skills development levy consists of 1% of an employer's payroll per month from April 1, 2001.

*Unemployment Insurance Fund*/Employers are required to contribute on a one-for-one basis for all employees to the Unemployment Insurance Fund at the rate of 1% of gross remuneration, but currently limited to a maximum of R88.36 per month or R1,060.32 per annum.

Workmen's compensation is payable by employers, by applying to the employee's earnings varying rates depending on the employer's industry.

*Value-added tax*/Value-added tax is levied on the supply or importation of goods and services on a broad basis at a rate of 14%. Goods exported and services supplied offshore are usually zero-rated. Other supplies, in certain circumstances, are specifically exempt from VAT.

*Transfer taxes*/Transfer taxes are levied on the sale or transfer of shares, calculated at 0.25% of the greater of the purchase consideration or market value of the shares on the date of transfer, and on the sale or transfer of land, calculated at 10% of the greater of the purchase price or market value of the land on the date of transfer. Transfers of immovable property that are subject to VAT are exempt from transfer taxes.

## Branch income

SA branches of foreign companies are not considered to be separate legal entities for tax purposes, and no tax is withheld on transfers of profits to the head office. Branches of foreign companies are taxed at a rate of 35% for tax years ending on or after April 1, 1996 and are also exempt from STC from that date.

## Income determination

*Inventory valuation*/Inventories are generally stated at the lower of cost or net realizable value. Write-downs of inventory for slow-moving and obsolete items must be justified, and a general policy on a percentage basis is not permitted. LIFO is not accepted for tax purposes.

*Capital gains*/A total of 50% of net capital gains realized on capital assets disposed of on or after October 1, 2001 is included in taxable income (for companies and trusts, other than special trusts). Special trusts and life assurance individual policyholder funds will include 25% of the realized net capital gains in taxable income. Capital gains tax does not apply to retirement funds until a holistic view of retirement fund taxation is complete.

*Intercompany dividends*/Dividends, other than foreign dividends, are not subject to tax in the hands of companies, but the company declaring the dividend is liable for STC. Qualifying foreign dividends received or accrued during years of assessment commencing on or after June 1, 2004 will be exempt.

*Foreign income*/Foreign income received by a SA resident company is subject to tax in SA. Double taxation may be avoided under certain double taxation agreements or by way of unilateral credit for foreign tax payable on foreign income.

*Stock dividends*/Stock dividends (capitalization issues of shares) are not subject to tax or STC, until the stock is realized.

*Other significant items*/Transfer pricing measures for any goods or services supplied from affiliated companies at a value that does not approximate that which would be obtained from an unrelated entity in an arm's length transaction could result in an adjustment to the income or expense taken into account for tax purposes. Related thin-capitalization provisions generally permit only a 3:1 ratio of foreign shareholder interest-bearing debt to equity.

## Deductions

*Depreciation and depletion*/A depreciation (wear and tear) allowance may be deducted on movable assets used for the purpose of trade. There are no statutory provisions relating to rates of wear and tear, but the SA Revenue Service has published a table of periods over which the assets should be written off in the absence of evidence to support another write off period. The rates of wear and tear, based on the cash cost, are calculated by the straight-line method. (See also "Capital investment" below.)

Buildings and other permanent structures may not be depreciated, apart from an annual allowance for each of the following.

1. Buildings used in a process of manufacture or a process similar to a process of manufacture—For buildings erected between July 1, 1996 and September 30, 1999, 10%; for buildings erected between January 1, 1989 and June 30, 1996 or after October 1, 1999, 5%; for buildings erected before January 1, 1989, 2%.

2. Hotel buildings—For buildings erected from June 4, 1988, 5% (previously 2%). For improvements within the existing building framework that commenced on or after March 17, 1993, 20%.

3. Agricultural cooperative storage buildings—For buildings erected from January 1, 1989, 5% (previously 2%).

4. Housing projects of not less than five units, 2%.

5. Buildings in urban development zones (see "Capital investment" below).

6. Specific allowances are also provided for pipelines, transmission lines and railway lines; aircraft, aircraft hangars, aprons, runways and taxiways; qualifying industrial assets; ships; and mining operations.

An allowance for assets disposed of or scrapped during a year of assessment is determined by reference to the cost less allowances already granted and the proceeds on disposal. Recoupments of allowances granted are taxable where disposal proceeds exceed tax written-down value on sale, subject to a maximum cost. Proceeds above cost will generally be taxed as a capital gain from October 1, 2001 (see above).

Book depreciation need not be the same as tax wear and tear. No cost or percentage depletion is available for natural resources.

*Net operating losses*/Losses may be carried forward indefinitely, provided a trade of a similar nature is carried on without interruption. There is no loss carryback.

*Payments to foreign affiliates*/Deductions may be claimed for royalties, managerial service fees, and interest charges paid to foreign affiliates, provided such amounts approximate those that would be paid to an unrelated entity in an arm's length transaction. Interest deductions may be limited where the paying company is thinly capitalized. Agreements relating to such payments require prior Foreign Exchange Control approval.

*Taxes*/Regional service levies are deductible from taxable income.

## Group taxation

Group taxation is not generally permitted in SA. However, tax relief is given for transactions between group companies to allow for reorganizations provided certain requirements are met.

## Tax incentives

*Inward investment*/Taxpayers with manufacturing operations or similar processes that receive cash grants in terms of a Government Incentive Scheme (see "Other incentives") are entitled to exemption from tax on such grants.

# South Africa

*Capital investment*/The available capital incentives are as follows.

1. Assets brought into use after December 15, 1989—A 20% per annum rate of depreciation applies to plant and machinery used in a process of manufacture or in a similar process, or to machinery and equipment used in the hotel trade. An accelerated rate of 33-1/3% per annum is applicable for new and unused plant and machinery acquired and brought into use in a process of manufacture under an agreement concluded during the period commencing on July 1, 1996 and ending on September 30, 1999. Plant and machinery brought into use after March 1, 2002 which was acquired in terms of an agreement concluded after March 1, 2002, will qualify for a 40% allowance in the first year and a 20% allowance in the following three years. Machinery and equipment used for farming are depreciated at the rate of 50% in the first year, 30% in the next year, and 20% in the final year.

2. Residential buildings, initial allowance—Housing projects of not less than five units qualify for an initial allowance of 10% of cost in the year in which they are completed and rented for the first time.

3. Buildings in urban development zones—Improvements to an existing building in an urban development zone where the existing structural or exterior framework is preserved and which commenced on or after a date still to be announced, qualify for an accelerated allowance of 20% per year. Buildings that are erected, extended or added to in an urban development zone (and which are not covered by the first-mentioned allowance) from the date to be announced from XXX, qualify for a 20% allowance in the first year and a 5% allowance in the following sixteen years.

*Other incentives*/As follows.

1. Small and Medium Enterprise Development Programme (SMEDP) replaces the Manufacturing Development Programme (MDP) that was available since October 1, 1996. The MDP will continue for the remainder of the contract period for already approved projects or expansions. The SMEDP has a significantly higher investment ceiling of R100 million and attracts lucrative cash based tax-free benefits. The incentive will consist of a tax-free establishment grant for two years paid quarterly on qualifying assets—ranging from 10% of the first R5 million investment to 1% on the R100 million ceiling. The project may qualify for a third year of the establishment grant subject to the attaining of a human resource remuneration ratio expressed in terms of the cost of manufacturing of at least 30%. A three-year cash grant of 50% of the cost of training new staff resulting from a new expansion or project will be payable in terms of the Skills Support Programme. This incentive is capped at 30% of the annual wage cost provided an approved training program is in place.

2. The Minister of Trade and Industry may approve special allowances for Strategic Industrial Projects where the costs of new qualifying industrial assets will exceed R50 million. The allowance may be either 100% (preferred status) or 50% (nonpreferred status) depending on the status granted to the project by the Minister, but is limited to either R600 million for preferred status projects and R300 million for nonpreferred status projects.

3. Tax holiday—The Tax Holiday was only available for applications made prior to October 1,1999 and is governed by section 37H of the Income Tax Act. The Tax Holiday takes the form of an exemption from income tax and STC. The Tax

Holiday is for two to six years depending on the elements for which the project qualified.

4. Applications for the reimbursement of the transfer cost of new plant, machinery, and equipment to SA from abroad will be considered on merit. The grant will be limited to US$150,000 for investments not exceeding R20 million, and US$50,000 for investments not exceeding R5 million.

## Withholding taxes

*Resident corporations and individuals*/No withholding taxes, other than payroll taxes, are leviable against payments to resident individuals and corporations.

*Nonresident corporations and individuals*/Tax is to be withheld from certain payments to foreign corporations, foreign companies, and nonresident persons as follows:

| Recipient | Dividends (1) | Interest (2) | Royalties and know-how (3) |
|---|---|---|---|
| | | | % |
| Nontreaty: | | | |
| Corporations and companies not resident in SA | | | 12 |
| Treaty: | | | |
| Algeria | | | 10 |
| Australia | | | 10 |
| Austria | | | Nil |
| Belarus | | | 10 or 12 (5) |
| Belgium | | | Nil |
| Botswana | | | 12 |
| Canada | | | 6 (4) or 10 |
| China, P.R. | | | 10 |
| China (Taiwan) | | | 10 |
| Croatia | | | 5 |
| Cypress | | | Nil or 12 (5) |
| Czech Republic | | | 10 |
| Denmark | | | Nil |
| Egypt | | | Nil or 12 (5) |
| Finland | | | Nil |
| France | | | Nil or 12 (5) |
| Germany | | | Nil or 12 (5) |
| Greece (Hellenic Republic) | | | 5, 7 or 12 (5) |
| Hungary | | | Nil |
| India | | | 10 |
| Indonesia | | | Nil or 10 (5) |
| Iran | | | Nil or 10 (5) |
| Ireland, Rep. of | | | Nil |
| Israel | | | Nil, 12 or 4.5 (6) |
| Italy | | | 6 or 12 (5) |
| Japan | | | 10 |
| Korea, Rep. of | | | 10 |
| Lesotho | | | 10 |
| Luxembourg | | | Nil |
| Malawi | | | Nil or 12 (5) |

# South Africa

| Recipient | Dividends (1) | Interest (2) | Royalties and know-how (3) |
|---|---|---|---|
| | | | % |
| Malta | | | 10 |
| Mauritius | | | Nil |
| Namibia | | | 10 |
| Netherlands | | | Nil |
| Norway | | | Nil |
| Oman | | | Details not available |
| Pakistan | | | Nil or 10 (5) |
| Poland | | | 10 |
| Romania | | | 12 |
| Russia | | | Nil |
| Seychelles | | | Nil or 12 (5) |
| Singapore | | | 5 |
| Slovakia | | | 10 |
| Swaziland | | | Nil or 12 (5) |
| Sweden | | | Nil or 12 (5) |
| Switzerland | | | Nil or 12 (5) |
| Thailand | | | 12 |
| Tunisia | | | 10 |
| Uganda | | | 10 |
| United Kingdom | | | Nil or 12 (5) (7) |
| United States | | | Nil |
| Zambia | | | Nil or 12 (5) |
| Zimbabwe | | | Nil or 12 (5) |

Notes:

1. SA does not levy a withholding tax on dividends.
2. SA does not levy a withholding tax on interest.
3. Individuals and companies may have to render annual returns of income and pay tax at normal rates, with credit being given for withholding tax deducted.
4. Maximum rate of normal tax is limited to 6% in respect of copyright royalties; other like payments in respect of the production or reproduction of any literary, dramatic, musical, or other artistic work; royalties for the use of or right to use computer software; or royalties for the use of or the right to use any patent or information concerning industrial, commercial, or scientific experience. In respect of all other royalties the maximum rate of normal tax is limited to 10%.
5. If not subject to tax in the hands of the recipient in country of residence, and/or if the recipient operates a permanent establishment effectively connected to the payment of the royalties in the country where the royalties arise, 12% rate applies.
6. As per Note 5, provided a withholding of 4.5% applies in the case of all royalties derived from the use of cinematographic or television film without regard to taxation of the recipient in country of residence.
7. If it was the main purpose of any person concerned with the creation or assignment of the rights in respect of which the royalties are paid to take advantage of the relevant Article in the tax treaty, the 12% rate applies.

At March 11, 2004, the following information holds.

The treaty with the United Kingdom includes Great Britain and Northern Ireland.

Comprehensive agreements have been ratified by SA with Botswana, Brazil, New Zealand, Nigeria, and Rwanda.

Comprehensive agreements have been signed but not ratified with Kuwait, Swaziland, and Ukraine.

Comprehensive agreements have been negotiated or renegotiated but not signed with Bulgaria, Cuba, Estonia, Ethiopia, Gabon, Germany, Ghana, Latvia, Lithuania, Malawi, Malaysia, Morocco, Mozambique, Namibia, Netherlands, Portugal, Qatar, Saudi Arabia, Spain, Sri Lanka, Tanzania, Turkey, United Arab Emirates, Zambia, and Zimbabwe.

A comprehensive agreement is being negotiated with Bangladesh.

There are limited sea and air transport agreements with Brazil, Portugal, and Spain.

## Tax administration

*Returns*/The corporate fiscal year is the same as the company's financial year. It may be changed upon application showing reasonable cause. Annual returns must be submitted within 60 days of the end of the company's fiscal year unless an extension has been allowed.

*Payments*/Payments are made with provisional returns filed at six-month intervals from the fiscal year-end and are generally based on the last issued assessment. Interest is charged on any underpayment outstanding for more than six months after the fiscal year-end except in the case of February year-ends, in which case it is seven months. Any balance (together with interest) is then paid following assessment.

# South Africa

## CORPORATION TAX CALCULATION

Financial year 2003-2004, April 1, 2003 to March 31, 2004

| | | |
|---|---:|---:|
| Net income per income statement before taxation | | R 1,000,000 |
| Add—Expenditure charged in income statement not allowable: | | |
|     Items of a capital nature | 110,000 | |
|     Donations | 5,000 | |
|     Depreciation per income statement | | |
|     (i.e., at rates applied by the company) | 110,800 | 225,800 |
| | | 1,225,800 |
| Deduct: | | |
|     Capital gains | 95,000 | |
|     Dividend—SA source | 160,000 | |
| Capital allowances claimed: | | |
|     Wear and tear allowance: | | |
|       Furniture and fittings—16.66% | 27,500 | |
|       Vehicles—20% | 15,500 | |
|     Depreciation allowance (first year): | | |
|       New plant and machinery | 20,000 | 318,000 |
| Taxable income before capital gains | | R 907,800 |
| Taxable capital gains (1) | | 47,500 |
| Total taxable income | | 955,300 |
| Tax payable at 30% | | R 286,590 |

Notes

1. Capital gains tax calculation

| | |
|---|---:|
|     Proceeds | 100,000 |
|     Less—Base cost | 5,000 |
|     Gain | 95,000 |
|     Taxable gain (at 50% inclusion rate) | 47,500 |

2. Exchange rate of the rand at March 18, 2004: US$1 = R6.7.

## PwC contact

For additional information on taxation in Spain, contact:

Jose Félix Gálvez
PricewaterhouseCoopers
Paseo de la Castellana, 53
28046 Madrid, Spain
Telephone: (34) (91) 5684530
Fax: (34) (91) 5684112
LN address: Jose Felix Galvez/ES/TLS/Pwc@ EMEA-ES
e-mail: jose.felix.galvez@es.landwellglobal.com

## General note

This entry also covers the Canary Islands, which has certain specific tax incentives.

Peculiarities for the Basque Country are covered under a specific heading.

As corporate tax, the discussion refers to direct tax on profits concerning resident entities. From 1999 onward, the direct tax on profits obtained by permanent establishments in Spain of foreign corporations/entities is called nonresident's tax (see "Branch income").

This nonresident's tax is also levied on income obtained in Spain by foreign entities without permanent establishment (see "Withholding tax").

## Significant developments

Since 1999, the statute-barred period for tax audits has been decreased to four years (instead of five). For tax periods beginning January 1, 2002, the carryforward period for tax losses is extended to 15 years. This applies also to tax losses that were pending offset in the first tax year beginning during the 2002 calendar year.

From the tax period beginning after June 26, 2000 onward, some of the tax credits available on foreign income have been replaced by participation exemption formulas, meaning a significant improvement with respect to the previous situation in some cases.

The income tax regime on Spanish companies holding foreign securities has been improved, and includes the above-mentioned changes on measures to avoid double taxation on foreign income.

Tax measures have been put in place to promote R&D and encourage investment in new technologies; some of them are of general application, while others are restricted to small companies.

Beginning in 2002, R&D tax benefits are enhanced by allowance of a 10% tax credit for investments in certain qualifying assets. For tax periods beginning after January 1, 2004 onward, the additional tax credit rate in R&D has been increased from 10% to 20% for some staff expenses (qualified researchers assigned exclusively to R&D activities) or expenses on projects contracted with universities, public organisms or centers of innovation and technology legally recognized.

The maximum base on which the 10% deduction applies in the case of acquisition of advanced technology in the form of patents, licenses, "know-how" and designs have been increased from €500,000 to €1,000,000.

Beginning in the first tax year commencing within 2002, tax consolidation requirements are softened (75% minimum participation – 90% before). Permanent establishments of foreign entities may also be dominant entities in tax consolidation groups as long as certain requirements are met.

The European Union (EU) approved the regime of the "Canary Islands Special Zone" (*Zona Especial Canaria* (ZEC)) that is applicable from June 25, 2000.

The special tax regime for entities engaged in hydrocarbons activities is no longer applicable except for those entitled to it for 2001.

Beginning in the first tax period as of January 1, 2002, the acquisition of a 5% or greater stake in a foreign entity meeting certain requirements could allow the investor to depreciate the goodwill part of its investment at a maximum 5% annual rate. By way of clarification, it appears that such finance goodwill may only be fiscally depreciable in direct holdings.

There is available a 10% tax credit for contributions to pension plans meeting certain requirements. A similar tax credit is given as of the first tax period beginning during 2003 over the facilities given directly or indirectly by an employer to its employees' kindergarten.

For tax periods beginning after January 1, 2003 nonresident companies operating in Spain through a permanent establishment are entitled to foreign tax credits against their Spanish tax on their taxable income, if the investments in subsidiaries are allocated to such Spanish permanent establishments.

In force since January 1, 2003, partnerships and similar entities incorporated abroad which develop activities in Spain in permanent establishment format are liable to income taxes in Spain as separate taxpayers, but just for the part of their income allocated to foreign partners.

For tax years commencing after January 1, 2004, thin capitalization rules (3:1 ratio) are not applicable when the lending nonresident related entity is resident in another EU member state (except tax havens). In the same way, controlled foreign corporations (CFC) rules are not longer applicable to companies resident in the EU.

Another innovation applicable to tax periods commencing January 1, 2004, regards to the tax credit on domestic dividends. Up until January 1, 2004, dividends obtained from companies resident in Spain enjoyed a full tax credit, provided that the shareholding held in the company concerned was at least 5% and the investment had been maintained without interruption for the year preceding the date on which dividends were demandable. After January 1, 2004 this time requirement may now be met after the dividend is distributed whereby the minimum stake must be maintained during the necessary time to complete a year.

For tax year beginning January 1, 2004, new tax benefits for venture capital companies have been introduced. Those include a 99% exemption on capital gains realized on dispositions of subsidiaries after the second year and up to the 15th year inclusive, as well as the extension of the participation exemption to nonresident shareholders.

## Taxes on corporate income

The current maximum corporate income tax rate is 35%, although other tax rates (40%, 25%, 20%, 10%, 1%, and 0%) may apply depending mainly on the type of business/type of entity.

Spain applies a reduced rate of 30% on the first €90,151.82 of tax profit earned by a qualifying small company. The justification for applying reduced rates to lower slices of income is ostensibly to provide benefit to small businesses. However, if an entity is obliged not to be taxed on its income but instead to have its resident shareholders taxed, the individual tax rates apply (imputation method).

Permanent establishments in Spain of foreign entities are also subject to nonresident's tax, ordinarily at a 35% rate on their tax profit.

Nonestablished foreign entities/individuals obtaining income in Spain may also be subject to nonresident's tax (see "Withholding tax").

## Corporate residence

Entities incorporated according to Spanish legislation, or having their domicile or place of management in Spanish territory, are resident and are subject to corporate income tax on their worldwide income.

Permanent establishments opened in Spain are subject to nonresident's tax. The same happens to partnership and partnership-like formats in certain cases (see the end of "Significant developments in recent years" section).

## Other taxes

*Value-added tax*/VAT is payable on supplies of goods and services deemed made in Spanish territory for purposes of this tax (according to its rules) and on the import/intra EU acquisition of goods. There are three rates for the different types of goods or services, as follows.

1. "Ordinary" rates of 16%—Applied to regular supplies of goods and services.
2. "Reduced" rate of 7%—Applied to basic necessities (food and agricultural products not covered under the "super reduced" rate of 4%, dwellings, and certain qualifying services). Among others, hairdressing services and works carried out by bricklayers or personal homes were granted such VAT rate as of January 1, 2000.
3. "Super-reduced" rate of 4%—In force since January 1, 2003, Spanish VAT taxpayers supplying services to non-EU recipients which previously were treated as supplied abroad (therefore out of the scope of Spanish VAT) must, in certain cases, charge Spanish VAT as long as such services are utilized/exploited in Spanish VAT territory. This may end up in the Spanish VAT charged, implying an increase of the cost for the service in question. This rate is appliod to basic necessities other than those classified under the "reduced" rate of 7% (bread, milk, books, medicine, etc.).

In the Canary Islands the *impuesto general Indirecto canario* (IGIC) applies in lieu of VAT. The "ordinary" IGIC rate is 5%, while other IGIC rates are 0%, 2%, 9%, and 13% (15% or 25% for tobacco). IGIC is similar to VAT, although some relevant differences should be considered, and there are also relevant exemptions, for example, for telecommunications services. Imports of tangible goods into the Canary Islands are subject to this tax.

In Ceuta and Melilla, sales tax is applied in lieu of VAT.

*Transfer tax*/Transfer tax is levied on transfers "*inter vivos*" when the transaction is not subject to VAT or exempt from this tax (in case of real estate supplies or leases). Transfers of quoted or unquoted securities are exempt from transfer tax and VAT under certain conditions.

In the Canary Islands there are exemptions available to new business with reference to the purchase of assets under certain conditions.

*Capital tax*/Capital tax is mainly levied on incorporations/liquidations of entities, capital increases, reductions, and contributions by shareholders to offset losses. It is incompatible with transfer tax and stamp duty in certain cases, but not with VAT.

*Stamp duty*/Stamp duty is mostly levied on notary deeds documenting valuable transactions subject to be entered in certain Public Registries (mercantile, property, industrial property). In this case, it is incompatible with transfer tax and capital tax, but compatible with VAT.

It is also levied on certain mercantile documents (e.g., bills of exchange, promissory notes) and on certain court and administrative documents.

*Property tax*/Property tax is levied on nonresident entities.

Nonresident entities that are owners of Spanish real estate, or in any way possess real property rights in Spain, are subject to a special levy accruing at December 31 each year, which is to be declared and paid during January of the year following accrual, in the place and manner established by law. The tax is 3% on the ratable value of the real property. This special levy does not apply to entities resident in a country signatory of a tax treaty including an exchange of information clause inasmuch as the ultimate shareholders of such entity are resident in Spain or in a country signatory of a tax treaty with Spain with such a clause.

Other exceptions to this levy apply.

*Other taxes*/There are many other taxes, such as the business activity tax (*Impuesto de Actividades Economicas* (IAE)) levied locally on the mere exercise of entrepreneurial professional activities (since January 2003 only companies with more than €1 million turnover [in the case of corporate groups the consolidated turnover figure will be applied to all the companies] are subject to this tax), and the real estate tax (levied by local authorities on the ownership of real-estate).

## Branch income

Income obtained by a resident entity through a branch in another jurisdiction is treated as income in the head office, and taxed accordingly. Currently an exemption regime is available under certain conditions; if those conditions are not met, an imputation method applies.

Likewise, income obtained by branches in Spain of foreign entities is taxed at the standard corporate income tax rate of 35% (or 40% in specific case of oil exploring, exploiting activities) applying in most cases the rules of resident entities.

Peculiarly for branches, payments to their head offices or other permanent establishments of the same entity for royalties, interest, commissions or technical assistance fees are nondeductible. Likewise, management and general administrative expenses incurred by the foreign head office are deductible to the extent that they are allocable to the branch, follow criteria of continuity and reasonability and meet some documentary and formal requirements.

Income remitted by a branch is subject to a withholding tax at source at the rate of 15% (in general), as per internal legislation in force since January 1, 2003. EU head offices in any case and on the other hand non-EU head offices resident in countries with a tax treaty signed with Spain and applying no branch tax to Spanish head offices are exempt from taxes in repatriation as per internal rules. Tax treaties signed by Spain generally mention nothing in this respect; therefore, it is understood that no branch tax is applicable also from a pure tax treaty side. Notwithstanding, there are some tax treaty exceptions to this rule, such as the treaties with Canada, Indonesia, and the United States, which expressly cover branch tax. In this last respect, it must be mentioned that U.S. head offices are taxed at a 10% rate on a Spanish branch's profit repatriation according to treaty provisions.

## Income determination

The general rule in corporate taxation is that, to determine the tax profit, accounting rules must be followed unless an express provision in tax legislation says anything on the contrary or establishes a special criterion for tax purposes.

Consequently, corporate income tax/permanent establishments' nonresident tax returns include some pages in which accounting/mercantile balance sheet and profit and loss account must be entered.

However, the tax authorities are expressly authorized to modify the accounting result exclusively for purposes of determining the tax result, in as much as they see that such accounting result has not been calculated following Spanish GAAP.

*Inventory valuation*/Inventory is valued at the acquisition or production cost. The average, FIFO and LIFO methods are accepted; replacement and base-stock methods are not, unless exceptional circumstances appear. As mentioned above, there is no special tax rule in this area; therefore, accounting rules are applied for both valuation and obsolescence provisions on inventory.

*Capital gains*/Capital gains are taxable in the tax period in which they arise. They are treated as normal income and taxed at the standard corporate income tax rate of 35%, after considering an uplift in the cost base for indexation tax purposes in case of real state.

If the proceeds of the sale of tangible and intangible assets, and at least a 5% participation in other entities held for more than a year, are reinvested in similar kinds of assets within a time frame established by law, tax on the gains realized on such sales allows the application of a tax credit determined generally by applying a 20% rate to the above-mentioned capital gains.

*Intercompany domestic dividends*/Dividends must be included gross for the purpose of determining taxable income. As long as certain requirements are met, a related tax credit Is then granted against the corporate tax liability, equivalent to the tax rate multiplied by dividends received. The tax credit generally allowed is equal to 100% of the dividends received from taxable domestic corporations where the recipient corporate entity holding is a 5% or more interest, provided that such percent has been held for at least one year or during the necessary time to complete a year (applicable as from January 1, 2004). As can be seen, this regime is to some extent equivalent to an exemption one; where such an entity holding is less than 5% or it is held for less than one year, the tax credit is equivalent to 35% of 50% of the dividends received.

Taxation on capital gains deriving from the sale of shares by an entity owning prior to the transfer at least 5% of the subsidiary for at least a year can be reduced by means of a tax credit amounting to the tax rate multiplied by the corresponding part of net undistributed profits of the subsidiary originated during the shareholder's period of tenure.

The reason for such a relief is that such gain is understood as an underlying dividend.

*Foreign income*/Resident entities are taxable on all income accruing to them, whether or not arising in Spain. For foreign-source income, total or partial tax relief in the form of credits or exemptions is given if the income is subject to tax in both Spain and the foreign country.

Such relief is granted in two cases, as follows.

1. Economic double taxation, where the same profits are taxed (a) in the foreign entity obtaining them and (b) in the hands of the Spanish-resident shareholder receiving dividends or obtaining capital gains from share transfers.
2. Juridical double taxation, where the same income is taxed in two countries in the hands of the same taxpayer, one where it is obtained (withholding tax at source) and the other where the recipient is resident.

Both relieves are developed below.

1. Dividends or profit-sharing income received by a Spanish company from a foreign entity are exempt, directly or indirectly, when the following requirements are met.
   a. The Spanish company holds at least 5% of the share capital of the nonresident company continuously throughout the fiscal year before the date of payment of the dividend. This one-year holding period is deemed to be complied with if such ownership is completed after actual dividend distribution.
   b. The foreign entity is subject to a tax similar to the Spanish corporate income tax, and is not resident in a listed tax-haven country. The similarity of the foreign tax is presumed if the foreign entity is resident in a country with which Spain has concluded a double taxation treaty incorporating an exchange-of-information provision.
   c. The income out of which the dividend is paid arises from the business activities of the foreign entity carried out abroad, as defined.

This exemption regime replaces that of full tax credit with seven-year carry forward for tax periods beginning June 26, 2000 onward.

Capital gains arising from the sale of shares of foreign entities are also entitled to such exemption as long as the above requirements are met in all holding periods and the acquiring entity is not resident in a tax haven.

Limitations on full exemption apply in certain cases.

This exemption regime replaced that of tax credit over just the net underlying dividends during the seller's holding period as of the tax period beginning June 26, 2000 onward.

As an alternative to this "exemption" regime just for dividend distribution, it is foreseen a tax credit based on imputation, that allows the crediting of the foreign tax paid abroad on the profits from which dividends come from together with the foreign withholding tax on such profit distribution, with the limit of the tax that would have been paid on the gross amount in Spain.

The only requirement to apply this "imputation" method is 1.a. above.

In this case of imputation, tax credit relief is extended to the underlying taxes considered to second- and third–tier foreign subsidiaries.

A carryforward of up to ten years is available.

2. As mentioned above as one of the possible systems, Spanish international legislation provides corporate tax relief on "juridical" double taxation by applying the imputation "method," that is, gross foreign income (including foreign withholding taxes) is considered for Spanish tax calculation purposes, and then a tax credit for the foreign withholding tax is applied, limited to the corporate tax that it would have paid if such gross income (with the deduction of all associated costs, leaving then the profit figure) had been obtained in Spain. The tax credit can be carried forward up to ten years.

For tax periods beginning before January 1, 2003 nonresident companies operating in Spain through permanent establishment were not entitled to foreign tax credits against their Spanish tax on its taxable income, even if the investments in subsidiaries are allocated to such Spanish permanent establishment but since that date foreign tax credits are available.

Under Spanish tax treaties and implemented EU tax directives, several methods have been established to avoid double taxation; the main one is the traditional deduction of a tax credit from the tax effectively paid. However, some treaties provide for the method of exemption or the exclusive right to tax; also, the tax-sparing clause is included in some treaties in order to deduct not only the tax actually paid but a higher amount.

*Stock dividends*/Bonus shares (partially or totally given to shareholders in a capital increase charged against distributable reserves) are not subject to corporate income tax; however, they must be taken into account in the computation of average cost of stock held (tax being paid at the time of disposal of the stock).

*Other significant items*/The following items, among others, are excluded or deferred from taxable income.

1. Dividend distribution corresponding to profits obtained by subsidiaries in tax periods in which the international transparency regime or the passive holding company regime applied.

2. A credit of 20% on capital gains deriving from the sale of assets which proceeds are reinvested in qualifying assets is discussed above in this section.

3. The writing-up of assets according to revaluation laws and tax-protected restructuring transactions involving accounting capital gains.

4. A reduction for an amount equivalent to the investment in majority stakes in foreign entities developing business abroad can be made to the tax base and then reintegrated in the following four years. This tax benefit is subject to meeting certain requirements among which are that the foreign entity cannot be resident in either the EU or a tax haven. Also, limitations in the amount of reduction (for instance, it cannot exceed 25% of the tax profit of the company before this reduction) may apply.

## Deductions

*Depreciation and depletion*/All fixed assets, except land, are depreciable for tax purposes. There are guideline rates of tax depreciation by both industry sector and asset type, expressing a maximum per annum rate and a maximum number of years of useful life. The straight-line method over the useful life is normally used, and it is applied on the cost of the asset or the written-up value (if such writing up was fiscally accepted). Out-of-book adjustments must be included in the tax return if the accounting depreciation exceeds that according to tax rules.

New qualifying assets that have an effective life over one year may be depreciated according to the two following declining-balance methods.

- By applying a constant percentage over the net book value of the assets multiplied by 1.5, 2, or 2.5 depending on the useful life of the asset (below five years, between five and eight years and over eight years, respectively).
- By using the sum-of-digits method: The asset's acquisition value is multiplied by a ratio consisting of the number of the year on a decreased basis (i.e., 3 for the first year, 2 for the second and 1 for the third in a three-year useful life) divided by the numbers for such years of useful life of the asset (i.e., 1 + 2 + 3 = 6 for three years useful life).

Buildings, furniture, and fittings cannot be depreciated under any of these declining-balance methods.

Special depreciation plans can be approved upon request for new assets, when they are subject to wear-and-tear at a rate higher than normal.

Depreciation booked will be fully deductible even if higher than the result of applying any of the above tax methods, if the taxpayer is able to evidence that such depreciation is real.

Mining assets and those used for research and development (R&D) (excluding buildings), among others, can be freely depreciated fiscally.

Mining entities, and also those involved in exploring/investigating oil natural resources, are allowed depletion in the terms and conditions established in applicable legislation.

However, intangibles are also depreciable, but such depreciation is not deductible if no consideration was paid or if related parties are involved unless such loss of value is undoubtedly evidenced.

The general rule for depreciation on intangibles in case useful life is not determined is a deemed useful life of ten years, but application of simple 10% annually will not be valid if the depreciation actually booked for these assets was lower.

***Net operating losses***/Tax losses may be carried forward for 15 years, but they cannot be carried back. There are no tax loss "baskets" (operating/capital) in Spanish legislation. Complex rules may limit the utilization of tax losses belonging to an entity dissolved as a result of a restructuring process. Also, the use of such tax losses in the company originating them in case of a change of shareholder is also restricted under certain circumstances.

***Payments to foreign affiliates***/Supplies of goods and/or services from a foreign group entity not established in Spain to a Spanish one must be valued at arm's length. Excess expense recorded over market value could be rejected corporate tax deductibility. Tax haven expense charges are disallowed in full unless proper evidence of an actual supply at arm's length is provided.

Management services from abroad imputed under the format of cost distribution from a group center must be mandatorily documented in a contract in writing signed previously to the effective start of service supply for the deductibility of the expenses. Notarization is highly recommended. In the rest of cases, having such a notarized contract is not mandatory, but extremely convenient. The same can be said about contributions to R&D programs.

As regards taxation in Spain for the foreign entity not established in Spain supplying services, the internal withholding tax rate to be applied on the gross income is 25%. Dividends, interest and gains on sale of interests in collective investment institutions are subject to withholding tax at a 15% rate since January 1, 2003. A 35% rate is applied for the rest of capital gains. If management services, technical assistance or the performance of studies are solely used outside Spanish territory and are linked to business abroad, then no withholding tax would apply.

Tax treaty provisions mostly allow exemption of amounts characterized as business profits. It must be reminded that this is a residual category. For instance, if the fee obtained qualifies as royalty, then withholding tax would apply at reduced tax treaty rates as long as the foreign entity obtains a tax residence certificate in its country. If no tax treaty applies, then the above 25% rate is applicable (see "Withholding Tax").

*Taxes*/Taxes other than corporate income tax that are entered as an expense due to their nature (for instance, IAE but not, for instance withholding) are deductible expenses. In some cases, indirect taxes such as nondeductible VAT or transfer tax could be added to the value of assets for depreciation purposes. In other cases, for instance, capital tax on incorporation, taxes are included in formation expenses and written off over a period of up to five years.

However, penalties imposed for failure to pay taxes and surcharges for late filing/ payment or for other tax infringements are not tax deductible.

Late payment interest booked as an expense is, in principle, deductible.

*Other significant items*/Other deductible items include certain gifts and donations (gifts made for purposes of promoting sales could be deducted in full, while some restrictions apply if donations are made to certain kind of institutions, such as charities duly registered in Spain in which the "deduction" is instrumented by means of a tax credit technique), bad and doubtful debts (the collection period needed to allow deductibility of the expense is reduced from one year to six months for tax periods beginning January 1, 2002 onward), portfolio depreciation, extraordinary repairs and overhauls, certain provisions that cover risk and expenses (for which the general rule is no deductibility) such as liabilities that could arise in court cases, warranty repair provisions, contributions to pension plans and similar formulae, and so on. They will be deductible if they meet certain conditions and are adequately supported by documentation.

Arm's length rules for transactions between resident related entities only apply if the result of using prices different from the market ones implies less taxation or a determent of tax in the transaction considered as a whole (i.e., taking into account all parties involved).

Interest expense is deductible but thin capitalization rules apply (3:1 ratio). For tax periods beginning January 1, 2002 and onward, the increase of this ratio can be negotiated with the Tax Authorities in all cases except when tax havens were involved (prior to that change in legislation, an increase in such ratio could only be requested when the borrower was resident in a country with a tax treaty signed with Spain). As from January 1, 2004, these rules are not applicable to nonresident lending related entities when they are resident in another EU member state.

## Group taxation

Group taxation (consolidation) of resident entities is permitted, provided that a formal election is made, but only affects corporation tax (not VAT, for instance) and withholdings on account of this tax. To file a consolidated income tax return, the election must be made before the beginning of the tax year for which the group taxation regime applies. The main requirement is that the consolidating corporation own directly or indirectly (in this last case, through other resident entities qualifying as consolidated) at least 75% of a Spanish resident dependent corporation at the beginning of the tax period for which the taxation regime is intended to be applied. Nonresident permanent establishments in Spain could be considered, for this purpose, as dominant entities, as long as certain requirements are met. Tax losses and tax credits prior to consolidation can be offset only against tax profits/tax due of the same corporation that generated them.

## Tax incentives

There are no tax incentives specifically for the foreign investor. Incentives may be granted to Spanish and foreign-owned corporations alike. Corporate tax legislation grants certain tax incentives, as follows.

Incentives concerning the activity/the place of the activity, as follows.

- A 50% credit on the corporate tax deriving from income obtained in Ceuta and Melilla through entities formally established there and actually carrying on activities comprising a full business cycle.
- A 99% credit on the corporate tax deriving from income obtained from the supply of local public services, except where the corporation in question has partially or totally a private shareholding.
- A 99% credit on the corporate tax deriving from income obtained from exports of films, books, and similar cultural items, subject to profit reinvestment in the acquisition of assets linked to such activities.

Incentives to promote certain kind of investments (subject to limits calculated as a 35% over the tax quota, raised to a 50% rate (this tax credit limit has been increased from 45% to 50% since the first tax year beginning after January 1, 2004) if R&D and technology information credits exceed 10% of such tax quota), as follows.

- For R&D expenses, a tax credit of 30% for R&D expenses equivalent to the average of the previous two years, and 50% for the excess.
- An additional 20% tax credit is foreseen if the project is carried out through certain qualifying centers/individuals. This tax credit has an extended carryforward period of 10 years for those credits generated up to first year finalizing after June 25, 2000, and 15 years from that tax period onward.
- A 10% credit over the investment in assets affected to R&D, compatible with those credits above, is also granted with the same carryforward criteria.
- For technology innovation, a new tax credit from year 2000 onward calculated over expenses incurred for this purpose. The rate applied is 15% or 10% depending on the concept. This tax credit has the same extended carryforward period as that of R&D.
- Antipollution investments are granted a 10% tax credit. From year 2000 onward, this tax credit is extended to acquisition of commercial vehicles (vans, trucks, etc.) as long as it is considered that they contribute to such antipollution purposes. For tax periods beginning in January 1, 2002, onward, such tax credit benefit is also granted to investments in certain alternative energy sources.
- Beginning in the first tax year within 2002, employer may apply a 10% tax credit over their contributions to their employees' Pension plans, if they earn annual

salary below €27,000. For salaries on or over that figure, such 10% is applied proportionally.

- Beginning in the first tax year within 2003, companies' investments expenses in kindergarten for their employees are granted a 10% tax credit.
- A 25% tax credit on an investment relating to the opening of a branch abroad or the acquisition of at least a 25% participation in a foreign entity linked to export activities or to tourist services in Spain.
- A 25% tax credit on publicity and promotion expenses incurred on an over-a-year basis for launching products or expanding markets abroad. Those expenses linked to commercial exhibitions and fairs abroad (or in Spain, if they have an international profile) also qualify.
- A 15% tax credit on the investment in cultural assets protected under applicable legislation. Said assets must be kept for a period of at least four years in order to qualify. Maintenance and repair expenses may also be considered. The same tax credit applies to investment in films and book releases.

*Other incentives*/Other incentives that will be applicable, include the following, among others.

- Tax credit of 5% to 10% may be obtained on expenditure incurred in, or related to, financing employees' continuing education programs. Expenses incurred by the company employer to familiarize employees in the use of new technologies (even if such use can take place out of the company's premises and out of the work timetable) also qualify for this tax credit. These expenses will not be deemed to be a benefit in kind for the employee.
- A €6,000 tax credit is granted per unit increase in the number of disabled workers per year hired on an indefinite and full-time basis. This increase is calculated by taking the average of company workers meeting these requirements in the tax year in question and comparing it with the average of the previous tax year.

*Special tax regimes*/Special tax regimes will be applicable under certain conditions, as follows.

1. Spanish and European Economic interest grouping.
2. Temporary consortia of companies.
3. Restructuring transactions (implementation of 90/434 EU Directive). As a general rule, this regime provides for tax neutrality in this type of transaction, so that the asset transfers that are necessarily involved do not trigger any tax implications (either from a direct, indirect or other Spanish tax perspective) for the parties involved (transferor, beneficiary and shareholder), until a subsequent transfer not protected by this regime takes place.

   Transactions covered by this regime are mergers, global cessions, spin-offs of business units/majority portfolio stakes, splits, share-to-share transactions, contribution of business units and contribution of assets (this last transaction is not fully tax-protected). Each of them must meet a series of requirements to qualify for the regime.

   The following briefly outlines some significant features of this regime.

   a. The tax credit position of an entity dissolved as a consequence of a tax-protected restructuring transaction is "acquired" in full by the beneficiary entity in case of universal succession.

Such "acquisition" would only refer to those credits linked to the assets transferred in case of transactions where the transferor is not dissolved or the succession cannot be deemed full from a Spanish mercantile perspective.

Regarding tax losses, the Spanish state tax authorities hold the view that no transfer of such tax losses may take place when the transferring entity is not dissolved. In case of dissolution of the transferring entity, tax losses may be applied by the beneficiary entity, but subject to limitations and restrictions.

b. Financial goodwill arising as a consequence of a merger transaction is tax depreciable at a maximum 5% annual rate (depreciation booked acting as a deduction limit) at the level of the Spanish entity beneficiary of the merger inasmuch as the seller of the shares which gives rise to such "merger" goodwill has been actually taxed for the equivalent capital gain in Spain or any other EU country (excluding tax havens).

Depreciation on goodwill arising in a merger resulting from the acquisition of shares previously owned by an individual who is resident in Spain and who had not included in his personal Income Tax capital gains generated in the sale of such shares, will not be deductible (before the first tax period beginning within 2002, it was also required that such resident individuals be related parties).

c. This tax regime cannot be applied if the main purpose behind the transaction is tax fraud or evasion (antiabuse clause). For tax periods beginning January 1, 2001 onward, a clarification of this antiabuse clause in line with that covered by in the EU Directive is added, so that if the transaction is not carried on for valid economic reasons, such as rationalization of activities or group restructuring to gain efficiency, but for obtaining a tax advantage, again the transaction in question will not qualify for this regime.

Application of this regime must be communicated to the tax authorities.

4. Fiscal transparency (internal and international-controlled foreign corporation rules). As for the first year beginning within 2003, internal transparency has disappeared, and a new regime for entities holding securities (in certain cases) and for entities purely holding assets has been set up.

Such new regime refers, in general terms, to personal income tax rules to determine the tax base, and applies a 40% rate over ordinary income, while a 15% rate applies to gains generated over one-year period.

5. Industrial development corporations.

6. Venture capital companies and funds and collective investment institutions.

7. Special leasing transactions.

8. Spanish holding company of foreign entities. For tax periods beginning June 26, 2000 onward, this regime has been modified. Under these new features, Spanish resident entities—the corporate purposes of which include the holding and management of foreign entities' shares—are granted some tax benefits if they meet certain requirements. One new requirement consists of the obligation that shares of the Spanish holding company be nominative.

The option for the application of this regime must be communicated to the tax authorities.

Entities under this regime are granted participation exemption on dividends and capital gains in the terms stated under "Foreign income" above even for below 5% direct stakes when the acquisition value of the participation is, at least, €6 million.

However, indirect participation, that is, in second-tier and further-tier foreign subsidiaries, will qualify when the 5% participation threshold is complied with.

However, the distribution of profits by the holding company to nonresident entities or individual shareholders is also not taxable in Spain (except for tax havens). Resident company shareholders are now entitled to internal tax credit on dividends subject to ordinary Spanish rules.

Contributions of shares in foreign subsidiaries qualifying for dividend/capital gain participation exemption made to the Spanish holding entity are granted the benefit of full tax neutrality under the regime for restructuring transactions (see 3. above).

9. Small- and medium-size business are eligible for incentives such as accelerated depreciation and amortization, more favorable bad debt provision treatment, as well as exemption from tax on capital gains upon the exemption upon the disposal of trading assets. From January 1, 1999 this exemption regime has been changed by the accelerated depreciation of the assets acquired with the amount received from the sale of trading assets. To be considered eligible for these incentives, for taxable periods beginning from June 25, 2000 onward, total company revenues should not exceed €3 million or €5 million for tax periods beginning January 1, 2002 and onward (group of companies' turnover figures must be also considered for this purpose). As from April 27, 2003 the limit has been increased up to €6 million.

   A reduced corporate tax rate of 30% applies on the first €91,151.81of tax profit taken on an annual basis.

   Small- and medium-size businesses are granted a tax credit amounting to 10% of investments and expenses incurred to improve the company's capabilities in Internet access and business information management, as well as to improve the efficiency of internal processes thanks to new technologies. This tax credit has a carryforward period of ten years.

10. Special tax regime for entities which activity consists on housing renting.

***Special tax regime of the Basque Country/***The three provinces that make up the Autonomous Region of the Basque Country (Alava, Guipúzcoa, and Vizcaya) have an "economic agreement" (*Concierto Económico*) with the central government (governed by Law 12 of May 23, 2002) whereby these provinces are granted the right to regulate their tax regimes

Coincident with the corporation tax reform in the country as a whole, the provincial authorities of the Basque Country have altered their regulations to incorporate certain provisions that make the area more attractive to taxpayers than the standard corporate tax regulations. These include the following.

1. The general tax rate has been reduced to 32.5%.

2. A reduced rate of 30% applies in the three provinces to small companies, provided that more than 50% of their share capital is owned by individuals (provision required only in Guipúzcoa).

3. A rate of 25% applies to companies that are officially listed on the Bilbao Stock Exchange, to brokerages and to companies that become officially listed on the

Bilbao Stock Exchange (in this case, the special rate only applies for the first three years onward the year of listing).

To calculate the tax base, the following must be taken into account.

1. Tax loss carryforwards may be offset over a 15-year period. In the case of creating a new company in the Basque Country, the tax loss carryforward period starts from the first year the company would earn profits.
2. Goodwill, brands, transfer rights, and so on, may be written off over a 20-year period.
3. "Financial goodwill" may be deducted through a provision over five years.
4. There are shorter depreciation periods for fixed assets.
5. Exemption regime for capital gains realized on sales of tangible and intangible assets and on sales of an at least 5% participation in other entities, instead of the deferring/tax credit regime previously mentioned for Spanish territory.

A 10% tax credit applies to investments in new tangible fixed assets, subject to certain requirements regarding the amount of investment. Software qualifies for an investment tax credit. A 10% tax credit applies to expenditures in access and management of commercial transfers through the internet. This tax credit is not compatible with the "investment in new tangible assets" tax credit. Subject to certain requirements, appropriation of profits to a special reserve for productive investment (SRPI) entitles the taxpayer to a credit of 10% of the amount appropriated.

The tax incentives for investing in securities, subject to certain requirements, are as follows.

1. Tax credit of 5% of the investment.
2. Investments in quoted companies and capital increases in any company qualify for a tax credit of 6.5%.
3. The credit increases to 8.5% for purchase of securities of companies listed on the Bilbao Stock Exchange since January 1, 1996, and applies only for the next three years that the company is quoted in that stock exchange.

Incentives for other activities and investments include the following.

1. R&D expenses—30%; 50% if the expenses exceed the average expenses for the previous two years.
2. Expenditure for environmental conservation and improvement and for conservation of energy—15%.
3. Investment to promote exports (e.g., foreign advertising, formation of companies and branches abroad)—25%.
4. Staff training—10%; 15% if the expenses exceed the average expenses for the previous two years.
5. Employment creation:
   a. €3,606.07 for each post created and for each year in which the average workforce is increased, provided that indefinite employment contracts are concluded (this requirement does not apply in Álava, temporary job posts can also be taken into account) and the increase is maintained for two years;
   b. €6,611.13 for each position created and for each year in which the average workforce is increased, provided that indefinite employment contracts are

concluded (this requirement does not apply in Álava, temporary job posts can also be taken into account) and persons who have special difficulties in finding employment are engaged.

6. Reduction of working hours. Companies that agree to a 10% reduction in working hours and a 10% increase in the workforce, to be maintained over three years, are granted the following.

   a. Free depreciation of existing and new tangible fixed assets.

   b. A 35% tax credit for new fixed asset investments, rather than 10%.

   c. A total of €4,507.59 for each position created and for each year in which the average workforce is increased, provided that indefinite employment contracts are concluded and the increase is maintained for two years.

7. There is also available a 10% tax credit for contributions to pension plans meeting certain requirements.

8. There is available a new 15% tax credit for investments on the exploitation of renewable energy resources. Only small- and medium-sized businesses are eligible for this special tax credit.

**Special tax regime of the Canary Islands**/This islands have a "special tax and economic regime" (*Regimen Económico y Fiscal* (REF)), whereby they are granted the right to special better conditions with reference to Spanish general tax system, and specific tax incentives mostly conditioned to some direct or indirect investments being made in the Canaries.

With reference to direct taxes, REF includes the following regarding companies and business domiciled in the Canaries or permanent establishments' activities therein.

1. Up to 90% of each year's undistributed accounting profits is allowed to be allocated into a special investment reserve (RIC), thus getting no corporate tax on such allocations, providing that they are invested within a five-year term (including the period of the obtaining of the profit) in qualified new assets in the Canaries (second hand assets may also qualify under certain conditions), or stake in other companies operating in the Canaries that invest in above referred qualified assets (until December 2003, the taxpayers were also allowed to invest the RIC allocations in certain public debt titles. Such option has disappeared from January 2004 on, although it remains for those allocations into the RIC that have been carried out until December 31, 2003). According to the regulation in force since January 2003, taxpayers may invest in advance, the amounts corresponding to future allocations into the RIC, provided that such allocations correspond to accounting profits to be obtained until December 31, 2005.

2. Most Spanish corporate tax incentives are 80% higher for companies and business in the Canaries, regarding both the incentives granted and their conditions to be used. Deduction of 25% for investments in new tangible fixed assets is available and second hand assets may also qualify under certain conditions.

3. A 50% allowance of corporate tax quota is granted regarding the taxable base arising from production activities of tangible goods from agricultural, farming, industrial, and fishing activities.

4. A 90% allowance of corporate tax quota is granted regarding profits of shipping companies arising from ships registered in the Canary Islands Special Ships and Shipping Companies Register. Sailors on those ships are

granted a 50% exemption on their personal income tax arising from their related wages while Social Security contributions to be made by the employer are reduced by 90%.

With reference to indirect taxes, apart from general lower taxation under IGIC compared to VAT and specific IGIC exemptions, the following should be noted.

1. There are incentives for new activities or improving existing activities and newly incorporated companies domiciled in the Canary Islands, or those companies which have already been incorporated and carry out a capital increase. The following exemptions are applicable for a period of three years as from the date on which the relevant formation or capital increase deed is executed.

   a. Exemption from transfer tax on their incorporation and any capital increases and acquisitions of capital goods (Share capital subscribed in respect of the formation of a company or a capital increase will be exempt from transfer tax on corporate operations only in the part of the amount that is dedicated to the importation or acquisition of capital goods). For IGIC purposes, capital goods are (article 40.8 and 9 of the law 20/1991) tangible goods, movables, livestock, immovables, which due to their nature and purpose are usually intended to be used for a period of time longer than one year as work instruments or means of exploitation.

   b. Exemption from the general indirect Canary Islands tax on supplies and imports of capital goods.

The above mentioned incentives (direct/indirect taxation) are going to be reviewed by the EU at the end of 2005, and they will probably be amended (the authorization obtained from the EU expires at December 2005). It is expected that the most of them will be extended.

2. Shipping companies are granted exemption form transfer tax regarding any contract related to ships registered in the Canary Islands Special Ships and Shipping Companies Register.

3. There are custom free areas available.

4. There is an indirect tax called "*Arbitrio sobre la Importación y Entrega de Mercancías*" (AIEM), that is levied on the import of determinate goods (included in a fixed list) into the Canary Islands (including products coming form EU countries), and on the fabrication and further selling of those goods in the Canary Islands territory. The applicable tax rates range between 5 and 15% (except for 25% for cigarettes). It should be noted that most of the products contained in the mentioned list are currently tax exempt in the inner sale of the same, so that the mentioned AIEM, in practice, just taxes the importation of the said goods.

Note: Upon EU demand there are restrictions on the application of some incentives (RIC, allowance for production and new business' indirect taxes incentives) regarding the following industrial sectors which are considered "sensitive", such as shipbuilding, synthetic fibers, automobile industry, iron and steel and coal industry.

**Special Canary Islands' Zone (ZEC)/**This was approved in January 2000 by the EU, and Spanish main regulation was passed in June 2000. The main regulations are the following:

1. New companies might qualify as ZEC entities and, subject to authorization from ZEC authorities, may be registered as such until December 31, 2006,

therefore enjoying the special ZEC tax regime until December 31, 2008. The EU could extend the regime under revision.

2. ZEC entity registration requires the promise to do the following.
    a. Make an investment in fixed assets for at least €100,000 within the first two years of activity.
    b. Create at least five new jobs in the Canaries.

3. ZEC territory includes all the Canaries except for those ZEC entities that intend to carry out industrial or commercial activities involving tangible goods, which must be located in specific controlled areas.

4. ZEC entities might be allowed to operate outside the Canaries through branches conditioned to keeping separate accounting books, but the special tax regime will not be applicable to such branches' activities.

5. ZEC allowed activities have included a wide range of industrial and commercial activities, most services and holdings. Credit and insurance entities are excluded and no stock exchanges are allowed.

6. ZEC entities enjoy reduced Spanish corporate tax rates for the taxable base arising from the allowed ZEC activities carried out within the ZEC. Such rates range from 1% to 5%, depending on the year of the ZEC entity registration, type of activity and job creation. The referred tax rates are limited up to certain taxable base amounts also depending on type of activities and job creation. The rest of their taxable base will be subject to general corporate tax rates.

7. ZEC entities enjoy relevant exemptions regarding IGIC and transfer tax (stamp duty also) as well as relevant reductions and simplified rules for local taxes.

8. Interest and some other returns from moveable goods paid by ZEC entities are exempt from Spanish tax on nonresidents, except when paid to residents in tax havens.

9. Benefits from the EU Parent-Subsidiary Directive are extended to non-EU residents. These benefits are not applicable when the income is paid to residents in tax havens.

10. ZEC entities are subject to fees payable to the ZEC registration authorities (€600 for registration application and €900 as annual maintenance fee).

## Withholding taxes

Ordinarily, the withholding tax is the mechanism by which the Spanish tax authorities collect the final tax on nonresidents. In case of resident beneficiaries, however, it is simply an advanced payment of a tax that then is normally self-assessed by the resident taxpayer on a final basis.

Bear in mind that the advance-payment profile of withholding tax described for resident beneficiaries also applies if nonresident entity/individuals not established in Spain transfer their ownership in Spanish real estate. In this case, the acquirer is obliged to withhold 5% on the sale price on account of the 35% that the seller is to pay on the resulting capital gain. Other capital gains (for instance, a transfer by a nonresident of a substantial participation in a Spanish entity where neither a tax treaty nor internal rules provides exemption) are liable to tax in the hands of the nonresident's transferors, but the mechanics of levying the tax are not those of withholding, but those of the nonresident having the tax paid directly, through its representative or by the depositor or manager of the assets in question, if any.

# Spain

The following chart shows general withholding rates on income obtained by resident/nonresident entities. Such rates must be taken as the maximum ones when recipients are nonresident entities. Where a significant peculiarity applies, reference is made in footnotes.

| Recipient | Dividends | Interest | Royalties |
|---|---|---|---|
| | % | % | % |
| Resident corporations and individuals......... | 15/(1) | 15 (2) | 15 (3) |
| Nonresident corporations and individuals: | | | |
| Nontreaty................................................. | 15 (4) | 15 (5) | 25 (6) |
| Treaty: | | | |
| Argentina ............................................. | 10 (7a) | 12.5 (8) (9) (10) (11) | 15 (12) |
| Australia................................................ | 15 | 10 | 10 (13) |
| Austria ................................................. | 10 (4) (7b) | 5 (5) | 5 |
| Belgium................................................. | 15 (4) | 10 (5) | 5 (14) |
| Bolivia................................................... | 10 (7a) | 15 (8) (9) (10) (11) | 15 (15) |
| Brazil ................................................... | 10 (7a) | 15 (16) (17) | 12.5 (18) |
| Bulgaria ................................................ | 5 (19) | Nil (20) | Nil (20) |
| Canada.................................................. | 15 | 15 | 10 (15) |
| China, P.R. ............................................ | 10 | 10 | 10 |
| Cuba...................................................... | 5 (7a) | 10 | 5 |
| Czechoslovakia (former) ....................... | 5 (7a) | Nil (20) | 5 (20) (21) |
| Denmark................................................ | 10 (4) (7b) | 10 (5) | 6 |
| Ecuador ................................................ | 15 | 10 (22) | 10 (23) |
| Finland.................................................. | 10 (4) (7a) | 10 (5) | 5 |
| France................................................... | 15 (4) (24) | 10 (5) (25) | 5 |
| Germany................................................ | 10 (4) (26) | 10 (27) | 5 |
| Greece.................................................. | 5(55) | 8(8) | 6 |
| Hungary................................................. | 5 (7a) | Nil (20) | Nil (20) |
| Iceland.................................................. | 5(56) | 5 | 5 |
| India...................................................... | 15 | 15 (9) (28) | 20 (29) |
| Indonesia .............................................. | 10 (7a) | 10 (9) | 10 |
| Ireland, Rep. of ..................................... | 15 (4) | Nil | 10 (30) |
| Israel..................................................... | 10 | 10 (9) (62) | 7 (31) |
| Italy....................................................... | 15 (4) | 12 (5) (8) (9) (28) | 8 (32) |
| Japan.................................................... | 10 (33) | 10 | 10 |
| Korea, Rep. of ...................................... | 10 (7a) | 10 (34) | 10 |
| Luxembourg........................................... | 10 (4) (7a) | 10 (5) (9) (35) | 10 (36) |
| Mexico .................................................. | 5 (7a) | 15 (37) | 10 (21) (38) |
| Morocco................................................ | 10 (7a) | 10 | 10 (39) |
| Netherlands .......................................... | 15 (4) (40) | 10 (5) | 6 (41) |
| Norway.................................................. | 10 (42) | 10 (8) (9) (10) (11) | |
| Philippines ............................................ | 10 (43) | 10 (44) | 15 (45) |
| Poland................................................... | 5 (7a) | Nil (20) | 10 (15) |
| Portugal ................................................ | 10 (3) (7a) | 15 (5) | 5 |
| Romania ................................................ | 10 (7a) | 10 (46) | 10 |
| Russian Federation ............................... | 15 (47) | 5 (9) (48) | 5 |

| Recipient | Dividends | Interest | Royalties |
|---|---|---|---|
| | % | % | % |
| Slovenia | 5(56) | 5(8) | 5 |
| Sweden | 10 (3) (49) | 15 (5) | 10 |
| Switzerland | 10 (7a) | 10 (50) | 5 |
| Thailand | 10 | 15 (51) | 15 (52) |
| Tunisia | 5 (7b) | 10 (53) | 10 |
| USSR (applied to former USSR entities except for Russian Federation) | 18 | Nil | 5 |
| United Kingdom | 10 (4) (43) | 12 (5) | 10 |
| United States | 10 (7a) | 10 (9) (11) (54) | 10 (30) |
| New tax treaties | | | |
| Chile | 5 (57) | 15 (58) | 10 (59) |
| Lithuania | 5 (60) | 10 (9) (61) | 10 (59) |

Notes:

1. As long as a corporate taxpayer, as shareholder, is entitled to full tax credit relief on the dividend received, no withholding would apply. Also, dividends out-of-profits originated in periods in which the subsidiary was transparent and dividends distributed between companies taxed under the combination regime are also exempt from withholding.

2. The 15% rate does not apply, among other cases, if the recipient is a resident bank, savings association, or other financial institution subject to corporate tax, provided such income does not represent portfolio income. For interest arising between companies taxed under combination rules, withholding is also excluded.

3. A 15% withholding is applied on income arising under royalty and technical assistance agreements, from rentals or through the granting of rights when title is not passed, except when such income constitutes the habitual business activity of the recipient. 25% will be applicable to fees received by an entity for the assignment of image rights or consent or authorization of such use.

4. The Spanish implementation of the EU Parent/Subsidiary Directive would allow EU shareholders withholding tax exemption on dividends from Spanish entities meeting certain conditions. Luxembourgian income recipients being entities under paragraph 1 of the protocol to the tax treaty with Spain (holding entities) are not allowed this exemption.

5. Spanish internal legislation provides withholding tax exemption on interest obtained by EU lenders not established in Spain meeting certain conditions. Luxembourgian income recipients being entities under paragraph 1 of the protocol to the tax treaty with Spain (holding entities) are not allowed this exemption.

6. The taxable base in cases of service supply, technical assistance or assembly/installation work connected to engineering contracts, carried out by nonresident entities with no permanent establishment does not follow the general rule of gross income. In such cases, total income can be reduced in related staff costs, certain supplies (water, electricity, telephone, etc.) and materials applied to the works, as long as, for staff costs, evidence is provided that they were actually taxed in Spain.

7. (a) Applied if the recipient is a company holding directly at least 25% of the paying company's capital; if not, a 15% rate applies.

    (b) Applied if the recipient is a company holding directly at least 50% of the paying company's capital; if not, a 15% rate applies.

8. Interest paid by certain public institutions is exempt.

9. Interest paid to certain public institutions is exempt.

10. For beneficiaries other than those described in (9), the regime would be of exemption, when both states so agree and the term of the loan is not less than five years.

11. Interest deriving from the acquisition or commercial, industry, or scientific equipment is exempt.

12. Royalty for the use or right to use news uses a 3% rate. Royalties for literary, cinematographic works, radio, TV, and so on, use a 5% rate. Royalties for the use or right to use copyright, industrial property, know how or scientific, commercial, or industrial equipment, uses a 10% rate.

13. Fees for supplies of services ancillary to those on which consideration is royalty are also characterized as such. Fees obtained for partial/total renounce to the use of those rights or assets whose consideration is characterized as royalties are also treated as such.

14. Commercial, industrial, and scientific equipment cannot be regarded as real estate. Otherwise, the fees in question will not be treated as royalties, but as consideration for rentals of real estate.

15. Royalties from copyright on literary, theatre, musical, or artistic work, except for films and TV programs, are exempt inasmuch as the recipient is resident in the other contracting state.

16. The maximum rate is 10% if interest is paid to financial institutions for loans and credits granted for a minimum term of ten years for the purchase of capital equipment.

17. Interest derived from securities issued by a contracting state can only be taxed in such state.

18. Royalties for copyright on films, TV, or radio programs released by an entity of a contracting party are taxed at a 10% rate. Fees for technical assistance and services supplied in connection with commercial, industrial, or scientific information are treated as royalties. A tax sparing clause is available.

19. Applied if the beneficial owner is a company (excluding persons' companies) holding directly or indirectly at least 25% of the paying company's capital; if not, a 15% rate applies.

20. Unless the beneficiary possesses a permanent establishment in Spain for which the loan/intangible was agreed.

21. Royalties from copyright on literary, theatre, musical, or artistic work, except for films and TV programs, are exempt inasmuch as the recipient is resident in the other contracting state subject to tax on such income.

22. Interest deriving from loans for the acquisition of industrial, commercial, or scientific equipment, for the sale of goods between companies or for the construction, installation, assembly works are subject to tax at a 5% rate.

23. Royalties from copyright on literary, theatre, musical, or artistic work, except for films or TV programs, are subject to tax at a 5% rate.

24. No withholding tax applies if the French shareholder owns directly or indirectly at least a 10% on the capital.

25. No withholding tax applies if the French entity receives interest (i) from the other contracting State or any of its territorial entities, (ii) or from a resident in the other State from an underlying commercial or industrial activity, or (iii) in connection with a credit sale of industrial, commercial or scientific equipment, or (iv) for a loan granted by a financial entity.

26. Applied if the recipient is a company holding at least 25% of the paying company's capital or dividend provides from a persons' company; if not, a 15% rate applies.

27. Interest payments to the *Deutsche Bundesbank* or to the *Kreditanstalt für Wiederaufbau* in Germany are exempt from Spanish tax.

28. For beneficiaries other than those described in (9) above the regime would be of exemption, when both states so agree.

29. Royalties for use of industrial, commercial, or scientific equipment are subject to tax at a 10% rate. Technical services and other royalties are levied at the general rate of 20%.

30. Royalties for copyright on literary, theatre, musical, or artistic work are taxed at a 5% rate. Royalties on films or other means of audio or video transmission, for the use or right to use industrial, commercial, or scientific equipment or over scientific works or under agreements between both states are taxed at an 8% rate.

31. Royalties derived from literary, dramatic, musical, or artistic works or from the leasing of industrial, commercial, or scientific equipment are taxed at 5% rate.

32. Royalties from copyright on literary, theatre, musical, or artistic work, except for films or TV programs, are subject to tax at a 4% rate.

33. Applied if the recipient is a company holding directly at least 25% of the paying company's capital during the six months previous to the dividend payment; if not, a 15% rate applies.

34. Interest paid to the other state, to any local entity within it to the Central Bank or any financial agency as agreed between both states is withholding tax-exempt. The same regime applies in connection with loans guaranteed or indirectly financed by any of the above, or with loans connected to financed acquisitions of industrial, commercial, or scientific equipment or of goods between entrepreneurs of both states.

35. Interest derived from a loan guaranteed by state is exempt.

36. The fee for renouncing totally or partially the use or right to use any of the concepts on which consideration qualify as royalty is also treated as such.

37. Interest received by financial and insurance entities is taxed at a 10% rate. Interest from loans granted by the government, central bank, or certain institutions is tax-exempt.

38. Capital gains from the transfer of assets/rights whose consideration for use qualifies as royalty are exempt from withholding tax unless the acquirer of such assets/rights is committed to resell them.

39. Royalties from copyright on literary, artistic, or scientific work, except for films and TV programs, are subject to tax at a 5% rate.

40. If the recipient is a Dutch company holding directly at least 50% of the paying company's capital or if the recipient holds 25% of this capital and the other 25% is held by another Dutch company, tax rate is reduced to 10%. Also,

under these conditions, the rate is limited to 5% if the recipient is not subject to Dutch tax on these dividends.

41. Capital gains from the transfer of assets/rights whose consideration for use qualifies as royalty are exempt from withholding tax unless the acquirer of such assets/rights is committed to resell them.

42. This is applied if the recipient is a company holding directly or indirectly at least 25% of the paying company's capital; if not, a 15% rate applies.

43. This is applied if the recipient is a company holding directly at least 10% of the paying company's capital; if not, a 15% rate applies.

44. Interest paid for bonds, obligations of similar securities generally offered to investors as well as related to the transfer of industrial, commercial, or scientific equipment, is subject to a 10% rate. Interest from bonds, obligations or similar securities issued by the state or local entity, or from loans given or guaranteed by any of both states, central banks or financial entities as agreed between states is exempt.

45. Royalties from films or audio or TV tapes are taxed at a 20% rate.

46. Interest from loans granted or guaranteed by a contracting state are tax exempt.

47. If the recipient has invested more than €100,000 in the company that pays the dividend or is tax exempt in its residence country, dividend is taxed at 10% rate. If both conditions are met, tax rate is reduced to 5%.

48. Interest from loans over seven-year maturity is tax exempt.

49. Applied if the recipient is a company (excluding persons' companies) holding at least 50% of the paying company's capital during the year before the dividend payment; if not, a 15% rate applies.

50. Interest paid to a Swiss bank for a long-term loan not repayable wholly or in part within five years is subject to tax only in Switzerland (exempt in Spain).

51. Interest received by financial and insurance entities is taxed at a 10% rate. Interest from loans granted by the government, central bank or certain institutions is tax-exempt.

52. Royalties from copyright (excluding films) are taxed at a 5% rate, while leasing fees from industrial, commercial, or scientific equipment are levied tax at an 8% withholding rate.

53. Interest from loans over seven-year maturity is taxed at a 5% rate.

54. Interest on long-term loans (five or more years) granted by banks or other financial institutions is exempt.

55. If the beneficial owner is not a company (other than a partnership) which holds directly at least 25% of the capital of the company paying the dividends the dividend is taxed at 10% rate.

56. If the beneficial owner is not a company (other than a partnership) which holds directly at least 25% of the capital of the company paying the the dividend is taxed at 15% rate.

57. This is applied if the beneficial owner is a company holding directly or indirectly at least 20% of the paying company's capital. If not, a 10% rate applies.

58. Interest derived from loans granted by financial and insurance entities, bonds and obligations valued at a stock market, or loans connected to financed acquisitions of machinery and equipment are subject to tax at a 5% rate.

59. Royalties for the use of industrial, commercial, or scientific equipment are subject to tax at a 5% rate.

60. Applied if the beneficial owner is a company (different than a persons' company) holding directly at least 25% of the paying company's capital. If not, a 15% rate applies.

61. Interest deriving from loans granted by public institutions or for the acquisition of industrial, commercial, or scientific equipment between companies (excluding related companies) are tax exempt.

62. A 5% rate applies for sales of industrial, commercial, and scientific equipment, sales of equipment between companies and on credit/interest from loans granted by a finance company.

## Tax administration

*Returns*/The system is one of self-assessment, which the tax authorities may audit. The tax year for corporation tax purposes is coincident with the entity's accounting year. The tax year cannot exceed 12 months, and therefore commencement (ordinarily), termination or change of a tax year-end gives rise to a period of less than one year.

*Payment of tax*/Three payments on account of the current year's tax must be made in the first 20 calendar days of April, October, and December. A large-entity taxpayer must compute these advances as a percentage of the current-year tax profit at March 31, September 30, and November 30 at a rate currently of 25% (some allowances and the tax year's advance payments can be credited against this 25% of tax profit). A small taxpayer has the option of computing these advance payments using the above option or taking the tax paid (increased by the associated payments on account credited) of the last final corporate tax return filed by April 1, October 1, and December 1 (respectively for each payment on account) and applying currently an 18% rate.

The final corporate tax return must be filed within the 25 calendar days following the six-month period after the accounting year-end, that is, for business years coincident with the calendar ones the filing period is July 1 through 25 of the following year.

Permanent establishments must file their income tax return within one month in certain cases, among which include the change of head office or its liquidation.

# Spain

## *CORPORATION TAX CALCULATION*

Calendar year 2003

| | | |
|---|---:|---:|
| Net income before taxes................................................................. | | € 2,000,000 |
| (Including 100,000 in domestic dividends coming from below 5% participation, 400,000 in capital gains from the sale of machinery re-investing the whole proceeds [600,000] in new machinery during the same year) | | |
| Add back: | | |
| Gifts to non-qualifying entities and penalties........................ | 10,000 | |
| Depreciation recorded in excess of tax-deductible amounts ............................................... | 100,000 | |
| Internal employees' pension plan expense not allocated to workers .................................................. | 200,000 | |
| Excess bad debt provision ................................................ | 150,000 | |
| | | 2,460,000 |
| Less: | | |
| Tax losses from prior years (1): | | |
| 1999.......................................................................... | 600,000 | (600,000) |
| Net tax profit................................................................................. | | € 1,860,000 |
| Tax due (standard rate of 35%).............................................. | | €   651,000 |
| Less: | | |
| Tax withheld on dividend income—15%............................. | 15,000 | |
| Tax relief on dividend income—17.5% (2)......................... | 17,500 | |
| Reinvestment tax credit—20% (3) ..................................... | 80,000 | |
| Tax credit on antipollution investments 90,000 originated in 2000—10% (4) .............................. | 9,000 | |
| Net tax payable............................................................................... | | €   529,500 |

Net tax payable expressed as a percentage of net tax profit—28.47%

Net tax payable expressed as a percentage of net accounting profit before tax—26.48%

Notes:

1. The corporation has the right to carry forward and freely offset past tax losses against net taxable income for future tax periods within the following maximum of years. Loss carryback is not contemplated.
2. The investment is one in which the corporation has less than a 5% interest and thus is entitled to relief at only 50% of the rate of corporate tax of the paying corporation, in this case 35%.
3. Since January 1, 2003, capital gains arising upon sale of certain tangible or intangible assets originate a 20% (17% for tax periods beginning before January 1, 2003) tax credit over the capital gain when the proceeds are reinvested in similar assets.
4. This 10% tax credit for antipollution investments has been in force since the 2000 tax year. The amount of the tax credit is limited to 35% of the tax quota; the excess may be carried forward and applied in the ten following financial periods.
5. Exchange rate of the Euro at January 1, 2004: US$1 = €0.793903.

## PwC contact

For additional information on taxation in Sri Lanka, contact:

Hiranthi Ratnayake
PricewaterhouseCoopers
100, Braybrooke Place
Colombo 2
Sri Lanka
Telephone: (94) (11) 2304282
Fax: (94) (11) 2304286
e-mail: hiranthi@pwc.lanka.net
LN: Hiranthi C Ratnayake/TLS/C&L/LK@C&L LK

## Significant developments

- Uniform single value-added tax (VAT) rate of 15% will apply from January 1, 2004, replacing the standard rate of 20% and the concessionary rate of 10%, which hitherto prevailed.
- Economic Service Charge (ESC) at 1%, which is in the nature of a minimum tax, will apply from April 1, 2004 to all business and professional entities who have been in operation for more than two years, other than those whose annual turnover does not exceed Rs 30 million, or whose total assets do not exceed Rs 10 million in value.
- Tax at 15% will be levied on profits from sale of shares held for less than two years by corporate entities (but not offshore funds) and resident individuals who derive net profits in excess of Rs 300,000 in any tax year from such sales.
- The standard corporate tax rate will be 30% for listed companies and 32.5% for other companies. A part of the tax amounting to 2.5% of the taxable income would be credited to a Human Resources Endowment Fund.
- Effective from April 1, 2004, the depreciation rates have been revised to accord with the economic depreciation of the respective capital assets.
- The tax treatment of losses will be amended, effective from April 1, 2004, to allow any business to set off losses, both current and brought forward, against income earned in a tax year only to the extent of 35% of that year's statutory income.

## Taxes on corporate income

Resident companies and public corporations are subject to income tax on their worldwide taxable incomes. From the tax year 2003/2004, the standard rate of tax will be 30% for listed companies, and 32.5% for other companies. Lower rates apply to some specified categories of income and institutions. The corporate income tax rate schedule applicable from tax year 2003/2004 is as follows.

# Sri Lanka

| | Tax Rate |
|---|---|
| Companies for nontraditional exports, agricultural undertakings, promotion of tourism, construction work, and for overseas management activities paid for in foreign currency............................................................. | 15%* |
| Companies with taxable income not exceeding Rs 5 million (other than a unit trust, mutual fund or venture capital company)................. | 20% |
| Specialized housing banks .......................................................................... | 20% |
| Existing venture capital companies or new venture capital companies not qualified for tax exemption...................................................................... | 20% |
| Unit trusts and mutual funds investing in specific areas.................................... | 10% |
| Other unit trusts and mutual funds.................................................................. | 20% |
| All other companies  – quoted public (with 300 shareholders or more) ........... | 30%** |
| – others ...................................................................... | 32.5%** |

(Marginal relief is available for companies with taxable income in the range of Rs 5 million to Rs 5.714 million, approximately.)

* The 15% rate applicable to the construction industry is restricted to resident companies only.

**A part of the tax amounting to 2.5% of the taxable income will be credited to a Human Resources Endowment Fund.

In addition, where dividends are distributed out of profits on which taxable income is computed, income tax is payable at 10% of the gross dividends.

Public corporations are also subject to tax of an additional amount, being the excess (if any) of 25% of the balance of profits left after deduction of the tax payable at 32.5% over the amount of gross dividends distributed out of profits on which taxable income is computed.

Unit trusts and mutual funds are treated like resident companies for income tax purposes. Units of investment are treated like company shares, and returns thereon to investors are treated like company dividends.

Nonresident companies are subject to income tax at 32.5% of their Sri Lanka-source taxable income, and at 10% (from 2003/2004) on their remittances of profits.

## Corporate residence

Where a company has its registered or principal office in Sri Lanka, or where the control and management of its business are exercised in Sri Lanka, the company is treated as resident for tax purposes.

## Other taxes

*Value-added tax*/VAT is in force from August 1, 2002. The VAT in force is a consumption based tax on the destination principle, and applies the tax credit method for deduction from the output tax of taxes paid on inputs.

VAT consists of two rate bands, as follows.

1. Zero rate, which applies to export of goods, services connected with international transportation of goods and passengers, and also any services consumed outside Sri Lanka for which payment is received in foreign currency through a bank.

2. Standard rate of 15%, which applies to all other goods and services, other than exempt and excluded supplies.

   Exemption is available to a limited range of supplies of goods and services.

Presently, the scope of VAT is limited to importation, manufacturing, and service sectors. VAT is also payable, from January 1, 2003, by banks, finance companies, specialized banks and other persons carrying on the business of supplying financial services, on their respective total value addition computed by reference to employee remuneration and the net profit or loss subject to an adjustment for economic depreciation.

***Port and Airport Development Levy***/This tax is charged at 1% on the declared customs value of all imported cargo. For articles imported for the purpose of processing and re-export, a lower rate of 0.50% applies.

***Debits tax***/A debits tax of 0.1% applies to the following.

- Debits to current accounts in a commercial bank.
- Debits to savings accounts in a commercial bank or specialized bank.
- Encashment of certificates of deposit and travelers' checks.

***Turnover tax***/A turnover tax, largely at 1%, is levied on wholesale and retail trade by the provincial councils.

***Stamp duties***/Stamp duties are levied only on transfers of immovable property by provincial councils. Stamp duties on other instruments and documents have been abolished.

***Excise duties***/Excise duties and special excise levies are charged on tobacco, cigarettes, liquor, motor vehicles, and selected petroleum products.

***Local taxes***/Taxes (more usually called rates) are currently assessed annually and collected from the owners of land and premises by the local authorities of the areas in which the properties are located. These authorities also charge and collect annual license fees from certain businesses, as well as "taxes" based on the annual gross takings of certain businesses such as hotels.

## Branch income

Foreign companies are permitted to register branches under local company law for the purpose of functioning merely as liaison offices or, subject to certain conditions, for the purpose of trade.

The Sri Lanka-source income of foreign companies from branches or projects is taxed at the nonresident company rates mentioned above. However, under most double-taxation-avoidance treaties which Sri Lanka has entered into, the income of a turnkey or service project will not be subject to income tax if its duration is less than the period specified in the treaty concerned. Where branch or project income is liable to income tax but the income is not readily ascertainable, the tax authority may prescribe that the income be computed on a fair percentage of the branch or project turnover in Sri Lanka.

## Income determination

Business accounting for income tax purposes should, unless otherwise specified by the tax statute, conform to Sri Lanka Accounting Standards, which have been given statutory force by legislation enacted in 1995.

*Inventory valuation*/Inventories should be measured at the lower of cost or net realizable value.

*Dividends*/Resident company dividends paid on shares held by resident or nonresident companies are not assessable on the recipients if income tax is withheld on such dividends, or the dividends are exempt from income tax, or the dividends are paid out of dividends received.

*Stock dividends*/Stock dividends (or bonus shares, in local parlance) are not taxable in the hands of a shareholder at the time of issue, but where such shares are capitalized out of company profits, and there is a return of this capital to the shareholder within six years from the date of issue, the amount of capital returned to the extent of the paid-up value of the bonus shares is treated by definition as a dividend and is taxable in the hands of the shareholder. However, if the shareholder is a company, this dividend may not be assessable, as explained above.

## Deductions

In ascertaining the total income subject to income tax from the financial accounts filed by a company, deductions from revenue are permitted for outgoings and matching expenses incurred in producing the income, including special deductions for the following.

1. Effective from April 1, 2004, an allowance for depreciation by wear and tear, calculated at 25% of the cost of information technology equipment and software, 20% per annum of the cost of any motor vehicle, lorry, bus, tractor, trailer, or office furniture, at 12.5% per annum of the cost of acquisition of plant, machinery or fixtures, 10% per annum of the cost of acquisitions, intangible assets (other than goodwill) and 6 2/3% per annum of the cost of any qualified building constructed, any industrial or hotel building purchased, bridges, railways, reservoirs, electricity or water distribution lines, and toll roads will be granted.

2. Cost of renewal of any capital asset, if no allowance is deductible for depreciation of that asset.

3. A total of 25% of the consideration paid for a license to use a manufacturing process.

4. Bad and doubtful debts.

5. Interest paid or payable on borrowings for purposes of business.

6. Turnover tax payable at the provincial level.

7. Development expenditure incurred on scientific, industrial or agricultural research.

8. Formation expenses of a company.

9. Termination gratuities paid to employees on cessation of business and annual payments made to an approved fund, held for payment under compulsory legislation of gratuities to employees upon termination of their services.

Deductions not permitted for certain expenses or allowances in the determination of total income are itemized below.

1. Any expenditure of a capital nature or any loss of capital, including book depreciation of capital assets.

2. Sri Lanka income tax payable, or any income tax or other similar tax payable in any country with which Sri Lanka has a double taxation avoidance treaty, other than the excess of the foreign-country tax on doubly taxed income over the maximum amount of the credit allowed in that country for the Sri Lanka income tax on that income.

3. Depreciation allowances or rentals or annual payments or renewals in respect of vehicles used on travel for purposes of business, or capital assets provided for the use of employees at their places of residence, other than motorcycles or bicycles used by nonexecutive staff and motor coaches used to transport employees to and from their places of work.

4. Input VAT, which is creditable against output VAT.

Relief is available as a deduction for contributions in money to an approved charity and contributions in money or kind to the government of Sri Lanka. The deduction for the former is subject to a ceiling of Rs 75,000. In the case of the latter, there is no limit to the deduction in respect of contribution in cash, but a limit of Rs 2 million applies to contributions in kind in any year. Any unrecouped excess of such contributions to government over the statutory income is available for carryforward deduction from the following year's statutory income, and so on. The residue of statutory income, called taxable income, is charged to income tax at the rates mentioned above.

Deductions from the total income from all sources of a company are allowed for any interest paid to a bank or financial institution on loans taken, or for any annuity, ground rent, or royalty paid; or for a business loss incurred in the tax year in determining the residual balance income which would be assessable for income tax. Where such deductions exceed the total income, any unrelieved excess is carried forward for deduction in the succeeding tax year from its total income for that tax year and so on without limitation. Effective from tax year 2004/2005, any business could set off losses, both current and brought, against income earned in any year only to the extent of 35% that year's statutory income. Any balance could be carried forward, but set off is subject to the same 35% limitation.

However, no deduction is allowed for a royalty paid by a person outside Sri Lanka to another person outside Sri Lanka. Further, no deduction from total income is allowed in a tax year for a business loss if at any time in that year more than one-third of the issued share capital of the loss-making company is held by persons who did not hold such share capital at any time in the year in which the loss was incurred. In such circumstances, the loss is deferred for deduction only from profits of the particular business in which the loss was incurred.

## Group taxation

There are no special provisions for taxation of companies in a group. Each company is taxed independently of others in the group.

## Tax incentives

Several tax exemptions and concessions are offered under the tax statute.

1. *Agricultural and industrial projects*—For agriculture, animal husbandry, agro processing, manufacture of machinery, industrial and machine tools, deep sea

fishing, information technology and allied services, electronics, export of nontraditional products including deemed export of goods, export or deemed export of services, with a minimum investment of Rs 10 million for a new company and Rs 50 million for an existing company, for any designated project with a minimum investment of Rs 2.5 million, and for any pioneering project in which the investment is in excess of Rs 250 million, a five year tax holiday is offered, followed by a 10% tax rate for the sixth and seventh year, and from the eighth year onward a 15% rate for agriculture and nontraditional exports and 20% for others.

2. *Infrastructure projects (large scale)*—For development of any airport, seaport, highway, or railway, development of any industrial park, development of any warehouse or store, provision of any sanitation facility or solid waste management system, power generation, transmission or distribution, development of water services, urban housing or town center development, tax exemption on profits and income will be granted in relation to the quantum of investment, as follows.

| Amount of minimum investment Rs million | Exemption period Years |
|---|---|
| 1,000 | 6 |
| 2,500 | 8 |
| 5,000 | 10 |
| 7,500 | 12 |

After the exemption period, a 15% rate will apply.

3. *Infrastructure projects (small scale)*—With an investment of not less than Rs 10 million for generation of power, tourism, recreation, warehousing and cold storage, garbage collection and disposal, construction of houses, or construction of hospitals, a five year tax holiday will be granted, followed by a 10% tax rate for the sixth and seventh year, and a 20% rate from the eighth year onward.

4. *Expansion of industrial undertakings for export of nontraditional products*— A company which has an undertaking for the manufacture and export of nontraditional goods and undertake the expansion of such goods by making an investment of not less than Rs 10 million prior to January 1, 2005 will be entitled to a two year tax holiday.

5. *Expansion of industrial undertakings for traditional exports and nonexportable goods*—Any company which undertakes the expansion of an undertaking for manufacture of goods (other than nontraditional goods for export) by making as investment of not less than Rs 10 million prior to January 1, 2005 will be entitled to a two year tax holiday on the incremental profits. The incremental profits mean the excess of the trade profits of that undertaking for the given tax year over the average annual profits of that undertaking of the immediately preceding three tax years.

6. *Companies engaged in research and development*—For such companies, a five year tax holiday, and 15% tax rate from sixth year is offered.

7. *New venture capital companies*—For such companies, a five year tax holiday from commencement of business is offered.

8. *Rehabilitation of nonperforming or under-performing industries*—For such companies, a three year tax holiday, and 15% tax rate from the fourth year depending on the nature of activity is offered.

9. Exemption from income tax is granted on the profits and income earned in foreign currency, remitted to Sri Lanka net of expenses considered reasonable by the tax authority, by a resident company in respect of any offshore business.

10. New or existing companies that export nontraditional goods are entitled to be taxed on the profits from these exports or services at a concessionary rate of 15%.

11. Corporate profits from agriculture, fisheries, livestock, construction, tourism, and provision of overseas management services are taxed at 15%. A company that produces or manufactures nontraditional goods and supplies these to a company for export or for use in the production or manufacture of goods for export by the latter company is entitled to be taxed on the profits from such supplies at a concessionary rate of 15%, provided the exporting company to which the goods are supplied is entitled to be taxed as mentioned above and the tax authority is satisfied that the goods supplied have been exported.

## Withholding taxes

Resident companies are entitled to withhold income tax at 10% of gross dividends payable to shareholders out of taxable profits

Any person in Sri Lanka who pays or credits to a person or partnership out of Sri Lanka any sum due as interest, rent, ground rent, royalty, or annuity is required to withhold income tax at 20% of the sum, but the requirement to withhold income tax does not apply to interest not sourced in Sri Lanka, or to interest on any loan or advance made by a banker or to interest paid on foreign currency held in an account with a foreign currency banking unit.

In particular instances, the tax authority may prescribe that income tax be withheld at a rate other than 20%, or the rate may be reduced for sums falling due as interest or royalties in respect of persons resident in countries with which Sri Lanka has double taxation treaties in force. Sri Lanka-source income from loan interest or royalties accruing to a nonresident company is taxed at a flat 15%, in the absence of a lower rate in the tax treaty with the home country of the nonresident.

Every bank and financial institution is required to withhold income tax at 10% on the amount of any interest paid on any sum of money deposited with it by any person in excess of Rs 9,000 per month, or Rs 108,000 per annum, from all deposits made by such person in any individual bank or financial institution. Withholding tax at 10% also applies to interest on Treasury bills and bonds and also on corporate debt securities.

Every person or partnership that pays a fee to another person or partnership in consideration for services rendered by the latter in the course of any business, profession, vocation or activity of an independent character is required to withhold income tax at 5% of such fee and furnish a certificate to the payee. The withholding requirement is extended to any commission, brokerage fee or other income of a like nature.

# Sri Lanka

The withholding tax rates in the double tax treaties entered into by Sri Lanka are as follows:

| Treaty countries | Dividends | Interest | Royalties |
|---|---|---|---|
| | % | % | % |
| Australia | 15 | 10 | 10 |
| Bangladesh | 15 | 15 | 15 |
| Belgium | 15 | 10 | 10 |
| Canada | 15 | 15 | 10 |
| Denmark | 15 | 10 | 10 |
| Finland | 15 | 10 | 10 |
| France | 15 | 10 | 10, 0 (1) |
| Germany | 15 | 10 | 10 |
| India | 15 | 10 | 10 |
| Indonesia | 15 | 15 | 15 |
| Iran | 10 | 10 | 8 |
| Italy | 15 | 10 | 10 |
| Japan | 15 | (2) | 0 (1, 3) |
| Korea, Rep. of | 15, 10 | 10 | 10 |
| Malaysia | 15 | 10 | 10 |
| Mauritius | 15, 10 | 15, 10 | 10 |
| Nepal | 15 | 10, 15 | 15 |
| Netherlands | 15, 10 | 15, 10 | 10 |
| Norway | 15 | 10 | 10, 0 (1) |
| Oman (4) | — | — | — |
| Pakistan | 15 | 10 | 20 |
| Poland | 15 | 10 | 10 |
| Romania | 12.5 | 10 | 10 |
| Russia | 10, 15 | 10 | 10 |
| Saudi Arabia | — | — | — |
| Singapore | 15 | 10 | 15 |
| Sweden | 15 | 10 | 10 |
| Switzerland | 15, 10 | 10 | 10 |
| Thailand | 15 | 10 | 15 |
| United Arab Emirates (4) | — | — | — |
| United Kingdom | 15 | 10 | 10 |

The numbers in parentheses refer to the following numbered Notes.

Notes:

1. A rate of 0% for copyright royalties.
2. A rate of 0% in certain circumstances.
3. A rate of 50% of normal tax.
4. These treaties are limited to the avoidance of double taxation of income from international transport by air.

The withholding tax rate on dividends, under the domestic tax statute, is 10%. Therefore, the statute rate of 10%, being lower, will prevail over the treaty rate of 15% in case of dividends distributed to nonresident shareholders.

Tax treaties with the following countries, which are in different stages of negotiation or finalization, await entry into force: Austria, Bulgaria, China, Egypt, Hong Kong, Jordan, Kuwait, New Zealand, Philippines, Qatar, the United States, and Vietnam.

## Tax administration

A tax year is any period of 12 consecutive months reckoned from April 1 in any calendar year to March 31 of the following year.

Sri Lanka has a pay-and-file system under which the income tax payable for each tax year is required to be paid in four installments on or before August 15, November 15, and February 15 of the tax year and the May 15 immediately following the end of the tax year. If each installment is not less than one-quarter of the income tax payable for the tax year immediately preceding, the balance of any income tax payable may be paid on or before September 30 immediately following the end of the tax year without incurring penalties.

The income tax of 10% on dividends payable or withheld by a resident company (see "Taxes on corporate income" and "Withholding taxes" above) must be paid within 30 days of the distribution of such dividends.

A company is required to file its income tax return in a prescribed format, with the financial statements and supporting schedules, on or before November 30 immediately following the end of the tax year.

## *CORPORATION TAX CALCULATION*

Tax year 2004/2005

|  | Resident company | Nonresident company |
| --- | --- | --- |
|  | **Rs** | **Rs** |
| Adjusted taxable profits | 100.00 | 100.00 |
| Income tax payable (32.5%) | (32.5) | (32.5) |
| Profits available for dividends/remittance | 67.50 | 67.50 |
| Dividend tax at 10% | 6.75 | Nil |
| Income tax on remittances— |  |  |
| 10% of remittance (assumed full after-tax profits) | N/A | (6.75) |
| Net returns to shareholders | 60.75 | 60.75 |

Notes:

1. It is assumed that profits are remitted in the tax year.
2. Average exchange rate (buying/selling) of the rupee at March 19, 2004: US$1 = Rs 97.9001.

# Swaziland

## PwC contact

For additional information on taxation in Swaziland, contact:

Theo Mason
PricewaterhouseCoopers
Smuts Street
P.O. Box 569 or 2513
Mbabane, Swaziland
Telephone: (268) 404-3143, 404-0658, 404-2861
Fax: (268) 404-5015
e-mail: theo.mason@sz.pwc.com

## Significant developments

The Income Tax (Amendment) Act 2000 has received royal assent and was published in the Swaziland Government Gazette on November 17, 2000.

The Act is effective July 1, 2001.

## Taxes on corporate income

Company income tax from July 1, 2001 will be assessed at a uniform rate of 30%.

## Corporate residence

Income tax is chargeable on all income derived from a source within or deemed to be within the country, irrespective of whether the recipient of the income is actually resident in Swaziland.

## Other taxes

There are no capital gains taxes or estate taxes.

Sales tax is assessed at the rate of 14%.

From July 1, 2001, there is a 14% sales tax (25% in respect of liquor and cigarettes) on goods imported into Swaziland and on the first sale of goods manufactured for sale in Swaziland in addition to customs and excise duties. Also, a 14% tax is applicable to most professional services.

## Branch income

Income tax on registered branch profits is calculated as for a resident company. In practice, branches are rare, as most foreign companies incorporate local subsidiary companies.

## Income determination

*Inventory valuation*/Inventory valuation is not specific but is effectively at the lower of cost (FIFO or average cost) and net realizable value.

*Capital gains*/Capital gains are not subject to income tax, provided it can be demonstrated that they are of a capital and not an income nature, that is, recurring transactions.

*Intercompany dividends*/Intercompany dividends are not subject to income tax. (But see "Withholding taxes" below.)

*Foreign income*/Foreign income is not subject to income tax unless it is deemed to be from a Swaziland source.

*Stock dividends*/Stock dividends are paid out of taxed profits. They are not subject to income tax when received by a company but are subject to taxation in the hands of individual taxpayers

## Deductions

*Depreciation*/Depreciation (wear-and-tear) allowances calculated by the net-reducing-balance method are available as follows.

| Asset | Rate % |
|---|---|
| Aircraft | 25 |
| Casino equipment | 15 |
| Construction equipment | 25 |
| Computer hardware | 33.33 |
| Computer software | 33.33 |
| Furniture and fittings | 10 |
| Hotel soft furnishings, including carpets | 10 |
| Legal and professional libraries | 5 |
| Lifts and elevators | 25 |
| Motor vehicles: | |
|     Cars | 20 |
|     Light delivery vehicles | 25 |
|     Lorries | 33.33 |
|     Buses | 33.3 |
| Office equipment | 10 |
| Plant and machinery | 10 |
| Sound and projection equipment | 20 |
| Television sets | 20 |
| Tractors | 25 |
| Trailers | 20 |
| Video recorders | 33.33 |
| Videotapes | 25 |

In the first year of an addition, the wear-and-tear allowance is calculated on a monthly basis. In respect of leased assets the lessors' claim for wear-and-tear allowance is usually spread over the lease period.

An initial allowance of 50% is granted in respect of plant and machinery used in a manufacturing process, including hotel equipment. A building initial allowance of 50% is granted in respect of industrial buildings used for manufacturing purposes and hotels, together with a 4% annual allowance.

An initial allowance of 50% is granted in respect of infrastructural machinery and plant (including transmission equipment) which was brought into use by the taxpayer for the first time. This allowance is known as "infrastructural initial allowance" and applies to new installations after July 1, 2001.

*Net operating losses*/Losses can only be carried forward.

# Swaziland

**Payments to foreign affiliates**/Deductions may be claimed for payments of management service fees, interest and royalties to foreign affiliates, provided they are made under a written agreement, are reasonable and receive exchange control approval in respect of transfers outside the rand monetary area. This approval is routinely given without any significant delay for bona fide transactions.

## Group taxation

There is no specific group taxation legislation. All companies are assessed on individual assessable profits and losses.

## Tax incentives

**Tax holidays**/A new manufacturing business or a new business engaged predominantly in exporting goods may, subject to the approval of the Minister for Finance, be granted a five-year period of exemption from normal taxation, provided cumulative taxable income in this period less cumulative remuneration paid to Swaziland citizens is less than 150% of the value of the fixed assets of the business at the end of each year of assessment.

**Development enterprises**/The Minister for Finance, with the prior consent of the Cabinet, can nominate a business as a development enterprise, granting additional tax concessions, for example, a lower rate of company income tax.

**Training expenditures**/In addition to normal deductible training expenses, a further deduction of 100% of expenses for training Swaziland citizens may be deducted under an approved training scheme.

## Withholding taxes

Nonresident taxes are levied as follows.

**Management and administration fees**/Management fees, administration fees, and so on, are taxed at the rate of 15% by way of a withholding tax.

**Dividends**/Tax is payable at the rate of 15% (12.5% in respect of companies registered in Botswana, Lesotho, and South Africa). Nonresident shareholders' tax is payable within 30 days of the date on which the dividend is payable.

**Interest**/Tax is payable at the rate of 10% withholding tax.

**Entertainers and sportsmen**/Tax is payable at the rate of 15%. This tax relates only to public entertainers and sportsmen not ordinarily resident in Swaziland. The person making the payment is required to deduct the tax and pay it within 15 days.

**Contractors or professionals**/Tax is payable at the rate of 15%. The Commissioner of Taxes must be notified of an agreement relating to construction operations or professional services under which payments are made to nonresident persons within 30 days of the agreement's being entered into. It is required that the tax be paid within 15 days from the date of payment.

## Tax administration

**Returns**/The tax year runs from July 1 to June 30. Companies are required theoretically to have a June 30 year-end, unless another year-end is approved by the Commissioner of Taxes. Such approval is routinely given. Income tax returns should be submitted within 30 days of June 30, unless an extension of time for submission is granted, which also is routinely given.

**Payment of tax**/Notice of the date of payment is usually given on the tax assessment.

**Provisional tax**/In respect of companies, provisional tax is payable in two installments, one within six months of the company's financial year, and the other no later than the last day of the company's financial year.

The estimate of taxable income for provisional tax purposes, should not be less than the taxable income assessed for the latest preceding year of assessment in respect of which an assessment has been issued not less than 21 days before the date the estimate is made, unless the taxpayer can satisfy the Commissioner of Taxes that the taxable income for the current year will be less than the taxable income for that preceding year.

A provisional taxpayer becomes liable to a penalty if the estimate of taxable income for the purposes of the second payment of provisional tax is found to be less than 90% of the taxable income as finally determined and is also less than the taxable income as assessed for the immediately preceding tax year.

# Swaziland

## *CORPORATION TAX CALCULATION*

Tax year ending June 30, 2003 (based on annual financial statements for year to December 31, 2003)

| | | | |
|---|---|---|---|
| Net income per accounts before taxation | | E | 1,000,000 |
| Add nondeductible items: | | | |
| Depreciation | 50,000 | | |
| Charitable donations | 5,000 | | |
| General bad debt provision | 45,000 | | 100,000 |
| Deduct: | | | |
| Capital profits included in income | 100,000 | | |
| Initial allowances | 60,000 | | |
| Wear-and-tear allowances | 40,000 | | 200,000 |
| Taxable income | | E | 900,000 |
| | | | |
| Tax payable | | | |
| Income tax payable at 33% | | E | 297,000 |
| *Less*—Provisional tax payments | | | |
| 1st installment | 133,650 | | |
| 2nd installment | 133,650 | | (267,300) |
| Balance of tax payable | | E | 29,700 |

Note:

Exchange rate of the Emalangeni at March 25, 2004: US$1 = E6.54329.

Note the following included in the Income Tax Amendment Act 2000.

Management charges paid by any person, ordinarily resident or carrying on business in Swaziland will be deemed to be income from a Swaziland source.

Royalties and management fees payable to nonresidents will be subject to a withholding tax of 15% such tax being a final tax.

Income from the use or right of use in Swaziland of video or audio material transmitted by satellite, cable, optic fiber, and so on, for use in television or broadcasting shall be deemed to have accrued from a source in Swaziland, and subject to taxation accordingly. A similar provision has also been introduced in respect of plant, machinery, equipment, vehicles, and other moveable property.

The introduction of an "infrastructural initial allowance" amounting to 50% of the cost incurred by the taxpayer on infrastructural machinery, plant and transmission equipment used in the provision of infrastructural services on or after July 1, 2000. The taxpayer will be entitled to deduct the aforementioned 50% in determining his taxable income.

Building societies, mutual loan associations, and parastatal organizations will no longer be exempt from normal tax.

## PwC contact

For additional information on taxation in Sweden, contact:

Peter Nortoft
Öhrlings PricewaterhouseCoopers
(visiting address: Kungsgatan 18)
SE–113 97 Stockholm, Sweden
Telephone: (46) (8) 555 330 00
Fax: (46) (8) 555 330 02
e-mail: peter.nortoft@se.pwc.com

## Significant developments

There have been significant developments with regard to Swedish corporate taxation during 2003 implying that new legislation has been enforced with regard to capital gains exemption as from July 1, 2003 and controlled foreign corporations (CFC) legislation as from January 1, 2004.

## Taxes on corporate income

*State (national) income tax*/Taxable income is subject to tax at a rate of 28%.

## Corporate residence

A company is considered to be resident if it is incorporated in Sweden.

## Other taxes

*Value-added tax*/VAT is 25% on the price charged (exclusive of VAT) and is chargeable on the sale of most goods and services. A reduced rate applies to a few goods and services.

*Stamp tax*/Stamp tax is payable on a transfer of real estate. Stamp tax on an intra-group transfer of real estate may be deferred as long as the real estate remains within the group

*Miscellaneous taxes*/There is a payroll tax (social security charges) of about 33% of cash and benefits-in-kind. Payroll tax is deductible for corporation tax purposes.

*Real estate tax*/Real estate tax is paid by the owner. The tax is 1% of a specific tax value and is deductible. For properties taxed as industrial estates, the tax is 0.5% of the tax value and is also deductible; for blocks of flats it is 0.5% and for rental apartments it is 1%.

## Branch income

Branch income (permanent establishment income) is taxed at corporate tax rates. No withholding tax is levied on the repatriation of taxed profits. The term "permanent establishment" is defined as a fixed place of business through which the business is carried on from a specific establishment, such as a place of management, branch, office, factory, or workshop. Places where entrepreneurial work is carried on are also regarded as permanent establishments.

# Sweden

## Income determination

*Inventory valuation*/Inventories are valued at acquisition cost or market value, whichever is lower. As an alternative, inventories may be valued at 97% of the total acquisition cost, which is determined on a FIFO basis. LIFO is not permitted.

Inventories should normally be stated at the same amount for tax and accounting purposes.

*Capital gains*/Capital gains tax exemption applies as from July 1, 2003 for Swedish corporate entities for gains related to the disposal of shares held for business reasons. The same applies to foreign companies resident in the European Economic Area (EEA) and conducting business from a permanent establishment (PE) in Sweden when the shares are allocated to the PE. Companies resident outside the EEA may by application of the nondiscrimination clause in a tax treaty also benefit from the participation exemption.

An exemption from the capital gains tax exemption applies for the sale of shares in a "shell "company, that is, a company where the market value of cash, shares and other marketable instruments (other than shares held for business reasons) and similar assets exceeds 50% of the consideration paid for the shares. The sale of a shell company results in a taxation of the seller of the gross consideration. Provided certain formalities are fulfilled it is, however, possible to avoid such gross taxation.

A consequence of the participation exemption is that capital losses on shares held for business reasons no longer will be deductible.

Shares in Swedish as well as in foreign companies can qualify as shares held for business reasons. Unquoted shares will always be considered as held for business reasons. Quoted shares are considered held for business reasons provided that the company has a holding corresponding to at least 10% of the voting rights, or the shares are held in the course of the business. An additional condition regarding quoted shares is that the shares must be held for a period of at least one year.

Capital losses on portfolio holdings of shares, share options, convertible debentures, and similar financial instruments are allowed only as an offset to capital gains on the same group of financial instruments. Certain special rules apply to computation of capital gains and losses on real estate.

*Intercompany dividends*/Participation exemption will also apply for dividends received on shares held for business reasons (see above). For dividend distributions purposes the requirement of a minimum holding period for a holding of quoted shares could be fulfilled retroactively.

*Foreign income*/Companies resident in Sweden are taxed on their worldwide income. Nonresident companies are taxed on income that is deemed to have its source within Sweden.

A Swedish corporation is taxed on foreign branch income. Double taxation is normally avoided by means of foreign tax credits.

Dividends from foreign subsidiaries are generally exempt from taxation according to the domestic provisions (tax exemption for dividends on shares held for business reasons).

A 13% tax credit, apart from the withholding tax credit, applies to dividends from foreign subsidiaries that are not tax exempt.

## Deductions

*Depreciation and depletion*/The following allowances are available.

1. Depreciation on fixed assets:
   a. Land improvements—5% per annum on acquisition cost;
   b. Buildings—2% to 5% per annum, depending on type and usage. The maximum allowance is 100%.
2. Machinery, equipment, motor vehicles, patents, leaseholds, and goodwill:
   Book depreciation—The depreciation charged in the books and accounts, as long as the total net value of the assets is not less than the following amounts:
   a. 70% of net value in previous accounts plus additions less proceeds of sales; or
   b. Cost less 20% per annum.
3. Direct charge—The cost of assets having an expected life of not more than three years and the cost of assets not exceeding SEK 5,000 (for large companies, SEK 20,000) may be charged directly against income.
4. Mines, quarries—100% depletion of cost over expected exploitation period.

*Net operating losses*/Losses may be carried forward without limitation, but they may not be carried back. Restrictions may apply after a change of ownership has occurred (more than 50% of the voting rights).

*Payments to foreign affiliates*/Transactions with an affiliate not liable to tax in Sweden must be at arm's length.

*Taxes*/Other than the national income tax on corporate profits, taxes are either directly deductible or added to the cost base for depreciation. Recoverable VAT is not treated as an expense or cost.

## Group taxation

Income taxes are assessed on companies individually, not on consolidated results. To enable the leveling of profits within a Swedish group, so-called group contributions can under qualifying conditions be exchanged between related companies.

## Tax incentives

The following incentives are available.

1. Accelerated depreciation of machinery and equipment—30% of declining balance.
2. Accruals reserves—Accruals reserves allow for a tax deductible appropriation for corporations of 25% of the taxable profit before appropriation to a reserve. Each year's appropriation forms a separate reserve that must be reversed to income no later than the sixth year following the appropriation.

## Withholding taxes

There are no Swedish taxes on interest and service fees paid to nonresident corporations or individuals. Such payments to resident corporations and individuals are taxed as ordinary income. Only resident banks and similar entities are required to withhold tax on interest payments to resident individuals, that is, 30% preliminary standard tax.

# Sweden

Withholding taxes on cash dividends, royalties, and certain rentals vary according to domestic law and tax treaties, as shown below.

| Recipient | Cash dividends (1, 2) | Royalties, certain rentals (3) |
|---|---|---|
| | % | % |
| Resident corporations | Nil (4) | Nil (5) |
| Resident individuals | 30 (4) | Nil (5) |
| Nonresident corporations and individuals: | | |
| Nontreaty: | 30 | Nil (5) |
| Treaty: | (6) | |
| Albania | 15/5 | 5 |
| Argentina | 15/10 (7) | 3/5/10/15 (7) |
| Australia | 15 | 10 |
| Austria | 10/Nil (6) | 10/Nil (8) |
| Bangladesh | 15/10 | 10 |
| Barbados | 15/5 | 5/Nil (9) |
| Belarus | 10/5/Nil | 10/5/3 (10) |
| Belgium | 15/Nil (6) | Nil |
| Bolivia | 15/Nil | 15 |
| Botswana | 15 | 15 |
| Brazil | 25 | 25 |
| Bulgaria | 10 | 5 |
| Canada | 15/5 | 10/Nil (11) |
| China, P.R (12) | 10/5 | 10 |
| Cyprus | 15/5 | Nil |
| Czech Republic (13) | 10/Nil | 5/Nil (9) |
| Denmark (14, 15) | 15/Nil (6, 15) | Nil (15) |
| Egypt | 20/5 | 14 |
| Estonia | 15/5 | 10/5 (16) |
| Faroe Islands (14, 15) | 15/Nil (15) | Nil (15) |
| Finland (14, 15) | 15/Nil (6) | Nil |
| France | 15/Nil (6) | Nil |
| Gambia | 15/5/0 | 12.5/5 (17) |
| Germany | 15/Nil (6) | Nil |
| Greece | Nil (6) | 5 |
| Hungary | 15/5 | Nil |
| Iceland (14, 15) | 15/Nil (15) | Nil (15) |
| India | 10 | 10/Nil |
| Indonesia | 15/10 | 15/10 (18) |
| Ireland, Rep. of | 15/5 (6) | Nil |
| Israel | 15/5 | Nil |
| Italy | 15/10 (6) | 5 |
| Jamaica | 22.5/10 | 10 |
| Japan | 15/5/0 | 10 |
| Kazakhstan | 15/5 | 10 |
| Kenya | 25/15 | 20 |
| Korea, Rep. of | 15/10 | 15/10 (19) |
| Latvia | 15/5 | 10/5 (16) |
| Lithuania | 15/5 | 10/5 (16) |
| Luxembourg | 15/Nil (6) | Nil |

| Recipient | Cash dividends (1, 2) | Royalties, certain rentals (3) |
|---|---|---|
| | % | % |
| Macedonia | 15/Nil | Nil |
| Malaysia | Nil | Nil |
| Malta | 15/Nil | Nil |
| Mauritius | 15/5 | 15 |
| Mexico | 15/5 | 10 |
| Morocco | Nil | Nil |
| Namibia | 15/5/Nil | 15/5 (20) |
| Netherlands | 15/Nil (6) | Nil |
| New Zealand | 15 | 10 |
| Norway (14, 15) | 15/Nil (15) | Nil (15) |
| Pakistan | 30/15 | 10 |
| Peru | 30 | 20 |
| Philippines | 25/15 | 25/15 (21) |
| Poland | 15/5 | 10 |
| Portugal | 10/0 | 10 |
| Romania | 10 | 10 |
| Russia | 15/5/Nil | Nil |
| Singapore | 15/10 | Nil |
| Slovak Republic (13) | 10/Nil | 5/Nil (9) |
| South Africa | 15/7.5/Nil | Nil |
| Spain | 15/10 (6) | 10 |
| Sri Lanka | 15 | 10 |
| Switzerland | 15/Nil | Nil |
| Tanzania | 25/15 | 20 |
| Thailand | 30/20/15 | 15 |
| Trinidad and Tobago | 20/10 | 20/Nil (22) |
| Tunisia | 20/15 | 15/5 (23) |
| Turkey | 20/15 | 10 |
| Ukraine | 10/5/Nil | 10/Nil |
| United Kingdom | 5/Nil (6) | Nil |
| United States | 15/5 | Nil |
| Venezuela | 10/5 | 10/7 (24) |
| Vietnam | 15/10/5 | 15/5 (25) |
| Yugoslavia (former) (26) | 15/5 | Nil |
| Zambia | 15/5 | 10 |
| Zimbabwe | 20/15 | 10 |

Notes:

1. According to domestic law there is no coupon (withholding) tax on dividends to a foreign company on shares held for business purposes, provided that the foreign company is similar to a Swedish limited liability company (and some other legal entites). For the definition of shares held for business purposes, see above.

2. The reduced rate shown after a stroke (/) refers to payments to corporations having requisite control. Where appropriate, the particular treaty should be consulted to see whether the reduced rate is applicable. Note also the domestic provision stating a 0% withholding tax for dividends distributed on

shares held for buisness reasons by a foreign entity similar to a Swedish limlited liability company and some other legal entities.

3. Swedish source royalties are treated as a special form of income from a PE, subject to treaty reduction or waiver. According to a recent proposal from the government, royalties paid from Sweden to a company within the EC should not be taxed in Sweden if one of the companies holds at least 25% (capital) of the other, or where there are two companies concerned, at least 25% are held by another company within the EC. Indirect participation does not benefit from the proposed legislation. Both the payer and the recipient must be legal entities under the EC-directive.

4. Payments to resident corporations and individuals are taxed as ordinary income. Only resident banks and similar entities are required to withhold tax on payments of cash dividends to resident individuals.

5. Royalties and certain rentals paid by Swedish licensees are treated as earned income taxable in Sweden and do not incur withholding taxes (see also Note 3 above).

6. Note also the domestic provision stating a 0% withholding tax on dividends distributed on shares held for business reasons to qualified entities (see Note 1).

7. Dividends—10% of the gross amount if the company receiving the dividends owns at least 25% of the foreign company's capital. Interest is exempt in certain cases.
   Royalties—Of the gross amount paid for the use of, or the right to use:
   a. News—3%;
   b. Copyright of literary, dramatic, musical, or other artistic work—5%;
   c. Any patent, trademark, design or model, plan, or secret formula or process; industrial or scientific equipment or information concerning industrial, commercial, or scientific experience; payments for the rendering of technical assistance—10%;
   d. All other cases—15%.

8. Royalties are normally taxable only in the recipient's home country. However, where the royalty is paid by a Swedish legal entity that is more than 50% owned by one Austrian recipient, entity or individual, the tax in Sweden is a maximum of 10%.

9. Literary, artistic, or scientific royalties—Nil; other royalties—5%.

10. Royalties for use of industrial, commercial, or scientific equipment—5%; with respect to patents, secret formulas or processes, or for information concerning industrial, commercial, or scientific experience—3%; other royalties—10%.

11. Royalties for use of copyright and literary, dramatic, musical, and artistic royalties—nil. Other royalties—10%. (Treaty should be consulted.)

12. The double taxation treaty does not include Hong Kong.

13. The same treaty is applicable to the Czech Republic and the Slovak Republic.

14. Signatory to the Nordic multilateral tax treaty.

15. Dividends are exempt from tax if the receiver of the dividends is a company directly owning at least 10% of the capital of the company paying out the dividends. Certain rentals are subject to tax if there is a permanent establishment in a state other than the home state and the claim is connected with the business carried on from the permanent establishment. Concerning

Iceland, dividends are normally exempt from tax for companies, but the tax rate is 15% if the dividends have been deducted from the income of the distributing company.

16. Royalties for the use of industrial, commercial, or scientific equipment—5%; other royalties—10%.

17. Royalties with respect to patents, secret formulas or processes or for information concerning industrial, commercial, or scientific experience—5%; other royalties—12.5%.

18. Royalties for the use of industrial, commercial, or scientific equipment or for information concerning industrial, commercial, or scientific experience—10%; other royalties—15%. (Treaty should be consulted.)

19. Literary, artistic, or scientific royalties, including films—15%; other royalties—10%. (Treaty should be consulted.)

20. Royalties with respect to patents, secret formulas or processes or for information concerning industrial or scientific experience—5%; other royalties—15%.

21. Literary, artistic, scientific, film, or other specially preferred royalties—15%; other royalties—25%. (Treaty should be consulted.)

22. Commercial royalties, including films—20%; copyright, literary, dramatic, musical, or artistic royalties—Nil.

23. Commercial royalties, including films—15%; literary, dramatic, musical, or artistic royalties—5%.

24. Literary, artistic, scientific, or film royalties—10%; other royalties—7%.

25. Royalties with respect to patents, designs or models, secret formulas or processes or for information concerning industrial or scientific experience or for the use of industrial, commercial, or scientific equipment involving a transfer of know-how—5%; other royalties—15%.

26. On Sweden's part the treaty is applicable to all republics and autonomous provinces of the former Yugoslavia with the exception of Macedonia, with which Sweden has concluded a bilateral treaty. However, it is not clear whether these states consider it applicable.

## Tax administration

**Returns**/The tax year coincides with the calendar year. Normally, the basis for tax assessment is the financial year. The year-end for a company may be fixed at any of the following dates—April 30, June 30, August 31, or December 31. Another year-end can be used by permission from the Swedish Tax Agency. Swedish subsidiaries of foreign parents are generally permitted to adopt the same year-end as the parent company, provided that the fiscal year corresponds to 12 whole months.

Every limited company or registered branch must file an annual tax return, which should be filed by May 2 each year. The annual assessments are made by the local tax offices in the calendar year following the income year.

**Payment of tax**/Income taxes are collected during the year in which the income is earned, under a preliminary tax system. A company's preliminary tax liability is determined by a preliminary tax assessment based either on the latest available final tax assessment or on a preliminary tax return filed by the company. The preliminary taxes are payable in equal installments every month, starting in

# Sweden

February of the tax year. Any balance due by the taxpayer is payable in 90 days after the assessment is made. Any balance due to the taxpayer is normally refunded in December of the assessment year.

## *CORPORATION TAX CALCULATION*

Calendar year 2003

| | | |
|---|---:|---:|
| Income before taxes | | SEK 1,000,000 |
| Less—Income tax provision | | 185,010 |
| Net income reported in statutory accounts | | 814,990 |
| Add: | | |
| Income taxes charged | 185,010 | |
| Depreciation charged | 250,000 | |
| Provision for doubtful accounts | 50,000 | |
| Gifts and donations | 2,000 | |
| Membership fees | 1,000 | |
| Entertainment expenses disallowed | 13,000 | |
| | | 501,010 |
| | | 1,316,000 |
| Deduct: | | |
| Dividends from subsidiaries | 150,000 | |
| Depreciation allowed: | | |
| Buildings | 40,000 | |
| Other fixed assets | 200,000 | |
| Losses on account of bad and doubtful accounts | 45,000 | 435,000 |
| | | 881,000 |
| Appropriation to an accruals reserve (25%) | | 220,250 |
| Taxable income | | SEK 660,750 |
| Income tax payable—660,750 at 28% | | SEK 185,010 |

Note:

Exchange rate of the krona at January 1, 2004: US$1 = SEK 7.18418.

## PwC contact

For additional information on taxation in Switzerland, contact:

Andrin Waldburger
PricewaterhouseCoopers AG
Stampfenbachstrasse 73
8035 Zurich, Switzerland
Telephone: (41) (1) 630 11 11
Fax: (41) (1) 630 44 15
LN address: Andrin Waldburger@PwC@EMEA-CH
e-mail: andrin.waldburger@ch.pwc.com

## Significant developments

The new federal act on mergers, demergers, transformation of legal entities under private law as well as asset transfer (Merger Act) is effective from July 1, 2004.

The new provisions will supersede the Swiss Contract/Company Law provisions pertaining to mergers and acquisitions and should close key loopholes in the current law, which in the past have been filled based on a practical approach by the relevant authorities. The Merger Act should provide for provisions that cover all commercial enterprises and cooperatives as well as associations and foundations.

Even though the Swiss tax legislation has already introduced specific rules for tax neutral company reorganizations in previous years, the Merger Act has an effect on the current tax legislation by explicitly including further possibilities of tax neutral reorganizations and confirming the current possibilities in a more consistent terminology.

## Taxes on corporate income

The Swiss Federation levies direct federal income tax at a flat rate of 8.5% on profits after tax. In addition, each canton has its own tax law and levies cantonal and communal income taxes at different rates. Therefore, the tax burden of income (and capital) varies from canton to canton. Cantonal and communal taxes are imposed at progressive rates, based on the ratio of profit to capital and reserves or at flat rates. As a general rule, the approximate range of the maximum effective income tax rate on profit for federal, cantonal, and communal taxes is between 17% and 30%, depending on the company's place of residence.

## Corporate residence

A company is considered resident in Switzerland if its place of incorporation is in Switzerland. Residency is also linked to the place of effective management, which may be the center from which day-to-day activities are directed or the place where decisions of a managerial nature are taken.

## Other taxes

*Capital tax*/Only cantons levy a capital tax, which is based on the corporation's capital and reserves. The tax rates vary from 0.0675% to 0.76%.

*Value-added tax*/Proceeds of sales and services effected in Switzerland are subject to VAT at the standard rate of 7.6%, 2.4% on goods for basic needs, and 3.6% on services in connection with the provision of accommodation. The registered taxpayer is generally entitled to offset against the VAT payable the amount of such tax charged by suppliers or paid on imports.

## Branch income

The same principles apply as for corporations, provided transactions with the head office or other branches are at arm's length. There is no withholding tax on profit transfers to the head office.

## Income determination

*Inventory valuation*/Inventories may not be valued in excess of the lower of cost or market for tax and financial accounting purposes. The FIFO or average method generally determines cost. LIFO is hardly found in practice.

As a concession, a reserve against stock contingencies may be set up in the books. It is admissible to the extent that it does not exceed one-third of cost or lower market value at the balance sheet date. If the reserve amounts to more than one-third, the special risks (e.g., obsolescence, slow-moving stocks) connected with the inventory must be substantiated to the satisfaction of the tax authorities.

*Capital gains*/Under the direct federal tax law and the cantonal tax laws, all income earned (and losses suffered) by a company are generally classified as business income (or losses), with the following exceptions.

1. Capital gains on real estate—Certain cantons assess capital gains on the sale of real estate partly by ordinary taxes on income (difference between carrying amount and cost, i.e., recaptured depreciation) and partly by a real estate gains tax (difference between cost and intrinsic sales value). Tax rates for the real estate gains tax vary considerably from canton to canton (Zurich— between 5% and 60%, depending on the duration of ownership and the amount of the taxable gain).

2. Capital gains on investments—For federal income tax purposes and in all cantons, a capital gain from the sale of a substantial participation (i.e., at least 20%) acquired after January 1, 1997, will, in effect, be free of income tax after a minimum holding period of one year. A capital gain from the sale of a substantial participation held prior to January 1, 1997, will be subject to income tax at ordinary rates. After January 1, 2007, a capital gain resulting from a sale of a participation held prior to January 1, 1997, can be sold free of federal income tax.

   In certain circumstances, a capital gain realized by a member of a Swiss group from the sale of a substantial participation held prior to January 1, 1997, to a foreign group company can be set off against a provision in the same amount. This provision must be dissolved and the gain becomes subject to tax if, prior to January 1, 2007, the participation is transferred out of the group, major parts of the assets and liabilities are sold, or the participation is liquidated. After January 1, 2007, the provision set against the capital gain may be dissolved income tax neutrally.

*Intercompany dividends*/For direct federal tax and for all of the cantonal and communal taxes, dividends received by a Swiss corporation holding at least 20% or CHF2 million in a domestic or foreign corporation's shares are, in effect, exempt from tax or taxed at reduced rates.

*Foreign income*/Resident corporations are basically taxed on their worldwide income. However, income attributable to foreign branches (bona fide permanent establishments outside Switzerland) is not taxed in Switzerland but is taken into account only to determine the rate of tax applicable to taxable income. The same rule applies for income from real estate situated abroad.

Dividends, interest, and royalties from Swiss or foreign sources are included in assessable income. However, in certain cantons, special methods of assessment may apply for dividend and other income originating outside Switzerland. For dividends, a relief is generally available as described above under "Intercompany dividends." The irrecoverable portion of foreign withholding taxes of most treaty countries can be credited against the related Swiss income taxes on the same income. Foreign withholding taxes of all nontreaty countries and those of Pakistan are not creditable, but they are deductible for income tax purposes.

Undistributed income of foreign subsidiaries is not taxed in Switzerland.

**Stock dividends**/Stock dividends received by a Swiss corporation are not taxable if the book value of the investment is left at original cost. Stock dividends distributed by a Swiss corporation will be treated like cash dividends.

## Deductions

**Depreciation and depletion**/Depreciation of tangible and intangible fixed assets is allowed to the extent it is "commercially justified." For tax purposes, the straight-line or the declining-balance method may be used. Depreciation and amortization not recorded in the statutory accounts are not deductible for tax purposes. The following are the maximum annual rates of amortization and depreciation permitted for direct federal tax purposes. (Most cantons have adopted them for cantonal and communal tax purposes; some cantons have higher rates.)

| | Rate per annum | |
| --- | --- | --- |
| | Straight line | Declining balance |
| | % | % |
| **Immovable assets** | | |
| Vacant plots, land without structures | Nil | Nil |
| Dwelling houses of real estate companies and worker colonies | 1 | 2 |
| Office, shop, or cinema theater buildings | 2 | 4 |
| Buildings of the restaurant and hotel trade | 3 | 6 |
| Factories, warehouses, and industrial immovable property | 4 | 8 |
| Railroad sidings; water, gas, and electricity mains for industrial purposes; storage tanks; containers | 10 | 20 |
| **Movable assets** | | |
| Office furniture and machines, workshop and storeroom equipment | 12.5 | 25 |
| Machinery, equipment, and vehicles (excluding motorcars) | 15 | 30 |
| Machinery and equipment used in more than one shift or used under heavy conditions (e.g., road-construction machines), automobiles | 20 | 40 |
| Machine tools, larger hand tools; hotel and restaurant crockery, cutlery, and linen | 22.5 | 45 |
| IT (hardware and software), automatic control systems, security equipment, and electronic instruments | 20 | 40 |
| **Intangible assets** | | |
| Goodwill, patent license, and other rights of use | 20 | 40 |

Special (higher) rates of depreciation may be allowed for assets used only for short periods or for assets under intensive use (e.g., shift work). These rates must, in general, be agreed on with the competent tax authority. Some cantons allow special accelerated depreciation on a case-by-case basis.

Recaptured depreciation on the sale of depreciated property is classified as normal business income.

*Net operating losses*/For federal and cantonal tax purposes, losses may be carried forward for seven years. Apart from the Canton of Thurgau, there is no loss carryback.

*Payments to foreign affiliates*/Interest, royalties, and license and other fees to foreign affiliates are allowable as deductions to the extent that they meet the arm's length test, that is, are equivalent to charges that would be made by an unrelated third party. The debt-to-equity ratio should in general not exceed 6:1. The Federal Tax Authorities issued more detailed guidelines with respect to safe-harbor debt-to-equity ratios for different types of assets. Any interest paid on excessive debts is basically not deductible for tax purposes.

*Taxes*/All taxes paid or due are deductible for direct federal, as well as cantonal and communal, tax purposes.

## Group taxation

Tax is levied on each corporation as a separate entity, that is, a parent company and its Swiss subsidiaries are taxed separately, and only the dividends from, but not the profits of, the subsidiaries are taxed in the parent company's hands and form the basis of relief.

## Tax incentives

*Inward and capital investment*/Many cantons offer a great variety of incentives for newly established companies or for expansion investments, such as financial grants, favorable credit facilities and real property, tax holidays, or significant tax relief for cantonal and communal tax purposes for up to ten years. In some cantons, a tax holiday even for federal tax purposes may be granted if certain conditions are met. In practice, tailor-made agreements with would-be investors are concluded with the cantonal authorities concerned.

*Other incentives*/Holding corporations may in most instances be entirely exempt from cantonal and communal income taxes. Significant relief from cantonal and communal income taxes may be obtained for corporations not performing business activities within Switzerland or for other special-purpose corporations, such as research, management, or auxiliary corporations.

## Withholding taxes

The statutory rate of Swiss withholding tax is 35%. Relief, if any, is generally granted by refund. The following table shows the remaining tax for the recipient. Credit for the unrelieved portion of Swiss withholding tax may be available in the country of the recipient.

*Treaties in force*

| Recipient | Dividends | | Interest (2) | Royalties (3) |
|---|---|---|---|---|
| | Portfolio | Substantial holdings (1) | | |
| | % | % | % | % |
| Resident corporations and individuals.................. | Nil (4) | Nil (5) | Nil (4) | Nil |
| Nonresident corporations and individuals: | | | | |
| Nontreaty............................. | 35 | 35 | 35 | Nil |
| Treaty: | | | | |
| Albania ............................. | 15 | 5 | 5 | |
| Australia ........................... | 15 | 15 | 10 | |
| Austria ............................. | 15 (6) | Nil (6) | 5 | |
| Belarus............................. | 15 | 5 | 8/5 (7) | |
| Belgium ............................ | 15 | 10 | 10 | |
| Bulgaria............................ | 15 | 5 | 10 | |
| Canada.............................. | 15 | 5 | 10 | |
| China, P.R. ........................ | 10 | 10 | 10 | |
| Croatia.............................. | 15 | 5 | 5 | |
| Czech Republic ................. | 15 | 5 | Nil | |
| Denmark............................ | Nil | Nil | Nil | |
| Ecuador............................. | 15 | 15 | 10/0 (8) | |
| Egypt................................ | 15 | 5 | 15 (9) | |
| Finland ............................. | 10 | 5 | Nil | |
| France ............................. | 15 | 0/15 (10) | Nil | |
| Germany............................ | 15 | Nil | Nil | |
| Profit sharing bonds....... | | | 30 | |
| Greece ............................. | 15 | 5 | 10 | |
| Hungary............................. | 10 | 10 | 10 | |
| Iceland.............................. | 15 | 5 | Nil | |
| India ................................. | 10 | 10 | 10 | |
| Indonesia.......................... | 15 | 10 | 10 | |
| Iran................................... | 15 | 5 | 10 | |
| Ireland, Rep. of ................. | 15 | 10 | Nil | |
| Israel ............................... | 15 | 5 | 10/5 (11) | |
| Italy  ................................ | 15 | 15 | 12.5 | |
| Ivory Coast (Côte d'Ivoire).. | 15 | 16 | 15 | |
| Jamaica.............. ............... | 15 | 10 | 5/10 (12) | |
| Japan ............................... | 15 | 10 | 10 | |
| Kazakhstan........................ | 15 | 5 | 10 | |
| Korea, Rep. of.................... | 15 | 10 | 10 | |
| Kuwait .............................. | 15 | 15 | 10 | |
| Kyrgysztan........................ | 15 | 5 | 5 | |
| Latvia ............................... | 15 | 5 | 10 (13) | |
| Lithuania........................... | 15 | 5 | 10 (13) | |
| Luxembourg....................... | 15 | 0/5 (14) | 10 | |
| Macedonia......................... | 15 | 5 | 10 | |
| Malaysia ........................... | 15 | 5 | 10 | |
| Mexico.............................. | 15 | 5 | 15/10 (15) | |
| Moldova............................. | 15 | 5 | 10 | |

# Switzerland

| Recipient | Dividends | | Interest (2) | Royalties (3) |
|---|---|---|---|---|
| | Portfolio | Substantial holdings (1) | | |
| | % | % | % | % |
| Mongolia........................... | 15 | 5 | 10 | |
| Morocco ........................... | 15 | 7 | 10 | |
| Netherlands...................... | 15 | Nil | 5 | |
| New Zealand .................... | 15 | 15 | 10 | |
| Norway ............................ | 15 | 5 (16) | NIL | |
| Pakistan........................... | 35 | 15 | 15 | |
| Philippines....................... | 15 | 10 | 10 | |
| Poland ............................. | 15 | 5 | 10 | |
| Portugal........................... | 15 | 10 | 10 | |
| Romania........................... | 10 | 10 | 10 | |
| Russia ............................. | 15 | 5 (17) | 5/10 (18) | |
| Singapore........................ | 15 | 10 | 10 | |
| Slovak Republic................ | 15 | 5 | 10/0 (19) | |
| Slovenia........................... | 15 | 5 | 5 | |
| South Africa..................... | 7.5 | 7.5 | 10 | |
| Spain............................... | 15 | 10 | 10 | |
| Sri Lanka......................... | 15 | 10 | 10/5 (20) | |
| Sweden ........................... | 15 | Nil | 5 | |
| Thailand .......................... | 15 | 10 | 15/10 (21) | |
| Trinidad and Tobago ......... | 20 | 10 | 10 | |
| Tunisia............................. | 10 | 10 | 10 | |
| Ukraine............................ | 15 | 5 | 10 | |
| USSR (former).................. | (22) | (22) | (22) | |
| United Kingdom................ | 15 | 5 | Nil | |
| United States................... | 15 | 5 | 0 | |
| Uzbekistan....................... | 15 | 5 | 10 | |
| Venezuela........................ | 10 | Nil | 5 | |
| Vietnam ........................... | 15 | 7/10 (23) | 10 | |

### New treaties not yet in force (date of signature)

| Recipient | Dividends | | Interest (2) | Royalties (3) |
|---|---|---|---|---|
| | Portfolio | Substantial holdings (1) | | |
| | % | % | % | % |
| Argentina (April 23, 1997/ November 23, 2000).......... | 15 | 10 | 12 | Nil |
| Estonia (June 11, 2002) ........ | 15 | 5 | 10 (12) | Nil |

### With the following countries new treaties have been initialed:

Armenia, Georgia, and Zimbabwe.

Notes:

1. A substantial holding is considered to arise where the recipient company holds at least the following percentages in the Swiss company's voting power or shares.

|  | % |
|---|---|
| Canada, France, Israel, Jamaica, Kazakhstan, Philippines, Thailand, Trinidad and Tobago, United States | 10 |
| Iran | 15 |
| Austria, Finland, Germany, Latvia, Lithuania, Russia, Ukraine, Uzbekistan | 20 |
| Albania, Argentina (not yet in force), Belarus, Belgium, Bulgaria, Croatia, Czech Republic, Egypt, Greece, Iceland, Indonesia, Republic of Ireland, Japan, Republic of Korea, Kyrgysztan, Luxembourg, Macedonia, Malaysia, Mexico, Moldova, Mongolia, Morocco, Netherlands, Norway, Poland, Portugal, Singapore, Slovak Republic, Slovenia, Spain, Sri Lanka, Sweden, United Kingdom, Venezuela | 25 |
| Pakistan | 33.33 |

2. Withholding tax is levied only on interest on bonds, bond-like loans, and interest paid by banking institutions to nonbanks. There is no withholding tax on interest of normal loan agreements.

3. There is no withholding tax on royalties, licenses, and similar fees payable by Swiss individuals or corporations.

4. The statutory rate of 35% is levied but refunded, provided the respective earnings are declared as income for tax purposes.

5. No withholding tax is levied; tax liability may be met by notification procedure.

6. Rates indicated are based on the assumption that the revision of the treaty will be ratified. Otherwise, the old tax rate of 5% for both portfolio and substantial holdings remains applicable.

7. A rate of 5% on interest of bank loans, otherwise, 8%.

8. Full relief is granted for bank loans and credit sales, as well as governmental bonds and loans guaranteed by export promotion agencies.

9. Full relief is granted for interest paid in connection with sales on credit and for interest on loans granted by a bank.

10. Relief is 20%, leaving a tax of 15% in the case where one or several persons that are not residents of France or member states of the EU have a substantial interest in the French company receiving the dividend in the form of a participation or in any other form and if neither the shares of the Swiss nor the French company are quoted or traded on a recognized stock market.

11. The 5% rate is applicable for bank loans

12. The lower rate applies to interest on bank loans and interest paid to financial institutions or insurance companies.

13. Full relief is granted for interest paid in connection with sales on credit between independent third parties.

14. Relief is 30%, leaving a tax of 5% if the holding period of the dividend-paying Swiss company is less than two years.

15. A rate of 10% tax on interest paid to a bank.

16. Likely to be 0% as from January 1, 2004.

17. Participation of more than 20% and more than CHF 200,000 of the nominal capital.
18. The 5% rate is applicable for bank loans.
19. The 0% rate is applicable for bank loans.
20. The 5% rate is applicable if the recipient of interest is a bank or other financial institution resident in Sri Lanka.
21. The 10% rate is applicable on interest paid to financial institutions, including insurance companies.
22. The treaty is not applicable to the Baltic states. Applicability to Commonwealth of Independent States (CIS) member states should be verified individually.
23. A rate of 7% for participation of more than 50%, 10% for participation of more than 25%, but less than 50%.

## Tax administration

The tax year is the business year. This means the basis for corporate taxation is the applicable accounting period, which may end at any date within a calendar year.

The tax system is based on taxpayers' declarations, with subsequent assessments being issued by the tax authorities on the basis of the returns filed. Companies are initially assessed on a provisional basis, the final assessments being issued after the tax base has been either the subject of a tax audit or declared final by the authorities.

*Payment of tax*/Unless payments on account are specifically requested, federal, cantonal, and communal taxes on income and capital are, in most cantons and for federal tax purposes, payable only upon receipt of a demand based on a provisional or final assessment. About one month before the due date, a provisional tax bill based on the latest return filed or the assessment of the preceding period is sent to the taxpayer. Payment is usually in two or three installments. If the entire amount is paid up front, a discount may be granted.

*CORPORATION TAX CALCULATIONS*

## I—Industrial and commercial corporations:
## Canton and City of Zurich

Tax year 2004 equaling business year 2004 (business year ending at any date in 2004)

### Assessable profit

|  | Profit for 2004 |
|---|---|
|  | CHF |
| Reported profit (loss) after tax.................................................... | 1,529,000 |
| Adjustments for tax purposes: |  |
|    Excessive depreciation (adjustment in the tax return) ......................... | 113,000 |
|    Release of excessive inventory reserve (adjustment in the tax return) . | (42,000) |
| Other adjustments............................................................................... | 0 |
|  | 1,600,000 |
| Deduct: |  |
|    Loss carryforward (if any)—Allowed as a deduction............................ | 0 |
| Profit after tax/taxable profit (including adjustments in tax return) ............ | 1,600,000 |

### Assessable capital

|  | End of business year |
|---|---|
|  | CHF |
| Paid-in capital ................................................................................. | 4,000,000 |
| Disclosed reserves............................................................................ | 2,000,000 |
| Retained earnings (deficit): |  |
|    Brought forward.............................................................................. | 5,001,000 |
|    Profit (loss) for the year*................................................................ | 1,529,000 |
|    Gross dividend declared................................................................. | (2,076,000) |
| Excess depreciation reserve ............................................................. | 377,000 |
| Excess inventory reserve .................................................................. | 169,000 |
| Other undisclosed reserves................................................................ | 0 |
| Taxable capital | 11,000,000 |

*Statutory profit less taxes paid or due at closing date.

### Tax payable for 2004

|  | Profit | Rate of tax | Tax payable |
|---|---|---|---|
|  | CHF | % | CHF |
| Taxable profit ............................................... | 1,600,000 | 4 | 64,000 |
| Less—4% of taxable capital (11,000,000) ................. | 440,000 |  |  |
| Profit in excess of 4% yield ...................................... | 1,160,000 | 5 | 58,000 |
| Less—4% of taxable capital (11,000,000) ................. | 440,000 |  |  |
| Profit in excess of 8% yield ...................................... | 720,000 | 5 | 36,000 |
| Maximum (10% of 1,600,000 = 160,000) |  |  |  |
|    not reached ............................................................................. |  |  | 158,000 |

# Switzerland

| | On profit | On capital | Together |
|---|---|---|---|
| | CHF | CHF | CHF |
| Basic tax | | | |
| On profit.................................................................. | 158,000 | | |
| On capital (0.15% of 11,000,000)............................... | | 16,500 | 174,500 |
| Cantonal tax—100% of basic tax........................... | 158,000 | 16,500 | 174,500 |
| Communal tax—122% of basic tax........................ | 192,760 | 20,130 | 212,890 |
| Parish tax—11% of basic tax................................ | 17,380 | 1,815 | 19,195 |
| Total Zurich cantonal and communal tax payable ....... | 368,140 | 38,445 | 406,585 |

## Federal tax

Tax year 2004 equaling business year 2004 (business year ending at any date in 2004)

### Assessable profit

| | Profit for 2004 |
|---|---|
| | CHF |
| Reported profit or (loss) after tax................................................ | 1,529,000 |
| Adjustments for tax purposes: | |
| Excessive depreciation ........................................................ | 113,000 |
| Release of excessive inventory reserve.................................. | (42,000) |
| | 1,600,000 |
| Deduct: | |
| Loss carryforward (if any)—Allowed as a deduction .............................. | 0 |
| Profit after tax/taxable profit (including adjustments in tax return)............... | 1,600,000 |

### Federal tax payable for the year 2004

| | CHF |
|---|---|
| Total taxable profit ................................................................. | 1,600,000 |
| Tax at 8.5% ............................................................................ | 136,000 |

Note:

The effective tax burden is calculated by adding the 2004 direct federal tax to the 2004 Zurich cantonal and communal income taxes, that is, CHF 368,140 + CHF 136,000 = CHF 504,140. Accordingly, the profit before tax in Zurich would amount to CHF 2,104,140. Thus, the effective federal and cantonal income tax on profit before tax is 23.96%.

## II—Industrial and commercial corporations: Canton and City of Geneva

Tax year 2004 equaling business year 2004 (business year ending at any date in 2004)

### Assessable profit

|  | Profit for 2004 |
|---|---|
|  | CHF |
| Reported profit (or loss) after tax | 1,529,000 |
| Adjustments for tax purposes: |  |
| Excessive depreciation (adjustment in the tax return) | 113,000 |
| Release of excessive inventory reserve (adjustment in the tax return) | (42,000) |
| Profit after tax/taxable profit (including adjustments in tax return) | 1,600,000 |

### Assessable capital

|  | End of business year |
|---|---|
|  | CHF |
| Paid-in capital | 4,000,000 |
| Legal reserves | 2,000,000 |
| Retained earnings (deficit): |  |
| Brought forward | 5,001,000 |
| Profit (loss) for the year* | 1,529,000 |
| Gross dividend declared | (2,076,000) |
| Excess depreciation reserve | 377,000 |
| Excess inventory reserve | 169,000 |
| Other undisclosed reserves | 0 |
| Taxable capital for 2004 | 11,000,000 |

*Statutory profit less taxes paid or due at closing date.

### Geneva cantonal/communal taxes payable for the year 2004

| | |
|---|---|
| Rate of tax for net income | 10% |
| Rate of tax for capital (unless loss, then 0.2%) | 0.18% |
| Cantonal/communal multiplier for net income | 2.349 |
| Cantonal/communal multiplier for capital | 2.239 |
| Rate of tax for net income (including the cantonal/communal multiplier) | 23.49% |
| Rate of tax for the capital (including the cantonal/communal multiplier) | 0.40302% |

|  | Profit | Rate of tax | Tax payable |
|---|---|---|---|
|  | CHF | % | CHF |
| Total income tax payable for 2004 | 1,600,000 | 23.49 | 375,840 |
| Total capital tax payable for 2004 | 11,000,000 | 0.40302 | 44,332 |
| Total tax payable |  |  | 420,172 |

***Federal tax payable for the year 2004***

|  | CHF |
|---|---|
| Total taxable profit | 1,600,000 |
| Tax at 8.5% | 136,000 |

Notes:

1. The effective tax burden is calculated by adding the 2004 direct federal tax to the 2004 Geneva cantonal and communal taxes, that is, CHF 375,840 + CHF 136,000 = CHF 511,840. Accordingly, the profit before tax in Geneva would amount to CHF 2,111,840. Thus, the effective Geneva and federal income tax rate on profit before tax is 24.24%.

2. Geneva also levies a "*taxe professionnelle*" at the communal level that is based on the annual turnover achieved, rental costs and engaged staff. The rate applicable depends on the industry or business activity.

3. Exchange rate of the Swiss franc at January 1, 2004: US$1 = CHF 1.23720.

## PwC contact

For additional information on taxation in Tahiti, contact:

Christophe Parion
PricewaterhouseCoopers–FITEC
Fiduciaire tahitienne
d'expertise comptable
Centre Vaima
B.P. 608
98713 Papeete
Tahiti
Telephone: (689) 50 86 00
Fax: (689) 43 99 32
e-mail: christophe.parion@pwc.pf

## Note

This information also applies to French Polynesia.

## Significant developments

Investments in certain construction-related activities are eligible for tax credits at varying rates. See "Tax incentives" below.

Transaction tax rates has increased.

Specifics taxes on insurance business has increased.

## Taxes on corporate income

*General income tax*/Income tax rates range from 35% to 45%, plus an additional tax if the taxable income is greater than XPF50 million.

The rate varies according to a ratio computed as follows.

(Net value of certain assets + Deductible personnel expenses) ÷ Taxable income

Where the ratio is more than 5.5, the tax rate is 35%. If the ratio is less than 1.0, the rate is 45%. The rate increases by one percentage point for every decrease in ratio of one-half point.

"Net value of assets" includes depreciable fixed assets held within French Polynesia and included in the balance sheet. "Deductible personnel expenses" do not include salaries for chairmen and executive directors or managers.

To determine taxable income, the accrual method of accounting must be used.

*Minimum tax*/A minimum tax, levied on a lump-sum basis, is equal to 0.5% of the turnover, with a minimum of XPF50,000 and a maximum of XPF4 million.

New companies are exempt from the minimum tax for the first two financial years.

The additional tax due when a company has a taxable income of more than XPF50 million is calculated as follows, by slices.

| | |
|---|---|
| From XPF0 to XPF100,000,000 | 6% |
| From XPF100,000,000 to XPF200,000,000 | 9% |
| From XPF200,000,000 to XPF400,000,000 | 11% |
| Over XPF400,000,000 | 13% |

## Other taxes

***Transaction tax***/A transaction tax is levied on any business that is not liable to corporate income tax (mainly unlimited liability entities). It is computed as a percentage of turnover, according to the following scales that were increased in 2003.

| Turnover | | % |
|---|---|---|
| **Over** | **Not over** | |

**Services except regulated activities:**

| Over | Not over | % |
|---|---|---|
| 0 | XPF 5,000,000 | 2.2 |
| XPF 5,000,000 | 10,000,000 | 4.9 |
| 10,000,000 | 20,000,000 | 6.0 |
| 20,000,000 | 50,000,000 | 7.4 |
| 50,000,000 | 75,000,000 | 8.6 |
| 75,000,000 | | 11.8 |

**Regulated activities (architect, notary, chartered accountant, etc.):**

| Over | Not over | % |
|---|---|---|
| 0 | XPF 5,000,000 | 3.0 |
| XPF 5,000,000 | 10,000,000 | 6.0 |
| 10,000,000 | 20,000,000 | 7.25 |
| 20,000,000 | 50,000,000 | 8.50 |
| 50,000,000 | 75,000,000 | 11.0 |
| 75,000,000 | | 17.5 |

**Trading activities:**

| Over | Not over | % |
|---|---|---|
| 0 | XPF 20,000,000 | 1.1 |
| XPF 20,000,000 | 40,000,000 | 2.0 |
| 40,000,000 | 80,000,000 | 3.23 |
| 80,000,000 | 200,000,000 | 4.1 |
| 200,000,000 | 300,000,000 | 5.2 |
| 300,000,000 | 500,000,000 | 6.3 |
| 500,000,000 | 750,000,000 | 8.25 |
| 750,000,000 | 900,000,000 | 9.25 |
| 900,000,000 | | 10.25 |

Rate reductions are possible for certain activities with low profitability or subject to profit limitations.

***Value-added tax***/As of January 1, 1998, VAT applies to sales of goods and supply of services. Regulations governing the scope of the tax are overall the same as those applicable in mainland France.

For corporations, the basic principle is that the supplier (taxable person) must charge VAT on goods and services supplied, and get a tax credit for VAT paid on business expenditures. The net tax is paid to the authorities.

Unless goods or services are outside the scope of or exempt from VAT, the tax is charged at the following rates, unchanged since 2002.

| | 2004 % |
|---|---|
| Standard rate (services) | 10 |
| Intermediate rate (products not charged at lower rate) | 16 |
| Lower rate (most food products, books, etc.) | 6 |

Exemptions apply to certain banking, insurance and financial services, property transactions, education and health services, water distribution, and the oil products trade. Nonexempt supplies are referred to as "taxable supplies."

VAT is due on goods imported into French Polynesia, but all exported goods and services are exempt.

**Movable property income tax**/A withholding tax at the rate of 10% (12% on premiums) is levied on the following.
1. Dividends and any type of profit distribution.
2. Interest paid to shareholders.
3. Profit shares, attendance fees, etc.
4. Premiums paid to creditors and bondholders.
5. Redemptions and repayments of business capital.

A tax of 2.5% is retained on interest paid by local banks on term deposits. Certain exemptions from this tax are provided by law.

**Real property tax**/Owners of certain buildings and land (see below) must file a declaration each time there is a 10% change in the rental value of their properties. The tax is levied annually at the rate of 10% of 75% of the annual rental value. Municipalities may levy an additional surtax of up to 50%, resulting in a maximum tax burden of 15%.

The tax is levied on the following real property.
1. Buildings located in Tahiti.
2. Land used for industrial or commercial purposes.
3. Any industrial or commercial installations that represent a construction site.
4. Boats situated at a fixed place.

The law provides several permanent and temporary exemptions. A five-year temporary exemption applies to new construction and reconstructions or additions. This temporary exemption does not apply to land used for commercial or industrial purposes.

**Trade tax**/A trade tax applies to commercial or industrial activities and the exercise of a profession. Exemptions apply to certain professional activities.

The trade tax generally is composed of two major elements.
1. A fixed tax (*droit fixe*), which is determined by the type of activity and other factors, of which the number of employees is the most important.
2. A proportional tax (*droit proportionnel*), which is based on the rental value of any professional premises.

The tax rates vary according to type of activity and the location of the activity. For example, a hotel in Papeete is liable to a fixed tax of XPF200,000 and a 2% proportional tax.

Municipalities and the Chamber of Commerce may levy additional taxes based on the trade tax paid by a company. The minimum tax rates are 80% for municipalities, and 22% for the Chamber of Commerce. Municipalities may levy another tax at the rate of 10% of the rental value used in the calculation of the proportional tax.

The trade tax itself was suppressed in 2001, but the additional taxes remain.

# Tahiti

*Beverage license duty*/Individuals and legal entities possessing a license to deal commercially with beverages are liable for an annual beverage license duty, regardless of any activity. The amount of duty is determined by the level of the beverage license and its location. For example, a first-class license in Tahiti costs XPF70,000 per year.

*Local taxes*/Minor taxes are levied by the municipalities, such as the tax on real property and taxes based on the trade tax (see above).

*Capital gains taxes*/Capital gains are usually included in taxable income. There are exceptions, however, for certain types, according to how long the assets were owned and, under special conditions, how the capital gains were used (see below).

## Income determination

*Capital gains*/Gains on sales of real property and shares of real property companies, which apply only to unconstructed land (or if the value of the construction is less than 50% of the value of the land), are determined after deducting costs incurred for the sale, the purchase costs (except interest) and expenses incurred to increase the value of the property. Historical costs may be converted to a present value by an official index if the property was owned for more than three years. Real property capital gains exceeding XPF200,000 are taxed at rates determined by the length of possession. If the property was owned for three years or less the tax rate is 20%. Possession for more than three and up to five years incurs a tax rate of 10%.

Exemptions from real property capital gains tax are granted for the following.

1. Capital gains taxable under other tax laws in French Polynesia. (This includes capital gains received by companies subject to income tax.)
2. Capital gains realized in the case of expropriation.
3. Capital gains realized by an individual upon the sale of a personal residence.

## Deductions

*General expenses*/Expenses incurred to carry on business may be deducted from taxable income. Nondeductible expenses include the following.

1. Penalties and fines.
2. Cost of houses, yachts, planes.
3. Expenses incurred on the Windward Islands to provide personnel accommodations (except hotels).
4. Salaries received by persons not subject to the social security regime and retirement insurance expenses that exceed certain limits.
5. Management salaries exceeding normal level, and in any case exceeding XPF2 million per month.

*Depreciation and depletion*/Depreciation on fixed assets is allowed as a deductible expense for purposes of computing income tax. The straight-line method may be applied to all depreciable assets. The declining-balance method may be applied to equipment with a useful life of at least three years, and to industrial buildings with a useful life of not more than 15 years. The rate of depreciation is determined by applying the following coefficients to the straight-line rate.

| Useful life | Coefficient |
|---|---|
| (Years) | |
| 3–4 | 1.5 |
| 5–6 | 2.0 |
| More than 6 | 2.5 |

Deductible amortization is limited to a maximum basis of XPF6 million for cars, and XPF5 million for software.

***Net operating losses***/An enterprise may deduct a loss incurred during a financial year from the profits of the following year. Unused losses may be carried forward for the five years following the year in which incurred. Unused depreciation may be carried forward indefinitely.

***Payments to foreign affiliates***/Day-to-day management fees in Tahiti are deductible from taxable income. Fees for other management services provided from abroad are deductible under justification, and up to a maximum amount linked to a ratio calculated as follows.

General management costs x (Local turnover ÷ General turnover)

Only those fees corresponding to effective work are deductible.

See also the discussion of interest under "Other significant items."

***Other significant items***/The creation of reserves is recognized as a deductible expense if the following conditions are met.

1. An occurrence may result in a loss or decrease in value of an asset that normally should fall into the financial year in question.
2. The reason or origin of the event occurred within the financial year in question.
3. The loss or decrease in value is sufficiently concrete.
4. The loss or decrease in value is explained in a separate statement.

Royalties are deductible in computing taxable income.

Interest paid to banks or other financial institutions is deductible. Interest paid to shareholders for loans is deductible up to a rate fixed annually by the territorial authorities. In 2003 the rate was 6%. Deductible interest cannot exceed four times the share capital amount (this limitation does not apply to loans granted by a parent company to a subsidiary).

Net income on sales of fixed assets is taxable in the amount of only 2/3 if the asset has been hold between five and ten years, and in the amount of only 2/5 if the asset has been hold or more than ten years.

Dividends received from a local company that have supported the 10% withholding tax (see below) are deductible from taxable income.

## Tax incentives

***DOM/TOM investments***/Certain investments in French Polynesia's DOMs (overseas departments) or TOMs (overseas territories, such as Tahiti) are eligible for this program.

Beneficiaries must be liable to French tax laws; that is, they must be residents of metropolitan France or a DOM. Beneficiaries may be corporations (liable to the corporate tax or the actual profits tax) or individuals (liable to the individual tax on revenue).

For corporations subject to corporate tax, the qualifying amount may be deducted in full from taxable income during the accounting year, applying before all other deductions, such as loss carryovers. Any amount not used in the current accounting year may be carried forward. The deduction may be applied in the year the investment is made and in the following four years.

For individuals and corporations not subject to corporate tax (IRPP), the percentage of the total investment that is deductible is limited to 50% of the investment, 60% of which must be given to the renter if the investor rents the activity.

The investments must have a productive capacity and either create or extend business in the following areas.

| | |
|---|---|
| Agriculture | Hotels |
| Audio, video, and movie production | Industry |
| Construction | Public works |
| Cottage industries | Tourism |
| Energy sources, new | Transportation |
| Fisheries | |

Investments in maintenance activities, if they relate to a productive activity, are eligible for the tax benefits.

Qualified investments by individuals also include investment to acquire or construct buildings for primarily residential use, whether for owners or leaseholders. The percentage of the total investment that is deductible is limited to 5% per year for five years for investments made in the years 2001 through 2006.

For some activities, companies must obtain agreement from the Budget Minister before direct investment.

*Investment Code*/Investments in excess of stated amounts in certain activities located in specified areas that have been approved by the Council of Ministers of the Territories are eligible for tax and monetary advantages. The following activities are eligible.

| | |
|---|---|
| Agriculture | Manufacturing, more than 50% for export |
| Agroindustry | Marine activities |
| Cattle farming | Production and processing |
| Communications, inter-island | Tourism |
| Energy, renewable | Video and television |

Benefits include the following.

1. Under certain conditions, exemptions for a maximum period of three to seven years from the following.
   a. Entry duty on equipment and materials to be used as part of the investment.
   b. Registration duty.
   c. Trade tax (except for the additional tax levied by municipalities or the Chamber of Commerce).
   d. Income tax on movable property.
   e. Real property tax.
   f. Corporate income tax.
2. A partial reimbursement of employer's social charges for three years.

3. Temporary protective measures for the domestic market.

4. Partial reimbursement (up to 75%) of staff training costs.

The total benefits granted may not exceed 30% of the total investment, less eventual costs for acquiring property and buildings and the amount of duties levied. In calculating the threshold for eligibility and benefits, projections for three years must be taken into account.

The benefits granted under the Investment Code are subject to government decision (decree) that defines the obligations of the Territory and the beneficiary.

*Other incentives/*Investments in construction or in a company that invests in construction that exceed XPF100,000 and are realized in 1998 and 1999 are eligible for a 30% tax credit (20% for investments realized in 2000 and 2001). Investments in hotel construction or in a company that invests in hotel construction that exceed XPF200,000 for an extension or XPF500,000 for a new hotel are eligible for a 50% tax credit.

## Withholding taxes

A 10% tax is now withheld from payments to nonresidents for the following services or activities.

1. Use of industrial or commercial property, trademarks, and similar items.

2. Services rendered by a parent company for administration, management, holding expenses, and so on.

3. Technical assistance, services from advisers and engineers, studies of any kind.

4. Insurance premiums.

## Specific tax on insurance business

A 3% tax is due on the turnover (increased in 2004).

A 6% tax is due on the annual increase of the technical reserves (increased in 2004).

## Tax administration

An annual tax return (declaration) must be filed, indicating taxable income or loss of the preceding financial year. The return must be filed before April 30 of the following year if the income tax applies, and before April 1 if the transaction tax applies.

## Notes

Exchange rate (selling) of the Pacific franc at January 1, 2004: US$1 = XPF95.18.

The Pacific franc is pegged to the Euro at €1 = XPF119.89.

# Taiwan

## PwC contact

For additional information on taxation in Taiwan, contact:

Wen-Horng Kao
PricewaterhouseCoopers
23/F Int'l Trade Building
333 Keelung Rd., Sec. 1
Taipei 110, Taiwan, ROC
Telephone: (886) (2) 2729 5209
Fax: (886) (2) 8780 0342 (Tax)
e-mail: wen-horng.kao@tw.pwc.com

## Significant developments

A new regulation in relation to transfer pricing was introduced on January 2, 2004. The new regulation empowers the tax authorities to adjust the transfer prices of the group companies by the following methods in the following order: comparable uncontrolled price method, resale-price method, cost-plus method, and other methods stipulated by the Ministry of Finance. The advanced pricing agreement mechanism is also introduced for group companies that conduct related parties transactions to obtain prior approval from the tax authorities for the relevant transfer prices and acceptable pricing methods before the end of the financial year that the related parties transactions incurred.

## Taxes on corporate income

*Income tax*/Income is taxed as follows.

| Taxable income | Tax thereon |
|---|---|
| Up to NT$50,000 ............................................. | Exempt |
| NT$50,001 to NT$71,428................................. | 50% of taxable income less NT$25,000 |
| NT$71,429 to NT$100,000.............................. | 15% of taxable income |
| NT$100,001 and over ...................................... | 25% of taxable income less NT$10,000 |

Taxable income of certain qualified high-tech companies located in the Science-based Industrial Park is subject to a maximum rate of 20%.

*Taxation of interest*/Interest received on commercial paper, Treasury bills and certain other interest-bearing financial instruments is subject to a withholding tax of 20%. However, such income is not subject to any other form of income tax and is effectively taxed separately from other income referred to above.

*Tax on retained earnings*/For earnings before January 1, 1998, if undistributed earnings as reported on the corporation's tax return exceed 100% (200% for government-approved important industries) of the par value of the capital stock, capital must be increased or dividends declared; otherwise, shareholders will be assessed dividends tax applicable to their shares of all undistributed earnings. Alternatively, the corporation may choose to pay a 10% income tax on the excess portion and retain the earnings indefinitely. For earnings on or after January 1, 1998, an additional 10% tax will be imposed on any current earnings that remain undistributed by the end of the following year.

## Corporate residence

According to the Company Law in Taiwan the principal office of a company must be registered with the government. Corporate residence is determined by the place of registration, which normally is the place of central management.

## Other taxes

*Value-added tax*/The VAT rate is 5% for standard VAT entities. For banks, insurance companies, trust operators, security and futures firms, short-term commercial paper operators, and pawnshops, the rate is 2% for exclusively authorized business and 5% for others. The rate for re-insurance operators is 1%.

*Securities transaction tax*/Tax is levied on securities transactions at the rate of 0.3% on gross proceeds from the sale of stocks. Trading in corporate bonds, financial bonds and government bonds is exempt from securities transaction tax.

## Branch income

A foreign corporation whose head office is outside Taiwan must keep separate books for each branch within Taiwan. Head office administrative expenses may be allocated to the branch under certain conditions. Income tax is assessed only on the branch's profits.

Corporations with a branch in Taiwan should complete an annual income tax return. The rates of taxation are as shown in the table above. If no branch is maintained in Taiwan, revenues or proceeds are subject to a 20% withholding tax unless the Ministry of Finance has given approval to adopt the basis of estimating taxable income as 10% or 15% of gross revenue, effectively reducing withholding tax to 2.5% or 3.75%.

*Branch income from international transport, construction, technical services, and leasing*/Where it proves complicated to compute accurately the proportion of a branch's taxable income derived in Taiwan from these sources, the Ministry of Finance may direct that the taxable income be estimated as 10% of the gross revenue derived from Taiwan for international transportation business and 15% for construction engineering, technical services, or machinery and equipment leasing; alternatively, a branch may apply to the Ministry to adopt this basis, but the application must be made before the beginning of the financial period affected.

*Motion picture leasing*/A branch in Taiwan can deem 45% of the revenue from leasing of motion pictures as cost. However, if a foreign enterprise with no branch office in Taiwan leases motion pictures through agents, 50% of the revenues can be deemed as cost.

## Income determination

*Inventory and marketable securities valuation*/Inventory must be valued at cost. If cost exceeds market, the latter may be used as the valuation basis except when LIFO is used. Cost may be determined by the actual-cost, LIFO, FIFO, moving-average, weighted-average, simple-average, or any other method if approved by the tax authorities in advance. If no application has been made to adopt one of these methods, the weighted-average method must be used. Conformity between financial and tax reporting is not required.

*Capital gains*/Gains on disposal of fixed assets are taxable as current-year income, with the exception of gain on the sale of land. The capital gains tax on marketable securities has been replaced by the securities transaction tax (see "Other taxes" above).

*Intercompany dividends*/Starting January 1, 1998, dividends received from investee companies by a corporate shareholder are not included in the taxable income of the shareholder. In addition, tax paid by the investee corporation can be distributed to the domestic corporate shareholders as tax credits, but the tax credit cannot be used to offset its own income tax liability. The tax credits must be recorded in a separate book to be treated as tax credits available to its own shareholders. Dividends from foreign subsidiaries are taxable, but credit is given for foreign withholding tax, limited to the local company's effective rate of tax.

*Foreign income*/Foreign income received by a Taiwan corporation is taxed. Double taxation is avoided by means of foreign tax credits.

*Stock dividends*/Stock dividends paid out of the current profits or earned surplus are paid after deducting the withholding tax, which can then be used as a credit in the personal income tax return of the stockholder.

## Imputation tax system

The main purpose of the imputation tax system is to eliminate double taxation on earnings of a corporation. Corporations are taxed at 25% on profits. Furthermore, any undistributed current earnings of investee companies derived on or after January 1, 1998 are subject to an additional 10% corporate income tax. This tax can be distributed to the domestic individual shareholders to offset their individual income tax. However, the tax credits distributable to shareholders are subject to certain upper limitations.

A record of an account called "tax credits available to shareholders" must be kept separately from the books. The purpose of this nonbook account is to keep track of the tax credits that are distributable to the stockholders for offsetting their individual income taxes.

## Deductions

*Depreciation and depletion*/Straight-line, reducing-balance and machine-hour methods are acceptable to the tax administration. With the approval of the Tax Authority, a company may revalue its fixed assets each time the government's wholesale price index increases by 25% over a base period. A company's base period is established at the time of purchase of fixed assets or at such time as a company revalues its fixed assets. Any increase in fixed assets may then be depreciated for tax purposes.

Under the Statute for Upgrading Industries, accelerated depreciation may be applicable to machinery for exclusive use for research and development, experiments, quality control, and energy saving purposes.

*Net operating losses*/Losses may be carried over for five years but cannot be carried back.

*Payments to foreign affiliates*/Royalties, interest, and service fees paid to a foreign affiliate are subject to withholding of income tax. Royalties or service fees paid to a foreign entity may be tax exempt if certain requirements are met and prior approval is obtained.

*Taxes*/All taxes other than income tax are deductible, except for taxes associated with capital acquisitions (such as taxes on purchases of land).

*Other significant items*/If a company invests in a foreign entity and holds at least 20% equity ownership (this limitation is not applied if special approval is obtained from the Executive Yuan), the company can attribute 20% of the investment amount to a "reserve for foreign investment loss."

## Group taxation

After a qualified merger, spin-off, or acquisition, a company can choose to file a single consolidated corporate income tax return with its subsidiaries if the company continuously holds over 90% shares of the subsidiaries for 12 months in a tax year.

## Tax incentives

*Inward investment*/Companies that invest in emerging, important and strategic enterprises may claim 20% of the investment amount as a tax credit. An entity qualified as an emerging, important and strategic enterprise may elect the shareholders' investment credit described above, or a five-year income tax holiday for the enterprise itself. The election must be made by a resolution of the shareholders' meeting within two years from the date when payment for stock purchase is initiated.

*Capital investment*/A company can claim as a tax credit within five years 5% to 20% of the expenditures incurred in the following areas.

1. Automated production equipment or technology.
2. Resource recycling, pollution-control equipment or technology.
3. Equipment and technology used in energy saving, clean energy, and recycling of industrial wastewater.
4. Equipment and technology of reducing greenhouse gas remission and improving energy utilization.
5. Hardware, software and technology of internet, broadcasting capacity, enterprise resource planning, communication and telecommunication products, electronics, video conference equipment, and digital content that would promote the efficiency of corporate information transmission.

A company may credit 30% of the amount of expenditure on research and development (R&D) and personnel training individually against the amount of the corporate income tax payable. When the R&D and personnel training expenditures of the current year individually exceed 50% of the total R&D expenditures and the total personnel training expenditures of the preceding two years, a company can claim 50% of the exceeding portion as a tax credit. However, a company can only claim the total R&D and personnel training tax credits up to 50% of the current year's income tax if the credits exceed 50% of the current year's income tax. The R&D and personnel training tax credits can be claimed within five years from the year the expenditures are incurred. If a company located in the science-based industrial park expands its plant with a concurrent capital increase, the company qualifies for a four-year income tax holiday on additional income generated from newly added machinery and equipment. Alternatively, such a company can choose to deduct 15% of the cost of the newly added production equipment from tax otherwise due on the increased income generated by the expansion.

When an emerging, important and strategic enterprise expands with a concurrent capital increase, the entity is entitled to a five-year income tax holiday on additional income generated from newly added machinery and equipment. However, the entity may choose to elect either this income tax holiday or a shareholders' investment tax credit.

An enterprise listed under the classification of scientific industry is eligible for exemption from assessments of import duty and business tax for imported machinery and equipment provided that they cannot be fabricated locally.

An enterprise engaged in the manufacturing and the pertinent technological service industries is eligible for exemption from income tax assessment for a period of five years if it is incorporated or expands its current business capacity with additional capital contribution during the period from January 1, 2002 to December 31, 2003.

*Tax concession on mergers*/A merger or consolidation of companies can be exempt from stamp tax, deed tax, securities transaction tax and business tax incurred from the merger or consolidation. After the merger or consolidation, most tax concessions previously enjoyed by the merged entities will continue to be applicable to the surviving company (or new company) after the merger or consolidation. However, the surviving company (or new company) is required to manufacture the same products or provide services which were approved by the Ministry of Economic Affairs (MOEA) for tax concessions engaged by the merged entities in order to continue the concessions obtained previously.

The net operating losses (NOL) of each participating entity incurred in five years prior to the merger or consolidation may be carried over to the surviving or the newly created entity according to the percentage of shares in the surviving or the newly-created entity held by all shareholders of each participating entity.

*Logistics and distribution center*/Foreign companies or their branches that establish logistics and distribution centers within Taiwan, which will handle warehousing and simple processing of goods, and deliver goods to domestic customers on behalf of the foreign companies, may be exempt from income tax for the sales transaction in Taiwan. The tax exemption treatment may also apply to the foreign companies or its Taiwan branch if they commission a domestic profit-seeking enterprise in Taiwan to establish a logistics center to carry on such activities.

*Operation headquarters*/For enterprises that establish operation headquarters within the territory of Taiwan reaching a specific size and bring about significant economic benefit, the following categories of income shall be exempted from income tax.

1. The income derived from provision of management services or R&D services to affiliates abroad.
2. The income in terms of royalty payment received from affiliates abroad.
3. The investment return and assets disposal profits received under investments in affiliates abroad.

## Withholding taxes

Domestic corporations paying certain types of income are required to withhold as follows.

| Recipient | Dividends | Interest | Royalties |
|---|---|---|---|
| | % | % | % |
| Resident corporations and individuals ............ | N/A | 10 (1) | 15 |
| Nontreaty....................................................... | 30/25/20 (2) | 20 | 20 |
| Treaty: | | | |
| Australia .................................................. | 15/10 (3) | 10 | 12.5 |
| Gambia..................................................... | 10 | 10 | 10 |
| Indonesia.................................................. | 10 | 10 | 10 |
| Macedonia (F.Y.R.O)................................. | 10 | 10 | 10 |
| Malaysia (4).............................................. | 12.5 | 10 | 10 |
| Netherlands............................................... | 10 | 10 | 10 |
| New Zealand ............................................. | 15 | 10 | 10 |
| Singapore.................................................. | (5) | 20 | 15 |
| South Africa............................................... | 15/5 (6) | 10 | 10 |
| Swaziland.................................................. | 10 | 10 | 10 |
| United Kingdom......................................... | 10 | 10 | 10 |
| Vietnam .................................................... | 15 | 10 | 15 |

Notes:

1. Bank interest—10%; short-term commercial paper—20%.
2. For an investment project under the Statute for Investment by Overseas Chinese or the Statute for Investment by Foreign Nationals that has been approved by the MOEA, the withholding rate is 20%. The withholding tax on dividends paid to a non-Foreign Investment Approved (FIA) company by a resident company is 25%. For nonresident individuals the withholding tax rate is 30%.
3. A rate of 10% for shareholders that are companies (other than partnerships) with at least a 25% shareholding.
4. The withholding tax rate on technical service fee payments is reduced to 7.5%.
5. The total tax burden of corporate income tax and dividends tax is not to exceed 40% of the total profits of the company.
6. A rate of 5% for shareholders with at least a 10% shareholding.

*Tax treaties*/Double taxation treaties with Australia, Gambia, Indonesia, New Zealand, Singapore, South Africa, Swaziland, the Former Yugoslav Republic of Macedonia, Malaysia, Vietnam, the Netherlands, and the United Kingdom relate to corporate and individual income tax. Treaties with Canada, European Union, Germany, Israel, Japan, the Republic of Korea, Luxembourg, Macau, the Netherlands, Norway, Sweden, Thailand, and the United States relate to certain earnings from the operation of ships and/or aircraft.

## Tax administration

*Returns*/The tax year ends on December 31. Tax returns are filed on a self-assessment basis. Businesses may request approval from the local collection authority to file income tax returns using a fiscal date other than December 31. Income tax returns are due in the fifth month of the following tax year. Interest is charged on the delayed payment.

# Taiwan

*Payment of tax*/Tax is paid on a self-assessment basis in two installments. The first payment is based on 50% of the tax liability of the prior year's tax return and is made in the ninth month of the enterprise's fiscal year. However, if the taxpayer meets certain requirements, it may self-assess this provisional tax based on the taxable income of the first half of the fiscal year. The second payment is made at the time of filing the annual tax return. The returns are subsequently reviewed by the tax authorities, and a final assessment is issued.

## CORPORATION TAX CALCULATION

Calendar year ending December 31, 2003

| | | |
|---|---:|---:|
| Gross profits | | NT$ 10,000,000 |
| Other income (1) | | 2,000,000 |
| Total income | | 12,000,000 |
| Less: | | |
| Deductible operating expenses (2) | 7,000,000 | |
| Other expenses (3) | 1,000,000 | 8,000,000 |
| Net income | | 4,000,000 |
| Less: | | |
| Net loss carried over | 400,000 | |
| Tax-free interest (government bonds) | 100,000 | 500,000 |
| Taxable income (4) | | NT$ 3,500,000 |
| Tax payable—(3,500,000 x 25%) – 10,000 | | NT$ 865,000 |
| Distributable earnings | | NT$ 2,635,000 |
| Tax credits distributable to shareholders | | NT$ 865,000 |

Notes:

1. Includes income from dividends, interest, royalties, capital gains, and other sources.
2. Only expenses allowable under the rules governing assessment of income tax returns of profit-seeking enterprises are deductible here.
3. Includes interest expense, capital, and casualty losses.
4. Separate provisions may apply to companies that conform with the Statute for Upgrading Industries.
5. Exchange rate of the Taiwan dollar at January 1, 2004: US$1 = NT$33.964.

## PwC contacts

For additional information on taxation in Tanzania, contact:

Vinoo Somaiya
David Tarimo
PricewaterhouseCoopers
International House
Garden Avenue
PO Box 45
Dar-es-Salaam, Tanzania
Telephone: (255) (22) 2133100
Fax: (255) (22) 2133200
LN address: Information@tz.pwc.com
Attn: Vinoo Somaiya/David Tarimo

## Significant developments

In the 2003 Budget speech, the Minister for Finance announced that a new Income Tax Act was to be introduced with effect from January 1, 2004. He requested stakeholders to make representations on the Act before it is tabled in Parliament. The latest draft of the Income Tax Act 2004, which is set out in a Bill dated January 30, 2004, has gone to Parliament for a first reading, and the commencement date is now set for July 1, 2004. As the new Income Tax Act 2004 has yet to be passed into law, and as the current Income Tax Act 1973 continues to apply for years of income starting prior to commencement date, the information below relates to the current Income Tax Act 1973.

## Taxes on corporate income

*Income tax*/A resident corporation is subject to income tax on its worldwide income at the corporate rate of income tax of 30%.

## Corporate residence

A corporation is resident in Tanzania if it is incorporated in Tanzania, or if the management and control of its affairs are exercised in Tanzania during any period in the relevant year of income.

## Branch income

Income derived from Tanzania by a nonresident corporation having a permanent establishment in Tanzania is taxable at the corporate rate of income tax of 30%.

Where branch profits after tax are not reinvested in Tanzania, whether or not remitted, a "branch dividend" is deemed to be paid.

## Income determination

*Inventory valuation*/The normal inventory valuation method is the lower of cost and net realizable value. Special inventory valuation provisions apply only in relation to farming stock (i.e., livestock, produce, and harvested crops).

*Capital gains*/Capital gains tax applies to capital gains arising from the disposal of real property or financial assets (e.g., shares) where such property is registered in Tanzania. The rate of capital gains tax is 10%. Before obtaining a legal transfer of the property being sold, capital gains tax clearance must be obtained.

***Intercompany dividends**/*Any intercorporate dividends are not subject to withholding tax, provided that both companies are resident, and provided that the holding of the recipient represents at least 25% of the voting power of the corporation paying the dividend. If these conditions are not satisfied, then withholding tax on dividends applies at a rate of 10%.

***Foreign income**/*Provision is made for relief by way of credit from the tax chargeable in Tanzania, where overseas tax has been charged on income derived outside Tanzania.

***Stock dividends**/*Bonus shares do not constitute income chargeable to tax on the recipient, unless they are issued out of retained profits or realized capital reserves and their ownership is transferred from one shareholder to another, with or without consideration.

***Rental income**/*Income in respect of any rent in excess of TZS500,000 is taxed at source at the rates of 15% for residents, and 20% for nonresidents, as a final tax.

## Deductions

***Depreciation**/*Depreciation allowances are calculated as follows.

| Type of asset | Allowance | Method | Rate |
|---|---|---|---|
| | Industrial building allowance | Straight-line | % |
| Industrial buildings, hotels.......................................................... | | | 5 |
| Expenditure other than on buildings | | | |
| First year...................................................................................... | | | 50 |
| Subsequent years (reducing balance)........................................... | | | 37.5, 25, 12.5 |

Capital expenditure on mining is eligible for capital deduction at the following rates.

| | % |
|---|---|
| Prospecting and development capital expenditure.................................... | 100 |
| Annual additional capital allowance on the balance of unredeemed qualifying capital expenditure ..................................... | 15 |

Note:

"Qualifying capital expenditure" for the purpose of additional capital allowances means capital expenditure incurred wholly and exclusively for the purpose of development operations, and does not include expenditure incurred for the purpose of prospecting or for acquisition of mineral rights or any interest or finance charges.

Losses can be carried forward indefinitely. Losses from mining operations may only be offset against income from mining operations.

***Payments to foreign affiliates**/*Charges from foreign affiliates must be on an arm's length basis in order to be deductible. Where the payment is by a permanent establishment to its head office, then there is no relief for interest, royalties, or management or professional fees paid to the head office.

***Taxes**/*Taxes other than taxes on income are generally deductible when calculating taxable profits.

## Group taxation

There are no provisions for tax consolidation/group relief.

## Tax incentives

*Inward investment*/There are no incentives specifically for inward investment; see "Other incentives" below.

*Capital investment*/Investment deductions are granted in addition to any other capital deductions (see "Depreciation" above) in respect of the following categories of capital expenditure.

|  | Rate % |
|---|---|
| Industrial buildings and machinery installed therein by any business that manufactures or processes goods | 20 |
| Hotels (and machinery installed therein) | 20 |
| Certain expenditure on agricultural or livestock development farms | 20 |
| Telecommunications equipment and telecommunications towers | 20 |
| Ships | 40 |

*Other incentives*/In the past, registration with the Tanzania Investment Centre (TIC) (formerly Investment Promotion Centre) guaranteed specific tax incentives. This is no longer the case, and with effect from July 1, 2000, the tax treatment is harmonized for all investors. However, a corporation holding a certificate of incentives granted by the TIC prior to July 1, 2002 will still continue to get 100% immediate deduction on eligible capital expenditure.

## Withholding taxes

There is no distinction between withholding rates relating to corporate and to individual recipients. Likewise, the treaty rates cited below are applicable to nonresident corporate and individual recipients alike.

| Nature of payment | Residents % | Nonresidents % |
|---|---|---|
| Dividends | 10 | 10 |
| Interest | 15 | 15 |
| Royalties | — | 20 |
| Management or professional fees | — | 20 |
| Rent, premiums, or like considerations | 15 | 20 |
| Pensions or retirement annuities, | — | 15 |
| Income from leased aircraft | — | 0 |
| Considerations for carriage of goods by road (n/a to TIN (taxpayer identification number) registered payees) | 4 | — |
| Fee, charge, or like consideration for goods supplied or services rendered (n/a to TIN registered payers) | 2 | — |
| Any dividend payable by companies listed on the Dar-es-Salaam Stock Exchange | 5 | — |

Withholding taxes applicable to payments to residents by a person carrying on mining operations are as above, except if the payment is for technical services, in which case the rate is 3%. Where the payment is to a nonresident by a person carrying on mining operations, then the rates are as follows.

| Nature of payment | Nonresidents % |
|---|---|
| Management fees whose total in any year does not exceed 2% of the amount claimed as a deduction from income in respect of the operating expenses incurred in mining operations | 3 |
| Management fees in excess of the above amount | 20 |
| Rent, premiums, or like considerations for the use or protection of property | 20 |
| Interest on loans in foreign currency from third parties | 0 |
| Interest other than interest on loans in foreign currency other than from third parties | 15 |
| Pensions or retirement annuities | 15 |
| Dividends | 10 |
| Professional fees | 20 |
| Technical service fees | 3 |

Note:

The resident withholding tax rates also apply to nonresidents that have a permanent establishment in Tanzania.

*Tax treaties*/The following treaty rates are specified.

| Country | Dividends % | Interest % | Royalties % | Management, professional fees % |
|---|---|---|---|---|
| Canada | 20/25 (1) | 15.0 | 20 | 20 |
| Denmark | 15 | 12.5 | 20 | 20 |
| Finland | 20 | 15.0 | 20 | 20 |
| India | 10/15 (2) | 12.5 | 20 | 20 |
| Italy | 10 | 15.0 | 15 | 30 |
| Norway | 20 | 15.0 | 20 | 20 |
| Sweden | 15/25 (3) | 12.5 | 20 | 20 |
| Zambia | 20 | 20.0 | 30 | 30 |

| Country | Rent premiums, or like considerations % | Pensions % | Shipping % | Air transportation % |
|---|---|---|---|---|
| Canada | 0 | 15 | 0 | 0 |
| Denmark | 40 | 12.5 | 1.375 | 0 |
| Finland | 40 | 12.5 | 1.375 | 0 |
| India | 40 | 12.5 | 1.375 | 0 |
| Italy | 40 | 12.5 | 1.375 | 0 |
| Norway | 40 | 12.5 | 1.375 | 0 |
| Sweden | 40 | 12.5 | 1.375 | 0 |
| Zambia | 40 | 12.5 | 0 | 0 |

Notes:

1. The lower rate applies where the recipient holds 15% of the voting power.
2. The lower rate applies when the recipient has held 10% of the shares for six months.
3. The lower rate applies when the recipient has held 25% of the voting shares for six months.

## Tax administration

***Returns***/A provisional return, containing an estimate of the chargeable income and the tax payable thereon is due for submission within three months from the beginning of the accounting period to which the return relates.

The final return, containing a full and true statement of the company's income from all sources chargeable to corporation tax in Tanzania, must be furnished within six months from the end of the accounting period to which the return relates.

***Payment of tax***/Any provisional tax is payable in four equal installments not later than 3 months, 6 months, 9 months, and 12 months from the beginning of the accounting period. Final tax is payable in a lump sum on the date on which the return is due for submission to the tax authorities.

## CORPORATION TAX CALCULATION

For year of income ending December 31, 2003

Income tax computation

| | | |
|---|---:|---:|
| Net income before taxation | | TZS 10,000,000 |
| Add: | | |
| Depreciation | 1,000,000 | |
| Charitable donations | 20,000 | |
| Unapproved pension contributions | 30,000 | |
| Unrealized exchange losses | | |
| (including year-end translations) | 300,000 | |
| Loss on disposal of machinery | 150,000 | |
| Leave passage provision | 60,000 | 1,560,000 |
| | | 11,560,000 |
| Less: | | |
| Dividend income | 200,000 | |
| Capital expenditure other than on buildings | 900,000 | |
| Industrial building allowance | 150,000 | |
| Leave passage paid | 40,000 | |
| Losses brought forward | 800,000 | 2,090,000 |
| Chargeable income | | TZS 9,470,000 |
| Tax thereon at 30% (resident corporation rate) | | TZS 2,841,000 |
| Tax on dividend income (200,000) at 10% | | |
| (resident withholding tax rate) | | 20,000 |
| Total tax | | TZS 2,861,000 |

Note:

Exchange rate of the Tanzanian shilling at January 1, 2004: US$1 = TZS 1,080.

# Thailand

## PwC contact

For additional information on taxation in Thailand, contact:

Janist Aphornratana
PricewaterhouseCoopers Legal & Tax Consultants Ltd.
Bangkok City Tower, 15th Floor
179 South Sathorn Road
Bangkok 10120, Thailand
Telephone: (66) (2) 286 9999
Fax: (66) (2) 286 2666
e-mail: janist.aphornratana@th.pwc.com

## Significant developments

There are no significant developments to tax on corporate income.

## Taxes on corporate income

Corporate income tax (CIT) is generally paid at a flat rate of 30% on net taxable profits.

However, a reduction is given to listed companies, that is, companies listed with the Stock Exchange of Thailand (SET) and the Market for Alternative Investment (MAI), the newly established trading board by the SET, as follows.

- Companies listed on the SET before September 6, 2001:
  - net profits: Bht0-300 million: 25%;
  - net profits: Bht301 million or more: 30%.
- Companies listed on the SET from September 6, 2001: net profits, 25%;
- Listed companies on the MAI from September 6, 2001: net profits, 20%.

The reduced rates for existing listed companies will be applied for only five accounting periods starting from the accounting period beginning on or after September 6, 2001. As for newly-listed registered companies on the SET and the MAI, the rates will be applied for five accounting periods as well but commencing from the accounting period starting on or after the listing day. Note that the concession rate will be granted to a newly listed company on the SET from September 6, 2001 to September 5, 2004 only.

A company listed either on the SET or MAI on or after September 6, 2001 will not be granted the above reduced rate if it contains any of the following characteristics.

1. The company is delisted from the SET during the period of three years before relisting on the SET or MAI.
2. The company is amalgamated by another existing listed company or acquiring business in whole or in part from the existing listed companies during the period of three years before listing on the SET or MAI.
3. The company acquires whole or part of the business of an existing listed company during the period in which the company is entitled to tax rate reduction. Otherwise, the entitlement to tax reduction shall be terminated, starting from the accounting period in which the acquisition of business occurs.

Moreover, starting from the accounting period commencing on or after 1 January 2002, SMEs (defined as a juristic company or partnership with paid up capital not exceeding Baht 5 million at the end of any accounting period) is also granted reduced CIT rates as follows:

| Net profits | Rate |
| --- | --- |
| Not more than Baht 1 million | 20% |
| Baht 1,000,000–3,000,000 | 25% |
| Baht 3,000,000 or more | 30% |

## Corporate residence

Corporate residence is determined by the place of incorporation. A company incorporated under the laws of Thailand is a domestic corporation. A company incorporated abroad is resident in Thailand if it carries on business in Thailand. Place of management and control is not statutorily defined. The term "carrying on business in Thailand" is broad and, subject to the provisions of double taxation treaties, includes the presence of an employee, representative, or go-between that results in a foreign corporation's deriving income or gains in Thailand.

## Other taxes

*Value-added tax*/VAT is levied at a rate of 10%, but currently reduced to 7% until September 30, 2005, except on exports, which are zero-rated, and a number of exempt goods and services, for example, basic groceries, education, health care, interest, leasing of immovable property, and sale of real estate.

*Specific business tax*/Specific business tax is levied on the gross receipts of certain businesses. Among the more significant items are the interest and foreign exchange gains of banks and other financial institutions, life insurance premiums, and dealing in real estate, where the rate of tax is 3%.

*Municipal tax*/An additional surcharge of 10% of the specific business tax is levied as municipal tax.

*Local taxes*/There are three major local taxes.

1. Household and Land tax—12.5% of assessable economic rental income.
2. Signboard tax—Rates vary according to size; minimum of Bht200 per annum.
3. Local Development tax—Rates range between 0.25% and 0.95% of the appraised value of land assessed by local authorities. This tax does not apply if the property is subject to household and land tax.

*Capital taxes*/There are no capital taxes in Thailand.

*Branch income*/Branches of foreign corporations pay income taxes at corporate tax rates on locally earned profits only. Branch profits remitted to the foreign head office are subject to additional tax at the rate of 10%. However, this is a tax on disposition of profits abroad, and is not limited to remittances. For example, a credit of profits to the head office account in the books is held to be a disposition of profits abroad, even though no remittance of funds takes place, and the additional 10% tax is payable at the time of the entry in the books.

## Income determination

*Inventory valuation*/Inventory is valued at the lower of cost or market price. Any recognized method of ascertaining the cost price may be used, including LIFO, but a change in the method can be made only with the prior approval of the Director-General of the Revenue Department. Conformity between book and tax reporting is required.

*Capital gains*/Capital gains are taxed as ordinary income.

*Intercompany dividends*/Dividends received from a Thai company by a company listed on the Stock Exchange of Thailand are exempt from tax. Dividends received by a nonlisted company from other Thai companies are also exempt from tax, provided the company receiving the dividends holds at least 25% of the total voting shares without any cross-shareholding. In other cases where one Thai company receives dividends from another Thai company, one-half of the dividends are exempt from tax. The above tax exemption is on the condition that the shares must be held for at least three months before and three months after the dividends are received.

*Foreign income*/Only Thailand-incorporated companies are taxed on worldwide income. A foreign-incorporated company is taxed on profits arising from or in consequence of business carried on in Thailand. A foreign company not carrying on business in Thailand is subject to a withholding tax on certain types of assessable income (e.g., interest, dividends, royalties, rentals, and service fees) paid from or in Thailand.

The Revenue Code does not describe how foreign income received by a Thailand-incorporated company is taxed, but it is believed that the Revenue Department regards foreign branch income as taxable when earned, and foreign dividend income as taxable when received. Double taxation is relieved by way of a credit against the tax chargeable in Thailand.

*Stock dividends*/Stock dividends are taxable to the recipient as ordinary income.

## Deductions

*Depreciation and depletion*/Deduction for wear and tear and depreciation is allowed as a percentage of cost. If the rate of deduction adopted by a company under its own accounting method is lower than the percentage of cost, deduction will be allowed only at the rate adopted by the company. The straight-line basis is the method most commonly used by companies, but any generally accepted basis, such as the reducing-balance or sum-of-the-years-digits method, is permitted. Certain assets (e.g., machines for research and development (R&D)) are allowed to be initially deducted at a special rate (e.g., 40% in case of machines for R&D

research) of the cost, with the remaining depreciated at the prescribed rate. Rates are as follows.

|  | % |
|---|---|
| Buildings: | |
| Durable buildings ........................................................................ | 5 |
| Temporary buildings ..................................................................... | 100 |
| Cost of acquisition of depletable natural resources ................................ | 5 |
| Cost of acquisition of lease rights: | |
| If there is no written lease agreement or if there is a written lease agreement containing a renewal clause whereby continual renewals are permitted.......................... | 10 |
| If there is a written lease agreement containing no renewal clause or containing a renewal clause but restricting renewable periods to a definitely limited duration............................... | (1) |
| Cost of acquisition of the right in a process, formula, goodwill, trademark, business license, patent, copyright, or any other right: | |
| If the period of use is not limited....................................... | 10 |
| If the period of use is limited.......................................... | (2) |
| Any properties not above mentioned, excluding land and inventory........................ | 20 |
| Machinery and equipment used in technological R&D............................. | 40 |

Notes:

1. Percentage rate equals 100 divided by the sum of years of the original and renewable lease periods.

2. Percentage rate equals 100 divided by the number of years of use.

*Net operating losses*/Losses may be carried forward for the following five accounting periods. Carryback of losses is not permitted.

*Payments to foreign affiliates*/A Thailand-incorporated company can claim a deduction for royalties, management service fees, and interest charges, provided they are expended exclusively for the purpose of acquiring profits or for the purposes of business in Thailand and do not exceed a reasonable amount.

*Taxes*/In general, all taxes are deductible except corporate income tax.

*Other significant items*/Deductions for allowable charitable contributions and certain other donations may not exceed 2% of the net taxable profits.

## Group taxation

Group taxation is not permitted.

## Tax incentives

*Inward investment*/Tax incentives in certain industries eligible for promotion include the following.

1. Exemption or reduction of import duties on imported machinery.

2. Reduction of import duties on imported raw materials and components.

3. Exemption from corporate income taxes for three to eight years.

4. Exemption of up to five years from withholding tax on goodwill, royalties, or fees remitted abroad.

5. Exclusion from taxable income of dividends derived from promoted enterprises during the income tax holiday period.

Additional incentives to encourage exports include the following.

1. Exemption from import duties on imported raw materials and components.
2. Exemption from import duties on re-export items.
3. Allowance to deduct from corporate taxable income the amount equivalent to 5% of an increase in income derived from export over the previous year, excluding costs of insurance and transportation.

Additional incentives for enterprises located in investment promotion zones include the following.

1. Reduction of 50% of corporate income tax for five years after the termination of a normal income tax holiday, or from the date of earning income if no tax holiday is granted.
2. Allowance to double the cost of transportation, electricity, and water supply for deduction from corporate taxable income.

**Capital investment**/There are no tax incentives for capital investment.

**Other incentives**/Commercial banks granted a license to undertake international banking facilities business in Thailand are entitled to the following privileges.

1. A corporate income tax rate of 10% on the net profit from the international banking facilities business.
2. Exemption from withholding tax on interest paid to a foreign depositor or lender where the funds are used for offshore lending.
3. Withholding tax exemption on interest income paid to foreign depositors or lenders where the funds are used for lending to a state enterprise under the approval of the Ministry of Finance.
4. Exemption from profit remittance tax for offshore lending businesses.
5. Exemption from specific business and municipal tax on gross income.
6. Stamp duty exemption for international banking facilities businesses.

**Tax Incentives for Regional Operating Headquaters (ROH)**/Tax incentives to attract foreign firms to establish regional headquarters in Thailand came into effect on August 16, 2002. These new ROH rules should make Thailand, with its wide tax treaty network, an attractive headquarters location for multinational companies.

ROH means a juristic company organized under Thai law and providing administrative, technical assistance or supporting services to its domestic or overseas affiliated enterprises or branches.

The tax incentives available are as follows.

- A 10% CIT on service income from affiliated enterprise and branches, for services including administrative services, technical assistance, management, research and development (R&D), or training. The ROH must provide such services in at least three other countries.
- A 10% CIT on interest income received as a result of re-lending to affiliated enterprises or branches funds borrowed by the ROH.
- A 10% CIT on royalty income derived from affiliated enterprises and branches including its related companies and generated from R&D work performed in Thailand.

- A CIT exemption on dividends received from domestic and overseas affiliated enterprises and branches.
- Personal income tax exemption for expatriate employees for services undertaken outside Thailand, provided the relevant employment costs are not deducted by the ROH or an affiliated enterprise in Thailand.
- Expatriate employees may elect to pay personal income tax at a rate of 15% for a period of two years, provided they forego withholding tax credits for interest and dividend income.

To qualify for the tax incentives the ROH must meet the following conditions.

- The ROH must be formed as a corporation under Thai law.
- The ROH must have paid-up capital of at least Baht 10 million (US$250,000) on the last day of any accounting period.
- Provide services to affiliated enterprise or branches in at least three other countries.

Income from services provided must form at least 50% of ROH income (reduced to 1/3 for the first three years).

## Withholding taxes

| Recipient | Dividends % | Interest % | Royalties % |
|---|---|---|---|
| Resident corporations | Nil/10 (1) | Nil/1 (2) | 3 |
| Resident individuals | 10 | 15 | (3) |
| Nonresident corporations and individuals: | | | |
| Non-treaty | 10 | 15 | 15 |
| Treaty: | | | |
| Australia | 10 | 10/15 (4) | 15 |
| Austria | 10 | 10/15 (4) | 15 |
| Bahrain | 10 | 10/15 (4) | 15 |
| Bangladesh | 10 | 10/15 (4) | 15 |
| Belgium | 10 | 10/15 (4) | 5/15 (5) |
| Canada | 10 | 10/15 (4) | 5/15 (5) |
| China, P.R. | 10 | 10/15 (4) | 15 |
| Cyprus | 10 | 10/15 | 5/10/15 |
| Czech Republic | 10 | 10/15 (4) | 5/10/15 (6) |
| Denmark | 10 | 15 | 15 |
| Finland | 10 | 10/15 (4) | 15 |
| France | 10 | 3/10/15 (7) | 0/5/15 (8) |
| Germany | 10 | 10/15 (4) | 5/15 (5) |
| Hungary | 10 | 10/15 (4) | 15 |
| India | 10 | 10/15 (4) | 15 |
| Indonesia | 10 | 10/15 (4) | 15 |
| Israel | 10 | 10/15 (4) | 5/15 (5) |
| Italy | 10 | 10/15 (4) | 5/15 (5) |
| Japan | 10 | 10/15 (4) | 15 |
| Korea, Rep. of | 10 | 10/15 (4) | 15 |
| Laos | 10 | 10/15 (4) | 15 |
| Luxembourg | 10 | 10/15 (4) | 15 |
| Malaysia | 10 | 10/15 (4) | 15 |

# Thailand

| Recipient | Dividends | Interest | Royalties |
|---|---|---|---|
| | % | % | % |
| Mauritius | 10 | 10/15 (4) | 5/15 (5) |
| Nepal | 10 | 10/15 (4) | 15 |
| Netherlands | 10 | 10/15 (4) | 5/15 (5) |
| New Zealand | 10 | 10/15 (4) | 10/15 (6) |
| Norway | 10 | 10/15 (4) | 5/10/15 (6) |
| Pakistan | 10 | 10/15 (4) | 10/15 (9) |
| Philippines | 10 | 10/15 (4) | 15 |
| Poland | 10 | 10/15 (4) | 5/15 (5) |
| Romania | 10 | 10/15 (4) | 15 |
| Singapore | 10 | 10/15 (4) | 15 |
| South Africa | 10 | 10/15 (4) | 15 |
| Spain | 10 | 10/15 (4) | 5/8/15 (10) |
| Sri Lanka | 10 | 10/15 (4) | 15 |
| Sweden | 10 | 10/15 (4) | 15 |
| Switzerland | 10 | 10/15 (4) | 5/10/15 (6) |
| United Arab Emirates | 10 | 10/15 | 15 |
| United Kingdom | 10 | 10/15 (4) | 5/15 (5) |
| United States | 10 | 10/15 (11) | 5/8/15 (10) |
| Uzbekistan | 10 | 10/15 | 8/15 (10) |
| Vietnam | 10 | 10/15 (4) | 15 |

The numbers in parentheses refer to the following numbered Notes.

Notes:

1. The nil rate applies to a recipient company listed on the Stock Exchange of Thailand.
2. The 1% rate applies to interest payments made to all resident corporations other than banks or finance companies except where interest arises from bonds or debentures.
3. Deduction is made according to the graduated scale of personal income tax rates.
4. The 10% rate applies to interest paid to a recipient that is a bank or financial institution (including an insurance company).
5. The 5% rate applies to royalties paid for the use of any copyright of literary, artistic, or scientific work.
6. The 5% rate applies for the use of any copyright of literary, artistic, or scientific work excluding cinematograph films or films or tapes used for radio or television broadcasting, and the 10% rate to any patent, trademark, design, or model, plan, secret formula, or process.
7. The 3% rate applies to interest paid on loans or credits granted for a period of four years or more with the participation of a public finance organization to a public authority, or to an enterprise in France that is tied to the sale of plant and machinery or studies relating to the equipping or supply of industrial, commercial, or scientific installations, as well as public works. The 10% rate applies to interest paid to any financial establishment in France.
8. The zero rate applies to royalties paid in respect of films or works registered on magnetic tapes, and the 5% rate to royalties for the use of any copyright of literary, artistic, or scientific work.

9. The 10% rate applies to royalties paid for the use of any copyright of literary, artistic, or scientific work.

10. The 5% rate applies to royalties paid for the use of any copyright of literary, artistic, or scientific work, including software, motion pictures and works on film, tape or other means of reproduction for use in connection with radio or television broadcasting. The 8% rate applies to royalties paid for the use of industrial, commercial, or scientific equipment.

11. The 10% rate applies to (a) interest paid to a bank or financial institution (including an insurance company) and (b) interest paid under a sale on credit.

## Tax administration

*Returns*/The tax year for a company is its accounting period, which must be of 12 months' duration. However, it may be less than 12 months in the case of the first accounting period after incorporation, or after prior approval from the Revenue and Commercial Registration Departments has been received for a change in the closing date.

The system is one of self-assessment. A company prepares and files its tax returns by the due dates, and at the same time pays the taxes calculated to be due.

*Withholding tax returns*/Withholding tax returns (except for the sale of immovable property) must be filed within seven days from the last day of the month in which income has been paid. The withheld tax could then be used to credit against corporate income tax payable of the payee.

*Payment of tax*/Corporate income tax is paid semiannually. A half-year return must be filed within two months after the end of the first six months of an accounting period. The tax to be paid is computed on one-half of the estimated profits for the full accounting period, except for listed companies, banks, certain other financial institutions, and other companies under prescribed conditions, where the tax is based on the actual net profit for the first six months. The annual tax return is filed within 150 days from the close of an accounting period. The tax due is payable at that time. Credit is given for the amount of tax paid at the half-year.

### CORPORATION TAX CALCULATION

Year ended December 31, 2003

| | | |
|---|---:|---:|
| Net profit according to the income statement of the company ............................................................................ | | Bht 1,000,000 |
| Add—Items not to be taken as expenses: | | |
|    Provision for inventory obsolescence................................... | 100,000 | |
|    Provision for doubtful debts ................................................ | 50,000 | |
|    Expenses of a personal character, gifts ............................. | 15,000 | 165,000 |
| | | 1,165,000 |
| Less: | | |
|    Dividend from subsidiary company ..................................... | 100,000 | |
|    Bad debts written off (1) ...................................................... | 40,000 | |
|    Inventory written off (1)....................................................... | 150,000 | 290,000 |
| Taxable profit ........................................................................... | Bht | 875,000 |
| Tax thereon at 30% ................................................................. | Bht | 262,500 |

Notes:

1. It is presumed that the bad debt and inventory write-off procedures are in accordance with the rules and conditions under the Revenue Code.

2. Exchange rate of the Baht at January 1, 2004: US$1 = Bht 39.60. (Source: Revenue Department Notification.)

## PwC contact

For additional information on taxation in Trinidad and Tobago, contact:

Peter R. Inglefield
PricewaterhouseCoopers
11–13 Victoria Avenue
Port-of-Spain, Trinidad
Telephone: (1) (868) 623 1361
Fax: (1) (868) 623 1512
LN address: Peter Inglefield@Price Waterhouse-CARIB
e-mail: peter.inglefield@tt.pwc.com

## Significant developments

There have been some legislative amendments to the Corporation Tax and related enactments in the past year but no major changes to the existing fiscal regime. The amendments cover an increase in the total amount that may be claimed in respect of contributions made to local art and culture, sport and audio visual and video productions from TT$450,000 to TT$1,000,000 per annum.

## Taxes on corporate income

*Corporation tax*/With effect from January 1, 2004 the standard rate of tax is 30%, but this varies significantly in the case of certain classes of companies (e.g., life insurance companies). The tax rates are as follows.

|  | % |
|---|---|
| Ordinary companies | 30 |
| Life insurance companies | 15 |
| Companies engaged in liquefaction of natural gas, manufacture of petrochemicals, physical separation of liquids from a natural gas stream, transmission and distribution of natural gas, wholesale distribution and marketing of petroleum products | 35 |
| Petroleum companies (petroleum profits tax) | 50 |

The 2002 Budget also proposed changes to the dates for the payment of quarterly installments of tax from the last day of March, June, September, and December to the 25th day of March, June, and September, and the 22nd day of December. No Act of Parliament has as yet been passed to give effect to this proposal.

## Corporate residence

Corporate residence is determined by reference to the location of the central management and control of the business of a company. The place of incorporation is regarded as merely one of the factors to be taken into account in determining where central management and control are located.

## Other taxes

*Business levy*/With effect from January 1, 2001, corporations are subject to a business levy at the rate of 0.2% of gross revenue or receipts. Exemption is available for certain companies, including petroleum companies and companies whose annual turnover is less than TT$200,000. This levy is payable quarterly, and the taxpayer is entitled to a tax credit of corporate tax up to a maximum of the business levy liability.

*Green Fund Levy*/Effective January 1, 2001, a Green Fund Levy of 0.1% is applicable to companies doing business in Trinidad and Tobago and having gross income or receipts in excess of TT$200,000 per annum. This levy is payable quarterly and is neither a deduction in computing chargeable income nor a credit against corporation tax due.

*Unemployment levy*/Only petroleum companies remain liable to the unemployment levy, at the rate of 5% of taxable profits.

*Supplemental petroleum tax*/The supplemental petroleum tax (SPT) is chargeable on the gross income (derived from the sale of crude oil) less certain allowances at scale rates, which increase with the price of crude. The tax is computed separately in respect of land and marine operations.

Incentives are available in the form of enhanced allowances for workovers and repair costs, and include a deduction for geological and geophysical costs.

The SPT is deductible in arriving at profits subject to petroleum profits tax.

*Value-added tax*/VAT is applicable to a wide range of goods and services. The standard rate applicable to commercial supplies is 15%.

Certain basic unprocessed foods and agricultural supplies are zero rated, as are crude oil, natural gas, and all exported goods and services. Effective January 1, 1995, hotel accommodations and yachting services to nonresidents are zero-rated.

A number of services, including financial services, real estate brokerage, residential rentals, and educational services, are exempt. However, with effect from January 1, 1994, financial services (as specified) are subject to a transaction tax at a rate of 15%. From January 1, 1993, imported inputs of highly capital-intensive manufacturers are exempt from VAT.

*Hotel accommodation tax*/With effect from January 1, 1995 hotels are subject to a hotel accommodation tax at a rate of 10% of the value of the accommodation.

*Insurance premium tax*/Also effective January 1, 1995 a tax at the rate of 6% has been imposed on insurance premiums in respect of general insurance contracts. Life insurance and reinsurance premiums are exempt.

## Branch income

The tax rates applicable on branch profits are the same as on corporate profits. In addition, branch profits, after deduction of corporation tax and reinvestments, are subject to withholding tax annually at varying rates on profits remitted/deemed remitted to the head office.

## Income determination

*Inventory valuation*/Inventories are generally stated at the lower of cost or market value. Cost may be determined by FIFO or the average-cost method. The LIFO and base-stock methods are not generally accepted for tax purposes.

*Capital gains*/Gains on the disposal of chargeable assets within 12 months of acquisition or reacquistion within 12 months of disposal are subject to tax at standard corporate rates. (See "Depreciation and depletion" below.)

*Intercompany dividends*/Dividends received from both domestic subsidiaries and other domestic corporations are fully exempt from tax.

*Foreign income*/A Trinidad and Tobago corporation is taxed on worldwide income. Foreign branch income is taxed as earned, and foreign dividends are taxed when received. Double taxation is avoided by means of foreign tax credits.

*Stock dividends*/A Trinidad and Tobago corporation can distribute tax-free a dividend of common stock (bonus issue) proportionately to all common stockholders.

## Deductions

*Depreciation and depletion*/With effect from January 1, 1995 tax depreciation rates (wear-and-tear allowances) have been standardized by statute. Fixed assets are to be classified into one of four classes.

|  | Rate % |
|---|---|
| Class A—Furniture and fittings | 10 |
| Class B—Motor vehicles | 25 |
| Class C—Heavy equipment, motor lorries, trucks, computer equipment | 33.3 |
| Class D—Extra heavy equipment | 40 |

The allowance will be calculated at the rate applying to aggregate expenditure incurred on assets within the class acquired after January 1, 1995 on a declining-balance basis.

A wear-and-tear allowance at the rate of 10% (calculated on a declining-balance basis) has also been introduced for new buildings and structures and capital improvements completed on or after January 1, 1995. This allowance will apply to all buildings or structures, as well as capital improvements thereto, that are used in the trade, business, profession, or vocation for the production of income. However, companies currently enjoying benefits under the Income Tax (In Aid of Industry) Act or under the Fiscal Incentives Act, the Free Zones Act will be unable to claim this allowance.

For buildings constructed between January 1, 1993 and December 31, 1995 that qualify for tax exemption in respect of the profit, sale or rental income therefrom, an election must be made to claim either the tax exemption or the wear-and-tear allowance.

Accelerated tax depreciation is allowed to all manufacturing trades in the form of an initial allowance in the year of acquisition on capital expenditure, including expenditure on industrial buildings. The rates are 10% for industrial buildings and 60% for machinery and equipment. For those companies engaged in the production of sugar, petroleum, or petrochemicals or enjoying concessions under the Fiscal Incentives Act, the rate is 20% An annual allowance of 2% on cost (petroleum operations, 5%) is granted on industrial buildings referred to above, subject to the provisions relating to buildings or structures completed after January 1, 1995.

In addition to the initial allowance, companies engaged in petroleum production operations enjoy a first-year allowance of 20% of the capital expenditure incurred on plant and machinery, with the remaining cost being written off on a straight-line basis over five years.

Gains on sale of tax-depreciable assets are taxable as ordinary income (i.e., a balancing charge). Where the gain is not a short-term capital gain (see "Capital gains"), the taxable gain is limited to the tax depreciation received. Tax depreciation is not required to conform to book depreciation.

A depletion allowance (an annual allowance) is granted on certain expenditures incurred on winning access to the mineral source. The allowance includes a first-year allowance, an initial allowance and an annual allowance.

*Net operating losses*/A loss may be carried forward indefinitely to be set off against future profits.

Loss carrybacks are not permitted.

Effective January 1, 1997 a limited form of group loss relief has been introduced, whereby losses may be surrendered to a claimant company within the group, except that the claimant's tax liability cannot be reduced by more than 25%. Companies must be resident in Trinidad and Tobago. Only losses incurred after January 1, 1997 qualify for this relief.

*Payments to foreign affiliates*/A Trinidad and Tobago corporation may claim a deduction for royalties and interest charges paid to foreign affiliates, provided the amounts are paid at arm's length and the appropriate withholding tax is deducted and properly accounted for. For interest to be deductible for tax purposes the recipient must be subject to tax in Trinidad and Tobago or otherwise specifically exempt therefrom. Deduction for management charges is restricted to the amount of the management charges or 1% of outgoings and expenses exclusive of the charges, whichever is the lower. Tax depreciation allowances may not be treated as an expense for this purpose. Withholding tax may also be applicable to management charges.

*Taxes*/Other than the supplementary petroleum tax, no taxes or levies are deductible in arriving at taxable profit (see "Other taxes" above).

*Other significant items*/Charitable contributions to approved charities under a deed of covenant are deductible

Expenditure on the promotion of artistic works, the sponsoring of sports or sportsmen, the sponsoring of works promoting local culture are deductible at 150% of the actual expenditure subject to a maximum annual deduction of TT$1 million. In addition, where a production company incurs expenditure on its own audio, audio visual, or video productions for educational purposes these are deductible at 150% of actual expenditure subject to an annual maximum of TT$1 million.

From 1994, contributions by local insurance companies to Catastrophe Reserve Funds become deductible for tax purposes up to the value of 20% of net premium income from property insurance business.

## Group taxation

There is no provision for group taxation in Trinidad and Tobago, but with effect from January 1, 1997 a limited form of group loss relief has been introduced (see "Net operating losses" above).

## Tax incentives

*Tax holidays*/Incentives are as follows.

1. Fiscal Incentives Act, 1979: An approved enterprise, which must be a locally incorporated resident corporation, may be granted an exemption from

corporation tax for a period of up to ten years, depending on the category under which it is approved. Exemption may be total or partial. Subject to approval, profits may be distributed tax free to shareholders except in the case of certain nonresident shareholders, where the relief is restricted to so much of the tax as exceeds their liability in their country of residence. Net losses during the tax holiday period (i.e., the excess of total losses over total profits) may be carried forward for setoff without limitation for five years from the end of the tax holiday period, after which the normal setoff provisions for losses apply.

2. Approved Tourism Projects: Under the Tourism Development Act 2000, approved tourism development projects including hotels are granted a tax holiday for periods of up to seven years. In addition, a carryover from a tax exemption period, if any, is permitted of any loss arising out of the operation or renting of an approved tourism project written off against profits in accordance with normal income tax loss provisions, subsequent to the tax holiday period. An approved tourism project means a project declared to be so by the government.

3. Approved mortgage and other companies: The profits of an approved company are exempt from corporation tax. The exempt profits when distributed to shareholders are exempt from corporation tax and income tax.

4. Business expansion scheme: The business expansion scheme was introduced in 1988 to allow approved small companies carrying on business in a regional development area and companies carrying out certain approved activities a tax credit of 15% of their chargeable profit. This scheme is to be restructured to encourage both individual and corporate investors to invest in venture capital companies by allowing a "tax rebate" on their investment.

5. Construction companies: Profits and income derived from trading in properties constructed between January 1, 1993 and December 31, 1996 are exempt from income and corporate taxes until the year 2000. However, from January 1, 1995 such companies may elect to claim the 10% wear-and-tear allowance applicable to newly constructed buildings, in which case the profits and income will become chargeable to tax in the normal manner (see "Deductions" above).

***Export incentives/***These incentives are as follows.

Customs duty rebate—Effective July 1, 1995, the 5% customs duty payable on raw material inputs by manufacturers has been removed.

Promotional expenses—Promotional expenses incurred by local firms to promote the expansion of existing markets and/or the creation of new ones for the export of specified services or locally produced goods will be tax deductible as an expense at 150% of the actual outlay.

Tax-deductible promotional expenses are defined as those expenses incurred in respect of specified services or goods produced in Trinidad and Tobago. This includes such items as advertising in foreign markets and participation in trade fairs and missions.

Employment allowance—An allowance of 200% of the cost of employing additional workers has been reintroduced with effect from January 1, 1997. The allowance will be granted in respect of the net increase of workers in a year of income. This applies only in respect of workers earning TT$4,000 per month or less and for the initial 12 months of unbroken employment of each additional worker.

Scholarship allowance—From the year 2001, companies can deduct the actual expenses incurred in granting scholarships to nationals who are not employees, directors, or associates of directors of the company for tertiary education.

Market development grants—An Export Development Corporation was established to manage government export-development programs and also to do all things necessary and appropriate for the encouragement, promotion, and expansion of export-oriented business. The Corporation was empowered to give financial assistance to exporters by way of market development grants. In 1994 the Tourism and Industrial Development Corporation was formed to incorporate in a single entity the functions of the Export Development Corporation, the Tourism Development Authority, and the Industrial Development Corporation. This is now the authority responsible for administering the grants.

These grants are not exempt from taxation unless (1) they have been made in respect of expenses incurred by an exporter prior to the export of the first commercial shipment of goods produced in Trinidad and Tobago and (2) the foreign market is not in a country specified as an "excluded country."

Market development grants will be awarded to exporters that meet the criteria set out by the Corporation. Qualifying expenses include costs incurred in research in foreign markets, product design and testing abroad.

Training—An allowance of up to 150% of expenses may be claimed in respect of expenses incurred in the training or retraining of staff.

## Withholding taxes

Withholding tax is imposed at varying rates up to 20%, depending on the nature of the payment, the status of the payee and the applicability of double taxation treaties. From January 1995, as a result of a reduction in the withholding tax rate, the tax treaty rate in some instances is now higher than the statutory rate. In such cases the lower statutory rate applies. The rates below have been adjusted to reflect these reductions.

| | | Dividends | | |
|---|---|---|---|---|
| | | Portfolio | Substantial holdings | Interest |
| Recipient | | % | % | % |
| Resident corporations and individuals...................................... | | Nil | Nil | Nil |
| Nonresident corporations and individuals: | | | | |
| Nontreaty.............................................. | (1) | 15 | 15 | 20 |
| | (2) | 10/15 | 10/15 | 20 |
| Treaty: | | | | |
| Canada (3) ......................................... | (1) | 15 | 15 | 15 |
| | (2) | 15 | 10 | 15 |
| CARICOM countries ............................ | (1) | 0 | 0 | 0 |
| | (2) | 0 | 0 | 0 |
| Denmark............................................... | (1) | 15 | 15 | 15 |
| | (2) | 15 | 10 | 15 |
| France ................................................. | (1) | 15 | 15 | 10 |
| | (2) | 15 | 10 | 10, Nil (4) |
| Germany............................................... | (1) | 15 | 15 | 10, Nil, 15 (5) |
| | (2) | 15 | 10 | 10, Nil, 15 (5) |
| India ..................................................... | (1) | 10 | 10 | 10 |
| | (2) | 10 | 10 | 10 |
| Italy ..................................................... | (1) | 15 | 15 | 10 |
| | (2) | 15 | 10 | 10 |
| Luxembourg......................................... | (1) | 10 | 5 | 7.5, 10 (11) |
| | (2) | 10 | 5 | 7.5, 10 (11) |
| Norway ................................................ | (1) | 15 | 15 | 15 |
| | (2) | 15 | 10 | 15 |
| Sweden ................................................ | (1) | 15 | 15 | 15 |
| | (2) | 15 | 10 | 10, Nil, 15 (6) |
| Switzerland...... .................................. | (1) | 15 | 15 | 10 |
| | (2) | 15 | 10 | 10 |
| United Kingdom .................................. | (1) | 15 | 15 | 10 |
| | (2) | 15 | 10 | 10 |
| United States....................................... | (1) | 15 | 15 | 20 |
| | (2) | 15 | 10 | 15, Nil, 20 (7) |
| Venezuela............................................ | (1) | 10 | 5 | 15 |
| | (2) | 10 | 10 | 15 |

# Trinidad and Tobago

|  | Royalties | | |
|---|---|---|---|
| **Recipient** | **(8)** | **(9)** | **(10)** |
|  | % | % | % |
| Resident corporations, individuals .................................................. |  | Nil |  |
| Nonresident corporations, individuals: |  |  |  |
| Nontreaty.......................................................................................... | 20 | 20 | 20 |
| Treaty: |  |  |  |
| Canada.......................................................................................... | 15 | Nil | 20 |
| CARICOM countries ..................................................................... | 15 | 15 | 20 |
| Denmark........................................................................................ | 15 | Nil | 20 |
| France .......................................................................................... | 10 | Nil | 20 |
| Germany........................................................................................ | 10 | Nil | 20 |
| India.............................................................................................. | 10 | 10 | 10 |
| Italy............................................................................................... | 5 | Nil | 20 |
| Luxembourg................................................................................... | 10 | 10 | 20 |
| Norway .......................................................................................... | 15 | Nil | 20 |
| Sweden.......................................................................................... | 20 | Nil | 20 |
| Switzerland ................................................................................... | 10 | Nil | 20 |
| United Kingdom ............................................................................ | 10 | Nil | 20 |
| United States ................................................................................ | 15 | Nil | 20 |
| Venezuela...................................................................................... | 10 | 10 | 20 |

The numbers in parentheses refer to the following numbered Notes.

Notes:

1. Individuals.

2. Corporations. The lesser rate applies to parent companies.

3. The treaty between Canada and Trinidad and Tobago has been renegotiated, but has not yet been ratified by the respective territories.

4. The rate is 10% of the gross amount if interest is paid to a resident of France; it is nil if the interest is paid to the French government or to any agency or instrumentality of the French government.

5. The rate is 10% of the gross amount if the interest is paid to a bank that is a resident of Germany, nil where interest is paid to certain stated governmental institutions and 15% of the gross amount in all other cases.

6. The rate is 10% of the gross amount if the interest is paid to a bank that is a resident of Sweden, nil where interest is paid to certain specified governmental institutions and 15% of the gross amount in all other cases.

7. The rate is 15% of the gross amount if the interest is paid to a bank or financial institution in the United States that does not have a permanent establishment in Trinidad and Tobago, nil where the interest is paid to the U.S. government or to any agency or instrumentality wholly owned by the U.S. government, and 20% of the gross amount in all other cases.

8. The rate applies to patent royalties.

9. The rate applies to copyright royalties and similar payments.

10. The rate applies to royalties paid in respect of the operations of mines or quarries or of the extraction or removal of natural resources.

11. A total of 7.5% of the gross amount of interest on loans, commercial paper and deposits, and 10% of the gross amount of interest in all other cases. Interest derived from loans paid by or guaranteed by the government is exempt.

## Tax administration

*Returns*/The tax system in force is a self-assessment system, which requires the taxpayer to make a return to the Board of Inland Revenue by the April 30 following the end of the fiscal period. A six-month grace period is allowed, following which a penalty (effective October 1995) of TT$1,000 for every six months or part thereof accrues.

*Payment of tax*/Corporation tax and business levy are payable quarterly in advance on March 31, June 30, September 30, and December 31. Installments are based on an estimate of the current year's liability or the actual tax payable for the previous year, whichever is greater.

## CORPORATION TAX CALCULATION

Fiscal year ended December 31, 2004

| | | |
|---|---:|---:|
| Net income before taxes | | TT$ 1,000,000 |
| Add: | | |
| Depreciation | 285,000 | |
| Nonallowable expenses: | | |
| Increase in the general provision for bad debts (1) | 10,000 | |
| Charitable donations not under covenant | 5,000 | |
| Entertainment expenses (25% nondeductible) | 5,000 | 305,000 |
| | | 1,305,000 |
| Deduct: | | |
| Wear-and-tear allowance (2) | 225,000 | |
| Ordinary dividend (100%) from resident company | 160,000 | 385,000 |
| | | 920,000 |
| Taxable income | | TT$ 920,000 |
| Tax due: | | |
| Corporation tax thereon at 30% | | TT$ 276,000 |
| Less—Business levy paid (0.2% of 5 million) | | (10,000) |
| | | TT$ 266,000 |

Notes:

1. Only specific write-offs are allowed for tax purposes.
2. A wear-and-tear allowance is granted in the place of depreciation at rates prescribed by statute.
3. The effects of promotional expenses and market development grants have not been included in the corporation tax calculation.
4. Exchange rate as of March 1, 2004: US$1 = TT$6.20.

# Turkey

## PwC contacts

For additional information on taxation in Turkey, contact:

Adnan Nas
Kadir Bas
PricewaterhouseCoopers (Basaran Nas Yeminli Mali Müsavirlik AS)
BJK Plaza Süleyman Seba Caddesi, No. 48
B Blok, Kat 9 Akaretler
Besiktas 34357
Istanbul, Turkey
Telephone: (90) (212) 326 6060
Fax: (90) (212) 326 6050
e-mail: adnan.nas@tr.pwc.com
        kadir.bas@tr.pwc.com

## Significant developments

Effective April 24, 2003, investment allowance application has been amended and is no longer tied to an Investment Incentive Certificate.

Effective January 1, 2004, inflationary accounting has been introduced, eliminating the applications of revaluation of fixed assets, cost revision mechanism, LIFO method for inventory valuation and financial expense restrictions, and offering amendments on depreciation of fixed assets and restatement of certain nonmonetary items. Effective January 1, 2004, statutory fund application, which was effectively a surcharge on the corporate and income tax rate, has been abolished and new corporate and income tax rates have been defined. Moreover, filing and payment dates for corporate tax have been changed as indicated below.

## Taxes on corporate income

Corporations are liable to taxation as described below.

1.  Phase I: Profits generated in 2004, as adjusted by exemptions and deductions, including prior-year losses carried forward, are subject to corporation tax at 33%. Note that this is a temporary rate applicable for 2004 only. The corporate income tax rate is to be 30% from 2005 onward.

2.  Phase II: Dividend distribution to individual and nonresident corporate shareholders is subject to withholding tax (WHT) at the rate of 10%. If profits are not distributed or added to paid-in capital, they will not be subject to WHT. Note that dividend distributions to the resident entities and branches of nonresident corporations are not subject to dividend withholding tax.

Corporations are required to pay advance corporation tax based on their quarterly profits at the rate of 33% for the year 2004 (rate of 30% would be applicable for the year 2005 and onward). This is due to be filed by the 10th and to be paid by the 17th of the second month following the quarter. Advance corporation tax paid during the year is offset against the corporate tax liability calculated over the annual corporate tax return. The balance of advance tax can be refunded or used to offset other tax liabilities.

## Corporate residence

If both the legal and the business headquarters of a company are located outside Turkey, the company is regarded as a nonresident entity. If one of these headquarters is located within Turkey, the company is regarded as a resident entity. Resident entities are subject to tax on their worldwide income, whereas nonresident entities are taxed solely on the income derived from activities in Turkey.

## Other taxes

*Value-added tax*/An (European Union) EU-type VAT is levied varying from 1% to 18%. The standard rate is 18%. A 1% rate is applicable for certain agricultural products, newspapers, magazines and goods subject to financial leasing (except for some luxury items). A rate of 8% applies to basic food and books. Telecommunication services, normal petrol, super petrol (including unleaded petrol), diesel fuel and kerosene and fuel oil are subject to 18% VAT.

Special consumption tax is applied mainly on four different groups of products at different tax rates. These are petroleum products, natural gas, lubricating oil, solvents and derivatives of solvents (Group I), automobiles and other vehicles, motorcycles, planes, helicopters, yachts (Group II), tobacco and tobacco products, alcoholic beverages (Group III), and luxury products (Group IV). Unlike VAT, which is applied on each delivery, the Special Consumption Tax is levied only once, in general, on the delivery of these goods by the manufacturers or during the importation by importers.

*Banking and insurance transactions tax*/Banking and insurance companies' fees (e.g., bank charges and insurance premiums) are exempt from VAT but are subject to banking and insurance transactions tax (BITT) at a rate of 1% or 5%. The purchase of goods and services by banking and insurance companies is subject to VAT. This is not deductible from BITT but is charged as an expense.

*Stamp tax*/Stamp duty applies to a wide range of documents, including but not limited to contracts, agreements, financial statements, and payrolls. Stamp duty is levied as a percentage of the value stated on the contract or payroll at rates varying between 0.15% and 0.75% and at an insignificant fixed amount where there is no monetary value on the contract. For financial statements and some other documents a lump sum stamp tax is levied. There is no capital duty in Turkey.

## Branch income

Branch profits are subject to corporation tax at the rate of 33% (30% for 2005 and onward). The profit which is transferred to the headquarters is subject to corporate withholding tax at the rate of 10%.

## Income determination

*Inventory valuation*/The methods used in calculating the value of year-end stock or goods sold are weighted average and FIFO. Stock-count deficits are recorded as legally disallowable expenses, whereas stock-count surpluses are treated as income at year-end for corporation tax purposes.

*Fixed assets*/With the introduction of the inflationary accounting system in Turkey, fixed assets would be adjusted against the effects of inflation using a monthly inflation rate (wholesale price index).

*Capital gains*/Capital gains and losses are included in the determination of corporate income. There is no separate capital gains taxation in Turkey. For residents there is a tax-planning tool to reduce the corporate tax burden on capital gains arising from the disposal of real estates or participation shares, that is, temporary corporate tax exemption as explained below.

Under temporary Article 28 of the Corporate Income Tax Law, if capital gains arising from the disposal of real estate or participation shares are added to paid-in capital, they are exempt from corporation tax at 33% until December 31, 2004. To benefit from this exemption, the real estate or participation shares must have been held for more than two years. For nonresidents, where so stated in related tax treaties, an exemption may be available in the event of disposal of participation shares after a holding period exceeding one year from the date of acquisition. Foreign exchange gains arising during the calculation of capital gains from the sale of securities or capital shares purchased by nonresidents (individuals or corporations) in exchange for foreign currency funds (capital in cash or in-kind) that have been brought directly into Turkey are not treated as taxable income. However, such capital gains will be considered as taxable income if the nonresidents regularly engage in the selling and purchasing of Turkish securities and capital shares.

Interest gains from treasury and government bonds held by a business entity as assets are subject to corporation tax.

*Intercompany dividends*/Domestic-source dividend income is free from tax in the hands of a Turkish corporation.

*Foreign income*/Foreign-source income such as dividends, royalties and interest is fully taxable in Turkey. Partial relief from taxation is granted insofar as the tax paid overseas does not exceed the rate of tax payable for similar income in Turkey. Undistributed income of foreign subsidiaries is not taxable in Turkey.

*Stock dividends*/A Turkish corporation may increase its paid-in capital via retained earnings. Shares issued in this manner are not taxable for the recipient.

## Deductions

*Depreciation and depletion*/With the introduction of the inflation accounting system in Turkey, the application of depreciation has been amended. Under these amendments, fixed assets acquired after January 1, 2004 are subject to depreciation over rates to be determined by the Ministry of Finance, based on their useful life. However, the Ministry of Finance has not announced the useful lives yet, as of March 18, 2004. The fixed assets acquired before January 1, 2004 would continue to be depreciated over the former application, in which the maximum rate applicable is 20% per year. The taxpayer may choose either the straight-line method or the declining-balance method and may change the option from declining-balance to straight-line (but not vice versa) at any time during the life of the asset. The applicable rate for the declining-balance method is twice the rate of straight-line method.

Goodwill is depreciated in equal installment over five years. Leasehold improvements are depreciated in equal installments over the lease period.

Natural resources (mainly oil and minerals) are the property of the state, and therefore cannot be acquired or depreciated by private taxpayers. However, on individual application, license values for each natural resource are subject to depreciation at the rates determined jointly by the Ministry of Finance and the

Ministry of Industry and Trade. Mine and oil-well installations are depreciated as tangible fixed assets, and any remaining book value may be written off at any time extraction ceases for economic reasons. The costs of dry or unsuccessful exploratory drillings are expensed as incurred.

Profits or losses on disposal of fixed assets (i.e., the difference between the proceeds and the written-down value) are included in taxable income in the year of disposal. If renewal of disposed-of assets is considered necessary by the owners of the business concern, the profit accrued therefrom can be retained for up to three years without being taxed. After a purchase of new fixed assets the profits may be offset against the depreciation of the new assets.

*Losses*/Corporate losses may be carried forward for five years. Losses may not be carried back.

*Payments to foreign affiliates*/Charges for royalties and interest by foreign affiliates may be deductible for tax purposes, provided that transfer pricing and thin capitalization rules are adhered to, respectively.

*Taxes*/Essentially, income taxes and VAT (with some exceptions) are not tax deductible. Fees and duties paid in relation to assets of the company are deductible in determining taxable income.

*Pensions and employees' leaving indemnities*/These expenses are deductible only when paid and are subject to an upper limit.

*Bad debts*/Bad and doubtful accounts receivable are deductible under certain circumstances. Amounts of the receivables subsequently collected are added to the profits of the year in which they are collected.

## Group taxation

Tax consolidation is not permitted in Turkey.

## Tax incentives

The major tax incentives available are the investment incentive allowance, exemption for portfolio management activities of investment funds and a participation exemption for dividends from resident corporations paid to resident corporations or Turkish branches of foreign corporations.

Under the investment incentive regulations, investors are required to receive a specific approval (an Investment Incentive Certificate) from the Undersecretariat of Treasury in order to benefit from incentives such as VAT, customs taxes and stamp tax exemption and credit allocation. In order to be granted an investment incentive certificate, a predetermined minimum amount of investment is required (TL 200 billion in priority development regions; TL 400 billion in developed and normal regions).

*Investment incentive allowance*/Due to the recent amendments, an Investment Incentive Certificate is not required in order to benefit from investment allowance.

Under the amended application, companies can deduct 40% of the cost of the depreciable equipment that is acquired or produced for utilization in their activities from their tax base as investment allowance. Only the cost of fixed assets purchased or produced for the purpose of the activities of the company come under the scope of investment allowance. Investment allowance is not applicable for machinery or equipment whose cost is less than TL 6 billion (approximately US$4,500 at the current foreign exchange rate). The application of the investment allowance will be available in the year the investment expenditures are initiated and denominated in Turkish lira. In the event of it not being immediately utilized as a tax deduction from taxable profits, due to the absence or lack of taxable income in the related year, it may be carried forward until it is totally netted off against the taxable base and indexed against inflation. Moreover, investment allowance figures calculated and exempted from corporation tax as such are also exempt from withholding tax. In addition to the tax exemption due to the investment allowance, the related assets are also depreciated for tax purposes.

***Portfolio management income***/Portfolio management income from "A" type, real estate and venture capital investment funds is exempt from both corporation tax and corporate withholding tax. However, "B" type investment funds are exempt from corporation tax, but subject to 10% corporate withholding tax.

## Withholding taxes

There are no withholding taxes on payments to resident corporations by other resident corporations, except for a 5% withholding tax on progress payments to contractors, both domestic and foreign, within the scope of construction business spanning more than one calendar year. However, interest income and repo income paid by banks to corporations is subject to WHT.

Withholding taxes on payments by a domestic corporation to a foreign corporation in a nontreaty country are as shown below.

|  | % |
|---|---|
| Rentals from immovable assets | 22 |
| Leasing of goods | 1 |
| Sales and transfer of intangible assets such as patents and copyrights | 25 |
| Payments for the use of patents, copyrights and licenses | 22 |
| Professional services | 22 |
| Petroleum services | 5 |
| Interest on foreign bank loans | Nil |
| Dividend distribution over after-tax profit (excluding Turkish branches of foreign corporations) | 10 |
| Interest on deposits | |
| Interest income derived from foreign currency time deposits with a maturity of | |
| Up to one year | 24 |
| One year and over | 18 |
| Interest income derived from bearer deposit accounts | |
| Demand deposits and callable accounts | 18 |
| Time deposits of up to three months (including three months) | 18 |
| Time deposits of up to six months (including six months) | 16 |
| Time deposits of up to one year | 12 |
| Time deposits of one year and over | 7 |
| Repo income | 22 |

Withholding taxes on payments to nonresident individuals are as follows.

|  | % |
|---|---|
| Rentals from immovable assets | 22 |
| Sales and transfer of intangible assets such as patents and copyrights | 25 |
| Payments for the use of patents, copyrights and licenses | 22 |
| Professional services (depending on the type of service provided) | 17 or 22 |
| Wages and salaries | 15–40 |
| Interest on deposits | |
| Interest income derived from foreign currency time deposits with a maturity of | |
| Up to one year | 24 |
| One year and over | 18 |
| Interest income derived from bearer deposit accounts | |
| Demand deposits and callable accounts | 18 |
| Time deposits of up to three months (including three months) | 18 |
| Time deposits of up to six months (including six months) | 16 |
| Time deposits of up to one year | 12 |
| Time deposits of one year and over | 7 |
| Repo income | 22 |

### Nontreaty/treaty withholding

| | Dividends (1) (2) | Interest (2) (3) | Royalties | Technical assistance fees (4) (5) |
|---|---|---|---|---|
| | % | % | % | % |
| Nontreaty countries | 10 | 10 | 22 | 22 |
| Treaty: | | | | |
| Albania | 5-15 (6) | 10 | 10 | 22 (7) |
| Algeria | 12 | 10 | 10 | 22 |
| Austria | 25-35 (8) | 15 | 10 | 10-22 (9) |
| Azerbaijan | 10 | 10 | 10 | 22 |
| Bangladesh | 10 | 10 | 10 | 22 |
| Belarus | 10-15 (10) | 10 (11) | 10 | 22 |
| Belgium | 15-20 (12) | 15 | 10 | 22 |
| Bulgaria | 10-15 (13) | 10 | 10 | 22 |
| Czech Republic | 10 | 10 | 10 | 22 |
| China (Taiwan) | 10 | 10 | 10 | 22 |
| Croatia | 10 | 10 | 10 | 22 (7) |
| Denmark | 15-20 (14) | 15 | 10 | 22 |
| Egypt | 5-15 (6) | 10 | 10 | 22 |
| Finland | 15-20 (14) | 15 | 10 | 22 |
| France | 15-20 (15) | 15 | 10 | 22 |
| Germany | 15-20 (15) | 15 | 10 | 22 |
| Hungary | 10-15 (13) | 10 | 10 | 22 |
| India | 15 | 10-15 (16) | 15 | 22 |
| Indonesia | 10-15 (17) | 10 | 10 | 22 |
| Israel | 10 | 10 (18) | 10 | 22 |
| Italy | 15 | 15 | 10 | 22 |
| Japan | 10-15 (19, 20) | 10-15 (21) | 10 | 15 |
| Jordan | 10-15 (19) | 10 | 12 | 22 (7) |

| | Dividends (1) (2) | Interest (2) (3) | Royalties | Technical assistance fees (4) (5) |
|---|---|---|---|---|
| | % | % | % | % |
| Kazakhstan | 10 | 10 (22) | 10 (22) | 22 (7) |
| Korea, Republic of | 15-20 (14) | 10-15 (23) | 10 | 22 |
| Kuwait | 10 | 10 | 10 | 22 (7) |
| Kyrgyzstan | 10 | 10 | 10 | 22 |
| Latvia | 10 | 10 | 5-10 (24) | 22 |
| Lithuania | 10 | 10 | 5-10 (24) | — |
| Macedonia | 5-10 (6) | 10 | 10 | 22 (7) |
| Malaysia | 10-15 (25) | 15 | 10 | 22 |
| Moldova | 10-15 (26) | 10 | 10 | 22 (7) |
| Mongolia | 10 | 10 | 10 | 22 (7) |
| The Netherlands | 15-20 (27) | 10-15 (23) | 10 | 22 |
| Northern Cyprus | 15-20 (14) | 10 | 10 | 5-22 (40) |
| Norway | 20-30 (28) | 15 | 10 | 22 |
| Pakistan | 10-15 (29) | 10 | 10 | 22 |
| Poland | 10-15 (19) | 10 | 10 | 22 |
| Romania | 15 | 10 | 10 | 22 |
| Russian Federation | 10 | 10 | 10 | 22 (7) |
| Saudi Arabia (30) | — | — | — | — |
| Singapore | 10-15 (31) | 7.5-10 (32) | 10 | 22 |
| Slovak Republic | 5-10 (33) | 10 | 10 | 22 |
| Slovenia | 10 | 10 | 10 | 22 (7) |
| Spain | 5-15 (6)/ 5-15 (38) | 10-15 (39) | 10 | 22 |
| Sudan | 10 | 10 | 10 | 22 (7) |
| Sweden | 15-20 (14) | 15 | 10 | 22 |
| Tajikistan | 10 | 10 | 10 | 22 (7) |
| Tunisia | 12-15 (34) | 10 | 10 | 22 (7) |
| Turkmenistan | 10 | 10 | 10 | 22 |
| Ukraine | 10 | 10 | 10 | 22 |
| United Arab Emirates | 10-12 (35) | 10 | 10 | 22 |
| United Kingdom | 15-20 (36) | 15 | 10 | 22 |
| United States | 15-20 (37) | 15 | 5-10 (24) | 22 |
| Uzbekistan | 10 | 10 | 10 | 22 |

The numbers in parentheses above refer to the following numbered Notes.

Notes:

1. Dividend taxation refers to the corporate withholding tax.
2. Reduced to local rate by Turkish law if it is lower than the treaty rate.
3. Generally, tax withheld from interest is 10%. In certain circumstances, such as bank credits and loans from abroad, the rates are nil.
4. Technical assistance fees are considered as independent professional service income. If a bilateral tax treaty exists, they are taxed only in certain circumstances in Turkey. If the tax is applied, with the exception of Austria and Northern Cyprus, the rate is 22%. In general, under the tax treaties of Turkey, if the duration of services does not exceed 183 days in aggregate in any continuous 12-month period, Turkey does not tax technical assistance fees.

5. In certain circumstances, individuals who are not considered as seconded under technical assistance contracts and who establish residence (over 183 days) may be subject to normal income tax withholding on salaries (25% to 55%). For entities that employ labor under such contracts, which is not considered as falling under the classification of independent professional services, the changes made under the contract are subject to 25% withholding tax, including levy.

6. A rate of 5% if the recipient company owns at least 25% of the shares of the payer company; otherwise 15%.

7. Taxed only if there is a fixed place of business; there is no 183-day rule.

8. A rate of 25% if the recipient company owns at least 25% of the payer company; otherwise 35%.

9. A rate of 10% if the services are not rendered in Turkey.

10. A rate of 10% if the recipient company holds at least 25% of the payer company; otherwise 15%.

11. If the interest is paid to the Central Bank of Belarus, the interest obtained will be exempt from withholding tax.

12. By an amending protocol, 10% if the recipient is a company and the dividend is not subject to tax in Belgium. Otherwise, 20%, or 15% if the recipient is a company and owns at least 10% of the payer company.

13. A rate of 10% if the recipient company owns at least 25% of the payer company; otherwise 15%.

14. A rate of 15% if the recipient company owns at least 25% of the payer company; otherwise 20%.

15. A rate of 15% if the recipient company owns at least 10% of the payer company; otherwise 20%.

16. A rate of 10% if the interest is paid to a bank or financial institution; otherwise 15%.

17. A rate of 10% if the recipient company holds at least 25% of the payer company; otherwise 15%.

18. If the interest is paid to the Central Bank of Israel, the interest obtained will be exempt from withholding tax.

19. A rate of 10% if the recipient company owns at least 25% of the payer company, otherwise 15%.

20. If the Turkish tax on the income is less than 40%, the rates are 15% and 20%, respectively.

21. A rate of 10% if the recipient is a financial institution (bank or insurance company), otherwise 15%.

22. If Kazakhstan accepts a lower rate in its bilateral tax treaties with any Organization for Economic Cooperation and Development (OECD) countries concluded after its treaty with Turkey, this lower rate will be applied.

23. A rate of 10% if debt matures in more than two years, otherwise 15%.

24. A rate of 5% if the royalty fees are paid in return for utilization rights of industrial, commercial and scientific equipment. Otherwise 10% will apply.

25. A rate of 0% if undistributed dividends are not taxed in Malaysia. 10% if the recipient company holds at least 25% of the payer company; otherwise 15%.

26. A rate of 10% if the recipient company holds at least 25% of the payer company; otherwise 15%.

27. If the recipient company owns at least 25% of the payer company, 15% or, by an amending protocol, 10% if the recipient is a company and the dividend is not subject to tax in the Netherlands. Otherwise, 20%.

28. A rate of 25% in Turkey; 20% in Norway if the recipient company owns at least 25% of the payer company; otherwise 30% and 25%, respectively.

29. A rate of 10% if the recipient owns at least 25% of the payer company and if the payer company engages in industrial activities; otherwise 15%.

30. Agreement covers income derived from air transport between Turkey and Saudi Arabia.

31. A rate of 10% if the recipient company holds at least 25% of the payer company; otherwise 15%.

32. A rate of 7.5% if the interest recipient is a financial institution, otherwise 10%.

33. A rate of 5% if the recipient company holds at least 25% of the payer company; otherwise 10%.

34. A rate of 12% if the recipient owns at least 25% of the payer company, otherwise 15%.

35. A rate of 10% if the recipient company holds at least 25% of the voting rights in the payer company, otherwise 12%. Note that if the recipient is a state institute of United Arab Emirates the applicable rate would be 5%.

36. A rate of 15% if the recipient company holds at least 25% of the voting rights in the payer company, otherwise 20%.

37. A rate of 15% if the recipient company holds at least 10% of the voting rights in the payer company, otherwise 20%.

38. Profits of a Spanish company carrying on business in Turkey through a permanent establishment situated therein may, after having been taxed under the provisions of business profits, be taxed on the remaining amount in Turkey in accordance with the provision of Turkish domestic law, but the tax so charged shall not exceed 5% of the remaining amount where profits of a company are subject to the full rate of corporation tax in Turkey; otherwise 15%.

39. A rate of 10% of the gross amount of such interest, if the interest is derived from a loan of whatever kind granted by a bank or if the interest is paid in connection with the sale on credit of merchandise or equipment to an enterprise of a Contracting State (i.e., Spain or Turkey); otherwise 15%.

40. A rate of 5% if the service provider is present in Turkey for less than 183 days.

Note that the bilateral tax treaties with Greece and Iran are also signed and approved by Turkey. The treaties would be enforced once the relevant actions are taken by the other contacting states.

## Tax administration

***Returns***/Resident entities and nonresident entities having a permanent establishment are obliged to file annual corporate income tax returns (on a calendar-year basis unless permission to the contrary is specifically obtained from the Ministry of Finance). These returns are to be submitted within the first

15 days of April of the following year. Foreign corporations having no permanent establishment are subject only to withholding tax, where applicable.

In 1995 the Ministry of Finance announced that taxpayers whose tax returns have not been certified by a sworn financial advisor (*Yeminli Mali Musavir* (YMM)) and whose assets and/or net turnover exceed the thresholds defined by the Ministry of Finance will be a higher priority when annual tax audits by the Ministry's tax auditors are carried out.

***Payment of tax***/Corporation tax must be paid by April 30 of the year of filing. A total of 33% (30% would be applied for 2005 and onward) of taxable income declared on a quarterly basis is filed as advance tax by the 10th day, and is payable by the 17th of the second month following each quarter. Advance corporate tax paid is offset against corporation tax calculated in the tax return.

## *CORPORATION TAX CALCULATION*

Calendar year 2004

|  | | (In TL millions) |
|---|---:|---:|
| Book income before taxes | | 10,000,000 |
| Add: | | |
|   Increase in pension reserves | 200,000 | |
|   Increase in general provision for bad debts | 100,000 | 300,000 |
| | | 10,300,000 |
| Deduct—Investment incentive allowance (1) | | 700,000 |
| Taxable income | | 9,600,000 |
| Corporation tax thereon at 33% | | 3,168,000 |

## Withholding tax calculation

### *Computation of taxable income*

|  | (In TL millions) |
|---|---:|
| Corporate income before taxes | 10,000,000 |
| Deduct—corporation tax (2) | 3,168,000 |
| After tax corporate income | 6,832,000 |

### *Computation of withholding tax when profits are distributed* (3)

|  | (In TL millions) |
|---|---:|
| Withholding tax base | 6,832,000 |
| Withholding tax on dividends (6,832,000 x 10%) | 683,200 |

The profit distribution is subject to 10% withholding tax for nontreaty countries, after allocation of first and second level legal reserves.

### *Totals*

|  | (In TL millions) |
|---|---:|
| Total Tax Burden | 3,851,200 |
|   Corporation tax | 3,168,000 |
|   Amount withheld against dividends | 683,200 |

Notes:

1. Investment expenditure is assumed as TL 1,750,000 million. Due to the new investment allowance regulations, 40% of this amount (TL 700,000 million) is deductible from the corporate income tax base. No withholding tax is calculated over the allowance figure.

2. Corporation tax is 33%. After corporation tax, profit is not subject to any withholding tax unless distributed. Profit to be distributed is subject to withholding tax at 10%.

3. Assuming that 100% of the profit after tax is distributed and ignoring the effects of legal reserves. No withholding tax is calculated if there is no profit distribution.

4. Exchange rate of Turkish lira at March 18, 2004: US$1 = TL 1,315,866.

## PwC contact

For additional information on taxation in Uganda, contact:

Russell Eastaugh
PricewaterhouseCoopers
Communications House
1 Colville Street
(P.O. Box 8053)
Kampala, Uganda
Telephone: (256) (41) 236018
Fax: (256) (41) 230153
e-mail: russell.eastaugh@ug.pwc.com

## Taxes on corporate income

The corporation tax rate is 30%.

## Corporate residence

A resident company is one that is incorporated in Uganda, one whose management and control are exercised in Uganda, or one that undertakes a majority of its operations in Uganda during the year of income.

## Other taxes

*Value-added tax*/VAT is charged at 17% on the supply of goods and services. The following supplies are zero-rated.

1. Goods or services exported from Uganda.
2. International transportation of passengers or goods and related services.
3. Drugs and medicines.
4. Educational materials.
5. Locally produced cereals.
6. Milk.

Some supplies are exempt, the main categories being unprocessed foodstuffs, agricultural products and livestock; machinery for processing of agricultural and diary products, financial and insurance services; education services; medical, dental and nursing goods and services; passenger transportation services (other than tour and travel operators); accommodation in tourist lodges and hotels outside of Kampala and Entebbe, petroleum fuels; computers, printers and accessories in heading 84.71 of the Harmonised Commodity Code , computer software, mobile toilets, life jackets, insecticides, certain land and property transactions, and gambling services. VAT on imported services applies.

Where a person's VAT credit exceeds UShs5 million, the credit may be offset against a future VAT liability or any other taxes due from that person.

## Branch income

Branch income is taxed at 30%.

## Income determination

*Inventory valuation*/Trading stock should be stated in accordance with the prime-cost or absorption-cost method. If not readily identifiable, FIFO or average cost can be used.

*Capital gains*/A tax on capital gains has been introduced on business assets other than assets subject to capital allowances and trading stock. No indexation of costs is allowed. Capital gains are in principle calculated on the basis of the market value as at March 31, 1998. The tax rate is the normal income tax rate on corporate profits, 30%. In addition, if sales proceeds of assets for which capital allowances have been claimed exceed the tax written-down value of those assets, the excess is treated as trading income.

*Intercompany dividends*/Dividends received by a resident company that controls 25% or more of the company paying the dividend are deemed not to be income chargeable to tax.

*Foreign income*/A resident company is taxed on worldwide income. Foreign tax credit is available up to the average Ugandan tax rate.

*Stock dividends*/Bonus issues of stock are permissible and are not taxable.

## Deductions

*Depreciation and depletion*/Capital allowances consist of an initial allowance on plant and machinery in the first year of service, followed by writing-down allowances calculated after deduction of the initial allowances and on a reducing-balance basis.

|  | % |
| --- | --- |
| Initial allowance in the following areas: | |
|    Entebbe, Jinja, Kampala, Namanve, Njeru | 50 |
|    Other areas | 75 |
| Writing-down allowances: | |
|    Computers, data-handling equipment | 40 |
|    Cars, small buses, and goods vehicles; construction and earth-moving equipment | 35 |
|    Large buses and goods vehicles; specialized trucks, tractors, trailers, and trailer-mounted containers; plant and machinery used in farming, manufacturing or mining | 30 |
|    Railroad equipment, vessels, barges, tugs, aircraft, office furniture and fixtures, any depreciable asset not included in any other class | 20 |

Fixed assets are aggregated for each of the above categories. Sales proceeds of an asset are deducted from the reduced balance of its category, and any excess is taxable as trading income.

For road vehicles other than commercial vehicles, the expenditure on which capital allowances can be claimed is restricted to Ushs30 million for each vehicle.

Capital allowances on new buildings used in manufacturing, research and development into improved methods of manufacture or mining and approved hotels and hospitals and approved commercial buildings are calculated on a straight-line basis at 5%. The cost base is reduced by the initial allowance of 20%. Note that initial allowance is 20% on new industrial buildings (other than approved commercial buildings).

Mineral exploration expenditure is wholly written off in the year in which it is incurred.

*Net operating losses*/Losses may be carried forward and offset against future profits without time limit. Farming losses can be offset only against future farming income. Only final losses on long-term contracts can be carried back.

*Payments to foreign affiliates*/Royalties and management and professional fees can be paid to foreign affiliates after deduction of 15% withholding tax. In respect of interest, there is a restriction related to thin capitalization. The allowed ratio is 2:1 foreign debt (to the foreign controller) to foreign equity. Interest on the excess debt is not allowed. Interest is also subject to 15% withholding tax.

*Other significant items*/Other significant items are as follows.

1. Bad debts written off are deductible, but provisions (except specific provisions for banks) are not.
2. Entertainment outlays, contributions to retirement funds, pensions paid, and National Social Security Fund (NSSF) company contributions are not allowable expenses for tax purposes.
3. Insurance companies are permitted to make reserves for unexpired risks.
4. Expenses incurred by companies on their initial public offerings, and any other start up costs, are allowable at a flat rate of 25%.
5. The expenses incurred by the employer on housing provided to the employee are now tax deductible to the employer.
6. The interest on treasury bills is no longer tax-exempt income.
7. Under a finance lease, the lessee is treated as the owner of the property, and the lessor is treated as having made a loan to the lessee. The interest component of a finance lease payment made by a lessee is treated as an allowable expense. The lessee can claim capital allowances on the leased property.

## Group taxation

No offset of losses between affiliated companies is permitted.

## Tax incentives

*Inward investment*/Tax incentives are the same for local and foreign investors.

*Other incentives*/None.

## Withholding taxes

On all payments for goods and services in excess of UShs1 million in aggregate, tax of 4% should be withheld where the government is the payer or owns shares in the payer.

On payments of dividends and interest to resident individuals or companies, or to companies having a permanent establishment in Uganda, withholding tax should be deducted at the rate of 15%. Note that for dividends, where a resident company owns at least 25% of the shares of another resident company that is paying the dividend, no withholding tax should be deducted. Also note that, subject to certain conditions, interest paid to a nonresident person in respect of a "widely" issued debenture is exempt from tax. The tax authorities unfortunately have not given a definition of what is a "widely" issued debenture.

Withholding tax is deducted on payments to nonresident road transport operators at a rate of 2% of the gross amount derived by the person from carriage.

On any payment to a nonresident person for rent derived from sources in Uganda tax should be withheld at a rate of 15% on the gross payment, unless the amount is attributable to a branch. Uganda-sourced services contract suffer 15% withholding tax if payable to nonresidents.

Double taxation treaties have been ratified with Denmark, Norway, South Africa, the United Kingdom, and Zambia. The United Kingdom treaty provides for 15% withholding from dividends, interest, royalties, and technical fees; the Zambian treaty does not provide for withholding taxes. The South Africa treaty provides for a withholding tax rate of 10% on management or professional fees and royalties. The East African double tax agreement has not been ratified.

## Tax administration

*Returns*/The tax year runs from July 1 to June 30. Corporations are taxed on their accounting period ending during the tax year. A final return is due within four months from the end of the accounting period.

*Payment of tax*/Credit is now allowed for any tax withheld prior to the due date for the payment of the installments If the finally calculated tax exceeds the provisional tax, the excess is payable on the due date for furnishing the final tax return. Additional tax should be paid within 45 days from the date of service of the notice of assessment.

Penalties are levied in the event of late submission of returns, or late payment of tax due, or if the final tax charge exceeds the provisional estimate by more than 10%.

## CORPORATION TAX CALCULATION

Accounting period ending June 30, 2003

| | | |
|---|---:|---:|
| Net income before taxes | | UShs 1,000,000 |
| Add: | | |
| Depreciation | 250,000 | |
| Donations | 150,000 | |
| Provision for bad debts | 70,000 | |
| Legal expenses on property purchase | 80,000 | |
| Entertainment | 10,000 | |
| Contributions to retirement fund, | | |
| NSSF company contribution | 300,000 | 860,000 |
| | | 1,860,000 |
| Deduct: | | |
| Capital allowances: | | |
| Wear and tear | 160,000 | |
| Industrial building | 40,000 | |
| Dividends received from a subsidiary | 60,000 | |
| Profit on sale of depreciable assets | 100,000 | 360,000 |
| Taxable income | | UShs 1,500,000 |
| Tax thereon at 30% | | UShs 450,000 |

Note:

Exchange rate of the Uganda new shilling at January 1, 2004: US$1 = Ushs 1937.

# Ukraine

## PwC contact

For additional information on taxation in Ukraine, contact:

Jorge E. Intriago
PricewaterhouseCoopers
38 Turgenevska, 5th floor
Kyiv 01054
Ukraine
Telephone: (380) (44) 490 6777
Fax: (380) (44) 216 4558
e-mail: jorge.e.intriago@ua.pwc.com

## Significant developments

Ukraine's tax system began undergoing major reforms in 1997. The reforms are aimed at increasing government revenues by reducing the number of special tax exemptions, as well as simplifying and streamlining compliance procedures. The reforms are expected to be completed when a new tax code is introduced.

## Taxes on corporate income

Ukraine's corporate profits tax, which has a uniform rate of 25%, applies to taxable profits earned by resident entities and permanent establishments of foreign companies. Profits derived by a nonresident can be computed by the tax authorities based on a 30% notional margin method. Special tax regime applies to Ukrainian insurance companies. Net insurance premiums (gross premium less amounts paid to reinsurance company) are taxed at a 3% rate, except for long-term life insurance premiums, which are taxed at a 0% rate. Profits earned by insurance company from activities other than insurance are taxed at standard rate.

## Corporate residence

Corporate residence is determined by the place of incorporation. Resident entities are taxed on their worldwide income. Nonresident entities are taxed on their Ukrainian-source income.

## Other taxes

Other principal corporate taxes and compulsory payments in Ukraine are the value-added tax (VAT), social security contributions, excise tax, land tax, tax on owners of motor vehicles, and import duties. In addition, there are 14 different local taxes that may be levied at the discretion of local authorities.

*Value-added tax*/VAT payers, whether residents or nonresidents, include entities whose volume of transactions subject to VAT exceeded 3,600 nontaxable allowances (currently approximately US$11,500) in any period during the previous 12 months. In addition, VAT payers include importers of goods, services or works, entities that engage in trade for cash, regardless of their sales turnover, and entities that engage in the transport of cargoes or passengers through the territory of Ukraine. Any entity qualifying as a VAT payer is required to obtain a VAT registration number.

Transactions that are subject to VAT include the sale of goods, works, or services in Ukraine, import of goods, works or services into Ukraine, and export of goods, works and services from Ukraine.

The main exempted items include educational services, health care services, pharmaceuticals registered in Ukraine, sale of goods and services to diplomatic missions on a reciprocal basis, and charitable activities.

- Transactions that are not subject to VAT include the following.
- The issue, sale, and exchange of securities.
- Depository, clearing, and registrar activities in respect of securities.
- The provision of property by a lessor to a lessee under an operating lease, and return of property upon expiry of the operating lease.
- Interest element of lease payments under financial lease agreements.
- Provision of financial loans and bank guarantees.
- Exchange of foreign currency.
- Insurance and reinsurance services specified in the Law on Insurance.
- Contribution of fixed assets to the statutory fund of a Ukrainian legal entity, whether a domestic or cross-border entity.
- Payment of dividends and royalties in cash.
- Funds under loan, deposit, insurance, or proxy agreements.
- Brokerage and dealer services in respect of securities transaction.
- Transfer of a taxpayer's assets to another taxpayer in the course of merger or acquisition.
- Transit of cargoes and passengers through Ukraine.

VAT is levied at 20% on domestic sales and the import of goods, works, and services. A 0% VAT applies to the export of goods and provision of works and services for use outside Ukraine, sales through duty-free shops, and international transport services.

Entities engaged in supplying goods or services that are taxable are allowed full credit for VAT paid on their purchases and expenses that are deductible for corporate profits tax purposes (input tax). Entities that supply taxable goods or services, plus exempt goods or services, are subject to a limitation for recovery of VAT paid on their purchases and expenses. An entity that provides only exempt goods or services cannot obtain a refund for VAT purposes.

*Excise tax*/Excise tax is applied to certain goods imported into or produced in Ukraine. The list of excisable goods includes alcoholic beverages, beer, tobacco and tobacco products, gasoline and diesel fuel and cars. Export of excisable goods from Ukraine is exempt from excise tax where payment is effected in foreign currency. Currently excise tax rates are specific (in monetary units per commodity item) except for cigarettes where combined (i.e., specific and ad valorem) rate applies.

*Import duty*/Import duty is levied at various rates in accordance with the Ukraine's Customs Tariff. There are relieved and full rates of import duty. Relieved rates of duty apply to goods originating from countries that enjoy most-favored-nation trade status, or which have concluded free trade agreements with Ukraine. Full rates of duty apply to goods originating from other countries. Most-favored-nation trade status applies to more than 60 countries (e.g., the EU and Economic Commission for Europe (ECE) countries, United States). Ukraine has concluded free trade agreements with most of the ex-USSR countries, allowing duty-free import of goods originating in those countries.

## Branch income

A foreign company can set up a representative office in Ukraine, which would be similar to an unincorporated branch. The representative office does not constitute a legal entity. A nonresident company operating a representative office is deemed to carry on business in Ukraine through a permanent establishment, and may be subject to 25% corporate profits tax unless protected by a double taxation treaty.

## Income determination

*Inventory valuation*/The book and tax inventory valuations must conform. Accounting rules permit the use of FIFO, LIFO, weighted-average, individual costing, normative costs, and selling price methods. Inventories are valued at the lower of initial cost or net realizable value.

*Capital gains*/Capital gains are taxed as part of ordinary income.

*Intercompany dividends*/Dividends from domestic subsidiaries are fully excluded from the tax base. No ownership threshold is required for exclusion. Upon remittance of dividends, the payer has to pay to the state from its own funds advance tax at the standard rate (i.e., 25%), which can be used to offset its future corporate profits tax liability. Tax liability on net insurance premiums cannot be used for such offset.

*Stock dividends*/The 25% advance tax does not apply where dividends are paid by way of new shares, provided that allocation of holding between shareholders remains unchanged, and where dividends are paid to domestic investment funds.

*Foreign income*/Companies resident in Ukraine are taxed on their worldwide income. Credit relief may be available for foreign tax paid, up to the amount of Ukrainian tax that would have been due.

Credit relief may not be available for the following foreign taxes—capital tax and tax on capital gains, post duty, tax on sales, other indirect taxes, and taxes paid from passive income (dividends, interests, insurance, and royalties).

## Deductions

*Depreciation and depletion*/Quarterly depreciation charges are computed on the basis of the reducing-balance method at the following quarterly rates.

| Description of assets | Assets purchased prior to January 1, 2004 | New assets purchased after January 1, 2004 |
|---|---|---|
| | % | % |
| Group 1 (buildings, constructions, premises) | 1.25 | 2 |
| Group 2 (transport vehicles, furniture, office equipment, household equipment, optical, electronic and electric appliances) | 6.25 | 10 |
| Group 3 (all other assets) | 3.75 | 6 |

Group 4 assets (computers, devices for automatic processing of information, software, devices for scanning and printing, other information systems, telephone sets (including mobile), microphones and portable radio transmitters purchased after January 1, 2003) are subject to quarterly depreciation at a 15% rate. Those assets purchased prior to January 1, 2003 belong to Group 2 assets, and are depreciated at 6.25% rate.

The value of land cannot be depreciated.

Intangible assets may be amortized by using the straight-line method over the asset's useful economic life, up to a maximum of ten years.

*Net operating losses*/Tax losses recorded prior to January 1, 2003 can be carried forward up to three years. Tax losses recorded after January 1, 2003 can be carried forward indefinitely. Losses cannot be carried back.

*Payments to foreign affiliates*/Where interest is payable between entities, 50% or more of the charter fund of which is owned or managed (directly or indirectly) by nonresidents, deductibility of interest expense is limited for the Ukrainian borrower. There are no special restrictions on the deductibility of royalties and service fees paid to foreign affiliates. Payments to related entity should be at arm's length.

*Taxes*/Mandatory taxes and levies are deductible for corporate profits tax purposes.

*Exchange gains*/Exchange gains and losses on debt denominated in foreign currency in respect of loans or financial leasing are taxable or deductible, accordingly.

*Nondeductible expenses*/Examples of nondeductible items include the following.

- Expenses that do not relate to the taxpayer's business.
- Expenses that are not supported by relevant document (e.g., voucher, receipt, check, etc.).
- Expenses in relation to the financing of management bodies, including holding companies, which are separate legal entities.
- Service fees paid to related entities, unless there is documentary evidence that fees are paid in relation to services actually performed.
- Payments in respect of goodwill.
- Expenses in respect of car parking, 50% of expenses in respect of purchase of fuel and lubricants for cars and operating lease of cars.
- Expenses relating to the provision of employees with uniform, safety clothes and shoes, as well as food, if the amount exceeds the norms established by the Cabinet of Ministers of Ukraine.
- Expenses in respect of personnel education in a nonresident educational institution. This includes expenses in respect of education of individuals who are a related entity to the company (e.g., shareholders who control at least 20% of a company's capital, or a company's directors)
- Expenses relating to receptions, presentations, entertainment, sampling and provisions of goods and services free of charge within the scope of an advertising campaign, if the amount exceeds 2% of the taxpayer's taxable profits for the previous year.
- Expenses in respect of business trips of the taxpayer's employees and members of its management bodies, where the purpose of such a trip does not correspond to the business of the taxpayer.
- Expenses in respect of the purchase of goods, works or services from nonresident entities based in tax haven jurisdictions that exceed the allowable amount equal to 85% of the amounts actually paid.

- Expenses in respect of warranty services, if the amount exceeds 10% of the total value of the goods sold, which have valid warranty terms.

## Group taxation

In Ukraine each company is taxed individually. However, companies that have domestic unincorporated branches may pay consolidated corporate profits tax.

## Tax incentives

A capital contribution into a Ukrainian entity is not subject to any local tax. In-kind contributions of foreign shareholders to the charter funds of Ukrainian companies are exempt from import duty. In addition, fixed assets (e.g., equipment designed for use in business) contributed into a local entity in return for corporate rights are exempt from VAT.

Special tax exemptions are available to local manufacturers of automobiles and spare parts, where in-cash contributions to the statutory fund of a local entity equal at least US$150 million for manufacturers of cars, US$30 million for manufacturers of trucks and buses, and US$10 million for manufacturers of spare parts for automobiles and buses.

Various tax incentives are available for agricultural entities.

Business entities operating in special economic zones and areas of priority development throughout various regions of Ukraine can be entitled to exemption from import duty and import VAT; exemption from corporate profits tax or taxation at reduced rates; and reduced rates of withholding tax on income derived by nonresidents and on dividends. Special economic zones and areas of priority development include the following.

- Zakarpattia (Zakarpatsky region).
- Azov and Donetsk (Donetsk region).
- Slavutych (Kiev Region).
- Kurortopolis Truskavets and Yavoriv (Lviv region).
- Porto-franco and Reni (Odessa region).
- Mykolayiv.
- Interport Kovel (Volyn region).
- Port Crimea (Kerch).
- Kharkiv.
- Certain areas in the Chernigiv, Crimea, Donetsk, Lugansk, Sumy, Volyn, Zakarpatsky, and Zhytomyr regions.

## Withholding taxes

The payment of dividends to nonresident shareholders attracts withholding tax at the rate of 15%, unless the relevant double taxation treaty provides otherwise.

Interest, royalties, and technical service fees (wherever qualifying as an engineering type income) payable to nonresidents are subject to 15% withholding tax, which can be reduced or eliminated under effective double taxation treaties. As of January 1, 2004, double taxation treaties are in effect with the following countries.

| Recipient | Dividends | Interest | Royalties |
|---|---|---|---|
| | % | % | % |
| Nontreaty | 15 | Nil/15 | 15 |
| Treaty: | | | |
| Armenia | 5/15 | Nil/10 | Nil |
| Austria | 5/10 | Nil/2/5 | Nil/5 |
| Azerbaijan | 10 | Nil/10 | 10 |
| Belarus | 15 | 10 | 15 |
| Belgium | 5/15 | Nil/2/5 | Nil/5 |
| Bulgaria | 5/15 | Nil/10 | 10 |
| Canada | 5/15 | Nil/10 | Nil/10 |
| China, P.R. | 5/10 | Nil/10 | 10 |
| Croatia | 5/10 | Ni/10 | 10 |
| Cyprus (1) | Nil | Nil | Nil |
| Czech Republic | 5/15 | Nil/5 | 10 |
| Denmark | 5/15 | Nil/10 | Nil/10 |
| Egypt | 12 | Nil/12 | 12 |
| Estonia | 5/15 | Nil/10 | 10 |
| Finland | Nil/5/15 | Nil/5/10 | Nil/5/10 |
| France | Nil/5/15 | Nil/2/10 | Nil/10 |
| Georgia | 5/10 | Nil/10 | 10 |
| Germany | 5/10 | Nil/2/5 | Nil/5 |
| Greece | 5/10 | Nil/10 | 10 |
| Hungary | 5/15 | Nil/10 | 5 |
| India | 10/15 | Nil/10 | 10 |
| Indonesia | 10/15 | Nil/10 | 10 |
| Iran | 10 | Nil/10 | 10 |
| Italy | 5/15 | Nil/10 | 7 |
| Japan (1) | 15 | Nil/10 | Nil/10 |
| Kazakhstan | 5/15 | Nil/10 | 10 |
| Korea | 5/15 | Nil/5 | 5 |
| Kyrgyzstan | 5/15 | Nil/10 | 10 |
| Latvia | 5/15 | Nil/10 | 10 |
| Lebanon | 5/15 | Nil/10 | 10 |
| Lithuania | 5/15 | Nil/10 | 10 |
| Macedonia | 5/15 | Nil/10 | 10 |
| Malaysia (1) | 15 | Nil/15 | 10/15 |
| Moldova | 5/15 | Nil/10 | 10 |
| Mongolia (1) | Nil | Nil | Nil |
| Netherlands | Nil/5/15 | Nil/2/10 | Nil/10 |
| Norway | 5/15 | Nil/10 | 5/10 |
| Poland | 5/25 | Nil/10 | 10 |
| Portugal | 10/15 | Nil/10 | 10 |
| Romania | 10/15 | Nil/10 | 10/15 |
| Russia | 5/15 | Nil/10 | 10 |
| Serbia and Montenegro | 5/10 | Nil/10 | 10 |
| Slovak Republic | 10 | 10 | 10 |
| Spain (1) | 18 | Nil | Nil/5 |
| Sweden | Nil/5/10 | Nil/10 | Nil/10 |
| Switzerland | 5/15 | Nil/10 | Nil/10 |
| Tajikistan | 10 | Nil/10 | 0 |

# Ukraine

| Recipient | Dividends | Interest | Royalties |
|---|---|---|---|
| | % | % | % |
| Turkey | 10/15 | Nil/10 | 10 |
| Turkmenistan | 10 | Nil/10 | 10 |
| United Kingdom | 5/10 | Nil | Nil |
| United States | 5/15 | Nil | 10 |
| Uzbekistan | 10 | Nil/10 | 10 |
| Vietnam | 10 | Nil/10 | 10 |

Note:

1. The treaty with the former USSR still applies.

## Tax administration

**Returns/**Tax returns must be filed both by resident and nonresident taxpayers on a quarterly basis within 40 calendar days following the last day of the reporting quarter (i.e., by May 10, August 9, November 9, and February 9).

*Payment of tax/*Tax should be paid quarterly within ten calendar days following the date when the tax return has to be filed.

## *CORPORATION TAX CALCULATION*

Calendar year ending December 31, 2003

(Under legislation in force as at December 31, 2003)

| | | | |
|---|---|---|---|
| Income | | UAH | 800,000 |
| Add: | | | |
| Royalties and service fees | 100,000 | | |
| Capital gains | 100,000 | | 200,000 |
| Gross income | | | 1,000,000 |
| Less: | | | |
| Gross expenses | 400,000 | | |
| Depreciation expenses | 200,000 | | 600,000 |
| Profit | | | 400,000 |
| Loss carryforward | | | 100,000 |
| Taxable profit | | UAH | 300,000 |
| Corporate profits tax at 25% | | UAH | 75,000 |

Note:

Exchange rate of the Hryvnia at January 1, 2004: US$1 = UAH 5.4245 (UAH is an abbreviation for the Ukrainian Hryvnia).

## PwC contact

For additional information on taxation in the United Kingdom, contact:

David Prosser
PricewaterhouseCoopers
1 Embankment Place
London WC2N 6NN, England
Telephone: (44) (20) 7583 5000, [44] [20] 7804 5852 (direct)
Fax: (44) (20) 7804 6622
LN domain: David Prosser/UK/TLS/PwC@EMEA-UK
e-mail: david.prosser@uk.pwc.com

## Significant developments

Recent changes include legislation to give relief, broadly on an accounts basis, for the amortization and other costs associated with intellectual property (from April 2002), to introduce an exemption relief from tax on the sale of substantial shareholdings (also from April 2002), to tax most profits and losses associated with foreign exchange and financial instruments on a basis closely aligned with the accounts, as has been the case since 1996 for other financing costs (from October 2002), to modernize the taxation of U.K. presences of overseas entities (from January 2003) to overhaul the corporate tax deductions allowed in respect of employee share schemes (from January 2003), and to introduce a new "stamp duty land tax" in place of the old stamp duty payable on land transactions (from December 2003).

The most important legislation proposed for 2004 will completely revise the United Kingdom's thin capitalization regime, by bringing it into the transfer pricing rules rather than (as is currently the case) dealing with it via the rules on distributions of profit. The essential elements of the rules will, however, remain. In particular, there are to be no safe harbors, so that interest disallowances will continue to be given by reference to an unclear "arm's length" standard. New rules will also update the deductions for "expenses of management" allowed to nontrading companies; in some respects the new rules will be more generous and in others less so, and the changes will end up broadly revenue-neutral

The United Kingdom has no general antiavoidance rule, and in the Budget of March 17, 2004 the Chancellor said one was not contemplated, despite press speculation. However, the Chancellor said that legislation based on the U.S. tax shelter regulations would shortly be introduced, broadly to require promoters of certain types of generic tax planning arrangements to register them with the Inland Revenue, and users of such arrangements to disclose their use in their corporate tax returns. Little detail was given as to the timing or scope of the new rules.

## Taxes on corporate income

*Corporation tax*/The normal rate is 30% for all three years ending March 31, 2003, 2004, and 2005. For companies with tax-adjusted profits below £300,000, the rate is 19% for the year to March 31, 2005. For companies with tax-adjusted profits between £300,000 and £1,500,000, there is a sliding scale of tax rates. For corporate entities with associated companies, both profit limits are divided by the number of active companies worldwide.

*Advance corporation tax*/Distributions still carry a (generally nonrepayable) tax credit in the hands of U.K. resident noncorporate shareholders, even after the abolition of ACT in April 1999, but the amount is reduced to one-ninth of the distribution. In consequence of this, shareholders resident in certain countries may be entitled to claim a payable tax credit under the relevant double taxation treaty with the United Kingdom. In practice, however, as explained in "Withholding taxes" below, the reduction in the rate of the credit makes the potential payment either nil or minimal.

*Petroleum revenue tax (PRT)*/A tax of 50% is levied on profits accruing from oil and gas extracted in the United Kingdom and in the U.K. territorial sea and continental shelf in respect of fields given development consent before March 16, 1993. PRT has effectively been abolished, together with associated relief and allowances, for fields that received development consent after March 15, 1993. PRT paid is deductible in computing corporation tax on the company's total profits.

## Corporate residence

U.K. incorporated companies are generally treated as U.K. resident. However, companies resident in the United Kingdom under domestic law, but treated as solely resident in a different country under that country's double taxation treaty with the United Kingdom, are no longer treated as U.K. resident for the purposes of U.K. domestic tax law either.

Again subject to the above exception, companies incorporated overseas are also treated as U.K. resident if their central management and control are situated in the United Kingdom, that is, the place where the directors make policy decisions as opposed to decisions on the day-to-day running of the business.

Tax residence is important because resident companies are taxable in the United Kingdom on their worldwide profits, while nonresident companies are subject to U.K. corporation tax only on the trading profits of a U.K. permanent establishment, plus U.K. income tax (generally by way of withholding) on certain U.K. source income.

Until 2003, the liability to corporation tax depended on the existence of a branch or agency in the United Kingdom. From January 1, 2003, the liability is slightly extended to cover any kind of permanent establishment (PE) through which a trade is carried on. For the first time, rules have also been introduced to explain how the PE's profits should be evaluated, including a form of thin capitalization limitation.

## Other taxes

*Value-added tax*/VAT is charged at 17.5% on the supply of most goods and services in the course of business, apart from domestic fuel and power, and certain other reduced rate supplies, which are subject to VAT at 5%. Most exports, most food, most public transport, books and publications, and certain other essential goods and services are zero-rated. Some supplies are exempt, the main categories being the grant of certain interests in land, insurance, financial services, education, and health and welfare. Zero rating is preferable to exemption, because the VAT incurred on making a zero rated supply can be recovered, while that incurred in making an exempt supply cannot.

*Local municipal taxes*/Local taxes are not based on income, but rather are levied on the occupiers of business property by reference to a deemed annual rental value for the property concerned.

*Customs and excise duties*/Many goods imported into the United Kingdom from outside the European Union (EU) are subject to customs duties. The rates of duty are provided by the EU's Common Customs Tariff.

Excise duties are chargeable on most hydrocarbon oil products, alcoholic drinks, and tobacco products imported into or produced in the United Kingdom.

*Employers' national insurance contributions*/Employers are obliged to pay National Insurance Contributions based on a percentage of each employee's earnings. For the year ending April 5, 2003, the rate was 11.8% on all earnings above £89 a week, and for the year ending April 5, 2004, it is 12.8% on all earnings above £89 a week. There is some reduction for employees "contracted out" of the state pension scheme into a private scheme.

*Insurance premium tax (IPT)*/IPT at 5% applies to premiums for most general insurance, such as for buildings and contents and motor insurance, where the insured risk is in the United Kingdom. To prevent "fragmentation", the rate increases to 17.5% where the insurance is in effect part of a supply of goods or services chargeable to VAT at 17.5%.

*Airport passenger duty*/Individuals leaving the United Kingdom by air are obliged to pay a duty of between £5 and £40, which in practice is invariably included in the cost of the air ticket. For flights within the United Kingdom, the maximum rate of duty is £10.

*Stamp duty*/Stamp duty is charged at 0.5% on sales of shares, and at graduated rates up to 4% on certain other types of property, until recently including land and buildings. Stamp duty is not charged on transfers of debt instruments or certain intellectual property; nor, as from April 23, 2002, is it charged on transfers of goodwill, and from December 1, 2003, transfers of land and buildings are instead charged stamp duty land tax (at the same graduated rates). Agreements to sell shares can attract "stamp duty reserve tax" at 0.5%. This is offset against the stamp duty due on the later transfer. Stamp duty is not usually charged on the issue of shares, but is chargeable at 1.5% on an issue or transfer of shares in Depository Receipt form or into certain "clearance systems." Transfers of assets within worldwide groups are generally exempt from stamp duty.

*Environmental taxes*/There are several environmental taxes as below, that is, "Landfill tax," "Climate change levy," and "Aggregates levy."

*Landfill tax*/This is a tax on waste disposal in landfill sites. The standard rate for the year to March 31, 2004 is thus £14 per ton, and is due to increase to £15 per ton from April 1, 2004. The reduced rate for inert waste remains at £2 per ton. There are proposals to increase the rate to £18 per ton in 2005, and eventually to increase the rate to £35 per ton by 2011

*Climate change levy*/This is a tax on energy used in the United Kingdom such as electricity, gas, coal, and so on. It came into effect on April 1, 2001, and is charged at rates that depend on the nature of the fuel used. There are reduced rates and exclusions from the charge, for example, supplies to domestic or charitable users, and to those who carry out specific energy-saving measures.

*Aggregates levy*/This tax is levied from April 1, 2002 on the extraction or importation of sand, gravel, and crushed rock for commercial exploitation in the United Kingdom. The rate of tax is £1.60 per ton.

## Branch income

Tax rates on branch profits are the same as for domestic corporations, except that the 19% small profits rate is not available to non-U.K. resident corporations unless under the terms of a double taxation treaty. No tax is withheld on transfers of profits to the head office.

## Income determination

*Inventory valuation*/In general, the book and tax methods of inventory valuation will conform. In practice, inventories are normally valued for tax purposes at the lower of cost or net realizable value. A FIFO basis of determining cost where items cannot be identified is acceptable, but not the base-stock or the LIFO method.

*Capital gains*/Gains on capital assets are taxed at the normal corporation tax rates. Gains and losses arising upon the disposal of assets held on March 31, 1982 are computed on the assumption that the assets were acquired at their market value on that date (but not where using the March 31, 1982 market value produces a greater gain or loss than that arising from using historic cost). The costs deducted from gross proceeds on the disposal of an asset are the costs of acquisition and subsequent improvements, plus the incidental costs of sale, and indexation. Indexation represents an increase in costs based on the percentage rise (if any) in the U.K. retail prices index over the relevant period, that is, from March 31, 1982, the date of acquisition or the dates improvements were carried out, as appropriate, to the date of disposal. Indexation cannot create or increase a capital loss. It can only reduce or eliminate a chargeable gain. Most acquisitions and disposals between U.K. group companies are treated as made on a no gain no loss basis (i.e., at base cost plus indexation). Otherwise acquisitions from, or disposals to, affiliates are treated as made at fair market value, as are other acquisitions or disposals not at arm's length.

Capital losses are allowed only as an offset to capital gains. An excess of capital losses over capital gains in a company's accounting period may be carried forward without limitation but may not be carried back. There is a good deal of antiavoidance legislation concerning the computation of chargeable gains, notably to stop losses being created or gains avoided where assets are depreciated by intra-group transactions, or where losses are "bought in" from third parties.

Gains realized on certain types of assets can be deferred where all or most of the proceeds are reinvested in other assets of those types within a specified period (generally three years). The "rolled-over" gain then reemerges as and when the latter assets are sold. At present the main asset categories qualifying for rollover are land and buildings, and goodwill. Goodwill acquired after April 1, 2002 will not be eligible for this sort of rollover, as "new" goodwill and intellectual property will be dealt with on an accounts basis rather than as capital gains assets.

From April 1, 2002, most disposals of shareholdings of 10% or more are exempt from tax. The main exceptions will be those of nontrading subsidiaries or subgroups, or of companies acquired within the previous year.

*Intercompany dividends*/All dividends from U.K. companies are excluded from the taxable income of the recipient company.

*Foreign income*/A U.K. resident company is taxed on its worldwide income. It is taxed on foreign branch income as earned and, generally, on foreign dividends when received. Double taxation is avoided by means of foreign tax credits or by deducting the foreign tax against income. The United Kingdom has an extensive network of double taxation treaties.

Under the "controlled foreign companies" (CFC) regime, a U.K. resident company may be taxed on a proportion of the undistributed profits of certain United Kingdom-controlled nonresident companies in which the resident company has an interest. No liability arises where one of a number of tests (e.g., the "acceptable distribution" or the "exempt activities" test) can be satisfied.

*Stock dividends*/A U.K. company can distribute tax-free a dividend of new share capital proportionately to all shareholders. If there is a right to elect for cash, all distributions to all individual shareholders, including trustees, are taxable as dividend income whether cash or capital stock is taken.

## Deductions

*Depreciation and depletion*/In the period of expenditure, tax depreciation (known as capital allowances) is available, generally at 25% of the cost of machinery and equipment acquired for use in a trade or property rental business; thereafter, tax depreciation is taken generally at 25% per annum on the reducing balance basis. With some exceptions (notably cars, ships and machinery and equipment in offices and other nonindustrial buildings), the rate of tax depreciation for machinery and equipment with an expected useful life when new of at least 25 years, and purchased after November 25, 1996, is reduced to 6%. The rate of tax depreciation of most plant leased to nonresidents is 10% (6% for long-life assets). Industrial buildings and certain hotels qualify for tax depreciation at 4% per annum (straight-line basis) on cost. No tax depreciation is normally allowed on other commercial buildings, apart from certain machinery and equipment embodied in the fabric of the buildings. In certain areas (enterprise zones), tax depreciation at 100% is available for all types of commercial buildings. Tax depreciation of machinery and equipment, and of industrial buildings, can be disclaimed in whole or in part, thereby deferring allowances.

Depreciation allowances of 10% per annum of the cost of acquisition of mineral assets, and 25% per annum of other qualifying expenditures relating to mineral extraction, are available. These allowances are given on the reducing balance basis.

Excess depreciation allowances are generally recaptured on disposal. This is done on an asset by asset basis for industrial buildings, but on a "pool" basis for most machinery and equipment—in which case there is no recapture unless the sale proceeds exceed the total tax written down value of the pooled assets.

*Net operating losses*/Losses may be carried forward indefinitely, but losses of a particular trade can be carried forward only against profits of the same trade. Loss carryback is available for trading losses against total profits of (normally) the previous 12 months (provided the same trade was being carried on in that period). There is a more limited facility to carry back certain losses of investment companies, also normally for 12 months.

*Payments to foreign affiliates*/Generally, deductions can be claimed for royalties, management service fees and interest charges paid to foreign affiliates, provided the amounts do not exceed what would be paid to unrelated entities. Interest deductions may be limited where the paying company is thinly capitalized; the United Kingdom has no explicit "safe harbor" limits, and this will continue to be so when the thin capitalization rules become part of the transfer pricing regime in 2004.

# United Kingdom

*Taxes*/Local municipal taxes (business rates) may be deducted from taxable income. These rates are based on property values. There are no local taxes on income. In addition, National Insurance Contributions (social security taxes) paid by an employer in respect of employees may also be deducted. Indirect taxes such as irrecoverable VAT or landfill tax are normally deductible, as is Petroleum Revenue Tax.

## Group taxation

Operating profits and losses (and, since 2000, capital gains and losses, though subject to some restrictions) arising in the same period can be offset between U.K. resident 75% affiliates within a worldwide group. Intra-group transfer of assets is normally tax-free. Group companies can generally elect to account for VAT as if they were one person, and where this is done, no VAT is charged on intra-group supplies of goods or services

## Tax incentives

*Capital investment*/See "Depreciation and depletion." Small- and medium-sized companies are entitled to accelerated capital allowances on purchases of most types of machinery and equipment after July 2, 1997. A full write-off in the first year is also given in respect of expenditure by small companies on information and communications technology between April 1, 2000 and March 31, 2004 inclusive.

*Other incentives*/There are special tax reliefs for expenditure on U.K. films and on scientific research and development. A system of tax credits for certain research and development (R&D) expenditure by small- and medium-sized companies was introduced for expenditure incurred on or after April 1, 2000. This allows a deduction against profits equal to 150% of the expenditure, and for tax credit payments for be made to companies which have not yet started to trade or are trading at a loss. This R&D scheme was extended to larger companies in 2002, although with a smaller uplift of 25%, rather than 50%, to the deduction, and no option of a cash payment as an alternative.

## Withholding taxes

Domestic corporations paying certain types of income must withhold as follows.

| Recipient | Dividends (1) | Interest (2) | Royalties (3) |
|---|---|---|---|
| | % | % | % |
| Resident corporations | Nil | 20/Nil (4) | 22/Nil (4) |
| Resident individuals | Nil | 20 | 22 |
| Nonresident corporations and individuals: | | | |
| Nontreaty | Nil | 20 | 22 |
| Treaty (5): | | | |
| Antigua and Barbuda | | 20 | Nil |
| Argentina | | 12 (6, 7) | 15 (8) |
| Australia | | 10 (6) | 5 (34) |
| Austria | * | Nil | Nil |
| Azerbaijan | | 10 (7) | 10 (10) |
| Bangladesh | | 10 (11) | 10 |
| Barbados | * | 15 | Nil |
| Belarus (12) | | 5 (6) | Nil |
| Belgium | * (14) | 15 | Nil |

| Recipient | Dividends (1) | Interest (2) | Royalties (3) |
|---|---|---|---|
| | % | % | % |
| Belize | * | 20 | Nil |
| Bolivia | | 15 (7) | 15 |
| Botswana | * | 15 (7) | 15 |
| Brunei | * | 20 | Nil |
| Bulgaria | | Nil | Nil |
| Burma (Myanmar) | | 20 | Nil |
| Canada | * (14) | 10 (7) | 10 (15) |
| Channel Islands: | | | |
| Guernsey | | 20 | 22 |
| Jersey | | 20 | 22 |
| China, P.R. | | 10 | 10 (22) |
| Croatia (16) | * | 10 | 10 |
| Cyprus | * | 10 | Nil |
| Czech Republic (17) | | Nil | 10 (18) |
| Denmark | | Nil | Nil |
| Egypt | | 15 | 15 |
| Estonia | | 10 (6) | 10 |
| Falkland Islands | | Nil | Nil |
| Fiji | * | 10 (7) | 15 (15) |
| Finland | | Nil (7) | Nil |
| France | * | Nil | Nil |
| Gambia | * | 15 | 12.5 |
| Germany | | Nil | Nil |
| Ghana | | 12.5 (7) | 12.5 |
| Greece | | Nil | Nil |
| Grenada | | 20 | Nil |
| Guyana | | 15 (7) | 10 |
| Hungary | | Nil | Nil |
| Iceland | * | Nil | Nil |
| India | * (9) | 15 (7, 19) | 15 (20) |
| Indonesia | * | 10 | 15 |
| Ireland, Rep. of | | Nil | Nil |
| Isle of Man | | 20 | 22 |
| Israel | | 15 | Nil (21) |
| Italy | * (14) | 10 (6) | 8 |
| Ivory Coast (Côte d'Ivoire) | | 15 | 10 |
| Jamaica | * | 12.5 (7) | 10 |
| Japan | * | 10 (7) | 10 |
| Jordan | | 10 | 10 |
| Kazakhstan | | 10 (7) | 10 |
| Kenya | * | 15 | 15 |
| Kiribati | * | 20 | Nil |
| Korea, Rep. of | | 10 (7) | 10 |
| Kuwait | | Nil | 10 |
| Latvia | | 10 | 10 |
| Lesotho | | 10 (7) | 10 |
| Lithuania | | 10(6) | 10(23) |
| Luxembourg | * (14) | Nil | 5 |
| Macedonia (16) | * | 10 | 10 |
| Malawi | * | Nil (24) | Nil (24) |

# United Kingdom

| Recipient | Dividends (1) | Interest (2) | Royalties (3) |
|---|---|---|---|
| | % | % | % |
| Malaysia | | 10 | 8 |
| Malta | * | 10 | 10 |
| Mauritius | * | 20 (6) | 15 |
| Mexico | | 15 (6, 15, 25) | 10 |
| Mongolia | | 10 (7, 26) | 5 |
| Montserrat | | 20 | Nil |
| Morocco | | 10 | 10 |
| Namibia | | 20 | 5 (15) |
| Netherlands | * (14) | Nil | Nil |
| New Zealand | * (9) | 10 | 10 |
| Nigeria | | 12.5 | 12.5 |
| Norway | | Nil | Nil |
| Oman | | Nil | Nil |
| Pakistan | | 15 | 12.5 |
| Papua New Guinea | | 10 | 10 |
| Philippines | * | 15 (27) | 22 (28) |
| Poland | * | Nil | 10 |
| Portugal | | 10 | 5 |
| Romania | * | 10 | 15 (29) |
| Russian Federation | | Nil | Nil |
| St. Kitts and Nevis | | 20 | Nil |
| Sierra Leone | | 20 | Nil |
| Singapore | | 10 | 10 |
| Slovak Republic (17) | | Nil | 10 (18) |
| Slovenia (16) | * | 10 | 10 |
| Solomon Islands | * | 20 | Nil |
| South Africa | | Nil | Nil |
| Spain | * | 12 (7) | 10 |
| Sri Lanka | | 10 (6) | 10 (18) |
| Sudan | * | 15 | 10 |
| Swaziland | | 20 | Nil |
| Sweden | * (14) | Nil | Nil |
| Switzerland | * (14) | Nil | Nil |
| Taiwan | | 10 | 10 (13) |
| Thailand | * | 20 (30) | 15 (31) |
| Trinidad and Tobago | * | 10 | 10 (15) |
| Tunisia | | 12 (30) | 15 |
| Turkey | | 15 | 10 |
| Tuvalu | * | 20 | Nil |
| Uganda | | 15 | 15 |
| Ukraine | | Nil | Nil |
| USSR (former) (12) | | Nil | Nil |
| United States (32) | | Nil | Nil |
| Uzbekistan | | 5 (33) | 5 (33) |
| Venezuela | | 5 | 7 (22) |
| Vietnam | | 10 | 10 |
| Yugoslavia (former) (16) | * | 10 | 10 |
| Zambia | * | 10 | 10 |
| Zimbabwe | * | 10 | 10 |

Notes:

1. A tax credit is available to U.K. resident individual shareholders on dividends received, as described above. Some double taxation treaties allow a half or full tax credit (less, normally, a 5% to 15% notional withholding tax) also to nonresident individuals and usually to corporate portfolio investors. Treaties that allow a payable credit are indicated by an asterisk (*). However, since April 6, 1999 the credit has been reduced from one quarter to one ninth, which has the result that unless note 14 below applies, the tax credit indicated by the asterisk is now in effect useless, since it is wholly eliminated by the (usually 15%) withholding tax allowed by the treaty.

2. Withholding tax applies only to "annual interest" (i.e., excluding interest on certain short-term loans). Banks and similar financial institutions are also normally able to pay annual interest to non-U.K. residents free of withholding tax. In addition, most of the U.K. treaties provide for a nil rate of withholding on interest paid to governmental and quasigovernmental lenders. Such exemptions are not separately indicated in the table below.

3. Some types of royalties are not subject to U.K. withholding tax, including film royalties and equipment royalties. Treaty provisions specifically relating to these are therefore not mentioned here.

4. From April 6, 2001, payments to any U.K. resident company (not just banks, as before) can be made free of withholding tax if the recipient is chargeable to tax on the interest or royalty. Discussions continue as to whether this provision will be extended to recipients who are exempt from U.K. tax on the interest or royalty.

5. Where a reduced rate of withholding is allowed by any treaty, whether on interest or royalties, it is usual for this reduced rate to be stated not to apply to amounts which are in excess of a normal commercial rate of interest/royalty, or where the interest/royalty is effectively connected to a PE in the United Kingdom of the recipient or where the debt/license was created primarily to obtain the advantage of the treaty; such general limitations are not specifically indicated in the table below.

6. Nil on certain loans.

7. Treaty rate not applicable to certain loans held by tax-exempt holders and resold within three months of acquisition.

8. Lower rates, primarily of 5% on copyright royalties and 10% on patents and know-how, will in practice apply in almost all cases.

9. No tax credit for companies.

10. A 5% rate on literary/artistic copyright royalties.

11. A 7.5% rate on interest paid to banks and other financial institutions.

12. The United Kingdom has announced that the old UK/USSR treaty ceased to apply to Armenia, Georgia, Kyrgyzstan, or Moldova on April 5, 2002, so that there was from that date no treaty in force with any of those countries. However, the old UK/USSR treaty will continue to apply to Belarus, Tajikistan, and Turkmenistan until new treaties are concluded. A treaty with Belarus has been signed but is not yet in force.

13. Treaty effective from April 1, 2003.

14. Half tax credit payable by the U.K. Exchequer to nonresident companies possessing 10% or more of the voting power of the paying company, subject to a 5% withholding tax (10% for Canada) on the aggregate of the dividend and

the half credit, and subject to antiabuse provisions in the case of the Netherlands and Switzerland. From April 6, 1999 the tax credit has been reduced to a level where the repayment after 5% withholding tax will be only about 0.3% of the dividend.

15. Nil on literary/artistic copyright royalties.
16. The United Kingdom's treaty with the former Yugoslavia is regarded as still in force between the United Kingdom and Croatia, Macedonia, Slovenia, and the Federal Republic of Yugoslavia (Serbia and Montenegro). The position with regard to the remainder of the former Yugoslavia is undetermined.
17. The independent states of the Czech Republic and the Slovak Republic have confirmed that they will honor the treaty between the United Kingdom and the former Czechoslovakia.
18. Nil on copyright royalties.
19. A rate of 10% on certain bank loans.
20. A rate of 10% or 20% in certain limited cases.
21. A rate of 15% of the corporate income tax rate on film and TV royalties.
22. A rate of 7% on royalties for use of industrial, commercial, or scientific equipment.
23. A rate of 5% on royalties for use of industrial, commercial, or scientific equipment.
24. A rate of 20%/22% if paid to a company controlling more than 50% of the voting power of the paying company.
25. Nil on government and local authority loans. The rate is 5% where the beneficial owner is a bank or insurance company or the interest is derived from bonds and securities that are regularly and substantially traded on a recognized securities market. The rate is 10% where the beneficial owner is not a bank or insurance company but the interest is paid by a bank or by the purchaser of machinery and equipment to a person who sold that equipment on credit.
26. A rate of 7% on interest paid to banks.
27. A rate of 10% on interest on bonds issued to the public.
28. A rate of 15% on royalties on tapes for TV or radio broadcasting.
29. A rate of 10% on copyright royalties.
30. A rate of 10% on interest paid to banks and other financial institutions.
31. A rate of 5% on literary/artistic/scientific copyright royalties.
32. New treaty effective from May 1, 2003 in respect of withholding taxes.
33. Lower rate may be substituted to match any lower rate agreed in a treaty between Uzbekistan and a third Organization for Economic Cooperation and Development (OECD) country.
34. When the revised treaty comes into force on April 1, 2004, but 10% until then.

## Tax administration

**Returns**/Companies are assessed by reference to accounting periods. Normally, the accounting period is the period for which the company makes up its accounts. An accounting period for corporation tax purposes cannot exceed 12 months. Companies must file their statutory accounts and tax return within one year from the end of the accounting period; the return must include a self-assessment of the tax payable, eliminating the need for assessment by the Revenue.

*Payment of tax*/For most companies corporation tax has been payable annually, nine months after the end of the accounting period to which it relates (so, normally before the return is filed). For larger companies and groups a system of quarterly payments on account, based on estimated profits, has been introduced, the first payment being due in the seventh month of the accounting period. This system will not apply to companies with taxable profits below £1,500,000 (that limit being shared between the companies in a group, where relevant).

## *CORPORATION TAX CALCULATION*

For year ending December 31, 2003

Schedule D, Case I (trading income):

| | | |
|---|---:|---:|
| Net profit before taxation shown by the accounts for the year ending December 31, 2003............................................. | | £ 1,000,000 |
| Add: | | |
| Depreciation amounts charged in accounts.......................... | 400,000 | |
| Interest payable on loan used to fund the purchase of a subsidiary ................................................ | 100,000 | |
| Various other disallowable items ......................................... | 40,000 | 540,000 |
| | | 1,540,000 |
| Less: Amounts credited in accounts: | | |
| Dividends received from UK-resident companies (not liable to corporation tax in recipient company's hands) ..................................................... | 10,000 | |
| Research & development costs uplift at 25% on £20,000...... | 5,000 | |
| Interest income receivable on investments (gross)............... | 120,000 | |
| Capital allowances: | | |
| Industrial buildings at 4% ................................................. | 120,000 | |
| Machinery and equipment: Writing down allowances at 25% ..................................................... | 360,000 | |
| Research and development allowance at 100% ............... | 5,000 | 620,000 |
| | | 920,000 |
| Add: | | |
| Schedule D, Case III: Interest income receivable (gross)....... | 120,000 | |
| Less: Nontrading loan interest payable ................... ............... | (100,000) | |
| Chargeable gains: Capital gains (net of capital losses) ... ........ | 46,500 | 66,500 |
| Profits chargeable to corporation tax....................................... | | £ 986,500 |
| Corporation tax at 30% (1) ........................................................ | | 295,950 |
| Interest received under deduction of tax at 20% ...................... | 105,000 | |
| *Less*—Interest paid on which 20% withholding tax due ........... | (79,000) | |
| | 26,000 | |
| Income tax borne on net receipt of £26,000 at 20% ................................ | | (5,200) |
| Corporation tax payable (2)....................................................... | | £ 290,750 |

Notes:

1. It is assumed that the company is associated with at least one other company: as a result it cannot benefit from the small profits rate, and it is also liable to pay tax by installments.

2. The new system of quarterly payments has now been phased in, so for an accounting period ending on December 31, 2003, 25% of the total liability is due on each of July 14, 2003, October 14, 2003, January 14, 2004, and April 14, 2004.

3. It is assumed that the capital gains are not included in the accounts profit of £1,000,000. To the extent that they are, they would be deducted before the £46,500 is added back.

4. Interest is taxed or allowed on an accruals basis; the withholding tax associated with it is paid or credited on a receipts and payments basis.

5. Exchange rate of the pound sterling at February 28, 2004: US$1 = £0.536.

## PwC contact

For additional information on taxation in the United States, contact:

Rick Stamm
PricewaterhouseCoopers LLP
1177 Avenue of the Americas
New York, New York 10036
email: rick.stamm@us.pwc.com

## Significant developments

Treasury finalized regulations requiring disclosure of abusive tax shelter transactions.

The personal holding company and accumulated earnings rates were reduced to 15%.

Availability of bonus depreciation was extended to property acquired until January 1, 2005, and the first year depreciation rate was increased to 50% on certain property.

Section 179 was temporarily expanded to include a deduction for off-the-shelf computer software, the Section 179 limit was temporarily increased to $100,000 and the phase-out was increased to $400,000.

Tax benefits for exports (DISC/FSC/ETI) remain an open issue. The World Trade Organization (WTO) found that the extraterritorial income (ETI) regime was an illegal export subsidy. The U.S. has not repealed the ETI regime and certain United States goods are subject to European Union (EU) sanctions upon import into the EU.

The individual capital gains rate was reduced, there was a reduction in the amount of gain recognized from the sale of small business stock, and capital gains treatment may be available for individual's dividend income.

## Taxes on corporate income

*Regular federal income tax*/The current maximum federal corporate tax rate is 35%. Regular federal income tax is levied at the following rates.

| Taxable income | | Tax on | Percentage |
|---|---|---|---|
| Over | Not over | Column 1 | on excess |
| (Column 1) | | | |
| 0 | $ 50,000 | — | 15 |
| $ 50,000 | 75,000 | $ 7,500 | 25 |
| 75,000 | 100,000 | 13,750 | 34 |
| 100,000 | 335,000 | 22,250 | 39 |
| 335,000 | 10,000,000 | 113,900 | 34 |
| 10,000,000 | 15,000,000 | 3,400,000 | 35 |
| 15,000,000 | 18,333,333 | 5,150,000 | 38 |
| 18,333,333 | | 6,416,667 | 35 |

The 39% tax rate applies to taxable income between $100,000 and $335,000 to eliminate the benefit of the 15% and 25% rates, and the 38% tax rate applies to taxable income between $15,000,000 and $18,333,333 to eliminate the benefit of the 34% rate. Personal service corporations are subject to a flat income tax rate of 35%.

Generally, a corporation is required to prepay 100% of its estimated tax liability for the year in four equal installments.

Estimated tax includes regular tax, alternative minimum tax, environmental tax, and (for foreign corporations) the tax on gross transportation income. To avoid a penalty, small corporations may estimate the installments on the basis of the prior year's tax liability. Corporations that had taxable income of at least $1 million (before utilization of net operating loss or capital loss carryforwards) in any of the three preceding years can rely on the prior-year liability method for the first quarter estimated payment only. Such corporations must thereafter satisfy the requirement on the basis of their estimate of the current year's tax liability.

## Corporate residence

A corporation organized or created in the United States or under the law of the United States is a domestic corporation. A domestic corporation is a resident corporation even though it does no business or owns no property in the United States. A foreign corporation engaged in trade or business within the United States is a resident foreign corporation.

## Other taxes

In addition to the regular federal income tax, the following taxes may apply.

**Top rate on net capital gains**/On current sales, the long-term capital gains tax rate is the same as the tax rates applicable to ordinary income. However, differences may arise where the alternative minimum tax is imposed.

**Federal alternative minimum tax**/An alternative minimum tax (AMT) is imposed on corporations other than S corporations (see below) and small C corporations (generally those with no three-year average annual gross receipts exceeding $7.5 million). The tax is 20% of alternative minimum taxable income (AMTI). AMTI is computed by adjusting the corporation's regular taxable income by specified adjustments and "tax preference" items. Tax preference or adjustment items could arise, for example, if a corporation has substantial accelerated depreciation, percentage depletion, intangible drilling costs, or nontaxable income.

**Accumulated earnings tax**/Corporations (other than S corporations, domestic and foreign personal holding companies, corporations exempt from tax under Subchapter F of the Internal Revenue Code, and passive foreign investment companies) accumulating earnings and profits for the purpose of avoiding share-holder personal income tax are subject to this penalty tax, in addition to any other tax that may be applicable. The accumulated earnings tax is equal to 15% of "accumulated taxable income." Generally, accumulated taxable income is the excess of taxable income with certain adjustments, including a deduction for regular income taxes, over the dividends paid deduction and the accumulated earnings credit. The credit allows most corporations to accumulate $250,000 of prior and current-period earnings before the tax may be imposed.

**Personal holding company tax**/U.S. corporations and certain foreign corporations that receive substantial "passive income" and are "closely held" (both as defined) may be subject to personal holding company tax. The personal holding company tax is 15% of undistributed personal holding company income and is levied in addition to the regular tax. A foreign personal holding company (as defined) is subject only to the regular corporate income tax, but its U.S. shareholders are taxable on their respective shares of the corporation's income, whether distributed or not.

Corporations with 75 or fewer shareholders, none of whom can be corporations, that meet certain other requirements may elect to be taxed under Subchapter S. S corporations are taxed in a manner similar but not identical to partnerships and are generally not subject to federal income tax.

*State and municipal taxes*/Corporate income tax rates vary from state to state and generally range from 1% to 12% (although some states impose no income tax). The most common taxable base is income, which is generally allocated to a state on the basis of a three-factor formula: tangible assets, sales and other receipts, and payroll. Other taxes that states may impose in lieu of or in addition to taxes based on income include franchise taxes, and taxes on the capital of a corporation. State and municipal taxes are deductible expenses for federal income tax purposes.

*Other*/Most states and some cities impose sales or use taxes and a variety of property taxes. The federal government and many state governments also impose miscellaneous excise taxes on various products at either the manufacturing, wholesale or retail level.

## Branch income

Tax rates on branch profits are the same as on corporate profits. The law also imposes a 30% branch level tax (BLT) in addition to U.S. corporate-level income taxes on a foreign corporation's U.S. branch earnings and profits for the year that are effectively connected with a U.S. business. The taxable base for the BLT is increased (decreased) by any decrease (increase) in the U.S. net equity of the branch. The BLT on profits can be replaced by the secondary withholding tax or, if a relevant treaty so provides (subject to strict "treaty shopping" rules), eliminated entirely. If the BLT is eliminated by treaty, the secondary withholding rules will generally apply instead. Under these rules, a portion of any dividend paid by the foreign corporation will be treated as U.S.-source income (subject to withholding) if 25% or more of the corporation's total gross income for the three years preceding the year of payment was effectively connected with a U.S. business.

With certain exceptions, a 30% (or lower treaty rate) branch-level tax will also be imposed on interest payments by the U.S. branch to foreign lenders. In addition, the tax will apply if the amount of interest deducted by the branch on its U.S. tax return exceeds the amount of interest actually paid during the year.

## Income determination

*Inventory valuation*/Inventories are generally stated at the lower of cost or market on a FIFO basis. LIFO, on a cost basis only, can be elected for tax purposes, with book and tax conformity generally required.

The tax law requires capitalization for tax purposes of several costs allocable to the manufacturing process that are frequently expensed as current operating costs for financial reporting (e.g., the excess of tax over financial statement depreciation).

*Capital gains*/Gains or losses on the sale or exchange of capital assets held for more than 12 months are treated as long-term capital gains or losses. Gains or losses on the sale or exchange of capital assets held for 12 months or less are treated as short-term capital gains or losses. The excess of net long-term capital gain over net short-term capital loss is considered net capital gain. Capital losses are allowed only as an offset to capital gains. An excess of capital losses over capital gains in a taxable year may be carried back three years and carried forward five years to be utilized against (offset) capital gains.

For dispositions of personal property and certain nonresidential real property used in a trade or business, net gains are first taxable as ordinary income to the extent of the depreciation/cost recovery, with any remainder generally treated as capital gain. For other trade or business real property, net gains are generally taxed as ordinary income to the extent that the depreciation or cost recovery claimed exceeds the straight-line amount, with any remainder treated as capital gain.

An exception to capital gain treatment exists to the extent that losses on business assets were recognized in prior years. A net loss from the sale of business assets is treated as an ordinary loss. Future gains, however, will be treated as ordinary income to the extent of such losses recognized in the five immediately preceding years.

*Intercompany dividends*/A U.S. corporation can generally deduct 70% of dividends received from other U.S. corporations. The dividends-received deduction is increased from 70% to 80% if the recipient of the dividend distribution owns at least 20% but less than 80% of the distributing corporation. Generally, 100% of dividends received from U.S. corporations in which there is at least 80% ownership is deductible. With minor exceptions, a U.S. corporation cannot deduct dividends it receives from a foreign corporation.

*Foreign income*/Generally, a U.S. corporation is taxed on its worldwide income, including foreign branch income as earned and foreign dividends when received. Double taxation is avoided by means of foreign tax credits. Alternatively, a deduction may be claimed for actual foreign taxes. In the case of foreign subsidiaries more than 50% owned by U.S. shareholders (controlled foreign corporations, or CFCs), Subpart F provides that certain types of undistributed income will be currently taxed to the U.S. shareholders. Generally, Subpart F income includes (1) passive income, such as dividends, interest, rents, royalties, net foreign currency and commodities gains, and gains from the sale of certain investment property; (2) certain insurance income; (3) shipping income; (4) oil-related income; and (5) certain related-party sales and services income. In addition, investments in U.S. property by CFCs (including loans to U.S. shareholders) can result in a deemed dividend to the U.S. shareholder. "Active financing income" is not Subpart F income for tax years beginning before 2007.

Income from certain passive foreign investment companies (where 75% or more of the income is passive or at lest 50% of the assets held produce passive income) is also subject to current taxation. Current taxation occurs if the corporation elects to be a qualified electing fund (QEF) or there are actual distributions. If the QEF election is not made and the corporation makes an actual distribution, the distribution will be treated as an excess distribution to the extent it exceeds 125% of the average of the distributions made with respect to the stock over the three immediately preceding years. The excess distribution is spread over the taxpayer's holding period, and subject to tax at the highest marginal tax rates in effect. (This deferred tax amount is also subject to an interest charge.)

*Stock dividends*/A U.S. corporation can distribute a tax-free dividend of common stock proportionately to all common stock shareholders. If the right to elect cash is given, all distributions to all shareholders are taxable as dividend income whether cash or stock is taken. There are exceptions to these rules, and extreme caution must be observed before making such distributions.

## Deductions/net operating losses

*Depreciation and depletion*/For property placed in service after 1986, capital costs must be recovered by using the Modified Accelerated Cost Recovery System (MACRS) method. The general cost recovery periods are 3, 5, 7, 10, 15, 20, 27.5, and 39 years (31.5 years for property placed in service before May 13, 1993). Most tangible personal property is in the 3-, 5-, or 7-year class. (Automobiles are placed in the 5-year class.) Property placed in the 3-, 5-, 7-, or 10-year class is depreciated by using the 200% declining-balance method, then switching to straight-line at a time that will maximize the depreciation deduction. Property in the 15- or 20-year class is depreciated by using the 150% declining-balance method with a later switch to the straight-line method. An election may be made to use the Alternative Depreciation System (basically, the straight-line method over prescribed lives). Residential rental property is generally depreciated by the straight-line method over 27.5 years. Nonresidential real property is depreciated by the straight-line method over 39 years (31.5 years for property placed in service before May 13, 1993).

A 30% special first-year depreciation allowance applies (unless an election-out is made) for new MACRS property acquired after September 10, 2001 and before January 1, 2005 (subject to transition rules) with a recovery period of 20 years or less, certain computer software, water utility property, and certain leasehold improvements. The special allowance applies for regular income tax and AMT purposes. No AMT adjustment is made if the special allowance is used. The property must be placed in service before 2005 (before 2006 for certain longer-lived property). The special allowance does not apply to property that must be depreciated using the Alternative Depreciation System, or to "listed property" not used predominantly for business. The special allowance reduces basis before regular depreciation is figured. A similar, but somewhat broader, 30% special first-year allowance applies to certain property placed in service in the "Liberty Zone" in lower Manhattan.

For most tangible personal and real property placed in service in the United States after 1980 but before January 1, 1987, capital costs must be recovered by the Accelerated Cost Recovery System (ACRS), which applies accelerated methods of cost recovery over periods specified by statute. The general ACRS recovery periods are 3, 5, 10, 15, 18, and 19 years.

Special rules apply to automobiles and certain other "listed" property. Accelerated depreciation deductions can be claimed only if the automobile is used 50% or more for qualified business use (as defined). Further, for automobiles placed in service after 1986, the yearly allowable depreciation deduction cannot exceed specific dollar limitations. For example, for automobiles placed in service in 2004 the limits are: for the first year, $2,960; second year, $4,800; third year, $2,850; and subsequent years, $1,675. However, for autos that qualify for the special 30% first-year depreciation allowance described above, the first-year limit is increased by 50% so that the $4,690, to $7,650, Special rules also apply to automobiles and certain other property to the extent they are used less than 50% for business purposes.

The cost recovery methods and periods are the same for both new and used property. An election to use the straight-line method over the regular recovery period or a longer recovery period is also available. Or, taxpayers may elect to use the 150% declining-balance method over the regular recovery period for all property other than real property. This method is required for alternative minimum tax purposes, except for property for which the special 30% first-year depreciation allowance, described above, is claimed.

Corporations can elect to expense up to a statutory amount per year ($100,000 for 2003; $100,000 for 2004, $100,000 for 2005, and $100,000 for 2006) of the cost of certain eligible property used in the active conduct of a trade or business. The maximum deduction amount is reduced dollar for dollar where the corporation places in service during the tax year qualified tangible personal property in excess of $400,000 for tax years 2003, 2004, 2005 and 2006. In addition, the deduction under this election is limited to the taxable income of the business. The annual expensing limit is increased by the lesser of $35,000 or the lesser of the cost of the New York Liberty Zone property for that property acquired after September 10, 2001 that is placed in service before 2007 and used in the "Liberty Zone" of lower Manhattan. Furthermore, only 50% of the cost of the Liberty Zone Property is taken into account when applying the $400,000 limit.

Separate methods and periods of cost recovery are specified by statute for certain tangible personal and real property used outside the United States.

Rapid amortization may be allowable for certain pollution control facilities.

Tax depreciation is not required to conform to book depreciation.

For natural resource properties other than timber and certain oil and gas properties, depletion may be computed on a cost or a percentage basis.

Cost depletion is based on the adjusted basis of the property. Each year, the adjusted basis of the property is reduced, but not below zero, by the amount of depletion calculated for that year. The current-year cost depletion deduction is based on an estimate of the number of units that make up the deposit and the number of units extracted and sold during the year.

Percentage depletion is deductible at rates varying from 5% to 25% of gross income, depending on the mineral and certain other conditions, and may be deducted even after the total depletion deductions have exceeded the cost basis. However, percentage depletion is limited to 50% (100% for oil and gas properties) of taxable income from the property, computed without allowance for depletion. (The income limit doesn't apply to production from marginal oil and gas properties, for tax years beginning before 2004.) Percentage depletion for certain "small producers" (as defined) is allowable at 15%. Where the latter exemption applies, oil and gas percentage depletion is limited to 65% of taxable income in addition to the other limitations on percentage depletion noted above.

**Net operating losses**/Generally, a two-year carryback is allowed for federal income tax purposes. If the loss is not fully utilized, it may be carried forward 20 years. A five-year carryback applies to net operating losses (NOLs) arising in tax years ending in 2001 or 2002. For tax years beginning before August 6, 1997, a loss may be carried back three years, and, if not fully utilized, it may be carried forward 15 years. An irrevocable election to forgo a carryback period is permitted. For state tax purposes carryback and carryforward provisions are often similar to the federal provisions, except that several states do not permit any carrybacks or carryforwards.

Complex rules may limit the utilization of net operating losses after a reorganization or other change in corporate ownership. Generally, if the ownership of more than 50% in value of the stock of the loss corporation changes, a limit is placed on the amount of future income that may be offset by losses carried forward.

*Payments to foreign affiliates*/A U.S. corporation can generally claim a deduction for royalties, management service fees, and interest charges paid to foreign affiliates, to the extent the amounts are actually paid and are not in excess of what it would pay an unrelated entity, that is, are at arm's length. In addition, U.S. withholding on these payments may be required.

*Taxes*/See, for example, "State and municipal taxes" above.

*Other significant items*/Deductions for allowable charitable contributions may not exceed 10% of taxable income computed without regard to certain deductions, including charitable contributions themselves. Deductions for contributions so limited may be carried over to the five succeeding years, subject to the 10% limitation annually, as noted above. Organizational expenditures and new business start-up costs may be amortized over a period of not less than 60 months. Depending on the taxpayer's tax accounting method, research and experimental expenditures may be deducted as incurred or treated as deferred expenses and amortized over a period of not less than 60 months; however, in general, the method used must be consistently applied.

The deduction for business meal and entertainment expenses is 50% of the expenses incurred. There are also limitations on the deductibility of international and domestic business travel expenses.

## Group taxation

An affiliated group of U.S. corporations consisting of a parent and subsidiaries directly or indirectly 80% owned (as defined) can offset the profits of one affiliate against the losses of another affiliate within the group by electing to file a consolidated federal income tax return. A foreign-incorporated subsidiary cannot be consolidated into the U.S. group, except for certain Mexican- and Canadian-incorporated entities. Filing on a consolidated (combined) basis is also allowed (or may be required) in certain states

## Tax incentives

*Inbound investment*/There are generally no specific incentives related to inbound investment at the federal level, other than the portfolio debt and bank deposit exceptions. The portfolio debt exception enables nonresidents and foreign corporations to invest in certain obligations (which must meet certain statutory requirements to qualify as "portfolio debt") in the United States without being subject to U.S. income (or withholding) tax on the interest income. Certain state and local benefits may also be available.

*Capital investment*/An energy investment credit is allowed for 10% of investments in qualified energy property. Qualified energy property is solar and geothermal property (as defined). A similar credit is allowed for electricity-production facilities using certain renewable resources, including wind and closed-loop biomass, placed in service before 2004.

A credit is available for certain qualified expenditures in connection with the rehabilitation of older business real estate. The allowable credit is from 10% to 20% of qualifying expenditures for buildings built before 1936 and for certified historic structures. The basis of the property is reduced for all of the credit claimed.

Generally, property used outside the United States and its possessions does not qualify for the credit. Unused credits can be carried back one year and carried forward 20 years. Part of the credit may be lost if the property is sold before the end of its recovery period (recapture of investment credit).

*Exports (FSC/DISC)/*The domestic international sales company (DISC) and foreign sales corporation (FSC) regimes were replaced as of October 1, 2000 with the extraterritorial income (ETI) regime. Under the ETI regime, gross income does not include ETI to the extent that such income is qualifying foreign trade income, which is the amount of gross income which (if excluded) would result in a reduction of taxable income by the greatest of 15% of foreign trade income, 1.2% of foreign trading gross receipts, 30% of foreign sale and lease income. Taxpayers are required to allocate deductions between excluded and nonexcluded foreign trade income because deductions attributable to excluded ETI are not allowed. Also, no foreign tax credit against U.S. income taxes will be allowed for any income taxes paid or accrued to any foreign country or U.S. possession (including taxes paid in lieu of tax) with respect to excluded ETI.

In January 2002, the WTO ruled that the ETI regime was an illegal export subsidy, just as it had ruled against the previous DISC and FSC regimes. As a sanction, the EU was given authority to impose up to $4 billion in trade sanctions against U.S. manufacturing and agricultural exports. The EU has begun imposition of these trade sanctions, which will not be removed until the ETI regime is repealed. In the interim, taxpayers will be subject to the EU sanctions, but must continue to comply with the ETI regime.

*U.S. possessions/*The Puerto Rico and possessions tax credit allowed by Section 936 are terminated for years beginning after December 31, 1995. However, a U.S. corporation that was actively engaged in business in a U.S. possession on October 13, 1995 and that made a Section 936 election for the taxable year including that date can limit U.S. tax on active business income earned by a possessions business, certain investment income earned in the possession and gain from the sale of substantially all of the assets used in the possessions business. Such corporations are considered "existing credit claimants" as of the effective date of the repeal of Section 936 and therefore may continue to claim benefits, subject to a ten-year phase-out period.

Existing credit claimants must limit the credit to either a percentage of the otherwise allowable credit (applicable percentage limitation) or the amount of the credit determined under a formula that reflects economic activity in the possession (economic activity limitation). The amount of income that is eligible for the credit is further limited to the specially defined adjusted base period income for tax years beginning after December 31, 2001 and before January 1, 2006 if the claimant applies the economic activity limitation, and for tax years beginning after December 31, 1997 and before January 1, 2006 for claimants that apply the applicable percentage limitation. The credit does not apply to qualified possession source investment income (QPSII) earned after June 30, 1996.

*Employment*/Credits against the tax ("work opportunity tax credit") are available for employment of certain types of workers who began work for an employer before January 1, 2004. "Creditable" wages are generally the first $6,000 of wages paid to each qualified employee for the year. The credit is 40% of creditable wages, for a maximum credit of $2,400. A similar "welfare-to-work" credit is available for 35% of the first $10,000 of certain workers' first-year wages, and 50% of the first $10,000 of their second-year wages. A similar credit for employers in the New York Liberty Zone was available for tax years 2002 and 2003. Under the common general rule, unused credits can be carried back one year and forward 20 years.

*Qualified private activity bonds*/Interest income received on certain qualified private activity bonds (as defined) is generally exempt from federal income tax. This enables a business enterprise to issue the bonds at a lower interest rate.

*Research and development*/A credit against the federal tax equal to 20% of the sum of qualified research expenses in excess of the base amount (as defined) and basic research payments (as defined) may be obtained for the period from July 1, 1996 through June 30, 2004, but special filing requirements apply to research expenditures paid or incurred between July 1, 1999 and September 30, 2001. The base amount cannot be less than 50% of the current year's qualified research expenditures.

Those taxpayers that, despite significant R&D investments, are unable to claim the standard R&D credit because their current R&D intensity is lower than during the credit's 1984–88 "fixed base" period may utilize an elective "alternative incremental research credit" (AIRC). Under the AIRC, a graduated-rate system applies to the extent that the taxpayer's current-year qualified research expenses (QREs) exceed a specified percentage of its average gross receipts for the prior four years (the "base amount"). This election to be subject to the alternative incremental credit regime applies to the tax year for which it is made and all later years unless the IRS consents to its revocation.

The deduction for research and development expenditures must be reduced by the entire amount of the credit unless an election is made to reduce the amount of the credit.

## Withholding taxes

As of May 2004.

| | Interest | Dividends | | |
| | paid by U.S. | Paid by U.S. | Qualifying for | |
| | obligors— | corporations— | direct dividend | |
| Country of residence | general | general (1) | rate (1) | Royalties (2) |
|---|---|---|---|---|
| | % | % | % | % |
| Nontreaty | 30 | 30 | 30 | 30 |
| Australia | 10 (4, 24, 25) | 15 (4, 22) | 5 (3, 4, 22, 28) | 0 (4)/5 (4)/5 (4) |
| Austria | 0 (4, 7) | 15 (4, 11) | 5 (4, 11) | 0 (4)/10 (4)/0 (4) |
| Barbados | 5 (4) | 15 (4, 11) | 5 (3, 4, 11) | 5 (4) |
| Belgium | 15 (4) | 15 (4) | 5 (3, 4) | 0 (4)/0 (5)/0 (4) |
| Canada | 10 (4) | 15 (4, 11) | 5 (4, 11) | 0 (4)/10 (4)/0 (4) |
| China, People's Rep. of | 10 (4) | 10 (4) | 10 (4) | 10 (4, 10)/10 (4)/10 (4) |

# United States

| Country of residence | Interest paid by U.S. obligors— general | Dividends | | Royalties (2) |
|---|---|---|---|---|
| | | Paid by U.S. corporations— general (1) | Qualifying for direct dividend rate (1) | |
| | % | % | % | % |
| Commonwealth of Independent States .. | 0 (8) | 30 | 30 | 0 |
| Cyprus ........................ | 10 (4) | 15 (4) | 5 (3, 4) | 0 (4) |
| Czech Republic ............ | 0 (4) | 15 (4, 11) | 5 (3, 4, 11) | 10 (4)/0 (4)/0 (4) |
| Denmark ...................... | 0 (4, 21) | 15 (4, 22) | 5 (3, 4, 22) | 0 (4) |
| Egypt............................ | 15 (5) | 15 (5) | 5 (3,5) | 0 (5)/0 (5)/15 (4) |
| Estonia........................ | 10 (4, 21) | 15 (4, 11) | 5 (3, 4, 11) | 5 (4, 14)/10 (4)/10 (4) |
| Finland ....................... | 0 (4) | 15 (4, 11) | 5 (3, 4, 11) | 5 (4)/0 (4)/0 (4) |
| France........................ | 0 (4) | 15 (3, 4, 11) | 5 (4, 11) | 5 (4)/0 (4)/0 (4) |
| Germany ..................... | 0 (4) | 15 (4, 11) | 5 (3, 4, 11) | 0 (4)/0 (4, 15)/0 (4) |
| Greece ........................ | 0 (5) | 30 | 30 | 0 (5)/30/0 (5) |
| Hungary ...................... | 0 (4) | 15 (4) | 5 (3, 4) | 0 (4) |
| Iceland ........................ | 0 (4) | 15 (4) | 5 (3, 4) | 0 (4)/30 /0 (4) |
| India............................ | 15 (4, 13) | 25 (4, 11) | 15 (3, 4, 11) | 10 (4, 14)/15 (4)/15 (4) |
| Indonesia .................... | 10 (4) | 15 (4) | 10 (4) | 10 (4, 14)/10 (4)/10 (4) |
| Ireland, Rep. of............ | 0 (4) | 15 (4, 11) | 5 (4, 11) | 0 (4) |
| Israel............................ | 17.5 (4, 13, 17) | 25 (4, 11) | 12.5 (3, 4, 11) | 15 (4)/10 (4)/10 (4) |
| Italy ............................ | 15 (4) | 15 (4) | 5 (3, 4) | 10 (4, 9)/8 (4)/5 (4) |
| Jamaica........................ | 12.5 (4) | 15 (4) | 10 (3, 4) | 10 (4) |
| Japan .......................... | 10 (4) | 15 (4) | 10 (3, 4) | 10 (4) |
| Japan (New Treaty)....... | 10 (4, 27) | 10 (4, 22, 27) | 5 (3, 4, 22, 27, 28) | 0 (4, 27)/0 (4, 27)/0 (4, 27) |
| Kazakhstan ................. | 10 (4) | 15 (4, 16) | 5 (3, 4, 16) | 10 (4, 18)/10 (4)/10 (4) |
| Korea, Rep. of ............. | 12 (4) | 15 (4) | 10 (3, 4) | 15 (4)/10 (4)/10 (4) |
| Latvia .......................... | 10 (4, 21) | 15 (4, 11) | 5 (3, 4, 11) | 5 (4, 14)/10 (4)/10 (4) |
| Lithuania ..................... | 10 (4, 21) | 15 (4, 11) | 5 (3, 4, 11) | 5 (4, 14)/10 (4)/10 (4) |
| Luxembourg ................ | 0 (4, 5) | 15 (4, 11) | 5 (3, 4, 11) | 0 (4) |
| Mexico.......................... | 15 (4, 23) | 10 (4, 22, 26) | 5 (3, 4, 22, 26, 28) | 10 (4) |
| Morocco ...................... | 15 (4) | 15 (4) | 10 (3, 4) | 10 (5)/10 (4)/10 (4) |
| Netherlands................. | 0 (4) | 15 (4, 11) | 5 (3, 4, 11) | 0 (4)/0 (4, 15)/0 (4) |
| New Zealand ............... | 10 (4) | 15 (4) | 15 (4) | 10 (4) |
| Norway ........................ | 0 (4) | 15 (4) | 15 (4) | 0 (4)/0 (5)/0 (4) |
| Pakistan........................ | 30 | 30 | 15 (3, 5) | 0 (5)/30/0 (5) |

| Country of residence | Interest paid by U.S. obligors— general | Dividends | | Royalties (2) |
| --- | --- | --- | --- | --- |
| | | Paid by U.S. corporations— general (1) | Qualifying for direct dividend rate (1) | |
| | % | % | % | % |
| Philippines.................... | 15 (4) | 25 (4) | 20 (3, 4) | 15 (4) |
| Poland......................... | 0 (4) | 15 (4) | 5 (3, 4) | 10 (4) |
| Portugal....................... | 10 (4) | 15 (4, 11) | 5 (3, 4, 11) | 10 (4) |
| Romania...................... | 10 (4) | 10 (4) | 10 (4) | 15 (4)/10 (4)/10 (4) |
| Russia......................... | 0 (4) | 10 (4, 16) | 5 (3, 4, 16) | 0 (4) |
| Slovak Republic............ | 0 (4) | 15 (4, 11) | 5 (3, 4, 11) | 10 (4)/0 (4)/0 (4) |
| Slovenia ...................... | 5 (4) | 15 (4, 22) | 5 (3, 4, 22) | 5 (4) |
| South Africa ................. | 0 (4, 7) | 15 (4, 11) | 5 (4, 11) | 0 (4) |
| Spain.......................... | 10 (4) | 15 (4, 11) | 10 (3, 4, 11) | 8 (4, 12)/8 (4, 12)/5 (4, 12) |
| Sweden ....................... | 0 (4) | 15 (4, 11) | 5 (4, 11) | 0 (4) |
| Switzerland ................. | 0 (4, 7) | 15 (4, 11) | 5 (4, 11) | 0 (4) |
| Thailand ...................... | 15 (4, 13) | 15 (4, 11) | 10 (4, 11) | 8 (14)/5/15 (19) |
| Trinidad and Tobago ..... | 30 | 30 | 30 | 15 (4)/30/0 (4) |
| Tunisia......................... | 15 (4) | 20 (4, 11) | 14 (3, 4, 11) | 10 (4, 14)/15 (4)/15 (4) |
| Turkey ......................... | 15 (4, 6, 13) | 20 (4, 11) | 15 (4, 11) | 5 (14)/10/10 |
| Ukraine........................ | 0 (4) | 15 (4, 16) | 5 (3, 4, 16) | 10 (4) |
| United Kingdom............ | 0 (4) | 15 (4) | 5 (3, 4) | 0 (4)/0 (5)/0 (4) |
| United Kingdom (New Treaty) ............ | 0 (4, 21, 27) | 15 (4, 22, 27) | 5 (3, 4, 22, 27, 28) | 0 (4, 27)/0 (4, 27)/0 (4, 27) |
| Venezuela ................... | 10(4, 20, 21) | 15 (4, 22) | 5 (3, 4, 22) | 5 (4, 14)/10 (4)/10 (4) |

Notes:

1. No U.S. tax is imposed on a dividend paid by a U.S. corporation that received at least 80% of its gross income from an active foreign business for the three-year period before the dividend is declared.

2. Royalties: The rate is different if the royalties are industrial/motion pictures and television/other.

3. The reduced rate applies to dividends paid by a subsidiary to a foreign parent corporation that has the required percentage of stock ownership. In some cases, the income of the subsidiary must meet certain requirements (e.g., a certain percentage of its total income must consist of income other than dividends and interest). For Italy, the reduced rate is 10% if the foreign corporation owns 10% to 50% of the voting stock (for a 12-month period) of the company paying the dividends.

4. The exemption or reduction in rate does not apply if the recipient has a permanent establishment in the United States and the property giving rise to the income is effectively connected with this permanent establishment. Under certain treaties, exemption or reduction in rate also does not apply if the property producing the income is effectively connected with a fixed base in the United States from which the recipient performs independent personal

services. Even with the treaty, if the income is not effectively connected with a trade or business in the United States by the recipient, the recipient will be considered as not having a permanent establishment in the United States under Internal Revenue Code section 894(b).

5. The exemption or reduction in rate does not apply if the recipient is engaged in a trade or business in the United States through a permanent establishment that is in the United States. However, if the income is not effectively connected with a trade or business in the United States by the recipient, the recipient will be considered as not having a permanent establishment in the United States to apply the reduced treaty rate to that item of income.

6. Contingent interest that does not qualify as portfolio interest is treated as a dividend and is subject to the rate for dividends.

7. The rate is 15% (30% for Switzerland) for contingent interest that does not qualify as portfolio interest.

8. The exemption applies only to interest on credits, loans, and other indebtedness connected with the financing of trade between the United States and the Commonwealth of Independent States member. It does not include interest from the conduct of a general banking business.

9. The rate for royalties with respect to tangible personal property is 7%.

10. Tax imposed on 70% of gross royalties for rentals of industrial, commercial, or scientific equipment.

11. The rate for dividends paid by U.S. corporations—general column applies to dividends paid by a regulated investment company (RIC) or a real estate investment trust (REIT). However, that rate applies to dividends paid by a REIT only if the beneficial owner of the dividends is an individual holding less than a 10% interest (25% in the case of Netherlands, Portugal, Spain, and Tunisia) in the REIT.

12. Royalties not taxed at the 5% or 8% rate are taxed at a 10% rate, unless note 7 applies.

13. The rate is 10% if the interest is paid on a loan granted by a bank or similar financial institution. For Thailand, the 10% rate also applies to interest from an arm's length sale on credit of equipment, merchandise, or services.

14. This is the rate for royalties for the use of, or the right to use, industrial, commercial, and scientific equipment. The rate for royalties for information concerning industrial, commercial, and scientific know-how is subject to the rate on copyright royalties-other.

15. The exemption does not apply to cinematographic items, or works on film, tape, or other means of reproduction for use in radio or television broadcasting.

16. The rate on dividends paid by U.S. corporations-general applies to dividends paid by a RIC. Dividends paid by a REIT are subject to a 30% rate.

17. An election can be made to treat this interest income as if it were industrial and commercial profits taxable under article 8 of the treaty.

18. If the payments were for the use of, or the right to use, industrial, commercial, or scientific equipment, an election may be made to compute the tax on a net basis as if such income were attributable to a permanent establishment or fixed base in the United States.

19. The rate is 5% for royalties on the use of any copyright of literary, artistic, or scientific work, including software.

20. The rate is 4.95% if the interest is beneficially owned by a financial institution (including an insurance company).

21. The rate is 15% for interest determined with reference to (a) receipts, sales, income, profits or other cash flow of the debtor or a related person, (b) any change in the value of any property of the debtor or a related person, or (c) any dividend, partnership distribution or similar payment made by the debtor or related person.

22. The rate for dividends paid by U.S. corporations – general column applies to dividends paid by a RIC or REIT. However, that rate applies to dividends paid by a REIT only if the beneficial owner of the dividends is (a) an individual holding not more than a 10% interest in the REIT, (b) a person holding not more than 5% of any class of the REIT's stock and the dividends are paid on stock that is publicly traded, or (c) a person holding not more than a 10% interest in the REIT and the REIT is diversified.

23. The rate is 4.9% for interest derived from (1) loans granted by banks and insurance companies and (2) bonds or securities that are regularly and substantially traded on a recognized securities market. The rate is 10% for interest not described in the preceding sentence and paid (i) by banks or (ii) by the buyer of machinery and equipment to the seller due to a sale on credit.

24. Interest determined with reference to the profits of the issuer or one of its associated enterprises is taxed at 15%.

25. Interest received by a financial institution is exempt.

26. Dividends received by a trust, company, or other organization operated exclusively to administer or provide pension, retirement, or other employee benefits generally are exempt if certain conditions are met.

27. Exemption does not apply to amount paid under, or as part of, a conduit arrangement.

28. Dividends received from an 80%-owned corporate subsidiary are exempt if certain conditions are met.

## Foreign tax credit

Generally, credit is allowed, subject to limitations, against U.S. corporate taxes for foreign income taxes paid, including income taxes "deemed paid" on income of affiliates from which dividends are paid.

## Tax administration

*Returns*/The U.S. tax system is based on the principle of self-assessment. A corporate taxpayer is required to file an annual tax return (generally Form 1120) by the 15th day of the third month following the close of its tax year. A taxpayer can obtain an additional six-month extension of time to file its tax return. Failure to timely file may result in penalties.

*Payment of tax*/A taxpayer's tax liability is generally required to be paid throughout the year (by estimated taxes) and fully paid by the date its tax return is initially due. For corporations, the tax is required to be fully paid by the 15th day of the third month following the close of the tax year; generally, no extensions to pay are allowed. Failure to pay the tax by the due dates as indicated above can result in estimated tax and late payment penalties.

*Tax shelter*/Treasury issued final regulations requiring taxpayers to disclose transactions determined to be abusive or possibly abusive. Current information on

# United States

these transactions, known as listed and reportable transactions, is available from the IRS web site (www.irs.gov).

## CORPORATION TAX CALCULATION

Year ending December 31, 2004

### Taxable income

| | | |
|---|---:|---:|
| Net income before taxes (including $300,000 net long-term capital gain) | | $ 1,000,000 |
| Add: | | |
| Foreign dividend gross-up (Note) | 50,000 | |
| Charitable contributions (excess over limitation) | 200,000 | 250,000 |
| | | 1,250,000 |
| Deduct: | | |
| Deductions allowed for tax purposes not claimed against book income | 100,000 | |
| 100% of dividend from wholly owned domestic subsidiary | 150,000 | 250,000 |
| Taxable income | | $ 1,000,000 |

### Regular tax

| | |
|---|---:|
| On first 50,000 (0–50,000) at 15% | $ 7,500 |
| On next 25,000 (50,001–75,000) at 25% | 6,250 |
| On next 25,000 (75,001–100,000) at 34% | 8,500 |
| On next 235,000 (100,001–335,000) at 39% | 91,650 |
| On excess over 335,000 (335,001–1,000,000) at 34% | 226,100 |
| Total regular corporate tax | 340,000 |
| Less—Foreign tax credit (1) | (80,000) |
| Federal tax payable (excluding alternative minimum tax) | $ 260,000 |

Note:

1. The foreign tax credit is determined as follows.

| | $ |
|---|---:|
| Foreign pretax income of a wholly owned foreign subsidiary | 250,000 |
| Foreign income tax imposed on subsidiary | (50,000) |
| Dividend paid | 200,000 |
| Gross-up for deemed paid (indirect) tax [200,000 (A) x 50,000 (B)] ÷ 200,000 (C) | 50,000 |
| Foreign tax credit: | |
| Deemed paid tax | 50,000 |
| Withholding tax—15% of 200,000 | 30,000 |
| | $ 80,000 |

A: Dividend;
B: Foreign tax;
C: E&P after tax.

## PwC contact

For additional information on taxation in Uruguay, contact:

Daniel Garcia
PricewaterhouseCoopers
Cerrito 461, Piso 4
11000 Montevideo, Uruguay
Telephone: (598) (2) 916 0463
Fax: (598) (2) 916 0605, 916 0653
e-mail: garcia.daniel@uy.pwc.com

## General note

This entry is repeated from the 2003/2004 edition. For more up-to-date
information consult the contact listed above or Jacqueline Collette at
jacqueline.collete@us.pwc.com.

## Significant developments

There have been no significant regulatory or tax developments in the past year.

## Taxes on corporate income

Annual tax at 35% is imposed on income from industrial or commercial activities of
Uruguayan source as well as on income from farms and properties in rural areas.
A 35% withholding tax is imposed on dividends paid or credited to individuals and
legal entities domiciled abroad in cases where these payments are taxed in the
country of the recipient and that country recognizes a tax credit in respect of the
withholding tax paid in Uruguay. However, when the foreign legal entity cannot
use such tax credit because it has suffered fiscal losses, the dividends are exempt
from Uruguayan withholding.

The annual 35% tax applies to exploration and exploitation income of petroleum
companies and is the sole tax payable by these companies in Uruguay.

## Corporate residence

Corporate residence is based on the principal location where the corporation's
activities are performed.

## Other taxes

*Value-added tax*/The basic rate for VAT is 23%. A few items are either subject to
a special 14% rate or exempt from the tax.

*Capital tax*/All types of legal entity and business enterprise owners are subject
to capital tax at a 1.5% rate. Income taxpayers can reduce their capital tax liability
up to the corporate income tax of the fiscal year. Such reduction cannot exceed
1% of the capital tax amount.

*Tax on commissions*/Commissions and similar income obtained by
commissioners, consignees, foreign trade agents, auctioneers, brokers,
mandataries, mediators, and customs agents are subject to a 10.5% tax on gross
income when such income is more than 50% of their total gross income.
Net income corresponding to commissions is exempt from the annual 35%
corporate tax.

# Uruguay

## Branch income

Annual tax at 35% is imposed on income from industrial and commercial activities. Withholding tax is imposed on profits remitted or credited to a home office where these profits are taxed in the home office's country and where this country recognizes a tax credit in respect of the withholding tax paid in Uruguay. The withholding tax rate is a rate that, added to the 35% annual tax rate, equals the tax credit rate obtainable in the country of the recipient, with an upper limit of 21%.

## Income determination

*Inventory valuation*/Replacement cost is permitted, as well as FIFO, LIFO, or average, irrespective of the inventory valuation method elected for accounting purposes. Adjustments for price-level changes cannot be made.

*Capital gains*/Capital gains are treated as ordinary income, except for capital gains on property in rural areas, which are exempt from tax.

*Intercompany dividends*/Dividends from subsidiaries are exempt.

*Foreign income*/Tax on income from industrial and commercial activities is levied only on income from Uruguayan sources.

Income derived from activities performed, assets located, or rights utilized for economic purposes abroad is not subject to income tax.

As a general rule, duly documented expenses that are necessary to obtain and preserve gross taxable income are tax deductible. Conversely, those expenses associated with deriving or preserving income not subject to income tax are not deductible from the taxable base.

*Stock dividends*/Stock dividends are not taxable.

*Other significant items*/An income adjustment for inflation has been in force since January 1, 1981, calculated by multiplying the increase in the wholesalers' price index for the financial year by the difference between the following.
1. Total assets at the beginning of the year, excluding fixed assets.
2. Total liabilities at the beginning of the year.

If (1) is greater than (2), an inflation loss adjustment is deducted from gross income. However, if (2) is greater than (1), an inflation gain adjustment is added.

## Deductions

*Depreciation and depletion*/Straight-line depreciation over useful life is mandatory. Rates of write-offs allowed are 2% per year for urban buildings, 3% per year for rural buildings and no more than 10% per year for new vehicles. Other rates are accepted if economically justified. No conformity between book and tax depreciation is required. The excess of sale price over the fiscal value of depreciated property, restated for inflation, is considered taxable income.

Percentages for depletion computed on the cost of natural resource properties are allowed in accordance with generally accepted criteria.

Depreciation and depletion percentages are computed on the historical cost of fixed assets revalued at year-end on the basis of the increase in the wholesalers' price index. Capital gains derived from the revaluation of fixed assets are not taxable income.

*Net operating losses*/Losses may be carried forward and deducted from the net taxable income of the following three years, once adjusted for inflation. There are no loss carrybacks.

*Payments to foreign affiliates*/Royalties, interest, and service fees paid to foreign affiliates are deductible. Payments to the head office or other branches of the head office are not deductible. However, the portion of the expenses incurred by the head office when developing trademarks, patents, and industrial processes as well as technical know-how that is allocated to the local branch is deductible.

*Taxes*/Income and capital taxes are not deductible.

## Group taxation

Group taxation is not permitted.

## Tax incentives

*Capital investment*/Incentives for capital investment are as follows.

1. Income reinvested in fixed assets

   40% of capital expenditure in industrial machinery, vehicles and installations, agricultural machinery, computers, and telecommunications equipment and 20% of capital expenditure in construction and enlargement of industrial buildings are exempt from income tax, up to 40% of net taxable income.

2. Fixed assets

   Industrial machinery acquired from January 1, 1991 to January 1, 1998 is exempt from capital tax for the five years following the year of acquisition. Industrial machinery and computers acquired after January 1, 1998 are exempt from capital tax.

3. Accelerated depreciation

   Industrial machinery and installations, trucks, agricultural machinery, and computers acquired between January 1, 2001 and December 31, 2002 are subject to accelerated depreciation. The taxpayer has the option of depreciating these assets over a period of two to four years.

4. Income tax exemption

   Investment law provides for a promotion declaration benefiting manufacturing undertakings. If an investment project is declared promoted, tax benefits are granted. Among these benefits, an amount equivalent to the investment made through self-funding is exempted from income tax.

Other incentives include the following.

1. Free trade zones

   Companies operating as users of free-trade zones are not subject to tax. Social security taxes as well as withholding taxes on dividends or profits remitted abroad are excluded from this exemption.

2. Holding companies

   Uruguayan corporations whose principal activity is to invest abroad in securities, bonds, shares, commercial paper, debentures, commodities, and property or to develop commercial activities abroad are exempt from all taxes under certain conditions. They are subject only to an annual tax of 0.3% on their net worth.

3. Printing industry

   Companies that print books and educational material are exempt from capital tax and value-added tax.

4. Shipping industry

   Imports of material, supplies, and equipment required for the construction, maintenance, and repair of shipyards or vessels are exempt.

5. Income of water and air transportation companies

   This income is tax exempt. In the case of foreign companies, the exemption is subject to reciprocal treatment. The government may exempt from income tax companies engaged in transportation by land, subject also to the conditions of reciprocal treatment.

6. Forestry and citriculture

   Companies engaged in forestry and citriculture are exempt from income tax, and forests and land so employed are exempt from capital tax and real estate contributions.

7. Software industry

   Income derived from the production of software is exempt from income tax for fiscal years ending from January 1, 2001 to December 31, 2004.

## Withholding taxes

Royalties as well as fees for technical services paid or credited to individuals and legal entities domiciled abroad are subject to a withholding tax rate of 35% on the gross amount. Fees for technical services are exempt in cases where the beneficiaries are subject to income tax in their country and do not receive a tax credit for the withholding tax paid in Uruguay.

*Tax treaties*/Uruguay has signed tax treaties with Germany and Hungary.

## Tax administration

*Returns*/Returns are filed on a fiscal-year basis. Income and capital taxes are self-assessed.

*Payment of tax*/Income and capital taxes are paid in monthly installments, calculated on the basis of the previous year's tax. The difference between the installments paid and the total annual tax is paid four months after the fiscal year-end.

## *CORPORATION TAX CALCULATION*

Fiscal year ending December 31, 2002

| | | |
|---|---|---|
| Net income before taxes | | $ 1,000,000 |
| Add: | | |
| Provision for capital tax | 40,000 | |
| Provision for dismissal indemnities | 30,000 | |
| Provision for bad and doubtful debts | | |
| in excess of allowed amount | 20,000 | |
| Donations other than to public entities | 10,000 | 100,000 |
| | | 1,100,000 |
| Less: | | |
| Tax losses of prior years (1) | 50,000 | |
| Inflation adjustment (2) | 50,000 | 100,000 |
| Net taxable income | | $ 1,000,000 |
| Tax on income from industrial and commercial | | |
| activities—35% of 1,000,000 | | $350,000 |

Notes:

1.  Although technically the deduction of prior years' tax losses should be computed as a final deduction, the law provides for the deduction of these tax losses in determining the total net income.

2.  The inflation adjustment is calculated on the basis of balances at the beginning of the financial year, as follows.

| | | |
|---|---|---|
| Total assets at fiscal value | | $ 10,000,000 |
| Less: | | |
| Assets that produce exempted income | — | |
| Investments in other enterprises | — | |
| Fixed assets | 3,000,000 | 3,000,000 |
| | | 7,000,000 |
| Total liabilities at fiscal value | | (6,500,000) |
| | $ | 500,000 |

Assumed increase in the wholesalers' price index = 10%

Inflation adjustment (loss): 500,000 x 0.1 = 50,000

3.  Exchange rate of the peso at December 31, 2002: US$1 = Ps27.17.

# Uzbekistan, Republic of

## PwC contact

For additional information on taxation in Uzbekistan, contact:

Abdulkhamid Muminov
PricewaterhouseCoopers
5 Ivlev Street
Tashkent 700090, Uzbekistan
Telephone: (998) (71) 120 6101
Fax: (998) (71) 120 6645
e-mail: abdulkhamid.muminov@uz.pwc.com

## Significant developments

Legislation in the Republic of Uzbekistan is constantly evolving during the period of economic transition from the preindependence socialist economy. On April 14, 1997 Uzbekistan introduced a consolidated tax code, which in certain cases represents a significant change from the previous laws, regulations, and decrees. The code became effective on January 1, 1998. Since that time the tax authorities have issued a number of regulations and procedures on how to apply the provisions of the tax code. The information presented below is based on laws, regulations, and practices as of March 15, 2004.

Noteworthy changes in the tax and regulatory legislation subsequent to the adoption of the tax code, which are effective from January 1, 2004, include the following.

1. Reduction in the corporate profits tax rate from 24% in 2002 to 20% in 2003, and again down to 18% in 2004.
2. The rate of mandatory conversion of foreign currency receipts is likely to be maintained at 50%.

## Taxes on corporate income

*Profits tax*/Enterprises (i.e., legal persons) are subject to profits tax at the rate of 18%. Legal entities receiving income from lotteries, auctions, and casino are taxed at the 20% from revenue. Significant tax concessions may be available to certain types of enterprise (see below).

*Local taxes*/Prior to January 1, 2002, there were two local taxes based on accounting profit (less profits tax), the social infrastructure development tax and a maintenance levy. Maximum rates for these taxes were 6% and 2%, respectively. With effect from the mentioned date, these two taxes were replaced by one single "infrastructure development tax" which is charged at a maximum rate of 8% on the same base. Actual rates may vary from region to region on the basis of decisions of the local authorities, but, in fact, are currently set at the maximum rates.

## Corporate residence

For Uzbek tax purposes, corporations are classified as resident or nonresident. A resident corporation is one established in accordance with Uzbek legislation.

## Other taxes

*Sales (value-added) tax*/Legal entities are subject to VAT, which is applied to taxable turnover and taxable imports. The rate for taxable turnover is 20%. This rate also applies to taxable imports, for which the tax base is determined as the customs value plus any customs duties, tariffs and excise tax payable upon import. Exports are generally zero-rated. Insurance and most types of financial services are exempt.

VAT is generally paid once each month.

***Natural resource tax***/All legal enterprises and individuals engaged in the extraction or other use of natural resources are subject to natural resource tax, which usually is based on the volume of the resource extracted.

***Other taxes***/The most important of the other taxes imposed in Uzbekistan are as follows.

1. Property tax. Prior to January 1, 2002, the tax was imposed at a rate of 5% of an enterprise's tangible and intangible fixed assets at their historic value. However, effective from the mentioned date the tax would be assessed at a 2% rate on the residual value of property with effect of revaluation. The tax rate has been increased to 3% in 2003 and further increased to 3.5% as of January 1, 2004. The revaluation should now on be performed on an annual basis as of January 1.

2. Road fund tax—Generally imposed at a rate of 1.5% of an enterprise's turnover.

3. Ecology tax—Generally imposed at a rate of 1% of an enterprise's production costs and period expenses, except for mandatory payments to the state budget, taxes, levies and contributions to the state special purpose funds.

4. Pension fund tax—Generally imposed at a rate of 0.7% of an enterprise's turnover.

5. Payroll taxes—Prior to January 1, 2004 imposed at a cumulative rate of 37.2% of gross salaries of employees and allocated as follows.
   - 35%—Pension Fund
   - 1.5%—Employment Fund
   - 0.7%—Professional Union Fund

Effective from January 1, 2004 a unified social security contribution with the rate of 33% (applied to the gross salaries of employees) was introduced instead of an array of the abovementioned mandatory social security contributions.

Other taxes include water tax, land tax, excise tax, fixed tax on income of legal entities and individuals from certain entrepreneurial activities (with effect from January 1, 2004), and other local taxes. Export duties have been abolished.

## Branch income

Uzbek legislation does not allow investments through representative offices, on the basis that representative offices are prohibited from carrying out commercial, income-generating activity. Branches of foreign legal entities are in theory possible. However, from a practical perspective, they are treated by the Uzbek authorities as a full Uzbek legal entity, and thus offer no distinct advantage for foreign investors.

Branches of foreign corporations are taxed on their profits from Uzbek activities. Foreign legal entities carrying on activities or deriving income from sources in Uzbekistan are subject to profits tax at the standard rate of 18%.

Branches of foreign legal entities carrying on business in the country may also be subject to an additional 10% branch profits tax upon repatriation of income.

## Income determination

*Inventory valuation*/Uzbek legislation permits the application of FIFO and the average cost method for the valuation of inventory for tax purposes.

*Capital gains*/No special treatment of capital gains has been legislated. They are taxed under the standard profits tax rules.

*Intercompany dividends*/Dividends paid by domestic subsidiaries will be subject to a 15% withholding tax at source. The net income received by the parent company will then be excluded from its profits tax base.

*Foreign income*/Relief is provided for foreign taxes paid to countries with which Uzbekistan has a double taxation treaty.

## Deductions

In certain cases the tax base for profits tax purposes varies significantly from the computation of taxable profits as in most Western jurisdictions. Expenditures, such as advertising, entertaining, international and long-distance telephone calls, labor, and debt servicing, are either nondeductible or restricted to very low levels.

*Depreciation and depletion*/Fixed assets are pooled into five classes and subject to straight-line depreciation at rates ranging from 5% to 20%. Certain geological exploration expenses are subject to a separate 15% depreciation rate.

*Net operating losses*/Tax losses cannot be carried forward or back, unless permitted by a special governmental decree.

*Payments to foreign affiliates*/The tax code introduces transfer pricing for international transactions between a parent company and its Uzbek branch and/or subsidiary. The mechanism for determining independent transfer prices has yet to be announced.

*Taxes*/Generally, taxes are deductible for corporate profits tax purposes. The exception is the infrastructure development tax based on after tax profits.

*Other significant items*/There are several noteworthy restrictions on the deductibility of expenses for corporate profits tax. Examples include the following.

- Entertaining, advertising, and telephone (long distance and international) expenses, most of which are restricted to very low limits based on the company's turnover.
- Interest on long-term debt is not deductible. Currently, in respect of bank loans received for capital investment purposes it is unclear whether interest on such bank loans should either be capitalized in the cost of capital investment or deductible for profits tax purposes.

## Group taxation

There is no provision for consolidation of income or losses by related companies for tax purposes.

## Tax incentives

There are significant tax incentives for investing in strategically important sectors of the Uzbek economy. These concessions are constantly changing, but the most important are granted a seven-year tax holiday for production-oriented companies included in the government's investment program. At present, significant tax concessions may be available to enterprises with foreign equity, agricultural enterprises, export-oriented enterprises, and enterprises producing children's and women's hygiene goods.

For major projects the scope and duration of a range of tax and currency incentives are likely to be subject to a specific project agreement with the government, written into legislation by decree and settled only after protracted and detailed negotiations.

Effective 2003, local producers of consumer goods are entitled to a 20% reduced profits tax rate with respect to income received from production of consumer goods.

## Withholding taxes

**General**/The domestic withholding tax rates are as follows.

|  | % |
|---|---|
| Dividends and interest | 15 |
| Insurance and reinsurance payments | 10 |
| Freight | 6 |
| Royalties, services (including management, consulting services), rents, other income except wages | 20 |

**Double taxation treaty relief**/Foreign legal entities that do not carry on activities in Uzbekistan through a PE are subject to withholding tax on income from sources in Uzbekistan, subject to the terms of a relevant double taxation treaty. Uzbekistan generally does not recognize the tax treaties of the former Soviet Union. Double taxation treaties in force establish withholding rates as follows.

| Recipient | Dividends | Interest | Royalties |
|---|---|---|---|
| Austria | 5 (1)/15 | 10 | 5 |
| Azerbaijan | 10 | 10 | 10 |
| Belarus | 15 | 10 | 15 |
| Belgium | 5 (2)/15 | 10 | 5 |
| Canada | 5 (1)/15 | 10 | 5 (3, 4)/10 |
| Czech Republic | 10 | 5 | 10 |
| China, P.R. | 10 | 10 | 10 |
| Finland | 5 (1)/15 | 5 | 5 (3)/10 (4) |
| France | 5(1)/10 | 5 | 0 |
| Georgia | 5/15 | 10 | 10 |
| Germany | 5 (5)/15 | 5 (6) | 3 (3, 7)/5 (4) |
| Greece | 8 | 10 | 8 |
| India | 15 | 15 | 15 |
| Indonesia | 10 | 10 | 10 |
| Israel | 10 | 10 | 5 (4)/10 |
| Japan | 15 | 10 | 10/20 |
| Kazakhstan | 10 | 10 | 10 |
| Kyrgyzstan | 5 | 5 | 15 |
| Latvia | 10 | 10 | 10 |
| Luxembourg | 5 (5)/15 | 10 | 5 |
| Malaysia | 10 | 10 | 10 |
| Moldova | 5/15 | 10 | 15 |
| Netherlands | 5 (5)/15 | 10 | 15 |
| Pakistan | 10 | 10 | 15 |
| Poland | 5/15 | 10 | 10 |

# Uzbekistan, Republic of

| Recipient | Dividends | Interest | Royalties |
|---|---|---|---|
| Romania | 10 | 10 | 10 |
| Russia | 10 | 10 | 0 |
| South Korea | 5 (5)/15 | 5 | 2 (7)/5 |
| Switzerland | 5(9)/15 | 5 | 5 |
| Thailand | 10 | 10 (8)/15 | 15 |
| Turkey | 10 | 10 | 10 |
| Turkmenistan | 10 | 10 | 10 |
| United Kingdom | 5 (9)/10 | 5 | 5 |
| Ukraine | 10 | 10 | 10 |
| Vietnam | 15 | 10 | 15 |

Notes:

1. Where the beneficial shareholder owns not less than 10% of the voting shares.
2. Where the beneficial owner holds at least 10% of the capital of the paying entity.
3. Where royalties are paid for patents, trademarks, know-how, and so on.
4. Where royalties are paid for copyrights on literature, cinema, musical works, and so on.
5. Where the beneficial shareholder owns not less than 25% of the capital of the paying entity.
6. Where one state has identified specific types of interest income which may be subject to a 0% withholding tax, the same treatment is taken by the other state.
7. Where royalties are paid in respect of use or the right to use industrial, commercial, or scientific equipment.
8. Where the interest is received by any financial institution (including insurance companies).
9. Where the beneficial shareholder owns not less than 20% of the voting shares.

## Tax administration

Uzbek enterprises, including entities with foreign investment, are required to make three advance installments of profits tax in each quarter based on estimated profits in the quarter. The installments are payable by the 15th day of each month. Final quarterly payments based on actual profit figures are payable no later than five days after the filing deadline for the quarterly tax returns (which is the 25th day of the month following the period of assessment). The final annual payment must be made within five days of the filing deadline for the final year end declaration (which is February 15 of the year following the year of assessment for Uzbek entities and March 25 for enterprises with foreign investment).

## Exchange control

There is a strictly enforced system of currency controls and regulations. In addition, there is a mandatory requirement to convert 50% of all hard-currency earnings into the national currency of Uzbekistan, the Soum. Although, many restrictions has been lifted with respect to currency convertibility it still remains one of the major issues faced by all businesses and foreign nationals operating in Uzbekistan.

The exchange rate of the Soum at January 1, 2004: US$1 = UZS980.00.

## PwC contact

For additional information in Venezuela, contact:

Luis Fernando Miranda
Elys Aray
Espiñeira, Sheldon y Asociados
Edificio Del Rio
Avenida Principal de Chuao
Caracas 1061-A, Venezuela
Espiñeira, Sheldon y Asociados
c/o Jet International-M347
P.O. Box 020010
Miami, Florida 33102-0010
U.S.A.
Telephone (58) (0212) 7006124, 7006339
Fax (58) (0212) 7006280
e-mail: fernando.miranda@ve.pwc.com
         Elys.Aray@ve.pwc.com

## Significant developments

The following information is updated at March 8, 2004.

The Bank Debit Tax Law was amended on March 11, 2004, thereby extending the application of this tax until December 31, 2004 at the 0.5% rate.

In November 2004 the Income Tax Regulation was published for the main purpose of regulating those regimes that were incorporated in the Income Tax Law, published in December 2002, namely worldwide income regime, international fiscal transparency regime, and dividend tax, as well as basic provisions regarding fiscal inflation adjustment.

## Taxes on corporate income

Corporate income is taxed at the following rates (Tariff 2/).

| Taxable income | | | Ordinary income tax | |
|---|---|---|---|---|
| Over | Not over | | % Rate | Subtract |
| TU 0 | TU 2,000 | ............................................................ | 15 | 0 |
| TU 2,000 | TU 3,000 | ............................................................ | 22 | TU 140 |
| TU 3,000 | | ............................................................ | 34 | TU 500 |

*Tax units/*The 1994 Income Tax Law Reform established the concept of a taxable unit as an element that reduces the negative effects created by inflation on the determination of the tax rates. The Tax Code established the initial tax unit (TU) at Bs 1,000, with annual basis adjustments according to the variation of the consumer price index (CPI) from the previous year. During 2003 the TU was Bs 19,400 and for 2004 is Bs 24,700.

Oil exploitation and certain related income is taxed at a flat rate of 50%, except when earned by corporations created under congressionally approved association agreements and companies engaged in the exploration and exploitation of nonassociated gas and the processing, refining, transportation, distribution, commercialization and exportation of the gas and its components, and for the execution of vertically integrated projects associated with exploitation, refining, industrialization, emulsification, transport, and commercialization of extra heavy crude and natural bitumen, in which case such income is subject to the tax set forth in Tariff 2.

*Minimum tax*/Corporations and other legal entities, as well as unincorporated businesses, are subject to a minimum tax referred to as the Business Asset Tax. The rental of residential property, charitable and exempt organizations, government organizations and primary-level agricultural and fishing activities are exempt from the application of the Business Asset Tax. New businesses are exempt during the preoperating phase and for the first two years of operations.

The taxable basis is determined by calculating an average of beginning- and end-of-year tangible and intangible asset values after accumulated depreciation and amortization and inflation adjustments required by the income tax law. The tax is calculated on 1% of the taxable base, and is payable only when it exceeds ordinary income tax on regular taxable income for the same year. The Business Asset Tax paid may be carried forward to three years and used to reduce income tax liabilities for those years.

Excluded from the calculation are investments in shares of other companies, assets entirely used in the production of exempt income, certain monetary assets of financial institutions and insurance companies, and new assets not yet placed in service. Exporters are entitled to a pro rata reduction in the amount of calculated Business Asset Tax based on the ratio of export sales to total sales.

*Municipal business license tax*/Corporate and business entities as well as individuals and unincorporated societies are subject to municipal tax on gross income from industrial or trade activities carried on in the municipality during the fiscal year. The rates range from 0.1% to 10.0%, depending on the activity and the municipality.

## Corporate residence

According to the Venezuelan Tax Code the following companies are regarded as domiciled.

1. Companies incorporated in Venezuela and registered with the Mercantile Registry as established by commercial law.
2. Foreign companies registered with the Superintendence of Foreign Investments (SIEX) to be domiciled in Venezuela as branches duly registered with the Mercantile Registry.

The following companies are nondomiciled but are subject to Venezuelan taxes.

1. Foreign companies registered with SIEX to provide from abroad technical assistance, technological services, royalty items and professional services.
2. Foreign banks granting loans to local companies.
3. Foreign companies leasing goods to local companies.
4. Foreign companies deriving income from economic activities carried out in Venezuela or from assets in Venezuela.

## Value-added tax

Federal VAT (IVA in Spanish) is a one-time tax payable by the ultimate consumer of all types of products and services. However, each business entity involved in the process from the sale of raw materials, to the production and distribution of finished products, to the ultimate consumer, is required to bill its customers the tax on its products (output tax) and to pay the tax on its purchases or imports of goods and services (input tax), crediting the amounts so paid against the amounts due on its own activities. The net amount payable by each entity is considered to represent a tax on the value added.

In general, VAT does not represent an additional cost to business enterprises, because even though all types of business enterprises, including government departments and agencies, with some exceptions, are required to accept charges of the tax by suppliers on their purchases of goods and services, such amounts are normally deductible from the liability of the business enterprises for the tax on their billings to customers.

There are some exceptions, principally when the sales of an enterprise are exempt from VAT, in which case the enterprise is treated as the final consumer and must absorb any VAT charges on its purchases except insofar as its activities are subject to the zero rate (see below). However, input tax paid on goods or services used to produce items that are exempt from VAT may be deducted for corporate income tax purposes.

*Taxable transactions*/In general, VAT is payable on all sales and rental of goods rendering of services and the importation of goods and services, although a number of significant exceptions are provided by law.

*Sales of goods*/The law defines a sale as any transmission of corporal or tangible goods, including those made on a conditional basis or through irrevocable trust. The taxable amount of a sale includes the sale price as well as other amounts charged to the purchaser for other taxes, duties, interest, or surcharges of whatever nature. VAT becomes payable when the goods are invoiced or shipped to the customers or when the price is paid in full or in part.

Exempt sales include the following.

1. Certain foods and other products for human consumption.
2. Fertilizers as well as any natural gas used in the manufacturing thereof.
3. Some products for animal consumption.
4. Medicines.
5. Products derived from hydrocarbons and some raw materials intended to improve the quality of gasoline.
6. Wheelchairs.
7. Books, magazines, newspapers, and the paper used in producing these products.
8. Vehicles, aircraft, and trains for passenger transport.
9. Machinery and equipment for agribusiness.
10. Scientific equipment purchased by the government (as of June 1, 1999).

*Services*/Taxable services are those rendered within Venezuela by one person to another on an independent basis, transportation passengers or goods, agency activities, technical assistance, and transfer of technology. VAT is payable to service providers at the time a charge becomes due or at the time advance payments are received. The taxable amount includes not only the price of services, but also charges to the customers for other taxes, interest, and so on.

Exempt services include the following.

1. Domestic land and maritime transportation of passengers.
2. Educational services.
3. Accommodations for students and the disabled.
4. Professional services rendered to the government (e.g., public power).
5. Healthcare and dental services, surgery, and hospitalization, offered by public and nonprofit entities.
6. Theaters, sports, and cultural events.
7. Food services for employees and students.
8. Certain utilities (e.g., electricity, water, telephone).
9. Housecleaning.

***Exports***/Exports are zero rated. Consequently, VAT is not payable on exports, including exports of in-bond processing companies, technical fees to foreign residents and sales to in-bond processing companies and companies that export their entire production. Though exporters do not collect VAT on export sales, they can recover VAT charges on their purchases of goods and services by means of a refund certificate. This certificate may be use to pay other tax obligations.

Additionally, a zero rate applies to independent personal services provided by residents in Venezuela that are used solely by and for the benefit of persons abroad without a permanent establishment or fixed base in Venezuela.

***Tax rates***/The rate may change every year, within the range of 8% to 16.5%. As of September 1, 2002, the general VAT rate is 16%.

An additional tax rate of 10% is applicable to the sale and imports of luxury products, such as vehicles valued at over US$30,000, motorcycles with a cylinder capacity of 500 cc, nickel or token game machines, aircraft used for recreational or sport purposes, fighting bulls, trained horses, caviar, jewelry with precious stones valued at a price exceeding US$500.

As of January 1, 2003 an 8% VAT rate will apply to the following transactions.

1. Imports and sales of the following items: (a) livestock for slaughter, (b) beef and dairy cattle, goats, sheep, and swine for breeding purposes, (c) meats in their natural state, or refrigerated, frozen or salted meats, or meats in brine, (d) vegetable fats and oils, whether or not refined, for use only in the production of edible oils.
2. Rendering of professional services to any government entity, in any level or branch of government, provided such services do not involve any commercial transactions but rather predominantly intellectual work or efforts.
3. Domestic air passenger transportation.

***Payment and collection***/The excess of VAT charged or chargeable to customers over VAT paid to vendors (or customs authorities—*Servicio Nacional Integrado de Administración, Aduanera y Tributaria* (SENIAT)), including the corresponding payment, must be remitted to SENIAT within the first 15 days of the following month.

***VAT exoneration***/In March 1997, the Venezuelan government issued a VAT exoneration for taxpayers developing hydrocarbon projects (among other things) during the preoperating stage. The above described VAT exoneration was substituted by an exemption set forth in the VAT Law, which is (in general terms) similar to the derogated exoneration and includes the "preoperating stage."

In order to be able to claim the VAT exemption, taxpayers must follow a registration process with the Tax Administration, which requires the submission of certain detailed information related to each project.

*Refunds*/Refunds of an overpayment shown by a monthly return may be requested, or the overpayment may be offset against VAT payable with the returns of subsequent months. The tax credit produced in export sales can be offset against VAT in taxable operations or against certain other federal taxes, or a refund may be requested. VAT paid by tourists is not refundable upon departure.

Taxpayers qualified by the Tax Administration as special taxpayers were designated as liable parties in their capacity as withholding agents in regard to payment of VAT generated in their purchase of movable property or services received by providers that are regular taxpayers for VAT purposes.

## Bank debit tax

The law establishing the bank debit tax will be effective as of March 16, 2002 and until December 31, 2004. This is applicable to debits or withdrawals made to financial instruments qualified by the aforementioned standard, in which the financial institution or entity administrating the accounts or financial instruments constitutes the collection or withholding agent, as the case might be.

Among the tax liable parties, the law includes individuals or companies, in their capacity as holders of accounts or financial instruments or parties ordering payments, for the operations which constitute the taxable activities set forth in the law carried out in banks and other financial institutions. Likewise, banks and other financial institutions are considered as taxpayers.

In this connection, a tax rate is established equivalent to 0.50% of the amount of each debit or withdrawal made. However, certain fiscal benefits are established by means of exemption.

## Branch income

Branches of foreign corporations are subject to the same tax rules as Venezuelan corporations. Interbranch income and deductions must be eliminated. Branches of foreign entities are deemed to remit the positive difference between their annual book and fiscal income to their head office (branch profits tax). Such remittances are subject to the 34% flat dividend tax regardless of whether there is actual payment unless the branch provides proof of reinvestment of its profits for a five years period. If such proof is established, no deemed remittance is assumed. A Venezuelan taxpayer has to recognize annually on an accrual basis income generated in a company or other legal entity located in a JLFT (Jurisdiction with Low Fiscal Taxation) that it controls. Further, investments in JLFT must be declared to the tax authorities (SENIAT).

## Income determination

*Inventory valuation*/Inventories can be valued at cost or the lower of cost or market. Any method generally accepted for accounting purposes can be accepted for tax purposes.

# Venezuela

*Capital gains*/Capital gains are taxable as ordinary income and capital losses are deductible from ordinary income. Capital losses resulting from the sale of stock, capital reduction, or liquidation of a company are deductible under the following conditions.

1. The cost of acquisition of the capital stock was not in excess of the price quoted on a stock exchange or an amount with a reasonable relationship to the book value of the capital stock.
2. The holding period of the investment was for at least two years immediately preceding the date of the sale.
3. The stockholder proves that the company selling the shares carried on economic activities for at least the two years preceding the date of sale.

Conditions 2 and 3 are not required in the case of stock quoted on the Venezuelan Stock Exchange.

At present, the tax law contains two different rulings as to the deductibility of losses incurred through operations on the Venezuelan Stock Market. For the first, see above. As to the second, income obtained from operations on the local market is subject to a final 1% tax that is withheld at the source. Losses in this kind of operation are not deductible against other income (but see above). Corporate shareholders not domiciled in Venezuela cannot deduct such losses from other taxable income other than dividends arising from Venezuelan sources.

*Intercompany dividends*/Until the year 2000, dividends were exempt from tax, regardless of recipient. A 34% dividend tax applies beginning January 1, 2001. Gains upon liquidation or reduction of capital are taxable to the liquidating entity.

The dividend tax is levied at a flat rate of 34% on the positive difference between book income and tax income generated after 2000. Book income is understood to be that approved at a shareholders' meeting and based on the financial statements prepared pursuant to GAAP. To determine this difference a LIFO method applies. The 34% (domestic) rate can be mitigated under tax treaties to 10%, 5%, or even 0%. Withholding is to be made at the moment a dividend is declared or credited to an account of the recipient.

Dividends obtained from companies incorporated or domiciled abroad or incorporated abroad and domiciled in Venezuela are taxed at a flat 34% rate.

*Foreign income*/Until the year 2000 only income derived from activities or property in Venezuela was subject to tax. Income earned outside the country was not subject to Venezuelan taxation, with the exception of fees for technical assistance and technological services rendered from abroad to Venezuela (see below). Beginning January 1, 2001 extraterritorial income is subject to Venezuelan income tax. The broadening of the territoriality regime is based on the concept of worldwide income taxation, according to which the following.

1. Domiciled companies must pay a tax on total income whether from national or foreign source.
2. Companies domiciled abroad with permanent establishment in the country will pay tax on their income, whether of national or foreign source, attributable to that establishment.
3. Nondomiciled companies will pay taxes on their income originated or caused in the country.
4. Domiciled companies as well as companies domiciled abroad with permanent establishment in the country may credit the tax paid abroad for earnings of

extraterritorial source against the income tax payable in the country, subject to limitations.

*Foreign technical assistance and services*/Taxable income of foreign taxpayers providing technical assistance or technological services from abroad to individuals or entities that use them in Venezuela, or assign them to third parties, is established at 30% of gross income for technical assistance fees, and at 50% of gross income for technological service fees. The law provides that 60% of technical assistance and technological service fees is deemed rendered abroad, and the other 40% in Venezuela if the contract does not specify the proportion in which the services are rendered. It also provides that 75% of the entire income related to technological services and 25% of that related to technological assistance is rendered abroad if not otherwise specified in the contract. (See also "Withholding taxes.")

*International fiscal transparency*/A regime of international fiscal transparency is created for the purpose of establishing special standards of fiscal control governing capital investments in countries classified as Jurisdictions with Low Fiscal Taxation (JLFT or tax havens). Under certain conditions a Venezuelan taxpayer may be required to recognize income generated in its JLFT subsidiary on an accrual basis in its tax return.

*Stock dividends*/Beginning January 1, 2001, dividends of stock will be subject to payment of the aforementioned dividend tax. Moreover, as of January 1, 2002, said stock dividends will be subject to an advanced payment of dividend tax equivalent to 1% of the dividend distributed. Stock dividends will have no cost for tax purposes, whether they are paid out of liquid and collected income or as a result of asset revaluation.

*Transfer pricing*/Taxpayers that carry out operations with related parties must calculate their income, costs and deductions by applying a defined methodology of transfer pricing. This regime is applicable to imports, exports, and interest paid to recipients abroad and technical assistance, technological services, and royalties fees.

## Inflation adjustment

A system for the adjustment of nonmonetary assets, nonmonetary liabilities, and shareholder's equity has been established. "Nonmonetary assets" include land, construction, machinery, vehicles, installations, inventories, and investment other than in securities (e.g., bonds and stocks). There are two phases to the adjustments, which are as follows.

1. Initial adjustment (catch-up)/The initial adjustment on depreciable fixed assets requires a registration tax of 3% on the amount of the adjustment.
2. Annual adjustment/The annual adjustment is applied each year in determining the taxable income.

Both adjustments are mandatory for taxpayers engaged in commercial, industrial, financial, and insurance operations and in exploitation of mines and hydrocarbons. The annual adjustment is optional for taxpayers performing non-business activities.

*Initial adjustment*/This document must be filed at the closing date of any fiscal year ended after January 1, 1993. This adjustment is applicable to all nonmonetary assets and nonmonetary liabilities.

# Venezuela

The initial adjustment is calculated by applying the variations between the CPI of the Caracas metropolitan area prevailing in the month in which the nonmonetary assets were acquired and the month corresponding to the initial adjustment. Assets acquired before 1950 are deemed to have been acquired in January 1950.

A registry tax of 3% is applied exclusively to the initial revaluation adjustment of depreciable fixed assets. For payment, taxpayers must be registered in the Asset Revaluation Registry, maintained by the Tax Administration. The resulting tax can be paid in three consecutive annual installments, beginning at the date of registration.

Companies in the preoperating stage, which is deemed ended with the first invoice, must determine and pay a 3% tax once the preoperating period has ended.

Depreciation or amortization (see below) on the revaluation adjustment is allowed, based on the original estimated life of the asset.

***Annual adjustment***/This adjustment, effective as of January 1, 1993, applies to fiscal periods begun after that date. The adjustment factor must be applied to the following balance sheet items at the closing date of the fiscal year. The resulting adjustment will increase or decrease taxable income.

| Balance sheet items | Adjustment factor | Tax effect |
|---|---|---|
| Nonmonetary assets: | | |
| Inventories, including inventories in transit (1) | Annual variation of the CPI | Increase taxable income |
| Fixed assets (2) | Annual variation of the CPI | Increase taxable income |
| Other assets, trademarks, patents, production licenses, other rights, and investments in stock not registered in the Constructa Nacional de Vavulas (CNV), deferred charges (except interest). | Annual variation of the CPI | Increase taxable income |
| Investments in shares registered in the CNV | Adjusted to the share's market value at the end of the year | Increase taxable income |
| Nonmonetary liabilities: | | |
| Deferred credits (except interest) | Annual variation of the CPI | Decrease taxable income |
| Equity: | | |
| Tax initial equity (3) | Annual variation of the CPI | Decrease taxable income |

Notes:

1. Inventories are to be valued at historical cost for purposes of applying the CPI. The provisions of the Income Tax Law detail the procedures for applying the CPI. The revaluation of inventories in the tax year is to be included as part of the initial inventories of the following year.

2. The annual revaluation adjustment of fixed assets is considered part of the cost when the assets are sold.

3. Tax initial equity is defined as the difference between assets and liabilities at the beginning of the tax year, less accounts receivable from administrators, affiliated and related companies. In order to determine the initial tax equity, assets not located in the country as well as goods, debts, and liabilities entirely applied to the production of deemed, exempt or exonerated income are excluded.

Net losses arising from this adjustment that have not been offset may only be carried forward to the next tax period (one year).

Gains or losses originating from the adjustment of accounts receivable or investments, as well as debts and liabilities in foreign currency or with a readjustability clause pending at the closing date of the taxable period, will be deemed realized.

## Deductions

**Depreciation and depletion**/Depreciation is generally computed on a straight-line basis, although any other generally accepted method for accounting purposes is also accepted. Depreciation is not allowed on real estate used as rental property. Depreciation on the stepped-up portion of assets revalued by any method other than the inflation adjustments noted above is not permitted.

**Net operating losses**/Losses may be carried forward to three years. There is no loss carryback. Losses from inflation adjustment can only be carried forward one year.

Foreign losses can only be offset against foreign profits.

**Payments to foreign affiliates**/A Venezuelan corporation can claim a deduction for royalties and technical assistance and for technical service fees paid to foreign affiliates, subject to the following conditions.

1. The contract is registered within 60 days of execution with the Superintendent of Foreign Investments.
2. Income tax payable by the recipient is withheld at source.
3. The transfer pricing requirements are met.

Foreign companies domiciled in Venezuela are allowed to deduct royalties paid to parent companies or foreign affiliates. Companies must notify the Superintendence of Foreign Investments of payments made within 60 days. See also "Withholding taxes" below. Branches of foreign companies, however, may not deduct such payments to head offices or related parties.

**Taxes**/Municipal, state, and local taxes are deductible in determining taxable income. Corporate and business asset taxes are not deductible.

**Other significant items**/Deductions for allowable charitable contributions are limited to 10% of taxable income (before deducting contributions) when taxable income does not exceed TU 10,000 and to 8% when it exceeds that amount. For oil extraction companies the deduction is limited to 1% of the precontribution tax amount.

Also deductible are payments required by the labor law, such as profit sharing (generally between 15 days' and 4 months' salary) and severance indemnity accruals (five days' salary per month of employee service, calculated at the employee's last monthly salary, plus interest on prior accruals). In cases of

# Venezuela

unjustified dismissals, double severance indemnities must be paid. However, accruals for such additional indemnities are generally not deductible until paid.

## Group taxation

Effective January 1, 2000, group taxation is no longer possible.

## Tax incentives

*Capital investment*/A tax credit of 10% of the value of new investments in fixed assets, excluding land, for those legal entities deriving income from approved industrial activities carried out within the five first years following the effective date of this law. Approved industrial activities include the following: industrials, agro-industrials, construction, electricity, telecommunications, and scientific technology.

Likewise, an additional tax rebate of 10% is available for investments in assets, programs and activities aimed at the conservation and protection of the environment.

These tax rebates will be granted to companies that are incorporated under association agreements for the execution of vertically integrated projects associated with exploitation, refining, industrialization, emulsification, transport, and commercialization of extra heavy crude and natural bitumen. Similarly, companies engaged in exploration and exploitation of associated gas or related activities (integrated or not) are entitled to this tax rebate.

However, activities associated with tourism will be granted a 75% tax rebate on the amount of new investment. The agricultural, cattle, fishing, and fish farming activities will be entitled to an 80% tax rebate.

Investment tax credits can be carried forward to three years.

*Other incentives*/Some customs duty incentives are available, such as drawback upon re-export of materials for the production of exports. This may take the form of a tax refund certificate issued by the Ministry of Finance. The certificate is a negotiable bond and will be accepted by the Treasury Funds Office for payment of national taxes if presented within two years of the date of receipt. Determination of the amount of the refund will take into account the import duties effectively paid at the time the materials used in the manufacture of the exported product were received in Venezuela.

During the year 2000, two Exoneration Decrees were issued in regard to income tax.

The first Decree establishes exoneration from tax payment for net earnings of Venezuelan source derived from primary exploitation of activities associated with agriculture, forestry, livestock, poultry breeding, fishing, and fish farming.

The second Decree stipulates an exoneration of income tax for net earnings of Venezuelan source obtained by companies incorporated or to be incorporated in the states of Amazonas, Apure, Delta Amacuro, Sucre, and Trujllo and small and medium enterprises engaged in business, services and manufacturing, which are incorporated or to be incorporated in certain industrial parks.

The beneficiaries of these exonerations must comply with certain formal requirements and must designate 100% of the amount of exonerated tax to investments aimed at areas comprising their regular activities.

## Withholding taxes

Resident corporations making certain types of payments must withhold taxes. T2 refers to Tariff 2. These include the following.

| | Resident (1) | | Nonresident | |
|---|---|---|---|---|
| | Corporation | Individual | Corporation | Individual |
| Commissions (2) | 5% | 3% | 5% | 34% |
| Royalties (3) | 5% | 3% | T2 on 90% | 34% on 90% |
| Interest to foreign financial institutions | N/A | N/A | 4.95% | N/A |
| Other interest | 5% | 3% | T2 on 95% | 34% on 95% |
| Professional fees | 5% | 3% | T2 on 90% | 34% on 90% |
| Technical assistance fees (3) | 5% | 3% | T2 on 30% | 34% on 30% |
| Technological service fees (3) | 5% | 3% | T2 on 50% | 34% on 50% |
| Real estate rentals | 5% | 3% | 5% | 34% |
| Tangible personal property rentals | 5% | 3% | 5% | 34% |
| Contractor and subcontractor services | 2% | 1% | T2 | 34% |
| Film and TV exhibition rights | 5% | 3% | T2 on 25% | 34% on 25% |
| Insurance and reinsurance premiums | N/A | N/A | 10% on 30% | N/A |
| Payments to international media organizations | 5% | 3% | T2 on 15% | N/A |
| Acquisition of Venezuela commercial funds | 5% | 3% | 5% | 34% |
| Payments to nondomiciled international transportation companies (4) | N/A | N/A | T2 on 5% | N/A |

The numbers in parentheses refer to the following numbered Notes.

Notes:

1. Withholding taxes constitute prepayments against final tax liability as determined by the income tax return when filed.
2. Includes commissions earned in other than a dependent relationship (e.g., employer/employee). Commissions are subject to withholding in the same manner as salaries and wages.
3. The rates for nonresidents are those for payments to a nondomiciled corporation not resident in a treaty country and rendering services from abroad with no permanent establishment in Venezuela.
4. Excludes payments exempted under international shipping agreements.

# Venezuela

*Tax treaties*/There are currently comprehensive treaties for the avoidance of double taxation with the following countries, which are mainly based on the Organization for Economic Cooperation and Development (OECD) model.

| | | |
|---|---|---|
| Barbados | Indonesia | Sweden |
| Belgium | Italy | Switzerland |
| Czech Republic | Netherlands | Trinidad and Tobago |
| Denmark | Norway | United Kingdom |
| France | Portugal | United States |
| Germany | | |

Treaties with other countries are being negotiated.

## Tax administration

*Returns*/Final tax returns must be filed within three months following the end of the tax year. The system is one of self-assessment.

*Payment of tax*/The total amount of tax due must be paid at the time of filing the annual return. Estimated tax payments can be paid in nine equal monthly installments beginning with the sixth month of the taxable year. Companies engaged in mining, hydrocarbon exploitation and related activities must make 12 equal monthly estimated tax payments.

## Exchange control

On January 2003 the Venezuelan government and the Venezuelan Central Bank (VCB) restricted the free foreign currency trade and established an exchange control regime, which is characterized by the following aspects.

The VCB centralizes the purchase and sales of foreign currency.

All foreign currency derived from the export of goods, services, and technology must be sold to the VCB, through the financial system and at the official exchange rate. Exporters are to be registered with the Users Registry. For such purposes, exporters are to consign certain documentation certifying good fiscal status. Likewise, the sale of every foreign currency introduced in the country for various concepts, including direct foreign investment, to the VCB is mandatory. In such case, said foreign currency is to be registered with the Superintendence of Foreign Investment (SIEX), for re-exportation and remittance purposes. The acquisition of foreign currency for imports is also subject to application for "Foreign Currency Authorization," which is bound to certain conditions.

## CORPORATE TAX CALCULATION

Calendar year 2004

| | | |
|---|---|---:|
| Taxable income (manufacturing company) ......................................... | Bs | 160,000,000 |
| Divided by the value of the TU (Bs 24,700/1TU)................................ | | 24,700 |
| Taxable income in TU ....................................................................... | TU | 6,478 |
| Tax thereon: | | |
| Tariff 2—34% ................................................................................ | TU | 2,203 |
| Subtract (per tax table)................................................................... | TU | (500) |
| Total tax ......................................................................................... | TU | 1,703 |
| *Less*—Credit for investment in fixed assets: | | |
| Net fixed assets adjusted for inflation acquired during the year— | | |
|   Bs.8,000,000 equal to TU 324 (Bs.8,000,000/TU 24,700) | | |
|   Tax credit of 10% over new investments in fixed assets | | |
|   (TU 323 at 10%)........................................................................... | TU | (32) |
| Net income tax................................................................................ | TU | 1,671 |
| *Less*—Withholding taxes ................................................................ | TU | (100) |
| *Less*—Advance payments ............................................................... | TU | (100) |
| Net income tax payable in TU........................................................... | TU | 1,471 |
| Net income tax payable in Bs ........................................................... | Bs | 36,333,700 |
| Net income tax payable in US$ at exchange rate of 1920:1................ | $ | 18,924 |

Note:

Exchange rate of the Bolivar at March 8, 2004: US$1 = Bs 1,920.00.

# Vietnam

## PwC contact

For additional information on taxation in Vietnam, contact:

Richard J. Irwin
Partner
Tax and Consulting
PricewaterhouseCoopers (Vietnam) Ltd.
Fourth Floor, Saigon Tower
29 Le Duan, District 1
Ho Chi Minh City
Vietnam
Telephone: (84) (8) 823 0796
Fax: (84) (8) 825 1947
e-mail: r.j.irwin@vn.pwc.com

## Significant developments

Effective from January 1, 2004, the standard corporate income tax (known as business income tax, or BIT) in Vietnam will be 28% for both foreign and local enterprises, as compared with the previous rates of 25% for foreign enterprises 32% for local enterprises. See also "Tax incentives" below.

## Taxes on corporate income

*Standard rates*/As of January 1, 2004, the standard BIT rate is 28% for foreign-invested companies and domestic companies, branches of foreign companies and foreign contractors not governed by the Foreign Investment Law. Incentive BIT rates vary from 10%, 15% to 20%. For Build-Operate-Transfer (BOT) enterprises the normal rate is 10%.

For oil and gas enterprises the standard rate is 50% for both local and foreign companies. Incentive rates range down to 32%, on a case-by-case basis.

*Preferential rates*/Preferential rates of 20%, 15%, and 10% for foreign invested companies and domestic companies are available where certain criteria are met. See "Tax incentives."

## Corporate residence

The concept of permanent establishment (PE) has been introduced in the BIT regime. However, all foreign investments must be approved (licensed) by the authorities, and the BIT status will be decided as a part of the overall approval process. Residence becomes relevant with regard to foreign-exchange control and tax treaties.

## Other taxes

*Value-added tax*/VAT is a tax imposed on the value added of goods and services. VAT is applied to all business establishments in Vietnam (whether local or foreign). Depending on the category of goods or services, the VAT rates are 0%, 5%, and 10% (the standard rate), with a wide range of exemptions. Effective from January 1, 2004, the 20% VAT rate is no longer applicable. Exports of manufactured and processed goods, and exported services are subject to the 0% rate. A concessionary deemed input VAT is abolished effective January 1, 2004.

*Special sales tax*/A special sales tax (SST) applies to only a few goods and services, such as alcohol, imported automobiles, petroleum, cigarettes, playing cards, and discotheque, massage, karaoke, casino, jackpot, golf clubs, and entertainment with betting and lotteries. For goods, SST is charged only at the production or importation stage. Rates range from 15% to 100%. Effective from January 1, 2004, goods that are subject to SST are also VATable. Temporary SST reductions are available in two cases, which are losses due to natural disasters, and special treatment for motor car assemblers.

*Production royalties*/Production royalties in the form of a natural resource tax (NRT) are payable in industries exploiting natural resources such as oil and gas, other minerals, forests, fisheries, and importantly, natural water. The tax applicable is based on production value. NRT rates range from 0% to 40%.

*Property taxes*/Where land or water surfaces are used, a rental is charged. The annual charges can be as low as US$150 per square kilometer for certain sea areas, and as high as US$12 per square meter in prime city areas such as Ho Chi Minh City and Hanoi. Exemptions are granted subject to certain conditions, for example, to BOT enterprises.

*Import and export duties*/Import duty rates generally range from 0% to 50%. However, for certain products, such as liquor and cigarettes, the rates can be as high as 100%. Exemptions are generally granted for goods brought in as capital in a foreign investment or goods brought in for processing for re-export or goods imported under ODA fund. As a result of Vietnam's entry into ASEAN (Association of South East Asian Nations), there is a requirement for its tariff rates to be reduced to no more than 5% by 2006. The government is currently revising the rates and partially implementing the revised lower rates with imports from and exports to ASEAN countries.

Export duties are charged basically on natural resources. Rates range from 0% to 45%.

## Branch income

Tax is levied at 28% on profits of branches of foreign banks, tobacco companies, law firms and other branches. Branches of foreign entities are currently permitted to operate in Vietnam, but are subject to many limitations.

## Income determination

*Inventory valuation*/There are at present no provisions for valuing inventories or determining inventory flows. The tax treatment will follow the accounting treatment. Accounting policies generally follow Vietnamese Accounting Standards.

*Capital gains*/Capital gains are subject to BIT. The definition of deductible cost base is unclear. Sale proceeds may also be subject to VAT, depending on the nature of the asset.

Gains made by a foreign investor on a transfer of an interest in a Vietnam-licensed enterprise are subject to BIT at the 28% standard rate.

*Intercompany dividends*/Intercompany dividends are generally nontaxable.

*Foreign income*/In practice, only Vietnam-source income is likely to be booked in the Vietnam investment vehicle. However, there are more cases where Vietnam resident companies are making investments overseas. The foreign income, under the domestic tax law, is subject to Vietnam BIT with tax credits available.

# Vietnam

*Stock dividends*/Stock dividends are not encountered in practice at present.

## Deductions

*Depreciation and depletion*/Effective from January 1, 2004, tax depreciation is different from accounting depreciation. Depreciation in excess of the rates specified in the regulations on tax depreciation is not deductible. These regulations specify maximum and minimum permissible effective lives for various classes of assets, including intangibles. . In addition to straight line method, business enterprises are allowed to use double declining balance method and units of production method in certain cases. Current permissible rates are as follows.

|  | % |
|---|---|
| Buildings | 2–4 |
| Office equipment | 10–20 |
| Automobiles | 10–16.66 |
| Machinery and equipment | 3.33–6.66 |

*Net operating losses*/Losses may be carried forward for five years. Carryback is not permitted.

*Payments to foreign affiliates*/There are no special restrictions on the deductibility of royalties and service fees paid to foreign affiliates. However, the regulations on the transfer of technology impose certain limits on royalty rates and other technology transfer fees. There is a 70:30 debt/equity limitation.

*Taxes*/Special sales tax is deductible for BIT purposes.

*Other significant items*/The following are specifically stated to be nondeductible.
1. Fines.
2. Loss of any asset due to natural disasters, theft, and so on.
3. Loss as a result of disruption of production, regardless of cause.
4. Depreciation in excess of the rates set by the Ministry of Finance.
5. Noncategorized expenditure in excess of the set limits (10%) as a percentage of total expenditure.

## Group taxation

There is no provision for any form of consolidated filing or group loss relief.

## Tax incentives

*Inward investment*/Preferential BIT rates of 10%, 15%, and 20% are available where certain criteria are met, and in fields or locations in which investment is encouraged. Preferential rates are available for a period of between ten years and the duration of the project, starting from the commencement of operating activities. When the preferential rate expires, the rate generally reverts to the standard rate.

Investors may be considered for tax holidays. These take the form of a complete exemption from BIT for a certain period beginning immediately after the project becomes profitable (before the offset of losses), followed by a further period during which tax is charged at half the agreed rate. The duration of these holiday periods relates directly to the tax rate applicable to the individual project and may continue for up to eight years.

*Other incentives*/Other tax incentives apply to foreign-invested enterprises located in export-processing zones, industrial zones, and hi-tech zones, and to BOT enterprises if certain conditions are met.

## Withholding taxes

*Interest*/An interest withholding tax of 10% was introduced on January 1, 1999, and applies to any loan agreement signed after December 31, 1998. However, offshore loans provided by certain government or semi-governmental institutions may obtain an exemption from the interest withholding tax where a relevant double taxation agreement (DTA) applies.

*Royalties, license fees, etc.*/What might broadly be termed as payments in respect of intellectual property are taxed at a flat rate of 10%.

*Management fees, etc.*/Under the latest regulations, management fees are only acceptable in certain circumstances. For example, simple allocation of general head office charges would not be acceptable. In addition to this, a withholding tax is very likely to be charged on management fees and head office charges if they fall within the definition of payments to foreign contractors (see below).

*Payments to foreign contractors*/A withholding tax on payments to "foreign contractors" applies where a Vietnamese party (including a foreign-invested enterprise licensed under the Law on Foreign Investment) contracts with a foreign party that does not have a licensed investment in Vietnam. This withholding tax applies in many cases and can be a very significant cost for businesses.

Foreign contractors can apply to be deduction-method VAT payers if they adopt the Vietnamese accounting system, or a system that is internationally recognized and acceptable to the authorities. If accounting records are adequate, the foreign contractor will pay BIT on actual profits, but otherwise on a deemed-profit basis.

For direct (non-deduction-method) foreign contractors, VAT and BIT will be withheld by the contracting party at a deemed percentage of taxable turnover. Various rates are specified according to the nature of the contract performed. For BIT the withholding tax rate varies from 1% to 10%. For VAT, the effective withholding tax rate can also range from 1% to 10%. The VAT withheld by the contracting party is an allowable input credit in its VAT return. The VAT and BIT rates are summarized below.

| Business activities | Effective VAT rate (%) | Deemed BIT rate (%) |
|---|---|---|
| Trading (including supply of water, food, and foodstuffs; supplies and chemical materials to petroleum contractors) | 1 | 1 |
| Services | 5 or 10 | 5 |
| Construction, installation without supply of materials and/or machinery and equipment; exploration, design, and supervision | 2.5 | 2 |
| Construction, installation with supply of materials and/or machinery and equipment | 1.5 | 2 |
| Other manufacturing and transportation | 2.5 or 1.25 | 2 |
| Interest | Exempt | 10 |
| Royalties | Exempt | 10 |

# Vietnam

Where a contractor subcontracts out part of the contract, taxable turnover does not include the value of the subcontract, provided evidence is produced that the subcontractor has paid tax on the value of the subcontract.

The obligation to withhold and pay the BIT and VAT rests with the Vietnamese party to the contract. DTA relief may be available in certain circumstances (see below).

***Cross-border leases**/*A Vietnam-based lessee is required to withhold tax from payments to an offshore lessor. The rate is 10%, comprising a deemed BIT rate of 5% and VAT at 5%.

***Summary of withholding tax rates**/*The rates of tax to be withheld from various forms of income are as follows. Note that at press time, substantial revisions to the foreign corporation withholding tax regime are being proposed and considered.

| Recipient | Interest | Royalties |
|---|---|---|
| | % | % |
| Domestic corporations | Nil | 10 |
| Vietnamese individuals | Nil | 10 |
| Foreign corporations (1) | 10 | 10 |
| Foreign individuals | 10 | 10 |
| Treaty: | | |
| Australia | 10 | 10 |
| Belarus (1, 2) | 10 | 15 |
| Belgium (1, 2, 3) | 10 | 5/10/15 |
| Bulgaria (1, 2, *) | 10 | 15 |
| Canada (3) | 10 | 7.5/10 |
| China, P.R. (2) | 10 | 10 |
| Cuba (*) | 10 | 10 |
| Czech Republic (2) | 10 | 10 |
| Denmark (1, 2, 3) | 10 | 5/15 |
| France | Nil | 10 |
| Finland | 10 | 10 |
| Germany (2, 3) | 10 | 7.5/10 |
| Hungary | 10 | 10 |
| Iceland (2) | 10 | 10 |
| India (2) | 10 | 10 |
| Indonesia (1, 2) | 15 | 15 |
| Italy (2, 3) | 10 | 7.5/10 |
| Japan (2) | 10 | 10 |
| Korea (South) (1, 2, 3) | 10 | 5/15 |
| Korea (North) | 10 | 10 |
| Laos | 10 | 10 |
| Luxembourg | 10 | 10 |
| Malaysia (2) | 10 | 10 |
| Mongolia (3) | 10 | 10 |
| Myanmar (2, *) | 10 | 10 |
| Netherlands (1, 2, 3) | 7/10 | 5/10/15 |
| Norway | 10 | 10 |
| Philippines (1) | 15 | 15 |
| Poland (1, 3) | 10 | 10/15 |
| Romania (1, 2) | 10 | 15 |
| Russia (1) | 10 | 15 |

| Recipient | Interest | Royalties |
|---|---|---|
| | % | % |
| Singapore (1, 2, 3) | 10 | 5/15 |
| Sweden (1, 2, 3) | 10 | 5/15 |
| Switzerland | 10 | 10 |
| Thailand (2) | 10/15 | 15 |
| Ukraine (2) | 10 | 10 |
| United Kingdom | 10 | 10 |
| Uzbekistan (1, 2) | 10 | 15 |

*Agreements signed but not ratified.

Notes:

1. In some cases the limits set by the treaty are higher than the present withholding rate under domestic law. Therefore, the domestic rates will apply.

2. Interest derived by certain government bodies is exempt from withholding tax.

3. Royalty withholding tax rates vary for certain types of royalties.

## Tax administration

***VAT returns and payments/***Taxpayers must file VAT returns monthly by the 10th day of the following month. The taxpayer must remit the VAT payable at the same time when submitting the VAT return, and no later than by the 25th of the month. At the end of the year the taxpayer must complete an annual tax finalization.

***BIT returns and payments/***BIT returns are filed annually. Provisional quarterly payments are also required. The standard tax year is the calendar year. The Ministry of Finance has approved different accounting year-ends in a number of cases. Tax is collected each year in four quarterly provisional installments according to the provisional declaration submitted. Payment must be made at the same time of submission BIT return, but not later than the last day of the quarter. The annual tax return and the audited financial statements should be filed within 90 days of the end of the financial year.

# Vietnam

## CORPORATION TAX CALCULATION

Fiscal year ending December 31, 2003

|  | | (In VND millions) |
|---|---:|---:|
| Net income before taxes | | 3,360 |
| Add: | | |
| Fines | 50 | |
| Expenses without supporting documentation | 100 | |
| Advertising, promotion and marketing expenditure in excess of limit | 200 | 350 |
|  | | 3,710 |
| Deduct: Loss carried over from previous years (wholly foreign owned and joint venture companies) | | 450 |
| Taxable income | | 3,260 |
| Tax at 28% (standard rate, foreign invested enterprises) | | 912.8 |

Note:

Exchange rate of the Vietnamese Dong at January 1, 2004: US$1 = VND16,156.

## PwC contact

For additional information on taxation in Zambia, contact:

Eileen Duncan
PricewaterhouseCoopers
National Savings and Credit Bank Building
Seventh Floor
North End, Cairo Road
(P.O. Box 30942)
Lusaka, Zambia
Telephone: (260) (1) 228809–10, 220782, 220778
Fax: (260) (1) 220768
Internet: pwclsk@ zamnet.zm, office@zm.pwc.com
e-mail: eileen.duncan@zm.pwc.com

## General note

This entry is repeated from the 2003/2004 edition. For more up-to-date information consult the contact listed above or Jacqueline Collette at jacqueline.collete@us.pwc.com.

The information in this entry is current as of January 2003. For subsequent developments consult the contact listed above.

## Taxes on corporate income

The standard rate of corporate tax is 35%. The tax on income from banking is 35% for profits not exceeding ZK250 million and 45% for profits in excess of ZK250 million. With effect from April 1, 2002 mining companies involved in the production of copper or cobalt are subject to tax at a reduced rate of 25%. Income derived from farming activities, chemical fertilizer manufacture, and export of nontraditional products is taxed at 15%. The rate of tax for a company whose shares are listed on the Lusaka Stock Exchange will be increased from 30% to 33% from April 1, 2003 in accordance with the announcements made in the National Budget 2003.

## Corporate residence

Zambian residence is determined to exist where a company is incorporated in Zambia or where control and management of the corporation are exercised within Zambia.

## Other taxes

*Value-added tax*/VAT was introduced with effect from July 1, 1995, and sales tax was abolished on the same date. The standard rate of tax is 17.5% of the value of the taxable goods and services. There are some zero-rated and exempt goods and services. The zero rate applies to goods and services that are destined for the export market and to medicines, medical drugs, farm produce, uncooked meat and poultry, and related products.

*Property transfer tax*/Currently, transfers of land or shares other than transfers between related resident companies or persons are subject to a property transfer tax, payable by the transferor, of 3% of the realized value. Transfers of company shares that are listed on any stock exchange in Zambia are exempt from property transfer tax.

# Zambia

*Mineral royalty tax/* Mineral royalty is based on the open market gross sales and the current rates are 0.6% for certain successor companies to Zambia Consolidated Copper Mines Ltd. (ZCCM), 2% for natural resources such as base or precious metals and industrial minerals, and 5% for gemstones. These changes to the rates apply from April 1, 2003.

*Equity levy/*The equity levy has been replaced by a dividend policy for parastatals. They are now required to pay annual dividends equal to at least 10% of the inflation-adjusted government equity.

## Branch income

Tax rates on branch profits are the same as those on corporate profits, but no tax is withheld on transfers of profits to the head office.

## Income determination

*Inventory valuation/*Inventories are generally stated at the lower of cost or market on the FIFO basis. LIFO may be accepted by the Commissioner of Taxes, provided it is used regularly thereafter. Conformity of book and tax reporting is required.

*Capital gains/*There is no capital gains tax in Zambia.

*Intercompany dividends/*All dividends paid by a Zambian corporation to another Zambian corporation are subject to a withholding tax. The rate of withholding tax on amounts payable to resident companies is 15%. The recipient company may set off the withholding tax payable upon declaration of a dividend against the withholding tax already paid in respect of the same dividend. Income tax is not charged on such dividends in Zambia and therefore the 15% is the final tax for Zambian tax purposes.

With effect from April 1, 2002 payments of dividends by a mining company involved in copper or cobalt production are subject to withholding tax at 0%.

*Foreign income/*A Zambian corporation is taxed on foreign branch income as earned except where this income cannot be remitted to the republic. In those circumstances it is taxed when it can be remitted to the republic. Foreign dividends are taxed when received. Double taxation is avoided by foreign tax credits.

*Stock dividends/*A Zambian corporation may issue bonus shares tax free.

## Deductions

*Depreciation and depletion/*Capital allowances are as follows.

| | Wear-and-tear allowance % |
|---|---|
| Industrial buildings | 5* |
| Commercial buildings | 2* |
| Plant and machinery, implements, commercial vehicles | 25* |
| Other vehicles | 20* |
| Manufacturing industries | 50* |
| Tourism industries | 50* |
| Farming | 50* |
| Leased assets | 50* |
| Farm works and improvements | 100 |

*Straight-line method.

For industrial buildings only, an initial allowance and an investment allowance, each of 10%, are available only in the year in which the buildings are first brought into use. The investment allowance is not deductible from the value of the asset and is for manufacturers only.

There are special provisions for capital expenditure relating to mining operations.

For industrial organizations, accelerated depreciation rates may be negotiated with the Commissioner of Taxes in certain circumstances.

Expenditure for the construction of, addition to or alteration of any industrial building used in a manufacturing business qualifies for an investment allowance of 10%. There is no investment allowance on plant and machinery. Investment allowances are not deducted from the cost when calculating initial or wear-and-tear allowances.

Proceeds from disposals are deducted from the income tax written-down value brought forward; therefore, effectively no adjustment is made for profits or losses until the cessation of the business. However, if the total of capital recoveries (i.e., sales proceeds) in any tax year on all implements, machinery and equipment exceeds the residue of the income tax written-down value at the end of the year, the excess amount is treated as income.

If the disposal proceeds exceed the income tax written-down value, then the excess is treated as income, but the excess that is liable to tax in respect of each asset is to be restricted to the total of capital allowances claimed and allowed in previous years.

Capital allowances are not required to conform to book depreciation.

*Employee fringe benefits*/The cost of providing fringe benefits to employees in forms other than direct cash payments is no longer allowed as a deduction for company tax purposes.

*Net operating losses*/For income tax purposes a loss can be carried forward for a maximum period of five years (or ten years in the case of the former Zambia Consolidated Copper Mines (ZCCM) Ltd), but it may be set off only against income from the source from which the loss was incurred. Certain former ZCCM mining companies can carry a loss forward for a maximum period of 20 years. Losses resulting from a farming activity may be carried back to a previous charge year, provided an application is made to the Commissioner of Taxes within 18 months of the loss's being incurred.

*Payments to foreign affiliates*/A Zambian corporation can claim a deduction for royalties, management service fees, and interest charges paid to foreign affiliates.

*Inducement allowance*/From April 1, 1993 the inducement allowance has been subject to tax in the hands of the recipient. The employer is allowed a tax deduction for the cost of the inducement allowance.

*Taxes*/No taxes are deductible in determining assessable income for tax purposes.

*Expenses relating to approved share option schemes*/Expenditure incurred by an employer in setting up an approved share scheme and the costs incurred in administering the same are deductible.

## Group taxation

Group taxation is not permitted.

## Tax incentives

A preferential rate of 15% applies to that portion of profits arising from the export of nontraditional products, which are defined as anything produced or manufactured in the country other than minerals and electricity.

*Industrial development*/Investment incentives under the Investment Act of 1993 apply to any investor that holds an investment certificate and does one of the following.

1. Exports nontraditional products or services.
2. Produces inputs to or products from an agricultural export business.
3. Engages in the tourist industry and has foreign exchange earnings that exceed 25% of gross annual earnings.
4. Has an import substitution business that provides net foreign exchange savings.
5. Operates in a rural area.
6. Engages in mining in any part of the republic.

*General incentives*/A qualifying investor is entitled to the following.

1. Income from farming and from the manufacture of chemical fertilizer is taxed at a rate of 15%.
2. Income from the export of nontraditional products is taxed at a rate of 15%.
3. Tax on income from a rural enterprise is to be reduced by one-seventh for each of the first five years.
4. Entitlement to appropriate capital allowances.
5. Entitlement to 10% development allowance on new orchards and similar plantations.
6. Losses incurred by an investor are carried forward to be deducted from future profits from the same source.
7. Revenue expenditure on experiments and research will be allowed as a deduction.
8. Dividends from farming income are exempt from tax for the first five years of operations.
9. Where a tax treaty exists, tax paid by investors on their foreign income will be allowed as a credit against their Zambian tax liability.
10. An investor in mining will be entitled to special capital allowances.
11. An investor may apply to the Controller of Customs to operate a bonded factory.
12. A small-scale enterprise is eligible for the following.
    a. Exemption from tax for the first three years if operating in an urban area and for the first five years if operating in a rural area.
    b. Exemption from customs duties on imported mining equipment, including specialized motor vehicles for a mining enterprise.
    c. Exemption from the payment of rates on factory premises for the first five years.
    d. Permission to operate a manufacturing enterprise without a manufacturing license for the first five years.
13. Right of repatriation of the proceeds of the sale or liquidation of the enterprise attributable to the foreign investment.

14. From April 1, 2002, the tax rate for mining companies involved in copper and cobalt production is 25%.
15. The withholding tax rate on dividends paid by any mining company in Zambia involved in copper and cobalt production is reduced to 0%.
16. The withholding tax rate on the payment of any interest, royalties, or management fees paid by any mining company involved in copper and cobalt production to its shareholders or affiliates or any lender of money is 0% per annum.

**Special incentives**/Investors that invest a minimum of US$250,000 or the equivalent and employ a minimum of ten employees are entitled to a self-employment permit or resident permit, provided they do the following.

1. Export nontraditional products that result in net foreign exchange earnings.
2. Produce products for use locally in agriculture and/or other agro-related products for export.
3. Engage in tourism, earning at least 25% of their gross income in foreign exchange.
4. Engage in an import-substitution industry using substantially local raw materials.
5. Are located in a rural area.

The Investment Centre will assist the investor meeting these requirements to obtain work permits for up to five expatriate employees.

**Services**/The Investment Centre will assist investors in identifying suitable land for investment and in obtaining it. It will also assist them in obtaining water, electricity, transport, and communication services and similar facilities required for the investment. In addition, the Centre will assist an investor in obtaining any license, permit or registration.

**Investment guarantees**/No interest in or right over property of any description of an investor is to be compulsorily acquired except for public purposes under an Act of Parliament providing for compensation thereof. Any compensation payable under this section is to be made promptly at the market value and is to be fully transferable at the applicable exchange rate in the currency in which the investment was originally made, without deductions for taxes, levies and other duties except where those are due.

**Petroleum industry**/The Petroleum (Exploration and Production) Act of 1985 regulates petroleum exploration, development and production in Zambia. It also grants exemptions and incentives through tax, customs duty, and other rebates. The Income Tax (Petroleum Operations) Regulations of 1985 govern the assessment of income from petroleum operations.

**Agricultural development**/A development allowance of 10% of the expenditure incurred in planting tea, coffee, bananas, and other approved plants will be allowed as a deduction. If not utilized, it may be carried forward for a maximum of three years. The full cost of farm improvements and farm works is allowed as a deduction in the charge year in which it is incurred.

**Job credit**/The job credit has been introduced as an incentive to the manufacturing industry to create new jobs. An amount between 5% and 10% of the total wages payable to additional Zambian citizens employed is available for offset against assessable income for four consecutive years.

# Zambia

*Capital investment*/See the description of investment allowances under "Depreciation and depletion."

## Withholding taxes

Resident companies making certain types of payments are required to withhold tax as follows.

| Recipient | Dividends | Interest | Royalties |
|---|---|---|---|
| | % | % | % |
| Resident corporations............................ | 15 | 15 | 15 |
| Resident individuals................................ | 15 | 15 | 15 |
| Nonresident corporations, individuals: | | | |
| Paid by the former ZCCM Ltd .................. | 0 | 0 | 0 |
| Paid by a mining company in copper | | | |
| and cobalt production (1)..................... | 0 | 0 | 0 |
| Nontreaty................................................ | 15 | 15 | 15 |
| Treaty: ................................................... | | | |
| Denmark............................................. | 15 (2) | 15 (2) | 10 |
| France ................................................ | 20 (2) | 30 (2) | Nil |
| Germany.............................................. | 15 (2) | 10 | 10 |
| Ireland, Rep. of .................................. | Nil | Nil | Nil |
| Italy .................................................... | 15 (2, 3) | 10 | 10 |
| Japan.................................................. | Nil | 10 | 10 |
| Netherlands ........................................ | 20 (2) | Nil | 10 |
| Norway ............................................... | 15 (2) | 15 (2) | 10 |
| Sweden ............................................... | 15 (2) | 15 (2) | 10 |
| Switzerland......................................... | 20 (2) | Nil | Nil |
| United Kingdom .................................. | 15 (2, 3) | 10 | 10 |
| United States (4)................................. | Nil/20 (5) | Nil | Nil |

| Recipient | Management, professional fees | Rents |
|---|---|---|
| | % | % |
| Resident corporations, individuals ......................................... | 15 | 15 |
| Nonresident corporations, individuals: | | |
| Mining company in copper and | | |
| cobalt production (5) ............................................................ | 0 | 0 |
| Nontreaty.......................................................................... | 15 | 15 |
| Treaty: | | |
| Denmark ........................................................................ | Nil | 15 |
| France............................................................................. | 30 (2) | 15 |
| Germany.......................................................................... | Nil | 15 |
| Ireland, Rep. of .............................................................. | Nil | 15 |
| Italy................................................................................. | Nil | 15 |
| Japan.............................................................................. | Nil | 15 |
| Netherlands .................................................................... | Nil | 15 |
| Norway............................................................................ | Nil | 15 |
| Sweden............................................................................ | Nil | 15 |
| Switzerland ..................................................................... | 30 (2) | 15 |
| United Kingdom .............................................................. | Nil | 15 |
| United States (4)............................................................. | 30 (2) | 15 |

The numbers in parentheses refer to the following numbered Notes.

Notes:

1. The withholding tax rate is reduced to 0% where the payment is made by a mining company involved in copper and cobalt production in Zambia to its shareholders or affiliates or any lender of money.
2. The lesser of the local rate or treaty rate will apply. From April 1, 1996 the withholding tax rate on dividends payable to all nonresidents is 15%, but residents of countries that have tax treaties with Zambia can apply to the Commissioner of Taxes for a direction to use the rates of tax laid down in the tax treaties involved.
3. Or 5% where recipient controls 25% or more of the voting equity of the payer.
4. There is no formal tax treaty between Zambia and the United States, but Zambia has been applying the preindependence treaty on an informal basis; a specific approval must be obtained from the Zambia Revenue Authority (ZRA).
5. Nil rate applies to individuals; 20% rate applies to others.

## Tax administration

***Returns***/Taxpayers are required to self-assess themselves and submit to the authorities the self-assessment return, together with the settlement of any outstanding tax, by the following September 30. The tax year is the fiscal year to March 31. With effect from April 1, 1995 a specific penalty has been introduced for failure to submit tax returns on or before September 30 or any specified due date.

***Payment of tax***/Taxpayers are required to submit to the Zambia Revenue Authority (ZRA) an estimate of their profits for the year to March 31 by July 14 of that year, when the first installment of one-quarter of the tax falls due. The remaining installments must be paid on or before October 14 of that year and January 14 and April 14 of the following year. There is a 5% penalty if the final estimate differs from the actual by more than one-third. This was reintroduced following the January 2001 Budget and is subject to confirmation by legislation.

# Zambia

## CORPORATION TAX CALCULATION

| | | |
|---|---:|---:|
| Profit before taxation for calendar year<br>ended December 31, 2002 | | ZK 350,000,000 |
| Add: | | |
| Depreciation | 12,000,000 | |
| Net loss on sale of fixed assets | 1,500,000 | |
| Increase in general provision for doubtful debts | 2,000,000 | |
| Entertainment expenses | 750,000 | |
| Noncash fringe benefits | 1,500,000 | |
| Legal expenses (1) | 1,000,000 | |
| Disallowable subscriptions and donations | 400,000 | 19,150,000 |
| | | 369,150,000 |
| Less: | | |
| Investment allowances | 1,000,000 | |
| Initial allowances | 600,000 | |
| Wear-and-tear allowances | 9,400,000 | |
| Commercial buildings allowance | 460,000 | |
| Industrial buildings allowances | 1,150,000 | |
| Dividend received from resident corporation | 20,000,000 | |
| Realized exchange gain on long-term loan<br>for purchase of capital equipment | 50,540,000 | 83,150,000 |
| Taxable income | | ZK 286,000,000 |
| Tax thereon: | | |
| Farming companies—Tax at 15% | | ZK   42,900,000 |
| Manufacturing, services, and other companies—<br>Tax at 35% | | ZK 100,100,000 |
| Banks (2): | | |
| Tax at 35% | | ZK   87,500,000 |
| Tax at 45% | | 16,200,000 |
| | | ZK 103,700,000 |

Notes:

1.  Legal expenses of ZK1,000,000 include:

    | | ZK |
    |---|---:|
    | Property purchase | 300,000 |
    | Short lease negotiation | 150,000 |
    | Stamp tax | 450,000 |
    | Valuation expense | 100,000 |
    | Total | 1,000,000 |

2.  Taxable income from banking in excess of ZK250 million is taxed at 45%.

3.  Exchange rate of the kwacha at March 25, 2003: US$1 = ZK4896.

## PwC contact

For additional information on taxation in Zimbabwe, contact:

Manuel Lopes
PricewaterhouseCoopers
P.O. Box 453
Harare, Zimbabwe
Telephone: (263) (4) 307213–19
Fax: (263) (4) 332724/332495
e-mail: manuel.lopes@pwc.com

## General note

This entry is repeated from the 2003/2004 edition. For more up-to-date information consult the contact listed above or Jacqueline Collette at jacqueline.collete@us.pwc.com.

## Significant developments

A bank levy of 5% on net profits of banking institutions was introduced as from the year ended December 31, 2001.

## Taxes on corporate income

*Income tax/* Tax on corporate taxable income is levied at a rate of 30%, plus an AIDS levy of 3%, giving an effective rate of 30.9%.

## Corporate residence

A corporation is regarded as ordinarily resident in the country where the central management and control of the policy of the corporation are exercised.

## Other taxes

*Sales tax/* A four-tier sales tax rate is in effect, as follows:

|  | % |
|---|---|
| Specified luxury goods | 25 |
| Electricity | 5 |
| Other goods and services | 15 |
| Local sales of motor vehicles (passenger) | 15 |
| Local sales of motor vehicles (commercial) | 10 |

Basic goods are exempt from sales tax.

## Branch income

Branch income is subject to income tax at the same rates as domestic corporations. Branch profits tax has been abolished as of January 1,1999. Tax is payable at the rate of 20% on remittances to headquarters by Zimbabwean branches of foreign corporations in respect of foreign expenses allocated to the branch operation.

## Income determination

*Inventory valuation/* The value of inventory is stated at the lower of cost or market value. LIFO is not permitted. Book and tax reporting need not conform.

# Zimbabwe

*Capital gains*/Gains on specified capital assets (immovable property and marketable securities, including shares in private companies) are taxed at a flat rate of 20%. Shares quoted on the Zimbabwe Stock Exchange are tax exempt. Acquisition costs are subject to a 50% annual allowance for inflation. Capital losses are set off against capital gains for the same year, and overall losses are carried forward for setoff against future capital gains. There is no carryback and no limitation on the period of ownership.

*Intercompany dividends*/Dividends from Zimbabwean sources are tax exempt.

*Foreign income*/Resident corporations are taxed only on income from sources within or deemed to be within Zimbabwe, rather than on worldwide income. In this context interest earned from sources outside Zimbabwe is deemed to be Zimbabwean income. Foreign dividends are subject to income tax at the rate of 20% on the gross dividend. Relief in the form of tax credits is granted to the extent of the lower of the Zimbabwean and the foreign tax applicable to that income.

*Stock dividends*/Stock dividends (bonus shares) may be issued by Zimbabwean corporations. Capitalization issues of this nature are not subject to income tax in the hands of recipients and are excluded from withholding taxes on dividends.

## Deductions

Depreciation is computed on either the straight-line or the reducing-balance basis. The following allowances are available.

1. Special initial allowance
   a. Businesses in all areas—The allowance is computed on expenditure incurred on the construction of or additions to industrial buildings (e.g., hotels with liquor or casino licenses), farm improvements (restricted to Z$10,000,000 for schools, hospitals, and clinics), and staff housing (up to Z$1,000,000 per residential unit); and on the purchase of machinery, equipment, and motor vehicles (restricted to Z$1,000,000 for passenger vehicles). The rate is 50% effective from January 1, 2001. Industrial buildings, hotels, farm improvements, and staff housing do not qualify for this allowance unless constructed by the taxpayer.
   b. Business in growth-point areas—Commercial buildings constructed in growth-point areas qualify for a special initial allowance of 50% of expenditure incurred on the construction.

2. Wear-and-tear allowance—A wear-and-tear allowance is available to the extent of the balance remaining after the special initial allowance (which is optional) and on purchased buildings, as follows:

| Asset | Rate |
|---|---|
| Commercial buildings purchased or constructed (construction in the 1975/1976 fiscal year and onward) | 2.5% on cost |
| Industrial buildings, hotels, farm improvements, and staff housing, purchased or constructed | 5% on cost |
| Machinery, equipment, and furniture | Generally 10% on reducing balance |
| Motor vehicles | Generally 20% on reducing balance |

Accelerated rates will be allowed on machinery, equipment, furniture, and motor vehicles, if justified.

Where the special initial allowance of 50% is claimed, an accelerated wear-and-tear allowance of 25% is allowed in each of the second and third years.

3. Mining allowances — Capital expenditure can be claimed on a life-of-mine basis, or, alternatively, current capital expenditure can be deducted in full each year. Special concessions apply to new mines, including reopened or reequipped mining enterprises.

4. Recoupments of capital allowances on sales of depreciated property are subject to income tax as ordinary income.

5. Book and tax reporting need not conform.

*Net operating losses*/Loss carryover is restricted to six years, with limitations to prevent trading in losses. Mining losses are not restricted. There is no loss carryback.

*Payments to foreign affiliates*/There are no special restrictions on the deductibility of royalties and service fees paid to foreign affiliates, subject to the general provisions that the expenditure must have been incurred for the purposes of trade or in the production of income and that the amounts are no greater than would be determined on an arm's-length basis. In the case of mining operations, a debt to equity ratio of 3:1 was introduced from January 1, 2001. Interest on excess debt is not deductible. From the same date any allowance or deduction shall only be claimed in respect of expenditure or losses attributable to a particular mining location and shall not be claimed in respect of any other mining location. Royalties and interest received are normally taxable in Zimbabwe. Service fees are taxable in Zimbabwe only if the services for which payment is made were rendered in Zimbabwe.

*Taxes*/No taxes on income are deductible in determining taxable income. All other taxes are deductible, for example, sales tax and property tax.

## Group taxation

Group taxation is not permitted.

## Tax incentives

*Investment allowances*/Corporations operating in export processing zones pay corporate tax at 15% after a five-year tax holiday. They are exempt from withholding taxes on dividends and fees, and they are allowed duty-free importation of raw materials and capital goods.

Manufacturers exporting 50% of their manufactured or processed output (by quantity or volume rather than value) are subject to a corporate rate of 20% only.

The operator of a tourist facility in an approved tourist development zone enjoys a five year tax holiday, and is taxable at 15% over the next five years and at 20% thereafter.

For business operations in rural growth-point areas there is a 15% deduction in respect of expenditure incurred in the erection of or additions to commercial buildings, industrial buildings, hotels with liquor or casino licenses, and staff housing; and the purchase of new or unused articles, implements, machinery, and utensils (other than vehicles intended or adapted for use on roads) used in a growth-point area. Recapture of investment allowance is not taxable.

# Zimbabwe

## Withholding taxes

Domestic corporations paying the types of income indicated are required to withhold tax as shown below.

| Recipient | Dividends | Interest | Royalties and fees (1) |
|---|---|---|---|
| | % | % | % |
| Resident corporations | Nil | 20 (2, 3) | Nil |
| Resident individuals | 15, 20 (4) | 20 (2, 3) | Nil |
| Nonresident corporations and individuals: | | | |
| Nontreaty | 15, 20 (4) | 10 | 20 |
| Treaty | | | |
| Bulgaria | 15, 20 (4, 5) | 10 | 10 |
| Canada | 15, 20 (4, 5) | 10 | 10 |
| France | 15, 20 (4, 5) | 10 | 10 |
| Germany | 15, 20 (4, 5) | 10 | 7.5 |
| Mauritius | 15, 20 (4, 5) | 10 | 15 |
| Netherlands | 15, 20 (4, 5) | 10 | 10 |
| Norway | 15, 20 (4, 6) | 10 | 10 |
| Poland | 15 (5) | 10 | 10 |
| South Africa | 15, 20 (4) | 10 | 20 |
| Sweden | 15, 20 (4, 6) | 10 | 10 |
| United Kingdom | 15, 20 (4, 7) | 10 | 10 |

The numbers in parentheses refer to the following numbered Notes.

Notes:

1. Fees, including directors' fees, payable to nonresidents for services of a technical, managerial, administrative, or consultative nature are subject to withholding tax.
2. A rate of 20% applies to local interest from any bank, discount house, financial institution, or building society.
3. A rate of 20% applies to local treasury bills.
4. The 15% rate applies to quoted shares, the 20% rate to unquoted shares.
5. A reduced rate of 10% applies to dividends on substantial holdings (25% or more) under the Bulgarian, Canadian, French, German, Mauritian, Netherlands, and Polish tax treaties.
6. A reduced rate of 15% applies to dividends in substantial holdings (25% or more) under the Norwegian and Swedish treaties.
7. A reduced rate of 5% applies to dividends on substantial holdings (25% or more) under the U.K. tax treaty.

## Tax administration

*Returns/*The statutory year of assessment is the period of 12 months commencing on January 1. The tax year ends on December 31 in terms of income tax legislation, with effect from December 31, 1997.

The system is one of information filing, under which corporations must file annual returns of income and capital gains as well as other prescribed information. Assessments are made by the tax authorities after examination of returns and supporting information by assessors.

*Payment of tax/*Payment of tax by corporations is made through provisional tax payments. The responsibility of estimating the amount of provisional tax payable rests on the corporation. The tax in respect of each assessment year is payable in three installments on the annual payment dates fixed by the Commissioner General and communicated to the corporation. The payments must constitute 50% of the estimated provisional tax on the first annual payment date (February 28 each year) and 25% on each of the two remaining dates (June 30 and November 30 of the same year).

# Zimbabwe

## CORPORATION TAX CALCULATION

Fiscal year ending December 31, 2003

| | | | |
|---|---:|---:|---:|
| Profit per accounts before taxation | | | Z$ 1,000,000 |
| Deduct: | | | |
| Foreign dividends of 40,000, less | | | |
| foreign withholding of 6,000 | 34,000 | | |
| Zimbabwe dividend (not taxable) | 26,000 | | 60,000 |
| Profit from trading and other operations | | | 940,000 |
| Add: | | | |
| Depreciation charged in the accounts (i.e., at | | | |
| rates applied by the company) | 220,000 | | |
| Recoupment of capital allowances previously | | | |
| granted on assets sold | 13,500 | | |
| Expenditure charged in accounts but not incurred | | | |
| in the production of income or for the purposes | | | |
| of trade or expenditure of a capital nature: | | | |
| Charitable donations and expenses | | | |
| applicable to dividends | 4,900 | | |
| Entertainment allowance paid to director | | | |
| and employees | 10,000 | | |
| Other entertainment expenditure | 15,100 | | |
| Items of a capital nature | 8,000 | | 271,500 |
| | | | 1,211,500 |
| Deduct: | | | |
| Capital allowances (statutory rates) | | | 400,000 |
| Taxable income (trading operations) | | | Z$ 811,500 |
| | | | |
| Income tax payable: | | | |
| Trading operations: 811,500 at 30% | | | Z$ 243,450 |
| 3% AIDS levy | | | 73,035 |
| | | | Z$ 316,485 |
| | | | |
| Tax payable by a locally registered company: | | | |
| On trading operations calculated as above | | | Z$ 316,485 |
| On foreign dividends—40,000 (gross dividend) at 20% | | | 8,000 |
| Total tax payable by a locally registered company | | | 324,485 |
| Less—Double taxation relief (foreign withholding tax paid) | | | (6,000) |
| Tax payable by locally registered company and | | | |
| foreign corporation | | | Z$ 318,485 |

Note:

Exchange rate of the Zimbabwe dollar at December 31, 2002: US$1 = Z$55.00.